BERNSTEIN'S HANDBOOK OF ARBITRATION AND DISPUTE RESOLUTION PRACTICE
VOLUME 2: APPENDICES

BY

John Tackaberry, Q.C., FCIArb
and
Arthur Marriott, Q.C., FCIArb

WITH CONTRIBUTIONS FROM

Agricultural Property Arbitrations
    Derek Wood, C.B.E., Q.C., FCIArb, MRICS, F.A.A.V.
Adjudication   Rowan Planterose, M.A., LL.B., Barrister, FCIArb
Construction Industry Arbitrations   John Sims, FRICS, FCIArb, MAE
Dispute Boards   Pierre M. Genton, Ing.dipl EPFL/SIA-IMD, C.Eng.FICE
Documents-Only Arbitrations in Consumer Disputes
    Margaret Rutherford, Q.C, LL.B., FCIArb
International Commercial Arbitrations   Constantine Partasides
Investment Treaty Arbitration   Nigel Blackaby and Lluís Paradell
Maritime Arbitrations   Bruce Harris, FCIArb, F.R.S.A.
Online Dispute Resolution   Julia Hörnle
Rent Review and Property Valuation Arbitration   Geoffrey Dale, M.A., FRICS, FCIArb
Small Claims in the County Court   R. G. Greenslade, C.B.E., LL.B
Sport   Murray Rosen, Q.C., FCIArb
Commodity Trade Arbitration   Graham Perry, M.A., FCIArb
Dispute Settlement in WTO Law   Philippe Ruttley, M.A. (Oxon), Solicitor
Disciplinary Tribunals for the Legal Profession
    Karen Gough, LL.B., FCIArb, Dip. ICArb

Foreword by Lord Phillips
Introduction by the Lord Saville of Newdigate

PUBLISHED BY
SWEET & MAXWELL
IN CONJUNCTION WITH
THE CHARTERED INSTITUTE OF ARBITRATORS
LONDON 2003

Published in 2003 by
Sweet and Maxwell Limited of
100 Avenue Road
Swiss Cottage
London NW3 3PF
in conjunction with
The Chartered Institute of Arbitrators
Typeset by Wyvern 21, Bristol
Printed and bound in Great Britain by MPG Books Ltd, Bodmin, Cornwall

No natural forests were destroyed to make this product;
only farmed timber was used and replanted

First edition	1987
Second edition	1993
Third edition	1998
Reprinted	2000
Fourth edition	2003

A CIP catalogue record is available from the British Library

ISBN 0421 75760 4

All rights reserved. Crown copyright material is reproduced with the permission of the controller of HMSO and the Queen's Printer for Scotland.

No part of this publication may be reproduced or transmitted in any form or by any means, or stored in any retrieval system of any nature without prior written permission, except for permitted fair dealing under the Copyright, Designs and Patents Act 1988, or in accordance with the terms of a licence issued by the Copyright Licensing Agency in respect of photocopying and/or reprographic reproduction. Application for permission for other use of copyright material including permission to reproduce extracts in other published works shall be made to the publishers. Full acknowledgment of author, publisher and source must be given.

© John Tackaberry Q.C.

HEERE Learning sits, a comely Dame in yeares;
    Upon whose head, a heavenly dew doth fall;
Within her lap, an opened booke appeares:
Her right hand shewes, a sunne that shines to all;
    Blind Ignorance, expelling with that light:
    The Scepter shewes, her power and soveraigne might.

Her out spread Armes, and booke hear readines
T'imbrace all men, and entertaine their love:
The shower, those sacred graces doth expresse
By Science, that do flow from heaven above.
    Her age declares the studie, and the paine;
    Of many yeares, ere we our knowledge gaine.

Via ad Deura est Scientia quœ ad institutionem recre et honeste vivendi pertinct

Extracts from: Henry Peacham's 'Minerva Britanna' on which the moulded panels of the Long Gallery Ceiling were based. With thanks to the National Trust, Blickling Hall

Table of Contents

Volume 2

APPENDIX 1: STATUTORY MATERIALS AND RULES OF COURT

	PARA.
1. Unfair Contract Terms Act 1977 (1997, c.50)	A1–001
2. Agricultural Holdings Act 1986, Sch.11 (1986, c.5)	A2–001
3. Agricultural Holdings (Form of Award in Arbitration Proceedings) Order 1990 (SI 1990/1472)	A3–001
4. Civil Procedure Rules, Part 62—Arbitration Claims	A4–001
5. Civil Procedure Rules, Practice Direction—Arbitration	A5–001
6. Arbitration Act 1996 (1996, c.23)	A6–001
7. The Arbitration Act 1996 (Commencement No.1) Order 1996 (SI 1996/3146)	A7–001
8. High Court and County Courts (Allocation of Arbitration Proceedings) Order 1996 (SI 1996/3215)	A8–001
9. The Housing Grants, Construction and Regeneration Act 1996, ss.104–117 (1996, c.53)	A9–001
10. The Scheme for Construction Contracts (England and Wales) Regulations 1998 (SI 1998/649)	A10–001
11. Human Rights Act 1998 (1998, c.42)	A11–001
12. The Unfair Terms in Consumer Contracts Regulations 1999 (SI 1999/2083)	A12–001

APPENDIX 2: INTERNATIONAL CONVENTIONS AND RELATED MATERIALS

13. Article 6 of the Convention for the Protection of Human Rights and Fundamental Freedoms, as amended by Protocol No. 11 (European Treaty Series No.5, 1950).	A13–001
14. UNCITRAL Model Law on International Commercial Arbitration	A14–001

15. UNCITRAL Arbitration Rules A15–001
16. UNCITRAL Notes on Organizing Arbitral Proceedings A16–001
17. The New York Convention on the Recognition and Enforcement of Foreign Arbitral Awards A17–001

APPENDIX 3: INSTITUTIONAL RULES

18. AAA International Arbitration Rules (as Amended and Effective November 1, 2001) A18–001
19. CEDR Rules for Adjudication A19–001
20. The Chartered Institute of Arbitrators Arbitration Rules 2000 Edition (incorporating the Short Form Rules) A20–001
21. The Chartered Institute of Arbitrators Arbitration Scheme for the Travel Industry Rules (2001 Edition) A21–001
22. Arbitration and ADR Dispute Resolution Procedures offered by the Chartered Institute of Arbitrators A22–001
23. The Chartered Institute of Arbitrators Commercial Arbitration Scheme (2000 Edition)... A23–001
24. The Chartered Institute of Arbitrators Rules of the Mortgage Code Arbitration Scheme (Second Edition May 2000) A24–001
25. The Chartered Institute of Arbitrators "Surveyors Arbitration Scheme" Rules A25–001
26. City Disputes Panel Arbitration Rules A26–001
27. City Disputes Panel Mediation Rules A27–001
28. The Construction Industry Model Arbitration Rules (1st Edition, February 1998) A28–001
29. The Construction Industry Model Arbitration Rules (1st Edition, February 1998—Notes Issued by the Society of Construction Arbitrators) A29–001
30. Court of Arbitration for Sport Code of Sports–related Arbitration Statutes of the Bodies Working for the Settlement of Sports–related Disputes and Procedural Rules A30–001
31. Court of Arbitration for Sport Mediation Rules A31–001
32. International Federation of Consulting Engineers General Conditions of Contract for Construction (for Building and Engineering Works designed by the Employer), Clause 20—Claims, Disputes and Arbitration A32–001
33. International Federation of Consulting Engineers General Conditions of Contract for Construction (for Building and Engineering Works designed by the Employer) —General Conditions of Dispute Adjudication Agreement and Procedural Rules A33–001
34. Grain and Feed Trade Association Form 125 Arbitration Rules . A34–001
35. Grain and Feed Trade Association Form 126 Simple Dispute Rules A35–001
36. Grain and Feed Trade Association Form 127 Charter Party Arbitration Rules A36–001

37. Grain and Feed Trade Association Form 128 Mediation Rules ... A37–001
38. International Bar Association Rules on the Taking of Evidence in International Commercial Arbitration (June 1999) A38–001
39. Rules of Arbitration of the International Chamber of Commerce A39–001
40. International Chamber of Commerce ADR Rules A40–001
41. International Chamber of Commerce DOCDEX Rules A41–001
42. International Chamber of Commerce Rules for Expertise A42–001
43. The Institution of Civil Engineers' Arbitration Procedure (1997) A43–001
44. The London Court of International Arbitration Rules A44–001
45. The London Court of International Arbitration Mediation Procedure A45–001
46. The LMAA Terms (2002) A46–001
47. The LMAA Small Claims Procedure (Revised January 1, 2002) A47–001
48. The LMAA Mediation Terms (2002) A48–001
49. The Permanent Court of Arbitration List of Basic Documents A49–001
50. The Permanent Court of Arbitration Procedures for Cases under the UNCITRAL Arbitration Rules A50–001
51. The Permanent Court of Arbitration Procedural Guidelines for Requesting Designation of an Appointing Authority by the Secretary-General of the Permanent Court of Arbitration under the UNCITRAL Arbitration Rules A51–001
52. World Intellectual Property Organization Arbitration Rules A52–001
53. Annex 2 of the World Trade Organisation Agreement—Understanding on rules and procedures governing the settlement of disputes A53–001

APPENDIX 4: PRECEDENTS AND DRAFTING SUGGESTIONS

Arbitration Agreements—Before a Dispute has arisen
1. General arbitration clause—short form A54–003
2. Another longer form of general arbitration clause A54–004
3. Tailoring the powers of the tribunal to the wishes of the parties A54–005
4. Diminishing or enhancing the role of the court A54–006
5. *Scott v Avery* clause A54–007
6. Time limit A54–008
7. Place and law of the arbitration A54–009
8. Incorporating institutional rules A54–010
9. Chartered Institute of Arbitrators' Association clauses A54–011
10. London Court of International Arbitration clauses A54–012
11. BIMCO/London Maritime Arbitrators' Association clauses A54–013
12. Clause referring disputes to arbitration by the Court of Arbitration of the International Chamber of Commerce A54–014
13. UNCITRAL Arbitration Rules—model clause A54–015
14. "Ad hoc" agreement A54–016
15. American Arbitration Association A54–017
16. Kuala Lumpur Regional Centre for Arbitration A54–018

17. Indian Council of Arbitration A54–019
18. Singapore International Arbitration Centre A54–020
19. Hong Kong International Arbitration Centre A54–021

Arbitration Agreements—After a Dispute has Arisen
20. General form A54–022
21. To tailor an arbitration agreement to the wishes of the parties ... A54–023
22. To diminish or enhance the role of the court in the contract for arbitration A54–024
23. Agreement in advance (but post-dispute) for equal sharing of costs A54–025
24. Agreement varying the existing arbitration agreement A54–026

Appointments——Forms
25. Joint appointment of a sole arbitrator A54–027
26. Appointment of an arbitrator by a party A54–028
27. Notice to concur in the appointment of a sole arbitrator A54–029
28. Notice requiring other party to appoint an arbitrator in the situation where the third arbitrator is an umpire A54–030
29. Appointment as sole arbitrator where other party fails to appoint to determine disputes currently existing A54–031
30. Appointment by two arbitrators of umpire or third arbitrator A54–032
31. Joint appointment of a substitute sole arbitrator A54–033
32. Appointment by an appointing body or person A54–034

Topics for Consideration
33. List of matters for possible consideration in organising arbitral proceedings A54–035

General—Initial Steps
34. Initial letter from sole arbitrator to the parties A54–036
35. Schedule of Fees A54–037
36. Letter appointing a preliminary meeting A54–038

Examples of Initial Sets of Directions
37. Order for Directions No. 1 .... A54–039
38. Another Order for Directions No. 1 .... A54–040
39. Draft directions for consideration at preliminary meeting A54–053
40. Specimen letter following preliminary meeting sending [draft] directions A54–061
41. Notice to arbitrator of an application for leave to amend pleading or statement of case A54–063
42. Notice of intention to proceed *ex parte* after failure to comply with directions A54–064
43. Notice of intention to proceed *ex parte* after failure to attend hearing A54–065
44. Possible statement of case directions A54–066

Table of Contents

Construction Cases
45. Clause for main or principal contract which also provides for determination of related sub–contract issues A54–067
46. Provision in sub–contract requiring concurrence with head arbitration if required A54–068
47. Construction directions A54–069
48. Another form of construction directions A54–070
49. Construction Scott Schedule Claim for extra work—stage one ... A54–071
50. Checklist for preliminary meeting A54–072
51. Construction Scott Schedule of defects—stage two A54–073
52. Claimant's Scott Schedule of defects A54–074

Arbitration Clauses relevant to Rent Review
53. Provision enabling rent review under underlease to be referred to same arbitrator (in appendix) A54–075
54. Provision in underlease of part enabling rent review to be referred to same arbitrator as rent review under head lease A54–076
55. Suggested draft directions for a rent review arbitration by written representation A54–077
56. Suggested draft directions for a rent review arbitration involving an oral hearing A54–078
57. Agreement to refer point of law for the decision of counsel A54–079

Awards
58. Final award without reasons A54–080
59. Final award with reasons A54–081
60. Final award—reasons to be annexed—consumer dispute A54–082
61. Interim award A54–083
62. Interim awards reserving costs for later decision A54–084
63. Clause reserving costs and giving directions A54–085
64. Clause reserving costs but making an award "nisi" as to costs and giving directions A54–086
65. Final award incorporating alternative final award A54–087
66. Award by umpire A54–088
67. Clauses for awards—rent review—declaration that landlord has unreasonably withheld consent A54–089
68. Award for the delivery up of property, with alternative money award A54–090
69. Letter publishing award A54–091

Court Forms
Arbitration Award
70. N322A Application to enforce an award............................ A54–092
71. PF 166 Certificate as to Finality A54–093

Arbitration Claims
72. N15 Acknowledgment of Service A54–094

73. N8 Claim Form A54–095
74. N8A Notes for the Claimant A54–096
75. N8B Notes for the Defendant A54–097

Arbitration Proceedings
76. No.15A Acknowledgment of Service A54–098
77. No.8A Claim Form A54–099
78. PF 167 Order to Stay Proceedings A54–102
79. Specimen letter—arbitrator's charges A54–103

Miscellaneous
80. ICC—Arbitrator's Declaration of Acceptance and Statement of Independence A54–104
81. ICC Terms of Reference A54–105
82. Possible terms of engagement for a barrister/arbitrator A54–117
83. Dispute Board—Mediation—Arbitration clause A54–128
84. Communications Protocols A54–129

ADR Clauses
85. Suggested ICC ADR clauses A54–130
86. ADR clause combined with arbitration clause A54–131
87. Model Contract Clauses A54–132
88. Mediation UK Standards for Mediators (general mediation) A54–149

APPENDIX 5: MISCELLANEOUS

55. Chess Clock Arbitrations—Factors to consider when setting up and running time controls A55–001
56. The Role of the Courts in Arbitrations A56–001
57. Departmental Advisory Committee on Arbitration Law—Report on the Arbitration Bill (February 1996) A57–001
58. The Departmental Advisory Committee on Arbitration Law—Supplementary Report on the Arbitration Act 1996 (January 1997) A58–001
59. United Nations Compensation Commission Governing Council—Report and Recommendations made by the Panel of Commissioners concerning the twenty–third instalment of "E3" claims; Annex: Summary of general propositions A59–001
60. Convention on the settlement of investment disputes between States and Nationals of other States A60–001
61. Arbitration Act 1950 (14 Geo. 6 c.27) A61–001
62. Arbitration Act 1975 (1975 c.3) A62–001
63. Arbitration Act 1979 (1979 c.42) A63–001
64. Late Payment of Commercial Debts (Interest) Act 1998 (1998 c.20) A64–001
65. Contracts (Rights of Third Parties) Act 1999 (1999 c.31) A65–001
66. Federation of Oils, Seeds and Fats Associations Ltd (FOSFA International) Rules of Arbitration and Appeal A66–001

67. Sports Dispute Resolution Panel ("SDRP") Arbitration Rules ... A67–001
68. Consumer ODR Schemes A68–001
69. Online Dispute Resolution Providers A69–001
70. The World Bank, Washington, D.C. Standard Bidding Documents, Procurement of Works (May 2000, Revised March 2002) —Section XIII. Disputes Settlement Procedure A70–001
71. The Refined Sugar Association Rules Relating to Arbitration A71–001
72. AAA Supplementary Procedures for Online Arbitration of July 1, 2001 .... A72–001
73. Hong Kong International Arbitration Centre Electronic Transaction Arbitration Rules A73–001
74. China International Economic and Trade Arbitration Commission Arbitration Rules A74–001
75. B v Dentists Disciplinary Tribunal A75–001
76. ICSID Rules of Procedure for the Institution of Conciliation and Arbitration Proceedings (Institution Rules) A76–001
77. ICSID Rules of Procedure for Arbitration Proceedings (Arbitration Rules) A77–001
78. ICSID Rules of Procedure for Conciliation Proceedings (Conciliation Rules) A78–001

                                                 PAGE

INDEX 1037

APPENDIX 1

STATUTORY MATERIALS AND RULES OF COURT

Unfair Contract Terms Act 1977

(1977, c.50)

An Act to impose further limits on the extent to which under the law of England and Wales and Northern Ireland civil liability for breach of contract, or for negligence or other breach of duty, can be avoided by means of contract terms and otherwise, and under the law of Scotland civil liability can be avoided by means of contract terms.
[26TH OCTOBER 1977]

A1–001

PART I

AMENDMENT OF LAW FOR ENGLAND AND WALES AND NORTHERN IRELAND

Introductory

Scope of Part I

1.—(1) For the purposes of this Part of this Act, "negligence" means the breach— A1–002

(a) of any obligation, arising from the express or implied terms of a contract, to take reasonable care or exercise reasonable skill in the performance of the contract;

(b) of any common law duty to take reasonable care or exercise reasonable skill (but not any stricter duty);

(c) of the common duty of care imposed by the Occupiers' Liability Act 1957 or the Occupiers' Liability Act (Northern Ireland) 1957.

(2) This Part of this Act is subject to Part III; and in relation to contracts, the operation of sections 2 to 4 and 7 is subject to the exceptions made by Schedule 1.

(3) In the case of both contract and tort, sections 2 to 7 apply (except where the

contrary is stated in section 6(4)) only to business liability, that is liability for breach of obligations or duties arising—

(a) from things done or to be done by a person in the course of a business (whether his own business or another's); or

(b) from the occupation of premises used for business purposes of the occupier;

and references to liability are to be read accordingly [but liability of an occupier of premises for breach of an obligation or duty towards a person obtaining access to the premises for recreational or educational purposes, being liability for loss or damage suffered by reason of the dangerous state of the premises, is not a business liability of the occupier unless granting that person that access for the purposes concerned falls within the business purposes of the occupier.]

(4) In relation to any breach of duty or obligation, it is immaterial for any purpose of this Part of this Act whether the breach was inadvertent or intentional, or whether liability for it arises directly or vicariously.

Avoidance of liability for negligence, breach of contract, etc.

Negligence liability

A1–003 2.—(1) A person cannot by reference to any contract term or to a notice given to persons generally or to particular persons exclude or restrict his liability for death or personal injury resulting from negligence.

(2) In the case of other loss or damage, a person cannot so exclude or restrict his liability for negligence except in so far as the term or notice satisfies the requirement of reasonableness.

(3) Where a contract term or notice purports to exclude or restrict liability for negligence a person's agreement to or awareness of it is not of itself to be taken as indicating his voluntary acceptance of any risk.

Liability arising in contract

A1–004 3.—(1) This section applies as between contracting parties where one of them deals as consumer or on the other's written standard terms of business.

(2) As against that party, the other cannot by reference to any contract term—

(a) when himself in breach of contract, exclude or restrict any liability of his in respect of the breach; or

(b) claim to be entitled—

(i) to render a contractual performance substantially different from that which was reasonably expected of him, or

(ii) in respect of the whole or any part of his contractual obligation, to render no performance at all,

except in so far as (in any of the cases mentioned above in this subsection) the contract term satisfies the requirement of reasonableness.

Unreasonable indemnity clauses

4.—(1) A person dealing as consumer cannot by reference to any contract term be made to indemnify another person (whether a party to the contract or not) in respect of liability that may be incurred by the other for negligence or breach of contract, except in so far as the contract term satisfies the requirement of reasonableness.

(2) This section applies whether the liability in question—

   (a) is directly that of the person to be indemnified or is incurred by him vicariously;

   (b) is to the person dealing as consumer or to someone else.

A1–005

Liability arising from sale or supply of goods

"Guarantee" of consumer goods

5.—(1) In the case of goods of a type ordinarily supplied for private use or consumption, where loss or damage—

   (a) arises from the goods proving defective while in consumer use; and

   (b) results from the negligence of a person concerned in the manufacture or distribution of the goods,

liability for the loss or damage cannot be excluded or restricted by reference to any contract term or notice contained in or operating by reference to a guarantee of the goods.

(2) For these purposes—

   (a) goods are to be regarded as "in consumer use" when a person is using them, or has them in his possession for use, otherwise than exclusively for the purposes of a business; and

   (b) anything in writing is a guarantee if it contains or purports to contain some promise or assurance (however worded or presented) that defects will be made good by complete or partial replacement, or by repair, monetary compensation or otherwise.

(3) This section does not apply as between the parties to a contract under or in pursuance of which possession or ownership of the goods passed.

A1–006

Sale and hire-purchase

6.—(1) Liability for breach of the obligations arising from—

   (a) [section 12 of the Sale of Goods Act 1979] (seller's implied undertakings as to title, etc.);

   (b) section 8 of the Supply of Goods (Implied Terms) Act 1973 (the corresponding thing in relation to hire-purchase),

cannot be excluded or restricted by reference to any contract term.

(2) As against a person dealing as consumer, liability for breach of the obligations arising from—

A1–007

(a) [section 13, 14 or 15 of the 1979 Act] (seller's implied undertakings as to conformity of goods with description or sample, or as to their quality or fitness for a particular purpose);

(b) section 9, 10 or 11 of the 1973 Act (the corresponding things in relation to hire-purchase),

cannot be excluded or restricted by reference to any contract term.

(3) As against a person dealing otherwise than as consumer, the liability specified in subsection (2) above can be excluded or restricted by reference to a contract term, but only in so far as the term satisfies the requirement of reasonableness.

(4) The liabilities referred to in this section are not only the business liabilities defined by section 1(3), but include those arising under any contract of sale of goods or hire-purchase agreement.

Miscellaneous contracts under which goods pass

A1–008 7.—(1) Where the possession or ownership of goods passes under or in pursuance of a contract not governed by the law of sale of goods or hire-purchase, subsections (2) to (4) below apply as regards the effect (if any) to be given to contract terms excluding or restricting liability for breach of obligation arising by implication of law from the nature of the contract.

(2) As against a person dealing as consumer, liability in respect of the goods' correspondence with description or sample, or their quality or fitness for any particular purpose, cannot be excluded or restricted by reference to any such term.

(3) As against a person dealing otherwise than as a consumer, that liability can be excluded or restricted by reference to such a term, but only in so far as the term satisfies the requirement of reasonableness.

[(3A) Liability for breach of the obligations arising under section 2 of the Supply of Goods and Services Act 1982 (implied terms about title etc. in certain contracts for the transfer of the property in goods) cannot be excluded or restricted by reference to any such term.]

(4) Liability in respect of—

(a) the right to transfer ownership of the goods, or give possession; or

(b) the assurance of quiet possession to a person taking goods in pursuance of the contract,

cannot [(in a case to which subsection (3A) above does not apply)] be excluded or restricted by reference to any such term except in so far as the term satisfies the requirement of reasonableness.

(5) This section does not apply in the case of goods passing on a redemption of trading stamps within the Trading Stamps Act 1964 or the Trading Stamps Act (Northern Ireland) 1965.

Other provisions about contracts

Misrepresentation

A1–009 8.—(1) In the Misrepresentation Act 1967, the following is substituted for section 3—

"Avoidance of provision excluding liability for misrepresentation

3. If a contract contains a term which would exclude or restrict—

(a) any liability to which a party to a contract may be subject by reason of any misrepresentation made by him before the contract was made; or

(b) any remedy available to another party to the contract by reason of such a misrepresentation,

that term shall be of no effect except in so far as it satisfies the requirement of reasonableness as stated in section 11(1) of the Unfair Contract Terms Act 1977; and it is for those claiming that the term satisfies that requirement to show that it does."

(2) The same section is substituted for section 3 of the Misrepresentation Act (Northern Ireland) 1967.

Effect of breach

9.—(1) Where for reliance upon it a contract term has to satisfy the requirement of reasonableness, it may be found to do so and be given effect accordingly notwithstanding that the contract has been terminated either by breach or by a party electing to treat it as repudiated.

(2) Where on a breach the contract is nevertheless affirmed by a party entitled to treat it as repudiated, this does not of itself exclude the requirement of reasonableness in relation to any contract term.

Evasion by means of secondary contract

10. A person is not bound by any contract term prejudicing or taking away rights of his which arise under, or in connection with the performance of, another contract, so far as those rights extend to the enforcement of another's liability which this Part of this Act prevents that other from excluding or restricting.

Explanatory provisions

The "reasonableness" test

11.—(1) In relation to a contract term, the requirement of reasonableness for the purposes of this Part of this Act, section 3 of the Misrepresentation Act 1967 and section 3 of the Misrepresentation Act (Northern Ireland) 1967 is that the term shall have been a fair and reasonable one to be included having regard to the circumstances which were, or ought reasonably to have been, known to or in the contemplation of the parties when the contract was made.

(2) In determining for the purposes of section 6 or 7 above whether a contract term satisfies the requirement of reasonableness, regard shall be had in particular to the matters specified in Schedule 2 to this Act; but this subsection does not prevent the court or arbitrator from holding, in accordance with any rule of law, that a term which purports to exclude or restrict any relevant liability is not a term of the contract.

(3) In relation to a notice (not being a notice having contractual effect), the requirement of reasonableness under this Act is that it should be fair and reasonable to allow reliance on it, having regard to all the circumstances obtaining when the liability arose or (but for the notice) would have arisen.

(4) Where by reference to a contract term or notice a person seeks to restrict liability to a specified sum of money, and the question arises (under this or any other Act) whether the term or notice satisfies the requirement of reasonableness, regard shall be had in particular (but without prejudice to subsection (2) above in the case of contract terms) to—

(a) the resources which he could expect to be available to him for the purpose of meeting the liability should it arise; and

(b) how far it was open to him to cover himself by insurance.

(5) It is for those claiming that a contract term or notice satisfies the requirement of reasonableness to show that it does.

"Dealing as consumer"

A1–013   12.— (1) A party to a contract "deals as consumer" in relation to another party if—

(a) he neither makes the contract in the course of a business nor holds himself out as doing so; and

(b) the other party does make the contract in the course of a business; and

(c) in the case of a contract governed by the law of sale of goods or hire-purchase, or by section 7 of this Act, the goods passing under or in pursuance of the contract are of a type ordinarily supplied for private use or consumption.

(2) But on a sale by auction or by competitive tender the buyer is not in any circumstances to be regarded as dealing as consumer.

(3) Subject to this, it is for those claiming that a party does not deal as consumer to show that he does not.

Varieties of exemption clause

A1–014   13.—(1) To the extent that this Part of this Act prevents the exclusion or restriction of any liability it also prevents—

(a) making the liability or its enforcement subject to restrictive or onerous conditions;

(b) excluding or restricting any right or remedy in respect of the liability, or subjecting a person to any prejudice in consequence of his pursuing any such right or remedy;

(c) excluding or restricting rules of evidence or procedure;

and (to that extent) sections 2 and 5 to 7 also prevent excluding or restricting liability by reference to terms and notices which exclude or restrict the relevant obligation or duty.

(2) But an agreement in writing to submit present or future differences to arbitration is not to be treated under this Part of this Act as excluding or restricting any liability.

Unfair Contract Terms Act 1977

Interpretation of Part I

14. In this Part of this Act—

"business" includes a profession and the activities of any government department or local or public authority;

"goods" has the same meaning as in the [Sale of Goods Act 1979];

"hire-purchase agreement" has the same meaning as in the Consumer Credit Act 1974;

"negligence" has the meaning given by section 1(1);

"notice" includes an announcement, whether or not in writing, and any other communication or pretended communication; and

"personal injury" includes any disease and any impairment of physical or mental condition.

Part II

Amendment of Law for Scotland

15.—(1) This Part of this Act [...], is subject to Part III of this Act and does not affect the validity of any discharge or indemnity given by a person in consideration of the receipt by him of compensation in settlement of any claim which he has.

(2) Subject to subsection (3) below, sections 16 to 18 of this Act apply to any contract only to the extent that the contract—

(a) relates to the transfer of the ownership or possession of goods from one person to another (with or without work having been done on them);

(b) constitutes a contract of service or apprenticeship;

(c) relates to services of whatever kind, including (without prejudice to the foregoing generality) carriage, deposit and pledge, care and custody, mandate, agency, loan and services relating to the use of land;

(d) relates to the liability of an occupier of land to persons entering upon or using that land;

(e) relates to a grant of any right or permission to enter upon or use land not amounting to an estate or interest in the land.

(3) Notwithstanding anything in subsection (2) above, sections 16 to 18—

(a) do not apply to any contract to the extent that the contract—

(i) is a contract of insurance (including a contract to pay an annuity on human life);

(ii) relates to the formation, constitution or dissolution of any body corporate or unincorporated association or partnership;

(b) apply to—

a contract of marine salvage or towage;

a charter party of a ship or hovercraft;

a contract for the carriage of goods by ship or hovercraft; or

a contract to which subsection (4) below relates,

only to the extent that—

(i) both parties deal or hold themselves out as dealing in the course of a business (and then only in so far as the contract purports to exclude or restrict liability for breach of duty in respect of death or personal injury); or
(ii) the contract is a consumer contract (and then only in favour of the consumer).

(4) This subsection relates to a contract in pursuance of which goods are carried by ship or hovercraft and which either—

(a) specifies ship or hovercraft as the means of carriage over part of the journey to be covered; or
(b) makes no provision as to the means of carriage and does not exclude ship or hovercraft as that means,

in so far as the contract operates for and in relation to the carriage of the goods by that means.

Liability for breach of duty

A1–017 16.—(1) [Subject to subsection (1A) below] where a term of a contract [, or a provision of a notice given to persons generally or to particular persons] purports to exclude or restrict liability for breach of duty arising in the course of any business or from the occupation of any premises used for business purposes of the occupier, that term [or provision]—

(a) shall be void in any case where such exclusion or restriction is in respect of death or personal injury;
(b) shall, in any other case, have no effect if it was not fair and reasonable to incorporate the term in the contract [or, as the case may be, if it is not fair and reasonable to allow reliance on that provision.]

[(1A) Nothing in paragraph (b) of subsection (1) above shall be taken as implying that a provision of a notice has effect in circumstances where, apart from that paragraph, it would not have effect.]

(2) Subsection (1)(a) above does not affect the validity of any discharge and indemnity given by a person, on or in connection with an award to him of compensation for pneumoconiosis attributable to employment in the coal industry, in respect of any further claim arising from his contracting that disease.

(3) Where under subsection (1) above a term of a contract [or a provision of a notice] is void or has no effect, the fact that a person agreed to, or was aware of, the term [or provision] shall not of itself be sufficient evidence that he knowingly and voluntarily assumed any risk.

Control of unreasonable exemptions in consumer or standard form contracts

17.—(1) Any term of a contract which is a consumer contract or a standard form contract shall have no effect for the purpose of enabling a party to the contract—

(a) who is in breach of a contractual obligation, to exclude or restrict any liability of his to the consumer or customer in respect of the breach;

(b) in respect of a contractual obligation, to render no performance, or to render a performance substantially different from that which the consumer or customer reasonably expected from the contract;

if it was not fair and reasonable to incorporate the term in the contract.

(2) In this section "customer" means a party to a standard form contract who deals on the basis of written standard terms of business of the other party to the contract who himself deals in the course of a business.

Unreasonable indemnity clauses in consumer contracts

18.—(1) Any term of a contract which is a consumer contract shall have no effect for the purpose of making the consumer indemnify another person (whether a party to the contract or not) in respect of liability which that other person may incur as a result of breach of duty or breach of contract, if it was not fair and reasonable to incorporate the term in the contract.

(2) In this section "liability" means liability arising in the course of any business or from the occupation of any premises used for business purposes of the occupier.

"Guarantee" of consumer goods

19.—(1) This section applies to a guarantee—

(a) in relation to goods which are of a type ordinarily supplied for private use or consumption; and

(b) which is not a guarantee given by one party to the other party to a contract under or in pursuance of which the ownership or possession of the goods to which the guarantee relates is transferred.

(2) A term of a guarantee to which this section applies shall be void in so far as it purports to exclude or restrict liability for loss or damage (including death or personal injury)—

(a) arising from the goods proving defective while—

(i) in use otherwise than exclusively for the purposes of a business; or
(ii) in the possession of a person for such use; and

(b) resulting from the breach of duty of a person concerned in the manufacture or distribution of the goods.

(3) For the purposes of this section, any document is a guarantee if it contains or purports to contain some promise or assurance (however worded or presented) that defects will be made good by complete or partial replacement, or by repair, monetary compensation or otherwise.

Obligations implied by law in sale and hire-purchase contracts

A1–021   20.—(1) Any term of a contract which purports to exclude or restrict liability for breach of the obligations arising from—

    (a) section 12 of the Sale of Goods Act [1979] (seller's implied undertakings as to title etc.);

    (b) section 8 of the Supply of Goods (Implied Terms) Act 1973 (implied terms as to title in hire-purchase agreements),

shall be void.

(2) Any term of a contract which purports to exclude or restrict liability for breach of the obligations arising from—

    (a) section 13, 14 or 15 of the said Act of [1979] (seller's implied undertakings as to conformity of goods with description or sample, or as to their quality or fitness for a particular purpose);

    (b) section 9, 10 or 11 of the said Act of 1973 (the corresponding provisions in relation to hire-purchase),

shall—

    (i) in the case of a consumer contract, be void against the consumer;

    (ii) in any other case, have no effect if it was not fair and reasonable to incorporate the term in the contract.

Obligations implied by law in other contracts for the supply of goods

A1–022   21.—(1) Any term of a contract to which this section applies purporting to exclude or restrict liability for breach of an obligation—

    (a) such as is referred to in subsection (3)(a) below—

        (i) in the case of a consumer contract, shall be void against the consumer, and

        (ii) in any other case, shall have no effect if it was not fair and reasonable to incorporate the term in the contract;

    (b) such as is referred to in subsection (3)(b) below, shall have no effect if it was not fair and reasonable to incorporate the term in the contract.

(2) This section applies to any contract to the extent that it relates to any such matter as is referred to in section 15(2)(a) of this Act, but does not apply to—

    (a) a contract of sale of goods or a hire-purchase agreement; or

    (b) a charterparty of a ship or hovercraft unless it is a consumer contract (and then only in favour of the consumer).

(3) An obligation referred to in this subsection is an obligation incurred under a contract in the course of a business and arising by implication of law from the nature of the contract which relates—

  (a) to the correspondence of goods with description or sample, or to the quality or fitness of goods for any particular purpose; or

  (b) to any right to transfer ownership or possession of goods, or to the enjoyment of quiet possession of goods.

(4) Nothing in this section applies to the supply of goods on a redemption of trading stamps within the Trading Stamps Act 1964.

Consequence of breach

22. For the avoidance of doubt, where any provision of this Part of this Act requires that the incorporation of a term in a contract must be fair and reasonable for that term to have effect—   **A1–023**

  (a) if that requirement is satisfied, the term may be given effect to notwithstanding that the contract has been terminated in consequence of breach of that contract;

  (b) for the term to be given effect to, that requirement must be satisfied even where a party who is entitled to rescind the contract elects not to rescind it.

Evasion by means of secondary contract

23. Any term of any contract shall be void which purports to exclude or restrict, or has the effect of excluding or restricting—   **A1–024**

  (a) the exercise, by a party to any other contract, of any right or remedy which arises in respect of that other contract in consequence of breach of duty, or of obligation, liability for which could not by virtue of the provisions of this Part of this Act be excluded or restricted by a term of that other contract;

  (b) the application of the provisions of this Part of this Act in respect of that or any other contract.

The "reasonableness" test

24.—(1) In determining for the purposes of this Part of this Act whether it was fair and reasonable to incorporate a term in a contract, regard shall be had only to the circumstances which were, or ought reasonably to have been, known to or in the contemplation of the parties to the contract at the time the contract was made.   **A1–025**

(2) In determining for the purposes of section 20 or 21 of this Act whether it was fair and reasonable to incorporate a term in a contract, regard shall be had in particular to the matters specified in Schedule 2 to this Act; but this subsection shall not prevent a court or arbiter from holding in accordance with any rule of law, that a term which purports to exclude or restrict any relevant liability is not a term of the contract

[(2A) In determining for the purposes of this Part of this Act whether it is fair and reasonable to allow reliance on a provision of a notice (not being a notice having contractual effect) regard shall be had to all the circumstances obtaining when the liability arose or (but for the provision) would have arisen.]

(3) Where a term in a contract [or a provision of a notice] purports to restrict liability to a specified sum of money, and the question arises for the purposes of this Part of this Act whether it was fair and reasonable to incorporate the term in the contract [or whether it is fair and reasonable to allow reliance on the provision], then, without prejudice to subsection (2) above [in the case of a term in a contract], regard shall be had in particular to—

> (a) the resources which the party seeking to rely on that term [or provision] could expect to be available to him for the purpose of meeting the liability should it arise;
>
> (b) how far it was open to that party to cover himself by insurance.

(4) The onus of proving that it was fair and reasonable to incorporate a term in a contract [or that it is fair and reasonable to allow reliance on a provision of a notice] shall lie on the party so contending.

Interpretation of Part II

A1–026　25.—(1) In this Part of this Act—

> "breach of duty" means the breach—
>> (a) of any obligation, arising from the express or implied terms of a contract, to take reasonable care or exercise reasonable skill in the performance of the contract;
>> (b) of any common law duty to take reasonable care or exercise reasonable skill;
>> (c) of the duty of reasonable care imposed by section 2(1) of the Occupiers' Liability (Scotland) Act 1960;
>
> "business" includes a profession and the activities of any government department or local or public authority;
> "consumer" has the meaning assigned to that expression in the definition in this section of "consumer contract";
> "consumer contract" means a contract (not being a contract of sale by auction or competitive tender) in which—
>> (a) one party to the contract deals, and the other party to the contract ("the consumer") does not deal or hold himself out as dealing, in the course of a business, and
>> (b) in the case of a contract such as is mentioned in section 15(2)(a) of this Act, the goods are of a type ordinarily supplied for private use or consumption;
>>
>> and for the purposes of this Part of this Act the onus of proving that a contract is not to be regarded as a consumer contract shall lie on the party so contending;
>
> "goods" has the same meaning as in the [Sale of Goods Act 1979];
>
> "hire-purchase agreement" has the same meaning as in section 189(1) of the Consumer Credit Act 1974;
> ["notice" includes an announcement, whether or not in writing, and any other communication or pretended communication;]

"personal injury" includes any disease and any impairment of physical or mental condition.

(2) In relation to any breach of duty or obligation, it is immaterial for any purpose of this Part of this Act whether the act or omission giving rise to that breach was inadvertent or intentional, or whether liability for it arises directly or vicariously.

(3) In this Part of this Act, any reference to excluding or restricting any liability includes—

(a) making the liability or its enforcement subject to any restrictive or onerous conditions;

(b) excluding or restricting any right or remedy in respect of the liability, or subjecting a person to any prejudice in consequence of his pursuing any such right or remedy;

(c) excluding or restricting any rule of evidence or procedure;

(d) [. . .]

but does not include an agreement to submit any question to arbitration.

(4) [. . .]

(5) In sections 15 and 16 and 19 to 21 of this Act, any reference to excluding or restricting liability for breach of an obligation or duty shall include a reference to excluding or restricting the obligation or duty itself.

Part III

Provisions applying to whole of United Kingdom

Miscellaneous

International supply contracts

26.—(1) The limits imposed by this Act on the extent to which a person may exclude or restrict liability by reference to a contract term do not apply to liability arising under such a contract as is described in subsection (3) below.

(2) The terms of such a contract are not subject to any requirement of reasonableness under section 3 or 4; and nothing in Part II of this Act shall require the incorporation of the terms of such a contract to be fair and reasonable for them to have effect.

(3) Subject to subsection (4), that description of contract is one whose characteristics are the following—

(a) either it is a contract of sale of goods or it is one under or in pursuance of which the possession or ownership of goods passes; and

(b) it is made by parties whose places of business (or, if they have none, habitual residences) are in the territories of different States (the Channel Islands and the Isle of Man being treated for this purpose as different States from the United Kingdom).

(4) A contract falls within subsection (3) above only if either—

(a) the goods in question are, at the time of the conclusion of the contract, in the course of carriage, or will be carried, from the territory of one State to the territory of another; or

(b) the acts constituting the offer and acceptance have been done in the territories of different States; or

(c) the contract provides for the goods to be delivered to the territory of a State other than that within whose territory those acts were done.

Choice of law clauses

A1–028   27.—(1) Where the [law applicable to] a contract is the law of any part of the United Kingdom only by choice of the parties (and apart from that choice would be the law of some country outside the United Kingdom) sections 2 to 7 and 16 to 21 of this Act do not operate as part [of the law applicable to the contract].

(2) This Act has effect notwithstanding any contract term which applies or purports to apply the law of some country outside the United Kingdom, where (either or both)—

(a) the term appears to the court, or arbitrator or arbiter to have been imposed wholly or mainly for the purpose of enabling the party imposing it to evade the operation of this Act; or

(b) in the making of the contract one of the parties dealt as consumer, and he was then habitually resident in the United Kingdom, and the essential steps necessary for the making of the contract were taken there, whether by him or by others on his behalf.

(3) In the application of subsection (2) above to Scotland, for paragraph (b) there shall be substituted—

"(b) the contract is a consumer contract as defined in Part II of this Act, and the consumer at the date when the contract was made was habitually resident in the United Kingdom, and the essential steps necessary for the making of the contract were taken there, whether by him or by others on his behalf.".

Temporary provision for sea carriage of passengers

A1–029   28.—(1) This section applies to a contract for carriage by sea of a passenger or of a passenger and his luggage where the provisions of the Athens Convention (with or without modification) do not have, in relation to the contract, the force of law in the United Kingdom.

(2) In a case where—

(a) the contract is not made in the United Kingdom, and

(b) neither the place of departure nor the place of destination under it is in the United Kingdom,

a person is not precluded by this Act from excluding or restricting liability for loss or damage, being loss or damage for which the provisions of the Convention would, if they had the force of law in relation to the contract, impose liability on him.

(3) In any other case, a person is not precluded by this Act from excluding or restricting liability for that loss or damage—

(a) in so far as the exclusion or restriction would have been effective in that case had the provisions of the Convention had the force of law in relation to the contract; or

(b) in such circumstances and to such extent as may be prescribed, by reference to a prescribed term of the contract.

(4) For the purposes of subsection (3)(a), the values which shall be taken to be the official values in the United Kingdom of the amounts (expressed in gold francs) by reference to which liability under the provisions of the Convention is limited shall be such amounts in sterling as the Secretary of State may from time to time by order made by statutory instrument specify.

(5) In this section—

(a) the references to excluding or restricting liability include doing any of those things in relation to the liability which are mentioned in section 13 or section 25(3) and (5); and

(b) "the Athens Convention" means the Athens Convention relating to the Carriage of Passengers and their Luggage by Sea, 1974; and

(c) "prescribed" means prescribed by the Secretary of State by regulations made by statutory instrument;

and a statutory instrument containing the regulations shall be subject to annulment in pursuance of a resolution of either House of Parliament.

Saving for other relevant legislation

29.—(1) Nothing in this Act removes or restricts the effect of, or prevents reliance upon, any contractual provision which—

(a) is authorised or required by the express terms or necessary implication of an enactment; or

(b) being made with a view to compliance with an international agreement to which the United Kingdom is a party, does not operate more restrictively than is contemplated by the agreement.

(2) A contract term is to be taken—

(a) for the purposes of Part I of this Act, as satisfying the requirement of reasonableness; and

(b) for those of Part II, to have been fair and reasonable to incorporate,

if it is incorporated or approved by, or incorporated pursuant to a decision or ruling of, a competent authority acting in the exercise of any statutory jurisdiction or function and is not a term in a contract to which the competent authority is itself a party.

(3) In this section—

"competent authority" means any court, arbitrator or arbiter, government department or public authority;

"enactment" means any legislation (including subordinate legislation) of the United Kingdom or Northern Ireland and any instrument having effect by virtue of such legislation; and

"statutory" means conferred by an enactment.

Obligations under Consumer Protection Acts

A1–031   30. [. . .]

General

Commencement; amendments; repeals

A1–032   31.—(1) This Act comes into force on 1st February 1978.

(2) Nothing in this Act applies to contracts made before the date on which it comes into force; but subject to this, it applies to liability for any loss or damage which is suffered on or after that date.

(3) The enactments specified in Schedule 3 to this Act are amended as there shown.

(4) The enactments specified in Schedule 4 to this Act are repealed to the extent specified in column 3 of that Schedule.

Citation and extent

A1–033   32.—(1) This Act may be cited as the Unfair Contract Terms Act 1977.

(2) Part I of this Act extends to England and Wales and to Northern Ireland; but it does not extend to Scotland.

(3) Part II of this Act extends to Scotland only.

(4) This Part of this Act extends to the whole of the United Kingdom.

SCHEDULES

Section 1(2)   SCHEDULE 1

Scope of sections 2 to 4 and 7

A1–034   1. Sections 2 to 4 of this Act do not extend to—

(a) any contract of insurance (including a contract to pay an annuity on human life);

(b) any contract so far as it relates to the creation or transfer of an interest in land, or to the termination of such an interest, whether by extinction, merger, surrender, forfeiture or otherwise;

(c) any contract so far as it relates to the creation or transfer of a right or interest in any patent, trade mark*, copyright or design right, registered design, technical

---

* This includes a reference to a registered service mark: Patents, Designs and Marks Act 1986, s.2 and Sch. 2, Pt I, para.1(2)(f).

Unfair Contract Terms Act 1977

or commercial information or other intellectual property, or relates to the termination of any such right or interest;

(d) any contract so far as it relates—

(i) to the formation or dissolution of a company (which means any body corporate or unincorporated association and includes a partnership), or
(ii) to its constitution or the rights or obligations of its corporators or members;

(e) any contract so far as it relates to the creation or transfer of securities or of any right or interest in securities.

2. Section 2(1) extends to—

(a) any contract of marine salvage or towage;

(b) any charterparty of a ship or hovercraft; and

(c) any contract for the carriage of goods by ship or hovercraft;

but subject to this sections 2 to 4 and 7 do not extend to any such contract except in favour of a person dealing as consumer.

3. Where goods are carried by ship or hovercraft in pursuance of a contract which either—

(a) specifies that as the means of carriage over part of the journey to be covered, or

(b) makes no provision as to the means of carriage and does not exclude that means,

then sections 2(2), 3 and 4 do not, except in favour of a person dealing as consumer, extend to the contract as it operates for and in relation to the carriage of the goods by that means.

4. Section 2(1) and (2) do not extend to a contract of employment, except in favour of the employee.

5. Section 2(1) does not affect the validity of any discharge and indemnity given by a person, on or in connection with an award to him of compensation for pneumoconiosis attributable to employment in the coal industry, in respect of any further claim arising from his contracting that disease.

. . . .

Sections 11(2) and 24(2) SCHEDULE 2

"Guidelines" for Application of Reasonableness Test

The matters to which regard is to be had in particular for the purposes of sections 6(3), 7(3) and (4), 20 and 21 are any of the following which appear to be relevant— **A1–035**

(a) the strength of the bargaining positions of the parties relative to each other, taking into account (among other things) alternative means by which the customer's requirements could have been met;

(b) whether the customer received an inducement to agree to the term, or in accepting it had an opportunity of entering into a similar contract with other persons, but without having to accept a similar term;

(c) whether the customer knew or ought reasonably to have known of the existence and extent of the term (having regard, among other things, to any custom of the trade and any previous course of dealing between the parties);

(d) where the term excludes or restricts any relevant liability if some condition is not complied with, whether it was reasonable at the time of the contract to expect that compliance with that condition would be practicable;

(e) whether the goods were manufactured, processed or adapted to the special order of the customer.

Section 31(3)   SCHEDULE 3

AMENDMENT OF ENACTMENTS

A1–036 [...]
In the Supply of Goods (Implied Terms) Act 1973 (as originally enacted and as substituted by the Consumer Credit Act 1974)—

(a) in section 14(1) for the words from "conditional sale" to the end substitute "a conditional sale agreement where the buyer deals as consumer within Part I of the Unfair Contract Terms Act 1977 [...]"

(b) in section 15(1), in the definition of "business", for "local authority or statutory undertaker" substitute "or local or public authority".

Section 31(4)   SCHEDULE 4

REPEALS

A1–037

Chapter	Short Title	Extent of repeal
56 & 57 Vict. c.71.	Sale of Goods Act 1893.	In section 55, subsections (3) to (11). Section 55A. Section 61(6). In section 62(1) the definition of "contract for international sale of goods".
1962 c.46.	Transport Act 1962.	Section 43(7).
1967 c.45.	Uniform Laws on International Sales Act 1967.	In section 1(4), the words "55 and 55A".
1972 c.33.	Carriage by Railway Act 1972.	In section 1(1), the words from "and shall have" onwards. Section 5(1).

Chapter	Short Title	Extent of repeal
1973 c.13.	Supply of Goods (Implied Terms) Act 1973.	Section 6. In section 7(1), the words from "contract for the international sale of goods" onwards. In section 12, subsections (2) to (9). Section 13. In section 15(1), the definition of "consumer sale".

The repeals in sections 12 and 15 of the Supply of Goods (Implied Terms) Act 1973 shall have effect in relation to those sections as originally enacted and as substituted by the Consumer Credit Act 1974.

Agricultural Holdings Act 1986, Sch. 11

(1986, c.5)

SCHEDULES

. . .

Sections 84 and 94   SCHEDULE 11

Arbitrations

Appointment and remuneration of arbitrator

A2–001   **1.**—(1) The arbitrator shall be a person appointed by agreement between the parties or, in default of agreement, a person appointed on the application of either of the parties by the President of the Royal Institution of Chartered Surveyors (referred to in this Schedule as "the President") from among the members of the panel constituted for the purposes of this paragraph.

(2) No application may be made to the President for an arbitrator to be appointed by him under this paragraph unless the application is accompanied by such fee as may be prescribed as the fee for such an application; but once the fee has been paid in connection with any such application no further fee shall be payable in connection with any subsequent application for the President to exercise any function exercisable by him in relation to the arbitration by virtue of this Schedule (including an application for the appointment by him in an appropriate case of a new arbitrator).

(3) Any such appointment by the President shall be made by him as soon as possible after receiving the application; but where the application is referable to a demand for arbitration made under section 12 of this Act any such appointment shall in any event not be made by him earlier than four months before the next termination date following the date of the demand (as defined by subsection (4) of that section).

(4) A person appointed by the President as arbitrator shall, where the arbitration relates to an agricultural holding in Wales, be a person who possesses a knowledge of Welsh agricultural conditions, and, if either party to the arbitration so requires, a knowledge also of the Welsh language.

(5) For the purposes of this Schedule there shall be constituted a panel consisting of such number of persons as the Lord Chancellor may determine, to be appointed by him.

[(6) A member of the panel constituted for the purposes of this Schedule shall vacate his office on the day on which he attains the age of seventy years; but this sub-paragraph is subject to section 26(4) to (6) of the Judicial Pensions and Retirement Act 1993 (power to authorise continuance in office up to the age of seventy-five years).]

2. If the arbitrator dies, or is incapable of acting, or for seven days after notice from either party requiring him to act fails to act, a new arbitrator may be appointed as if no arbitrator had been appointed.

3. In relation to an arbitrator who is appointed in place of another arbitrator (whether under paragraph 2 above or otherwise) the reference in section 12(2) of this Act to the date of the reference shall be construed as a reference to the date when the original arbitrator was appointed.

4. Neither party shall have power to revoke the appointment of the arbitrator without the consent of the other party; and his appointment shall not be revoked by the death of either party.

5. Every appointment, application, notice, revocation and consent under the foregoing paragraphs must be in writing.

6. The remuneration of the arbitrator shall be—

(a) where he is appointed by agreement between the parties, such amount as may be agreed upon by him and the parties or, in default of agreement, fixed by the registrar of the county court (subject to an appeal to the judge of the court) on an application made by the arbitrator or either of the parties,

(b) where he is appointed by the President, such amount as may be agreed upon by the arbitrator and the parties or, in default of agreement, fixed by the President,

and shall be recoverable by the arbitrator as a debt due from either of the parties to the arbitration.

Conduct of proceedings and witnesses

7. The parties to the arbitration shall, within thirty-five days from the appointment of the arbitrator, deliver to him a statement of their respective cases with all necessary particulars and—

(a) no amendment or addition to the statement or particulars delivered shall be allowed after the expiry of the said thirty-five days except with the consent of the arbitrator,

(b) a party to the arbitration shall be confined at the hearing to the matters alleged in the statement and particulars delivered by him and any amendment or addition duly made.

8. The parties to the arbitration and all persons claiming through them respectively shall, subject to any legal objection, submit to be examined by the arbitrator, on oath or affirmation, in relation to the matters in dispute and shall, subject to any such objection, produce before the arbitrator all samples and documents within their possession or power respectively which may be required or called for, and do all other things which during the proceedings the arbitrator may require.

9. Witnesses appearing at the arbitration shall, if the arbitrator thinks fit, be examined on oath or affirmation, and the arbitrator shall have power to administer oaths to, or to take the affirmation of, the parties and witnesses appearing.

10. The provisions of county court rules as to the issuing of witness summonses shall, subject to such modifications as may be prescribed by such rules, apply for the purposes of the arbitration as if it were an action or matter in the county court.

11.—(1) Subject to sub-paragraphs (2) and (3) below, any person who—

(a) having been summoned in pursuance of county court rules as a witness in the arbitration refuses or neglects, without sufficient cause, to appear or to produce any documents required by the summons to be produced, or

(b) having been so summoned or being present at the arbitration and being required to give evidence, refuses to be sworn or give evidence,

A2–002

shall forfeit such fine as the judge of the county court may direct.

(2) A judge shall not have power under sub-paragraph (1) above to direct that a person shall forfeit a fine of an amount exceeding £10.

(3) No person summoned in pursuance of county court rules as a witness in the arbitration shall forfeit a fine under this paragraph unless there has been paid or tendered to him at the time of the service of the summons such sum in respect of his expenses (including, in such cases as may be prescribed by county court rules, compensation for loss of time) as may be so prescribed for the purposes of section 55 of the County Courts Act 1984.

(4) The judge of the county court may at his discretion direct that the whole or any part of any such fine, after deducting costs, shall be applicable towards indemnifying the party injured by the refusal or neglect.

12.—(1) Subject to sub-paragraph (2) below, the judge of the county court may, if he thinks fit, upon application on affidavit by either party to the arbitration, issue an order under his hand for bringing up before the arbitrator any person (in this paragraph referred to as a "prisoner") confined in any place under any sentence or under committal for trial or otherwise, to be examined as a witness in the arbitration.

(2) No such order shall be made with respect to a person confined under process in any civil action or matter.

(3) Subject to sub-paragraph (4) below, the prisoner mentioned in any such order shall be brought before the arbitrator under the same custody, and shall be dealt with in the same manner in all respects, as a prisoner required by a writ of habeas corpus to be brought before the High Court and examined there as a witness.

(4) The person having the custody of the prisoner shall not be bound to obey the order unless there is tendered to him a reasonable sum for the conveyance and maintenance of a proper officer or officers and of the prisoner in going to, remaining at, and returning from, the place where the arbitration is held.

13. The High Court may order that a writ of habeas corpus ad testificandum shall issue to bring up a prisoner for examination before the arbitrator, if the prisoner is confined in any prison under process in any civil action or matter.

Award

A2–003 **14.**—(1) Subject to sub-paragraph (2) below, the arbitrator shall make and sign his award within fifty-six days of his appointment.

(2) The President may from time to time enlarge the time limited for making the award, whether that time has expired or not.

15. The arbitrator may if he thinks fit make an interim award for the payment of any sum on account of the sum to be finally awarded.

16. The arbitrator shall—

(a) state separately in the award the amounts awarded in respect of the several claims referred to him, and

(b) on the application of either party, specify the amount awarded in respect of any particular improvement or any particular matter the subject of the award.

17. Where by virtue of this Act compensation under an agreement is to be substituted for compensation under this Act for improvements or for any such matters as are specified in Part II of Schedule 8 to this Act, the arbitrator shall award compensation in accordance with the agreement instead of in accordance with this Act.

18. The award shall fix a day not later than one month after the delivery of the award for the payment of the money awarded as compensation, costs or otherwise.

19. The award shall be final and binding on the parties and the persons claiming under them respectively.

20. The arbitrator shall have power to correct in the award any clerical mistake or error arising from any accidental slip or omission.

Reasons for award

21. [Section 10 of the Tribunals and Inquiries Act 1992] (reasons to be given for decisions of tribunals etc) shall apply in relation to the award of an arbitrator appointed under this Schedule by agreement between the parties as it applies in relation to the award of an arbitrator appointed under this Schedule otherwise than by such agreement.

A2–004

Interest on awards

22. Any sum directed to be paid by the award shall, unless the award otherwise directs, carry interest as from the date of the award and at the [same rate as that specified in section 17 of the Judgments Act 1838 at the date of the award].

A2–005

Costs

23. The costs of, and incidental to, the arbitration and award shall be in the discretion of the arbitrator who may direct to and by whom and in what manner the costs, or any part of the costs, are to be paid.

A2–006

24. On the application of either party, any such costs shall be taxable in the county court according to such of the scales prescribed by county court rules for proceedings in the county court as may be directed by the arbitrator under paragraph 23 above, or, in the absence of any such direction, by the county court.

25.—(1) The arbitrator shall, in awarding costs, take into consideration—

(a) the reasonableness or unreasonableness of the claim of either party, whether in respect of amount or otherwise,

(b) any unreasonable demand for particulars or refusal to supply particulars, and

(c) generally all the circumstances of the case.

(2) The arbitrator may disallow the costs of any witness whom he considers to have been called unnecessarily and any other costs which he considers to have been unnecessarily incurred.

Special case, setting aside award and remission

26. The arbitrator may, at any stage of the proceedings, and shall, upon a direction in that behalf given by the judge of the county court upon an application made by either party, state in the form of a special case for the opinion of the county court any question of law arising in the course of the arbitration and any question as to the jurisdiction of the arbitrator.

A2–007

27.—(1) Where the arbitrator has misconducted himself, the county court may remove him.

(2) Where the arbitrator has misconducted himself, or an arbitration or award has been improperly procured, or there is an error of law on the face of the award, the county court may set the award aside.

28.—(1) The county court may from time to time remit the award, or any part of the award, to the reconsideration of the arbitrator.

(2) In any case where it appears to the county court that there is an error of law on the face of the award, the court may, instead of exercising its power of remission under sub-paragraph (1) above, vary the award by substituting for so much of it as is affected by the error such award as the court considers that it would have been proper for the arbitrator to make in the circumstances; and the award shall thereupon have effect as so varied.

(3) Where remission is ordered under that sub-paragraph, the arbitrator shall, unless the order otherwise directs, make and sign his award within thirty days after the date of the order.

(4) If the county court is satisfied that the time limited for making the said award is for any good reason insufficient, the court may extend or further extend that time for such period as it thinks proper.

Miscellaneous

A2–008 29. Any amount paid, in respect of the remuneration of the arbitrator by either party to the arbitration, in excess of the amount, if any, directed by the award to be paid by him in respect of the costs of the award shall be recoverable from the other party.

30. The provisions of this Schedule relating to the fixing and recovery of the remuneration of an arbitrator and the making and enforcement of an award as to costs, together with any other provision in this Schedule applicable for the purposes of or in connection with those provisions, shall apply where the arbitrator has no jurisdiction to decide the question referred to him as they apply where the arbitrator has jurisdiction to decide that question.

31. For the purposes of this Schedule, an arbitrator appointed by the President shall be taken to have been so appointed at the time when the President executed the instrument of appointment; and in the case of any such arbitrator the periods mentioned in paragraphs 7 and 14 above shall accordingly run from that time.

32. Any instrument of appointment or other document purporting to be made in the exercise of any function exercisable by the President under paragraph 1, 6 or 14 above and to be signed by or on behalf of the President shall be taken to be such an instrument or document unless the contrary is shown.

Agricultural Holdings (Form of Award in Arbitration Proceedings) Order 1990

(SI 1990/1472)

Made	*4th July 1990*
Laid before Parliament	*16th October 1990*
Coming into force	*19th July 1990*

The Lord Chancellor, in exercise of the powers conferred on him by section 84(2) and (3)(c) of, and paragraph 15 of Schedule 13 to, the Agricultural Holdings Act 1986, after consultation with the Council on Tribunals as required by section 10 of the Tribunals and Inquiries Act 1971, hereby makes the following Order:— A3–001

Citation and commencement

1. This Order may be cited as the Agricultural Holdings (Form of Award in Arbitration Proceedings) Order 1990 and shall come into force on 19th July 1990. A3–002

Saving

2. Articles 3 and 4 below shall not apply in relation to an arbitration where the arbitrator was appointed under the Agricultural Holdings Act 1948 before 18th June 1986. A3–003

Form of award

3. An award in proceedings on an arbitration under the Agricultural Holdings Act 1986 shall be made in the form set out in the Schedule to this Order, or in a form to the like effect, with such omissions or modifications as the circumstances may require. A3–004

Revocation

4. The Agricultural Holdings (England and Wales) Rules 1948, the Agricultural Holdings (England and Wales) (Amendment) Rules 1978 and the Agricultural Holdings (England and Wales) Rules (Variation) Order 1985 are hereby revoked. A3–005

Article 3　　　　　　　　THE SCHEDULE

Agricultural Holdings Act 1986 (*Note 1*)

Form of Award

Arbitrator:　　　[name and address]　　　　　　　　　　　　　　　　A3–006
Date of appointment:
Time for making award extended to:
Present landlord:　　　[name and address]
Present tenant:　　　[name and address]
Rent payable prior to arbitration:

Award of the Arbitrator

The claims or questions set out in the Schedule to this award have been referred to arbitration and, having considered the evidence and the submissions of the parties, I, the arbitrator, award as follows: (*Note 2*)

    1. The landlord is to pay to the tenant in respect of the claims set out in Column 1 of Part I of the Schedule the sum(s) set out in Column 2 thereof.

    2. The tenant is to pay to the landlord in respect of the claims set out in Column 1 of Part II of the Schedule the sum(s) set out in Column 2 thereof.

    3. As from   (the next day on which the tenancy could have been brought to an end by notice to quit given at the date of the notice demanding arbitration under section 12 of the Act) the rent previously payable [is [increased] [reduced] to £   ] [continues unchanged at £   ] being the rent properly payable in respect of the holding at the date of the reference to arbitration.

    4. The notice to quite referred to in Part IV of the Schedule shall [not] have effect. [I postpone the termination of the tenancy until   ].

    5. My award in respect of the claims set out in Column 1 of Part V of the Schedule is set out in Column 2 thereof.

    6. The landlord must pay to the tenant the sum(s) awarded by me to the tenant on the   day (*Note 3*) after delivery of this award, and the tenant must pay to the landlord the sum(s) awarded by me to the landlord on the same day.

    7. The costs of and incidental to the arbitration and the award shall be dealt with as follows:

    (a) My costs of the award amounting of £   must be paid by the [landlord] [tenant] [landlord and the tenant in the following proportions]:

    (b) As respects the costs of and incidental to this arbitration [each party must bear his own costs] [the landlord must pay [% of] the costs of the tenant] [the tenant must pay [% of] the costs of the landlord] [to be taxed in the County Court] [according to Scale [   ] as prescribed by the County Court Rules] [[the landlord] [the tenant] must pay £   to the [tenant] [landlord] on account of his costs]:

    (c) All costs ordered by me to be paid shall be paid on the day (*Note 3*) after delivery of this award.

Signed by the arbitrator in the presence of:

(*Note 4*)

Date:

This award was delivered to the [landlord] [tenant] on [date].

PART I

Column 1	Column 2
Claims made by the landlord	Sum(s) awarded

Part II

Column 1	Column 2
Claims made by the tenant	Sum(s) awarded

Part III

Rent

Part IV

Question(s) arising out of a notice to quit

Part V

Column 1	Column 2
Other claims	Award

Appendix

Statement of Reasons for Award (*Note 5*)

Notes for the arbitrator

1. This form must be followed as closely as possible, with only such omissions or modifications as circumstances may require. Paragraphs 1 to 6 inclusive will not all be relevant in every case, and any which are not relevant should be omitted.

2. The arbitrator must state separately in the ward the amounts awarded in respect of the several claims referred to him. If either party applies to him to specify the amount awarded in respect of any particular improvement or any particular matter, he must do so.

3. The day on which payment is to be made must not be later than one month after the delivery of the award. Paragraph 22 of Schedule 11 to the Act provides for interest to be payable on sums directed by the award to be paid.

4. The award must be endorsed with the date of delivery so that there is no doubt as to the date upon which payments are to be made under paragraphs 6 and 8, and upon the date from which interest runs.

5. The arbitrator must furnish a statement of his reasons for the award if the landlord or the tenant so requests "on or before the giving or notification of the decision"—see section 12 of the Tribunals and Inquiries Act 1971. The statement may deal with different matters under different headings as appropriate; for example—

> the facts he found to be admitted or proved;
>
> the submissions of the parties and his rulings on them;
>
> the method of valuation he applied to the facts found so as to arrive at his determination;
>
> the costs of, and incidental to, the arbitration and award.

Civil Procedure Rules, Part 62—Arbitration Claims

Scope of this part and interpretation

A4–001 62.1—(1) This Part contains rules about arbitration claims.
(2) In this Part—

(a) "the 1950 Act" means the Arbitration Act 1950;

(b) "the 1975 Act" means the Arbitration Act 1975;

(c) "the 1979 Act" means the Arbitration Act 1979;

(d) "the 1996 Act" means the Arbitration Act 1996;

(e) references to—

(i) the 1996 Act; or
(ii) any particular section of that Act

include references to that Act or to the particular section of that Act as applied with modifications by the ACAS Arbitration Scheme (England and Wales) Order 2001; and

(f) "arbitration claim form" means a claim form in the form set out in the practice direction.

(3) Part 58 (Commercial Court) applies to arbitration claims in the Commercial Court, Part 59 (Mercantile Court) applies to arbitration claims in the Mercantile Court and Part 60 (Technology and Construction Court claims) applies to arbitration claims in the Technology and Construction Court, except where this Part provides otherwise.

I Claims Under the 1996 Act

Interpretation

A4–002 62.2—(1) In this Section of this Part "arbitration claim" means—

(a) any application to the court under the 1996 Act;

(b) a claim to determine—

(i) whether there is a valid arbitration agreement;
(ii) whether an arbitration tribunal is properly constituted; or

what matters have been submitted to arbitration in accordance with an arbitration agreement;

(c) a claim to declare that an award by an arbitral tribunal is not binding on a party; and

(d) any other application affecting—

(i) arbitration proceedings (whether started or not); or
(ii) an arbitration agreement.

(2) This Section of this Part does not apply to an arbitration claim to which Sections II or III of this Part apply.

Starting the claim

62.3—(1) Except where paragraph (2) applies an arbitration claim must be started by the issue of an arbitration claim form in accordance with the Part 8 procedure.

(2) An application under section 9 of the 1996 Act to stay legal proceedings must be made by application notice to the court dealing with those proceedings.

(3) The courts in which an arbitration claim may be started are set out in the practice direction.

(4) Rule 30.5(3) applies with the modification that a judge of the Technology and Construction Court may transfer the claim to any other court or specialist list.

A4–003

Arbitration claim form

62.4—(1) An arbitration claim form must—

(a) include a concise statement of—

  (i) the remedy claimed; and

  (ii) any questions on which the claimant seeks the decision of the court;

(b) give details of any arbitration award challenged by the claimant, identifying which part or parts of the award are challenged and specifying the grounds for the challenge;

(c) show that any statutory requirements have been met;

(d) specify under which section of the 1996 Act the claim is made;

(e) identify against which (if any) defendants a costs order is sought; and

(f) specify either—

  (i) the persons on whom the arbitration claim form is to be served, stating their role in the arbitration and whether they are defendants; or

  (ii) that the claim is made without notice under section 44(3) of the 1996 Act and the grounds relied on.

A4–004

(2) Unless the court orders otherwise an arbitration claim form must be served on the defendant within 1 month from the date of issue and rules 7.5 and 7.6 are modified accordingly.

(3) Where the claimant applies for an order under section 12 of the 1996 Act (extension of time for beginning arbitral proceedings or other dispute resolution procedures), he may include in his arbitration claim form an alternative application for a declaration that such an order is not needed.

Service out of the jurisdiction

62.5—(1) The court may give permission to serve an arbitration claim form out of the jurisdiction if—

(a) the claimant seeks to—

  (i) challenge; or

  (ii) appeal on a question of law arising out of,

  an arbitration award made within the jurisdiction;

A4–005

(The place where an award is treated as made is determined by section 53 of the 1996 Act.)

    (b) the claim is for an order under section 44 of the 1996 Act; or

    (c) the claimant—

        (i) seeks some other remedy or requires a question to be decided by the court affecting an arbitration (whether started or not), an arbitration agreement or an arbitration award; and

        (ii) the seat of the arbitration is or will be within the jurisdiction or the conditions in section 2(4) of the 1996 Act are satisfied.

(2) An application for permission under paragraph (1) must be supported by written evidence—

    (a) stating the grounds on which the application is made; and

    (b) showing in what place or country the person to be served is, or probably may be found.

(3) Rules 6.24 to 6.29 apply to the service of an arbitration claim form under paragraph (1).

(4) An order giving permission to serve an arbitration claim form out of the jurisdiction must specify the period within which the defendant may file an acknowledgment of service.

Notice

A4–006   62.6—(1) Where an arbitration claim is made under section 24, 28 or 56 of the 1996 Act, each arbitrator must be a defendant.

(2) Where notice must be given to an arbitrator or any other person it may be given by sending him a copy of—

    (a) the arbitration claim form; and

    (b) any written evidence in support.

(3) Where the 1996 Act requires an application to the court to be made on notice to any other party to the arbitration, that notice must be given by making that party a defendant.

Case management

A4–007   62.7—(1) Part 26 and any other rule that requires a party to file an allocation questionnaire does not apply.

(2) Arbitration claims are allocated to the multi-track.

(3) Part 29 does not apply.

(4) The automatic directions set out in the practice direction apply unless the court orders otherwise.

CIVIL PROCEDURE RULES

Stay of legal proceedings

62.8—(1) An application notice seeking a stay of legal proceedings under section 9 of the 1996 Act must be served on all parties to those proceedings who have given an address for service.

(2) A copy of an application notice under paragraph (1) must be served on any other party to the legal proceedings (whether or not he is within the jurisdiction) who has not given an address for service, at—

(a) his last known address; or

(b) a place where it is likely to come to his attention.

(3) Where a question arises as to whether—

(a) an arbitration agreement has been concluded; or

(b) the dispute which is the subject-matter of the proceedings falls within the terms of such an agreement,

the court may decide that question or give directions to enable it to be decided and may order the proceedings to be stayed pending its decision.

Variation of time

62.9—(1) The court may vary the period of 28 days fixed by section 70(3) of the 1996 Act for—

(a) challenging the award under section 67 or 68 of the Act; and

(b) appealing against an award under section 69 of the Act.

(2) An application for an order under paragraph (1) may be made without notice being served on any other party before the period of 28 days expires.

(3) After the period of 28 days has expired—

(a) an application for an order extending time under paragraph (1) must—

(i) be made in the arbitration claim form; and
(ii) state the grounds on which the application is made;

(b) any defendant may file written evidence opposing the extension of time within 7 days after service of the arbitration claim form; and

(c) if the court extends the period of 28 days, each defendant's time for acknowledging service and serving evidence shall start to run as if the arbitration claim form had been served on the date when the court's order is served on that defendant.

Hearings

62.10—(1) The court may order that an arbitration claim be heard either in public or in private.

(2) Rule 39.2 does not apply.

(3) Subject to any order made under paragraph (1)—

(a) the determination of—

(i) a preliminary point of law under section 45 of the 1996 Act; or

(ii) an appeal under section 69 of the 1996 Act on a question of law arising out of an award,

will be heard in public; and

(b) all other arbitration claims will be heard in private.

(4) Paragraph (3)(a) does not apply to—

(a) the preliminary question of whether the court is satisfied of the matters set out in section 45(2)(b); or

(b) an application for permission to appeal under section 69(2)(b).

II OTHER ARBITRATION CLAIMS

Scope of this section

A4–011 62.11—(1) This Section of this Part contains rules about arbitration claims to which the old law applies.

(2) In this Section

(a) "the old law" means the enactments specified in Schedules 3 and 4 of the 1996 Act as they were in force before their amendment or repeal by that Act; and

(b) "arbitration claim" means any application to the court under the old law and includes an appeal (or application for permission to appeal) to the High Court under section 1(2) of the 1979 Act.

(3) This Section does not apply to—

(a) a claim to which Section III of this Part applies; or

(b) a claim on the award.

Applications to judge

A4–012 62.12 A claim—

(a) seeking permission to appeal under section 1(2) of the 1979 Act;

(b) under section 1(5) of that Act (including any claim seeking permission); or

(c) under section 5 of that Act,

must be made in the High Court and will be heard by a judge of the Commercial Court unless any such judge directs otherwise.

Starting the claim

62.13—(1) Except where paragraph (2) applies an arbitration claim must be started by the issue of an arbitration claim form in accordance with the Part 8 procedure.

(2) Where an arbitration claim is to be made in existing proceedings—

    (a) it must be made by way of application notice; and

    (b) any reference in this Section of this Part to an arbitration claim form includes a reference to an application notice.

(3) The arbitration claim form in an arbitration claim under section 1(5) of the 1979 Act (including any claim seeking permission) must be served on—

    (a) the arbitrator or umpire; and

    (b) any other party to the reference.

A4–013

Claims in district registries

62.14 If—

    (a) a claim is to be made under section 12(4) of the 1950 Act for an order for the issue of a witness summons to compel the attendance of the witness before an arbitrator or umpire; and

    (b) the attendance of the witness is required within the district of a District Registry,

the claim may be started in that Registry.

A4–014

Time limits and other special provisions about arbitration claims

62.15—(1) An arbitration claim to

    (a) remit an award under section 22 of the 1950 Act;

    (b) set aside an award under section 23(2) of that Act or otherwise; or

    (c) direct an arbitrator or umpire to state the reasons for an award under section 1(5) of the 1979 Act,

must be made, and the arbitration claim form served, within 21 days after the award has been made and published to the parties.

(2) An arbitration claim to determine any question of law arising in the course of a reference under section 2(1) of the Arbitration Act 1979 must be made, and the arbitration claim form served, within 14 days after—

    (a) the arbitrator or umpire gave his consent in writing to the claim being made; or

    (b) the other parties so consented.

(3) An appeal under section 1(2) of the 1979 Act must be filed, and the arbitration claim form served, within 21 days after the award has been made and published to the parties.

A4–015

(4) Where reasons material to an appeal under section 1(2) of the 1979 Act are given on a date subsequent to the publication of the award, the period of 21 days referred to in paragraph (3) will run from the date on which reasons are given.

(5) In every arbitration claim to which this rule applies—

(a) the arbitration claim form must state the grounds of the claim or appeal;

(b) where the claim or appeal is based on written evidence, a copy of that evidence must be served with the arbitration claim form; and

(c) where the claim or appeal is made with the consent of the arbitrator, the umpire or the other parties, a copy of every written consent must be served with the arbitration claim form.

(6) In an appeal under section 1(2) of the 1979 Act—

(a) a statement of the grounds for the appeal specifying the relevant parts of the award and reasons; and

(b) where permission is required, any written evidence in support of the contention that the question of law concerns—

(i) a term of a contract; or
(ii) an event,

which is not a "one-off" term or event,

must be filed and served with the arbitration claim form.

(7) Any written evidence in reply to written evidence under paragraph (6)(b) must be filed and served on the claimant not less than 2 days before the hearing.

(8) A party to a claim seeking permission to appeal under section 1(2) of the 1979 Act who wishes to contend that the award should be upheld for reasons not expressed or fully expressed in the award and reasons must file and serve on the claimant, a notice specifying the grounds of his contention not less than 2 days before the hearing.

Service out of the jurisdiction

A4–016 62.16—(1) Subject to paragraph (2)—

(a) any arbitration claim form in an arbitration claim under the 1950 Act or the 1979 Act; or

(b) any order made in such a claim,

may be served out of the jurisdiction with the permission of the court if the arbitration to which the claim relates—

(i) is governed by the law of England and Wales; or

(ii) has been, is being, or will be, held within the jurisdiction.

(2) An arbitration claim form seeking permission to enforce an award may be served out of the jurisdiction with the permission of the court whether or not the arbitration is governed by the law of England and Wales.

(3) An application for permission to serve an arbitration claim form out of the jurisdiction must be supported by written evidence—

(a) stating the grounds on which the application is made; and

(b) showing in what place or country the person to be served is, or probably may be found.

Rules 6.24 to 6.29 apply to the service of an arbitration claim form under paragraph (1).

(5) An order giving permission to serve an arbitration claim form out of the jurisdiction must specify the period within which the defendant may file an acknowledgment of service.

III ENFORCEMENT

Scope of this section

62.17—This Section of this Part applies to all arbitration enforcement proceedings other than by a claim on the award.

A4–017

Enforcement of awards

62.18—(1) An application for permission under—

A4–018

(a) section 66 of the 1996 Act;

(b) section 101 of the 1996 Act;

(c) section 26 of the 1950 Act; or

(d) section 3(1)(a) of the 1975 Act,

to enforce an award in the same manner as a judgment or order may be made without notice in an arbitration claim form.

(2) The court may specify parties to the arbitration on whom the arbitration claim form must be served.

(3) The parties on whom the arbitration claim form is served must acknowledge service and the enforcement proceedings will continue as if they were an arbitration claim under Section I of this Part.

(4) With the permission of the court the arbitration claim form may be served out of the jurisdiction irrespective of where the award is, or is treated as, made.

(5) Where the applicant applies to enforce an agreed award within the meaning of section 51(2) of the 1996 Act—

(a) the arbitration claim form must state that the award is an agreed award; and

(b) any order made by the court must also contain such a statement.

(6) An application for permission must be supported by written evidence—

(a) exhibiting—

(i) where the application is made under section 66 of the 1996 Act or under

section 26 of the 1950 Act, the arbitration agreement and the original award (or copies);
  (ii) where the application is under section 101 of the 1996 Act, the documents required to be produced by section 102 of that Act; or
  (iii) where the application is under section 3(1)(a) of the 1975 Act, the documents required to be produced by section 4 of that Act;

(b) stating the name and the usual or last known place of residence or business of the claimant and of the person against whom it is sought to enforce the award; and

(c) stating either—

  (i) that the award has not been complied with; or
  (ii) the extent to which it has not been complied with at the date of the application.

(7) An order giving permission must—

(a) be drawn up by the claimant; and

(b) be served on the defendant by—

  (i) delivering a copy to him personally; or
  (ii) sending a copy to him at his usual or last known place of residence or business.

(8) An order giving permission may be served out of the jurisdiction—

(a) without permission; and

(b) in accordance with rules 6.24 to 6.29 as if the order were an arbitration claim form.

(9) Within 14 days after service of the order or, if the order is to be served out of the jurisdiction, within such other period as the court may set—

(a) the defendant may apply to set aside the order; and

(b) the award must not be enforced until after—

  (i) the end of that period; or
  (ii) any application made by the defendant within that period has been finally disposed of.

(10) The order must contain a statement of—

(a) the right to make an application to set the order aside; and

(b) the restrictions on enforcement under rule 62.18(9)(b).

(11) Where a body corporate is a party any reference in this rule to place of residence or business shall have effect as if the reference were to the registered or principal address of the body corporate.

Interest on awards

62.19—(1) Where an applicant seeks to enforce an award of interest the whole or any part of which relates to a period after the date of the award, he must file a statement giving the following particulars—

    (a) whether simple or compound interest was awarded;

    (b) the date from which interest was awarded;

    (c) where rests were provided for, specifying them;

    (d) the rate of interest awarded; and

    (e) a calculation showing—

        (i) the total amount claimed up to the date of the statement; and
        (ii) any sum which will become due on a daily basis.

(2) A statement under paragraph (1) must be filed whenever the amount of interest has to be quantified for the purpose of—

    (a) obtaining a judgment or order under section 66 of the 1996 Act (enforcement of the award); or

    (b) enforcing such a judgment or order.

Registration in High Court of foreign awards

62.20—(1) Where—

    (a) an award is made in proceedings on an arbitration in any part of a United Kingdom Overseas Territory (within the meaning of rule 6.18(f)) or other territory to which Part I of the Foreign Judgments (Reciprocal Enforcement) Act 1933 ("the 1933 Act") extends;

    (b) Part II of the Administration of Justice Act 1920 extended to that part immediately before Part I of the 1933 Act was extended to that part; and

    (c) an award has, under the law in force in the place where it was made, become enforceable in the same manner as a judgment given by a court in that place,

RSC Order 71, Part I applies in relation to the award as it applies in relation to a judgment given by the court subject to the modifications in paragraph (2).

(2) The modifications referred to in paragraph (1) are as follows—

    (a) for references to the country of the original court are substituted references to the place where the award was made; and

    (b) the written evidence required by RSC Order 71, rule 3 must state (in addition to the matters required by that rule) that to the best of the information or belief of the maker of the statement the award has, under the law in force in the place where it was made, become enforceable in the same manner as a judgment given by a court in that place.

Registration of awards under the Arbitration (International Investment Disputes) Act 1966

A4–021   62.21—(1) In this rule—

(a) "the 1966 Act" means the Arbitration (International Investment Disputes) Act 1966;

(b) "award" means an award under the Convention;

(c) "the Convention" means the Convention on the settlement of investment disputes between States and nationals of other States which was opened for signature in Washington on 18th March 1965;

(d) "judgment creditor" means the person seeking recognition or enforcement of an award; and

(e) "judgment debtor" means the other party to the award.

(2) Subject to the provisions of this rule, the following provisions of RSC Order 71 apply with such modifications as may be necessary in relation to an award as they apply in relation to a judgment to which Part II of the Foreign Judgments (Reciprocal Enforcement) Act 1933 applies—

(a) rule 1;

(b) rule 3(1) (except sub-paragraphs (c)(iv) and (d));

(c) rule 7 (except paragraph (3)(c) and (d)); and

(d) rule 10(3).

(3) An application to have an award registered in the High Court under section 1 of the 1966 Act must be made in accordance with the Part 8 procedure.

(4) The written evidence required by RSC Order 71, rule 3 in support of an application for registration must—

(a) exhibit the award certified under the Convention instead of the judgment (or a copy of it); and

(b) in addition to stating the matters referred to in rule 3(1)(c)(i) and (ii), state whether—

(i) at the date of the application the enforcement of the award has been stayed (provisionally or otherwise) under the Convention; and

(ii) any, and if so what, application has been made under the Convention, which, if granted, might result in a stay of the enforcement of the award.

(5) Where, on granting permission to register an award or an application made by the judgment debtor after an award has been registered, the court considers—

(a) that the enforcement of the award has been stayed (whether provisionally or otherwise) under the Convention; or

(b) that an application has been made under the Convention which, if granted, might result in a stay of the enforcement of the award,

the court may stay the enforcement of the award for such time as it considers appropriate.

Civil Procedure Rules, Practice Direction—Arbitration

This Practice Direction Supplements Part 62

SECTION I

A5–001 1.1 This Section of this Practice Direction applies to arbitration claims to which Section I of Part 62 applies.
1.2 In this Section "the 1996 Act" means the Arbitration Act 1996.
1.3 Where a rule provides for a document to be sent, it may be sent—

(1) by first class post;

(2) through a document exchange; or

(3) by fax, electronic mail or other means of electronic communication.

62.3—Starting the claim

A5–002 2.1 An arbitration claim under the 1996 Act (other than under section 9) must be started in accordance with the High Court and County Courts (Allocation of Arbitration Proceedings) Order 1996 by the issue of an arbitration claim form.
2.2 An arbitration claim form must be substantially in the form set out in Appendix A to this practice direction.
2.3 Subject to paragraph 2.1, an arbitration claim form may be issued at the courts set out in column 1 of the table below and will be entered in the list set out against that court in column 2.

Court	List
Admiralty and Commercial Registry at the Royal Courts of Justice, London	Commercial list
Technology and Construction Court Registry, St. Dunstan's House, London	TCC list
District Registry of the High Court (where mercantile court established)	Mercantile list
District Registry of the High Court (where arbitration claim form marked "Technology and Construction Court" in top right hand corner)	TCC list
Central London County Court	Mercantile list

62.4—Arbitration claim form

Service

A5–003 3.1 The court may exercise its powers under rule 6.8 to permit service of an arbitration claim form at the address of a party's solicitor or representative acting for him in the arbitration.
3.2 Where the arbitration claim form is served by the claimant he must file a certificate of service within 7 days of service of the arbitration claim form. (Rule 6.10 specifies what a certificate of service must show).

Civil Procedure Rules

Acknowledgment of service or making representations by arbitrator or ACAS

4.1 Where— A5–004

(1) an arbitrator; or

(2) ACAS (in a claim under the 1996 Act as applied with modifications by the ACAS Arbitration Scheme (England and Wales) Order 2001)

is sent a copy of an arbitration claim form (including an arbitration claim form sent under rule 62.6(2)), that arbitrator or ACAS (as the case may be) may—

(a) apply to be made a defendant; or

(b) make representations to the court under paragraph 4.3.

4.2 An application under paragraph 4.1(2)(a) to be made a defendant—

(1) must be served on the claimant; but

(2) need not be served on any other party.

4.3 An arbitrator or ACAS may make representations by filing written evidence or in writing to the court.

Supply of documents from court records

5.1 An arbitration claim form may only be inspected with the permission of the court. A5–005

62.7—Case management

6.1 The following directions apply unless the court orders otherwise. A5–006

6.2 A defendant who wishes to rely on evidence before the court must file and serve his written evidence—

(1) within 21 days after the date by which he was required to acknowledge service; or,

(2) where a defendant is not required to file an acknowledgement of service, within 21 days after service of the arbitration claim form.

6.3 A claimant who wishes to rely on evidence in reply to written evidence filed under paragraph 6.2 must file and serve his written evidence within 7 days after service of the defendant's evidence.

6.4 Agreed indexed and paginated bundles of all the evidence and other documents to be used at the hearing must be prepared by the claimant.

6.5 Not later than 5 days before the hearing date estimates for the length of the hearing must be filed together with a complete set of the documents to be used.

6.6 Not later than 2 days before the hearing date the claimant must file and serve—

(1) a chronology of the relevant events cross-referenced to the bundle of documents;

(2) (where necessary) a list of the persons involved; and

(3) a skeleton argument which lists succinctly—

   (a) the issues which arise for decision;
   (b) the grounds of relief (or opposing relief) to be relied upon;
   (c) the submissions of fact to be made with the references to the evidence; and
   (d) the submissions of law with references to the relevant authorities.

6.7 Not later than the day before the hearing date the defendant must file and serve a skeleton argument which lists succinctly—

(1) the issues which arise for decision;

(2) the grounds of relief (or opposing relief) to be relied upon;

(3) the submissions of fact to be made with the references to the evidence; and

(4) the submissions of law with references to the relevant authorities.

Securing the attendance of witnesses

A5–007 7.1 A party to arbitral proceedings being conducted in England or Wales who wishes to rely on section 43 of the 1996 Act to secure the attendance of a witness must apply for a witness summons in accordance with Part 34.

7.2 If the attendance of the witness is required within the district of a district registry, the application may be made at that registry.

7.3 A witness summons will not be issued until the applicant files written evidence showing that the application is made with—

(1) the permission of the tribunal; or

(2) the agreement of the other parties.

Interim remedies

A5–008 8.1 An application for an interim remedy under section 44 of the 1996 Act must be made in an arbitration claim form.

Applications under sections 32 and 45 of the 1996 Act

A5–009 9.1 This paragraph applies to arbitration claims for the determination of—

(1) a question as to the substantive jurisdiction of the arbitral tribunal under section 32 of the 1996 Act; and

(2) a preliminary point of law under section 45 of the 1996 Act.

9.2 Where an arbitration claim is made without the agreement in writing of all the other parties to the arbitral proceedings but with the permission of the arbitral tribunal, the written evidence or witness statements filed by the parties must set out any evidence relied on by the parties in support of their contention that the court should, or should not, consider the claim.

9.3 As soon as practicable after the written evidence is filed, the court will decide whether or not it should consider the claim and, unless the court otherwise directs, will so decide without a hearing.

Decisions without a hearing

10.1 Having regard to the overriding objective the court may decide particular issues without a hearing. For example, as set out in paragraph 9.3, the question whether the court is satisfied as to the matters set out in section 32(2)(b) or section 45(2)(b) of the 1996 Act.

10.2 The court will generally decide whether to extend the time limit under section 70(3) of the 1996 Act without a hearing. Where the court makes an order extending the time limit, the defendant must file his written evidence within 21 days from service of the order.

A5–010

62.9—Variation of time

11.1 An application for an order under rule 62.9(1)—

A5–011

(1) before the period of 28 days has expired, must be made in a Part 23 application notice; and

(2) after the period of 28 days has expired, must be set out in a separately identified part in the arbitration claim form.

Applications for permission to appeal

12.1 Where a party seeks permission to appeal to the court on a question of law arising out of an arbitration award, the arbitration claim form must—

A5–012

(1) identify the question of law; and

(2) state the grounds

on which the party alleges that permission should be given.

12.2 The written evidence in support of the application must set out any evidence relied on by the party for the purpose of satisfying the court—

(1) of the matters referred to in section 69(3) of the 1996 Act; and

(2) that permission should be given.

12.3 The written evidence filed by the respondent to the application must—

(1) state the grounds on which the respondent opposes the grant of permission;

(2) set out any evidence relied on by him relating to the matters mentioned in section 69(3) of the 1996 Act; and

(3) specify whether the respondent wishes to contend that the award should be upheld for reasons not expressed (or not fully expressed) in the award and, if so, state those reasons.

SECTION II

13.1 This Section of this Practice Direction applies to arbitration claims to which Section II of Part 62 applies.

A5–013

62.13—Starting the claim

A5–014 14.1 An arbitration claim must be started in the Commercial Court and, where required to be heard by a judge, be heard by a judge of that court unless he otherwise directs.

Section III

A5–015 15.1 This Section of this Practice Direction applies to enforcement proceedings to which Section III of Part 62 applies.

62.21—Registration of awards under the Arbitration (International Investment Disputes) Act 1966

A5–016 16.1 Awards ordered to be registered under the 1966 Act and particulars will be entered in the Register kept for that purpose at the Admiralty and Commercial Registry.

CIVIL PROCEDURE RULES

A5–017

Claim Form (arbitration)

In the

Claim No.

Issue date

for court use only

In an arbitration claim between

Claimant

SEAL

Defendant(s)

In the matter of an [intended] arbitration between

Claimant

Respondent(s) *Set out the names and addresses of persons to be served with the claim form stating their role in the arbitration and whether they are defendants.*

Defendant's name and address

☐ This claim will be heard on:

at   am/pm

☐ This claim is made without notice.

The court office at

When corresponding with the court, please address forms or letters to the Court Manager and quote the case number.

N8 Claim form (arbitration)

Statutory Materials and Rules of Court

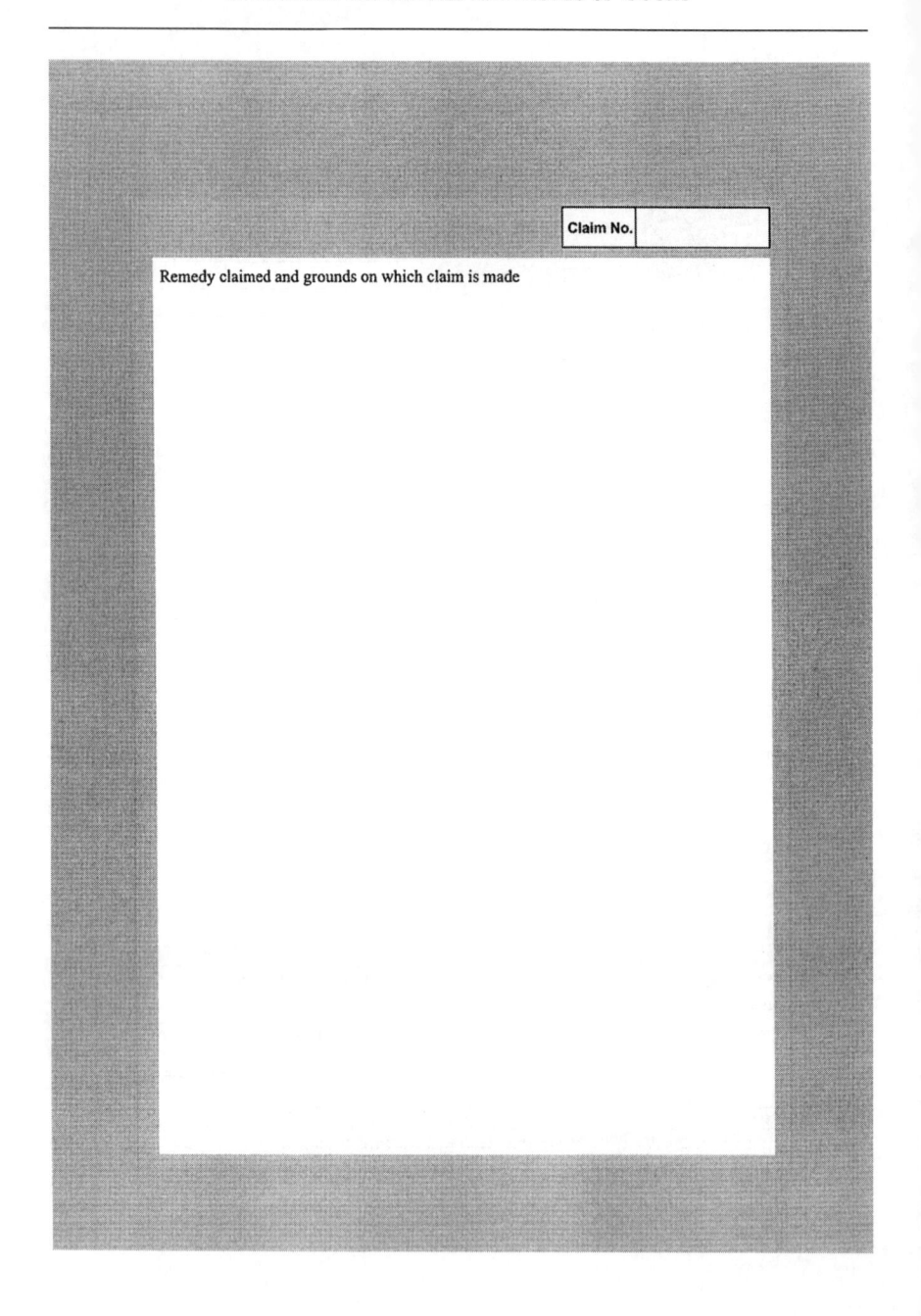

| Claim No. | |

Remedy claimed and grounds on which claim is made

	Claim No.	

The claimant seeks an order for costs against

Statement of Truth
*(I believe)(The Claimant believes) that the facts stated in these particulars of claim are true.
* I am duly authorised by the claimant to sign this statement

Full name _____

Name of claimant's solicitor's firm _____

signed_____ position or office held _____
        *(Claimant)(Claimant's solicitor)   (if signing on behalf of firm or company)
*delete as appropriate

Claimant's or claimant's solicitor's address to which documents should be sent if different from overleaf. If you are prepared to accept service by DX, fax or e-mail, please add details.

STATUTORY MATERIALS AND RULES OF COURT

Arbitration Claim - notes for the claimant
Please read these guidance notes before you begin completing the claim form

The arbitration claim form may be used to start proceedings and make an application in existing proceedings. Where an application is being made in existing proceedings, an acknowledgment of service form is not required and the references to an acknowledgment of service form in the Notes for the Defendant should be deleted.

With the exception of:
- applications under section 9 of the Arbitration Act 1996; and
- certain proceedings which may be started only in the High Court or only in a county court - see High Court and County Courts (Allocation of Arbitration Proceedings) Order 1996, arbitration proceedings may be started in the courts set out in the table opposite.

Court	List
Admiralty and Commercial Registry at the Royal Courts of Justice, London	Commercial
Technology and Construction Court Registry, St Dunstan's House, London	TCC
District Registry of the High Court *(where Mercantile court established)*	Mercantile
District Registry of the High Court *(where the Claim form marked 'Technology and Construction Court' in top right hand corner)*	TCC
Central London County Court	Mercantile

Heading
You must fill in the heading of the claim form with:
- the name of the court (High Court or county court); and
- if issued in a District Registry, the name of the District Registry

Claimant and defendant details
You must provide your full name and address and the full names and addresses of the defendants to be served. If a defendant is to be served outside England and Wales, the court's permission may need to be sought *(see Rule 62.5)*.

Remedy claimed and grounds on which claim is made
You must:
- include a concise statement of - the remedy claimed; and - any questions on which you seek the decision of the court;
- give details of any arbitration award which you challenge, identifying which part or parts of the award are challenged and the grounds for the challenge;
- show that any statutory requirements have been met;

- specify under which section of the Act the claim is made;

Respondents
- if on notice, give the names and addresses of the persons on whom the arbitration claim form is to be served, stating their role in the arbitration and whether they are defendants; or
- state that the claim is made without notice under section 44(3) of the 1966 Act, and the grounds relied on.

Acknowledgment of service form
An acknowledgment of service form N15 must accompany the arbitration claim form. You should complete the heading on this form. Where the claim form is to be served out of the jurisdiction, you must amend the Notes for the Defendant to give the time within which the defendant must acknowledge service and file evidence. The claim form is valid for one month beginning with the date of its issue or, where required to be served out of the jurisdiction, for such period as the court may fix.

Address for documents
You must provide an address for service within England and Wales to which documents should be sent. That address must be either the business address of your solicitor, or your residential or business address.

Statement of Truth
The statement of truth must be signed by you or by your solicitor. Where the statement of truth is not signed by the solicitor and the claimant is a registered company or corporation, the statement of truth must be signed by either a director, the treasurer, secretary, chief executive, manager or other officer of the company and (in the case of a corporation) the mayor, chairman, president or town clerk.

You may rely on the matters set out in the claim form as evidence only if the claim form is verified by a statement of truth. You may also file an affidavit or witness statement in support of the arbitration claim, which must be served with the claim form.

N8A Arbitration claim - notes for claimant (03.02)

Civil Procedure Rules

Arbitration Claim - notes for the defendant

Please read these guidance notes carefully before you respond to the arbitration claim form

Court staff can help you with procedures but they cannot give legal advice. If you need legal advice, you should contact a solicitor or a Citizens Advice Bureau immediately.

Responding to the claim

If you are:
- named as a defendant in the claim form; and
- served with a copy of it,

you should respond by completing and returning to the court office the acknowledgment of service form which was enclosed with the claim form, within *(14 days) (   ) of the date it was served on you. At the same time you must serve a copy on the claimant and any other party shown on the claim form.

If the claim form was:
- sent by post, the *(14 days) (   ) starts 2 days from the date of the postmark on the envelope;
- delivered or left at your address, the *(14 days) (   ) starts on the day it was given to you;
- handed to you personally, the *(14 days) (   ) starts on the day it was given to you.

The acknowledgment of service

If you:
- fail to complete and file the acknowledgment of service within the time specified; or
- if you indicate that you do not intend to contest the claim,

If you later change your mind, you will not be entitled to contest the claim without the court's permission.

Evidence

If you wish to rely on evidence before the court, you must file and serve your written evidence within *(21 days) (   ) of the date the claim form was served on you.

Statement of truth

The acknowledgment of service must be signed by you or by your solicitor. Where the acknowledgment of service is not signed by your solicitor and you are a registered company or corporation, it must be signed by either a director, the treasurer, secretary, chief executive, manager or other officer of the company and (in the case of a corporation) the mayor, Chairman, president or town clerk.

Notes for arbitrators

If you are:
- an arbitrator; or
- ACAS (in a claim under the 1996 Act as applied with modification by the ACAS (England and Wales) Order 2001),

who has been named as a defendant in the claim form, the above notes apply to you as they do to any other defendant.

If you were, or are:
- an arbitrator in the arbitration which led to this claim; and
- if you are not named as a defendant;

this claim form is sent to you for information

You may either:
- make a request (with notice only to the claimant) to be made a defendant
- may make representations to the court *(see paragraph 4.3 of practice direction to Part 62)*

Claimant should alter where appropriate if the claim form is to be served out of the jurisdiction (see CPR Part 6)

N8B Arbitration claim - notes for defendant (03.02)

49

STATUTORY MATERIALS AND RULES OF COURT

A5–018

Acknowledgment of Service
(arbitration claim)

In the	
Claim No.	
Claimant (including ref)	
Defendant	

You should read the 'notes for defendant' attached to the claim form which will tell you how to complete this form, and when and where to send it.

Tick and complete sections A - D as appropriate.
In all cases you must complete sections E and F

Section A

☐ I do **not** intend to contest this claim

Section B

☐ I intend to contest this claim

Give brief details of any different remedy you are seeking.

Section C

☐ I intend to dispute the court's jurisdiction
(Please note, any application must be filed within 14 days of the date on which you file this acknowledgment of service)

The court office at

When corresponding with the court, please address forms or letters to the Court Manager and quote the claim number.
N15 Acknowledgment of Service (arbitration) (03.02)

CIVIL PROCEDURE RULES

Claim No. [   ]

Section D

☐ I intend to rely on written evidence

My written evidence:
☐ is filed with this form
☐ will be filed and served within 21 days after the date by which I am required to file this acknowledgment of service.

Section E

Full name of defendant filing this acknowledgment

Section F

Signed
(To be signed by you or by your solicitor)

*(I believe)(The defendant believes) that the facts stated in this form are true. *I am duly authorised by the defendant to sign this statement

*delete as appropriate

Position or office held
(if signing on behalf of firm or company)

Date

Give an address in England or Wales to which notices about this case can be sent to you

Postcode

Tel. no.

	if applicable
Ref. no.	
fax. no.	
DX no.	
e-mail	

51

Arbitration Act 1996

(1996 c.23)

A6–001　An Act to restate and improve the law relating to arbitration pursuant to an arbitration agreement; to make other provision relating to arbitration and arbitration awards; and for connected purposes.

[17TH JUNE 1996]

PART I

ARBITRATION PURSUANT TO AN ARBITRATION AGREEMENT

Introductory

General principles

A6–002　1. The provisions of this Part are founded on the following principles, and shall be construed accordingly—

> (a) the object of arbitration is to obtain the fair resolution of disputes by an impartial tribunal without unnecessary delay or expense;
>
> (b) the parties should be free to agree how their disputes are resolved, subject only to such safeguards as are necessary in the public interest;
>
> (c) in matters governed by this Part the court should not intervene except as provided by this Part.

Scope of application of provisions

A6–003　2.—(1) The provisions of this Part apply where the seat of the arbitration is in England and Wales or Northern Ireland.

(2) The following sections apply even if the seat of the arbitration is outside England and Wales or Northern Ireland or no seat has been designated or determined—

> (a) sections 9 to 11 (stay of legal proceedings, &c.), and
>
> (b) section 66 (enforcement of arbitral awards).

(3) The powers conferred by the following sections apply even if the seat of the arbitration is outside England and Wales or Northern Ireland or no seat has been designated or determined—

> (a) section 43 (securing the attendance of witnesses), and
>
> (b) section 44 (court powers exercisable in support of arbitral proceedings);

but the court may refuse to exercise any such power if, in the opinion of the court, the fact that the seat of the arbitration is outside England and Wales or Northern Ireland, or that when designated or determined the seat is likely to be outside England and Wales or Northern Ireland, makes it inappropriate to do so.

(4) The court may exercise a power conferred by any provision of this Part not mentioned in subsection (2) or (3) for the purpose of supporting the arbitral process where—

   (a) no seat of the arbitration has been designated or determined, and

   (b) by reason of a connection with England and Wales or Northern Ireland the court is satisfied that it is appropriate to do so.

(5) Section 7 (separability of arbitration agreement) and section 8 (death of a party) apply where the law applicable to the arbitration agreement is the law of England and Wales or Northern Ireland even if the seat of the arbitration is outside England and Wales or Northern Ireland or has not been designated or determined.

The seat of the arbitration

3. In this Part "the seat of the arbitration" means the juridical seat of the arbitration designated— A6–004

   (a) by the parties to the arbitration agreement, or

   (b) by any arbitral or other institution or person vested by the parties with powers in that regard, or

   (c) by the arbitral tribunal if so authorised by the parties,

or determined, in the absence of any such designation, having regard to the parties' agreement and all the relevant circumstances.

Mandatory and non-mandatory provisions

4.—(1) The mandatory provisions of this Part are listed in Schedule 1 and have effect notwithstanding any agreement to the contrary. A6–005
(2) The other provisions of this Part (the "non-mandatory provisions") allow the parties to make their own arrangements by agreement but provide rules which apply in the absence of such agreement.
(3) The parties may make such arrangements by agreeing to the application of institutional rules or providing any other means by which a matter may be decided.
(4) It is immaterial whether or not the law applicable to the parties' agreement is the law of England and Wales or, as the case may be, Northern Ireland.
(5) The choice of a law other than the law of England and Wales or Northern Ireland as the applicable law in respect of a matter provided for by a non-mandatory provision of this Part is equivalent to an agreement making provision about that matter.
(6) For this purpose an applicable law determined in accordance with the parties' agreement, or which is objectively determined in the absence of any express or implied choice, shall be treated as chosen by the parties.

Agreements to be in writing

A6–006   5.—(1) The provisions of this Part apply only where the arbitration agreement is in writing, and any other agreement between the parties as to any matter is effective for the purposes of this Part only if in writing.
The expressions "agreement", "agree" and "agreed" shall be construed accordingly.
(2) There is an agreement in writing—

(a) if the agreement is made in writing (whether or not it is signed by the parties),

(b) if the agreement is made by exchange of communications in writing, or

(c) if the agreement is evidenced in writing.

(3) Where parties agree otherwise than in writing by reference to terms which are in writing, they make an agreement in writing.
(4) An agreement is evidenced in writing if an agreement made otherwise than in writing is recorded by one of the parties, or by a third party, with the authority of the parties to the agreement.
(5) An exchange of written submissions in arbitral or legal proceedings in which the existence of an agreement otherwise than in writing is alleged by one party against another party and not denied by the other party in his response constitutes as between those parties an agreement in writing to the effect alleged.
(6) References in this Part to anything being written or in writing include its being recorded by any means.

The arbitration agreement

Definition of arbitration agreement

A6–007   6.—(1) In this Part an "arbitration agreement" means an agreement to submit to arbitration present or future disputes (whether they are contractual or not).
(2) The reference in an agreement to a written form of arbitration clause or to a document containing an arbitration clause constitutes an arbitration agreement if the reference is such as to make that clause part of the agreement.

Separability of arbitration agreement

A6–008   7. Unless otherwise agreed by the parties, an arbitration agreement which forms or was intended to form part of another agreement (whether or not in writing) shall not be regarded as invalid, non-existent or ineffective because that other agreement is invalid, or did not come into existence or has become ineffective, and it shall for that purpose be treated as a distinct agreement.

Whether agreement discharged by death of a party

A6–009   8.—(1) Unless otherwise agreed by the parties, an arbitration agreement is not discharged by the death of a party and may be enforced by or against the personal representatives of that party.
(2) Subsection (1) does not affect the operation of any enactment or rule of law by virtue of which a substantive right or obligation is extinguished by death.

Arbitration Act 1996

Stay of legal proceedings

Stay of legal proceedings

9.—(1) A party to an arbitration agreement against whom legal proceedings are brought (whether by way of claim or counterclaim) in respect of a matter which under the agreement is to be referred to arbitration may (upon notice to the other parties to the proceedings) apply to the court in which the proceedings have been brought to stay the proceedings so far as they concern that matter.   **A6–010**

(2) An application may be made notwithstanding that the matter is to be referred to arbitration only after the exhaustion of other dispute resolution procedures.

(3) An application may not be made by a person before taking the appropriate procedural step (if any) to acknowledge the legal proceedings against him or after he has taken any step in those proceedings to answer the substantive claim.

(4) On an application under this section the court shall grant a stay unless satisfied that the arbitration agreement is null and void, inoperative, or incapable of being performed.

(5) If the court refuses to stay the legal proceedings, any provision that an award is a condition precedent to the bringing of legal proceedings in respect of any matter is of no effect in relation to those proceedings.

Reference of interpleader issue to arbitration

10.—(1) Where in legal proceedings relief by way of interpleader is granted and any issue between the claimants is one in respect of which there is an arbitration agreement between them, the court granting the relief shall direct that the issue be determined in accordance with the agreement unless the circumstances are such that proceedings brought by a claimant in respect of the matter would not be stayed.   **A6–011**

(2) Where subsection (1) applies but the court does not direct that the issue be determined in accordance with the arbitration agreement, any provision that an award is a condition precedent to the bringing of legal proceedings in respect of any matter shall not affect the determination of that issue by the court.

Retention of security where Admiralty proceedings stayed

11.—(1) Where Admiralty proceedings are stayed on the ground that the dispute in question should be submitted to arbitration, the court granting the stay may, if in those proceedings property has been arrested or bail or other security has been given to prevent or obtain release from arrest—   **A6–012**

(a) order that the property arrested be retained as security for the satisfaction of any award given in the arbitration in respect of that dispute, or

(b) order that the stay of those proceedings be conditional on the provision of equivalent security for the satisfaction of any such award.

(2) Subject to any provision made by rules of court and to any necessary modifications, the same law and practice shall apply in relation to property retained in pursuance of an order as would apply if it were held for the purposes of proceedings in the court making the order.

Commencement of arbitral proceedings

Power of court to extend time for beginning arbitral proceedings, etc.

A6–013

12.—(1) Where an arbitration agreement to refer future disputes to arbitration provides that a claim shall be barred, or the claimant's right extinguished, unless the claimant takes within a time fixed by the agreement some step—

(a) to begin arbitral proceedings, or

(b) to begin other dispute resolution procedures which must be exhausted before arbitral proceedings can be begun,

the court may by order extend the time for taking that step.

(2) Any party to the arbitration agreement may apply for such an order (upon notice to the other parties), but only after a claim has arisen and after exhausting any available arbitral process for obtaining an extension of time.

(3) The court shall make an order only if satisfied—

(a) that the circumstances are such as were outside the reasonable contemplation of the parties when they agreed the provision in question, and that it would be just to extend the time, or

(b) that the conduct of one party makes it unjust to hold the other party to the strict terms of the provision in question.

(4) The court may extend the time for such period and on such terms as it thinks fit, and may do so whether or not the time previously fixed (by agreement or by a previous order) has expired.

(5) An order under this section does not affect the operation of the Limitation Acts (see section 13).

(6) The leave of the court is required for any appeal from a decision of the court under this section.

Application of Limitation Acts

A6–014

13.—(1) The Limitation Acts apply to arbitral proceedings as they apply to legal proceedings.

(2) The court may order that in computing the time prescribed by the Limitation Acts for the commencement of proceedings (including arbitral proceedings) in respect of a dispute which was the subject matter—

(a) of an award which the court orders to be set aside or declares to be of no effect, or

(b) of the affected part of an award which the court orders to be set aside in part, or declares to be in part of no effect,

the period between the commencement of the arbitration and the date of the order referred to in paragraph (a) or (b) shall be excluded.

(3) In determining for the purposes of the Limitation Acts when a cause of action accrued, any provision that an award is a condition precedent to the bringing of legal

proceedings in respect of a matter to which an arbitration agreement applies shall be disregarded.

(4) In this Part "the Limitation Acts" means—

(a) in England and Wales, the Limitation Act 1980, the Foreign Limitation Periods Act 1984 and any other enactment (whenever passed) relating to the limitation of actions;

(b) in Northern Ireland, the Limitation (Northern Ireland) Order 1989, the Foreign Limitation Periods (Northern Ireland) Order 1985 and any other enactment (whenever passed) relating to the limitation of actions.

Commencement of arbitral proceeding

14.—(1) The parties are free to agree when arbitral proceedings are to be regarded as commenced for the purposes of this Part and for the purposes of the Limitation Acts. **A6–015**

(2) If there is no such agreement the following provisions apply.

(3) Where the arbitrator is named or designated in the arbitration agreement, arbitral proceedings are commenced in respect of a matter when one party serves on the other party or parties a notice in writing requiring him or them to submit that matter to the person so named or designated.

(4) Where the arbitrator or arbitrators are to be appointed by the parties, arbitral proceedings are commenced in respect of a matter when one party serves on the other party or parties notice in writing requiring him or them to appoint an arbitrator or to agree to the appointment of an arbitrator in respect of that matter.

(5) Where the arbitrator or arbitrators are to be appointed by a person other than a party to the proceedings, arbitral proceedings are commenced in respect of a matter when one party gives notice in writing to that person requesting him to make the appointment in respect of that matter.

The arbitral tribunal

The arbitral tribunal

15.—(1) The parties are free to agree on the number of arbitrators to form the tribunal and whether there is to be a chairman or umpire. **A6–016**

(2) Unless otherwise agreed by the parties, an agreement that the number of arbitrators shall be two or any other even number shall be understood as requiring the appointment of an additional arbitrator as chairman of the tribunal.

(3) If there is no agreement as to the number of arbitrators, the tribunal shall consist of a sole arbitrator.

Procedure for appointment of arbitrators

16.—(1) The parties are free to agree on the procedure for appointing the arbitrator or arbitrators, including the procedure for appointing any chairman or umpire. **A6–017**

(2) If or to the extent that there is no such agreement, the following provisions apply.

(3) If the tribunal is to consist of a sole arbitrator, the parties shall jointly appoint the arbitrator not later than 28 days after service of a request in writing by either party to do so.

(4) If the tribunal is to consist of two arbitrators, each party shall appoint one arbitrator not later than 14 days after service of a request in writing by either party to do so.

(5) If the tribunal is to consist of three arbitrators—

(a) each party shall appoint one arbitrator not later than 14 days after service of a request in writing by either party to do so, and

(b) the two so appointed shall forthwith appoint a third arbitrator as the chairman of the tribunal.

(6) If the tribunal is to consist of two arbitrators and an umpire—

(a) each party shall appoint one arbitrator not later than 14 days after service of a request in writing by either party to do so, and

(b) the two so appointed may appoint an umpire at any time after they themselves are appointed and shall do so before any substantive hearing or forthwith if they cannot agree on a matter relating to the arbitration.

(7) In any other case (in particular, if there are more than two parties) section 18 applies as in the case of a failure of the agreed appointment procedure.

Power in case of default to appoint sole arbitrator

A6–018 17.—(1) Unless the parties otherwise agree, where each of two parties to an arbitration agreement is to appoint an arbitrator and one party ("the party in default") refuses to do so, or fails to do so within the time specified, the other party, having duly appointed his arbitrator, may give notice in writing to the party in default that he proposes to appoint his arbitrator to act as sole arbitrator.

(2) If the party in default does not within 7 clear days of that notice being given—

(a) make the required appointment, and

(b) notify the other party that he has done so,

the other party may appoint his arbitrator as sole arbitrator whose award shall be binding on both parties as if he had been so appointed by agreement.

(3) Where a sole arbitrator has been appointed under subsection (2), the party in default may (upon notice to the appointing party) apply to the court which may set aside the appointment.

(4) The leave of the court is required for any appeal from a decision of the court under this section.

Failure of appointment procedure

A6–019 18.—(1) The parties are free to agree what is to happen in the event of a failure of the procedure for the appointment of the arbitral tribunal.

There is no failure if an appointment is duly made under section 17 (power in case of default to appoint sole arbitrator), unless that appointment is set aside.

(2) If or to the extent that there is no such agreement any party to the arbitration agreement may (upon notice to the other parties) apply to the court to exercise its powers under this section.

(3) Those powers are—

(a) to give directions as to the making of any necessary appointments;

(b) to direct that the tribunal shall be constituted by such appointments (or any one or more of them) as have been made;

(c) to revoke any appointments already made;

(d) to make any necessary appointments itself.

(4) An appointment made by the court under this section has effect as if made with the agreement of the parties.

(5) The leave of the court is required for any appeal from a decision of the court under this section.

Court to have regard to agreed qualifications

19. In deciding whether to exercise, and in considering how to exercise, any of its powers under section 16 (procedure for appointment of arbitrators) or section 18 (failure of appointment procedure), the court shall have due regard to any agreement of the parties as to the qualifications required of the arbitrators.

A6–020

Chairman

20.—(1) Where the parties have agreed that there is to be a chairman, they are free to agree what the functions of the chairman are to be in relation to the making of decisions, orders and awards.

A6–021

(2) If or to the extent that there is no such agreement, the following provisions apply.

(3) Decisions, orders and awards shall be made by all or a majority of the arbitrators (including the chairman).

(4) The view of the chairman shall prevail in relation to a decision, order or award in respect of which there is neither unanimity nor a majority under subsection (3).

Umpire

21.—(1) Where the parties have agreed that there is to be an umpire, they are free to agree what the functions of the umpire are to be, and in particular—

A6–022

(a) whether he is to attend the proceedings, and

(b) when he is to replace the other arbitrators as the tribunal with power to make decisions, orders and awards.

(2) If or to the extent that there is no such agreement, the following provisions apply.

(3) The umpire shall attend the proceedings and be supplied with the same documents and other materials as are supplied to the other arbitrators.

(4) Decisions, orders and awards shall be made by the other arbitrators unless and until they cannot agree on a matter relating to the arbitration.

In that event they shall forthwith give notice in writing to the parties and the umpire, whereupon the umpire shall replace them as the tribunal with power to make decisions, orders and awards as if he were sole arbitrator.

(5) If the arbitrators cannot agree but fail to give notice of that fact, or if any of them

fails to join in the giving of notice, any party to the arbitral proceedings may (upon notice to the other parties and to the tribunal) apply to the court which may order that the umpire shall replace the other arbitrators as the tribunal with power to make decisions, orders and awards as if he were sole arbitrator.

(6) The leave of the court is required for any appeal from a decision of the court under this section.

Decision-making where no chairman or umpire

A6–023   22.—(1) Where the parties agree that there shall be two or more arbitrators with no chairman or umpire, the parties are free to agree how the tribunal is to make decisions, orders and awards.

(2) If there is no such agreement, decisions, orders and awards shall be made by all or a majority of the arbitrators.

Revocation of arbitrator's authority

A6–024   23.—(1) The parties are free to agree in what circumstances the authority of an arbitrator may be revoked.

(2) If or to the extent that there is no such agreement the following provisions apply.

(3) The authority of an arbitrator may not be revoked except—

   (a) by the parties acting jointly, or

   (b) by an arbitral or other institution or person vested by the parties with powers in that regard.

(4) Revocation of the authority of an arbitrator by the parties acting jointly must be agreed in writing unless the parties also agree (whether or not in writing) to terminate the arbitration agreement.

(5) Nothing in this section affects the power of the court—

   (a) to revoke an appointment under section 18 (powers exercisable in case of failure of appointment procedure), or

   (b) to remove an arbitrator on the grounds specified in section 24.

Power of court to remove arbitrator

A6–025   24.—(1) A party to arbitral proceedings may (upon notice to the other parties, to the arbitrator concerned and to any other arbitrator) apply to the court to remove an arbitrator on any of the following grounds—

   (a) that circumstances exist that give rise to justifiable doubts as to his impartiality;

   (b) that he does not possess the qualifications required by the arbitration agreement;

   (c) that he is physically or mentally incapable of conducting the proceedings or there are justifiable doubts as to his capacity to do so;

   (d) that he has refused or failed—

       (i) properly to conduct the proceedings, or

(ii) to use all reasonable despatch in conducting the proceedings or making an award.

and that substantial injustice has been or will be caused to the applicant.

(2) If there is an arbitral or other institution or person vested by the parties with power to remove an arbitrator, the court shall not exercise its power of removal unless satisfied that the applicant has first exhausted any available recourse to that institution or person.

(3) The arbitral tribunal may continue the arbitral proceedings and make an award while an application to the court under this section is pending.

(4) Where the court removes an arbitrator, it may make such order as it thinks fit with respect to his entitlement (if any) to fees or expenses, or the repayment of any fees or expenses already paid.

(5) The arbitrator concerned is entitled to appear and be heard by the court before it makes any order under this section.

(6) The leave of the court is required for any appeal from a decision of the court under this section.

Resignation of arbitrator

25.—(1) The parties are free to agree with an arbitrator as to the consequences of his resignation as regards—　　　　　　　　　　　　　　　　　　　　　　　　　　　　　　　A6–026

(a) his entitlement (if any) to fees or expenses, and

(b) any liability thereby incurred by him.

(2) If or to the extent that there is no such agreement the following provisions apply.

(3) An arbitrator who resigns his appointment may (upon notice to the parties) apply to the court—

(a) to grant him relief from any liability thereby incurred by him, and

(b) to make such order as it thinks fit with respect to his entitlement (if any) to fees or expenses or the repayment of any fees or expenses already paid.

(4) If the court is satisfied that in all the circumstances it was reasonable for the arbitrator to resign, it may grant such relief as is mentioned in subsection (3)(a) on such terms as it thinks fit.

(5) The leave of the court is required for any appeal from a decision of the court under this section.

Death of arbitrator or person appointing him

26.—(1) The authority of an arbitrator is personal and ceases on his death.　　　　　A6–027

(2) Unless otherwise agreed by the parties, the death of the person by whom an arbitrator was appointed does not revoke the arbitrator's authority.

Filling of vacancy, etc.

27.—(1) Where an arbitrator ceases to hold office, the parties are free to agree—　　A6–028

(a) whether and if so how the vacancy is to be filled,

(b) whether and if so to what extent the previous proceedings should stand, and

(c) what effect (if any) his ceasing to hold office has on any appointment made by him (alone or jointly).

(2) If or to the extent that there is no such agreement, the following provisions apply.

(3) The provisions of sections 16 (procedure for appointment of arbitrators) and 18 (failure of appointment procedure) apply in relation to the filling of the vacancy as in relation to an original appointment.

(4) The tribunal (when reconstituted) shall determine whether and if so to what extent the previous proceedings should stand.

This does not affect any right of a party to challenge those proceedings on any ground which had arisen before the arbitrator ceased to hold office.

(5) His ceasing to hold office does not affect any appointment by him (alone or jointly) of another arbitrator, in particular any appointment of a chairman or umpire.

Joint and several liability of parties to arbitrators for fees and expenses

A6–029   28.—(1) The parties are jointly and severally liable to pay to the arbitrators such reasonable fees and expenses (if any) as are appropriate in the circumstances.

(2) Any party may apply to the court (upon notice to the other parties and to the arbitrators) which may order that the amount of the arbitrators' fees and expenses shall be considered and adjusted by such means and upon such terms as it may direct.

(3) If the application is made after any amount has been paid to the arbitrators by way of fees or expenses, the court may order the repayment of such amount (if any) as is shown to be excessive, but shall not do so unless it is shown that it is reasonable in the circumstances to order repayment.

(4) The above provisions have effect subject to any order of the court under section 24(4) or 25(3)(b) (order as to entitlement to fees or expenses in case of removal or resignation of arbitrator).

(5) Nothing in this section affects any liability of a party to any other party to pay all or any of the costs of the arbitration (see sections 59 to 65) or any contractual right of an arbitrator to payment of his fees and expenses.

(6) In this section references to arbitrators include an arbitrator who has ceased to act and an umpire who has not replaced the other arbitrators.

Immunity of arbitrator

A6–030   29.—(1) An arbitrator is not liable for anything done or omitted in the discharge or purported discharge of his functions as arbitrator unless the act or omission is shown to have been in bad faith.

(2) Subsection (1) applies to an employee or agent of an arbitrator as it applies to the arbitrator himself.

(3) This section does not affect any liability incurred by an arbitrator by reason of his resigning (but see section 25).

Jurisdiction of the arbitral tribunal

Competence of tribunal to rule on its own jurisdiction

A6–031   30.—(1) Unless otherwise agreed by the parties, the arbitral tribunal may rule on its own substantive jurisdiction, that is, as to—

(a) whether there is a valid arbitration agreement,

(b) whether the tribunal is properly constituted, and

(c) what matters have been submitted to arbitration in accordance with the arbitration agreement.

(2) Any such ruling may be challenged by any available arbitral process of appeal or review or in accordance with the provisions of this Part.

Objection to substantive jurisdiction of tribunal

31.—(1) An objection that the arbitral tribunal lacks substantive jurisdiction at the outset of the proceedings must be raised by a party not later than the time he takes the first step in the proceedings to contest the merits of any matter in relation to which he challenges the tribunal's jurisdiction.

A party is not precluded from raising such an objection by the fact that he has appointed or participated in the appointment of an arbitrator.

(2) Any objection during the course of the arbitral proceedings that the arbitral tribunal is exceeding its substantive jurisdiction must be made as soon as possible after the matter alleged to be beyond its jurisdiction is raised.

(3) The arbitral tribunal may admit an objection later than the time specified in subsection (1) or (2) if it considers the delay justified.

(4) Where an objection is duly taken to the tribunal's substantive jurisdiction and the tribunal has power to rule on its own jurisdiction, it may—

(a) rule on the matter in an award as to jurisdiction, or

(b) deal with the objection in its award on the merits.

If the parties agree which of these courses the tribunal should take, the tribunal shall proceed accordingly.

(5) The tribunal may in any case, and shall if the parties so agree, stay proceedings whilst an application is made to the court under section 32 (determination of preliminary point of jurisdiction).

Determination of preliminary point of jurisdiction

32.—(1) The court may, on the application of a party to arbitral proceedings (upon notice to the other parties), determine any question as to the substantive jurisdiction of the tribunal.

A party may lose the right to object (see section 73).

(2) An application under this section shall not be considered unless—

(a) it is made with the agreement in writing of all the other parties to the proceedings, or

(b) it is made with the permission of the tribunal and the court is satisfied—

(i) that the determination of the question is likely to produce substantial savings in costs,

(ii) that the application was made without delay, and

(iii) that there is good reason why the matter should be decided by the court.

(3) An application under this section, unless made with the agreement of all the other parties to the proceedings, shall state the grounds on which it is said that the matter should be decided by the court.

(4) Unless otherwise agreed by the parties, the arbitral tribunal may continue the arbitral proceedings and make an award while an application to the court under this section is pending.

(5) Unless the court gives leave, no appeal lies from a decision of the court whether the conditions specified in subsection (2) are met.

(6) The decision of the court on the question of jurisdiction shall be treated as a judgment of the court for the purposes of an appeal.

But no appeal lies without the leave of the court which shall not be given unless the court considers that the question involves a point of law which is one of general importance or is one which for some other special reason should be considered by the Court of Appeal.

The arbitral proceedings

General duty of the tribunal

A6–034

33.—(1) The tribunal shall—

(a) act fairly and impartially as between the parties, giving each party a reasonable opportunity of putting his case and dealing with that of his opponent, and

(b) adopt procedures suitable to the circumstances of the particular case, avoiding unnecessary delay or expense, so as to provide a fair means for the resolution of the matters falling to be determined.

(2) The tribunal shall comply with that general duty in conducting the arbitral proceedings, in its decisions on matters of procedure and evidence and in the exercise of all other powers conferred on it.

Procedural and evidential matters

A6–035

34.—(1) It shall be for the tribunal to decide all procedural and evidential matters, subject to the right of the parties to agree any matter.

(2) Procedural and evidential matters include—

(a) when and where any part of the proceedings is to be held;

(b) the language or languages to be used in the proceedings and whether translations of any relevant documents are to be supplied;

(c) whether any and if so what form of written statements of claim and defence are to be used, when these should be supplied and the extent to which such statements can be later amended;

(d) whether any and if so which documents or classes of documents should be disclosed between and produced by the parties and at what stage;

(e) whether any and if so what questions should be put to and answered by the respective parties and when and in what form this should be done;

(f) whether to apply strict rules of evidence (or any other rules) as to the admissibility, relevance or weight of any material (oral, written or other) sought to be tendered on any matters of fact or opinion, and the time, manner and form in which such material should be exchanged and presented;

(g) whether and to what extent the tribunal should itself take the initiative in ascertaining the facts and the law;

(h) whether and to what extent there should be oral or written evidence or submissions.

(3) The tribunal may fix the time within which any directions given by it are to be complied with, and may if it thinks fit extend the time so fixed (whether or not it has expired).

Consolidation of proceedings and concurrent hearings

35.—(1) The parties are free to agree— A6–036

(a) that the arbitral proceedings shall be consolidated with other arbitral proceedings, or

(b) that concurrent hearings shall be held,

on such terms as may be agreed.

(2) Unless the parties agree to confer such power on the tribunal, the tribunal has no power to order consolidation of proceedings or concurrent hearings.

Legal or other representation

36. Unless otherwise agreed by the parties, a party to arbitral proceedings may be represented in the proceedings by a lawyer or other person chosen by him. A6–037

Power to appoint experts, legal advisers or assessors

37.—(1) Unless otherwise agreed by the parties— A6–038

(a) the tribunal may—

(i) appoint experts or legal advisers to report to it and the parties, or
(ii) appoint assessors to assist it on technical matters,

and may allow any such expert, legal adviser or assessor to attend the proceedings; and

(b) the parties shall be given a reasonable opportunity to comment on any information, opinion or advice offered by any such person.

(2) The fees and expenses of an expert, legal adviser or assessor appointed by the tribunal for which the arbitrators are liable are expenses of the arbitrators for the purposes of this Part.

General powers exercisable by the tribunal

38.—(1) The parties are free to agree on the powers exercisable by the arbitral tribunal for the purposes of and in relation to the proceedings. A6–039

(2) Unless otherwise agreed by the parties the tribunal has the following powers.
(3) The tribunal may order a claimant to provide security for the costs of the arbitration.
This power shall not be exercised on the ground that the claimant is—

(a) an individual ordinarily resident outside the United Kingdom, or

(b) a corporation or association incorporated or formed under the law of a country outside the United Kingdom, or whose central management and control is exercised outside the United Kingdom.

(4) The tribunal may give directions in relation to any property which is the subject of the proceedings or as to which any question arises in the proceedings, and which is owned by or is in the possession of a party to the proceedings—

(a) for the inspection, photographing, preservation, custody or detention of the property by the tribunal, an expert or a party, or

(b) ordering that samples be taken from, or any observation be made of or experiment conducted upon, the property.

(5) The tribunal may direct that a party or witness shall be examined on oath or affirmation, and may for that purpose administer any necessary oath or take any necessary affirmation.
(6) The tribunal may give directions to a party for the preservation for the purposes of the proceedings of any evidence in his custody or control.

Power to make provisional awards

A6–040   39.—(1) The parties are free to agree that the tribunal shall have power to order on a provisional basis any relief which it would have power to grant in a final award.
(2) This includes, for instance, making—

(a) a provisional order for the payment of money or the disposition of property as between the parties, or

(b) an order to make an interim payment on account of the costs of the arbitration.

(3) Any such order shall be subject to the tribunal's final adjudication; and the tribunal's final award, on the merits or as to costs, shall take account of any such order.
(4) Unless the parties agree to confer such power on the tribunal, the tribunal has no such power.
This does not affect its powers under section 47 (awards on different issues, &c.).

General duty of parties

A6–041   40.—(1) The parties shall do all things necessary for the proper and expeditious conduct of the arbitral proceedings.
(2) This includes—

(a) complying without delay with any determination of the tribunal as to procedural or evidential matters, or with any order or directions of the tribunal, and

(b) where appropriate, taking without delay any necessary steps to obtain a decision of the court on a preliminary question of jurisdiction or law (see sections 32 and 45).

Powers of tribunal in case of party's default

41.—(1) The parties are free to agree on the powers of the tribunal in case of a party's failure to do something necessary for the proper and expeditious conduct of the arbitration.

(2) Unless otherwise agreed by the parties, the following provisions apply.

(3) If the tribunal is satisfied that there has been inordinate and inexcusable delay on the part of the claimant in pursuing his claim and that the delay—

    (a) gives rise, or is likely to give rise, to a substantial risk that it is not possible to have a fair resolution of the issues in that claim, or

    (b) has caused, or is likely to cause, serious prejudice to the respondent,

the tribunal may make an award dismissing the claim.

(4) If without showing sufficient cause a party—

    (a) fails to attend or be represented at an oral hearing of which due notice was given, or

    (b) where matters are to be dealt with in writing, fails after due notice to submit written evidence or make written submissions,

the tribunal may continue the proceedings in the absence of that party or, as the case may be, without any written evidence or submissions on his behalf, and may make an award on the basis of the evidence before it.

(5) If without showing sufficient cause a party fails to comply with any order or directions of the tribunal, the tribunal may make a peremptory order to the same effect, prescribing such time for compliance with it as the tribunal considers appropriate.

(6) If a claimant fails to comply with a peremptory order of the tribunal to provide security for costs, the tribunal may make an award dismissing his claim.

(7) If a party fails to comply with any other kind of peremptory order, then, without prejudice to section 42 (enforcement by court of tribunal's peremptory orders), the tribunal may do any of the following—

    (a) direct that the party in default shall not be entitled to rely upon any allegation or material which was the subject matter of the order;

    (b) draw such adverse inferences from the act of non-compliance as the circumstances justify;

    (c) proceed to an award on the basis of such materials as have been properly provided to it;

    (d) make such order as it thinks fit as to the payment of costs of the arbitration incurred in consequence of the non-compliance.

Powers of court in relation to arbitral proceedings

Enforcement of peremptory orders of tribunal

A6–043   **42.**—(1) Unless otherwise agreed by the parties, the court may make an order requiring a party to comply with a peremptory order made by the tribunal.

(2) An application for an order under this section may be made—

- (a) by the tribunal (upon notice to the parties),
- (b) by a party to the arbitral proceedings with the permission of the tribunal (and upon notice to the other parties), or
- (c) where the parties have agreed that the powers of the court under this section shall be available.

(3) The court shall not act unless it is satisfied that the applicant has exhausted any available arbitral process in respect of failure to comply with the tribunal's order.

(4) No order shall be made under this section unless the court is satisfied that the person to whom the tribunal's order was directed has failed to comply with it within the time prescribed in the order or, if no time was prescribed, within a reasonable time.

(5) The leave of the court is required for any appeal from a decision of the court under this section.

Securing the attendance of witnesses

A6–044   **43.**—(1) A party to arbitral proceedings may use the same court procedures as are available in relation to legal proceedings to secure the attendance before the tribunal of a witness in order to give oral testimony or to produce documents or other material evidence.

(2) This may only be done with the permission of the tribunal or the agreement of the other parties.

(3) The court procedures may only be used if—

- (a) the witness is in the United Kingdom, and
- (b) the arbitral proceedings are being conducted in England and Wales or, as the case may be, Northern Ireland.

(4) A person shall not be compelled by virtue of this section to produce any document or other material evidence which he could not be compelled to produce in legal proceedings.

Court powers exercisable in support of arbitral proceedings

A6–045   **44.**—(1) Unless otherwise agreed by the parties, the court has for the purposes of and in relation to arbitral proceedings the same power of making orders about the matters listed below as it has for the purposes of and in relation to legal proceedings.

(2) Those matters are—

- (a) the taking of the evidence of witnesses;
- (b) the preservation of evidence;

(c) making orders relating to property which is the subject of the proceedings or as to which any question arises in the proceedings—

   (i) for the inspection, photographing, preservation, custody or detention of the property, or
   (ii) ordering that samples be taken from, or any observation be made of or experiment conducted upon, the property;

and for that purpose authorising any person to enter any premises in the possession or control of a party to the arbitration;

(d) the sale of any goods the subject of the proceedings;

(e) the granting of an interim injunction or the appointment of a receiver.

(3) If the case is one of urgency, the court may, on the application of a party or proposed party to the arbitral proceedings, make such orders as it thinks necessary for the purpose of preserving evidence or assets.

(4) If the case is not one of urgency, the court shall act only on the application of a party to the arbitral proceedings (upon notice to the other parties and to the tribunal) made with the permission of the tribunal or the agreement in writing of the other parties.

(5) In any case the court shall act only if or to the extent that the arbitral tribunal, and any arbitral or other institution or person vested by the parties with power in that regard, has no power or is unable for the time being to act effectively.

(6) If the court so orders, an order made by it under this section shall cease to have effect in whole or in part on the order of the tribunal or of any such arbitral or other institution or person having power to act in relation to the subject-matter of the order.

(7) The leave of the court is required for any appeal from a decision of the court under this section.

Determination of preliminary point of law

45.—(1) Unless otherwise agreed by the parties, the court may on the application of a party to arbitral proceedings (upon notice to the other parties) determine any question of law arising in the course of the proceedings which the court is satisfied substantially affects the rights of one or more of the parties.

An agreement to dispense with reasons for the tribunal's award shall be considered an agreement to exclude the court's jurisdiction under this section.

A6–046

(2) An application under this section shall not be considered unless—

   (a) it is made with the agreement of all the other parties to the proceedings, or

   (b) it is made with the permission of the tribunal and the court is satisfied—

      (i) that the determination of the question is likely to produce substantial savings in costs, and
      (ii) that the application was made without delay.

(3) The application shall identify the question of law to be determined and, unless made with the agreement of all the other parties to the proceedings, shall state the grounds on which it is said that the question should be decided by the court.

(4) Unless otherwise agreed by the parties, the arbitral tribunal may continue the arbitral proceedings and make an award while an application to the court under this section is pending.

(5) Unless the court gives leave, no appeal lies from a decision of the court whether the conditions specified in subsection (2) are met.

(6) The decision of the court on the question of law shall be treated as a judgment of the court for the purposes of an appeal.

But no appeal lies without the leave of the court which shall not be given unless the court considers that the question is one of general importance, or is one which for some other special reason should be considered by the Court of Appeal.

The award

Rules applicable to substance of dispute

A6–047   46.—(1) The arbitral tribunal shall decide the dispute—

    (a) in accordance with the law chosen by the parties as applicable to the substance of the dispute, or

    (b) if the parties so agree, in accordance with such other considerations as are agreed by them or determined by the tribunal.

(2) For this purpose the choice of the laws of a country shall be understood to refer to the substantive laws of that country and not its conflict of laws rules.

(3) If or to the extent that there is no such choice or agreement, the tribunal shall apply the law determined by the conflict of laws rules which it considers applicable.

Awards on different issues, etc.

A6–048   47.—(1) Unless otherwise agreed by the parties, the tribunal may make more than one award at different times on different aspects of the matters to be determined.

(2) The tribunal may, in particular, make an award relating—

    (a) to an issue affecting the whole claim, or

    (b) to a part only of the claims or cross-claims submitted to it for decision.

(3) If the tribunal does so, it shall specify in its award the issue, or the claim or part of a claim, which is the subject matter of the award.

Remedies

A6–049   48.—(1) The parties are free to agree on the powers exercisable by the arbitral tribunal as regards remedies.

(2) Unless otherwise agreed by the parties, the tribunal has the following powers.

(3) The tribunal may make a declaration as to any matter to be determined in the proceedings.

(4) The tribunal may order the payment of a sum of money, in any currency.

(5) The tribunal has the same powers as the court—

    (a) to order a party to do or refrain from doing anything;

    (b) to order specific performance of a contract (other than a contract relating to land);

ARBITRATION ACT 1996

(c) to order the rectification, setting aside or cancellation of a deed or other document.

Interest

49.—(1) The parties are free to agree on the powers of the tribunal as regards the award of interest.

(2) Unless otherwise agreed by the parties the following provisions apply.

(3) The tribunal may award simple or compound interest from such dates, at such rates and with such rests as it considers meets the justice of the case—

- (a) on the whole or part of any amount awarded by the tribunal, in respect of any period up to the date of the award;
- (b) on the whole or part of any amount claimed in the arbitration and outstanding at the commencement of the arbitral proceedings but paid before the award was made, in respect of any period up to the date of payment.

(4) The tribunal may award simple or compound interest from the date of the award (or any later date) until payment, at such rates and with such rests as it considers meets the justice of the case, on the outstanding amount of any award (including any award of interest under subsection (3) and any award as to costs).

(5) References in this section to an amount awarded by the tribunal include an amount payable in consequence of a declaratory award by the tribunal.

(6) The above provisions do not affect any other power of the tribunal to award interest.

A6–050

Extension of time for making award

50.—(1) Where the time for making an award is limited by or in pursuance of the arbitration agreement, then, unless otherwise agreed by the parties, the court may in accordance with the following provisions by order extend that time.

(2) An application for an order under this section may be made—

- (a) by the tribunal (upon notice to the parties), or
- (b) by any party to the proceedings (upon notice to the tribunal and the other parties),

but only after exhausting any available arbitral process for obtaining an extension of time.

(3) The court shall only make an order if satisfied that a substantial injustice would otherwise be done.

(4) The court may extend the time for such period and on such terms as it thinks fit, and may do so whether or not the time previously fixed (by or under the agreement or by a previous order) has expired.

(5) The leave of the court is required for any appeal from a decision of the court under this section.

A6–051

Settlement

51.—(1) If during arbitral proceedings the parties settle the dispute, the following provisions apply unless otherwise agreed by the parties.

A6–052

(2) The tribunal shall terminate the substantive proceedings and, if so requested by the parties and not objected to by the tribunal, shall record the settlement in the form of an agreed award.

(3) An agreed award shall state that it is an award of the tribunal and shall have the same status and effect as any other award on the merits of the case.

(4) The following provisions of this Part relating to awards (sections 52 to 58) apply to an agreed award.

(5) Unless the parties have also settled the matter of the payment of the costs of the arbitration, the provisions of this Part relating to costs (sections 59 to 65) continue to apply.

Form of award

A6–053   52.—(1) The parties are free to agree on the form of an award.

(2) If or to the extent that there is no such agreement, the following provisions apply.

(3) The award shall be in writing signed by all the arbitrators or all those assenting to the award.

(4) The award shall contain the reasons for the award unless it is an agreed award or the parties have agreed to dispense with reasons.

(5) The award shall state the seat of the arbitration and the date when the award is made.

Place where award treated as made

A6–054   53. Unless otherwise agreed by the parties, where the seat of the arbitration is in England and Wales or Northern Ireland, any award in the proceedings shall be treated as made there, regardless of where it was signed, despatched or delivered to any of the parties.

Date of award

A6–055   54.—(1) Unless otherwise agreed by the parties, the tribunal may decide what is to be taken to be the date on which the award was made.

(2) In the absence of any such decision, the date of the award shall be taken to be the date on which it is signed by the arbitrator or, where more than one arbitrator signs the award, by the last of them.

Notification of award

A6–056   55.—(1) The parties are free to agree on the requirements as to notification of the award to the parties.

(2) If there is no such agreement, the award shall be notified to the parties by service on them of copies of the award, which shall be done without delay after the award is made.

(3) Nothing in this section affects section 56 (power to withhold award in case of non-payment).

Power to withhold award in case of non-payment

A6–057   56.—(1) The tribunal may refuse to deliver an award to the parties except upon full payment of the fees and expenses of the arbitrators.

(2) If the tribunal refuses on that ground to deliver an award, a party to the arbitral

ARBITRATION ACT 1996

proceedings may (upon notice to the other parties and the tribunal) apply to the court, which may order that—

(a) the tribunal shall deliver the award on the payment into court by the applicant of the fees and expenses demanded, or such lesser amount as the court may specify,

(b) the amount of the fees and expenses properly payable shall be determined by such means and upon such terms as the court may direct, and

(c) out of the money paid into court there shall be paid out such fees and expenses as may be found to be properly payable and the balance of the money (if any) shall be paid out to the applicant.

(3) For this purpose the amount of fees and expenses properly payable is the amount the applicant is liable to pay under section 28 or any agreement relating to the payment of the arbitrators.

(4) No application to the court may be made where there is any available arbitral process for appeal or review of the amount of the fees or expenses demanded.

(5) References in this section to arbitrators include an arbitrator who has ceased to act and an umpire who has not replaced the other arbitrators.

(6) The above provisions of this section also apply in relation to any arbitral or other institution or person vested by the parties with powers in relation to the delivery of the tribunal's award.

As they so apply, the references to the fees and expenses of the arbitrators shall be construed as including the fees and expenses of that institution or person.

(7) The leave of the court is required for any appeal from a decision of the court under this section.

(8) Nothing in this section shall be construed as excluding an application under section 28 where payment has been made to the arbitrators in order to obtain the award.

Correction of award or additional award

57.—(1) The parties are free to agree on the powers of the tribunal to correct an award or make an additional award.   **A6–058**

(2) If or to the extent there is no such agreement, the following provisions apply.

(3) The tribunal may on its own initiative or on the application of a party—

(a) correct an award so as to remove any clerical mistake or error arising from an accidental slip or omission or clarify or remove any ambiguity in the award, or

(b) make an additional award in respect of any claim (including a claim for interest or costs) which was presented to the tribunal but was not dealt with in the award.

These powers shall not be exercised without first affording the other parties a reasonable opportunity to make representations to the tribunal.

(4) Any application for the exercise of those powers must be made within 28 days of the date of the award or such longer period as the parties may agree.

(5) Any correction of an award shall be made within 28 days of the date the application was received by the tribunal or, where the correction is made by the tribunal on its own

initiative, within 28 days of the date of the award or, in either case, such longer period as the parties may agree.

(6) Any additional award shall be made within 56 days of the date of the original award or such longer period as the parties may agree.

(7) Any correction of an award shall form part of the award.

Effect of award

A6–059　58.—(1) Unless otherwise agreed by the parties, an award made by the tribunal pursuant to an arbitration agreement is final and binding both on the parties and on any persons claiming through or under them.

(2) This does not affect the right of a person to challenge the award by any available arbitral process of appeal or review or in accordance with the provisions of this Part.

Costs of the arbitration

Costs of the arbitration

A6–060　59.—(1) References in this Part to the costs of the arbitration are to—

(a) the arbitrators' fees and expenses,

(b) the fees and expenses of any arbitral institution concerned, and

(c) the legal or other costs of the parties.

(2) Any such reference includes the costs of or incidental to any proceedings to determine the amount of the recoverable costs of the arbitration (see section 63).

Agreement to pay costs in any event

A6–061　60. An agreement which has the effect that a party is to pay the whole or part of the costs of the arbitration in any event is only valid if made after the dispute in question has arisen.

Award of costs

A6–062　61.—(1) The tribunal may make an award allocating the costs of the arbitration as between the parties, subject to any agreement of the parties.

(2) Unless the parties otherwise agree, the tribunal shall award costs on the general principle that costs should follow the event except where it appears to the tribunal that in the circumstances this is not appropriate in relation to the whole or part of the costs.

Effect of agreement or award about costs

A6–063　62. Unless the parties otherwise agree, any obligation under an agreement between them as to how the costs of the arbitration are to be borne, or under an award allocating the costs of the arbitration, extends only to such costs as are recoverable.

The recoverable costs of the arbitration

A6–064　63.—(1) The parties are free to agree what costs of the arbitration are recoverable.

(2) If or to the extent there is no such agreement, the following provisions apply.

(3) The tribunal may determine by award the recoverable costs of the arbitration on such basis as it thinks fit.
If it does so, it shall specify—

(a) the basis on which it has acted, and

(b) the items of recoverable costs and the amount referable to each.

(4) If the tribunal does not determine the recoverable costs of the arbitration, any party to the arbitral proceedings may apply to the court (upon notice to the other parties) which may—

(a) determine the recoverable costs of the arbitration on such basis as it thinks fit, or

(b) order that they shall be determined by such means and upon such terms as it may specify.

(5) Unless the tribunal or the court determines otherwise—

(a) the recoverable costs of the arbitration shall be determined on the basis that there shall be allowed a reasonable amount in respect of all costs reasonably incurred, and

(b) any doubt as to whether costs were reasonably incurred or were reasonable in amount shall be resolved in favour of the paying party.

(6) The above provisions have effect subject to section 64 (recoverable fees and expenses of arbitrators).

(7) Nothing in this section affects any right of the arbitrators, any expert, legal adviser or assessor appointed by the tribunal, or any arbitral institution, to payment of their fees and expenses.

Recoverable fees and expenses of arbitrators

64.—(1) Unless otherwise agreed by the parties, the recoverable costs of the arbitration shall include in respect of the fees and expenses of the arbitrators only such reasonable fees and expenses as are appropriate in the circumstances.

(2) If there is any question as to what reasonable fees and expenses are appropriate in the circumstances, and the matter is not already before the court on an application under section 63(4), the court may on the application of any party (upon notice to the other parties)—

(a) determine the matter, or

(b) order that it be determined by such means and upon such terms as the court may specify.

(3) Subsection (1) has effect subject to any order of the court under section 24(4) or 25(3)(b) (order as to entitlement to fees or expenses in case of removal or resignation of arbitrator).

(4) Nothing in this section affects any right of the arbitrator to payment of his fees and expenses.

Power to limit recoverable costs

A6–066   65.—(1) Unless otherwise agreed by the parties, the tribunal may direct that the recoverable costs of the arbitration, or of any part of the arbitral proceedings, shall be limited to a specified amount.

(2) Any direction may be made or varied at any stage, but this must be done sufficiently in advance of the incurring of costs to which it relates, or the taking of any steps in the proceedings which may be affected by it, for the limit to be taken into account.

Powers of the court in relation to award

Enforcement of the award

A6–067   66.—(1) An award made by the tribunal pursuant to an arbitration agreement may, by leave of the court, be enforced in the same manner as a judgment or order of the court to the same effect.

(2) Where leave is so given, judgment may be entered in terms of the award.

(3) Leave to enforce an award shall not be given where, or to the extent that, the person against whom it is sought to be enforced shows that the tribunal lacked substantive jurisdiction to make the award.

The right to raise such an objection may have been lost (see section 73).

(4) Nothing in this section affects the recognition or enforcement of an award under any other enactment or rule of law, in particular under Part II of the Arbitration Act 1950 (enforcement of awards under Geneva Convention) or the provisions of Part III of this Act relating to the recognition and enforcement of awards under the New York Convention or by an action on the award.

Challenging the award: substantive jurisdiction

A6–068   67.—(1) A party to arbitral proceedings may (upon notice to the other parties and to the tribunal) apply to the court—

(a) challenging any award of the arbitral tribunal as to its substantive jurisdiction; or

(b) for an order declaring an award made by the tribunal on the merits to be of no effect, in whole or in part, because the tribunal did not have substantive jurisdiction.

A party may lose the right to object (see section 73) and the right to apply is subject to the restrictions in section 70(2) and (3).

(2) The arbitral tribunal may continue the arbitral proceedings and make a further award while an application to the court under this section is pending in relation to an award as to jurisdiction.

(3) On an application under this section challenging an award of the arbitral tribunal as to its substantive jurisdiction, the court may by order—

(a) confirm the award,

(b) vary the award, or

(c) set aside the award in whole or in part.

(4) The leave of the court is required for any appeal from a decision of the court under this section.

Challenging the award: serious irregularity

68.—(1) A party to arbitral proceedings may (upon notice to the other parties and to the tribunal) apply to the court challenging an award in the proceedings on the ground of serious irregularity affecting the tribunal, the proceedings or the award.
A party may lose the right to object (see section 73) and the right to apply is subject to the restrictions in section 70(2) and (3).

(2) Serious irregularity means an irregularity of one or more of the following kinds which the court considers has caused or will cause substantial injustice to the applicant—

    (a) failure by the tribunal to comply with section 33 (general duty of tribunal);

    (b) the tribunal exceeding its powers (otherwise than by exceeding its substantive jurisdiction: see section 67);

    (c) failure by the tribunal to conduct the proceedings in accordance with the procedure agreed by the parties;

    (d) failure by the tribunal to deal with all the issues that were put to it;

    (e) any arbitral or other institution or person vested by the parties with powers in relation to the proceedings or the award exceeding its powers;

    (f) uncertainty or ambiguity as to the effect of the award;

    (g) the award being obtained by fraud or the award or the way in which it was procured being contrary to public policy;

    (h) failure to comply with the requirements as to the form of the award; or

    (i) any irregularity in the conduct of the proceedings or in the award which is admitted by the tribunal or by any arbitral or other institution or person vested by the parties with powers in relation to the proceedings or the award.

(3) If there is shown to be serious irregularity affecting the tribunal, the proceedings or the award, the court may—

    (a) remit the award to the tribunal, in whole or in part, for reconsideration,

    (b) set the award aside in whole or in part, or

    (c) declare the award to be of no effect, in whole or in part.

The court shall not exercise its power to set aside or to declare an award to be of no effect, in whole or in part, unless it is satisfied that it would be inappropriate to remit the matters in question to the tribunal for reconsideration.

(4) The leave of the court is required for any appeal from a decision of the court under this section.

Appeal on point of law

69.—(1) Unless otherwise agreed by the parties, a party to arbitral proceedings may (upon notice to the other parties and to the tribunal) appeal to the court on a question of law arising out of an award made in the proceedings.

An agreement to dispense with reasons for the tribunal's award shall be considered an agreement to exclude the court's jurisdiction under this section.

(2) An appeal shall not be brought under this section except—

(a) with the agreement of all the other parties to the proceedings, or

(b) with the leave of the court.

The right to appeal is also subject to the restrictions in section 70(2) and (3).

(3) Leave to appeal shall be given only if the court is satisfied—

(a) that the determination of the question will substantially affect the rights of one or more of the parties,

(b) that the question is one which the tribunal was asked to determine,

(c) that, on the basis of the findings of fact in the award—

(i) the decision of the tribunal on the question is obviously wrong, or
(ii) the question is one of general public importance and the decision of the tribunal is at least open to serious doubt, and

(d) that, despite the agreement of the parties to resolve the matter by arbitration, it is just and proper in all the circumstances for the court to determine the question.

(4) An application for leave to appeal under this section shall identify the question of law to be determined and state the grounds on which it is alleged that leave to appeal should be granted.

(5) The court shall determine an application for leave to appeal under this section without a hearing unless it appears to the court that a hearing is required.

(6) The leave of the court is required for any appeal from a decision of the court under this section to grant or refuse leave to appeal.

(7) On an appeal under this section the court may by order—

(a) confirm the award,

(b) vary the award,

(c) remit the award to the tribunal, in whole or in part, for reconsideration in the light of the court's determination, or

(d) set aside the award in whole or in part.

The court shall not exercise its power to set aside an award, in whole or in part, unless it is satisfied that it would be inappropriate to remit the matters in question to the tribunal for reconsideration.

(8) The decision of the court on an appeal under this section shall be treated as a judgment of the court for the purposes of a further appeal.

But no such appeal lies without the leave of the court which shall not be given unless the court considers that the question is one of general importance or is one which for some other special reason should be considered by the Court of Appeal.

Challenge or appeal: supplementary provisions

70.—(1) The following provisions apply to an application or appeal under section 67, 68 or 69.

(2) An application or appeal may not be brought if the applicant or appellant has not first exhausted—

(a) any available arbitral process of appeal or review, and

(b) any available recourse under section 57 (correction of award or additional award).

(3) Any application or appeal must be brought within 28 days of the date of the award or, if there has been any arbitral process of appeal or review, of the date when the applicant or appellant was notified of the result of that process.

(4) If on an application or appeal it appears to the court that the award—

(a) does not contain the tribunal's reasons, or

(b) does not set out the tribunal's reasons in sufficient detail to enable the court properly to consider the application or appeal,

the court may order the tribunal to state the reasons for its award in sufficient detail for that purpose.

(5) Where the court makes an order under subsection (4), it may make such further order as it thinks fit with respect to any additional costs of the arbitration resulting from its order.

(6) The court may order the applicant or appellant to provide security for the costs of the application or appeal, and may direct that the application or appeal be dismissed if the order is not complied with.

The power to order security for costs shall not be exercised on the ground that the applicant or appellant is—

(a) an individual ordinarily resident outside the United Kingdom, or

(b) a corporation or association incorporated or formed under the law of a country outside the United Kingdom, or whose central management and control is exercised outside the United Kingdom.

(7) The court may order that any money payable under the award shall be brought into court or otherwise secured pending the determination of the application or appeal, and may direct that the application or appeal be dismissed if the order is not complied with.

(8) The court may grant leave to appeal subject to conditions to the same or similar effect as an order under subsection (6) or (7).

This does not affect the general discretion of the court to grant leave subject to conditions.

Challenge or appeal: effect of order of court

71.—(1) The following provisions have effect where the court makes an order under section 67, 68 or 69 with respect to an award.

(2) Where the award is varied, the variation has effect as part of the tribunal's award.

A6–071

A6–072

(3) Where the award is remitted to the tribunal, in whole or in part, for reconsideration, the tribunal shall make a fresh award in respect of the matters remitted within three months of the date of the order for remission or such longer or shorter period as the court may direct.

(4) Where the award is set aside or declared to be of no effect, in whole or in part, the court may also order that any provision that an award is a condition precedent to the bringing of legal proceedings in respect of a matter to which the arbitration agreement applies, is of no effect as regards the subject matter of the award or, as the case may be, the relevant part of the award.

Miscellaneous

Saving for rights of person who takes no part in proceedings

A6–073   72.—(1) A person alleged to be a party to arbitral proceedings but who takes no part in the proceedings may question—

(a) whether there is a valid arbitration agreement,

(b) whether the tribunal is properly constituted, or

(c) what matters have been submitted to arbitration in accordance with the arbitration agreement,

by proceedings in the court for a declaration or injunction or other appropriate relief.

(2) He also has the same right as a party to the arbitral proceedings to challenge an award—

(a) by an application under section 67 on the ground of lack of substantive jurisdiction in relation to him, or

(b) by an application under section 68 on the ground of serious irregularity (within the meaning of that section) affecting him;

and section 70(2) (duty to exhaust arbitral procedures) does not apply in his case.

Loss of right to object

A6–074   73.—(1) If a party to arbitral proceedings takes part, or continues to take part, in the proceedings without making, either forthwith or within such time as is allowed by the arbitration agreement or the tribunal or by any provision of this Part, any objection—

(a) that the tribunal lacks substantive jurisdiction,

(b) that the proceedings have been improperly conducted,

(c) that there has been a failure to comply with the arbitration agreement or with any provision of this Part, or

(d) that there has been any other irregularity affecting the tribunal or the proceedings,

he may not raise that objection later, before the tribunal or the court, unless he shows that, at the time he took part or continued to take part in the proceedings, he did not know and could not with reasonable diligence have discovered the grounds for the objection.

(2) Where the arbitral tribunal rules that it has substantive jurisdiction and a party to arbitral proceedings who could have questioned that ruling—

(a) by any available arbitral process of appeal or review, or

(b) by challenging the award,

does not do so, or does not do so within the time allowed by the arbitration agreement or any provision of this Part, he may not object later to the tribunal's substantive jurisdiction on any ground which was the subject of that ruling.

Immunity of arbitral institutions, etc.

74.—(1) An arbitral or other institution or person designated or requested by the parties to appoint or nominate an arbitrator is not liable for anything done or omitted in the discharge or purported discharge of that function unless the act or omission is shown to have been in bad faith.   **A6–075**

(2) An arbitral or other institution or person by whom an arbitrator is appointed or nominated is not liable, by reason of having appointed or nominated him, for anything done or omitted by the arbitrator (or his employees or agents) in the discharge or purported discharge of his functions as arbitrator.

(3) The above provisions apply to an employee or agent of an arbitral or other institution or person as they apply to the institution or person himself.

Charge to secure payment of solicitors' costs

75.—The powers of the court to make declarations and orders under section 73 of the Solicitors Act 1974 or Article 71H of the Solicitors (Northern Ireland) Order 1976 (power to charge property recovered in the proceedings with the payment of solicitors' costs) may be exercised in relation to arbitral proceedings as if those proceedings were proceedings in the court.   **A6–076**

Supplementary

Service of notices, etc.

76.—(1) The parties are free to agree on the manner of service of any notice or other document required or authorised to be given or served in pursuance of the arbitration agreement or for the purposes of the arbitral proceedings.   **A6–077**

(2) If or to the extent that there is no such agreement the following provisions apply.

(3) A notice or other document may be served on a person by any effective means.

(4) If a notice or other document is addressed, pre-paid and delivered by post—

(a) to the addressee's last known principal residence or, if he is or has been carrying on a trade, profession or business, his last known principal business address, or

(b) where the addressee is a body corporate, to the body's registered or principal office,

it shall be treated as effectively served.

(5) This section does not apply to the service of documents for the purposes of legal proceedings, for which provision is made by rules of court.

(6) References in this Part to a notice or other document include any form of communication in writing and references to giving or serving a notice or other document shall be construed accordingly.

Powers of court in relation to service of documents

A6–078   77.—(1) This section applies where service of a document on a person in the manner agreed by the parties, or in accordance with provisions of section 76 having effect in default of agreement, is not reasonably practicable.

(2) Unless otherwise agreed by the parties, the court may make such order as it thinks fit—

(a) for service in such manner as the court may direct, or

(b) dispensing with service of the document.

(3) Any party to the arbitration agreement may apply for an order, but only after exhausting any available arbitral process for resolving the matter.

(4) The leave of the court is required for any appeal from a decision of the court under this section.

Reckoning periods of time

A6–079   78.—(1) The parties are free to agree on the method of reckoning periods of time for the purposes of any provision agreed by them or any provision of this Part having effect in default of such agreement.

(2) If or to the extent there is no such agreement, periods of time shall be reckoned in accordance with the following provisions.

(3) Where the act is required to be done within a specified period after or from a specified date, the period begins immediately after that date.

(4) Where the act is required to be done a specified number of clear days after a specified date, at least that number of days must intervene between the day on which the act is done and that date.

(5) Where the period is a period of seven days or less which would include a Saturday, Sunday or a public holiday in the place where anything which has to be done within the period falls to be done, that day shall be excluded.

In relation to England and Wales or Northern Ireland, a "public holiday" means Christmas Day, Good Friday or a day which under the Banking and Financial Dealings Act 1971 is a bank holiday.

Power of court to extend time limits relating to arbitral proceedings

A6–080   79.—(1) Unless the parties otherwise agree, the court may by order extend any time limit agreed by them in relation to any matter relating to the arbitral proceedings or specified in any provision of this Part having effect in default of such agreement.

This section does not apply to a time limit to which section 12 applies (power of court to extend time for beginning arbitral proceedings, &c.).

(2) An application for an order may be made—

(a) by any party to the arbitral proceedings (upon notice to the other parties and to the tribunal), or

(b) by the arbitral tribunal (upon notice to the parties).

(3) The court shall not exercise its power to extend a time limit unless it is satisfied—

(a) that any available recourse to the tribunal, or to any arbitral or other institution or person vested by the parties with power in that regard, has first been exhausted, and

(b) that a substantial injustice would otherwise be done.

(4) The court's power under this section may be exercised whether or not the time has already expired.

(5) An order under this section may be made on such terms as the court thinks fit.

(6) The leave of the court is required for any appeal from a decision of the court under this section.

Notice and other requirements in connection with legal proceedings

80.—(1) References in this Part to an application, appeal or other step in relation to legal proceedings being taken "upon notice" to the other parties to the arbitral proceedings, or to the tribunal, are to such notice of the originating process as is required by rules of court and do not impose any separate requirement.

(2) Rules of court shall be made—

(a) requiring such notice to be given as indicated by any provision of this Part, and

(b) as to the manner, form and content of any such notice.

(3) Subject to any provision made by rules of court, a requirement to give notice to the tribunal of legal proceedings shall be construed—

(a) if there is more than one arbitrator, as a requirement to give notice to each of them; and

(b) if the tribunal is not fully constituted, as a requirement to give notice to any arbitrator who has been appointed.

(4) References in this Part to making an application or appeal to the court within a specified period are to the issue within that period of the appropriate originating process in accordance with rules of court.

(5) Where any provision of this Part requires an application or appeal to be made to the court within a specified time, the rules of court relating to the reckoning of periods, the extending or abridging of periods, and the consequences of not taking a step within the period prescribed by the rules, apply in relation to that requirement.

(6) Provision may be made by rules of court amending the provisions of this Part—

(a) with respect to the time within which any application or appeal to the court must be made,

(b) so as to keep any provision made by this Part in relation to arbitral proceedings in step with the corresponding provision of rules of court applying in relation to proceedings in the court, or

(c) so as to keep any provision made by this Part in relation to legal proceedings in step with the corresponding provision of rules of court applying generally in relation to proceedings in the court.

(7) Nothing in this section affects the generality of the power to make rules of court.

Saving for certain matters governed by common law

A6–082   81.—(1) Nothing in this Part shall be construed as excluding the operation of any rule of law consistent with the provisions of this Part, in particular, any rule of law as to—

(a) matters which are not capable of settlement by arbitration;

(b) the effect of an oral arbitration agreement; or

(c) the refusal of recognition or enforcement of an arbitral award on grounds of public policy.

(2) Nothing in this Act shall be construed as reviving any jurisdiction of the court to set aside or remit an award on the ground of errors of fact or law on the face of the award.

Minor definitions

A6–083   82.—(1) In this Part—

"arbitrator", unless the context otherwise requires, includes an umpire;
"available arbitral process", in relation to any matter, includes any process of appeal to or review by an arbitral or other institution or person vested by the parties with powers in relation to that matter;
"claimant", unless the context otherwise requires, includes a counterclaimant, and related expressions shall be construed accordingly;
"dispute" includes any difference;
"enactment" includes an enactment contained in Northern Ireland legislation;
"legal proceedings" means civil proceedings in the High Court or a county court;
"peremptory order" means an order made under section 41(5) or made in exercise of any corresponding power conferred by the parties;
"premises" includes land, buildings, moveable structures, vehicles, vessels, aircraft and hovercraft;
"question of law" means—

(a) for a court in England and Wales, a question of the law of England and Wales, and

(b) for a court in Northern Ireland, a question of the law of Northern Ireland;

"substantive jurisdiction", in relation to an arbitral tribunal, refers to the matters specified in section 30(1)(a) to (c), and references to the tribunal exceeding its substantive jurisdiction shall be construed accordingly.

(2) References in this Part to a party to an arbitration agreement include any person claiming under or through a party to the agreement.

Index of defined expressions: Part I

83. In this Part the expressions listed below are defined or otherwise explained by the provisions indicated— A6–084

agreement, agree and agreed	section 5(1)
agreement in writing	section 5(2) to (5)
arbitration agreement	sections 6 and 5(1)
arbitrator	section 82(1)
available arbitral process	section 82(1)
claimant	section 82(1)
commencement (in relation to arbitral proceedings)	section 14
costs of the arbitration	section 59
the court	section 105
dispute	section 82(1)
enactment	section 82(1)
legal proceedings	section 82(1)
Limitation Acts	section 13(4)
notice (or other document), party—	section 76(6)
– in relation to an arbitration agreement	section 82(2)
– where section 106(2) or (3) applies	section 106(4)
peremptory order	section 82(1) (and see section 41(5))
premises	section 82(1)
question of law	section 82(1)
recoverable costs	sections 63 and 64
seat of the arbitration	section 3
serve and service (of notice or other document)	section 76(6)
substantive jurisdiction (in relation to an arbitral tribunal)	section 82(1) (and see section 30(1)(a) to (c))
upon notice (to the parties or the tribunal)	section 80
written and in writing	section 5(6)

Transitional provisions

84.—(1) The provisions of this Part do not apply to arbitral proceedings commenced before the date on which this Part comes into force. A6–085

(2) They apply to arbitral proceedings commenced on or after that date under an arbitration agreement whenever made.

(3) The above provisions have effect subject to any transitional provision made by an order under section 109(2) (power to include transitional provisions in commencement order).

STATUTORY MATERIALS AND RULES OF COURT

PART II

OTHER PROVISIONS RELATING TO ARBITRATION

Domestic arbitration agreements

Modifications of Part I in relation to domestic arbitration agreement

A6–086   85.—(1) In the case of a domestic arbitration agreement the provisions of Part I are modified in accordance with the following sections.
(2) For this purpose a "domestic arbitration agreement" means an arbitration agreement to which none of the parties is—

>   (a) an individual who is a national of, or habitually resident in, a state other than the United Kingdom, or

>   (b) a body corporate which is incorporated in, or whose central control and management is exercised in, a state other than the United Kingdom,

and under which the seat of the arbitration (if the seat has been designated or determined) is in the United Kingdom.
(3) In subsection (2) "arbitration agreement" and "seat of the arbitration" have the same meaning as in Part I (see sections 3, 5(1) and 6).

Staying of legal proceedings

A6–087   86.—(1) In section 9 (stay of legal proceedings), subsection (4) (stay unless the arbitration agreement is null and void, inoperative, or incapable of being performed) does not apply to a domestic arbitration agreement.
(2) on an application under that section in relation to a domestic arbitration agreement the court shall grant a stay unless satisfied—

>   (a) that the arbitration agreement is null and void, inoperative, or incapable of being performed, or

>   (b) that there are other sufficient grounds for not requiring the parties to abide by the arbitration agreement.

(3) The court may treat as a sufficient ground under subsection (2)(b) the fact that the applicant is or was at any material time not ready and willing to do all things necessary for the proper conduct of the arbitration or of any other dispute resolution procedures required to be exhausted before resorting to arbitration.
(4) For the purposes of this section the question whether an arbitration agreement is a domestic arbitration agreement shall be determined by reference to the facts at the time the legal proceedings are commenced.

Effectiveness of agreement to exclude court's jurisdiction

A6–088   87.—(1) In the case of a domestic arbitration agreement any agreement to exclude the jurisdiction of the court under—

(a) section 45 (determination of preliminary point of law), or

(b) section 69 (challenging the award: appeal on point of law), is not effective unless entered into after the commencement of the arbitral proceedings in which the question arises or the award is made.

(2) For this purpose the commencement of the arbitral proceedings has the same meaning as in Part I (see section 14).

(3) For the purposes of this section the question whether an arbitration agreement is a domestic arbitration agreement shall be determined by reference to the facts at the time the agreement is entered into.

Power to repeal or amend sections 85 to 87

88.—(1) The Secretary of State may by order repeal or amend the provisions of sections 85 to 87.

(2) An order under this section may contain such supplementary, incidental and transitional provisions as appear to the Secretary of State to be appropriate.

(3) An order under this section shall be made by statutory instrument and no such order shall be made unless a draft of it has been laid before and approved by a resolution of each House of Parliament.

A6–089

Consumer arbitration agreements

Application of unfair terms regulations to consumer arbitration agreements

89.—(1) The following sections extend the application of the Unfair Terms in Consumer Contracts Regulations 1994 in relation to a term which constitutes an arbitration agreement.

For this purpose "arbitration agreement" means an agreement to submit to arbitration present or future disputes or differences (whether or not contractual).

(2) In those sections "the Regulations" means those regulations and includes any regulations amending or replacing those regulations.

(3) Those sections apply whatever the law applicable to the arbitration agreement.

A6–090

Regulations apply where consumer is a legal person

90. The Regulations apply where the consumer is a legal person as they apply where the consumer is a natural person.

A6–091

Arbitration agreement unfair where modest amount sought

91.—(1) A term which constitutes an arbitration agreement is unfair for the purposes of the Regulations so far as it relates to a claim for a pecuniary remedy which does not exceed the amount specified by order for the purposes of this section.

(2) Orders under this section may make different provision for different cases and for different purposes.

(3) The power to make orders under this section is exercisable—

(a) for England and Wales, by the Secretary of State with the concurrence of the Lord Chancellor,

A6–092

(b) for Scotland, by the Secretary of State [. . .], and

(c) for Northern Ireland, by the Department of Economic Development for Northern Ireland with the concurrence of the Lord Chancellor.

(4) Any such order for England and Wales or Scotland shall be made by statutory instrument which shall be subject to annulment in pursuance of a resolution of either House of Parliament.

(5) Any such order for Northern Ireland shall be a statutory rule for the purposes of the Statutory Rules (Northern Ireland) Order 1979 and shall be subject to negative resolution, within the meaning of section 41(6) of the Interpretation Act (Northern Ireland) 1954.

Small claims arbitration in the county court

Exclusion of Part I in relation to small claims arbitration in the county court

A6–093 92. Nothing in Part I of this Act applies to arbitration under section 64 of the County Courts Act 1984.

Appointment of judges as arbitrators

Appointment of judges as arbitrators

A6–094 93.—(1) A judge of the Commercial Court or an official referee may, if in all the circumstances he thinks fit, accept appointment as a sole arbitrator or as umpire by or by virtue of an arbitration agreement.

(2) A judge of the Commercial Court shall not do so unless the Lord Chief Justice has informed him that, having regard to the state of business in the High Court and the Crown Court, he can be made available.

(3) An official referee shall not do so unless the Lord Chief Justice has informed him that, having regard to the state of official referees' business, he can be made available.

(4) The fees payable for the services of a judge of the Commercial Court or official referee as arbitrator or umpire shall be taken in the High Court.

(5) In this section—

"arbitration agreement" has the same meaning as in Part I, and
"official referee" means a person nominated under section 68(1)(a) of the Supreme Court Act 1981 to deal with official referees' business.

(6) The provisions of Part I of this Act apply to arbitration before a person appointed under this section with the modifications specified in Schedule 2.

Statutory arbitrations

Application of Part I to statutory arbitrations

A6–095 94.—(1) The provisions of Part I apply to every arbitration under an enactment (a "statutory arbitration"), whether the enactment was passed or made before or after the commencement of this Act, subject to the adaptations and exclusions specified in sections 95 to 98.

(2) The provisions of Part I do not apply to a statutory arbitration if or to the extent that their application—

    (a) is inconsistent with the provisions of the enactment concerned, with any rules or procedure authorised or recognised by it, or

    (b) is excluded by any other enactment.

(3) In this section and the following provisions of this Part "enactment"—

    (a) in England and Wales, includes an enactment contained in subordinate legislation within the meaning of the Interpretation Act 1978;

    (b) in Northern Ireland, means a statutory provision within the meaning of section 1(f) of the Interpretation Act (Northern Ireland) 1954.

General adaptation of provisions in relation to statutory arbitrations

95.—(1) The provisions of Part I apply to a statutory arbitration—   **A6–096**

    (a) as if the arbitration were pursuant to an arbitration agreement and as if the enactment were that agreement, and

    (b) as if the persons by and against whom a claim subject to arbitration in pursuance of the enactment may be or has been made were parties to that agreement.

(2) Every statutory arbitration shall be taken to have its seat in England and Wales or, as the case may be, in Northern Ireland.

Specific adaptations of provisions in relation to statutory arbitrations

96.—(1) The following provisions of Part I apply to a statutory arbitration with the   **A6–097**
following adaptations.

(2) In section 30(1) (competence of tribunal to rule on its own jurisdiction), the reference in paragraph (a) to whether there is a valid arbitration agreement shall be construed as a reference to whether the enactment applies to the dispute or difference in question.

(3) Section 35 (consolidation of proceedings and concurrent hearings) applies only so as to authorise the consolidation of proceedings, or concurrent hearings in proceedings, under the same enactment.

(4) Section 46 (rules applicable to substance of dispute) applies with the omission of subsection (1)(b) (determination in accordance with considerations agreed by parties).

Provisions excluded from applying to statutory arbitrations

97.—(1) The following provisions of Part I do not apply in relation to a statutory   **A6–098**
arbitration—

    (a) section 8 (whether agreement discharged by death of a party);

    (b) section 12 (power of court to extend agreed time limits);

    (c) sections 9(5), 10(2) and 71(4) (restrictions on effect of provision that award condition precedent to right to bring legal proceedings).

Power to make further provision by regulations

A6–099   **98.**—(1) The Secretary of State may make provision by regulations for adapting or excluding any provision of Part I in relation to statutory arbitrations in general or statutory arbitrations of any particular description.

(2) The power is exercisable whether the enactment concerned is passed or made before or after the commencement of this Act.

(3) Regulations under this section shall be made by statutory instrument which shall be subject to annulment in pursuance of a resolution of either House of Parliament.

Part III

Recognition and Enforcement of Certain Foreign Awards

Enforcement of Geneva Convention awards

Continuation of Part II of the Arbitration Act 1950

A6–100   **99.** Part II of the Arbitration Act 1950 (enforcement of certain foreign awards) continues to apply in relation to foreign awards within the meaning of that Part which are not also New York Convention awards.

Recognition and enforcement of New York Convention awards

New York Convention awards

A6–101   **100.**—(1) In this Part a "New York Convention award" means an award made, in pursuance of an arbitration agreement, in the territory of a state (other than the United Kingdom) which is a party to the New York Convention.

(2) For the purposes of subsection (1) and of the provisions of this Part relating to such awards—

(a) "arbitration agreement" means an arbitration agreement in writing, and

(b) an award shall be treated as made at the seat of the arbitration, regardless of where it was signed, despatched or delivered to any of the parties.

In this subsection "agreement in writing" and "seat of the arbitration" have the same meaning as in Part I.

(3) If Her Majesty by Order in Council declares that a state specified in the Order is a party to the New York Convention, or is a party in respect of any territory so specified, the Order shall, while in force, be conclusive evidence of that fact.

(4) In this section "the New York Convention" means the Convention on the Recognition and Enforcement of Foreign Arbitral Awards adopted by the United Nations Conference on International Commercial Arbitration on 10th June 1958.

Recognition and enforcement of awards

A6–102   **101.**—(1) A New York Convention award shall be recognised as binding on the persons as between whom it was made, and may accordingly be relied on by those persons by way of defence, set-off or otherwise in any legal proceedings in England and Wales or Northern Ireland.

(2) A New York Convention award may, by leave of the court, be enforced in the same manner as a judgment or order of the court to the same effect.

As to the meaning of "the court" see section 105.

(3) Where leave is so given, judgment may be entered in terms of the award.

Evidence to be produced by party seeking recognition or enforcement

102.—(1) A party seeking the recognition or enforcement of a New York Convention award must produce—

(a) the duly authenticated original award or a duly certified copy of it, and

(b) the original arbitration agreement or a duly certified copy of it.

(2) If the award or agreement is in a foreign language, the party must also produce a translation of it certified by an official or sworn translator or by a diplomatic or consular agent.

Refusal of recognition or enforcement

103.—(1) Recognition or enforcement of a New York Convention award shall not be refused except in the following cases.

(2) Recognition or enforcement of the award may be refused if the person against whom it is invoked proves—

(a) that a party to the arbitration agreement was (under the law applicable to him) under some incapacity;

(b) that the arbitration agreement was not valid under the law to which the parties subjected it or, failing any indication thereon, under the law of the country where the award was made;

(c) that he was not given proper notice of the appointment of the arbitrator or of the arbitration proceedings or was otherwise unable to present his case;

(d) that the award deals with a difference not contemplated by or not falling within the terms of the submission to arbitration or contains decisions on matters beyond the scope of the submission to arbitration (but see subsection (4));

(e) that the composition of the arbitral tribunal or the arbitral procedure was not in accordance with the agreement of the parties or, failing such agreement, with the law of the country in which the arbitration took place;

(f) that the award has not yet become binding on the parties, or has been set aside or suspended by a competent authority of the country in which, or under the law of which, it was made.

(3) Recognition or enforcement of the award may also be refused if the award is in respect of a matter which is not capable of settlement by arbitration, or if it would be contrary to public policy to recognise or enforce the award.

(4) An award which contains decisions on matters not submitted to arbitration may be recognised or enforced to the extent that it contains decisions on matters submitted to arbitration which can be separated from those on matters not so submitted.

(5) Where an application for the setting aside or suspension of the award has been made to such a competent authority as is mentioned in subsection (2)(f), the court before which the award is sought to be relied upon may, if it considers it proper, adjourn the decision on the recognition or enforcement of the award.

It may also on the application of the party claiming recognition or enforcement of the award order the other party to give suitable security.

Saving for other bases of recognition or enforcement

A6–105   104. Nothing in the preceding provisions of this Part affects any right to rely upon or enforce a New York Convention award at common law or under section 66.

PART IV

GENERAL PROVISIONS

Meaning of "the court": jurisdiction of High Court and county court

A6–106   105.—(1) In this Act "the court" means the High Court or a county court, subject to the following provisions.

(2) The Lord Chancellor may by order make provision—

(a) allocating proceedings under this Act to the High Court or to county courts; or

(b) specifying proceedings under this Act which may be commenced or taken only in the High Court or in a county court.

(3) The Lord Chancellor may by order make provision requiring proceedings of any specified description under this Act in relation to which a county court has jurisdiction to be commenced or taken in one or more specified county courts.

Any jurisdiction so exercisable by a specified county court is exercisable throughout England and Wales or, as the case may be, Northern Ireland.

(4) An order under this section—

(a) may differentiate between categories of proceedings by reference to such criteria as the Lord Chancellor sees fit to specify, and

(b) may make such incidental or transitional provision as the Lord Chancellor considers necessary or expedient.

(5) An order under this section for England and Wales shall be made by statutory instrument which shall be subject to annulment in pursuance of a resolution of either House of Parliament.

(6) An order under this section for Northern Ireland shall be a statutory rule for the purposes of the Statutory Rules (Northern Ireland) Order 1979 which shall be subject to annulment in pursuance of a resolution of either House of Parliament in like manner as a statutory instrument and section 5 of the Statutory Instruments Act 1946 shall apply accordingly.

Crown application

106.—(1) Part I of this Act applies to any arbitration agreement to which Her Majesty, either in right of the Crown or of the Duchy of Lancaster or otherwise, or the Duke of Cornwall, is a party.

(2) Where Her Majesty is party to an arbitration agreement otherwise than in right of the Crown, Her Majesty shall be represented for the purposes of any arbitral proceedings—

> (a) where the agreement was entered into by Her Majesty in right of the Duchy of Lancaster, by the Chancellor of the Duchy or such person as he may appoint, and
>
> (b) in any other case, by such person as Her Majesty may appoint in writing under the Royal Sign Manual.

(3) Where the Duke of Cornwall is party to an arbitration agreement, he shall be represented for the purposes of any arbitral proceedings by such person as he may appoint.

(4) References in Part I to a party or the parties to the arbitration agreement or to arbitral proceedings shall be construed, where subsection (2) or (3) applies, as references to the person representing Her Majesty or the Duke of Cornwall.

Consequential amendments and repeals

107.—(1) The enactments specified in Schedule 3 are amended in accordance with that Schedule, the amendments being consequential on the provisions of this Act.

(2) The enactments specified in Schedule 4 are repealed to the extent specified.

Extent

108.—(1) The provisions of this Act extend to England and Wales and, except as mentioned below, to Northern Ireland.

(2) The following provisions of Part II do not extend to Northern Ireland—

> section 92 (exclusion of Part I in relation to small claims arbitration in the county court), and
>
> section 93 and Schedule 2 (appointment of judges as arbitrators).

(3) Sections 89, 90 and 91 (consumer arbitration agreements) extend to Scotland and the provisions of Schedules 3 and 4 (consequential amendments and repeals) extend to Scotland so far as they relate to enactments which so extend, subject as follows.

(4) The repeal of the Arbitration Act 1975 extends only to England and Wales and Northern Ireland.

Commencement

109.—(1) The provisions of this Act come into force on such day as the Secretary of State may appoint by order made by statutory instrument, and different days may be appointed for different purposes.

(2) An order under subsection (1) may contain such transitional provisions as appear to the Secretary of State to be appropriate.

Short title

A6–111   **110.** This Act may be cited as the Arbitration Act 1996.

SCHEDULES

SCHEDULE 1

MANDATORY PROVISIONS OF PART I

A6–112   sections 9 to 11 (stay of legal proceedings);
section 12 (power of court to extend agreed time limits);
section 13 (application of Limitation Acts);
section 24 (power of court to remove arbitrator);
section 26(1) (effect of death of arbitrator);
section 28 (liability of parties for fees and expenses of arbitrators);
section 29 (immunity of arbitrator);
section 31 (objection to substantive jurisdiction of tribunal);
section 32 (determination of preliminary point of jurisdiction);
section 33 (general duty of tribunal);
section 37(2) (items to be treated as expenses of arbitrators);
section 40 (general duty of parties);
section 43 (securing the attendance of witnesses);
section 56 (power to withhold award in case of non-payment);
section 60 (effectiveness of agreement for payment of costs in any event);
section 66 (enforcement of award);
sections 67 and 68 (challenging the award: substantive jurisdiction and serious irregularity), and sections 70 and 71 (supplementary provisions; effect of order of court) so far as relating to those sections;
section 72 (saving for rights of person who takes no part in proceedings);
section 73 (loss of right to object);
section 74 (immunity of arbitral institutions, &c.);
section 75 (charge to secure payment of solicitors' costs).

SCHEDULE 2

MODIFICATIONS OF PART I IN RELATION TO JUDGE-ARBITRATORS

Introductory

A6–113   **1.** In this Schedule "judge-arbitrator" means a judge of the Commercial Court or official referee appointed as arbitrator or umpire under section 93.

General

A6–114   **2.**—(1) Subject to the following provisions of this Schedule, references in Part I to the court shall be construed in relation to a judge-arbitrator, or in relation to the appointment of a judge-arbitrator, as references to the Court of Appeal.

(2) The references in sections 32(6), 45(6) and 69(8) to the Court of Appeal shall in such a case be construed as references to the House of Lords.

Arbitration Act 1996

Arbitrator's fees

3.—(1) The power of the court in section 28(2) to order consideration and adjustment of the liability of a party for the fees of an arbitrator may be exercised by a judge-arbitrator.

(2) Any such exercise of the power is subject to the powers of the Court of Appeal under sections 24(4) and 25(3)(b) (directions as to entitlement to fees or expenses in case of removal or resignation).

A6–115

Exercise of court powers in support of arbitration

4.—(1) Where the arbitral tribunal consists of or includes a judge-arbitrator the powers of the court under sections 42 to 44 (enforcement of peremptory orders, summoning witnesses, and other court powers) are exercisable by the High Court and also by the judge-arbitrator himself.

(2) Anything done by a judge-arbitrator in the exercise of those powers shall be regarded as done by him in his capacity as judge of the High Court and have effect as if done by that court.

Nothing in this sub-paragraph prejudices any power vested in him as arbitrator or umpire.

A6–116

Extension of time for making award

5.—(1) The power conferred by section 50 (extension of time for making award) is exercisable by the judge-arbitrator himself.

(2) Any appeal from a decision of a judge-arbitrator under that section lies to the Court of Appeal with the leave of that court.

A6–117

Withholding award in case of non-payment

6.—(1) The provisions of paragraph 7 apply in place of the provisions of section 56 (power to withhold award in the case of non-payment) in relation to the withholding of an award for non-payment of the fees and expenses of a judge-arbitrator.

(2) This does not affect the application of section 56 in relation to the delivery of such an award by an arbitral or other institution or person vested by the parties with powers in relation to the delivery of the award.

7.—(1) A judge-arbitrator may refuse to deliver an award except upon payment of the fees and expenses mentioned in section 56(1).

(2) The judge-arbitrator may, on an application by a party to the arbitral proceedings, order that if he pays into the High Court the fees and expenses demanded, or such lesser amount as the judge-arbitrator may specify—

(a) the award shall be delivered,

(b) the amount of the fees and expenses properly payable shall be determined by such means and upon such terms as he may direct, and

(c) out of the money paid into court there shall be paid out such fees and expenses as may be found to be properly payable and the balance of the money (if any) shall be paid out to the applicant.

(3) For this purpose the amount of fees and expenses properly payable is the amount

A6–118

the applicant is liable to pay under section 28 or any agreement relating to the payment of the arbitrator.

(4) No application to the judge-arbitrator under this paragraph may be made where there is any available arbitral process for appeal or review of the amount of the fees or expenses demanded.

(5) Any appeal from a decision of a judge-arbitrator under this paragraph lies to the Court of Appeal with the leave of that court.

(6) Where a party to arbitral proceedings appeals under sub-paragraph (5), an arbitrator is entitled to appear and be heard.

Correction of award or additional award

A6–119   8. Subsections (4) to (6) of section 57 (correction of award or additional award: time limit for application or exercise of power) do not apply to a judge-arbitrator.

Costs

A6–120   9. Where the arbitral tribunal consists of or includes a judge-arbitrator the powers of the court under section 63(4) (determination of recoverable costs) shall be exercised by the High Court.

10.—(1) The power of the court under section 64 to determine an arbitrator's reasonable fees and expenses may be exercised by a judge-arbitrator.

(2) Any such exercise of the power is subject to the powers of the Court of Appeal under sections 24(4) and 25(3)(b) (directions as to entitlement to fees or expenses in case of removal or resignation).

Enforcement of award

A6–121   11. The leave of the court required by section 66 (enforcement of award) may in the case of an award of a judge-arbitrator be given by the judge-arbitrator himself.

Solicitors' costs

A6–122   12. The powers of the court to make declarations and orders under the provisions applied by section 75 (power to charge property recovered in arbitral proceedings with the payment of solicitors' costs) may be exercised by the judge-arbitrator.

Powers of court in relation to service of documents

A6–123   13.—(1) The power of the court under section 77(2) (powers of court in relation to service of documents) is exercisable by the judge-arbitrator.

(2) Any appeal from a decision of a judge-arbitrator under that section lies to the Court of Appeal with the leave of that court.

Powers of court to extend time limits relating to arbitral proceedings

A6–124   14.—(1) The power conferred by section 79 (power of court to extend time limits relating to arbitral proceedings) is exercisable by the judge-arbitrator himself.

(2) Any appeal from a decision of a judge-arbitrator under that section lies to the Court of Appeal with the leave of that court.

SCHEDULE 3

Consequential Amendments

Merchant Shipping Act 1894 (c.60)

1. In section 496 of the Merchant Shipping Act 1894 (provisions as to deposits by owners of goods), after subsection (4) insert—

"(5) In subsection (3) the expression 'legal proceedings' includes arbitral proceedings and as respects England and Wales and Northern Ireland the provisions of section 14 of the Arbitration Act 1996 apply to determine when such proceedings are commenced.".

Stannaries Court (Abolition) Act 1896 (c.45)

2. In section 4(1) of the Stannaries Court (Abolition) Act 1896 (references of certain disputes to arbitration), for the words from "tried before" to "any such reference" substitute "referred to arbitration before himself or before an arbitrator agreed on by the parties or an officer of the court".

Tithe Act 1936 (c.43)

3. In section 39(1) of the Tithe Act 1936 (proceedings of Tithe Redemption Commission)—

(a) for "the Arbitration Acts 1889 to 1934" substitute "Part I of the Arbitration Act 1996";

(b) for paragraph (e) substitute—

"(e) the making of an application to the court to determine a preliminary point of law and the bringing of an appeal to the court on a point of law;";

(c) for "the said Acts" substitute "Part I of the Arbitration Act 1996".

Education Act 1944 (c.31)

4. [. . .]

Commonwealth Telegraphs Act 1949 (c.39)

5. In section 8(2) of the Commonwealth Telegraphs Act 1949 (proceedings of referees under the Act) for "the Arbitration Acts 1889 to 1934, or the Arbitration Act (Northern Ireland) 1937," substitute "Part I of the Arbitration Act 1996".

Lands Tribunal Act 1949 (c.42)

6. In section 3 of the Lands Tribunal Act 1949 (proceedings before the Lands Tribunal)—

(a) in subsection (6)(c) (procedural rules: power to apply Arbitration Acts), and

(b) in subsection (8) (exclusion of Arbitration Acts except as applied by rules),

for "the Arbitration Acts 1889 to 1934" substitute "Part I of the Arbitration Act 1996".

Wireless Telegraphy Act 1949 (c.54)

A6–131   7. In the Wireless Telegraphy Act 1949, Schedule 2 (procedure of appeals tribunal), in paragraph 3(1)—

(a) for the words "the Arbitration Acts 1889 to 1934" substitute "Part I of the Arbitration Act 1996";

(b) after the word "Wales" insert "or Northern Ireland"; and

(c) for "the said Acts" substitute "Part I of that Act".

Patents Act 1949 (c.87)

A6–132   8. In section 67 of the Patents Act 1949 (proceedings as to infringement of pre-1978 patents referred to comptroller), for "The Arbitration Acts 1889 to 1934" substitute "Part I of the Arbitration Act 1996".

National Health Service (Amendment) Act 1949 (c.93)

A6–133   9. In section 7(8) of the National Health Service (Amendment) Act 1949 (arbitration in relation to hardship arising from the National Health Service Act 1946 or the Act), for "the Arbitration Acts 1889 to 1934" substitute "Part I of the Arbitration Act 1996" and for "the said Acts" substitute "Part I of that Act".

Arbitration Act 1950 (c.27)

A6–134   10. In section 36(1) of the Arbitration Act 1950 (effect of foreign awards enforceable under Part II of that Act) for "section 26 of this Act" substitute "section 66 of the Arbitration Act 1996".

Interpretation Act (Northern Ireland) 1954 (c.33 (N.I.))

A6–135   11. In section 46(2) of the Interpretation Act (Northern Ireland) 1954 (miscellaneous definitions), for the definition of "arbitrator" substitute—

"'arbitrator' has the same meaning as in Part I of the Arbitration Act 1996;".

Agricultural Marketing Act 1958 (c.47)

A6–136   12. In section 12(1) of the Agricultural Marketing Act 1958 (application of provisions of Arbitration Act 1950)—

(a) for the words from the beginning to "shall apply" substitute "Sections 45 and 69 of the Arbitration Act 1996 (which relate to the determination by the court of questions of law) and section 66 of that Act (enforcement of awards) apply"; and

(b) for "an arbitration" substitute "arbitral proceedings".

Carriage by Air Act 1961 (c.27)

A6–137   13.—(1) The Carriage by Air Act 1961 is amended as follows.
(2) In section 5(3) (time for bringing proceedings)—

(a) for "an arbitration" in the first place where it occurs substitute "arbitral proceedings"; and

(b) for the words from "and subsections (3) and (4)" to the end substitute "and the provisions of section 14 of the Arbitration Act 1996 apply to determine when such proceedings are commenced.".

(3) In section 11(c) (application of section 5 to Scotland)—

(a) for "subsections (3) and (4)" substitute "the provisions of section 14 of the Arbitration Act 1996"; and

(b) for "an arbitration" substitute "arbitral proceedings".

Factories Act 1961 (c.34)

14. In the Factories Act 1961, for section 171 (application of Arbitration Act 1950), substitute— **A6–138**

"Application of the Arbitration Act 1996

171. Part I of the Arbitration Act 1996 does not apply to proceedings under this Act except in so far as it may be applied by regulations made under this Act.".

Clergy Pensions Measure 1961 (No. 3)

15. In the Clergy Pensions Measure 1961, section 38(4) (determination of questions), for the words "The Arbitration Act 1950" substitute "Part I of the Arbitration Act 1996". **A6–139**

Transport Act 1962 (c.46)

16.—(1) The Transport Act 1962 is amended as follows. **A6–140**

(2) In section 74(6)(f) (proceedings before referees in pension disputes), for the words "the Arbitration Act 1950" substitute "Part I of the Arbitration Act 1996".

(3) In section 81(7) (proceedings before referees in compensation disputes), for the words "the Arbitration Act 1950" substitute "Part I of the Arbitration Act 1996".

(4) In Schedule 7, Part IV (pensions), in paragraph 17(5) for the words "the Arbitration Act 1950" substitute "Part I of the Arbitration Act 1996".

Corn Rents Act 1963 (c.14)

17. In the Corn Rents Act 1963, section 1(5) (schemes for apportioning corn rents, &c.), for the words "the Arbitration Act 1950" substitute "Part I of the Arbitration Act 1996". **A6–141**

Plant Varieties and Seeds Act 1964 (c.14)

18. [. . .] **A6–142**

Lands Tribunal and Compensation Act (Northern Ireland) 1964 (c.29 (N.I.))

19. In section 9 of the Lands Tribunal and Compensation Act (Northern Ireland) 1964 (proceedings of Lands Tribunal), in subsection (3) (where Tribunal acts as arbitrator) for "the Arbitration Act (Northern Ireland) 1937" substitute "Part I of the Arbitration Act 1996". **A6–143**

Industrial and Provident Societies Act 1965 (c.12)

A6–144 20.—(1) Section 60 of the Industrial and Provident Societies Act 1965 is amended as follows.

(2) In subsection (8) (procedure for hearing disputes between society and member, &c.)—

> (a) in paragraph (a) for "the Arbitration Act 1950" substitute "Part I of the Arbitration Act 1996"; and
>
> (b) in paragraph (b) omit "by virtue of section 12 of the said Act of 1950".

(3) For subsection (9) substitute—

> "(9) The court or registrar to whom any dispute is referred under subsections (2) to (7) may at the request of either party state a case on any question of law arising in the dispute for the opinion of the High Court or, as the case may be, the Court of Session.".

Carriage of Goods by Road Act 1965 (c.37)

A6–145 21. In section 7(2) of the Carriage of Goods by Road Act 1965 (arbitrations: time at which deemed to commence), for paragraphs (a) and (b) substitute—

> "(a) as respects England and Wales and Northern Ireland, the provisions of section 14(3) to (5) of the Arbitration Act 1996 (which determine the time at which an arbitration is commenced) apply;".

Factories Act (Northern Ireland) 1965 (c.20 (N.I.))

A6–146 22. In section 171 of the Factories Act (Northern Ireland) 1965 (application of Arbitration Act), for "The Arbitration Act (Northern Ireland) 1937" substitute "Part I of the Arbitration Act 1996".

Commonwealth Secretariat Act 1966 (c.10)

A6–147 23. In section 1(3) of the Commonwealth Secretariat Act 1966 (contracts with Commonwealth Secretariat to be deemed to contain provision for arbitration), for "the Arbitration Act 1950 and the Arbitration Act (Northern Ireland) 1937" substitute "Part I of the Arbitration Act 1996".

Arbitration (International Investment Disputes) Act 1966 (c.41)

A6–148 24. In the Arbitration (International Investment Disputes) Act 1966, for section 3 (application of Arbitration Act 1950 and other enactments) substitute—

> **"Application of provisions of Arbitration Act 1996**
>
> 3.—(1) The Lord Chancellor may by order direct that any of the provisions contained in sections 36 and 38 to 44 of the Arbitration Act 1996 (provisions concerning the conduct of arbitral proceedings, &c.) shall apply to such proceedings pursuant to the Convention as are specified in the order with or without any modifications or exceptions specified in the order.

(2) Subject to subsection (1), the Arbitration Act 1996 shall not apply to proceedings pursuant to the Convention, but this subsection shall not be taken as affecting section 9 of that Act (stay of legal proceedings in respect of matter subject to arbitration).

(3) An order made under this section—

(a) may be varied or revoked by a subsequent order so made, and
(b) shall be contained in a statutory instrument.".

Poultry Improvement Act (Northern Ireland) 1968 (c.12 (N.I.))

25. In paragraph 10(4) of the Schedule to the Poultry Improvement Act (Northern Ireland) 1968 (reference of disputes), for "The Arbitration Act (Northern Ireland) 1937" substitute "Part I of the Arbitration Act 1996". **A6–149**

Industrial and Provident Societies Act (Northern Ireland) 1969 (c.24 (N.I.))

26.—(1) Section 69 of the Industrial and Provident Societies Act (Northern Ireland) 1969 (decision of disputes) is amended as follows. **A6–150**
(2) In subsection (7) (decision of disputes)—

(a) in the opening words, omit the words from "and without prejudice" to "1937";

(b) at the beginning of paragraph (a) insert "without prejudice to any powers exercisable by virtue of Part I of the Arbitration Act 1996,"; and

(c) in paragraph (b) omit "the registrar or" and "registrar or" and for the words from "as might have been granted by the High Court" to the end substitute "as might be granted by the registrar".

(3) For subsection (8) substitute—

"(8) The court or registrar to whom any dispute is referred under subsections (2) to (6) may at the request of either party state a case on any question of law arising in the dispute for the opinion of the High Court.".

Health and Personal Social Services (Northern Ireland) Order 1972 (N.I.14)

27. In Article 105(6) of the Health and Personal Social Services (Northern Ireland) Order 1972 (arbitrations under the Order), for "the Arbitration Act (Northern Ireland) 1937" substitute "Part I of the Arbitration Act 1996". **A6–151**

Consumer Credit Act 1974 (c. 39)

28.—(1) Section 146 of the Consumer Credit Act 1974 is amended as follows. **A6–152**
(2) In subsection (2) (solicitor engaged in contentious business), for "section 86(1) of the Solicitors Act 1957" substitute "section 87(1) of the Solicitors Act 1974".
(3) In subsection (4) (solicitor in Northern Ireland engaged in contentious business), for the words from "business done" to "Administration of Estates (Northern Ireland) Order 1979" substitute "contentious business (as defined in Article 3(2) of the Solicitors (Northern Ireland) Order 1976.".

Friendly Societies Act 1974 (c.46)

A6–153 29.—(1) The Friendly Societies Act 1974 is amended as follows.
(2) For section 78(1) (statement of case) substitute—

"(1) Any arbitrator, arbiter or umpire to whom a dispute falling within section 76 above is referred under the rules of a registered society or branch may at the request of either party state a case on any question of law arising in the dispute for the opinion of the High Court or, as the case may be, the Court of Session.".

(3) In section 83(3) (procedure on objections to amalgamations &c. of friendly societies), for "the Arbitration Act 1950 or, in Northern Ireland, the Arbitration Act (Northern Ireland) 1937" substitute "Part I of the Arbitration Act 1996".

Industry Act 1975 (c.68)

A6–154 30. In Schedule 3 to the Industry Act (arbitration of disputes relating to vesting and compensation orders), in paragraph 14 (application of certain provisions of Arbitration Acts)—

(a) for "the Arbitration Act 1950 or, in Northern Ireland, the Arbitration Act (Northern Ireland) 1937" substitute "Part I of the Arbitration Act 1996", and

(b) for "that Act" substitute "that Part".

Industrial Relations (Northern Ireland) Order 1976 (N.I.16)

A6–155 31. In Article 59(9) of the Industrial Relations (Northern Ireland) Order 1976 (proceedings of industrial tribunal), for "The Arbitration Act (Northern Ireland) 1937" substitute "Part I of the Arbitration Act 1996".

Aircraft and Shipbuilding Industries Act 1977 (c.3)

A6–156 32. In Schedule 7 to the Aircraft and Shipbuilding Industries Act 1977 (procedure of Arbitration Tribunal), in paragraph 2—

(a) for "the Arbitration Act 1950 or, in Northern Ireland, the Arbitration Act (Northern Ireland) 1937" substitute "Part I of the Arbitration Act 1996", and

(b) for "that Act" substitute "that Part".

Patents Act 1977 (c.37)

A6–157 33. In section 130 of the Patents Act 1977 (interpretation), in subsection (8) (exclusion of Arbitration Act) for "The Arbitration Act 1950" substitute "Part I of the Arbitration Act 1996".

Judicature (Northern Ireland) Act 1978 (c.23)

A6–158 34.—(1) The Judicature (Northern Ireland) Act 1978 is amended as follows.
(2) In section 35(2) (restrictions on appeals to the Court of Appeal), after paragraph (f) insert—

"(fa) except as provided by Part I of the Arbitration Act 1996, from any decision of the High Court under that Part;".

(3) In section 55(2) (rules of court) after paragraph (c) insert—

"(cc) providing for any prescribed part of the jurisdiction of the High Court in relation to the trial of any action involving matters of account to be exercised in the prescribed manner by a person agreed by the parties and for the remuneration of any such person;".

Health and Safety at Work (Northern Ireland) Order 1978 (N.I.9)

35. In Schedule 4 to the Health and Safety at Work (Northern Ireland) Order 1978 (licensing provisions), in paragraph 3, for "The Arbitration Act (Northern Ireland) 1937" substitute "Part I of the Arbitration Act 1996".   A6–159

County Courts (Northern Ireland) Order 1980 (N.I.3)

36.—(1) The County Courts (Northern Ireland) Order 1980 is amended as follows.   A6–160
(2) In Article 30 (civil jurisdiction exercisable by district judge)—

(a) for paragraph (2) substitute—

"(2) Any order, decision or determination made by a district judge under this Article (other than one made in dealing with a claim by way of arbitration under paragraph (3)) shall be embodied in a decree which for all purposes (including the right of appeal under Part VI) shall have the like effect as a decree pronounced by a county court judge.";

(b) for paragraphs (4) and (5) substitute—

"(4) Where in any action to which paragraph (1) applies the claim is dealt with by way of arbitration under paragraph (3)—

(a) any award made by the district judge in dealing with the claim shall be embodied in a decree which for all purposes (except the right of appeal under Part VI) shall have the like effect as a decree pronounced by a county court judge;

(b) the district judge may, and shall if so required by the High Court, state for the determination of the High Court any question of law arising out of an award so made;

(c) except as provided by sub-paragraph (b), any award so made shall be final; and

(d) except as otherwise provided by county court rules, no costs shall be awarded in connection with the action.

(5) Subject to paragraph (4), county court rules may

(a) apply any of the provisions of Part I of the Arbitration Act 1996 to arbitrations under paragraph (3) with such modifications as may be prescribed;

(b) prescribe the rules of evidence to be followed on any arbitration under paragraph (3) and, in particular, make provision with respect to the manner of taking and questioning evidence.

(5A) Except as provided by virtue of paragraph (5)(a), Part I of the Arbitration Act 1996 shall not apply to an arbitration under paragraph (3).".

(3) After Article 61 insert—

"Appeals from decisions under Part I of Arbitration Act 1996

61A.—(1) Article 61 does not apply to a decision of a county court judge made in the exercise of the jurisdiction conferred by Part I of the Arbitration Act 1996.

(2) Any party dissatisfied with a decision of the county court made in the exercise of the jurisdiction conferred by any of the following provisions of Part I of the Arbitration Act 1996, namely—

> (a) section 32 (question as to substantive jurisdiction of arbitral tribunal);
> (b) section 45 (question of law arising in course of arbitral proceedings);
> (c) section 67 (challenging award of arbitral tribunal: substantive jurisdiction);
> (d) section 68 (challenging award of arbitral tribunal: serious irregularity);
> (e) section 69 (appeal on point of law),

may, subject to the provisions of that Part, appeal from that decision to the Court of Appeal.

(3) Any party dissatisfied with any decision of a county court made in the exercise of the jurisdiction conferred by any other provision of Part I of the Arbitration Act 1996 may, subject to the provisions of that Part, appeal from that decision to the High Court.

(4) The decision of the Court of Appeal on an appeal under paragraph (2) shall be final.".

Supreme Court Act 1981 (c.54)

A6–161   **37.**—(1) The Supreme Court Act 1981 is amended as follows.
(2) In section 18(1) (restrictions on appeals to the Court of Appeal), for paragraph (g) substitute—

"(g) except as provided by Part I of the Arbitration Act 1996, from any decision of the High Court under that Part;".

(3) In section 151 (interpretation, &c.), in the definition of "arbitration agreement", for "the Arbitration Act 1950 by virtue of section 32 of that Act;" substitute "Part I of the Arbitration Act 1996;".

Merchant Shipping (Liner Conferences) Act 1982 (c.37)

A6–162   **38.** In section 7(5) of the Merchant Shipping (Liner Conferences) Act 1982 (stay of legal proceedings), for the words from "section 4(1)" to the end substitute "section 9 of the Arbitration Act 1996 (which also provides for the staying of legal proceedings).".

Agricultural Marketing (Northern Ireland) Order 1982 (N.I.12)

A6–163   **39.** In Article 14 of the Agricultural Marketing (Northern Ireland) Order 1982 (application of provisions of Arbitration Act (Northern Ireland) 1937)—

(a) for the words from the beginning to "shall apply" substitute "Section 45 and 69 of the Arbitration Act 1996 (which relate to the determination by the court of questions of law) and section 66 of that Act (enforcement of awards)" apply; and

(b) for "an arbitration" substitute "arbitral proceedings".

Mental Health Act 1983 (c.20)

40. In section 78 of the Mental Health Act 1983 (procedure of Mental Health Review Tribunals), in subsection (9) for "The Arbitration Act 1950" substitute "Part I of the Arbitration Act 1996". **A6–164**

Registered Homes Act 1984 (c.23)

41. [. . .] **A6–165**

Housing Act 1985 (c.68)

42. In section 47(3) of the Housing Act 1985 (agreement as to determination of matters relating to service charges) for "section 32 of the Arbitration Act 1950" substitute "Part I of the Arbitration Act 1996". **A6–166**

Landlord and Tenant Act 1985 (c.70)

43. [. . .] **A6–167**

Credit Unions (Northern Ireland) Order 1985 (N.I.12)

44.—(1) Article 72 of the Credit Unions (Northern Ireland) Order 1985 (decision of disputes) is amended as follows. **A6–168**

(2) In paragraph (7)—

(a) in the opening words, omit the words from "and without prejudice" to "1937";

(b) at the beginning of sub-paragraph (a) insert "without prejudice to any powers exercisable by virtue of Part I of the Arbitration Act 1996,"; and

(c) in sub-paragraph (b) omit "the registrar or" and "registrar or" and for the words from "as might have been granted by the High Court" to the end substitute "as might be granted by the registrar".

(3) For paragraph (8) substitute—

"(8) The court or registrar to whom any dispute is referred under paragraphs (2) to (6) may at the request of either party state a case on any question of law arising in the dispute for the opinion of the High Court.".

Agricultural Holdings Act 1986 (c.5)

45. In section 84(1) of the Agricultural Holdings Act 1986 (provisions relating to arbitration), for "the Arbitration Act 1950" substitute "Part I of the Arbitration Act 1996". **A6–169**

Insolvency Act 1986 (c.45)

A6–170 46. In the Insolvency Act 1986, after section 349 insert—

"**Arbitration agreements to which bankrupt is party**

349A.—(1) This section applies where a bankrupt had become party to a contract containing an arbitration agreement before the commencement of his bankruptcy.

(2) If the trustee in bankruptcy adopts the contract, the arbitration agreement is enforceable by or against the trustee in relation to matters arising from or connected with the contract.

(3) If the trustee in bankruptcy does not adopt the contract and a matter to which the arbitration agreement applies requires to be determined in connection with or for the purposes of the bankruptcy proceedings—

(a) the trustee with the consent of the creditors' committee, or

(b) any other party to the agreement,

may apply to the court which may, if it thinks fit in all the circumstances of the case, order that the matter be referred to arbitration in accordance with the arbitration agreement.

(4) In this section—

'arbitration agreement' has the same meaning as in Part I of the Arbitration Act 1996; and

'the court' means the court which has jurisdiction in the bankruptcy proceedings.".

Building Societies Act 1986 (c.53)

A6–171 47. In Part II of Schedule 14 to the Building Societies Act 1986 (settlement of disputes: arbitration), in paragraph 5(6) for "the Arbitration Act 1950 and the Arbitration Act 1979 or, in Northern Ireland, the Arbitration Act (Northern Ireland) 1937" substitute "Part I of the Arbitration Act 1996".

Mental Health (Northern Ireland) Order 1986 (N.I.4)

A6–172 48. In Article 83 of the Mental Health (Northern Ireland) Order 1986 (procedure of Mental Health Review Tribunal), in paragraph (8) for "The Arbitration Act (Northern Ireland) 1937" substitute "Part I of the Arbitration Act 1996".

Multilateral Investment Guarantee Agency Act 1988 (c.8)

A6–173 49. For section 6 of the Multilateral Investment Guarantee Agency Act 1988 (application of Arbitration Act) substitute—

"**Application of Arbitration Act**

6.—(1) The Lord Chancellor may by order made by statutory instrument direct that any of the provisions of sections 36 and 38 to 44 of the Arbitration Act 1996 (provisions in relation to the conduct of the arbitral proceedings, &c.) apply, with such modifications or exceptions as are specified in the order, to such arbitration proceedings pursuant to Annex II to the Convention as are specified in the order.

(2) Except as provided by an order under subsection (1) above, no provision of Part I of the Arbitration Act 1996 other than section 9 (stay of legal proceedings) applies to any such proceedings.".

Copyright, Designs and Patents Act 1988 (c.48)

50. In section 150 of the Copyright, Designs and Patents Act 1988 (Lord Chancellor's power to make rules for Copyright Tribunal), for subsection (2) substitute—   **A6–174**

"(2) The rules may apply in relation to the Tribunal, as respects proceedings in England and Wales or Northern Ireland, any of the provisions of Part I of the Arbitration Act 1996.".

Fair Employment (Northern Ireland) Act 1989 (c.32)

51. In the Fair Employment (Northern Ireland) Act 1989, section 5 (7) (procedure of Fair Employment Tribunal), for "The Arbitration Act (Northern Ireland) 1937" substitute "Part I of the Arbitration Act 1996".   **A6–175**

Limitation (Northern Ireland) Order 1989 (N.I.11)

52. In Article 2(2) of the Limitation (Northern Ireland) Order 1989 (interpretation), in the definition of "arbitration agreement", for "the Arbitration Act (Northern Ireland) 1937" substitute "Part I of the Arbitration Act 1996".   **A6–176**

Insolvency (Northern Ireland) Order 1989 (N.I.19)

53. In the Insolvency (Northern Ireland) Order 1989, after Article 320 insert—   **A6–177**

"*Arbitration agreements to which bankrupt is party*

320A.—(1) This Article applies where a bankrupt had become party to a contract containing an arbitration agreement before the commencement of his bankruptcy.

(2) If the trustee in bankruptcy adopts the contract, the arbitration agreement is enforceable by or against the trustee in relation to matters arising from or connected with the contract.

(3) If the trustee in bankruptcy does not adopt the contract and a matter to which the arbitration agreement applies requires to be determined in connection with or for the purposes of the bankruptcy proceedings—

    (a) the trustee with the consent of the creditors' committee, or
    (b) any other party to the agreement,

may apply to the court which may, if it thinks fit in all the circumstances of the case, order that the matter be referred to arbitration in accordance with the arbitration agreement.

(4) In this Article—

    'arbitration agreement' has the same meaning as in Part I of the Arbitration Act 1996; and
    'the court' means the court which has jurisdiction in the bankruptcy proceedings.".

Social Security Administration Act 1992 (c.5)

A6–178   54. [. . .]

Social Security Administration (Northern Ireland) Act 1992 (c.8)

A6–179   55. In section 57 of the Social Security Administration (Northern Ireland) Act 1992 (procedure for inquiries, &c.), in subsection (6) for "the Arbitration Act (Northern Ireland) 1937" substitute "Part I of the Arbitration Act 1996".

Trade Union and Labour Relations (Consolidation) Act 1992 (c.52)

A6–180   56. In sections 212(5) and 263(6) of the Trade Union and Labour Relations (Consolidation) Act 1992 (application of Arbitration Act) for "the Arbitration Act 1950" substitute "Part I of the Arbitration Act 1996".

Industrial Relations (Northern Ireland) Order 1992 (N.I.5)

A6–181   57. In Articles 84(9) and 92(5) of the Industrial Relations (Northern Ireland) Order 1992 (application of Arbitration Act) for "The Arbitration Act (Northern Ireland) 1937" substitute "Part I of the Arbitration Act 1996".

Registered Homes (Northern Ireland) Order 1992 (N.I.20)

A6–182   58. In Article 33(3) of the Registered Homes (Northern Ireland) Order 1992 (procedure of Registered Homes Tribunal) for "The Arbitration Act (Northern Ireland) 1937" substitute "Part I of the Arbitration Act 1996".

Education Act 1993 (c.35)

A6–183   59. [. . .]

Roads (Northern Ireland) Order 1993 (N.I.15)

A6–184   60.—(1) The Roads (Northern Ireland) Order 1993 is amended as follows.
(2) In Article 131 (application of Arbitration Act) for "the Arbitration Act (Northern Ireland) 1937" substitute "Part I of the Arbitration Act 1996".
(3) In Schedule 4 (disputes), in paragraph 3(2) for "the Arbitration Act (Northern Ireland) 1937" substitute "Part I of the Arbitration Act 1996".

Merchant Shipping Act 1995 (c.21)

A6–185   61. In Part II of Schedule 6 to the Merchant Shipping Act 1995 (provisions having effect in connection with Convention Relating to the Carriage of Passengers and Their Luggage by Sea), for paragraph 7 substitute—

"**7.** Article 16 shall apply to arbitral proceedings as it applies to an action; and, as respects England and Wales and Northern Ireland, the provisions of section 14 of the Arbitration Act 1996 apply to determine for the purposes of that Article when an arbitration is commenced.".

Arbitration Act 1996

Industrial Tribunals Act 1996 (c.17)

62. In section 6(2) of the Industrial Tribunals Act 1996 (procedure of industrial tribunals), for "The Arbitration Act 1950" substitute "Part I of the Arbitration Act 1996".

A6–186

SCHEDULE 4

Repeals

A6–187

Chapter	Short title	Extent of repeal
1892 c. 43.	Military Lands Act 1892.	In section 21(b), the words "under the Arbitration Act 1889".
1922 c. 51.	Allotments Act 1922.	In section 21(3), the words "under the Arbitration Act 1889".
1937 c. 8 (N.I.).	Arbitration Act (Northern Ireland) 1937.	The whole Act.
1949 c. 54.	Wireless Telegraphy Act 1949.	In Schedule 2, paragraph 3(3).
1949 c. 97.	National Parks and Access to the Countryside Act 1949.	In section 18(4), the words from "Without prejudice" to "England or Wales".
1950 c. 27.	Arbitration Act 1950.	Part I. Section 42(3).
1958 c. 47.	Agricultural Marketing Act 1958.	Section 53(8).
1962 c. 46.	Transport Act 1962.	In Schedule 11, Part II, paragraph 7.
1964 c. 14.	Plant Varieties and Seeds Act 1964.	In section 10(4) the words from "or in section 9" to "three arbitrators)". Section 39(3)(b)(i).
1964 c. 29 (N.I.).	Lands Tribunal and Compensation Act (Northern Ireland) 1964.	In section 9(3) the words from "so, however, that" to the end.
1965 c. 12.	Industrial and Provident Societies Act 1965.	In section 60(8)(b), the words "by virtue of section 12 of the said Act of 1950".
1965 c. 37.	Carriage of Goods by Road Act 1965.	Section 7(2)(b).
1965 c. 13 (N.I.).	New Towns Act (Northern Ireland) 1965.	In section 27(2), the words from "under and in accordance with" to the end.
1969 c. 24 (N.I.).	Industrial and Provident Societies Act (Northern Ireland) 1969.	In section 69(7)— (a) in the opening words, the words from "and without prejudice" to "1937"; (b) in paragraph (b) the words "the registrar or" and "registrar or".
1970 c. 31.	Administration of Justice Act 1970.	Section 4. Schedule 3.
1973 c. 41.	Fair Trading Act 1973.	Section 33(2)(d).
1973 N.I. 1.	Drainage (Northern Ireland) Order 1973.	In Article 15(4), the words from "under and in accordance" to the end.

Chapter	Short title	Extent of repeal
1974 c. 47.	Solicitors Act 1974.	Article 40(4). In Schedule 7, in paragraph 9(2), the words from "under and in accordance" to the end. In section 87(1), in the definition of "contentious business", the words "appointed under the Arbitration Act 1950".
1975 c. 3.	Arbitration Act 1975.	The whole Act.
1975 c. 74.	Petroleum and Submarine Pipe-Lines Act 1975.	In Part II of Schedule 2— (a) in model clause 40(2), the words "in accordance with the Arbitration Act 1950"; (b) in model clause 40(2B), the words "in accordance with the Arbitration Act (Northern Ireland) 1937". In Part II of Schedule 3, in model clause 38(2), the words "in accordance with the Arbitration Act 1950".
1976 N.I. 12.	Solicitors (Northern Ireland) Order 1976.	In Article 3(2), in the entry "contentious business", the words "appointed under the Arbitration Act (Northern Ireland) 1937". Article 71H(3).
1977 c. 37.	Patents Act 1977.	In section 52(4) the words "section 21 of the Arbitration Act 1950 or, as the case may be, section 22 of the Arbitration Act (Northern Ireland) 1937 (statement of cases by arbitrators); but". Section 131(e).
1977 c. 38.	Administration of Justice Act 1977.	Section 17(2).
1978 c. 23.	Judicature (Northern Ireland) Act 1978.	In section 35(2), paragraph (g)(v).
1979 c. 42.	Arbitration Act 1979.	The whole Act.
1980 c. 58.	Limitation Act 1980.	Section 34.
1980 N.I. 3.	County Courts (Northern Ireland) Order 1980.	Article 31(3).
1981 c. 54.	Supreme Court Act 1981.	Section 148. In Schedule 5, the amendment to the Arbitration Act 1950.
1982 c. 27.	Civil Jurisdiction and Judgments Act 1982.	Section 25(3)(c) and (5). In section 26— (a) in subsection (1), the words "to arbitration or";

Chapter	Short title	Extent of repeal
		(b) in subsection (1)(a)(i), the words "arbitration or";
		(c) in subsection (2), the words "arbitration or".
1982 c. 53.	Administration of Justice Act 1982.	Section 15(6).
		In Schedule 1, Part IV.
1984 c. 5.	Merchant Shipping Act 1984.	Section 4(8).
1984 c. 12.	Telecommunications Act 1984.	Schedule 2, paragraph 13(8).
1984 c. 16.	Foreign Limitation Periods Act 1984.	Section 5.
1984 c. 28.	County Courts Act 1984.	In Schedule 2, paragraph 70.
1985 c. 61.	Administration of Justice Act 1985.	Section 58. In Schedule 9, paragraph 15.
1985 c. 68.	Housing Act 1985.	In Schedule 18, in paragraph 6(2) the words from "and the Arbitration Act 1950" to the end.
1985 N.I. 12.	Credit Unions (Northern Ireland) Order 1985.	In Article 72(7)—
		(a) in the opening words, the words from "and without prejudice" to "1937";
		(b) in sub-paragraph (b), the words "the registrar or" and "registrar or".
1986 c. 45.	Insolvency Act 1986.	In Schedule 14, the entry relating to the Arbitration Act 1950.
1988 c. 8.	Multilateral Investment Guarantee Agency Act 1988.	Section 8(3).
1988 c. 21.	Consumer Arbitration Agreements Act 1988.	The whole Act.
1989 N.I. 11.	Limitation (Northern Ireland) Order 1989.	Article 72. In Schedule 3, paragraph 1.
1989 N.I. 19.	Insolvency (Northern Ireland) Order 1989.	In Part II of Schedule 9, paragraph 66.
1990 c. 41.	Courts and Legal Services Act 1990.	Sections 99 and 101 to 103.
1991 N.I. 7.	Food Safety (Northern Ireland) Order 1991.	In Articles 8(8) and 11(10), the words from "and the provisions" to the end.
1992 c. 40.	Friendly Societies Act 1992.	In Schedule 16, paragraph 30(1).
1995 c. 8.	Agricultural Tenancies Act 1995.	Section 28(4).
1995 c. 21.	Merchant Shipping Act 1995.	Section 96(10). Section 264(9).

Chapter	Short title	Extent of repeal
1995 c. 42.	Private International Law (Miscellaneous Provisions) Act 1995.	Section 3.

The Arbitration Act 1996 (Commencement No.1) Order 1996

(SI 1996/3146)

Made   16th December 1996

The Secretary of State, in exercise of the powers conferred on him by section 109 of the Arbitration Act 1996, hereby makes the following Order: **A7–001**

1. This Order may be cited as the Arbitration Act 1996 (Commencement No. 1) Order 1996.

2. The provisions of the Arbitration Act 1996 ("the Act") listed in Schedule 1 to this Order shall come into force on the day after this Order is made.

3. The rest of the Act, except sections 85 to 87, shall come into force on 31st January 1997.

4. The transitional provisions in Schedule 2 to this Order shall have effect.

Article 2   SCHEDULE 1

Section 91 so far as it relates to the power to make orders under the section. **A7–002**
Section 105.
Section 107(1) and paragraph 36 of Schedule 3, so far as relating to the provision that may be made by county court rules.
Section 107(2) and the reference in Schedule 4 to the County Courts (Northern Ireland) Order 1980 so far as relating to the above matter.
Sections 108 to 110.

Article 4   SCHEDULE 2

1. In this Schedule: **A7–003**

   (a) "the appointed day" means the date specified in Article 3 of this Order;

   (b) "arbitration application" means any application relating to arbitration made by or in legal proceedings, whether or not arbitral proceedings have commenced;

   (c) "the old law" means the enactments specified in section 107 as they stood before their amendment or repeal by the Act.

2. The old law shall continue to apply to:

   (a) arbitral proceedings commenced before the appointed day;

   (b) arbitration applications commenced or made before the appointed day;

   (c) arbitration applications commenced or made on or after the appointed day relating to arbitral proceedings commenced before the appointed day

and the provisions of the Act which would otherwise be applicable shall not apply.

3. The provisions of this Act brought into force by this Order shall apply to any other arbitration application.

4. In the application of paragraph (b) of subsection (1) of section 46 (provision for dispute to be decided in accordance with provisions other than law) to an arbitration agreement made before the appointed day, the agreement shall have effect in accordance with the rules of law (including any conflict of laws rules) as they stood immediately before the appointed day.

High Court and County Courts (Allocation of Arbitration Proceedings) Order 1996

(SI 1996/3215)

Made	*19th December 1996*
Laid before Parliament	*20th December 1996*
Coming into force	*31st January 1997*

The Lord Chancellor, in exercise of the powers conferred on him by section 105 of the Arbitration Act 1996, hereby makes the following Order:— **A8–001**

1.—(1) This Order may be cited as the High Court and County Courts (Allocation of Arbitration Proceedings) Order 1996 and shall come into force on 31st January 1997.

(2) In this Order, "the Act" means the Arbitration Act 1996.

2. Subject to articles 3 to 5, proceedings under the Act shall be commenced and taken in the High Court.

3. Proceedings under section 9 of the Act (stay of legal proceedings) shall be commenced in the court in which the legal proceedings are pending.

4. Proceedings under sections 66 and 101(2) (enforcement of awards) of the Act may be commenced in any county court.

5.—(1) Proceedings under the Act may be commenced and taken in the Central London County Court Mercantile List. **A8–002**

(2) Where, in exercise of the powers conferred by sections 41 and 42 of the County Courts Act 1984 the High Court or the judge in charge of the Central London County Court Mercantile List orders the transfer of proceedings under the Act which were commenced in the Central London County Court Mercantile List to the High Court, those proceedings shall be taken in the High Court.

(3) Where, in exercise of its powers under section 40(2) of the County Courts Act 1984 the High Court orders the transfer of proceedings under the Act which were commenced in the High Court to the Central London County Court Mercantile List, those proceedings shall be taken in the Central London County Court Mercantile List.

(4) In exercising the powers referred to in paragraphs (2) and (3) regard shall be had to the following criteria—

(a) the financial substance of the dispute referred to arbitration, including the value of any claim or counterclaim;

(b) the nature of the dispute referred to arbitration (for example, whether it arises out of a commercial or business transaction or relates to engineering, building or other construction work);

(c) whether the proceedings are otherwise important and, in particular, whether they raise questions of importance to persons who are not parties, and

(d) the balance of convenience points to having the proceedings taken in the Central London County Court Mercantile List,

and, where the financial substance of the dispute exceeds £200,000, the proceedings shall be taken in the High Court unless the proceedings do not raise questions of general importance to persons who are not parties.

(5) The value of any claim or counterclaim shall be calculated in accordance with rule 16.3(6) of the Civil Procedure Rules 1998.

[(6) In this article—

"the Central London County Court Mercantile List" means the Court established at the Central London County Court pursuant to Part 59 of the Civil Procedure Rules 1998.];

"value" shall be construed in accordance with articles 9 and 10 of the High Court and County Courts Jurisdiction Order 1991.

6. Nothing in this Order shall prevent the judge in charge of the commercial list (within the meaning of section 62(3) of the Supreme Court Act 1981) from transferring proceedings under the Act to another list, court or Division of the High Court to which he has power to transfer proceedings and, where such an order is made, the proceedings may be taken in that list, court or Division as the case may be.

The Housing Grants, Construction and Regeneration Act 1996, ss.104–117

(1996, c.53)

Part II

Construction Contracts

Introductory provisions

Construction contracts

104.—(1) In this Part a "construction contract" means an agreement with a person for any of the following—   **A9–001**

  (a) the carrying out of construction operations;

  (b) arranging for the carrying out of construction operations by others, whether under sub-contract to him or otherwise;

  (c) providing his own labour, or the labour of others, for the carrying out of construction operations.

(2) References in this Part to a construction contract include an agreement—

  (a) to do architectural, design, or surveying work, or

  (b) to provide advice on building, engineering, interior or exterior decoration or on the laying-out of landscape,

in relation to construction operations.

(3) References in this Part to a construction contract do not include a contract of employment (within the meaning of the Employment Rights Act 1996).

(4) The Secretary of State may by order add to, amend or repeal any of the provisions of subsection (1), (2) or (3) as to the agreements which are construction contracts for the purposes of this Part or are to be taken or not to be taken as included in references to such contracts.

No such order shall be made unless a draft of it has been laid before and approved by a resolution of each of House of Parliament.

(5) Where an agreement relates to construction operations and other matters, this Part applies to it only so far as it relates to construction operations.

An agreement relates to construction operations so far as it makes provision of any kind within subsection (1) or (2).

(6) This Part applies only to construction contracts which—

  (a) are entered into after the commencement of this Part, and

Statutory Materials and Rules of Court

(7) This Part applies whether or not the law of England and Wales or Scotland is otherwise the applicable law in relation to the contract.

Meaning of "construction operations"

A9–002   105.—(1) In this Part "construction operations" means, subject as follows, operations of any of the following descriptions—

   (a) construction, alteration, repair, maintenance, extension, demolition or dismantling of buildings, or structures forming, or to form, part of the land (whether permanent or not);

   (b) construction, alteration, repair, maintenance, extension, demolition or dismantling of any works forming, or to form, part of the land, including (without prejudice to the foregoing) walls, roadworks, power-lines, telecommunication apparatus, aircraft runways, docks and harbours, railways, inland waterways, pipe-lines, reservoirs, water-mains, wells, sewers, industrial plant and installations for purposes of land drainage, coast protection or defence;

   (c) installation in any building or structure of fittings forming part of the land, including (without prejudice to the foregoing) systems of heating, lighting, air-conditioning, ventilation, power supply, drainage, sanitation, water supply or fire protection, or security or communications systems;

   (d) external or internal cleaning of buildings and structures, so far as carried out in the course of their construction, alteration, repair, extension or restoration;

   (e) operations which form an integral part of, or are preparatory to, or are for rendering complete, such operations as are previously described in this subsection, including site clearance, earth-moving, excavation, tunnelling and boring, laying of foundations, erection, maintenance or dismantling of scaffolding, site restoration, landscaping and the provision of roadways and other access works;

   (f) painting or decorating the internal or external surfaces of any building or structure.

(2) The following operations are not construction operations within the meaning of this Part—

   (a) drilling for, or extraction of, oil or natural gas;

   (b) extraction (whether by underground or surface working) of minerals; tunnelling or boring, or construction of underground works, for this purpose;

   (c) assembly, installation or demolition of plant or machinery, or erection or demolition of steelwork for the purposes of supporting or providing access to plant or machinery, on a site where the primary activity is—

      (i) nuclear processing, power generation, or water or effluent treatment, or
      (ii) the production, transmission, processing or bulk storage (other than warehousing) of chemicals, pharmaceuticals, oil, gas, steel or food and drink;

   (d) manufacture or delivery to site of—

      (i) building or engineering components or equipment,

(ii) materials, plant or machinery, or

(iii) components for systems of heating, lighting, air-conditioning, ventilation, power supply, drainage, sanitation, water supply or fire protection, or for security or communications systems,

except under a contract which also provides for their installation;

(e) the making, installation and repair of artistic works, being sculptures, murals and other works which are wholly artistic in nature.

(3) The Secretary of State may by order add to, amend or repeal any of the provisions of subsection (1) or (2) as to the operations and work to be treated as construction operations for the purposes of this Part.

(4) No such order shall be made unless a draft of it has been laid before and approved by a resolution of each House of Parliament.

Provisions not applicable to contract with residential occupier

106.—(1) This Part does not apply— A9–003

(a) to a construction contract with a residential occupier (see below), or

(b) to any other description of construction contract excluded from the operation of this Part by order of the Secretary of State.

(2) A construction contract with a residential occupier means a construction contract which principally relates to operations on a dwelling which one of the parties to the contract occupies, or intends to occupy, as his residence.
In this subsection "dwelling" means a dwelling-house or a flat; and for this purpose—

"dwelling-house" does not include a building containing a flat; and

"flat" means separate and self-contained premises constructed or adapted for use for residential purposes and forming part of a building from some other part of which the premises are divided horizontally.

(3) The Secretary of State may by order amend subsection (2).

(4) No order under this section shall be made unless a draft of it has been laid before and approved by a resolution of each House of Parliament.

Provisions applicable only to agreements in writing

107.—(1) The provisions of this Part apply only where the construction contract is in A9–004
writing, and any other agreement between the parties as to any matter is effective for the purposes of this Part only if in writing.
The expressions "agreement", "agree" and "agreed" shall be construed accordingly.

(2) There is an agreement in writing—

(a) if the agreement is made in writing (whether or not it is signed by the parties),

(b) if the agreement is made by exchange of communications in writing, or

(c) if the agreement is evidenced in writing.

(3) Where parties agree otherwise than in writing by reference to terms which are in writing, they make an agreement in writing.

(4) An agreement is evidenced in writing if an agreement made otherwise than in writing is recorded by one of the parties, or by a third party, with the authority of the parties to the agreement.

(5) An exchange of written submissions in adjudication proceedings, or in arbitral or legal proceedings in which the existence of an agreement otherwise than in writing is alleged by one party against another party and not denied by the other party in his response constitutes as between those parties an agreement in writing to the effect alleged.

(6) References in this Part to anything being written or in writing include its being recorded by any means.

Adjudication

Right to refer disputes to adjudication

A9–005 108.—(1) A party to a construction contract has the right to refer a dispute arising under the contract for adjudication under a procedure complying with this section.
For this purpose "dispute" includes any difference.
(2) The contract shall—

(a) enable a party to give notice at any time of his intention to refer a dispute to adjudication;

(b) provide a timetable with the object of securing the appointment of the adjudicator and referral of the dispute to him within 7 days of such notice;

(c) require the adjudicator to reach a decision within 28 days of referral or such longer period as is agreed by the parties after the dispute has been referred;

(d) allow the adjudicator to extend the period of 28 days by up to 14 days, with the consent of the party by whom the dispute was referred;

(e) impose a duty on the adjudicator to act impartially; and

(f) enable the adjudicator to take the initiative in ascertaining the facts and the law.

(3) The contract shall provide that the decision of the adjudicator is binding until the dispute is finally determined by legal proceedings, by arbitration (if the contract provides for arbitration or the parties otherwise agree to arbitration) or by agreement.

The parties may agree to accept the decision of the adjudicator as finally determining the dispute.

(4) The contract shall also provide that the adjudicator is not liable for anything done or omitted in the discharge or purported discharge of his functions as adjudicator unless the act or omission is in bad faith, and that any employee or agent of the adjudicator is similarly protected from liability.

(5) If the contract does not comply with the requirements of subsections (1) to (4), the adjudication provisions of the Scheme for Construction Contracts apply.

(6) For England and Wales, the Scheme may apply the provisions of the Arbitration Act 1996 with such adaptations and modifications as appear to the Minister making the scheme to be appropriate.

THE HOUSING GRANTS, CONSTRUCTION AND REGENERATION ACT 1996

For Scotland, the Scheme may include provision conferring powers on courts in relation to adjudication and provision relating to the enforcement of the adjudicator's decision.

Payment

Entitlement to stage payments

109.—(1) A party to a construction contract is entitled to payment by instalments, stage payments or other periodic payments for any work under the contract unless— **A9–006**

(a) it is specified in the contract that the duration of the work is to be less than 45 days, or

(b) it is agreed between the parties that the duration of the work is estimated to be less than 45 days.

(2) The parties are free to agree the amounts of the payments and the intervals at which, or circumstances in which, they become due.

(3) In the absence of such agreement, the relevant provisions of the Scheme for Construction Contracts apply.

(4) References in the following sections to a payment under the contract include a payment by virtue of this section.

Dates for payment

110.—(1) Every construction contract shall— **A9–007**

(a) provide an adequate mechanism for determining what payments become due under the contract, and when, and

(b) provide for a final date for payment in relation to any sum which becomes due.

The parties are free to agree how long the period is to be between the date on which a sum becomes due and the final date for payment.

(2) Every construction contract shall provide for the giving of notice by a party not later than five days after the date on which a payment becomes due from him under the contract, or would have become due if—

(a) the other party had carried out his obligations under the contract, and

(b) no set-off or abatement was permitted by reference to any sum claimed to be due under one or more other contracts,

specifying the amount (if any) of the payment made or proposed to be made, and the basis on which that amount was calculated.

(3) If or to the extent that a contract does not contain such provision as is mentioned in subsection (1) or (2), the relevant provisions of the Scheme for Construction Contracts apply.

Notice of intention to withhold payment

A9–008   111.—(1) A party to a construction contract may not withhold payment after the final date for payment of a sum due under the contract unless he has given an effective notice of intention to withhold payment.

The notice mentioned in section 110(2) may suffice as a notice of intention to withhold payment if it complies with the requirements of this section.

(2) To be effective such a notice must specify—

(a) the amount proposed to be withheld and the ground for withholding payment, or

(b) if there is more than one ground, each ground and the amount attributable to it,

and must be given not later than the prescribed period before the final date for payment.

(3) The parties are free to agree what that prescribed period is to be.

In the absence of such agreement, the period shall be that provided by the Scheme for Construction Contracts.

(4) Where an effective notice of intention to withhold payment is given, but on the matter being referred to adjudication it is decided that the whole or part of the amount should be paid, the decision shall be construed as requiring payment not later than—

(a) seven days from the date of the decision, or

(b) the date which apart from the notice would have been the final date for payment,

whichever is the later.

Right to suspend performance for non-payment

A9–009   112.—(1) Where a sum due under a construction contract is not paid in full by the final date for payment and no effective notice to withhold payment has been given, the person to whom the sum is due has the right (without prejudice to any other right or remedy) to suspend performance of his obligations under the contract to the party by whom payment ought to have been made ("the party in default").

(2) The right may not be exercised without first giving to the party in default at least seven days' notice of intention to suspend performance, stating the ground or grounds on which it is intended to suspend performance.

(3) The right to suspend performance ceases when the party in default makes payment in full of the amount due.

(4) Any period during which performance is suspended in pursuance of the right conferred by this section shall be disregarded in computing for the purposes of any contractual time limit the time taken, by the party exercising the right or by a third party, to complete any work directly or indirectly affected by the exercise of the right.

Where the contractual time limit is set by reference to a date rather than a period, the date shall be adjusted accordingly.

Prohibition of conditional payment provisions

A9–010   113.—(1) A provision making payment under a construction contract conditional on the payer receiving payment from a third person is ineffective, unless that third person, or any other person payment by whom is under the contract (directly or indirectly) a condition of payment by that third person, is insolvent.

(2) For the purposes of this section a company becomes insolvent—

(a) on the making of an administration order against it under Part II of the Insolvency Act 1986,

(b) on the appointment of an administrative receiver or a receiver or manager of its property under Chapter I of Part III of that Act, or the appointment of a receiver under Chapter II of that Part,

(c) on the passing of a resolution for voluntary winding-up without a declaration of solvency under section 89 of that Act, or

(d) on the making of a winding-up order under Part IV or V of that Act.

(3) For the purposes of this section a partnership becomes insolvent—

(a) on the making of a winding-up order against it under any provision of the Insolvency Act 1986 as applied by an order under section 420 of that Act, or

(b) when sequestration is awarded on the estate of the partnership under section 12 of the Bankruptcy (Scotland) Act 1985 or the partnership grants a trust deed for its creditors.

(4) For the purposes of this section an individual becomes insolvent—

(a) on the making of a bankruptcy order against him under Part IX of the Insolvency Act 1986, or

(b) on the sequestration of his estate under the Bankruptcy (Scotland) Act 1985 or when he grants a trust deed for his creditors.

(5) A company, partnership or individual shall also be treated as insolvent on the occurrence of any event corresponding to those specified in subsection (2), (3) or (4) under the law of Northern Ireland or of a country outside the United Kingdom.

(6) Where a provision is rendered ineffective by subsection (1), the parties are free to agree other terms for payment.

In the absence of such agreement, the relevant provisions of the Scheme for Construction Contracts apply.

Supplementary provisions

The Scheme for Construction Contracts

114.—(1) The Minister shall by regulations make a scheme ("the Scheme for Construction Contracts") containing provision about the matters referred to in the preceding provisions of this Part.

(2) Before making any regulations under this section the Minister shall consult such persons as he thinks fit.

(3) In this section "the Minister" means—

(a) for England and Wales, the Secretary of State, and

(b) for Scotland, the Lord Advocate.

(4) Where any provisions of the Scheme for Construction Contracts apply by virtue of this Part in default of contractual provision agreed by the parties, they have effect as implied terms of the contract concerned.

(5) Regulations under this section shall not be made unless a draft of them has been approved by resolution of each House of Parliament.

Service of notices, etc.

A9–012 115.—(1) The parties are free to agree on the manner of service of any notice or other document required or authorised to be served in pursuance of the construction contract or for any of the purposes of this Part.

(2) If or to the extent that there is no such agreement the following provisions apply.

(3) A notice or other document may be served on a person by any effective means.

(4) If a notice or other document is addressed, pre-paid and delivered by post—

    (a) to the addressee's last known principal residence or, if he is or has been carrying on a trade, profession or business, his last known principal business address, or

    (b) where the addressee is a body corporate, to the body's registered or principal office,

it shall be treated as effectively served.

(5) This section does not apply to the service of documents for the purposes of legal proceedings, for which provision is made by rules of court.

(6) References in this Part to a notice or other document include any form of communication in writing and references to service shall be construed accordingly.

Reckoning periods of time

A9–013 116.—(1) For the purposes of this Part periods of time shall be reckoned as follows.

(2) Where an act is required to be done within a specified period after or from a specified date, the period begins immediately after that date.

(3) Where the period would include Christmas Day, Good Friday or a day which under the Banking and Financial Dealings Act 1971 is a bank holiday in England and Wales or, as the case may be, in Scotland, that day shall be excluded.

Crown application

A9–014 117.—(1) This Part applies to a construction contract entered into by or on behalf of the Crown otherwise than by or on behalf of Her Majesty in her private capacity.

(2) This Part applies to a construction contract entered into on behalf of the Duchy of Cornwall notwithstanding any Crown interest.

(3) Where a construction contract is entered into by or on behalf of Her Majesty in right of the Duchy of Lancaster, Her Majesty shall be represented, for the purposes of any adjudication or other proceedings arising out of the contract by virtue of this Part, by the Chancellor of the Duchy or such person as he may appoint.

(4) Where a construction contract is entered into on behalf of the Duchy of Cornwall, the Duke of Cornwall or the possessor for the time being of the Duchy shall be represented, for the purposes of any adjudication or other proceedings arising out of the contract by virtue of this Part, by such person as he may appoint.

The Scheme for Construction Contracts (England and Wales) Regulations 1998

(SI 1998/649)

Made 6th March 1998
Coming into force 1st May 1998

The Secretary of State, in exercise of the powers conferred on him by sections 108(6), **A10–001**
114 and 146(1) and (2) of the Housing Grants, Construction and Regeneration Act 1996, and of all other powers enabling him in that behalf, having consulted such persons as he thinks fit, and draft Regulations having been approved by both Houses of Parliament, hereby makes the following Regulations:

Citation, commencement, extent and interpretation

1.—(1) These Regulations may be cited as the Scheme for Construction Contracts **A10–002**
(England and Wales) Regulations 1998 and shall come into force at the end of the period of 8 weeks beginning with the day on which they are made (the "commencement date").

(2) These Regulations shall extend only to England and Wales.

(3) In these Regulations, "the Act" means the Housing Grants, Construction and Regeneration Act 1996.

The Scheme for Construction Contracts

2. Where a construction contract does not comply with the requirements of section **A10–003**
108(1) to (4) of the Act, the adjudication provisions in Part I of the Schedule to these Regulations shall apply.

3. Where—

(a) the parties to a construction contract are unable to reach agreement for the purposes mentioned respectively in sections 109, 111 and 113 of the Act, or

(b) a construction contract does not make provision as required by section 110 of the Act,

the relevant provisions in Part II of the Schedule to these Regulations shall apply.

4. The provisions in the Schedule to these Regulations shall be the Scheme for Construction Contracts for the purposes of section 114 of the Act.

Regulations 2, 3 and 4 SCHEDULE

THE SCHEME FOR CONSTRUCTION CONTRACTS

PART I

ADJUDICATION

Notice of Intention to seek Adjudication

1.—(1) Any party to a construction contract (the "referring party") may give written **A10–004**
notice (the "notice of adjudication") of his intention to refer any dispute arising under the contract, to adjudication.

(2) The notice of adjudication shall be given to every other party to the contract.

(3) The notice of adjudication shall set out briefly—

    (a) the nature and a brief description of the dispute and of the parties involved,

    (b) details of where and when the dispute has arisen,

    (c) the nature of the redress which is sought, and

    (d) the names and addresses of the parties to the contract (including, where appropriate, the addresses which the parties have specified for the giving of notices).

2.—(1) Following the giving of a notice of adjudication and subject to any agreement between the parties to the dispute as to who shall act as adjudicator—

    (a) the referring party shall request the person (if any) specified in the contract to act as adjudicator, or

    (b) if no person is named in the contract or the person named has already indicated that he is unwilling or unable to act, and the contract provides for a specified nominating body to select a person, the referring party shall request the nominating body named in the contract to select a person to act as adjudicator, or

    (c) where neither paragraph (a) nor (b) above applies, or where the person referred to in (a) has already indicated that he is unwilling or unable to act and (b) does not apply, the referring party shall request an adjudicator nominating body to select a person to act as adjudicator.

(2) A person requested to act as adjudicator in accordance with the provisions of paragraph (1) shall indicate whether or not he is willing to act within two days of receiving the request.

(3) In this paragraph, and in paragraphs 5 and 6 below, an "adjudicator nominating body" shall mean a body (not being a natural person and not being a party to the dispute) which holds itself out publicly as a body which will select an adjudicator when requested to do so by a referring party.

3. The request referred to in paragraphs 2, 5 and 6 shall be accompanied by a copy of the notice of adjudication.

4. Any person requested or selected to act as adjudicator in accordance with paragraphs 2, 5 or 6 shall be a natural person acting in his personal capacity. A person requested or selected to act as an adjudicator shall not be an employee of any of the parties to the dispute and shall declare any interest, financial or otherwise, in any matter relating to the dispute.

5.—(1) The nominating body referred to in paragraphs 2(1)(b) and 6(1)(b) or the adjudicator nominating body referred to in paragraphs 2(1)(c), 5(2)(b) and 6(1)(c) must communicate the selection of an adjudicator to the referring party within five days of receiving a request to do so.

(2) Where the nominating body or the adjudicator nominating body fails to comply with paragraph (1), the referring party may—

    (a) agree with the other party to the dispute to request a specified person to act as adjudicator, or

    (b) request any other adjudicator nominating body to select a person to act as adjudicator.

The Scheme for Construction Contracts Regulations 1998

(3) The person requested to act as adjudicator in accordance with the provisions of paragraphs (1) or (2) shall indicate whether or not he is willing to act within two days of receiving the request.

6.—(1) Where an adjudicator who is named in the contract indicates to the parties that he is unable or unwilling to act, or where he fails to respond in accordance with paragraph 2(2), the referring party may—

(a) request another person (if any) specified in the contract to act as adjudicator, or

(b) request the nominating body (if any) referred to in the contract to select a person to act as adjudicator, or

(c) request any other adjudicator nominating body to select a person to act as adjudicator.

(2) The person requested to act in accordance with the provisions of paragraph (1) shall indicate whether or not he is willing to act within two days of receiving the request.

7.—(1) Where an adjudicator has been selected in accordance with paragraphs 2, 5 or 6, the referring party shall, not later than seven days from the date of the notice of adjudication, refer the dispute in writing (the "referral notice") to the adjudicator.

(2) A referral notice shall be accompanied by copies of, or relevant extracts from, the construction contract and such other documents as the referring party intends to rely upon.

(3) The referring party shall, at the same time as he sends to the adjudicator the documents referred to in paragraphs (1) and (2), send copies of those documents to every other party to the dispute.

8.—(1) The adjudicator may, with the consent of all the parties to those disputes, adjudicate at the same time on more than one dispute under the same contract.

(2) The adjudicator may, with the consent of all the parties to those disputes, adjudicate at the same time on related disputes under different contracts, whether or not one or more of those parties is a party to those disputes.

(3) All the parties in paragraphs (1) and (2) respectively may agree to extend the period within which the adjudicator may reach a decision in relation to all or any of these disputes.

(4) Where an adjudicator ceases to act because a dispute is to be adjudicated on by another person in terms of this paragraph, that adjudicator's fees and expenses shall be determined in accordance with paragraph 25.

9.—(1) An adjudicator may resign at any time on giving notice in writing to the parties to the dispute.

(2) An adjudicator must resign where the dispute is the same or substantially the same as one which has previously been referred to adjudication, and a decision has been taken in that adjudication.

(3) Where an adjudicator ceases to act under paragraph 9(1)—

(a) the referring party may serve a fresh notice under paragraph 1 and shall request an adjudicator to act in accordance with paragraphs 2 to 7; and

(b) if requested by the new adjudicator and insofar as it is reasonably practicable, the parties shall supply him with copies of all documents which they had made available to the previous adjudicator.

(4) Where an adjudicator resigns in the circumstances referred to in paragraph (2), or

where a dispute varies significantly from the dispute referred to him in the referral notice and for that reason he is not competent to decide it, the adjudicator shall be entitled to the payment of such reasonable amount as he may determine by way of fees and expenses reasonably incurred by him. The parties shall be jointly and severally liable for any sum which remains outstanding following the making of any determination on how the payment shall be apportioned.

10. Where any party to the dispute objects to the appointment of a particular person as adjudicator, that objection shall not invalidate the adjudicator's appointment nor any decision he may reach in accordance with paragraph 20.

11.—(1) The parties to a dispute may at any time agree to revoke the appointment of the adjudicator. The adjudicator shall be entitled to the payment of such reasonable amount as he may determine by way of fees and expenses incurred by him. The parties shall be jointly and severally liable for any sum which remains outstanding following the making of any determination on how the payment shall be apportioned.

(2) Where the revocation of the appointment of the adjudicator is due to the default or misconduct of the adjudicator, the parties shall not be liable to pay the adjudicator's fees and expenses.

Powers of the adjudicator

12. The adjudicator shall—

(a) act impartially in carrying out his duties and shall do so in accordance with any relevant terms of the contract and shall reach his decision in accordance with the applicable law in relation to the contract; and

(b) avoid incurring unnecessary expense.

13. The adjudicator may take the initiative in ascertaining the facts and the law necessary to determine the dispute, and shall decide on the procedure to be followed in the adjudication. In particular he may—

(a) request any party to the contract to supply him with such documents as he may reasonably require including, if he so directs, any written statement from any party to the contract supporting or supplementing the referral notice and any other documents given under paragraph 7(2),

(b) decide the language or languages to be used in the adjudication and whether a translation of any document is to be provided and if so by whom,

(c) meet and question any of the parties to the contract and their representatives,

(d) subject to obtaining any necessary consent from a third party or parties, make such site visits and inspections as he considers appropriate, whether accompanied by the parties or not,

(e) subject to obtaining any necessary consent from a third party or parties, carry out any tests or experiments,

(f) obtain and consider such representations and submissions as he requires, and, provided he has notified the parties of his intention, appoint experts, assessors or legal advisers,

(g) give directions as to the timetable for the adjudication, any deadlines, or limits as to the length of written documents or oral representations to be complied with, and

(h) issue other directions relating to the conduct of the adjudication.

14. The parties shall comply with any request or direction of the adjudicator in relation to the adjudication.

15. If, without showing sufficient cause, a party fails to comply with any request, direction or timetable of the adjudicator made in accordance with his powers, fails to produce any document or written statement requested by the adjudicator, or in any other way fails to comply with a requirement under these provisions relating to the adjudication, the adjudicator may—

(a) continue the adjudication in the absence of that party or of the document or written statement requested,

(b) draw such inferences from that failure to comply as circumstances may, in the adjudicator's opinion, be justified, and

(c) make a decision on the basis of the information before him attaching such weight as he thinks fit to any evidence submitted to him outside any period he may have requested or directed.

16.—(1) Subject to any agreement between the parties to the contrary, and to the terms of paragraph (2) below, any party to the dispute may be assisted by, or represented by, such advisers or representatives (whether legally qualified or not) as he considers appropriate.

(2) Where the adjudicator is considering oral evidence or representations, a party to the dispute may not be represented by more than one person, unless the adjudicator gives directions to the contrary.

17. The adjudicator shall consider any relevant information submitted to him by any of the parties to the dispute and shall make available to them any information to be taken into account in reaching his decision.

18. The adjudicator and any party to the dispute shall not disclose to any other person any information or document provided to him in connection with the adjudication which the party supplying it has indicated is to be treated as confidential, except to the extent that it is necessary for the purposes of, or in connection with, the adjudication.

19.—(1) The adjudicator shall reach his decision not later than—

(a) twenty eight days after the date of the referral notice mentioned in paragraph 7(1), or

(b) forty two days after the date of the referral notice if the referring party so consents, or

(c) such period exceeding twenty eight days after the referral notice as the parties to the dispute may, after the giving of that notice, agree.

(2) Where the adjudicator fails, for any reason, to reach his decision in accordance with paragraph (1)—

(a) any of the parties to the dispute may serve a fresh notice under paragraph 1 and shall request an adjudicator to act in accordance with paragraphs 2 to 7; and

(b) if requested by the new adjudicator and insofar as it is reasonably practicable, the parties shall supply him with copies of all documents which they had made available to the previous adjudicator.

(3) As soon as possible after he has reached a decision, the adjudicator shall deliver a copy of that decision to each of the parties to the contract.

Adjudicator's decision

A10–006 20. The adjudicator shall decide the matters in dispute. He may take into account any other matters which the parties to the dispute agree should be within the scope of the adjudication or which are matters under the contract which he considers are necessarily connected with the dispute. In particular, he may—

(a) open up, revise and review any decision taken or any certificate given by any person referred to in the contract unless the contract states that the decision or certificate is final and conclusive,

(b) decide that any of the parties to the dispute is liable to make a payment under the contract (whether in sterling or some other currency) and, subject to section 111(4) of the Act, when that payment is due and the final date for payment,

(c) having regard to any term of the contract relating to the payment of interest decide the circumstances in which, and the rates at which, and the periods for which simple or compound rates of interest shall be paid.

21. In the absence of any directions by the adjudicator relating to the time for performance of his decision, the parties shall be required to comply with any decision of the adjudicator immediately on delivery of the decision to the parties in accordance with this paragraph.

22. If requested by one of the parties to the dispute, the adjudicator shall provide reasons for his decision.

Effects of the decision

A10–007 23.—(1) In his decision, the adjudicator may, if he thinks fit, order any of the parties to comply peremptorily with his decision or any part of it.

(2) The decision of the adjudicator shall be binding on the parties, and they shall comply with it until the dispute is finally determined by legal proceedings, by arbitration (if the contract provides for arbitration or the parties otherwise agree to arbitration) or by agreement between the parties.

24. Section 42 of the Arbitration Act 1996 shall apply to this Scheme subject to the following modifications—

(a) in subsection (2) for the word "tribunal" wherever it appears there shall be substituted the word "adjudicator",

(b) in subparagraph (b) of subsection (2) for the words "arbitral proceedings" there shall be substituted the word "adjudication",

(c) subparagraph (c) of subsection (2) shall be deleted, and

(d) subsection (3) shall be deleted.

25. The adjudicator shall be entitled to the payment of such reasonable amount as he may determine by way of fees and expenses reasonably incurred by him. The parties

shall be jointly and severally liable for any sum which remains outstanding following the making of any determination on how the payment shall be apportioned.

26. The adjudicator shall not be liable for anything done or omitted in the discharge or purported discharge of his functions as adjudicator unless the act or omission is in bad faith, and any employee or agent of the adjudicator shall be similarly protected from liability.

Part II

Payment

Entitlement to and amount of stage payments

1. Where the parties to a relevant construction contract fail to agree—   **A10–008**

    (a) the amount of any instalment or stage or periodic payment for any work under the contract, or

    (b) the intervals at which, or circumstances in which, such payments become due under that contract, or

    (c) both of the matters mentioned in sub-paragraphs (a) and (b) above,

the relevant provisions of paragraphs 2 to 4 below shall apply.

2.—(1) The amount of any payment by way of instalments or stage or periodic payments in respect of a relevant period shall be the difference between the amount determined in accordance with sub-paragraph (2) and the amount determined in accordance with sub-paragraph (3).

(2) The aggregate of the following amounts—

    (a) an amount equal to the value of any work performed in accordance with the relevant construction contract during the period from the commencement of the contract to the end of the relevant period (excluding any amount calculated in accordance with sub-paragraph (b)),

    (b) where the contract provides for payment for materials, an amount equal to the value of any materials manufactured on site or brought onto site for the purposes of the works during the period from the commencement of the contract to the end of the relevant period, and

    (c) any other amount or sum which the contract specifies shall be payable during or in respect of the period from the commencement of the contract to the end of the relevant period.

(3) The aggregate of any sums which have been paid or are due for payment by way of instalments, stage or periodic payments during the period from the commencement of the contract to the end of the relevant period.

(4) An amount calculated in accordance with this paragraph shall not exceed the difference between—

    (a) the contract price, and

    (b) the aggregate of the instalments or stage or periodic payments which have become due.

Dates for payment

A10–009 3. Where the parties to a construction contract fail to provide an adequate mechanism for determining either what payments become due under the contract, or when they become due for payment, or both, the relevant provisions of paragraphs 4 to 7 shall apply.

4. Any payment of a kind mentioned in paragraph 2 above shall become due on whichever of the following dates occurs later—

(a) the expiry of 7 days following the relevant period mentioned in paragraph 2(1) above, or

(b) the making of a claim by the payee.

5. The final payment payable under a relevant construction contract, namely the payment of an amount equal to the difference (if any) between—

(a) the contract price, and

(b) the aggregate of any instalment or stage or periodic payments which have become due under the contract,

shall become due on the expiry of—

(a) 30 days following completion of the work, or

(b) the making of a claim by the payee,

whichever is the later.

6. Payment of the contract price under a construction contract (not being a relevant construction contract) shall become due on—

(a) the expiry of 30 days following the completion of the work, or

(b) the making of a claim by the payee,

whichever is the later.

7. Any other payment under a construction contract shall become due—

(a) on the expiry of 7 days following the completion of the work to which the payment relates, or

(b) the making of a claim by the payee,

whichever is the later.

Final date for payment

A10–010 8.—(1) Where the parties to a construction contract fail to provide a final date for payment in relation to any sum which becomes due under a construction contract, the provisions of this paragraph shall apply.

(2) The final date for the making of any payment of a kind mentioned in paragraphs 2, 5, 6 or 7, shall be 17 days from the date that payment becomes due.

Notice specifying amount of payment

A10–011 9. A party to a construction contract shall, not later than 5 days after the date on which any payment—

(a) becomes due from him, or

(b) would have become due, if—

(i) the other party had carried out his obligations under the contract, and
(ii) no set-off or abatement was permitted by reference to any sum claimed to be due under one or more other contracts,

give notice to the other party to the contract specifying the amount (if any) of the payment he has made or proposes to make, specifying to what the payment relates and the basis on which that amount is calculated.

Notice of intention to withhold payment

10. Any notice of intention to withhold payment mentioned in section 111 of the Act shall be given not later than the prescribed period, which is to say not later than 7 days before the final date for payment determined either in accordance with the construction contract, or where no such provision is made in the contract, in accordance with paragraph 8 above. **A10–012**

Prohibition of conditional payment provisions

11. Where a provision making payment under a construction contract conditional on the payer receiving payment from a third person is ineffective as mentioned in section 113 of the Act, and the parties have not agreed other terms for payment, the relevant provisions of— **A10–013**

(a) paragraphs 2, 4, 5, 7, 8, 9 and 10 shall apply in the case of a relevant construction contract, and

(b) paragraphs 6, 7, 8, 9 and 10 shall apply in the case of any other construction contract.

Interpretation

12. In this Part of the Scheme for Construction Contracts— **A10–014**

"claim by the payee" means a written notice given by the party carrying out work under a construction contract to the other party specifying the amount of any payment or payments which he considers to be due and the basis on which it is, or they are calculated;

"contract price" means the entire sum payable under the construction contract in respect of the work;

"relevant construction contract" means any construction contract other than one—

(a) which specifies that the duration of the work is to be less than 45 days, or

(b) in respect of which the parties agree that the duration of the work is estimated to be less than 45 days;

"relevant period" means a period which is specified in, or is calculated by reference to the construction contract or where no such period is so specified or is so calculable, a period of 28 days;

"value of work" means an amount determined in accordance with the construction contract under which the work is performed or where the contract contains no such provision, the cost of any work performed in accordance with that contract together with an amount equal to any overhead or profit included in the contract price;

"work" means any of the work or services mentioned in section 104 of the Act.

Human Rights Act 1998

(1998, c.42)

A11–001 An Act to give further effect to rights and freedoms guaranteed under the European Convention on Human Rights; to make provision with respect to holders of certain judicial offices who become judges of the European Court of Human Rights; and for connected purposes.

[9TH NOVEMBER 1998]

BE IT ENACTED by the Queen's most Excellent Majesty, by and with the advice and consent of the Lords Spiritual and Temporal, and Commons, in this present Parliament assembled, and by the authority of the same, as follows:—

Introduction

The Convention rights

A11–002 **1.**—(1) In this Act "the Convention rights" means the rights and fundamental freedoms set out in—

(a) Articles 2 to 12 and 14 of the Convention,

(b) Articles 1 to 3 of the First Protocol, and

(c) Articles 1 and 2 of the Sixth Protocol,

as read with Articles 16 to 18 of the Convention.

(2) Those Articles are to have effect for the purposes of this Act subject to any designated derogation or reservation (as to which see sections 14 and 15).

(3) The Articles are set out in Schedule 1.

(4) The [Lord Chancellor] may by order make such amendments to this Act as he considers appropriate to reflect the effect, in relation to the United Kingdom, of a protocol.

(5) In subsection (4) "protocol" means a protocol to the Convention—

(a) which the United Kingdom has ratified; or

(b) which the United Kingdom has signed with a view to ratification.

(6) No amendment may be made by an order under subsection (4) so as to come into force before the protocol concerned is in force in relation to the United Kingdom.

Interpretation of Convention rights

A11–003 **2.**—(1) A court or tribunal determining a question which has arisen in connection with a Convention right must take into account any—

(a) judgment, decision, declaration or advisory opinion of the European Court of Human Rights,

(b) opinion of the Commission given in a report adopted under Article 31 of the Convention,

(c) decision of the Commission in connection with Article 26 or 27(2) of the Convention, or

(d) decision of the Committee of Ministers taken under Article 46 of the Convention,

whenever made or given, so far as, in the opinion of the court or tribunal, it is relevant to the proceedings in which that question has arisen.

(2) Evidence of any judgment, decision, declaration or opinion of which account may have to be taken under this section is to be given in proceedings before any court or tribunal in such manner as may be provided by rules.

(3) In this section "rules" means rules of court or, in the case of proceedings before a tribunal, rules made for the purposes of this section—

(a) by the Lord Chancellor or the Secretary of State, in relation to any proceedings outside Scotland;

(b) by the Secretary of State, in relation to proceedings in Scotland; or

(c) by a Northern Ireland department, in relation to proceedings before a tribunal in Northern Ireland—

(i) which deals with transferred matters; and
(ii) for which no rules made under paragraph (a) are in force.

Legislation

Intepretation of legislation

3.—(1) So far as it is possible to do so, primary legislation and subordinate legislation **A11–004** must be read and given effect in a way which is compatible with the Convention rights.

(2) This section—

(a) applies to primary legislation and subordinate legislation whenever enacted;

(b) does not affect the validity, continuing operation or enforcement of any incompatible primary legislation; and

(c) does not affect the validity, continuing operation or enforcement of any incompatible subordinate legislation if (disregarding any possibility of revocation) primary legislation prevents removal of the incompatibility.

Declaration of incompatibility

4.—(1) Subsection (2) applies in any proceedings in which a court determines whether **A11–005** a provision of primary legislation is compatible with a Convention right.

(2) If the court is satisfied that the provision is incompatible with a Convention right, it may make a declaration of that incompatibility.

(3) Subsection (4) applies in any proceedings in which a court determines whether a provision of subordinate legislation, made in the exercise of a power conferred by primary legislation, is compatible with a Convention right.

(4) If the court is satisfied—

(a) that the provision is incompatible with a Convention right, and

(b) that (disregarding any possibility of revocation) the primary legislation concerned prevents removal of the incompatibility,

it may make a declaration of that incompatibility.

(5) In this section "court" means—

(a) the House of Lords;

(b) he Judicial Committee of the Privy Council;

(c) the Courts-Martial Appeal Court;

(d) in Scotland, the High Court of Justiciary sitting otherwise than as a trial court or the Court of Session;

(e) in England and Wales or Northern Ireland, the High Court or the Court of Appeal.

(6) A declaration under this section ("a declaration of incompatibility")—

(a) does not affect the validity, continuing operation or enforcement of the provision in respect of which it is given; and

(b) is not binding on the parties to the proceedings in which it is made.

Right of Crown to intervene

A11–006 5.—(1) Where a court is considering whether to make a declaration of incompatibility, the Crown is entitled to notice in accordance with rules of court.

(2) In any case to which subsection (1) applies—

(a) a Minister of the Crown (or a person nominated by him),

(b) a member of the Scottish Executive,

(c) a Northern Ireland Minister,

(d) a Northern Ireland department,

is entitled, on giving notice in accordance with rules of court, to be joined as a party to the proceedings.

(3) Notice under subsection (2) may be given at any time during the proceedings.

(4) A person who has been made a party to criminal proceedings (other than in Scotland) as the result of a notice under subsection (2) may, with leave, appeal to the House of Lords against any declaration of incompatibility made in the proceedings.

(5) In subsection (4)—

"criminal proceedings" includes all proceedings before the Courts-Martial Appeal Court; and

"leave" means leave granted by the court making the declaration of incompatibility or by the House of Lords.

Public authorities

Acts of public authorities

6.—(1) It is unlawful for a public authority to act in a way which is incompatible with a Convention right.

(2) Subsection (1) does not apply to an act if—

- (a) as the result of one or more provisions of primary legislation, the authority could not have acted differently; or
- (b) in the case of one or more provisions of, or made under, primary legislation which cannot be read or given effect in a way which is compatible with the Convention rights, the authority was acting so as to give effect to or enforce those provisions.

(3) In this section "public authority" includes—

- (a) a court or tribunal, and
- (b) any person certain of whose functions are functions of a public nature,

but does not include either House of Parliament or a person exercising functions in connection with proceedings in Parliament.

(4) In subsection (3) "Parliament" does not include the House of Lords in its judicial capacity.

(5) In relation to a particular act, a person is not a public authority by virtue only of subsection (3)(b) if the nature of the act is private.

(6) "An act" includes a failure to act but does not include a failure to—

- (a) introduce in, or lay before, Parliament a proposal for legislation; or
- (b) make any primary legislation or remedial order.

Proceedings

7.—(1) A person who claims that a public authority has acted (or proposes to act) in a way which is made unlawful by section 6(1) may—

- (a) bring proceedings against the authority under this Act in the appropriate court or tribunal, or
- (b) rely on the Convention right or rights concerned in any legal proceedings, but only if he is (or would be) a victim of the unlawful act.

(2) In subsection (1)(a) "appropriate court or tribunal" means such court or tribunal as may be determined in accordance with rules; and proceedings against an authority include a counterclaim or similar proceeding.

(3) If the proceedings are brought on an application for judicial review, the applicant is to be taken to have a sufficient interest in relation to the unlawful act only if he is, or would be, a victim of that act.

(4) If the proceedings are made by way of a petition for judicial review in Scotland, the applicant shall be taken to have title and interest to sue in relation to the unlawful act only if he is, or would be, a victim of that act.

(5) Proceedings under subsection (1)(a) must be brought before the end of—

(a) the period of one year beginning with the date on which the act complained of took place; or

(b) such longer period as the court or tribunal considers equitable having regard to all the circumstances.

but that is subject to any rule imposing a stricter time limit in relation to the procedure in question.

(6) In subsection (1)(b) "legal proceedings" includes—

(a) proceedings brought by or at the instigation of a public authority; and

(b) an appeal against the decision of a court or tribunal.

(7) For the purposes of this section, a person is a victim of an unlawful act only if he would be a victim for the purposes of Article 34 of the Convention if proceedings were brought in the European Court of Human Rights in respect of that act.

(8) Nothing in this Act creates a criminal offence.

(9) In this section "rules" means—

(a) in relation to proceedings before a court or tribunal outside Scotland, rules made by the Lord Chancellor or the Secretary of State for the purposes of this section or rules of court,

(b) in relation to proceedings before a court or tribunal in Scotland, rules made by the Secretary of State for those purposes,

(c) in relation to proceedings before a tribunal in Northern Ireland—

(i) which deals with transferred matters; and
(ii) for which no rules made under paragraph (a) are in force,

rules made by a Northern Ireland department for those purposes, and includes provision made by order under section 1 of the Courts and Legal Services Act 1990.

(10) In making rules, regard must be had to section 9.

(11) The Minister who has power to make rules in relation to a particular tribunal may, to the extent he considers it necessary to ensure that the tribunal can provide an appropriate remedy in relation to an act (or proposed act) of a public authority which is (or would be) unlawful as a result of section 6(1), by order add to—

(a) the relief or remedies which the tribunal may grant; or

(b) the grounds on which it may grant any of them.

(12) An order made under subsection (11) may contain such incidental, supplemental, consequential or transitional provision as the Minister making it considers appropriate.

(13) "The Minister" includes the Northern Ireland department concerned.

Judicial remedies

A11–009   8.—(1) In relation to any act (or proposed act) of a public authority which the court finds is (or would be) unlawful, it may grant such relief or remedy, or make such order, within its powers as it considers just and appropriate.

(2) But damages may be awarded only by a court which has power to award damages, or to order the payment of compensation, in civil proceedings.

(3) No award of damages is to be made unless, taking account of all the circumstances of the case, including—

(a) any other relief or remedy granted, or order made, in relation to the act in question (by that or any other court), and

(b) the consequences of any decision (of that or any other court) in respect of that act,

the court is satisfied that the award is necessary to afford just satisfaction to the person in whose favour it is made.

(4) In determining—

(a) whether to award damages, or

(b) the amount of an award,

the court must take into account the principles applied by the European Court of Human Rights in relation to the award of compensation under Article 41 of the Convention.

(5) A public authority against which damages are awarded is to be treated—

(a) in Scotland, for the purposes of section 3 of the Law Reform (Miscellaneous Provisions) (Scotland) Act 1940 as if the award were made in an action of damages in which the authority has been found liable in respect of loss or damage to the person to whom the award is made;

(b) for the purposes of the Civil Liability (Contribution) Act 1978 as liable in respect of damage suffered by the person to whom the award is made.

(6) In this section—

"court" includes a tribunal;
"damages" means damages for an unlawful act of a public authority; and
"unlawful" means unlawful under section 6(1).

Judicial acts

9.—(1) Proceedings under section 7(1)(a) in respect of a judicial act may be brought only— **A11–010**

(a) by exercising a right of appeal;

(b) on an application (in Scotland a petition) for judicial review; or

(c) in such other forum as may be prescribed by rules.

(2) That does not affect any rule of law which prevents a court from being the subject of judicial review.

(3) In proceedings under this Act in respect of a judicial act done in good faith, damages may not be awarded otherwise than to compensate a person to the extent required by Article 5(5) of the Convention.

(4) An award of damages permitted by subsection (3) is to be made against the Crown; but no award may be made unless the appropriate person, if not a party to the proceedings, is joined.

(5) In this section—

"appropriate person" means the Minister responsible for the court concerned, or a person or government department nominated by him;
"court" includes a tribunal;
"judge" includes a member of a tribunal, a justice of the peace and a clerk or other officer entitled to exercise the jurisdiction of a court;
"judicial act" means a judicial act of a court and includes an act done on the instructions, or on behalf, of a judge; and
"rules" has the same meaning as in section 7(9).

Remedial action

Power to take remedial action

A11–011 10.—(1) This section applies if—

(a) a provision of legislation has been declared under section 4 to be incompatible with a Convention right and, if an appeal lies—

(i) all persons who may appeal have stated in writing that they do not intend to do so;
(ii) the time for bringing an appeal has expired and no appeal has been brought within that time; or
(iii) an appeal brought within that time has been determined or abandoned; or

(b) it appears to a Minister of the Crown or Her Majesty in Council that, having regard to a finding of the European Court of Human Rights made after the coming into force of this section in proceedings against the United Kingdom, a provision of legislation is incompatible with an obligation of the United Kingdom arising from the Convention.

(2) If a Minister of the Crown considers that there are compelling reasons for proceeding under this section, he may by order make such amendments to the legislation as he considers necessary to remove the incompatibility.

(3) If, in the case of subordinate legislation, a Minister of the Crown considers—

(a) that it is necessary to amend the primary legislation under which the subordinate legislation in question was made, in order to enable the incompatibility to be removed, and

(b) that there are compelling reasons for proceeding under this section,

he may by order make such amendments to the primary legislation as he considers necessary.

(4) This section also applies where the provision in question is in subordinate legislation and has been quashed, or declared invalid, by reason of incompatibility with a Convention right and the Minister proposes to proceed under paragraph 2(b) of Schedule 2.

(5) If the legislation is an Order in Council, the power conferred by subsection (2) or (3) is exercisable by Her Majesty in Council.

(6) In this section "legislation" does not include a Measure of the Church Assembly or of the General Synod of the Church of England.

(7) Schedule 2 makes further provision about remedial orders.

Other rights and proceedings

Safeguard for existing human rights

11. A person's reliance on a Convention right does not restrict— **A11–012**

   (a) any other right or freedom conferred on him by or under any law having effect in any part of the United Kingdom; or

   (b) his right to make any claim or bring any proceedings which he could make or bring apart from sections 7 to 9.

Freedom of expression

12.—(1) This section applies if a court is considering whether to grant any relief **A11–013** which, if granted, might affect the exercise of the Convention right to freedom of expression.

(2) If the person against whom the application for relief is made ("the respondent") is neither present nor represented, no such relief is to be granted unless the court is satisfied—

   (a) that the applicant has taken all practicable steps to notify the respondent; or

   (b) that there are compelling reasons why the respondent should not be notified.

(3) No such relief is to be granted so as to restrain publication before trial unless the court is satisfied that the applicant is likely to establish that publication should not be allowed.

(4) The court must have particular regard to the importance of the Convention right to freedom of expression and, where the proceedings relate to material which the respondent claims, or which appears to the court, to be journalistic, literary or artistic material (or to conduct connected with such material), to—

   (a) the extent to which—

      (i) the material has, or is about to, become available to the public; or
      (ii) it is, or would be, in the public interest for the material to be published;

   (b) any relevant privacy code.

(5) In this section—

   "court" includes a tribunal; and
   "relief" includes any remedy or order (other than in criminal proceedings).

Freedom of thought, conscience and religion

A11–014   13.—(1) If a court's determination of any question arising under this Act might affect the exercise by a religious organisation (itself or its members collectively) of the Convention right to freedom of thought, conscience and religion, it must have particular regard to the importance of that right.

(2) In this section "court" includes a tribunal.

Derogations and reservations

Derogations

A11–015   14.—(1) In this Act "designated derogation" means—

(a) the United Kingdom's derogation from Article 5(3) of the Convention; and

(b) any derogation by the United Kingdom from an Article of the Convention, or of any protocol to the Convention, which is designated for the purposes of this Act in an order made by the [Lord Chancellor].

(2) The derogation referred to in subsection (1)(a) is set out in Part I of Schedule 3.

(3) If a designated derogation is amended or replaced it ceases to be a designated derogation.

(4) But subsection (3) does not prevent the [Lord Chancellor] from exercising his power under subsection (1)(b) to make a fresh designation order in respect of the Article concerned.

(5) The [Lord Chancellor] must by order make such amendments to Schedule 3 as he considers appropriate to reflect—

(a) any designation order; or

(b) the effect of subsection (3).

(6) A designation order may be made in anticipation of the making by the United Kingdom of a proposed derogation.

Reservations

A11–016   15.—(1) In this Act "designated reservation" means—

(a) the United Kingdom's reservation to Article 2 of the First Protocol to the Convention; and

(b) any other reservation by the United Kingdom to an Article of the Convention, or of any protocol to the Convention, which is designated for the purposes of this Act in an order made by the [Lord Chancellor].

(2) The text of the reservation referred to in subsection (1)(a) is set out in Part II of Schedule 3.

(3) If a designated reservation is withdrawn wholly or in part it ceases to be a designated reservation.

(4) But subsection (3) does not prevent the [Lord Chancellor] from exercising his power under subsection (1)(b) to make a fresh designation order in respect of the Article concerned.

(5) The [Lord Chancellor] must by order make such amendments to this Act as he considers appropriate to reflect—

(a) any designation order; or

(b) the effect of subsection (3).

Period for which designated derogations have effect

16.—(1) If it has not already been withdrawn by the United Kingdom, a designated derogation ceases to have effect for the purposes of this Act— **A11–017**

(a) in the case of the derogation referred to in section 14(1)(a), at the end of the period of five years beginning with the date on which section 1(2) came into force;

(b) in the case of any other derogation, at the end of the period of five years beginning with the date on which the order designating it was made.

(2) At any time before the period—

(a) fixed by subsection (1)(a) or (b), or

(b) extended by an order under this subsection,

comes to an end, the [Lord Chancellor] may by order extend it by a further period of five years.

(3) An order under section 14(1)(b) ceases to have effect at the end of the period for consideration, unless a resolution has been passed by each House approving the order.

(4) Subsection (3) does not affect—

(a) anything done in reliance on the order; or

(b) the power to make a fresh order under section 14(1)(b).

(5) In subsection (3) "period for consideration" means the period of forty days beginning with the day on which the order was made.

(6) In calculating the period for consideration, no account is to be taken of any time during which—

(a) Parliament is dissolved or prorogued; or

(b) both Houses are adjourned for more than four days.

(7) If a designated derogation is withdrawn by the United Kingdom, the [Lord Chancellor] must by order make such amendments to this Act as he considers are required to reflect that withdrawal.

Periodic review of designated reservations

17.—(1) The appropriate Minister must review the designated reservation referred to in section 15(1)(a)— **A11–018**

(a) before the end of the period of five years beginning with the date on which section 1(2) came into force; and

(b) if that designation is still in force, before the end of the period of five years beginning with the date on which the last report relating to it was laid under subsection (3).

(2) The appropriate Minister must review each of the other designated reservations (if any)—

(a) before the end of the period of five years beginning with the date on which the order designating the reservation first came into force; and

(b) if the designation is still in force, before the end of the period of five years beginning with the date on which the last report relating to it was laid under subsection (3).

(3) The Minister conducting a review under this section must prepare a report on the result of the review and lay a copy of it before each House of Parliament.

Judges of the European Court of Human Rights

Appointment to European Court of Human Rights

A11–019   18.—(1) In this section "judicial office" means the office of—

(a) Lord Justice of Appeal, Justice of the High Court or Circuit judge, in England and Wales;

(b) judge of the Court of Session or sheriff, in Scotland;

(c) Lord Justice of Appeal, judge of the High Court or county court judge, in Northern Ireland.

(2) The holder of a judicial office may become a judge of the European Court of Human Rights ("the Court") without being required to relinquish his office.

(3) But he is not required to perform the duties of his judicial office while he is a judge of the Court.

(4) In respect of any period during which he is a judge of the Court—

(a) a Lord Justice of Appeal or Justice of the High Court is not to count as a judge of the relevant court for the purposes of section 2(1) or 4(1) of the Supreme Court Act 1981 (maximum number of judges) nor as a judge of the Supreme Court for the purposes of section 12(1) to (6) of that Act (salaries etc.);

(b) a judge of the Court of Session is not to count as a judge of that court for the purposes of section 1(1) of the Court of Session Act 1988 (maximum number of judges) or of section 9(1)(c) of the Administration of Justice Act 1973 ("the 1973 Act") (salaries etc.);

(c) a Lord Justice of Appeal or judge of the High Court in Northern Ireland is not to count as a judge of the relevant court for the purposes of section 2(1) or 3(1) of the Judicature (Northern Ireland) Act 1978 (maximum number of judges) nor as a judge of the Supreme Court of Northern Ireland for the purposes of section 9(1)(d) of the 1973 Act (salaries etc.);

(d) a Circuit judge is not to count as such for the purposes of section 18 of the Courts Act 1971 (salaries etc.);

(e) a sheriff is not to count as such for the purposes of section 14 of the Sheriff Courts (Scotland) Act 1907 (salaries etc.);

(f) a county court judge of Northern Ireland is not to count as such for the purposes of section 106 of the County Courts Act Northern Ireland 1959 (salaries etc.).

(5) If a sheriff principal is appointed a judge of the Court, section 11(1) of the Sheriff Courts (Scotland) Act 1971 (temporary appointment of sheriff principal) applies, while he holds that appointment, as if his office is vacant.

(6) Schedule 4 makes provision about judicial pensions in relation to the holder of a judicial office who serves as a judge of the Court.

(7) The Lord Chancellor or the Secretary of State may by order make such transitional provision (including, in particular, provision for a temporary increase in the maximum number of judges) as he considers appropriate in relation to any holder of a judicial office who has completed his service as a judge of the Court.

Parliamentary procedure

Statements of compatibility

19.—(1) A Minister of the Crown in charge of a Bill in either House of Parliament must, before Second Reading of the Bill— **A11–020**

(a) make a statement to the effect that in his view the provisions of the Bill are compatible with the Convention rights ("a statement of compatibility"); or

(b) make a statement to the effect that although he is unable to make a statement of compatibility the government nevertheless wishes the House to proceed with the Bill.

(2) The statement must be in writing and be published in such manner as the Minister making it considers appropriate.

Supplemental

Orders, etc. under this Act

20.—(1) Any power of a Minister of the Crown to make an order under this Act is exercisable by statutory instrument. **A11–021**

(2) The power of the Lord Chancellor or the Secretary of State to make rules (other than rules of court) under section 2(3) or 7(9) is exercisable by statutory instrument.

(3) Any statutory instrument made under section 14, 15 or 16(7) must be laid before Parliament.

(4) No order may be made by the Lord Chancellor or the Secretary of State under

section 1(4), 7(11) or 16(2) unless a draft of the order has been laid before, and approved by, each House of Parliament.

(5) Any statutory instrument made under section 18(7) or Schedule 4, or to which subsection (2) applies, shall be subject to annulment in pursuance of a resolution of either House of Parliament.

(6) The power of a Northern Ireland department to make—

(a) rules under section 2(3)(c) or 7(9)(c), or

(b) an order under section 7(11),

is exercisable by statutory rule for the purposes of the Statutory Rules (Northern Ireland) Order 1979.

(7) Any rules made under section 2(3)(c) or 7(9)(c) shall be subject to negative resolution; and section 41(6) of the Interpretation Act Northern Ireland) 1954 (meaning of "subject to negative resolution") shall apply as if the power to make the rules were conferred by an Act of the Northern Ireland Assembly.

(8) No order may be made by a Northern Ireland department under section 7(11) unless a draft of the order has been laid before, and approved by, the Northern Ireland Assembly.

Interpretation, etc.

A11–022 21.—(1) In this Act—

"amend" includes repeal and apply (with or without modifications);
"the appropriate Minister" means the Minister of the Crown having charge of the appropriate authorised government department (within the meaning of the Crown Proceedings Act 1947);
"the Commission" means the European Commission of Human Rights;
"the Convention" means the Convention for the Protection of Human Rights and Fundamental Freedoms, agreed by the Council of Europe at Rome on 4th November 1950 as it has effect for the time being in relation to the United Kingdom;
"declaration of incompatibility" means a declaration under section 4;
"Minister of the Crown" has the same meaning as in the Ministers of the Crown Act 1975;
"Northern Ireland Minister" includes the First Minister and the deputy First Minister in Northern Ireland;
"primary legislation" means any—

(a) public general Act;

(b) local and personal Act;

(c) private Act;

(d) Measure of the Church Assembly;

(e) Measure of the General Synod of the Church of England;

(f) Order in Council—

(i) made in exercise of Her Majesty's Royal Prerogative;

(ii) made under section 38(1)(a) of the Northern Ireland Constitution Act

1973 or the corresponding provision of the Northern Ireland Act 1998; or

(iii) amending an Act of a kind mentioned in paragraph (a), (b) or (c);

and includes an order or other instrument made under primary legislation (otherwise than by the National Assembly for Wales, a member of the Scottish Executive, a Northern Ireland Minister or a Northern Ireland department) to the extent to which it operates to bring one or more provisions of that legislation into force or amends any primary legislation;

"the First Protocol" means the protocol to the Convention agreed at Paris on 20th March 1952;

"the Sixth Protocol" means the protocol to the Convention agreed at Strasbourg on 28th April 1983;

"the Eleventh Protocol" means the protocol to the Convention (restructuring the control machinery established by the Convention) agreed at Strasbourg on 11th May 1994;

"remedial order" means an order under section 10;

"subordinate legislation" means any—

(a) Order in Council other than one—

   (i) made in exercise of Her Majesty's Royal Prerogative;
   (ii) made under section 38(1)(a) of the Northern Ireland Constitution Act 1973 or the corresponding provision of the Northern Ireland Act 1998; or
   (iii) amending an Act of a kind mentioned in the definition of primary legislation;

(b) Act of the Scottish Parliament;

(c) Act of the Parliament of Northern Ireland;

(d) Measure of the Assembly established under section 1 of the Northern Ireland Assembly Act 1973;

(e) Act of the Northern Ireland Assembly;

(f) order, rules, regulations, scheme, warrant, byelaw or other instrument made under primary legislation (except to the extent to which it operates to bring one or more provisions of that legislation into force or amends any primary legislation);

(g) order, rules, regulations, scheme, warrant, byelaw or other instrument made under legislation mentioned in paragraph (b), (c), (d) or (e) or made under an Order in Council applying only to Northern Ireland;

(h) order, rules, regulations, scheme, warrant, byelaw or other instrument made by a member of the Scottish Executive, a Northern Ireland Minister or a Northern Ireland department in exercise of prerogative or other executive functions of Her Majesty which are exercisable by such a person on behalf of Her Majesty;

"transferred matters" has the same meaning as in the Northern Ireland Act 1998; and

"tribunal" means any tribunal in which legal proceedings may be brought.

(2) The references in paragraphs (b) and (c) of section 2(1) to Articles are to Articles of the Convention as they had effect immediately before the coming into force of the Eleventh Protocol.

(3) The reference in paragraph (d) of section 2(1) to Article 46 includes a reference to Articles 32 and 54 of the Convention as they had effect immediately before the coming into force of the Eleventh Protocol.

(4) The references in section 2(1) to a report or decision of the Commission or a decision of the Committee of Ministers include references to a report or decision made as provided by paragraphs 3, 4 and 6 of Article 5 of the Eleventh Protocol (transitional provisions).

(5) Any liability under the Army Act 1955, the Air Force Act 1955 or the Naval Discipline Act 1957 to suffer death for an offence is replaced by a liability to imprisonment for life or any less punishment authorised by those Acts; and those Acts shall accordingly have effect with the necessary modifications.

Short title, commencement, application and extent

A11–023   22.—(1) This Act may be cited as the Human Rights Act 1998.

(2) Sections 18, 20 and 21(5) and this section come into force on the passing of this Act.

(3) The other provisions of this Act come into force on such day as the Secretary of State may by order appoint; and different days may be appointed for different purposes.

(4) Paragraph (b) of subsection (1) of section 7 applies to proceedings brought by or at the instigation of a public authority whenever the act in question took place; but otherwise that subsection does not apply to an act taking place before the coming into force of that section.

(5) This Act binds the Crown.

(6) This Act extends to Northern Ireland.

(7) Section 21(5), so far as it relates to any provision contained in the Army Act 1955, the Air Force Act 1955 or the Naval Discipline Act 1957, extends to any place to which that provision extends.

SCHEDULES

SCHEDULE 1   Section 1(3)

THE ARTICLES

PART I

THE CONVENTION

RIGHTS AND FREEDOMS

Article 2

Right to life

A11–024   1. Everyone's right to life shall be protected by law. No one shall be deprived of his life intentionally save in the execution of a sentence of a court following his conviction of a crime for which this penalty is provided by law.

2. Deprivation of life shall not be regarded as inflicted in contravention of this Article when it results from the use of force which is no more than absolutely necessary:

(a) in defence of any person from unlawful violence;

(b) in order to effect a lawful arrest or to prevent the escape of a person lawfully detained;

(c) in action lawfully taken for the purpose of quelling a riot or insurrection.

Article 3

Prohibition of torture

No one shall be subjected to torture or to inhuman or degrading treatment or punishment. **A11–025**

Article 4

Prohibition of slavery and forced labour

1. No one shall be held in slavery or servitude. **A11–026**
2. No one shall be required to perform forced or compulsory labour.
3. For the purpose of this Article the term "forced or compulsory labour" shall not include:

(a) any work required to be done in the ordinary course of detention imposed according to the provisions of Article 5 of this Convention or during conditional release from such detention;

(b) any service of a military character or, in case of conscientious objectors in countries where they are recognised, service exacted instead of compulsory military service;

(c) any service exacted in case of an emergency or calamity threatening the life or well-being of the community;

(d) any work or service which forms part of normal civic obligations.

Article 5

Right to liberty and security

1. Everyone has the right to liberty and security of person. No one shall be deprived **A11–027** of his liberty save in the following cases and in accordance with a procedure prescribed by law:

(a) the lawful detention of a person after conviction by a competent court;

(b) the lawful arrest or detention of a person for non-compliance with the lawful order of a court or in order to secure the fulfilment of any obligation prescribed by law;

(c) the lawful arrest or detention of a person effected for the purpose of bringing him before the competent legal authority on reasonable suspicion of having committed an offence or when it is reasonably considered necessary to prevent his committing an offence or fleeing after having done so;

(d) the detention of a minor by lawful order for the purpose of educational supervision or his lawful detention for the purpose of bringing him before the competent legal authority;

(e) the lawful detention of persons for the prevention of the spreading of infectious diseases, of persons of unsound mind, alcoholics or drug addicts or vagrants;

(f) the lawful arrest or detention of a person to prevent his effecting an unauthorised entry into the country or of a person against whom action is being taken with a view to deportation or extradition.

2. Everyone who is arrested shall be informed promptly, in a language which he understands, of the reasons for his arrest and of any charge against him.

3. Everyone arrested or detained in accordance with the provisions of paragraph 1(c) of this Article shall be brought promptly before a judge or other officer authorised by law to exercise judicial power and shall be entitled to trial within a reasonable time or to release pending trial. Release may be conditioned by guarantees to appear for trial.

4. Everyone who is deprived of his liberty by arrest or detention shall be entitled to take proceedings by which the lawfulness of his detention shall be decided speedily by a court and his release ordered if the detention is not lawful.

5. Everyone who has been the victim of arrest or detention in contravention of the provisions of this Article shall have an enforceable right to compensation.

Article 6

Right to a fair trial

A11–028 1. In the determination of his civil rights and obligations or of any criminal charge against him, everyone is entitled to a fair and public hearing within a reasonable time by an independent and impartial tribunal established by law. Judgment shall be pronounced publicly but the press and public may be excluded from all or part of the trial in the interest of morals, public order or national security in a democratic society, where the interests of juveniles or the protection of the private life of the parties so require, or to the extent strictly necessary in the opinion of the court in special circumstances where publicity would prejudice the interests of justice.

2. Everyone charged with a criminal offence shall be presumed innocent until proved guilty according to law.

3. Everyone charged with a criminal offence has the following minimum rights:

(a) to be informed promptly, in a language which he understands and in detail, of the nature and cause of the accusation against him;

(b) to have adequate time and facilities for the preparation of his defence;

(c) to defend himself in person or through legal assistance of his own choosing or, if he has not sufficient means to pay for legal assistance, to be given it free when the interests of justice so require;

(d) to examine or have examined witnesses against him and to obtain the attendance and examination of witnesses on his behalf under the same conditions as witnesses against him;

(e) to have the free assistance of an interpreter if he cannot understand or speak the language used in court.

Article 7

No punishment without law

1. No one shall be held guilty of any criminal offence on account of any act or omission which did not constitute a criminal offence under national or international law at the time when it was committed. Nor shall a heavier penalty be imposed than the one that was applicable at the time the criminal offence was committed.   **A11–029**

2. This Article shall not prejudice the trial and punishment of any person for any act or omission which, at the time when it was committed, was criminal according to the general principles of law recognised by civilised nations.

Article 8

Right to respect for private and family life

1. Everyone has the right to respect for his private and family life, his home and his correspondence.   **A11–030**

2. There shall be no interference by a public authority with the exercise of this right except such as is in accordance with the law and is necessary in a democratic society in the interests of national security, public safety or the economic well-being of the country, for the prevention of disorder or crime, for the protection of health or morals, or for the protection of the rights and freedoms of others.

Article 9

Freedom of thought, conscience and religion

1. Everyone has the right to freedom of thought, conscience and religion; this right includes freedom to change his religion or belief and freedom, either alone or in community with others and in public or private, to manifest his religion or belief, in worship, teaching, practice and observance.   **A11–031**

2. Freedom to manifest one's religion or beliefs shall be subject only to such limitations as are prescribed by law and are necessary in a democratic society in the interests of public safety, for the protection of public order, health or morals, or for the protection of the rights and freedoms of others.

Article 10

Freedom of expression

1. Everyone has the right to freedom of expression. This right shall include freedom to hold opinions and to receive and impart information and ideas without interference by public authority and regardless of frontiers. This Article shall not prevent States from requiring the licensing of broadcasting, television or cinema enterprises.   **A11–032**

2. The exercise of these freedoms, since it carries with it duties and responsibilities, may be subject to such formalities, conditions, restrictions or penalties as are prescribed by law and are necessary in a democratic society, in the interests of national security, territorial integrity or public safety, for the prevention of disorder or crime, for the protection of health or morals, for the protection of the reputation or rights of others, for preventing the disclosure of information received in confidence, or for maintaining the authority and impartiality of the judiciary.

Article 11

Freedom of assembly and association

A11–033 1. Everyone has the right to freedom of peaceful assembly and to freedom of association with others, including the right to form and to join trade unions for the protection of his interests.

2. No restrictions shall be placed on the exercise of these rights other than such as are prescribed by law and are necessary in a democratic society in the interests of national security or public safety, for the prevention of disorder or crime, for the protection of health or morals or for the protection of the rights and freedoms of others. This Article shall not prevent the imposition of lawful restrictions on the exercise of these rights by members of the armed forces, of the police or of the administration of the State.

Article 12

Right to marry

A11–034 Men and women of marriageable age have the right to marry and to found a family, according to the national laws governing the exercise of this right.

Article 14

Prohibition of discrimination

A11–035 The enjoyment of the rights and freedoms set forth in this Convention shall be secured without discrimination on any ground such as sex, race, colour, language, religion, political or other opinion, national or social origin, association with a national minority, property, birth or other status.

Article 16

Restrictions on political activity of aliens

A11–036 Nothing in Articles 10, 11 and 14 shall be regarded as preventing the High Contracting Parties from imposing restrictions on the political activity of aliens.

Article 17

Prohibition of abuse of rights

A11–037 Nothing in this Convention may be interpreted as implying for any State, group or person any right to engage in any activity or perform any act aimed at the destruction of any of the rights and freedoms set forth herein or at their limitation to a greater extent than is provided for in the Convention.

Article 18

Limitation on use of restrictions on rights

The restrictions permitted under this Convention to the said rights and freedoms shall not be applied for any purpose other than those for which they have been prescribed. **A11–038**

Part II

The first protocol

Article 1

Protection of property

Every natural or legal person is entitled to the peaceful enjoyment of his possessions. No one shall be deprived of his possessions except in the public interest and subject to the conditions provided for by law and by the general principles of international law. **A11–039**

The preceding provisions shall not, however, in any way impair the right of a State to enforce such laws as it deems necessary to control the use of property in accordance with the general interest or to secure the payment of taxes or other contributions or penalties.

Article 2

Right to education

No person shall be denied the right to education. In the exercise of any functions which it assumes in relation to education and to teaching, the State shall respect the right of parents to ensure such education and teaching in conformity with their own religious and philosophical convictions. **A11–040**

Article 3

Right to free elections

The High Contracting Parties undertake to hold free elections at reasonable intervals by secret ballot, under conditions which will ensure the free expression of the opinion of the people in the choice of the legislature. **A11–041**

Part III

The Sixth Protocol

Article 1

Abolition of the death penalty

The death penalty shall be abolished. No one shall be condemned to such penalty or executed. **A11–042**

Article 2

Death penalty in time of war

A11–043   A State may make provision in its law for the death penalty in respect of acts committed in time of war or of imminent threat of war; such penalty shall be applied only in the instances laid down in the law and in accordance with its provisions. The State shall communicate to the Secretary General of the Council of Europe the relevant provisions of that law.

SCHEDULE 2   Section 10

Remedial orders

Orders

A11–044   1.—(1) A remedial order may—

    (a) contain such incidental, supplemental, consequential or transitional provision as the person making it considers appropriate;

    (b) be made so as to have effect from a date earlier than that on which it is made;

    (c) make provision for the delegation of specific functions;

    (d) make different provision for different cases.

(2) The power conferred by sub-paragraph (1)(a) includes—

    (a) power to amend primary legislation (including primary legislation other than that which contains the incompatible provision); and

    (b) power to amend or revoke subordinate legislation (including subordinate legislation other than that which contains the incompatible provision).

(3) A remedial order may be made so as to have the same extent as the legislation which it affects.

(4) No person is to be guilty of an offence solely as a result of the retrospective effect of a remedial order.

Procedure

A11–045   2. No remedial order may be made unless—

    (a) a draft of the order has been approved by a resolution of each House of Parliament made after the end of the period of 60 days beginning with the day on which the draft was laid; or

    (b) it is declared in the order that it appears to the person making it that, because of the urgency of the matter, it is necessary to make the order without a draft being so approved.

Orders laid in draft

3.—(1) No draft may be laid under paragraph 2(a) unless— **A11–046**

    (a) the person proposing to make the order has laid before Parliament a document which contains a draft of the proposed order and the required information; and

    (b) the period of 60 days, beginning with the day on which the document required by this sub-paragraph was laid, has ended.

(2) If representations have been made during that period, the draft laid under paragraph 2(a) must be accompanied by a statement containing—

    (a) a summary of the representations; and

    (b) if, as a result of the representations, the proposed order has been changed, details of the changes.

Urgent cases

4.—(1) If a remedial order ("the original order") is made without being approved in draft, the person making it must lay it before Parliament, accompanied by the required information, after it is made. **A11–047**

(2) If representations have been made during the period of 60 days beginning with the day on which the original order was made, the person making it must (after the end of that period) lay before Parliament a statement containing—

    (a) a summary of the representations; and

    (b) if, as a result of the representations, he considers it appropriate to make changes to the original order, details of the changes.

(3) If sub-paragraph (2)(b) applies, the person making the statement must—

    (a) make a further remedial order replacing the original order; and

    (b) lay the replacement order before Parliament.

(4) If, at the end of the period of 120 days beginning with the day on which the original order was made, a resolution has not been passed by each House approving the original or replacement order, the order ceases to have effect (but without that affecting anything previously done under either order or the power to make a fresh remedial order).

Definitions

5. In this Schedule— **A11–048**

    "representations" means representations about a remedial order (or proposed remedial order) made to the person making (or proposing to make) it and includes any relevant Parliamentary report or resolution; and
    "required information" means—

        (a) an explanation of the incompatibility which the order (or proposed order) seeks to remove, including particulars of the relevant declaration, finding or order; and

(b) a statement of the reasons for proceeding under section 10 and for making an order in those terms.

Calculating periods

A11–049 6. In calculating any period for the purposes of this Schedule, no account is to be taken of any time during which—

(a) Parliament is dissolved or prorogued; or

(b) both Houses are adjourned for more than four days.

SCHEDULE 3

DEROGATION AND RESERVATION

PART I

DEROGATION

The 1988 notification

A11–050 The United Kingdom Permanent Representative to the Council of Europe presents his compliments to the Secretary General of the Council, and has the honour to convey the following information in order to ensure compliance with the obligations of Her Majesty's Government in the United Kingdom under Article 15(3) of the Convention for the Protection of Human Rights and Fundamental Freedoms signed at Rome on 4 November 1950.

There have been in the United Kingdom in recent years campaigns of organised terrorism connected with the affairs of Northern Ireland which have manifested themselves in activities which have included repeated murder, attempted murder, maiming, intimidation and violent civil disturbance and in bombing and fire raising which have resulted in death, injury and widespread destruction of property. As a result, a public emergency within the meaning of Article 15(1) of the Convention exists in the United Kingdom.

The Government found it necessary in 1974 to introduce and since then, in cases concerning persons reasonably suspected of involvement in terrorism connected with the affairs of Northern Ireland, or of certain offences under the legislation, who have been detained for 48 hours, to exercise powers enabling further detention without charge, for periods of up to five days, on the authority of the Secretary of State. These powers are at present to be found in Section 12 of the Prevention of Terrorism (Temporary Provisions) Act 1984, Article 9 of the Prevention of Terrorism (Supplemental Temporary Provisions) Order 1984 and Article 10 of the Prevention of Terrorism (Supplemental Temporary Provisions) (Northern Ireland) Order 1984.

Section 12 of the Prevention of Terrorism (Temporary Provisions) Act 1984 provides for a person whom a constable has arrested on reasonable grounds of suspecting him to be guilty of an offence under Section 1, 9 or 10 of the Act, or to be or to have been involved in terrorism connected with the affairs of Northern Ireland, to be detained in right of the arrest for up to 48 hours and thereafter, where the Secretary of State extends the detention period, for up to a further five days. Section 12 substantially re-enacted Section 12 of the Prevention of Terrorism (Temporary Provisions) Act 1976 which, in turn, substantially re-enacted Section 7 of the Prevention of Terrorism (Temporary Provisions) Act 1974.

Article 10 of the Prevention of Terrorism (Supplemental Temporary Provisions) (Northern Ireland) Order 1984 (SI 1984/417) and Article 9 of the Prevention of Terrorism (Supplemental Temporary Provisions) Order 1984 (SI 1984/418) were both made under Sections 13 and 14 of and Schedule 3 to the 1984 Act and substantially re-enacted powers of detention in Orders made under the 1974 and 1976 Acts. A person who is being examined under Article 4 of either Order on his arrival in, or on seeking to leave, Northern Ireland or Great Britain for the purpose of determining whether he is or has been involved in terrorism connected with the affairs of Northern Ireland, or whether there are grounds for suspecting that he has committed an offence under Section 9 of the 1984 Act, may be detained under Article 9 or 10, as appropriate, pending the conclusion of his examination. The period of this examination may exceed 12 hours if an examining officer has reasonable grounds for suspecting him to be or to have been involved in acts of terrorism connected with the affairs of Northern Ireland.

Where such a person is detained under the said Article 9 or 10 he may be detained for up to 48 hours on the authority of an examining officer and thereafter, where the Secretary of State extends the detention period, for up to a further five days.

In its judgment of 29 November 1988 in the Case of *Brogan and Others*, the European Court of Human Rights held that there had been a violation of Article 5(3) in respect of each of the applicants, all of whom had been detained under Section 12 of the 1984 Act. The Court held that even the shortest of the four periods of detention concerned, namely four days and six hours, fell outside the constraints as to time permitted by the first part of Article 5(3). In addition, the Court held that there had been a violation of Article 5(5) in the case of each applicant.

Following this judgment, the Secretary of State for the Home Department informed Parliament on 6 December 1988 that, against the background of the terrorist campaign, and the overriding need to bring terrorists to justice, the Government did not believe that the maximum period of detention should be reduced. He informed Parliament that the Government were examining the matter with a view to responding to the judgment. On 22 December 1988, the Secretary of State further informed Parliament that it remained the Government's wish, if it could be achieved, to find a judicial process under which extended detention might be reviewed and where appropriate authorised by a judge or other judicial officer. But a further period of reflection and consultation was necessary before the Government could bring forward a firm and final view.

Since the judgment of 29 November 1988 as well as previously, the Government have found it necessary to continue to exercise, in relation to terrorism connected with the affairs of Northern Ireland, the powers described above enabling further detention without charge for periods of up to 5 days, on the authority of the Secretary of State, to the extent strictly required by the exigencies of the situation to enable necessary enquiries and investigations properly to be completed in order to decide whether criminal proceedings should be instituted. To the extent that the exercise of these powers may be inconsistent with the obligations imposed by the Convention the Government has availed itself of the right of derogation conferred by Article 15(1) of the Convention and will continue to do so until further notice.

Dated 23 December 1988.

The 1989 notification

A11–051 The United Kingdom Permanent Representative to the Council of Europe presents his compliments to the Secretary General of the Council, and has the honour to convey the following information.

In his communication to the Secretary General of 23 December 1988, reference was made to the introduction and exercise of certain powers under section 12 of the Prevention of Terrorism (Temporary Provisions) Act 1984, Article 9 of the Prevention of Terrorism (Supplemental Temporary Provisions) Order 1984 and Article 10 of the Prevention of Terrorism (Supplemental Temporary Provisions) (Northern Ireland) Order 1984.

These provisions have been replaced by section 14 of and paragraph 6 of Schedule 5 to the Prevention of Terrorism (Temporary Provisions) Act 1989, which make comparable provision. They came into force on 22 March 1989. A copy of these provisions is enclosed.

The United Kingdom Permanent Representative avails himself of this opportunity to renew to the Secretary General the assurance of his highest consideration.

23 March 1989.

PART II

RESERVATION

A11–052 At the time of signing the present (First) Protocol, I declare that, in view of certain provisions of the Education Acts in the United Kingdom, the principle affirmed in the second sentence of Article 2 is accepted by the United Kingdom only so far as it is compatible with the provision of efficient instruction and training, and the avoidance of unreasonable public expenditure.

Dated 20 March 1952. Made by the United Kingdom Permanent Representative to the Council of Europe.

SCHEDULE 4

SECTION 18(6)

JUDICIAL PENSIONS

Duty to make orders about pensions

A11–053 **1.**—(1) The appropriate Minister must by order make provision with respect to pensions payable to or in respect of any holder of a judicial office who serves as an ECHR judge.

(2) A pensions order must include such provisions as the Minister making it considers is necessary to secure that—

  (a) an ECHR judge who was, immediately before his appointment as an ECHR judge, a member of a judicial pension scheme is entitled to remain as a member of that scheme;

  (b) the terms on which he remains a member of the scheme are those which would have been applicable had he not been appointed as an ECHR judge; and

(c) entitlement to benefits payable in accordance with the scheme continues to be determined as if, while serving as an ECHR judge, his salary was that which would (but for section 18(4)) have been payable to him in respect of his continuing service as the holder of his judicial office.

Contributions

2. A pensions order may, in particular, make provision—   A11–054

   (a) for any contributions which are payable by a person who remains a member of a scheme as a result of the order, and which would otherwise be payable by deduction from his salary, to be made otherwise than by deduction from his salary as an ECHR judge; and

   (b) for such contributions to be collected in such manner as may be determined by the administrators of the scheme.

Amendments of other enactments

3. A pensions order may amend any provision of, or made under, a pensions Act in such manner and to such extent as the Minister making the order considers necessary or expedient to ensure the proper administration of any scheme to which it relates.   A11–055

Definitions

4. In this Schedule—   A11–056

   "appropriate Minister" means—

   (a) in relation to any judicial office whose jurisdiction is exercisable exclusively in relation to Scotland, the Secretary of State; and

   (b) otherwise, the Lord Chancellor;

   "ECHR judge" means the holder of a judicial office who is serving as a judge of the Court;
   "judicial pension scheme" means a scheme established by and in accordance with a pensions Act;
   "pensions Act" means—

   (a) the County Courts Act Northern Ireland) 1959;

   (b) the Sheriffs' Pensions (Scotland) Act 1961;

   (c) the Judicial Pensions Act 1981; or

   (d) the Judicial Pensions and Retirement Act 1993; and

   "pensions order" means an order made under paragraph 1.

The Unfair Terms in Consumer Contracts Regulations 1999

(SI 1999/2083)

Made 22nd July 1999
Laid before Parliament 22nd July 1999
Coming into force 1st October 1999

A12–001 Whereas the Secretary of State is a Minister designated for the purposes of section 2(2) of the European Communities Act 1972 in relation to measures relating to consumer protection:

Now, the Secretary of State, in exercise of the powers conferred upon him by section 2(2) of that Act, hereby makes the following Regulations:—

Citation and commencement

A12–002 1. These Regulations may be cited as the Unfair Terms in Consumer Contracts Regulations 1999 and shall come into force on 1st October 1999.

Revocation

A12–003 2. The Unfair Terms in Consumer Contracts Regulations 1994 are hereby revoked.

Interpretation

A12–004 3.—(1) In these Regulations—

"the Community" means the European Community;
"consumer" means any natural person who, in contracts covered by these Regulations, is acting for purposes which are outside his trade, business or profession;
"court" in relation to England and Wales and Northern Ireland means a county court or the High Court, and in relation to Scotland, the Sheriff or the Court of Session;
"Director" means the Director General of Fair Trading;
"EEA Agreement" means the Agreement on the European Economic Area signed at Oporto on 2nd May 1992 as adjusted by the protocol signed at Brussels on 17th March 1993;
"Member State" means a State which is a contracting party to the EEA Agreement;
"notified" means notified in writing;
"qualifying body" means a person specified in Schedule 1;
"seller or supplier" means any natural or legal person who, in contracts covered by these Regulations, is acting for purposes relating to his trade, business or profession, whether publicly owned or privately owned;
"unfair terms" means the contractual terms referred to in regulation 5.

(2) In the application of these Regulations to Scotland for references to an "injunction" or an "interim injunction" there shall be substituted references to an "interdict" or "interim interdict" respectively.

The Unfair Terms in Consumer Contracts Regulations 1999

Terms to which these Regulations apply

4.—(1) These Regulations apply in relation to unfair terms in contracts concluded between a seller or a supplier and a consumer. **A12–005**
(2) These Regulations do not apply to contractual terms which reflect—

(a) mandatory statutory or regulatory provisions (including such provisions under the law of any Member State or in Community legislation having effect in the United Kingdom without further enactment);
(b) the provisions or principles of international conventions to which the Member States or the Community are party.

Unfair terms

5.—(1) A contractual term which has not been individually negotiated shall be regarded as unfair if, contrary to the requirement of good faith, it causes a significant imbalance in the parties' rights and obligations arising under the contract, to the detriment of the consumer. **A12–006**
(2) A term shall always be regarded as not having been individually negotiated where it has been drafted in advance and the consumer has therefore not been able to influence the substance of the term.
(3) Notwithstanding that a specific term or certain aspects of it in a contract has been individually negotiated, these Regulations shall apply to the rest of a contract if an overall assessment of it indicates that it is a pre-formulated standard contract.
(4) It shall be for any seller or supplier who claims that a term was individually negotiated to show that it was.
(5) Schedule 2 to these Regulations contains an indicative and non-exhaustive list of the terms which may be regarded as unfair.

Assessment of unfair terms

6.—(1) Without prejudice to regulation 12, the unfairness of a contractual term shall be assessed, taking into account the nature of the goods or services for which the contract was concluded and by referring, at the time of conclusion of the contract, to all the circumstances attending the conclusion of the contract and to all the other terms of the contract or of another contract on which it is dependent. **A12–007**
(2) In so far as it is in plain intelligible language, the assessment of fairness of a term shall not relate—

(a) to the definition of the main subject matter of the contract, or
(b) to the adequacy of the price or remuneration, as against the goods or services supplied in exchange.

Written contracts

7.—(1) A seller or supplier shall ensure that any written term of a contract is expressed in plain, intelligible language. **A12–008**
(2) If there is doubt about the meaning of a written term, the interpretation which is most favourable to the consumer shall prevail but this rule shall not apply in proceedings brought under regulation 12.

Effect of unfair term

A12–009   8.—(1) An unfair term in a contract concluded with a consumer by a seller or supplier shall not be binding on the consumer.

(2) The contract shall continue to bind the parties if it is capable of continuing in existence without the unfair term.

Choice of law clauses

A12–010   9. These Regulations shall apply notwithstanding any contract term which applies or purports to apply the law of a non-Member State, if the contract has a close connection with the territory of the Member States.

Complaints—consideration by Director

A12–011   10.—(1) It shall be the duty of the Director to consider any complaint made to him that any contract term drawn up for general use is unfair, unless—

(a) the complaint appears to the Director to be frivolous or vexatious; or

(b) a qualifying body has notified the Director that it agrees to consider the complaint.

(2) The Director shall give reasons for his decision to apply or not to apply, as the case may be, for an injunction under regulation 12 in relation to any complaint which these Regulations require him to consider.

(3) In deciding whether or not to apply for an injunction in respect of a term which the Director considers to be unfair, he may, if he considers it appropriate to do so, have regard to any undertakings given to him by or on behalf of any person as to the continued use of such a term in contracts concluded with consumers.

Complaints—consideration by qualifying bodies

A12–012   11.—(1) If a qualifying body specified in Part One of Schedule 1 notifies the Director that it agrees to consider a complaint that any contract term drawn up for general use is unfair, it shall be under a duty to consider that complaint.

(2) Regulation 10(2) and (3) shall apply to a qualifying body which is under a duty to consider a complaint as they apply to the Director.

Injunctions to prevent continued use of unfair terms

A12–013   12.—(1) The Director or, subject to paragraph (2), any qualifying body may apply for an injunction (including an interim injunction) against any person appearing to the Director or that body to be using, or recommending use of, an unfair term drawn up for general use in contracts concluded with consumers.

(2) A qualifying body may apply for an injunction only where—

(a) it has notified the Director of its intention to apply at least fourteen days before the date on which the application is made, beginning with the date on which the notification was given; or

(b) the Director consents to the application being made within a shorter period.

(3) The court on an application under this regulation may grant an injunction on such terms as it thinks fit.

(4) An injunction may relate not only to use of a particular contract term drawn up for general use but to any similar term, or a term having like effect, used or recommended for use by any person.

Powers of the Director and qualifying bodies to obtain documents and information

13.—(1) The Director may exercise the power conferred by this regulation for the purpose of— **A12–014**

    (a) facilitating his consideration of a complaint that a contract term drawn up for general use is unfair; or

    (b) ascertaining whether a person has complied with an undertaking or court order as to the continued use, or recommendation for use, of a term in contracts concluded with consumers.

(2) A qualifying body specified in Part One of Schedule 1 may exercise the power conferred by this regulation for the purpose of—

    (a) facilitating its consideration of a complaint that a contract term drawn up for general use is unfair; or

    (b) ascertaining whether a person has complied with—

        (i) an undertaking given to it or to the court following an application by that body, or
        (ii) a court order made on an application by that body,

as to the continued use, or recommendation for use, of a term in contracts concluded with consumers.

(3) The Director may require any person to supply to him, and a qualifying body specified in Part One of Schedule 1 may require any person to supply to it—

    (a) a copy of any document which that person has used or recommended for use, at the time the notice referred to in paragraph (4) below is given, as a pre-formulated standard contract in dealings with consumers;

    (b) information about the use, or recommendation for use, by that person of that document or any other such document in dealings with consumers.

(4) The power conferred by this regulation is to be exercised by a notice in writing which may—

    (a) specify the way in which and the time within which it is to be complied with; and

    (b) be varied or revoked by a subsequent notice.

(5) Nothing in this regulation compels a person to supply any document or information which he would be entitled to refuse to produce or give in civil proceedings before the court.

(6) If a person makes default in complying with a notice under this regulation, the court may, on the application of the Director or of the qualifying body, make such order as the court thinks fit for requiring the default to be made good, and any such order may provide that all the costs or expenses of and incidental to the application shall be borne by the person in default or by any officers of a company or other association who are responsible for its default.

Notification of undertakings and orders to Director

A12–015 14. A qualifying body shall notify the Director—

   (a) of any undertaking given to it by or on behalf of any person as to the continued use of a term which that body considers to be unfair in contracts concluded with consumers;

   (b) of the outcome of any application made by it under regulation 12, and of the terms of any undertaking given to, or order made by, the court;

   (c) of the outcome of any application made by it to enforce a previous order of the court.

Publication, information and advice

A12–016 15.—(1) The Director shall arrange for the publication in such form and manner as he considers appropriate, of—

   (a) details of any undertaking or order notified to him under regulation 14;

   (b) details of any undertaking given to him by or on behalf of any person as to the continued use of a term which the Director considers to be unfair in contracts concluded with consumers;

   (c) details of any application made by him under regulation 12, and of the terms of any undertaking given to, or order made by, the court;

   (d) details of any application made by the Director to enforce a previous order of the court.

(2) The Director shall inform any person on request whether a particular term to which these Regulations apply has been—

   (a) the subject of an undertaking given to the Director or notified to him by a qualifying body; or

   (b) the subject of an order of the court made upon application by him or notified to him by a qualifying body;

and shall give that person details of the undertaking or a copy of the order, as the case may be, together with a copy of any amendments which the person giving the undertaking has agreed to make to the term in question.

(3) The Director may arrange for the dissemination in such form and manner as he considers appropriate of such information and advice concerning the operation of these Regulations as may appear to him to be expedient to give to the public and to all persons likely to be affected by these Regulations.

The functions of the Financial Services Authority

16. The functions of the Financial Services Authority under these Regulations shall be treated as functions of the Financial Services Authority under the [Financial Services and Markets Act 2000].

A12–017

Regulation 3 SCHEDULE 1

QUALIFYING BODIES

PART ONE

[**1.** The Information Commissioner.]
[**2.** The Gas and Electricity Markets Authority.]
[**3.** The Director General of Electricity Supply for Northern Ireland.]
[**4.** The Director General of Gas for Northern Ireland.]
[**5.** The Director General of Telecommunications.]
[**6.** The Director General of Water Services.]
[**7.** The Rail Regulator.]
[**8.** Every weights and measures authority in Great Britain.]
[**9.** The Department of Enterprise, Trade and Investment in Northern Ireland.]
[**10.** The Financial Services Authority.]

A12–018

PART TWO

11. Consumers' Association.

A12–019

Regulation 5(5) SCHEDULE 2

INDICATIVE AND NON-EXHAUSTIVE LIST OF TERMS WHICH MAY BE REGARDED AS UNFAIR

1. Terms which have the object or effect of—

A12–020

(a) excluding or limiting the legal liability of a seller or supplier in the event of the death of a consumer or personal injury to the latter resulting from an act or omission of that seller or supplier;

(b) inappropriately excluding or limiting the legal rights of the consumer vis-à-vis the seller or supplier or another party in the event of total or partial non-performance or inadequate performance by the seller or supplier of any of the contractual obligations, including the option of offsetting a debt owed to the seller or supplier against any claim which the consumer may have against him;

(c) making an agreement binding on the consumer whereas provision of services by the seller or supplier is subject to a condition whose realisation depends on his own will alone;

(d) permitting the seller or supplier to retain sums paid by the consumer where the latter decides not to conclude or perform the contract, without providing for the consumer to receive compensation of an equivalent amount from the seller or supplier where the latter is the party cancelling the contract;

(e) requiring any consumer who fails to fulfil his obligation to pay a disproportionately high sum in compensation;

(f) authorising the seller or supplier to dissolve the contract on a discretionary basis where the same facility is not granted to the consumer, or permitting the seller or supplier to retain the sums paid for services not yet supplied by him where it is the seller or supplier himself who dissolves the contract;

(g) enabling the seller or supplier to terminate a contract of indeterminate duration without reasonable notice except where there are serious grounds for doing so;

(h) automatically extending a contract of fixed duration where the consumer does not indicate otherwise, when the deadline fixed for the consumer to express his desire not to extend the contract is unreasonably early;

(i) irrevocably binding the consumer to terms with which he had no real opportunity of becoming acquainted before the conclusion of the contract;

(j) enabling the seller or supplier to alter the terms of the contract unilaterally without a valid reason which is specified in the contract;

(k) enabling the seller or supplier to alter unilaterally without a valid reason any characteristics of the product or service to be provided;

(l) providing for the price of goods to be determined at the time of delivery or allowing a seller of goods or supplier of services to increase their price without in both cases giving the consumer the corresponding right to cancel the contract if the final price is too high in relation to the price agreed when the contract was concluded;

(m) giving the seller or supplier the right to determine whether the goods or services supplied are in conformity with the contract, or giving him the exclusive right to interpret any term of the contract;

(n) limiting the seller's or supplier's obligation to respect commitments undertaken by his agents or making his commitments subject to compliance with a particular formality;

(o) obliging the consumer to fulfil all his obligations where the seller or supplier does not perform his;

(p) giving the seller or supplier the possibility of transferring his rights and obligations under the contract, where this may serve to reduce the guarantees for the consumer, without the latter's agreement;

(q) excluding or hindering the consumer's right to take legal action or exercise any other legal remedy, particularly by requiring the consumer to take disputes exclusively to arbitration not covered by legal provisions, unduly restricting the evidence available to him or imposing on him a burden of proof which, according to the applicable law, should lie with another party to the contract.

2. Scope of paragraphs 1(g), (j) and (l)—

(a) Paragraph 1(g) is without hindrance to terms by which a supplier of financial services reserves the right to terminate unilaterally a contract of indeterminate duration without notice where there is a valid reason, provided that the supplier is required to inform the other contracting party or parties thereof immediately.

(b) Paragraph 1(j) is without hindrance to terms under which a supplier of financial services reserves the right to alter the rate of interest payable by the consumer or due to the latter, or the amount of other charges for financial services without notice where there is a valid reason, provided that the supplier is required to inform the other contracting party or parties thereof at the earliest opportunity and that the latter are free to dissolve the contract immediately.

Paragraph 1(j) is also without hindrance to terms under which a seller or supplier reserves the right to alter unilaterally the conditions of a contract of indeterminate duration, provided that he is required to inform the consumer with reasonable notice and that the consumer is free to dissolve the contract.

(c) Paragraphs 1(g), (j) and (l) do not apply to:
— transactions in transferable securities, financial instruments and other products or services where the price is linked to fluctuations in a stock exchange quotation or index or a financial market rate that the seller or supplier does not control;
— contracts for the purchase or sale of foreign currency, traveller's cheques or international money orders denominated in foreign currency;

(d) Paragraph 1(l) is without hindrance to price indexation clauses, where lawful, provided that the method by which prices vary is explicitly described.

Appendix 2

INTERNATIONAL CONVENTIONS AND RELATED MATERIALS

Article 6 of the Convention for the Protection of Human Rights and Fundamental Freedoms, as amended by Protocol No. 11[1]

(EUROPEAN TREATY SERIES NO. 5, 1950)

Rome, 4.XI.1950

Article 6. Right to a fair trial

1. In the determination of his civil rights and obligations or of any criminal charge against him, everyone is entitled to a fair and public hearing within a reasonable time by an independent and impartial tribunal established by law. Judgment shall be pronounced publicly but the press and public may be excluded from all or part of the trial in the interests of morals, public order or national security in a democratic society, where the interests of juveniles or the protection of the private life of the parties so require, or to the extent strictly necessary in the opinion of the court in special circumstances where publicity would prejudice the interests of justice.   **A13–001**

2. Everyone charged with a criminal offence shall be presumed innocent until proved guilty according to law.

3. Everyone charged with a criminal offence has the following minimum rights:

(a) to be informed promptly, in a language which he understands and in detail, of the nature and cause of the accusation against him;

(b) to have adequate time and facilities for the preparation of his defence;

(c) to defend himself in person or through legal assistance of his own choosing or, if he has not sufficient means to pay for legal assistance, to be given it free when the interests of justice so require;

---

1 Reproduced with the kind permission of the Council of Europe.

(d) to examine or have examined witnesses against him and to obtain the attendance and examination of witnesses on his behalf under the same conditions as witnesses against him;

(e) to have the free assistance of an interpreter if he cannot understand or speak the language used in court.

UNCITRAL Model Law on International Commercial Arbitration[1]

(United Nations Document A/40/17, Annex 1)

(As adopted by the United Nations Commission on International Trade Law on 21 June 1985)

Chapter I

General Provisions

Article 1. Scope of application[*]

(1) This Law applies to international commercial[**] arbitration, subject to any agreement in force between this State and any other State or States. **A14–001**
(2) The provisions of this Law, except articles 8, 9, 35 and 36, apply only if the place of arbitration is in the territory of this State.
(3) An arbitration is international if:

- (a) the parties to an arbitration agreement have, at the time of the conclusion of that agreement, their places of business in different States; or
- (b) one of the following places is situated outside the State in which the parties have their places of business:
    - (i) the place of arbitration if determined in, or pursuant to, the arbitration agreement;
    - (ii) any place where a substantial part of the obligations of the commercial relationship is to be performed or the place with which the subject-matter of the dispute is most closely connected; or
- (c) the parties have expressly agreed that the subject-matter of the arbitration agreement relates to more than one country.

---

[1] Reproduced with the kind permission of United Nations Commission on International Trade Law.
[*] Article headings are for reference purposes only and are not to be used for purposes of interpretation.
[**] The term "commercial" should be given a wide interpretation so as to cover matters arising from all relationships of a commercial nature, whether contractual or not. Relationships of a commercial nature include, but are not limited to, the following transactions: any trade transaction for the supply or exchange of goods or services; distribution agreement; commercial representation or agency; factoring; leasing; construction of works; consulting; engineering; licensing; investment; financing; banking; insurance; exploitation agreement or concession; joint venture and other forms of industrial or business cooperation; carriage of goods or passengers by air, sea, rail or road.

(4) For the purposes of paragraph (3) of this article:

  (a) if a party has more than one place of business, the place of business is that which has the closest relationship to the arbitration agreement;

  (b) if a party does not have a place of business, reference is to be made to his habitual residence.

(5) This Law shall not affect any other law of this State by virtue of which certain disputes may not be submitted to arbitration or may be submitted to arbitration only according to provisions other than those of this Law.)

Article 2. Definitions and rules of interpretation

A14–002 For the purposes of this Law:

  (a) "arbitration" means any arbitration whether or not administered by a permanent arbitral institution;

  (b) "arbitral tribunal" means a sole arbitrator or a panel of arbitrators;

  (c) "court" means a body or organ of the judicial system of a State;

  (d) where a provision of this Law, except article 28, leaves the parties free to determine a certain issue, such freedom includes the right of the parties to authorize a third party, including an institution, to make that determination;

  (e) where a provision of this Law refers to the fact that the parties have agreed or that they may agree or in any other way refers to an agreement of the parties, such agreement includes any arbitration rules referred to in that agreement;

  (f) where a provision of this Law, other than in articles 25(a) and 32(2)(a), refers to a claim, it also applies to a counter-claim, and where it refers to a defence, it also applies to a defence to such counter-claim.

Article 3. Receipt of written communications

A14–003 (1) Unless otherwise agreed by the parties:

  (a) any written communication is deemed to have been received if it is delivered to the addressee personally or if it is delivered at his place of business, habitual residence or mailing address; if none of these can be found after making a reasonable inquiry, a written communication is deemed to have been received if it is sent to the addressee's last-known place of business, habitual residence or mailing address by registered letter or any other means which provides a record of the attempt to deliver it;

  (b) the communication is deemed to have been received on the day it is so delivered.

(2) The provisions of this article do not apply to communications in court proceedings.

Article 4. Waiver of right to object

A party who knows that any provision of this Law from which the parties may derogate or any requirement under the arbitration agreement has not been complied with and yet proceeds with the arbitration without stating his objection to such non-compliance without undue delay or, if a time-limit is provided therefor, within such period of time, shall be deemed to have waived his right to object. **A14–004**

Article 5. Extent of court intervention

In matters governed by this Law, no court shall intervene except where so provided in this Law. **A14–005**

Article 6. Court or other authority for certain functions of arbitration assistance and supervision

The functions referred to in articles 11(3), 11(4), 13(3), 14, 16(3) and 34(2) shall be performed by .... [Each State enacting this model law specifies the court, courts or, where referred to therein, other authority competent to perform these functions.] **A14–006**

CHAPTER II

ARBITRATION AGREEMENT

Article 7. Definition and form of arbitration agreement

(1) "Arbitration agreement" is an agreement by the parties to submit to arbitration all or certain disputes which have arisen or which may arise between them in respect of a defined legal relationship, whether contractual or not. An arbitration agreement may be in the form of an arbitration clause in a contract or in the form of a separate agreement. **A14–007**

(2) The arbitration agreement shall be in writing. An agreement is in writing if it is contained in a document signed by the parties or in an exchange of letters, telex, telegrams or other means of telecommunication which provide a record of the agreement, or in an exchange of statements of claim and defence in which the existence of an agreement is alleged by one party and not denied by another. The reference in a contract to a document containing an arbitration clause constitutes an arbitration agreement provided that the contract is in writing and the reference is such as to make that clause part of the contract.

Article 8. Arbitration agreement and substantive claim before court

A14–008   (1) A court before which an action is brought in a matter which is the subject of an arbitration agreement shall, if a party so requests not later than when submitting his first statement on the substance of the dispute, refer the parties to arbitration unless it finds that the agreement is null and void, inoperative or incapable of being performed.

(2) Where an action referred to in paragraph (1) of this article has been brought, arbitral proceedings may nevertheless be commenced or continued, and an award may be made, while the issue is pending before the court.

Article 9. Arbitration agreement and interim measures by court

A14–009   It is not incompatible with an arbitration agreement for a party to request, before or during arbitral proceedings, from a court an interim measure of protection and for a court to grant such measure.

CHAPTER III

COMPOSITION OF ARBITRAL TRIBUNAL

Article 10. Number of arbitrators

A14–010   (1) The parties are free to determine the number of arbitrators.
(2) Failing such determination, the number of arbitrators shall be three.

Article 11. Appointment of arbitrators

A14–011   (1) No person shall be precluded by reason of his nationality from acting as an arbitrator, unless otherwise agreed by the parties.

(2) The parties are free to agree on a procedure of appointing the arbitrator or arbitrators, subject to the provisions of paragraphs (4) and (5) of this article.

(3) Failing such agreement,

> (a) in an arbitration with three arbitrators, each party shall appoint one arbitrator, and the two arbitrators thus appointed shall appoint the third arbitrator; if a party fails to appoint the arbitrator within thirty days of receipt of a request to do so from the other party, or if the two arbitrators fail to agree on the third arbitrator within thirty days of their appointment, the appointment shall be made, upon request of a party, by the court or other authority specified in article 6;

(b) in an arbitration with a sole arbitrator, if the parties are unable to agree on the arbitrator, he shall be appointed, upon request of a party, by the court or other authority specified in article 6.

(4) Where, under an appointment procedure agreed upon by the parties,

(a) a party fails to act as required under such procedure, or

(b) the parties, or two arbitrators, are unable to reach an agreement expected of them under such procedure, or

(c) a third party, including an institution, fails to perform any function entrusted to it under such procedure,

any party may request the court or other authority specified in article 6 to take the necessary measure, unless the agreement on the appointment procedure provides other means for securing the appointment.

(5) A decision on a matter entrusted by paragraph (3) or (4) of this article to the court or other authority specified in article 6 shall be subject to no appeal. The court or other authority, in appointing an arbitrator, shall have due regard to any qualifications required of the arbitrator by the agreement of the parties and to such considerations as are likely to secure the appointment of an independent and impartial arbitrator and, in the case of a sole or third arbitrator, shall take into account as well the advisability of appointing an arbitrator of a nationality other than those of the parties.

Article 12. Grounds for challenge

(1) When a person is approached in connection with his possible appointment as an arbitrator, he shall disclose any circumstances likely to give rise to justifiable doubts as to his impartiality or independence. An arbitrator, from the time of his appointment and throughout the arbitral proceedings, shall without delay disclose any such circumstances to the parties unless they have already been informed of them by him.

(2) An arbitrator may be challenged only if circumstances exist that give rise to justifiable doubts as to his impartiality or independence, or if he does not possess qualifications agreed to by the parties. A party may challenge an arbitrator appointed by him, or in whose appointment he has participated, only for reasons of which he becomes aware after the appointment has been made.

A14–012

Article 13. Challenge procedure

(1) The parties are free to agree on a procedure for challenging an arbitrator, subject to the provisions of paragraph (3) of this article.

(2) Failing such agreement, a party who intends to challenge an arbitrator shall, within fifteen days after becoming aware of the constitution of the arbitral tribunal or after becoming aware of any circumstance referred to in article 12(2), send a written statement of the reasons for the challenge to the arbitral tribunal. Unless the challenged arbitrator withdraws from his office or the other party agrees to the challenge, the arbitral tribunal shall decide on the challenge.

A14–013

(3) If a challenge under any procedure agreed upon by the parties or under the procedure of paragraph (2) of this article is not successful, the challenging party may request, within thirty days after having received notice of the decision rejecting the challenge, the court or other authority specified in article 6 to decide on the challenge, which decision shall be subject to no appeal; while such a request is pending, the arbitral tribunal, including the challenged arbitrator, may continue the arbitral proceedings and make an award.

Article 14. Failure or impossibility to act

A14–014 (1) If an arbitrator becomes *de jure* or *de facto* unable to perform his functions or for other reasons fails to act without undue delay, his mandate terminates if he withdraws from his office or if the parties agree on the termination. Otherwise, if a controversy remains concerning any of these grounds, any party may request the court or other authority specified in article 6 to decide on the termination of the mandate, which decision shall be subject to no appeal.

(2) If, under this article or article 13(2), an arbitrator withdraws from his office or a party agrees to the termination other mandate of an arbitrator, this does not imply acceptance of the validity of any ground referred to in this article or article 12(2).

Article 15. Appointment of substitute arbitrator

A14–015 Where the mandate of an arbitrator terminates under article 13 or 14 or because of his withdrawal from office for any other reason or because of the revocation of his mandate by agreement of the parties or in any other case of termination of his mandate, a substitute arbitrator shall be appointed according to the rules that were applicable to the appointment of the arbitrator being replaced.

CHAPTER IV

JURISDICTION OF ARBITRAL TRIBUNAL

Article 16. Competence of arbitral tribunal to rule on its jurisdiction

A14–016 (1) The arbitral tribunal may rule on its own jurisdiction, including any objections with respect to the existence or validity of the arbitration agreement. For that purpose, an arbitration clause which forms part of a contract shall be treated as an agreement independent of the other terms of the contract. A decision by the arbitral tribunal that the contract is null and void shall not entail *ipso jure* the invalidity of the arbitration clause.

(2) A plea that the arbitral tribunal does not have jurisdiction shall be raised not later than the submission of the statement of defence. A party is not precluded from raising

such a plea by the fact that he has appointed, or participated in the appointment of, an arbitrator. A plea that the arbitral tribunal is exceeding the scope of its authority shall be raised as soon as the matter alleged to be beyond the scope of its authority is raised during the arbitral proceedings. The arbitral tribunal may, in either case, admit a later plea if it considers the delay justified.

(3) The arbitral tribunal may rule on a plea referred to in paragraph (2) of this article either as a preliminary question or in an award on the merits. If the arbitral tribunal rules as a preliminary question that it has jurisdiction, any party may request, within thirty days after having received notice of that ruling, the court specified in article 6 to decide the matter, which decision shall be subject to no appeal; while such a request is pending, the arbitral tribunal may continue the arbitral proceedings and make an award.

Article 17. Power of arbitral tribunal to order interim measures

Unless otherwise agreed by the parties, the arbitral tribunal may, at the request of a party, order any party to take such interim measure of protection as the arbitral tribunal may consider necessary in respect of the subject-matter of the dispute. The arbitral tribunal may require any party to provide appropriate security in connection with such measure. **A14–017**

Chapter V

Conduct of Arbitral Proceedings

Article 18. Equal treatment of parties

The parties shall be treated with equality and each party shall be given a full opportunity of presenting his case. **A14–018**

Article 19. Determination of rules of procedure

(1) Subject to the provisions of this Law, the parties are free to agree on the procedure to be followed by the arbitral tribunal in conducting the proceedings. **A14–019**

(2) Failing such agreement, the arbitral tribunal may, subject to the provisions of this Law, conduct the arbitration in such manner as it considers appropriate. The power conferred upon the arbitral tribunal includes the power to determine the admissibility, relevance, materiality and weight of any evidence.

Article 20. Place of arbitration

A14–020 (1) The parties are free to agree on the place of arbitration. Failing such agreement, the place of arbitration shall be determined by the arbitral tribunal having regard to the circumstances of the case, including the convenience of the parties.

(2) Notwithstanding the provisions of paragraph (1) of this article, the arbitral tribunal may, unless otherwise agreed by the parties, meet at any place it considers appropriate for consultation among its members, for hearing witnesses, experts or the parties, or for inspection of goods, other property or documents.

Article 21. Commencement of arbitral proceedings

A14–021 Unless otherwise agreed by the parties, the arbitral proceedings in respect of a particular dispute commence on the date on which a request for that dispute to be referred to arbitration is received by the respondent.

Article 22. Language

A14–022 (1) The parties are free to agree on the language or languages to be used in the arbitral proceedings. Failing such agreement, the arbitral tribunal shall determine the language or languages to be used in the proceedings. This agreement or determination, unless otherwise specified therein, shall apply to any written statement by a party, any hearing and any award, decision or other communication by the arbitral tribunal.

(2) The arbitral tribunal may order that any documentary evidence shall be accompanied by a translation into the language or languages agreed upon by the parties or determined by the arbitral tribunal.

Article 23. Statements of claim and defence

A14–023 (1) Within the period of time agreed by the parties or determined by the arbitral tribunal, the claimant shall state the facts supporting his claim, the points at issue and the relief or remedy sought, and the respondent shall state his defence in respect of these particulars, unless the parties have otherwise agreed as to the required elements of such statements. The parties may submit with their statements all documents they consider to be relevant or may add a reference to the documents or other evidence they will submit.

(2) Unless otherwise agreed by the parties, either party may amend or supplement his claim or defence during the course of the arbitral proceedings, unless the arbitral tribunal considers it inappropriate to allow such amendment having regard to the delay in making it.

Article 24. Hearings and written proceedings

(1) Subject to any contrary agreement by the parties, the arbitral tribunal shall decide whether to hold oral hearings for the presentation of evidence or for oral argument, or whether the proceedings shall be conducted on the basis of documents and other materials. However, unless the parties have agreed that no hearings shall be held, the arbitral tribunal shall hold such hearings at an appropriate stage of the proceedings, if so requested by a party.

(2) The parties shall be given sufficient advance notice of any hearing and of any meeting of the arbitral tribunal for the purposes of inspection of goods, other property or documents.

(3) All statements, documents or other information supplied to the arbitral tribunal by one party shall be communicated to the other party. Also any expert report or evidentiary document on which the arbitral tribunal may rely in making its decision shall be communicated to the parties.

Article 25. Default of a party

Unless otherwise agreed by the parties, if, without showing sufficient cause,

(a) the claimant fails to communicate his statement of claim in accordance with article 23(1), the arbitral tribunal shall terminate the proceedings;

(b) the respondent fails to communicate his statement of defence in accordance with article 23(1), the arbitral tribunal shall continue the proceedings without treating such failure in itself as an admission of the claimant's allegations;

(c) any party fails to appear at a hearing or to produce documentary evidence, the arbitral tribunal may continue the proceedings and make the award on the evidence before it.

Article 26. Expert appointed by arbitral tribunal

(1) Unless otherwise agreed by the parties, the arbitral tribunal

(a) may appoint one or more experts to report to it on specific issues to be determined by the arbitral tribunal;

(b) may require a party to give the expert any relevant information or to produce, or to provide access to, any relevant documents, goods or other property for his inspection.

(2) Unless otherwise agreed by the parties, if a party so requests or if the arbitral tribunal considers it necessary, the expert shall, after delivery of his written or oral report, participate in a hearing where the parties have the opportunity to put questions to him and to present expert witnesses in order to testify on the points at issue.

Article 27. Court assistance in taking evidence

A14–027 The arbitral tribunal or a party with the approval of the arbitral tribunal may request from a competent court of this State assistance in taking evidence. The court may execute the request within its competence and according to its rules on taking evidence.

CHAPTER VI

MAKING OF AWARD AND TERMINATION OF PROCEEDINGS

Article 28. Rules applicable to substance of dispute

A14–028 (1) The arbitral tribunal shall decide the dispute in accordance with such rules of law as are chosen by the parties as applicable to the substance of the dispute. Any designation of the law or legal system of a given State shall be construed, unless otherwise expressed, as directly referring to the substantive law of that State and not to its conflict of laws rules.

(2) Failing any designation by the parties, the arbitral tribunal shall apply the law determined by the conflict of laws rules which it considers applicable.

(3) The arbitral tribunal shall decide *ex aequo et bono* or as *amiable compositeur* only if the parties have expressly authorized it to do so.

(4) In all cases, the arbitral tribunal shall decide in accordance with the terms of the contract and shall take into account the usages of the trade applicable to the transaction.

Article 29. Decision making by panel of arbitrators

A14–029 In arbitral proceedings with more than one arbitrator, any decision of the arbitral tribunal shall be made, unless otherwise agreed by the parties, by a majority of all its members. However, questions of procedure may be decided by a presiding arbitrator, if so authorized by the parties or all members of the arbitral tribunal.

Article 30. Settlement

A14–030 (1) If, during arbitral proceedings, the parties settle the dispute, the arbitral tribunal shall terminate the proceedings and, if requested by the parties and not objected to by the arbitral tribunal, record the settlement in the form of an arbitral award on agreed terms.

(2) An award on agreed terms shall be made in accordance with the provisions of article 31 and shall state that it is an award. Such an award has the same status and effect as any other award on the merits of the case.

Article 31. Form and contents of award

(1) The award shall be made in writing and shall be signed by the arbitrator or arbitrators. In arbitral proceedings with more than one arbitrator, the signatures of the majority of all members of the arbitral tribunal shall suffice, provided that the reason for any omitted signature is stated.

(2) The award shall state the reasons upon which it is based, unless the parties have agreed that no reasons are to be given or the award is an award on agreed terms under article 30.

(3) The award shall state its date and the place of arbitration as determined in accordance with article 20(1). This award shall be deemed to have been made at that place.

(4) After the award is made, a copy signed by the arbitrators in accordance with paragraph (1) of this article shall be delivered to each party.

Article 32. Termination of proceedings

(1) The arbitral proceedings are terminated by the final award or by an order of the arbitral tribunal in accordance with paragraph (2) of this article.

(2) The arbitral tribunal shall issue an order for the termination of the arbitral proceedings when:

- (a) the claimant withdraws his claim, unless the respondent objects thereto and the arbitral tribunal recognizes a legitimate interest on his part in obtaining a final settlement of the dispute;
- (b) the parties agree on the termination of the proceedings;
- (c) the arbitral tribunal finds that the continuation of the proceedings has for any other reason become unnecessary or impossible.

(3) The mandate of the arbitral tribunal terminates with the termination of the arbitral proceedings, subject to the provisions of articles 33 and 34(4).

Article 33. Correction and interpretation of award; additional award

(1) Within thirty days of receipt of the award, unless another period of time has been agreed upon by the parties:

- (a) a party, with notice to the other party, may request the arbitral tribunal to correct in the award any errors in computation, any clerical or typographical errors or any errors of similar nature;
- (b) if so agreed by the parties, a party, with notice to the other party, may request the arbitral tribunal to give an interpretation of a specific point or part of the award.

If the arbitral tribunal considers the request to be justified, it shall make the correction or give the interpretation within thirty days of receipt of the request. The interpretation shall form part of the award.

(2) The arbitral tribunal may correct any error of the type referred to in paragraph (1)(a) of this article on its own initiative within thirty days of the date of the award.

(3) Unless otherwise agreed by the parties, a party, with notice to the other party, may request, within thirty days a receipt of the award, the arbitral tribunal to make an additional award as to claims presented in the arbitral proceedings but omitted from the award. If the arbitral tribunal considers the request to be justified, it shall make the additional award within sixty days.

(4) The arbitral tribunal may extend, if necessary, the period of time within which it shall make a correction, intepretation or an additional award under paragraph (1) or (3) of this article.

(5) The provisions of article 31 shall apply to a correction or interpretation of the award or to an additional award.

Chapter VII

Recourse Against Award

Article 34. Application for setting aside as exclusive recourse against arbitral award

A14-034 (1) Recourse to a court against an arbitral award may be made only by an application for setting aside in accordance with paragraphs (2) and (3) of this article.

(2) An arbitral award may be set aside by the court specified in article 6 only if:

(a) the party making the application furnishes proof that:

(i) a party to the arbitration agreement referred to in article 7 was under some incapacity; or the said agreement is not valid under the law to which the parties have subjected it or, failing any indication thereon, under the law of this State; or

(ii) the party making the application was not given proper notice of the appointment of an arbitrator or of the arbitral proceedings or was otherwise unable to present his case; or

(iii) the award deals with a dispute not contemplated by or not falling within the terms of the submission to arbitration, or contains decisions on matters beyond the scope of the submission to arbitration, provided that, if the decisions on matters submitted to arbitration can be separated from those not so submitted, only that part of the award which contains decisions on matters not submitted to arbitration may be set aside; or

(iv) the composition of the arbitral tribunal or the arbitral procedure was not in accordance with the agreement of the parties, unless such agreement was in conflict with a provision of this Law from which the parties cannot derogate, or, failing such agreement, was not in accordance with this Law; or

(b) the court finds that:

    (i) the subject-matter of the dispute is not capable of settlement by arbitration under the law of this State; or

    (ii) the award is in conflict with the public policy of this State.

(3) An application for setting aside may not be made after three months have elapsed from the date on which the party making that application had received the award or, if a request had been made under article 33, from the date on which that request had been disposed of by the arbitral tribunal.

(4) The court, when asked to set aside an award, may, where appropriate and so requested by a party, suspend the setting aside proceedings for a period of time determined by it in order to give the arbitral tribunal an opportunity to resume the arbitral proceedings or to take such other action as in the arbitral tribunal's opinion will eliminate the grounds for setting aside.

Chapter VII

Recognition and Enforcement of Awards

Article 35. Recognition and enforcement

(1) An arbitral award, irrespective of the county in which it was made, shall be recognized as binding and, upon application in writing to the competent court, shall be enforced subject to the provisions of this article and of article 36.

(2) The party relying on an award or applying for its enforcement shall supply the duly authenticated original award or a duly certified copy thereof, and the original arbitration agreement referred to in article 7 or a duly certified copy thereof. If the award or agreement is not made in an official language of this State, the party shall supply a duly certified translation thereof into such language.***

Article 36. Grounds for refusing recognition or enforcement

(1) Recognition or enforcement of an arbitral award, irrespective of the country in which it was made, may be refused only:

  (a) at the request of the party against whom it is invoked, if that party furnishes to the competent court where recognition or enforcement is sought proof that:

    (i) a party to the arbitration agreement referred to in article 7 was under some incapacity; or the said agreement is not valid under the law to which the

---

*** The conditions set forth in this paragraph are intended to set maximum standards. It would, thus, not be contrary to the harmonization to be achieved by the model law if a State retained even less onerous conditions.

parties have subjected it or, failing any indication thereon, under the law of the country where the award was made; or

(ii) the party against whom the award is invoked was not given proper notice of the appointment of an arbitrator or of the arbitral proceedings or was otherwise unable to present his case; or

(iii) the award deals with a dispute not contemplated by or not falling within the terms of the submission to arbitration, or it contains decisions on matters beyond the scope of the submission to arbitration, provided that, if the decisions on matters submitted to arbitration can be separated from those not so submitted, that part of the award which contains decisions on matters submitted to arbitration may be recognized and enforced; or

(iv) the composition of the arbitral tribunal or the arbitral procedure was not in accordance with the agreement of the parties or, failing such agreement, was not in accordance with the law of the country where the arbitration took place; or

(v) the award has not yet become binding on the parties or has been set aside or suspended by a court of the country in which, or under the law of which, that award was made; or

(b) if the court finds that:

(i) the subject-matter of the dispute is not capable of settlement by arbitration under the law of this State; or

(ii) the recognition or enforcement of the award would be contrary to the public policy of this State.

(2) If an application for setting aside or suspension of an award has been made to a court referred to in paragraph (1)(a)(v) of this article, the court where recognition or enforcement is sought may, if it considers it proper, adjoun its decision and may also, on the application of the party claiming recognition or enforcement of the award, order the other party to provide appropriate security.

Explanatory note by the UNCITRAL secretariat on the Model Law on International Commercial Arbitration[*]

A14–037   1. The UNCITRAL Model Law on International Commercial Arbitration was adopted by the United Nations Commission on International Trade Law (UNCITRAL) on 21 June 1985, at the close of the Commission's 18th annual session. The General Assembly, in its resolution 40/72 of 11 December 1985, recommended "that all States give due consideration to the Model Law on International Commercial Arbitration, in view of the desirability of uniformity of the law of arbitral procedures and the specific needs of international commercial arbitration practice".

2. The Model Law constitutes a sound and promising basis for the desired harmonization and improvement of national laws. It covers all stages of the arbitral process from the arbitration agreement to the recognition and enforcement of the arbitral award and reflects a worldwide consensus on the principles and important issues of international

---

[*] This note has been prepared by the secretariat of the United Nations Commission on International Trade Law (UNCITRAL) for informational purposes only; it is not an official commentary on the Model Law. A commentary prepared by the Secretariat on an earlier draft of the Model Law appears in document A/CN.9/264, reproduced in *UNCITRAL Yearbook*, vol. XVI, 1985 (United Nations publication, Sales No. E.87.V.4).

arbitration practice. It is acceptable to States of all regions and the different legal or economic systems of the world.

3. The form of a model law was chosen as the vehicle for harmonization and improvement in view of the flexibility it gives to States in preparing new arbitration laws. It is advisable to follow the model as closely as possible since that would be the best contribution to the desired harmonization and in the best interest of the users of international arbitration, who are primarily foreign parties and their lawyers.

A. Background to the Model Law

4. The Model Law is designed to meet concerns relating to the current state of national laws on arbitration. The need for improvement and harmonization is based on findings that domestic laws are often inappropriate for international cases and that considerable disparity exists between them. **A14–038**

1. Inadequacy of domestic laws

5. A global survey of national laws on arbitration revealed considerable disparities not only as regards individual provisions and solutions but also in terms of development and refinement. Some laws may be regarded as outdated, sometimes going back to the nineteenth century and often equating the arbitral process with court litigation. Other laws may be said to be fragmentary in that they do not address all relevant issues. Even most of those laws which appear to be up-to-date and comprehensive were drafted with domestic arbitration primarily, if not exclusively, in mind. While this approach is understandable in view of the fact that even today the bulk of cases governed by a general arbitration law would be of a purely domestic nature, the unfortunate consequence is that traditional local concepts are imposed on international cases and the needs of modern practice are often not met. **A14–039**

6. The expectations of the parties as expressed in a chosen set of arbitration rules or a "one-off" arbitration agreement may be frustrated, especially by a mandatory provision of the applicable law. Unexpected and undesired restrictions found in national laws relate, for example, to the parties' ability effectively to submit future disputes to arbitration, to their power to select the arbitrator freely, or to their interest in having the arbitral proceedings conducted according to the agreed rules of procedure and with no more court involvement than is appropriate. Frustrations may also ensue from non-mandatory provisions which may impose undesired requirements on unwary parties who did not provide otherwise. Even the absence of non-mandatory provisions may cause difficulties by not providing answers to the many procedural issues relevant in an arbitration and not always settled in the arbitration agreement.

2. Disparity between national laws

7. Problems and undesired consequences, whether emanating from mandatory or non-mandatory provisions or from a lack of pertinent provisions, are aggravated by the fact **A14–040**

that national laws on arbitral procedure differ widely. The differences are a frequent source of concern in international arbitration, where at least one of the parties is, and often both parties are, confronted with foreign and unfamiliar provisions and procedures. For such a party it may be expensive, impractical or impossible to obtain a full and precise account of the law applicable to the arbitration.

8. Uncertainty about the local law with the inherent risk of frustration may adversely affect not only the functioning of the arbitral process but already the selection of the place of arbitration. A party may well for those reasons hesitate or refuse to agree to a place which otherwise, for practical reasons, would be appropriate in the case at hand. The choice of places of arbitration would thus be widened and the smooth functioning of the arbitral proceedings would be enhanced if States were to adopt the Model Law which is easily recognizable, meets the specific needs of international commercial arbitration and provides an international standard with solutions acceptable to parties from different States and legal systems.

B. Salient Features of the Model Law

1. Special procedural regime for international commercial arbitration

A14–041   9. The principles and individual solutions adopted in the Model Law aim at reducing or eliminating the above concerns and difficulties. As a response to the inadequacies and disparities of national laws, the Model Law presents a special legal regime geared to international commercial arbitration, without affecting any relevant treaty in force in the State adopting the Model Law. While the need for uniformity exists only in respect of international cases, the desire of updating and improving the arbitration law may be felt by a State also in respect of non-international cases and could be met by enacting modern legislation based on the Model Law for both categories of cases.

(a) Substantive and territorial scope of application

A14–042   10. The Model Law defines an arbitration as international if "the parties to an arbitration agreement have, at the time of the conclusion of that agreement, their places of business in different States" (article 1(3)). The vast majority of situations commonly regarded as international will fall under this criterion. In addition, an arbitration is international if the place of arbitration, the place of contract performance, or the place of the subject-matter of the dispute is situated in a State other than where the parties have their place of business, or if the parties have expressly agreed that the subject-matter of the arbitration agreement relates to more than one country.

11. As regards the term "commercial", no hard and fast definition could be provided. Article 1 contains a note calling for "a wide interpretation so as to cover matters arising from all relationships of a commercial nature, whether contractual or not". The footnote to article 1 then provides an illustrative list of relationships that are to be considered commercial, thus emphasizing the width of the suggested interpretation and indicating that the determinative test is not based on what the national law may regard as "commercial".

12. Another aspect of applicability is what one may call the territorial scope of application. According to article 1(2), the Model Law as enacted in a given State would apply

only if the place of arbitration is in the territory of that State. However, there is an important and reasonable exception. Articles 8(1) and 9 which deal with recognition of arbitration agreements, including their compatibility with interim measures of protection, and articles 35 and 36 on recognition and enforcement of arbitral awards are given a global scope, i.e. they apply irrespective of whether the place of arbitration is in that State or in another State and, as regards articles 8 and 9, even if the place of arbitration is not yet determined.

13. The strict territorial criterion, governing the bulk of the provisions of the Model Law, was adopted for the sake of certainty and in view of the following facts. The place of arbitration is used as the exclusive criterion by the great majority of national laws and, where national laws allow parties to choose the procedural law of a State other than that where the arbitration takes place, experience shows that parties in practice rarely make use of that facility. The Model Law, by its liberal contents, further reduces the need for such choice of a "foreign" law in lieu of the (Model) Law of the place of arbitration, not the least because it grants parties wide freedom in shaping the rules of the arbitral proceedings. This includes the possibility of incorporating into the arbitration agreement procedural provisions of a "foreign" law, provided there is no conflict with the few mandatory provisions of the Model Law. Furthermore, the strict territorial criterion is of considerable practical benefit in respect of articles 11, 13, 14, 16, 27 and 34, which entrust the courts of the respective State with functions of arbitration assistance and supervision.

(b) Delimitation of court assistance and supervision

14. As evidenced by recent amendments to arbitration laws, there exists a trend in **A14–043** favour of limiting court involvement in international commercial arbitration. This seems justified in view of the fact that the parties to an arbitration agreement make a conscious decision to exclude court jurisdiction and, in particular in commercial cases, prefer expediency and finality to protracted battles in court.

15. In this spirit, the Model Law envisages court involvement in the following instances. A first group comprises appointment, challenge and termination of the mandate of an arbitrator (articles 11, 13 and 14), jurisdiction of the arbitral tribunal (article 16) and setting aside of the arbitral award (article 34). These instances are listed in article 6 as functions which should be entrusted, for the sake of centralization, specialization and acceleration, to a specially designated court or, as regards articles 11, 13 and 14, possibly to another authority (e.g. arbitral institution, chamber of commerce). A second group comprises court assistance in taking evidence (article 27), recognition of the arbitration agreement, including its compatibility with court-ordered interim measures of protection (articles 8 and 9), and recognition and enforcement of arbitral awards (articles 35 and 36).

16. Beyond the instances in these two groups, "no court shall intervene, in matters governed by this Law". This is stated in the innovative article 5, which by itself does not take a stand on what is the appropriate role of the courts but guarantees the reader and user that he will find all instances of possible court intervention in this Law, except for matters not regulated by it (e.g. consolidation of arbitral proceedings, contractual relationship between arbitrators and parties or arbitral institutions, or fixing of costs and fees, including deposits). Especially foreign readers and users, who constitute the majority of potential users and may be viewed as the primary addressees of any special law on international commercial arbitration, will appreciate that they do not have to search outside this Law.

2. Arbitration agreement

A14–044 17. Chapter II of the Model Law deals with the arbitration agreement, including its recognition by courts. The provisions follow closely article 11 of the Convention on the Recognition and Enforcement of Foreign Arbitral Awards (New York, 1958) (hereafter referred to as "1958 New York Convention"), with a number of useful clarifications added.

(a) Definition and form of arbitration agreement

A14–045 18. Article 7(1) recognizes the validity and effect of a commitment by the parties to submit to arbitration an existing dispute (*"compromis"*) or a future dispute (*"clause compromissoire"*). The latter type of agreement is presently not given full effect under certain national laws.

19. While oral arbitration agreements are found in practice and are recognized by some national laws, article 7(2) follows the 1958 New York Convention in requiring written form. It widens and clarifies the definition of written form of article 11(2) of that Convention by adding "telex or other means of telecommunication which provide a record of the agreement, by covering the submission-type situation of "an exchange of statements of claim and defence in which the existence of an agreement is alleged by one party and not denied by another", and by providing that "the reference in a contract to a document" (e.g. general conditions) "containing an arbitration clause constitutes an arbitration agreement provided that the contract is in writing and the reference is such as to make that clause part of the contract".

(b) Arbitration agreement and the courts

A14–046 20. Articles 8 and 9 deal with two important aspects of the complex issue of the relationship between the arbitration agreement and resort to courts. Modelled on article II(3) of the 1958 New York Convention, article 8(1) of the Model Law obliges any court to refer the parties to arbitration if seized with a claim on the same subject-matter unless it finds that the arbitration agreement is null and void, inoperative or incapable of being performed. The referral is dependent on a request which a party may make not later than when submitting his first statement on the substance of the dispute. While this provision, where adopted by a State when it adopts the Model Law, by its nature binds merely the courts of that State, it is not restricted to agreements providing for arbitration in that State and, thus, helps to give universal recognition and effect to international commercial arbitration agreements.

21. Article 9 expresses the principle that any interim measures of protection that may be obtained from courts under their procedural law (e.g. pre-award attachments) are compatible with an arbitration agreement. Like article 8, this provision is addressed to the courts of a given State, insofar as it determines their granting of interim measures as being compatible with an arbitration agreement, irrespective of the place of arbitration. Insofar as it declares it to be compatible with an arbitration agreement for a party to request such measure from a court, the provision would apply irrespective of whether the request is made to a court of the given State or of any other country. Wherever such request may be made, it may not be relied upon, under the Model Law, as an objection against the existence or effect of an arbitration agreement.

3. Composition of arbitral tribunal

22. Chapter III contains a number of detailed provisions on appointment, challenge, **A14–047** termination of mandate and replacement of an arbitrator. The chapter illustrates the approach of the Model Law in eliminating difficulties arising from inappropriate or fragmentary laws or rules. The approach consists, first, of recognizing the freedom of the parties to determine, by reference to an existing set of arbitration rules or by an ad hoc agreement, the procedure to be followed, subject to fundamental requirements of fairness and justice. Secondly, where the parties have not used their freedom to lay down the rules of procedure or a particular issue has not been covered, the Model Law ensures, by providing a set of suppletive rules, that the arbitration may commence and proceed effectively to the resolution of the dispute.

23. Where under any procedure, agreed upon by the parties or based upon the suppletive rules of the Model Law, difficulties arise in the process of appointment, challenge or termination of the mandate of an arbitrator, Articles 11, 13 and 14 provide for assistance by courts or other authorities. In view of the urgency of the matter and in order to reduce the risk and effect of any dilatory tactics, instant resort may be had by a party within a short period of time and the decision is not appealable.

4. Jurisdiction of arbitral tribunal

(a) Competence to rule on own jurisdiction

24. Article 16(1) adopts the two important (not yet generally recognized) principles of **A14–048** *"Kompetenz-Kompetenz"* and of separability or autonomy of the arbitration clause. The arbitral tribunal may rule on its own jurisdiction, including any objections with respect to the existence or validity of the arbitration agreement. For that purpose, an arbitration clause shall be treated as an agreement independent of the other terms of the contract, and a decision by the arbitral tribunal that the contract is null and void shall not entail *ipso jure* the invalidity of the arbitration clause. Detailed provisions in paragraph (2) require that any objections relating to the arbitrators' jurisdiction be made at the earliest possible time.

25. The arbitral tribunal's competence to rule on his own jurisdiction, i.e. on the very foundation of its mandate and power, is, of course, subject to court control. Where the arbitral tribunal rules as a preliminary question that it has jurisdiction, article 16(3) provides for instant court control in order to avoid unnecessary waste of money and time. However, three procedural safeguards are added to reduce the risk and effect of dilatory tactics: short time-period for resort to court (30 days), court decision is not appealable, and discretion of the arbitral tribunal to continue the proceedings and make an award while the matter is pending with the court. In those less common cases where the arbitral tribunal combines its decision on jurisdiction with an award on the merits, judicial review on the question of jurisdiction is available in setting aside proceedings under article 34 or in enforcement proceedings under article 36.

(b) Power to order Interim measures

26. Unlike some national laws, the Model Law empowers the arbitral tribunal, **A14–049** unless otherwise agreed by the parties, to order any party to take an interim measure of protection in respect of the subject-matter of the dispute, if so requested by a

party (article 17). It may be noted that the article does not deal with enforcement of such measures; any State adopting the Model Law would be free to provide court assistance in this regard.

5. Conduct of arbitral proceedings

A14–050 27. Chapter V provides the legal framework for a fair and effective conduct of the arbitral proceedings. It opens with two provisions expressing basic principles that permeate the arbitral procedure governed by the Model Law. Article 18 lays down fundamental requirements of procedural justice and article 19 the rights and powers to determine the rules of procedure.

(a) Fundamental procedural rights of a party

A14–051 28. Article 18 embodies the basic principle that the parties shall be treated with equality and each party shall be given a full opportunity of presenting his case. Other provisions implement and specify the basic principle in respect of certain fundamental rights of a party. Article 24(1) provides that, unless the parties have validly agreed that no oral hearings for the presentation of evidence or for oral argument be held, the arbitral tribunal shall hold such hearings at an appropriate stage of the proceedings, if so requested by a party. It should be noted that article 24(1) deals only with the general right of a party to oral hearings (as an alternative to conducting the proceedings on the basis of documents and other materials) and not with the procedural aspects such as the length, number or timing of hearings.

29. Another fundamental right of a party of being heard and being able to present his case relates to evidence by an expert appointed by the arbitral tribunal. Article 26(2) obliges the expert, after having delivered his written or oral report, to participate in a hearing where the parties may put questions to him and present expert witnesses in order to testify on the points at issue, if such a hearing is requested by a party or deemed necessary by the arbitral tribunal. As another provision aimed at ensuring fairness, objectivity and impartiality, article 24(3) provides that all statements, documents and other information supplied to the arbitral tribunal by one party shall be communicated to the other party, and that any expert report or evidentiary document on which the arbitral tribunal may rely in making its decision shall be communicated to the parties. In order to enable the parties to be present at any hearing and at any meeting of the arbitral tribunal for inspection purposes, they shall be given sufficient notice in advance (article 24(2)).

(b) Determination of rules of procedure

A14–052 30. Article 19 guarantees the parties' freedom to agree on the procedure to be followed by the arbitral tribunal in conducting the proceedings, subject to a few mandatory provisions on procedure, and empowers the arbitral tribunal, failing agreement by the parties, to conduct the arbitration in such a manner as it considers appropriate. The power conferred upon the arbitral tribunal includes the power to determine the admissibility, relevance, materiality and weight of any evidence.

31. Autonomy of the parties to determine the rules of procedure is of special importance in international cases since it allows the parties to select or tailor the rules according to their specific wishes and needs, unimpeded by traditional domestic concepts and with-

out the earlier mentioned risk of frustration. The supplementary discretion of the arbitral tribunal is equally important in that it allows the tribunal to tailor the conduct of the proceedings to the specific features of the case without restraints of the traditional local law, including any domestic rules on evidence. Moreover, it provides a means for solving any procedural questions not regulated in the arbitration agreement or the Model Law.

32. In addition to the general provisions of article 19, there are some special provisions using the same approach of granting the parties autonomy and, failing agreement, empowering the arbitral tribunal to decide the matter. Examples of particular practical importance in international cases are article 20 on the place of arbitration and article 22 on the language of the proceedings.

(c) Default of a party

33. Only if due notice was given, may the arbitral proceedings be continued in the absence of a party. This applies, in particular, to the failure of a party to appear at a hearing or to produce documentary evidence without showing sufficient cause for the failure (article 25(c)). The arbitral tribunal may also continue the proceedings where the respondent fails to communicate his statement of defence, while there is no need for continuing the proceedings if the claimant fails to submit his statement of claim (article 25(a), (b)). **A14–053**

34. Provisions which empower the arbitral tribunal to carry out its task even if one of the parties does not participate are of considerable practical importance since, as experience shows, it is not uncommon that one of the parties has little interest in cooperating and in expediting matters. They would, thus, give international commercial arbitration its necessary effectiveness, within the limits of fundamental requirements of procedural justice.

6. Making of award and termination of proceedings

(a) Rules applicable to substance of dispute

35. Article 28 deals with the substantive law aspects of arbitration. Under paragraph (1), the arbitral tribunal decides the dispute in accordance with such rules of law as may be agreed by the parties. This provision is significant in two respects. It grants the parties the freedom to choose the applicable substantive law, which is important in view of the fact that a number of national laws do not clearly or fully recognize that right. In addition, by referring to the choice of "rules of law" instead of "law", the Model Law gives the parties a wider range of options as regards the designation of the law applicable to the substance of the dispute in that they may, for example, agree on rules of law that have been elaborated by an international forum but have not yet been incorporated into any national legal system. The power of the arbitral tribunal, on the other hand, follows more traditional lines. When the parties have not designated the applicable law, the arbitral tribunal shall apply the law, i.e. the national law, determined by the conflict of laws rules which it considers applicable. **A14–054**

36. According to article 28(3), the parties may authorize the arbitral tribunal to decide the dispute *ex aequo et bono* or as *amiables compositeurs*. This type of arbitration is currently not known or used in all legal systems and there exists no uniform understanding as regards the precise scope of the power of the arbitral tribunal. When parties anticipate an uncertainty in this respect, they may wish to provide a clarification in the arbitration agreement by a more specific authorization to the arbitral tribunal. Paragraph

(4) makes clear that in all cases, i.e. including an arbitration *ex aequo et bono*, the arbitral tribunal must decide in accordance with the terms of the contract and shall take into account the usages of the trade applicable to the transaction.

(b) Making of award and other decisions

A14–055   37. In its rules on the making of the award (articles 29–31), the Model Law pays special attention to the rather common case that the arbitral tribunal consists of a plurality of arbitrators (in particular, three). It provides that, in such case, any award and other decision shall be made by a majority of the arbitrators, except on questions of procedure, which may be left to a presiding arbitrator. The majority principle applies also to the signing of the award, provided that the reason for any omitted signature is stated.

38. Article 31(3) provides that the award shall state the place of arbitration and that it shall be deemed to have been made at that place. As to this presumption, it may be noted that the final making of the award constitutes a legal act, which in practice is not necessarily one factual act but may be done in deliberations at various places, by telephone conversation or correspondence; above all, the award need not be signed by the arbitrators at the same place.

39. The arbitral award must be in writing and state its date. It must also state the reasons on which it is based, unless the parties have agreed otherwise or the award is an award on agreed terms, i.e. an award which records the terms of an amicable settlement by the parties. It may be added that the Model Law neither requires nor prohibits "dissenting opinions".

7. Recourse against award

A14–056   40. National laws on arbitration, often equating awards with court decisions, provide a variety of means of recourse against arbitral awards, with varying and often long time-periods and with extensive lists of grounds that differ widely in the various legal systems. The Model Law attempts to ameliorate this situation, which is of considerable concern to those involved in international commercial arbitration.

(a) Application for setting aside as exclusive recourse

A14–057   41. The first measure of improvement is to allow only one type of recourse, to the exclusion of any other means of recourse regulated in another procedural law of the State in question. An application for setting aside under article 34 must be made within three months of receipt of the award. It should be noted that "recourse" means actively "attacking" the award; a party is, of course, not precluded from seeking court control by way of defence in enforcement proceedings (article 36). Furthermore, "recourse" means resort to a court, i.e. an organ of the judicial system of a State; a party is not precluded from resorting to an arbitral tribunal of second instance if such a possibility has been agreed upon by the parties (as is common in certain commodity trades).

(b) Grounds for setting aside

A14–058   42. As a further measure of improvement, the Model Law contains an exclusive list of limited grounds on which an award may be set aside. This list is essentially the same as the one in article 36(1), taken from article V of the 1958 New York Convention: lack of capacity of parties to conclude arbitration agreement or lack of valid arbitration agreement; lack of notice of appointment of an arbitrator or of the arbitral proceedings or inability of a party to present his case; award deals with matters not covered by submission to arbitration; composition of arbitral tribunal or conduct of arbitral proceedings contrary to effective agreement of parties or, failing agreement, to the Model Law; non-arbitrability of subject-matter of dispute and violation of public policy, which would include serious departures from fundamental notions of procedural justice.

43. Such a parallelism of the grounds for setting aside with those provided in article V of the 1958 New York Convention for refusal of recognition and enforcement was already adopted in the European Convention on International Commercial Arbitration (Geneva, 1961). Under its article IX, the decision of a foreign court setting aside an award for a reason other than the ones listed in article V of the 1958 New York Convention does not constitute a ground for refusing enforcement. The Model Law takes this philosophy one step further by directly limiting the reasons for setting aside.

44. Although the grounds for setting aside are almost identical to those for refusing recognition or enforcement, two practical differences should be noted. Firstly, the grounds relating to public policy, including non-arbitrability, may be different in substance, depending on the State in question (i.e. State of setting aside or State of enforcement). Secondly, and more importantly, the grounds for refusal of recognition or enforcement are valid and effective only in the State (or States) where the winning party seeks recognition and enforcement, while the grounds for setting aside have a different impact: The setting aside of an award at the place of origin prevents enforcement of that award in all other countries by virtue of article V(1)(e) of the 1958 New York Convention and article 36(1)(a)(v) of the Model Law.

8. Recognition and enforcement of awards

45. The eighth and last chapter of the Model Law deals with recognition and enforcement of awards. Its provisions reflect the significant policy decision that the same rules should apply to arbitral awards whether made in the country of enforcement or abroad, and that those rules should follow closely the 1958 New York Convention. **A14–059**

(a) Towards uniform treatment of all awards irrespective of country of origin

46. By treating awards rendered in international commercial arbitration in a uniform manner irrespective of where they were made, the Model Law draws a new demarcation line between "international" and "non-international" awards instead of the traditional line between "foreign" and "domestic" awards. This new line is based on substantive grounds rather than territorial borders, which are inappropriate in view of the limited importance of the place of arbitration in international cases. The place of arbitration is often chosen for reasons of convenience of the parties and the dispute may have little or no connection with the State where the arbitration takes place. Consequently, the recognition and enforcement of "international" awards, whether "foreign" or "domestic", should be governed by the same provisions. **A14–060**

47. By modelling the recognition and enforcement rules on the relevant provisions of the 1958 New York Convention, the Model Law supplements, without conflicting with, the regime of recognition and enforcement created by that successful Convention.

(b) Procedural conditions of recognition and enforcement

A14–061   48. Under article 35(1) any arbitral award, irrespective of the country in which it was made, shall be recognized as binding and enforceable, subject to the provisions of article 35(2) and of article 36 (which sets forth the grounds on which recognition or enforcement may be refused). Based on the above consideration of the limited importance of the place of arbitration in international cases and the desire of overcoming territorial restrictions, reciprocity is not included as a condition for recognition and enforcement.

49. The Model Law does not lay down procedural details of recognition and enforcement since there is no practical need for unifying them, and since they form an intrinsic part of the national procedural law and practice. The Model Law merely sets certain conditions for obtaining enforcement: application in writing, accompanied by the award and the arbitration agreement (article 35(2)).

(c) Grounds for refusing recognition or enforcement

A14–062   50. As noted earlier, the grounds on which recognition or enforcement may be refused under the Model Law are identical to those listed in article V of the New York Convention. Only, under the Model Law, they are relevant not merely to foreign awards but to all awards rendered in international commercial arbitration. While some provisions of that Convention, in particular as regards their drafting, may have called for improvement, only the first ground on the list i.e. "the parties to the arbitration agreement were, under the law applicable to them, under some incapacity" was modified since it was viewed as containing an incomplete and potentially misleading conflicts rule. Generally, it was deemed desirable to adopt, for the sake of harmony, the same approach and wording as this important Convention.

Further information may be obtained from:

UNCITRAL Secretariat
Vienna International Centre
P.O. Box 500
A-1400 Vienna, Austria

Telex: 135612
Tel.: (+43 1) 26060-4060
Fax: (+43 1) 26060-5813
Internet: http://www.uncitral.org
Email: uncitral@uncitral.org

UNCITRAL Arbitration Rules[1]

(RESOLUTION 31/98 ADOPTED BY THE GENERAL ASSEMBLY ON 15 DECEMBER 1976)

The General Assembly,
Recognizing the value of arbitration as a method of settling disputes arising in the context of international commercial relations,
Being convinced that the establishment of rules for *ad hoc* arbitration that are acceptable in countries with different legal, social and economic systems would significantly contribute to the development of harmonious international economic relations,
Bearing in mind that the Arbitration Rules of the United Nations Commission on International Trade Law have been prepared after extensive consultation with arbitral institutions and centres of international commercial arbitration,
Noting that the Arbitration Rules were adopted by the United Nations Commission on International Trade Law at its ninth session after due deliberation,
1. *Recommends* the use of the Arbitration Rules of the United Nations Commission of International Trade Law in the settlement of disputes arising in the context of international commercial relations, particularly by reference to the Arbitration Rules in commercial contracts;
2. *Requests* the Secretary-General to arrange for the widest possible distribution of the Arbitration Rules.

SECTION I. INTRODUCTORY RULES

Scope of application

Article 1

1. Where the parties to a contract have agreed in writing that disputes in relation to that contract shall be referred to arbitration under the UNCITRAL Arbitration Rules, then such disputes shall be settled in accordance with these Rules subject to such modification as the parties may agree in writing.
2. These Rules shall govern the arbitration except that where any of these Rules is in conflict with a provision of the law applicable to the arbitration from which the parties cannot derogate, that provision shall prevail.

Notice, calculation of periods of time

Article 2

1. For the purposes of these Rules, any notice, including a notification, communication or proposal, is deemed to have been received if it is physically delivered to the addressee or if it is delivered at his habitual residence, place of business or mailing address, or, if none of these can be found after making reasonable inquiry, then at the addressee's

---

[1] Reproduced with the kind permission of United Nations Commission on International Trade Law.

last-known residence or place of business. Notice shall be deemed to have been received on the day it is so delivered.

2. For the purposes of calculating a period of time under these Rules, such period shall begin to run on the day following the day when a notice, notification, communication or proposal is received. If the last day of such period is an official holiday or a non-business day at the residence or place of business of the addressee, the period is extended until the first business day which follows. Official holidays or non-business days occurring during the running of the period of time are included in calculating the period.

Notice of arbitration

Article 3

A15–004   **1.** The party initiating recourse to arbitration (hereinafter called the "claimant") shall give to the other party (hereinafter called the "respondent") a notice of arbitration.

2. Arbitral proceedings shall be deemed to commence on the date on which the notice of arbitration is received by the respondent.

3. The notice of arbitration shall include the following:

(a) A demand that the dispute be referred to arbitration;

(b) The names and addresses of the parties;

(c) A reference to the arbitration clause or the separate arbitration agreement that is invoked;

(d) A reference to the contract out of or in relation to which the dispute arises;

(e) The general nature of the claim and an indication of the amount involved, if any;

(f) The relief or remedy sought;

(g) A proposal as to the number of arbitrators (i.e. one or three), if the parties have not previously agreed thereon.

4. The notice of arbitration may also include:

(a) The proposals for the appointments of a sole arbitrator and an appointing authority referred to in article 6, paragraph 1;

(b) The notification of the appointment of an arbitrator referred to in article 7;

(c) The statement of claim referred to in article 18.

Representation and assistance

Article 4

A15–005   The parties may be represented or assisted by persons of their choice. The names and addresses of such persons must be communicated in writing to the other party; such communication must specify whether the appointment is being made for purposes of representation or assistance.

Section II. Composition of the Arbitral Tribunal

Number of arbitrators

Article 5

If the parties have not previously agreed on the number of arbitrators (i.e. one or three) and if within fifteen days after the receipt by the respondent of the notice of arbitration the parties have not agreed that there shall be only one arbitrator, three arbitrators shall be appointed.

A15–006

Appointment of Arbitrators (Articles 6 to 8)

Article 6

1. If a sole arbitrator is to be appointed, either party may propose to the other:

A15–007

  (a) The names of one or more persons, one of whom would serve as the sole arbitrator; and

  (b) If no appointing authority has been agreed upon by the parties, the name or names of one or more institutions or persons, one of whom would serve as appointing authority.

2. If within thirty days after receipt by a party of a proposal made in accordance with paragraph 1 the parties have not reached agreement on the choice of a sole arbitrator, the sole arbitrator shall be appointed by the appointing authority agreed on by the parties. If no appointing authority has been agreed upon by the parties, or if the appointing authority agreed upon refuses to act or fails to appoint the arbitrator within sixty days of the receipt of a party's request therefor, either party may request the Secretary-General of the Permanent Court of Arbitration at The Hague to designate an appointing authority.

3. The appointing authority shall, at the request of one of the parties, appoint the sole arbitrator as promptly as possible. In making the appointment the appointing authority shall use the following list-procedure, unless both parties agree that the list-procedure should not be used or unless the appointing authority determines in its discretion that the use of the list-procedure is not appropriate for the case:

  (a) At the request of one of the parties the appointing authority shall communicate to both parties an identical list containing at least three names;

  (b) Within fifteen days after the receipt of this list, each party may return the list to the appointing authority after having deleted the name or names to which he objects and numbered the remaining names on the list in the order of his preference;

  (c) After the expiration of the above period of time the appointing authority shall appoint the sole arbitrator from among the names approved on the lists returned to it and in accordance with the order of preference indicated by the parties;

  (d) If for any reason the appointment cannot be made according to this procedure, the appointing authority may exercise its discretion in appointing the sole arbitrator.

4. In making the appointment, the appointing authority shall have regard to such considerations as are likely to secure the appointment of an independent and impartial arbitrator and shall take into account as well the advisability of appointing an arbitrator of a nationality other than the nationalities of the parties.

Article 7

A15–008 **1.** If three arbitrators are to be appointed, each party shall appoint one arbitrator. The two arbitrators thus appointed shall choose the third arbitrator who will act as the presiding arbitrator of the tribunal.

2. If within thirty days after the receipt of a party's notification of the appointment of an arbitrator the other party has not notified the first party of the arbitrator he has appointed:

(a) The first party may request the appointing authority previously designated by the parties to appoint the second arbitrator; or

(b) If no such authority has been previously designated by the parties, or if the appointing authority previously designated refuses to act or fails to appoint the arbitrator within thirty days after receipt of a party's request therefor, the first party may request the Secretary-General of the Permanent Court of Arbitration at The Hague to designate the appointing authority. The first party may then request the appointing authority so designated to appoint the second arbitrator. In either case, the appointing authority may exercise its discretion in appointing the arbitrator.

3. If within thirty days after the appointment of the second arbitrator the two arbitrators have not agreed on the choice of the presiding arbitrator, the presiding arbitrator shall be appointed by an appointing authority in the same way as a sole arbitrator would be appointed under article 6.

Article 8

A15–009 **1.** When an appointing authority is requested to appoint an arbitrator pursuant to article 6 or article 7, the party which makes the request shall send to the appointing authority a copy of the notice of arbitration, a copy of the contract out of or in relation to which the dispute has arisen and a copy of the arbitration agreement if it is not contained in the contract. The appointing authority may require from either party such information as it deems necessary to fulfil its functions.

2. Where the names of one or more persons are proposed for appointment as arbitrators, their full names, addresses and nationalities shall be indicated, together with a description of their qualifications.

Challenge of arbitrators (Articles 9 to 12)

Article 9

A15–010 A prospective arbitrator shall disclose to those who approach him in connection with his possible appointment any circumstances likely to give rise to justifiable doubts as to his impartiality or independence. An arbitrator, once appointed or chosen, shall disclose such circumstances to the parties unless they have already been informed by him of these circumstances.

Article 10

1. Any arbitrator may be challenged if circumstances exist that give rise to justifiable doubts as to the arbitrator's impartiality or independence.
2. A party may challenge the arbitrator appointed by him only for reasons of which he becomes aware after the appointment has been made.

Article 11

1. A party who intends to challenge an arbitrator shall send notice of his challenge within fifteen days after the appointment of the challenged arbitrator has been notified to the challenging party or within fifteen days after the circumstances mentioned in articles 9 and 10 became known to that party.
2. The challenge shall be notified to the other party, to the arbitrator who is challenged and to the other members of the arbitral tribunal. The notification shall be in writing and shall state the reasons for the challenge.
3. When an arbitrator has been challenged by one party, the other party may agree to the challenge. The arbitrator may also, after the challenge, withdraw from his office. In neither case does this imply acceptance of the validity of the grounds for the challenge. In both cases the procedure provided in article 6 or 7 shall be used in full for the appointment of the substitute arbitrator, even if during the process of appointing the challenged arbitrator a party had failed to exercise his right to appoint or to participate in the appointment.

Article 12

1. If the other party does not agree to the challenge and the challenged arbitrator does not withdraw, the decision on the challenge will be made:

   (a) When the initial appointment was made by an appointing authority, by that authority;

   (b) When the initial appointment was not made by an appointing authority, but an appointing authority has been previously designated, by that authority;

   (c) In all other cases, by the appointing authority to be designated in accordance with the procedure for designating an appointing authority as provided for in article 6.

2. If the appointing authority sustains the challenge, a substitute arbitrator shall be appointed or chosen pursuant to the procedure applicable to the appointment or choice of an arbitrator as provided in articles 6 to 9 except that, when this procedure would call for the designation of an appointing authority, the appointment of the arbitrator shall be made by the appointing authority which decided on the challenge.

Replacement of an arbitrator

Article 13

1. In the event of the death or resignation of an arbitrator during the course of the arbitral proceedings, a substitute arbitrator shall be appointed or chosen pursuant to the procedure provided for in articles 6 to 9 that was applicable to the appointment or choice of the arbitrator being replaced.

2. In the event that an arbitrator fails to act or in the event of the *de jure* or *de facto* impossibility of his performing his functions, the procedure in respect of the challenge and replacement of an arbitrator as provided in the preceding articles shall apply.

Repetition of hearings in the event of the replacement of an arbitrator

Article 14

A15–015   If under articles 11 to 13 the sole or presiding arbitrator is replaced, any hearings held previously shall be repeated; if any other arbitrator is replaced, such prior hearings may be repeated at the discretion of the arbitral tribunal.

SECTION III. ARBITRAL PROCEEDINGS

General provisions

Article 15

A15–016   1. Subject to these Rules, the arbitral tribunal may conduct the arbitration in such manner as it considers appropriate, provided that the parties are treated with equality and that at any stage of the proceedings each party is given a full opportunity of presenting his case.
2. If either party so requests at any stage of the proceedings, the arbitral tribunal shall hold hearings for the presentation of evidence by witnesses, including expert witnesses, or for oral argument. In the absence of such a request, the arbitral tribunal shall decide whether to hold such hearings or whether the proceedings shall be conducted on the basis of documents and other materials.
3. All documents or information supplied to the arbitral tribunal by one party shall at the same time be communicated by that party to the other party.

Place of arbitration

Article 16

A15–017   1. Unless the parties have agreed upon the place where the arbitration is to be held, such place shall be determined by the arbitral tribunal, having regard to the circumstances of the arbitration.
2. The arbitral tribunal may determine the locale of the arbitration within the country agreed upon by the parties. It may hear witnesses and hold meetings for consultation among its members at any place it deems appropriate, having regard to the circumstances of the arbitration.
3. The arbitral tribunal may meet at any place it deems appropriate for the inspection of goods, other property or documents. The parties shall be given sufficient notice to enable them to be present at such inspection.
4. The award shall be made at the place of arbitration.

UNCITRAL ARBITRATION RULES

Language

Article 17

1. Subject to an agreement by the parties, the arbitral tribunal shall, promptly after its appointment, determine the language or languages to be used in the proceedings. This determination shall apply to the statement of claim, the statement of defence, and any further written statements and, if oral hearings take place, to the language or languages to be used in such hearings.

2. The arbitral tribunal may order that any documents annexed to the statement of claim or statement of defence, and any supplementary documents or exhibits submitted in the course of the proceedings, delivered in their original language, shall be accompanied by a translation into the language or languages agreed upon by the parties or determined by the arbitral tribunal.

A15–018

Statement of claim

Article 18

1. Unless the statement of claim was contained in the notice of arbitration, within a period of time to be determined by the arbitral tribunal, the claimant shall communicate his statement of claim in writing to the respondent and to each of the arbitrators. A copy of the contract, and of the arbitration agreement if not contained in the contract, shall be annexed thereto.

2. The statement of claim shall include the following particulars:

(a) The names and addresses of the parties;

(b) A statement of the facts supporting the claim;

(c) The points at issue;

(d) The relief or remedy sought.

The claimant may annex to his statement of claim all documents he deems relevant or may add a reference to the documents or other evidence he will submit.

A15–019

Statement of defence

Article 19

1. Within a period of time to be determined by the arbitral tribunal, the respondent shall communicate his statement of defence in writing to the claimant and to each of the arbitrators.

2. The statement of defence shall reply to the particulars (b), (c) and (d) of the statement of claim (article 18, para. 2). The respondent may annex to his statement the documents on which he relies for his defence or may add a reference to the documents or other evidence he will submit.

3. In his statement of defence, or at a later stage in the arbitral proceedings if the arbitral tribunal decides that the delay was justified under the circumstances, the respond-

A15–020

ent may make a counter-claim arising out of the same contract or rely on a claim arising out of the same contract for the purpose of a set-off.

4. The provisions of article 18, paragraph 3, shall apply to a counter-claim and a claim relied on for the purpose of a set-off.

Amendments to the claim or defence

Article 20

A15–021   During the course of the arbitral proceedings either party may amend or supplement his claim or defence unless the arbitral tribunal considers it inappropriate to allow such amendment having regard to the delay in making it or prejudice to the other party or any other circumstances. However, a claim may not be amended in such a manner that the amended claim falls outside the scope of the arbitrator clause or separate arbitration agreement.

Pleas as to the jurisdiction of the arbitral tribunal

Article 21

A15–022   **1.** The arbitral tribunal shall have the power to rule on objections that it has no jurisdiction, including any objections with respect to the existence or validity of the arbitration clause or of the separate arbitration agreement.

2. The arbitral tribunal shall have the power to determine the existence or the validity of the contract of which an arbitration clause forms a part. For the purposes of article 21, an arbitration clause which forms part of a contract and which provides for arbitration under these Rules shall be treated as an agreement independent of the other terms of the contract. A decision by the arbitral tribunal that the contract is null and void shall not entail *ipso jure* the invalidity of the arbitration clause.

3. A plea that the arbitral tribunal does not have jurisdiction shall be raised not later than in the statement of defence or, with respect to a counter-claim, in the reply to the counter-claim.

4. In general, the arbitral tribunal should rule on a plea concerning its jurisdiction as preliminary question. However, the arbitral tribunal may proceed with the arbitration and rule on such a plea in their final award.

Further written statements

Article 22

A15–023   The arbitral tribunal shall decide which further written statements, in addition to the statement of claim and the statement of defence, shall be required from the parties or may be presented by them and shall fix the periods of time for communicating such statements.

Periods of time

Article 23

The periods of time fixed by the arbitral tribunal for the communication of written statements (including the statement of claim and statement of defence) should not exceed forty-five days. However, the arbitral tribunal may extend the time-limits if it concludes that an extension is justified.

Evidence and hearings (Articles 24 and 25)

Article 24

1. Each party shall have the burden of proving the facts relied on to support his claim or defence.

2. The arbitral tribunal may, if it considers it appropriate, require a party to deliver to the tribunal and to the other party, within such a period of time as the arbitral tribunal shall decide, a summary of the documents and other evidence which that party intends to present in support of the facts in issue set out in his statement of claim or statement of defence.

3. At any time during the arbitral proceedings the arbitral tribunal may require the parties to produce documents, exhibits or other evidence within such a period of time as the tribunal shall determine.

Article 25

1. In the event of an oral hearing, the arbitral tribunal shall give the parties adequate advance notice of the date, time and place thereof.

2. If witnesses are to be heard, at least fifteen days before the hearing each party shall communicate to the arbitral tribunal and to the other party the names and addresses of the witnesses he intends to present, the subject upon and the languages in which such witnesses will give their testimony.

3. The arbitral tribunal shall make arrangements for the translation of oral statements made at a hearing and for a record of the hearing if either is deemed necessary by the tribunal under the circumstances of the case, or if the parties have agreed thereto and have communicated such agreement to the tribunal at least fifteen days before the hearing.

4. Hearings shall be held *in camera* unless the parties agree otherwise. The arbitral tribunal may require the retirement of any witness or witnesses during the testimony of other witnesses. The arbitral tribunal is free to determine the manner in which witnesses are examined.

5. Evidence of witnesses may also be presented in the form of written statements signed by them.

6. The arbitral tribunal shall determine the admissibility, relevance, materiality and weight of the evidence offered.

Interim measures of protection

Article 26

1. At the request of either party, the arbitral tribunal may take any interim measures it deems necessary in respect of the subject-matter of the dispute, including measures for the conservation of the goods forming the subject-matter in dispute, such as ordering their deposit with a third person or the sale of perishable goods.

2. Such interim measures may be established in the form of an interim award. The arbitral tribunal shall be entitled to require security for the costs of such measures.

3. A request for interim measures addressed by any party to a judicial authority shall not be deemed incompatible with the agreement to arbitrate, or as a waiver of that agreement.

Experts

Article 27

A15–028 **1.** The arbitral tribunal may appoint one or more experts to report to it, in writing, on specific issues to be determined by the tribunal. A copy of the expert's terms of reference, established by the arbitral tribunal, shall be communicated to the parties.

2. The parties shall give the expert any relevant information or produce for his inspection any relevant documents or goods that he may require of them. Any dispute between a party and such expert as to the relevance of the required information or production shall be referred to the arbitral tribunal for decision.

3. Upon receipt of the expert's report, the arbitral tribunal shall communicate a copy of the report to the parties who shall be given the opportunity to express, in writing, their opinion on the report. A party shall be entitled to examine any document on which the expert has relied in his report.

4. At the request of either party the expert, after delivery of the report, may be heard at a hearing where the parties shall have the opportunity to be present and to interrogate the expert. At this hearing either party may present expert witnesses in order to testify on the points at issue. The provisions of article 25 shall be applicable to such proceedings.

Default

Article 28

A15–029 **1.** If, within the period of time fixed by the arbitral tribunal, the claimant has failed to communicate his claim without showing sufficient cause for such failure, the arbitral tribunal shall issue an order for the termination of the arbitral proceedings. If, within the period of time fixed by the arbitral tribunal, the respondent has failed to communicate his statement of defence without showing sufficient cause for such failure, the arbitral tribunal shall order that the proceedings continue.

2. If one of the parties, duly notified under these Rules, fails to appear at a hearing, without showing sufficient cause for such failure, the arbitral tribunal may proceed with the arbitration.

3. If one of the parties, duly invited to produce documentary evidence, fails to do so within the established period of time, without showing sufficient cause for such failure, the arbitral tribunal may make the award on the evidence before it.

Closure of hearings

Article 29

1. The arbitral tribunal may inquire of the parties if they have any further proof to offer or witnesses to be heard or submissions to make and, if there are none, it may declare the hearings closed.

2. The arbitral tribunal may, if it considers it necessary owing to exceptional circumstances, decide, on its own motion or upon application of a party, to reopen the hearings at any time before the award is made.

Waiver of rules

Article 30

A party who knows that any provision of, or requirement under, these Rules has not been complied with and yet proceeds with the arbitration without promptly stating his objection to such non-compliance, shall be deemed to have waived his right to object.

SECTION IV. THE AWARD

Decisions

Article 31

1. When there are three arbitrators, any award or other decision of the arbitral tribunal shall be made by a majority of the arbitrators.

2. In the case of questions of procedure, when there is no majority or when the arbitral tribunal so authorises, the presiding arbitrator may decide on his own, subject to revision, if any, by the arbitral tribunal.

Form and effect of the award

Article 32

1. In addition to making a final award, the arbitral tribunal shall be entitled to make interim, interlocutory, or partial awards.

2. The award shall be made in writing and shall be final and binding on the parties. The parties undertake to carry out the award without delay.

3. The arbitral tribunal shall state the reasons upon which the award is based, unless the parties have agreed that no reasons are to be given.

4. An award shall be signed by the arbitrators and it shall contain the date on which and the place where the award was made. Where there are three arbitrators and one of them fails to sign, the award shall state the reason for the absence of the signature.

5. The award may be made public only with the consent of both parties.

6. Copies of the award signed by the arbitrators shall be communicated to the parties by the arbitral tribunal.

7. If the arbitration law of the country where the award is made requires that the award

be filed or registered by the arbitral tribunal, the tribunal shall comply with this requirement within the period of time required by law.

Applicable law, amiable compositeur

Article 33

A15–034   1. The arbitral tribunal shall apply the law designated by the parties as applicable to the substance of the dispute. Failing such designation by the parties, the arbitral tribunal shall apply the law determined by the conflict of laws rules which it considers applicable.

2. The arbitral tribunal shall decide as *amiable compositeur* or *ex aequo et bono* only if the parties have expressly authorized the arbitral tribunal to do so and if the law applicable to the arbitral procedure permits such arbitration.

3. In all cases, the arbitral tribunal shall decide in accordance with the terms of the contract and shall take into account the usages of the trade applicable to the transaction.

Settlement or other grounds for termination

Article 34

A15–035   1. If, before the award is made, the parties agree on a settlement of the dispute, the arbitral tribunal shall either issue an order for the termination of the arbitral proceedings or, if requested by both parties and accepted by the tribunal, record the settlement in the form of an arbitral award on agreed terms. The arbitral tribunal is not obliged to give reasons for such an award.

2. If, before the award is made, the continuation of the arbitral proceedings becomes unnecessary or impossible for any reason not mentioned in paragraph 1, the arbitral tribunal shall inform the parties of its intention to issue an order for the termination of the proceedings. The arbitral tribunal shall have the power to issue such an order unless a party raises justifiable grounds for objection.

3. Copies of the order for termination of the arbitral proceedings or of the arbitral award on agreed terms, signed by the arbitrators, shall be communicated by the arbitral tribunal to the parties. Where an arbitral award on agreed terms is made, the provisions of article 32, paragraphs 2 and 4 to 7, shall apply.

Interpretation of the award

Article 35

A15–036   1. Within thirty days after the receipt of the award, either party, with notice to the other party, may request that the arbitral tribunal give an interpretation of the award.

2. The interpretation shall be given in writing within forty-five days after the receipt of the request. The interpretation shall form part of the award and the provisions of article 32, paragraphs 2 to 7, shall apply.

Correction of the award

Article 36

1. Within thirty days after the receipt of the award, either party, with notice to the other party, may request the arbitral tribunal to correct in the award any errors in computation, any clerical or typographical errors, or any errors of similar nature. The arbitral tribunal may within thirty days after the communication of the award make such corrections on is own initiative. **A15–037**
2. Such corrections shall be in writing, and the provisions of article 32, paragraphs 2 to 7, shall apply.

Additional award

Article 37

1. Within thirty days after the receipt of the award, either party, with notice to the other party, may request the arbitral tribunal to make an additional award as to claims presented in the arbitral proceedings but omitted from the award. **A15–038**
2. If the arbitral tribunal considers the request for an additional award to be justified and considers that the omission can be rectified without any further hearings or evidence, it shall complete its award within sixty days after the receipt of the request.
3. When an additional award is made, the provisions of article 32, paragraphs 2 to 7, shall apply.

Costs (Articles 38–40)

Article 38

The arbitral tribunal shall fix the costs of arbitration in its award. The term "costs" includes only: **A15–039**

- (a) The fees of the arbitral tribunal to be stated separately as to each arbitrator and to be fixed by the tribunal itself in accordance with article 39;
- (b) The travel and other expenses incurred by the arbitrators;
- (c) The costs of expert advice and of other assistance required by the arbitral tribunal;
- (d) The travel and other expenses of witnesses to the extent such expenses are approved by the arbitral tribunal;
- (e) The costs for legal representation and assistance of the successful party if such costs were claimed during the arbitral proceedings, and only to the extent that the arbitral tribunal determines that the amount of such costs is reasonable;
- (f) Any fees and expenses of the appointing authority as well as the expenses of the Secretary-General of the Permanent Court of Arbitration at The Hague.

Article 39

A15–040 1. The fees of the arbitral tribunal shall be reasonable in amount, taking into account the amount in dispute. the complexity of the subject-matter, the time spent by the arbitrators and any other relevant circumstances of the case.

2. If an appointing authority has been agreed upon by the parties or designated by the Secretary-General of the Permanent Court of Arbitration at The Hague, and if that authority has issued a schedule of fees for arbitrators in international cases which it administers, the arbitral tribunal in fixing its fees shall take that schedule of fees into account to the extent that it considers appropriate in the circumstances of the case.

3. If such appointing authority has not issued a schedule of fees for arbitrators in international cases, any party may at any time request the appointing authority to furnish a statement setting forth the basis for establishing fees which is customarily followed in international cases in which the authority appoints arbitrators. If the appointing authority consents to provide such a statement, the arbitral tribunal in fixing its fees shall take such information into account to the extent that it considers appropriate in the circumstances of the case.

4. In cases referred to in paragraphs 2 and 3, when a party so requests and the appointing authority consents to perform the function, the arbitral tribunal shall fix its fees only after consultation with the appointing authority which may make any comment it deems appropriate to the arbitral tribunal concerning the fees.

Article 40

A15–041 1. Except as provided in paragraph 2, the costs of arbitration shall in principle be borne by the unsuccessful party. However, the arbitral tribunal may apportion each of such costs between the parties if it determines that apportionment is reasonable taking into account the circumstances of the case.

2. With respect to the costs of legal representation and assistance referred to in article 38, paragraph (e), the arbitral tribunal, taking into account the circumstances of the case, shall be free to determine which party shall bear such costs or may apportion such costs between the parties if it determines that apportionment is reasonable.

3. When the arbitral tribunal issues an order for the termination of the arbitral proceedings or makes an award on agreed terms, it shall fix the costs of arbitration referred to in article 38 and article 39, paragraph 1, in the text of that order or award.

4. No additional fees may be charged by an arbitral tribunal for interpretation or correction or completion of its award under articles 35–37.

Deposit of costs

Article 41

A15–042 1. The arbitral tribunal, on its establishment, may request each party to deposit an equal amount as an advance for the costs referred to in article 38, paragraphs (a), (b) and (c).

2. During the course of the arbitral proceedings the arbitral tribunal may request supplementary deposits from the parties.

3. If an appointing authority has been agreed upon by the parties or designated by the Secretary-General of the Permanent Court of Arbitration at The Hague, and when a party so requests and the appointing authority consents to perform the function, the arbitral

tribunal shall fix the amounts of any deposits or supplementary deposits only after consultation with the appointing authority which may make any comments to the arbitral tribunal which it deems appropriate concerning the amount of such deposits and supplementary deposits.

4. If the required deposits are not paid in full within thirty days after the receipt of the request, the arbitral tribunal shall so inform the parties in order that one or another of them may make the required payment. If such payment is not made, the arbitral tribunal may order the suspension or termination of the arbitral proceedings.

5. After the award has been made, the arbitral tribunal shall render an accounting to the parties of the deposits received and return any unexpended balance to the parties.

Further information may be obtained from:

UNCITRAL Secretariat
Vienna International Centre
P.O. Box 500
A-1400 Vienna, Austria

Telex: 135612
Telephone: (+43 1) 26060-4060
Telefax: (+43 1) 26060-5813
Internet: http://www.uncitral.org
E-mail: uncitral@uncitral.org

UNCITRAL Notes on Organizing Arbitral Proceedings[1]

(UNITED NATIONS, VIENNA, 1996)

PREFACE

A16–001 The United Nations Commission on International Trade Law (UNCITRAL) finalized the Notes at its twenty-ninth session (New York, May 28–June 14 1996). In addition to the 36 member States of the Commission, representatives of many other States and of a number of international organizations participated in the deliberations. In preparing the draft materials, the Secretariat consulted with experts from various legal systems, with national arbitration bodies and with international professional associations.

The Commission, after an initial discussion on the project in 1993, considered in 1994 a draft entitled "Draft Guidelines for Preparatory Conferences in Arbitral Proceedings". That draft was also discussed at several meetings of arbitration practitioners, including the XIIth International Arbitration Congress, held by the International Council for Commercial Arbitration (ICCA) at Vienna from 3 to 6 November 1994. On the basis of those discussions in the Commission and elsewhere, the Secretariat prepared draft Notes on Organizing Arbitral Proceedings. The Commission considered the draft Notes in 1995, and a revised draft in 1996, when the Notes were finalized.

INTRODUCTION

Purpose of the notes

A16–002 1. The purpose of the Notes is to assist arbitration practitioners by listing and briefly describing questions on which appropriately timed decisions on organizing arbitral proceedings may be useful. The text, prepared with a particular view to international arbitrations, may be used whether or not the arbitration is administered by an arbitral institution.

Non-binding character of the Notes

A16–003 2. No legal requirement binding on the arbitrators or the parties is imposed by the Notes. The arbitral tribunal remains free to use the Notes as it sees fit and is not required to give reasons for disregarding them.

3. The Notes are not suitable to be used as arbitration rules, since they do not establish any obligation of the arbitral tribunal or the parties to act in a particular way. Accordingly, the use of the Notes cannot imply any modification of the arbitration rules that the parties may have agreed upon.

---

[1] Reproduced with the kind permission of United Nations Commission on International Trade Law.

Discretion in conduct of proceedings and usefulness of timely decisions on organizing proceedings

4. Laws governing the arbitral procedure and arbitration rules that parties may agree upon typically allow the arbitral tribunal broad discretion and flexibility in the conduct of arbitral proceedings. This is useful in that it enables the arbitral tribunal to take decisions on the organization of proceedings that take into account the circumstances of the case, the expectations of the parties and of the members of the arbitral tribunal, and the need for a just and cost-efficient resolution of the dispute. **A16–004**

5. Such discretion may make it desirable for the arbitral tribunal to give the parties a timely indication as to the organization of the proceedings and the manner in which the tribunal intends to proceed. This is particularly desirable in international arbitrations, where the participants may be accustomed to differing styles of conducting arbitrations. Without such guidance, a party may find aspects of the proceedings unpredictable and difficult to prepare for. That may lead to misunderstandings, delays and increased costs.

Multi-party arbitration

6. These Notes are intended for use not only in arbitrations with two parties but also in arbitrations with three or more parties. Use of the Notes in multi-party arbitration is referred to below in paragraphs 86–88 (item 18). **A16–005**

Process of making decisions on organizing arbitral proceedings

7. Decisions by the arbitral tribunal on organizing arbitral proceedings may be taken with or without previous consultations with the parties. The method chosen depends on whether, in view of the type of the question to be decided, the arbitral tribunal considers that consultations are not necessary or that hearing the views of the parties would be beneficial for increasing the predictability of the proceedings or improving the procedural atmosphere. **A16–006**

8. The consultations, whether they involve only the arbitrators or also the parties, can be held in one or more meetings, or can be carried out by correspondence or telecommunications such as telefax or conference telephone calls or other electronic means. Meetings may be held at the venue of arbitration or at some other appropriate location.

9. In some arbitrations a special meeting may be devoted exclusively to such procedural consultations; alternatively, the consultations may be held in conjunction with a hearing on the substance of the dispute. Practices differ as to whether such special meetings should be held and how they should be organized. Special procedural meetings of the arbitrators and the parties separate from hearings are in practice referred to by expressions such as "preliminary meeting", "pre-hearing conference", "preparatory conference", "pre-hearing review", or terms of similar meaning. The terms used partly depend on the stage of the proceedings at which the meeting is taking place.

List of matters for possible consideration in organizing arbitral proceedings

A16–007   10. The Notes provide a list, followed by annotations, of matters on which the arbitral tribunal may wish to formulate decisions on organizing arbitral proceedings.

11. Given that procedural styles and practices in arbitration vary widely, that the purpose of the Notes is not to promote any practice as best practice, and that the Notes are designed for universal use, it is not attempted in the Notes to describe in detail different arbitral practices or express a preference for any of them.

12. The list, while not exhaustive, covers a broad range of situations that may arise in an arbitration. In many arbitrations, however, only a limited number of the matters mentioned in the list need to be considered. It also depends on the circumstances of the case at which stage or stages of the proceedings it would be useful to consider matters concerning the organization of the proceedings. Generally, in order not to create opportunities for unnecessary discussions and delay, it is advisable not to raise a matter prematurely, i.e. before it is clear that a decision is needed.

13. When the Notes are used, it should be borne in mind that the discretion of the arbitral tribunal in organizing the proceedings may be limited by arbitration rules, by other provisions agreed to by the parties and by the law applicable to the arbitral procedure. When an arbitration is administered by an arbitral institution, various matters discussed in the Notes may be covered by the rules and practices of that institution.

LIST OF MATTERS FOR POSSIBLE CONSIDERATION IN ORGANIZING ARBITRAL PROCEEDINGS

A16–008

	Paragraphs
1. Set of arbitration rules	14–16
If the parties have not agreed on a set of arbitration rules, would they wish to do so	14–16
2. Language of proceedings	17–20
(a) Possible need for translation of documents, in full or in part	18
(b) Possible need for interpretation of oral presentations	19
(c) Cost of translation and interpretation	20
3. Place of arbitration	21–23
(a) Determination of the place of arbitration, if not already agreed upon by the parties	21–22
(b) Possibility of meetings outside the place of arbitration	23
4. Administrative services that may be needed for the arbitral tribunal to carry out its functions	24–27
5. Deposits in respect of costs	28–30
(a) Amount to be deposited	28
(b) Management of deposits	29
(c) Supplementary deposits	30
6. Confidentiality of information relating to the arbitration; possible agreement thereon	31–32
7. Routing of written communications among the parties and the arbitrators ..	33–34
8. Telefax and other electronic means of sending documents	35–37
(a) Telefax	35

	(b) Other electronic means (e.g. electronic mail and magnetic or optical disk)	36–37
9.	Arrangements for the exchange of written submissions	38–41
	(a) Scheduling of written submissions	39–40
	(b) Consecutive or simultaneous submissions	41
10.	Practical details concerning written submissions and evidence (e.g. method of submission, copies, numbering, references)	42
11.	Defining points at issue; order of deciding issues; defining relief or remedy sought	43–46
	(a) Should a list of points at issue be prepared	43
	(b) In which order should the points at issue be decided	44–45
	(c) Is there a need to define more precisely the relief or remedy sought	46
12.	Possible settlement negotiations and their effect on scheduling proceedings	47
13.	Documentary evidence	48–54
	(a) Time-limits for submission of documentary evidence intended to be submitted by the parties; consequences of late submission	48–49
	(b) Whether the arbitral tribunal intends to require a party to produce documentary evidence	50–51
	(c) Should assertions about the origin and receipt of documents and about the correctness of photocopies be assumed as accurate	52
	(d) Are the parties willing to submit jointly a single set of documentary evidence	53
	(e) Should voluminous and complicated documentary evidence be presented through summaries, tabulations, charts, extracts or samples	54
14.	Physical evidence other than documents	55–58
	(a) What arrangements should be made if physical evidence will be submitted	56
	(b) What arrangements should be made if an on-site inspection is necessary	57–58
15.	Witnesses	59–68
	(a) Advance notice about a witness whom a party intends to present; written witnesses' statements	60–62
	(b) Manner of taking oral evidence of witnesses	63–65
	(i) Order in which questions will be asked and the manner in which the hearing of witnesses will be conducted	63
	(ii) Whether oral testimony will be given under oath or affirmation and, if so, in what form an oath or affirmation should be made	64
	(iii) May witnesses be in the hearing room when they are not testifying	65
	(c) The order in which the witnesses will be called	66
	(d) Interviewing witnesses prior to their appearance at a hearing	67
	(e) Hearing representatives of a party	68
16.	Experts and expert witnesses	69–73
	(a) Expert appointed by the arbitral tribunal	70–72
	(i) The expert's terms of reference	71
	(ii) The opportunity of the parties to comment on the expert's report, including by presenting expert testimony	72
	(b) Expert opinion presented by a party (expert witness)	73
17.	Hearings	74–85
	(a) Decision whether to hold hearings	74–75
	(b) Whether one period of hearings should be held or separate periods of hearings	76

213

    (c) Setting dates for hearings 77
    (d) Whether there should be a limit on the aggregate amount of time each 78–79
        party will have for oral arguments and questioning witnesses ....
    (e) The order in which the parties will present their arguments and evid- 80
        ence ....
    (f) Length of hearings 81
    (g) Arrangements for a record of the hearings 82–83
    (h) Whether and when the parties are permitted to submit notes summariz- 84–85
        ing their oral arguments ....
18. Multi-party arbitration 86–88
19. Possible requirements concerning filing or delivering the award 89–90
    Who should take steps to fulfil any requirement 90

ANNOTATIONS

1. Set of arbitration rules

If the parties have not agreed on a set of arbitration rules, would they wish to do so

A16–009   **14.** Sometimes parties who have not included in their arbitration agreement a stipulation that a set of arbitration rules will govern their arbitral proceedings might wish to do so after the arbitration has begun. If that occurs, the UNCITRAL Arbitration Rules may be used either without modification or with such modifications as the parties might wish to agree upon. In the alternative, the parties might wish to adopt the rules of an arbitral institution; in that case, it may be necessary to secure the agreement of that institution and to stipulate the terms under which the arbitration could be carried out in accordance with the rules of that institution.

15. However, caution is advised as consideration of a set of arbitration rules might delay the proceedings or give rise to unnecessary controversy.

16. It should be noted that agreement on arbitration rules is not a necessity and that, if the parties do not agree on a set of arbitration rules, the arbitral tribunal has the power to continue the proceedings and determine how the case will be conducted.

2. Language of proceedings

A16–010   **17.** Many rules and laws on arbitral procedure empower the arbitral tribunal to determine the language or languages to be used in the proceedings, if the parties have not reached an agreement thereon.

(a) Possible need for translation of documents, in full or in part

A16–011   **18.** Some documents annexed to the statements of claim and defence or submitted later may not be in the language of the proceedings. Bearing in mind the needs of the proceedings and economy, it may be considered whether the arbitral tribunal should order that any of those documents or parts thereof should be accompanied by a translation into the language of the proceedings.

(b) Possible need for interpretation of oral presentations

19. If interpretation will be necessary during oral hearings, it is advisable to consider whether the interpretation will be simultaneous or consecutive and whether the arrangements should be the responsibility of a party or the arbitral tribunal. In an arbitration administered by an institution, interpretation as well as translation services are often arranged by the arbitral institution. A16–012

(c) Cost of translation and interpretation

20. In taking decisions about translation or interpretation, it is advisable to decide whether any or all of the costs are to be paid directly by a party or whether they will be paid out of the deposits and apportioned between the parties along with the other arbitration costs. A16–013

3. Place of arbitration

(a) Determination of the place of arbitration, if not already agreed upon by the parties

21. Arbitration rules usually allow the parties to agree on the place of arbitration, subject to the requirement of some arbitral institutions that arbitrations under their rules be conducted at a particular place, usually the location of the institution. If the place has not been so agreed upon, the rules governing the arbitration typically provide that it is in the power of the arbitral tribunal or the institution administering the arbitration to determine the place. If the arbitral tribunal is to make that determination, it may wish to hear the views of the parties before doing so. A16–014

22. Various factual and legal factors influence the choice of the place of arbitration and their relative importance varies from case to case. Among the more prominent factors are: (a) suitability of the law on arbitral procedure of the place of arbitration: (b) whether there is a multilateral or bilateral treaty on enforcement of arbitral awards between the State where the arbitration takes place and the State or States where the award may have to be enforced; (c) convenience of the parties and the arbitrators, including the travel distances; (d) availability and cost of support services needed; and (e) location of the subject-matter in dispute and proximity of evidence.

(b) Possibility of meetings outside the place of arbitration

23. Many sets of arbitration rules and laws on arbitral procedure expressly allow the arbitral tribunal to hold meetings elsewhere than at the place of arbitration. For example, under the UNCITRAL Model Law on International Commercial Arbitration "the arbitral tribunal may, unless otherwise agreed by the parties, meet at any place it considers appropriate for consultation among its members, for hearing witnesses, experts or the parties, or for inspection of goods, other property or documents" (article 20(2)). The purpose of this discretion is to permit arbitral proceedings to be carried out in a manner that is most efficient and economical. A16–015

4. Administrative services that may be needed for the arbitral tribunal to carry out its functions

A16–016 24. Various administrative services (e.g. hearing rooms or secretarial services) may need to be procured for the arbitral tribunal to be able to carry out its functions. When the arbitration is administered by an arbitral institution, the institution will usually provide all or a good part of the required administrative support to the arbitral tribunal. When an arbitration administered by an arbitral institution takes place away from the seat of the institution, the institution may be able to arrange for administrative services to be obtained from another source, often an arbitral institution; some arbitral institutions have entered into cooperation agreements with a view to providing mutual assistance in servicing arbitral proceedings.

25. When the case is not administered by an institution, or the involvement of the institution does not include providing administrative support, usually the administrative arrangements for the proceedings will be made by the arbitral tribunal or the presiding arbitrator; it may also be acceptable to leave some of the arrangements to the parties, or to one of the parties subject to agreement of the other party or parties. Even in such cases, a convenient source of administrative support might be found in arbitral institutions, which often offer their facilities to arbitrations not governed by the rules of the institution. Otherwise, some services could be procured from entities such as chambers of commerce, hotels or specialized firms providing secretarial or other support services.

26. Administrative services might be secured by engaging a secretary of the arbitral tribunal (also referred to as registrar, clerk, administrator or rapporteur), who carries out the tasks under the direction of the arbitral tribunal. Some arbitral institutions routinely assign such persons to the cases administered by them. In arbitrations not administered by an institution or where the arbitral institution does not appoint a secretary, some arbitrators frequently engage such persons, at least in certain types of cases, whereas many others normally conduct the proceedings without them.

27. To the extent the tasks of the secretary are purely organizational (e.g. obtaining meeting rooms and providing or coordinating secretarial services), this is usually not controversial. Differences in views, however, may arise if the tasks include legal research and other professional assistance to the arbitral tribunal (e.g. collecting case law or published commentaries on legal issues defined by the arbitral tribunal, preparing summaries from case law and publications, and sometimes also preparing drafts of procedural decisions or drafts of certain parts of the award, in particular those concerning the facts of the case). Views or expectations may differ especially where a task of the secretary is similar to professional functions of the arbitrators. Such a role of the secretary is in the view of some commentators inappropriate or is appropriate only under certain conditions, such as that the parties agree thereto. However, it is typically recognized that it is important to ensure that the secretary does not perform any decision-making function of the arbitral tribunal.

5. Deposits in respect of costs

(a) Amount to be deposited

A16–017 28. In an arbitration administered by an institution, the institution often sets, on the basis of an estimate of the costs of the proceedings, the amount to be deposited as an advance for the costs of the arbitration. In other cases it is customary for the arbitral tribunal to make such an estimate and request a deposit. The estimate typically includes travel and other expenses by the arbitrators, expenditures for administrative assistance required by the arbitral tribunal, costs of any expert advice required by the arbitral tribunal, and the fees for the arbitrators. Many arbitration rules have provisions on this matter, including on whether the deposit should be made by the two parties (or all parties in a multi-party case) or only by the claimant.

(b) Management of deposits

29. When the arbitration is administered by an institution, the institution's services may include managing and accounting for the deposited money. Where that is not the case, it might be useful to clarify matters such as the type and location of the account in which the money will be kept and how the deposits will be managed. **A16–018**

(c) Supplementary deposits

30. If during the course of proceedings it emerges that the costs will be higher than anticipated, supplementary deposits may be required (e.g. because the arbitral tribunal decides pursuant to the arbitration rules to appoint an expert). **A16–019**

6. *Confidentiality of information relating to the arbitration; possible agreement thereon*

31. It is widely viewed that confidentiality is one of the advantageous and helpful features of arbitration. Nevertheless, there is no uniform answer in national laws as to the extent to which the participants in an arbitration are under the duty to observe the confidentiality of information relating to the case. Moreover, parties that have agreed on arbitration rules or other provisions that do not expressly address the issue of confidentiality cannot assume that all jurisdictions would recognize an implied commitment to confidentiality. Furthermore, the participants in an arbitration might not have the same understanding as regards the extent of confidentiality that is expected. Therefore, the arbitral tribunal might wish to discuss that with the parties and, if considered appropriate, record any agreed principles on the duty of confidentiality. **A16–020**

32. An agreement on confidentiality might cover, for example, one or more of the following matters: the material or information that is to be kept confidential (e.g. pieces of evidence, written and oral arguments, the fact that the arbitration is taking place, identity of the arbitrators, content of the award); measures for maintaining confidentiality of such information and hearings; whether any special procedures should be employed for maintaining the confidentiality of information transmitted by electronic means (e.g. because communication equipment is shared by several users, or because electronic mail over public networks is considered not sufficiently protected against unauthorized access); circumstances in which confidential information may be disclosed in part or in whole (e.g. in the context of disclosures of information in the public domain, or if required by law or a regulatory body).

7. Routing of written communications among the parties and the arbitrators

A16–021 33. To the extent the question how documents and other written communications should be routed among the parties and the arbitrators is not settled by the agreed rules, or, if an institution administers the case, by the practices of the institution, it is useful for the arbitral tribunal to clarify the question suitably early so as to avoid misunderstandings and delays.

34. Among various possible patterns of routing, one example is that a party transmits the appropriate number of copies to the arbitral tribunal, or to the arbitral institution, if one is involved, which then forwards them as appropriate. Another example is that a party is to send copies simultaneously to the arbitrators and the other party or parties. Documents and other written communications directed by the arbitral tribunal or the presiding arbitrator to one or more parties may also follow a determined pattern, such as through the arbitral institution or by direct transmission. For some communications, in particular those on organizational matters (e.g. dates for hearings), more direct routes of communication may be agreed, even if, for example, the arbitral institution acts as an intermediary for documents such as the statements of claim and defence, evidence or written arguments.

8. Telefax and other electronic means of sending documents

(a) Telefax

A16–022 35. Telefax, which offers many advantages over traditional means of communication, is widely used in arbitral proceedings. Nevertheless, should it be thought that, because of the characteristics of the equipment used, it would be preferable not to rely only on a telefacsimile of a document, special arrangements may be considered, such as that a particular piece of written evidence should be mailed or otherwise physically delivered, or that certain telefax messages should be confirmed by mailing or otherwise delivering documents whose facsimile were transmitted by electronic means. When a document should not be sent by telefax, it may, however, be appropriate, in order to avoid an unnecessarily rigid procedure, for the arbitral tribunal to retain discretion to accept an advance copy of a document by telefax for the purposes of meeting a deadline, provided that the document itself is received within a reasonable time thereafter.

(b) Other electronic means (e.g. electronic mail and magnetic or optical disk)

A16–023 36. It might be agreed that documents, or some of them, will be exchanged not only in paper-based form, but in addition also in an electronic form other than telefax (e.g. as electronic mail, or on a magnetic or optical disk), or only in electronic form. Since the use of electronic means depends on the aptitude of the persons involved and the availability of equipment and computer programs, agreement is necessary for such means to be used. If both paper-based and electronic means are to be used, it is advisable to decide which one is controlling and, if there is a time-limit for submitting a document, which act constitutes submission.

37. When the exchange of documents in electronic form is planned, it is useful, in order to avoid technical difficulties, to agree on matters such as: data carriers (e.g. electronic mail or computer disks) and their technical characteristics; computer programs to be used in preparing the electronic records; instructions for transforming the electronic

records into human-readable form; keeping of logs and back-up records of communications sent and received; information in human-readable form that should accompany the disks (e.g. the names of the originator and recipient, computer program, titles of the electronic files and the back-up methods used); procedures when a message is lost or the communication system otherwise fails; and identification of persons who can be contacted if a problem occurs.

9. Arrangements for the exchange of written submissions

38. After the parties have initially stated their claims and defences, they may wish, or the arbitral tribunal might request them, to present further written submissions so as to prepare for the hearings or to provide the basis for a decision without hearings. In such submissions, the parties, for example, present or comment on allegations and evidence, cite or explain law, or make or react to proposals. In practice such submissions are referred to variously as, for example, statement, memorial, counter-memorial, brief, counter-brief, reply, *réplique, duplique*, rebuttal or rejoinder; the terminology is a matter of linguistic usage and the scope or sequence of the submission.

(a) Scheduling of written submissions

39. It is advisable that the arbitral tribunal set time-limits for written submissions. In enforcing the time-limits, the arbitral tribunal may wish, on the one hand, to make sure that the case is not unduly protracted and, on the other hand, to reserve a degree of discretion and allow late submissions if appropriate under the circumstances. In some cases the arbitral tribunal might prefer not to plan the written submissions in advance, thus leaving such matters, including time-limits, to be decided in light of the developments in the proceedings. In other cases, the arbitral tribunal may wish to determine, when scheduling the first written submissions, the number of subsequent submissions.

40. Practices differ as to whether, after the hearings have been held, written submissions are still acceptable. While some arbitral tribunals consider post-hearing submissions unacceptable, others might request or allow them on a particular issue. Some arbitral tribunals follow the procedure according to which the parties are not requested to present written evidence and legal arguments to the arbitral tribunal before the hearings; in such a case, the arbitral tribunal may regard it as appropriate that written submissions be made after the hearings.

(b) Consecutive or simultaneous submissions

41. Written submissions on an issue may be made consecutively, i.e. the party who receives a submission is given a period of time to react with its counter-submission. Another possibility is to request each party to make the submission within the same time period to the arbitral tribunal or the institution administering the case; the received submissions are then forwarded simultaneously to the respective other party or parties. The approach used may depend on the type of issues to be commented upon and the time in which the views should be clarified. With consecutive submissions, it may take longer than with simultaneous ones to obtain views of the parties on a given issue. Consecutive submissions, however, allow the reacting party to comment on all points raised by the other party or parties, which simultaneous submissions do not; thus, simultaneous submissions might possibly necessitate further submissions.

10. Practical details concerning written submissions and evidence (e.g. method of submission, copies, numbering, references)

A16–027   42. Depending on the volume and kind of documents to be handled, it might be considered whether practical arrangements on details such as the following would be helpful:

- Whether the submissions will be made as paper documents or by electronic means, or both (see paragraphs 35-37);
- The number of copies in which each document is to be submitted;
- A system for numbering documents and items of evidence, and a method for marking them, including by tabs;
- The form of references to documents (e.g. by the heading and the number assigned to the document or its date);
- Paragraph numbering in written submissions, in order to facilitate precise references to parts of a text;
- When translations are to be submitted as paper documents, whether the translations are to be contained in the same volume as the original texts or included in separate volumes.

11. Defining points at issue; order of deciding issues; defining relief or remedy sought

(a) Should a list of points at issue be prepared

A16–028   43. In considering the parties' allegations and arguments, the arbitral tribunal may come to the conclusion that it would be useful for it or for the parties to prepare, for analytical purposes and for ease of discussion, a list of the points at issue, as opposed to those that are undisputed. If the arbitral tribunal determines that the advantages of working on the basis of such a list outweigh the disadvantages, it chooses the appropriate stage of the proceedings for preparing a list, bearing in mind also that subsequent developments in the proceedings may require a revision of the points at issue. Such an identification of points at issue might help to concentrate on the essential matters, to reduce the number of points at issue by agreement of the parties, and to select the best and most economical process for resolving the dispute. However, possible disadvantages of preparing such a list include delay, adverse effect on the flexibility of the proceedings, or unnecessary disagreements about whether the arbitral tribunal has decided all issues submitted to it or whether the award contains decisions on matters beyond the scope of the submission to arbitration. The terms of reference required under some arbitration rules, or in agreements of parties, may serve the same purpose as the above-described list of points at issue.

(b) In which order should the points at issue be decided

A16–029   44. While it is often appropriate to deal with all the points at issue collectively, the arbitral tribunal might decide to take them up during the proceedings in a particular order. The order may be due to a point being preliminary relative to another (e.g. a decision on the jurisdiction of the arbitral tribunal is preliminary to consideration of substantive issues, or the issue of responsibility for a breach of contract is preliminary to the issue of the resulting damages). A particular order may be decided also when the breach of various contracts is in dispute or when damages arising from various events are claimed.

45. If the arbitral tribunal has adopted a particular order of deciding points at issue, it might consider it appropriate to issue a decision on one of the points earlier than on the other ones. This might be done, for example, when a discrete part of a claim is ready for decision while the other parts still require extensive consideration, or when it is expected that after deciding certain issues the parties might be more inclined to settle the remaining ones. Such earlier decisions are referred to by expressions such as "partial", "interlocutory" or "interim" awards or decisions, depending on the type of issue dealt with and on whether the decision is final with respect to the issue it resolves. Questions that might be the subject of such decisions are, for example, jurisdiction of the arbitral tribunal, interim measures of protection, or the liability of a party.

(c) Is there a need to define more precisely the relief or remedy sought

46. If the arbitral tribunal considers that the relief or remedy sought is insufficiently definite, it may wish to explain to the parties the degree of definiteness with which their claims should be formulated. Such an explanation may be useful since criteria are not uniform as to how specific the claimant must be in formulating a relief or remedy. **A16–030**

12. Possible settlement negotiations and their effect on scheduling proceedings

47. Attitudes differ as to whether it is appropriate for the arbitral tribunal to bring up the possibility of settlement. Given the divergence of practices in this regard, the arbitral tribunal should only suggest settlement negotiations with caution. However, it may be opportune for the arbitral tribunal to schedule the proceedings in a way that might facilitate the continuation or initiation of settlement negotiations. **A16–031**

13. Documentary evidence

(a) Time-limits for submission of documentary evidence intended to be submitted by the parties; consequences of late submission

48. Often the written submissions of the parties contain sufficient information for the arbitral tribunal to fix the time-limit for submitting evidence. Otherwise, in order to set realistic time periods, the arbitral tribunal may wish to consult with the parties about the time that they would reasonably need. **A16–032**

49. The arbitral tribunal may wish to clarify that evidence submitted late will as a rule not be accepted. It may wish not to preclude itself from accepting a late submission of evidence if the party shows sufficient cause for the delay.

(b) Whether the arbitral tribunal intends to require a party to produce documentary evidence

50. Procedures and practices differ widely as to the conditions under which the arbitral tribunal may require a party to produce documents. Therefore, the arbitral tribunal might **A16–033**

consider it useful, when the agreed arbitration rules do not provide specific conditions, to clarify to the parties the manner in which it intends to proceed.

51. The arbitral tribunal may wish to establish time-limits for the production of documents. The parties might be reminded that, if the requested party duly invited to produce documentary evidence fails to do so within the established period of time, without showing sufficient cause for such failure, the arbitral tribunal is free to draw its conclusions from the failure and may make the award on the evidence before it.

(c) Should assertions about the origin and receipt of documents and about the correctness of photocopies be assumed as accurate

A16–034   **52.** It may be helpful for the arbitral tribunal to inform parties that it intends to conduct the proceedings on the basis that, unless a party raises an objection to any of the following conclusions within a specified period of time: (a) a document is accepted as having originated from the source indicated in the document; (b) a copy of a dispatched communication (e.g. letter, telex, telefax or other electronic message) is accepted without further proof as having been received by the addressee; and (c) a copy is accepted as correct. A statement by the arbitral tribunal to that effect can simplify the introduction of documentary evidence and discourage unfounded and dilatory objections, at a late stage of the proceedings, to the probative value of documents. It is advisable to provide that the time-limit for objections will not be enforced if the arbitral tribunal considers the delay justified.

(d) Are the parties willing to submit jointly a single set of documentary evidence

A16–035   **53.** The parties may consider submitting jointly a single set of documentary evidence whose authenticity is not disputed. The purpose would be to avoid duplicate submissions and unnecessary discussions concerning the authenticity of documents, without prejudicing the position of the parties concerning the content of the documents. Additional documents may be inserted later if the parties agree. When a single set of documents would be too voluminous to be easily manageable, it might be practical to select a number of frequently used documents and establish a set of "working" documents. A convenient arrangement of documents in the set may be according to chronological order or subject-matter. It is useful to keep a table of contents of the documents, for example, by their short headings and dates, and to provide that the parties will refer to documents by those headings and dates.

(e) Should voluminous and complicated documentary evidence be presented through summaries, tabulations, charts, extracts or samples

A16–036   **54.** When documentary evidence is voluminous and complicated, it may save time and costs if such evidence is presented by a report of a person competent in the relevant field (e.g. public accountant or consulting engineer). The report may present the information in the form of summaries, tabulations, charts, extracts or samples. Such presentation of evidence should be combined with arrangements that give the interested party the opportunity to review the underlying data and the methodology of preparing the report.

14. Physical evidence other than documents

A16–037   **55.** In some arbitrations the arbitral tribunal is called upon to assess physical evidence other than documents, for example, by inspecting samples of goods, viewing a video recording or observing the functioning of a machine.

(a) What arrangements should be made if physical evidence will be submitted

56. If physical evidence will be submitted, the arbitral tribunal may wish to fix the time schedule for presenting the evidence, make arrangements for the other party or parties to have a suitable opportunity to prepare itself for the presentation of the evidence, and possibly take measures for safekeeping the items of evidence.

(b) What arrangements should be made if an on-site inspection is necessary

57. If an on-site inspection of property or goods will take place, the arbitral tribunal may consider matters such as timing, meeting places, other arrangements to provide the opportunity for all parties to be present, and the need to avoid communications between arbitrators and a party about points at issue without the presence of the other party or parties.

58. The site to be inspected is often under the control of one of the parties, which typically means that employees or representatives of that party will be present to give guidance and explanations. It should be borne in mind that statements of those representatives or employees made during an on-site inspection, as contrasted with statements those persons might make as witnesses in a hearing, should not be treated as evidence in the proceedings.

15. Witnesses

59. While laws and rules on arbitral procedure typically leave broad freedom concerning the manner of taking evidence of witnesses, practices on procedural points are varied. In order to facilitate the preparations of the parties for the hearings, the arbitral tribunal may consider it appropriate to clarify, in advance of the hearings, some or all of the following issues.

(a) Advance notice about a witness whom a party intends to present; written witnesses' statements

60. To the extent the applicable arbitration rules do not deal with the matter, the arbitral tribunal may wish to require that each party give advance notice to the arbitral tribunal and the other party or parties of any witness it intends to present. As to the content of the notice, the following is an example of what might be required, in addition to the names and addresses of the witnesses: (a) the subject upon which the witnesses will testify; (b) the language in which the witnesses will testify; and (c) the nature of the relationship with any of the parties, qualifications and experience of the witnesses if and to the extent these are relevant to the dispute or the testimony, and how the witnesses learned about the facts on which they will testify. However, it may not be necessary to require such a notice, in particular if the thrust of the testimony can be clearly ascertained from the party's allegations.

61. Some practitioners favour the procedure according to which the party presenting witness evidence submits a signed witness's statement containing testimony itself. It should be noted, however, that such practice, which implies interviewing the witness by the party presenting the testimony, is not known in all parts of the world and, moreover, that some practitioners disapprove of it on the ground that such contacts between the party and the witness may compromise the credibility of the testimony and are therefore

improper (see paragraph 67). Notwithstanding these reservations, signed witness's testimony has advantages in that it may expedite the proceedings by making it easier for the other party or parties to prepare for the hearings or for the parties to identify uncontested matters. However, those advantages might be outweighed by the time and expense involved in obtaining the written testimony.

62. If a signed witness's statement should be made under oath or similar affirmation of truthfulness, it may be necessary to clarify by whom the oath or affirmation should be administered and whether any formal authentication will be required by the arbitral tribunal.

(b) Manner of taking oral evidence of witnesses

(i) Order in which questions will be asked and the manner in which the hearing of witnesses will be conducted

A16–042 63. To the extent that the applicable rules do not provide an answer, it may be useful for the arbitral tribunal to clarify how witnesses will be heard. One of the various possibilities is that a witness is first questioned by the arbitral tribunal, whereupon questions are asked by the parties, first by the party who called the witness. Another possibility is for the witness to be questioned by the party presenting the witness and then by the other party or parties, while the arbitral tribunal might pose questions during the questioning or after the parties on points that in the tribunal's view have not been sufficiently clarified. Differences exist also as to the degree of control the arbitral tribunal exercises over the hearing of witnesses. For example, some arbitrators prefer to permit the parties to pose questions freely and directly to the witness, but may disallow a question if a party objects; other arbitrators tend to exercise more control and may disallow a question on their initiative or even require that questions from the parties be asked through the arbitral tribunal.

(ii) Whether oral testimony will be given under oath or affirmation and, if so, in what form an oath or affirmation should be made

A16–043 64. Practices and laws differ as to whether or not oral testimony is to be given under oath or affirmation. In some legal systems, the arbitrators are empowered to put witnesses on oath, but it is usually in their discretion whether they want to do so. In other systems, oral testimony under oath is either unknown or may even be considered improper as only an official such as a judge or notary may have the authority to administer oaths.

(iii) May witnesses be in the hearing room when they are not testifying

A16–044 65. Some arbitrators favour the procedure that, except if the circumstances suggest otherwise, the presence of a witness in the hearing room is limited to the time the witness is testifying; the purpose is to prevent the witness from being influenced by what is said in the hearing room, or to prevent that the presence of the witness would influence another witness. Other arbitrators consider that the presence of a witness during the testimony of other witnesses may be beneficial in that possible contradictions may be readily clarified or that their presence may act as a deterrent against untrue statements. Other possible approaches may be that witnesses are not present in the hearing room before their testimony, but stay in the room after they have testified, or that the arbitral tribunal decides the question for each witness individually depending on what the arbitral tribunal considers most appropriate. The arbitral tribunal may leave the procedure to be decided during the hearings, or may give guidance on the question in advance of the hearings.

(c) The order in which the witnesses will be called

66. When several witnesses are to be heard and longer testimony is expected, it is likely to reduce costs if the order in which they will be called is known in advance and their presence can be scheduled accordingly. Each party might be invited to suggest the order in which it intends to present the witnesses, while it would be up to the arbitral tribunal to approve the scheduling and to make departures from it. **A16–045**

(d) Interviewing witnesses prior to their appearance at a hearing

67. In some legal systems, parties or their representatives are permitted to interview witnesses, prior to their appearance at the hearing, as to such matters as their recollection of the relevant events, their experience, qualifications or relation with a participant in the proceedings. In those legal systems such contacts are usually not permitted once the witness's oral testimony has begun. In other systems such contacts with witnesses are considered improper. In order to avoid misunderstandings, the arbitral tribunal may consider it useful to clarify what kind of contacts a party is permitted to have with a witness in the preparations for the hearings. **A16–046**

(e) Hearing representatives of a party

68. According to some legal systems, certain persons affiliated with a party may only be heard as representatives of the party but not as witnesses. In such a case, it may be necessary to consider ground rules for determining which persons may not testify as witnesses (e.g. certain executives, employees or agents) and for hearing statements of those persons and for questioning them. **A16–047**

16. Experts and expert witnesses

69. Many arbitration rules and laws on arbitral procedure address the participation of experts in arbitral proceedings. A frequent solution is that the arbitral tribunal has the power to appoint an expert to report on issues determined by the tribunal; in addition, the parties may be permitted to present expert witnesses on points at issue. In other cases, it is for the parties to present expert testimony, and it is not expected that the arbitral tribunal will appoint an expert. **A16–048**

(a) Expert appointed by the arbitral tribunal

70. If the arbitral tribunal is empowered to appoint an expert, one possible approach is for the tribunal to proceed directly to selecting the expert. Another possibility is to consult the parties as to who should be the expert; this may be done, for example, without mentioning a candidate, by presenting to the parties a list of candidates, soliciting proposals from the parties, or by discussing with the parties the "profile" of the expert the arbitral tribunal intends to appoint, i.e. the qualifications, experience and abilities of the expert. **A16–049**

(i) The expert's terms of reference

71. The purpose of the expert's terms of reference is to indicate the questions on which the expert is to provide clarification, to avoid opinions on points that are not for the expert to assess and to commit the expert to a time schedule. While the discretion to **A16–050**

appoint an expert normally includes the determination of the expert's terms of reference, the arbitral tribunal may decide to consult the parties before finalizing the terms. It might also be useful to determine details about how the expert will receive from the parties any relevant information or have access to any relevant documents, goods or other propeny, so as to enable the expert to prepare the report. In order to facilitate the evaluation of the expert's report, it is advisable to require the expert to include in the report information on the method used in arriving at the conclusions and the evidence and information used in preparing the report.

(ii) The opportunity of the parties to comment on the expert's report, including by presenting expert testimony

A16–051   72. Arbitration rules that contain provisions on experts usually also have provisions on the right of a party to comment on the report of the expert appointed by the arbitral tribunal. If no such provisions apply or more specific procedures than those prescribed are deemed necessary, the arbitral tribunal may, in light of those provisions, consider it opportune to determine, for example, the time period for presenting written comments of the parties, or, if hearings are to be held for the purpose of hearing the expert, the procedures for interrogating the expert by the parties or for the participation of any expert witnesses presented by the parties.

(b) Expert opinion presented by a party (expert witness)

A16–052   73. If a party presents an expert opinion, the arbitral tribunal might consider requiring, for example, that the opinion be in writing, that the expert should be available to answer questions at hearings, and that, if a party will present an expert witness at a hearing, advance notice must be given or that the written opinion must be presented in advance, as in the case of other witnesses (see paragraphs 60–62).

17. Hearings

(a) Decision whether to hold hearings

A16–053   74. Laws on arbitral procedure and arbitration rules often have provisions as to the cases in which oral hearings must be held and as to when the arbitral tribunal has discretion to decide whether to hold hearings.

75. If it is up to the arbitral tribunal to decide whether to hold hearings, the decision is likely to be influenced by factors such as, on the one hand, that it is usually quicker and easier to clarify points at issue pursuant to a direct confrontation of arguments than on the basis of correspondence and, on the other hand, the travel and other cost of holding hearings, and that the need of finding acceptable dates for the hearings might delay the proceedings. The arbitral tribunal may wish to consult the parties on this matter.

(b) Whether one period of hearings should be held or separate periods of hearings

A16–054   76. Attitudes vary as to whether hearings should be held in a single period of hearings or in separate periods, especially when more than a few days are needed to complete the hearings. According to some arbitrators, the entire hearings should normally be held in a single period, even if the hearings are to last for more than a week. Other arbitrators in such cases tend to schedule separate periods of hearings. In some cases issues to be decided are separated, and separate hearings set for those issues, with the aim that oral presentation on those issues will be completed within the allotted time. Among the advantages of one period of hearings are that it involves less travel costs, memory will not fade, and it is unlikely that people representing a party will change. On the other hand, the longer the hearings, the more difficult it may be to find early dates acceptable to all participants. Furthermore, separate periods of hearings may be easier to schedule, the subsequent hearings may be tailored to the development of the case, and the period between the hearings leaves time for analysing the records and negotiations between the parties aimed at narrowing the points at issue by agreement.

(c) Setting dates for hearings

77. Typically, firm dates will be fixed for hearings. Exceptionally, the arbitral tribunal may initially wish to set only "target dates" as opposed to definitive dates. This may be done at a stage of the proceedings when not all information necessary to schedule hearings is yet available, with the understanding that the target dates will either be confirmed or rescheduled within a reasonably short period. Such provisional planning can be useful to participants who are generally not available on short notice. **A16–055**

(d) Whether there should be a limit on the aggregate amount of time each party will have for oral arguments and questioning witnesses

78. Some arbitrators consider it useful to limit the aggregate amount of time each party has for any of the following: (a) making oral statements; (b) questioning its witnesses; and (c) questioning the witnesses of the other party or parties. In general, the same aggregate amount of time is considered appropriate for each party, unless the arbitral tribunal considers that a different allocation is justified. Before deciding, the arbitral tribunal may wish to consult the parties as to how much time they think they will need. **A16–056**

79. Such planning of time, provided it is realistic, fair and subject to judiciously firm control by the arbitral tribunal, will make it easier for the parties to plan the presentation of the various items of evidence and arguments, reduce the likelihood of running out of time towards the end of the hearings and avoid that one party would unfairly use up a disproportionate amount of time.

(e) The order in which the parties will present their arguments and evidence

80. Arbitration rules typically give broad latitude to the arbitral tribunal to determine the order of presentations at the hearings. Within that latitude, practices differ, for example, as to whether opening or closing statements are heard and their level of detail; the sequence in which the claimant and the respondent present their opening statements, arguments, witnesses and other evidence; and whether the respondent or the claimant has the last word. In view of such differences, or when no arbitration rules apply, it may foster efficiency of the proceedings if the arbitral tribunal clarifies to the parties, in advance of the hearings, the manner in which it will conduct the hearings, at least in broad lines. **A16–057**

(f) Length of hearings

81. The length of a hearing primarily depends on the complexity of the issues to be argued and the amount of witness evidence to be presented. The length also depends on the procedural style used in the arbitration. Some practitioners prefer to have written evidence and written arguments presented before the hearings, which thus can focus on the issues that have not been sufficiently clarified. Those practitioners generally tend to **A16–058**

plan shorter hearings than those practitioners who prefer that most if not all evidence and arguments are presented to the arbitral tribunal orally and in full detail. In order to facilitate the parties' preparations and avoid misunderstandings, the arbitral tribunal may wish to clarify to the parties, in advance of the hearings, the intended use of time and style of work at the hearings.

(g) Arrangements for a record of the hearings

A16–059   82. The arbitral tribunal should decide, possibly after consulting with the parties, on the method of preparing a record of oral statements and testimony during hearings. Among different possibilities, one method is that the members of the arbitral tribunal take personal notes. Another is that the presiding arbitrator during the hearing dictates to a typist a summary of oral statements and testimony. A further method, possible when a secretary of the arbitral tribunal has been appointed, may be to leave to that person the preparation of a summary record. A useful, though costly, method is for professional stenographers to prepare verbatim transcripts, often within the next day or a similarly short time period. A written record may be combined with tape-recording, so as to enable reference to the tape in case of a disagreement over the written record.

83. If transcripts are to be produced, it may be considered how the persons who made the statements will be given an opportunity to check the transcripts. For example, it may be determined that the changes to the record would be approved by the parties or, failing their agreement, would be referred for decision to the arbitral tribunal.

(h) Whether and when the parties are permitted to submit notes summarizing their oral arguments

A16–060   84. Some legal counsel are accustomed to giving notes summarizing their oral arguments to the arbitral tribunal and to the other party or parties. If such notes are presented, this is usually done during the hearings or shortly thereafter; in some cases, the notes are sent before the hearing. In order to avoid surprise, foster equal treatment of the parties and facilitate preparations for the hearings, advance clarification is advisable as to whether submitting such notes is accceptable and the time for doing so.

85. In closing the hearings the arbitral tribunal will normally assume that no further proof is to be offered or submission to be made. Therefore, if notes are to be presented to be read after the closure of the hearings, the arbitral tribunal may find it worthwhile to stress that the notes should be limited to summarizing what was said orally and in particular should not refer to new evidence or new argument.

18. Multi-party arbitration

A16–061   86. When a single arbitration involves more than two parties (multi-party arbitration), considerations regarding the need to organize arbitral proceedings, and matters that may be considered in that connection, are generally not different from two-party arbitrations. A possible difference may be that, because of the need to deal with more than two parties, multi-party proceedings can be more complicated to manage than bilateral proceedings. The Notes, notwithstanding a possible greater complexity of multi-party arbitration, can be used in multi-party as well as in two-party proceedings.

87. The areas of possibly increased complexity in multi-party arbitration are, for example, the flow of communications among the parties and the arbitral tribunal (see

paragraphs 33, 34 and 38–41); if points at issue are to be decided at different points in time, the order of deciding them (paragraphs 44–45); the manner in which the parties will participate in hearing witnesses (paragraph 63); the appointment of experts and the participation of the parties in considering their reports (paragraphs 70–72); the scheduling of hearings (paragraph 76); the order in which the parties will present their arguments and evidence at hearings (paragraph 80).

88. The Notes, which are limited to pointing out matters that may be considered in organizing arbitral proceedings in general, do not cover the drafting of the arbitration agreement or the constitution of the arbitral tribunal, both issues that give rise to special questions in multi-party arbitration as compared to two-party arbitration.

19. Possible requirements concerning filing or delivering the award

89. Some national laws require that arbitral awards be filed or registered with a court **A16–062** or similar authority, or that they be delivered in a particular manner or through a particular authority. Those laws differ with respect to, for example, the type of award to which the requirement applies (e.g. to all awards or only to awards not rendered under auspices of an arbitral institution); time periods for filing, registering or delivering the award (in some cases those time periods may be rather short); or consequences for failing to comply with the requirement (which might be, for example, invalidity of the award or inability to enforce it in a particular manner).

Who should take steps to fulfil any requirement

90. If such a requirement exists, it is useful, some time before the award is to be **A16–063** issued, to plan who should take the necessary steps to meet the requirement and how the costs are to be borne.

The New York Convention on the Recognition and Enforcement of Foreign Arbitral Awards[1]

(JUNE 10, 1958)

Article I

A17–001   1. This Convention shall apply to the recognition and enforcement of arbitral awards made in the territory of a State other than the State where the recognition and enforcement of such awards are sought, and arising out of differences between persons, whether physical or legal. It shall also apply to arbitral awards not considered as domestic awards in the State where their recognition and enforcement are sought.

2. The term "arbitral awards" shall include not only awards made by arbitrators appointed for each case but also those made by permanent arbitral bodies to which the parties have submitted.

3. When signing, ratifying or acceding to this Convention, or notifying extension under article X hereof, any State may on the basis of reciprocity declare that it will apply the Convention to the recognition and enforcement of awards made only in the territory of another Contracting State. It may also declare that it will apply the Convention only to differences arising out of legal relationships, whether contractual or not, which are considered as commercial under the national law of the State making such declaration.

Article II

A17–002   1. Each Contracting State shall recognize an agreement in writing under which the parties undertake to submit to arbitration all or any differences which have arisen or which may arise between them in respect of a defined legal relationship, whether contractual or not, concerning a subject-matter capable of settlement by arbitration.

2. The term "agreement in writing" shall include an arbitral clause in a contract or an arbitration agreement, signed by the parties or contained in an exchange of letters or telegrams.

3. The court of a Contracting State, when seized of an action in a matter in respect of which the parties have made an agreement within the meaning of this article shall, at the request of one of the parties, refer the parties to arbitration, unless it finds that the said agreement is null and void, inoperative or incapable of being performed.

Article III

A17–003   Each Contracting State shall recognize arbitral awards as binding and enforce them in accordance with the rules of procedure of the territory where the award is relied upon, under the conditions laid down in the following articles. There shall not be imposed

---

[1] Reproduced with the kind permission of United Nations Commission on International Trade Law.

substantially more onerous conditions or higher fees or charges on the recognition or enforcement of arbitral awards to which this Convention applies than are imposed on the recognition or enforcement of domestic arbitral awards.

Article IV

1. To obtain the recognition and enforcement mentioned in the preceding article, the party applying for recognition and enforcement shall, at the time of the application, supply:

    (a) The duly authenticated original award or a duly certified copy thereof;

    (b) The original agreement referred to in article II or a duly certified copy thereof.

2. If the said award or agreement is not made in an official language of the country in which the award is relied upon, the party applying for recognition and enforcement of the award shall produce a translation of these documents into such language. The translation shall be certified by an official or sworn translator or by a diplomatic or consular agent.

Article V

1. Recognition and enforcement of the award may be refused, at the request of the party against whom it is invoked, only if that party furnishes to the competent authority where the recognition and enforcement is sought, proof that:

    (a) The parties to the agreement referred to in article II were, under the law applicable to them, under some incapacity, or the said agreement is not valid under the law to which the parties have subjected it or, failing any indication thereon, under the law of the country where the award was made; or

    (b) The party against whom the award is invoked was not given proper notice of the appointment of the arbitrator or of the arbitration proceedings or was otherwise unable to present his case; or

    (c) The award deals with a difference not contemplated by or not falling within the terms of the submission to arbitration, or it contains decisions on matters beyond the scope of the submission to arbitration, provided that, if the decisions on matters submitted to arbitration can be separated from those not so submitted, that part of the award which contains decisions on matters submitted to arbitration may be recognized and enforced; or

    (d) The composition of the arbitral authority or the arbitral procedure was not in accordance with the agreement of the parties, or, failing such agreement, was not in accordance with the law of the country where the arbitration took place; or

(e) The award has not yet become binding on the parties, or has been set aside or suspended by a competent authority of the country in which, or under the law of which, that award was made.

2. Recognition and enforcement of an arbitral award may also be refused if the competent authority in the country where recognition and enforcement is sought finds that:

(a) The subject matter of the difference is not capable of settlement by arbitration under the law of that country; or

(b) The recognition or enforcement of the award would be contrary to the public policy of that country.

Article VI

A17–006 If an application for the setting aside or suspension of the award has been made to a competent authority referred to in article V(1)(e), the authority before which the award is sought to be relied upon may, if it considers it proper, adjourn the decision on the enforcement of the award and may also, on the application of the party claiming enforcement of the award, order the other party to give suitable security.

Article VII

A17–007 1. The provisions of the present Convention shall not affect the validity of multilateral or bilateral agreements concerning the recognition and enforcement of arbitral awards entered into by the Contracting States nor deprive any interested party of any right he may have to avail himself of an arbitral award in the manner and to the extent allowed by the law or the treaties of the country where such award is sought to be relied upon.

2. The Geneva Protocol on Arbitration Clauses of 1923 and the Geneva Convention on the Execution of Foreign Arbitral Awards of 1927 shall cease to have effect between Contracting States on their becoming bound and to the extent that they become bound, by this Convention.

Article VIII

A17–008 1. This Convention shall be open until 31 December 1958 for signature on behalf of any Member of the United Nations and also on behalf of any other State which is or hereafter becomes a member of any specialised agency of the United Nations, or which is or hereafter becomes a party to the Statute of the International Court of Justice, or any other State to which an invitation has been addressed by the General Assembly of the United Nations.

2. This Convention shall be ratified and the instrument of ratification shall be deposited with the Secretary-General of the United Nations.

Article IX

1. This Convention shall be open for accession to all States referred to in article VIII. **A17–009**
2. Accession shall be effected by the deposit of an instrument of accession with the Secretary-General of the United Nations.

Article X

1. Any State may, at the time of signature, ratification or accession, declare that this **A17–010** Convention shall extend to all or any of the territories for the international relations of which it is responsible. Such a declaration shall take effect when the convention enters into force for the State concerned.
2. At any time thereafter any such extension shall be made by notification addressed to the Secretary-General of the United Nations and shall take effect as from the ninetieth day after the day of receipt by the Secretary-General of the United Nations of this notification, or as from the date of entry into force of the Convention for the State concerned, whichever is the later.
3. With respect to those territories to which this Convention is not extended at the time of signature, ratification or accession, each State concerned shall consider the possibility of taking the necessary steps in order to extend the application of this Convention to such territories, subject, where necessary for constitutional reasons, to the consent of the Governments of such territories.

Article XI

In the case of a federal or non-unitary State, the following provisions shall apply: **A17–011**

(a) With respect to those articles of this Convention that come within the legislative jurisdiction of the federal authority, the obligations of the federal Government shall to this extent be the same as those of Contracting States which are not federal States;

(b) With respect to those articles of this Convention that come within the legislative jurisdiction of constituent states or provinces which are not, under the institutional system of the federation, bound to take legislative action, the federal Government shall bring such articles with a favourable recommendation to the notice of the appropriate authorities of constituent states or provinces at the earliest possible moment;

(c) A federal State Party to this Convention shall, at the request of any other Contracting State transmitted through the Secretary-General of the United Nations, supply a statement of the law and practice of the federation and its constituent units in regard to any particular provision of this Convention, showing the extent to which effect has been given to that provision by legislative or other action.

Article XII

A17–012 1. This Convention shall come into force on the ninetieth day following the date of deposit of the third instrument of ratification or accession.
2. For each State ratifying or acceeding [*sic*] to this Convention after the deposit of the third instrument of ratification or accession, this Convention shall enter into force on ninetieth day after deposit of such State of its instrument of ratification or accession.

Article XIII

A17–013 1. Any Contracting State may denounce this Convention by a written notification to the Secretary-General of the United Nations. Denunciation shall take effect one year after the date of receipt of the notification by the Secretary-General.
2. Any State which has made a declaration or notification under article X may, at any time thereafter, by notification to the Secretary-General of the United Nations, declare that this Convention shall cease to extend to the territory concerned one year after the date of the receipt of the notification by the Secretary-General.
3. This Convention shall continue to be applicable to arbitral awards in respect of which recognition or enforcement proceedings have been instituted before the denunciation takes effect.

Article XIV

A17–014 A Contracting State shall not be entitled to avail itself of the present Convention against other Contracting States except to the extent that it is itself bound to apply the Convention.

Article XV

A17–015 The Secretary-General of the United Nations shall notify the States contemplated in article VIII of the following:

(a) Signatures and ratifications in accordance with article VIII;

(b) Accessions in accordance with article IX;

(c) Declarations and notifications under articles I, X and XI;

(d) The date upon which this Convention enters into force in accordance with article XII;

(e) Denunciations and notifications in accordance with article XIII.

Article XVI

1. This Convention, of which the Chinese, English, French, Russian and Spanish texts **A17–016** shall be equally authentic, shall be deposited in the archives of the United Nations.

2. The Secretary-General of the United Nations shall transmit a certified copy of this Convention to the States contemplated in article VIII.

Note

1. The Convention went into force on 7 June 1959.

Appendix 3

INSTITUTIONAL RULES

AAA International Arbitration Rules[1]

(As Amended and Effective November 1, 2001)

Introduction

The world business community uses arbitration to resolve commercial disputes arising **A18–001** in the global marketplace. Supportive laws are in place. The New York Convention of 1958 has been widely adopted, providing a favorable legislative climate. Arbitration clauses are enforced. International commercial arbitration awards are recognized by national courts in most parts of the world, even more than foreign court judgments.

Arbitration institutions have been established in many countries to administer international cases. Many have entered into cooperative arrangements with the American Arbitration Association.

These International Arbitration Rules have been developed to encourage greater use of such services. By providing for arbitration under these rules, parties can avoid the uncertainty of having to petition a local court to resolve procedural impasses. These rules are intended to provide effective arbitration services to world business through the use of administered arbitration.

As the International Centre for Dispute Resolution (ICDR) is a division of the American Arbitration Association (AAA), parties can arbitrate future disputes under these rules by inserting either of the following clauses into their contracts:

> "Any controversy or claim arising out of or relating to this contract shall be determined by arbitration in accordance with the International Arbitration Rules of the International Centre for Dispute Resolution."

---

[1] Copyright: the American Arbitration Association 2001. Reprinted with permission of the American Arbitration Association.

or

"Any controversy or claim arising out of or relating to this contract shall be determined by arbitration in accordance with the International Arbitration Rules of the American Arbitration Association."

The parties may wish to consider adding:

(a) "The number of arbitrators shall be (one or three)";

(b) "The place of arbitration shall be (city and/or country)"; or

(c) "The language(s) of the arbitration shall be _____."

Parties are encouraged, when writing their contracts or when a dispute arises, to request a conference, in person or by telephone, with the ICDR, to discuss an appropriate method for selection of arbitrators or any other matter that might facilitate efficient arbitration of the dispute.

Under these rules, the parties are free to adopt any mutually agreeable procedure for appointing arbitrators, or may designate arbitrators upon whom they agree. Parties can reach agreements concerning appointing arbitrators either when writing their contracts or after a dispute has arisen. This flexible procedure permits parties to utilize whatever method they consider best suits their needs. For example, parties may choose to have a sole arbitrator or a tribunal of three or more. They may agree that arbitrators shall be appointed by the ICDR, or that each side shall designate one arbitrator and those two shall name a third, with the ICDR making appointments if the tribunal is not promptly formed by that procedure. Parties may mutually request the ICDR to submit to them a list of arbitrators from which each can delete names not acceptable to it, or the parties may instruct the ICDR to appoint arbitrators without the submission of lists, or may leave that matter to the sole discretion of the ICDR. Parties also may agree on a variety of other methods for establishing the tribunal. In any event, if parties are unable to agree on a procedure for appointing arbitrators or on the designation of arbitrators, the ICDR, after inviting consultation by the parties, will appoint the arbitrators. The rules thus provide for the fullest exercise of party autonomy, while assuring that the ICDR is available to act if the parties cannot reach mutual agreement.

Whenever a singular term is used in the rules, such as "party," "claimant" or "arbitrator," that term shall include the plural if there is more than one such entity.

Parties may choose to use the ICDR's mediation services. The ICDR can schedule the mediation for anywhere in the world and will propose a list of specialized international mediators.

Parties filing an international case with the American Arbitration Association's International Centre for Dispute Resolution may do so by contacting any one of the AAA's regional offices or by contacting the International Centre for Dispute Resolution's New York, N.Y. office which is supervised by multilingual attorneys and case managers who have the requisite expertise in international matters.

Further information about these rules can be secured by contacting the International Centre for Dispute Resolution at 888-855-9575.

AAA International Arbitration Rules

International Centre for Dispute Resolution

International Arbitration Rules

Article 1

1. Where parties have agreed in writing to arbitrate disputes under these International Arbitration Rules or have provided for arbitration of an international dispute by the International Centre for Dispute Resolution or the American Arbitration Association without designating particular rules, the arbitration shall take place in accordance with these rules, as in effect at the date of commencement of the arbitration, subject to whatever modifications the parties may adopt in writing.

2. These rules govern the arbitration, except that, where any such rule is in conflict with any provision of the law applicable to the arbitration from which the parties cannot derogate, that provision shall prevail.

3. These rules specify the duties and responsibilities of the administrator, the International Centre for Dispute Resolution, a division of the American Arbitration Association. The administrator may provide services through its Centre, located in New York City, or through the facilities of arbitral institutions with which it has agreements of cooperation.

I. Commencing the Arbitration

Notice of Arbitration and Statement of Claim

Article 2

1. The party initiating arbitration ("claimant") shall give written notice of arbitration to the administrator and at the same time to the party against whom a claim is being made ("respondent").

2. Arbitral proceedings shall be deemed to commence on the date on which the administrator receives the notice of arbitration.

3. The notice of arbitration shall contain a statement of claim including the following:

(a) a demand that the dispute be referred to arbitration;

(b) the names and addresses of the parties;

(c) a reference to the arbitration clause or agreement that is invoked;

(d) a reference to any contract out of or in relation to which the dispute arises;

(e) a description of the claim and an indication of the facts supporting it;

(f) the relief or remedy sought and the amount claimed; and

(g) may include proposals as to the means of designating and the number of arbitrators, the place of arbitration and the language (s) of the arbitration.

4. Upon receipt of the notice of arbitration, the administrator shall communicate with all parties with respect to the arbitration and shall acknowledge the commencement of the arbitration.

Statement of Defense and Counterclaim

Article 3

A18–004   1. Within 30 days after the commencement of the arbitration, a respondent shall submit a written statement of defense, responding to the issues raised in the notice of arbitration, to the claimant and any other parties, and to the administrator.

2. At the time a respondent submits its statement of defense, a respondent may make counterclaims or assert setoffs as to any claim covered by the agreement to arbitrate, as to which the claimant shall within 30 days submit a written statement of defense to the respondent and any other parties and to the administrator.

3. A respondent shall respond to the administrator, the claimant and other parties within 30 days after the commencement of the arbitration as to any proposals the claimant may have made as to the number of arbitrators, the place of the arbitration or the language(s) of the arbitration, except to the extent that the parties have previously agreed as to these matters.

4. The arbitral tribunal, or the administrator if the arbitral tribunal has not yet been formed, may extend any of the time limits established in this article if it considers such an extension justified.

Amendments to Claims

Article 4

A18–005   During the arbitral proceedings, any party may amend or supplement its claim, counterclaim or defense, unless the tribunal considers it inappropriate to allow such amendment or supplement because of the party's delay in making it, prejudice to the other parties or any other circumstances. A party may not amend or supplement a claim or counterclaim if the amendment or supplement would fall outside the scope of the agreement to arbitrate.

II. THE TRIBUNAL

Number of Arbitrators

Article 5

A18–006   If the parties have not agreed on the number of arbitrators, one arbitrator shall be appointed unless the administrator determines in its discretion that three arbitrators are appropriate because of the large size, complexity or other circumstances of the case.

Appointment of Arbitrators

Article 6

A18–007   1. The parties may mutually agree upon any procedure for appointing arbitrators and shall inform the administrator as to such procedure.

2. The parties may mutually designate arbitrators, with or without the assistance of the

administrator. When such designations are made, the parties shall notify the administrator so that notice of the appointment can be communicated to the arbitrators, together with a copy of these rules.

3. If within 45 days after the commencement of the arbitration, all of the parties have not mutually agreed on a procedure for appointing the arbitrator(s) or have not mutually agreed on the designation of the arbitrator(s), the administrator shall, at the written request of any party, appoint the arbitrator(s) and designate the presiding arbitrator. If all of the parties have mutually agreed upon a procedure for appointing the arbitrator(s), but all appointments have not been made within the time limits provided in that procedure, the administrator shall, at the written request of any party, perform all functions provided for in that procedure that remain to be performed.

4. In making such appointments, the administrator, after inviting consultation with the parties, shall endeavor to select suitable arbitrators. At the request of any party or on its own initiative, the administrator may appoint nationals of a country other than that of any of the parties.

5. Unless the parties have agreed otherwise no later than 45 days after the commencement of the arbitration, if the notice of arbitration names two or more claimants or two or more respondents, the administrator shall appoint all the arbitrators.

Impartiality and Independence of Arbitrators

Article 7

1. Arbitrators acting under these rules shall be impartial and independent. Prior to accepting appointment, a prospective arbitrator shall disclose to the administrator any circumstance likely to give rise to justifiable doubts as to the arbitrator's impartiality or independence. If, at any stage during the arbitration, new circumstances arise that may give rise to such doubts, an arbitrator shall promptly disclose such circumstances to the parties and to the administrator. Upon receipt of such information from an arbitrator or a party, the administrator shall communicate it to the other parties and to the tribunal. **A18–008**

2. No party or anyone acting on its behalf shall have any ex parte communication relating to the case with any arbitrator, or with any candidate for appointment as party-appointed arbitrator except to advise the candidate of the general nature of the controversy and of the anticipated proceedings and to discuss the candidate's qualifications, availability or independence in relation to the parties, or to discuss the suitability of candidates for selection as a third arbitrator where the parties or party-designated arbitrators are to participate in that selection. No party or anyone acting on its behalf shall have any ex parte communication relating to the case with any candidate for presiding arbitrator.

Challenge of Arbitrators

Article 8

1. A party may challenge any arbitrator whenever circumstances exist that give rise to justifiable doubts as to the arbitrator's impartiality or independence. A party wishing to challenge an arbitrator shall send notice of the challenge to the administrator within 15 days after being notified of the appointment of the arbitrator or within 15 days after the circumstances giving rise to the challenge become known to that party. **A18–009**

2. The challenge shall state in writing the reasons for the challenge.

3. Upon receipt of such a challenge, the administrator shall notify the other parties of the challenge. When an arbitrator has been challenged by one party, the other party or parties may agree to the acceptance of the challenge and, if there is agreement, the arbitrator shall withdraw. The challenged arbitrator may also withdraw from office in the absence of such agreement. In neither case does withdrawal imply acceptance of the validity of the grounds for the challenge.

Article 9

A18–010   If the other party or parties do not agree to the challenge or the challenged arbitrator does not withdraw, the administrator in its sole discretion shall make the decision on the challenge.

Replacement of an Arbitrator

Article 10

A18–011   If an arbitrator withdraws after a challenge, or the administrator sustains the challenge, or the administrator determines that there are sufficient reasons to accept the resignation of an arbitrator, or an arbitrator dies, a substitute arbitrator shall be appointed pursuant to the provisions of Article 6, unless the parties otherwise agree.

Article 11

A18–012   **1.** If an arbitrator on a three-person tribunal fails to participate in the arbitration for reasons other than those identified in Article 10, the two other arbitrators shall have the power in their sole discretion to continue the arbitration and to make any decision, ruling or award, notwithstanding the failure of the third arbitrator to participate. In determining whether to continue the arbitration or to render any decision, ruling or award without the participation of an arbitrator, the two other arbitrators shall take into account the stage of the arbitration, the reason, if any, expressed by the third arbitrator for such nonparticipation, and such other matters as they consider appropriate in the circumstances of the case. In the event that the two other arbitrators determine not to continue the arbitration without the participation of the third arbitrator, the administrator on proof satisfactory to it shall declare the office vacant, and a substitute arbitrator shall be appointed pursuant to the provisions of Article 6, unless the parties otherwise agree.

2. If a substitute arbitrator is appointed under either Article 10 or Article 11, the tribunal shall determine at its sole discretion whether all or part of any prior hearings shall be repeated.

III. GENERAL CONDITIONS

Representation

Article 12

A18–013   Any party may be represented in the arbitration. The names, addresses and telephone numbers of representatives shall be communicated in writing to the other parties and to

AAA International Arbitration Rules

the administrator. Once the tribunal has been established, the parties or their representatives may communicate in writing directly with the tribunal.

Place of Arbitration

Article 13

1. If the parties disagree as to the place of arbitration, the administrator may initially determine the place of arbitration, subject to the power of the tribunal to determine finally the place of arbitration within 60 days after its constitution. All such determinations shall be made having regard for the contentions of the parties and the circumstances of the arbitration. **A18–014**

2. The tribunal may hold conferences or hear witnesses or inspect property or documents at any place it deems appropriate. The parties shall be given sufficient written notice to enable them to be present at any such proceedings

Language

Article 14

If the parties have not agreed otherwise, the language(s) of the arbitration shall be that of the documents containing the arbitration agreement, subject to the power of the tribunal to determine otherwise based upon the contentions of the parties and the circumstances of the arbitration. The tribunal may order that any documents delivered in another language shall be accompanied by a translation into the language(s) of the arbitration. **A18–015**

Pleas as to Jurisdiction

Article 15

1. The tribunal shall have the power to rule on its own jurisdiction, including any objections with respect to the existence, scope or validity of the arbitration agreement. **A18–016**

2. The tribunal shall have the power to determine the existence or validity of a contract of which an arbitration clause forms a part. Such an arbitration clause shall be treated as an agreement independent of the other terms of the contract. A decision by the tribunal that the contract is null and void shall not for that reason alone render invalid the arbitration clause.

3. A party must object to the jurisdiction of the tribunal or to the arbitrability of a claim or counterclaim no later than the filing of the statement of defense, as provided in Article 3, to the claim or counterclaim that gives rise to the objection. The tribunal may rule on such objections as a preliminary matter or as part of the final award.

Conduct of the Arbitration

Article 16

1. Subject to these rules, the tribunal may conduct the arbitration in whatever manner it considers appropriate, provided that the parties are treated with equality and that each party has the right to be heard and is given a fair opportunity to present its case. **A18–017**

2. The tribunal, exercising its discretion, shall conduct the proceedings with a view to expediting the resolution of the dispute. It may conduct a preparatory conference with the parties for the purpose of organizing, scheduling and agreeing to procedures to expedite the subsequent proceedings.

3. The tribunal may in its discretion direct the order of proof, bifurcate proceedings, exclude cumulative or irrelevant testimony or other evidence, and direct the parties to focus their presentations on issues the decision of which could dispose of all or part of the case.

4. Documents or information supplied to the tribunal by one party shall at the same time be communicated by that party to the other party or parties.

Further Written Statements

Article 17

A18–018 1. The tribunal may decide whether the parties shall present any written statements in addition to statements of claims and counterclaims and statements of defense, and it shall fix the periods of time for submitting any such statements.

2. The periods of time fixed by the tribunal for the communication of such written statements should not exceed 45 days. However, the tribunal may extend such time limits if it considers such an extension justified.

Notices

Article 18

A18–019 1. Unless otherwise agreed by the parties or ordered by the tribunal, all notices, statements and written communications may be served on a party by air mail, air courier, facsimile transmission, telex, telegram, or other written forms of electronic communication addressed to the party or its representative at its last known address or by personal service.

2. For the purpose of calculating a period of time under these rules, such period shall begin to run on the day following the day when a notice, statement or written communication is received. If the last day of such period is an official holiday at the place received, the period is extended until the first business day which follows. Official holidays occurring during the running of the period of time are included in calculating the period.

Evidence

Article 19

A18–020 1. Each party shall have the burden of proving the facts relied on to support its claim or defense.

2. The tribunal may order a party to deliver to the tribunal and to the other parties a summary of the documents and other evidence which that party intends to present in support of its claim, counterclaim or defense.

3. At any time during the proceedings, the tribunal may order parties to produce other documents, exhibits or other evidence it deems necessary or appropriate.

Hearings

Article 20

1. The tribunal shall give the parties at least 30 days' advance notice of the date, time and place of the initial oral hearing. The tribunal shall give reasonable notice of subsequent hearings.

2. At least 15 days before the hearings, each party shall give the tribunal and the other parties the names and addresses of any witnesses it intends to present, the subject of their testimony and the languages in which such witnesses will give their testimony.

3. At the request of the tribunal or pursuant to mutual agreement of the parties, the administrator shall make arrangements for the interpretation of oral testimony or for a record of the hearing.

4. Hearings are private unless the parties agree otherwise or the law provides to the contrary. The tribunal may require any witness or witnesses to retire during the testimony of other witnesses. The tribunal may determine the manner in which witnesses are examined.

5. Evidence of witnesses may also be presented in the form of written statements signed by them.

6. The tribunal shall determine the admissibility, relevance, materiality and weight of the evidence offered by any party. The tribunal shall take into account applicable principles of legal privilege, such as those involving the confidentiality of communications between a lawyer and client.

Interim Measures of Protection

Article 21

1. At the request of any party, the tribunal may take whatever interim measures it deems necessary, including injunctive relief and measures for the protection or conservation of property.

2. Such interim measures may take the form of an interim award, and the tribunal may require security for the costs of such measures.

3. A request for interim measures addressed by a party to a judicial authority shall not be deemed incompatible with the agreement to arbitrate or a waiver of the right to arbitrate.

4. The tribunal may in its discretion apportion costs associated with applications for interim relief in any interim award or in the final award.

Experts

Article 22

1. The tribunal may appoint one or more independent experts to report to it, in writing, on specific issues designated by the tribunal and communicated to the parties.

2. The parties shall provide such an expert with any relevant information or produce for inspection any relevant documents or goods that the expert may require. Any dispute between a party and the expert as to the relevance of the requested information or goods shall be referred to the tribunal for decision.

3. Upon receipt of an expert's report, the tribunal shall send a copy of the report to all parties and shall give the parties an opportunity to express, in writing, their opinion on the report. A party may examine any document on which the expert has relied in such a report.

4. At the request of any party, the tribunal shall give the parties an opportunity to question the expert at a hearing. At this hearing, parties may present expert witnesses to testify on the points at issue.

Default

Article 23

A18–024 1. If a party fails to file a statement of defense within the time established by the tribunal without showing sufficient cause for such failure, as determined by the tribunal, the tribunal may proceed with the arbitration.

2. If a party, duly notified under these rules, fails to appear at a hearing without showing sufficient cause for such failure, as determined by the tribunal, the tribunal may proceed with the arbitration.

3. If a party, duly invited to produce evidence or take any other steps in the proceedings, fails to do so within the time established by the tribunal without showing sufficient cause for such failure, as determined by the tribunal, the tribunal may make the award on the evidence before it.

Closure of Hearing

Article 24

A18–025 1. After asking the parties if they have any further testimony or evidentiary submissions and upon receiving negative replies or if satisfied that the record is complete, the tribunal may declare the hearings closed.

2. The tribunal in its discretion, on its own motion or upon application of a party, may reopen the hearings at any time before the award is made.

Waiver of Rules

Article 25

A18–026 A party who knows that any provision of the rules or requirement under the rules has not been complied with, but proceeds with the arbitration without promptly stating an objection in writing thereto, shall be deemed to have waived the right to object.

Awards, Decisions and Rulings

Article 26

A18–027 1. When there is more than one arbitrator, any award, decision or ruling of the arbitral tribunal shall be made by a majority of the arbitrators. If any arbitrator fails to sign the award, it shall be accompanied by a statement of the reason for the absence of such signature.

2. When the parties or the tribunal so authorize, the presiding arbitrator may make decisions or rulings on questions of procedure, subject to revision by the tribunal.

Form and Effect of the Award

Article 27

1. Awards shall be made in writing, promptly by the tribunal, and shall be final and binding on the parties. The parties undertake to carry out any such award without delay.
2. The tribunal shall state the reasons upon which the award is based, unless the parties have agreed that no reasons need be given.
3. The award shall contain the date and the place where the award was made, which shall be the place designated pursuant to Article 13.
4. An award may be made public only with the consent of all parties or as required by law.
5. Copies of the award shall be communicated to the parties by the administrator.
6. If the arbitration law of the country where the award is made requires the award to be filed or registered, the tribunal shall comply with such requirement.
7. In addition to making a final award, the tribunal may make interim, interlocutory, or partial orders and awards.

Applicable Laws and Remedies

Article 28

1. The tribunal shall apply the substantive law(s) or rules of law designated by the parties as applicable to the dispute. Failing such a designation by the parties, the tribunal shall apply such law(s) or rules of law as it determines to be appropriate.
2. In arbitrations involving the application of contracts, the tribunal shall decide in accordance with the terms of the contract and shall take into account usages of the trade applicable to the contract.
3. The tribunal shall not decide as amiable compositeur or ex aequo et bono unless the parties have expressly authorized it to do so.
4. A monetary award shall be in the currency or currencies of the contract unless the tribunal considers another currency more appropriate, and the tribunal may award such pre-award and post-award interest, simple or compound, as it considers appropriate, taking into consideration the contract and applicable law.
5. Unless the parties agree otherwise, the parties expressly waive and forego any right to punitive, exemplary or similar damages unless a statute requires that compensatory damages be increased in a specified manner. This provision shall not apply to any award of arbitration costs to a party to compensate for dilatory or bad faith conduct in the arbitration.

Settlement or Other Reasons for Termination

Article 29

A18–030 1. If the parties settle the dispute before an award is made, the tribunal shall terminate the arbitration and, if requested by all parties, may record the settlement in the form of an award on agreed terms. The tribunal is not obliged to give reasons for such an award.

2. If the continuation of the proceedings becomes unnecessary or impossible for any other reason, the tribunal shall inform the parties of its intention to terminate the proceedings. The tribunal shall thereafter issue an order terminating the arbitration, unless a party raises justifiable grounds for objection.

Interpretation or Correction of the Award

Article 30

A18–031 1. Within 30 days after the receipt of an award, any party, with notice to the other parties, may request the tribunal to interpret the award or correct any clerical, typographical or computation errors or make an additional award as to claims presented but omitted from the award.

2. If the tribunal considers such a request justified, after considering the contentions of the parties, it shall comply with such a request within 30 days after the request.

Costs

Article 31

A18–032 The tribunal shall fix the costs of arbitration in its award. The tribunal may apportion such costs among the parties if it determines that such apportionment is reasonable, taking into account the circumstances of the case.

Such costs may include:

(a) the fees and expenses of the arbitrators;

(b) the costs of assistance required by the tribunal, including its experts;

(c) the fees and expenses of the administrator;

(d) the reasonable costs for legal representation of a successful party; and

(e) any such costs incurred in connection with an application for interim or emergency relief pursuant to Article 21.

Compensation of Arbitrators

Article 32

A18–033 Arbitrators shall be compensated based upon their amount of service, taking into account their stated rate of compensation and the size and complexity of the case. The administrator shall arrange an appropriate daily or hourly rate, based on such considerations, with the parties and with each of the arbitrators as soon as practicable after the commencement of the arbitration. If the parties fail to agree on the terms of compensation, the administrator shall establish an appropriate rate and communicate it in writing to the parties.

Deposit of Costs

Article 33

1. When a party files claims, the administrator may request the filing party to deposit appropriate amounts as an advance for the costs referred to in Article 31, paragraphs (a), (b) and (c).
2. During the course of the arbitral proceedings, the tribunal may request supplementary deposits from the parties.
3. If the deposits requested are not paid in full within 30 days after the receipt of the request, the administrator shall so inform the parties, in order that one or the other of them may make the required payment. If such payments are not made, the tribunal may order the suspension or termination of the proceedings.
4. After the award has been made, the administrator shall render an accounting to the parties of the deposits received and return any unexpended balance to the parties.

Confidentiality

Article 34

Confidential information disclosed during the proceedings by the parties or by witnesses shall not be divulged by an arbitrator or by the administrator. Unless otherwise agreed by the parties, or required by applicable law, the members of the tribunal and the administrator shall keep confidential all matters relating to the arbitration or the award.

Exclusion of Liability

Article 35

The members of the tribunal and the administrator shall not be liable to any party for any act or omission in connection with any arbitration conducted under these rules, except that they may be liable for the consequences of conscious and deliberate wrongdoing.

Interpretation of Rules

Article 36

The tribunal shall interpret and apply these rules insofar as they relate to its powers and duties. The administrator shall interpret and apply all other rules.

INSTITUTIONAL RULES

ADMINISTRATIVE FEES

A18–038 The administrative fees of the ICDR are based on the amount of the claim or counterclaim. Arbitrator compensation is not included in this schedule. Unless the parties agree otherwise, arbitrator compensation and administrative fees are subject to allocation by the arbitrator in the award.

Fees

A18–039 A nonrefundable initial filing fee is payable in full by a filing party when a claim, counterclaim or additional claim is filed.

A case service fee will be incurred for all cases that proceed to their first hearing. This fee will be payable in advance at the time that the first hearing is scheduled. This fee will be refunded at the conclusion of the case if no hearings have occurred.

However, if the administrator is not notified at least 24 hours before the time of the scheduled hearing, the case service fee will remain due and will not be refunded.

These fees will be billed in accordance with the following schedule:

Amount of Claim	Initial Filing Fee	Case Service Fee
Above $0 to $10,000	$500	N/A
Above $10,000 to $75,000	$750	N/A
Above $75,000 to $150,000	$1,250	$750
Above $150,000 to $300,000	$2,750	$1,000
Above $300,000 to $500,000	$4,250	$1,250
Above $500,000 to $1,000,000	$6,000	$2,000
Above $1,000,000 to $7,000,000	$8,500	$2,500
Above $7,000,000 to $10,000,000	$13,000	$3,000
Above $10,000,000	*	*
No Amount Stated**	$3,250	$750

*Contact the ICDR's New York office for fees for claims in excess of $10 million.
**This fee is applicable when no amount can be stated at the time of filing, or when a claim or counterclaim is not for a monetary amount. The fees are subject to increase or decrease when the claim or counterclaim is disclosed.

The minimum fees for any case having three or more arbitrators are $2,750 for the filing fee, plus a $1,000 case service fee.

Suspension for Nonpayment

A18–040 If arbitrator compensation or administrative charges have not been paid in full, the administrator may so inform the parties in order that one of them may advance the required payment. If such payments are not made, the tribunal may order the suspension or termination of the proceedings. If no arbitrator has yet been appointed, the ICDR may suspend the proceedings.

Hearing Room Rental

The fees described above do not cover the rental of hearing rooms, which are available on a rental basis. Check with the ICDR for availability and rates.

Rules, forms, procedures and guides, as well as information about applying for a fee reduction or deferral, are subject to periodic change and updating. To ensure that you have the most current information, see our Web site at www.adr.org.

International Centre for Dispute Resolution

1633 Broadway
Floor 10
New York, NY 10019-6708
1.212.484.4181
1.888.855.9575
aaainternational@adr.org

CEDR Rules for Adjudication[1]

Commencing adjudication and nomination of the Adjudicator

A19–001 1 A party to a contract (the "Referring Party") may at any time give notice (the "Notice") in writing to the other Party(ies) of its intention to refer a dispute arising under, out of, or in connection with, the contract to adjudication.
The Notice shall contain:

- names, addresses and full contact details of the Parties and of any representatives appointed by the Parties
- a copy of the relevant provisions of the contract providing for adjudication
- brief details of the dispute to be referred to adjudication
- details of remedy sought.

A copy of the Notice shall be sent by the Referring Party to the Adjudicator, if named in the contract, at the same time as it is sent to the other Party(ies). The Adjudicator shall, within 2 days of receiving the Notice, confirm in writing to the Parties that he or she is available to act.

2 If no Adjudicator is named in the contract, or if the named Adjudicator does not confirm his or her availability to act, then the Referring Party shall immediately apply to the Centre for Effective Dispute Resolution ("CEDR Solve") using CEDR Solve's application form to nominate an Adjudicator. CEDR Solve shall nominate an Adjudicator and communicate the nomination to all the Parties within 5 days of receipt of:

- the completed application form
- a copy of the Notice of Adjudication
- CEDR Solve's nomination fee.

3 The Adjudicator shall, within 24 hours of receipt of the nomination, confirm in writing to the Parties that he or she is available to act, whether in response to receiving the Notice or to a nomination by CEDR Solve. The Adjudicator shall provide to them, at the same time, a copy of the terms on which he or she is prepared to act including information regarding fees and expenses.

Conduct of the adjudication

A19–002 4 Within 7 days of the giving of the Notice, the Referring Party shall send to the Adjudicator, copied at the same time and by the same method to the other Party(ies), a concise statement of case which shall include:

- a copy of the Notice

---

[1] This document is reproduced with the kind permission of the copyright-holder, the Centre for Effective Dispute Resolution (CEDR). The CEDR Rules for Adjudication is one of the many model ADR documents from CEDR which can be found on their website at www.cedr.co.uk.

CEDR Rules for Adjudication

- a copy of the conditions of the contract and other provisions in the contract on which the Referring Party intends to rely
- details of the circumstances giving rise to the dispute
- the reasons for entitlement to the remedy sought
- the evidence, including relevant documentation, in support of its case.

5 Under these Rules the date of referral is the date on which both the Adjudicator and the other Party(ies) receive the concise statement of case from the Referring Party.

6 The Adjudicator shall reach a decision within 28 days of the date of referral. Subject to the Adjudicator's agreement, this period may be extended by 14 days with the consent of the Referring Party or longer if agreed by all the Parties.

7 The Adjudicator may take the initiative in ascertaining the facts and the law.

8 The Adjudicator shall establish the timetable and procedure for the adjudication which may include the consideration of:

- the extent, form and time limits applying to any documentary or oral submission of the Parties
- site visits or inspections
- meeting the Parties
- issuing particular directions
- the appointment of an Expert or Assessor subject to paragraph 13 of these rules.

9 Copies of all documents submitted by a Party to the Adjudicator shall be sent simultaneously and by the same method to the other Party(ies). Similarly, all documents issued by the Adjudicator shall be sent simultaneously to the Parties.

10 The Adjudicator shall not take into consideration any document or statement, whether of a Party or Witness, that has not been made available to the other Party(ies) for comment.

11 Any failure by any Party to respond to any request or direction by the Adjudicator shall not invalidate the adjudication or the Adjudicator's decision.

12 A party may at any time request additional Parties to be joined in the adjudication. Joinder of additional Parties shall be subject to the agreement of the Adjudicator, the existing Parties and additional Parties.

13 The Adjudicator may, at any time, obtain legal or technical advice on any matter provided that the Parties are informed with reasons beforehand. Prior to making the decision, the Adjudicator shall provide the Parties with copies of any written advice so obtained.

Decision of the Adjudicator

14 The Adjudicator shall decide the dispute acting impartially and in good faith. The Adjudicator shall have the power to open up, review and revise any certificate, decision, direction, instruction, notice, requirement or valuation made under the contract to which the dispute relates except where the contract precludes this. **A19–003**

15 The Adjudicator may decide any other matters which the Adjudicator determines should be taken into account in deciding the dispute.

16 The Adjudicator shall reach a decision and communicate the decision in writing to the Parties in accordance with the time limits in paragraph 6.

17 The Adjudicator shall give reasons with the decision unless the Parties agree to the contrary.

18 The Adjudicator may, on his or her own initiative or at the request of a Party made within 5 days of the date that the decision is communicated to the Parties, correct the decision in respect of any typographical or arithmetical error as a result of an accidental slip or omission.

19 The Adjudicator's decision shall be binding unless or until the dispute is finally determined by agreement, court proceedings or by reference to arbitration in accordance with the contract. Unless otherwise agreed by the Parties, the Court or the Arbitrator(s) shall not be bound by the Adjudicator's decision.

Enforcement

A19–004   20 The Parties shall implement the Adjudicator's decision without delay and shall be entitled to such relief or remedies as are set out in the decision.

21 Any payment to be made in accordance with the Adjudicator's decision shall be paid in full without the paying Party(ies) having a right of set-off, counterclaim or abatement.

Cost of the parties

A19–005   22 Each Party shall bear its own costs. The Adjudicator may not decide the Parties' legal and other costs arising out of or in connection with the adjudication unless the Parties otherwise agree.

Fees and expenses of the Adjudicator

A19–006   23 The Parties shall be jointly and severally responsible for the Adjudicator's fees and expenses including the fees and expenses of any legal or technical adviser instructed under paragraph 13.

24 In the decision, the Adjudicator shall have discretion to apportion liability with regard to the Adjudicator's fees and expenses referred to in paragraph 23.

Resignation of the Adjudicator

A19–007   25 The Adjudicator shall resign if:

- the dispute has already been referred to Adjudication and a decision has been made
- the Adjudicator is not competent to decide because the nature of the dispute is significantly different to the dispute referred in the Notice, or
- the Adjudicator becomes unable to give a decision in accordance with the timescales set out in paragraph 6.

26 The Adjudicator shall notify the Parties of his or her resignation in writing and the Parties shall be liable for the Adjudicator's fees and expenses up to the date of resignation in accordance with paragraph 23.

Mediation

A19–008   27 At any time before the issue of the Adjudicator's decision the Parties may agree to refer the dispute to mediation. In that case each Party shall notify the Adjudicator in writing and the adjudication shall be suspended. The time in which the Adjudicator must decide the dispute shall be extended by the period of suspension.

28 If the Parties are unable to agree a Mediator within 7 days from the date they agree to refer the dispute to mediation then any Party may apply to CEDR Solve to nominate the mediator.

29 The Adjudicator shall not act as the Mediator and shall not take part in any such mediation.

30 If the dispute is settled by mediation, the adjudication shall be at an end and the Parties shall promptly settle the Adjudicator's fees and expenses referred to in paragraph 23. If a settlement is not reached within 28 days from the date on which the Parties agree to refer the dispute to mediation, or if at any time a Party abandons the mediation, the adjudication shall recommence on written confirmation to the Parties by the Adjudicator that he or she is able to continue pursuant to a request in writing by any Party.

Other provisions

31 If at any time after the date of referral the Adjudicator is unable or unwilling to act or fails to reach a decision in accordance with the time limits in paragraph 6, a Party may apply to CEDR Solve to nominate a replacement Adjudicator. **A19–009**

32 The Adjudicator shall not be liable for anything done or omitted in the discharge of his or her functions unless the act or omission was in bad faith. The same immunity shall extend to CEDR Solve as the Adjudicator Nominating Body and any employee or agent of the Adjudicator or CEDR Solve.

33 The Adjudicator's decision may not be relied upon by third parties to whom the Adjudicator shall owe no duty of care.

Law

34 These rules shall be governed by English Law and under the jurisdiction of the English Courts. **A19–010**

The Chartered Institute of Arbitrators Arbitration Rules[1]

2000 EDITION (INCORPORATING THE SHORT FORM RULES)

For use in England Wales and Northern Ireland

A20–001   Where any agreement, submission or reference provides for arbitration under the Rules of the Chartered Institute of Arbitrators (the Institute), the parties shall be taken to have agreed that the arbitration shall be conducted in accordance with these Rules or any modified, amended or substituted Rules which the Institute may have adopted and which have come into effect before the commencement of that arbitration.

Article 1. Introductory

A20–002   **1.1** These Rules are intended to govern arbitrations under the Arbitration Act 1996 (the Act) and incorporate all the provisions of the Act (whether mandatory or non-mandatory) unless any such provision is non-mandatory and is expressly excluded or modified by these Rules or by the agreement of the parties.

1.2 The parties may not amend or modify these Rules or any procedure under them after the appointment of an arbitrator unless the arbitrator agrees to such amendment or modification.

1.3 All expressions used in these Rules which are also used in the Act have the same meaning as they do in the Act and any reference to a section number means the section of the Act having that number

Article 2. Commencement of the Arbitration

A20–003   **2.1** The arbitration shall be regarded as commenced in accordance with the provisions of section 14.

2.2 Any party wishing to commence an arbitration under these Rules (the Claimant) shall serve upon the other party (the Respondent) a written request for arbitration under these Rules (the arbitration notice) which shall include or be accompanied by:—

(a) the names and addresses of the parties to the arbitration;

(b) copies of the contractual documents (if any) in which the arbitration agreement is contained or under which the arbitration arises;

(c) a brief statement describing the nature and circumstances of the dispute and specifying the relief claimed;

(d) any proposal which the Claimant may have with regard to the identity, qualifications or number of arbitrators or the name of any Appointing Authority if such be needed;

(e) if the arbitration agreement provides for each party to appoint an arbitrator, the

---

[1] This document is reproduced with the kind permission of the copyright-holder, the Chartered Institute of Arbitrators.

name and address (and telephone and fax numbers and e-mail address if known) of the arbitrator appointed by the Claimant.

2.3 Within 14 days of the service of the arbitration notice the Respondent may serve upon the Claimant a response containing some or all of the following:—

(a) an admission or denial of all or any part of the claim;

(b) a brief statement of the nature and circumstances of any proposed counterclaim;

(c) confirmation or rejection of any proposals contained in the arbitration notice;

(d) if the arbitration agreement calls for each party to appoint an arbitrator, the name and address (and telephone and fax numbers and e-mail address if known) of the arbitrator appointed by the Respondent.

2.4 Failure to send a response or to include therein any of the matters referred to at Article 2.2 above shall not preclude the Respondent from denying any claim or raising any counterclaim in any Defence properly served subsequently in the arbitration, but failure to appoint an arbitrator within the 14 day period where each party is to appoint an arbitrator shall bring the provisions of section 17 into effect.

Article 3. Appointing Authority

3.1 The parties may agree to nominate an Appointing Authority, but if there is no such agreement the Appointing Authority shall be the President or a Vice President for the time being of the Institute.

A20–004

3.2 Any application to the Appointing Authority to act under the provisions of these Rules shall be accompanied by:—

(a) copies of the arbitration notice and any response or other related correspondence or documentation;

(b) confirmation that a copy of the application has been served upon the other party;

(c) particulars of any method of or criteria for selection of arbitrators agreed between the parties.

3.3 The Appointing Authority or the Institute if it is not the Appointing Authority may require payment of a fee by either or both parties for any services rendered under these Rules.

Article 4. Appointment of the Arbitrator

4.1 Any reference in these Rules to the arbitrator means and includes a sole arbitrator or all the arbitrators where two or more are appointed.

A20–005

4.2 The provisions of sections 15, 16 and 17 shall apply to the procedure for the appointment of the arbitrator but if no appointment is made under those provisions the arbitrator shall be appointed by the Appointing Authority on the application of either party.

4.3 Where a chairman is to be appointed (whether by agreement or under the provisions of section 15(2)) and no chairman has been appointed the chairman shall be appointed by the Appointing Authority on the application of either party.

4.4 If any arbitrator dies or is unable, or refuses, to act, the Appointing Authority will appoint another arbitrator on the application of either party or of the remaining arbitrators, if any.

4.5 In exercising or considering how to exercise any power of appointing an arbitrator under these Rules an Appointing Authority shall have due regard to any agreement of the parties as to the qualifications required of the arbitrator.

4.6 Arbitrators appointed under these Rules (whether or not appointed by the Institute) may be subject to monitoring, supervision or scrutiny by the Institute or by the Appointing Authority and by agreeing to arbitration under these Rules the parties agree that disclosure of documentation to the Institute or the Appointing Authority or any authorised representative of either of them for the purposes of such monitoring, supervision or scrutiny does not infringe any principle of confidentiality relating to the arbitration.

Article 5. Communications between Parties and the Arbitrator

5.1 When the Arbitrator sends any communication to one party he shall send a copy to the other party or parties.

5.2 Any communication sent by a party to the Arbitrator shall be copied by that party to the other party or parties and marked as having been so copied.

5.3 The addresses of the parties or their representatives for the purpose of communications during the course of the proceedings shall be as most recently notified to the arbitrator and the other party and the provisions of section 76 shall apply to all such communications.

5.4 With the agreement of the parties the arbitrator may appoint the Institute to act as arbitration administrator whether or not the Institute is the Appointing Authority under these Rules.

5.5 Where the Institute is so appointed all communications or notices in writing between a party and the arbitrator will be sent through the Institute and communications addressed to the arbitrator will be deemed to be received by him when received by the Institute.

Article 6. Arbitration Procedure

6.1 It shall be for the arbitrator to decide all procedural and evidential matters (including but not limited to the matters referred to in section 34(2)), subject to the right of the parties to agree any matter and subject also to Article 1.2 above.

6.2 Before making any application to the arbitrator for directions as to procedural or evidential matters a party must give the other party a reasonable opportunity (being not less than 14 days unless the Arbitrator directs otherwise) to agree the terms of the directions proposed and any agreement on directions must be communicated to the arbitrator promptly.

6.3 Where there is more than one arbitrator and a chairman has been appointed the chairman sitting alone may give directions on procedural or evidential matters after consulting the other arbitrators.

6.4 Any application for directions on procedural or evidential matters or response thereto must be accompanied by all such evidence or reasoned submissions as the applicant may consider appropriate in the circumstances or as directed by the arbitrator and the arbitrator may direct a time limit for making or responding to such applications.

6.5 Unless the arbitrator orders that a meeting shall take place or one is requested by the parties or either of them the arbitrator will give directions on any such application on receipt of the response thereto or, if there is no response, on expiry of the time allowed for such response or such other time as the arbitrator may direct.

Article 7. Powers of the Arbitrator

7.1 The arbitrator shall have all the powers given to an arbitrator by the Act (including, **A20–008** but limited as hereafter set out, those contained in section 35 (consolidation of proceedings and concurrent hearings) and 39 (provisional orders)).

7.2 In addition the arbitrator may limit the number of expert witnesses to be called by any party or may direct that no expert be called on any issue or issues or that expert evidence may be called only with the permission of the arbitrator.

7.3 Where the same arbitrator is appointed under these Rules in two or more arbitrations which appear to raise common issues of fact or law, whether or not involving the same parties, the arbitrator may direct that such two or more arbitrations or any specific claims or issues arising therein be consolidated or heard concurrently.

7.4 Where an arbitrator has ordered consolidation of proceedings or concurrent hearings he may give such further directions as are necessary or appropriate for the purposes of such consolidated proceedings or concurrent hearings and may exercise any powers given to him by these Rules or by the Act either separately or jointly in relation thereto

7.5 Where proceedings are consolidated the arbitrator will, unless the parties otherwise agree, deliver a consolidated award or awards in those proceedings which will be binding on all the parties thereto.

7.6 Where the arbitrator orders concurrent hearings the arbitrator will, unless the parties otherwise agree, deliver separate awards in each arbitration.

7.7 Where an arbitrator has ordered consolidation or concurrent hearings he may at any time revoke any orders so made and give such further orders or directions as may be appropriate for the separate hearing and determination of each arbitration.

7.8 The arbitrator has power to grant relief on a provisional basis in respect of the following matters:—

   (a) a provisional order for the payment of money or the disposition of property as between the parties;

   (b) a provisional order for interim payment on account of the costs of the arbitration;

   (c) a provisional order for the grant of any relief claimed in the arbitration.

7.9 The arbitrator may exercise the power of granting provisional relief set out in Article 7.8 above on the application of a party or of his own motion provided that he gives notice to all parties of his intention to do so and provides an opportunity to each party to make representations in respect thereof.

7.10 The arbitrator may order any money or property which is the subject of an order for provisional relief to be paid or delivered to a stakeholder on such terms as he considers appropriate.

7.11 An order for provisional relief may be confirmed, varied or revoked in whole or in part by the arbitrator who made it or any other arbitrator who may subsequently have jurisdiction over the dispute to which it relates.

Article 8. Form of Procedure

A20–009 8.1 Subject to the rights of the parties to agree to adopt a documents-only or some other simplified or expedited procedure (see the provisions of the First Schedule to these Rules) and subject to the arbitrator's right under section 41 to proceed in the absence of a party in default each party has the right to be heard before the arbitrator.

8.2 Unless the arbitrator otherwise directs the arbitration will proceed on the basis of pleadings exchanged as hereafter set out.

8.3 All pleadings should contain all allegations of fact or matters of opinion which it is intended to establish by evidence and set out all items of relief or other remedies sought together with the total value of all quantifiable sums claimed, and must be signed by or on behalf of the party advancing it. Where a Respondent denies any allegation (a) he must state his reasons for doing so; and (b) if he intends to put forward a different version of events from that given by the Claimant he must state his own version.

8.4 Parties may (i) include in any pleading statements of law or of evidence; (ii) give the name of any witnesses whom they propose to call; or (iii) attach or serve with any pleading a copy of any document which they consider necessary to their claim including any expert report, but are under no obligation to do any of these things.

8.5 Where a claim is based on a written agreement a copy of the contract or any documents constituting the agreement should be attached to or served with the Particulars of Claim.

8.6 Unless the arbitrator otherwise directs the parties will exchange pleadings as follows:—

- (a) Within 28 days of the receipt by the Claimant of the arbitrator's acceptance of the appointment the Claimant shall send to the arbitrator and to the other party Particulars of Claim;

- (b) Within 28 days of the receipt of the Particulars of Claim the Respondent will send to the arbitrator and to the other party a Defence but if no Defence is served within that time limit or such extended time limit as the arbitrator may allow then the Respondent will be debarred from serving a Defence and pleadings are deemed to be closed;

- (c) If the Respondent wishes to make any counterclaim then a Counterclaim shall be served with the Defence;

- (d) Within 28 days of the receipt of the Defence and Counterclaim (if any) the Claimant may send to the arbitrator and to the other party a Reply (and Defence to Counterclaim if any), but if no Defence to Counterclaim is served within that time limit or such extended time limit as the arbitrator may allow then the Claimant will be debarred from serving a Defence to Counterclaim and pleadings are deemed to be closed;

- (e) Within 14 days of the receipt of a Defence to Counterclaim (if any) the Respondent may send to the arbitrator and to the other party a Reply to Defence to Counterclaim and pleadings are closed on the expiry of that time limit or such extended time limit as the arbitrator may allow or on the service of a Reply to Defence to Counterclaim if sooner;

- (f) Any further pleadings may only be served with the leave of the Arbitrator;

- (g) When a party has been debarred from serving a Defence or Defence to Counterclaim under Article 8.5(b) or (d) above the other party or parties shall still be required to prove any allegations made in the Particulars of Claim or Counterclaim as the case may be.

8.7 Before or after close of pleadings the arbitrator may give detailed directions with any appropriate timetable for all further procedural steps in the arbitration, including (but not limited to) the following:—

  (a) Any amendment to, expansion of, summary of, or reproduction in some other format of, any pleading or any extension to or alteration of time limits for pleadings;

  (b) disclosure and production of documents as between the parties;

  (c) the exchange of statements of evidence of witnesses of fact;

  (d) the number and types of experts and exchange of their reports;

  (e) meetings between experts;

  (f) arrangements for any hearing;

  (g) the procedures to be adopted at any hearing;

  (h) any time limits to be imposed on the length of oral submissions or the examination or cross-examination of witnesses.

8.8 The arbitrator may at any time order any of the following to be delivered to him in writing:—

  (a) submissions to be advanced by or on behalf of any party;

  (b) questions intended to be put to any witness;

  (c) answers by any witness to identified questions.

Article 9. Awards

9.1 Any award shall be in writing, dated, and signed by the arbitrator (or, where there is more than one, all the arbitrators agreeing to the award), and shall contain sufficient reasons to show why the arbitrator has reached the decisions contained in it, unless the parties otherwise agree or the award is by consent.

9.2 The arbitrator may notify any award to the parties as a draft or proposal and may in his discretion consider any further submissions or proposals put to him by any party but subject to any time limit which he may impose.

9.3 Any award shall state the seat of the arbitration.

Article 10. Costs

10.1 The general Principle is that costs shall be paid by the losing party, but subject to the overriding discretion of the arbitrator as to which party will bear what proportion of the costs of the arbitration.

10.2 In the exercise of that discretion the arbitrator shall have regard to all the material circumstances, including such of the following as may be relevant:—

  (a) which of the issues raised in the arbitration has led to the incurring of substantial costs and which party succeeded in respect of such issues;

(b) whether any claim which succeeded was unreasonably exaggerated;

(c) the conduct of the party which succeeded on any claim and any concession made by the other party;

(d) the degree of success of each party;

(e) any admissible evidence of any offer of settlement or compromise made by any party.

10.3 In considering any admissible evidence of any offer of settlement or compromise by the Respondent (whether such offer was made before or after the commencement of the arbitration) the arbitrator shall normally follow the principle that a Claimant who is awarded the same as or less overall than was offered should recover the costs otherwise recoverable only up to the date when it was reasonable that the offer should have been accepted and the party making the offer should recover costs thereafter.

10.4 In considering any admissible evidence of any offer of settlement or compromise by the Claimant (whether such offer was made before or after the commencement of the arbitration) the arbitrator shall normally follow the principle that a Claimant who is awarded the same as or more than the sum at which he offered to settle or otherwise obtains a more advantageous award should recover his costs otherwise recoverable on an indemnity basis from the date when it was reasonable that the offer should have been accepted unless the arbitrator has good reason to depart from this principle.

Article 11. General

11.1 Any party may be represented by any one or more person or persons of their choice subject to such proof of authority as the arbitrator may require.

11.2 The arbitrator shall establish and record addresses and telephone numbers (including e-mail addresses or fax and telex numbers) of each party and their respective representatives.

11.3 Periods of time shall be reckoned as provided in section 78.

11.4 The parties shall inform the arbitrator promptly of any agreed settlement or compromise, and section 51 shall then apply thereto.

11.5 The parties shall inform the arbitrator promptly of any proposed application to the court and shall provide him with copies of all documentation intended to be used in any such application.

Article 12. Definitions

12.1 For the avoidance of doubt the following expressions have the following meanings:—

The Act	The Arbitration Act 1996 including any statutory modification or re-enactment thereof
Arbitration notice	the written notice which marks the commencement of the arbitration
Appointing Authority	the Authority specified under Article 3 hereof
Article	any article set out in these Rules
Claim	includes counterclaim
Claimant	includes counterclaimant
Concurrent hearing	any two or more arbitrations being heard together
Consolidation	any two or more arbitrations being treated as one

	proceeding
The Institute	The Chartered Institute of Arbitrators
Party	one of the parties to the arbitration
Provisional order	any order for provisional relief under section 39
Respondent	includes respondent to a counterclaim
Section	a section of the Act

12.2 In any event the provisions of the Interpretation Act 1978 apply hereto.

FIRST SCHEDULE

Short Form Procedure

Paragraph 1 Adoption of the Short Form Procedure

1.1 The parties may agree at any time prior to or during the course of the arbitration to adopt this Short Form Procedure, and in that event the Rules set out above shall be modified as hereafter provided;

1.2 Article 8 of the above Rules shall be deleted, and the alternative Article 8 set out in Paragraph 2 of this Schedule substituted.

Paragraph 2 Alternative Article 8

2.1 The arbitration will be conducted on a documents-only basis subject to the discretion of the Arbitrator to order an oral hearing in respect of any part (or the whole) of the arbitration, but in exercising that discretion the Arbitrator shall bear in mind his duties under section 33;

2.2 Unless the Arbitrator otherwise directs the arbitration will proceed on the basis of exchange of Statements of Case as hereafter set out;

2.3 All Statements of Case shall contain the following:—

(i) a full statement of the party's arguments of fact and law;

(ii) signed and dated statements of the evidence of any witness upon whose evidence the party relies;

(iii) copies of all documents the contents of which the party relies on;

(iv) a full statement of all relief or remedies claimed;

(v) detailed calculations of any sums claimed;

2.4 Unless the Arbitrator otherwise directs the parties will exchange Statements of Case as follows:—

(a) Within 28 days of the receipt by the Claimant of the Arbitrator's acceptance of the appointment the Claimant shall send to the Arbitrator and to the other party his Statement of Case;

(b) Within 28 days of the receipt of the Claimant's Statement of Case the Respondent will send to the Arbitrator and to the other party the Respondent's Statement of Case but if no Respondent's Statement of Case is served within that time limit or such extended time limit as the arbitrator may allow then the Respondent will be debarred from serving a Statement of Case and pleadings are deemed to be closed;

A20–014

A20–015

INSTITUTIONAL RULES

(c) If the Respondent wishes to make any counterclaim then his Statement of Case shall include that counterclaim;

(d) Within 28 days of the receipt of the Respondent's Statement of Case and Counterclaim (if any) the Claimant may send to the arbitrator and to the other party a further Statement of Case by way of Reply (and Defence to Counterclaim if any) but if no Reply is served within that time limit or such extended time limit as the arbitrator may allow the pleadings are deemed to be closed and if no Defence to Counterclaim is served then the Claimant will be debarred from serving a Defence to Counterclaim;

(e) Within 14 days of the receipt of a Statement of Case by way of Defence to Counterclaim (if any) the Respondent may send to the arbitrator and to the other party a further Statement of Case by way of Reply to Defence to Counterclaim and on the expiry of that time limit or such extended time limit as the arbitrator may allow or on the service of a Reply to Defence to Counterclaim if sooner pleadings are closed;

(f) When a Respondent or Claimant has been debarred from serving a Defence or Defence to Counterclaim under Article 2.4(b) or (d) above the other party or parties will still be required to prove any allegations made in his or their respective Statements of Case.

2.5 Before or after close of exchanges of Statements of Case the Arbitrator may give detailed directions with any appropriate timetable for all further procedural steps in the arbitration, including (but not limited to) the following:—

(a) Any amendment to, expansion of, summary of, or reproduction in some other format of, any Statement of Case or any extension to or alteration of time limits for service of Statements of Case;

(b) disclosure and production of documents as between the parties;

(c) the exchange of statements of evidence of witnesses of fact;

(d) the number and types of experts and exchange of their reports;

(e) meetings between experts;

(f) arrangements for any oral hearing if, in the exercise of his discretion he concludes that any oral hearing is necessary including any time limits to be imposed on the length of oral submissions or the examination or cross examination of witnesses.

2.6 The Arbitrator may at any time order any of the following to be delivered to him in writing:—

(a) submissions to be advanced by or on behalf of any party;

(b) questions intended to be put to any witness;

(c) answers by any witness to identified questions.

Paragraph 3 Rules of Evidence

A20–016   **3.1** In any arbitration under the Short Form Procedure the parties are deemed to have waived all rules and requirements in respect of the law relating to admissibility of evidence unless at any stage before publication of any award (whether or not the final or last award) any party notifies the Arbitrator in writing of that party's wish to withdraw such waiver.

3.2 In any event withdrawal of such waiver shall not take effect unless the Arbitrator in his absolute discretion consents thereto.

3.3 Before consenting to withdrawal of such waiver the Arbitrator shall permit the other party or parties to make such representations, whether orally or in writing, as he considers appropriate.

3.4 In the event of such withdrawal taking effect the Arbitrator shall give such directions, either in writing or by way of holding a preliminary meeting for the further conduct of the arbitration as he considers appropriate and may take into account the fact of the withdrawal of such waiver in considering the exercise of his discretion to award costs.

The Chartered Institute of Arbitrators Arbitration Scheme for the Travel Industry Rules[1]

(2001 Edition)

A21–001　This innovative Scheme has been developed to resolve consumer disputes within the travel industry. It is based upon the Consumer Dispute Resolution Scheme published by the Chartered Institute of Arbitrators ("the Institute"), in consultation with the Office of Fair Trading and the National Consumer Council.

1. Introduction and Scope of the Scheme

A21–002　**1.1** The Arbitration Scheme for the Travel Industry ("the Scheme") applies to claims for compensation sought in respect of disputes between members of the Association of British Travel Agents ("ABTA") and their customers. Where a contract exists claims may be made by or on behalf of any person named in the booking form or other contractual documents. In these Rules "customer" includes prospective customers of the ABTA member and includes all persons on whose behalf a claim is made.

1.2 These Rules apply to applications for arbitration received on or after 1st May 2001.

1.3 All claims for compensation under this Scheme must be made in pounds sterling only.

1.4 All claims made must be made in written English. Where video evidence is submitted any commentary must be in English.

1.5 Under the Scheme:

(a) Claims cannot be made where the amount claimed per person exceeds £5,000

(b) Claims cannot be made where the total amount claimed exceeds £15,000

(c) Any claims arising from the same booking will be consolidated and the limits in (a) and (b) above will apply.

1.6 The Scheme is not designed to deal with claims arising solely from personal injury or illness. The Scheme is designed to deal with claims for general compensation arising from breach of contract and/or negligence. However, if such a general compensation claim includes an element of minor illness or personal injury then this can also be considered by the Arbitrator, although for this specific element the Arbitrator cannot award more than £1,000 per person, such amount to be included within the total amounts allowable under the Scheme as set out in 1.5 above. The Scheme cannot be used for disputes concerning:

(a) Claims for compensation exceeding the limits above

(b) Serious personal injury, serious illness, nervous shock, death or the consequences of any of these other than as provided for above.

1.7 In considering the Parties' cases, the Arbitrator shall have regard to ABTA's Code

---

[1] This document is reproduced with the kind permission of the copyright-holder, the Chartered Institute of Arbitrators.

of Conduct. In the event of a conflict between a rule of law and a provision of the code, the interpretation most favourable to the customer shall prevail.

1.8 These Rules are designed primarily for arbitrations between two Parties, that is to say, between a travel agent or a tour operator and its customers. However, a customer may also apply for arbitration against both a travel agent and a tour operator.

1.9 The Claimant must confirm on the application form that every reasonable effort has been made to resolve the dispute through the Respondent's in-house complaints procedure.

2. Commencement of Arbitration Proceedings and Arbitration Procedure

2.1 The arbitration begins after the customer making the claim ("the Claimant") has signed and submitted an application form together with their full schedule and statement ("the Claim") to the Chartered Institute of Arbitrators ("the Institute"), in duplicate, accompanied by the appropriate registration fee. The application form is available from the Institute in hard copy or can be downloaded from the Institute's website at www.arbitrators.org. Specimen forms can also be downloaded from the ABTA website at www.abta.com.

2.2 The Claimant's application for arbitration must be received by the Institute within 9 months of completion of the return journey or of the events giving rise to the dispute, whichever the later. However, applications can still be made outside this time limit if the ABTA Member ("Respondent") agrees, but the ABTA Code does not require agreement from the Respondent.

2.3 The Claimants registration fees are charged on the scale set out in the application form. The Respondent is required to pay a separate fee direct to the Institute. But:

(a) Where two members of ABTA (for example, a travel agent and a tour operator) are joined in the same application, each shall pay half the fee

(b) Where the only Claimant is a child under the age of 12 at the date when the holiday was booked, a registration fee is payable by the person making the claim on that child's behalf.

2.4 Registration fees are non-returnable save for Rules 2.15 and 5.1.

2.5 Upon receipt of the application form, the schedule and Statement of Claim from the Claimant, the Institute will forward the documentation to the Respondent, giving the Respondent 21 days in which to submit to the Institute a Defence to Claim, in duplicate, accompanied by the signed application form and appropriate registration fees.

2.6 Upon receipt of the Respondent's Defence to Claim, the Institute will forward a copy of the Defence to Claim to the Claimant, who shall be given 7 days to submit final Comments on the Defence. The Comments on the Defence should not include any new claims, but simply reply to the Defence to Claim submitted, and shall be submitted in duplicate.

2.7 The Institute will send a copy of the Claimant's Comments on the Defence to the Respondent, who is not permitted to make any further comment without the express approval of the Arbitrator.

2.8 A single Arbitrator will then be appointed by the President or a Vice-President of the Institute. Subject to any Directions given by the Arbitrator, the arbitration procedure will be on documents only. The Arbitrators selected for appointment are Fellows of the Institute and all appointments are within the Institute's exclusive and unfettered control.

2.9 An award cannot be made for an amount of more than the amount claimed on the application form.

2.10 Payment ordered by an award must be made within 21 days of the date of the award, unless directed otherwise in the award. Payment of an award must be made directly between the Parties and not through the Arbitrator, the Institute or ABTA. Arbitration awards are directly enforceable through the courts. Enforcement is the Parties' responsibility and the Institute is unable to assist. Any queries concerning enforcement should in the first instance be addressed to ABTA.

2.11 Original documents will be returned to the Parties after six weeks have elapsed from the date of the award if requested by the Parties within this time, but only if a self-addressed envelope of suitable size and appropriate prepaid postage accompanies the request.

2.12 Arbitrator's may request the provision of any further documents, information or submissions that they consider would assist them in their decision. If these are not sent to the Institute or to the Arbitrator within the time prescribed, the Arbitrator will proceed on the basis only of the documents already before him.

2.13 Documents submitted by the Parties other than those contained within the Statement of Claim, the Defence to Claim or Comments on the Defence will not be admissible as of right but at the Arbitrator's sole discretion. Where a Party submits such documents, the Arbitrator will decide whether or not they are admissible. Where the documents are held to be admissible, the other Party will be sent copies and be entitled to comment on them before an award is made.

2.14 If a Respondent does not submit its Defence to Claim within the time allowed and does not send one within 14 days of a reminder by the Institute, the Arbitrator will be appointed and, subject to any Arbitrator's Directions given, the dispute will be decided by reference to the documents submitted by the Claimant.

2.15 If, in the Arbitrator's opinion (which shall be final), the dispute is not capable of proper resolution on documents only, the Arbitrator's appointment shall be revoked and the Parties registration fees will be reimbursed.

3. Content of Submissions for Arbitration

A21–004 **3.1** The Statement of Claim shall include:

> (a) A description of the claim made, which should not seek recovery for an amount above that stated upon the arbitration application form
>
> (b) All evidence that is available to support the claim, including, but not exclusively, complaints lodged prior to or during the holiday, or photographs, or a video taken during the holiday
>
> (c) All supporting documents and other evidence submitted in duplicate, or where there are two Respondents, in triplicate. Where videos are submitted the relevant extract shall be in VHS standard format, shall not exceed 15 minutes running time, but may include a commentary.

3.2 If the Claimant is unable to submit the documents which evidence the original contract or order, the Respondent shall submit a copy of such documents with the Defence.

3.3 The Defence to Claim should be in writing in the form defined for the Statement of Claim, i.e. in documentary form, in duplicate, and forwarded by post, and shall include;

(a) A copy of the booking conditions and the brochure, or advertisement from which the holiday was selected

(b) A copy of the signed booking form, where available

(c) A copy of the confirmation invoice, and any variations made to it

(d) What matters in the Claimant's documents are accepted or agreed

(e) What matters are disputed, with reasons why

(f) Any supporting documents relied on as evidence.

3.4 Comments on the Defence should be submitted on the prescribed form, in duplicate. The relevant Party may raise no new matters or points of claim at this stage in proceedings.

4. Powers of the Arbitrator

4.1 Any Arbitrator appointed shall be, and remain at all times during the arbitration, **A21–005** impartial and independent of the Parties and of ABTA, and shall decide the case in accordance with the relevant law.

4.2 Any Arbitrator should also act reasonably expeditiously, and in a way that provides a fair means for resolving the dispute.

4.3 The Arbitrator may, alternatively, in his/her absolute discretion, refuse to consider documents that are not submitted within timescales set down by these Rules.

4.4 When deciding on liability and amount of award, the Arbitrator must not take into account any offers of settlement that have been made by either Party, but it shall be open to the Arbitrator to have regard to such offers when awarding to any Party the reimbursement of the registration fee under Rule 5.1.

4.5 The Arbitrator shall have full jurisdiction to consider whether any claim made falls within his/her powers to determine, and, assuming such course is reasonable in all the circumstances, and having regard to cost, to request legal or expert assistance provided that the Parties should have had a full opportunity to comment upon such assistance.

4.6 Upon the application of the Claimant within the time limit in 2.2, the Arbitrator shall have the power to join a further party to the claim (provided that further party is an ABTA member) subject to an adjustment in the Respondent's fee as provided for in Rule 2.3(a).

4.7 The Arbitrator shall direct the procedure of the arbitration including the amendment of time limits and other procedural matters and have the power to:

(a) Allow submission of further evidence and the amendment of the Statement of Claim or Defence to Claim

(b) Order the Parties to produce goods, documents or property for inspection

(c) Conduct such enquiries as may be desirable

(d) Receive and take into account any relevant oral or written evidence

(e) Proceed with the arbitration if either Party:—

    (i) Fails to comply with these Rules or with any Direction or
    (ii) Fails, after receiving due notice, to attend any meeting or inspection ordered by the Arbitrator.

5. Costs

A21–006 **5.1** The maximum amount that may be awarded to either Party as recompense for costs expended in the arbitration shall be an amount equal to the Claimant's registration fee for the arbitration.

5.2 In exercising his/her discretion, the Arbitrator may have regard to offers made to settle the dispute prior to commencement of the arbitration.

5.3 No legal proceedings may be brought by one Party against the other for recovery of costs incurred during the arbitration, except as provided for in Rule 5.1 above.

5.4 The provisions for costs will not apply to any application for appeal against the Award.

5.5 Each Party shall bear its own costs of preparing and submitting its case (including legal costs). These shall include costs for preparing and submitting any subsequent application for Review, as specified in Rule 8.3.

6. Finality of the Award

A21–007 **6.1** Generally, the Award of the Arbitrator will be final and binding on both Parties, and any payments that the Arbitrator directs to be paid must be paid within 21 days of the date of the award.

6.2 If, however, either Party considers the Award is one that no reasonable Arbitrator should have reached on the basis of the documents presented, any payment ordered should still be made, but they may write requesting that the matter be referred to Review.

6.3 If no Application for Review is made within 21 days all Parties must comply with the terms of the original arbitration Award.

7. Review Procedures & Rules

A21–008 **7.1** Any Party to arbitration under this Scheme may appeal against the Award of the original Arbitrator. The Party requesting the Review is known as the "Appellant".

7.2 An Application for Review by the Appellant will only be considered if:

(a) The Institute receives it within 21 days of the date that the Award was dispatched to the Parties by the Institute.

(b) It is accompanied by a copy of the Arbitrator's Award together with a statement setting out the reasons why the Award is one that no reasonable Arbitrator should have reached on the basis of the documents presented.

(c) A cheque accompanies it for the sum of £300, made payable to *"The Chartered Institute of Arbitrators"*. This fee is known as the "Review Fee".

7.3 The Institute will acknowledge receipt of the Application for Review and will send the Appellant a "Review Request Form". The Institute will also notify the other Party or Parties ("the Review Respondent(s)") that the Application for Review has been made.

7.4 The Appellant shall return the completed Review Request Form to the Institute within 7 days together with additional copies of the form for each Review Respondent.

7.5 The Institute will send a copy of the Appellant's completed Review Request Form to the Review Respondent(s) who shall, within 14 days of receipt, send to the Institute a written response. The Institute will send a copy of each response to the Appellant and to every Review Respondent involved. No further representations shall be allowed except by leave of the Review Arbitrator.

7.6 The Institute shall appoint a sole senior Arbitrator (the "Review Arbitrator") to determine the dispute and shall notify the Parties of such appointment.

7.7 The Institute shall obtain from the original Arbitrator the documents submitted by the Parties to him/her and deliver those documents with a copy of the original Award to the Review Arbitrator. The Review Arbitrator shall not consider any new evidence presented by any Party in the Review and may either:

   (a) Confirm the original Award, or

   (b) Set aside the original Award in whole or part and substitute a new Award.

8. Costs of Review Procedure

8.1 The Appellant shall pay the Review Fee and shall not be entitled to recover this fee and no order shall be made in relation to this fee, regardless of the outcome of the Review.   **A21–009**

8.2 After the Review has been considered the Review Arbitrator shall also consider the costs order made under the original arbitration. In doing so, the Review Arbitrator may, within the absolute discretion exercised in accordance with Rules 5.1 and 5.2, order the reimbursement by one Party to the Review of any registration fee paid by any other Party.

8.3 Each Party shall bear its own costs of preparing and submitting its case for Review (including legal costs).

9. Miscellaneous Conditions of Review Procedure

9.1 The Rules relating to the conduct of arbitration at first instance shall apply to a Review except where such Rules are inconsistent with Rules 7 and 8.   **A21–010**

9.2 Once the Review Procedure has been completed, no further steps can be taken by any Party under these Rules. Any Party considering the possibility of an appeal to the courts, if indeed such an appeal is legally possible, is strongly advised to seek legal advice.

10. Confidentiality

10.1 No party involved in any arbitration under the Rules, or ABTA, the Institute or the Arbitrator, shall disclose explicit details of the proceedings, award, and reasons for the award to any stranger to the proceedings unless it is necessary to do so in order to enforce the Award.   **A21–011**

11. Miscellaneous

11.1 The law to apply (English, Scottish etc) shall be determined by the Arbitrator if the Parties fail to agree.   **A21–012**

11.2 The Institute reserves the right to appoint a substitute Arbitrator if the Arbitrator originally appointed dies, is incapacitated or is for any reason unable to deal expeditiously with the dispute. The Parties shall be notified of any substitution.

11.3 Awards made under the Scheme shall be final and binding on the Parties, subject to the conditions of the Review Procedure.

11.4 Subject to the right of either Party to request the Institute to draw the Arbitrator's attention to any accidental slip or omission which he/she has power to correct by law, neither the Institute nor the Arbitrator can enter into correspondence regarding an Award made under the Scheme.

11.5 Neither the Institute nor the Arbitrator shall be liable to any Party for any act or omission in connection with any arbitration conducted under these Rules, save that the Arbitrator (but not the Institute) shall be liable for any wrongdoing on his/her own part arising from bad faith.

Arbitration and ADR Dispute Resolution Procedures offered by the Chartered Institute of Arbitrators[1]

NON-CONSUMER OR COMMERCIAL DISPUTE RESOLUTION SCHEMES

Association of Newspapers & Magazine Wholesalers (2 schemes) **A22–001**

Chartered Institute of Housing

Chartered Institute of Arbitrators Commercial Arbitration Scheme (Includes Review Procedure)

Computer Software for Solicitors Arbitration Scheme

Esso Petroleum Limited

Federation of Engine Re-Manufacturers

Finance & Leasing Association (Commercial Mediation Scheme)

Honda Dealers (UK)

Institute of Field Archaeologists

Institute of Management Consultancy

Legal Services Commission

Meetings Industry Association

Musicians' Union (Mediation/Arbitration Scheme with Review Procedure)

National Association of Commercial Finance Brokers

Nationwide Football League

Park Home Pitch Fee

SAAB (GB)

Tile Association (Mediation/Arbitration Scheme with Review Procedure & Non-HGCRA Adjudication)

Timber Trade Federation

TotalFinaElf

JOINT CONSUMER AND COMMERCIAL DISPUTE RESOLUTION SCHEMES

British Institute of Architectural Technologists (Mediation & Arbitration **A22–002** Procedures)

British Wood Preserving & Damp proofing Association

---

[1] This document is reproduced with the kind permission of the copyright-holder, the Chartered Institute of Arbitrators.

Careers & Education Business Partnership

Coal Mining Subsidence (Statutory Regulations, 2 schemes)

National Approved Letting Scheme

National House-Building Council (2 schemes)

Recruitment & Employment Confederation (Mediation & Arbitration procedures)

Surveyors & Valuers Arbitration Scheme (2 schemes)

Consumer Dispute Resolution Schemes

Communications (Telecommunications & Postal Services)

A22–003

British Telecom

Consignia (formerly the Post Office)

Kingston Communications (Hull)

Manx Telecom

NTL

Page One

T-Mobile (formerly One2One)

Telewest

Orange

Vodafone

Construction, Building, Surveying & Architecture

Arbitration Scheme for the Flat Roofing Industry

British Blind & Shutter Association

Building Guarantee Scheme

Door & Shutter Manufacturers Association

Heating & Ventilation Contractors Association

Tile Association

E-Commerce

Ford Journey Dispute Resolution Procedure (Online Dispute Resolution procedure)

Web Trader (Online Dispute Resolution procedure)

Funeral Services

National Association of Funeral Directors (Conciliation/Arbitration with Review Procedure)

ARBITRATION AND ADR DISPUTE RESOLUTION PROCEDURES

>National Society of Allied & Independent Funeral Directors (Conciliation/Arbitration with Review Procedure)

Financial Services
> British Cheque Cashers Association
>
> Consumer Credit Trade Association
>
> Finance & Leasing Association
>
> Mortgage Code Arbitration Scheme

Glass & Plastics
> Glass & Glazing Federation
>
> Incorporation of Plastic Window Fabricators & Installers Limited and Craftsmans Guarantee Corporation
>
> Network VEKA

Household
> Association of Manufacturers of Domestic Appliances
>
> British Association of Removers

Insurance
> AON Home Assistance (formerly AA Home Assistance)
>
> Denplan

Leaseholder
> Brent Council Leaseholder Dispute Resolution Scheme (includes conciliation and arbitration)
>
> Tower Hamlets Leaseholders Dispute Resolution Scheme
>
> Waltham Forest Leaseholder Dispute Resolution Scheme (includes conciliation and arbitration)

Leisure/Travel
> Arbitration Scheme for the Travel Industry (includes Online Dispute Resolution and Review Procedure)
>
> Direct Holidays (Includes Review Procedure)
>
> Holiday Caravan Pitch Fee
>
> Holiday Caravan Arbitration Scheme
>
> Land Rover Adventure Holidays
>
> Passenger Shipping Association
>
> Peepul Ltd (t/a India Travel Direct)

Saga Holidays (Includes Review Procedure)

Seychelles Travel

The Mediterranean Experience

Miscellaneous Consumer Services

Chartered Institute of Arbitrators Consumer Dispute Resolution Scheme (Conciliation/Arbitration)

European Extra-Judicial Network Dispute Resolution Scheme

Mail Order Traders Association

Transport

Virgin Trains

Water

Dwr Cymru (Welsh Water)

Northumbrian Water

Other

The Chartered Institute of Arbitrators also

- Nominates arbitrators, adjudicators, mediators, evaluators, experts (for determination or witness) for party appointment
- Appoints the above where the Chartered Institute of Arbitrators is named as the appointing body within a contract, or where the parties agree to refer the matter to the President of the Chartered Institute of Arbitrators

MEDIATION

A22–004   The Chartered Institute of Arbitrators has a Panel of Civil & Commercial Mediators available for scheme, Presidential or party appointment.

It also administers several Med/Arb Schemes for consumer and commercial disputes (above).

ADJUDICATION

A22–005   The Chartered Institute of Arbitrators, as an Adjudicator Nominating Body, is responsible for nominating adjudicators to resolve disputes within 28 days from nomination under the terms of the Housing Grants Construction & Regeneration Act 1996 (Part Two).

Training & Accommodation

The Chartered Institute of Arbitrators provides training for professionals and those interested in dispute resolution, and has three suites of modern, fully equipped rooms suitable for meetings, hearings, seminars and small conferences. **A22–006**

For further information on any of the above, please refer to www.arbitrators.org

The Chartered Institute of Arbitrators Commercial Arbitration Scheme[1]

(2000 Edition)

A23–001 Where any agreement, submission or reference provides for arbitration under the Rules of the Commercial Arbitration Scheme (the Scheme), the Parties shall be taken to have agreed that the arbitration shall be conducted in accordance with these Rules or any modified, amended or substituted Rules which have come into effect before the commencement of that arbitration.

1. Introductory

A23–002 **1.1** These Rules are intended to govern arbitrations under the Rules of the Chartered Institute of Arbitrators' Commercial Arbitration Scheme, in conjunction with the Arbitration Act 1996 (the Act) and incorporate all the provisions of the Act (whether mandatory or non-mandatory) except for any provision that is not mandatory under the Act and is expressly excluded or modified by these Rules or by the agreement of the Parties.

1.2 These Rules are Institutional Rules for the purposes of section 4(3) of the Act.

1.3 The Parties may not amend or modify these Rules or any procedure under them after the appointment of an Arbitrator unless the Arbitrator agrees to such amendment or modification.

1.4 All expressions used in these Rules, which are also used in the Act, have the same meaning as they do in the Act.

2. Commencement of the Arbitration

A23–003 **2.1** The arbitration shall be regarded as commenced in accordance with the provisions of section 14 of the Act.

2.2 Any Party wishing to commence an arbitration under these Rules (the Claimant) shall serve on the Chartered Institute of Arbitrators ("the Institute"), using the prescribed form (the Arbitration Notice) with a copy to the other Party, a written request for arbitration under these Rules accompanied by:—

(a) The names, addresses, telephone and fax numbers and email addresses of the Parties to the arbitration;

(b) Copies of the Contractual documents (if any) in which the arbitration agreement is contained or under which the arbitration arises, or an agreement signed by all the Parties that the matter(s) in dispute should be referred to arbitration under these Rules;

(c) A brief statement describing the nature and circumstances of the dispute and specifying the relief claimed.

3. Appointing Authority/Appointment of the Arbitrator

A23–004 **3.1** The Appointing Authority under these Rules will be the Chartered Institute of Arbitrators.

---

[1] This document is reproduced with the kind permission of the copyright-holder, the Chartered Institute of Arbitrators.

The ciarb Rules of the Mortgage Code Arbitration Scheme

3.2 Upon receipt of the Arbitration Notice on the prescribed form, the President or a Vice-President of the Institute will appoint a suitable Arbitrator having due regard to any agreement between the Parties as to the qualifications required of the Arbitrator.

3.3 Upon receipt of the Arbitration Notice on the prescribed form, the Institute will also expect to have received from the Claimant the following:

(a) The names and addresses of all Parties to the arbitration;

(b) A brief statement of the nature and circumstances of the dispute(s);

(c) A copy of the arbitration clause in the Contract or agreement signed by all the Parties that the dispute(s) should be referred to arbitration;

(d) The appropriate fee;

(e) Confirmation that any conditions precedent to arbitration contained in the Contract or arbitration agreement have been complied with; and

(f) Any other relevant document.

3.4 Arbitrators appointed under these Rules may be subject to monitoring, supervision or scrutiny by the Institute, and by agreeing to arbitration under these Rules the Parties agree that disclosure of documentation, including any Award, to the Institute for the purposes of such monitoring, supervision or scrutiny does not infringe any principle of confidentiality relating to the arbitration.

3.5 If the Arbitrator dies or is unable, or refuses, to act, the Institute will appoint another Arbitrator on the application of any of the Parties.

4. Communications between Parties and the Arbitrator

4.1 When the Arbitrator sends any communication to one Party he shall send a copy to the other Party or Parties.

4.2 Any communication sent by a Party to the Institute prior to the Arbitrator's appointment, or to the Arbitrator once appointed, shall be copied by that Party to the other Party or Parties and marked as having been so copied.

4.3 The address of a Party or their representatives for the purpose of communications during the course of the proceedings shall be as most recently notified to the Arbitrator and the other Party or Parties and the provisions of section 76 of the Act shall apply.

4.4 The Institute shall act as administrator for the arbitration until the point where the Arbitrator is appointed. All communications or notices in writing between the Parties and the Institute prior to the Arbitrator's appointment will be forwarded by the Institute to the Arbitrator, and shall be deemed to be received by him at the time of his appointment by the Institute.

5. Arbitration Procedures

5.1 It shall be for the Arbitrator to decide all procedural and evidential matters (including but not limited to the matters referred to in section 34(2) of the Act), subject to Article 1.3 above. In deciding procedural matters the Arbitrator and the Parties may by consent take in to account the Institute's IT Protocol.

5.2 Before making any application to the Arbitrator for directions as to procedural or evidential matters a Party must give the other Party a reasonable opportunity (being not less than 15 days unless the Arbitrator otherwise directs) to agree the terms of the directions proposed. Any proposed agreement on directions must be communicated to the Arbitrator for his approval/consideration.

5.3 Any application for directions on procedural or evidential matters or response thereto must be accompanied by all such evidence or reasoned submissions as the applicant may consider appropriate in the circumstances or as directed by the Arbitrator and the Arbitrator may determine time limits for making or responding to such applications.

5.4 If in the event the Arbitrator orders that a meeting shall take place or if one is requested by one or each of Parties and the Arbitrator accedes to that request, the Arbitrator will give directions on the format and procedure for such a meeting.

6. Powers of the Arbitrator

A23–007   **6.1** The Arbitrator shall have all the powers given to an Arbitrator by the Act, including, those contained in section 35 (consolidation of proceedings and concurrent hearings) and section 39 (provisional orders).

6.2 The Arbitrator may limit the number of expert witnesses to be called by any Party or may direct that no expert be called on any issue or issues or that expert evidence may be called only with the permission of the Arbitrator.

6.3 Where the same Arbitrator is appointed under these Rules in two or more arbitrations which appear to raise common issues of fact or law, and at least one of the Parties is common to all the arbitrations, the Arbitrator may direct that such two or more arbitrations or any specific claims or issues arising therein be consolidated or heard concurrently.

6.4 Where an Arbitrator has ordered consolidation of proceedings or concurrent hearings he may give such further directions as are necessary or appropriate for the purposes of such consolidated proceedings or concurrent hearings and may exercise any powers given to him by these Rules or by the Act either separately or jointly in relation thereto.

6.5 Where proceedings are consolidated the Arbitrator will, unless the Parties otherwise agree, deliver a consolidated Award or Awards in those proceedings which will be binding on all the Parties thereto.

6.6 Where the Arbitrator orders concurrent hearings the Arbitrator will, unless the Parties otherwise agree, deliver separate Awards in each arbitration.

6.7 Where an Arbitrator has ordered consolidation or concurrent hearings he may at any time revoke any orders previously made and give such further orders or directions as may be appropriate for the separate hearing and determination of each arbitration.

6.8 The Arbitrator has power to grant relief on a provisional basis in respect of the following matters:—

(a) A provisional order for the payment of money or the disposition of property as between the Parties;

(b) A provisional order for interim payment on account of the costs of the arbitration;

(c) A provisional order for the grant of any relief claimed in the arbitration.

6.9 The Arbitrator may exercise the power of granting provisional relief set out in Article 6.8 above on the application of a Party or on his own volition provided that he gives an opportunity to each Party to make representations in respect thereof.

6.10 The Arbitrator may order any money or property that is the subject of an order for provisional relief to be paid or delivered to a stakeholder on such terms as he considers appropriate.

The CIArb RULES OF THE MORTGAGE CODE ARBITRATION SCHEME

6.11 An order for provisional relief may be confirmed, varied or revoked in whole or in part at any time by the Arbitrator who made it or by any other Arbitrator who may subsequently have jurisdiction over the dispute to which it relates.

7. Form of Procedure

7.1 Subject to the rights of the Parties to agree to adopt a documents-only or some **A23–008** other simplified or expedited procedure (see the provisions of the First Schedule to these Rules) and subject to the Arbitrator's right under section 41 to proceed in the absence of a Party in default each Party has the right to be heard before the Arbitrator.

7.2 Unless the Arbitrator otherwise directs the arbitration will proceed on the basis of statements exchanged as hereinafter set out.

7.3 Statements should contain all allegations of fact or matters of opinion which it is intended to establish by evidence and set out all items of relief or other remedies sought together with the total value of all quantifiable sums claimed, and must be signed by or on behalf of the Party submitting the statement. Where a Party denies any allegation it must state the reasons for doing so and provide its own version.

7.4 Parties should include in any Statements:—

(a) Details of the specific Acts or case law which they intend to cite;

(b) The names and statements of any witnesses of fact;

(c) Copies of any other documents that they consider necessary to their claim(s) including any experts' reports.

7.5 Where a claim is based on a written agreement a copy of the Contract or any documents constituting the agreement should be attached to or served with the Statement of Claim.

7.6 Unless the Arbitrator otherwise directs, the Parties will exchange statements as follows:—

(a) Within 28 days of the receipt by the Claimant of the Arbitrator's acceptance of the appointment the Claimant shall send to the Arbitrator and the Respondent its Statement of Claim;

(b) The Respondent shall within 28 days from receipt of the Statement of Claim send to the Arbitrator and to the Claimant a Statement of Defence. If no Statement of Defence is served within that time limit or such extended time limit as the Arbitrator may allow then the Respondent will be debarred from serving a Statement of Defence or having one considered;

(c) If the Respondent wishes to make any counterclaim then a Statement of Counterclaim shall be served with the Statement of Defence;

(d) The Claimant shall within 28 days from receipt of the Statement(s) of Defence and Counterclaim (if any) send to the Arbitrator and to the Respondent a Reply (and Statement of Defence to Counterclaim if any). If neither reply, nor a Statement of Defence to Counterclaim is served within that time limit or such extended time limit as the Arbitrator may allow then the Claimant will be debarred from serving a Reply or Statement of Defence to Counterclaim as the case may be;

(e) The Respondent shall within 14 days send to the Arbitrator and to the Claimant a Reply to the Statement of the Defence to Counterclaim. If no reply is served within that time limit or such extended time limit as the Arbitrator may allow, then the Respondent will be debarred from serving a Reply;

(f) Any further Statements may only be served with the leave of the Arbitrator;

(g) When a Party has been debarred from serving a Statement of Defence or Statement of Defence to Counterclaim, or Reply thereto, under Article 7.6(b), 7.6(d) or 7.6(e) above, the other Party or Parties shall still be required to prove any allegations made in the Statements of Claim or Counterclaim as the case may be.

7.7 At any time, the Arbitrator may give detailed directions with any appropriate timetable for all further procedural steps in the arbitration, including (but not limited to) the following:—

(a) Any amendment to, expansion of, summary of, or reproduction in some other format of any statement or any extension to or alteration of time limits for statements;

(b) Disclosure and production of documents between the Parties;

(c) The exchange of statements of evidence of witnesses of fact;

(d) The number and types of expert and exchange of their reports;

(e) Meetings between experts;

(f) Arrangements for any hearing;

(g) The procedures to be adopted at any hearing;

(h) Any time limits to be imposed on the length of oral submissions or the examination or cross-examination of witnesses.

7.8 The Arbitrator may at any time order any of the following to be delivered to him in writing:—

(a) Submissions to be advanced by or on behalf of any Party;

(b) Questions intended to be put to any witness;

(c) Answers by any witness to written questions.

8. Awards

8.1 Any Award shall be in writing, dated, and signed by the Arbitrator, and shall contain sufficient reasons to show why the Arbitrator has reached the decisions contained in it, unless the Parties otherwise agree or the Award is by consent.

8.2 In the first instance, the Arbitrator may submit an Award or a proposal to the Parties in draft form and may in his discretion consider any further written submissions or proposals put to him by any Party but subject to any time limit that he may impose.

8.3 Any Award shall state the seat of the arbitration.

THE CIARB RULES OF THE MORTGAGE CODE ARBITRATION SCHEME

9. Costs

9.1 The Arbitrator in his Award shall deal with the costs of the arbitration, which shall cover the Institute's fees and expenses, the Arbitrator's fees and expenses, and the legal or other costs of the Parties.

A23–010

9.2 The costs of the arbitration as far as the Institute and the Arbitrator are concerned, are in accordance with the table below. In addition, the Arbitrator in his Award will deal with the Parties' own costs:

LEVEL OF CLAIM	CIARB	ARBITRATOR
Total claim of £100,000 or less	Institute's fees and expenses of £300 + VAT payable by the Parties, with the application for arbitration.	Subject to Rule 9.3, the loser is responsible for the Arbitrator's fees, which are set at £70 per hour, plus VAT (if applicable), plus reasonable travel and out-of-pocket expenses.
Total claim of £100,001 up to £250,000	Institute's fees and expenses of £300 + VAT payable by the Parties, with the application for arbitration.	Subject to Rule 9.3, the loser is responsible for the Arbitrator's fees, which are set at £95 per hour, plus VAT (if applicable), plus reasonable travel and out-of-pocket expenses.
Total claim in excess of £250,001	Institute's fees and expenses of £300 + VAT payable by the Parties, with the application for arbitration.	Subject to Rule 9.3, the loser is responsible for the Arbitrator's fees, which are set at £120 per hour, plus VAT (if applicable), plus reasonable travel and out-of-pocket expenses.

9.3 The general principle is that the losing Party shall pay costs, but the Arbitrator has an overriding discretion to decide whether or not to apportion the costs of the arbitration in some other manner. In any exercise of his discretion the Arbitrator shall have regard to all the material circumstances, including such of the following as may be relevant:—

(a) Which (if any) of the issues raised in the arbitration has led to the incurring of substantial costs and which Party succeeded in respect of such issues;

(b) Whether any claim which succeeded was unreasonably exaggerated;

(c) The conduct of the Party which succeeded with any claim(s) and any concession(s) made by the other Party;

(d) The degree of success of each Party;

(e) Any admissible evidence of any offer or settlement or compromise made by any Party.

9.4 In considering any admissible evidence of any offer of settlement or compromise by any Party (whether such offer was made before or after the commencement of the arbitration) the Arbitrator shall normally follow the principle that a Party who is Awarded the same as or less than was offered overall or for any specific issue should recover the costs otherwise recoverable only up to the date when it was reasonable that such offer should have been accepted and the Party making the offer should recover its costs thereafter with respect to any matters covered by such offer.

10. Review of Award

A23–011   **10.1** The Arbitrator has the discretion if an application is made by either Party within 28 days of the date of the Award to:—

(a) Correct the Award so as to remove a clerical mistake or error arising from an accidental slip or omission or clarify or remove any ambiguity in the Award, or

(b) Make an additional Award in respect of any claim or counterclaim (including one for interest or costs), which was presented to the Arbitrator but was not dealt with in the Award.

10.2 Before exercising the discretion given in paragraph 10.1, the Arbitrator will give the other Party or Parties a reasonable opportunity to make representations on the application.

10.3 The Arbitrator shall make any necessary correction of Award within 28 days of the receipt of the application, whilst any additional Award will be made within 56 days of the receipt of such an application.

11. Appeal against Award to Appeal Tribunal

A23–012   **11.1** Any Party may Appeal the Arbitrator's Award subject to the following provisions:—

(a) The Applicant must have exhausted the Review of Award mechanism (if applicable) as provided by paragraph 10

(b) The Appeal must be made within 28 days of the date of Award or of the date of notification of the result of the review mechanism paragraph 10, which will be deemed for this purpose to be the date of publication of the Award

(c) An Appeal can only be made on a point of law and/or on the grounds that based on the findings of fact in the Award the decision of the Arbitrator is obviously wrong and/or on the grounds that there has been a serious irregularity affecting the Arbitrator, the proceedings or the Award.

11.2 The Party making the Appeal must deliver to the Institute five copies of the Appeal documents giving full and precise details of the point(s) of law and/or the grounds upon which the decision of the Arbitrator is obviously wrong having regard to the findings of fact in the Award and/or the grounds upon which it is alleged that there has been a serious irregularity affecting the Arbitrator, the proceedings or the Award.

11.3 On receipt of an Appeal the President or a Vice-President of the Institute will appoint an Appeal Tribunal of three Arbitrators one of whom will be a lawyer, who will Chair the Tribunal.

The CIArb Rules of the Mortgage Code Arbitration Scheme

11.4 The Appeal Tribunal will send to the other Party a copy of the Appeal document and allow them a reasonable period of time to submit a reply.

11.5 The Appeal Tribunal shall determine the Appeal without a hearing and shall have the power to:—

(a) Confirm the Award, or

(b) Set aside the Award in whole or in part and substitute a new Award

12. Costs of Appeal-To-Appeal Tribunal

12.1 The Party making the Appeal shall pay a registration fee of £500 plus VAT and a payment of £5,000 plus VAT as security for costs for the Appeal Tribunal.   **A23–013**

12.2 The Appeal Tribunal may make an Award allocating the costs of the Appeal as between the Parties but shall Award costs on the general principle that costs should follow the event. The recoverable costs of the Appeal shall be determined on the basis of a reasonable amount of costs reasonably incurred.

13. General

13.1 Any Party may be represented by any person or persons of their choice subject to such proof of authority as the Arbitrator may require.   **A23–014**

13.2 The Arbitrator shall establish and record the addresses telephone and fax numbers and e-mail addresses of each Party and their respective representatives.

13.3 Periods of time shall be reckoned as provided in section 78 of the Act.

13.4 The Parties shall inform the Arbitrator promptly of any agreed settlement or compromise, and section 51 of the Act shall then apply thereto.

13.5 The Parties shall inform the Arbitrator promptly of any proposed application to the court and shall provide him with copies of all documentation intended to be used in any such application.

14. Definitions

14.1 For the avoidance of doubt the following expressions have the following meanings:—   **A23–015**

The Act	The Arbitration Act 1996 including any statutory modification or re-enactment thereof
Arbitration notice	The written notice which marks the commencement of the arbitration
Article	Any article set out in these Rules
Claim	includes Counterclaim
Claimant	includes Counterclaimant
Concurrent hearing	any two or more arbitrations being heard together
Consolidation	any two or more arbitrations being treated as one proceeding
The Institute	The Chartered Institute of Arbitrators
Party	One of the Parties to the arbitration
Provisional order	any order for provisional relief under section 39 of the Act
Respondent	includes Respondent to a Counterclaim
Section	a section of the Act

14.2 In any event the provisions of the Interpretation Act 1978 apply hereto.

FIRST SCHEDULE

Short Form Procedure

Paragraph 1 Adoption of the Short Form Procedure

A23–016   **1.1** The Parties may agree at any time prior to or during the course of the arbitration to adopt this Short Form Procedure, and in that event the Rules set out above shall be modified as hereinafter provided;

1.2 Article 7 of the above Rules shall be deleted, and the alternative Article 7 set out in Paragraph 2 of this Schedule substituted.

Paragraph 2 Alternative to Article 7

A23–017   **2.1** The arbitration will be conducted on a documents-only basis subject to the discretion of the Arbitrator to order a meeting for clarification purposes of no more than one day in length in respect of the whole or any part of the arbitration, but in exercising that discretion the Arbitrator shall bear in mind his duties under section 33 of the Act;

2.2 Unless the Arbitrator otherwise directs the arbitration will proceed on the basis of exchange of Statements of Case as hereinafter set out;

2.3 All Statements of Case shall contain the following:—

(a) A full statement of the Party's arguments of fact and law;

(b) Signed and dated statements of the evidence of any witness upon whose evidence the Party relies;

(c) Copies of all documents upon which the Party relies;

(d) A full statement of all relief or remedies claimed;

(e) Detailed calculations of any sums claimed;

2.4 Unless the Arbitrator otherwise directs the Parties will exchange Statements of Case as follows:—

(a) Within 28 days of the receipt by the Claimant of the Arbitrator's acceptance of the appointment the Claimant shall send to the Arbitrator and the Respondent its Statement of Claim;

(b) The Respondent shall within 28 days from receipt of the Statement of Claim send to the Arbitrator and the Claimant a Statement of Defence. If no Statement of Defence is served within that time limit or such extended time limit as the Arbitrator may allow then the Respondent will be debarred from serving a Statement of Defence;

(c) If the Respondent wishes to make any Counterclaim then a Counterclaim shall be served with the Statement of Defence;

(d) The Claimant shall within 14 days from receipt of the Statement of Defence and within 28 days from receipt of the Statement of Counterclaim (if any) send to the Arbitrator and to the other Party a Reply and Defence to Counterclaim (if any). If no Statement of Defence to Counterclaim is served within that time limit or such extended time limit as the Arbitrator may allow then the Claimant will be debarred from serving a Defence to Counterclaim;

(e) The Respondent shall within 14 days from receipt of the Defence to Counterclaim send to the Arbitrator and to the other Party a Reply to Defence to Counterclaim;

(f) Any further statements may only be served with the leave of the Arbitrator;

(g) When a Party has been debarred from serving a Statement of Defence or Statement of Defence to Counterclaim under Article 2.4(b) or 2.4(d) above the other Party or Parties shall still be required to prove any allegations made in the Statements of Claim or Counterclaim as the case may be.

2.5 At any time, the Arbitrator may give detailed directions with any appropriate timetable for all further procedural steps in the arbitration, including (but not limited to) the following:—

(a) Any amendment to, expansion of, summary of, or reproduction in some other format of, any Statement or any extension to or alteration of time limits for service of Statements;

(b) Disclosure and production of documents as between the Parties;

(c) The exchange of statements of evidence of witnesses of fact;

(d) The number and types of expert and exchange of their reports;

(e) Meetings between experts;

(f) Arrangements for any oral hearing if, in the exercise of his discretion he concludes that an oral hearing is necessary including any time limits to be imposed on the length of oral submissions or the examination or cross examination of witnesses.

2.6 The Arbitrator may at any time order any of the following to be delivered to him in writing:—

(a) Submissions to be advanced by or on behalf of any Party;

(b) Questions intended to be put to any witness;

(c) Answers by any witness to written questions.

Paragraph 3 Rules of Evidence

3.1 In any arbitration under the Short Form Procedure the Parties are deemed to have waived all rules and requirements in respect of the law relating to admissibility of evidence unless at any stage before publication of any Award any Party notifies the Arbitrator in writing of that Party's wish to withdraw such waiver. Furthermore, the Arbitrator shall only make such an amendment to procedure with the agreement of the other Party.

3.2 In any event withdrawal of such waiver shall not take effect unless the Arbitrator in his absolute discretion consents thereto.

3.3 Before consenting to withdrawal of such waiver the Arbitrator shall permit the other Party or Parties to make such representations, whether orally or in writing, as he considers appropriate.

3.4 In the event of such withdrawal taking effect the Arbitrator shall give such directions, either in writing or by way of holding a preliminary meeting for the further conduct of the arbitration as he considers appropriate and may take into account the fact of the withdrawal of such waiver in considering the exercise of his discretion to Award costs.

3.5 The Arbitrator shall allow submissions by Parties in respect of the weight to be given to evidence heard if so requested by either Party.

The Chartered Institute of Arbitrators Rules of the Mortgage Code Arbitration Scheme[1]

(SECOND EDITION MAY 2000)

(to apply only to those disputes which arise on or after 30th April 1998)

1. Introduction

1.1 This Scheme is administered by the Chartered Institute of Arbitrators ("the Institute"). It applies to disputes between (a) members of the Council of Mortgage Lenders ("CML"), who are not currently members of an ombudsman scheme covering mortgage complaints, or mortgage intermediaries currently registered with the Mortgage Code Compliance Board ("MCCB"), and (b) their clients, in respect of any complaint of an alleged breach of the CML Code of Mortgage Lending Practice ("the Mortgage Code") by the client. If so requested by the client the reference to arbitration shall be mandatory for any such CML member, and also for any such intermediary registered with MCCB on or after 30th April 1998, provided that any internal complaints procedure has first been exhausted without resolution of the dispute. **A24–001**

1.2 In addition, if so requested by the borrower, any other mortgage lender or mortgage intermediary may refer a complaint by a residential borrower of an alleged breach of the Mortgage Code to arbitration under the Scheme, provided that any internal complaints procedure has first been exhausted without resolution of the dispute.

1.3 The Scheme does not apply to disputes where:—

(a) one or either of the Parties has already initiated legal action, unless that legal action is suspended by agreement,

(b) the claim concerns physical injury, illness, nervous shock or their consequences;

(c) disputes involve amounts claimed in excess of £100,000, or

(d) the lender or intermediary ("the Respondent") feels that an application made under the Rules of the Scheme is frivolous or vexations. In such circumstances they may challenge the validity of the application by following the procedure outlined on the application form.

1.4 Subject to Rule 1.3(d), if, after considering the documents or other representations submitted by the Parties, the Arbitrator believes that the dispute is not capable of resolution under these Rules, the Parties shall be so advised. In that event the Arbitrator's appointment will be cancelled, and the Parties' application for arbitration treated as withdrawn. The Parties will then be able to pursue the matter through the courts.

1.5 These Rules apply to disputes between two Parties but, if they and the Arbitrator agree, the Rules may be adapted for the same dispute involving three or more Parties.

1.6 A registration fee is payable by the Respondent when an application for arbitration is submitted. The registration fee is non-refundable in all circumstances.

---

[1] This document is reproduced with the kind permission of the copyright-holder, the Chartered Institute of Arbitrators.

2. Commencement of Arbitration Proceedings

A24–002 **2.1** To commence arbitration proceedings, a joint application by the Claimant and Respondent must first be submitted to the Institute through the Respondent, i.e. the relevant mortgage lender or mortgage intermediary on the Scheme application form, accompanied by the appropriate fee from the Respondent.

2.2 Subject to Rule 1.3(d), the arbitration commences when the Institute writes to the Parties telling them that their application has been accepted. At this stage the Claimant will be sent a Statement of Claim form.

2.3 The President or a Vice-President of the Institute will appoint an Arbitrator and will inform the Parties of his appointment.

2.4 The Institute may appoint a substitute Arbitrator, in the event of the Arbitrator resigning, dying or otherwise becoming incapacitated, or for any reason being unable to attend competently or expeditiously to his duties.

2.5 Once appointed the Arbitrator will communicate with or issue directions to the Parties through the Institute. Correspondence with the Arbitrator must be copied to all Parties.

3. Arbitration Procedure

A24–003 **3.1** The Arbitrator shall have the jurisdiction and power to direct the procedure of the arbitration in terms of Section 34 of the Arbitration Act 1996. The Arbitrator shall also have the power to:

    (a) allow submission of further evidence and the amendment of Claim or Defence;

    (b) order the Parties to produce goods, documents or property for inspection;

    (c) conduct such enquiries as may appear to the Arbitrator to be desirable;

    (d) receive and take into account any oral or written evidence as the Arbitrator shall decide to be relevant;

    (e) appoint an expert to report on specific issues or take legal advice;

    (f) award interest whether or not claimed;

    (g) proceed with the arbitration if either Party fails to comply with these Rules or with the Arbitrator's directions, or if either Party fails to attend any meeting or inspection ordered by the Arbitrator but only after giving that Party written notice;

    (h) terminate the arbitration if the Arbitrator considers the case to be incapable of resolution under the Scheme;

    (i) if the Parties settle their dispute prior to an Award they must immediately inform the Institute in writing of the terms of the settlement and the Arbitrator shall record them in a Consent Award enforceable under the Arbitration Act 1996.

3.2 In addition to the powers conferred by these Rules, the Arbitrator shall have the widest discretion permitted by law to resolve the dispute in relation to an alleged breach of the CML Code of Mortgage Lending Practice in a fair, just, speedy, economical and final manner in accordance with natural justice.

3.3 The arbitration will normally proceed on the basis of written argument only, which must be submitted in duplicate. However, if either Party requests it or if the Arbitrator considers it appropriate a meeting or inspection may be held. Any such meeting or inspection shall be made in the presence of both Parties who may be questioned by the Arbitrator in order to clarify matters in dispute. The costs of such a meeting/inspection shall be met by the Party who requests it.

3.4 Within 28 days of receipt of the Statement of Claim form, the Claimant shall send the completed form to the Institute together with all supporting documents. The Claimant may not raise issues or claim amounts not covered by the application form without the Arbitrator's consent.

3.5 A copy of the Statement of Claim and supporting documents will be sent by the Institute to the Respondent, who then has 28 days in which to submit a written Statement of Defence.

3.6 A copy of the Statement of Defence and supporting documents will be sent by the Institute to the Claimant, who is entitled to submit written Comments within a further 14 days. Such Comments must be restricted to points arising from the Respondent's Defence. The Claimant may not introduce any new matters or new Points of Claim, and if new evidence is produced it will be disregarded by the Arbitrator.

3.7 The Arbitrator will make an Award with reasons after considering all submissions and evidence. The Award may be for an amount up to and including a maximum of £100,000 inclusive of interest and costs.

3.8 The Institute will send a copy of the Award to each Party, and to the CML and MCCB for their private information.

3.9 Unless otherwise directed, any amount awarded shall be paid within 21 days of dispatch of the Award to the Parties. Such payments shall be made direct to the Party entitled to receive it.

3.10 Any Award made under this Scheme is final and binding under the Arbitration Act, 1996, and therefore, once published, it will not be open to review. If either Party wishes to appeal against the Award, leave must be sought within 28 days from the date of publication of the Award. It should be noted that Parties cannot appeal on a point of fact. Neither the Institute nor the Arbitrator can advise the Parties on how to seek leave to appeal.

3.11 The Arbitrator is not liable for anything done or omitted in the discharge or purported discharge of his functions as Arbitrator unless the act or omission is shown to have been in bad faith.

3.12 Any Party may request the return of its original documents but must do so within 42 days of the date of dispatch of the Award.

4. Content of Submissions for Arbitration

4.1 The Statement of Claim shall include:

    (a) nature and basis of the Claim;

    (b) the amount of compensation claimed or other remedy sought;

    (c) all supporting documents relied on as evidence.

4.2 If the Claimant is unable to submit any relevant document, the Respondent shall use reasonable endeavours to provide a copy of that document with the Defence.

4.3 The Statement of Defence shall include:

    (a) what matters in the opposing documents are accepted or agreed;

(b) what matters are disputed, with reasons;

(c) any supporting documents relied on as evidence.

4.4 The response by the Claimant to any Defence shall include:

(a) what matters in the opposing documents are accepted or agreed;

(b) what matters are disputed, with reasons;

(c) any supporting documents relied on as evidence.

4.5 If any Party fails to deliver anything required by these Rules and does not supply it within 14 days of a reminder by the Institute then:

(a) where a Claim or a Counterclaim is not delivered it shall be deemed to be abandoned;

(b) where a Claim is abandoned the arbitration will not proceed;

(c) where the failure concerns information requested by the Arbitrator, the arbitration shall proceed as the Arbitrator considers appropriate;

(d) where the failure is non-delivery of the Defence the Arbitrator may make the Award on the basis of documents received. Alternatively the Arbitrator may wish to allow the Respondent a further period in which to submit the Defence.

5. Arbitration Costs

A24–005   **5.1** The Arbitrator's fees and expenses and those of any expert or legal adviser appointed by him shall be paid by the Respondent.

5.2 The Institute's administration charges are also payable by the Respondent.

5.3 Subject to Rule 5.4 and 5.5 below, each Party shall bear its own costs of preparing and submitting its case and of attending any hearing.

5.4 The Arbitrator may also order one Party to pay any or any part of or all of the other's costs where the former has, in the view of the Arbitrator, acted unreasonably and caused the opposing Party unnecessary expense.

5.5 These provisions for costs will not apply to any application or appeal to the court.

6. Miscellaneous

A24–006   **6.1** Where not expressly addressed by the contract, the national law will apply unless the Parties otherwise agree. If Scots law applies, substitute Arbiter for Arbitrator throughout these Rules.

6.2 Neither the Institute nor the Arbitrator can enter into any correspondence regarding an Award issued under this Scheme.

6.3 Neither the Institute nor the Arbitrator shall be liable to any Party for any act or omission in connection with the arbitration conducted under these Rules.

6.4 Nothing herein shall prevent the Parties agreeing to settle the differences or dispute arising out of the agreement without recourse to arbitration.

6.5 Nothing herein shall prevent the Parties from appealing the Award to the High Court in terms of the Arbitration Act 1996, or any statutory modification or re-enactment thereof for the time being in force. This provision applies equally to the law of Scotland.

The CIArb Rules of the Mortgage Code Arbitration Scheme

Application for Arbitration

To: The Chartered Institute of Arbitrators ("the Institute") A24–007
The International Arbitration and Mediation Centre
12 Bloomsbury Square
London, WC1A 2LP

1. .... Claimant

   of ....

   ....

   .... Tel: ....

   and

   .... Respondent

   of ....

   ....

   .... Tel: ....

   hereby apply to the Institute for the following dispute to be resolved under the current Rules of the Mortgage Code Arbitration Scheme for determination by an Arbitrator appointed by the Institute. We confirm that we have exhausted the usual internal complaints procedure of the Respondent organisation.

2. The dispute concerns the following issues: (only a brief outline is required here—**do not** submit any other documentation)

   ....
   ....
   ....
   ....
   ....
   ....

3. The amount (if any) claimed is £ ....
4. We, the Parties to this application, have read the current Rules of the Scheme. We agree to be bound by them and by the Award of the Arbitrator appointed to determine the dispute.
5. Subject to point 6, a cheque for the sum of £881.25* (£750 plus VAT) is attached from the Respondent in payment of the Scheme fees.

* All cheques should be made in favour of the Chartered Institute of Arbitrators

6. Request to Proceed on a Preliminary Issue
   (a) If the Respondent wishes to claim that 'the application is not covered by the Rules', or is frivolous or vexatious, an fee for £146.87 (£125 plus VAT) must be enclosed, in order that the matter can be dealt with by an arbitrator as a preliminary issue.
   (b) If that arbitrator decides that the application for arbitration is invalid, the parties will be free to pursue the matter by litigation.
   (c) A decision to allow the application to proceed to arbitration does not, under any circumstances, indicate that the application will be successful.
   (d) If the matter proceeds to arbitration, the arbitrator making the preliminary ruling will not automatically be appointed to arbitrate.
   (e) If the matter proceeds the Respondent will be invoiced for the costs of the full arbitration process.

Signed: .... Date. ....
(by or for the Claimant)

Signed: .... Date: ....
(by or for the Respondent)

The Chartered Institute of Arbitrators "Surveyors Arbitration Scheme" Rules[1]

This Scheme is based upon the Consumer Dispute Resolution Scheme published by the Chartered Institute of Arbitrators (the ClArb) in consultation with the Office of Fair Trading and the National Consumer Council.

A25–001

1. Introduction

1.1 The Surveyors Arbitration Scheme applies to claims for compensation or other remedies sought in respect of any disputes between clients and members of the Royal Institution of Chartered Surveyors. The Scheme also applies to a third party to whom a liability in damages would be owed in negligence by reason of the breach by a member of an established duty of care.

A25–002

1.2 The Scheme does not apply to disputes concerning;

(i) sums for claims or counterclaims exceeding £50,000 exclusive of VAT;

(ii) dishonesty including fraud;

(iii) physical injury, illness, nervous shock or their consequences.

1.3 The Rules apply to disputes between two parties but, if the Parties and the Arbitrator agree, the Rules may be adapted for disputes involving three or more parties.

1.4 Registration fees are payable by each party when an application for arbitration is submitted.

1.5 For the purposes of this Scheme, a "Consumer" means a natural person who, in making the contract, or otherwise dealing with or relying on any work of the surveyor or valuer, does so for purposes outside the course of any business of his, and "consumer claim" shall be construed accordingly.

1.6 Confirmation is required on the application form that:

(i) the Claimant or Respondent is or is not a Consumer; and,

(ii) the Claimant has sought resolution of the dispute through the Respondent's in-house complaints procedure (if any); and,

(iii) the Parties have either taken part in or have specifically declined to take part in formal mediation; or,

(iv) the application is following an adjudicator's decision.

2. Commencement of Arbitration Proceedings

2.1 Where the conditions as set out under paragraph 1.6 above are fulfilled the matter can be referred to arbitration.

A25–003

2.2 The arbitration begins after both parties have signed and submitted an application form to the ClArb accompanied by the appropriate registration fees.

2.3 The ClArb will then write to the Parties telling them that their application has been accepted.

---

[1] This document is reproduced with the kind permission of the copyright-holder, the Chartered Institute of Arbitrators.

2.4 The CIArb will proceed with the administration of the arbitration.

2.5 The President or a Vice-President of the CIArb will appoint an Arbitrator and the CIArb will inform the Parties of the Arbitrator's name at the appropriate time.

3. Arbitration Procedure

A25–004 **3.1** The arbitration will normally proceed on the basis of written argument and evidence which must be submitted in duplicate and in accordance with the following procedure:—

  (i) The CIArb shall notify the person making the claim (the Claimant) that he has 28 days to send, in duplicate, the Statement of Case to the CIArb together with all supporting documents to prove that case. The Claimant may not raise issues or claim amounts not covered by the application form without first obtaining the Arbitrator's consent. Upon application by the Claimant the CIArb may grant one 14 day extension of time.

  (ii) A copy of the claim documents will be sent by the CIArb to the other party (the Respondent) who then has 28 days in which to submit, in duplicate, a written defence. Providing notice was given on the application form, the Respondent shall submit details and all necessary supporting documents to prove any counterclaim. Upon application by the Respondent the CIArb may grant one 14 day extension of time.

  (iii) A copy of the defence documents, and any counterclaim, will be sent by the CIArb to the Claimant, who is entitled to submit, in duplicate, written comments on the defence to the claim restricted to points arising from the Respondent's defence only and a defence to the counterclaim within a further 14 days. The Claimant may not introduce any new matters or new points of claim.

  (iv) A copy of the Claimant's comments and the defence to the counterclaim will be sent by the CIArb to the Respondent who is entitled to submit, in duplicate, written comments on the defence to the counterclaim within a further 14 days. Such comments must be restricted to points arising from the Claimant's defence to the counterclaim if any. A copy of these written comments, when received by the CIArb will be sent to the Claimant. The Claimant is not permitted to make any further comment.

3.2 The Arbitrator will consider all submissions and evidence. If the Arbitrator considers it appropriate, meeting(s) with the Parties and/or site visit(s) will be held. The Arbitrator will then make an award with reasons and provide the CIArb with five copies of the Award.

3.3 The CIArb will then:—

  (i) notify the parties that the Award has been published and is available on payment of the amount due in respect of the Arbitrator's fees and expenses; and

  (ii) upon receipt of payment of the Arbitrator's fees and expenses, send a copy of the Award to each party and to RICS.

3.4 Unless otherwise directed, any amount awarded shall be paid within 21 days of dispatch of the Award to the Parties. Such payments shall be made direct to the party entitled to receive it.

3.5 Any Award made under this Scheme is final and legally binding on all parties.

3.6 Any party may request the return of its original documents but must do so within 42 days of the date of dispatch of the Award.

3.7 If any party fails to deliver anything required by these Rules and does not supply it within 14 days of a reminder by the CIArb then:

  (i) a claim or a counterclaim not delivered shall be deemed to be abandoned;

  (ii) where a claim is abandoned the arbitration will not proceed and the Respondent's registration fee will be refunded;

  (iii) where a counterclaim is abandoned the arbitration will proceed with the original claim;

  (iv) where the failure concerns information requested by the Arbitrator, the arbitration shall proceed as the Arbitrator considers appropriate;

  (v) where the failure is non-delivery of the defence (or the Claimant's response to a counterclaim) the Arbitrator may make the award on the basis of documents received.

3.8 If the case is settled the Parties must immediately inform the CIArb by submitting a joint statement in writing signed by them both stating the terms of the settlement. If the Parties so require the Arbitrator shall record those terms in an Agreed Award.

4. Arbitrator's Powers

4.1 The Arbitrator shall have the jurisdiction and power to direct the procedure of the arbitration including the amendment of time limits and other procedural requirements and have the power to:

  (i) allow submission of further evidence and the amendment of claim, counterclaim or defence;

  (ii) order the Parties to produce goods, documents or property for inspection;

  (iii) conduct such enquiries as may be desirable;

  (iv) receive and take into account any oral or written evidence as deemed to be relevant;

  (v) award simple interest whether or not claimed;

  (vi) proceed with the arbitration if either party fails to comply with these Rules or with any Directions, or if either party fails to attend any meeting or inspection ordered by the Arbitrator but only after giving that party written notice;

  (vii) terminate the arbitration if the case is considered to be incapable of resolution under the Scheme or if the Parties settle their dispute prior to an award.

4.2 In consumer claims, the Arbitrator will have the power to award costs in accordance with 6.1 below.

4.3 In non-consumer claims the Arbitrator will have the power to assess and award in whole or in part the parties' costs if properly detailed and submitted in accordance with 5.1, 5.3, 5.4 and 5.5 below. This power shall only apply up to the claim limits prescribed at 6.1 and for costs that do not exceed the limits shown at 6.9.

5. Content of Submissions for Arbitration

A25–006 5.1 The claim shall include:

(i) nature and basis of the claim;

(ii) the amount of compensation claimed or other remedy sought;

(iii) all supporting documents relied on as evidence;

(iv) details of costs of preparing the claim in non-consumer disputes only.

5.2 If the Claimant is unable to submit a copy of any original contract or order, the Respondent shall submit a copy of that document with the defence.
5.3 The defence shall include:

(i) what matters in the opposing documents are accepted or agreed;

(ii) what matters are disputed, with reasons why;

(iii) any supporting documents relied on as evidence;

(iv) details of costs of preparing the defence in non-consumer disputes only.

5.4 Any counterclaim shall include

(i) the nature and basis of the counterclaim;

(ii) the amount of compensation claimed or other remedy sought;

(iii) any supporting documents relied on as evidence;

(iv) details of costs of preparing the counterclaim, in non-consumer disputes only.

5.5 The response by the Claimant to any defence and/or counterclaim shall include:

(i) what matters in the opposing documents are accepted or agreed;

(ii) what matters are disputed, with reasons why;

(iii) any supporting documents relied on as evidence;

(iv) details of costs of preparing the response to the defence and/or any counterclaim in non-consumer disputes only.

6. Arbitration Costs

A25–007 6.1 The allocation of costs is normally in accordance with the table shown below but in all cases, the Arbitrator has the discretion to award costs against:—

(i) any party whose claim, counterclaim or defence is judged to be frivolous or vexatious in whole or in part; or

(ii) any party who has conducted the case in such a way as to put the other party to unnecessary expenditure; or

(iii) a successful party who has failed to accept an offer of settlement which equals or exceeds the Arbitrator's Award.

Type of Claim	COSTS		
	CIARB	**ARBITRATOR**	**PARTY**
Consumer claim less than £3,000	Each party initially pays its own registration fee. If Claimant wins, Respondent is liable for Claimant's registration fee. If Respondent wins, Claimant's registration fee is forfeited.	If Claimant wins, Respondent is liable for arbitrator's costs. If Respondent wins, RICS pays arbitrator's costs.	Each party bears its own costs.
Consumer claim £3,000 or over but not exceeding £50,000	Each party initially pays its own registration fee. If Claimant wins, Respondent is liable for Claimant's registration fee. If Respondent wins, Claimant is liable for Respondent's registration fee.	If Claimant wins, Respondent is liable for arbitrator's costs. If Respondent wins, Claimant is liable for arbitrator's costs.	Each party bears its own costs.
Non-consumer claim not exceeding £50,000. This includes any RICS member who is acting as Claimant. If there is also a counterclaim not exceeding £50,000, then the costs are assessed on either the claim or the counterclaim whichever is the greater.	Each party initially pays its own registration fee. If Claimant wins, Respondent is liable for Claimant's registration fee. If Respondent wins, Claimant is liable for Respondent's registration fee.	If Claimant wins, Respondent is liable for arbitrator's costs. If Respondent wins, Claimant is liable for arbitrator's costs.	If Claimant wins, Respondent is liable for his own and Claimant's costs. If Respondent wins, Claimant is liable for his own and Respondent's costs. (see also 6.9)

6.2 In a non-consumer claim the Parties' recoverable costs shall be limited to the sums stated at 6.9 below.

6.3 The registration fee is £200 plus VAT per party.

6.4 If a party wishes to amend its claim or counterclaim to a sum of £3,000 or above having firstly claimed a sum of less than £3,000 then that party shall pay a further registration fee of £100 plus VAT.

6.5 A party cannot amend its claim or counterclaim to a sum greater than £50,000.

6.6 The Arbitrator's fees and expenses will be as indicated in the award and paid directly to the CIArb

6.7 The Arbitrator will charge a fee in accordance with the table shown below:—

Type of Claim	Amount of Claim or Counterclaim whichever is the greater (excluding VAT).	Fee rate (plus VAT if applicable)	Maximum chargeable hours
Consumer	Less than £3,000	Fixed fee of £400	N/A
Consumer	£3,000 – £50,000	£75 per hour	15 hours
Non-consumer	Less than £15,000	£75 per hour	15 hours
Non-consumer	£15,000 – £30,000	£100 per hour	25 hours
Non-consumer	£30,000 – £50,000	£100 per hour	30 hours

6.8 If in exceptional circumstances the Arbitrator decides to hold meeting(s) with the Parties and/or site visit(s), a maximum additional fee of £100 plus VAT if applicable will be charged.

6.9 In a non-consumer claim, the Arbitrator will determine in his award the Parties' recoverable costs on such basis as he thinks fit but in no case shall the costs exceed the following maximum sums:—

Amount of Claim or Counterclaim whichever is the greater (excluding VAT).	Limit on Parties' Costs (plus VAT if applicable)
Less than £15,000	£5,000 per party
£15,000–£30,000	£7,500 per party
£30,000–£50,000	£10,000 per party

6.10 The provisions for costs will not apply to any application for appeal against the Award.

7. Review of Award

7.1 The Arbitrator has the discretion if an application is made by either party within 28 days of the date of the Award to:—

>   (i) correct the Award so as to remove a clerical mistake or error arising from an accidental slip or omission or clarify or remove any ambiguity in the Award, or

(ii) make an additional Award in respect of any claim or counterclaim (including one for interest or costs) which was presented to the Arbitrator but was not dealt with in the Award.

7.2 Before exercising the discretion given in paragraph 7.1 the Arbitrator will give the other party a reasonable opportunity to make representations on the application.

7.3 The Arbitrator shall endeavour to make any necessary correction of the Award or make any additional Award within 28 days of the receipt of such application.

8. Appeal Against Award to Appeal Tribunal

8.1 Any party may appeal the Arbitrator's Award subject to the following provisions: **A25–009**

(i) The Applicant must have exhausted the Review of Award mechanism (if applicable) as provided by paragraph 7.

(ii) The Appeal must be made within 28 days of the date of the Award or the date of notification of the result of the review mechanism in paragraph 7, which will be deemed for this purpose to be the date of publication of the Award.

(iii) An appeal can only be made on a point of law and/or on the grounds that based on the findings of fact in the Award the decision of the Arbitrator is obviously wrong and/or on the grounds that there has been a serious irregularity affecting the Arbitrator, the proceedings or the Award.

8.2 The Party making the Appeal must deliver to the CIArb five copies of the appeal documents giving full and precise details of the point(s) of law and/or the grounds upon which the decision of the Arbitrator is obviously wrong having regard to the findings of fact in the Award and/or the grounds upon which it is alleged that there has been a serious irregularity affecting the Arbitrator, the proceedings or the Award.

8.3 On receipt of an appeal the President or a Vice-President of the CIArb will appoint an Appeal Tribunal of three arbitrators none of whom will be on the approved RICS Scheme panel and one of whom will be a lawyer.

8.4 The Appeal Tribunal will send to the other Party a copy of the appeal document and allow them a reasonable period of time to submit a reply.

8.5 The Appeal Tribunal shall determine the Appeal without a hearing and shall have the power to:—

(i) confirm the Award, or

(ii) set aside the Award in whole or in part and substitute a new Award.

9. Costs of Appeal to Appeal Tribunal

9.1 The Party making the Appeal shall pay a registration fee of £250 plus VAT and a **A25–010** payment of £2,250 plus VAT as security for costs of the Appeal Tribunal.

9.2 The Appeal Tribunal may make an Award allocating the costs of the Appeal as between the Parties but shall award costs on the general principle that costs should follow the event. The recoverable costs of the Appeal shall be determined on the basis of a reasonable amount of costs reasonably incurred.

10. Appeal to Court

A25–011 Once the appeal procedure in paragraph 8 is exhausted, that is finality so far as the rules and provisions of the scheme are concerned. Any party considering the possibility of a further appeal to the Courts, if indeed any such appeal is legally possible, is strongly advised to seek the advice of a solicitor.

11. Miscellaneous

A25–012 **11.1** The national law to be applied shall be determined by the Arbitrator if the Parties fail to agree. If Scottish law applies, substitute arbiter for arbitrator throughout these rules. The seat of the arbitration shall be determined by the Arbitrator if the parties fail to agree.

11.2 If necessary the ClArb shall appoint a substitute arbitrator and shall notify the Parties accordingly.

11.3 Neither the ClArb nor the Arbitrator nor the Appeal Tribunal can enter into any correspondence regarding any Award, Review of Award or Appeal against Award.

11.4 Neither the ClArb nor the Arbitrator shall be liable to any party for any act or omission in connection with an arbitration conducted under these Rules.

City Disputes Panel Arbitration Rules[1]

April 1997

The Aim

1 The aim of every tribunal appointed under these Rules shall be to resolve the dispute fairly, within the shortest time commensurate with the nature of the dispute and the wishes of the parties. To facilitate this aim these Rules (rule 22) empower the parties to request the tribunal to adjourn or stay the proceedings at any time should they wish to consider alternative procedures.

Request for Arbitration

2 Where parties to a dispute in the financial services sector (other than a dispute to which rule 3 applies) have agreed that it shall be referred to the City Disputes Panel ("the CDP") for arbitration any party may request the CDP to appoint a tribunal under this rule. Where it is desired that the dispute shall be determined within a certain period the request shall so state. The requesting party shall confirm that copies of the request have been served on the other parties.

3 Where all the parties to a dispute are agreed that rapid decision is required they may jointly request the CDP to appoint a tribunal, stating that the request is made under this rule and specifying why rapid resolution of the dispute is needed and the date by which a decision is sought.

4 A request under rules 2 or 3 above shall be in writing and shall comprise the names, addresses, telephone and fax numbers of the parties, and brief details of the nature of the dispute and the relief claimed.

Commencement of the Arbitration

5 An arbitration shall be deemed to commence on the date when the request for arbitration is received by the CDP.

The Arbitral Tribunal

6 On receipt of a request for arbitration the CDP will appoint a tribunal from its panel of arbitrators. The tribunal will usually consist of a legally qualified chairman and two experienced financial services practitioners. However, a sole arbitrator may be appointed if the circumstances of the case so warrant.

7 Where the request for arbitration has been made under rule 2, the CDP will appoint a tribunal and notify the parties of its membership within 7 days of the commencement of the arbitration. Where the request has been made under rule 3 the CDP will appoint a tribunal and notify the parties of its membership within the shortest time possible.

Impartiality of Arbitrators

8 Before agreeing to be appointed to a tribunal under these Rules each arbitrator shall sign a declaration to the effect that to the best of his knowledge and belief no circumstances exist which might give rise to justified doubts as to his impartiality or independ-

---

[1] This document is reproduced with the kind permission of the City Disputes Panel.

ence and if such circumstances arise subsequently the arbitrator concerned shall at once disclose them to the CDP and to the parties.

Completion of the Tribunal's Appointment

A26–006   9 As soon as the CDP has received the declarations required by rule 8 it shall send to the parties for signature an agreement to submit their dispute to arbitration and on receipt from the parties of this agreement the CDP will notify them that the tribunal is duly constituted.

Communications

A26–007   10 The parties shall communicate with the tribunal through the CDP unless the parties, the tribunal and the CDP otherwise agree.

Challenge, Revocation or Cessation of an Arbitrator's Authority

A26–008   11 If, at any time after the tribunal has been duly constituted under rule 9, a party believes that there are justifiable reasons to doubt the impartiality or independence of one or more of its members, or believes that he has some other reasonable ground for objecting to the continued involvement of that member or those members, he shall so inform the CDP within 7 days of becoming aware of such reasons or ground. The member or members thus challenged may thereupon withdraw, and shall do so if another party agrees with the challenge, but if he or they do not the CDP will rule upon the validity of the challenge as soon as possible and in any event within 3 working days. If the CDP accepts the validity of the challenge, the challenged member or members shall withdraw and the CDP will thereupon fill the vacancy or vacancies on the tribunal. Any decision of the CDP under this rule shall be final, subject to rule 12 below.

12 The provisions of rule 11 are subject to any statutory rights a party may have to apply to a court to remove an arbitrator.

13 The CDP shall have power to revoke the authority of an arbitrator and remove and replace him if justifiable doubts arise as to his impartiality, or he becomes physically or mentally incapable of conducting the proceedings or there are justifiable doubts as to his capacity to do so, or if he has refused or failed properly to conduct the proceedings or to use all reasonable despatch in so doing or in making an award. On the death of an arbitrator his authority ceases and the CDP shall thereupon appoint a successor to him.

14 If during the course of the proceedings a member of the tribunal is replaced, no hearing which has already taken place shall be repeated save in so far as the new tribunal considers repetition is necessary.

Jurisdiction of the Tribunal

A26–009   15 The tribunal shall have power to rule on any question regarding its own jurisdiction or the existence or validity of the arbitration agreement, as to whether the tribunal is properly constituted, and as to what matters have been submitted to arbitration in accordance with the agreement. Where the arbitration agreement forms part of a contract it shall be treated as an agreement independent of the contract. A challenge to the tribunal's jurisdiction made at the outset of the proceedings must be raised by a party not later than the time when he takes the first step in the proceedings to contest the merits of the matter in relation to which the challenge arises and a challenge during the proceedings must be made as soon as possible after the matter giving rise to the challenge is raised. The tribunal will rule on the objection in an award as to jurisdiction unless the parties expressly request it to deal with the objection in its award on the merits.

Additional Powers of the Tribunal

16 In addition to the powers conferred on the tribunal by any other rule, and unless the parties at any time agree otherwise, the tribunal shall have the power to: A26–010

(a) order the rectification of any mistake which the tribunal determines to be common to the parties in any contract or arbitration agreement;

(b) give directions to a party for the preservation for the purposes of the proceedings of any evidence in his custody or control;

(c) give directions for the inspection, photographing, preservation, custody or detention by the tribunal, an expert, or a party of any property the subject of the proceedings and which is owned by or in the possession of a party;

(d) direct the parties to provide security for the costs of the arbitration in one or more payments and in such proportions as it deems just. This power shall not be exercised on the ground that the party is ordinarily resident outside the United Kingdom or is a corporation or association incorporated or formed under the law of a country outside the United Kingdom, or whose central management or control is outside the United Kingdom. Any sums provided by way of security shall be deposited with the CDP and may be drawn on by the tribunal as required. Any interest earned on deposits will be added to those deposits;

(e) direct any party to provide security for any other party's costs of the reference, to the extent permitted by the applicable procedural law.

Duty of the Tribunal

17 The tribunal shall adopt procedures appropriate to the case and to the aim of achieving the just, speedy, economical and final resolution of the dispute. To that end it shall act fairly and impartially between the parties, giving each party a reasonable opportunity of presenting his case and dealing with that of his opponent including the opportunity if he so desires of an oral hearing for the presentation of evidence and argument. A26–011

Procedural Freedom of the Tribunal

18 Subject to the tribunal's duty under rule 17 the parties may agree on the arbitral procedure or any part thereof. When they do not, the tribunal shall determine all procedural matters in its absolute discretion including in particular the admissibility, relevance, materiality and weight of any evidence. In a three-member tribunal the Chairman alone may give directions and make procedural rulings and orders provided he is authorised to do so by the other members. A26–012

Duty of the Parties

19 It shall be the duty of the parties to do all things necessary for the proper and expeditious conduct of the proceedings. If a Claimant fails to prosecute his claim within the time laid down by the tribunal without showing sufficient cause for such failure, the tribunal may make an award dismissing the claim. If a party fails to participate in the proceedings at any stage without showing sufficient cause, the tribunal may direct that A26–013

the proceedings shall continue despite his failure and may make an award on the basis of the evidence before it.

First Management Meeting

A26–014　20 This rule shall apply except where the parties have requested rapid decision under rule 3, when rule 21 shall apply. Immediately after the tribunal has been duly constituted each party shall be invited to make written representations regarding appropriate procedures for the future conduct of the arbitration. The tribunal shall then call the parties to a meeting ("the first management meeting") to consider such procedures within 14 days after it has been duly constituted or within such further time as the tribunal shall determine, unless all the parties and the tribunal agree that such a meeting is not required. At this meeting, or following the parties' written representations if no meeting is required, the tribunal may give directions upon the following specific matters and any other matters, including those referred to in rule 22 below, upon which any party may request the tribunal or the tribunal may deem it desirable to give directions:

(a) the manner in which and the times within which the issues in the arbitration shall be defined;

(b) whether a simplified hearing procedure, such as that set out in Appendix I, should be adopted;

(c) whether, with the agreement of the parties, the dispute should be determined upon the basis of documents only under the procedure set out in Appendix II;

(d) the production of documents;

(e) a timetable.

At the first management meeting the tribunal shall also ask the parties whether they wish to exclude any right of appeal.

First Management Meeting (rapid decision)

A26–015　21 Where the parties have requested a rapid decision under rule 3 a first management meeting shall be called immediately after the tribunal has been duly constituted under rule 9 unless all the parties and the tribunal agree that such a meeting is not required. Having considered any representations made by the parties, at the first management meeting or otherwise, the tribunal shall give such directions for the future conduct of the proceedings as may be appropriate to secure the rapid determination of the dispute.

Alternative Resolution Procedures

A26–016　22 The tribunal itself will not employ alternative dispute resolution procedures. However, should the parties at any stage of the proceedings wish to consider the possibility of resolving the dispute, or certain issues, by alternative procedures they may request the tribunal to adjourn or stay the proceedings and to give appropriate directions, if required. The tribunal will enquire at the first management meeting and at any subsequent management meeting whether any possibilities exist for the settlement of the dispute, or of some part of it, and whether the parties wish to consider resolving the dispute, or certain issues, by alternative procedures.

Defining the Issues

23 Unless the parties agree or the tribunal directs otherwise, the parties shall set out their cases in writing in accordance with (a) to (d) below: **A26–017**

- (a) within 14 days of the directions referred to in rule 20 the Claimant shall serve a statement setting out the substance of his case and the contentions of law on which he relies and the damages or other relief he claims.

- (b) within 21 days of receipt of the Claimant's statement the Respondent shall serve a statement setting out the substance of his defence and the contentions of law on which he relies by way of defence to the claim and including any counterclaim.

- (c) within 21 days of receipt of the statement of the Respondent the Claimant may serve a statement in reply which shall include a defence to counterclaim, if appropriate.

- (d) all such statements shall be accompanied by copies of the documents upon which the party relies or, if these are numerous, by copies of the principal documents on which he relies together with a list of his further documents. "Documents" includes transcripts of tapes, disks or computer records and any other record which is capable of being printed out or transcribed.

Further Management Meetings

24 Whenever subsequently to the first management meeting the tribunal considers it appropriate to do so, the tribunal may invite the parties to make written representations as to the future conduct of the arbitration and the directions to be given and may call a further management meeting to consider such directions. **A26–018**

25 At the further management meeting the tribunal will give directions for the further conduct of the arbitration and will consider among other matters:

- (a) whether any matters hitherto at issue may now be agreed;
- (b) whether any party should give more details of his case on any issue;
- (c) whether there should be discovery of documents either generally or in relation to any issue;
- (d) whether there should be a hearing to determine whether any allegation should be struck out as disclosing no reasonable cause of action or defence;
- (e) whether any issue should be determined by way of interim award;
- (f) whether an expert or adviser should be appointed to investigate and report to the tribunal on any matter or issue of fact or law.

Witnesses

26 The tribunal may require each party to notify the tribunal and the other parties of the identities of all witnesses the party intends to call and may require the parties to exchange signed witnesses' statements and experts' reports before the hearing. A party may request the attendance at the hearing of a witness whose evidence has been submitted in written form and any witness who gives oral evidence may be questioned by or **A26–019**

on behalf of the party which calls him and any other party. The testimony of witnesses may be presented in affidavit form, with the leave of the tribunal. Unless the parties agree the contrary, evidence shall not be on oath.

Experts Appointed by the Tribunal

A26–020   27 The tribunal may appoint an expert or experts to report to it on specific issues. The parties shall give such expert any relevant information, document or thing he may require of them. The tribunal shall provide the parties with a copy of any expert's report and of any document referred to therein and shall give the parties an opportunity to comment upon such report and to question the expert thereon.

Hearings

A26–021   28 The tribunal shall fix the date, time and place of any meeting or hearing, of which the parties will be given reasonable notice.

29 Hearings shall take place in London or Edinburgh as appropriate unless the parties, with the leave of the tribunal, or the tribunal, choose otherwise. All the parties and their representatives shall be entitled to be present throughout but, save with the consent of the tribunal and the parties, persons not involved in the proceedings shall not be admitted. The proceedings and any award shall remain confidential unless the tribunal, with the consent of the parties, directs otherwise or disclosure is required by law, by a court of competent jurisdiction or by any governmental agency or regulatory authority to which a party making disclosure is subject.

30 Any party may be legally represented or may, with the leave of the tribunal, appear by some other representative.

The Award

A26–022   31 Unless the parties expressly agree otherwise the tribunal shall make any award in writing and shall state the reasons upon which it is based.

32 Any award or other decision of a tribunal of three may be made by a majority of the members of the tribunal and failing a majority decision on any issue the chairman of the tribunal shall make the award alone, as if he were the sole arbitrator.

33 If any member of the tribunal should fail to join in the making of an award, having been given a reasonable opportunity to do so, the remaining member or members of the tribunal may proceed in his absence.

34 The award shall be made on the date when the CDP sends it to the parties.

35 If at any time the parties settle their differences it shall be their joint and several duty to inform the tribunal immediately in writing. The tribunal shall thereupon be discharged and the reference to arbitration concluded, subject to the payment by the parties of any outstanding fees and costs. However, the tribunal will render an award recording the settlement if requested by any party to do so.

36 The tribunal may add to, vary or amend an award to correct any clerical or arithmetical mistake or error arising from any accidental slip or omission. The tribunal may also add to, vary or amend an award to clarify any aspect of the award or to remove any ambiguity in its wording, provided the parties have been given an opportunity to make representations regarding the proposed addition, variation or amendment and all parties have assented thereto.

37 The tribunal shall decide all matters according to law, unless expressly authorised in writing by the parties to decide in accordance with such other considerations as are agreed by the parties or determined by the tribunal.

City Disputes Panel Arbitration Rules

Remedies

38 Unless the parties expressly agree otherwise the tribunal may: A26–023

    (a) make a declaration as to any matter to be determined in the proceedings;

    (b) order the payment of a sum of money in any currency;

    (c) to the extent permitted by the applicable procedural law, (i) order a party to do or refrain from doing anything, (ii) order specific performance of a contract, (iii) order the rectification, setting aside or cancellation of a deed or other document.

Interest

39 Unless the parties expressly agree otherwise the tribunal may award simple or compound interest from such dates at such rates and with such rests as it considers appropriate: A26–024

    (a) on the whole or part of any amount awarded by the tribunal, in respect of any period up to the date of the award;

    (b) on the whole or part of any amount claimed in the arbitration and outstanding at the commencement of the proceedings but paid before the award was made, in respect of any period up to the date of payment;

    (c) from the date of the award until payment on the outstanding amount of any award, including any award of interest under (a) or (b) above and any award as to costs.

Costs

40 The tribunal will specify in its award the costs of the arbitration which shall include the fees and expenses of the tribunal and of any experts employed by the tribunal under rule 27 and the registration fees of the CDP.   A26–025

41 The tribunal will direct in its award whether a party shall pay the whole or any part of another party's costs, which may include legal fees and disbursements, experts' fees and disbursements and witnesses' expenses and the tribunal shall determine the amount of the recoverable costs if these are not agreed, unless the parties are agreed that the costs shall be determined in some other way.

42 If the arbitration is abandoned, suspended or concluded by agreement or otherwise before an award is made, the parties shall be jointly and severally liable for all the costs of the arbitration as determined by the tribunal.

Exclusion of Liability

43 Neither the CDP nor any arbitrator shall be liable for anything done or omitted in purported discharge of its or his functions unless the act or omission is shown to have been in bad faith.   A26–026

Scotland

44 Where the place of arbitration is in Scotland: A26–027

    (a) the tribunal may, unless the parties expressly agree otherwise, make an award in respect of delictual damages, if appropriate, and may award interest in respect of the whole or any part of any award for such period prior to the date of the award as it considers just;

(b) the parties will not, unless they expressly agree otherwise, apply at any stage to the tribunal to state a case for the opinion of the Court of Session.

APPENDIX I

The Simplified Hearing Procedure

A26–028   1 Where the tribunal has directed that the simplified hearing procedure shall be followed:

(a) the Claimant shall, within such period as the tribunal may direct, formulate his case in writing in sufficient detail to identify the matters in dispute and serve it together with copies of any documents on which he relies upon the Respondent and the members of the tribunal;

(b) the Respondent shall, within such period as the tribunal may direct, formulate his defence, and counterclaim if any, in sufficient detail to identify which matters if any in the Claimant's case he accepts and which matters he denies and shall serve it together with copies of any documents on which he relies upon the Respondent and the members of the tribunal; and

(c) the tribunal shall give directions as to service of a reply to any counterclaim under paragraph 2 below.

2 If any party requires further directions he shall specify his requirements in writing to the tribunal within 7 days of the date for service of the Respondent's defence and after this 7 day period has elapsed the tribunal shall give directions either in writing or at an oral hearing as to the future conduct of the arbitration or, if no further directions are required, shall so state.

3 Subject to any directions given under paragraph 2, the tribunal shall, within 21 days of service by the Respondent of his defence, proceed to a hearing of the dispute at which no evidence shall be adduced save for the documents appended to the statements of case and defence, except as the tribunal may otherwise direct or permit.

4 The tribunal shall publish its award within 7 days of the hearing.

APPENDIX II

Decision without a Hearing

A26–029   1 Where parties agree that their dispute shall be decided on the basis of documents only the issues shall be defined in accordance with rule 23, unless the parties agree that they shall be defined in accordance with a different procedure or in some other way.

2 The tribunal will thereafter hold a management meeting, unless the parties and the tribunal agree that such a meeting is not required, and will give such directions as may be required, including:

(a) directions as to any submissions as to fact and law which the parties may wish to make before the tribunal proceeds to its award;

(b) the time within which such submissions are to be made; and

(c) the time after the expiry of which the tribunal may make its award.

City Disputes Panel Mediation Rules[1]

April 1997

Approach to the CDP

1 Where one party to a dispute or difference seeks mediation, that party may ask the CDP to take steps to seek the agreement thereto of the other party or parties.

2 Any costs incurred by the CDP in seeking to obtain the agreement of all parties to participate in the mediation process shall, if the mediation takes place, be borne in equal shares by the parties to the mediation and otherwise by the party making the initial mediation request.

3 Where both or all the parties to a dispute or difference agree to mediation they shall jointly request that the CDP appoint a mediator.

Appointment of a Mediator

4 The mediator shall be appointed by the CDP following consultation with the parties, and shall be a member of the CDP.

5 Such appointment shall be subject to the parties to the mediation entering in to a written agreement with the CDP regulating the terms and conditions of the mediation. This agreement shall be in the CDP standard form unless otherwise agreed and the parties shall in the agreement jointly and severally agree to pay the CDP's and the mediator's costs, fees, disbursements and expenses.

Mediation Procedure

6 The mediator shall be responsible for the conduct of the mediation. The mediator's aim will be to achieve a settlement which the parties consider to be appropriate to their particular circumstances.

7 If the mediator considers it helpful, a preliminary meeting may be held with the parties to discuss the conduct of the mediation, to give directions and to deal with any other matters that may be relevant.

8 The mediator may if requested to do so by all the parties give a non-binding evaluation of the respective merits of the dispute or any aspect of it.

9 At the request of all parties the mediator may make a written recommendation as to terms of settlement. Such recommendation may differ from the decision a court or arbitrator would have reached.

Legal Advisers

10 A party may be legally represented provided that a party intending to be so represented shall inform the mediator and all other parties accordingly.

11 Legal advisers acting for parties may participate in the mediation process to such an extent as the mediator may consider useful and appropriate.

Confidentiality and Privilege

12 The mediation shall be conducted on the same basis as "without prejudice" negotiations in an action in the courts of England or Scotland as the case may be. Mediation

---

[1] This document is reproduced with the kind permission of the City Disputes Panel.

proceedings shall be regarded as privileged except insofar as the parties agree otherwise.

13 The parties and the mediator agree to maintain confidentiality subject only to the need to disclose any matters in proceedings to enforce any agreement for settlement.

14 Any documents and written or oral statements produced or made for the purpose of the mediation shall not be admissible or subject to disclosure in any other proceedings. "Documents" includes transcripts of tapes, disks or computer records and any other record which is capable of being printed out or transcribed.

15 No party shall have access to the mediator's notes or call the mediator as a witness in any proceedings relating to any aspect of the mediation.

Recording Agreements

A27–006   **16** The parties may record any agreed settlement which results from the mediation as a binding and enforceable contract. No agreement as to the terms of any settlement reached in the mediation shall be legally binding unless in writing and signed by the parties or their authorised representatives.

17 Where the mediation is conducted in the context of court or arbitration proceedings, the court or arbitral tribunal may be requested to render the agreement as a consent order or consent award.

Exclusion of Liability

A27–007   **18** Neither the CDP nor any mediator appointed under these Rules shall be liable to the parties for any act or omission whatsoever in connection with the mediation.

Termination of Mediation

A27–008   **19** Mediation may be discontinued at any time should any party so wish. If the mediator considers it appropriate he or she may bring the mediation to an end.

Post-mediation Functions

A27–009   **20** The mediator may, if requested, assist in agreeing terms of settlement.

21 A mediator under these Rules shall not act as an arbitrator in relation to the same dispute or difference unless the parties agree. Alternatively, he or she may agree to determine the matter as an expert after the mediation has come to an end if all the parties at that stage so request.

The Construction Industry Model Arbitration Rules[1]

(1st Edition, February 1998)

For use with Arbitration Agreements under the Arbitration Act 1996

Rule 1: Objective and Application

1.1 These Rules are to be read consistently with the Arbitration Act 1996 (the Act), **A28–001** with common expressions having the same meaning. Appendix 1 contains definitions of terms. Section numbers given in these Rules are references to the Act.

1.2 The objective of the Rules is to provide for the fair, impartial, speedy, cost-effective and binding resolution of construction disputes, with each party having a reasonable opportunity to put his case and to deal with that of his opponent. The parties and the arbitrator are to do all things necessary to achieve this objective: see Sections 1 (General principles), 33 (General duty of the tribunal) and 40 (General duty of parties).

1.3 After an arbitrator has been appointed under these Rules, the parties may not, without the agreement of the arbitrator, amend the Rules or impose procedures in conflict with them.

1.4 The arbitrator has all the powers and is subject to all the duties under the Act except where expressly modified by the Rules.

1.5 Sections of the Act which need to be read with the Rules are printed with the text. Other Sections referred to are printed in Appendix II.

1.6 These Rules apply where:

(a) a single arbitrator is to be appointed, and

(b) the seat of the arbitration is in England and Wales or Northern Ireland.

1.7 These Rules do not exclude the powers of the Court in respect of arbitral proceedings, nor any agreement between the parties concerning those powers.

Rule 2: Beginning and Appointment

2.1 Arbitral proceedings are begun in respect of a dispute when one party serves on **A28–002** the other a written notice of arbitration identifying the dispute and requiring him to agree to the appointment of an arbitrator: but see Rule 3.6 and Section 13 (Application of Limitation Acts).

2.2 The party serving notice of arbitration should name any persons he proposes as arbitrator with the notice or separately. The other party should respond and may propose other names.

2.3 If the parties fail to agree on the name of an arbitrator within 14 days (or any agreed extension) after:

(i) the notice of arbitration is served, or

(ii) a previously appointed arbitrator ceases to hold office for any reason,

---

[1] This document is reproduced with the kind permission of the Society of Construction Arbitrators.

either party may apply for the appointment of an arbitrator to the person so empowered.

2.4 In the event of a failure in the procedure for the appointment of an arbitrator under Rule 2.3 and in the absence of agreement, Section 18 (Failure of appointment procedure) applies. In this event the court shall seek to achieve the objectives in Rules 2.6 to 2.8.

2.5 The arbitrator's appointment takes effect upon his agreement to act or his appointment under Rule 2.3, whether or not his terms have been accepted.

2.6 Where two or more related arbitral proceedings on the same project fall under separate arbitration agreements (whether or not between the same parties) any person who is required to appoint an arbitrator must give due consideration as to whether

(i) the same arbitrator, or

(ii) a different arbitrator

should be appointed in respect of those arbitral proceedings and should appoint the same arbitrator unless sufficient grounds are shown for not doing so.

2.7 Where different persons are required to appoint an arbitrator in relation to arbitral proceedings covered by Rule 2.6, due consideration includes consulting with every other such person. Where an arbitrator has already been appointed in relation to one such arbitral proceeding, due consideration includes considering the appointment of that arbitrator.

2.8 As between any two or more persons who are required to appoint, the obligation to give due consideration under Rules 2.6 or 2.7 may be discharged by making arrangements for some other person or body to make the appointment in relation to disputes covered by Rule 2.6.

2.9 The provisions in Rules 2 and 3 concerning related arbitral proceedings and disputes and joinder apply in addition to other such provisions contained in any contract between the parties in question.

Rule 3: Joinder

3.1 A notice of arbitration may include two or more disputes if they fall under the same arbitration agreement.

3.2 A party served with a notice of arbitration may, at any time before an arbitrator is appointed, himself give a notice of arbitration in respect of any other disputes which fall under the same arbitration agreement and those other disputes shall be consolidated with the arbitral proceedings.

3.3 After an arbitrator has been appointed, either party may give a further notice of arbitration to the other and to the arbitrator referring any other dispute which falls under the same arbitration agreement to those arbitral proceedings. If the other party does not consent to the other dispute being so referred, the arbitrator may, as he considers appropriate, order either:

(i) that the other dispute should be referred to and consolidated with the same arbitral proceedings, or

(ii) that the other dispute should not be so referred.

3.4 If the arbitrator makes an order under Rule 3.3(ii), Rules 2.3 and 2.4 then apply.

3.5 In relation to a notice of arbitration in respect of any other dispute under Rules 3.2 or 3.3, the arbitrator is empowered to:

(i) decide any matter which may be a condition precedent to bringing the other dispute before the arbitrator;

(ii) abrogate any condition precedent to the bringing of arbitral proceedings in respect of the other dispute.

3.6 Arbitral proceedings in respect of any other dispute are begun when the notice of arbitration for that other dispute is served: see Section 13 (Application of Limitation Acts).

3.7 Where the same arbitrator is appointed in two or more related arbitral proceedings on the same project each of which involves some common issue, whether or not involving the same parties, the arbitrator may, if he considers it appropriate, order the concurrent hearing of any two or more such proceedings or of any claim or issue arising in such proceedings: see Section 35 and see also Rule 2.9.

3.8 If the arbitrator orders concurrent hearings he may give such other directions as are necessary or desirable for the purpose of such hearings but shall, unless the parties otherwise agree, deliver separate awards in each of such proceedings, see also Rule 2.9.

3.9 Where the same arbitrator is appointed in two or more arbitral proceedings each of which involves some common issue, whether or not involving the same parties, the arbitrator may, if all the parties so agree, order that any two or more such proceedings shall be consolidated.

3.10 If the arbitrator orders the consolidation of two or more arbitral proceedings he may give such other directions as are appropriate for the purpose of such consolidated proceedings and shall, unless the parties otherwise agree, deliver a single award which shall be final and binding on all the parties to the consolidated proceedings.

3.11 Where an arbitrator has ordered concurrent hearings or consolidation under the foregoing rules he may at any time revoke any orders so made and may give such further orders or directions as are appropriate for the separate hearing and determination of the matters in issue.

3.12 Where two or more arbitral proceedings are ordered to be heard concurrently or to be consolidated, the arbitrator may exercise any or all of the powers in these Rules either separately or jointly in relation to the proceedings to which such order relates.

Rule 4: Particular Powers

4.1 The arbitrator has the power set out in Section 30(1) (Competence of the tribunal **A28–004** to rule on its own jurisdiction). This includes power to rule on what matters have been submitted to arbitration.

4.2 The arbitrator has the powers set out in Section 37(1) (Power to appoint experts, legal advisers or assessors). This includes power to:

(i) appoint experts or legal advisers to report to him and to the parties;

(ii) appoint assessors to assist him on technical matters.

4.3 The arbitrator has the powers set out in Section 38(4) to (6) (General powers exercisable by the tribunal). This includes power to give directions for:

(a) the inspection, photographing, preservation, custody or detention of property by the arbitrator, an expert or a party;

(b) ordering samples to be taken from, or any observation be made of or experiment conducted upon, property;

(c) a party or witness to be examined on oath or affirmation and to administer any necessary oath or take any necessary affirmation;

(d) the preservation for the purposes of the proceedings of any evidence in the custody or control of a party.

4.4 The arbitrator may order the preservation of any work, goods or materials even though they form part of work which is continuing.

4.5 The arbitrator may direct the manner in which, by whom and when any test or experiment is to be carried out. The arbitrator may himself observe any test or experiment and in the absence of one or both parties provided that they have the opportunity to be present.

4.6 The arbitrator may order a claimant to give security for the whole or part of the costs likely to be incurred by his opponent in defending a claim if satisfied that the claimant is unlikely to be able to pay those costs if the claim is unsuccessful. In exercising this power, the arbitrator shall consider all the circumstances including the strength of the claim and any defence, and the stage at which the application is made. This power is subject to Section 38(3).

4.7 The arbitrator may give reasons for any decision under Rule 4.6 if the parties so request and the arbitrator considers it appropriate.

4.8 The arbitrator has the power to order a claimant to give security for the arbitrator's costs: see Section 38(3).

4.9 If, without showing sufficient cause, a claimant fails to comply with an order for security for costs under Rule 4.6, the arbitrator may make a peremptory order to the same effect prescribing such time for compliance as he considers appropriate. If the peremptory order is not complied with, the arbitrator may make an award dismissing the claim: see Rules 11.4 and 11.6.

Rule 5: Procedure and Evidence

A28–005 **5.1** Subject to these Rules, the arbitrator shall decide all procedural and evidential matters including those set out in Section 34(2) (Procedural and evidential matters), subject to the right of the parties to agree any matter. This includes the power to direct:

(a) when and where any part of the proceedings is to be held;

(b) the languages to be used in the proceedings and whether translations are to be supplied;

(c) the use of written statements and the extent to which they can be later amended.

5.2 The arbitrator shall determine which documents or classes of documents should be disclosed between and produced by the parties and at what stage.

5.3 Whether or not there are oral proceedings the arbitrator may determine the manner in which the parties and their witnesses are to be examined.

5.4 The arbitrator is not bound by the strict rules of evidence and shall determine the admissibility, relevance or weight of any material sought to be tendered on any matters of fact or opinion by any party.

5.5 The arbitrator may himself take the initiative in ascertaining the facts and the law.

The Construction Industry Model Arbitration Rules

5.6 The arbitrator may fix the time within which any order or direction is to be complied with and may extend or reduce the time at any stage.

5.7 In any of the following cases:

    (a) an application for security for costs;

    (b) an application to strike out for want of prosecution;

    (c) an application for an order for provisional relief;

    (d) any other instance where he considers it appropriate,

the arbitrator shall require that evidence be put on affidavit or that some other formal record of the evidence be made.

Rule 6: Form of Procedure and Directions

6.1 As soon as he is appointed the arbitrator must consider the form of procedure which is most appropriate to the dispute: see Section 33 (General duty of the tribunal). **A28–006**

6.2 For this purpose the parties shall, as soon as practicable after the arbitrator is appointed, provide to each other and to the arbitrator:

    (a) a note stating the nature of the dispute with an estimate of the amounts in issue;

    (b) a view as to the need for and length of any hearing;

    (c) proposals as to the form of procedure appropriate to the dispute.

6.3 The arbitrator shall convene a procedural meeting with the parties or their representatives at which, having regard to any information that may have been submitted under Rule 6.2, he shall give a direction as to the procedure to be followed. The direction may:

    (a) adopt the procedure in Rules 7, 8 or 9;

    (b) adopt any part of one or more of these procedures;

    (c) adopt any other procedure which he considers to be appropriate;

    (d) impose time limits

and may be varied or amended by the arbitrator from time to time.

6.4 The arbitrator shall give such directions as he considers appropriate in accordance with the procedure adopted. He shall also give such other directions under these Rules as he considers appropriate: see particularly Rules 4, 5 and 13.4.

6.5 In deciding what directions are appropriate the arbitrator shall have regard to any advisory procedure and give effect to any supplementary procedure issued for use under any contract to which the dispute relates.

6.6 The matters under Rules 6.3 and 6.4 may be dealt with without a meeting if the parties so agree and the arbitrator considers a meeting to be unnecessary.

Rule 7: Short Hearing

7.1 This procedure is appropriate where the matters in dispute are to be determined principally by the arbitrator inspecting work, materials, machinery or the like. **A28–007**

7.2 The parties shall, either at the same time or in sequence as the arbitrator may direct, submit written statements of their cases, including any documents and statements of witnesses relied on.

7.3 There shall be a hearing of not more than one day at which each party will have a reasonable opportunity to address the matters in dispute. The arbitrator's inspection may take place before or after the hearing or may be combined with it. The parties may agree to extend the hearing.

7.4 The arbitrator may form his own opinion on the matters in dispute and need not inform the parties of his opinion before delivering his award.

7.5 Either party may adduce expert evidence but may recover any costs so incurred only if the arbitrator decides that such evidence was necessary for coming to his decision.

7.6 The arbitrator shall make his award within one month of the last of the foregoing steps or within such further time as he may require and notify to the parties.

7.7 The recovery of costs is subject to Rule 13.4: see Section 65 (Power to limit recoverable costs).

Rule 8: Documents Only

8.1 This procedure is appropriate where there is to be no hearing, for instance, because the issues do not require oral evidence, or because the sums in dispute do not warrant the cost of a hearing.

8.2 The parties shall, either at the same time or in sequence as the arbitrator may direct, submit written statements of their cases including:

  (a) an account of the relevant facts or opinions relied on;

  (b) statements of witnesses concerning those facts or opinions, signed or otherwise confirmed by the witness;

  (c) the remedy or relief sought, for instance, a sum of money with interest.

8.3 Each party may submit a statement in reply to that of the other party.

8.4 After reading the parties' written statements, the arbitrator may:

  (a) put questions to or request a further written statement from either party;

  (b) direct that there be a hearing of not more than one day at which he may put questions to the parties or to any witness. In this event the parties will also have a reasonable opportunity to comment on any additional information given to the arbitrator.

8.5 The arbitrator shall make his award within one month of the last of the foregoing steps, or within such further time as he may require and notify to the parties.

8.6 The recovery of costs is subject to Rule 13.4: see Section 65 (Power to limit recoverable costs).

Rule 9: Full Procedure

9.1 Where neither the Documents Only nor the Short Procedure is appropriate, the Full Procedure should be adopted, subject to such modification as is appropriate to the particular matters in issue.

9.2 The parties shall exchange statements of claim and defence in accordance with the following guidelines:

The Construction Industry Model Arbitration Rules

    (a) each statement should contain the facts and matters of opinion which are intended to be established by evidence and may include a statement of any relevant point of law which will be contended for;

    (b) a statement should contain sufficient particulars to enable the other party to answer each allegation without recourse to general denials;

    (c) a statement may include or refer to evidence to be adduced if this will assist in defining the issues to be determined;

    (d) the reliefs or remedies sought, for instance, specific monetary losses, must be stated in such a way that they can be answered or admitted;

    (e) all statements should adopt a common system of numbering or identification of sections to facilitate analysis of issues. Particulars given in schedule form should anticipate the need to incorporate replies.

9.3 The arbitrator may permit or direct the parties at any stage to amend, expand, summarise or reproduce in some other format any of the statements of claim or defence so as to identify the matters essentially in dispute, including preparing a list of the matters in issue.

9.4 The arbitrator should give detailed directions, with times or dates for all steps in the proceedings including:

    (a) further statements or particulars required;

    (b) disclosure and production of documents between the parties: see Rule 5.2;

    (c) service of statements of witnesses of fact;

    (d) the number of experts and service of their reports;

    (e) meetings between experts and/or other persons;

    (f) arrangements for any hearing.

9.5 The arbitrator should fix the length of each hearing including the time which will be available to each party to present its case and answer that of its opponent.

9.6 The arbitrator may at any time order the following to be delivered to him and to the other party in writing:

    (a) any submission or speech by an advocate;

    (b) questions intended to be put to any witness;

    (c) answers by any witness to identified questions.

Rule 10: Provisional Relief

10.1 The arbitrator has power to order the following relief on a provisional basis: see **A28–010** Section 39 (Power to make provisional awards)

    (a) payment of a reasonable proportion of the sum which is likely to be awarded finally in respect of the claims to which the payment relates, after taking account of any defence or counterclaim that may be available;

(b) payment of a sum on account of any costs of the arbitration, including costs relating to an order under this Rule;

(c) any other relief claimed in the arbitral proceedings.

10.2 The arbitrator may exercise the powers under this Rule after application by a party or of his own motion after giving due notice to the parties.

10.3 An order for provisional relief under this Rule must be based on formal evidence: see Rule 5.7. The arbitrator may give such reasons for his order as he thinks appropriate.

10.4 The arbitrator may order any money or property which is the subject of an order for provisional relief to be paid to or delivered to a stakeholder on such terms as he considers appropriate.

10.5 An order for provisional relief is subject to the final adjudication of the arbitrator who makes it, or of any arbitrator who subsequently has jurisdiction over the dispute to which it relates.

Rule 11: Default Powers and Sanctions

11.1 The arbitrator has the power set out in Section 41(3) (Powers of tribunal in case of party's default) to make an award dismissing a claim.

11.2 The arbitrator has the power set out in Section 41(4) to proceed in the absence of a party or without any written evidence or submission from a party.

11.3 The arbitrator may by any order direct that if a party fails to comply with that order he will:

(a) refuse to allow the party in default to rely on any allegation or material which was the subject of the order;

(b) draw such adverse inferences from the act of non-compliance as the circumstances justify;

and may, if that party fails to comply without showing sufficient cause, refuse to allow such reliance or draw such adverse inferences and may proceed to make an award on the basis of such materials as have been properly provided, and may make any order as to costs in consequence of such non-compliance.

11.4 In addition to his power under Rule 11.3 the arbitrator has the powers set out in Section 41(5), (6) and (7) (peremptory orders).

11.5 An application to the court for an order requiring a party to comply with a peremptory order may be made only by or with the permission of the arbitrator: see Section 42(2) (Enforcement of peremptory orders of tribunal).

11.6 An application to dismiss a claim for inordinate and inexcusable delay or failure to comply with a peremptory order to provide security for costs must be based on formal evidence: see Rule 5.7. Where a claim is dismissed on such a ground, the claim shall be barred and may not be rearbitrated.

Rule 12: Awards and Remedies

12.1 The arbitrator has the powers set out in Section 47 (Awards on different issues, &c).

12.2 Where the arbitrator directs or the parties agree to a hearing dealing with part of a dispute, then whether or not there is any agreement between the parties as to such matters, the arbitrator may do any of the following:

(a) decide what are the issues or questions to be determined;

(b) decide whether or not to give an award on part of the claims submitted;

(c) make an order for provisional relief: but see Rule 10.2.

12.3 At the conclusion of a hearing, where the arbitrator is to deliver an award he shall inform the parties of the target date for its delivery. The arbitrator must take all possible steps to complete the award by that date and inform the parties of any reason which prevents him doing so. The award shall not deal with the allocation of costs and/or interest unless the parties have been given an opportunity to address these issues.

12.4 An award shall be in writing, dated and signed by the arbitrator. The award must comply with any other requirements of the contract under which it is given. Section 58 (Effect of award) applies but see Rule 10.

12.5 An award should contain sufficient reasons to show why the arbitrator has reached the decisions contained in it unless the parties otherwise agree or the award is agreed.

12.6 The arbitrator has the powers set out in Section 48(3), (4) and (5) (Remedies).

12.7 Where an award orders that a party should do some act, for instance carry out specified work, the arbitrator has the power to supervise the performance or, if he thinks it appropriate, to appoint (and to reappoint as may be necessary) a suitable person so to supervise and to fix the terms of his engagement and retains all powers necessary to ensure compliance with the award.

12.8 The arbitrator has the powers set out in Section 49(3) and (4) (Interest). This is in addition to any power to award contractual interest.

12.9 The arbitrator has the powers set out in Section 57(3) to (6) (Correction of award or additional award) which are to be exercised subject to the time limits stated.

12.10 The arbitrator may notify an award or any part of an award to the parties as a draft or proposal. In such case unless the arbitrator otherwise directs no further evidence shall be admitted and the arbitrator shall consider only such comments of the parties as are notified to him within such time as he may specify and thereafter the arbitrator shall issue the award.

12.11 Where an award is made and there remains outstanding a claim by the other party, the arbitrator may order that the whole or part of the amount of the award be paid to a stakeholder on such terms as he considers appropriate.

Rule 13: Costs

13.1 The general principle is that costs should be borne by the losing party: see Section 61 (Award of costs). Subject to any agreement between the parties, the arbitrator has the widest discretion in awarding which party should bear what proportion of the costs of the arbitration.

13.2 In allocating costs the arbitrator shall have regard to all material circumstances, including such of the following as may be relevant:

(a) which of the claims has led to the incurring of substantial costs and whether they were successful;

(b) whether any claim which has succeeded was unreasonably exaggerated;

(c) the conduct of the party who succeeded on any claim and any concession made by the other party;

(d) the degree of success of each party.

See also Rule 13.9.

13.3 Where an award deals with both a claim and a counterclaim, the arbitrator should deal with the recovery of costs in relation to each of them separately unless he considers them to be so interconnected that they should be dealt with together.

13.4 The arbitrator may impose a limit on recoverable costs of the arbitration or any part of the proceedings: see Section 65 (Power to limit recoverable costs). In determining such limit the arbitrator shall have regard primarily to the amounts in dispute.

13.5 In determining a limit on recoverable costs the arbitrator shall also have regard to any advisory procedure and give effect to any supplementary procedure issued for use under any contract to which the dispute relates.

13.6 A direction under Rule 13.4 may impose a limit on part of the costs of the arbitration: see Section 59 (Costs of the arbitration).

13.7 Where proceedings include claims which are not claims for money, the arbitrator shall take these into account as he thinks appropriate when fixing a limit under Rule 13.4.

13.8 A direction under Rule 13.4 may be varied at any time, subject to Section 65(2). For this purpose the arbitrator may require the parties to submit at any time statements of costs incurred and foreseen.

13.9 In allocating costs the arbitrator shall have regard to any offer of settlement or compromise from either party, whatever its description or form. The general principle which the arbitrator should follow is that a party who recovers less overall than was offered to him in settlement or compromise should recover the costs which he would otherwise have been entitled to recover only up to the date on which it was reasonable for him to have accepted the offer, and the offeror should recover his costs thereafter.

13.10 Section 63(3) to (7) (The recoverable costs of the arbitration) applies to the determination of the recoverable costs of the arbitration (determination by the arbitrator or by the court). Where the arbitrator is to determine recoverable costs, he may do so on such basis as he thinks fit. Section 59 (Costs of the arbitration) also applies.

Rule 14: Miscellaneous

A28–014 **14.1** A party may be represented in the proceedings by any one or more persons of his choice and by different persons at different times: see Section 36 (Legal or other representation).

14.2 The arbitrator shall establish and record postal addresses and other means, including facsimile or telex, by which communication in writing may be effected for the purposes of the arbitration. Section 76(3) to (6) (Service of notices, &c) shall apply in addition.

14.3 Section 78(3) to (5) (Reckoning periods of time) apply to the reckoning of periods of time.

14.4 The parties shall promptly inform the arbitrator of any settlement. Section 51 (Settlement) then applies.

14.5 The parties shall promptly inform the arbitrator of any intended application to the court and provide copies of any proceedings issued in relation to any such matter.

APPENDIX I

Definition of Terms

Act	means the Arbitration Act 1996 (cap 23) including any amendment or reenactment.
claim	includes counterclaim.
claimant	includes counterclaimant.
concurrent hearing	means two or more arbitral proceedings being heard together: see Rules 3.7 and 3.8.
consolidation	means two or more arbitral proceedings being treated as one proceeding: see Rules 3.9 and 3.10.
dispute	includes a difference which is subject to a condition precedent to arbitral proceedings being brought: see Rule 3.5.
notice of arbitration	means the written notice which begins arbitral proceedings: see Rules 2.1 and 3.6.

The Construction Industry Model Arbitration Rules[1]

(1st Edition, February 1998)

Notes Issued by the Society of Construction Arbitrators

(Updated January 2002)

Introduction

A29–001   1. In response to the Bill which was to become the Arbitration Act 1996, the Society of Construction Arbitrators (SCA) initiated the production of Model Arbitration Rules for adoption by all construction institutions and other bodies having interests in construction arbitration. A series of committees was established under the Chairmanship of Lord Justice Auld, including a plenary group, a steering group and a drafting sub-committee which adopted the acronym CIMAR.

2. In the course of its work, the CIMAR steering group published a framework document with suggested draft rules in September 1996. A full draft of the rules was issued in February 1997 and, after wide consultation, the Rules were published as consultation document in April 1997.

3. After further extensive consultation the Rules were recirculated in draft in October 1997 and offered for formal endorsement to all the relevant construction institutions and bodies. This resulted in requests for a number of additions and amendments, while many bodies were prepared to endorse the Rules as printed. This first edition of the Rules, printed in February 1998, lists the bodies who have endorsed the Rules.

4. The drafting and production of the first edition was [sic] been undertaken principally by John Uff, FEng QC, Peter Aeberli, RIBA barrister, and Christopher Dancaster, FRICS, the then Secretary, SCA. The Rules will be kept under review and further editions produced by a cross-industry review body which was established under the auspices of the SCA shortly after the publication of the first edition.

5. The Review Body was set up under the chairmanship of His Honour Judge Humphrey LLoyd QC. Feedback has been received from the bodies who endorsed the Rules and from users. There has been no evidence of particular problems with wording or content of the Rules themselves to justify any change but comment has been received as to the need for additional guidance in respect of certain of the Rules. This guidance has been incorporated within these updated Notes.

Drafting

A29–002   6. The Arbitration Act 1996 (the Act) dictates a radically different approach to arbitration Rules. While the 1950 Arbitration Act contained only general measures and required

---

[1] This document is reproduced with the kind permission of the Society of Construction Arbitrators.

that Rules should be fully drafted, the 1996 Act contains extensive powers which, in most cases, require contracting in.

7. The drafting team had to decide between incorporation by reference and extensive repetition of sections of the Act within the Rules. The steering group was in favour of the former and decided that, in the interest of efficiency, sections of the Act of immediate relevance should be printed after the Rule in question, with other sections necessary to the working of the Rules being printed as an appendix. As at January 2002 the Act is no longer novel and this decision has been modified in the version of CIMAR included on the SCA web site (see note 10 below).

8. Apart from incorporating powers direct from the Act, the Rules have two other purposes:

(1) to extend or amend the provisions of the Act where necessary; and
(2) to add a general framework to the specific powers and duties in order to provide guidance to users as well as to arbitrators.

Objective (2) gives rise to the issue of "user friendliness" which has been much debated. One question was whether the Rules should set out extensive procedures or whether they should be as brief as was consistent with their overall purpose. The approach adopted is essentially one of brevity coupled with clarity, which has generally commanded wide support.

9. The Rules are divided into fourteen sections called Rules with numbering within each Rule running to one decimal place only. In addition, having considered various appendices which might be helpful, the choice has narrowed to two, namely definition of terms (Appendix I) and Sections of the Act referred to but not printed in the Rules (Appendix II).

10. In the year 2000 CIMAR was included on the SCA web site (www.arbitrators-society.org) in the same form as it appeared in print. It has become apparent in the course of use on the web that the Rules would be far more user friendly on the screen if the sections of the Act that are appended to each Rule were to be replaced with a link to the appropriate section of the Act as it appears in the Government web site (www.open.gov). This has now been done. There is one small caveat to this decision and that relates to the occasional fragility of links on the web. If any difficulty is found with these links please inform the site webmaster as identified on the opening page of the SCA website.

Adoption of CIMAR

A29–003 11. The importance of having the same Rules adopted by all relevant construction institutions and bodies is generally accepted. A large proportion of construction work now spans more than one professional body and disputes necessarily do likewise. There is no good reason for different arbitration rules to exist within the same industry. Specifically, in the light of Section 86 of the 1996 Act not being brought into force, there is no longer an ability to bring Court proceedings in respect of multi-party disputes. If arbitration is to play a proper role in construction disputes, it is imperative that a workable system of joinder should be created. Common Rules are the only way to achieve this in practice (see Rule 3). There are many other aspects of the Rules where a common approach across the industry is highly desirable (for instance, orders for provisional relief, Rule 10).

12. Where any of the contract producing bodies within the industry considers that individual procedural Rules are required, the Rules make express provision for the incorporating of such Rules, for instance in the form of "advisory or model procedures" under Rule 6. There are other express provisions in CIMAR which invite additional Rules. Conversely, however, some Rules will operate only if they are incorporated as drafted by all the relevant institutions. This applies in the case of joinder under Rule 2, where appointment of a common arbitrator must be considered by the persons individually charged with making the appointment.

Notes on the Rules

A29–004   **13.** These Notes are based on the Notes that have accompanied CIMAR since publication which have been edited and updated to provide the guidance that has been identified as being necessary by the Review Body.

Rule 1

A29–005   **14.** This is largely declaratory, serving to recall the now express requirements as to the basic rules of arbitration.

15. It is in the nature of arbitration that the parties will wish to agree (to the extent that the law allows) how they wish their arbitration to be conducted and it has been suggested in relation to Rule 1.3 that the principle of party autonomy requires that the parties should be at liberty to alter the Rules. While this argument is recognised, the achievement of uniformity throughout the construction industry requires that general amendment of the Rules should be discouraged. Consequently, the Rule is drafted so as to prohibit amendment (save with the agreement of the arbitrator) after the arbitrator has been appointed.

16. Before the arbitrator is appointed, the parties are clearly free to amend CIMAR if they find that this is really necessary. The arbitrator appointed will be accepting to serve on the amended basis. After an arbitrator has been appointed, if the parties wish for some good reason to agree an amendment to the Rules or a procedure in conflict with them, they will have to gain the agreement also of the arbitrator (otherwise, as a worst case scenario, the arbitrator would be compelled to resign). Parties should therefore be careful to consult, together, with the arbitrator before seeking to agree such amendments or procedures. (See also Rule 5.1)

17. Rule 1.6 limits the application of these Rules to a single arbitrator and to arbitrations in England and Wales or Northern Ireland. Any wider applications could be the subject of special Rules issued by individual institutions (for instance the ICE has Rules for Scotland).

18. Rule 1.7 was added late in the drafting process at the request of the JCT whose Standard Form of Building Contract contains an agreement to the bringing of an appeal pursuant to Section 69(2)(a) of the Act. The Rule is declaratory of what is otherwise the clear effect of CIMAR.

Rule 2

19. This Rule sets out a uniform procedure for beginning arbitral proceedings for the purpose of the Limitation Acts. To the extent the standard forms differ, they should be brought into line with Rule 2.1. It is also provided that the arbitrator's appointment takes effect from his agreement to act or appointment, even if this is conditional upon acceptance of his terms.

A29–006

20. The important question of appointing an arbitrator in two or more related disputes is dealt with under Rules 2.5 to 2.7. These impose duties on persons having the function of appointing arbitrators to give consideration to whether the same or a different arbitrator should be appointed. This will be a matter of considerable importance to the parties involved. It is questionable whether these Rules would be capable of enforcement against the person empowered to appoint. A powerful sanction exists, however, through possible challenge to an arbitrator who is appointed otherwise than in accordance with these Rules.

21. The term "related arbitral proceedings" in Rule 2.6 refers to those concerning disputes or differences that raise issues that are substantially the same as or connected with the issues that are already the subject of arbitral proceedings.

22. Rule 2.9 makes it clear that the provisions in Rules 2 and 3 concerning related disputes apply in addition to any contract provisions in this regard, which may exist in the Standard Forms.

Rule 3

23. This Rule deals both with joinder of disputes and joinder of parties in related disputes. Rules 3.1 to 3.4 permit either party to raise disputes in addition to the initial dispute which is referred. This may be done as a matter of right by the respondent before an arbitrator is appointed.

A29–007

24. After an arbitrator has been appointed, either party may give notice of another dispute. CIMAR do not preclude the parties from agreeing to consolidate a further dispute with existing arbitration proceedings. The arbitrator should be consulted before this is done. If the arbitrator's position were compromised or otherwise affected the parties should not insist on their right.

25. If one party does not agree that a further dispute should be consolidated with existing arbitration proceedings the arbitrator is empowered to decide whether or not this should be done. In such a situation the arbitrator should always obtain submissions from both parties before making his decision.

26. The arbitrator should not order consolidation of the two disputes if there is a likelihood that a party will be prejudiced as a result, for example by the hearing and the award in the first arbitration being delayed.

27. Consolidation should be ordered if the overall costs of resolving the two disputes will be reduced as a result without detriment to a party, for example by reducing the time needed for the hearing if the same witnesses are involved.

28. In the event that the arbitrator decides that the dispute should not be referred to the same arbitral proceedings, it continues as a separate dispute, there then being no agreement as to the appointment of an arbitrator for that dispute.

29. A party initiating arbitration must normally take into account any matter which is a condition precedent to arbitration. For example, it may be necessary first to refer the matter in question to the Engineer under the contract, and arbitral proceedings may not be available until this has been done. Rule 3.5 applies to a situation where the original notice of arbitration is validly given but a condition precedent potentially applies to the "other" dispute to be referred under Rules 3.2 or 3.3. If the condition precedent has to be satisfied, this may either hold up the proceedings or effectively prevent the other dispute from being joined. Rule 3.5, therefore, empowers the arbitrator to take whatever steps are necessary to resolve the matter, so that the other dispute may be joined (or the arbitrator may decide that it should not be joined on other grounds).

30. Rule 3.5 is expressed in wide terms so as to cover any foreseeable type of condition precedent. In the example of reference to the Engineer, the arbitrator is empowered under Rule 3.5(i) to "decide any matter which may be a condition precedent". Thus, if there is disagreement as to whether the matter in question has been referred to the Engineer, the arbitrator may decide whether or not it has been so referred.

31. Rule 3.5(ii) contains an even wider power to "abrogate any condition precedent". In the example in paragraph 29, the arbitrator could decide that the requirement for the dispute to be referred to the Engineer should no longer apply, if he has already decided that the matter in question had not been referred.

32. Another example of the application of Rule 3.5 is where the contract requires a dispute first to be the subject of mediation or conciliation proceedings within a fixed timescale. One party may allege that the condition precedent has not been satisfied. Sub-Rule (i) empowers the arbitrator to decide whether or not this is so, and, if not, Sub-Rule (ii) empowers him to abrogate the condition precedent. In either event, the arbitrator is empowered to allow the additional disputes to be brought within the arbitral proceedings without further delay.

33. Clause 3.5 thus empowers the arbitrator to short-circuit what may otherwise become a time-consuming and unnecessary procedural argument, which may be unrelated to the true merits of the disputes.

34. Note that the definition of "dispute" in Appendix I to the Rules includes a difference which is subject to a condition precedent to arbitral proceedings being brought.

35. Some bodies commenting on the Rules have suggested that the arbitrator should be empowered to order consolidation of separate proceedings in which he is appointed. The consensus view was to the contrary, but any adopting body may itself include such a power by additional Rules.

Rule 4

36. This Rule concerns the powers of the arbitrator to rule on jurisdiction (Section 30) and to appoint experts, advisers or assessors (Section 37); also the power to give directions in relation to property, examination of witnesses and preservation of evidence.

37. Where experts, advisers or assessors are appointed by the arbitrator the parties must be provided with full copies of any information, opinion or advice that is given so that they have the reasonable opportunity to comment set out in s37(1)(b) of the Act.

38. Specific power is given to order the preservation of work, goods or materials which form part of the ongoing construction work. The arbitrator is also given the power to order any test or experiment, which he may observe with or without the presence of the parties.

39. When operating Rule 4.4 the arbitrator should be careful to avoid unnecessary delay to the progress of the work on site resulting from an order for the preservation of work. Such an order will generally result from a need to take evidence that would otherwise disappear and such evidence should be taken at the earliest opportunity in order that the contract works may proceed without delay. The arbitrator should also bear in mind any provisions in the contract for the continuation of work when quality disputes arise.

40. The circumstances in which the arbitrator is empowered to make an order for security for costs (Section 38) are set out in Rule 4.6. The question whether the arbitrator should give reasons for his order has given rise to a range of views. Rule 4.7 represents a compromise which may be amended by the parties subject to Rule 1.3. The Review Body has prepared detailed guidance on the question of security for costs and this is included as Appendix 1 to these Notes.

41. Although Rule 4.7 is conditioned on a request by a party, an arbitrator is always entitled to give reasons for any decision. Compliance with the general duties in section 33 of the Act may require reasons to be given on any application. An application for security is mentioned in Rule 5.7 as a type of application where the evidence may need to be on affidavit. An arbitrator, before dealing with an application for security for costs, ought to ask if reasons are required. The consequences of non-compliance with an order for security can be severe—see Rule 4.9. If reasons are given the Parties will know that the decision does not go beyond the recorded evidence and was made on the right basis. In addition, as set out above, where a sealed or other offer has been made, the arbitrator may need to demonstrate how the application has been decided. Confidence in the arbitral process is served by openness, so that parties should have no doubt that the arbitrator has acted fairly and impartially, even if the decision may not be that which a party wishes.

42. The arbitrator would be entitled to decline to give reasons if a request for reasons for a decision was made after the decision was given unless there was good reason for the request not having been made beforehand.

43. Under Rule 4.8: 1) the arbitrator may agree terms with the parties to the effect that he will receive security from both of them and 2) a Respondent is a Claimant as far as a Counter-Claim is concerned *(see the definitions in Appendix 1 to the Rules)*.

Rule 5

44. This Rule incorporates the powers provided under Section 34, ensuring that the arbitrator has full discretion as to the adoption of rules of evidence, disclosure of documents and the conducting of oral proceedings.

45. Rule 5.1 is intended to make clear the right of the parties to agree any procedural and evidential matter that is not already addressed in the Rules. (If it is in the Rules then Rule 1.3 governs their amendment.) Subject to that party autonomy, the arbitrator also has to decide procedural and evidential matters to the extent that they are not already set forth in the Rules.

46. Some have suggested that by reading Rules 1.3 and 5.1 together it could be argued that CIMAR requires that the parties' autonomy has to yield to the arbitrator's ultimate control. Such an interpretation is not intended. For the reasons set out above, Rule 1.3 requires the agreement of the arbitrator after appointment. So, a solution for any parties concerned by such an argument may be to consider (before appointing the arbitrator) the deletion of the opening phrase "Subject to these Rules" in Rule 5.1 or substituting it with "To the extent that such matters are not already set out in these Rules". It may be appropriate for parties when agreeing a consensual appointment to raise these matters with the arbitrator beforehand or at the preliminary meeting.

47. The power to grant permission to amend in Rule 5.1(c) should be exercised unless there is such injustice to one party that cannot be dealt with by the award of costs. There are three different categories of written statement in an arbitration:

> *Written Statements of Case*: Amendment should always be allowed save where the prejudice to the other party will not be remedied by an award of costs.

Written statements by Counsel: Can be amended at any time as may be required by the handling of the case.

Written witness statements of fact or opinion: If the witness finds that he is not telling the truth in an original written statement he must be allowed to amend or possibly he will be considered to have committed perjury. Where the amendment arises for reasons other than an original genuine mistake the credibility of the witness may come into question as a result.

48. Any order for disclosure of documents should relate to those that are relevant to the issues before the arbitrator. Disclosure may usefully be limited by identifying specific issues that are to be put to the arbitrator beforehand. There is merit in staged disclosure, *e.g.* a party first discloses the documents upon which it principally relies. Preliminary disclosure by lists of files often saves time and cost (provided that the contents are properly identified to avoid dispute about the contents). Inspection follows.

49. Once a party has made all the disclosure that it intends to give without prompting, the other party can then make requests for any documents or classes of documents that have not been disclosed. If they are not disclosed voluntarily the arbitrator may order their disclosure but should only do so if persuaded of the reasonableness and justification of the request.

50. Rule 5.4 is formulated to give the arbitrator discretion as to the way in which he will deal with evidence. He must however ensure that the parties are not taken by surprise by the way in which he administers this rule. He ought therefore at the outset of the proceedings to invite the parties to consider and to agree (and if necessary to decide) whether and to what extent rules of evidence are or are not to be followed. The arbitrator may, for example, decide to accept hearsay evidence without requiring that prior notice is given. In that event he must ensure that the parties are aware that he will be doing this so that no disadvantage is caused to a party who might otherwise expect hearsay evidence adduced without notice to be excluded. If subsequently he were to decide to admit apparently irrelevant or hearsay evidence he must ensure that the parties are aware that he will do so and allow them the opportunity to make submissions as to the weight (if any) that he should give to that evidence.

51. In considering whether to admit evidence that a party submits is irrelevant the arbitrator should be aware that he may run the risk of a challenge under s68 should he admit truly irrelevant evidence.

52. Whatever rules are adopted as to evidence for the purpose of the hearing, Rule 5.7 requires formal evidence in relation to particular matters, including an application for provisional relief. The reason for this provision is that construction arbitration has become increasingly informal. While in general this is to be encouraged, the matters listed are considered to require at least a degree of evidential formality, so that a party may know the basis on which an order has been made against him. "Some other formal record" will include a written statement of the evidence attested by the witness before the arbitrator or an agreed written record of any evidence taken orally in the presence of the arbitrator, *e.g.* by a transcript or electronic record. The arbitrator must be prepared to make his own record available to the parties, provided that this is agreed beforehand. A party may well make its own record but must, of course, not give it to the arbitrator without giving a copy to the other party.

53. It is generally appropriate for the arbitrator to require that pleadings or statements of case are verified by the party in person, or, in the case of a Company, by a director or manager with knowledge of the facts.

The Construction Industry Model Arbitration Rules

Rule 6

54. This Rule deals with the initial stages in the arbitration where the form of procedure must be determined. The parties are required initially to submit information relevant to the choice of procedure. A29–010

55. Rule 6.2 has been found to be a valuable initial step in the arbitration. It is for the parties to comply with this Rule without prompting by the arbitrator. In practice this seldom happens and the arbitrator should remind the parties of this requirement immediately on appointment.

56. The arbitrator will normally convene a procedural meeting at which the decision as to procedure will be made and other appropriate directions given. A meeting is to be held unless the parties and the arbitrator consider it unnecessary. An arbitrator who considers that his obligations under Section 33 would be best served by issuing procedural directions without incurring the cost of a preliminary meeting should not be dissuaded by this Rule from making such a suggestion to the parties.

57. A preliminary meeting held with the parties themselves present can often however create a climate encouraging the settlement of the dispute. A preliminary meeting can also be of significant assistance to the arbitrator in understanding the dispute and determining the appropriate procedure.

58. In appropriate circumstances a preliminary meeting or any other procedural meeting can be held by telephone or video conference call.

59. Subject to the parties' right to agree procedural matters (see Rule 5.1), the arbitrator is given wide powers by Rule 6.3, including adopting procedures that may curtail oral hearings. For the reasons in the note to Rule 9.6, an arbitrator must exercise such powers with great care and only after considering the parties' submissions (and hopefully their agreement to the procedure).

60. Rule 6.5 provides that, in giving directions, the arbitrator is to have regard to "any advisory procedure and give effect to any supplementary procedure issued for use under any contract to which the dispute relates". This allows any body responsible for issuing forms of contract to draw up its own special procedure containing requirements for particular types of dispute. A similar provision is contained in Rule 13.5 in relation to costs.

Rule 7

61. It may on occasion be appropriate for the arbitrator to utilise elements of Rules 7, 8 and 9 in a single arbitration. A29–011

62. Rule 7 is a procedure designed for use where there is to be a hearing of short duration with the arbitrator inspecting the relevant work, materials, etc. The parties exchange Statements of Case either at the same time or sequentially as the arbitrator may order. This is followed by a hearing normally of one day's duration. The inspection may be combined with the hearing.

63. Under this Rule the parties are discouraged from adducing expert evidence, which will normally be at their own cost. It is of the essence of the procedure that the arbitrator forms his own opinion and Rule 7.4 provides that he is not bound to communicate this to the parties, reversing the effect of *Fox v PG Wellfair* (1982) 19 BLR 52.

Rule 8

64. This is an alternative short procedure involving documents only where the parties are required, either at the same time or sequentially as the arbitrator may direct, to submit full written statements of their case. A29–012

65. The arbitrator should always carefully consider whether a documents only procedure is appropriate. He should in all normal circumstances accede to any request that he operates Rule 8.4 in terms of further written statements and/or there be a hearing of not more than one day in duration.

66. Where statements of witnesses are submitted it is important for the arbitrator to know that they contain the words of the witness and not some other person who may have composed the statement. Rule 8.2(b) therefore allows for statements to be signed or otherwise confirmed, for instance by a letter to this effect. The arbitrator retains the right to put either written questions to the parties or to direct a short hearing.

Rule 9

67. This sets out a full procedure where there is a need for the parties to exchange pleadings (the term is not used as such in the Rules). Rule 9.2 sets out guidelines intended to facilitate an efficient exchange of the parties' respective cases.

68. A statement of defence which does not include the following will not comply with Rule 9.2:

- which of the allegations in the statement of claim are denied
- which allegations the respondent is for good reason unable to deny or to admit but which he requires the claimant to prove
- which allegations are admitted.

Where a respondent denies or does not admit an allegation

- he must state his reasons for doing so
- if he intends to put forward a different version of events from that given by the claimant, he must state his own version.

69. These requirements apply equally to the defence of a counter-claim (see the definitions) and to any reply or other answer which the claimant may submit to the defence. If these requirements are not satisfied the arbitrator should issue an order requiring compliance at an early juncture. Failure to comply with such an order may result in the making of a peremptory order under Section 41(5) in the same terms and, if this is not complied with, the operation of the sanctions in Section 41(7).

70. The existence of the provisions for amendment of a statement of claim or defence, disclosure and the like is not a reason for non-compliance with Rule 9.2.

71. Rule 9.6 is included to encourage the reduction of unnecessary and costly oral proceedings. The arbitrator should, however, carefully consider the ramifications of precluding oral submissions or speeches by an advocate before deciding to do so unless this has been agreed by both parties. In any event if written opening or closing submissions are ordered in writing the advocates should be offered the opportunity to make brief oral submissions in clarification.

72. The arbitrator should always bear in mind that Rule 9 gives the parties the right to a hearing and he should not deprive a party of this right without submissions from the parties first.

73. The arbitrator is required to give detailed directions for the preparation and conduct of a hearing, for which he must also fix the overall length and times available to each party. In fixing the length of any hearing or the time available to the parties he should

always take into account the interests of the parties. The arbitrator is empowered to require any matters to be submitted in writing.

Rule 10

74. A principal intention of this section is to preserve the claimant's cash flow in proceedings which he is bound to win but in which the amount of his entitlement has not been ascertained at the stage of the proceedings at which the provisional relief is considered and/or granted. **A29–014**

75. The side note to Section 39 of the Act is wrong and does not form a part of the section. In the absence of specific agreement there is no power to make a provisional *award*. The arbitrator's power is limited to the making of an order for provisional *relief*. The arbitrator is given this power by Rule 10.

76. An order for provisional relief may be made on application from a party and after hearing any objections from the other party.

77. The arbitrator may decide that his obligations under Sections 1 and 33 suggest that an order for provisional relief is appropriate. He should in this event give notice that he intends to make such an order and he must allow the parties to make such submissions as they desire before he does so.

78. An order for provisional relief must be based upon formal evidence in accordance with Rule 5.7. In making such an order the arbitrator should note the provisions of Rule 10.3 regarding the giving of reasons. The arbitrator should remember that compliance with the general duties in section 33 of the Act may require reasons to be given. An arbitrator, before making an order for provisional relief ought to ask if reasons are required. If reasons are given the Parties will know that the decision was made on the right basis. (See also paragraph 40 above).

79. An order for provisional relief is subject to the final adjudication either of the arbitrator who makes it or of any other arbitrator who may have jurisdiction over the dispute to which the order relates.

80. There is an alternative to an order for provisional relief. If it is self evident, having taken into account any defence, set-off or counterclaim, that sums are unquestionably due from one party to the other the arbitrator should, on application, order payment in an award under Section 47 rather than as provisional relief. The arbitrator must however be absolutely certain that he is not deciding something prematurely in doing this.

Rule 11

81. This Rule incorporates powers under Section 41 to dismiss a claim on the ground of inordinate and inexcusable delay or to proceed with the arbitration where one party is in default. **A29–015**

82. The power to make a peremptory order is given under Rule 11.4, where a failure to comply allows the arbitrator to debar the party in default, draw adverse inferences and proceed on the basis of the materials properly provided. A peremptory order may be made only after a party has failed without sufficient cause to comply with an earlier order to the same effect (Section 41(5)).

83. Alternatively, Rule 11.3 empowers the arbitrator to achieve the effect of a peremptory order directly through a single order, providing that a party will be debarred or adverse inferences drawn in the event of non-compliance with the original order. This Rule reflects the present practice of many arbitrators.

84. The final sentence of Rule 11.6 makes clear that an award dismissing a claim for inordinate and inexcusable delay will bar the claim from being re-arbitrated. So, by

333

agreement (unless the parties provide otherwise: see note to Rule 1.3), the parties are here removing the doubt in law whether such an arbitral award which has not addressed the merits of the claim would preclude the claimant from re-commencing proceedings. However, preventing a party from re-commencing while the applicable limitation period has not expired would seem to conflict with the statutory policy allowing the period of limitation in which to pursue one's rights: *Lazenby (James) & Co v McNicholas Construction Co Ltd* [1995] 3 All ER 820. Therefore, it is suggested that a claim should not be dismissed for delay within the limitation period for that claim.

Rule 12

A29–016   85. This Rule deals with a variety of matters leading to the award. While the term "interim award" has been dropped from the legislation, Rule 12.1 incorporates the powers under Section 47 to make awards on different issues. It is the practice of many arbitrators to enumerate their awards in the same arbitration sequentially, identifying the matter(s) dealt with in each award as is required by Section 47(3).

86. For the purpose of a hearing on part of the dispute, the arbitrator is specifically empowered to decide what issues are to be determined. Where there is a hearing on part of the dispute, the arbitrator retains the discretion not to give an award or alternatively to make an order for provisional relief under Rule 10.

87. The arbitrator has the widest discretion as to the remedies he may order. Where this includes an order that a party should do some act, the arbitrator has power to supervise or if he thinks fit, appoint some other person to supervise the performance.

88. As a general rule the arbitrator should avoid making an award of specific performance of construction works. An award in damages is normally an alternative. It is far less likely to cause subsequent problems regarding the adequacy of the performance of those works if the cost is ascertained and a money award made, even if this means that the arbitrator has to base his award on an estimate rather than the actual cost of carrying out the work. Some detailed considerations concerning the award of specific performance if both parties are agreed that such an award is appropriate are included in Appendix 2 to these Notes.

89. The powers under Section 49 to award simple or compound interest, and under Section 57 to correct an accidental slip or ambiguity, are incorporated. Rule 12.10 gives the arbitrator the power to notify an award or part as a draft or proposal. Such a notification should be clearly identified as being a draft or a proposal as it may be phrased in such a way that could otherwise create the inference that it should be binding. There is no obligation to do so, but the practice of issuing parts of an award in draft is not uncommon. Issuing an award in draft may lead to the proffering of additional evidence and submissions, as to which the arbitrator is given express powers.

90. The arbitrator should, before making his award on the substantive issues, indicate to the parties that it is his intention, unless the parties agree to the contrary, to reserve his award of costs to be dealt with in a later award and after the parties have been given the opportunity to address him orally or in writing upon his award of costs.

91. The award of interest is at the arbitrator's discretion. He should not make such an award without allowing the parties to make submissions beforehand. He should always tell the parties if he is considering the award of compound interest so that they may make submissions on this point.

92. The arbitrator should ensure that every conclusion that he reaches is supported by and follows logically from the reasons that he gives. Reasons should be given in respect of all matters that are put to the arbitrator for his decision. The award must not deal with any matters that the parties have not asked the arbitrator to decide.

93. Rule 12.11 gives the arbitrator a discretion to deal with a monetary award where there remains outstanding a cross-claim by the other party which may have the effect of reducing or extinguishing the award in question. In such circumstances, and in order to pre-empt a costly dispute as to enforcement, the arbitrator may order payment of the whole or part of the amount of the award to a stakeholder on terms. The arbitrator may thus seek to achieve summary and substantial justice as between the parties pending his decision on the cross-claim. This should be reflected in the terms upon which the money is ordered to be paid. The arbitrator is not bound to exercise this power and would normally encourage the parties to seek agreement.

Rule 13

94. The general principles to be adopted in regard to the apportionment of costs are set out in Rules 13.1 to 13.3, while preserving the widest discretion to the arbitrator. Rule 13.1 adopts the more direct wording of the UNCITRAL Rules, rather than of Section 61 (costs to follow the event). More detailed guidance on the apportionment of costs is included in Appendix 3 to these Notes.   **A29–017**

95. The power to impose a limit on recoverable costs of the arbitration (Section 65) is dealt with [in] the Rules 13.4 to 13.8. The complexity of the dispute should always be considered in addition to the amount in dispute. "Recoverable Costs" includes the arbitrator's fees (Section 59). An order under Section 65 limits what may be recovered from the other party and has no effect on liability to pay fees incurred. More detailed guidance on the limitation of recoverable costs is included in Appendix 4 to these Notes.

96. Earlier drafts of CIMAR incorporated fixed limits on recoverable costs of 25% of the amount in dispute, and 10% in the case of an arbitration adopting the Short Hearing or Documents Only procedures. While these limits were not in themselves contentious, the general view was that they were insufficiently flexible for the wide range of disputes which might be covered by CIMAR. The Rules, accordingly, empower the arbitrator to fix any limit, having regard to any model procedure issued under the relevant contract (see also notes to Rule 6 above).

97. The effect of an "offer of settlement" is expressly provided for under Rule 13.9, in accordance with established practice. The determinations of recoverable costs by the arbitrator himself is dealt with in Rule 13.10.

Rule 14

98. This Rule incorporates provisions dealing with representation (Section 36), notifications (Section 76) and reckoning of time (Section 78). The parties are required promptly to inform the arbitrator of any settlement or application to the Court.   **A29–018**

APPENDIX 1

Guidance on Security for Costs

Rule 4.6 does not follow either section 726(1) of the Companies Act 1985 (see now Rules 25.12 and 25.13 of the CPR), or the former Order 23 of the Rules of the Supreme Court. It applies to any claimant and not just a company. It will apply to a counterclaimant (see the definitions in Appendix 1 to the Act). Section 38(3) of the Act provides no positive guidance as to the way in which the arbitrator should deal with an application that security for costs is ordered but in most cases the principles developed by the courts   **A29–019** on applications under the Companies Act should be followed. Thus the arbitrator should split the application into two stages. The first will be addressed to the question: is the claimant unlikely to be able to pay? If that is answered: Yes, then the next stage will concern the questions: should security be ordered and in what amount? If the arbitrator is satisfied that the claimant is likely to be able to pay the costs, the application ought to be dismissed without starting on the second stage. (Note—the Companies Act is however predicated upon the requirement that the tribunal is satisfied that the claimant *will* be unable to pay which is not the position in CIMAR which sets the test at the level of being unlikely to be able to pay).

Stage 1 requires the arbitrator to assume that the defence will be successful and an award will be made in favour of the applicant. (This assumption may be reviewed, if required by the claimant, but only under the second stage.) An application may be made before the applicant has set out its defence. In such circumstances the arbitrator should require evidence on affidavit of the defence, as provided by Rule 5.7, in order to ensure the bona fides of the applicant. Where the applicant has a counterclaim which raises the same issues as the claim (e.g. where the defence is that the work is defective or that delay makes the claimant liable to the defendant), then the applicant must at the outset agree not to pursue the counterclaim if security is ordered and not provided, so that the claim is stayed. Otherwise no practical purpose will be served by an order for security since the arbitration will continue on the counterclaim (see *BJ Crabtree (Insulation) Ltd v GPT Communication Systems Ltd* (1990) 59 BLR 43).

Stage 1 will however require the arbitrator to establish the probable amount of costs for which the claimant might be liable, were the claim unsuccessful. The arbitrator has also to take into account any orders for costs that have already been made and not satisfied, since costs which the applicant would not be able to recover must be excluded. The arbitrator may also have to consider whether Rule 13 might be exercised (this gives the arbitrator latitude to depart from the ordinary rule that the loser should pay) if identifiable circumstances exist which make it probable that the claimant would not be required to pay all the applicant's costs. Under Stage 2, the arbitrator may fix a lower amount (the courts frequently do so—see later) so there need be no concern that the costs assessed or assumed for the purposes of Stage 1 will be those for which security is ordered under Stage 2. Under the first stage the arbitrator has to make a common sense forecast about ability to pay at the time when the award might have to be honoured. (If the claimant is insolvent no forecast is needed.) The question is not whether the claimant *might* be unable to pay the costs, but whether the claimant is unlikely to be able to pay them, which is a higher degree of probability.

If the claimant is a company then the applicant's evidence will usually be the latest accounts filed at Companies House. They are rarely up to date and may either not be representative of the present position of the company or be uninformative. A pragmatic approach is justified e.g. if a reputable claimant has always paid its debts then it may be likely to meet its obligations under the award, especially if the alternative is to go out of business. If accounts have not been filed by the date required then some very good reason should be provided, a company ought to be able to file accounts within the time limit required. Companies that do not comply with their statutory obligations may have a reason not to do so, especially if the default is not corrected once the application is made. A company that wishes to rely upon management accounts to dispel the inferences to be drawn from the filed accounts (or the absence of such accounts) will usually need to have such accounts vouched for by the company's auditors or some other reputable source, as they may contain unjustifiable assumptions, e.g. in the treatment of sales or in the valuation of assets.

If the claimant is likely to be able to pay the costs and if the application is dismissed, the arbitrator may leave open the possibility of a further application, should the claimant's circumstances change. In such event the arbitrator should make it clear that the applicant cannot rely upon evidence which was or ought to have been available at the time of the original application which was dismissed.

The second stage requires two fundamental questions to be answered: is the application being made genuinely to protect the interest of the applicant, or is it being made for an ulterior purpose, namely to oppress the claimant and to stifle the claimant's claim? Useful guidance is given in *Keary Developments Ltd v Tarmac Construction Ltd* [1995] 3 All ER 534. Although Rule 4.6 gives the arbitrator a wide discretion to take all circumstances into account the policy of CIMAR must be observed. A claimant who has agreed to arbitrate under CIMAR must be taken to have accepted the risk of the application of Rule 4.6 and its consequence, namely that security for costs will be ordered if *actual or probable* inability to pay the costs is established. A defence that the applicant has not shown that the claimant *will* not be able to pay is insufficient. If, therefore, the conditions are satisfied, an arbitrator must protect the interests of the applicant.

A29–020

If the claimant argues the claim will be successful in whole or in part, the arbitrator is not required to decide on the likely outcome and ought only to take account of the claim as it is presented. The arbitrator should not pre-empt the decision on the merits. Normally, the arbitrator ought not to consider evidence that might support or undermine either the claim or the defence unless it is incontrovertible, such as plain admissions in documents. Some claims or defences may need to be examined sceptically, e.g. where the claim has not been properly quantified. A defendant should not have to incur costs in dealing with an ill-thought out claim. An applicant who has not completely revealed its defence to an apparently good claim is at risk in having its bona fides doubted, especially where the application is made early in the proceedings. The inclusion of a reference to the strength or weakness of a party's case emphasises that the arbitrator must consider whether to order security is going to be oppressive to the claimant or whether it is reasonably necessary to protect the applicant since the pursuit of a claim by a claimant which will not be able to honour its obligations (if unsuccessful) is also oppressive to an applicant.

An application for security may require an assessment of the cases of each party. Since the arbitrator will ultimately have to decide the case on its merits, an arbitrator ought to be very careful about investigating the supposed merits of any case and, preferably, ought only to do so with the open and informed consent of the parties, for they may not want the arbitrator to delve into the case, as the views then formed may not be reversed later. If the application does require a decision on the merits it is strongly recommended that reasons are given for the decision, whether or not a request is made under Rule 4.7. The parties can then be sure that the arbitrator is not prejudging the ultimate case.

Sealed offers (variously calderbank or without predjudice offers) may cause difficulties for the parties where an application for security is made. A claimant may wish to reveal the existence of a sealed offer made by the respondent in support of the merit of its case but the respondent does not want the offer made known to the arbitrator as it considers that it may be prejudiced as a result. This point was considered by the DAC (Departmental Advisory Committee on Arbitration Law) and its conclusions were set out in paragraph 196 of its Report on the Arbitration Bill dated February 1996. Paragraph 196 reads "*We are not disturbed by this.* (the disclosure of an offer) *It seems to us that a tribunal, properly performing its duties under Clause* (Section) *33 could and should not be influenced by such matters if the case proceeds to a hearing on the merits, nor do we accept that the disclosure of such information could somehow disqualify the*

337

tribunal from acting." The arbitrator should not therefore be concerned that an application for his removal might be successful if he is made aware of an offer that a party considers is privileged and alleges bias as a result. Arbitrators will in any event be aware that offers to settle made by respondents are very often set at a figure that is in excess of that which the respondent considers to be the entitlement of the claimant on a commercial basis in an endeavour to obtain a settlement.

If an arbitrator considers the claimant's impecuniosity has been caused by the conduct of the applicant then the application may be oppressive and security ought not to be ordered. Such assertions about the conduct of the applicant must however be supported by evidence.

The stage at which the application is made may be another symptom of oppression. A party that is legally represented will almost always have carried out a search at Companies House as soon as the arbitration has started. Late applications tend to be made to fend off the inevitability that a claim is likely to succeed unless it is stopped dead in its tracks. It can be unfair to defer an application since a claimant may reasonably believe that its available resources can be used to prosecute the claim. If the arbitrator considers that the application could and should have been made earlier, then a lower amount of security or even a relatively nominal order might be appropriate.

A29–021 *Amount of Security:* In order not to stifle a bona fide claim that might be settled it is customary to require security to be provided in stages. For example, the first order might be up to and including disclosure of documents, the next might be up to and including the exchange of experts' reports or up to and including the pre-hearing review, i.e. any crucial stage which might lead to a resolution of the case. The order should cover both the costs already incurred and those to be incurred. An order up to a given stage must clearly define that stage. An order that does not refer to a stage may be taken to be for the whole proceedings up to award. The amount is in the discretion of the arbitrator but the overall objective of arbitration must always be observed, namely to try to resolve the dispute, if at all possible without a hearing. To require a claimant to provide a substantial amount of security for costs may defeat those ends and bring about an injustice.

The applicant ought to present the arbitral tribunal with a clear, detailed (but without revealing privileged matters) and apparently justified statement of the amount of costs that have been incurred, so that they may be seen to be both tangible and justifiable, and the costs that will be incurred, in each case, making a clear difference between the types of cost, e.g. those of lawyers, experts etc. A legally represented party may retain a costs draftsman to prepare a model bill of costs but it is not necessary to do so, provided it is clear what has been or will be incurred, when, by whom and for what purpose. Arbitrators should view statements of costs with some care as they are not likely to be understated. Although the costs of lawyers and experts can be high it does not follow that they or the hours envisaged will actually be incurred. The amount of security ordered should not be used as an instrument of oppression, although it must give the applicant reasonable protection. It should be the arbitrator's conservative estimate of the minimum costs which the defendant is likely to incur and to recover. An order for security is not in the nature of an indemnity.

It is sometimes said that a claimant cannot possibly meet the amount that ought to be provided, so its bona fide claim will be not heard. However, if the company cannot provide the amount itself, it may be provided by the shareholders or other backers of a company or the claimant, but at the price of fettering the working capital of the claimant. In turn, it raises the question whether as a result the claimant will have the ability to pay the costs at the end of the day. A balance will therefore have to be struck by the arbitrator.

An arbitrator may wish to be persuaded by the claimant that a company or an individual claimant (e.g. the claimant's family) has no assets before tempering the order that should be made.

A sealed offer is material and may affect the outcome of an application. (See earlier discussion on revealing such offers). The arbitrator must decide whether it may be admitted in evidence, having regard to its terms. If it is admissible an arbitrator should give reasons for the decision so as to ensure that neither party has any reason to question his overall independence and impartiality. The arbitrator may take the view that the amount offered was sensible and that the claimant will be unlikely to receive an award for more and, taking into account Rule 13.9, will thereby be exposed to an award for costs in favour of the applicant. On the other hand, the arbitrator may take the view that the claimant will do better than the amount of the offer, and that the application for security is being made in order to stifle a claim, the merits of which are undoubted, so that in reality the only question is the amount to which the claimant is entitled.

If security is required, the usual order is that the claimant must provide the security within 21 days, failing which the claim is stayed. Security can be in any form satisfactory to the applicant or, in default, to the arbitrator (and the order should say so). Thus it need not be by way of payment to a stakeholder but might be by the provision of a guarantee or bond from a reputable source. If the arbitrator has to decide then he or she will wish to be sure that the security will be immediately enforceable. If the security is not given in the form ordered it is for the respondent to seek a peremptory order under s41(5). (See Rule 4.9). If the security is still not given it is then for the respondent to decide whether an application to dismiss under s41(6) is appropriate. (See Rule 11.6)

APPENDIX 2

Specific Performance

If both parties are agreed that an award of specific performance is appropriate or if **A29–022** the arbitrator is for some reason unable to ascertain the cost, such an award should never be a final award. Performance of the award may itself be the subject of dispute between the parties and the arbitrator should not disqualify himself from dealing with those disputes.

The award should deal with the way in which the work is to be supervised. The arbitrator may supervise the work himself but if he does so should ensure that his position as arbitrator is in no way compromised thereby.

An independent supervisor may be appropriate but the method of appointment of this individual must be resolved beforehand. Is it to be an appointment by the arbitrator or a joint appointment by the parties? The terms of reference, fees and the method of payment of the supervisor must also be decided beforehand. The arbitrator must make clear his own overall function with regard to the work as it is always possible that one party may take issue with a decision of the supervisor.

When making an award of specific performance the arbitrator should always endeavour to include an alternative award in damages if the award of specific performance is not honoured by a specific date. Similar considerations apply to an award for the specific delivery or handing over of goods, when the arbitrator must be very careful about the rights to the property or to use the property.

It is not normally considered that the completion of construction works is an appropriate subject for an award of specific performance.

APPENDIX 3

The Allocation of Costs

A29–023 Rules 13.1 and 13.2 entitle an arbitrator to allocate the costs of issues and evidence. It is not necessary to await the overall result of the arbitration and then to award costs to follow the ultimate event, i.e. to the "winner", although in complex cases this may still be fair. An issue that is heard separately may decide the outcome of a dispute or claim, e.g. on jurisdiction, limitation, or the admissibility of a contractual claim. An issue may be one which clears the ground (e.g. on the effect of exclusion clause) and avoids other costs being incurred (e.g. issues of liability alone). An issue may however simply be about part of a case. Before an issue is ordered or accepted on the proposal of the parties the arbitrator should be satisfied that it will be or is likely to be cost-effective. The arbitrator may wish to know the amount of the costs likely to be affected. Seemingly attractive proposals can save relatively small amounts. The arbitrator may also wish to ask a party suggesting or opposing a course whether it accepts liability for the costs of the issue of the arbitration (where the issue is pivotal). In these ways later argument about liability for the costs may be avoided.

Generally a party who proposes an issue of any kind but is unsuccessful on it is liable to bear the costs (as provided by section 61). Similarly a party who tenders evidence or makes a submission that takes up a significant amount of resources and time but which is not accepted (e.g. about a specific head of loss) may be deprived of the costs involved and may be required to meet the costs of the other party, even if otherwise successful. The possibility of such a costs sanction helps to decide whether a part of a claim or a defence is really essential.

Before making an order which applies the general principle to an issue or to part of a case an arbitrator will need to be satisfied both of the amount of costs at stake and that they can be relatively easily assessed.

A29–024 *Summary Assessment:* An arbitrator may adopt the modern practice of the courts. Where a hearing of an application or an issue does not last more than a day and the outcome is that a party must pay the costs in any event the amount of those costs can be assessed immediately by the tribunal. However section 63(3) of the Act requires costs to be dealt with by an award so, unless the parties have agreed to a special procedure for the summary assessment of costs, it is thought that a summary assessment following an application will not be effective since the subject-matter of applications are not usually dealt with by an award (i.e. they do not fall within section 47 of the Act). A summary assessment following the hearing of an issue may be the subject of an award.

If the arbitrator intends to make summary assessments then it is essential that a suitable procedure is adopted at the outset of the proceedings [see section 33(1)(b)]. It should not be introduced thereafter without the consent of the parties. The procedure should follow the model used by the courts, e.g. it should provide for a party only to be able to obtain a summary assessment if a properly verified statement of the costs claimed is served on the other party and on the arbitrator not less than 24 hours before the hearing.

In making a summary assessment the arbitrator should receive submissions from every party. The principles are set out in section 63(5). Section 63(3) must be observed (unless otherwise agreed by the parties). In general it is convenient to inquire first whether the rates claimed are or are not agreed. In many cases the rates are not disputed (especially where the paying party submitted a statement with comparable rates). Guideline rates for lawyers are published by the Senior Costs Judge and by TecSA (www.tecsa.org) and TECBAR. The inquiry may then turn to the time spent and work done. The arbitrator should not need to spend much time for otherwise it will not be a summary assessment.

APPENDIX 4

THE LIMITATION OF RECOVERABLE COSTS

The arbitrator may limit recoverable costs in respect of a part or the whole of the reference. He may set a limit on the application of a party or by his own motion. If by his own motion he must allow the parties to make submissions to him before making the order.

The arbitrator may set the limit at the outset of the proceedings or at any stage of the arbitration. If he limits recoverable costs during the course of the proceedings he may only do so in respect of costs not yet incurred. It cannot be done retrospectively.

When a limit is set the arbitrator must have regard primarily to the amount in dispute but must always remember that "Proportionality" does not relate just to money. The matters in dispute may involve complex issues of law the resolution of which may be of such importance to the parties that it may be inappropriate to relate the costs of resolution to the amount of money at stake.

The dispute may not involve any money at all, a declaration may be all that is sought. In that event any limit that is set to costs has to relate to what would be a reasonable sum for resolving the matter.

If the arbitrator has set a limit to recoverable costs it is vital that any award of costs specifically refers to the limit that has been set. It is insufficient for the arbitrator to award, for example, "75% of the Claimant's costs to be paid by the Respondent" in a situation where a limit has been set without stating that it is 75% of the costs up to the limit or that it is 75% of the limit.

Where a limit of recoverable costs has been set the arbitrator must also be very careful in framing his award of costs to consider the application of a subsequent determination of the quantum of recoverable costs under s 63. The successful party may have incurred costs in excess of the limit. The maximum costs that he is entitled to recover is set at the limit but the amount of the costs he is entitled to recover under s 63(5) may actually be less than the limit.

A suitable form of words in this situation would be:

"The Respondent shall pay the Claimant's costs up to (the limit). Where the paying party considers that (the limit) exceeds the amount that should properly be paid in accordance with s 63(5), those costs shall [be determined by award by me under the provisions of s 63.3] or [be determined by the court under s 63(4)]".

A29–025

Court of Arbitration for Sport Code of Sports-related Arbitration Statutes of the Bodies Working for the Settlement of Sports-related Disputes and Procedural Rules[1]

A JOINT DISPOSITIONS

A30–001   S1 In order to settle, through arbitration, sports-related disputes, two bodies are hereby created:

- the International Council of Arbitration for Sport (ICAS) and
- the Court of Arbitration for Sport (CAS).

The disputes referred to in the preceding paragraph include, in particular, those connected with doping. The disputes to which a federation, association or other sports body is party are a matter for arbitration in the sense of this Code, only insofar as the statutes or regulations of the said sports bodies or a specific agreement so provide.

The seat of the ICAS and the CAS is established in Lausanne, Switzerland.

S2 The task of the ICAS is to facilitate the settlement of sports-related disputes through arbitration or mediation and to safeguard the independence of the CAS and the rights of the parties. To this end, it looks after the administration and financing of the CAS.

S3 The CAS, which has a list of arbitrators, procures the arbitral resolution of disputes arising within the field of sport through the intermediary of arbitration provided by Panels composed of one or three arbitrators.

It comprises an Ordinary Arbitration Division and an Appeals Arbitration Division.

The CAS can also procure the resolution of sports-related disputes through mediation. The mediation procedure is governed by separate rules.

B THE INTERNATIONAL COUNCIL OF ARBITRATION FOR SPORT (ICAS)

1 Composition

A30–002   S4 The ICAS is composed of twenty members, namely high-level jurists appointed in the following manner:

(a) four members are appointed by the International Sports Federations ("IFs"), viz. three by the Summer Olympic IFs (ASOIF), one by the Winter Olympic IFs ("AIWF"), chosen from within or from outside their membership;

(b) four members are appointed by the Association of the National Olympic Committees ("ANOC"), chosen from within or from outside its membership;

(c) four members are appointed by the International Olympic Committee ("IOC"), chosen from within or from outside its membership;

---

1 This document is reproduced with the kind permission of Court of Arbitration for Sport.

(d) four members are appointed by the twelve members of the ICAS listed above, after appropriate consultation with a view to safeguarding the interests of the athletes;

(e) four members are appointed by the sixteen members of the ICAS listed above and chosen from among personalities independent of the bodies designating the other members of the ICAS.

S5 The members of the ICAS are appointed for a renewable period of four years.

Upon their appointment, the members of the ICAS sign a declaration undertaking to exercise their function in a personal capacity, with total objectivity and independence, in conformity with this Code. They are, in particular, bound by the confidentiality obligation which is provided in Article R43.

The members of the ICAS may not appear on the list of arbitrators of the CAS nor act as counsel to one of the parties in proceedings before the CAS.

If a member of the ICAS resigns, dies or is prevented from carrying out his functions for any other reason, he is replaced, for the remaining period of his mandate, in conformity with the terms applicable to his appointment.

2 Attributions

S6 The ICAS exercises the following functions:

1. It adopts and amends this Code;
2. It elects from among its members for a renewable period of four years:
    - the President proposed by the IOC,
    - two Vice-Presidents (one proposed by the IFs and one by the National Olympic Committees [NOCs]), responsible for deputizing for the President if necessary, by order of seniority in age,
    - the President of the Ordinary Arbitration Division and the President of the Appeals Arbitration Division of the CAS,
    - the deputies of the two Division Presidents;
3. It appoints the personalities who are to constitute the list of arbitrators and the list of mediators of CAS (Article S3);
4. It exercises those functions concerning the challenge and removal of arbitrators, and any other functions which the Procedural Rules confer upon it;
5. It looks after the financing of the CAS. To this end, inter alia:
    5.1 it receives and manages, in conformity with the financial regulations of the CAS, the funds allocated to its operations;
    5.2 it approves the ICAS budget prepared by the Court Office of the CAS;
    5.3 it approves the annual accounts of the CAS established by the Court Office of the CAS;
6. It appoints the Secretary General of the CAS and terminates his duties upon proposal of the President;

7. It supervises the activities of the Court Office of the CAS;
8. If it deems such action appropriate, it sets up regional or local, permanent or ad hoc arbitration structures;
9. If it deems such action appropriate, it creates a legal aid fund to facilitate access to CAS arbitration and determines the terms of implementation;
10. It may take any other action which it deems likely to protect the rights of the parties and, in particular, to best guarantee the total independence of the arbitrators and to promote the settlement of sports-related disputes through arbitration;
11. It may create a mediation system.

S7 The ICAS exercises its functions either itself, or through the intermediary of its Board, made up of the President and two Vice-Presidents of the ICAS, the President of the Ordinary Arbitration Division and the President of the Appeals Arbitration Division of the CAS.

The ICAS may not delegate to the Board the functions listed under Article S6, paragraphs 1, 2, 5.2 and 5.3.

3 Operation

S8 The ICAS meets whenever the activity of the CAS so requires, but at least once a year.

The ICAS constitutes a quorum when at least half of its members participate in taking a decision. Decisions are taken during meetings or by correspondence by a simple majority of the voting members, the President having the casting vote in the event of a tie. However, any modification of this Code requires a majority of two-thirds of the members of ICAS. ICAS members may not act by proxy.

The Secretary General of the CAS takes part in the decision-making with a consultative voice, and acts as Secretary to the ICAS.

S9 The President of the ICAS is also President of the CAS. He is also responsible for the ordinary administrative tasks within the remit of the ICAS.

S10 The Board of the ICAS meets at the invitation of the ICAS President.

The CAS Secretary General participates in the decision-making with a consultative voice, and acts as Secretary to the Board.

The Board constitutes a quorum if three of its members participate in taking a decision. Decisions are taken during meetings or by correspondence with a simple majority of those voting; the President has the casting vote in the event of a tie.

S11 A member of the ICAS or the Board may be challenged when circumstances allow legitimate doubt to be cast on his independence vis-à-vis one of the parties to an arbitration which must be the subject of a decision by the ICAS or the Board pursuant to Article S6, paragraph 4. He shall spontaneously disqualify himself when the subject of a decision is an arbitration procedure in which appears, as a party, a sports body to which he belongs or in which a member of the law firm to which he belongs is an arbitrator or counsel.

The member disqualified shall not take part in the deliberations concerning the arbitration in question and shall not receive any information on the activities of the ICAS and the Board concerning such arbitration.

C THE COURT OF ARBITRATION FOR SPORT (CAS)

1 Mission

S12 The CAS sets in operation Panels which have the task of providing for the resolution by arbitration of disputes arising within the field of sport in conformity with the Procedural Rules (Articles R27 et seq.).

To this end, the CAS attends to the constitution of Panels and the smooth running of the proceedings. It places at the disposal of the parties the necessary infrastructure.

The responsibility of such Panels is, inter alia:

a. to resolve the disputes that are referred to them through ordinary arbitration;

b. to resolve through the appeals arbitration procedure disputes, (including doping-related disputes) concerning the decisions of disciplinary tribunals or similar bodies of federations, associations or other sports bodies, insofar as the statutes or regulations of the said sports bodies or a specific agreement so provide;

c. to give non-binding advisory opinions at the request of the IOC, the IFs, the NOCs, the associations recognized by the IOC and the Olympic Games Organizing Committees ("OCOGs").

2 Arbitrators

S13 The personalities designated by the ICAS, in conformity with Article S6, paragraph 3, appear on the list of arbitrators for a renewable period of four years.

There are at least one hundred and fifty of these arbitrators.

S14 In establishing the list of CAS arbitrators, the ICAS shall call upon personalities with a legal training and who possess recognized competence with regard to sport and respect, in principle, the following distribution:

- 1/5th of the arbitrators selected from among the persons proposed by the IOC, chosen from within its membership or from outside;

- 1/5th of the arbitrators selected from among the persons proposed by the IFs, chosen from within their membership or outside;

- 1/5th of the arbitrators selected from among the persons proposed by the NOCs, chosen from within their membership or outside;

- 1/5th of the arbitrators chosen after appropriate consultations with a view to safeguarding the interests of the athletes;

- 1/5th of the arbitrators chosen from among persons independent of the bodies responsible for proposing arbitrators in conformity with the present article.

S15 The proposals for designating such arbitrators that shall constitute the list referred to in Article S14, shall be notified to the ICAS within the time limit which the latter shall establish.

Institutional Rules

The list of CAS arbitrators and all modifications to such list are published.

S16 In appointing the personalities who appear on the list of arbitrators, the ICAS shall, wherever possible, ensure fair representation of the different continents.

S17 Subject to the provisions of the Procedural Rules (Articles R27 et seq.), if a CAS arbitrator resigns, dies or is prevented from carrying out his functions for any other reason, he may be replaced, for the remaining period of his mandate, in conformity with the terms applicable to his appointment.

S18 The personalities who appear on the list of arbitrators may be called upon to serve on Panels constituted by either one of the CAS Divisions.

Upon their appointment, the CAS arbitrators and the CAS mediators sign a declaration undertaking to exercise their functions personally with total objectivity and independence, and in conformity with the provisions of this Code.

S19 CAS arbitrators are bound by the duty of confidentiality, which is provided in Article R43.

3 Organisation of the CAS

A30–007   **S20** The CAS is composed of two divisions, the Ordinary Arbitration Division and the Appeals Arbitration Division.

  a. **The Ordinary Arbitration Division** constitutes Panels, the mission of which is to resolve disputes submitted to the ordinary procedure, and performs, through the intermediary of its President, all other functions in relation to the smooth running of the proceedings conferred upon it by the Procedural Rules (Articles R27 et seq.).

  b. **The Appeals Arbitration Division** constitutes Panels, the mission of which is to resolve disputes (including doping-related disputes) concerning the decisions of disciplinary tribunals or similar bodies of federations, associations or other sports bodies insofar as the statutes or regulations of the said sports bodies or a specific agreement so provide. It performs, through the intermediary of its President, all other functions in relation to the smooth running of the proceedings conferred upon it by the Procedural Rules (Articles R27 et seq.).

Arbitration proceedings submitted to the CAS are assigned by the Court Office to one of these two Divisions according to their nature. Such assignment may not be contested by the parties or raised by them as a cause of irregularity.

S21 The President of one or other of the two Divisions of the CAS may be challenged if circumstances exist that give rise to legitimate doubts with regard to his independence vis-à-vis one of the parties to an arbitration assigned to his Division. He shall spontaneously disqualify himself when, in arbitration proceedings assigned to his Division, one of the parties is a sports body to which he belongs, or when a member of the law firm to which he belongs is acting as arbitrator or counsel.

When the President of one of the two Divisions is challenged, the functions relating to the smooth running of the proceedings conferred upon him by the Procedural Rules (Articles R27 et seq.), are performed by the President of the CAS and the President of the Division may not receive any information concerning the activities of the CAS regarding the arbitration proceedings which led to the disqualification.

S22 The CAS includes a Court Office composed of a Secretary General and Counsels, who replace the Secretary General when required.
The Court Office performs the functions which are assigned to it by this Code.

D MISCELLANEOUS PROVISIONS

S23 The present Statutes are supplemented by the Procedural Rules adopted by the ICAS. **A30–008**
S24 The English text and the French text are authentic. In the event of any divergence, the French text shall prevail.
S25 The present Statutes may be amended by decision of the ICAS, in conformity with Article S8.
S26 The present Statutes and Procedural Rules come into force through the decision of the twelve members of the ICAS, nominated for the first time by the IOC, the IFs and the NOCs taken by a two-thirds majority.

Procedural Rules

A GENERAL PROVISIONS

Application of the Rules

R27 These Procedural Rules apply whenever the parties have agreed to refer a sports-related dispute to the CAS. Such disputes may arise out of a contract containing an arbitration clause or be the subject of a later arbitration agreement (ordinary arbitration proceedings) or involve an appeal against a decision given by the disciplinary tribunals or similar bodies of a federation, association or sports body where the statutes or regulations of such bodies, or a specific agreement provides for an appeal to the CAS (appeal arbitration proceedings). **A30–009**

Such disputes may involve matters of principle relating to sport or matters of pecuniary or other interests brought into play in the practice or the development of sport and, generally speaking, any activity related or connected to sport.

These Procedural Rules also apply where the CAS is called upon to give an advisory opinion (consultation proceedings).

Seat

R28 The seat of the CAS and of each Arbitration Panel ("Panel") is in Lausanne, Switzerland. However, should circumstances so warrant, and after consultation with all parties, the President of the Panel or, failing him, the President of the relevant Division may decide to hold a hearing in another place. **A30–010**

Language

R29 The CAS working languages are French and English. In the absence of agreement between the parties, and taking into account all pertinent circumstances, the President of the Panel shall select one of these two languages as the language of the arbitration at the start of the proceedings before the Panel. **A30–011**

The parties may choose another language provided that the Arbitration Panel agrees. The parties shall advise the CAS of such a choice. In the event of such a choice, the Panel may order that the parties bear all or part of the translation and interpreting costs.

Representation and Assistance

A30–012   R30 The parties may be represented or assisted by persons of their choice. The names, addresses, telephone and facsimile numbers of the persons representing the parties shall be communicated to the Court Office, the other party and the Panel after its formation.

Notifications and Communications

A30–013   R31 All notifications and communications that the CAS or the Panel intend for the parties shall be made through the Court Office. The notifications and communications shall be written in French or in English and sent to the address shown in the arbitration request, statement of appeal or application for an opinion, or to any other address specified at a later date.

All arbitration awards, orders, and other decisions made by the CAS and the Panel shall be notified by any means permitting proof of receipt.

All communications from the parties intended for the CAS or the Panel, including the arbitration request, statement of appeal, application for an opinion and request for participation of a third party, as well as the reply shall be sent to the CAS in as many copies as there are parties, counsel and arbitrators, together with one additional copy for the CAS itself.

Time-limit

A30–014   R32 The time limits fixed under the present Code shall begin from the day after that on which notification by the CAS is received. Official holidays and non-working days are included in the calculation of time limits. The time limits fixed under the present Code are respected if the communications by the parties are sent before midnight on the last day on which such time limits expire. If the last day of the time limit is an official holiday or a non-business day in the country where the notification has been made, the time limit shall expire at the end of the first following business day.

Upon application on justified grounds, either the President of the Panel or, failing him, the President of the relevant Division, may extend the time-limits provided in these Procedural Rules, if the circumstances so warrant.

Independence and Qualifications of Arbitrators

A30–015   R33 Every arbitrator shall be and remain independent of the parties and shall immediately disclose any circumstances likely to affect independence with respect to any of the parties.

Every arbitrator shall appear on the list drawn up by the ICAS in accordance with the Statutes which are part of this Code and shall have the availability required to expeditiously complete the arbitration.

Challenge

A30–016   R34 An arbitrator may be challenged if the circumstances give rise to legitimate doubts over his independence. The challenge shall be brought immediately after the ground for the challenge has become known.

Challenges are in the exclusive power of the ICAS which may exercise such power through its Board in accordance with the Statutes which are part of this Code. The petition setting forth the facts giving rise to the challenge shall be lodged by a party. The ICAS or its Board shall rule on the challenge after the other parties, the challenged arbitrator and the other arbitrators have been invited to submit written comments. It shall give brief reasons for its decision.

Removal

R35 An arbitrator may be removed by the ICAS if he refuses to or is prevented from carrying out his duties or if he fails to fulfil his duties pursuant to the present Code. The ICAS may delegate this function to its Board. The Board shall invite the parties, the arbitrator in question and the other arbitrators to submit written comments and shall render a brief reasoned decision. **A30–017**

Replacement

R36 In the event of resignation, death, challenge or removal of an arbitrator, such arbitrator shall be replaced in accordance with the provisions applicable to his appointment. Unless otherwise agreed by the parties or otherwise decided by the Panel, the proceedings shall continue without repetition of the procedure which took place prior to the replacement. **A30–018**

Provisional and Conservatory Measures

R37 No party may apply for provisional or conservatory measures under these Procedural Rules before the request for arbitration or the statement of appeal, which implies the exhaustion of internal remedies, has been filed with the CAS. **A30–019**

The President of the relevant Division, prior to the transfer of the file to the Panel, or thereafter the Panel may, upon application by one of the parties, make an order for provisional or conservatory measures. In agreeing to submit to these Procedural Rules any dispute subject to appeal arbitration proceedings, the parties expressly waive their rights to request such measures from state authorities. This waiver does not apply to provisional or conservatory measures in connection with disputes subject to ordinary arbitration proceedings.

If an application for provisional measures is filed, the President of the relevant Division or the Panel invites the opponent to express his position within fifteen days or within a shorter time-limit if circumstances so require. The President of the relevant Division or the Panel shall issue an order within a short time. In case of utmost urgency, the President of the relevant Division, prior to the transfer of the file to the Panel, or thereafter the President of the Panel may issue an order upon mere presentation of the application, provided that the opponent shall be heard subsequently.

Temporary and conservatory measures may be made conditional upon the provision of security.

B SPECIAL PROVISIONS APPLICABLE TO THE ORDINARY ARBITRATION PROCEDURE

Request for Arbitration

R38 The party intending to submit a reference to arbitration under these Procedural Rules shall file a request with the CAS containing: **A30–020**

- the name and address of the respondent;
- a brief statement of the facts and legal argument, including a statement of the issue to be submitted to the CAS for determination;
- the claimant's request for relief;
- a copy of the contract containing the arbitration agreement or of any document providing for arbitration in accordance with these Procedural Rules;
- any relevant information about the number and choice of the arbitrator(s), in particular if the arbitration agreement provides for three arbitrators, the name and address of the arbitrator chosen by the claimant from the CAS list of names.

Upon filing its request, the claimant shall pay the Court Office fee provided in Article R64.1.

Initiation of the Arbitration by the CAS and Answer

A30–021   **R39** Unless it is apparent from the outset that there is manifestly no agreement to arbitrate referring to the CAS, the Court Office shall take all appropriate actions to set the arbitration in motion. To this effect, it in particular communicates the request to the respondent, calls upon the parties to express themselves on the law applicable to the merits of the dispute and sets time-limits for the respondent to submit any relevant information about the number and choice of the arbitrator(s), in particular to appoint an arbitrator from the CAS list, as well as to file an answer to the request for arbitration. The answer shall contain:

- a brief statement of the defence;
- any defence of lack of jurisdiction;
- any counterclaim.

R40 Formation of the Panel

Number of Arbitrators

A30–022   **R40.1** The Panel is composed of one or three arbitrators. If the arbitration agreement does not specify the number of arbitrators, the President of the Division shall determine the number taking into account the amount in litigation and the complexity of the dispute.

Appointment of the Arbitrators

A30–023   **R40.2** The parties may agree on the method of appointment of the arbitrators. In the absence of an agreement, the arbitrators shall be appointed in accordance with the following paragraphs.

If, by virtue of the arbitration agreement or a decision of the President of the Division, a sole arbitrator is to be appointed, the parties may select him by mutual agreement within a time-limit of twenty days set by the Court Office upon receipt of the request. In the absence of an agreement within such time-limit, the President of the Division shall proceed with the appointment.

If, by virtue of the arbitration agreement or of a decision of the President of the

Division, three arbitrators are to be appointed, the claimant shall appoint its arbitrator in the request or within the time-limit set in the decision on the number of arbitrators and the respondent shall appoint its arbitrator within the time-limit set by the Court Office upon receipt of the request. In the absence of such appointment, the President of the Division shall proceed with the appointment in lieu of the parties. The two arbitrators so appointed shall select the President of the Panel by mutual agreement within a time-limit set by the Court Office. In the absence of an agreement within such time-limit, the President of the Division shall appoint the President of the Panel in lieu of the two arbitrators.

Confirmation of the Arbitrators and Transfer of the File

R40.3 Any arbitrator selected by the parties or by other arbitrators shall only be deemed appointed after confirmation by the President of the Division. Before proceeding with such confirmation, the latter shall ascertain that the arbitrator fulfils the requirements of Article R33.

Once the Panel is formed, the Court Office takes notice of the formation and transfers the file to the arbitrators.

A30–024

R41 Multiparty Arbitration

Plurality of Claimants/Respondents

R41.1 If the request for arbitration names several claimants and/or respondents, the CAS shall proceed with the formation of the Panel in accordance with the number of arbitrators and the method of appointment agreed by all parties. In the absence of such an agreement, the President of the Division shall decide on the number of arbitrators in accordance with Article R40.1.

If a sole arbitrator is to be appointed, Article R40.2 shall apply. If three arbitrators are to be appointed and there are several claimants, the claimants shall jointly appoint an arbitrator. If three arbitrators are to be appointed and there are several respondents, the respondents shall jointly appoint an arbitrator. In the absence of such a joint appointment, the President of the Division shall proceed with the appointment in lieu of the claimants/respondents. If (i) three arbitrators are to be appointed, (ii) there are several claimants and several respondents, and (iii) either the claimants or the respondents fail to jointly appoint an arbitrator, then both coarbitrators shall be appointed by the President of the Division in accordance with Article R40.2. In all cases, the coarbitrators shall select the President of the Panel in accordance with Article R40.2.

A30–025

Joinder

R41.2 If a respondent intends to cause a third party to participate in the arbitration, it shall so state in its answer, together with the reasons therefor, and file an additional copy of its answer. The Court Office shall communicate this copy to the person the participation of which is requested and set such person a time-limit to state its position on its participation and to submit a response pursuant to Article R39. It shall also set a time-limit for the claimant to express its position on the participation of the third party.

A30–026

Intervention

R41.3 If a third party intends to participate as a party in the arbitration, it shall file with the CAS an application to this effect, together with the reasons therefore within the

A30–027

time-limit set for the respondent's answer to the request for arbitration. To the extent applicable, such application shall have the same contents as a request for arbitration. The Court Office shall communicate a copy of this application to the parties and set a time-limit for them to express their position on the participation of the third party and to file, to the extent applicable, an answer pursuant to Article R39.

Joint Provisions on Joinder and Intervention

A30–028   R41.4 A third party may only participate in the arbitration if it is bound by the arbitration agreement or if itself and the other parties agree in writing.

Upon expiration of the time-limit set in Articles R41.2 and R41.3, the President of the Division shall decide on the participation of the third party, taking into account, in particular, the prima facie existence of an arbitration agreement as referred to in Article R39 above. Such decision shall be without prejudice to the decision of the Panel on the same matter.

If the President of the Division accepts the participation of the third party, the CAS shall proceed with the formation of the Panel in accordance with the number of arbitrators and the method of appointment agreed by all parties. In the absence of such an agreement, the President of the Division shall decide on the number of arbitrators in accordance with Article R40.1. If a sole arbitrator is to be appointed, Article R40.2 shall apply. If three arbitrators are to be appointed, the coarbitrators shall be appointed by the President of the Division and shall choose the President of the Panel in accordance with Article R40.2.

Regardless of the decision of the Panel on the participation of the third party, the formation of the Panel cannot be challenged. In the event that the Panel accepts the participation, it shall, if required, issue related procedural directions.

Conciliation

A30–029   R42 The President of the Division, before the transfer of the file to the Panel, and thereafter the Panel may at any time seek to resolve the dispute by conciliation. Any settlement may be embodied in an arbitral award rendered by consent of the parties.

Confidentiality

A30–030   R43 Proceedings under these Procedural Rules are confidential. The parties, the arbitrators and the CAS undertake not to disclose to any third party any facts or other information relating to the dispute or the proceedings. Awards shall not be made public unless the award itself so provides or all parties agree.

R44 Procedure before the Panel

Written Submissions

A30–031   R44.1 The procedure before the Panel comprises written submissions and, if the Panel deems it appropriate, an oral hearing. Upon the receipt of the file, the President of the Panel, if appropriate, shall issue directions in connection with the written submissions. As a general rule, there shall be one statement of claim, one response and, if the circumstances so require, one reply and one second response. The parties may, in the statement of claim and in the response, raise claims not contained in the request for arbitration and in the answer to the request. Thereafter, no party may raise any new claim without the consent of the other party.

Together with their written submissions, the parties shall produce all written evidence upon which they intend to rely. After the exchange of the written submissions, the parties shall not be authorized to produce further written evidence, except by mutual agreement or if the Panel so permits on the basis of exceptional circumstances.

In their written submissions, the parties shall specify any witnesses and experts which they intend to call and state any other evidentiary measure which they request.

Hearing

R44.2 Once the exchange of pleadings is closed, the President of the Panel shall issue directions with respect to the hearing and in particular set the hearing date. As a general rule, there shall be one hearing during which the Panel hears the parties, the witnesses and the expert as well as the parties' final oral arguments, for which the respondent has the floor last.

The President of the Panel shall conduct the hearing and ascertain that the statements made are concise and limited to the subject of the written presentations, to the extent that these presentations are relevant. Except if the parties agree otherwise, the hearings are not public. There shall be minutes of the hearing. Any person heard by the Panel may be assisted by an interpreter at the cost of the party which called such upon.

The parties may call to be heard by the Panel such witnesses and experts which they have specified in their written submissions.

Before hearing any witness, expert or interpreter, the Panel shall solemnly invite such persons to tell the truth, subject to the sanctions of perjury.

Once the hearing is closed, the parties shall not be authorized to produce further written pleadings, except if the Panel so orders.

After consulting the parties, the Panel may, if it deems itself to be sufficiently well informed, decide not to hold a hearing.

A30–032

Evidentiary Proceedings Ordered by the Panel

R44.3 A party may request the Panel to issue an order that the other party produces documents in its custody or under its control. The party seeking such production shall demonstrate that the documents are likely to exist and to be relevant.

If it deems it appropriate to supplement the presentations of the parties, the Panel may at any time order the production of additional documents or the examination of witnesses, appoint and hear experts, and proceed with any other procedural act.

The Panel shall consult the parties with respect to the appointment and terms of reference of such expert. The expert appointed by the Panel shall be and remain independent of the parties and shall immediately disclose any circumstances likely to affect independence with respect to any of the parties.

A30–033

Expedited Procedure

R44.4 With the consent of the parties, the Panel may proceed in an expedited manner for which it shall issue appropriate directions.

A30–034

Default

R44.5 If the Claimant fails to submit its statement of claim in accordance with art. R44.1 of the Code, the request for arbitration shall be deemed withdrawn.

If the Respondent fails to submit its response in accordance with art. R44.1 of the Code, the Panel may nevertheless proceed with the arbitration and deliver an award.

A30–035

If any of the parties is duly summoned yet fails to appear at the hearing, the Panel may nevertheless proceed with the hearing.

Law Applicable to the Merits

A30–036 R45 The Panel shall decide the dispute according to the rules of law chosen by the parties or, in the absence of such a choice, according to Swiss law. The parties may authorize the Panel to decide ex aequo et bono.

Award

A30–037 R46 The award shall be made by a majority decision, or, in the absence of a majority, by the President alone. The award shall be written, dated and signed. Unless the parties agree otherwise, it shall briefly state reasons. The signature of the President of the Panel shall suffice.

The award shall be final and binding upon the parties. It may not be challenged by way of an action for setting aside to the extent that the parties have no domicile, habitual residence, or business establishment in Switzerland and that they have expressly excluded all setting aside proceedings in the arbitration agreement or in an agreement entered into subsequently, in particular at the outset of the arbitration.

C SPECIAL PROVISIONS APPLICABLE TO THE APPEAL ARBITRATION PROCEEDINGS

Appeal

A30–038 R47 A party may appeal from the decision of a disciplinary tribunal or similar body of a federation, association or sports body, insofar as the statutes or regulations of the said body so provide or as the parties have concluded a specific arbitration agreement and insofar as the appellant has exhausted the legal remedies available to him prior to the appeal, in accordance with the statutes or regulations of the said sports body.

Statement of Appeal

A30–039 R48 The appellant shall submit to the CAS a statement of appeal containing:

- the name and address of the respondent;
- a copy of the decision appealed from;
- the appellant's request for relief;
- the appointment of the arbitrator chosen by the appellant from the CAS list, unless the parties have agreed to a Panel composed of a sole arbitrator;
- if applicable, an application to stay the execution of the decision appealed from, together with reasons;
- a copy of the provisions of the statutes or regulations or the specific agreement providing for appeal to the CAS.

Upon filing the statement, the appellant shall pay the Court Office fee provided for under Article R65.2.

Time-limit for Appeal

R49 In the absence of a time-limit set in the statutes or regulations of the federation, association, sports body concerned, or of a previous agreement, the time-limit for appeal shall be twenty one days from the communication of the decision which is appealed from.   **A30–040**

Number of Arbitrators

R50 The appeal shall be submitted to a Panel of three arbitrators, except if the appellant establishes at the time of the statement of appeal that the parties have agreed to a Panel composed of a sole arbitrator or if the President of the Division considers that the matter is an emergency and the appeal should be submitted to a sole arbitrator.   **A30–041**

Appeal Brief

R51 Within ten days following the expiration of the time-limit for the appeal, the appellant shall file with the CAS a brief stating the facts and legal arguments giving rise to the appeal, together with all exhibits and specification of other evidence upon which he intends to rely, failing which the appeal shall be deemed withdrawn.   **A30–042**

Initiation of the Arbitration by the CAS

R52 Unless it is apparent from the outset that there is manifestly no agreement to arbitrate referring to the CAS, the CAS shall take all appropriate actions to set the arbitration in motion. To this effect, the Court Office shall, in particular, communicate the statement of appeal to the respondent, and the President of the Division shall proceed with the formation of the Panel in accordance with Articles R53 and R54. If applicable, he shall also decide promptly on an application for a stay.   **A30–043**

Appointment of Arbitrator by Respondent

R53 Unless the parties have agreed to a Panel composed of a sole arbitrator or the President of the Division considers that the appeal is an emergency and must be submitted to a sole arbitrator, the respondent shall appoint an arbitrator within ten days after the receipt of the statement of appeal. In the absence of an appointment within such time-limit, the President of the Division shall proceed with the appointment in lieu of the respondent.   **A30–044**

Appointment of the Sole Arbitrator or of the President and Confirmation of the Arbitrators by the CAS

R54 If, by virtue of the parties' agreement or of a decision of the President of a Division, a sole arbitrator is to be appointed, the President of the Division shall appoint the sole arbitrator upon receipt of the motion for appeal.   **A30–045**

If three arbitrators are to be appointed, the President of the Division shall appoint the President of the Panel upon appointment of the arbitrator by the respondent. The arbitrators selected by the parties shall only be deemed appointed after confirmation by the President of the Division. Before proceedings with such confirmation, the President of the Division shall ascertain that the arbitrators fulfil the requirements of Article R33.

Once the Panel is formed, the Court Office takes notice of the formation of the Panel and transfers the file to the arbitrators.

Answer of Respondent

A30–046 R55 Within twenty days from the receipt of the grounds for the appeal, the respondent shall submit to the CAS an answer containing:

- a statement of defence;
- any defence of lack of jurisdiction;
- any exhibits or specification of other evidence upon which the respondent intends to rely.

If the Respondent fails to submit its response by the given time limit, the Panel may nevertheless proceed with the arbitration and deliver an award.

Appeal and answer complete

A30–047 R56 Unless the parties agree otherwise or the President of the Panel orders otherwise on the basis of exceptional circumstances, the parties shall not be authorized to supplement their argumentation, nor to produce new exhibits, nor to specify further evidence on which they intend to rely after the submission of the grounds for the appeal and of the answer.

Scope of Panel's Review, Hearing

A30–048 R57.1 The Panel shall have full power to review the facts and the law. Upon transfer of the file, the President of the Panel shall issue directions in connection with the hearing for the examination of the parties, the witnesses and the experts, as well as for the oral arguments. He may also request communication of the file of the disciplinary tribunal or similar body, the decision of which is subject to appeal. Articles R44.2 and R44.3 shall apply.

After consulting the parties, the Panel may, if it deems itself to be sufficiently well informed, decide not to hold a hearing. At the hearing, the proceedings take place in camera, unless the parties agree otherwise.

If any of the parties is duly summoned yet fails to appear, the Panel may nevertheless proceed with the hearing.

Law Applicable

A30–049 R58 The Panel shall decide the dispute according to the applicable regulations and the rules of law chosen by the parties or, in the absence of such a choice, according to the law of the country in which the federation, association or sports body which has issued the challenged decision is domiciled.

Award

A30–050 R59 The award shall be rendered by a majority decision, or in the absence of a majority, by the President alone. It shall be written, dated and signed. The award shall state brief reasons. The signature of the President shall suffice.

The Panel may decide to communicate the holding of the award to the parties, prior to the reasons.

The award shall be final from such written communication.

The award shall be final and binding upon the parties. It may not be challenged by way of an action for setting aside to the extent that the parties have no domicile, habitual residence, or business establishment in Switzerland and that they have expressly excluded all setting aside proceedings in the arbitration agreement or in an agreement entered into subsequently, in particular at the outset of the arbitration.

The holding of the award shall be communicated to the parties within four months after the filing of the statement of appeal. Such time-limit may be extended by the President of the Appeals Arbitration Division upon a motivated request from the President of the Panel.

The award or a summary setting forth the results of the proceedings shall be made public by the CAS, unless both parties agree that they should remain confidential.

D Special Provisions Applicable to the Consultation Proceedings

Request for Opinion

R60 The IOC, the IFs, the NOCs, the associations recognized by the IOC, the OCOGs, may request an advisory opinion from the CAS about any legal issue with respect to the practice or development of sports or any activity related to sports. The request for an opinion shall be addressed to the CAS and accompanied by any document likely to assist the Panel entrusted with giving the opinion. **A30–051**

Initiation by the CAS

R61 When a request is filed, the CAS President shall review whether it may be the subject of an opinion. In the affirmative, he shall proceed with the formation of a Panel of one or three arbitrators from the CAS list and designate the President. He shall formulate, in his own discretion, the questions submitted to the Panel and forward these questions to the Panel. **A30–052**

Opinion

R62 Before rendering its opinion, the Panel may request additional information. The opinion may be published with the consent of the party which requested it. It does not constitute a binding arbitral award. **A30–053**

E Interpretation

R63 A party may apply to the CAS for the interpretation of an award issued in an ordinary or appeals arbitration, whenever the holding of the award is unclear, incomplete, ambiguous or whenever its components are contradictory among themselves or contrary to the reasons, or whenever it contains clerical mistakes or a miscalculation of figures. **A30–054**

When an application for interpretation is filed, the President of the relevant Division shall review whether there is ground for interpretation. If there is ground, he shall submit the request to the Panel which has rendered the award for interpretation. The arbitrators of the Panel who are unable to act shall be replaced in accordance with Article R36. The Panel shall rule on the request within one month following the submission of the request to the Panel.

F Costs of the Proceedings

R64 Ordinary Arbitration

A30–055 **R64.1** Upon filing of the request, the claimant shall pay a minimum Court Office fee of Swiss francs 500.—, without which the CAS shall not proceed. The CAS shall in any event keep this fee. The Panel shall take it into account when assessing the final amount of the fees.

R64.2 Upon formation of the Panel, the Court Office shall fix, subject to later changes, the amount and the method of payment of the advance of costs. The filing of a counterclaim or a new claim shall result in the determination of separate advances.

To determine the amount of the advance, the Court Office shall fix an estimate of the costs of arbitration, which shall be borne by the parties in accordance with Article R64.4. The advance shall be paid in equal shares by the claimant and the respondent. If a party fails to pay its share, the other may substitute for it; in the absence of substitution, the claim to which the unpaid share relates shall be deemed withdrawn.

R64.3 Each party shall advance the cost of its own witnesses, experts and interpreters.

If the Panel appoints an expert, retains an interpreter or orders the examination of a witness, it shall issue directions with respect to an advance of costs, if appropriate.

R64.4 At the end of the proceedings, the Court Office shall determine the final amount of the cost of arbitration, which shall include the CAS Court Office fee, the costs and fees of the arbitrators computed in accordance with the CAS fee scale, the contribution towards the costs and expenses of the CAS, and the costs of witnesses, experts and interpreters.

R64.5 The foregoing costs shall be stated in the arbitral award, which shall also determine which party shall bear such costs or in which portion the parties shall share them. As a general rule, the award shall grant the prevailing party a contribution towards its legal fees and other expenses incurred in connection with the proceedings and, in particular, the costs of witnesses and interpreters. When granting such contribution, the Panel shall take into account the outcome of the proceedings, as well as the conduct and the financial resources of the parties.

R65 Appeals Arbitration

A30–056 **R65.1** Subject to Articles R65.2 and R65.4, the proceedings shall be free.

The fees and costs of the arbitrators, calculated in accordance with the CAS fee scale, together with the costs of the CAS are borne by the CAS.

R65.2 Upon submission of the statement of appeal, the appellant shall pay a minimum Court Office fee of Swiss francs 500.— without which the CAS shall not proceed and the appeal shall be deemed withdrawn. The CAS shall in any event keep this fee.

R65.3 The costs of the parties, witnesses, experts and interpreters shall be advanced by the parties. In the award, the Panel shall decide which party shall bear them or in what proportion the parties shall share them, taking into account the outcome of the proceedings, as well as the conduct and financial resources of the parties.

R65.4 If all circumstances so warrant, the President of the Appeals Arbitration Division may decide to apply Articles R64.4 and R64.5, 1st sentence, to an appeals arbitration, either ex officio or upon request of the President of the Panel.

Consultation Proceedings

A30–057 **R66** The Court Office shall determine, after consultation with the person requesting the opinion, to what extent and upon what terms such person shall contribute towards the costs of the consultation procedure.

G Miscellaneous Provisions

R67 The arbitration agreements entered into prior to November 22, 1994 shall be deemed to refer to the present Rules, unless both parties request the application of the Rules in force prior to November 22, 1994. **A30–058**

R68 The French text and the English text are authentic. In the event of any discrepancy, the French text shall prevail.

R69 The Procedural Rules may be amended by the decision of the Council, in conformity with Article S8.

Court of Arbitration for Sport Mediation Rules[1]

A31–001 Pursuant to Articles S2 and S6 paragraph 10 of the Code of Sports-related Arbitration, the International Council of Arbitration for Sport adopts the present Mediation Rules.

A. DEFINITIONS

Article 1

A31–002 CAS mediation is a non binding and informal procedure, based on a mediation agreement in which each party undertakes to attempt in good faith to negotiate with the other party, and with the assistance of a CAS mediator, with a view to settling a sports-related dispute.

CAS mediation is provided solely for the resolution of disputes related to the CAS ordinary procedure. A decision passed by the organ of a sports organization cannot be the subject of mediation proceedings before the CAS. All disputes related to disciplinary matters, as well as doping issues, are expressly excluded from CAS mediation.

Article 2

A31–003 A mediation agreement is one whereby the parties agree to submit to mediation a sports-related dispute which has arisen or which may arise between them.

A mediation agreement may take the form of a mediation clause inserted in a contract or that of a separate agreement.

B. SCOPE OF APPLICATION OF RULES

Article 3

A31–004 Where a mediation agreement provides for mediation under the CAS Mediation Rules, these Rules shall be deemed to form an integral part of such mediation agreement. Unless the parties have agreed otherwise, the version of these Rules in force on the date when the mediation request is filed shall apply.

The parties may however agree to apply other rules of procedure.

---

[1] This document is reproduced with the kind permission of Court of Arbitration for Sport.

C. Commencement of the Mediation

Article 4

A party wishing to institute mediation proceedings shall address a request to that effect in writing to the CAS Court Office, and at the same time send a copy of this to the other party. **A31–005**

The request shall contain: the identity of the parties and their representatives (name, address, telephone and fax numbers), a copy of the mediation agreement and a brief description of the dispute.

Upon filing its request, the party shall pay the administrative fee stipulated in Article 14 of the present Rules.

The day on which the mediation request is received by the CAS Court Office shall be considered as the date on which the mediation proceedings commence. The CAS Court Office shall immediately inform the parties of the date on which the mediation commences, and shall fix the time limit by which the other party shall pay its share of the administrative costs pursuant to Article 14 of the present Rules.

D. Appointment of the Mediator

Article 5

The ICAS draws up the list of mediators chosen from the list of CAS arbitrators or from outside. **A31–006**

The personalities whom the ICAS chooses appear on the list of mediators for a four-year period, and are thereafter eligible for reselection.

Article 6

Unless the parties have agreed between themselves on who the mediator will be, he shall be chosen by the CAS President from among the list of CAS mediators and appointed after consultation with the parties. **A31–007**

In accepting such appointment, the mediator undertakes to devote sufficient time to the mediation proceedings as will allow these to be conducted expeditiously.

The mediator shall be and must remain independent of the parties, and is bound to disclose any circumstances likely to compromise his independence with respect to any of the parties.

Having duly been informed thereof, the parties may however authorize the mediator to continue his mandate, by means of a signed separate or joint declaration.

In the event of an objection by any of the parties, or at his own discretion if he deems himself unable to bring the mediation to a successful conclusion, the mediator shall cease his mandate and inform the CAS President accordingly, whereupon the latter will make arrangements to replace him, after consulting the parties.

E. Representation of Parties

Article 7

A31–008 The parties may be represented or assisted in their meetings with the mediator.

If a party is being represented, the other party and the CAS must be informed beforehand as to the identity of such representative.

The representative must have full authority to settle the dispute alone, without consulting the party he is representing.

F. Conduct of Mediation

Article 8

A31–009 The mediation shall be conducted in the manner agreed by the parties. Failing such agreement between the parties, the mediator shall determine the manner in which the mediation will be conducted.

As soon as possible, the mediator shall establish the terms and timetable for submission by each party to the mediator and to the other party of a statement summarizing the dispute, including the following details:

— a brief description of the facts and points of law, including a list of the issues submitted to the mediator with a view to resolution;

— a copy of the mediation agreement.

Each party shall cooperate in good faith with the mediator and shall guarantee him the freedom to perform his mandate to advance the mediation as expeditiously as possible. The mediator may make any suggestions he deems appropriate in this regard. He may meet with separately with one of the parties, if he deems it necessary to do so.

G. Role of the Mediator

Article 9

A31–010 The mediator shall promote the settlement of the issues in dispute in any manner that he believes to be appropriate. To achieve this, he will:

a. identify the issues in dispute;

b. facilitate discussion of the issues by the parties;

c. propose solutions.

However, the mediator may not impose a solution of the dispute on either party.

H. Confidentiality

Article 10

The mediator, the parties, their representatives and advisers, experts and any other persons present during the meetings between the parties may not disclose to any third party any information given to them during the mediation, unless required by law to do so.

Under their own responsibility, the parties undertake not to compel the mediator to divulge records, reports or other documents, or to testify in regard to the mediation in any arbitral or judicial proceedings.

Any information given by one party may be disclosed by the mediator to the other party only with the consent of the former.

No record of any kind shall be made of the meetings. All the written documents shall be returned to the party providing these upon termination of the mediation, and no copy thereof shall be retained.

The parties shall not rely on, or introduce as evidence in any arbitral or judicial proceedings:

a. views expressed or suggestions made by a party with respect to a possible settlement of the dispute;

b. admissions made by a party in the course of the mediation proceedings;

c. documents, notes or other information obtained during the mediation proceedings;

d. proposals made or views expressed by the mediator; or

e. the fact that a party had or had not indicated willingness to accept a proposal.

I. Termination

Article 11

Either party or the mediator may terminate the mediation at any time. The mediation shall be terminated:

a. by the signing of a settlement by the parties;

b. by a written declaration of the mediator to the effect that further efforts at mediation are no longer worthwhile; or

c. by a written declaration of a party or the parties to the effect that the mediation proceedings are terminated.

J. Settlement

Article 12

A31–013   The settlement is drawn up by the mediator and signed by the mediator and the parties. Each party shall receive a copy thereof. In the event of any breach, a party may rely on such copy before an arbitral or judicial authority.

A copy of the settlement is submitted for inclusion in the records of the CAS Court Office.

K. Failure to Settle

Article 13

A31–014   The parties may have recourse to arbitration when a dispute has not been resolved by mediation, provided that an arbitration agreement or clause exists between the parties.

The arbitration clause may be included in the mediation agreement. In such a case, the expedited procedure provided for under article 44, paragraph 4 of the Code of Sports-related Arbitration may be applied.

In the event of failure to resolve a dispute by mediation, the mediator shall not accept an appointment as an arbitrator in any arbitral proceedings concerning the parties involved in the same dispute.

L. Costs

Article 14

A31–015   Each party shall pay the CAS Court Office the administrative fees fixed by the Court within the time limit provided in Article 4 of the present Rules. In the absence of such payment, the mediation proceedings will not be not set in motion.

The parties will pay their own mediation costs.

Unless otherwise agreed between the parties, the final costs of the mediation, which include the CAS fee, the fees of the mediator calculated on the basis of the CAS fee scale, a contribution towards the costs of the CAS, and the costs of witnesses, experts and interpreters, will be borne by the parties in equal measure.

The CAS Court Office may require the parties to deposit an equal amount as an advance towards the costs of the mediation.

Recommended clause for CAS mediation to be inserted in a contract

> "Any dispute, any controversy or claim arising under, out of or relating to this contract and any subsequent amendments of or in relation to this contract, including, but not limited to, its formation, validity, binding effect, interpretation, performance,

breach or termination, as well as non-contractual claims, shall be submitted to mediation in accordance with the CAS Mediation Rules. The language to be used in the mediation shall be . . . "

Additional clause in the absence of settlement of the dispute

"If, and to the extent that, any such dispute has not been settled within 90 days of the commencement of the mediation, or if, before the expiration of the said period, either party fails to participate or continue to participate in the mediation, the dispute shall, upon the filing of a Request for Arbitration by either party, be referred to and finally settled by CAS arbitration pursuant to the Code of Sports-related Arbitration. When the circumstances so require, the mediator may, at his own discretion or at the request of a party, seek an extension of the time limit from the CAS President."

International Federation of Consulting Engineers General Conditions of Contract for Construction (for Building and Engineering Works designed by the Employer), Clause 20—Claims, Disputes and Arbitration[1]

Contractor's Claims

A32–001   20.1 If the Contractor considers himself to be entitled to any extension of the Time for Completion and/or any additional payment, under any Clause of these Conditions or otherwise in connection with the Contract, the Contractor shall give notice to the Engineer, describing the event or circumstance giving rise to the claim. The notice shall be given as soon as practicable, and not later than 28 days after the Contractor became aware, or should have become aware, of the event or circumstance.

If the Contractor fails to give notice of a claim within such period of 28 days, the Time for Completion shall not be extended, the Contractor shall not be entitled to additional payment, and the Employer shall be discharged from all liability in connection with the claim. Otherwise, the following provisions of this Sub-Clause shall apply.

The Contractor shall also submit any other notices which are required by the Contract, and supporting particulars for the claim, all as relevant to such event or circumstance.

The Contractor shall keep such contemporary records as may be necessary to substantiate any claim, either on the Site or at another location acceptable to the Engineer. Without admitting the Employer's liability, the Engineer may, after receiving any notice under this Sub-Clause, monitor the record-keeping and/or instruct the Contractor to keep further contemporary records. The Contractor shall permit the Engineer to inspect all these records, and shall (if instructed) submit copies to the Engineer.

Within 42 days after the Contractor became aware (or should have become aware) of the event or circumstance giving rise to the claim, or within such other period as may be proposed by the Contractor and approved by the Engineer, the Contractor shall send to the Engineer a fully detailed claim which includes full supporting particulars of the basis of the claim and of the extension of time and/or additional payment claimed. If the event or circumstance giving rise to the claim has a continuing effect:

(a) this fully detailed claim shall be considered as interim;

(b) the Contractor shall send further interim claims at monthly intervals, giving the accumulated delay and/or amount claimed, and such further particulars as the Engineer may reasonably require; and

(c) the Contractor shall send a final claim within 28 days after the end of the effects resulting from the event or circumstance, or within such other period as may be proposed by the Contractor and approved by the Engineer.

Within 42 days after receiving a claim or any further particulars supporting a previous claim, or within such other period as may be proposed by the Engineer and approved by

---

[1] This document is reproduced with the kind permission of the copyright-holder, FIDIC, the International Federation of Consulting Engineers. It may not be copied in any way or by any means without prior permission of FIDIC. The Conditions of Contract, including the Dispute Adjudication Agreement and the Procedural Rules, may be purchased from FIDIC, PO Box 311, CH-1215, Geneva 20, Switzerland; Tel.: +41 (0)22 799 49 00; Fax: +41 (0)22 799 49 01; Email: fidic.pub@fidic.org.

the Contractor, the Engineer shall respond with approval, or with disapproval and detailed comments. He may also request any necessary further particulars, but shall nevertheless give his response on the principles of the claim within such time.

Each Payment Certificate shall include such amounts for any claim as have been reasonably substantiated as due under the relevant provision of the Contract. Unless and until the particulars supplied are sufficient to substantiate the whole of the claim, the Contractor shall only be entitled to payment for such part of the claim as he has been able to substantiate.

The Engineer shall proceed in accordance with Sub-Clause 3.5 [*Determinations*] to agree or determine (i) the extension (if any) of the Time for Completion (before or after its expiry) in accordance with Sub-Clause 8.4 [*Extension of Time for Completion*], and/or (ii) the additional payment (if any) to which the Contractor is entitled under the Contract.

The requirements of this Sub-Clause are in addition to those of any other Sub-Clause which may apply to a claim. If the Contractor fails to comply with this or another Sub-Clause in relation to any claim, any extension of time and/or additional payment shall take account of the extent (if any) to which the failure has prevented or prejudiced proper investigation of the claim, unless the claim is excluded under the second paragraph of this Sub-Clause.

Appointment of the Dispute Adjudication Board

20.2 Disputes shall be adjudicated by a DAB in accordance with Sub-Clause 20.4 **A32–002** [*Obtaining Dispute Adjudication Board's Decision*]. The Parties shall jointly appoint a DAB by the date stated in the Appendix to Tender.

The DAB shall comprise, as stated in the Appendix to Tender, either one or three suitably qualified persons ("the members"). If the number is not so stated and the Parties do not agree otherwise, the DAB shall comprise three persons.

If the DAB is to comprise three persons, each Party shall nominate one member for the approval of the other Party. The Parties shall consult both these members and shall agree upon the third member, who shall be appointed to act as chairman.

However, if a list of potential members is included in the Contract, the members shall be selected from those on the list, other than anyone who is unable or unwilling to accept appointment to the DAB.

The agreement between the Parties and either the sole member ("adjudicator") or each of the three members shall incorporate by reference the General Conditions of Dispute Adjudication Agreement contained in the Appendix to these General Conditions, with such amendments as are agreed between them.

The terms of the remuneration of either the sole member or each of the three members, including the remuneration of any expert whom the DAB consults, shall be mutually agreed upon by the Parties when agreeing the terms of appointment. Each Party shall be responsible for paying one-half of this remuneration.

If at any time the Parties so agree, they may jointly refer a matter to the DAB for it to give its opinion. Neither Party shall consult the DAB on any matter without the agreement of the other Party.

If at any time the Parties so agree, they may appoint a suitably qualified person or persons to replace (or to be available to replace) any one or more members of the DAB. Unless the Parties agree otherwise, the appointment will come into effect if a member declines to act or is unable to act as a result of death, disability, resignation or termination of appointment.

If any of these circumstances occurs and no such replacement is available, a replacement shall be appointed in the same manner as the replaced person was required to have been nominated or agreed upon, as described in this Sub-Clause.

The appointment of any member may be terminated by mutual agreement of both Parties, but not by the Employer or the Contractor acting alone. Unless otherwise agreed by both Parties, the appointment of the DAB (including each member) shall expire when the discharge referred to in Sub-Clause 14.12 [*Discharge*] shall have become effective.

Failure to Agree Dispute Adjudication Board

A32–003   20.3 If any of the following conditions apply, namely:

(a) the Parties fail to agree upon the appointment of the sole member of the DAB by the date stated in the first paragraph of Sub-Clause 20.2,

(b) either Party fails to nominate a member (for approval by the other Party) of a DAB of three persons by such date,

(c) the Parties fail to agree upon the appointment of the third member (to act as chairman) of the DAB by such date, or

(d) the Parties fail to agree upon the appointment of a replacement person within 42 days after the date on which the sole member or one of the three members declines to act or is unable to act as a result of death, disability, resignation or termination of appointment,

then the appointing entity or official named in the Appendix to Tender shall, upon the request of either or both of the Parties and after due consultation with both Parties, appoint this member of the DAB. This appointment shall be final and conclusive. Each Party shall be responsible for paying one-half of the remuneration of the appointing entity or official.

Obtaining Dispute Adjudication Board's Decision

A32–004   20.4 If a dispute (of any kind whatsoever) arises between the Parties in connection with, or arising out of, the Contract or the execution of the Works, including any dispute as to any certificate, determination, instruction, opinion or valuation of the Engineer, either Party may refer the dispute in writing to the DAB for its decision, with copies to the other Party and the Engineer. Such reference shall state that it is given under this Sub-Clause.

For a DAB of three persons, the DAB shall be deemed to have received such reference on the date when it is received by the chairman of the DAB.

Both Parties shall promptly make available to the DAB all such additional information, further access to the Site, and appropriate facilities, as the DAB may require for the purposes of making a decision on such dispute. The DAB shall be deemed to be not acting as arbitrator(s).

Within 84 days after receiving such reference, or within such other period as may be proposed by the DAB and approved by both Parties, the DAB shall give its decision, which shall be reasoned and shall state that it is given under this Sub-Clause. The decision shall be binding on both Parties, who shall promptly give effect to it unless and until it shall be revised in an amicable settlement or an arbitral award as described below. Unless the Contract has already been abandoned, repudiated or terminated, the Contractor shall continue to proceed with the Works in accordance with the Contract.

If either Party is dissatisfied with the DAB's decision, then either Party may, within 28 days after receiving the decision, give notice to the other Party of its dissatisfaction. If the DAB fails to give its decision within the period of 84 days (or as otherwise approved) after receiving such reference, then either Party may, within 28 days after this period has expired, give notice to the other Party of its dissatisfaction.

In either event, this notice of dissatisfaction shall state that it is given under this Sub-Clause, and shall set out the matter in dispute and the reason(s) for dissatisfaction. Except as stated in Sub-Clause 20.7 [*Failure to Comply with Dispute Adjudication Board's Decision*] and Sub-Clause 20.8 [*Expiry of Dispute Adjudication Board's Appointment*], neither Party shall be entitled to commence arbitration of a dispute unless a notice of dissatisfaction has been given in accordance with this Sub-Clause.

If the DAB has given its decision as to a matter in dispute to both Parties, and no notice of dissatisfaction has been given by either Party within 28 days after it received the DAB's decision, then the decision shall become final and binding upon both Parties.

Amicable Settlement

20.5 Where notice of dissatisfaction has been given under Sub-Clause 20.4 above, both Parties shall attempt to settle the dispute amicably before the commencement of arbitration. However, unless both Parties agree otherwise, arbitration may be commenced on or after the fifty-sixth day after the day on which notice of dissatisfaction was given, even if no attempt at amicable settlement has been made.

A32–005

Arbitration

20.6 Unless settled amicably, any dispute in respect of which the DAB's decision (if any) has not become final and binding shall be finally settled by international arbitration. Unless otherwise agreed by both Parties:

A32–006

(a) the dispute shall be finally settled under the Rules of Arbitration of the International Chamber of Commerce,

(b) the dispute shall be settled by three arbitrators appointed in accordance with these Rules, and

(c) the arbitration shall be conducted in the language for communications defined in Sub-Clause 1.4 [*Law and Language*].

The arbitrator(s) shall have full power to open up, review and revise any certificate, determination, instruction, opinion or valuation of the Engineer, and any decision of the DAB, relevant to the dispute. Nothing shall disqualify the Engineer from being called as a witness and giving evidence before the arbitrator(s) on any matter whatsoever relevant to the dispute.

Neither Party shall be limited in the proceedings before the arbitrator(s) to the evidence or arguments previously put before the DAB to obtain its decision, or to the reasons for dissatisfaction given in its notice of dissatisfaction. Any decision of the DAB shall be admissible in evidence in the arbitration.

Arbitration may be commenced prior to or after completion of the Works. The obligations of the Parties, the Engineer and the DAB shall not be altered by reason of any arbitration being conducted during the progress of the Works.

Failure to Comply with Dispute Adjudication Board's Decision

A32–007 20.7 In the event that:

(a) neither Party has given notice of dissatisfaction within the period stated in Sub-Clause 20.4 [*Obtaining Dispute Adjudication Board's Decision*],

(b) the DAB's related decision (if any) has become final and binding, and

(c) a Party fails to comply with this decision,

then the other Party may, without prejudice to any other rights it may have, refer the failure itself to arbitration under Sub-Clause 20.6 [*Arbitration*]. Sub-Clause 20.4 [*Obtaining Dispute Adjudication Board's Decision*] and Sub-Clause 20.5 [*Amicable Settlement*] shall not apply to this reference.

Expiry of Dispute Adjudication Board's Appointment

A32–008 20.8 If a dispute arises between the Parties in connection with, or arising out of, the Contract or the execution of the Works and there is no DAB in place, whether by reason of the expiry of the DAB's appointment or otherwise:

(a) Sub-Clause 20.4 [*Obtaining Dispute Adjudication Board's Decision*] and Sub-Clause 20.5 [*Amicable Settlement*] shall not apply, and

(b) the dispute may be referred directly to arbitration under Sub-Clause 20.6 [*Arbitration*].

International Federation of Consulting Engineers General Conditions of Contract for Construction (for Building and Engineering Works designed by the Employer)—General Conditions of Dispute Adjudication Agreement and Procedural Rules[1]

Definitions

1 Each "Dispute Adjudication Agreement" is a tripartite agreement by and between: **A33–001**

(a) the "Employer";

(b) the "Contractor"; and

(c) the "Member" who is defined in the Dispute Adjudication Agreement as being:

    (i) the sole member of the "DAB" (or "adjudicator") and, where this is the case, all references to the "Other Members" do not apply, or

    (ii) one of the three persons who are jointly called the "DAB" (or "dispute adjudication board") and, where this is the case, the other two persons are called the "Other Members".

The Employer and the Contractor have entered (or intend to enter) into a contract, which is called the "Contract" and is defined in the Dispute Adjudication Agreement, which incorporates this Appendix. In the Dispute Adjudication Agreement, words and expressions which are not otherwise defined shall have the meanings assigned to them in the Contract.

General Provisions

2 Unless otherwise stated in the Dispute Adjudication Agreement, it shall take effect **A33–002** on the latest of the following dates:

(a) the Commencement Date defined in the Contract,

(b) when the Employer, the Contractor and the Member have each signed the Dispute Adjudication Agreement, or

(c) when the Employer, the Contractor and each of the Other Members (if any) have respectively each signed a dispute adjudication agreement.

When the Dispute Adjudication Agreement has taken effect, the Employer and the Contractor shall each give notice to the Member accordingly. If the Member does not receive either notice within six months after entering into the Dispute Adjudication Agreement, it shall be void and ineffective.

This employment of the Member is a personal appointment. At any time, the Member may give not less than 70 days' notice of resignation to the Employer and to the Con-

---

[1] This document is reproduced with the kind permission of the copyright-holders, FIDIC, the International Federation of Consulting Engineers. It may not be copied in any way or by any means without prior permission of FIDIC. The Conditions of Contract, including the Dispute Adjudication Agreement and the Procedural Rules, may be purchased from FIDIC, PO Box 311, CH-1215, Geneva 15, Switzerland; Tel.: +41 (0)22 799 49 00; Fax: +41 (0)22 799 49 01; Email: fidic.pub@fidic.org.

tractor, and the Dispute Adjudication Agreement shall terminate upon the expiry of this period.

No assignment or subcontracting of the Dispute Adjudication Agreement is permitted without the prior written agreement of all the parties to it and of the Other Members (if any).

Warranties

A33–003   3 The Member warrants and agrees that he/she is and shall be impartial and independent of the Employer, the Contractor and the Engineer. The Member shall promptly disclose, to each of them and to the Other Members (if any), any fact or circumstance which might appear inconsistent with his/her warranty and agreement of impartiality and independence.

When appointing the Member, the Employer and the Contractor relied upon the Member's representations that he/she is:

(a) experienced in the work which the Contractor is to carry out under the Contract,

(b) experienced in the interpretation of contract documentation, and

(c) fluent in the language for communications defined in the Contract.

General Obligations of the Member

A33–004   4 The Member shall:

(a) have no interest financial or otherwise in the Employer, the Contractor or the Engineer, nor any financial interest in the Contract except for payment under the Dispute Adjudication Agreement;

(b) not previously have been employed as a consultant or otherwise by the Employer, the Contractor or the Engineer, except in such circumstances as were disclosed in writing to the Employer and the Contractor before they signed the Dispute Adjudication Agreement;

(c) have disclosed in writing to the Employer, the Contractor and the Other Members (if any), before entering into the Dispute Adjudication Agreement and to his/her best knowledge and recollection, any professional or personal relationships with any director, officer or employee of the Employer, the Contractor or the Engineer, and any previous involvement in the overall project of which the Contract forms part;

(d) not, for the duration of the Dispute Adjudication Agreement, be employed as a consultant or otherwise by the Employer, the Contractor or the Engineer, except as may be agreed in writing by the Employer, the Contractor and the Other Members (if any);

(e) comply with the annexed procedural rules and with Sub-Clause 20.4 of the Conditions of Contract;

(f) not give advice to the Employer, the Contractor, the Employer's Personnel or the Contractor's Personnel concerning the conduct of the Contract, other than in accordance with the annexed procedural rules;

(g) not while a Member enter into discussions or make any agreement with the

Employer, the Contractor or the Engineer regarding employment by any of them, whether as a consultant or otherwise, after ceasing to act under the Dispute Adjudication Agreement;

(h) ensure his/her availability for all site visits and hearings as are necessary;

(i) become conversant with the Contract and with the progress of the Works (and of any other parts of the project of which the Contract forms part) by studying all documents received which shall be maintained in a current working file;

(j) treat the details of the Contract and all the DAB's activities and hearings as private and confidential, and not publish or disclose them without the prior written consent of the Employer, the Contractor and the Other Members (if any); and

(k) be available to give advice and opinions, on any matter relevant to the Contract when requested by both the Employer and the Contractor, subject to the agreement of the Other Members (if any).

General Obligations of the Employer and the Contractor

5 The Employer, the Contractor, the Employer's Personnel and the Contractor's Personnel shall not request advice from or consultation with the Member regarding the Contract, otherwise than in the normal course of the DAB's activities under the Contract and the Dispute Adjudication Agreement, and except to the extent that prior agreement is given by the Employer, the Contractor and the Other Members (if any). The Employer and the Contractor shall be responsible for compliance with this provision, by the Employer's Personnel and the Contractor's Personnel respectively.

The Employer and the Contractor undertake to each other and to the Member that the Member shall not, except as otherwise agreed in writing by the Employer, the Contractor, the Member and the Other Members (if any):

(a) be appointed as an arbitrator in any arbitration under the Contract;

(b) be called as a witness to give evidence concerning any dispute before arbitrator(s) appointed for any arbitration under the Contract; or

(c) be liable for any claims for anything done or omitted in the discharge or purported discharge of the Member's functions, unless the act or omission is shown to have been in bad faith.

The Employer and the Contractor hereby jointly and severally indemnify and hold the Member harmless against and from claims from which he/she is relieved from liability under the preceding paragraph.

Whenever the Employer or the Contractor refers a dispute to the DAB under Sub-Clause 20.4 of the Conditions of Contract, which will require the Member to make a site visit and attend a hearing, the Employer or the Contractor shall provide appropriate security for a sum equivalent to the reasonable expenses to be incurred by the Member. No account shall be taken of any other payments due or paid to the Member.

Payment

6 The Member shall be paid as follows, in the currency named in the Dispute Adjudication Agreement:

(a) a retainer fee per calendar month, which shall be considered as payment in full for:
  (i) being available on 28 days' notice for all site visits and hearings;
  (ii) becoming and remaining conversant with all project developments and maintaining relevant files;
  (iii) all office and overhead expenses including secretarial services, photocopying and office supplies incurred in connection with his duties; and
  (iv) all services performed hereunder except those referred to in sub-paragraphs (b) and (c) of this Clause.

The retainer fee shall be paid with effect from the last day of the calendar month in which the Dispute Adjudication Agreement becomes effective; until the last day of the calendar month in which the Taking-Over Certificate is issued for the whole of the Works.

With effect from the first day of the calendar month following the month in which Taking-Over Certificate is issued for the whole of the Works, the retainer fee shall be reduced by 50%. This reduced fee shall be paid until the first day of the calendar month in which the Member resigns or the Dispute Adjudication Agreement is otherwise terminated.

(b) a daily fee which shall be considered as payment in full for:
  (i) each day or part of a day up to a maximum of two days' travel time in each direction for the journey between the Member's home and the site, or another location of a meeting with the Other Members (if any);
  (ii) each working day on site visits, hearings or preparing decisions; and
  (iii) each day spent reading submissions in preparation for a hearing.

(c) all reasonable expenses incurred in connection with the Member's duties, including the cost of telephone calls, courier charges, faxes and telexes, travel expenses, hotel and subsistence costs: a receipt shall be required for each item in excess of five percent of the daily fee referred to in sub-paragraph (b) of this Clause;

(d) any taxes properly levied in the Country on payments made to the Member (unless a national or permanent resident of the Country) under this Clause 6.

The retainer and daily fees shall be as specified in the Dispute Adjudication Agreement. Unless it specifies otherwise, these fees shall remain fixed for the first 24 calendar months, and shall thereafter be adjusted by agreement between the Employer, the Contractor and the Member, at each anniversary of the date on which the Dispute Adjudication Agreement became effective.

The Member shall submit invoices for payment of the monthly retainer and air fares quarterly in advance. Invoices for other expenses and for daily fees shall be submitted following the conclusion of a site visit or hearing. All invoices shall be accompanied by a brief description of activities performed during the relevant period and shall be addressed to the Contractor.

The Contractor shall pay each of the Member's invoices in full within 56 calendar days after receiving each invoice and shall apply to the Employer (in the Statements under the Contract) for reimbursement of one-half of the amounts of these invoices. The Employer shall then pay the Contractor in accordance with the Contract.

If the Contractor fails to pay to the Member the amount to which he/she is entitled under the Dispute Adjudication Agreement, the Employer shall pay the amount due to the Member and any other amount which may be required to maintain the operation of the DAB; and without prejudice to the Employer's rights or remedies. In addition to all other rights arising from this default, the Employer shall be entitled to reimbursement of all sums paid in excess of one-half of these payments, plus all costs of recovering these sums and financing charges calculated at the rate specified in Sub-Clause 14.8 of the Conditions of Contract.

If the Member does not receive payment of the amount due within 70 days after submitting a valid invoice, the Member may (i) suspend his/her services (without notice) until the payment is received, and/or (ii) resign his/her appointment by giving notice under Clause 7.

Termination

7 At any time: (i) the Employer and the Contractor may jointly terminate the Dispute Adjudication Agreement by giving 42 days' notice to the Member; or (ii) the Member may resign as provided for in Clause 2.   **A33–007**

If the Member fails to comply with the Dispute Adjudication Agreement, the Employer and the Contractor may, without prejudice to their other rights, terminate it by notice to the Member. The notice shall take effect when received by the Member.

If the Employer or the Contractor fails to comply with the Dispute Adjudication Agreement, the Member may, without prejudice to his/her other rights, terminate it by notice to the Employer and the Contractor. The notice shall take effect when received by them both.

Any such notice, resignation and termination shall be final and binding on the Employer, the Contractor and the Member. However, a notice by the Employer or the Contractor, but not by both, shall be of no effect.

Default of the Member

8 If the Member fails to comply with any obligation under Clause 4, he/she shall not be entitled to any fees or expenses hereunder and shall, without prejudice to their other rights, reimburse each of the Employer and the Contractor for any fees and expenses received by the Member and the Other Members (if any), for proceedings or decisions (if any) of the DAB which are rendered void or ineffective.   **A33–008**

Disputes

9 Any dispute or claim arising out of or in connection with this Dispute Adjudication Agreement, or the breach, termination or invalidity thereof, shall be finally settled under the Rules of Arbitration of the International Chamber of Commerce by one arbitrator appointed in accordance with these Rules of Arbitration.   **A33–009**

PROCEDURAL RULES

1 Unless otherwise agreed by the Employer and the Contractor, the DAB shall visit the site at intervals of not more than 140 days, including times of critical construction events, at the request of either the Employer or the Contractor. Unless otherwise agreed   **A33–010**

by the Employer, the Contractor and the DAB, the period between consecutive visits shall not be less than 70 days, except as required to convene a hearing as described below.

2 The timing of and agenda for each site visit shall be as agreed jointly by the DAB, the Employer and the Contractor, or in the absence of agreement, shall be decided by the DAB. The purpose of site visits is to enable the DAB to become and remain acquainted with the progress of the Works and of any actual or potential problems or claims.

3 Site visits shall be attended by the Employer, the Contractor and the Engineer and shall be co-ordinated by the Employer in co-operation with the Contractor. The Employer shall ensure the provision of appropriate conference facilities and secretarial and copying services. At the conclusion of each site visit and before leaving the site, the DAB shall prepare a report on its activities during the visit and shall send copies to the Employer and the Contractor.

4 The Employer and the Contractor shall furnish to the DAB one copy of all documents which the DAB may request, including Contract documents, progress reports, variation instructions, certificates and other documents pertinent to the performance of the Contract. All communications between the DAB and the Employer or the Contractor shall be copied to the other Party. If the DAB comprises three persons, the Employer and the Contractor shall send copies of these requested documents and these communications to each of these persons.

5 If any dispute is referred to the DAB in accordance with Sub-Clause 20.4 of the Conditions of Contract, the DAB shall proceed in accordance with Sub-Clause 20.4 and these Rules. Subject to the time allowed to give notice of a decision and other relevant factors, the DAB shall:

(a) act fairly and impartially as between the Employer and the Contractor, giving each of them a reasonable opportunity of putting his case and responding to the other's case, and

(b) adopt procedures suitable to the dispute, avoiding unnecessary delay or expense.

6 The DAB may conduct a hearing on the dispute, in which event it will decide on the date and place for the hearing and may request that written documentation and arguments from the Employer and the Contractor be presented to it prior to or at the hearing.

7 Except as otherwise agreed in writing by the Employer and the Contractor, the DAB shall have power to adopt an inquisitorial procedure, to refuse admission to hearings or audience at hearings to any persons other than representatives of the Employer, the Contractor and the Engineer, and to proceed in the absence of any party who the DAB is satisfied received notice of the hearing; but shall have discretion to decide whether and to what extent this power may be exercised.

8 The Employer and the Contractor empower the DAB, among other things, to:

(a) establish the procedure to be applied in deciding a dispute,

(b) decide upon the DAB's own jurisdiction, and as to the scope of any dispute referred to it,

(c) conduct any hearing as it thinks fit, not being bound by any rules or procedures other than those contained in the Contract and these Rules,

(d) take the initiative in ascertaining the facts and matters required for a decision,

(e) make use of its own specialist knowledge, if any,

(f) decide upon the payment of financing charges in accordance with the Contract,

(g) decide upon any provisional relief such as interim or conservatory measures, and

(h) open up, review and revise any certificate, decision, determination, instruction, opinion or valuation of the Engineer, relevant to the dispute.

9 The DAB shall not express any opinions during any hearing concerning the merits of any arguments advanced by the Parties. Thereafter, the DAB shall make and give its decision in accordance with Sub-Clause 20.4, or as otherwise agreed by the Employer and the Contractor in writing. If the DAB comprises three persons:

(a) it shall convene in private after a hearing, in order to have discussions and prepare its decision;

(b) it shall endeavour to reach a unanimous decision: if this proves impossible the applicable decision shall be made by a majority of the Members, who may require the minority Member to prepare a written report for submission to the Employer and the Contractor; and

(c) if a Member fails to attend a meeting or hearing, or to fulfil any required function, the other two Members may nevertheless proceed to make a decision, unless:

   (i) either the Employer or the Contractor does not agree that they do so, or
   (ii) the absent Member is the chairman and he/she instructs the other Members to not make a decision.

Grain and Feed Trade Association Form 125 Arbitration Rules[1]

(EFFECTIVE FOR CONTRACTS DATED FROM 1ST JANUARY 2003)

Any dispute arising out of a contract or arbitration agreement, which incorporates or refers to these Rules, shall be referred to arbitration, and arbitrator(s) or board of appeal, as the case may be, will proceed to determine all issues put before them, in accordance with the following provisions:—

1. PRELIMINARY

A34–001   1:1 The provisions of the Arbitration Act 1996, and of any statutory amendment, modification or re-enactment thereof for the time being in force, shall apply to every arbitration and/or appeal under these Rules save insofar as such provisions are expressly modified by, or are inconsistent with, these Rules.
1:2 The juridical seat of the arbitration shall be, and is hereby designated pursuant to section 4 of the Arbitration Act 1996 as, England.
1:3 Arbitration shall take place at the registered offices of The Grain and Feed Trade Association (GAFTA), London, or (but without prejudice to Rules 1:1 and 1:2 above), elsewhere if agreed by the parties in writing.

2. PROCEDURE AND TIME LIMITS FOR CLAIMING ARBITRATION

A34–002   The claimant shall serve on the respondent a notice stating his intention to refer a dispute to arbitration within the following time limits. (The appointment of arbitrators shall be in accordance with Rule 3).

Disputes as to Quality and/or Condition

A34–003   2:1 (a) In respect of disputes arising out of the "Rye Terms" clause not later than the 10th consecutive day after the date of completion of final discharge. (See Rule 6).

(b) In respect of claims arising out of certificates of analysis in respect of which allowances are not fixed by the terms of the contract, not later than the 21st consecutive day after the date on which the claimant receives the final certificate of analysis.

(c) In respect of all other quality and/or condition disputes, not later than the 21st consecutive day after the date of completion of final discharge, or delivery, or the unstuffing of the container(s), as the case may be.

---

[1] This document is reproduced with the kind permission of the Grain and Feed Trade Association.

Other Disputes

2:2 In respect of all other disputes relating to the sale of goods:— **A34–004**

(a) arising out of CIF, CIFFO, C & F and similar shipment contract terms, not later than one year after (i) the expiry of the contract period of shipment, including extension if any, or (ii) the date of completion of final discharge of the ship at port of destination, whichever period shall last expire,

(b) arising out of FOB terms, not later than one year after (i) the date of the last bill of lading or (ii) the expiry of the contract period of delivery, including extension if any, whichever period shall first expire,

(c) on any other terms, not later than one year after the last day of the contractual delivery, collection or arrival period, as the case may be.

(d) Irrespective of the time limits in (a), (b) and (c) above, in the event of non-payment of amounts payable, not later than 60 consecutive days from the notice that a dispute has arisen as provided for in the Payment Clause of the contract.

2:3 No award by the tribunal shall be questioned or set aside on appeal or otherwise on the ground that the claim was not made within the time limits stipulated in this Rule if the respondent to the claim did not raise the matter in their submissions, so as to enable the tribunal to consider whether or not to exercise the discretion vested in it by Rule 21.

3. Appointment of the Tribunal

The dispute shall be heard and determined by a tribunal of three arbitrators (appointed **A34–005** in accordance with Rule 3:2) or, if both parties agree, by a sole arbitrator (appointed in accordance with clause 3:1). This rule is without prejudice to Rule 6, which governs the appointment of the tribunal in relation to disputes arising out of the Rye Terms clause, and Rule 5.3, which governs the appointment of a tribunal for examination of samples.

Procedure for the Appointment of a Sole Arbitrator

3:1 (a) If he requires the appointment of a sole arbitrator the claimant shall, before **A34–006** expiry of the time limit for claiming arbitration, serve a notice on the respondent seeking his agreement to the appointment of a sole arbitrator by GAFTA.

(b) Not later than the 9th consecutive day after service of the notice referred to in (a) above, the respondent shall either; (i) serve a notice on the claimant stating that he agrees to the appointment of a sole arbitrator by GAFTA, or (ii) appoint an arbitrator to a tribunal of three arbitrators and serve on the claimant a notice of the arbitrator so appointed, in which case Rule 3:2(c) shall apply.

(c) Where the parties have agreed to the appointment of a sole arbitrator, GAFTA shall appoint an arbitrator on receipt of the first statements and evidence submitted in accordance with Rule 4, or, where interlocutory or interim decisions are required of the tribunal, upon the application of either party.

Institutional Rules

Procedure for the Appointment of a Tribunal of Three Arbitrators

A34–007 3:2 (a) The claimant shall before the expiry of the time limit for claiming arbitration appoint an arbitrator and serve a notice on the respondent of the name of the arbitrator so appointed.

(b) The respondent shall, not later than the 9th consecutive day after service of the notice of the name of the claimant's arbitrator, appoint a second arbitrator and serve a notice on the claimant of the name of the arbitrator so appointed.

(c) If the respondent does not agree to the appointment of a sole arbitrator and has instead appointed an arbitrator and given written notice thereof pursuant to Rule 3:1(b), the claimant shall not later than the 9th consecutive day after service of such notice of appointment, appoint a second arbitrator and serve a notice on the respondent of the name of the arbitrator so appointed.

(d) Where two arbitrators have been appointed, GAFTA shall appoint a third arbitrator on receipt of the first statements and evidence submitted in accordance with Rule 4, or, where interlocutory or interim decisions are required of a tribunal, upon the application of either party. The third arbitrator shall be the chairman of the tribunal so formed and his name shall be notified to the parties by GAFTA.

Procedure for the Appointments of Arbitrators by GAFTA

A34–008 3:3 If either party fails to appoint an arbitrator or to give notice thereof within the above time limits, the other party may apply to GAFTA for the appointment of an arbitrator. Notice of such application must be served on the party who has failed to appoint. Upon such application being made, GAFTA will appoint an arbitrator on behalf of the party who has failed to do so, and give notice of the name of the arbitrator appointed to the parties.

Where the claimant has already sought the respondent's agreement to the appointment of a sole arbitrator pursuant to Rule 3:1, then GAFTA will appoint a sole arbitrator. Where either party has already appointed an arbitrator, pursuant to Rule 3:1(b) or Rule 3:2, then GAFTA will appoint the second arbitrator of the tribunal.

3:4 Applications to GAFTA for the appointment of an arbitrator shall be accompanied by:—

(a) prima facie evidence that the parties have entered into a contract subject to these Rules,

(b) copies of the notices (i) claiming arbitration and (ii) stating that an application has been made to GAFTA for the appointment of an arbitrator,

(c) the appropriate fee ruling at the date of application.

3:5 Appointments of arbitrators by GAFTA shall be made by any three of its Officers.

3:6 Any party making an application to GAFTA for the appointment of an arbitrator, may be required by GAFTA to pay a deposit of such sum as it may require on account of any fees and expenses thereafter arising.

3:7 An arbitrator appointed under these Rules shall be a GAFTA Qualified Arbitrator and shall not be interested in the transaction nor directly interested as a member of a company or firm named as a party to the arbitration, nor financially retained by any such

GRAIN AND FEED TRADE ASSOCIATION ARBITRATION RULES

company or firm, nor a member of nor financially retained by any company or firm financially associated with any party to the arbitration.

3:8 An appointment of an arbitrator shall be valid and effective for all purposes provided that he has signified his acceptance of the appointment to the party appointing him, or to GAFTA, as the case may be, at any time prior to the discharge of any arbitral function.

3:9 (a) If an arbitrator dies, refuses to act, resigns, or becomes incapable of acting, or if he fails to proceed with the arbitration, or is found to be ineligible, or his authority is revoked by the GAFTA pursuant to the GAFTA Rules and Regulations and Code of Conduct for Qualified Arbitrators, the party, or GAFTA as the case may be, who originally appointed that arbitrator shall forthwith appoint a substitute and serve notice thereof on the other party.

(b) If a party fails, contrary to (a) above, to appoint a substitute arbitrator and to give notice thereof within 5 consecutive days of learning of the arbitrator's death, refusal to act, resignation, incapacity, failure to proceed, finding of ineligibility or revocation of authority, as the case may be, GAFTA shall, upon the application of either party, have the power to appoint a substitute arbitrator.

4. ARBITRATION PROCEDURE

4:1 The claimant shall draw up a clear and concise statement of his case, which, together with a copy of the contract and any supporting documents, shall be served as set out in Rule 4.4. The Claimant shall deposit with GAFTA such sum, as GAFTA considers appropriate on account of the costs, fees and expenses of the arbitration.

4:2 The respondent shall, on receipt of the claimant's case and documents, draw up a clear and concise statement of his defence (and counterclaim, if any) which, together with any supporting documents, shall be served as set out in Rule 4.4.

4:3 The claimant may submit further written comments and/or documents in reply, such to be served as set out in Rule 4.4.

4:4 All statements and evidence shall be served by sending them to the other party, with copies to GAFTA. In the case of a sole arbitrator 2 sets, or in the case of a tribunal of three arbitrators, 4 sets of statements and evidence, shall be delivered to GAFTA. Failure to send all sets to GAFTA will render the party responsible liable for the costs of copying such documents for forwarding to the arbitrators.

4:5 The tribunal may vary or depart from the above procedure in order to give each party a reasonable opportunity of putting his case and dealing with that of his opponent, and shall adopt procedures suitable to the circumstances of the particular case, avoiding unnecessary delay or expense, so as to provide a fair means for the resolution of the matters falling to be determined.

4:6 The timetable for the proceedings, including any steps to be taken pursuant to Rule 4 and/or determined by the tribunal, will be advised to the parties by GAFTA. It shall be the duty of the tribunal to ensure the prompt progress of the arbitration, including the making of orders where appropriate. Any delay in the proceedings may be notified to GAFTA.

4:7 Nothing in this Rule shall prevent the respondent from delivering his statement and documentary evidence before receiving documents/statements from the claimant.

4:8 Where the tribunal considers that an oral hearing is necessary, the date, time and place will be arranged by GAFTA. In which event the parties may be represented by one of their employees, or by a GAFTA Qualified Arbitrator or other representative, but they may not be represented by a solicitor or barrister, or other legally qualified advocate, wholly or principally engaged in private practice, unless legal representation is expressly agreed. The tribunal may call upon either party to deposit with GAFTA such sum or sums as the tribunal considers appropriate on account of fees, costs and expenses.

Lapse of Claim

A34–010   **4:9** If neither party submits any documentary evidence or submissions as set out in this Rule or as ordered by the tribunal, within 1 year from the date of the notice claiming arbitration, then, the claimant's claim shall be deemed to have lapsed on the expiry of the said period of 1 year unless before that date the claim is renewed:

   (a) by a notice served by either party on the other, such notice to be served during the 30 consecutive days prior to the expiry date, or

   (b) by the service of documentary evidence or submissions by either party,

in which case the claim and counterclaim are each renewed for a further year.

The claim may be thus renewed for successive periods of 1 year, but not to exceed more than 6 years from the date of the first notice served in accordance with Rule 2. Wherever a claim is renewed any counterclaim is also deemed to be renewed.

4:10 If the arbitration is abandoned, suspended or concluded, by agreement or otherwise, before the final award is made, the parties shall be jointly and severally liable to pay to GAFTA the tribunal's and GAFTA costs, fees and expenses.

5. SAMPLES

A34–011   **5:1** If either party wishes to submit samples for examination by the tribunal, those samples shall be drawn, sealed and despatched to GAFTA in accordance with the provisions of the GAFTA Sampling Rules No. 124, and shall be held at the disposal of the tribunal.

5:2 As soon as possible after receipt (and if necessary prior to the completion of the exchange of submissions and documents pursuant to Rule 4 and/or the order of the tribunal), the samples shall be examined by the tribunal. In particular,

   (a) in the case of claims arising out of the "rye terms" clause, the samples shall be examined not later than 21 consecutive days after the date of completion of final discharge of the ship at port of destination, and

   (b) where the claim involves comparison with a f.a.q. (fair average quality) standard, the samples shall be examined not later than 21 consecutive days after the date of publication by GAFTA that the standard has been, or will not be, made.

5:3 Upon the joint application of both parties, GAFTA may arrange for the examination of the contract goods to take place at the port of destination, by a sole arbitrator or (in the case of a dispute arising out of the "rye terms" clause) three arbitrators, such arbitrator or arbitrators to be appointed by GAFTA. This provision does not over-ride the parties' obligations to take, seal and despatch samples where required by the GAFTA Sampling Rules No. 124. The tribunal so appointed shall determine all matters in dispute between the parties.

5:4 All samples sent to GAFTA for arbitration, testing and/or other purposes shall become and be the absolute property of GAFTA.

6. Arbitration Procedure for Claims Arising out of the "Rye Terms" Clause

6:1 When the claimant has served on the respondent notice of its intention to refer the dispute to arbitration in accordance with Rule 2:1(a) he shall send a copy of the notice to GAFTA, together with sufficient information to identify the samples relating to the claim.   **A34–012**

6:2 Notwithstanding anything to the contrary in these Rules, upon receipt of the notice as above, GAFTA shall appoint a tribunal of three arbitrators.

6:3 Any documentary submissions or evidence to be submitted by the parties shall be provided in accordance with Rule 4.

6:4 An award made pursuant to this Rule shall be final and binding and no appeal shall lie to a board of appeal.

7. String Arbitrations—Consolidated Arbitrations and Concurrent Hearings

Quality and Condition

7:1 If a contract forms part of a string of contracts which contain materially identical terms (albeit that the price may vary under each contract), a single arbitration determining a dispute as to quality and/or condition may be held between the first seller and the last buyer in the string as though they were parties who had contracted with each other.   **A34–013**

Any award made in such proceedings shall, subject only to any right of appeal pursuant to Rule 10, be binding on all the parties in the string and may be enforced by an intermediate party against his immediate contracting party as though a separate award had been made pursuant to each contract.

Other Cases

7:2 In all other cases, if all parties concerned expressly agree, the tribunal may conduct arbitral proceedings concurrently with other arbitral proceedings, and, in particular, concurrent hearings may be held, but separate awards shall be made pursuant to each contract.

8. Issues of Substantive Jurisdiction, Provisional Orders and Awards on Different Aspects

Issues of Substantive Jurisdiction

8:1 (a) The tribunal may rule on its own jurisdiction, that is, as to whether there is a   **A34–014**

Institutional Rules

valid arbitration agreement, whether the tribunal is properly constituted and what matters have been submitted to arbitration in accordance with the arbitration agreement.

(b) In the event that the tribunal determines it has no jurisdiction, GAFTA will notify the parties of the tribunal's decision. Such decision shall be final and binding upon the parties subject to any right of appeal to a board of appeal pursuant to Rule 10. GAFTA will invoice the claimant for any costs, fees and expenses incurred. In the event that the tribunal determines that it has jurisdiction, no appeal shall lie to a board of appeal.

(c) If the board of appeal upholds the tribunal's determination that it has no jurisdiction, the board of appeal shall order accordingly and GAFTA shall notify the parties and the tribunal and will invoice the appellants for any costs, fees and expenses incurred.

(d) If the board of appeal reverses the tribunal's determination that it has no jurisdiction, the board of appeal shall order accordingly, and GAFTA shall notify the parties and the tribunal, and shall order that the dispute be referred to arbitration afresh, whereupon:-

   (i) The dispute shall be deemed to be one arising out of a contract embodying these Rules.
   (ii) The tribunal formerly appointed shall thereupon cease to act and shall not be re-appointed when the dispute is referred as aforesaid.
   (iii) The provisions of Rule 3 shall apply, the time limits for appointment running from the date of the board of appeal's order.
   (iv) The board of appeal may in its absolute discretion extend the time limits in these Rules, and no objection that time has expired shall be taken if the requirements of Rules were previously complied with.

Provisional Orders

A34–015 8:2 Where the tribunal decides at any time to order on a provisional basis any relief which it would have power to grant in a final award, no appeal shall lie to a board of appeal until the tribunal has issued a final award determining the issues between the parties.

Awards on Different Aspects

A34–016 8:3 Where the tribunal decides during the course of an arbitration to make an award dealing finally with one or more aspects of the dispute, but which leaves to be decided by the tribunal other aspect(s) of the dispute, it may make an award which shall be final and binding as to the aspect(s) with which it deals, subject to any right of appeal pursuant to Rule 10.

9. Awards of Arbitration

A34–017 9:1 All awards shall be in writing and shall be signed by the sole arbitrator or, in the case of an award made by a three-man tribunal, by all three arbitrators. The tribunal shall have the power to assess and award the costs of and connected with the reference, including the fees and/or expenses of GAFTA, (which shall be those for the time being in force as prescribed by the Council of GAFTA) and also the fees and/or expenses incurred by the tribunal. The tribunal will assess and award costs at the conclusion of the arbitration.

9:2 The tribunal shall, on the application of either party, made before the arbitration award is made, have the power to extend the time for appealing in any case in which it considers it just or necessary so to do. Any such extension must be stated in the award.

9:3 The tribunal shall submit the award to GAFTA. Upon receipt of the signed award GAFTA shall give notice to the parties named in the award that the award is at their disposal upon payment of the fees and expenses incurred by the tribunal and GAFTA. If payment is not received by GAFTA within 14 days from such notice, GAFTA may call upon any one or more of the parties to take up the award and in such case the party or parties so called upon shall pay the fees and expenses as directed. Upon receipt of the fees and/or expenses, GAFTA shall date and issue the award to the parties, which date shall for the purpose of the Arbitration Act 1996 and these Rules be deemed to be the date on which the award was made.

9:4 Subject to any right of appeal pursuant to Rule 10 awards of arbitration shall be conclusive and binding on the parties with respect both to the matters in dispute and as to costs.

9:5 No award shall be questioned or invalidated on the ground that an arbitrator was not qualified to act unless such objection was made at the outset of the arbitration.

10. Right of Appeal

10:1 Save as provided in Rules 6:4, 8:1(b), 8:2, and 21, either party may appeal against an award to a board of appeal provided that the following conditions are complied with:—

(a) Not later than 12 noon on the 30th consecutive day after the date on which the award was made the appellant shall:—
   (i) ensure that a written notice of appeal is received by GAFTA,
   (ii) serve a notice of his intention to appeal on the other party and ensure receipt of a copy by GAFTA,
   (iii) and (subject to the provisions of Rule 19) make payment to GAFTA of the appeal deposit stated on the award of arbitration on account of the costs, fees and expenses of the appeal.

(b) The fees and expenses of the arbitration award incurred by the tribunal and/or GAFTA shall be paid to GAFTA before the appeal is heard.

(c) The appellants shall pay such further sum or sums on account of fees, costs and expenses as may be called for by GAFTA or the board of appeal at any time after the lodging of the appeal (as defined in (a) and (b) above) and prior to the publication of the award by the board of appeal. The fees charged by the board of appeal shall be in accordance with the scale of fees laid down by the Council from time to time.

10:2 If appeals are lodged by both parties to the award GAFTA shall have the power to consolidate such appeals for hearing by the same board of appeal.

10:3 If neither the appeal fee required under Rule 10:1 nor evidence from a bank as required by Rule 19 has been received by GAFTA within 35 consecutive days of receipt of the notice of appeal, such notice shall be deemed to have been withdrawn and the right of appeal waived unless, prior to the expiry of that period of 35 consecutive days, the appellant has applied to the board of appeal for an extension, in which case the board of appeal may, in its absolute discretion on hearing evidence and/or submissions from each party, grant an extension.

11. Boards of Appeal

A34–019   **11:1** Boards of appeal shall be elected and constituted in accordance with the GAFTA Rules and Regulations and Code of Conduct for Qualified Arbitrators and each board of appeal shall, when so elected, appoint one of its members to be chairman. Where the first tier arbitration award was made by a sole arbitrator the board of appeal will comprise of three members. Where the first tier award was made by a tribunal of three arbitrators, then the board of appeal shall comprise of five members. GAFTA will notify the parties of the names of the members of the board of appeal.

11:2 If a member of the board of appeal dies, refuses to act, resigns, or becomes incapable of acting, or if he fails to proceed with the appeal, or is found to be ineligible, or his authority is revoked by GAFTA pursuant to the GAFTA Rules and Regulations and Code of Conduct for Qualified Arbitrators, the next member of the Committee of Appeal duly appointed for this purpose shall thereupon become a member of the board of appeal in his place.

12. Appeal Procedure

A34–020   **12:1** The parties shall, in conformity with Rule 12:2, serve their statements of case and documentary evidence in accordance with the timetable which will be notified to the parties by GAFTA on behalf of the Appeal Board. The timetable will require the service of pleadings in the following order:—

(a) The Appellant shall issue a concise statement of his case together with supporting documents.

(b) The Respondent shall, on receipt of the Appellant's statement and any documents, issue a concise statement of his case together with supporting documents.

(c) The Appellant then has the right, on receipt of Respondent's statement and documents, to issue a statement in reply.

12:2 Statements of case and documentary evidence (which may include new evidence not before the arbitrators) shall be served by sending them to the other party with copies to GAFTA. Where the appeal is against the award of a sole arbitrator 3 copies, or where the appeal is against the award of a tribunal of three arbitrators 5 copies, shall be sent to GAFTA. Failure to send all copies to GAFTA will render the party responsible liable to GAFTA for the costs of copying such documents for forwarding to the board of appeal.

12:3 GAFTA will set down the appeal for hearing having due regard to the above timetable or any other timetable which the board of appeal may decide. In the event of an oral hearing the parties may be represented by one of their employees, or by a qualified arbitrator (who has not previously acted in the case) or by a representative, but they may not be represented by a solicitor or barrister, or other legally qualified advocate, wholly or principally engaged in private practice, unless legal representation is expressly agreed.

12:4 An appeal involves a new hearing of the dispute and the board of appeal may confirm, vary, amend or set-aside the award of the tribunal. In particular (but not by way of restriction), the board of appeal may;

   (a) vary an award by increasing or reducing the liability of either party,

   (b) correct any errors in the award or otherwise alter or amend it,

   (c) award the payment of interest,

   (d) award the payment of costs, fees and expenses of and incidental to the hearing of the arbitration and the appeal. Such costs, fees and expenses will normally follow the event.

12:5 An award shall be confirmed unless the board of appeal decides by a majority to vary, amend or set it aside.

12:6 The award of the board of appeal, whether confirming, varying, amending or setting aside the original award of arbitration, shall be signed by the chairman of the board of appeal, and, when so signed, shall be deemed to be the award of the board of appeal, and shall be final, conclusive and binding. Rule 9:3 shall apply to awards of the board of appeal.

12:7 (a) If the appellant, on receiving notice of the date fixed for the hearing of the appeal, requests a postponement of more than 14 days, or at the first or any subsequent hearing of the appeal requests an adjournment, then in such event the board of appeal may in its absolute discretion direct that as a condition of granting an adjournment all or any part of the money required by the terms of the award of arbitration to be paid by either party to the other shall be deposited in such bank and in such currency (either in the United Kingdom or abroad) as the board of appeal may direct. Such money shall be held by such bank in an account in the name of GAFTA, or on such terms as the board of appeal may direct. The board of appeal shall, where such money has been deposited, direct in its award how and to which of the parties the amount so held shall be paid out.

   (b) If the appellant fails to make such payment as aforesaid in accordance with the directions of the board of appeal, and within such time as the board of appeal stipulates, then (subject to the provisions of Rule 19) the appeal shall be deemed to be withdrawn.

   (c) If in the opinion of the board of appeal the appellant has been guilty of undue delay in proceeding with his appeal the board of appeal shall give due warning to the appellant that he should proceed with due despatch. If the appellant continues, thereafter, to delay the progress of the appeal, the board of appeal may (after giving both parties a reasonable opportunity to make submissions) order that the appeal is deemed to have been withdrawn, in which event the money on deposit (with interest if any, less any tax deductible) shall immediately become due and payable to the party and/or parties entitled thereto under the terms of the award of arbitration.

Institutional Rules

12:8 No award of a board of appeal or decision by a board of appeal on any issue or aspect, shall be questioned or invalidated on the ground that any of its members was not qualified to act unless objection is made within a reasonable period of the notification of the members of the board of appeal.

13. Withdrawals of Appeals

A34–021   **13:1** The appellant shall have the right, at any time before the board of appeal makes an award, to withdraw his appeal by giving notice of such withdrawal to GAFTA, and in such case GAFTA shall forthwith notify all parties to the arbitration that the appeal has been withdrawn. If notice of withdrawal is received by the Association within 10 consecutive days of the date on which the appeal was lodged in accordance with Rule 10:1, two thirds of the deposit shall be returned. If notice of withdrawal is received by GAFTA not later than 48 hours before the time of the first scheduled hearing of the appeal a third of the deposit shall be returned. No part of the deposit shall be returned following receipt of notice of withdrawal at any later date.

13:2 In the event of withdrawal the respondent shall continue to have the right of appeal against the award to a board of appeal in accordance with the provisions of Rule 10, save that the time limit laid down in Rule 10:1 shall be 12 noon on the 30th consecutive day after the date of service of notice by GAFTA to that party of the aforesaid withdrawal.

14. Appeals on String Contracts—Quality and/or Condition

A34–022   **14:1** Where a "string" award is made pursuant to Rule 7:1, then, unless it is an award determining a dispute arising out of the "Rye Terms" clause, each party in the string shall be entitled to appeal against that award to a board of appeal, provided that each of the following provisions, in addition to the provisions of Rule 10, are complied with:—

    (a) If the appellant is an intermediate party he shall state in his notice of appeal whether he is appealing as a buyer or as seller.

    (b) If the appellant is the first seller or the last buyer he shall, within the time limits set out in Rule 10:1(a)(ii), serve written notice of his intention to appeal on the party in immediate contractual relationship with him.

    (c) If the appellant is an intermediate party and is appealing as buyer or seller he shall, within the time limits set out in Rule 10:1(a)(ii), serve notice of his intention to appeal on both the respondent to the appeal and also his own immediate seller or buyer.

    (d) The recipient of a notice served pursuant to the above provisions may, if it wishes to commence appeal proceedings against its own immediate contracting party, pass on a like notice upon the next party in the string. Such notice shall be passed on with due despatch, in which case the time limit in Rule 10 shall be deemed to have been complied with.

14:2 All appeals to which this Rule applies and to all awards made pursuant to this Rule shall be binding on every appellant and respondent. Non-compliance with any provisions of Rule 14:1(d) shall in no way limit or affect the jurisdiction of the board of appeal.

15. Appeal Awards

GAFTA may call upon either of the disputing parties to take up the award of the board of appeal and in such case the party so called upon shall take up the award and pay the fees, costs and expenses of the board of appeal and/or GAFTA. Upon receipt of the fees, costs and expenses, GAFTA shall then date and issue the award to the parties, which date shall, for the purposes of the Arbitration Act 1996, be deemed to be the date upon which the award is made. **A34–023**

16. Legal Representation and Costs

16:1 The parties may expressly agree that they may engage legal representatives (i.e. solicitors, and/or a barrister and/or other legally qualified advocate or advisor wholly or principally engaged in private practice) to represent them in the arbitration and/or in any appeal proceedings and to appear on their behalf at any oral hearings. The tribunal, and/or the board of appeal, shall determine the recoverable costs of engaging legal representatives. **A34–024**

16:2 Where there is no such agreement between the parties they are nevertheless free to engage legal representatives to represent them in the written proceedings but not to appear on their behalf at oral hearings. The costs of engaging legal representatives in such circumstances shall not be recoverable.

17. Tribunal's or Board of Appeal's Own Evidence

If at any time prior to the close of the proceedings the tribunal or the board of appeal deem it appropriate, they may take steps to ascertain the facts and the law on their own initiative, provided that they give both parties reasonable opportunity to comment on and/or provide evidence in response. **A34–025**

18. Fees and Expenses

Each party engaging in an arbitration or an appeal pursuant to these Rules, whether or not a Member of GAFTA, is deemed thereby to agree to abide by these Rules and to **A34–026** agree with the Association to be liable to GAFTA (jointly and severally with the other parties to the arbitration or appeal) for all fees and expenses incurred in connection with the arbitration or appeal or any remissions, which said fees and expenses shall, upon notification by GAFTA be and become a debt due to GAFTA.

19. Currency Regulations

A34–027 If an appellant is precluded by currency regulations from paying any money due to be paid by him as required under Rule 10, and notifies GAFTA in writing (a) in the case of inability to pay the appeal fee when giving notice of appeal, and (b) in the case of inability to pay any further sum directed to be paid under Rules 10 and/or 12, within 9 consecutive days of the money being demanded, accompanied in every case by evidence from a bank that he has already made application for the transfer of the required sum, he shall be entitled to an extension of up to 35 consecutive days from the date when the said payment became due in which to pay such sum.

20. Notices

Service on parties

A34–028 **20:1** All notices to be served on the parties pursuant to these Rules shall be served by letter, telex, telegram or by other method of rapid written communication. For the purposes of time limits, the date of despatch shall, unless otherwise stated, be deemed to be the date of service.

Service on the brokers or agents named in the contract shall be deemed proper service under these Rules. So far as concerns such notices, this Rule over-rides any other provisions of the contract.

Service on Tribunals and Appeal Boards

A34–029 **20:2** Unless the tribunal or board of appeal otherwise directs, all notices, proceedings and documents to be served on arbitrators and members of a board of appeal pursuant to these Rules shall be served by letter, telex, telegram or other method of rapid written communication on the Secretary of the Association at the offices of GAFTA. For the purposes of any time limits receipt of such notices by GAFTA shall be deemed to be the date of service.

Computation of Time

A34–030 **20:3** Where these Rules require service not later than a specified number of consecutive days after a specified date or occurrence, that specified date or occurrence shall not count as one of the consecutive days.

21. Non-Compliance with Time Limits and Rules

A34–031 If any time limit or provisions imposed by these Rules are not complied with, and when such matters are raised as a defence to the arbitration claim, then, subject only to the discretion of the tribunal or board of appeal conferred by this Rule, the claimant's claims and/or appellant's appeal as the case may be, shall be deemed to be waived and absolutely barred, except:—

(a) where the tribunal may in its discretion admit a claim if satisfied that the circumstances were outside the reasonable contemplation of the parties when they entered into the contract and that it would be just to extend the time, or when the conduct of one party makes it unjust to hold the other party to the strict terms of the time limit in question. Otherwise the tribunal may determine that the claim is waived and barred and refuse to admit it. There shall be no appeal to the board of appeal against the decision of the tribunal to exercise its discretion to admit a claim. If a tribunal decides not to admit the claim, then the claimant shall have the right to appeal pursuant to Rule 10, and the board of appeal shall have the power in its absolute discretion to overturn that decision and to admit the claim;

(b) upon appeal if any of the provisions of Rules 10 to 20 have not been complied with, then the board of appeal may, in its absolute discretion, extend the time for compliance (notwithstanding that the time may already have expired) or dispense with the necessity for compliance and may proceed to hear and determine the appeal as if each and all of those Rules had been complied with. Any decision made pursuant to this Rule shall be final, conclusive and binding.

22. DEFAULTERS

22:1 In the event of any party to an arbitration or an appeal held under these Rules neglecting or refusing to carry out or abide by a final award of the tribunal or board of appeal made under these Rules, the Council of GAFTA may post on the GAFTA Notice Board, Web-site, and/or circulate amongst Members in any way thought fit notification to that effect. The parties to any such arbitration or appeal shall be deemed to have consented to the Council taking such action as aforesaid.

22:2 In the event that parties do not pay the costs, fees or expenses of the arbitration or appeal when called upon to do so by GAFTA in accordance with these Rules, the Council may post on the GAFTA Notice Board, Web-site, and/or circulate amongst Members in any way thought fit notification to that effect. The parties to any such arbitration or appeal shall be deemed to have consented to the Council taking such action as aforesaid.

References to the masculine include references to the feminine and also to companies, corporations or other legal persons.

Grain and Feed Trade Association Form 126
Simple Dispute Rules[1]

(EFFECTIVE FOR CONTRACTS DATED FROM 1ST JANUARY 2003)

1: PLACE OF ARBITRATION

A35–001 Arbitration shall take place in the domicile of the Arbitrator, or elsewhere when considered appropriate with the agreement of the Parties, in which case, any travel expenses or related costs incurred by the Arbitrator shall be added to the costs, fees and expenses of the arbitration.

2: CLAIM

A35–002 In the event of non-compliance with the time limit for claiming arbitration as laid down in GAFTA Arbitration Rules No.125 and of such non-compliance being raised by the Respondents as a defence, claims shall be deemed to be waived and absolutely barred, unless the Arbitrator shall in his absolute discretion, otherwise determine.

3: ARBITRATOR: APPOINTMENT AND PROCEDURE

A35–003 **3:1** Where the Parties agree that the arbitration shall be held in accordance with the GAFTA Simple Dispute Arbitration Rules Form No: 126, they shall send to GAFTA the signed Arbitration Agreement, together with a copy of the Contract and a note of the issue at dispute, by letter, post or by hand, and/or by facsimile, and where agreed the name of the sole arbitrator.

3:2 Upon receipt, unless otherwise agreed by the Parties, GAFTA will appoint an arbitrator who shall be the sole Arbitrator. GAFTA will notify the Arbitrator, and the Parties, of his appointment, together with the date of the Arbitration.

3:3 An Arbitrator appointed under these Rules shall be a GAFTA Qualified Arbitrator and shall not be interested in the transaction nor directly interested as a member of a company or firm named as a party to the Arbitration, nor financially retained by any such company or firm, nor a member of nor financially retained by any company or firm financially associated with any party to the arbitration.

3:4 If an Arbitrator dies, or refuses to act, or becomes incapable of acting, or fails to proceed with the arbitration, or is found to be ineligible, GAFTA shall forthwith appoint a substitute.

---

[1] This document is reproduced with the kind permission of the Grain and Feed Trade Association.

4: Arbitration and Hearing

4:1 Not later than 7 business days from receipt of the notice of the appointment of the Arbitrator, the Claimants shall submit a clear and concise statement of his case and supporting documents to GAFTA and to the Respondents.   **A35–004**

4:2 Not later than 7 business days from receipt of the Claimants statement and documents, the Respondents shall submit a clear and concise statement of his case and supporting documents to GAFTA and to the Claimants.

4:3 The Claimants have 7 business days from receipt of the Respondents' case to respond in writing to the Respondents and to GAFTA on any new points which had been raised.

4:4 The Arbitrator will consider the documents submitted as above and will proceed with the Arbitration on the date set down by GAFTA.

4:5 If either Party wishes to present their case at an oral hearing, they should notify the other party and GAFTA that they will attend on the date notified by the Association under Rule 3:2.

4:6 The Arbitrator has discretion to re-schedule the date of the arbitration, or oral hearing and GAFTA will notify the Parties accordingly.

5: Representation

The Parties may be represented at the arbitration by an agent engaged in the Trade, but they may not be represented by, nor may they engage for the purposes of the presentation or preparation of their case, a solicitor/barrister or other legally qualified advocate or advisor wholly or principally engaged in private practice.   **A35–005**

6: Costs, Fees and Expenses

The total costs and fees for the Arbitration shall be laid down by the Council from time to time, and will be published by GAFTA. In the event that the Arbitrator and/or GAFTA anticipate incurring expenses in connection with the Arbitration, GAFTA will notify the Parties accordingly.   **A35–006**

7: Award

At the conclusion of the Arbitration, the Arbitrator's decision, including brief reasons, will be available for publication to the Parties, and will be dated and issued to the Parties wherever possible within 7 days. Or, if not previously paid to GAFTA, upon receipt of the costs, fees and expenses. The Arbitrator's Award will be final and binding on the Parties with no right of appeal either to GAFTA or to the Courts.   **A35–007**

8: General

Arbitrators Appointed Under Form No: 125

A35–008   **8:1** If prior to the Agreement to refer the dispute to the GAFTA Simple Disputes Arbitration, either Party had appointed an Arbitrator as required by the rules in GAFTA Arbitration Rules No.125; such appointment(s) shall be rendered void upon the signing of the Simple Disputes Agreement.

Definition of a Simple Dispute

A35–009   **8:2** Any issue of disagreement between the contracting Parties, which to the best of their knowledge does not contain complicated legal issues, lengthy contentions or arguments, and which they also consider requires a quick, simple answer without a fully reasoned award.

If, however, during the course of the arbitration, the Arbitrator finds that the contentions before him contain more complicated issues than he considers falls within the simple dispute definition, he will proceed with the arbitration, but will notify GAFTA. In which event GAFTA may re-assess the costs and fees laid down for the arbitration and notify the Parties accordingly.

8:3 Notices

A35–010   **8:3:1** All notices to be given under these Rules shall be given by letter, telex, telegram or by facsimile or by other method of rapid written communication and shall be deemed to be properly given if proved to have been despatched within the required time limits.

A notice to the Brokers or Agents named in the contract shall be deemed a notice under these Rules. So far as concerns such notices, this Rule over-rides, in relation to them, any provisions as to notices that may be contained in the contract.

8:3:2 All Notices, Proceedings and Documents to be served on the Arbitrator shall be given by the means specified in Rule 8:3:1 to the Secretary of the Association at the GAFTA offices and when so given shall be deemed to be properly served. For the purposes of any time limits receipt of such notices by the Association shall be deemed to be the date of receipt by the Arbitrator.

GRAIN AND FEED TRADE ASSOCIATION SIMPLE DISPUTE RULES

ARBITRATION AGREEMENT

A35–011

TO: The Grain & Feed Trade Association Telephone: +44 20 7814 9666
GAFTA House, Facsimile: +44 20 7814 8383
6 Chapel Place, Telex: 886984
Rivington Street,
LONDON EC2A 3SH

CLAIMANTS:

Name ....

Address ....

Telephone .... Facsimile .... Telex ....

RESPONDENTS:

Name ....

Address ....

....

Telephone .... Facsimile .... Telex ....

The above Parties agree that for the purposes of arbitration, resulting from a dispute which has arisen from their contract .... dated, ... incorporating the terms and conditions of a GAFTA standard form of Contract and/or GAFTA Arbitration Rules Form No: 125, that the GAFTA Simple Dispute Arbitration Rules shall apply (in place of the arbitration rules contained in Form No: 125), as set out in detail in the Simple Dispute Arbitration Rules Form No: 126.

The parties further agree to exclude recourse to the English Courts for a possible Judicial Review and to exclude the right of appeal to the GAFTA Committee of Appeal as provided in Form No. 125.

Up to such time as the parties enter into this Agreement the time limits in Form No: 125 shall apply.

Sellers .... Buyers ....

Signed .... Signed ....

Dated ....

Grain and Feed Trade Association Form 127
Charter Party Arbitration Rules[1]

(EFFECTIVE FOR CHARTER PARTIES DATED FROM 1ST JANUARY 2003)

References to the masculine include references to the feminine and also to companies, corporations or other legal persons.

Any dispute arising out of a charter-party, which incorporates these Rules, shall be referred to arbitration in accordance with the following provisions:—

1. PRELIMINARY

A36–001 **1:1** The provisions of the Arbitration Act 1996, and of any statutory amendment, modification or re-enactment thereof for the time being in force, shall apply to every arbitration under these Rules save insofar as such provisions are expressly modified by, or are inconsistent with, these Rules.

1:2 The juridical seat of the arbitration shall be, and is hereby designated pursuant to section 4 of the Arbitration Act 1996 as, England.

1:3 Arbitration shall take place at the registered offices of The Grain and Feed Trade Association (GAFTA), London, or (but without prejudice to Rules 1:1 and 1:2 above), elsewhere if agreed by the parties in writing.

2. PROCEDURE AND TIME LIMITS FOR CLAIMING ARBITRATION

A36–002 The claimant shall serve on the respondent a written notice stating his intention to refer a dispute to arbitration within 12 months of the last day of discharge, or in the case of non-performance, from the date of the charter-party.

3. APPOINTMENT OF THE TRIBUNAL

A36–003 The dispute shall be heard and determined by a tribunal of three arbitrators (appointed in accordance with Rule 3:2) or, if both parties agree, by a sole arbitrator (appointed in accordance with clause 3:1). The time limits imposed by this Rule for the appointment of the tribunal shall run from the date of service pursuant to Rule 2 of a notice referring a dispute to arbitration.

Procedure for the Appointment of a Sole Arbitrator

A36–004 **3:1** (a) If he requires the appointment of a sole arbitrator the claimant shall, not later

---

[1] This document is reproduced with the kind permission of the Grain and Feed Trade Association.

than the 9th consecutive day after service of the notice referring a claim to arbitration, serve a notice on the respondent seeking his agreement to the appointment of a sole arbitrator by GAFTA.

(b) Not later than the 9th consecutive day after service of the notice referred to in (a) above, the respondent shall either; (i) serve a notice on the claimant stating that he agrees to the appointment of a sole arbitrator by GAFTA, or (ii) appoint an arbitrator to a tribunal of three arbitrators and serve on the claimant a notice of the arbitrator so appointed, in which case Rule 3:2(c) shall apply.

(c) Where the parties have agreed to the appointment of a sole arbitrator by GAFTA, the Association shall then appoint an arbitrator on receipt of the first statements and evidence submitted in accordance with Rule 4, or, where interlocutory or interim decisions are required of the tribunal, upon the application of either party.

Procedure for the Appointment of a Tribunal of Three Arbitrators

3:2 (a) The claimant shall not later than the 9th consecutive day after service of the notice referring a claim to arbitration appoint an arbitrator and serve a notice on the respondent of the name of the arbitrator so appointed. **A36–005**

(b) The respondent shall, not later than the 9th consecutive day after service of the notice with the name of the claimants' arbitrator, appoint a second arbitrator and serve a notice on the claimant of the name of the arbitrator so appointed.

(c) If the respondent does not agree to the appointment of a sole arbitrator and has instead appointed an arbitrator and given written notice thereof pursuant to Rule 3:1(b), the claimant shall not later than the 9th consecutive day after service of such notice of appointment, appoint a second arbitrator and serve a notice on the respondent of the name of the arbitrator so appointed.

(d) Where two arbitrators have been appointed, GAFTA shall appoint a third arbitrator on receipt of the first statements and evidence submitted in accordance with Rule 4, or, where interlocutory or interim decisions are required of a tribunal, upon the application of either party. The third arbitrator shall be the chairman of the tribunal so formed and his name shall be notified to the parties by GAFTA.

Appointments of Arbitrators by GAFTA

3:3 If either party fails to appoint an arbitrator or to give notice thereof within the above time limits, the other party may apply to GAFTA for the appointment of an arbitrator. Notice of such application must be served on the party who has failed to appoint. Upon such application being made, GAFTA will appoint an arbitrator on behalf of the party who has failed to do so, and give notice of the arbitrator appointed to the parties. **A36–006**

Where the claimant has already sought the respondent's agreement to the appointment of a sole arbitrator pursuant to Rule 3:1 then GAFTA will appoint a sole arbitrator. Where either party has already appointed an arbitrator, pursuant to Rule 3:1(b) or Rule 3:2, then GAFTA will appoint the second arbitrator of the tribunal.

Applications to GAFTA for the appointment of an arbitrator shall be accompanied by,

A36–007 3:4 (a) prima facie evidence that the parties have entered into a contract subject to these Rules,

(b) copies of the notices to the other party (i) claiming arbitration and (ii) stating that an application has been made to GAFTA for the appointment of an arbitrator,

(c) the appropriate fee ruling at the date of application.

3:5 An arbitrator appointed under these rules shall be a Qualified Maritime Arbitrator Member of the GAFTA, and shall not be interested in the transaction nor directly interested as a member of a company or firm named as a party to the arbitration, nor financially retained by any such company or firm, nor a member of nor financially retained by any company or firm financially associated with any party to the arbitration.

3:6 An appointment of an arbitrator shall be valid and effective for all purposes provided that he has signified his acceptance of the appointment to the party appointing him, or to GAFTA, as the case may be, at any time prior to the discharge of any arbitral function.

3:7 (a) If an arbitrator dies, refuses to act, resigns, or becomes incapable of acting, or if he fails to proceed with the arbitration, or is found to be ineligible, or his authority is revoked by GAFTA pursuant to the Association's Rules and Regulations, the party, or GAFTA as the case may be, who originally appointed that arbitrator shall forthwith appoint a substitute and serve notice thereof on the other party.

(b) If a party fails, contrary to (a) above, to appoint a substitute arbitrator and to give notice thereof within 5 consecutive days of learning of the arbitrator's death, refusal to act, resignation, incapacity, failure to proceed, finding of ineligibility or revocation of authority, as the case may be, GAFTA shall, upon the application of either party, have the power to appoint a substitute arbitrator.

3:8 Any party making an application to GAFTA for the appointment of an arbitrator may be required by the Association to pay a deposit of such sum as GAFTA may require on account of any fees and expenses thereafter arising. In addition the tribunal may call upon either party to deposit with GAFTA such sum or sums as it considers appropriate on account of fees, costs and expenses prior to the commencement of the arbitration hearing.

4. Arbitration Procedure

A36–008 **4:1** The claimant shall draw up a clear and concise statement of his case, which, together with a copy of the contract and any supporting documents, shall be served as set out in Rule 4.4.

4:2 The respondent shall, on receipt of the claimant's case and documents, draw up a clear and concise statement of his defence (and counterclaim, if any) which, together with any supporting documents, shall be served as set out in Rule 4.4.

4:3 The claimant may submit further written comments and/or documents in reply, such to be served as set out in Rule 4.4.

4:4 All statements and evidence shall be served by sending them to the other party, with copies to GAFTA. In the case of sole arbitrator 2 sets, or in the case of a tribunal of three arbitrators, 4 sets of statements and evidence shall be delivered to GAFTA. Failure to send all sets to GAFTA will render the party responsible liable to GAFTA for the costs of copying such documents for forwarding to the arbitrators.

4:5 The tribunal may vary or depart from the above procedure in order to give each party a reasonable opportunity of putting his case and dealing with that of his opponent, and shall adopt procedures suitable to the circumstances of the particular case, avoiding unnecessary delay or expense, so as to provide a fair means for the resolution of the matters falling to be determined.

4:6 The timetable for the proceedings, including any steps to be taken pursuant to Rule 4 and/or determined by the tribunal, will be advised to the parties by GAFTA. It shall be the duty of the tribunal to ensure the prompt progress of the arbitration, including the making of orders where appropriate. Any delay in the proceedings may be notified to GAFTA.

4:7 Nothing in this Rule shall prevent the respondent from delivering his statement and documentary evidence before receiving documents/statements from the claimant.

4:8 Where the tribunal considers that an oral hearing is necessary, the date, time and place will be arranged by GAFTA. In which event the parties may be represented by one of their employees, or by a GAFTA Qualified Maritime Arbitrator, or other representative, but they may not be represented by a solicitor or barrister or qualified advocate, wholly or principally engaged in private practice, unless legal representation is expressly agreed.

4:9 If the arbitration is abandoned, suspended or concluded, by agreement or otherwise, before the final award is made, the parties shall be jointly and severally liable to pay to GAFTA the tribunals and the Association's costs, fees and expenses.

5. Consolidated Arbitrations and Concurrent Hearings

If all parties concerned expressly agree, the tribunal may conduct arbitral proceedings concurrently with other arbitral proceedings, and, in particular, concurrent hearings may be held, but separate awards shall be made pursuant to each contract.

6. Issues of Substantive Jurisdiction, Provisional Orders and Awards on Different Aspects

Issues of Substantive Jurisdiction

6:1 (a) The tribunal may rule on its own jurisdiction, that is, as to whether there is a valid arbitration agreement, whether the tribunal is properly constituted and what matters have been submitted to arbitration in accordance with the arbitration agreement.

(b) In the event that the tribunal determines it has no jurisdiction, GAFTA will notify the parties of the tribunal's decision. Such decision shall be final and binding upon the parties. GAFTA will invoice the claimant for any costs, fees and expenses incurred. In the event that the tribunal determines that it has jurisdiction there will be no appeal against that decision.

Provisional Orders

A36–011   6:2 The tribunal may decide at any time to order on a provisional basis any relief, which it would have power to grant in a final award.

Awards on Different Aspects

A36–012   6:3 Where the tribunal decides during the course of an arbitration to make an award dealing finally with one or more aspects of the dispute, but which leaves to be decided by it other aspect(s) of the dispute, it may make an award which shall be final and binding as to the aspect(s) with which it deals.

7. Awards of Arbitration

A36–013   All awards shall be in writing and shall be signed by the sole arbitrator or, in the case of an award made by a three-man tribunal, by all three arbitrators. The tribunal shall have the power to assess and award the costs of and connected with the reference, including GAFTA's fees and/or expenses (which shall be those for the time being in force as prescribed by the Council) and also the fees and/or expenses incurred by the tribunal. The tribunal will assess and award costs at the conclusion of the arbitration.

8. Legal Representation and Costs

A36–014   8:1 The parties may expressly agree that they may engage legal representatives (i.e. solicitors and/or a barrister and/or other legally qualified advocate or advisor wholly or principally engaged in private practice) to represent them in the arbitration proceedings and to appear on their behalf at any oral hearings.

8:2 Where there is no such agreement between the parties they are nevertheless free to engage legal representatives to represent them in the written proceedings but not to appear on their behalf at oral hearings. The costs of engaging legal representatives in such circumstances shall not be recoverable unless the tribunal considers that such costs were reasonably incurred.

9. Tribunal's Own Evidence

A36–015   If at any time prior to the close of the proceedings the tribunal deem it appropriate, it may take steps to ascertain the facts and the law on its own initiative, provided that both parties are given reasonable opportunity to comment on and/or provide evidence in response.

10. Fees and Expenses

Each party engaging in an arbitration pursuant to these Rules, whether or not a Member of the Association, is deemed thereby to agree to abide by these Rules and to agree with GAFTA to be liable to GAFTA (jointly and severally with the other parties to the arbitration) for all fees and expenses incurred in connection with the arbitration or any remissions, which said fees and expenses shall, upon notification by GAFTA be and become a debt due to the Association. **A36–016**

11. Notices

Service on parties

11:1 All notices to be served on the parties pursuant to these Rules shall be served by letter, telex, telegram or by other method of rapid written communication. For the purposes of time limits, the date of despatch shall, unless otherwise stated, be deemed to be the date of service. Service on the brokers or agents named in the charter-party shall be deemed proper service under these Rules. So far as concerns such notices, this Rule over-rides any other provisions of the contract. **A36–017**

Service on Tribunals

11:2 Unless the tribunal otherwise directs, all notices, proceedings and documents to be served on arbitrators pursuant to these Rules shall be served by letter, telex, telegram or other method of rapid written communication on the Secretary of the Association at GAFTA's Offices. For the purposes of any time limits receipt of such notices by the Association shall be deemed to be the date of service. **A36–018**

Computation of Time

11:3 Where these Rules require service not later than a specified number of consecutive days after a specified date or occurrence, that specified date or occurrence shall not count as one of the consecutive days. **A36–019**

12. Non-Compliance with Time Limits and Rules

If any time limit or provisions imposed by these Rules are not complied with then, subject only to the discretion of the tribunal conferred by this Rule, the claimant's claims shall be deemed to be waived and absolutely barred, except that such matters shall be raised as a defence to the arbitration claim, whereupon the tribunal may in its absolute discretion admit a claim upon such terms as it may think fit, or it may determine that the claim is waived and barred and refuse to admit it. **A36–020**

13. Defaulters

13:1 In the event of any party to an arbitration held under these Rules neglecting or refusing to carry out or abide by a final award of the tribunal made under these Rules, **A36–021**

the Council of the Association may post on GAFTA's Notice Board and/or circulate amongst Members in any way thought fit notification to that effect. The parties to any such arbitration shall be deemed to have consented to the Council taking such action as aforesaid.

13:2 In the event that parties do not pay the costs, fees or expenses of the arbitration when called upon to do so by GAFTA in accordance with these Rules, the Council may post on GAFTA's Notice Board and/or circulate amongst Members in any way thought fit notification to that effect. The parties to any such arbitration shall be deemed to have consented to the Council taking such action as aforesaid.

Grain and Feed Trade Association Form 128
Mediation Rules[1]

(Effective for Contracts Dated From 1st January 2003)

1. General

Upon receipt by GAFTA of the parties' written agreement to refer their dispute and/ or differences to mediation, the Association shall appoint a GAFTA Qualified Mediator.

A37–001

2. Place of Mediation

Mediation shall take place at GAFTA's offices or such place, as the parties shall agree.

A37–002

3. Appointment of Mediator

3:1 GAFTA shall notify the Mediator, and the Parties, of his/her appointment.
3:2 A Mediator shall not be interested in the transaction nor directly interested as a member of a company or firm named as a party to the mediation, nor financially retained by any such company or firm, nor a member of nor financially retained by any company or firm financially associated with any party to the mediation.
3:3 If the Mediator dies, or refuses to act, or becomes incapable of acting, or fails to proceed with the mediation, or is found to be ineligible, GAFTA shall forthwith appoint a substitute.

A37–003

4. Procedure

4:1 The Mediator will be responsible for progressing the mediation, which shall be completed no later than 45 days, or by such extended period as the parties may agree, from the date of receipt of the on account payment by the Association.
4:2 The parties agree to commence the mediation session with all parties present, and by each party submitting 5 days in advance, a succinct opening statement in writing, summarising their position with regard to the dispute in question.
4:3 The parties agree that their representatives at the mediation session will be authorised to commit and bind that party to any agreement that may result from the mediation session.
4:4 The parties may expressly agree that they may engage legal representatives (i.e. solicitors, and/or a barrister or other legally qualified advocate) to assist them in the mediation session.

A37–004

---

[1] This document is reproduced with the kind permission of the Grain and Feed Trade Association.

4:5 Where there is no such express agreement between the parties they are nevertheless free to engage legal representatives to assist them, but such representatives will not be allowed to be present at the mediation session.

4:6 The Mediator may at his sole discretion meet with either or both parties separately if and when he decides that private meetings are appropriate.

4:7 Any information made available to the Mediator in a private session shall be treated in strict confidence, and will only be disclosed if it is information that is already in the public domain, or, if the Mediator is expressly permitted to disclose that information to the other party.

4:8 The whole of the mediation session is held on a without prejudice basis and is therefore without prejudice to the rights of either party. All and any information, statements, documentation or material exchanged, made available or disclosed in any form within the mediation session by either party shall remain private and confidential and be exchanged, made available or disclosed for the use of that mediation process only and shall not prejudice the rights of either party if the mediation process fails. Accordingly, on the termination of the mediation all such information, statements, documentation and materials shall be returned to the originating party unless otherwise agreed in writing.

4:9 The Mediator shall cause the fact that the Mediation has failed to be entered on the record by date and time at GAFTA. It is then up to the Claimant to resolve the dispute by completing the arbitration if already claimed or, if the arbitration has not yet been claimed, to claim arbitration in accordance with the GAFTA Arbitration Rules. However, where under the GAFTA Arbitration Rules the period left for claiming arbitration is 14 days or less, arbitration can be claimed within 14 days from the date the mediator has caused the fact that the mediation failed to be entered on the record by date and time at GAFTA.

5. Costs, Fees and Expenses

A37–005   **5:1** The costs and fees for the mediation shall be laid down by the Council from time to time, and will be published by GAFTA.

5:2 With the notification of the appointment of the Mediator, the Association will call on each party to deposit such sums as GAFTA may require on account of the costs, fees and expenses of the mediation.

5:3 If the parties agree to hold the mediation at a place other than London, GAFTA shall subsequently call for additional deposits as may be required from time to time.

6. Agreement Resulting from Mediation

A37–006   At the conclusion of the Mediation session, the Mediator will draw up the Parties' settlement agreement in writing, which will be signed by the parties. A copy of the agreement will be lodged with GAFTA by the Mediator.

All correspondence to be given under these Rules shall be given by letter, telex, telegram or by facsimile or by other method of rapid written communication.

References to the masculine include references to the feminine and also to companies, corporations or other legal persons.

GRAIN AND FEED TRADE ASSOCIATION MEDIATION RULES

MEDIATION AGREEMENT

A37–007

To: The Grain & Feed Trade Association,
GAFTA House,
6 Chapel Place,
Rivington Street.
LONDON EC2A 3SH.

Telephone: + 44 20 7814 9666
Facsimile: + 44 20 7814 8383
Telex: 886984
E-mail: post@gafta.com

CLAIMANTS:

Name ....

Address ....

Telephone .... Facsimile ....

Telex .... E-mail ....

RESPONDENTS:

Name ....

Address ....

Telephone .... Facsimile ....

Telex .... E-mail ....

With regard to their dispute arising out of:-

Contract dated ....

Tonnage Commodity ....

incorporating the terms and conditions of the Grain & Feed Trade Association, (GAFTA) standard contract form .... and/or GAFTA Arbitration Rules form No. 125, or 127, the Parties hereby agree to refer the same to mediation and hereby apply to the Association for the appointment of a mediator for resolution in accordance with the GAFTA Mediation Rules No. 128.

The Parties agree that the arbitration will be stayed for a period of 45 days from the date when GAFTA receives payment on account of the costs, fees and expenses of the mediation.

Should the mediation not result in a settlement agreement within this period of 45 days or such extended period as the Parties may agree before the mediator, it is up to the Claimant, after the Mediator has declared that the mediation failed within such period, to resolve the dispute by completing the arbitration if already claimed, or if arbitration has not yet been claimed to claim arbitration within 14 days, in accordance with the GAFTA Arbitration Rules.

Signatures:–

Sellers .... Buyers ....

Dated ....

International Bar Association Rules on the Taking of Evidence in International Commercial Arbitration[1]

JUNE 1999

MEMBERS OF THE WORKING PARTY

David W Rivkin
Chair, SBL Committee D (Arbitration and ADR); Debevoise & Plimpton, New York, USA
Wolfgang Kühn
Former Chair, SBL Committee D; Heuking Kühn Lüer Heussen Wojtek, Düsseldorf, Germany
Giovanni M Ughi
Chair, SBL Committee D Working Party; Studio Legale Ughi e Nunziante, Milan, Italy
Hans Bagner
Vinge, Stockholm, Sweden
John Beechey
Clifford Chance, London, England
Jacques Buhart
Coudert Frères, Paris, France
Peter S Caldwell
Hong Kong
Bernardo M Cremades
B Cremades y Asociados, Madrid, Spain

Emmanuel Gaillard
Shearman & Sterling, Paris, France
Paul A Gelinas
Paris, France
Hans van Houtte
Stibbe Simont Monahan Duhot, Brussels, Belgium
Pierre A Karrer
Pestalozzi Gmuer & Patry, Zurich, Switzerland
Jan Paulsson
Freshfields, Paris, France
Hilmar Raeschke-Kessler
Rechtsanwaelte Beim Bundesgerichtshof, Karlsruhe-Ettlingen, Germany
Van Vechten Veeder QC
Essex Court Chambers, London, England
O L O de Witt Wijnen
Nauta Dutilh, Rotterdam, Netherlands

A38–001

ABOUT THE ARBITRATION AND ADR COMMITTEE (D)

Established as the Committee in the International Bar Association's Section on Business Law (SBL) which contributes to the development of the law and practice of international arbitration and other forms of dispute resolution, the Committee currently has over 1,800 members in 115 countries, and membership is increasing steadily.

A38–002

Links

Relations are maintained with all of the prominent international Arbitration institutions worldwide.

A38–003

---

[1] Reproduced with the permission of the International Bar Association. Copyright: International Bar Association.

Activities

A38–004
- The Committee provides programmes at IBA and SBL Conferences. Conference programmes are discussed in advance with members, who are encouraged to suggest topics for discussion and debate.

- Members may be appointed to attend law-making sessions such as those which led to the UNCITRAL Model Law on International Commercial Arbitration.

- The Committee produces regular newsletters giving news of members and updates on topics in this field of law. Contributions from members are essential for the continuing success of these newsletters.

- Any member of the Committee who wishes to pursue a line of private enquiry, or to encourage public debate of an issue within the Committee's remit, should ask the Committee Officers to circulate enquiries amongst the membership and to encourage co-operative endeavour.

Subcommittee on Recognition and Enforcement of Arbitral Awards (D1)

A38–005 The Convention on the Recognition and Enforcement of Foreign Arbitration Awards made in New York in 1958 to which more than 100 countries have acceded has demanded the establishment of a special Subcommittee. Practitioners attend the annual workshop of this Subcommittee in order to learn of the experience of various countries with this Convention.

Subcommittee on Alternative Dispute Resolution Systems (D2)

A38–006 This Subcommittee is devoted to the procedures and development of ADR. The subject has demanded far more attention from lawyers in recent years, and the Subcommittee provides a forum for studying and sharing experience of practitioners in various jurisdictions.

FOREWORD

A38–007 These IBA Rules on the Taking of Evidence in International Commercial Arbitration ("IBA Rules of Evidence") have been prepared by a Working Party of Committee D (Arbitration and ADR) of the Section on Business Law of the International Bar Association. The IBA has issued these Rules as a resource to parties and to arbitrators in order to enable them to conduct the evidence phase of international arbitration proceedings in an efficient and economical manner. The Rules provide mechanisms for the presentation of documents, witnesses of fact, expert witnesses and inspections, as well as for the conduct of evidentiary hearings. The Rules are designed to be used in conjunction with, and adopted together with, institutional or *ad hoc* rules or procedures governing international commercial arbitrations.

These IBA Rules of Evidence replace the IBA Supplementary Rules Governing the Presentation and Reception of Evidence in International Commercial Arbitration, originally issued in 1983. The IBA Rules of Evidence reflect procedures in use in many different legal systems, and they may be particularly useful when the parties come from different legal cultures.

If the parties wish to adopt the IBA Rules of Evidence in their arbitration clause, it is recommended that they add the following additional language to the clause:

> "In addition to the [institutional or *ad hoc* rules chosen by the parties], the parties agree that the arbitration shall be conducted according to the IBA Rules of Evidence."

In addition, parties and Arbitral Tribunals may adopt the IBA Rules of Evidence, in whole or in part, at the time in conduct of the arbitration, or they may vary them or use them as guidelines in developing their own procedures.

The IBA Rules of Evidence were adopted by the resolution of the IBA Council on 1 June 1999.

David W Rivkin
Chair, Committee on Arbitration and ADR
Section on Business Law

August 1999

The Rules

Preamble

1. These IBA Rules on the Taking of Evidence in International Commercial Arbitration (the "IBA Rules of Evidence") are intended to govern in an efficient and economical manner the taking of evidence in international commercial arbitrations, particularly those between Parties from different legal traditions. They are designed to supplement the legal provisions and the institutional or *ad hoc* rules according to which the Parties are conducting their arbitration.

2. Parties and Arbitral Tribunals may adopt the IBA Rules of Evidence, in whole or in part, to govern arbitration proceedings, or they may vary them or use them as guidelines in developing their own procedures. The Rules are not intended to limit the flexibility that is inherent in, and an advantage of, international arbitration, and Parties and Arbitral Tribunals are free to adapt them to the particular circumstances of each arbitration.

3. Each Arbitral Tribunal is encouraged to identify to the Parties, as soon as it considers it to be appropriate, the issues that it may regard as relevant and material to the outcome of the case, including issues where a preliminary determination may be appropriate.

4. The taking of evidence shall be conducted on the principle that each Party shall be entitled to know, reasonably in advance of any Evidentiary Hearing, the evidence on which the other Parties rely.

The Rules

Article 1

Definitions

In the IBA Rules of Evidence:

"*Arbitral Tribunal*" means a sole arbitrator or a panel of arbitrators validly deciding by majority or otherwise;

"*Claimant*" means the Party or Parties who commenced the arbitration and any Party who, through joinder or otherwise, becomes aligned with such Party or Parties;

"*Document*" means a writing of any kind, whether recorded on paper, electronic means, audio or visual recordings or any other mechanical or electronic means of storing or recording information;

"*Evidentiary Hearing*" means any hearing, whether or not held on consecutive days, at which the Arbitral Tribunal receives oral evidence;

"*Expert Report*" means a written statement by a Tribunal-Appointed Expert or a Party-Appointed Expert submitted pursuant to the IBA Rules of Evidence;

"*General Rules*" mean the institutional or *ad hoc* rules according to which the Parties are conducting their arbitration;

"*Party*" means a party to the arbitration;

"*Party-Appointed Expert*" means an expert witness presented by a Party;

"*Request to Produce*" means a request by a Party for a procedural order by which the Arbitral Tribunal would direct another Party to produce documents.

"*Respondent*" means the Party or Parties against whom the Claimant made its claim, and any Party who, through joinder or otherwise, becomes aligned with such Party or Parties, and includes a Respondent making a counter-claim;

"*Tribunal-Appointed Expert*" means a person or organization appointed by the Arbitral Tribunal in order to report to it on specific issues determined by the Arbitral Tribunal.

Article 2

Scope of Application

A38–010 **1.** Whenever the Parties have agreed or the Arbitral Tribunal has determined to apply the IBA Rules of Evidence, the Rules shall govern the taking of evidence, except to the extent that any specific provision of them may be found to be in conflict with any mandatory provision of law determined to be applicable to the case by the Parties or by the Arbitral Tribunal.

2. In case of conflict between any provisions of the IBA Rules of Evidence and the General Rules, the Arbitral Tribunal shall apply the IBA Rules of Evidence in the manner that it determines best in order to accomplish the purposes of both the General Rules and the IBA Rules of Evidence, unless the Parties agree to the contrary.

3. In the event of any dispute regarding the meaning of the IBA Rules of Evidence, the Arbitral Tribunal shall interpret them according to their purpose and in the manner most appropriate for the particular arbitration.

4. Insofar as the IBA Rules of Evidence and the General Rules are silent on any matter concerning the taking of evidence and the Parties have not agreed otherwise, the Arbitral Tribunal may conduct the taking of evidence as it deems appropriate, in accordance with the general principles of the IBA Rules of Evidence.

Article 3

Documents

A38–011 **1.** Within the time ordered by the Arbitral Tribunal, each Party shall submit to the Arbitral Tribunal and to the other Parties all documents available to it on which it relies, including public documents and those in the public domain, except for any documents that have already been submitted by another Party.

2. Within the time ordered by the Arbitral Tribunal, any Party may submit to the Arbitral Tribunal a Request to Produce.

3. A Request to Produce shall contain:

   (a) (*i*) a description of a requested document sufficient to identify it, or (*ii*) a description in sufficient detail (including subject matter) of a narrow and specific requested category of documents that are reasonably believed to exist;

   (b) a description of how the documents requested are relevant and material to the outcome of the case; and

   (c) a statement that the documents requested are not in the possession, custody or control of the requesting Party, and of the reason why that Party assumes the documents requested to be in the possession, custody or control of the other Party.

4. Within the time ordered by the Arbitral Tribunal, the Party to whom the Request to Produce is addressed shall produce to the Arbitral Tribunal and to the other Parties all the documents requested in its possession, custody or control as to which no objection is made.

5. If the Party to whom the Request to Produce is addressed has objections to some or all of the documents requested, it shall state them in writing to the Arbitral Tribunal within the time ordered by the Arbitral Tribunal. The reasons for such objections shall be any of those set forth in Article 9.2.

6. The Arbitral Tribunal shall, in consultation with the Parties and in timely fashion, consider the Request to Produce and the objections. The Arbitral Tribunal may order the Party to whom such Request is addressed to produce to the Arbitral Tribunal and to the other Parties those requested documents in its possession, custody or control as to which the Arbitral Tribunal determines that (*i*) the issues that the requesting Party wishes to prove are relevant and material to the outcome of the case, and (*ii*) none of the reasons for objection set forth in Article 9.2 apply.

7. In exceptional circumstances, if the propriety of an objection can only be determined by review of the document, the Arbitral Tribunal may determine that it should not review the document. In that event, the Arbitral Tribunal may, after consultation with the Parties, appoint an independent and impartial expert, bound to confidentiality, to review any such document and to report on the objection. To the extent that the objection is upheld by the Arbitral Tribunal, the expert shall not disclose to the Arbitral Tribunal and to the other Parties the contents of the document reviewed.

8. If a Party wishes to obtain the production of documents from a person or organization who is not a Party to the arbitration and from whom the Party cannot obtain the documents on its own, the Party may, within the time ordered by the Arbitral Tribunal, ask it to take whatever steps are legally available to obtain the requested documents. The Party shall identify the documents in sufficient detail and state why such documents are relevant and material to the outcome of the case. The Arbitral Tribunal shall decide on this request and shall take the necessary steps if in its discretion it determines that the documents would be relevant and material.

9. The Arbitral Tribunal, at any time before the arbitration is concluded, may request a Party to produce to the Arbitral Tribunal and to the other Parties any documents that it believes to be relevant and material to the outcome of the case. A Party may object to

such a request based on any of the reasons set forth in Article 9.2. If a Party raises such an objection, the Arbitral Tribunal shall decide whether to order the production of such documents based upon the considerations set forth in Article 3.6 and, if the Arbitral Tribunal considers it appropriate, through the use of the procedures set forth in Article 3.7.

10. Within the time ordered by the Arbitral Tribunal, the Parties may submit to the Arbitral Tribunal and to the other Parties any additional documents which they believe have become relevant and material as a consequence of the issues raised in documents, Witness Statements or Expert Reports submitted or produced by another Party or in other submissions of the Parties.

11. If copies are submitted or produced, they must conform fully to the originals. At the request of the Arbitral Tribunal, any original must be presented for inspection.

12. All documents produced by a Party pursuant to the IBA Rules of Evidence (or by a non-Party pursuant to Article 3.8) shall be kept confidential by the Arbitral Tribunal and by the other Parties, and they shall be used only in connection with the arbitration. The Arbitral Tribunal may issue orders to set forth the terms of this confidentiality. This requirement is without prejudice to all other obligations of confidentiality in arbitration.

Article 4

Witnesses of Fact

1. Within the time ordered by the Arbitral Tribunal, each Party shall identify the witnesses on whose testimony it relies and the subject matter of that testimony.

2. Any person may present evidence as a witness, including a Party or a Party's officer, employee or other representative.

3. It shall not be improper for a Party, its officers, employees, legal advisors or other representatives to interview its witnesses or potential witnesses.

4. The Arbitral Tribunal may order each Party to submit within a specified time to the Arbitral Tribunal and to the other Parties a written statement by each witness on whose testimony it relies, except for those witnesses whose testimony is sought pursuant to Article 4.10 (the "Witness Statement"). If Evidentiary Hearings are organized on separate issues (such as liability and damages), the Arbitral Tribunal or the Parties by agreement may schedule the submission of Witness Statements separately for each Evidentiary Hearing.

5. Each Witness Statement shall contain:

(a) the full name and address of the witness, his or her present and past relationship (if any) with any of the Parties, and a description of his or her background, qualifications, training and experience, if such a description may be relevant and material to the dispute or to the contents of the statement;

(b) a full and detailed description of the facts, and the source of the witness's information as to those facts, sufficient to serve as that witness's evidence in the matter in dispute;

(c) an affirmation of the truth of the statement; and

(d) the signature of the witness and its date and place.

6. If Witness Statements are submitted, any Party may, within the time ordered by the

Arbitral Tribunal, submit to the Arbitral Tribunal and to the other Parties revised or additional Witness Statements, including statements from persons not previously named as witnesses, so long as any such revisions or additions only respond to matters contained in another Party's Witness Statement or Expert Report and such matters have not been previously presented in the arbitration.

7. Each witness who has submitted a Witness Statement shall appear for testimony at an Evidentiary Hearing, unless the Parties agree otherwise.

8. If a witness who has submitted a Witness Statement does not appear without a valid reason for testimony at an Evidentiary Hearing, except by agreement of the Parties, the Arbitral Tribunal shall disregard that Witness Statement unless, in exceptional circumstances, the Arbitral Tribunal determines otherwise.

9. If the Parties agree that a witness who has submitted a Witness Statement does not need to appear for testimony at an Evidentiary Hearing, such an agreement shall not be considered to reflect an agreement as to the correctness of the content of the Witness Statement.

10. If a Party wishes to present evidence from a person who will not appear voluntarily at its request, the Party may, within the time ordered by the Arbitral Tribunal, ask it to take whatever steps are legally available to obtain the testimony of that person. The Party shall identify the intended witness, shall describe the subjects on which the witness's testimony is sought and shall state why such subjects are relevant and material to the outcome of the case. The Arbitral Tribunal shall decide on this request and shall take the necessary steps if in its discretion it determines that the testimony of that witness would be relevant and material.

11. The Arbitral Tribunal may, at any time before the arbitration is concluded, order any Party to provide, or to use its best efforts to provide, the appearance for testimony at an Evidentiary Hearing of any person, including one whose testimony has not yet been offered.

Article 5

Party-Appointed Experts

1. A Party may rely on a Party-Appointed Expert as a means of evidence on specific issues. Within the time ordered by the Arbitral Tribunal, a Party-Appointed Expert shall submit an Expert Report.

2. The Expert Report shall contain:

(a) the full name and address of the Party-Appointed Expert, his or her present and past relationship (if any) with any of the Parties, and a description of his or her background, qualifications, training and experience;

(b) a statement of the facts on which he or she is basing his or her expert opinions and conclusions;

(c) his or her expert opinions and conclusions, including a description of the method, evidence and information used in arriving at the conclusions;

(d) an affirmation of the truth of the Expert Report; and

(e) the signature of the Party-Appointed Expert and its date and place.

3. The Arbitral Tribunal in its discretion may order that any Party-Appointed Experts who have submitted Expert Reports on the same or related issues meet and confer on such issues. At such meeting, the Party-Appointed Experts shall attempt to reach agreement on those issues as to which they had differences of opinion in their Expert Reports, and they shall record in writing any such issues on which they reach agreement.

4. Each Party-Appointed Expert shall appear for testimony at an Evidentiary Hearing, unless the Parties agree otherwise and the Arbitral Tribunal accepts this agreement.

5. If a Party-Appointed Expert does not appear without a valid reason for testimony at an Evidentiary Hearing, except by agreement of the Parties accepted by the Arbitral Tribunal, the Arbitral Tribunal shall disregard his or her Expert Report unless, in exceptional circumstances, the Arbitral Tribunal determines otherwise.

6. If the Parties agree that a Party-Appointed Expert does not need to appear for testimony at an Evidentiary Hearing, such an agreement shall not be considered to reflect an agreement as to the correctness of the content of the Expert Report.

Article 6

Tribunal-Appointed Experts

A38–014   1. The Arbitral Tribunal, after having consulted with the Parties, may appoint one or more independent Tribunal-Appointed Experts to report to it on specific issues designated by the Arbitral Tribunal. The Arbitral Tribunal shall establish the terms of reference for any Tribunal-Appointed Expert report after having consulted with the Parties. A copy of the final terms of reference shall be sent by the Arbitral Tribunal to the Parties.

2. The Tribunal-Appointed Expert shall, before accepting appointment, submit to the Arbitral Tribunal and to the Parties a statement of his or her independence from the Parties and the Arbitral Tribunal. Within the time ordered by the Arbitral Tribunal, the Parties shall inform the Arbitral Tribunal whether they have any objections to the Tribunal-Appointed Expert's independence. The Arbitral Tribunal shall decide promptly whether to accept any such objection.

3. Subject to the provisions of Article 9.2, the Tribunal-Appointed Expert may request a Party to provide any relevant and material information or to provide access to any relevant documents, goods, samples, property or site for inspection. The authority of a Tribunal-Appointed Expert to request such information or access shall be the same as the authority of the Arbitral Tribunal. The Parties and their representatives shall have the right to receive any such information and to attend any such inspection. Any disagreement between a Tribunal-Appointed Expert and a Party as to the relevance, materiality or appropriateness of such a request shall be decided by the Arbitral Tribunal, in the manner provided in Articles 3.5 through 3.7. The Tribunal-Appointed Expert shall record in the report any non-compliance by a Party with an appropriate request or decision by the Arbitral Tribunal and shall describe its effects on the determination of the specific issue.

4. The Tribunal-Appointed Expert shall report in writing to the Arbitral Tribunal. The Tribunal-Appointed Expert shall describe in the report the method, evidence and information used in arriving at the conclusions.

5. The Arbitral Tribunal shall send a copy of such Expert Report to the Parties. The Parties may examine any document that the Tribunal-Appointed Expert has examined and any correspondence between the Arbitral Tribunal and the Tribunal-Appointed Expert. Within the time ordered by the Arbitral Tribunal, any Party shall have the opportunity to respond to the report in a submission by the Party or through an Expert Report

by a Party-Appointed Expert. The Arbitral Tribunal shall send the submission or Expert Report to the Tribunal-Appointed Expert and to the other Parties.

6. At the request of a Party or of the Arbitral Tribunal, the Tribunal-Appointed Expert shall be present at an Evidentiary Hearing. The Arbitral Tribunal may question the Tribunal-Appointed Expert, and he or she may be questioned by the Parties or by any Party-Appointed Expert on issues raised in the Parties' submissions or in the Expert Reports made by the Party-Appointed Experts pursuant to Article 6.5.

7. Any Expert Report made by a Tribunal-Appointed Expert and its conclusions shall be assessed by the Arbitral Tribunal with due regard to all circumstances of the case.

8. The fees and expenses of a Tribunal-Appointed Expert, to be funded in a manner determined by the Arbitral Tribunal, shall form part of the costs of the arbitration.

Article 7

On Site Inspection

Subject to the provisions of Article 9.2, the Arbitral Tribunal may, at the request of a Party or on its own motion, inspect or require the inspection by a Tribunal-Appointed Expert of any site, property, machinery or any other goods or process, or documents, as it deems appropriate. The Arbitral Tribunal shall, in consultation with the Parties, determine the timing and arrangement for the inspection. The Parties and their representatives shall have the right to attend any such inspection.

Article 8

Evidentiary Hearing

1. The Arbitral Tribunal shall at all times have complete control over the Evidentiary Hearing. The Arbitral Tribunal may limit or exclude any question to, answer by or appearance of a witness (which term includes, for the purposes of this Article, witnesses of fact and any Experts), if it considers such question, answer or appearance to be irrelevant, immaterial, burdensome, duplicative or covered by a reason for objection set forth in Article 9.2. Questions to a witness during direct and redirect testimony may not be unreasonably leading.

2. The Claimant shall ordinarily first present the testimony of its witnesses, followed by the Respondent presenting testimony of its witnesses, and then by the presentation by Claimant of rebuttal witnesses, if any. Following direct testimony, any other Party may question such witness, in an order to be determined by the Arbitral Tribunal. The Party who initially presented the witness shall subsequently have the opportunity to ask additional questions on the matters raised in the other Parties' questioning. The Arbitral Tribunal, upon request of a Party or on its own motion, may vary this order of proceeding, including the arrangement of testimony by particular issues or in such a manner that witnesses presented by different Parties be questioned at the same time and in confrontation with each other. The Arbitral Tribunal may ask questions to a witness at any time.

3. Any witness providing testimony shall first affirm, in a manner determined appropriate by the Arbitral Tribunal, that he or she is telling the truth. If the witness has submitted a Witness Statement or an Expert Report, the witness shall confirm it. The Parties may agree or the Arbitral Tribunal may order that the Witness Statement or Expert Report shall serve as that witness's direct testimony.

4. Subject to the provisions of Article 9.2, the Arbitral Tribunal may request any person to give oral or written evidence on any issue that the Arbitral Tribunal considers to be relevant and material. Any witness called and questioned by the Arbitral Tribunal may also be questioned by the Parties.

Article 9

Admissibility and Assessment of Evidence

A38–017   1. The Arbitral Tribunal shall determine the admissibility, relevance, materiality and weight of evidence.

2. The Arbitral Tribunal shall, at the request of a Party or on its own motion, exclude from evidence or production any document, statement, oral testimony or inspection for any of the following reasons:

   (a) lack of sufficient relevance or materiality;

   (b) legal impediment or privilege under the legal or ethical rules determined by the Arbitral Tribunal to be applicable;

   (c) unreasonable burden to produce the requested evidence;

   (d) loss or destruction of the document that has been reasonably shown to have occurred;

   (e) grounds of commercial or technical confidentiality that the Arbitral Tribunal determines to be compelling;

   (f) grounds of special political or institutional sensitivity (including evidence that has been classified as secret by a government or a public international institution) that the Arbitral Tribunal determines to be compelling; or

   (g) considerations of fairness or equality of the Parties that the Arbitral Tribunal determines to be compelling.

3. The Arbitral Tribunal may, where appropriate, make necessary arrangements to permit evidence to be considered subject to suitable confidentiality protection.

4. If a Party fails without satisfactory explanation to produce any document requested in a Request to Produce to which it has not objected in due time or fails to produce any document ordered to be produced by the Arbitral Tribunal, the Arbitral Tribunal may infer that such document would be adverse to the interests of that Party.

5. If a Party fails without satisfactory explanation to make available any other relevant evidence, including testimony, sought by one Party to which the Party to whom the request was addressed has not objected in due time or fails to make available any evidence, including testimony, ordered by the Arbitral Tribunal to be produced, the Arbitral Tribunal may infer that such evidence would be adverse to the interests of that Party.

Rules of Arbitration of the International Chamber of Commerce[1]

(in force as from 1 January 1998)

FOREWORD

The closing decades of the twentieth century saw international commercial arbitration **A39–001**
gain worldwide acceptance as the normal means of resolving international commercial disputes. National laws on arbitration have been modernized on all continents. International treaties on arbitration have been signed or adhered to with impressive success. Arbitration has become part of the curricula of large numbers of law schools. With the gradual removal of political and trade barriers and the rapid globalization of the world economy, new challenges have been created for arbitration institutions in response to the growing demand of parties for certainty and predictability, greater rapidity and flexibility as well as neutrality and efficacy in the resolution of international disputes.

Since the International Court of Arbitration was established in 1923, ICC arbitration has been constantly nourished by the experience gathered by the ICC International Court of Arbitration in the course of administering more than eleven thousand international arbitration cases, now involving each year parties and arbitrators from over 100 countries and from a diversity of legal, economic, cultural and linguistic backgrounds.

The present ICC Rules of Arbitration came into effect on 1 January 1998. They are the result of an intensive, worldwide consultation process and constitute the first major revision of the Rules in more than 20 years. The changes made are designed to reduce delays and ambiguities and to fill certain gaps, taking into account the evolution of arbitration practice. The basic features of the ICC arbitration system have not been altered, however, notably its universality and flexibility, as well as the central role played by the ICC Court in the administration of arbitral cases.

Every ICC arbitration is conducted by an arbitral tribunal with responsibility for examining the merits of the case and rendering a final award. Each year, ICC arbitrations are held in some 40 countries, in most major languages and with arbitrators of some 60 different nationalities. The work of those arbitral tribunals is monitored by the ICC Court, which meets weekly all year round. Currently composed of 112 members from 73 countries, the Court organizes and supervises arbitrations held under the ICC Rules of Arbitration. The Court must remain constantly alert to changes in the law and the practice of arbitration in all parts of the world and must adapt its working methods to the evolving needs of parties and arbitrators. For the day-to-day management of cases in many languages, the ICC Court is supported by a Secretariat based at the headquarters of the International Chamber of Commerce, in Paris.

---

[1] The Rules of Arbitration of the International Chamber of Commerce are published in their official English version by the International Chamber of Commerce ICC Publication No 808— ISBN 92.842.1302.0. Copyright © 1997, 2001 International Chamber of Commerce. Available from: ICC International Court of Arbitration, 38 cours Albert 1er, 75008 Paris, France, and on the web site: www.iccarbitration.org. Please also see the International Chamber of Commerce model arbitration clause at para. A54 014 of this Volume.

Although the ICC Rules of Arbitration have been especially designed for arbitrations in an international context, they may also be used for non-international cases.

The present publication contains only the 1998 ICC Rules of Arbitration. The 1988 ICC Rules of Optional Conciliation, with which they were previously published, have been replaced, as from 1 July 2001, by the ICC ADR Rules, which are published separately. This reedition of the 1998 Rules of Arbitration has allowed a number of typographical, syntactical and grammatical corrections to be made to the text as previously published. In addition, for the sake of consistency with the French version of the Rules, in the second sentence of Article 2(9) of Appendix III, the words "are expected" have been replaced by "have a duty".

August 2001

Standard ICC Arbitration Clause

A39–002 The ICC recommends that all parties wishing to make reference to ICC arbitration in their contracts use the following standard clause.

Parties are reminded that it may be desirable for them to stipulate in the arbitration clause itself the law governing the contract, the number of arbitrators and the place and language of the arbitration. The parties' free choice of the law governing the contract and of the place and language of the arbitration is not limited by the ICC Rules of Arbitration.

Attention is called to the fact that the laws of certain countries require that parties to contracts expressly accept arbitration clauses, sometimes in a precise and particular manner.

English

"All disputes arising out of or in connection with the present contract shall be finally settled under the Rules of Arbitration of the International Chamber of Commerce by one or more arbitrators appointed in accordance with the said Rules."

Rules of Arbitration of the International Chamber of Commerce

Introductory Provisions

Article 1

International Court of Arbitration

A39–003 1 The International Court of Arbitration (the "Court") of the International Chamber of Commerce (the "ICC") is the arbitration body attached to the ICC. The statutes of the Court are set forth in Appendix I. Members of the Court are appointed by the World Council of the ICC. The function of the Court is to provide for the settlement by arbitration of business disputes of an international character in accordance with the Rules of Arbitration of the International Chamber of Commerce (the "Rules"). If so empowered by an arbitration agreement, the Court shall also provide for the settlement by arbitration in accordance with these Rules of business disputes not of an international character.

2 The Court does not itself settle disputes. It has the function of ensuring the application of these Rules. It draws up its own Internal Rules (Appendix II).

3 The Chairman of the Court or, in the Chairman's absence or otherwise at his request, one of its Vice-Chairmen shall have the power to take urgent decisions on behalf of the Court, provided that any such decision is reported to the Court at its next session.

4 As provided for in its Internal Rules, the Court may delegate to one or more committees composed of its members the power to take certain decisions, provided that any such decision is reported to the Court at its next session.

5 The Secretariat of the Court (the "Secretariat") under the direction of its Secretary General (the "Secretary General") shall have its seat at the headquarters of the ICC.

Article 2

Definitions

In these Rules: A39–004

(i) "Arbitral Tribunal" includes one or more arbitrators.

(ii) "Claimant" includes one or more claimants and "Respondent" includes one or more respondents.

(iii) "Award" includes, *inter alia*, an interim, partial or final Award.

Article 3

Written Notifications or Communications; Time Limits

1 All pleadings and other written communications submitted by any party, as well as A39–005 all documents annexed thereto, shall be supplied in a number of copies sufficient to provide one copy for each party, plus one for each arbitrator, and one for the Secretariat. A copy of any communication from the Arbitral Tribunal to the parties shall be sent to the Secretariat.

2 All notifications or communications from the Secretariat and the Arbitral Tribunal shall be made to the last address of the party or its representative for whom the same are intended, as notified either by the party in question or by the other party. Such notification or communication may be made by delivery against receipt, registered post, courier, facsimile transmission, telex, telegram or any other means of telecommunication that provides a record of the sending thereof.

3 A notification or communication shall be deemed to have been made on the day it was received by the party itself or by its representative, or would have been received if made in accordance with the preceding paragraph.

4 Periods of time specified in or fixed under the present Rules shall start to run on the day following the date a notification or communication is deemed to have been made in accordance with the preceding paragraph. When the day next following such date is an official holiday, or a non-business day in the country where the notification or communication is deemed to have been made, the period of time shall commence on the first following business day. Official holidays and non-business days are included in the calculation of the period of time. If the last day of the relevant period of time granted is an official holiday or a non-business day in the country where the notification or communication is deemed to have been made, the period of time shall expire at the end of the first following business day.

COMMENCING THE ARBITRATION

Article 4

Request for Arbitration

A39–006   **1** A party wishing to have recourse to arbitration under these Rules shall submit its Request for Arbitration (the "Request") to the Secretariat, which shall notify the Claimant and Respondent of the receipt of the Request and the date of such receipt.

2 The date on which the Request is received by the Secretariat shall, for all purposes, be deemed to be the date of the commencement of the arbitral proceedings.

3 The Request shall, *inter alia*, contain the following information:

(a) the name in full, description and address of each of the parties;

(b) a description of the nature and circumstances of the dispute giving rise to the claim(s);

(c) a statement of the relief sought, including, to the extent possible, an indication of any amount(s) claimed;

(d) the relevant agreements and, in particular, the arbitration agreement;

(e) all relevant particulars concerning the number of arbitrators and their choice in accordance with the provisions of Articles 8, 9 and 10, and any nomination of an arbitrator required thereby; and

(f) any comments as to the place of arbitration, the applicable rules of law and the language of the arbitration.

4 Together with the Request, the Claimant shall submit the number of copies thereof required by Article 3(1) and shall make the advance payment on administrative expenses required by Appendix III ("Arbitration Costs and Fees") in force on the date the Request is submitted. In the event that the Claimant fails to comply with either of these requirements, the Secretariat may fix a time limit within which the Claimant must comply, failing which the file shall be closed without prejudice to the right of the Claimant to submit the same claims at a later date in another Request.

5 The Secretariat shall send a copy of the Request and the documents annexed thereto to the Respondent for its Answer to the Request once the Secretariat has sufficient copies of the Request and the required advance payment.

6 When a party submits a Request in connection with a legal relationship in respect of which arbitration proceedings between the same parties are already pending under these Rules, the Court may, at the request of a party, decide to include the claims contained in the Request in the pending proceedings provided that the Terms of Reference have not been signed or approved by the Court. Once the Terms of Reference have been signed or approved by the Court, claims may only be included in the pending proceedings subject to the provisions of Article 19.

Article 5

Answer to the Request; Counterclaims

1 Within 30 days from the receipt of the Request from the Secretariat, the Respondent shall file an Answer (the "Answer") which shall, *inter alia*, contain the following information:

(a) its name in full, description and address;

(b) its comments as to the nature and circumstances of the dispute giving rise to the claim(s);

(c) its response to the relief sought;

(d) any comments concerning the number of arbitrators and their choice in light of the Claimant's proposals and in accordance with the provisions of Articles 8, 9 and 10, and any nomination of an arbitrator required thereby; and

(e) any comments as to the place of arbitration, the applicable rules of law and the language of the arbitration.

2 The Secretariat may grant the Respondent an extension of the time for filing the Answer, provided the application for such an extension contains the Respondent's comments concerning the number of arbitrators and their choice and, where required by Articles 8, 9 and 10, the nomination of an arbitrator. If the Respondent fails to do so, the Court shall proceed in accordance with these Rules.

3 The Answer shall be supplied to the Secretariat in the number of copies specified by Article 3(1).

4 A copy of the Answer and the documents annexed thereto shall be communicated by the Secretariat to the Claimant.

5 Any counterclaim(s) made by the Respondent shall be filed with its Answer and shall provide:

(a) a description of the nature and circumstances of the dispute giving rise to the counterclaim(s); and

(b) a statement of the relief sought, including, to the extent possible, an indication of any amount(s) counterclaimed.

6 The Claimant shall file a Reply to any counterclaim within 30 days from the date of receipt of the counterclaim(s) communicated by the Secretariat. The Secretariat may grant the Claimant an extension of time for filing the Reply.

A39–007

Article 6

Effect of the Arbitration Agreement

A39–008 1 Where the parties have agreed to submit to arbitration under the Rules, they shall be deemed to have submitted *ipso facto* to the Rules in effect on the date of commencement of the arbitration proceedings, unless they have agreed to submit to the Rules in effect on the date of their arbitration agreement.

2 If the Respondent does not file an Answer, as provided by Article 5, or if any party raises one or more pleas concerning the existence, validity or scope of the arbitration agreement, the Court may decide, without prejudice to the admissibility or merits of the plea or pleas, that the arbitration shall proceed if it is *prima facie* satisfied that an arbitration agreement under the Rules may exist. In such a case, any decision as to the jurisdiction of the Arbitral Tribunal shall be taken by the Arbitral Tribunal itself. If the Court is not so satisfied, the parties shall be notified that the arbitration cannot proceed. In such a case, any party retains the right to ask any court having jurisdiction whether or not there is a binding arbitration agreement.

3 If any of the parties refuses or fails to take part in the arbitration or any stage thereof, the arbitration shall proceed notwithstanding such refusal or failure.

4 Unless otherwise agreed, the Arbitral Tribunal shall not cease to have jurisdiction by reason of any claim that the contract is null and void or allegation that it is non-existent, provided that the Arbitral Tribunal upholds the validity of the arbitration agreement. The Arbitral Tribunal shall continue to have jurisdiction to determine the respective rights of the parties and to adjudicate their claims and pleas even though the contract itself may be non-existent or null and void.

THE ARBITRAL TRIBUNAL

Article 7

General Provisions

A39–009 1 Every arbitrator must be and remain independent of the parties involved in the arbitration.

2 Before appointment or confirmation, a prospective arbitrator shall sign a statement of independence and disclose in writing to the Secretariat any facts or circumstances which might be of such a nature as to call into question the arbitrator's independence in the eyes of the parties. The Secretariat shall provide such information to the parties in writing and fix a time limit for any comments from them.

3 An arbitrator shall immediately disclose in writing to the Secretariat and to the parties any facts or circumstances of a similar nature which may arise during the arbitration.

4 The decisions of the Court as to the appointment, confirmation, challenge or replacement of an arbitrator shall be final and the reasons for such decisions shall not be communicated.

5 By accepting to serve, every arbitrator undertakes to carry out his responsibilities in accordance with these Rules.

6 Insofar as the parties have not provided otherwise, the Arbitral Tribunal shall be constituted in accordance with the provisions of Articles 8, 9 and 10.

Article 8

Number of Arbitrators

1 The disputes shall be decided by a sole arbitrator or by three arbitrators.

2 Where the parties have not agreed upon the number of arbitrators, the Court shall appoint a sole arbitrator, save where it appears to the Court that the dispute is such as to warrant the appointment of three arbitrators. In such case, the Claimant shall nominate an arbitrator within a period of 15 days from the receipt of the notification of the decision of the Court, and the Respondent shall nominate an arbitrator within a period of 15 days from the receipt of the notification of the nomination made by the Claimant.

3 Where the parties have agreed that the dispute shall be settled by a sole arbitrator, they may, by agreement, nominate the sole arbitrator for confirmation. If the parties fail to nominate a sole arbitrator within 30 days from the date when the Claimant's Request for Arbitration has been received by the other party, or within such additional time as may be allowed by the Secretariat, the sole arbitrator shall be appointed by the Court.

4 Where the dispute is to be referred to three arbitrators, each party shall nominate in the Request and the Answer, respectively, one arbitrator for confirmation. If a party fails to nominate an arbitrator, the appointment shall be made by the Court. The third arbitrator, who will act as chairman of the Arbitral Tribunal, shall be appointed by the Court, unless the parties have agreed upon another procedure for such appointment, in which case the nomination will be subject to confirmation pursuant to Article 9. Should such procedure not result in a nomination within the time limit fixed by the parties or the Court, the third arbitrator shall be appointed by the Court.

Article 9

Appointment and Confirmation of the Arbitrators

1 In confirming or appointing arbitrators, the Court shall consider the prospective arbitrator's nationality, residence and other relationships with the countries of which the parties or the other arbitrators are nationals and the prospective arbitrator's availability and ability to conduct the arbitration in accordance with these Rules. The same shall apply where the Secretary General confirms arbitrators pursuant to Article 9(2).

2 The Secretary General may confirm as co-arbitrators, sole arbitrators and chairmen of Arbitral Tribunals persons nominated by the parties or pursuant to their particular agreements, provided they have filed a statement of independence without qualification or a qualified statement of independence has not given rise to objections. Such confirmation shall be reported to the Court at its next session. If the Secretary General considers that a co-arbitrator, sole arbitrator or chairman of an Arbitral Tribunal should not be confirmed, the matter shall be submitted to the Court.

3 Where the Court is to appoint a sole arbitrator or the chairman of an Arbitral Tribunal, it shall make the appointment upon a proposal of a National Committee of the ICC that it considers to be appropriate. If the Court does not accept the proposal made, or if the National Committee fails to make the proposal requested within the time limit fixed by the Court, the Court may repeat its request or may request a proposal from another National Committee that it considers to be appropriate.

4 Where the Court considers that the circumstances so demand, it may choose the sole arbitrator or the chairman of the Arbitral Tribunal from a country where there is no

National Committee, provided that neither of the parties objects within the time limit fixed by the Court.

5 The sole arbitrator or the chairman of the Arbitral Tribunal shall be of a nationality other than those of the parties. However, in suitable circumstances and provided that neither of the parties objects within the time limit fixed by the Court, the sole arbitrator or the chairman of the Arbitral Tribunal may be chosen from a country of which any of the parties is a national.

6 Where the Court is to appoint an arbitrator on behalf of a party which has failed to nominate one, it shall make the appointment upon a proposal of the National Committee of the country of which that party is a national. If the Court does not accept the proposal made, or if the National Committee fails to make the proposal requested within the time limit fixed by the Court, or if the country of which the said party is a national has no National Committee, the Court shall be at liberty to choose any person whom it regards as suitable. The Secretariat shall inform the National Committee, if one exists, of the country of which such person is a national.

Article 10

Multiple Parties

A39–012   **1** Where there are multiple parties, whether as Claimant or as Respondent, and where the dispute is to be referred to three arbitrators, the multiple Claimants, jointly, and the multiple Respondents, jointly, shall nominate an arbitrator for confirmation pursuant to Article 9.

2 In the absence of such a joint nomination and where all parties are unable to agree to a method for the constitution of the Arbitral Tribunal, the Court may appoint each member of the Arbitral Tribunal and shall designate one of them to act as chairman. In such case, the Court shall be at liberty to choose any person it regards as suitable to act as arbitrator, applying Article 9 when it considers this appropriate.

Article 11

Challenge of Arbitrators

A39–013   **1** A challenge of an arbitrator, whether for an alleged lack of independence or otherwise, shall be made by the submission to the Secretariat of a written statement specifying the facts and circumstances on which the challenge is based.

2 For a challenge to be admissible, it must be sent by a party either within 30 days from receipt by that party of the notification of the appointment or confirmation of the arbitrator, or within 30 days from the date when the party making the challenge was informed of the facts and circumstances on which the challenge is based if such date is subsequent to the receipt of such notification.

3 The Court shall decide on the admissibility and, at the same time, if necessary, on the merits of a challenge after the Secretariat has afforded an opportunity for the arbitrator concerned, the other party or parties and any other members of the Arbitral Tribunal to comment in writing within a suitable period of time. Such comments shall be communicated to the parties and to the arbitrators.

Article 12

Replacement of Arbitrators

1 An arbitrator shall be replaced upon his death, upon the acceptance by the Court of the arbitrator's resignation, upon acceptance by the Court of a challenge, or upon the request of all the parties.

2 An arbitrator shall also be replaced on the Court's own initiative when it decides that he is prevented *de jure* or *de facto* from fulfilling his functions, or that he is not fulfilling his functions in accordance with the Rules or within the prescribed time limits.

3 When, on the basis of information that has come to its attention, the Court considers applying Article 12(2), it shall decide on the matter after the arbitrator concerned, the parties and any other members of the Arbitral Tribunal have had an opportunity to comment in writing within a suitable period of time. Such comments shall be communicated to the parties and to the arbitrators.

4 When an arbitrator is to be replaced, the Court has discretion to decide whether or not to follow the original nominating process. Once reconstituted, and after having invited the parties to comment, the Arbitral Tribunal shall determine if and to what extent prior proceedings shall be repeated before the reconstituted Arbitral Tribunal.

5 Subsequent to the closing of the proceedings, instead of replacing an arbitrator who has died or been removed by the Court pursuant to Articles 12(1) and 12(2), the Court may decide, when it considers it appropriate, that the remaining arbitrators shall continue the arbitration. In making such determination, the Court shall take into account the views of the remaining arbitrators and of the parties and such other matters that it considers appropriate in the circumstances.

The Arbitral Proceedings

Article 13

Transmission of the File to the Arbitral Tribunal

The Secretariat shall transmit the file to the Arbitral Tribunal as soon as it has been constituted, provided the advance on costs requested by the Secretariat at this stage has been paid.

Article 14

Place of the Arbitration

1 The place of the arbitration shall be fixed by the Court unless agreed upon by the parties.

2 The Arbitral Tribunal may, after consultation with the parties, conduct hearings and meetings at any location it considers appropriate unless otherwise agreed by the parties.

3 The Arbitral Tribunal may deliberate at any location it considers appropriate.

Article 15

Rules Governing the Proceedings

A39–017   **1** The proceedings before the Arbitral Tribunal shall be governed by these Rules and, where these Rules are silent, by any rules which the parties or, failing them, the Arbitral Tribunal may settle on, whether or not reference is thereby made to the rules of procedure of a national law to be applied to the arbitration.

2 In all cases, the Arbitral Tribunal shall act fairly and impartially and ensure that each party has a reasonable opportunity to present its case.

Article 16

Language of the Arbitration

A39–018   In the absence of an agreement by the parties, the Arbitral Tribunal shall determine the language or languages of the arbitration, due regard being given to all relevant circumstances, including the language of the contract.

Article 17

Applicable Rules of Law

A39–019   **1** The parties shall be free to agree upon the rules of law to be applied by the Arbitral Tribunal to the merits of the dispute. In the absence of any such agreement, the Arbitral Tribunal shall apply the rules of law which it determines to be appropriate.

2 In all cases the Arbitral Tribunal shall take account of the provisions of the contract and the relevant trade usages.

3 The Arbitral Tribunal shall assume the powers of an *amiable compositeur* or decide *ex aequo et bono* only if the parties have agreed to give it such powers.

Article 18

Terms of Reference; Procedural Timetable

A39–020   **1** As soon as it has received the file from the Secretariat, the Arbitral Tribunal shall draw up, on the basis of documents or in the presence of the parties and in the light of their most recent submissions, a document defining its Terms of Reference. This document shall include the following particulars:

   (a) the full names and descriptions of the parties;

   (b) the addresses of the parties to which notifications and communications arising in the course of the arbitration may be made;

   (c) a summary of the parties' respective claims and of the relief sought by each party, with an indication to the extent possible of the amounts claimed or counterclaimed;

   (d) unless the Arbitral Tribunal considers it inappropriate, a list of issues to be determined;

(e) the full names, descriptions and addresses of the arbitrators;

(f) the place of the arbitration; and

(g) particulars of the applicable procedural rules and, if such is the case, reference to the power conferred upon the Arbitral Tribunal to act as *amiable compositeur* or to decide *ex aequo et bono*.

2 The Terms of Reference shall be signed by the parties and the Arbitral Tribunal. Within two months of the date on which the file has been transmitted to it, the Arbitral Tribunal shall transmit to the Court the Terms of Reference signed by it and by the parties. The Court may extend this time limit pursuant to a reasoned request from the Arbitral Tribunal or on its own initiative if it decides it is necessary to do so.

3 If any of the parties refuses to take part in the drawing up of the Terms of Reference or to sign the same, they shall be submitted to the Court for approval. When the Terms of Reference have been signed in accordance with Article 18(2) or approved by the Court, the arbitration shall proceed.

4 When drawing up the Terms of Reference, or as soon as possible thereafter, the Arbitral Tribunal, after having consulted the parties, shall establish in a separate document a provisional timetable that it intends to follow for the conduct of the arbitration and shall communicate it to the Court and the parties. Any subsequent modifications of the provisional timetable shall be communicated to the Court and the parties.

Article 19

New Claims

After the Terms of Reference have been signed or approved by the Court, no party shall make new claims or counterclaims which fall outside the limits of the Terms of Reference unless it has been authorized to do so by the Arbitral Tribunal, which shall consider the nature of such new claims or counterclaims, the stage of the arbitration and other relevant circumstances.

Article 20

Establishing the Facts of the Case

1 The Arbitral Tribunal shall proceed within as short a time as possible to establish the facts of the case by all appropriate means.

2 After studying the written submissions of the parties and all documents relied upon, the Arbitral Tribunal shall hear the parties together in person if any of them so requests or, failing such a request, it may of its own motion decide to hear them.

3 The Arbitral Tribunal may decide to hear witnesses, experts appointed by the parties or any other person, in the presence of the parties, or in their absence provided they have been duly summoned.

4 The Arbitral Tribunal, after having consulted the parties, may appoint one or more experts, define their terms of reference and receive their reports. At the request of a party, the parties shall be given the opportunity to question at a hearing any such expert appointed by the Tribunal.

5 At any time during the proceedings, the Arbitral Tribunal may summon any party to provide additional evidence.

6 The Arbitral Tribunal may decide the case solely on the documents submitted by the parties unless any of the parties requests a hearing.

7 The Arbitral Tribunal may take measures for protecting trade secrets and confidential information.

Article 21

Hearings

A39–023   **1** When a hearing is to be held, the Arbitral Tribunal, giving reasonable notice, shall summon the parties to appear before it on the day and at the place fixed by it.

2 If any of the parties, although duly summoned, fails to appear without valid excuse, the Arbitral Tribunal shall have the power to proceed with the hearing.

3 The Arbitral Tribunal shall be in full charge of the hearings, at which all the parties shall be entitled to be present. Save with the approval of the Arbitral Tribunal and the parties, persons not involved in the proceedings shall not be admitted.

4 The parties may appear in person or through duly authorized representatives. In addition, they may be assisted by advisers.

Article 22

Closing of the Proceedings

A39–024   **1** When it is satisfied that the parties have had a reasonable opportunity to present their cases, the Arbitral Tribunal shall declare the proceedings closed. Thereafter, no further submission or argument may be made, or evidence produced, unless requested or authorized by the Arbitral Tribunal.

2 When the Arbitral Tribunal has declared the proceedings closed, it shall indicate to the Secretariat an approximate date by which the draft Award will be submitted to the Court for approval pursuant to Article 27. Any postponement of that date shall be communicated to the Secretariat by the Arbitral Tribunal.

Article 23

Conservatory and Interim Measures

A39–025   **1** Unless the parties have otherwise agreed, as soon as the file has been transmitted to it, the Arbitral Tribunal may, at the request of a party, order any interim or conservatory measure it deems appropriate. The Arbitral Tribunal may make the granting of any such measure subject to appropriate security being furnished by the requesting party. Any such measure shall take the form of an order, giving reasons, or of an Award, as the Arbitral Tribunal considers appropriate.

2 Before the file is transmitted to the Arbitral Tribunal, and in appropriate circumstances even thereafter, the parties may apply to any competent judicial authority for interim or conservatory measures. The application of a party to a judicial authority for such measures or for the implementation of any such measures ordered by an Arbitral Tribunal shall not be deemed to be an infringement or a waiver of the arbitration agreement and shall not affect the relevant powers reserved to the Arbitral Tribunal. Any such application and any measures taken by the judicial authority must be notified without delay to the Secretariat. The Secretariat shall inform the Arbitral Tribunal thereof.

Awards

Article 24

Time Limit for the Award

1 The time limit within which the Arbitral Tribunal must render its final Award is six months. Such time limit shall start to run from the date of the last signature by the Arbitral Tribunal or by the parties of the Terms of Reference or, in the case of application of Article 18(3), the date of the notification to the Arbitral Tribunal by the Secretariat of the approval of the Terms of Reference by the Court.

2 The Court may extend this time limit pursuant to a reasoned request from the Arbitral Tribunal or on its own initiative if it decides it is necessary to do so.

Article 25

Making of the Award

1 When the Arbitral Tribunal is composed of more than one arbitrator, an Award is given by a majority decision. If there be no majority, the Award shall be made by the chairman of the Arbitral Tribunal alone.

2 The Award shall state the reasons upon which it is based.

3 The Award shall be deemed to be made at the place of the arbitration and on the date stated therein.

Article 26

Award by Consent

If the parties reach a settlement after the file has been transmitted to the Arbitral Tribunal in accordance with Article 13, the settlement shall be recorded in the form of an Award made by consent of the parties if so requested by the parties and if the Arbitral Tribunal agrees to do so.

Article 27

Scrutiny of the Award by the Court

Before signing any Award, the Arbitral Tribunal shall submit it in draft form to the Court. The Court may lay down modifications as to the form of the Award and, without affecting the Arbitral Tribunal's liberty of decision, may also draw its attention to points of substance. No Award shall be rendered by the Arbitral Tribunal until it has been approved by the Court as to its form.

Article 28

Notification, Deposit and Enforceability of the Award

A39–030 **1** Once an Award has been made, the Secretariat shall notify to the parties the text signed by the Arbitral Tribunal, provided always that the costs of the arbitration have been fully paid to the ICC by the parties or by one of them.

2 Additional copies certified true by the Secretary General shall be made available on request and at any time to the parties, but to no one else.

3 By virtue of the notification made in accordance with Paragraph 1 of this Article, the parties waive any other form of notification or deposit on the part of the Arbitral Tribunal.

4 An original of each Award made in accordance with the present Rules shall be deposited with the Secretariat.

5 The Arbitral Tribunal and the Secretariat shall assist the parties in complying with whatever further formalities may be necessary.

6 Every Award shall be binding on the parties. By submitting the dispute to arbitration under these Rules, the parties undertake to carry out any Award without delay and shall be deemed to have waived their right to any form of recourse insofar as such waiver can validly be made.

Article 29

Correction and Interpretation of the Award

A39–031 **1** On its own initiative, the Arbitral Tribunal may correct a clerical, computational or typographical error, or any errors of similar nature contained in an Award, provided such correction is submitted for approval to the Court within 30 days of the date of such Award.

2 Any application of a party for the correction of an error of the kind referred to in Article 29(1), or for the interpretation of an Award, must be made to the Secretariat within 30 days of the receipt of the Award by such party, in a number of copies as stated in Article 3(1). After transmittal of the application to the Arbitral Tribunal, the latter shall grant the other party a short time limit, normally not exceeding 30 days, from the receipt of the application by that party, to submit any comments thereon. If the Arbitral Tribunal decides to correct or interpret the Award, it shall submit its decision in draft form to the Court not later than 30 days following the expiration of the time limit for the receipt of any comments from the other party or within such other period as the Court may decide.

3 The decision to correct or to interpret the Award shall take the form of an addendum and shall constitute part of the Award. The provisions of Articles 25, 27 and 28 shall apply *mutatis mutandis*.

Costs

Article 30

Advance to Cover the Costs of the Arbitration

A39–032 **1** After receipt of the Request, the Secretary General may request the Claimant to pay a provisional advance in an amount intended to cover the costs of arbitration until the Terms of Reference have been drawn up.

2 As soon as practicable, the Court shall fix the advance on costs in an amount likely to cover the fees and expenses of the arbitrators and the ICC administrative costs for the claims and counterclaims which have been referred to it by the parties. This amount may be subject to readjustment at any time during the arbitration. Where, apart from the claims, counterclaims are submitted, the Court may fix separate advances on costs for the claims and the counterclaims.

3 The advance on costs fixed by the Court shall be payable in equal shares by the Claimant and the Respondent. Any provisional advance paid on the basis of Article 30(1) will be considered as a partial payment thereof. However, any party shall be free to pay the whole of the advance on costs in respect of the principal claim or the counterclaim should the other party fail to pay its share. When the Court has set separate advances on costs in accordance with Article 30(2), each of the parties shall pay the advance on costs corresponding to its claims.

4 When a request for an advance on costs has not been complied with, and after consultation with the Arbitral Tribunal, the Secretary General may direct the Arbitral Tribunal to suspend its work and set a time limit, which must be not less than 15 days, on the expiry of which the relevant claims, or counterclaims, shall be considered as withdrawn. Should the party in question wish to object to this measure, it must make a request within the aforementioned period for the matter to be decided by the Court. Such party shall not be prevented, on the ground of such withdrawal, from reintroducing the same claims or counterclaims at a later date in another proceeding.

5 If one of the parties claims a right to a set-off with regard to either claims or counterclaims, such set-off shall be taken into account in determining the advance to cover the costs of arbitration in the same way as a separate claim insofar as it may require the Arbitral Tribunal to consider additional matters.

Article 31

Decision as to the Costs of the Arbitration

1 The costs of the arbitration shall include the fees and expenses of the arbitrators and the ICC administrative expenses fixed by the Court, in accordance with the scale in force at the time of the commencement of the arbitral proceedings, as well as the fees and expenses of any experts appointed by the Arbitral Tribunal and the reasonable legal and other costs incurred by the parties for the arbitration. **A39–033**

2 The Court may fix the fees of the arbitrators at a figure higher or lower than that which would result from the application of the relevant scale should this be deemed necessary due to the exceptional circumstances of the case. Decisions on costs other than those fixed by the Court may be taken by the Arbitral Tribunal at any time during the proceedings.

3 The final Award shall fix the costs of the arbitration and decide which of the parties shall bear them or in what proportion they shall be borne by the parties.

MISCELLANEOUS

Article 32

Modified Time Limits

1 The parties may agree to shorten the various time limits set out in these Rules. Any such agreement entered into subsequent to the constitution of an Arbitral Tribunal shall become effective only upon the approval of the Arbitral Tribunal. **A39–034**

INSTITUTIONAL RULES

2 The Court, on its own initiative, may extend any time limit which has been modified pursuant to Article 32(1) if it decides that it is necessary to do so in order that the Arbitral Tribunal or the Court may fulfil their responsibilities in accordance with these Rules.

Article 33

Waiver

A39–035 A party which proceeds with the arbitration without raising its objection to a failure to comply with any provision of these Rules, or of any other rules applicable to the proceedings, any direction given by the Arbitral Tribunal, or any requirement under the arbitration agreement relating to the constitution of the Arbitral Tribunal, or to the conduct of the proceedings, shall be deemed to have waived its right to object.

Article 34

Exclusion of Liability

A39–036 Neither the arbitrators, nor the Court and its members, nor the ICC and its employees, nor the ICC National Committees shall be liable to any person for any act or omission in connection with the arbitration.

Article 35

General Rule

A39–037 In all matters not expressly provided for in these Rules, the Court and the Arbitral Tribunal shall act in the spirit of these Rules and shall make every effort to make sure that the Award is enforceable at law.

APPENDIX I

STATUTES OF THE INTERNATIONAL COURT OF ARBITRATION OF THE ICC

Article 1

Function

A39–038 1 The function of the International Court of Arbitration of the International Chamber of Commerce (the "Court") is to ensure the application of the Rules of Arbitration of the International Chamber of Commerce, and it has all the necessary powers for that purpose.

2 As an autonomous body, it carries out these functions in complete independence from the ICC and its organs.

3 Its members are independent from the ICC National Committees.

Article 2

Composition of the Court
The Court shall consist of a Chairman, Vice-Chairmen, and members and alternate members (collectively designated as members). In its work it is assisted by its Secretariat (Secretariat of the Court).

Article 3

Appointment
1 The Chairman is elected by the ICC World Council upon the recommendation of the Executive Board of the ICC.
2 The ICC World Council appoints the Vice-Chairmen of the Court from among the members of the Court or otherwise.
3 Its members are appointed by the ICC World Council on the proposal of National Committees, one member for each Committee.
4 On the proposal of the Chairman of the Court, the World Council may appoint alternate members.
5 The term of office of all members is three years. If a member is no longer in a position to exercise his functions, his successor is appointed by the World Council for the remainder of the term.

Article 4

Plenary Session of the Court
The Plenary Sessions of the Court are presided over by the Chairman or, in his absence, by one of the Vice-Chairmen designated by him. The deliberations shall be valid when at least six members are present. Decisions are taken by a majority vote, the Chairman having a casting vote in the event of a tie.

Article 5

Committees
The Court may set up one or more Committees and establish the functions and organization of such Committees.

Article 6

Confidentiality
The work of the Court is of a confidential nature which must be respected by everyone who participates in that work in whatever capacity. The Court lays down the rules regarding the persons who can attend the meetings of the Court and its Committees and who are entitled to have access to the materials submitted to the Court and its Secretariat.

Article 7

Modification of the Rules of Arbitration
Any proposal of the Court for a modification of the Rules is laid before the Commis-

sion on International Arbitration before submission to the Executive Board and the World Council of the ICC for approval.

APPENDIX II

Internal Rules of the International Court of Arbitration of the ICC

Article 1

Confidential Character of the Work of the International Court of Arbitration

A39–045   1 The sessions of the Court, whether plenary or those of a Committee of the Court, are open only to its members and to the Secretariat.

2 However, in exceptional circumstances, the Chairman of the Court may invite other persons to attend. Such persons must respect the confidential nature of the work of the Court.

3 The documents submitted to the Court, or drawn up by it in the course of its proceedings, are communicated only to the members of the Court and to the Secretariat and to persons authorized by the Chairman to attend Court sessions.

4 The Chairman or the Secretary General of the Court may authorize researchers undertaking work of a scientific nature on international trade law to acquaint themselves with Awards and other documents of general interest, with the exception of memoranda, notes, statements and documents remitted by the parties within the framework of arbitration proceedings.

5 Such authorization shall not be given unless the beneficiary has undertaken to respect the confidential character of the documents made available and to refrain from any publication in their respect without having previously submitted the text for approval to the Secretary General of the Court.

6 The Secretariat will in each case submitted to arbitration under the Rules retain in the archives of the Court all Awards, Terms of Reference and decisions of the Court, as well as copies of the pertinent correspondence of the Secretariat.

7 Any documents, communications or correspondence submitted by the parties or the arbitrators may be destroyed unless a party or an arbitrator requests in writing within a period fixed by the Secretariat the return of such documents. All related costs and expenses for the return of those documents shall be paid by such party or arbitrator.

Article 2

Participation of Members of the International Court of Arbitration in ICC Arbitration

A39–046   1 The Chairman and the members of the Secretariat of the Court may not act as arbitrators or as counsel in cases submitted to ICC arbitration.

2 The Court shall not appoint Vice-Chairmen or members of the Court as arbitrators. They may, however, be proposed for such duties by one or more of the parties, or pursuant to any other procedure agreed upon by the parties, subject to confirmation.

3 When the Chairman, a Vice-Chairman or a member of the Court or of the Secretariat is involved in any capacity whatsoever in proceedings pending before the Court, such person must inform the Secretary General of the Court upon becoming aware of such involvement.

4 Such person must refrain from participating in the discussions or in the decisions of the Court concerning the proceedings and must be absent from the courtroom whenever the matter is considered.

5 Such person will not receive any material documentation or information pertaining to such proceedings.

Article 3

Relations between the Members of the Court and the ICC National Committees
1 By virtue of their capacity, the members of the Court are independent of the ICC National Committees which proposed them for appointment by the ICC World Council.

2 Furthermore, they must regard as confidential, vis-à-vis the said National Committees, any information concerning individual cases with which they have become acquainted in their capacity as members of the Court, except when they have been requested by the Chairman of the Court or by its Secretary General to communicate specific information to their respective National Committees.

Article 4

Committee of the Court
1 In accordance with the provisions of Article 1(4) of the Rules and Article 5 of its Statutes (Appendix I), the Court hereby establishes a Committee of the Court.

2 The members of the Committee consist of a Chairman and at least two other members. The Chairman of the Court acts as the Chairman of the Committee. If absent, the Chairman may designate a Vice-Chairman of the Court or, in exceptional circumstances, another member of the Court as Chairman of the Committee.

3 The other two members of the Committee are appointed by the Court from among the Vice-Chairmen or the other members of the Court. At each Plenary Session the Court appoints the members who are to attend the meetings of the Committee to be held before the next Plenary Session.

4 The Committee meets when convened by its Chairman. Two members constitute a quorum.

5 (a) The Court shall determine the decisions that may be taken by the Committee.

(b) The decisions of the Committee are taken unanimously.

(c) When the Committee cannot reach a decision or deems it preferable to abstain, it transfers the case to the next Plenary Session, making any suggestions it deems appropriate.

(d) The Committee's decisions are brought to the notice of the Court at its next Plenary Session.

Article 5

Court Secretariat
1 In case of absence, the Secretary General may delegate to the General Counsel and Deputy Secretary General the authority to confirm arbitrators, to certify true copies of Awards and to request the payment of a provisional advance, respectively provided for in Articles 9(2), 28(2) and 30(1) of the Rules.

2 The Secretariat may, with the approval of the Court, issue notes and other documents for the information of the parties and the arbitrators, or as necessary for the proper conduct of the arbitral proceedings.

Article 6

Scrutiny of Arbitral Awards

A39–050 When the Court scrutinizes draft Awards in accordance with Article 27 of the Rules, it considers, to the extent practicable, the requirements of mandatory law at the place of arbitration.

APPENDIX III

ARBITRATION COSTS AND FEES

Article 1

Advance on Costs

A39–051 **1** Each request to commence an arbitration pursuant to the Rules must be accompanied by an advance payment of US$ 2,500 on the administrative expenses. Such payment is non-refundable, and shall be credited to the Claimant's portion of the advance on costs.

2 The provisional advance fixed by the Secretary General according to Article 30(1) of the Rules shall normally not exceed the amount obtained by adding together the administrative expenses, the minimum of the fees (as set out in the scale hereinafter) based upon the amount of the claim and the expected reimbursable expenses of the Arbitral Tribunal incurred with respect to the drafting of the Terms of Reference. If such amount is not quantified, the provisional advance shall be fixed at the discretion of the Secretary General. Payment by the Claimant shall be credited to its share of the advance on costs fixed by the Court.

3 In general, after the Terms of Reference have been signed or approved by the Court and the provisional timetable has been established, the Arbitral Tribunal shall, in accordance with Article 30(4) of the Rules, proceed only with respect to those claims or counterclaims in regard to which the whole of the advance on costs has been paid.

4 The advance on costs fixed by the Court according to Article 30(2) of the Rules comprises the fees of the arbitrator or arbitrators (hereinafter referred to as "arbitrator"), any arbitration-related expenses of the arbitrator and the administrative expenses.

5 Each party shall pay in cash its share of the total advance on costs. However, if its share exceeds an amount fixed from time to time by the Court, a party may post a bank guarantee for this additional amount.

6 A party that has already paid in full its share of the advance on costs fixed by the Court may, in accordance with Article 30(3) of the Rules, pay the unpaid portion of the advance owed by the defaulting party by posting a bank guarantee.

7 When the Court has fixed separate advances on costs pursuant to Article 30(2) of the Rules, the Secretariat shall invite each party to pay the amount of the advance corresponding to its respective claim(s).

8 When, as a result of the fixing of separate advances on costs, the separate advance fixed for the claim of either party exceeds one half of such global advance as was previously fixed (in respect of the same claims and counterclaims that are the subject of separate advances), a bank guarantee may be posted to cover any such excess amount. In the event that the amount of the separate advance is subsequently increased, at least one half of the increase shall be paid in cash.

9 The Secretariat shall establish the terms governing all bank guarantees which the parties may post pursuant to the above provisions.

10 As provided in Article 30(2) of the Rules, the advance on costs may be subject to readjustment at any time during the arbitration, in particular to take into account fluctuations in the amount in dispute, changes in the amount of the estimated expenses of the arbitrator, or the evolving difficulty or complexity of arbitration proceedings.

11 Before any expertise ordered by the Arbitral Tribunal can be commenced, the parties, or one of them, shall pay an advance on costs fixed by the Arbitral Tribunal sufficient to cover the expected fees and expenses of the expert as determined by the Arbitral Tribunal. The Arbitral Tribunal shall be responsible for ensuring the payment by the parties of such fees and expenses.

Article 2

Costs and Fees

1 Subject to Article 31(2) of the Rules, the Court shall fix the fees of the arbitrator in accordance with the scale hereinafter set out or, where the sum in dispute is not stated, at its discretion.

2 In setting the arbitrator's fees, the Court shall take into consideration the diligence of the arbitrator, the time spent, the rapidity of the proceedings, and the complexity of the dispute, so as to arrive at a figure within the limits specified or, in exceptional circumstances (Article 31(2) of the Rules), at a figure higher or lower than those limits.

3 When a case is submitted to more than one arbitrator, the Court, at its discretion, shall have the right to increase the total fees up to a maximum which shall normally not exceed three times the fees of one arbitrator.

4 The arbitrator's fees and expenses shall be fixed exclusively by the Court as required by the Rules. Separate fee arrangements between the parties and the arbitrator are contrary to the Rules.

5 The Court shall fix the administrative expenses of each arbitration in accordance with the scale hereinafter set out or, where the sum in dispute is not stated, at its discretion. In exceptional circumstances, the Court may fix the administrative expenses at a lower or higher figure than that which would result from the application of such scale, provided that such expenses shall normally not exceed the maximum amount of the scale. Further, the Court may require the payment of administrative expenses in addition to those provided in the scale of administrative expenses as a condition to holding an arbitration in abeyance at the request of the parties or of one of them with the acquiescence of the other.

6 If an arbitration terminates before the rendering of a final Award, the Court shall fix the costs of the arbitration at its discretion, taking into account the stage attained by the arbitral proceedings and any other relevant circumstances.

7 In the case of an application under Article 29(2) of the Rules, the Court may fix an advance to cover additional fees and expenses of the Arbitral Tribunal and may make the transmission of such application to the Arbitral Tribunal subject to the prior cash payment in full to the ICC of such advance. The Court shall fix at its discretion any possible fees of the arbitrator when approving the decision of the Arbitral Tribunal.

8 When an arbitration is preceded by an attempt at amicable resolution pursuant to the ICC ADR Rules, one half of the administrative expenses paid for such ADR proceedings shall be credited to the administrative expenses of the arbitration.

9 Amounts paid to the arbitrator do not include any possible value added taxes (VAT) or other taxes or charges and imposts applicable to the arbitrator's fees. Parties have a duty to pay any such taxes or charges; however, the recovery of any such charges or taxes is a matter solely between the arbitrator and the parties.

A39–052

Article 3

Appointments of Arbitrators

A39–053 **1** A registration fee normally not exceeding US$ 2,500 is payable by the requesting party in respect of each request made to the ICC to appoint an arbitrator for any arbitration not conducted under the Rules. No request for appointment of an arbitrator will be considered unless accompanied by the said fee, which is not recoverable and becomes the property of the ICC.

2 The said fee shall cover any additional services rendered by the ICC regarding the appointment, such as decisions on a challenge of an arbitrator and the appointment of a substitute arbitrator.

Article 4

Scales of Administrative Expenses and Arbitrator's Fees

A39–054 **1** The Scales of Administrative Expenses and Arbitrator's Fees set forth below shall be effective as of 1 January 1998 in respect of all arbitrations commenced on or after such date, irrespective of the version of the Rules applying to such arbitrations.

2 To calculate the administrative expenses and the arbitrator's fees, the amounts calculated for each successive slice of the sum in dispute must be added together, except that where the sum in dispute is over US$ 80 million, a flat amount of US$ 75,800 shall constitute the entirety of the administrative expenses.

A. ADMINISTRATIVE EXPENSES

Sum in dispute (in US Dollars)			Administrative expenses[*]
up to	50 000		$ 2 500
from	50 001 to	100 000	3.50%
from	100 001 to	500 000	1.70%
from	500 001 to	1 000 000	1.15%
from	1 000 001 to	2 000 000	0.60%
from	2 000 001 to	5 000 000	0.20%
from	5 000 001 to	10 000 000	0.10%
from	10 000 001 to	50 000 000	0.06%
from	50 000 001 to	80 000 000	0.06%
over	80 000 000		$ 75 800

[*] *For illustrative purposes only, the table on the following page indicates the resulting administrative expenses in US when the proper calculations have been made.*

B. ARBITRATOR'S FEES

Sum in dispute (in US Dollars)			Fees[**]	
			minimum	maximum
up to	50 000		$2 500	17.00%
from	50 001 to	100 000	2.00%	11.00%
from	100 001 to	500 000	1.00%	5.50%
from	500 001 to	1 000 000	0.75%	3.50%
from	1 000 001 to	2 000 000	0.50%	2.50%
from	2 000 001 to	5 000 000	0.25%	1.00%
from	5 000 001 to	10 000 000	0.10%	0.55%
from	10 000 001 to	50 000 000	0.05%	0.17%
from	50 000 001 to	80 000 000	0.03%	0.12%
from	80 000 001 to	100 000 000	0.02%	0.10%
over	100 000 000		0.01%	0.05%

[**] *For illustrative purposes only, the table on the following page indicates the resulting range of fees when the proper calculations have been made.*

SUM IN DISPUTE (in US Dollars)		A. ADMINISTRATIVE EXPENSES(*) (in US Dollars)	B. ARBITRATOR'S FEES(**) (in US Dollars)	
			Minimum	Maximum
up to	50 000	2 500	2 500	17.00% of amount in dispute
from 50 001 to	100 000	2 500 + 3.50% of amt. over 50 000	2 500 + 2.00% of amt. over 50 000	8 500 + 11.00% of amt. over 50 000
from 100 001 to	500 000	4 250 + 1.70% of amt. over 100 000	3 500 + 1.00% of amt. over 100 000	14 000 + 5.50% of amt. over 100 000
from 500 001 to	1 000 000	11 050 + 1.15% of amt. over 500 000	7 500 + 0.75% of amt. over 500 000	36 000 + 3.50% of amt. over 500 000
from 1 000 001 to	2 000 000	16 800 + 0.60% of amt. over 1 000 000	11 250 + 0.50% of amt. over 1 000 000	53 500 + 2.50% of amt. over 1 000 000
from 2 000 001 to	5 000 000	22 800 + 0.20% of amt. over 2 000 000	16 250 + 0.25% of amt. over 2 000 000	78 500 + 1.00% of amt. over 2 000 000
from 5 000 001 to	10 000 000	28 800 + 0.10% of amt. over 5 000 000	23 750 + 0.10% of amt. over 5 000 000	108 500 + 0.55% of amt. over 5 000 000
from 10 000 001 to	50 000 000	33 800 + 0.06% of amt. over 10 000 000	28 750 + 0.05% of amt. over 10 000 000	136 000 + 0.17% of amt. over 10 000 000
from 50 000 001 to	80 000 000	57 800 + 0.06% of amt. over 50 000 000	48 750 + 0.03% of amt. over 50 000 000	204 000 + 0.12% of amt. over 50 000 000
from 80 000 001 to	100 000 000	75 800	57 750 + 0.02% of amt. over 80 000 000	240 000 + 0.10% of amt. over 80 000 000
over	100 000 000	75 800	61 750 + 0.01% of amt. over 100 000 000	260 000 + 0.05% of amt. over 100 000 000

(*)(**) *See preceding page*

International Chamber of Commerce ADR Rules[1]

(In force as from 1 July 2001)

FOREWORD

ICC has almost eight decades of experience in devising rules to govern and facilitate the conduct of international business. These include those designed to resolve the conflicts that inevitably arise in trading relations. The present ADR Rules represent ICC's most recent initiative in this field.   **A40–001**

The ICC ADR Rules are the result of discussions between dispute resolution experts and representatives of the business community from 75 countries. Their purpose is to offer business partners a means of resolving disputes amicably, in the way best suited to their needs. A distinctive feature of the Rules is the freedom the parties are given to choose the technique they consider most conducive to settlement. Failing agreement on the method to be adopted, the fallback shall be mediation.

As an amicable method of dispute resolution, ICC ADR should be distinguished from ICC arbitration. They are two alternative means of resolving disputes, although in certain circumstances they may be complementary. For instance, it is possible for parties to provide for ICC arbitration in the event of failure to reach an amicable settlement. Similarly, parties engaged in an arbitration may turn to ICC ADR if their dispute seems to warrant a different, more consensual approach. The two services remain distinct, however, each administered by a separate secretariat based at ICC headquarters in Paris.

The ICC ADR Rules replace the 1988 ICC Rules of Optional Conciliation and join the Rules of Arbitration, the Rules for Expertise and the Docdex Rules as an important component in ICC's range of dispute resolution services.

The ICC ADR Rules, which are effective as of 1 July 2001, may be used in domestic as well as international contexts.

June 2001

SUGGESTED ICC ADR CLAUSES

Optional ADR

"The parties may at any time, without prejudice to any other proceedings, seek to settle any dispute arising out of or in connection with the present contract in accordance with the ICC ADR Rules."   **A40–002**

---

[1] ADR Rules of the International Chamber of Commerce & Guide to ICC ADR are published in their official English version by the International Chamber of Commerce ICC Publication No. 809—ISBN 92.842.1303.7. Copyright © 2001 International Chamber of Commerce. Available from: ICC Dispute Resolution Services–ADR, 38 cours Albert 1 er, 75008 Paris, France, and on the web site: www.iccadr.org. Please see also the International Chamber of Commerce Suggested ADR clauses at paras A54–130 of this Volume.

Obligation to consider ADR

"In the event of any dispute arising out of or in connection with the present contract, the parties agree in the first instance to discuss and consider submitting the matter to settlement proceedings under the ICC ADR Rules."

Obligation to submit dispute to ADR with an automatic expiration mechanism

"In the event of any dispute arising out of or in connection with the present contract, the parties agree to submit the matter to settlement proceedings under the ICC ADR Rules. If the dispute has not been settled pursuant to the said Rules within 45 days following the filing of a Request for ADR or within such other period as the parties may agree in writing, the parties shall have no further obligations under this paragraph."

Obligation to submit dispute to ADR, followed by ICC arbitration as required

"In the event of any dispute arising out of or in connection with the present contract, the parties agree to submit the matter to settlement proceedings under the ICC ADR Rules. If the dispute has not been settled pursuant to the said Rules within 45 days following the filing of a Request for ADR or within such other period as the parties may agree in writing, such dispute shall be finally settled under the Rules of Arbitration of the International Chamber of Commerce by one or more arbitrators appointed in accordance with the said Rules of Arbitration."

ADR RULES OF THE INTERNATIONAL CHAMBER OF COMMERCE

Preamble

A40–003   Amicable settlement is a desirable solution for business disputes and differences. It can occur before or during the litigation or arbitration of a dispute and can often be facilitated through the aid of a third party (the "Neutral") acting in accordance with simple rules. The parties can agree to submit to such rules in their underlying contract or at any other time.

The International Chamber of Commerce ("ICC") sets out these amicable dispute resolution rules, entitled the ICC ADR Rules (the "Rules"), which permit the parties to agree upon whatever settlement technique they believe to be appropriate to help them settle their dispute. In the absence of an agreement of the parties on a settlement technique, mediation shall be the settlement technique used under the Rules. The Guide to ICC ADR, which does not form part of the Rules, provides an explanation of the Rules and of various settlement techniques which can be used pursuant to the Rules.

INTERNATIONAL CHAMBER OF COMMERCE ADR RULES

Article 1

Scope of the ICC ADR Rules

All business disputes, whether or not of an international character, may be referred to ADR proceedings pursuant to these Rules. The provisions of these Rules may be modified by agreement of all of the parties, subject to the approval of ICC.

Article 2

Commencement of the ADR Proceedings

A Where there is an agreement to refer to the Rules
1 Where there is an agreement between the parties to refer their dispute to the ICC ADR Rules, any party or parties wishing to commence ADR proceedings pursuant to the Rules shall send to ICC a written Request for ADR, which shall include:

(a) the names, addresses, telephone and facsimile numbers and e-mail addresses of the parties to the dispute and their authorized representatives, if any;

(b) a description of the dispute including, if possible, an assessment of its value;

(c) any joint designation by all of the parties of a Neutral or any agreement of all of the parties upon the qualifications of a Neutral to be appointed by ICC where no joint designation has been made;

(d) a copy of any written agreement under which the Request for ADR is made; and

(e) the registration fee of the ADR proceedings, as set out in the Appendix hereto.

2 Where the Request for ADR is not filed jointly by all of the parties, the party or parties filing the Request shall simultaneously send the Request to the other party or parties. Such Request may include any proposal regarding the qualifications of a Neutral or any proposal of one or more Neutrals to be designated by all of the parties. Thereafter, all of the parties may jointly designate a Neutral or may agree upon the qualifications of a Neutral to be appointed by ICC. In either case, the parties shall promptly notify ICC thereof.

3 ICC shall promptly acknowledge receipt of the Request for ADR in writing to the parties.

B Where there is no agreement to refer to the Rules
1 Where there is no agreement between the parties to refer their dispute to the ICC ADR Rules, any party or parties wishing to commence ADR proceedings pursuant to the Rules shall send to ICC a written Request for ADR, which shall include:

(a) the names, addresses, telephone and facsimile numbers and e-mail addresses of the parties to the dispute and their authorized representatives, if any;

(b) a description of the dispute including, if possible, an assessment of its value; and

(c) the registration fee of the ADR proceedings, as set out in the Appendix hereto.

The Request for ADR may also include any proposal regarding the qualifications of a Neutral or any proposal of one or more Neutrals to be designated by all of the parties.

2 ICC shall promptly inform the other party or parties in writing of the Request for ADR. Such party or parties shall be asked to inform ICC in writing, within 15 days of receipt of the Request for ADR, as to whether they agree or decline to participate in the ADR proceedings. In the former case, they may provide any proposal regarding the qualifications of a Neutral and may propose one or more Neutrals to be designated by the parties. Thereafter, all of the parties may jointly designate a Neutral or may agree upon the qualifications of a Neutral to be appointed by ICC. In either case, the parties shall promptly notify ICC thereof.

In the absence of any reply within such 15-day period, or in the case of a negative reply, the Request for ADR shall be deemed to have been declined and ADR proceedings shall not be commenced. ICC shall promptly so inform in writing the party or parties which filed the Request for ADR.

Article 3

Selection of the Neutral

A40–006 1 Where all of the parties have jointly designated a Neutral, ICC shall take note of that designation, and such person, upon notifying ICC of his or her agreement to serve, shall act as the Neutral in the ADR proceedings. Where a Neutral has not been designated by all of the parties, or where the designated Neutral does not agree to serve, ICC shall promptly appoint a Neutral, either through an ICC National Committee or otherwise, and notify the parties thereof. ICC shall make all reasonable efforts to appoint a Neutral having the qualifications, if any, which have been agreed upon by all of the parties.

2 Every prospective Neutral shall promptly provide ICC with a *curriculum vitae* and a statement of independence, both duly signed and dated. The prospective Neutral shall disclose to ICC in the statement of independence any facts or circumstances which might be of such nature as to call into question his or her independence in the eyes of the parties. ICC shall provide such information to the parties in writing.

3 If any party objects to the Neutral appointed by ICC and notifies ICC and the other party or parties thereof in writing, stating the reasons for such objection, within 15 days of receipt of notification of the appointment, ICC shall promptly appoint another Neutral.

4 Upon agreement of all of the parties, the parties may designate more than one Neutral or request ICC to appoint more than one Neutral, in accordance with the provisions of these Rules. In appropriate circumstances, ICC may propose the appointment of more than one Neutral to the parties.

Article 4

Fees and Costs

A40–007 1 The party or parties filing a Request for ADR shall include with the Request a non-refundable registration fee, as set out in the Appendix hereto. No Request for ADR shall be processed unless accompanied by the requisite payment.

2 Following the receipt of a Request for ADR, ICC shall request the parties to pay a deposit in an amount likely to cover the administrative expenses of ICC and the fees and expenses of the Neutral for the ADR proceedings, as set out in the Appendix hereto. The

ADR proceedings shall not go forward until payment of such deposit has been received by ICC.

3 In any case where ICC considers that the deposit is not likely to cover the total costs of the ADR proceedings, the amount of such deposit may be subject to readjustment. ICC may stay the ADR proceedings until the corresponding payments are made by the parties.

4 Upon termination of the ADR proceedings, ICC shall settle the total costs of the proceedings and shall, as the case may be, reimburse the parties for any excess payment or bill the parties for any balance required pursuant to these Rules.

5 All above deposits and costs shall be borne in equal shares by the parties, unless they agree otherwise in writing. However, any party shall be free to pay the unpaid balance of such deposits and costs should another party fail to pay its share.

6 A party's other expenditure shall remain the responsibility of that party.

Article 5

Conduct of the ADR Procedure

1 The Neutral and the parties shall promptly discuss, and seek to reach agreement upon, the settlement technique to be used, and shall discuss the specific ADR procedure to be followed.

2 In the absence of an agreement of the parties on the settlement technique to be used, mediation shall be used.

3 The Neutral shall conduct the procedure in such manner as the Neutral sees fit. In all cases the Neutral shall be guided by the principles of fairness and impartiality and by the wishes of the parties.

4 In the absence of an agreement of the parties, the Neutral shall determine the language or languages of the proceedings and the place of any meetings to be held.

5 Each party shall cooperate in good faith with the Neutral.

A40–008

Article 6

Termination of the ADR Proceedings

1 ADR proceedings which have been commenced pursuant to these Rules shall terminate upon the earlier of:

(a) the signing by the parties of a settlement agreement;

(b) the notification in writing to the Neutral by one or more parties, at any time after the discussion referred to in Article 5(1) has occurred, of a decision no longer to pursue the ADR proceedings;

(c) the completion of the procedure established pursuant to Article 5 and the notification in writing thereof by the Neutral to the parties;

(d) the notification in writing by the Neutral to the parties that the ADR proceedings will not, in the Neutral's opinion, resolve the dispute between the parties;

(e) the expiration of any time limit set for the ADR proceedings, if not extended by all of the parties, such expiration to be notified in writing by the Neutral to the parties;

A40–009

(f) the notification in writing by ICC to the parties and the Neutral, not less than 15 days after the due date for any payment by one or more parties pursuant to these Rules, stating that such payment has not been made; or

(g) the notification in writing by ICC to the parties stating, in the judgment of ICC, that there has been a failure to designate a Neutral or that it has not been reasonably possible to appoint a Neutral.

2 The Neutral, upon any termination of the ADR proceedings pursuant to Article 6(1), (a)–(e), shall promptly notify ICC of the termination of the ADR proceedings and shall provide ICC with a copy of any notification referred to in Article 6(1), (b)–(e). In all cases ICC shall confirm in writing the termination of the ADR proceedings to the parties and the Neutral, if a Neutral has already been designated or appointed.

Article 7

General Provisions

A40–010 **1** In the absence of any agreement of the parties to the contrary and unless prohibited by applicable law, the ADR proceedings, including their outcome, are private and confidential. Any settlement agreement between the parties shall similarly be kept confidential except that a party shall have the right to disclose it to the extent that such disclosure is required by applicable law or necessary for purposes of its implementation or enforcement.

2 Unless required to do so by applicable law and in the absence of any agreement of the parties to the contrary, a party shall not in any manner produce as evidence in any judicial, arbitration or similar proceedings:

(a) any documents, statements or communications which are submitted by another party or by the Neutral in the ADR proceedings, unless they can be obtained independently by the party seeking to produce them in the judicial, arbitration or similar proceedings;

(b) any views expressed or suggestions made by any party within the ADR proceedings with regard to the possible settlement of the dispute;

(c) any admissions made by another party within the ADR proceedings;

(d) any views or proposals put forward by the Neutral; or

(e) the fact that any party had indicated within the ADR proceedings that it was ready to accept a proposal for a settlement.

3 Unless all of the parties agree otherwise in writing, a Neutral shall not act nor shall have acted in any judicial, arbitration or similar proceedings relating to the dispute which is or was the subject of the ADR proceedings, whether as a judge, as an arbitrator, as an expert or as a representative or advisor of a party.

4 The Neutral, unless required by applicable law or unless all of the parties agree otherwise in writing, shall not give testimony in any judicial, arbitration or similar proceedings concerning any aspect of the ADR proceedings.

5 Neither the Neutral, nor ICC and its employees, nor the ICC National Committees shall be liable to any person for any act or omission in connection with the ADR proceedings.

APPENDIX

Schedule of ADR Costs

A The party or parties filing a Request for ADR shall include with the Request a non-refundable registration fee of US$ 1,500 to cover the costs of processing the Request for ADR. No Request for ADR shall be processed unless accompanied by the requisite payment.

B The administrative expenses of ICC for the ADR proceedings shall be fixed at ICC's discretion depending on the tasks carried out by ICC. Such administrative expenses shall not exceed the maximum sum of US$ 10,000.

C The fees of the Neutral shall be calculated on the basis of the time reasonably spent by the Neutral in the ADR proceedings, at an hourly rate fixed for such proceedings by ICC in consultation with the Neutral and the parties. Such hourly rate shall be reasonable in amount and shall be determined in light of the complexity of the dispute and any other relevant circumstances. The amount of reasonable expenses of the Neutral shall be fixed by ICC.

D Amounts paid to the Neutral do not include any possible value added taxes (VAT) or other taxes or charges and imposts applicable to the Neutral's fees. Parties are required to pay any such taxes or charges; however, the recovery of any such taxes or charges is a matter solely between the Neutral and the parties.

International Chamber of Commerce DOCDEX Rules[1]

FIRST REVISION, EFFECTIVE FROM MARCH 15, 2002

REPUBLISHED JULY 2002 WITH GRAMMATICAL AND TYPOGRAPHICAL CORRECTIONS

Article 1

Dispute Resolution Service

A41-001 **1.1** These Rules concern a service called Documentary Instruments Dispute Resolution Expertise (DOCDEX) which is available in connection with any dispute related to:

- a documentary credit incorporating the ICC Uniform Customs and Practice for Documentary Credits (UCP), and the application of the UCP and/or of the ICC Uniform Rules for Bank-to-Bank Reimbursement under Documentary Credits (URR),

- a collection incorporating the ICC Uniform Rules for Collections (URC), and the application of the URC,

- a demand guarantee incorporating the ICC Uniform Rules for Demand Guarantees (URDG), and the application of the URDG.

Its objective is to provide an independent, impartial and prompt expert decision (DOCDEX Decision) on how the dispute should be resolved on the basis of the terms and conditions of the documentary credit, the collection instruction, or the demand guarantee and the applicable ICC Rules, be it the UCP, the URR, the URC or the URDG (ICC Rules).

Any reference to DOCDEX will be deemed to apply to the latest version of the DOCDEX Rules and the applicable version of the ICC Rules, unless otherwise stipulated in the documentary credit, the collection instruction or the demand guarantee.

1.2 DOCDEX is made available by the International Chamber of Commerce (ICC) through its International Centre for Expertise (Centre) under the auspices of the ICC Commission on Banking Technique and Practice (Banking Commission).

1.3 When a dispute is submitted to the Centre in accordance with these rules, the Centre shall appoint three experts from a list of experts maintained by the Banking Commission. These three experts (Appointed Experts) shall make a decision which, after consultation with the Technical Adviser of the Banking Commission, shall be rendered by the Centre as a DOCDEX Decision in accordance with these Rules. The DOCDEX Decision is not intended to conform with any legal requirements of an arbitration award.

---

[1] ICC Rules for Documentary Instruments Dispute Resolution Expertise are published in their official English version by the International Chamber of Commerce ICC Publication No. 811. Copyright © 2002 International Chamber of Commerce. Available from: ICC International Centre for Expertise, 38 cours Albert 1er, 75008 Paris, France, and on the web site: www.iccdocdex.org. Users are reminded that under Article 1.4 of the DOCDEX Rules, unless otherwise agreed, a DOCDEX decision shall not be binding upon the parties. Should the parties wish to make the DOCDEX decision binding, they should therefore make provision for this, either in a joint request or otherwise.

INTERNATIONAL CHAMBER OF COMMERCE DOCDEX RULES

1.4 Unless otherwise agreed, a DOCDEX Decision shall not be binding upon the parties.

1.5 In the DOCDEX procedure the communication with the Centre shall be conducted exclusively in writing, *i.e.* by communication received in a form that provides a complete record thereof, via teletransmission or other expeditious means.

Article 2

Request

2.1 The Initiator shall apply for a DOCDEX Decision by submission of a request (Request). The Initiator may be one of the parties to the dispute applying individually, or more or all parties to the dispute submitting jointly a single Request. The Request, including all documents annexed thereto, shall be supplied to the Centre in Paris, France, in four copies.

2.2 A Request shall be concise and contain all necessary information clearly presented, in particular the following:

- **2.2.1** full name and address of the Initiator, clearly stating such Initiator's function(s) in connection with the documentary credit, the collection, or the demand guarantee, and

- **2.2.2** full name and address of any other party to the dispute (Respondent), clearly stating such Respondent's function(s) in connection with the documentary credit, the collection, or the demand guarantee, where the Request is not submitted jointly by all parties to the dispute, and

- **2.2.3** a statement of the Initiator formally requesting a DOCDEX Decision in accordance with the ICC DOCDEX Rules, ICC Publication No. 811, and

- **2.2.4** a summary of the dispute and of the Initiator's claims, clearly identifying all issues related to the documentary credit, the collection, or the demand guarantee and the applicable ICC Rules to be determined, and

- **2.2.5** copies of the documentary credit, the collection instruction, or the demand guarantee in dispute, all amendments thereto, and all documents deemed necessary to establish the relevant circumstances, and

- **2.2.6** a statement by the Initiator that a copy of such Request, including all documents annexed thereto, has been sent to each Respondent named in the Request.

2.3 The Request must be accompanied by the payment of the Standard Fee as per the Appendix hereto. No Request shall be processed unless accompanied by the requisite payment.

Article 3

Answer

3.1 The Respondent may submit an Answer to the Initiator's Request. The Respondent may be one or more of the parties to the dispute named in the Request as Respondent, each submitting an individual Answer or submitting jointly a single Answer. The Answer must be received by the Centre within the period stipulated in the Centre's Acknowledgement of the Request (see Article 5). The Answer, including all documents annexed thereto, shall be supplied to the Centre in Paris, France, in four copies.

3.2 An Answer shall be concise and contain all necessary information clearly presented, in particular the following:

    3.2.1 name and address of the Initiator, and

    3.2.2 date of the relevant Request, and

    3.2.3 a statement of the Respondent formally requesting a DOCDEX Decision in accordance with the ICC DOCDEX Rules, ICC Publication No. 811, and

    3.2.4 a summary of the Respondent's claims, clearly referring to all issues related to the documentary credit, the collection, or the demand guarantee and the applicable ICC Rules to be determined, and

    3.2.5 copies of all additional documents deemed necessary to establish the relevant circumstances, and

    3.2.6 a statement of the Respondent that a copy of such Answer, including all documents annexed thereto, has been sent in writing to the Initiator and to the other Respondent named in the Request.

3.3 If the Respondent does not provide a statement pursuant to Article 3.2.3, then the final DOCDEX Decision will not be made available to him.

Article 4

Supplements

A41–004   4.1 Request, Answers and Supplements shall be final as received.

4.2 The Centre may ask the Initiator and Respondent, by way of an Invitation, to submit specific supplementary information, including copies of documents, relevant to the DOCDEX Decision (Supplement).

4.3 Supplements must be received by the Centre in four copies within the period stipulated in the Invitation. The Supplement shall be concise and contain all necessary information clearly presented and include copies of relevant documents. It shall also contain:

    4.3.1 date and reference as stated in the Invitation, and

    4.3.2 name and address of the issuer of such Supplement, and

    4.3.3 a statement of the issuer of such Supplement that a copy of the Supplement, including all documents annexed thereto, has been sent to the Initiator or Respondent.

4.4 Supplements shall only be submitted to the Centre upon and in accordance with an Invitation issued by the Centre.

Article 5

Acknowledgements and Rejections

5.1 The Centre shall confirm the receipt of Requests, Answers and Supplements to the Initiator and Respondent (Acknowledgement).

5.2 The Centre will stipulate a reasonable period of time within which each Answer or Supplement must be received by the Centre. The stipulated time should not exceed 30 days after the date of the Acknowledgement of the receipt of a Request or 14 days after the date of an Invitation to submit a Supplement.

5.3 Any Answer or Supplement received by the Centre after expiry of the period of time specified in the relevant Acknowledgement or Invitation, or any communication not solicited by the Centre, shall be disregarded.

5.4 By advice to the Initiator and Respondent, the Centre may reject at any time, before or after its Acknowledgement, any Request, Answer or Supplement, in whole or part,

5.4.1 where the Centre or Appointed Experts deem any issue to be determined to be unrelated to the applicable ICC Rules, or

5.4.2 which in other respects, in particular regarding form and/or substance, does not fulfil the requirements of these Rules, or

5.4.3 in respect of which the Standard Fee has not been received by the Centre within 14 days after the date of the Request.

5.5 Periods of time specified in these Rules or in any Acknowledgement or Invitation referring to days shall be deemed to refer to consecutive calendar days and shall start to run on the day following the date of issuance stated in the relevant Acknowledgement or Invitation. If the last day of the relevant period of time is, or any fixed day falls on, a non-business day in Paris, France, then the period of time shall expire at the end of the first following business day in Paris.

Article 6

Appointment of Experts

6.1 The Banking Commission will maintain internal lists of experts having profound experience and knowledge of the applicable ICC Rules.

6.2 Upon receipt of a Request, the Centre shall appoint three independent experts from the list. Each Appointed Expert shall declare his independence of the parties indicated in the Request. The Centre shall designate one of the three Appointed Experts to act as their Chair.

6.3 An Appointed Expert shall at all times keep strictly confidential all information and documents related to any DOCDEX case.

6.4 Where an Appointed Expert deems that he is unable to carry out his functions, he shall immediately give notice of termination to the Centre. Where the Centre deems that an Appointed Expert is unable to carry out his functions, it shall immediately give notice of termination to such Appointed Expert. In either case, such Appointed Expert shall immediately return to the Centre the Request, Answer(s) and Supplement(s) received, including all documents annexed thereto, and the Centre shall inform the other Appointed Experts of such termination.

6.5 The Centre shall, without delay, replace an Appointed Expert whose appointment is prematurely terminated pursuant to Article 6.4 of these Rules and the Centre shall inform the other Appointed Experts accordingly.

Article 7

Appointed Experts' Procedure

A41–007 **7.1** The Centre shall submit to the Appointed Experts the Request, Answer(s) and Supplement(s) received in connection therewith.

7.2 The Appointed Experts shall render their decision impartially and exclusively on the basis of the Request, Answer(s) and Supplement(s) thereto, and the documentary credit and the UCP and/or URR, or the collection and the URC, or the demand guarantee and the URDG.

7.3 Where it is deemed necessary by the Appointed Experts, their Chair may ask the Centre to invite the Initiator and Respondent, pursuant to Article 4 of these Rules, to provide additional information and/or copies of documents.

7.4 Within 30 days after they have received all information and documents deemed by them to be necessary and appropriate to the issues to be determined, and provided that the Additional Fee as mentioned in Article 10.1 is paid, the Appointed Experts shall draft a decision and their Chair shall submit the decision to the Centre.

7.5 Neither the Initiator nor the Respondent shall

— seek an oral hearing in front of the Appointed Experts,

— request ICC to reveal the name of any Appointed Expert,

— seek to have an Appointed Expert or officer of the Banking Commission called as witness, expert or in any similar function to an arbitral tribunal or a court of law hearing the dispute in connection with which such Appointed Expert or officer of the Banking Commission participated by rendering a DOCDEX Decision.

Article 8

DOCDEX Decision

A41–008 **8.1** Upon receipt of the decision of the Appointed Experts, the Centre shall consult with the Technical Adviser of the Banking Commission or his nominated delegate, to ascertain that the DOCDEX Decision will be in line with the applicable ICC Rules and their interpretation by the Banking Commission. Amendments suggested by the Technical Adviser (or his delegate) shall be subject to the consent of the majority of the Appointed Experts.

8.2 Subject to Article 10.2 of these Rules, the Centre will issue and make available the DOCDEX Decision without delay to

8.2.1 the Initiator and

8.2.2 the Respondent who has requested, pursuant to Article 3.2.3, a DOCDEX

International Chamber of Commerce DOCDEX Rules

Decision in accordance with the ICC DOCDEX Rules, ICC Publication No. 811.

8.3 The DOCDEX Decision shall be issued by the Centre in the English language, unless Appointed Experts decide otherwise, and shall contain, *inter alia*, the following:

8.3.1 names of the Initiator and Respondent, and

8.3.2 summary of the representations relevant to the issues determined, and

8.3.3 determination of the issues and the decisions taken with succinctly stated reasons therefor, and

8.3.4 date of issuance and signature for and on behalf of the Centre.

8.4 The DOCDEX Decision shall be deemed to be made at Paris, France, and on the date of its issuance by the Centre.

Article 9

Deposit and publication of the DOCDEX Decision

9.1 An original of each DOCDEX Decision shall be deposited with the Centre and shall be kept there for 10 years. **A41–009**
9.2 The ICC may publish any DOCDEX Decision, provided always the identities of the parties to the dispute are not disclosed.

Article 10

Costs of DOCDEX

10.1 The costs of the DOCDEX service shall be the Standard Fee set out in the Appendix. The Standard Fee shall not be recoverable. In exceptional circumstances, an Additional Fee may be payable which shall be fixed by the Centre at its discretion, taking into account the complexity of the issue and subject to the ceiling set out in the Appendix under 'Additional Fee'. Such Additional Fee shall be invoiced to the Initiator within a reasonable time, at the latest within 45 days after the date of the Acknowledgement of the Request. The Centre will fix a time limit for the payment of the Additional Fee. The Centre may stay the procedure at any time, and instruct the Appointed Experts to suspend their work on the case, until the Additional Fee is paid by the Initiator. No Additional Fee will be charged where the amount of the letter of credit, the collection, or the demand guarantee in dispute does not exceed the minimum amount stated in the Appendix. **A41–010**
10.2 The DOCDEX Decision shall not be issued until the Centre has received the Additional Fee, if invoiced.

Article 11

General

A41–011 **11.1.** In all matters not expressly provided for in these Rules, the Centre, experts, Appointed Experts, officers, officials and employees of ICC shall adhere to strict confidentiality and shall act in the spirit of these Rules.

11.2 Appointed Experts, officers, officials and employees of ICC assume no liability or responsibility for the consequences arising out of delay and/or loss in transit of any message(s), letter(s) or document(s), or for delay, mutilation or other error(s) arising in the transmission of any telecommunication, or for errors in translation and/or interpretation of technical terms.

11.3 Appointed Experts, officers, officials and employees of ICC assume no liability or responsibility for the discharge or purported discharge of their functions in connection with any DOCDEX Decision, unless the act or omission is shown not to have been in good faith.

APPENDIX TO THE ICC RULES FOR DOCUMENTARY INSTRUMENTS DISPUTE RESOLUTION EXPERTISE

1. Standard Fee

A41–012 The Standard Fee, which includes administrative expenses and expert fees, is US$ 5000.

2. Additional Fee

A41–013 Pursuant to Article 10.1 of these Rules the Centre may, if the amount of the letter of credit, of the collection, or of the demand guarantee exceeds US$ 500 000, charge an Additional Fee of up to 100% of the Standard Fee.

3. Payment

A41–014 Any payment made towards such fees shall be made in United States dollars to the International Chamber of Commerce in Paris, clearly marked with the reference of DOCDEX

☐ by bank transfer to
UBS SA
35 rue des Noirettes
P.O. Box 2600
CH – 1211 Geneva 2
Switzerland
Account No.: 240-224534.61R
Swift code: UBSWCHZH12A
or
☐ by cheque payable to the International Chamber of Commerce,
or
☐ by Visa card stating
Expiry date
Visa card number
Name on card
Signature
Date

4. Transmission

Any such payment shall be accompanied by an advice in writing to: **A41–015**

International Chamber of Commerce
International Centre for Expertise
38 cours Albert 1er
F – 75008 Paris
France
Fax: +33 1 49 53 29 29
E-mail: docdex@iccwbo.org

stating the following data:
Name:
Business title:
Company:
Address:
Code/postal code:
Date of Request:

5. General

This Appendix is subject to change without notice. Please enquire with the International Chamber of Commerce as to the applicable version of this Appendix. **A41–016**

International Chamber of Commerce Rules for Expertise[1]

(in force as from 1 January 2003)

FOREWORD

A42-001 Experts with specialized knowledge in technical, legal, financial and other fields may be useful in a variety of situations. The ICC International Centre for Expertise responds to this need by offering three distinct services: the proposal of experts, the appointment of experts, and the administration of expertise proceedings.

The selection of competent experts, especially in an international context, is a delicate task. The Centre's privileged position at the heart of a worldwide business organization makes it particularly well-placed to fulfil this role. The Centre has proposed and appointed experts to give opinions on a wide range of subjects from accounting and contractual matters to the assessment of industrial processes and equipment.

Business needs and expertise have evolved since the ICC International Centre for Expertise was created in 1976. This makes it necessary periodically to revise the ICC Rules for Expertise under which the Centre operates. The present Rules, in force as from 1 January 2003, replace the previous revision of 1993 and introduce greater clarity and flexibility in the conduct of proceedings. Each of the Centre's three services is clearly distinguished and systematically described. Two appendices deal respectively with the Standing Committee of the International Centre for Expertise and costs.

ICC expertise is part of the wide-ranging services offered by the world business organization to facilitate international commercial relations. Expertise may be used in a variety of contexts: to remove uncertainty in business operations, to assist the amicable settlement of disputes, or in connection with litigation or arbitration. It is valuable both as a service in its own right and as a complement to other dispute resolution services. In this regard, a notable feature of the new Rules is the waiver of the non-refundable charge for the proposal of an expert when requested by an arbitral tribunal acting under the ICC Rules of Arbitration.

December 2002

SECTION I

GENERAL PROVISIONS

Article 1

The International Centre for Expertise

A42-002 **1.** The International Centre for Expertise (the "Centre") is a service centre of the International Chamber of Commerce (ICC). The Centre can perform one or more of the following functions in connection with domestic or international business matters:

---

[1] Rules for Expertise of the International Chamber of Commerce. Published in their official English version by the International Chamber of Commerce (ICC). ICC Publication No. 649 — ISBN 92-842-1318-5. Copyright © 2002 International Chamber of Commerce. Available from ICC International Centre for Expertise, 38 cours Albert 1er, 75008 Paris, France and on the website www.iccexpertise.org.

International Chamber of Commerce Rules for Expertise

A) Proposal of Experts

Upon the request of any physical or legal person(s) or any court or tribunal (a "Person"), the Centre can provide the name of one or more experts in a particular field of activity, pursuant to Section II of these Rules. The Centre's role is limited to proposing the name of one or more experts. The Person requesting a proposal may then contact directly the proposed expert(s), and, as the case may be, agree with such expert(s) on the scope of the appropriate mission and fees. There is no obligation to make use of the services of an expert proposed by the Centre. The proposal of an expert may be useful in many different contexts. A person may require an expert in connection with its ongoing business activities or in connection with contractual relations. A party to an arbitration may wish to obtain the name of a potential expert witness. A court or arbitral tribunal which has decided to appoint an expert may seek a proposal from the Centre.

B) Appointment of Experts

The Centre will appoint an expert, pursuant to Section III of these Rules, in situations where the parties have agreed to the appointment of an Expert and have agreed to use the Centre as the appointing authority or where the Centre is otherwise satisfied that there is a sufficient basis for appointing an expert. In such cases the appointment by the Centre shall be binding on the parties. The Centre's role is limited to appointing the expert in question.

C) Administration of Expertise Proceedings

When the parties have agreed upon the administration of expertise proceedings by the Centre or when the Centre is otherwise satisfied that there is a sufficient basis for administering expertise proceedings, the Centre will administer the proceedings pursuant to Section IV of these Rules.

2. The Centre consists of a Standing Committee and a Secretariat which is provided by ICC. The statutes of the Standing Committee are set forth in Appendix I.

Section II

Proposal of Experts

Article 2

Recourse to the Centre

1. Any Person may ask the Centre to propose one or more experts by submitting a Request for Proposal of Experts (the "Request for Proposal") to the Centre at the ICC International Secretariat in Paris.

2. The Request for Proposal shall include:

(a) the name, address, telephone and facsimile numbers and e-mail address of each Person filing the Request for Proposal;

A42–003

(b) a statement that the requesting Person is seeking the proposal of an Expert by the Centre;

(c) a description of the field of activity of the Expert to be proposed along with any desired qualifications of the Expert, including but not limited to education, language skills and professional experience, and any undesired attributes of the Expert;

(d) a description of any matters which would disqualify a potential Expert; and

(e) a description of the work to be carried out by the Expert and the desired time frame for completing such work.

3. Unless requested to do so by the person seeking the proposal of an expert, the Centre will not notify any other person of the filing of a Request for Proposal.

Article 3

The Expert

A42–004 **1.** Any proposal of an Expert by the Centre shall be made by the Centre either through an ICC National Committee or otherwise. The Centre's role normally ends on notification of the proposal unless the the Centre is asked to appoint the proposed Expert and/or administer the procedure pursuant to Sections III and IV.

2. Prior to the proposal of an Expert, the Centre shall consider in particular the prospective Expert's qualifications relevant to the circumstances of the case, and the Expert's availability, place of residence, and language skills.

3. Before a proposal, a prospective Expert shall sign a statement of independence and disclose in writing to the Centre any facts or circumstances which might be of such a nature as to call into question the Expert's independence in the eyes of the Person filing the Request for Proposal. The Centre shall provide such information in writing to such Person and shall fix a time limit for any comments from such Person.

Article 4

Costs for the Proposal of an Expert

A42–005 **1.** Each Request for Proposal must be accompanied by the non-refundable amount specified in Article 1 of Appendix II. This amount represents the total cost for the proposal of one Expert by the Centre. No Request for Proposal shall be processed unless accompanied by the requisite payment.

2. When the Centre is requested to propose more than one Expert, the non-refundable amount accompanying the Request for Proposal and to be paid by the requesting Person is the amount specified in the preceding paragraph multiplied by the number of Experts requested.

Section III

Appointment of Experts

Article 5

Recourse to the Centre

1. Any request for the appointment of an expert (the "Request for Appointment") shall be submitted to the Centre at the ICC International Secretariat in Paris. Any such request shall be processed by the Centre only when it is based upon an agreement between the parties for the appointment of an expert by the Centre or when the Centre is otherwise satisfied that there is a sufficient basis for appointing an expert.

2. The date on which the Request for Appointment is received by the Centre shall, for all purposes, be deemed to be the date of the commencement of the agreed or required expertise.

3. The Request for Appointment shall include:

   (a) the name, address, telephone and facsimile numbers and e-mail address of each Person filing the Request for Appointment and of any other persons involved in the expertise;

   (b) a statement that the requesting Person is seeking the appointment of an Expert by the Centre;

   (c) a description of the field of activity of the Expert to be appointed along with any desired qualifications of the Expert, including but not limited to education, language skills and professional experience, and any undesired attributes of the Expert;

   (d) a description of any matters which would disqualify a potential Expert;

   (e) a description of the work to be carried out by the Expert and the desired time frame for completing such work; and

   (f) a copy of any agreement for the appointment of an expert by the Centre and/or of any other elements which form the basis for the Request for Appointment.

4. The Centre shall promptly inform the other party or parties in writing of the Request for Appointment once the Centre has sufficient copies of the Request and has received the non-refundable amount required under Article 8.

5. When the Request for Appointment is not made jointly by all of the parties, and/or when the parties do not agree on the qualifications of the Expert, and/or when the parties do not agree on the Expert's work, the Centre shall send a copy of the Request for Appointment to the other party or parties who may make observations within a time limit fixed by the Centre.

Observations received shall be communicated by the Centre to the other party or parties for comments within a time limit fixed by the Centre.

6. The Centre shall proceed with the Request for Appointment as it sees fit and will inform the parties of how it will proceed.

Article 6

Written Notifications or Communications

A42–007 1. All written communications submitted to the Centre by any party to the Expertise, as well as all documents annexed thereto, shall be supplied in a number of copies sufficient to provide one copy for the Centre, one copy for each party and one copy for each Expert.

2. All notifications or communications from the Centre shall be made to the last address of the party or its representative for whom the same are intended, as notified by the party in question or by the other party. Such notification may be made by delivery against receipt, registered post, courier, facsimile transmission, telex, telegram or any other means of telecommunication that provides a record of the sending thereof.

3. A notification or communication shall be deemed to have been made on the day it was received by the party itself or by its representative, or would have been received if made in accordance with the preceding paragraph.

Article 7

The Expert

A42–008 1. Any appointment of an Expert by the Centre shall be made by the Centre either through an ICC National Committee or otherwise.

2. Prior to the appointment of an Expert, the Centre shall consider in particular the prospective Expert's qualifications relevant to the circumstances of the case, the Expert's availability, place of residence and relevant language skills, and any observations, comments or requests made by the parties. In appointing the Expert the Centre shall apply any agreement of the parties related to the appointment.

3. Every Expert must be independent of the parties involved in the expertise proceedings, unless otherwise agreed in writing by such parties.

4. Before an appointment, a prospective Expert shall sign a statement of independence and disclose in writing to the Centre any facts or circumstances which might be of such a nature as to call into question the Expert's independence in the eyes of the parties. The Centre shall provide such information to the parties in writing and fix a time limit for any comments from them.

Article 8

Costs for the Appointment of an Expert

A42–009 1. Each Request for Appointment must be accompanied by the non-refundable amount specified in Article 2 of Appendix II. This amount represents the total cost for the appointment of one Expert by the Centre. No Request for Appointment shall be processed unless accompanied by the requisite payment.

2. When the Centre is requested to appoint more than one Expert, the non-refundable amount accompanying the Request for Appointment and to be paid by the requesting Person is the amount specified in the preceding paragraph multiplied by the number of Experts requested.

3. When the Centre is requested to appoint an Expert who has already been proposed by the Centre in connection with the same matter, the Centre shall charge half of the non-refundable amount specified in Article 2 of Appendix II in addition to the already paid amount specified in Article 1 of Appendix II.

Section IV

Administration of Expertise Proceedings

Article 9

Recourse to the Centre

1. Any request for the administration of expertise proceedings (the "Request for Administration") shall be submitted to the Centre at the ICC International Secretariat in Paris. Any such request shall be processed by the Centre only when it is based upon an agreement for the administration of expertise proceedings by the Centre or when the Centre is otherwise satisfied that there is a sufficient basis for administering expertise proceedings.

2. The date on which the Request for Administration is received by the Centre shall, for all purposes, be deemed to be the date of the commencement of the expertise proceedings.

3. The Request for Administration shall include:

(a) the name, address, telephone and facsimile numbers and e-mail address of each Person filing the Request for Administration and of any other persons involved in the expertise proceedings;

(b) a statement that the requesting Person is seeking the administration of expertise proceedings by the Centre;

(c) a description of the field of activity of the Expert along with any desired qualifications of the Expert, including but not limited to education, language skills and professional experience, and any undesired attributes of the Expert;

(d) a description of any matters which would disqualify a potential Expert;

(e) a description of the work to be carried out by the Expert and the desired time frame for completing such work; and

(f) a copy of any agreement for the administration of expertise proceedings by the Centre and/or of any other elements which form the basis for the Request for Administration.

4. The Centre shall promptly inform the other party or parties in writing of the Request for Administration once the Centre has sufficient copies of the Request for Administration and has received the non-refundable amount required under Article 14.

5. The administration of the expertise proceedings by the Centre shall consist *inter alia* of:

(a) coordination between the parties and the Expert;

(b) initiating the appropriate steps to encourage the expeditious completion of the expertise proceedings;

(c) supervising the financial aspects of the proceedings;

(d) appointment of an expert using the procedure referred to in Section III or confirmation of an expert agreed to by all of the parties;

(e) review of the form of the Expert's report;

(f) notification of the Expert's final report to the parties; and

(g) notification of the termination of the expertise proceedings.

Article 10

Written Notifications or Communications

A42–011   **1.** All written communications submitted to the Centre by any party to the expertise proceedings, as well as all documents annexed thereto, shall be supplied in a number of copies sufficient to provide one copy for the Centre, one copy for each party and one copy for each Expert.

2. All notifications or communications from the Centre and the Expert shall be made to the last address of the party or its representative for whom the same are intended, as notified either by the party in question or by the other party. Such notification may be made by delivery against receipt, registered post, courier, facsimile transmission, telex, telegram or any other means of telecommunication that provides a record of the sending thereof.

3. A notification or communication shall be deemed to have been made on the day it was received by the party itself or by its representative, or would have been received if made in accordance with the preceding paragraph.

Article 11

Independence of the Expert — Replacement of the Expert

A42–012   **1.** Every Expert must remain independent of the parties involved in the expertise proceeding, unless otherwise agreed in writing by such parties.

2. An Expert appointed by the Centre, who has died or resigned or is unable to carry out the Expert's functions, shall be replaced.

3. An Expert appointed by the Centre shall be replaced upon the written request of all of the parties.

4. If any party objects that the Expert does not have the necessary qualifications or is not fulfilling the Expert's functions in accordance with the Rules or in a timely fashion, the Centre may replace the Expert after having considered the observations of the Expert and the other party or parties.

5. When an Expert is to be replaced, the Centre has discretion to decide whether or not to follow the original appointing process.

Article 12

The Expert's Mission

1. The Expert, after having consulted the parties, shall set out the Expert's Mission in a written document. That document shall not be inconsistent with anything in these Rules and shall be communicated to the parties and to the Centre. Such document shall include:

   (a) the names, addresses, telephone and facsimile numbers and e-mail addresses of the parties;

   (b) a list of issues to be treated in the Expert's Report;

   (c) the name(s), address(es), telephone and facsimile numbers and e-mail addresses of the Expert or Experts;

   (d) the procedure to be followed by the Expert and the place where the expertise should be conducted; and

   (e) a statement indicating the language in which the proceedings will be conducted.

Modifications to the Expert's Mission may be made by the Expert, in writing, only after full consultation with the parties. Any such written modifications shall be communicated to the parties and to the Centre.

2. Upon preparing the document setting out the Expert's Mission or as soon as possible thereafter, the Expert, after having consulted the parties, shall prepare a provisional timetable for the conduct of the expertise proceedings. The timetable shall be communicated to the parties and to the Centre. Any subsequent modifications of the provisional timetable shall be promptly communicated to the parties and to the Centre.

3. The Expert's main task is to make findings in a written Expert's Report within the limits set by the Expert's Mission after giving the parties the opportunity to be heard and/or to make written submissions. Unless otherwise agreed by all of the parties, the findings of the Expert shall not be binding upon the parties.

4. Unless otherwise agreed by the parties, the Expert's Report shall be admissible in any judicial or arbitral proceeding in which all of the parties thereto were parties to the expertise proceedings in which such Report was prepared.

5. Any information given to the Expert by the Centre or any party during the course of the expertise shall be used by the Expert only for the purposes of the expertise and shall be treated by the Expert as confidential.

6. The Expert's Report shall be submitted in draft form to the Centre before it is signed. The Centre may lay down modifications only as to the form of the Report. No Report shall be communicated to the parties by the Expert. No Report shall be signed by the Expert prior to the Centre's approval of such Report.

7. The Centre may waive the requirements laid down in Article 12(6) if expressly requested to do so in writing by all the parties and if the Centre considers that such a waiver is appropriate under the circumstances of the case.

8. The Expert's Report, after it is signed by the Expert, shall be sent to the Centre in as many copies as there are parties plus one for the Centre. Thereafter, the Centre shall

notify the Expert's Report to the party or parties and declare in writing that the expertise proceedings have been terminated.

Article 13

Duties and Responsibilities of the Parties

A42–014 1. The non-participation of a party in the expertise proceedings does not deprive the Expert of the power to make findings and render the Expert's Report, provided that such party has been given the opportunity to participate.

2. In agreeing to the application of the Rules the parties undertake to provide the Expert with all facilities in order to implement the Expert's Mission and, in particular, to make available all documents the Expert may consider necessary and also to grant the Expert free access to any place where the Expert may be required to go for the proper completion of the Expert's Mission.

Article 14

Costs for the Administration of Expertise Proceedings

A42–015 1. Each Request for Administration must be accompanied by the non-refundable amount specified in Article 3 of Appendix II. This amount will be credited to the requesting party's or parties' portion of the deposit pursuant to Article 14(3).

2. When the Centre is requested to administer an expertise proceeding where the Expert has already been proposed or appointed by the Centre in connection with the same matter, the non-refundable amount specified in Article 3 of Appendix II shall not be paid in addition to the non-refundable amounts paid for the proposal or the appointment of an Expert and specified in Articles 1 and 2 of Appendix II.

3. Following the receipt of a Request for Administration the Centre shall request the parties to pay a deposit in an amount likely to cover the administrative costs of the Centre and the fees and expenses of the Expert for the expertise proceedings, as set out in Article 3, paragraphs (2) and (3), of Appendix II. The expertise proceedings shall not go forward until payment of such deposit has been received by the Centre.

4. In any case where the Centre considers that the deposit is not likely to cover the total costs of the expertise proceedings, the amount of such deposit may be subject to readjustment. When the request for the corresponding payments has not been complied with, the Centre may suspend the expertise proceedings and set a time limit, on the expiry of which the expertise proceedings may be considered withdrawn.

5. Upon termination of administered expertise proceedings, the Centre shall settle the total costs of the proceedings and shall, as the case may be, reimburse the party or parties for any excess payment or bill the party or parties for any balance required pursuant to these Rules. The balance, if any, shall be payable before the notification of the final Expert's Report to the party or parties.

6. All above deposits and costs shall be borne in equal shares by the parties, unless they agree otherwise in writing. However, any party shall be free to pay the unpaid balance of such deposits and costs should the other party or parties fail to pay its or their share.

SECTION V

MISCELLANEOUS

Article 15

Waiver

A party which proceeds with the expertise proccedings without raising an objection to a failure to comply with any provision of these Rules, any direction given by the Centre or by the Expert, or any requirement of the Expert's Mission, or any requirement relating to the appointment of an Expert or to the conduct of the expertise proceedings, shall be deemed to have waived its right to object. **A42–016**

Article 16

Exclusion of Liability

Neither the Experts, nor the Centre, nor ICC and its employees, nor the ICC National Committees shall be liable to any person for any act or omission in connection with the expertise procedure. **A42–017**

Article 17

General Rule

In all matters not expressly provided for in these Rules, the Centre and the Experts shall act in the spirit of these Rules. **A42–018**

APPENDIX I

STATUTES OF THE STANDING COMMITTEE OF THE ICC INTERNATIONAL CENTRE FOR EXPERTISE

Article 1

Composition of the Standing Committee

The Standing Committee is composed of a maximum of eleven members (a Chairman, two Vice-Chairmen and up to eight members) appointed by ICC for a three-year renewable term. **A42–019**

Article 2

Meetings

A42–020   A meeting of the Standing Committee shall be convened by its Chairman whenever necessary.

Article 3

Function and Duties of the Standing Committee

A42–021   1. The function of the Standing Committee is to assist the Secretariat in reviewing the qualifications of the Experts to be proposed and/or appointed by the ICC International Centre for Expertise. The Standing Committee shall advise the Secretariat concerning all aspects of expertise to help to assure the quality of the Centre.

2. In the absence of the Chairman, or otherwise at the Chairman's request, one of the two Vice-Chairmen shall be appointed by the Chairman or by the Secretariat in the absence of an appointment by the Chairman to fulfil the tasks of the Chairman, including taking decisions pursuant to these Statutes.

3. The Secretariat shall inform the members of the Standing Committee about all Requests for Proposal or Requests for Appointment and ask the members for their advice.

The Chairman of the Standing Committee shall make the final decision on the proposal or appointment of the Expert.

4. In the case of a Request for Administration pursuant to Section IV:

(A) the Standing Committee shall be informed of the death or resignation of an Expert as well as of any objection by the party or parties or the Centre concerning an Expert, or of any other matter requiring the replacement of the Expert. It shall advise the Secretariat whether the objection of the party or parties pursuant to Article 11(3) or of the Centre pursuant to Article 11(4) of the Rules for Expertise is justified and make recommendations to the Chairman. The Chairman shall decide on the justification of any objection and/or on the manner in which the replacement will be made;

(B) the Chairman shall fix the expert or experts' fees and expenses in accordance with Article 3(3) of Appendix II to the Rules for Expertise; and

(C) upon the premature termination of the Expertise the Chairman shall fix the costs of the expertise pursuant to Article 3(4) of Appendix II to the Rules for Expertise.

Article 4

Confidentiality

A42–022   The work of the Standing Committee and the Secretariat is of a confidential nature which must be respected by everyone who participates in that work in whatever capacity.

Appendix II

Schedule of Expertise Costs

Article 1

Costs for Proposal

The non-refundable amount for the proposal of an Expert pursuant to the Rules for Expertise is US$ 2,500, provided, however, that the proposal of an Expert made at the request of an arbitral tribunal acting pursuant to the ICC Rules of Arbitration shall be free of charge. The non-refundable amount is payable by the requesting Person(s). No Request shall be processed unless accompanied by the requisite payment.

Article 2

Costs for Appointment

The non-refundable amount for the appointment of an Expert pursuant to the Rules for Expertise is US$ 2,500. This amount is payable by the requesting Person(s).

Article 3

Costs for Administration

1. The non-refundable amount for sole administration of the expertise proceedings pursuant to the Rules for Expertise is US$ 2,500. This amount is payable by the requesting Person(s). No Request shall be processed unless accompanied by the requisite payment.

2. The administrative expenses of the Centre for the Expertise proceedings shall be fixed at the Centre's discretion depending on the tasks carried out by the Centre. They shall not exceed 15% of the total Expert's fees and not be less than US$ 2,500.

3. The fees of the Expert shall be calculated on the basis of the time reasonably spent by the Expert in the expertise proceedings, at a daily rate fixed for such proceedings by the Centre in consultation with the Expert and the party or parties. Such daily rate shall be reasonable in amount and shall be determined in light of the complexity of the dispute and any other relevant circumstances. The amount of reasonable expenses of the Expert shall be fixed by the Centre.

4. If an expertise terminates before the notification of the final report, the Centre shall fix the costs of the expertise at its discretion, taking into account the stage attained by the expertise proceedings and any other relevant circumstances.

5. Amounts paid to the Expert do not include any possible value-added taxes (VAT) or other taxes or charges and imposts applicable to the Expert's fees. Parties have a duty to pay any such taxes or charges; however, the recovery of any such charges or taxes is a matter solely between the Expert and the party or parties.

The Institution of Civil Engineers' Arbitration Procedure (1997)[1]

PART A. OBJECTIVES, REFERENCE AND APPOINTMENT

Rule 1. Aims and objectives

A43–001   1.1 The object of arbitration is to obtain the fair resolution of disputes by an impartial arbitrator without unnecessary delay or expense. The Parties and the Arbitrator shall do all things necessary to achieve this object. The Arbitrator shall give each party a reasonable opportunity of putting its case and dealing with that of its opponent. This Procedure shall be interpreted and the proceedings shall be conducted in a manner most conducive to achieving these objectives.

1.2 Where the Act applies the Rules of this Procedure are institutional rules for the purposes of s4(3).

1.3 Where the Act does not apply, no alterations shall be made to this Procedure without the consent of the Arbitrator, except where there are express modifications in the Contract, or in the arbitration agreement.

Rule 2. Commencement of arbitration

A43–002   2.1 Unless otherwise provided in the Contract a dispute or difference shall be deemed to arise when a claim or assertion made by one party is rejected by the other party and that rejection is not accepted, or no response is received within a period of 28 days. Subject only to the due observance of any condition precedent in the Contract or the arbitration agreement either party may then invoke arbitration by serving a Notice to Refer on the other party.

2.2 The date upon which the Notice to Refer is served shall be regarded as the date upon which the arbitral proceedings are commenced.

2.3 The Notice to Refer shall list the matters which the Party serving the Notice to Refer wishes to be referred to arbitration. Nothing stated in the Notice shall restrict that party as to the manner in which it subsequently presents its case.

Rule 3. Appointment of sole arbitrator by agreement

A43–003   3.1 At the same time as or after serving the Notice to Refer either party may serve upon the other a Notice to Concur in the appointment of an Arbitrator listing therein the names addresses of one or more persons it proposes as Arbitrator.

3.2 Within 14 days thereafter the other party shall:

---

[1] This Procedure (approved February 1997) has been prepared by The Institution of Civil Engineers principally for use with the ICE family of Conditions of Contract and the NEC family of Documents in England and Wales for arbitrations conducted under the Arbitration Act 1996. It may be suitable for use with other contracts and in other jurisdictions. For the purposes of the ICE family of Conditions of Contract this Procedure shall be deemed to be an amendment or modification to the ICE Procedure (1983).

Copies of the Arbitration Procedure are available, priced £10, from Thomas Telford Services Ltd, 1 Heron Quay, London E14 4JD Tel. 0171 665 2464; Fax. 0171 537 3631.

This document is reproduced with the kind permission of the Institution of Civil Engineers.

(a) agree in writing to the appointment of one of the persons listed in the Notice to Concur or

(b) propose in like manner an alternative person or persons.

3.3 Once agreement has been reached either party may write to the person so selected inviting him to accept the appointment enclosing a copy of the Notice to Refer and documentary evidence of the other party's agreement to his appointment.

3.4 If the person so invited accepts the appointment he shall notify both parties simultaneously in writing. The date of posting or service as the case may be of this notification shall be deemed to be the date on which the Arbitrator's appointment is completed.

Rule 4. Appointment of sole arbitrator by the President

4.1 If within one calendar month from the service of the Notice to Concur the parties fail to appoint an Arbitrator in accordance with Rule 3 either party may apply to the President to appoint an Arbitrator. Alternatively the parties may agree to apply to the President without a Notice to Concur.

4.2 The application shall be in writing and shall include:

(a) a copy of the Notice to Refer;

(b) a copy of the Notice to Concur or the agreement to dispense with same;

(c) the names and addresses of all parties to the arbitration;

(d) a brief statement of the nature and circumstances of the dispute;

(e) a copy of the arbitration clause in the Contract or of the arbitration agreement;

(f) the appropriate fee;

(g) confirmation that any conditions precedent to arbitration contained in the Contract or arbitration agreement have been complied with and

(h) any other relevant document.

A copy of the application, but not supporting documentation, shall be sent at the same time to the other party.

4.3 The President will within 28 days of receiving the application or within such further time as may be necessary make the appointment and the Arbitrator's appointment shall thereby be completed. The Institution will notify both parties and the Arbitrator in writing as soon as possible thereafter.

Provided always that no such appointment shall be invalidated merely because the time limits set out herein have not been observed.

Rule 5. Notice of further disputes or differences

5.1 At any time before the Arbitrator's appointment is completed either party may put forward further disputes or differences to be referred to him. This shall be done by serving upon the other party an additional Notice to Refer in accordance with Rule 2.

5.2 Once his appointment is completed the Arbitrator shall have jurisdiction over any issue connected with and necessary to the determination of any dispute or difference already referred to him whether or not any condition precedent to referring the matter to arbitration had been complied with.

Part B. Arrangements for the Arbitration

Rule 6. The preliminary meeting

6.1 As soon as possible after his appointment the Arbitrator may summon the parties to a preliminary meeting for the purpose of giving such directions about the procedure to be adopted in the arbitration as he considers necessary and to deal with the matters referred to in Rule 6.4.

6.2 The Arbitrator may require the parties to submit to him short statements expressing their perceptions of the disputes or differences. Such statements shall give sufficient detail of the nature of the issues to enable the Arbitrator and the parties to discuss procedures appropriate for their settlement at the preliminary meeting.

6.3 The parties shall designate the seat of the arbitration. In default of such designation it shall be designated by the Arbitrator.

6.4 The parties and the Arbitrator shall consider whether and to what extent:

(a) Part F (Short Procedure) or Part G (Special Procedure for Experts) of these Rules shall apply;

(b) the arbitration should proceed on documents only;

(c) progress may be facilitated and costs saved by determining some of the issues in advance of the main hearing;

(d) evidence of Experts may be necessary, or desirable;

(e) disclosure of documents should be ordered;

(f) there should be a limit put on recoverable costs;

(g) where the Act applies to the Arbitration, the parties should enter into an agreement (if they have not already done so) excluding the right to appeal in accordance with the Act;

and in general shall consider such other steps as may achieve the speedy and cost effective resolution of the disputes.

Part C. Powers of the Arbitrator

Rule 7. Power to rule on his own jurisdiction

7.1 The Arbitrator shall have power to rule on his own substantive jurisdiction as to:

(a) whether there is a valid arbitration agreement;

(b) whether he is properly appointed;

(c) whether there is a dispute or difference capable of being referred to arbitration, and whether it has been validly referred;

(d) whether and to what extent the Procedure applies to the conduct of the arbitration;

(e) what matters have been submitted to him in accordance with the contract or the arbitration agreement and this Procedure.

7.2 Should any party refer a ruling under Rule 7.1 to the court the Arbitrator shall direct whether or not the arbitral proceedings shall continue pending a decision by the court.

Procedural and evidential matters

7.3 The Arbitrator shall have power to decide all procedural and evidential matters **A43–008** including, but not limited to:

(a) whether any and if so what form of written statements of claim and defence are to be used, when these should be supplied and the extent to which such statements can be later amended;

(b) whether any and if so which documents or classes of document should be disclosed between and produced by the parties and at what stage;

(c) whether any and if so what questions should be put to and answered by the respective parties in advance of a hearing and when and in what form this should be done;

(d) whether to apply the strict rules of evidence (or any other rules) as to the admissibility, relevance or weight of any material (oral, written or other) sought to be tendered on any matters of fact or opinion, and the time, manner and form in which such material should be exchanged and presented;

(e) whether and to what extent the Arbitrator should himself take the initiative in ascertaining the facts and the law;

(f) whether and to what extent he should rely upon his own knowledge and expertise;

(g) whether and to what extent there should be oral or written evidence or submissions;

(h) whether and to what extent expert evidence should be adduced;

(j) whether and to what extent evidence should be given under oath or affirmation;

(k) the manner in which the evidence of witnesses shall be taken;

(l) whether translations of any relevant documents are to be supplied;

(m) whether and to what extent enquiries tests or investigations should be conducted

and in default of agreement between the parties, shall have power to decide:

(n) when and where any part of the proceedings is to be held;

(p) the language or languages to be used in the proceedings.

The Arbitrator may fix the time within which any directions given by him are to be complied with and may if he thinks fit extend the time so fixed whether or not it has expired.

Power to limit recoverable costs

A43–009 7.4 The Arbitrator may direct that the recoverable Costs of the Arbitration, or any part of the arbitral proceedings shall be limited to a specific amount. Any such direction shall be given in advance of incurring the costs to which it relates.

Power to order security

A43–010 7.5 The Arbitrator shall have power to:

(a) make an order for security for costs in favour of one or more of the parties and

(b) order his own costs to be secured.

Money ordered to be paid under this Rule shall be paid as directed by the Arbitrator into a separate bank account in the name of a stakeholder to be appointed by and subject to the directions of the Arbitrator.

Power to order protective measures

A43–011 7.6 The Arbitrator (and in the case of urgency the courts also) shall have power to:

(a) order the preservation of evidence;

(b) make orders relating to property which is the subject of the proceedings or as to which any question arises in the proceedings:

(i) for the inspection, photographing, preservation, custody or detention of the property, or

(ii) ordering that samples be taken from, or any observation be made of or experiment conducted upon, the property;

(c) give directions for the detention storage sale or disposal of the whole or any part of the subject matter of the dispute at the expense of one or both of the parties.

PART D. PROCEDURES BEFORE THE HEARING

Rule 8. Statements of case and disclosure of documents

A43–012 8.1 To the extent that the Arbitrator directs, each party shall prepare in writing and shall serve upon the other party or parties and the Arbitrator a statement of its case comprising:

(a) a summary of that party's case;

(b) a summary of that party's evidence;

(c) a statement or summary of the issues between the parties;

(d) a list and/or a summary of the documents relied upon;

(e) any points of law with references to any authorities relied upon;

(f) a statement or summary of any other matters likely to assist the resolution of the disputes or differences between the parties;

(g) any other document or statement that the Arbitrator considers necessary.

The Arbitrator may order any party to answer the other party's case and to give reasons for any disagreement therewith.

8.2 The Arbitrator shall determine which documents or classes of documents should be disclosed between the parties and produced by the parties and at what stage.

8.3 Statements or answers shall contain sufficient detail for the other party to know the case it has to answer. If sufficient detail is not provided the Arbitrator may of his own motion or at the request of the other party order the provision of such further information, clarification or elaboration as the Arbitrator may think fit.

8.4 (a) If a party fails to comply with any order made under this Rule the Arbitrator may make a peremptory order to the same effect providing such time for compliance with it as the Arbitrator considers appropriate.

(b) If the defaulting party fails to comply with a peremptory order the Arbitrator shall have power to:

  (i) debar that party from relying on the matters in respect of which it is in default;
  (ii) draw such adverse inferences from the act of noncompliance as the circumstances justify;
  (iii) proceed to an award on the basis of such materials as have been properly provided to him.

Provided that the Arbitrator shall first give notice to the party in default that he intends to proceed under this Rule.

8.5 If the Arbitrator is satisfied that there has been inordinate and inexcusable delay by either party in pursuing its claim and that delay:

(a) gives rise, or is likely to give rise, to substantial risk that it is not possible to have a fair resolution of the issues in that claim or

(b) has caused, or is likely to cause, serious prejudice to the other party

the Arbitrator may make an award dismissing the claim.

Rule 9. Power to order concurrent hearings

9.1 Where disputes or differences have arisen under two or more contracts each concerned wholly or mainly with the same subject matter and the resulting arbitrations have been referred to the same Arbitrator he may with the agreement of all the parties concerned or upon the application of one of the parties being a party to all the contracts involved order that the whole or any part of the matters at issue shall be heard together upon such terms or conditions as the Arbitrator thinks fit.

9.2 Where an order for concurrent hearings has been made under Rule 9.1 the Arbitrator shall nevertheless make separate awards unless all the parties otherwise agree but the Arbitrator may if he thinks fit prepare one combined set of reasons to cover all the awards.

Rule 10. Procedural meetings

A43–014 10.1 The Arbitrator may at any time call such procedural meetings as he deems necessary to identify or clarify the issues to be decided and the procedures to be adopted. For this purpose the Arbitrator may request particular persons to attend on behalf of the parties.

10.2 Either party may at any time apply to the Arbitrator for leave to appear before him on any interlocutory matter. The Arbitrator may call a procedural meeting for the purpose or deal with the application in correspondence or otherwise as he thinks fit.

10.3 At any procedural meeting or otherwise the Arbitrator may give such directions as he thinks fit for the proper conduct of the arbitration.

Rule 11. Power to appoint assessors or to seek outside advice

A43–015 11.1 The Arbitrator may:

(a) appoint a legal technical or other assessor to assist him in the conduct of the arbitration. The Arbitrator shall direct when such assessor is to attend hearings of the arbitration;

(b) seek legal technical or other advice on any matter arising out of or in connection with the proceedings.

11.2 The parties shall be given reasonable opportunity to comment on any information, opinion or advice offered by any such person.

Rule 12. Preparation for the hearing

A43–016 12.1 In addition to his other powers the Arbitrator shall also have power to:

(a) order that the parties shall agree facts as facts and figures as figures where possible;

(b) order the parties to prepare an agreed and paginated bundle of all documents relied upon by the parties. The agreed bundle shall thereby be deemed to have been entered in evidence without further proof and without being read out at the hearing. Provided always that either party may at the hearing challenge the admissibility of any document in the agreed bundle;

(c) order that any Experts whose reports have been exchanged should meet and prepare a joint report identifying the points in issue and any other matters covered by their reports upon which they are in agreement and those upon which they disagree, stating the reasons for any disagreement.

12.2 Before the hearing the Arbitrator may and if so requested by the parties shall read the documents to be used at the hearing. For this or any other purpose the Arbitrator may require all such documents to be delivered to him at such time and place as he may specify.

Part E. Procedure at the Hearing

Rule 13. Powers at the hearing

13.1 The Arbitrator may hear the parties their representatives and/or witnesses at any time or place and may adjourn the arbitration for any period on the application of any party or as he thinks fit.

13.2 Any party may be represented by any person including in the case of a company or other legal entity a director officer employee or beneficiary of such company or entity. In particular, a person shall not be prevented from representing a party because he is or may be also a witness in the proceedings. Nothing shall prevent a party from being represented by different persons at different times.

13.3 Nothing in these Rules or in any other rule custom or practice shall prevent the Arbitrator from starting to hear the arbitration once his appointment is completed or at any time thereafter.

13.4 Any meeting with or summons before the Arbitrator at which both parties are represented may if the Arbitrator so directs be treated as part of the hearing.

13.5 At or before the hearing and after hearing representations on behalf of each party the Arbitrator may determine the order in which:

(a) the parties will present their cases;

(b) the order in which the issues will be heard and determined.

13.6 The Arbitrator may order any submission or speech by or on behalf of any party to be put into writing and delivered to him and to the other party. A party so ordered shall be entitled if it so wishes to enlarge upon or vary any such submission orally.

13.7 The Arbitrator may at any time (whether before or after the hearing has commenced) allocate the time available for the hearing between the parties and those representing the parties shall then adhere strictly to that allocation. Should a party's representative fail to complete the presentation of that party's case within the time so allowed further time shall only be afforded at the sole discretion of the Arbitrator and upon such conditions as to costs as the Arbitrator may see fit to impose.

13.8 The Arbitrator may on the application of either party or of his own motion hear and determine any issue or issues separately.

13.9 If a party fails to appear at the hearing and provided that the absent party has had notice of the hearing or the Arbitrator is satisfied that all reasonable steps have been taken to notify it of the hearing the Arbitrator may proceed with the hearing in its absence. The Arbitrator shall nevertheless take all reasonable steps to ensure that the disputes between the parties are determined justly and fairly.

Rule 14. Evidence

14.1 The Arbitrator may order a party to submit in advance of the hearing a list of the witnesses it intends to call. That party shall not thereby be bound to call any witness so listed and may add to the list so submitted at any time.

14.2 No expert evidence shall be admissible except by leave of the Arbitrator. Leave may be given on such terms and conditions as the Arbitrator thinks fit. Unless the Arbitrator otherwise orders such terms shall be deemed to include a requirement that a report from each Expert containing the substance of the evidence to be given shall be served upon the other party within a reasonable time before the hearing.

14.3 The Arbitrator may order that Experts appear before him separately or concurrently at the hearing or otherwise so that he may examine them inquisitorially provided always that at the conclusion of the questioning by the Arbitrator the parties or its representatives shall have the opportunity to put such further questions to any Expert as they may reasonably require.

14.4 The Arbitrator may order disclosure or exchange of proofs of evidence relating to factual issues. The Arbitrator may also order any party to prepare and disclose in writing in advance a list of points or questions to be put in cross-examination of any witness.

14.5 Where a list of questions is disclosed whether pursuant to an order of the Arbitrator or otherwise the party making disclosure shall not be bound to put any question therein to the witness unless the Arbitrator so orders. Where the party making disclosure puts a question not so listed in cross-examination the Arbitrator may disallow the costs thereby occasioned.

14.6 The Arbitrator may order that any witness statement or Expert's report which has been disclosed shall stand as the evidence in chief of that witness or Expert. The Arbitrator may also at any time before cross-examination order the witness or Expert to deliver written answers to questions arising out of any statement or report.

PART F. SHORT PROCEDURE

Rule 15. Short Procedure

15.1 Where the parties so agree (either of their own motion or at the invitation of the Arbitrator) the arbitration shall be conducted in accordance with the following Short Procedure or any variations thereto which the parties and the Arbitrator so agree.

15.2 Within 30 days after the preliminary meeting held under Rule 6.1 the claiming party shall set out its case in the form of a file containing:

(a) a statement as to the orders or awards it seeks;

(b) a statement of its reasons for being entitled to such orders or awards;

(c) copies of any documents on which it relies (including statements) identifying the origin and date of each document;

and shall deliver of the said file to the other party and to the Arbitrator in such manner and within such time as the Arbitrator may direct.

15.3 The other party shall either at the same time or within 30 days of receipt of the claiming party's statement as the Arbitrator may direct deliver to the claiming party and the Arbitrator its statement in the same form as in Rule 15.2.

15.4 The Arbitrator may view the site or the works and may in his sole discretion order, permit or require either or both parties to:

(a) submit further documents or information in writing;

(b) prepare or deliver further files by way of reply or response. Such files may include witness statements or expert reports.

Provided always that such further files shall not raise any issue not already included expressly or by necessary inference unless ordered by the Arbitrator in the files delivered in accordance with Rules 15.2 & 15.3.

15.5 Within 30 days of completing the foregoing steps the Arbitrator shall fix a day to meet the parties for the purpose of:

(a) receiving any oral submissions which either party may wish to make;

(b) the Arbitrator putting questions to the parties their representatives or witnesses.

For this purpose the Arbitrator shall give notice of any particular person he wishes to question but no person shall be bound to appear before him.

15.6 The time periods in Rules 15.2, 15.3 and 15.5 may be varied as the Arbitrator may think fit.

Documents only

15.7 Alternatively with the agreement of the parties the Arbitrator may dispense with the meeting and upon receipt of any further files or information under Rule 15.4 proceed directly to the award in accordance with Rule 15.8. **A43–020**

15.8 Within 30 days following the conclusion of the meeting under Rule 15.5, or in the absence of a meeting 30 days following receipt of the further files or information under Rule 15.4, or such further period as the Arbitrator may reasonably require the Arbitrator shall make his award.

Rule 16. Other matters

16.1 Unless the parties otherwise agree the Arbitrator shall have no power to award costs to either party and the Arbitrator's own fees and expenses shall be paid in equal shares by the parties. Where one party has agreed to the Arbitrator's fees and expenses the other party by agreeing to this Short Procedure shall be deemed to have agreed likewise to the Arbitrator's fees and expenses. **A43–021**

Provided always that this Rule shall not apply to any dispute which arises after the Short Procedure has been adopted or imposed by the Contract.

16.2 Either party may at any time before the Arbitrator has made his award under this Short Procedure require by written notice served on the Arbitrator and the other party that the arbitration shall cease to be conducted in accordance with this Short Procedure. Save only for Rule 16.3 the Short Procedure shall thereupon no longer apply or bind the parties but any evidence already laid before the Arbitrator shall be admissible in further proceedings as if it had been submitted as part of those proceedings and without further proof.

16.3 The party giving written notice under Rule 16.2 shall thereupon in any event become liable to pay:

(a) the whole of the Arbitrator's fees and expenses incurred up to the date of such notice and

(b) a sum to be assessed by the Arbitrator as reasonable compensation for the costs (including any legal costs) incurred by the other party up to the date of such notice.

Payment in full of such expenses shall be a condition precedent to that party's proceeding further in the arbitration unless the Arbitrator otherwise directs. Provided that non-payment of the said expenses shall not prevent the other party from proceeding in the arbitration.

Part G. Special Procedure For Experts

Rule 17. Special Procedure for Experts

A43–022 **17.1** Where the parties so agree (either of their own motion or at the invitation of the Arbitrator) the hearing and determination of any issues of fact which depend upon the evidence of Experts shall be conducted in accordance with the following Special Procedure.

17.2 Each party shall set out its case on such issues in the form of a file containing:

(a) a statement of the factual findings it seeks;

(b) a report or statement from and signed by each Expert upon whom that party relies;

(c) copies of any other documents referred to in each Expert's report or statement or on which the party relies identifying the origin and date of each document;

and shall deliver copies of the said file to the other party and to the Arbitrator in such manner and within such time as the Arbitrator may direct.

17.3 After reading the parties cases the Arbitrator may view the site or the works and may require either or both parties to submit further documents or information in writing.

17.4 Thereafter the Arbitrator shall fix a day when he shall meet the Experts whose reports or statements have been submitted. At the meeting each Expert may address the Arbitrator and put questions to any other Expert representing the other party. The Arbitrator shall so direct the meeting as to ensure that each Expert has an adequate opportunity to explain his opinion and to comment upon any opposing opinion. No other person shall be entitled to address the Arbitrator or question any Expert unless the parties and the Arbitrator so agree.

17.5 Thereafter the Arbitrator may make an award setting out with such details or particulars as may be necessary his decision upon the issues dealt with.

Rule 18. Costs

A43–023 **18.1** The Arbitrator may in his award make orders as to the payment of any costs relating to the foregoing matters including his own fees and expenses in connection therewith.

18.2 Unless the parties otherwise agree and so notify the Arbitrator neither party shall be entitled to any costs in respect of legal representation assistance or other legal work relating to the hearing and determination of factual issues by this Special Procedure.

Part H. Awards

Rule 19. Awards

A43–024 **19.1** The Arbitrator may at any time make an award, and may make more than one award at different times on different aspects of the matters to be determined.

19.2 An award may:

(a) order the payment of money to one or more of the parties;

(b) order a party to do or refrain from doing anything;

The Institution of Civil Engineers' Arbitration Procedure

    (c) order specific performance;

    (d) make a declaration as to any matter to be determined;

    (e) order rectification, setting aside or cancellation of a deed or other document;

    (f) be a consent award in the event of a settlement, which shall include an allocation of the Costs of the Arbitration.

Provisional relief

19.3 The Arbitrator may also make a provisional order and for this purpose the Arbitrator shall have power to award payment by one party to another of a sum representing a reasonable proportion of the final net amount which in his opinion that party is likely to be ordered to pay after determination of all the issues in the arbitration and after taking into account any defence or counterclaim upon which the other party may be entitled to rely.

19.4 The Arbitrator shall have power to order the party against whom a provisional order is made to pay part or all of the sum awarded to a stakeholder. In default of compliance with such an order the Arbitrator may order payment of the whole sum in the provisional order to the other party.

19.5 A provisional order shall be final and binding upon the parties unless and until it is varied by any subsequent award made by the same Arbitrator or by any other Arbitrator having jurisdiction over the matters in dispute. Any such subsequent award may order repayment of monies paid in accordance with the provisional order.

Interest

19.6 In any award the Arbitrator shall have power to award interest either simple or compound at such rate and between such dates or such events as he thinks fit.

Costs

19.7 Unless otherwise provided in this Procedure, the Arbitrator shall have power to:

    (a) make an award allocating the Costs of the Arbitration between the parties in such manner as he considers appropriate;

    (b) direct the basis upon which the costs are to be determined;

    (c) in default of agreement by the parties, determine the amount of the recoverable costs;

    (d) order payment of costs in relation to a provisional order including power to order that such costs shall be paid forthwith.

Rule 20. Reasons

20.1 The Arbitrator shall include in his award reasons for the award unless it is a consent award or the parties have agreed to dispense with reasons.

Rule 21. Making the award

21.1 Upon the closing of the hearing (if any) and after having considered all the evidence and submissions the Arbitrator shall prepare and make his award.

21.2 When the Arbitrator has made his award (including a provisional order under Rule 19.3) he shall so inform the parties in writing and shall specify how and where it may be taken up upon full payment of his fees and expenses.

Power to correct an award

A43–030 **21.3** The Arbitrator may, within 28 days of the date of the award, correct an award so as to remove any clerical mistake, error or ambiguity, and may also make an additional award in respect of any matter which was not dealt with in the award.

Rule 22. Appeals

A43–031 **22.1** If any party applies to the court for leave to appeal against any award or decision or for any other purpose that party shall forthwith notify the Arbitrator of the application.

The Arbitrator may continue the arbitral proceedings, including making further awards, pending a decision by the court.

22.2 Once any award or decision has been made and taken up the Arbitrator shall be under no obligation to make any statement in connection therewith other than in compliance with an order of the court.

Part J. Miscellaneous

Rule 23. Definitions

A43–032 **23.1** In these Rules the following definitions shall apply:

(a) "Arbitrator" includes a tribunal of two or more Arbitrators, an Umpire or Chairman;

(b) "Institution" means The Institution of Civil Engineers;

(c) "President" means the President for the time being of the Institution or any Vice-President acting on his behalf or such other person as may have been nominated in the arbitration agreement to appoint the Arbitrator in default of agreement between the Parties;

(d) "Procedure" means The Institution of Civil Engineers' Arbitration Procedure (1997) unless the context otherwise requires;

(e) "Contract" means the Contract between the parties which incorporates the arbitration agreement under which the dispute arises;

(f) "Expert" means an expert witness or person called to give expert opinion evidence;

(g) The "Act" means the Arbitration Act 1996 and when the Act applies words defined in it shall have the same meanings in this Procedure;

(h) "Costs of the Arbitration" shall include:

(i) the Arbitrator's fees and expenses;
(ii) the fees and expenses of any arbitral institution concerned;
(iii) the legal or other costs of the parties and
(iv) the costs of or incidental to any proceedings to determine the amount of the recoverable costs of the arbitration.

The Institution of Civil Engineers' Arbitration Procedure

Rule 24. Application of the ICE Procedure

24.1 This Procedure shall apply to the conduct of the arbitration if: A43–033

(a) the Contract so provides;

(b) the parties at any time so agree or

(c) the Arbitrator so stipulates at the time of his appointment.

Provided that where this Procedure applies by virtue of the Arbitrator's stipulation under (c) above the parties may within 14 days of that appointment agree otherwise in which event the Arbitrator's appointment shall be terminated.

24.2 This Procedure shall not apply to arbitrations under the law of Scotland for which a separate ICE Arbitration Procedure (Scotland) is available.

24.3 Where the seat of the arbitration is in a country other than England and Wales or Northern Ireland this Procedure shall apply to the extent that the applicable law permits.

24.4 If after the appointment of the Arbitrator any agreement is reached between the parties which is inconsistent with this Procedure the Arbitrator shall be entitled upon giving reasonable notice to terminate his appointment, and shall be entitled to payment of his reasonable fees and expenses incurred up to the date of the termination.

Rule 25. Exclusion of liability

25.1 Neither the Institution nor its servants or agents nor the President shall be liable   A43–034
to any party for any act omission or misconduct in connection with any appointment made or any arbitration conducted under this Procedure.

The London Court of International Arbitration Rules

(ADOPTED TO TAKE EFFECT FOR ARBITRATIONS COMMENCING ON OR AFTER JANUARY 1, 1998)[1]

A44–001 Where any agreement, submission or reference provides in writing and in whatsoever manner for arbitration under the rules of the LCIA or by the Court of the LCIA ("the LCIA Court"), the parties shall be taken to have agreed in writing that the arbitration shall be conducted in accordance with the following rules ("the Rules") or such amended rules as the LCIA may have adopted hereafter to take effect before the commencement of the arbitration. The Rules include the Schedule of Costs in effect at the commencement of the arbitration, as separately amended from time to time by the LCIA Court.

Article 1

The Request for Arbitration

A44–002 1.1 Any party wishing to commence an arbitration under these Rules ("the Claimant") shall send to the Registrar of the LCIA Court ("the Registrar") a written request for arbitration ("the Request"), containing or accompanied by:

(a) the names, addresses, telephone, facsimile, telex and e-mail numbers (if known) of the parties to the arbitration and of their legal representatives;

(b) a copy of the written arbitration clause or separate written arbitration agreement invoked by the Claimant ("the Arbitration Agreement"), together with a copy of the contractual documentation in which the arbitration clause is contained or in respect of which the arbitration arises;

(c) a brief statement describing the nature and circumstances of the dispute, and specifying the claims advanced by the Claimant against another party to the arbitration ("the Respondent");

(d) a statement of any matters (such as the seat or language(s) of the arbitration, or the number of arbitrators, or their qualifications or identities) on which the parties have already agreed in writing for the arbitration or in respect of which the Claimant wishes to make a proposal;

(e) if the Arbitration Agreement calls for party nomination of arbitrators, the name, address, telephone, facsimile, telex and e-mail numbers (if known) of the Claimant's nominee;

(f) the fee prescribed in the Schedule of Costs (without which the Request shall be treated as not having been received by the Registrar and the arbitration as not having been commenced);

---

[1] This document is reproduced with the kind permission of the London Court of International Arbitration.

(g) confirmation to the Registrar that copies of the Request (including all accompanying documents) have been or are being served simultaneously on all other parties to the arbitration by one or more means of service to be identified in such confirmation.

1.2 The date of receipt by the Registrar of the Request shall be treated as the date on which the arbitration has commenced for all purposes. The Request (including all accompanying documents) should be submitted to the Registrar in two copies where a sole arbitrator should be appointed, or, if the parties have agreed or the Claimant considers that three arbitrators should be appointed, in four copies.

Article 2

The Response

2.1 Within 30 days of service of the Request on the Respondent, (or such lesser period fixed by the LCIA Court), the Respondent shall send to the Registrar a written response to the Request ("the Response"), containing or accompanied by: **A44–003**

(a) confirmation or denial of all or part of the claims advanced by the Claimant in the Request;

(b) a brief statement describing the nature and circumstances of any counterclaims advanced by the Respondent against the Claimant;

(c) comment in response to any statements contained in the Request, as called for under Article 1.1(d), on matters relating to the conduct of the arbitration;

(d) if the Arbitration Agreement calls for party nomination of arbitrators, the name, address, telephone, facsimile, telex and e-mail numbers (if known) of the Respondent's nominee; and

(e) confirmation to the Registrar that copies of the Response (including all accompanying documents) have been or are being served simultaneously on all other parties to the arbitration by one or more means of service to be identified in such confirmation.

2.2 The Response (including all accompanying documents) should be submitted to the Registrar in two copies, or if the parties have agreed or the Respondent considers that three arbitrators should be appointed, in four copies.

2.3 Failure to send a Response shall not preclude the Respondent from denying any claim or from advancing a counterclaim in the arbitration. However, if the Arbitration Agreement calls for party nomination of arbitrators, failure to send a Response or to nominate an arbitrator within time or at all shall constitute an irrevocable waiver of that party's opportunity to nominate an arbitrator.

Article 3

The LCIA Court and Registrar

3.1 The functions of the LCIA Court under these Rules shall be performed in its name by the President or a Vice-President of the LCIA Court or by a division of three or five **A44–004**

members of the LCIA Court appointed by the President or a Vice-President of the LCIA Court, as determined by the President.

3.2 The functions of the Registrar under these Rules shall be performed by the Registrar or any deputy Registrar of the LCIA Court under the supervision of the LCIA Court.

3.3 All communications from any party or arbitrator to the LCIA Court shall be addressed to the Registrar.

Article 4

Notices and Periods of Time

A44–005   **4.1** Any notice or other communication that may be or is required to be given by a party under these Rules shall be in writing and shall be delivered by registered postal or courier service or transmitted by facsimile, telex, e-mail or any other means of telecommunication that provide a record of its transmission.

4.2 A party's last-known residence or place of business during the arbitration shall be a valid address for the purpose of any notice or other communication in the absence of any notification of a change to such address by that party to the other parties, the Arbitral Tribunal and the Registrar.

4.3 For the purpose of determining the date of commencement of a time limit, a notice or other communication shall be treated as having been received on the day it is delivered or, in the case of telecommunications, transmitted in accordance with Articles 4.1 and 4.2.

4.4 For the purpose of determining compliance with a time limit, a notice or other communication shall be treated as having been sent, made or transmitted if it is dispatched in accordance with Articles 4.1 and 4.2 prior to or on the date of the expiration of the time-limit.

4.5 Notwithstanding the above, any notice or communication by one party may be addressed to another party in the manner agreed in writing between them or, failing such agreement, according to the practice followed in the course of their previous dealings or in whatever manner ordered by the Arbitral Tribunal.

4.6 For the purpose of calculating a period of time under these Rules, such period shall begin to run on the day following the day when a notice or other communication is received. If the last day of such period is an official holiday or a non-business day at the residence or place of business of the addressee, the period is extended until the first business day which follows. Official holidays or non-business days occurring during the running of the period of time are included in calculating that period.

4.7 The Arbitral Tribunal may at any time extend (even where the period of time has expired) or abridge any period of time prescribed under these Rules or under the Arbitration Agreement for the conduct of the arbitration, including any notice or communication to be served by one party on any other party.

Article 5

Formation of the Arbitral Tribunal

A44–006   **5.1** The expression "the Arbitral Tribunal" in these Rules includes a sole arbitrator or all the arbitrators where more than one. All references to an arbitrator shall include the masculine and feminine. (References to the President, Vice-President and members of

THE LONDON COURT OF INTERNATIONAL ARBITRATION RULES

the LCIA Court, the Registrar or deputy Registrar, expert, witness, party and legal representative shall be similarly understood).

5.2 All arbitrators conducting an arbitration under these Rules shall be and remain at all times impartial and independent of the parties; and none shall act in the arbitration as advocates for any party. No arbitrator, whether before or after appointment, shall advise any party on the merits or outcome of the dispute.

5.3 Before appointment by the LCIA Court, each arbitrator shall furnish to the Registrar a written resume of his past and present professional positions; he shall agree in writing upon fee rates conforming to the Schedule of Costs; and he shall sign a declaration to the effect that there are no circumstances known to him likely to give rise to any justified doubts as to his impartiality or independence, other than any circumstances disclosed by him in the declaration. Each arbitrator shall thereby also assume a continuing duty forthwith to disclose any such circumstances to the LCIA Court, to any other members of the Arbitral Tribunal and to all the parties if such circumstances should arise after the date of such declaration and before the arbitration is concluded.

5.4 The LCIA Court shall appoint the Arbitral Tribunal as soon as practicable after receipt by the Registrar of the Response or after the expiry of 30 days following service of the Request upon the Respondent if no Response is received by the Registrar (or such lesser period fixed by the LCIA Court). The LCIA Court may proceed with the formation of the Arbitral Tribunal notwithstanding that the Request is incomplete or the Response is missing, late or incomplete. A sole arbitrator shall be appointed unless the parties have agreed in writing otherwise, or unless the LCIA Court determines that in view of all the circumstances of the case a three-member tribunal is appropriate.

5.5 The LCIA Court alone is empowered to appoint arbitrators. The LCIA Court will appoint arbitrators with due regard for any particular method or criteria of selection agreed in writing by the parties. In selecting arbitrators consideration will be given to the nature of the transaction, the nature and circumstances of the dispute, the nationality, location and languages of the parties and (if more than two) the number of parties.

5.6 In the case of a three-member Arbitral Tribunal, the chairman (who will not be a party-nominated arbitrator) shall be appointed by the LCIA Court.

Article 6

Nationality of Arbitrators

6.1 Where the parties are of different nationalities, a sole arbitrator or chairman of the Arbitral Tribunal shall not have the same nationality as any party unless the parties who are not of the same nationality as the proposed appointee all agree in writing otherwise. **A44–007**

6.2 The nationality of parties shall be understood to include that of controlling shareholders or interests.

6.3 For the purpose of this Article, a person who is a citizen of two or more states shall be treated as a national of each state; and citizens of the European Union shall be treated as nationals of its different Member States and shall not be treated as having the same nationality.

Article 7

Party and Other Nominations

7.1 If the parties have agreed that any arbitrator is to be appointed by one or more of them or by any third person, that agreement shall be treated as an agreement to nominate **A44–008**

485

an arbitrator for all purposes. Such nominee may only be appointed by the LCIA Court as arbitrator subject to his prior compliance with Article 5.3. The LCIA Court may refuse to appoint any such nominee if it determines that he is not suitable or independent or impartial.

7.2 Where the parties have howsoever agreed that the Respondent or any third person is to nominate an arbitrator and such nomination is not made within time or at all, the LCIA Court may appoint an arbitrator notwithstanding the absence of the nomination and without regard to any late nomination. Likewise, if the Request for Arbitration does not contain a nomination by the Claimant where the parties have howsoever agreed that the Claimant or a third person is to nominate an arbitrator, the LCIA Court may appoint an arbitrator notwithstanding the absence of the nomination and without regard to any late nomination.

Article 8

Three or More Parties

A44–009   **8.1** Where the Arbitration Agreement entitles each party howsoever to nominate an arbitrator, the parties to the dispute number more than two and such parties have not all agreed in writing that the disputant parties represent two separate sides for the formation of the Arbitral Tribunal as Claimant and Respondent respectively, the LCIA Court shall appoint the Arbitral Tribunal without regard to any party's nomination.

8.2 In such circumstances, the Arbitration Agreement shall be treated for all purposes as a written agreement by the parties for the appointment of the Arbitral Tribunal by the LCIA Court.

Article 9

Expedited Formation

A44–010   **9.1** In exceptional urgency, on or after the commencement of the arbitration, any party may apply to the LCIA Court for the expedited formation of the Arbitral Tribunal, including the appointment of any replacement arbitrator under Articles 10 and 11 of these Rules.

9.2 Such an application shall be made in writing to the LCIA Court, copied to all other parties to the arbitration; and it shall set out the specific grounds for exceptional urgency in the formation of the Arbitral Tribunal.

9.3 The LCIA Court may, in its complete discretion, abridge or curtail any time-limit under these Rules for the formation of the Arbitral Tribunal, including service of the Response and of any matters or documents adjudged to be missing from the Request. The LCIA Court shall not be entitled to abridge or curtail any other time-limit.

Article 10

Revocation of Arbitrator's Appointment

A44–011   **10.1** If either (a) any arbitrator gives written notice of his desire to resign as arbitrator to the LCIA Court, to be copied to the parties and the other arbitrators (if any) or (b) any arbitrator dies, falls seriously ill, refuses, or becomes unable or unfit to act, either upon challenge by a party or at the request of the remaining arbitrators, the LCIA Court may revoke that arbitrator's appointment and appoint another arbitrator. The LCIA Court shall decide upon the amount of fees and expenses to be paid for the former arbitrator's services (if any) as it may consider appropriate in all the circumstances.

10.2 If any arbitrator acts in deliberate violation of the Arbitration Agreement (including these Rules) or does not act fairly and impartially as between the parties or does not conduct or participate in the arbitration proceedings with reasonable diligence, avoiding unnecessary delay or expense, that arbitrator may be considered unfit in the opinion of the LCIA Court.

10.3 An arbitrator may also be challenged by any party if circumstances exist that give rise to justifiable doubts as to his impartiality or independence. A party may challenge an arbitrator it has nominated, or in whose appointment it has participated, only for reasons of which it becomes aware after the appointment has been made.

10.4 A party who intends to challenge an arbitrator shall, within 15 days of the formation of the Arbitral Tribunal or (if later) after becoming aware of any circumstances referred to in Article 10.1, 10.2 or 10.3, send a written statement of the reasons for its challenge to the LCIA Court, the Arbitral Tribunal and all other parties. Unless the challenged arbitrator withdraws or all other parties agree to the challenge within 15 days of receipt of the written statement, the LCIA Court shall decide on the challenge.

Article 11

Nomination and Replacement of Arbitrators

11.1 In the event that the LCIA Court determines that any nominee is not suitable or independent or impartial or if an appointed arbitrator is to be replaced for any reason, the LCIA Court shall have a complete discretion to decide whether or not to follow the original nominating process. **A44–012**

11.2 If the LCIA Court should so decide, any opportunity given to a party to make a re-nomination shall be waived if not exercised within 15 days (or such lesser time as the LCIA Court may fix), after which the LCIA Court shall appoint the replacement arbitrator.

Article 12

Majority Power to Continue Proceedings

12.1 If any arbitrator on a three-member Arbitral Tribunal refuses or persistently fails to participate in its deliberations, the two other arbitrators shall have the power, upon their written notice of such refusal or failure to the LCIA Court, the parties and the third arbitrator, to continue the arbitration (including the making of any decision, ruling or award), notwithstanding the absence of the third arbitrator. **A44–013**

12.2 In determining whether to continue the arbitration, the two other arbitrators shall take into account the stage of the arbitration, any explanation made by the third arbitrator for his non-participation and such other matters as they consider appropriate in the circumstances of the case. The reasons for such determination shall be stated in any award, order or other decision made by the two arbitrators without the participation of the third arbitrator.

12.3 In the event that the two other arbitrators determine at any time not to continue the arbitration without the participation of the third arbitrator missing from their deliberations, the two arbitrators shall notify in writing the parties and the LCIA Court of such determination; and in that event, the two arbitrators or any party may refer the matter to the LCIA Court for the revocation of that third arbitrator's appointment and his replacement under Article 10.

Article 13

Communications between Parties and the Arbitral Tribunal

A44–014 **13.1** Until the Arbitral Tribunal is formed, all communications between parties and arbitrators shall be made through the Registrar.

13.2 Thereafter, unless and until the Arbitral Tribunal directs that communications shall take place directly between the Arbitral Tribunal and the parties (with simultaneous copies to the Registrar), all written communications between the parties and the Arbitral Tribunal shall continue to be made through the Registrar.

13.3 Where the Registrar sends any written communication to one party on behalf of the Arbitral Tribunal, he shall send a copy to each of the other parties. Where any party sends to the Registrar any communication (including Written Statements and Documents under Article 15), it shall include a copy for each arbitrator; and it shall also send copies direct to all other parties and confirm to the Registrar in writing that it has done or is doing so.

Article 14

Conduct of the Proceedings

A44–015 **14.1** The parties may agree on the conduct of their arbitral proceedings and they are encouraged to do so, consistent with the Arbitral Tribunal's general duties at all times:

  (i) to act fairly and impartially as between all parties, giving each a reasonable opportunity of putting its case and dealing with that of its opponent; and

  (ii) to adopt procedures suitable to the circumstances of the arbitration, avoiding unnecessary delay or expense, so as to provide a fair and efficient means for the final resolution of the parties' dispute.

Such agreements shall be made by the parties in writing or recorded in writing by the Arbitral Tribunal at the request of and with the authority of the parties.

14.2 Unless otherwise agreed by the parties under Article 14.1, the Arbitral Tribunal shall have the widest discretion to discharge its duties allowed under such law(s) or rules of law as the Arbitral Tribunal may determine to be applicable; and at all times the parties shall do everything necessary for the fair, efficient and expeditious conduct of the arbitration.

14.3 In the case of a three-member Arbitral Tribunal the chairman may, with the prior consent of the other two arbitrators, make procedural rulings alone.

Article 15

Submission of Written Statements and Documents

15.1 Unless the parties have agreed otherwise under Article 14.1 or the Arbitral Tribunal should determine differently, the written stage of the proceedings shall be as set out below.

15.2 Within 30 days of receipt of written notification from the Registrar of the formation of the Arbitral Tribunal, the Claimant shall send to the Registrar a Statement of Case setting out in sufficient detail the facts and any contentions of law on which it relies, together with the relief claimed against all other parties, save and insofar as such matters have not been set out in its Request.

15.3 Within 30 days of receipt of the Statement of Case or written notice from the Claimant that it elects to treat the Request as its Statement of Case, the Respondent shall send to the Registrar a Statement of Defence setting out in sufficient detail which of the facts and contentions of law in the Statement of Case or Request (as the case may be) it admits or denies, on what grounds and on what other facts and contentions of law it relies. Any counterclaims shall be submitted with the Statement of Defence in the same manner as claims are to be set out in the Statement of Case.

15.4 Within 30 days of receipt of the Statement of Defence, the Claimant shall send to the Registrar a Statement of Reply which, where there are any counterclaims, shall include a Defence to Counterclaim in the same manner as a defence is to be set out in the Statement of Defence.

15.5 If the Statement of Reply contains a Defence to Counterclaim, within 30 days of its receipt the Respondent shall send to the Registrar a Statement of Reply to Counterclaim.

15.6 All Statements referred to in this Article shall be accompanied by copies (or, if they are especially voluminous, lists) of all essential documents on which the party concerned relies and which have not previously been submitted by any party, and (where appropriate) by any relevant samples and exhibits.

15.7 As soon as practicable following receipt of the Statements specified in this Article, the Arbitral Tribunal shall proceed in such manner as has been agreed in writing by the parties or pursuant to its authority under these Rules.

15.8 If the Respondent fails to submit a Statement of Defence or the Claimant a Statement of Defence to Counterclaim, or if at any point any party fails to avail itself of the opportunity to present its case in the manner determined by Article 15.2 to 15.6 or directed by the Arbitral Tribunal, the Arbitral Tribunal may nevertheless proceed with the arbitration and make an award.

Article 16

Seat of Arbitration and Place of Hearings

16.1 The parties may agree in writing the seat (or legal place) of their arbitration. Failing such a choice, the seat of arbitration shall be London, unless and until the LCIA Court determines in view of all the circumstances, and after having given the parties an opportunity to make written comment, that another seat is more appropriate.

16.2 The Arbitral Tribunal may hold hearings, meetings and deliberations at any convenient geographical place in its discretion; and if elsewhere than the seat of the arbitration, the arbitration shall be treated as an arbitration conducted at the seat of the arbitration and any award as an award made at the seat of the arbitration for all purposes.

16.3 The law applicable to the arbitration (if any) shall be the arbitration law of the seat of arbitration, unless and to the extent that the parties have expressly agreed in writing on the application of another arbitration law and such agreement is not prohibited by the law of the arbitral seat.

Article 17

Language of Arbitration

A44–018 **17.1** The initial language of the arbitration shall be the language of the Arbitration Agreement, unless the parties have agreed in writing otherwise and providing always that a non-participating or defaulting party shall have no cause for complaint if communications to and from the Registrar and the arbitration proceedings are conducted in English.

17.2 In the event that the Arbitration Agreement is written in more than one language, the LCIA Court may, unless the Arbitration Agreement provides that the arbitration proceedings shall be conducted in more than one language, decide which of those languages shall be the initial language of the arbitration.

17.3 Upon the formation of the Arbitral Tribunal and unless the parties have agreed upon the language or languages of the arbitration, the Arbitration Tribunal shall decide upon the language(s) of the arbitration, after giving the parties an opportunity to make written comment and taking into account the initial language of the arbitration and any other matter it may consider appropriate in all the circumstances of the case.

17.4 If any document is expressed in a language other than the language(s) of the arbitration and no translation of such document is submitted by the party relying upon the document, the Arbitral Tribunal or (if the Arbitral Tribunal has not been formed) the LCIA Court may order that party to submit a translation in a form to be determined by the Arbitral Tribunal or the LCIA Court, as the case may be.

Article 18

Party Representation

A44–019 **18.1** Any party may be represented by legal practitioners or any other representatives.

18.2 At any time the Arbitral Tribunal may require from any party proof of authority granted to its representative(s) in such form as the Arbitral Tribunal may determine.

Article 19

Hearings

A44–020 **19.1** Any party which expresses a desire to that effect has the right to be heard orally before the Arbitral Tribunal on the merits of the dispute, unless the parties have agreed in writing on documents-only arbitration.

19.2 The Arbitral Tribunal shall fix the date, time and physical place of any meetings and hearings in the arbitration, and shall give the parties reasonable notice thereof.

19.3 The Arbitral Tribunal may in advance of any hearing submit to the parties a list of questions which it wishes them to answer with special attention.

19.4 All meetings and hearings shall be in private unless the parties agree otherwise in writing or the Arbitral Tribunal directs otherwise.

19.5 The Arbitral Tribunal shall have the fullest authority to establish time-limits for meetings and hearings, or for any parts thereof.

Article 20

Witnesses

20.1 Before any hearing, the Arbitral Tribunal may require any party to give notice of the identity of each witness that party wishes to call (including rebuttal witnesses), as well as the subject matter of that witness's testimony, its content and its relevance to the issues in the arbitration.   **A44–021**

20.2 The Arbitral Tribunal may also determine the time, manner and form in which such materials should be exchanged between the parties and presented to the Arbitral Tribunal; and it has a discretion to allow, refuse, or limit the appearance of witnesses (whether witness of fact or expert witness).

20.3 Subject to any order otherwise by the Arbitral Tribunal, the testimony of a witness may be presented by a party in written form, either as a signed statement or as a sworn affidavit.

20.4 Subject to Article 14.1 and 14.2, any party may request that a witness, on whose testimony another party seeks to rely, should attend for oral questioning at a hearing before the Arbitral Tribunal. If the Arbitral Tribunal orders that other party to produce the witness and the witness fails to attend the oral hearing without good cause, the Arbitral Tribunal may place such weight on the written testimony (or exclude the same altogether) as it considers appropriate in the circumstances of the case.

20.5 Any witness who gives oral evidence at a hearing before the Arbitral Tribunal may be questioned by each of the parties under the control of the Arbitral Tribunal. The Arbitral Tribunal may put questions at any stage of his evidence.

20.6 Subject to the mandatory provisions of any applicable law, it shall not be improper for any party or its legal representatives to interview any witness or potential witness for the purpose of presenting his testimony in written form or producing him as an oral witness.

20.7 Any individual intending to testify to the Arbitral Tribunal on any issue of fact or expertise shall be treated as a witness under these Rules notwithstanding that the individual is a party to the arbitration or was or is an officer, employee or shareholder of any party.

Article 21

Experts to the Arbitral Tribunal

21.1 Unless otherwise agreed by the parties in writing, the Arbitral Tribunal: **A44–022**

    (a) may appoint one or more experts to report to the Arbitral Tribunal on specific issues, who shall be and remain impartial and independent of the parties throughout the arbitration proceedings; and

(b) may require a party to give any such expert any relevant information or to provide access to any relevant documents, goods, samples, property or site for inspection by the expert.

21.2 Unless otherwise agreed by the parties in writing, if a party so requests or if the Arbitral Tribunal considers it necessary, the expert shall, after delivery of his written or oral report to the Arbitral Tribunal and the parties, participate in one or more hearings at which the parties shall have the opportunity to question the expert on his report and to present expert witnesses in order to testify on the points at issue.

21.3 The fees and expenses of any expert appointed by the Arbitral Tribunal under this Article shall be paid out of the deposits payable by the parties under Article 24 and shall form part of the costs of the arbitration.

Article 22

Additional Powers of the Arbitral Tribunal

22.1 Unless the parties at any time agree otherwise in writing, the Arbitral Tribunal shall have the power, on the application of any party or of its own motion, but in either case only after giving the parties a reasonable opportunity to state their views:

(a) to allow any party, upon such terms (as to costs and otherwise) as it shall determine, to amend any claim, counterclaim, defence and reply;

(b) to extend or abbreviate any time-limit provided by the Arbitration Agreement or these Rules for the conduct of the arbitration or by the Arbitral Tribunal's own orders;

(c) to conduct such enquiries as may appear to the Arbitral Tribunal to be necessary or expedient, including whether and to what extent the Arbitral Tribunal should itself take the initiative in identifying the issues and ascertaining the relevant facts and the law(s) or rules of law applicable to the arbitration, the merits of the parties' dispute and the Arbitration Agreement;

(d) to order any party to make any property, site or thing under its control and relating to the subject matter of the arbitration available for inspection by the Arbitral Tribunal, any other party, its expert or any expert to the Arbitral Tribunal;

(e) to order any party to produce to the Arbitral Tribunal, and to the other parties for inspection, and to supply copies of, any documents or classes of documents in their possession, custody or power which the Arbitral Tribunal determines to be relevant;

(f) to decide whether or not to apply any strict rules of evidence (or any other rules) as to the admissibility, relevance or weight of any material tendered by a party on any matter of fact or expert opinion; and to determine the time, manner and form in which such material should be exchanged between the parties and presented to the Arbitral Tribunal;

(g) to order the correction of any contract between the parties or the Arbitration Agreement, but only to the extent required to rectify any mistake which the Arbitral Tribunal determines to be common to the parties and then only if and to the extent to which the law(s) or rules of law applicable to the contract or Arbitration Agreement permit such correction; and

(h) to allow, only upon the application of a party, one or more third persons to be joined in the arbitration as a party provided any such third person and the applicant party have consented thereto in writing, and thereafter to make a single final award, or separate awards, in respect of all parties so implicated in the arbitration.

22.2 By agreeing to arbitration under these Rules, the parties shall be treated as having agreed not to apply to any state court or other judicial authority for any order available from the Arbitral Tribunal under Article 22.1, except with the agreement in writing of all parties.

22.3 The Arbitral Tribunal shall decide the parties' dispute in accordance with the law(s) or rules of law chosen by the parties as applicable to the merits of their dispute. If and to the extent that the Arbitral Tribunal determines that the parties have made no such choice, the Arbitral Tribunal shall apply the law(s) or rules of law which it considers appropriate.

22.4 The Arbitral Tribunal shall only apply to the merits of the dispute principles deriving from "ex aequo et bono", "amiable composition" or "honourable engagement" where the parties have so agreed expressly in writing.

Article 23

Jurisdiction of the Arbitral Tribunal

23.1 The Arbitral Tribunal shall have the power to rule on its own jurisdiction, including any objection to the initial or continuing existence, validity or effectiveness of the Arbitration Agreement. For that purpose, an arbitration clause which forms or was intended to form part of another agreement shall be treated as an arbitration agreement independent of that other agreement. A decision by the Arbitral Tribunal that such other agreement is non-existent, invalid or ineffective shall not entail ipso jure the non-existence, invalidity or ineffectiveness of the arbitration clause.

23.2 A plea by a Respondent that the Arbitral Tribunal does not have jurisdiction shall be treated as having been irrevocably waived unless it is raised not later than the Statement of Defence; and a like plea by a Respondent to Counterclaim shall be similarly treated unless it is raised no later than the Statement of Defence to Counterclaim. A plea that the Arbitral Tribunal is exceeding the scope of its authority shall be raised promptly after the Arbitral Tribunal has indicated its intention to decide on the matter alleged by any party to be beyond the scope of its authority, failing which such plea shall also be treated as having been waived irrevocably. In any case, the Arbitral Tribunal may nevertheless admit an untimely plea if it considers the delay justified in the particular circumstances.

23.3 The Arbitral Tribunal may determine the plea to its jurisdiction or authority in an award as to jurisdiction or later in an award on the merits, as it considers appropriate in the circumstances.

23.4 By agreeing to arbitration under these Rules, the parties shall be treated as having agreed not to apply to any state court or other judicial authority for any relief regarding

Institutional Rules

the Arbitral Tribunal's jurisdiction or authority, except with the agreement in writing of all parties to the arbitration or the prior authorisation of the Arbitral Tribunal or following the latter's award ruling on the objection to its jurisdiction or authority.

Article 24

Deposits

A44–025   **24.1** The LCIA Court may direct the parties, in such proportions as it thinks appropriate, to make one or several interim or final payments on account of the costs of the arbitration. Such deposits shall be made to and held by the LCIA and from time to time may be released by the LCIA Court to the arbitrator(s), any expert appointed by the Arbitral Tribunal and the LCIA itself as the arbitration progresses.

24.2 The Arbitral Tribunal shall not proceed with the arbitration without ascertaining at all times from the Registrar or any deputy Registrar that the LCIA is in requisite funds.

24.3 In the event that a party fails or refuses to provide any deposit as directed by the LCIA Court, the LCIA Court may direct the other party or parties to effect a substitute payment to allow the arbitration to proceed (subject to any award on costs). In such circumstances, the party paying the substitute payment shall be entitled to recover that amount as a debt immediately due from the defaulting party.

24.4 Failure by a claimant or counterclaiming party to provide promptly and in full the required deposit may be treated by the LCIA Court and the Arbitral Tribunal as a withdrawal of the claim or counterclaim respectively.

Article 25

Interim and Conservatory Measures

A44–026   **25.1** The Arbitral Tribunal shall have the power, unless otherwise agreed by the parties in writing, on the application of any party:

    (a) to order any respondent party to a claim or counterclaim to provide security for all or part of the amount in dispute, by way of deposit or bank guarantee or in any other manner and upon such terms as the Arbitral Tribunal considers appropriate. Such terms may include the provision by the claiming or counterclaiming party of a cross-indemnity, itself secured in such manner as the Arbitral Tribunal considers appropriate, for any costs or losses incurred by such respondent in providing security. The amount of any costs and losses payable under such cross-indemnity may be determined by the Arbitral Tribunal in one or more awards;

    (b) to order the preservation, storage, sale or other disposal of any property or thing under the control of any party and relating to the subject matter of the arbitration; and

    (c) to order on a provisional basis, subject to final determination in an award, any relief which the Arbitral Tribunal would have power to grant in an award, including a provisional order for the payment of money or the disposition of property as between any parties.

25.2 The Arbitral Tribunal shall have the power, upon the application of a party, to order any claiming or counterclaiming party to provide security for the legal or other costs of any other party by way of deposit or bank guarantee or in any other manner and upon such terms as the Arbitral Tribunal considers appropriate. Such terms may include the provision by that other party of a cross-indemnity, itself secured in such manner as the Arbitral Tribunal considers appropriate, for any costs and losses incurred by such claimant or counterclaimant in providing security. The amount of any costs and losses payable under such cross-indemnity may be determined by the Arbitral Tribunal in one or more awards. In the event that a claiming or counterclaiming party does not comply with any order to provide security, the Arbitral Tribunal may stay that party's claims or counterclaims or dismiss them in an award.

25.3 The power of the Arbitral Tribunal under Article 25.1 shall not prejudice howsoever any party's right to apply to any state court or other judicial authority for interim or conservatory measures before the formation of the Arbitral Tribunal and, in exceptional cases, thereafter. Any application and any order for such measures after the formation of the Arbitral Tribunal shall be promptly communicated by the applicant to the Arbitral Tribunal and all other parties. However, by agreeing to arbitration under these Rules, the parties shall be taken to have agreed not to apply to any state court or other judicial authority for any order for security for its legal or other costs available from the Arbitral Tribunal under Article 25.2.

Article 26

The Award

26.1 The Arbitral Tribunal shall make its award in writing and, unless all parties agree in writing otherwise, shall state the reasons upon which its award is based. The award shall also state the date when the award is made and the seat of the arbitration; and it shall be signed by the Arbitral Tribunal or those of its members assenting to it.

26.2 If any arbitrator fails to comply with the mandatory provisions of any applicable law relating to the making of the award, having been given a reasonable opportunity to do so, the remaining arbitrators may proceed in his absence and state in their award the circumstances of the other arbitrator's failure to participate in the making of the award.

26.3 Where there are three arbitrators and the Arbitral Tribunal fails to agree on any issue, the arbitrators shall decide that issue by a majority. Failing a majority decision on any issue, the chairman of the Arbitral Tribunal shall decide that issue.

26.4 If any arbitrator refuses or fails to sign the award, the signatures of the majority or (failing a majority) of the chairman shall be sufficient, provided that the reason for the omitted signature is stated in the award by the majority or chairman.

26.5 The sole arbitrator or chairman shall be responsible for delivering the award to the LCIA Court, which shall transmit certified copies to the parties provided that the costs of arbitration have been paid to the LCIA in accordance with Article 28.

26.6 An award may be expressed in any currency. The Arbitral Tribunal may order that simple or compound interest shall be paid by any party on any sum awarded at such rates as the Arbitral Tribunal determines to be appropriate, without being bound by legal rates of interest imposed by any state court, in respect of any period which the Arbitral Tribunal determines to be appropriate ending not later than the date upon which the award is complied with.

26.7 The Arbitral Tribunal may make separate awards on different issues at different times. Such awards shall have the same status and effect as any other award made by the Arbitral Tribunal.

26.8 In the event of a settlement of the parties' dispute, the Arbitral Tribunal may render an award recording the settlement if the parties so request in writing (a "Consent Award"), provided always that such award contains an express statement that it is an award made by the parties' consent. A Consent Award need not contain reasons. If the parties do not require a consent award, then on written confirmation by the parties to the LCIA Court that a settlement has been reached, the Arbitral Tribunal shall be discharged and the arbitration proceedings concluded, subject to payment by the parties of any outstanding costs of the arbitration under Article 28.

26.9 All awards shall be final and binding on the parties. By agreeing to arbitration under these Rules, the parties undertake to carry out any award immediately and without any delay (subject only to Article 27); and the parties also waive irrevocably their right to any form of appeal, review or recourse to any state court or other judicial authority, insofar as such waiver may be validly made.

Article 27

Correction of Awards and Additional Awards

A44–028   **27.1** Within 30 days of receipt of any award, or such lesser period as may be agreed in writing by the parties, a party may by written notice to the Registrar (copied to all other parties) request the Arbitral Tribunal to correct in the award any errors in computation, clerical or typographical errors or any errors of a similar nature. If the Arbitral Tribunal considers the request to be justified, it shall make the corrections within 30 days of receipt of the request. Any correction shall take the form of separate memorandum dated and signed by the Arbitral Tribunal or (if three arbitrators) those of its members assenting to it; and such memorandum shall become part of the award for all purposes.

27.2 The Arbitral Tribunal may likewise correct any error of the nature described in Article 27.1 on its own initiative within 30 days of the date of the award, to the same effect.

27.3 Within 30 days of receipt of the final award, a party may by written notice to the Registrar (copied to all other parties), request the Arbitral Tribunal to make an additional award as to claims or counterclaims presented in the arbitration but not determined in any award. If the Arbitral Tribunal considers the request to be justified, it shall make the additional award within 60 days of receipt of the request. The provisions of Article 26 shall apply to any additional award.

Article 28

Arbitration and Legal Costs

A44–029   **28.1** The costs of the arbitration (other than the legal or other costs incurred by the parties themselves) shall be determined by the LCIA Court in accordance with the Schedule of Costs. The parties shall be jointly and severally liable to the Arbitral Tribunal and the LCIA for such arbitration costs.

28.2 The Arbitral Tribunal shall specify in the award the total amount of the costs of the arbitration as determined by the LCIA Court. Unless the parties agree otherwise in writing, the Arbitral Tribunal shall determine the proportions in which the parties shall bear all or part of such arbitration costs. If the Arbitral Tribunal has determined that all or any part of the arbitration costs shall be borne by a party other than a party which has already paid them to the LCIA, the latter party shall have the right to recover the appropriate amount from the former party.

28.3 The Arbitral Tribunal shall also have the power to order in its award that all or part of the legal or other costs incurred by a party be paid by another party, unless the parties agree otherwise in writing. The Arbitral Tribunal shall determine and fix the amount of each item comprising such costs on such reasonable basis as it thinks fit.

28.4 Unless the parties otherwise agree in writing, the Arbitral Tribunal shall make its orders on both arbitration and legal costs on the general principle that costs should reflect the parties' relative success and failure in the award or arbitration, except where it appears to the Arbitral Tribunal that in the particular circumstances this general approach is inappropriate. Any order for costs shall be made with reasons in the award containing such order.

28.5 If the arbitration is abandoned, suspended or concluded, by agreement or otherwise, before the final award is made, the parties shall remain jointly and severally liable to pay to the LCIA and the Arbitral Tribunal the costs of the arbitration as determined by the LCIA Court in accordance with the Schedule of Costs. In the event that such arbitration costs are less than the deposits made by the parties, there shall be a refund by the LCIA in such proportion as the parties may agree in writing, or failing such agreement, in the same proportions as the deposits were made by the parties to the LCIA.

Article 29

Decisions by the LCIA Court

29.1 The decisions of the LCIA Court with respect to all matters relating to the arbitration shall be conclusive and binding upon the parties and the Arbitral Tribunal. Such decisions are to be treated as administrative in nature and the LCIA Court shall not be required to give any reasons. **A44–030**

29.2 To the extent permitted by the law of the seat of the arbitration, the parties shall be taken to have waived any right of appeal or review in respect of any such decisions of the LCIA Court to any state court or other judicial authority. If such appeals or review remain possible due to mandatory provisions of any applicable law, the LCIA Court shall, subject to the provisions of that applicable law, decide whether the arbitral proceedings are to continue, notwithstanding an appeal or review.

Article 30

Confidentiality

30.1 Unless the parties expressly agree in writing to the contrary, the parties undertake as a general principle to keep confidential all awards in their arbitration, together with all materials in the proceedings created for the purpose of the arbitration and all other documents produced by another party in the proceedings not otherwise in the public domain—save and to the extent that disclosure may be required of a party by legal duty, to protect or pursue a legal right or to enforce or challenge an award in bona fide legal proceedings before a state court or other judicial authority. **A44–031**

30.2 The deliberations of the Arbitral Tribunal are likewise confidential to its members, save and to the extent that disclosure of an arbitrator's refusal to participate in the arbitration is required of the other members of the Arbitral Tribunal under Articles 10, 12 and 26.

30.3 The LCIA Court does not publish any award or any part of an award without the prior written consent of all parties and the Arbitral Tribunal.

Article 31

Exclusion of Liability

A44–032 **31.1** None of the LCIA, the LCIA Court (including its President, Vice-Presidents and individual members), the Registrar, any deputy Registrar, any arbitrator and any expert to the Arbitral Tribunal shall be liable to any party howsoever for any act or omission in connection with any arbitration conducted by reference to these Rules, save where the act or omission is shown by that party to constitute conscious and deliberate wrongdoing committed by the body or person alleged to be liable to that party.

31.2 After the award has been made and the possibilities of correction and additional awards referred to in Article 27 have lapsed or been exhausted, neither the LCIA, the LCIA Court (including its President, Vice-Presidents and individual members), the Registrar, any deputy Registrar, any arbitrator or expert to the Arbitral Tribunal shall be under any legal obligation to make any statement to any person about any matter concerning the arbitration, nor shall any party seek to make any of these persons a witness in any legal or other proceedings arising out of the arbitration.

Article 32

General Rules

A44–033 **32.1** A party who knows that any provision of the Arbitration Agreement (including these Rules) has not been complied with and yet proceeds with the arbitration without promptly stating its objection to such non-compliance, shall be treated as having irrevocably waived its right to object.

32.2 In all matters not expressly provided for in these Rules, the LCIA Court, the Arbitral Tribunal and the parties shall act in the spirit of these Rules and shall make every reasonable effort to ensure that an award is legally enforceable.

The London Court of International Arbitration Mediation Procedure[1]

EFFECTIVE 1 OCTOBER, 1999

Where any agreement provides for mediation of existing or future disputes under the procedure or rules of the LCIA, the parties shall be taken to have agreed that the mediation shall be conducted in accordance with the following procedure (the "Procedure") or such amended procedure as the LCIA may have adopted hereafter to take effect before the commencement of the mediation. The Procedure includes the Schedule of Mediation Fees and Expenses (the "Schedule") in effect at the commencement of the mediation, as separately amended from time to time by the LCIA Court.   A45–001

Article 1

Commencing Mediation—Prior existing agreements to mediate

1.1 Where there is a prior existing agreement to mediate under the Procedure (a "Prior Agreement"), any party or parties wishing to commence a mediation shall send to the Registrar of the LCIA Court ("the Registrar") a written request for mediation (the "Request for Mediation"), which shall briefly state the nature of the dispute and the value of the claim, and should include, or be accompanied by a copy of the Prior Agreement, the names, addresses, telephone, facsimile, telex and e-mail numbers (if known) of the parties to the mediation, and of their legal representatives (if known) and of the mediator proposed (if any) by the party or parties requesting mediation.   A45–002

1.2 If the Request for Mediation is not made jointly by all parties to the Prior Agreement, the party commencing the mediation shall, at the same time, send a copy of the Request for Mediation to the other party or parties.

1.3 The Request for Mediation shall be accompanied by the registration fee prescribed in the Schedule.

1.4 The LCIA Court shall appoint a mediator as soon as practicable after receipt by the Registrar of the Request for Mediation, with due regard for any nomination, or method or criteria of selection agreed in writing by the parties, and subject always to Article 8 of the Procedure.

1.5 Where there is a Prior Agreement, the date of commencement of the mediation shall be the date of receipt by the Registrar of the Request for Mediation.

Article 2

Commencing Mediation—no Prior Agreement

2.1 Where there is no Prior Agreement, any party or parties wishing to commence a mediation under the Procedure shall send to the Registrar a Request for Mediation, which shall briefly state the nature of the dispute and the value of the claim, and should include,   A45–003

---

[1] This document is reproduced with the kind permission of the London Court of International Arbitration.

or be accompanied by, the names, addresses, telephone, facsimile, telex and e-mail numbers (if known) of the parties to the mediation, and of their legal representatives (if known) and of the mediator proposed (if any) by the party or parties requesting mediation.

2.2 The Request for Mediation shall be accompanied by the registration fee prescribed in the Schedule.

2.3 If the Request for Mediation is not made jointly by all parties to the dispute,

a) the party wishing to commence the mediation shall, at the same time, send a copy of the Request for Mediation to the other party or parties; and

b) the other party or parties shall, within 14 days of receiving the Request for Mediation, advise the Registrar in writing whether or not they agree to the mediation of the dispute.

2.4 In the event that the other party or parties either declines mediation, or fails to agree to mediation within the 14 days referred to at Article 2.3b), there shall be no mediation under the Procedure and the Registrar shall so advise the parties, in writing.

2.5 The LCIA Court shall appoint a mediator as soon as practicable after agreement to mediate has been reached between the parties, with due regard for any nomination, or method or criteria of selection agreed in writing by the parties, and subject always to Article 8 of the Procedure.

2.6 Where there is no Prior Agreement, the date of commencement of the mediation shall be the date that agreement to mediate is reached in accordance with Article 2.3(b).

Article 3

Appointment of Mediator

A45–004   **3.1** Before appointment by the LCIA Court, pursuant to Article 1.4 or Article 2.5, the mediator shall furnish the Registrar with a written résumé of his or her past and present professional positions; and he or she shall sign a declaration to the effect that there are no circumstances known to him or her likely to give rise to any justified doubts as to his or her impartiality or independence, other than any circumstances disclosed by him or her in the declaration. A copy of the mediator's résumé and declaration shall be provided to the parties.

3.2 Where the mediator has made a disclosure, pursuant to Article 3.1, or where a party independently knows of circumstances likely to give rise to justified doubts as to his or her impartiality or independence, a party shall be at liberty to object to his or her appointment; in which case the LCIA Court shall appoint another mediator.

Article 4

Statements by the Parties

A45–005   **4.1** The parties are free to agree how, and in what form, they will inform the mediator of their respective cases, provided that, unless they have agreed otherwise, each party shall submit to the mediator, no later than 7 days before the date agreed between the mediator and the parties for the first scheduled mediation session, a brief written statement summarising his case; the background to the dispute; and the issues to be resolved.

4.2 Each written statement should be accompanied by copies of any documents to which it refers.

4.3 Each party shall, at the same time, submit a copy of his written statement and supporting documents to the other party or parties.

Article 5

Conduct of the Mediation

5.1 The mediator may conduct the mediation in such manner as he or she sees fit, having in mind at all times the circumstances of the case and the wishes of the parties.

5.2 The mediator may communicate with the parties orally or in writing, together, or individually, and may convene a meeting or meetings at a venue to be determined by the mediator after consultations with the parties.

5.3 Nothing which is communicated to the mediator in private during the course of the mediation shall be repeated to the other party of parties, without the express consent of the party making the communication.

5.4 Each party shall notify the other party and the mediator of the number and identity of those persons who will attend any meeting convened by the mediator.

5.5 Each party shall identify a representative of that party who is authorised to settle the dispute on behalf of that party, and shall confirm that authority in writing.

5.6 Unless otherwise agreed by the parties, the mediator will decide the language(s) in which the mediation will be conducted.

Article 6

Conclusion of the Mediation

The mediation will be at an end when, either

(a) a settlement agreement is signed by the parties; or

(b) the parties advise the mediator that it is their view that a settlement cannot be reached and that it is their wish to terminate the mediation; or

(c) the mediator advises the parties that, in his or her judgement, the mediation process will not resolve the issues in dispute; or

(d) the time limit for mediation provided in a Prior Agreement has expired and the parties have not agreed to extend that time limit.

Article 7

Settlement Agreement

7.1 If terms are agreed in settlement of the dispute, the parties, with the assistance of the mediator if the parties so request, shall draw up and sign a settlement agreement, setting out such terms.

7.2 By signing the settlement agreement, the parties agree to be bound by its terms.

Article 8

Costs

A45–009   **8.1** The costs of the mediation (the "Costs") shall include the fees and expenses of the mediator and the administrative charges of the LCIA, as set out in the Schedule.

8.2 The Costs shall be borne equally by the parties (or in such other proportions as they have agreed in writing).

8.3 As soon as practicable after receipt of the Request for Mediation, pursuant to Article 1 of the Procedure, or after the parties have agreed to mediate, pursuant to Article 2 of the Procedure, the LCIA will request the parties to file a deposit to be held on account of the Costs ("the Deposit"). The Deposit shall be paid by the parties in equal shares (or in such other proportions as they have agreed) prior to the appointment of the mediator.

8.4 A mediator shall not be appointed and the mediation shall not proceed until and unless the Deposit has been paid in full.

8.5 At the conclusion of the mediation, the LCIA, in consultation with the mediator, will fix the Costs of the mediation.

8.6 If the Deposit exceeds the Costs, the excess will be reimbursed to the parties in the proportions in which they paid the deposit. If the Costs exceed the Deposit, the shortfall will be invoiced to the parties for immediate payment in equal shares (or in such other proportions as they have agreed).

8.7 Any other costs incurred by the parties, whether in regard to legal fees, experts' fees or expenses of any other nature will not be part of the Costs for the purposes of the Procedure.

Article 9

Judicial or Arbitral Proceedings

A45–010   Unless they have agreed otherwise, and notwithstanding the mediation, the parties may initiate or continue any arbitration or judicial proceedings in respect of the dispute which is the subject of the mediation.

Article 10

Confidentiality and Privacy

A45–011   **10.1** All mediation sessions shall be private, and shall be attended only by the mediator, the parties and those individuals identified pursuant to Article 5.4.

10.2 The mediation process and all negotiations, and statements and documents prepared for the purposes of the mediation, shall be confidential and covered by "without prejudice" or negotiation privilege.

10.3 The mediation shall be confidential. Unless agreed among the parties, or required by law, neither the mediator nor the parties may disclose to any person any information regarding the mediation or any settlement terms, or the outcome of the mediation.

10.4 All documents or other information produced for or arising in relation to the mediation will be privileged and will not be admissible in evidence or otherwise discoverable in any litigation or arbitration in connection with the dispute referred to mediation, except for any documents or other information which would in any event be admissible or discoverable in any such litigation or arbitration.

10.5 There shall be no formal record or transcript of the mediation.

10.6 The parties shall not rely upon, or introduce as evidence in any arbitral or judicial proceedings, any admissions, proposals or views expressed by the parties or by the mediator during the course of the mediation.

Article 11

Exclusion of Liability

11.1 None of the LCIA, the LCIA Court (including its President, Vice-Presidents and individual members), the Registrar, any Deputy Registrar and any mediator shall be liable to any party howsoever for any act or omission in connection with any mediation conducted by reference to the Procedure, save where the act or omission is shown by that party to constitute conscious and deliberate wrongdoing committed by the body or person alleged to be liable to that party.

11.2 None of the LCIA, the LCIA Court (including its President, Vice-Presidents and individual members), the Registrar, any Deputy Registrar, or the Mediator shall be under any legal obligation to make any statement to any person about any matter concerning the mediation, nor shall any party seek to make any of these persons a witness in any legal or other proceedings arising out of the mediation.

The LMAA Terms (2002)[1]

EFFECTIVE FOR APPOINTMENTS ON AND AFTER 1 JANUARY, 2002

Preliminary

A46–001
1. These Terms may be referred to as "the L.M.A.A Terms (2002)".
2. In these Terms, unless the context otherwise requires,

(i) "the Association" means the London Maritime Arbitrators Association;

"Member of the Association" includes full, retired and supporting members;

"President" means the President for the time being of the Association

(ii) "tribunal" includes a sole arbitrator, a tribunal of two or more arbitrators, and an umpire

(iii) "original arbitrator" means an arbitrator appointed (whether initially or by substitution) by or at the request of a party as its nominee and any arbitrator duly appointed so to act following failure of a party to make its own nomination.

3. The purpose of arbitration according to these Terms is to obtain the fair resolution of maritime and other disputes by an impartial tribunal without unnecessary delay or expense. The arbitrators at all times are under a duty to act fairly and impartially between the parties and an original arbitrator is in no sense to be considered as the representative of his appointor.

Application

A46–002
4. These Terms apply to arbitral proceedings commenced on or after 1st January 2002. Section 14 of the Arbitration Act 1996 ("the Act") shall apply for the purpose of determining on what date arbitral proceedings are to be regarded as having commenced.

5. These Terms shall apply to an arbitration agreement whenever the parties have agreed that they shall apply and the parties shall in particular be taken to have so agreed:

(a) whenever the dispute is referred to a sole arbitrator who is a full Member of the Association and whenever both the original arbitrators appointed by the parties are full Members of the Association, unless both parties have agreed or shall agree otherwise;

(b) whenever a sole arbitrator or both the original arbitrators have been appointed on the basis that these Terms apply to their appointment.

Whenever a sole arbitrator or both the original arbitrators have been appointed on the basis referred to at (b), such appointments or the conduct of the parties in taking part in the arbitration thereafter shall constitute an agreement between the parties that the arbitration agreement governing their dispute has been made or varied so as to incorporate these Terms and shall further constitute authority to their respective arbitrators so to confirm in writing on their behalf.

[1] This document is reproduced with the kind permission of the London Maritime Arbitrators Association.

The LMAA Terms

6. In the absence of any agreement to the contrary the parties to all arbitral proceedings to which these Terms apply agree:

(a) that the law applicable to their arbitration agreement is English law; and

(b) that the seat of the arbitration is in England.

7. (a) Subject to paragraph (b), the arbitral proceedings and the rights and obligations of the parties in connection therewith shall be in all respects governed by the Act save to the extent that the provisions of the Act are varied, modified or supplemented by these Terms.

(b) Where the seat of the arbitration is outside England and Wales the provisions of these Terms shall nevertheless apply to the arbitral proceedings, save to the extent that any mandatory provisions of the law applicable to the arbitration agreement otherwise provide.

The Arbitral Tribunal

8. If the tribunal is to consist of three arbitrators: A46–003

(a) each party shall appoint one arbitrator not later than 14 days after service of a request in writing by either party to do so;

(b) the two so appointed may at any time thereafter appoint a third arbitrator so long as they do so before any substantive hearing or forthwith if they cannot agree on any matter relating to the arbitration;

(c) the third arbitrator shall be the chairman unless the parties shall agree otherwise;

(d) before the third arbitrator has been appointed or if the position has become vacant, the two original arbitrators, if agreed on any matter, shall have the power to make decisions, orders and awards in relation thereto;

(e) after the appointment of the third arbitrator decisions, orders or awards shall be made by all or a majority of the arbitrators;

(f) the view of the chairman shall prevail in relation to a decision, order or award in respect of which there is neither unanimity nor a majority under paragraph (e).

9. If the tribunal is to consist of two arbitrators and an umpire:

(a) each party shall appoint one arbitrator not later than 14 days after service of a request in writing by either party to do so;

(b) the two so appointed may appoint an umpire at any time after they themselves are appointed and shall do so before any substantive hearing or forthwith if they cannot agree on any matter relating to the arbitration;

(c) the umpire shall attend any substantive hearing and shall following his appointment be supplied with the same documents and other materials as are supplied to the other arbitrators;

(d) the umpire may take part in the hearing and deliberate with the original arbitrators;

(e) decisions, orders and awards shall be made by the original arbitrators unless and until they cannot agree on a matter relating to the arbitration. In that event they shall forthwith give notice in writing to the parties and the umpire, whereupon the umpire shall replace them as the tribunal with power to make decisions, orders and awards as if he were the sole arbitrator.

Jurisdiction

A46–004   10. The jurisdiction of the tribunal shall extend to determining all disputes arising under or in connection with the transaction the subject of the reference, and each party shall have the right before the tribunal has given notice of its intention to proceed to its award to refer to the tribunal for determination any further dispute(s) arising subsequent to the commencement of the arbitral proceedings.

Tribunal's Fees

A46–005   11. Provisions regulating fees payable to the tribunal and other related matters are set out in the First Schedule. Save as therein or herein otherwise provided, payment of the tribunal's fees and expenses is the joint and several responsibility of the parties. An arbitrator or umpire shall be entitled to resign from a reference in the circumstances set out in paragraph (C) of the First Schedule.

Arbitration Procedure

A46–006   12. (a) It shall be for the tribunal to decide all procedural and evidential matters subject to the right of the parties to agree any matter. However, the normal procedure to be adopted is as set out in the Second Schedule.

(b) In the absence of agreement it shall be for the tribunal to decide whether and to what extent there should be oral or written evidence or submissions in the arbitration. The parties should however attempt to agree at an early stage whether the arbitration is to be on documents alone (i.e. without a hearing) or whether there is to be an oral hearing.

Interlocutory Proceedings

A46–007   13. (a) In all cases the procedure set out in paragraphs 1 to 4 of the Second Schedule should be adopted.

(b) Applications for directions should not be necessary but, if required, they should be made in accordance with the Second Schedule.

(c) *Arbitrations on documents alone*
Following completion of the steps covered by paragraphs 1 to 4 of the Second Schedule, if it has been or is then determined by the tribunal or agreed by the parties that the case is to be dealt with on documents alone, the tribunal will then give notice to the parties of its intention to proceed to its award and will so proceed unless either party within seven days requests, and is thereafter granted, leave to serve further submissions and/or documents.

(d) *Oral hearings*
If it is determined or agreed that there shall be an oral hearing, then following the fixing of the hearing date a booking fee will be payable in accordance with the provisions of the First Schedule.

The LMAA Terms

Powers of the Tribunal

14. In addition to the powers set out in the Act, the tribunal shall have the following specific powers to be exercised in a suitable case so as to avoid unnecessary delay or expense, and so as to provide a fair means for the resolution of the matters falling to be determined:

    (a) The tribunal may limit the number of expert witnesses to be called by any party or may direct either that no expert be called on any issue(s) or that no expert evidence shall be called save with the leave of the tribunal.

    (b) Where two or more arbitrations appear to raise common issues of fact or law, the tribunals may direct that the two or more arbitrations shall be heard concurrently. Where such an order is made, the tribunals may give such directions as the interests of fairness, economy and expedition require including:

        (i) that the documents disclosed by the parties in one arbitration shall be made available to the parties to the other arbitration upon such conditions as the tribunals may determine;
        (ii) that the evidence given in one arbitration shall be received and admitted in the other arbitration, subject to all parties being given a reasonable opportunity to comment upon it and subject to such other conditions as the tribunals may determine.

    (c) If a party fails to comply with a peremptory order of the tribunal to provide security for costs, then without prejudice to the power granted by section 41(6) of the Act, the tribunal shall have power to stay that party's claim or such part of it as the tribunal thinks fit in its sole discretion.

A46–008

Preliminary Meetings

15. (a) The tribunal may decide at any stage that the circumstances of the arbitration require that there should be a preliminary meeting to enable the parties and the tribunal to review the progress of the case; to reach agreement so far as possible upon further preparation for, and the conduct of the hearing; and, where agreement is not reached, to enable the tribunal to give such directions as it thinks fit.

    (b) A preliminary meeting should be held in complex cases including most cases involving a hearing of more than five days' duration. Exceptionally more than one preliminary meeting may be required.

    (c) All preliminary meetings (whether required by the tribunal or held on the application of the parties) should be preceded by a discussion between the parties' representatives who should attempt to identify matters for discussion with the tribunal, attempt to reach agreement so far as possible on the directions to be given, and prepare for submission to the tribunal an agenda of matters for approval or determination by it.

    (d) Before the preliminary meeting takes place the parties should provide the tribunal with a bundle of appropriate documents, together with information sheets setting out the steps taken and to be taken in the arbitration, a list of any proposed directions whether agreed or not and an agenda of matters for discussion at the hearing. The information sheets should include estimates of readiness for the hearing and the likely duration of the hearing.

A46–009

(e) There is set out in the Third Schedule a guidance document indicating topics which may be appropriate for consideration before and at the preliminary hearing.

Settlement

A46–010 16. It is the duty of the parties (a) to notify the tribunal immediately if the arbitration is settled or otherwise terminated (b) to make provision in any settlement for payment of the fees and expenses of the tribunal and (c) to inform the tribunal of the parties' agreement as to the manner in which payment will be made of any outstanding fees and expenses of the tribunal, e.g. for interlocutory work not covered by any booking fee paid. The same duty arises if the settlement takes place after an interim award has been made. Upon being notified of the settlement or termination of any matter the tribunal may dispose of the documents relating to it.

17. Any booking fee paid will be dealt with in accordance with the provisions of paragraph (D)(1)(d) of the First Schedule. Any other fees and expenses of the tribunal shall be settled promptly and at latest within 28 days of presentation of the relevant account(s). Notwithstanding the terms of any settlement between them the parties shall remain jointly and severally responsible for all such fees and expenses of the tribunal until they have been paid in full.

Adjournment

18. If a case is for any reason adjourned part-heard, the tribunal will be entitled to an interim payment, payable in equal shares or otherwise as the tribunal may direct, in respect of fees and expenses already incurred, appropriate credit being given for the booking fee.

Availability of Arbitrators

A46–011 19. (a) In cases where it is known at the outset that an early hearing is essential, the parties should consult and ensure the availability of the arbitrator(s) to be appointed by them.

(b) If, in cases when the tribunal has already been constituted, the fixture of an acceptable hearing date is precluded by the commitments of the original appointee(s), the provisions of the Fourth Schedule shall apply.

The Award

A46–012 20. The time required for preparation of an award must vary with the circumstances of the case. The award should normally be available within not more than six weeks from the close of the proceedings. In many cases, and in particular where the matter is one of urgency, the interval should be substantially shorter.

21. The members of a tribunal need not meet together for the purpose of signing their award or of effecting any corrections thereto.

22.
(a) If before the award is made one or more parties to the reference shall give notice to the tribunal that a reasoned award is required, the award shall contain the reasons for the award.

(b) The parties agree to dispense with reasons in all cases where no notice shall have been given to the tribunal under paragraph (a) before the award is made.

[Note: the effect of such agreement is to exclude the court's jurisdiction under Section 69 of the Act to determine an appeal on a question of law arising out of the award; see Section 69(1)]

(c) Where in accordance with paragraph (b) the parties have agreed to dispense with reasons the tribunal will issue an award without reasons together with a document which does not form part of the award but which gives, on a confidential basis, an outline of the reasons for the tribunal's decision (hereafter called "privileged reasons").

(d) Unless the court shall otherwise determine, the document containing privileged reasons (referred to in paragraph (c)) may not be relied upon or referred to by either party in any proceedings relating to the award.

23. As soon as possible after an award has been made it shall be notified to the parties by the tribunal serving on them a notice in writing which shall inform the parties of the amount of the fees and expenses of the tribunal and which shall indicate that the award is available for sending to or collection by the parties upon full payment of such amount. At the stage of notification neither the award nor any copy thereof need be served on the parties and the tribunal shall be entitled thereafter to refuse to deliver the award or any copy thereof to the parties except upon full payment of its fees and expenses.

24. If any award has not been paid for and collected within one month of the date of publication, the tribunal may give written notice to either party requiring payment of the costs of the award, whereupon such party shall be obliged to pay for and collect the award within fourteen days.

25.

(a) In addition to the powers set out in Section 57 of the Act, the tribunal shall have the following powers to correct an award or to make an additional award:

(i) The tribunal may on its own initiative or on the application of a party correct any accidental mistake, omission or error of calculation in its award.

(ii) The tribunal may on the application of a party give an interpretation of a specific point or part of the award.

(b) An application for the exercise of the powers set out above and in Section 57 of the Act must be made within 28 days of the award unless the tribunal shall think fit to extend the time.

(c) The powers set out above shall not be exercised without first affording the other parties a reasonable opportunity to make representations to the tribunal.

(d) Any correction or interpretation of an award may be effected in writing on the original award or in a separate memorandum which shall become part of the award. It shall be effected within 90 days of the date of the original award unless all parties shall agree a longer period.

26. If the tribunal considers that an arbitration decision merits publication and gives notice to the parties of its intention to release the award for publication, then unless either or both parties inform the tribunal of its or their objection to publication within 21 days of the notice, the award may be publicised under such arrangements as the Association may effect from time to time. The publication will be so drafted as to preserve anonymity as regards the identity of the parties, of their legal or other representatives, and of the tribunal.

Service of Documents

A46–013 27. Where a party is represented by a lawyer or other agent in connection with any arbitral proceedings, all notices or other documents required to be given or served for the purposes of the arbitral proceedings together with all decisions, orders and awards made or issued by the tribunal shall be treated as effectively served if served on that lawyer or agent.

General

A46–014 28. Three months after the publication of a final award the tribunal may notify the parties of its intention to dispose of the documents and to close the file, and it will act accordingly unless otherwise requested within 21 days of such notice being given.

29. In relation to any matters not expressly provided for herein the tribunal shall act in accordance with the tenor of these Terms.

THE FIRST SCHEDULE

Tribunal's Fees

(A) Appointment fee

A46–015 An appointment fee is payable on appointment by the appointing party or by the party at whose request the appointment is made. The appointment fee shall be a standard fee fixed by the Committee of the Association from time to time. Unless otherwise agreed, the appointment fee of an umpire or third arbitrator shall in the first instance be paid by the claimant, and the appointment fee of an agreed sole arbitrator shall be paid by each party in equal shares.

(B) Interim fees

A46–016 An arbitrator may in his discretion require payment of his fees to date (which expression shall for these purposes include any expenses) at appropriate intervals (which shall be not less than three months). Any such demand for payment shall be addressed to the arbitrator's appointing party and shall be copied to any other member of the tribunal and other parties. A third arbitrator or umpire shall require payment from the parties in equal shares. Any such demand for payment is without prejudice (a) to ultimate liability for the fees in question and (b) to the parties' joint and several liability therefor.

(C) Right to resign for non-payment

A46–017 If any amount due under (A) or (B) above remains unpaid for more than 28 days after payment has been demanded, the arbitrator in his sole discretion may give written notice to his appointor and to the other parties and arbitrators that he will resign his appointment if such amount still remains unpaid 14 days after such notification. Without prejudice to ultimate liability for the fees in question, any other party may prevent such resignation by paying the amount demanded within the said 14 days. Upon any resignation under this paragraph the arbitrator will be entitled to immediate payment of his fees to date, and shall be under no liability to any party for any consequences of his resignation.

(D) Booking fees

A46–018 (1) (a) For a hearing of up to ten days' duration there shall be payable to the tribunal a booking fee of £350 per person or such other sum as the Committee of the Association may from time to time decide, for each day reserved. The booking fee will be invoiced to the party asking for the hearing date to be fixed or to the parties in equal shares if both parties ask for the hearing date to be fixed as the case may be and shall become due and shall be paid within 14 days of confirmation of the reservation or six months in advance of the first day reserved ("the start date"), whichever date be the later. If the fee is not paid in full by the due date the tribunal will be entitled to cancel the reservation forthwith without prejudice to its entitlement to be paid the fee in question or the appropriate proportion thereof in accordance with sub-paragraph (d) below. In the event of a cancellation under this provision either party may secure reinstatement of the reservation by payment within seven days of any balance outstanding.

(b) For hearings over ten days' duration the booking fee in sub-paragraph (1)(a) above shall for each day reserved be increased by 30% in the case of a hearing of up to 15 days and 60% in the case of a hearing of up to 20 days and may, at the discretion of the tribunal, be subscribed in non-returnable instalment payments. For hearings in excess of 20 days the booking fee shall be at the rate for a hearing of 20 days plus such additional sum as may be agreed with the parties in the light of the length of the proposed hearing.

(c) The booking fee for any third arbitrator or umpire shall be due and payable as above, save that the booking fee due to any third arbitrator or umpire appointed less than six months before the start date shall be due forthwith upon his appointment and payable within 14 days thereof.

(d) Where, (i) at the request of one or both of the parties, or (ii) by reason of settlement of any dispute, or (iii) by reason of cancellation pursuant to sub-paragraph (a) above or (iv) by reason of the indisposition or death of any arbitrator or umpire a hearing is adjourned or a hearing date vacated prior to or on or after the start date, then, unless non-returnable instalment or other payments have been agreed, the booking fee will be retained by (or, if unpaid, shall be payable to) the tribunal (i) in full if the date is adjourned or vacated less than three months before the start date or on or after that date, (ii) as to 50 per cent if the date is adjourned or vacated three months or more before the start date. Any interlocutory fees and expenses incurred will also be payable or, as the case may be, deductible from any refund under (ii).

(e) Where, at the request of one or both of the parties, or by reason of the indisposition or death of any arbitrator or umpire a hearing is adjourned or a hearing date is vacated and a new hearing date is fixed, a further booking fee will be payable in accordance with sub-paragraphs (a) and (b) above.

(2) An arbitrator or umpire who, following receipt of his booking fee or any part thereof, is for any reason replaced is, upon settlement of his fees for any interlocutory work, responsible for the transfer of his booking fee to the person appointed to act in his place. In the event of death the personal representative shall have corresponding responsibility.

(E) Security for costs of awards

(1) Without prejudice to the rights provided for in paragraphs (A), (B) and (D) above, **A46–019** a tribunal is entitled to reasonable security for its estimated costs (including its fees and

expenses) up to the making of an award. In calculating such amount credit will be given for any booking fees paid. Such security is to be provided no later than 21 days before the start of any oral hearing intended to lead to an award or, in the case of a documents-only arbitration, no later than immediately before the tribunal starts reading and drafting with a view to producing an award.

(2) If a tribunal exercises the right to request security under sub-paragraph (1) above, it shall advise the parties of its total estimated costs (a) in the case of an oral hearing, usually when such hearing is fixed and in any event no later than 28 days before the security must be in place, and (b) in the case of a documents-only arbitration 28 days before the tribunal intends to start reading and/or drafting with a view to producing an award.

(3) Requests for security hereunder shall be addressed to the party requesting any oral hearing, and to the claimant in the case of a documents-only arbitration. If such party fails to provide such security within the time set any other party will be given 7 days' notice in which to provide it, failing which the tribunal may vacate any hearing dates or, in the case of a documents-only arbitration, refrain from reading and/or drafting.

(4) In any case where time does not allow for the periods in sub-paragraphs (1)–(3) above, the tribunal shall be entitled at its discretion to set such shorter periods as are reasonable in the circumstances.

(5) The form of such security shall be in the tribunal's discretion. Normally an undertaking from an appropriate firm of lawyers or a P&I or Defence Association will be acceptable. However, a tribunal may require a cash deposit or bank guarantee. Any undertaking or guarantee must undertake to pay the sum covered no later than 5 weeks after publication of the relevant award and shall not be conditional upon the award being released unless the costs thereof are wholly covered by the relevant security.

(6) No estimate given hereunder shall prejudice the tribunal's entitlement to its reasonable fees and expenses.

(7) Any security provided or payment made in accordance with these provisions shall be without prejudice to ultimate liability as between the parties for the fees and expenses in question, and to the parties' joint and several liability to the tribunal until all outstanding fees and expenses have been paid in full.

(F) Accounting for payments made on account

A46–020 Where the case proceeds to an award, or is settled subsequent to the start of the hearing, appropriate credit will be given for any amounts paid under paragraphs (B), (D) or (E) above in calculating the amount to be paid in order to collect the award, or as the case may be, the amount payable to the tribunal upon settlement of the case.

Accommodation

A46–021 (1) If accommodation and/or catering is arranged by the tribunal, the cost will normally be recovered as part of the cost of the award, but where a case is adjourned part-heard or in other special circumstances, the tribunal reserves the right to direct that the cost shall be provisionally paid by the parties in equal shares (or as the tribunal may direct) promptly upon issue of the relevant account. Prior to booking accommodation and/or catering the tribunal may, if it thinks fit, request that it be provided with security sufficient to cover its prospective liabilities in respect thereof.

(2) If accommodation is reserved and paid for by the parties and it is desired that the cost incurred be the subject of directions in the award, the information necessary for that purpose must be furnished promptly to the tribunal.

THE SECOND SCHEDULE

Arbitration Procedure

1. The normal procedure (which shall apply unless the parties agree otherwise) requires service of claim submissions. If, exceptionally, formal pleadings are thought appropriate (e.g. in more complicated references) special permission must be obtained from the tribunal. Whether claim submissions or points of claim are served, they must set out the position of the claimants in respect of the issues that have arisen between the parties as clearly, concisely and comprehensively as possible, and must always be accompanied by all supporting documentation relevant to the issues between the parties.

2. Except in unusual cases (e.g. applications for interim final awards for sums which are said to be indisputably due and owing) defence submissions or, if the tribunal has permitted formal pleadings, points of defence (and counterclaim, if any) with all documentation relevant to the issues between the parties (other than that disclosed by the claimants) are to be served 28 days after receipt of the claim submissions or points of claim. An allegation that all relevant documentation has not been disclosed with the claim submissions or points of claim will not normally be a reason for allowing additional time for service of defence submissions or points of defence. However a failure to disclose all relevant documentation at an appropriate stage may be penalised in costs.

3. Submissions in reply or, if the tribunal has permitted formal pleadings, points of reply are to be served 14 days after service of submissions or points of defence unless there is also a defence to a counterclaim, in which case the submissions or pleadings are to be served within 28 days from receipt of the submissions or points of defence and counterclaim. Any reply to the defence to counterclaim must be served within 14 days thereafter.

4. A party serving supporting documentation must check with the tribunal whether it wishes to receive copies of all or some of the documentation at that stage. The aim should be for a tribunal to see enough documentation to be able to identify the issues in the case but not to be burdened with, for instance, copy invoices at the commencement of a reference.

5. All submissions and pleadings must be set out in numbered paragraphs.

6. Bare denials in response to an allegation will not be acceptable. If an allegation is denied, reasons must be given and if appropriate a positive contrary case put forward.

7. Applications for security for costs will not be considered until after service of defence submissions (or points of defence, if formal pleadings have been permitted). Any application must be accompanied by a justification for it and a breakdown of the costs which it is reasonably anticipated will be incurred up to the stage of the reference for which security is sought. In the light of paragraph (E) of the First Schedule it will not be appropriate for security for costs to include any provision for the fees of a tribunal.

8. Unless the parties agree that the reference is ready to proceed to an award on the exclusive basis of the written submissions that have already been served, both parties must complete the Questionnaire set out at the end of this Schedule within 14 days of the service of the final submissions or pleadings as set out in paragraph 4 above. Unless the parties agree, the tribunal will then establish the future procedural course of the reference, either on the basis of the Questionnaires and any other applications made to it in writing or, if appropriate, after a preliminary meeting.

9. Subject to any specific agreement between the parties or ruling from the tribunal, both parties are entitled at any stage to ask each other for any documentation that they consider to be relevant which has not previously been disclosed. Parties will not generally be required to provide broader disclosure than is required by the courts. Generally a party will only be required to disclose the documents on which it relies or which adversely affect its own case, as well as documents which either support or affect the other party's case.

10. If a party wishes to obtain disclosure of certain documents prior to service of submissions or a pleading, it must seek the agreement of the other party, failing which it should make an appropriate written application to the tribunal, explaining the rival positions of the parties in question.

11. In appropriate cases the tribunal may order the service of a statement of truth signed by an officer or by the legal representative of a party confirming the accuracy of any submissions or of any declarations that a reasonable search for relevant documentation has been carried out.

12. Subject to contrary agreement of the parties or an appropriate ruling by the tribunal, the parties will be required to exchange statements of evidence of fact (whether to be adduced in evidence under the Civil Evidence Acts or to stand as evidence in chief) as well as expert evidence covering areas agreed by the parties or ordered by the tribunal within a time scale agreed by the parties or ordered by the tribunal. Statements of evidence of fact or expert evidence that have not been exchanged in accordance with these provisions will not be admissible at a hearing without leave of the tribunal which will only be granted in exceptional circumstances.

13. Any application to a tribunal for directions as to procedural or evidential matters should, save in exceptional circumstances, be made only after the other party has been afforded an opportunity to agree, within three working days, the terms of the directions proposed. Any application that has not previously been discussed with the representatives of such other party and that does not fully record the rival positions of the parties will normally simply be rejected by a tribunal. If a party has been requested by another party to discuss and agree any application, but has failed to respond within three working days (or such other time as may be allowed by the tribunal), the tribunal will not elicit the comments of that party or make orders conditional on objections not being received.

14. Communications regarding procedural matters should be made expeditiously.

15. Tribunals will not acknowledge receipt of correspondence despite any request to that effect unless there is particular reason to do so.

16. Only in the most exceptional circumstances can it be appropriate for a party to question the terms of any procedural order made or seek a review of it by the tribunal.

17. If a tribunal considers that unnecessary costs have been incurred at any stage of a reference, it may of its own volition or on the application of a party make rulings as to the liability for the relevant discrete costs. Unnecessary costs may be incurred by, e.g., inappropriate applications having been made or not agreed, excessive photocopying or unnecessary communications being generated by the same message being sent by fax and/or e-mail, and mail and/or courier. Tribunals may order such costs to be assessed and paid immediately.

Questionnaire

A46–023 (Information to be provided as required in paragraph 8 of the Second Schedule to the LMAA Terms)

As many as possible of the procedural issues should be agreed by the parties. If agreement has been possible, then please make that clear in the answers to the Questionnaire.

> 1. A brief note of the nature of the claim (e.g. "unsafe port" or "balance of accounts dispute").

2. Approximate quantum of the claim.

3. Approximate quantum of any counterclaim.

4. The principal outstanding issues requiring determination raised by the claim and any counterclaim.

5. Are any amendments to the claim, defence or counterclaim required?

6. Are any of the issues in the reference suitable for determination as a preliminary issue?

7. Are there any areas of disclosure that remain to be dealt with?

8. Would a preliminary meeting be useful, and if so at what stage?

9. What statement evidence is it intended to adduce and by when; and (if there is to be a hearing) what oral evidence will be adduced?

10. What expert evidence is it intended to adduce by way of reports and/or oral testimony and by when will experts reports be exchanged? Generally a meeting of experts will be useful. Unless the parties agree or the tribunal rules that such a meeting would not be appropriate, when should the meeting take place?

11. Suggested timetable for preparation for the close of submissions if the case is to go ahead on documents alone or for a hearing if that is appropriate.

12. Estimated length of the hearing, if any.

13. Which witnesses of fact and experts is it anticipated will be called at the hearing, if there is to be one?

14. Is it appropriate for a hearing date to be fixed now? (Save in exceptional circumstances, a hearing date will not be fixed until the preparation of the case is sufficiently advanced to enable the duration of the hearing to be properly estimated; this will normally be after disclosure of documents has been substantially completed.)

15. Estimated costs of each party
    (i) up to completion of this Questionnaire; and
    (ii) through to the end of the reference.

16. Does either party consider that it is entitled to security for costs and, if so, in what amount?

17. Have the parties considered whether mediation might be worthwhile?

THE THIRD SCHEDULE

Preliminary Meetings

This Schedule sets out, in check-list form, the topics which may be appropriate for consideration when a preliminary meeting is to be held in accordance with paragraph 15 of the Terms. **A46–024**

The circumstances in which a preliminary meeting may be held vary very considerably. In some cases (including the more complex arbitrations and most cases involving a hearing of more than five days) a preliminary meeting is necessary and will be held on the initiative of the tribunal or at the request of the parties, after much of the preparatory work has been done, to review the progress of the case and to enable directions to be made or agreed for further preparation for, and the conduct of, the hearing. In other cases a dispute may have arisen as to some procedural matter (e.g. a failure to serve submissions or a pleading or to give adequate disclosure of documents) and a party may seek to persuade the tribunal to give appropriate directions (including, in a proper case, a peremptory order under Section 41(5) of the Act) so as to resolve the matter.

Whatever the occasion for a preliminary meeting with the arbitrators, two general principles apply; first, that an application to the arbitrators for a particular order should normally be made only after the other party has been afforded a reasonable opportunity to agree the terms of the directions proposed (see paragraph 13 of the Second Schedule); second, that, wherever possible, a preliminary meeting should be preceded by a discussion between the parties' representatives as to the future conduct of the case along the lines indicated in paragraph 15 of the Terms.

The check-list sets out some of the most important matters for consideration. However, many of the points mentioned will not arise unless the parties have agreed or the tribunal has ordered some procedure other than that contemplated by the Second Schedule. Such points, which are marked*, are included to cover cases of this kind.

The check-list cannot attempt to be comprehensive. Inevitably, certain matters must be left to the discretion of the tribunal and the parties' advisers. The opportunity is taken to list the procedural matters which may need to be considered in a logical order from the commencement of the arbitration. It should however be possible in cases where, for whatever reason, the Second Schedule is not followed, for the directions relating to at least the earlier stages of the arbitration to be agreed with the other party, or failing agreement to be dealt with on a written application to the arbitrators and without the need for a preliminary meeting (see paragraph 8 of the Second Schedule).

1. *Can the arbitration be decided on documents only?*

A46–025
        The parties and their advisers should consider at the outset whether the case is suitable to be decided without an oral hearing (see paragraph 12(c) of the Terms).

2. *Submissions and pleadings**

    (i) A time-table should be ordered or agreed for the service of submissions or pleadings.

    (ii) Once an initial exchange has taken place, it should be considered whether a reply is necessary and whether requests for further details (including particulars) of the other party's case are necessary and if made whether all such requests have been properly dealt with.

    (iii) As the case proceeds and further documents become available, the submissions or pleadings should be reviewed to see:

        (a) whether amendments are required;

        (b) whether all issues are still alive.

3. *Disclosure of documents**

    (i) A time-table should be ordered or agreed either for the disclosure of all relevant documents or for the initial disclosure of such specified categories of documents as may be ordered or agreed.

(ii) Applications for further disclosure should initially be made to the opposing party, and if not complied with, by application to the tribunal.
(iii) Disputes as to outstanding disclosure should not normally require a specific meeting with the arbitrators and applications can often best be reserved until a preliminary meeting is to take place in any event.
(iv) Consideration should always be given to whether it can be ordered or agreed that the ambit of disclosure be limited so as to avoid unnecessary delay and expense.

4. *Factual evidence*

   (i) Can some facts/figures be agreed or admitted?
   (ii) A time-table should be ordered or agreed for the exchange of statements (or affidavits) of witnesses of fact.
   (iii) It should be ordered or agreed:

   (a) whether the statements or affidavits are to be admitted without calling the maker to give oral evidence at the hearing or
   (b) whether the statements are to stand as the evidence in chief of the witnesses subject to their attending to give oral evidence; and
   (c) whether the evidence of any witness is to be taken in advance or by means of a live telephone or video link or by use of a video recording.

   (iv) In any case where it may be desired to seek the assistance of a Court (whether within or outside the United Kingdom) to secure the attendance of witnesses at the hearing, to obtain documentary or other evidence, to record oral testimony for presentation to the tribunal or to exercise other powers in support of the arbitral proceedings, the party intending to invoke the assistance of the Court should first where practicable seek the agreement of the other parties to the making of the application to the Court or, if agreement cannot be reached, should apply to the tribunal for permission to make the application (see Sections 43 and 44 of the Act) and for directions as to when and how it is to be made.

5. *Expert evidence*

   (i) It should be ordered or agreed whether or not the case requires expert evidence to be adduced and, if so, the subjects on which expert evidence is necessary and the number and disciplines of the experts.
   (ii) If it is ordered or agreed that the case is one requiring expert evidence the order or agreement should provide

   (a) whether each party is to adduce expert evidence; and/or
   (b) whether the tribunal should appoint experts or assessors to assist it on technical matters (see Section 37 of the Act);

   (iii) Where expert evidence is to be adduced by the parties a time-table should be ordered or agreed for the following:

   (a) the exchange of experts' reports;
   (b) any "without prejudice" meeting of experts held to agree or narrow the issues;
   (c) the drawing up of a memorandum by the experts setting out what has been agreed and what remains in issue;
   (d) the service of supplementary experts' reports;

(iv) It should be ordered or agreed whether the tribunal will deal with the technical issues on the basis of the experts' reports, without the need for the authors to give oral evidence.

6. *Preliminary Issues/Interim Awards*

Both the tribunal and the parties should consider at any preliminary meeting:

(i) what are the important matters in issue between the parties;
(ii) how are those issues best decided;
(iii) whether time and expense will be saved if one or more issues (e.g. interpretation of contract) are decided as preliminary issues;
(iv) whether liability and damages should be decided at one hearing or separately.

7. *Questions to the parties*

It may be considered whether one of the parties (or the tribunal) should put questions to a party and in what form this should be done.

8. *Procedure at the hearing*

A46–026   Directions may be given as to:

(i) what if any rules of evidence will apply and generally as to the manner and form in which the evidence is to be presented at the hearing;
(ii) the length of time available for witnesses to give their evidence or for parties or their representatives to present their arguments;
(iii) whether arguments are to be in written or oral form or a combination of the two.

9. *Investigations by the Tribunal*

Would any investigations by the tribunal assist in ascertaining the facts?

10. *Inspection*

Would the tribunal be assisted by attending trials or experiments, or inspecting any object featuring in the dispute?

11. *Documents*

(i) If possible provide agreed chronology and dramatis personae;
(ii) arrangements of documents (e.g. different bundles for different topics, or as appropriate) and dates by which bundles to be produced;
(iii) unnecessary inclusion of documents to be avoided;
(iv) when documents are voluminous, consider copying only key bundles and providing a core bundle.

12. *Advance reading*

(i) Provision of pleadings and other suitable material (e.g. experts' reports) to the tribunal as far in advance of the hearing as possible.

(ii) Should time be set aside during the hearing, after appropriate opening, for private reading of any documents by tribunal (to reduce time otherwise involved in reading documents out)?

13. *Multi-party disputes*

(i) Concurrent or consecutive hearings (see paragraph 14 (b) of the Terms);
(ii) procedure generally.

14. *Representation*

Level of representation at the hearing to be appropriate to the case.

15. *Hearing dates*

(The fixing of dates will, in the majority of cases, be most usefully considered after discovery has been substantially completed. An application for a date to be fixed should not, however, be made until the parties are able to make a realistic estimate of how long the hearing is likely to last, and when the parties will be ready.)

(i) Estimated duration of hearing.
(ii) When can parties realistically be expected to be ready?
(iii) Any problems re availability of witnesses? (If so, can these be mitigated by taking evidence in advance, using proofs/affidavits at the hearing, by means of a live telephone or video link, or by use of a video recording?)
(iv) Availability of tribunal (see paragraph 19 of the Terms and the Fourth Schedule).
(v) Accommodation required and numbers attending.
(vi) Any special facilities (e.g. transcripts, interpreters, etc.).
(vii) Arrangements for accommodation, etc.: who to book/pay for?

16. *Costs*

Estimates should be given of the parties' respective costs up to the date of the meeting, and through to the end of the hearing.

THE FOURTH SCHEDULE

Reconstitution of the Tribunal

The following provisions are directed to avoiding delay which the parties or either of them consider unacceptable, but if both parties prefer to retain a tribunal as already constituted they remain free so to agree.

1. The governing factor will be the ability of the tribunal to fix a hearing date within a reasonable time of the expected readiness date as notified by the parties on application for a date or, if they are not agreed as to the expected readiness date, within a reasonable time of whichever forecast date the tribunal considers more realistic.

2. For hearings of up to 10 days' estimated duration, what constitutes a reasonable time will (unless the parties apply for a date further ahead) be determined by reference to the estimated length of hearing as follows:

ESTIMATED DURATION	REASONABLE TIME
(i) Up to 2 days	3 months
(ii) 3–5 days	6 months
(iii) 6–10 days	10 months

"Relevant time-scale" is used below to mean whichever of the foregoing periods is applicable and, in cases of more than 10 days' duration, such corresponding time-scale as the tribunal may consider appropriate.

3. A sole arbitrator who is unable to offer a date within the relevant time-scale will offer to retire and, if so requested by the parties or either of them, will retire upon being satisfied that an appropriate substitute appointment has been effected by the parties; in event of their disagreement, either party may request the President to make the necessary substitute appointment.

4. In all other cases, unless all members of the tribunal are able to offer a matching date within the relevant time-scale:

(A) the tribunal will have regard to any agreed preference of the parties, but if there is no agreed preference the tribunal will fix:

   (i) the earliest hearing date that can be given by any member(s) able to offer a guaranteed date within the relevant time-scale;

   (ii) if a guaranteed date within the relevant time-scale cannot be offered by any member of the tribunal, the earliest date thereafter which can be guaranteed by any member(s) of the tribunal; on the basis, in either case, that any member then unable (by reason of a prior commitment) to guarantee the date so fixed will (unless that prior commitment has meanwhile cleared) retire by notice given six clear weeks prior to the start date.

(B) Upon notification of any such retirement an appropriate substitution will be effected as follows:

   (i) If an original arbitrator retires the substitute shall be promptly appointed by his appointer; or failing such appointment at least 21 days prior to the start date the substitute will then be appointed by the umpire or third arbitrator or, if an umpire or third arbitrator has not yet been appointed, the substitute will be appointed by the President;

   (ii) If an umpire or third arbitrator retires the substitute will be appointed by the original arbitrators.

5. For the purpose of Paragraph (4):

(A) "appropriate substitution" means appointment of a substitute able to match the hearing date established in accordance with sub-paragraph (A);

(B) "start date" means the first date reserved for the hearing;

(C) An umpire or third arbitrator will retain power to make any necessary substitution under sub-paragraph (B)(i) notwithstanding that he may himself have given notice of retirement under sub-paragraph (A) and an original arbitrator will retain the like power under sub-paragraph (B)(ii).

6. An arbitrator or umpire who retires as mentioned above shall:

(i) be entitled to immediate payment of his fees and expenses incurred up to the date of his retirement; and

(ii) incur no liability to any party by reason thereof.

Commentary

The LMAA Terms were last amended in parallel with, and came into effect at the same time as, the 1996 Act. The new revision (the LMAA Terms (2002)), which applies to all references commenced on or after 1st January, 2002, is designed to meet needs which have become apparent since 1997.

* * *

The most important changes are to be found in the *Second Schedule*. That reflects, with a number of alterations, what were previously the Procedural Guidelines. However, it is important to note that the provisions of this Schedule are not merely indicative. As paragraph 12(c) of the Terms says: " ... the normal procedure to be adopted is as set out in the Second Schedule." Henceforth, therefore, in the absence of some agreement of the parties or particular direction by the tribunal to the contrary, the Second Schedule procedure is to apply to all LMAA arbitrations under the 2002 Terms.

It provides, in the usual case, for submissions (not formal pleadings) accompanied by documents, and it contains a timetable for the exchange of such submissions.

Provision is also made for other interlocutory matters. A detailed survey is not appropriate here: the Schedule will repay a careful study by arbitrators and practitioners alike. However, it may be appropriate to highlight just a few matters.

Paragraph 7 deals with security for costs (not normally to be ordered until after service of defence submissions) and paragraph 8 requires the parties to complete a questionnaire in all cases to enable proper procedure to be laid down or agreed, unless the case is ready for an award on the exclusive basis of the written submissions that have already been served. Of frequent practical importance will be paragraph 13, which requires a party making an application to seek the other party's agreement, and which should reduce the amount of interlocutory correspondence by making it unnecessary in most cases for tribunals to seek comments on such applications.

Paragraph 17 makes it clear that special orders may be made when costs are wasted.

The new Second Schedule has meant that substantial passages from paragraphs 12, 13 and 14 of the 1997 Terms have been omitted.

* * *

Where once London arbitrators generally experienced only insignificant problems in recovering fees and expenses, the situation has changed considerably in recent years. Accordingly it has been felt necessary to alter the *First Schedule* substantially so as (a) to give arbitrators the right to seek interim payments of their fees and expenses (not more often than once every three months), (b) to give them the right (though not the obligation) to resign if such payments are not made and (c) to give tribunals the right to require security for their costs before embarking on a hearing or on the work required to prepare an award in a documents-only case.

Apart from offering necessary protection to arbitrators, these provisions are thought likely to be welcomed by users who will be kept better informed about the actual and likely future costs of their cases.

The opportunity has also been taken to clarify matters such as the right to booking fees and the right to cancel a hearing where they are not paid (paragraph (D)(1)(a); the entitlement of third arbitrators and umpires to booking fees ((D)(1)(c)), and the position concerning booking fees in the event of various matters leading to an adjournment or vacation of dates ((D)(1)(d) and (e)).

* * *

Other changes to the Terms are largely consequential, or of a tidying-up nature, or to modernise the language, but two particular points may usefully be mentioned. Paragraph 14(c) of the Terms reinstates the power to stay a claim for want of provision of security for costs, rather than simply to dismiss it; and paragraph 17 makes it clear that parties remain jointly and severally responsible for arbitrators' costs notwithstanding the terms of any settlement they may reach between themselves.

The LMAA Small Claims Procedure[1]

(REVISED JANUARY 1, 2002)

Introduction

1. These provisions shall be known as the LMAA Small Claims Procedure 2002 effective 1st January 2002. **A47–001**

Appointment of arbitrator

2. (a) If a dispute has arisen and the parties have agreed that it should be referred to arbitration under the Small Claims Procedure, then, unless a sole arbitrator has already been agreed on, either party may start the arbitration by giving notice to the other requiring him to join in appointing a sole arbitrator. If within fourteen days the parties have agreed on a sole arbitrator and the intended arbitrator has accepted the appointment, the Claimant shall within a further fourteen days send to the Respondent (with copies to the arbitrator) a letter of claim accompanied by copies of all relevant documents including experts' reports and shall further send to the arbitrator a remittance in his favour for the small claims fee as defined in para 3(b). **A47–002**

(b) If the parties have not within fourteen days agreed on a sole arbitrator, either party may apply in writing to the Honorary Secretary, London Maritime Arbitrators Association for the appointment of a sole arbitrator by the President. Such application shall be copied to the other party and shall be accompanied by a copy of the letter of claim together with copies of all said relevant documents and a remittance for the said small claims fee plus £100 plus VAT where applicable in favour of the L.M.A.A. Where appropriate a party applying to the President should provide a concise explanation of the issues which are likely to arise and an indication as to whether any particular expertise on the part of the arbitrator is required. The President, having considered the nature of the dispute shall appoint an appropriate arbitrator and shall give notice to the parties. The L.M.A.A. shall send to the arbitrator the letter of claim and the documents together with the said small claims fee, and shall retain the balance in respect of administrative expenses.

The arbitrator's fee

3. (a) The fixed fee includes the appointment fee, interlocutories, a hearing not exceeding one day (if required by the arbitrator pursuant to para 5 (g)), the writing of the Award and the assessment of costs (if any). It does not include expenses, such as the hire of an arbitration room, which shall in the first instance be paid by the Claimant on demand. **A47–003**

(b) The Small Claims fee shall be £1,250 (plus VAT where applicable) or such standard fee as shall be fixed from time to time by the Committee of the LMAA.

---

[1] This document is reproduced with the kind permission of the London Maritime Arbitrators Association.

Payment of the Small Claims fee shall be a condition precedent to the valid commencement of proceedings under the Small Claims Procedure.

(c) In the event of the Respondents putting forward a counterclaim which exceeds the amount of the claim an additional fixed fee in the amount of £500 (plus VAT where applicable) is payable by the Respondents. Such fee is to be paid within fourteen days of service of defence and counterclaim submissions failing which the arbitrator may, at his discretion, stay the counterclaim and proceed with the original claim.

(d) If the case is settled amicably before an award has been written, the arbitrator may retain out of the Small Claims fee a sum sufficient to compensate him for services thus far rendered and any balance shall be repaid.

Right of appeal excluded

A47–004   **4.** The right of appeal to the Courts is excluded under this procedure. By adopting the Small Claims Procedure the parties shall be deemed to have agreed to waive all rights of appeal.

Procedure

A47–005   **5.** (a) A letter of defence and details of counterclaim (if any) accompanied in each case by copies of all relevant documents including any experts' reports shall be delivered to the Claimant within twenty-eight days from receipt of the letter of claim or from the date of the appointment of the arbitrator, whichever shall be the later.

(b) A letter of reply and defence to counterclaim (if any) shall be delivered to the Respondent within a further twenty-one days. The arbitrator shall be entitled to refuse to admit evidence submitted at the stage of reply and defence to counterclaim (if any) if it should properly have been served with the letter of claim.

(c) Where there is a counterclaim, the Claimant shall deliver a letter of reply to defence to counterclaim (if he wishes to do so) within a further fourteen days.

(d) Any extension to the above time limits must be applied for before expiry of the existing time limit. If a party fails to serve its pleading within the time limit set, the arbitrator, on the application of the other party or of his own motion, will notify the defaulting party that unless the outstanding communication is received within a fixed period (maximum 14 days) he will proceed to the award on the basis of the submissions and documents before him to the exclusion of all others. Any pleading submitted by the defaulting party subsequent to expiry of the time limit set by the arbitrator's notice shall not be admissible. The time allowed by the arbitrator's notice, added to any extension of time previously allowed in respect of the same pleading shall not in total exceed 28 days.

(e) Following the service of the letter of reply, or, where there is a counterclaim, following service of the letter of reply to defence to counterclaim, the arbitrator may declare to the parties that pleadings have closed. No further pleadings shall be considered by the arbitrator following such a declaration.

(f) Copies of all the above letters and documents shall be sent to the arbitrator and to the other party, or if the other party is acting through a solicitor or representative, to that solicitor or representative.

(g) There shall be no hearing unless, in exceptional circumstances, the arbitrator requires this.

(h) In the case of an oral hearing the arbitrator shall have power to allocate the time available (which shall be limited to one working day) between the parties in such manner that each party has an equal opportunity in which to present his case.

(i) All communications or notifications under this procedure may be by letter, telex, telefax or e-mail.

Disclosure of documents

6. (a) There shall be no Discovery, but, if in the opinion of the arbitrator a party has failed to produce any relevant document(s) he may order the production of such document(s) and may indicate to the party to whom the order is directed that, if without adequate explanation he fails to produce the document(s), the arbitrator may proceed on the assumption that the contents of such document(s) do not favour that party's case. **A47–006**

(b) The expression "relevant documents" includes all documents relevant to the dispute, whether or not favourable to the party holding them. It includes witness statements, experts' reports and the like on which he intends to rely, but does not include documents which are not legally disclosable.

The award

7. The arbitrator will make every effort to publish the award within one month, in a documents only case, from the date when the arbitrator has received all relevant documents and submissions, or, where there is an oral hearing, from the close of the hearing. **A47–007**

Costs

8. The power of an arbitrator to award costs has been retained as an important feature of London arbitration. Such assessment shall be on a commercial basis having regard to the nature of the reference. Unless the parties otherwise agree, the amount which one party may be ordered to pay to the other in respect of legal costs (including disbursements) shall be assessed at a sum in the arbitrator's discretion up to £1,750, or such other maximum figure as shall be fixed from time to time by the Committee of the L.M.A.A. A party seeking to have its costs assessed must provide a breakdown of such costs. The successful party will normally be awarded the Small Claims fee (including the fee of £100.00 payable to the L.M.A.A. in cases where the President is requested to appoint an arbitrator) in addition to any legal costs which he has incurred, provided always that any award of costs shall be in the sole discretion of the arbitrator. **A47–008**

General

9. The arbitrator may in exceptional cases depart from or vary the above provisions at his entire discretion, save that he shall not be entitled to vary the maximum figure which can be awarded under the Small Claims Procedure in respect of legal costs. **A47–009**

COMMENTARY ON THE L.M.A.A. SMALL CLAIMS PROCEDURE

Introduction

A47–010   1. The Small Claims Procedure has been introduced to provide a simplified, quick and inexpensive procedure for the resolution of small claims. It is supplementary to the Documents Only procedure contained in the Third Schedule to the L.M.A.A. Terms (2002).

It is suggested that it should be used where neither the claim nor any counterclaim exceeds the sum of $50,000. It is not suitable for use where there are complex issues or where there is likely to be examination of witnesses. On the other hand, the Procedure may be suitable for handling larger claims where there is a single issue at stake.

There has been a regrettable tendency to apply the Procedure regardless of the complexity of the issues involved in a particular dispute (and occasionally, regardless of the amounts involved). This is likely to lead to dissatisfaction with and criticism of the Procedure since the constraints on the arbitrator and the parties imposed by the limited financial remuneration for their services (which is an essential part of the Procedure) may mean that a particular dispute is not dealt with as the parties envisage. Parties proposing to use the Procedure are therefore encouraged to consider at the outset as to whether it is appropriate to vary the terms of the Procedure (for example, by mutually agreeing to increase the maximum amount of recoverable costs). The position of the arbitrator is dealt with further in the context of discretion at paragraph 9 below.

Attention is drawn to the following features:

Reference to a sole arbitrator

A47–011   2. This will provide a saving both in time and expense. It is expected and hoped that in most cases the parties will be able to agree on the sole arbitrator. Where they cannot agree, application may be made to the L.M.A.A. and the President will then make the appointment. There will be a charge of £100 to cover the administrative expenses. The attention of the parties is drawn to the fact that payment of the fixed fee in full (including the additional element when the appointment is made by the President) is a condition precedent to the commencement of proceedings. In requesting the President to make an appointment under the Procedure, the appointing party should provide as full an explanation as is practicable as to the issues which he expects to arise. He should also draw the attention of the President to the fact that particular expertise on the part of the arbitrator may be desirable (for example, engineering expertise in the case of a performance dispute). Parties should also be aware that it is the practice of the President not to consider for appointment in a particular case any arbitrator whose name has been put forward by the appointing party. The objective of this practice is to avoid any perception on the part of the other party that the appointing party has secured an advantage by having the President appoint as arbitrator one of the individuals whom he has proposed. A party asking the President to make an appointment should not therefore disclose the names of the arbitrators proposed to the other party at the time of initiating proceedings.

Arbitrator to receive a fixed fee

A47–012   3. So that the parties know where they stand at an early stage it is provided that the arbitrator will receive a fixed fee. The fee for a claim has now been assessed at £1,250. In the case of a counterclaim which exceeds the amount of the claim there is an additional fixed fee of £500. This additional fee is charged because a counterclaim that exceeds the claim will normally involve different issues. No additional charge is made in respect of counterclaims which do not in total exceed the amount of the claim. Members of the LMAA have agreed to deal with disputes under the LMAA Small Claims Procedure as a service to the industry, though it will be appreciated that, having regard to current rates of remuneration, it may in many cases involve some financial sacrifice. Any expenses must be paid in addition.

Exclusion of appeal

4. Under the Arbitration Act 1996 there is no restriction on the parties to exclude the right of appeal. An agreement to arbitrate under the LMAA Small Claims Procedure will automatically be treated as an agreement to exclude the right of appeal. In view of this a Reasoned Award will not be published, but the arbitrator will give brief, privileged, reasons for his decision. **A47–013**

Informal procedure

5. There will be no formal pleadings and no discovery as such. Each party will be informed of the case against him by a simple exchange of letters accompanied by copies of all relevant documents, including witness statements. A strict but reasonable timetable is imposed, and, if a party fails to comply with a final time limit set by the arbitrator, the arbitrator will proceed to his award on the basis of the documents already received. There is substituted for discovery (a procedure frequently used to gain time) an obligation on the parties to disclose all relevant documents with their letters of claim or defence. Should a party fail in this obligation, the arbitrator is given power to order production of any missing documents and to give warning to that party that, if he fails to produce them without adequate explanation, the arbitrator may proceed on the basis that those documents do not favour that party's case. Claimants should note that any attempt to secure a tactical advantage by withholding production of evidence which should properly accompany the claim submissions until the stage of a reply may be met with a refusal on the part of the arbitrator to admit such further evidence. **A47–014**

Legal representation

6. The use of lawyers is not excluded, but it is thought that in many cases they will not be necessary. But it should be borne in mind that advice from a lawyer can often indicate to a party the strength or weakness of his case and can assist in reaching an amicable settlement; also, if settlement cannot be reached, the case may be presented by a lawyer in a more orderly and concise manner. **A47–015**

The award

7. The arbitrator will normally make his Award within one month from the date on which he has received all the papers. **A47–016**

The costs

8. The power of an arbitrator to award costs has been retained as an important feature of London arbitration. It operates to deter spurious claims or defences and may assist in promoting an amicable settlement. The arbitrator is given power to tax or assess legal costs, but on a commercial and strict basis. The amount recoverable will be assessed at a sum in the arbitrator's discretion not to exceed £1,750 or such other sum as may be fixed by the Committee of the LMAA. Although the arbitrator has a discretion to vary **A47–017**

or depart from the provisions of the Procedure in exceptional cases (see paragraph 9 below) this discretion does not extend to varying the amount of legal costs recoverable under this Procedure. It is regarded as being of fundamental importance so far as the Procedure is concerned that a party agreeing to arbitrate disputes according to the Procedure can be certain at the outset of his maximum liability in terms of costs.

Discretion

A47–018 9. It is expected that in the great majority of cases the strict timetable and provisions of the Procedure will be observed and enforced, but in exceptional cases there is discretion for the arbitrator to vary or depart from them. The success of the Procedure in promoting cost-effective arbitration in London has led to a regrettable number of cases in which disputes have been referred to arbitration according to the Procedure which are not appropriate for determination in accordance with the spirit, if not the letter, of that Procedure. Such situations can arise simply as the result of the fact that parties to a contract agreed in that contract to apply the Procedure to all disputes involving less than a certain sum of money, regardless of the nature of such disputes. In such cases the parties should be aware that the arbitrator may at the outset or at any time thereafter inform them that in his opinion the dispute referred to him cannot be dealt with satisfactorily according to the Procedure. He will then be entitled to invite the parties either to agree to an appropriate variation of the Procedure or, alternatively, to agree to his continuing to act on the basis of the LMAA Terms in force for the time being. In the event of a refusal by the parties so to agree the arbitrator shall be entitled to resign from the reference whilst retaining out of the Small Claims fee a sum sufficient to remunerate him for services thus far rendered.

The LMAA Mediation Terms (2002)[1]

(REVISED JANUARY 1, 2002)

Article 1

Preliminary

1.1 These terms may be referred to as "the LMAA Mediation Terms (2002)". **A48–001**
1.2 In these Terms unless the context otherwise requires:—

(a) "Association" means the London Maritime Arbitrators Association;

(b) "President" means the President for the time being of the Association;

(c) "Mediation" means and includes mediation, conciliation and any form of dispute resolution other than litigation and arbitration;

(d) "Mediator" means and includes one or more persons appointed or nominated for the purpose of mediation.

Article 2

Application and Purpose of the Terms

2.1 These Terms apply to mediation of disputes arising out of or relating to a contractual or other legal relationship, whether commercial or maritime, where the parties seeking an amicable settlement of their disputes have agreed that the Terms shall apply. **A48–002**
2.2 The parties may agree to exclude or vary any of these Terms at any time.

Article 3

Number of Mediators

Unless the parties otherwise agree there shall be one Mediator who shall be appointed within 14 days from the commencement of the mediation procedure as mentioned in Article 4 below. **A48–003**

Article 4

Commencement of the Mediation Procedure

4.1 The party initiating mediation shall send to the other party or parties a written invitation to mediate under these Terms, briefly setting out the matters in dispute. **A48–004**

---

[1] This document is reproduced with the kind permission of the London Maritime Arbitrators Association.

4.2 The mediation procedure shall be deemed to have commenced when the other party or parties accept in writing the invitation to mediation.

4.3 If the other party, or if one of the other parties, rejects the invitation to mediation, or if the other party or parties fail to respond to the invitation within 14 days or any other period that may be stated in the invitation, there will be no mediation procedure for the time being. Provided that, if there are more than two parties and one accepts but the other or others do not, then mediation in accordance with these Terms between the party making the invitation and the party accepting shall take place if they so agree.

Article 5

Appointment of Mediator

A48–005　**5.1** If the parties agree to mediate but are unable to agree on the appointment of a Mediator they may make an application in writing to the President, or such other person nominated for this purpose by the President, for the appointment of a Mediator. Such application shall be accompanied by a brief summary of the matters in dispute. A copy of the application and summary shall be sent to the other parties to the mediation. The President, or such other person nominated for this purpose by the President, may call for such further information as he may require. He shall then appoint the Mediator and shall notify the parties of his name and address.

5.2 Where the parties have agreed that each party should appoint a Mediator and one or more of the parties has failed to make the appointment, the party or parties who have made the appointment may apply in writing to the President, or such other person nominated for this purpose by the President, for the appointment of a Mediator on behalf of the defaulting party or parties and the procedure indicated in the preceding paragraph shall be followed.

Article 6

Exchange of Information

A48–006　**6.1** Each party will send to the Mediator within 14 days of his appointment, or such other period as may be agreed, copies of a concise Summary of its case in the dispute and all documents to which the Summary refers and any other documents to which it may wish to refer in the Mediation. A copy of the Summary and documents will be sent simultaneously to any other party to the Mediation.

6.2 In addition, each party may send to the Mediator and/or bring to the Mediation further documentation which it wishes to disclose in confidence to the Mediator but not the other party or parties, clearly stating that such documentation is confidential to the Mediator.

6.3 The parties shall endeavour to agree a joint summary and set of documents or, if this is not possible, the maximum number of pages for each Summary and set of documents to accompany each Summary.

Article 7

Duties and Powers of the Mediator

7.1 The Mediator shall assist the parties in an independent and impartial manner in their attempt to reach an amicable settlement of their dispute. He shall be guided by the principle of objectivity, fairness and justice, giving consideration to, among other things, the rights and obligations of the parties, the usages of the trade in question and the circumstances surrounding the dispute including any previous business practices between the parties or some of them.

A48–007

7.2 The Mediator shall conduct the mediation in such manner as he considers appropriate, taking into account the circumstances of the case, any wishes the parties may express, including any request that the Mediator hear oral statements, and the need for a speedy settlement of the dispute.

7.3 The Mediator may at any time make proposals for the settlement of disputes. Such proposal may be oral or in writing and need not be accompanied by any reasons therefor.

7.4 The Mediator may invite the parties to meet with him or may communicate with them orally or in writing. He may meet or communicate with the parties together or any of them separately. Where the Mediator receives factual information concerning the dispute from a party, he may disclose the substance of that information to the other party or parties so that that other party or those other parties may have the opportunity to present any explanation which it or they may consider appropriate. However, when a party gives information to the Mediator subject to the specific condition that it be kept confidential the Mediator shall not disclose that information to any other party.

7.5 The Mediator may, with the consent of the parties, call any witness he thinks may be able to assist in the mediation.

Article 8

Co-operation of Parties with Mediator

The parties will in good faith co-operate with the Mediator and in particular will endeavour to comply with requests by him to submit written materials, provide evidence and attend meetings.

A48–008

Article 9

Settlement Agreement

9.1 Where it appears to the Mediator that there are elements of a settlement which would be acceptable to the parties, he may formulate the terms of a possible settlement and submit them to the parties for their observations. He may reformulate the terms in the light of such observations.

A48–009

9.2 If the parties reach agreement on the settlement of the dispute they shall draw up and sign a written agreement. The Mediator may draw up, or assist the parties in drawing up, the settlement agreement.

9.3 The parties, by signing the settlement agreement, put an end to the dispute and are bound by the agreement.

9.4 The Mediator may, if so requested by the parties, draw up the settlement agreement in the form of an arbitration award or, where the matter has been referred to arbitration before the commencement of the mediation, the parties may agree that the settlement agreement be drawn up in the form of an arbitration award by the arbitration tribunal already appointed.

Article 10

Confidentiality

A48–010   The Mediator and the parties must keep confidential all matters relating to the mediation proceedings. Confidentiality extends also to the settlement agreement (or any arbitration award made) except where its disclosure is necessary for the purposes of implementation and enforcement.

Article 11

Termination of Mediation Procedure

A48–011   11.1 The mediation procedure is terminated:—

(a) By the signing of the settlement agreement by the parties or by the signing of an arbitration award, on the date of such agreement or award;

(b) By a written declaration of the parties to the effect that further efforts in mediation are no longer justified, on the date of the declaration;

(c) By a written declaration by a party to the other party or parties to the effect that the mediation procedure is terminated, on the date of the declaration;

(d) By a written declaration of the Mediator to the effect that further efforts at mediation are no longer justified, on the date of the declaration.

Article 12

Resort of Arbitration or Judicial proceedings

A48–012   Where the disputes referred to mediation are the subject of any arbitration or judicial proceedings either party may advise the arbitration tribunal or Court that they have agreed to mediation. The arbitration or judicial proceedings shall however continue during the conduct of the mediation subject to any right the arbitration tribunal or Court may exercise to take the mediation timetable into account when setting any timetable in those proceedings. The mediation procedure may not interrupt time limits and either party may initiate arbitration or judicial proceedings at any time where in his opinion such proceedings are necessary for preserving his rights.

Article 13

Costs

13.A The Mediator's costs

13.A.1 An appointment fee shall be payable to the Mediator by each party to the mediation procedure. The appointment fee shall be £250 per party or such other sum as the Committee of the Association may from time to time decide.

13.A.2 Upon termination of the mediation procedure the Mediator shall fix the costs of the mediation and shall give written notice thereof to the parties who shall, unless otherwise ordered by the Mediator, be liable to pay the same in equal proportions. Such costs shall include the Mediator's fees, which, unless agreed beforehand, shall be reasonable in amount, having regard to the time involved, the amount in dispute and the complexity of the case, any out of pocket expenses and the expenses of any witnesses called by the Mediator with the consent of the parties.

13.A.3 If any party fails to pay the Mediator's costs or its proportion thereof within 30 days from the termination of the mediation procedure, the other party or parties shall be jointly and severally liable to indemnify the Mediator in respect of such failure.

13.A.4 The Mediator may, on his appointment or at any time or times thereafter, order the parties to pay to him a deposit on account of his costs.

13.B The Parties' Costs

13.B.1 Normally each party shall bear its own costs.

13.B.2 However, if the Mediator should be of the opinion that any party has not genuinely tried to co-operate in the mediation or has been obstructive so that the mediation procedure has been thwarted or has been made more expensive, he may order that that party shall pay all or part of the costs of any other party; and, if such costs cannot be amicably agreed, the Mediator may assess and decide the amount to be paid and a certificate signed by the Mediator shall be conclusive and binding on the parties.

Article 14

Role of the Mediator in other proceedings

The parties and the Mediator undertake that the Mediator shall not act as arbitrator, witness, lawyer, adviser or representative of any party in arbitration or judicial proceedings in respect of the dispute that is the subject of the mediation procedure.

Article 15

Admissibility of evidence in other proceedings

15.1 Unless all parties to the mediation procedure otherwise agree, the parties undertake not to reveal, introduce or rely on the following as evidence in any arbitration or judicial proceedings, whether or not those proceedings relate to the dispute that is the subject of the mediation procedure:—

(a) Views expressed or proposals made by any party with a view to possible settlement of the dispute;

(b) Admissions made by the party in the course of the mediation procedure;

(c) Proposals made by the Mediator;

(d) The fact that a party has indicated its willingness to accept a proposal to settle made by the Mediator.

15.2 The parties further undertake, unless all other parties otherwise agree, not to refer to or rely on any documents which might have been disclosed during the mediation procedure, whether voluntarily or at the request of the Mediator or other party but which would otherwise have been privileged and to return all such documents and copies thereof to the party disclosing them.

The Permanent Court of Arbitration
List of Basic Documents[1]

PCA Conventions

- 1899 Convention for the Pacific Settlement of International Disputes **A49–001**
- 1907 Convention for the Pacific Settlement of International Disputes

PCA Rules of Procedure

- Permanent Court of Arbitration Optional Rules for Arbitration of Disputes **A49–002** Relating to Natural Resources and the Environment
- Permanent Court of Arbitration Optional Rules for Arbitrating Disputes between Two States
- Permanent Court of Arbitration Optional Rules for Arbitrating Disputes between Two Parties of Which Only One Is a State
- Permanent Court of Arbitration Optional Rules for Arbitration Involving International Organizations and States
- Permanent Court of Arbitration Optional Rules for Arbitration between International Organizations and Private Parties
- Permanent Court of Arbitration Optional Conciliation Rules
- Permanent Court of Arbitration Optional Rules for Fact-finding Commissions of Inquiry
- Guidelines for Adapting the Permanent Court of Arbitration Rules to Disputes Arising Under Multilateral Agreements and Multiparty Contracts

PCA Model Clauses

- Model Arbitration Clauses for Use in Connection with the Permanent Court of **A49–003** Arbitration Optional Rules for Arbitrating *Disputes between Two States*
- Model Arbitration Clauses for Use in Connection with the Permanent Court of Arbitration Optional Rules for Arbitrating *Disputes between Two Parties of Which Only One Is a State*
- Model Arbitration Clauses for Use in Connection with the Permanent Court of Arbitration Optional Rules for Arbitration *Involving International Organizations and States*

---

[1] This document is reproduced with the kind permission of the Permanent Court of Arbitration.

- Model Arbitration Clauses for Use in Connection with the Permanent Court of Arbitration Optional Rules for Arbitration *between International Organizations and Private Parties*
- Model Arbitration Clauses for Use in Connection with the Permanent Court of Arbitration *Optional Conciliation Rules*

UNCITRAL Rules and Procedures

A49–004
- Procedural Guidelines for Requesting Designation of an Appointing Authority by the Secretary-General of the Permanent Court of Arbitration under the UNCITRAL Arbitration Rules
- Permanent Court of Arbitration Procedures for Cases under the UNCITRAL Arbitration Rules
- Model Clauses for Permanent Court of Arbitration Services under the UNCITRAL Arbitration Rules
- UNCITRAL Arbitration Rules (1976)

Other PCA Rules and Procedures

A49–005
- Permanent Court of Arbitration Financial Assistance Fund for Settlement of International Disputes
- Rules of Procedure of the Administrative Council of the Permanent Court of Arbitration
- Rules Concerning the Organization and Internal Working of the International Bureau of the Permanent Court of Arbitration
- Schedule of Fees

The Permanent Court of Arbitration Procedures for Cases under the UNCITRAL Arbitration Rules[1]

Introduction

The UNCITRAL Arbitration Rules were adopted in 1976, after extensive deliberations by the United Nations Commission on International Trade Law. This Commission consists of thirty-six member States representing the different legal, economic and social systems and geographic regions of the world. In the preparation of these Rules, various interested international organizations and leading arbitration experts were consulted. The General Assembly of the United Nations has recommended the use of the UNCITRAL Arbitration Rules for inclusion in international commercial contracts. The universality and flexibility of the UNCITRAL Rules have prompted a number of arbitral institutions, including the PCA, to adapt them for use as their own institutional arbitration rules. All of the various sets of Permanent Court of Arbitration (PCA) arbitration rules are closely based on the UNCITRAL Arbitration Rules, and the PCA Conciliation Rules follow the 1980 UNCITRAL Conciliation Rules.

A50–001

In addition to these situations involving the preparation and adoption of an institution's own rules, UNCITRAL has noted the willingness of a number of arbitral institutions to act as appointing authority and to provide administrative services in arbitrations under the UNCITRAL Arbitration Rules. In 1982, UNCITRAL issued "Recommendations to Assist Arbitral Institutions and Other Interested Bodies with Regard to Arbitrations under the UNCITRAL Arbitration Rules", in order to assist institutions both in adapting the UNCITRAL Rules, and in offering to provide administrative and appointing authority services.

Although the PCA was established in 1899 to facilitate arbitration and other forms of dispute resolution between States only, it has evolved, in its over hundred-year existence, into a modern, multi-faceted arbitral institution that provides a wide variety of dispute resolution services to the international community. In addition to administering, pursuant to its own rules, arbitration involving States or intergovernmental organizations involved in disputes with one another or with private parties, the International Bureau of the PCA offers hearing facilities and ancillary administrative services to tribunals operating ad-hoc or under the auspices of another institution, and is available to facilitate arbitrations conducted under the UNCITRAL Arbitration Rules. The UNCITRAL Rules expressly provide that in the absence of an agreed "appointing authority", a party may request the Secretary-General of the PCA designate the appointing authority. In addition, when properly requested or designated by agreement, the Secretary-General, or the International Bureau, of the PCA will act as the appointing authority under the UNCITRAL Arbitration Rules.

The International Bureau will also provide administrative services to help parties and arbitrators conduct cases under the UNCITRAL Arbitration Rules.

---

[1] This document is reproduced with the kind permission of the Permanent Court of Arbitration.

Acting as Appointing Authority

A50–002 The International Bureau, or the Secretary-General, as the case may be,[2] will act as appointing authority if so designated by the parties. Administrative services may be requested by the parties or the arbitral tribunal, with the consent of the parties.

When requested to appoint a sole or the presiding arbitrator, the International Bureau will follow the list-procedure set forth in article 6 of the UNCITRAL Arbitration Rules, if appropriate. In accordance with the UNCITRAL Arbitration Rules, the International Bureau will exercise its discretion when requested to appoint a second arbitrator.

Article 12 of the UNCITRAL Arbitration Rules requires that all contested challenges be decided by the appointing authority. When deciding challenges at the request of any party, the International Bureau will appoint a special committee to make the decision, consisting of three persons, a majority of whom will be of nationalities different from that of any party.

The UNCITRAL Arbitration Rules provide that the fees of arbitrators shall be reasonable in amount, taking into consideration the amount in dispute, the complexity of the subject-matter, the time spent by the arbitrators, and other relevant circumstances of the case (art. 39, para. 2). The rules provide that parties may request the appointing authority to provide to the arbitrators and the parties a statement setting forth the basis for establishing fees that is customarily followed in cases in which the appointing authority acts (art. 39, para. 3). The International Bureau has no schedule of fees for arbitrators, but it will furnish a statement concerning customary fees based on its experience in administering dispute resolution.

Administrative Services

A50–003 When the International Bureau of the PCA is appointed as the administrator, it will, upon the request of all parties or the arbitral tribunal, provide the following administrative services:

Communications

A50–004 Transmitting—except at hearings—all oral and written communications from the parties to the arbitral tribunal and vice versa and between the parties. When transmitting communications to a party, the International Bureau will use the address set forth in the notice of arbitration or any other address that has been furnished by a party in writing to the International Bureau.

Hearings

A50–005 Upon request, the International Bureau will assist the arbitral tribunal to establish the date, time and place of hearings, giving such advance notice thereof to the parties as the tribunal determines pursuant to the UNCITRAL Arbitration Rules (art. 25, para. 1). The

---

[2] Parties are free to provide for either the International Bureau or the Secretary-General of the PCA as the appointing authority. Subsequent references herein to the International Bureau acting in the capacity of appointing authority shall apply *mutatis mutandis* to situations in which the Secretary-General performs this function.

International Bureau will provide a room for hearings at the Peace Palace in The Hague on a rental basis. If a hearing room is not available at the Peace Palace, the International Bureau will arrange a hearing room elsewhere. The cost of hearing rooms will be billed separately and excluded from the fees for administrative services.

Stenographic Transcripts, Tape Recording and Interpretation

Upon request, the International Bureau will make arrangements for stenographic transcripts, for tape recordings of hearings, and for the services of interpreters at hearings. The cost of these services will be billed separately and excluded from the fees for administrative services. **A50–006**

Fees of Arbitrators and Deposits

Upon request, the International Bureau will make all arrangements concerning the amounts of the arbitrators' fees, and advance deposits to be made on account of such fees in consultation with the parties and the arbitrators. The International Bureau does not fix the amount of fees of arbitrators and has no fee schedule for arbitrators. Upon request, the International Bureau will hold deposits from the parties and account for the same. **A50–007**

Registration of Awards

Upon request, the International Bureau will assist in the filing or registration of arbitral awards in countries where such filing or registration is required by law. **A50–008**

Other Services

Upon request, the International Bureau will consider providing other appropriate administrative services, including arranging for the services of a legally-trained tribunal secretary. **A50–009**

The Permanent Court of Arbitration Procedural Guidelines for Requesting Designation of an Appointing Authority by the Secretary-General of the Permanent Court of Arbitration under the UNCITRAL Arbitration Rules[1]

Appointing Authority

A51–001 Pursuant to the UNCITRAL Arbitration Rules, the parties may require the intervention of an "appointing authority":

- In cases in which there is to be a sole arbitrator, and the parties have not reached agreement on the choice of that arbitrator within the prescribed period of time (art. 6);
- In cases in which there are to be three arbitrators, and the respondent does not proceed, within the prescribed period of time, with the appointment of the arbitrator that he is entitled to appoint (art. 7, paras. 2 and 3), or the two party-appointed arbitrators do not agree on the choice of the presiding arbitrator within the prescribed period of time (art. 7, para. 3);
- In the event an arbitrator is challenged (art. 12);
- In connection with the fixing of the fees of an arbitrator (art. 39).

Secretary-General

A51–002 If the parties have not agreed on the name of the appointing authority or this authority refuses to act or fails to appoint the arbitrator within thirty days after receipt of a party's request therefore, the UNCITRAL Rules provide for the designation of an appointing authority by the Secretary-General of the Permanent Court of Arbitration (arts. 6–8). The Secretary-General does not, under the UNCITRAL Rules, directly appoint the arbitrator, unless the parties expressly invite him to do so (for example, by designating the Secretary-General as appointing authority in their arbitration agreement).

Procedure

A51–003 The request for designation of an appointing authority should be directed to the Secretary-General at the Permanent Court of Arbitration, Peace Palace, 2517 KJ The Hague, The Netherlands, and should be accompanied by:

(1) A copy of the arbitration clause or agreement establishing the applicability of the UNCITRAL Arbitration Rules;

---

[1] This document is reproduced with the kind permission of the Permanent Court of Arbitration.

Procedural Guidelines for Requesting Designation

(2) A copy of the Notice of Arbitration served upon the respondent, as well as the date of such service;

(3) An indication of the nationalities of the parties;

(4) The names and nationalities of the arbitrators already appointed, if any;

(5) The names of any institutions or persons that the parties had considered selecting as appointing authority but which have been rejected;

(6) A power of attorney evidencing the authority of the person making the request.

Before proceeding to designate the appointing authority, the Secretary-General conducts a *prima facie* screening of the documents submitted, and solicits the views of the opposing party. The entire process, from request to designation of an appointing authority, generally takes from 3–6 weeks.

There is an administrative charge for the designation of an appointing authority, which is payable in advance and is non-refundable.

World Intellectual Property Organisation Arbitration Rules[1]

(EFFECTIVE FROM OCTOBER 1, 1994)

I. GENERAL PROVISIONS

Abbreviated Expressions

Article 1

A52–001   In these Rules:

"Arbitration Agreement" means an agreement by the parties to submit to arbitration all or certain disputes which have arisen or which may arise between them; an Arbitration Agreement may be in the form of an arbitration clause in a contract or in the form of a separate contract;

"Claimant" means the party initiating an arbitration;

"Respondent" means the party against which the arbitration is initiated, as named in the Request for Arbitration;

"Tribunal" includes a sole arbitrator or all the arbitrators where more than one is appointed;

"WIPO" means the World Intellectual Property Organization;

"Center" means the WIPO Arbitration Center, a unit of the International Bureau of WIPO;

Words used in the singular include the plural and vice versa, as the context may require.

Scope of Application of Rules

Article 2

A52–002   Where an Arbitration Agreement provides for arbitration under the WIPO Arbitration Rules, these Rules shall be deemed to form part of that Arbitration Agreement and the dispute shall be settled in accordance with these Rules, as in effect on the date of the commencement of the arbitration, unless the parties have agreed otherwise.

Article 3

A52–003   (a) These Rules shall govern the arbitration, except that, where any of these Rules is in conflict with a provision of the law applicable to the arbitration from which the parties cannot derogate, that provision shall prevail.

---

[1] Material originally provided by the World Intellectual Property Organization (WIPO), the owner of the copyright. This material is reproduced with the kind permission of WIPO. The Secretariat of WIPO assumes no liability or responsibility with regard to the transformation or translation of this data.

(b) The law applicable to the arbitration shall be determined in accordance with Article 59(b).

Notices, Periods of Time

Article 4

(a) Any notice or other communication that may or is required to be given under these Rules shall be in writing and shall be delivered by expedited postal or courier service, or transmitted by telex, telefax or other means of telecommunication that provide a record thereof.

(b) A party's last known residence or place of business shall be a valid address for the purpose of any notice or other communication in the absence of any notification of a change by that party. Communications may in any event be addressed to a party in the manner stipulated or, failing such a stipulation, according to the practice followed in the course of the dealings between the parties.

(c) For the purpose of determining the date of commencement of a time limit, a notice or other communication shall be deemed to have been received on the day it is delivered or, in the case of telecommunications, transmitted in accordance with paragraphs (a) and (b) of this Article.

(d) For the purpose of determining compliance with a time limit, a notice or other communication shall be deemed to have been sent, made or transmitted if it is dispatched, in accordance with paragraphs (a) and (b) of this Article, prior to or on the day of the expiration of the time limit.

(e) For the purpose of calculating a period of time under these Rules, such period shall begin to run on the day following the day when a notice or other communication is received. If the last day of such period is an official holiday or a non-business day at the residence or place of business of the addressee, the period is extended until the first business day which follows. Official holidays or non-business days occurring during the running of the period of time are included in calculating the period.

(f) The parties may agree to reduce or extend the periods of time referred to in Articles 11, 15(b), 16(b), 17(b), 17(c), 18(b), 19(b)(iii), 41(a) and 42(a).

(g) The Center may, at the request of a party or on its own motion, extend the periods of time referred to in Articles 11, 15(b), 16(b), 17(b), 17(c), 18(b), 19(b)(iii), 67(d), 68(e) and 70(e).

Documents Required to Be Submitted to the Center

Article 5

(a) Until the notification by the Center of the establishment of the Tribunal, any written statement, notice or other communication required or allowed under Articles 6 to 36 shall be submitted by a party to the Center and a copy thereof shall at the same time be transmitted by that party to the other party.

(b) Any written statement, notice or other communication so sent to the Center shall be sent in a number of copies equal to the number required to provide one copy for each envisaged arbitrator and one for the Center.

(c) After the notification by the Center of the establishment of the Tribunal, any written statements, notices or other communications shall be submitted by a party directly to the Tribunal and a copy thereof shall at the same time be supplied by that party to the other party.

(d) The Tribunal shall send to the Center a copy of each order or other decision that it makes.

II. COMMENCEMENT OF THE ARBITRATION

Request for Arbitration

Article 6

A52–006   The Claimant shall transmit the Request for Arbitration to the Center and to the Respondent.

Article 7

A52–007   The date of commencement of the arbitration shall be the date on which the Request for Arbitration is received by the Center.

Article 8

A52–008   The Center shall inform the Claimant and the Respondent of the receipt by it of the Request for Arbitration and of the date of the commencement of the arbitration.

Article 9

A52–009   The Request for Arbitration shall contain:

(i) a demand that the dispute be referred to arbitration under the WIPO Arbitration Rules;

(ii) the names, addresses and telephone, telex, telefax or other communication references of the parties and of the representative of the Claimant;

(iii) a copy of the Arbitration Agreement and, if applicable, any separate choice-of-law clause;

(iv) a brief description of the nature and circumstances of the dispute, including an indication of the rights and property involved and the nature of any technology involved;

(v) a statement of the relief sought and an indication, to the extent possible, of any amount claimed;

(vi) any appointment that is required by, or observations that the Claimant considers useful in connection with, Articles 14 to 20.

Article 10

The Request for Arbitration may also be accompanied by the Statement of Claim referred to in Article 41.   A52–010

Answer to the Request

Article 11

Within 30 days from the date on which the Respondent receives the Request for Arbitration from the Claimant, the Respondent shall address to the Center and to the Claimant an Answer to the Request which shall contain comments on any of the elements in the Request for Arbitration and may include indications of any counterclaim or setoff.   A52–011

Article 12

If the Claimant has filed a Statement of Claim with the Request for Arbitration pursuant to Article 10, the Answer to the Request may also be accompanied by the Statement of Defense referred to in Article 42.   A52–012

Representation

Article 13

(a) The parties may be represented by persons of their choice, irrespective of, in particular, nationality or professional qualification. The names, addresses and telephone, telex, telefax or other communication references of representatives shall be communicated to the Center, the other party and, after its establishment, the Tribunal.   A52–013

(b) Each party shall ensure that its representatives have sufficient time available to enable the arbitration to proceed expeditiously.

(c) The parties may also be assisted by persons of their choice.

III. COMPOSITION AND ESTABLISHMENT OF THE TRIBUNAL

Number of Arbitrators

Article 14

(a) The Tribunal shall consist of such number of arbitrators as has been agreed by the parties.   A52–014

(b) Where the parties have not agreed on the number of arbitrators, the Tribunal shall consist of a sole arbitrator, except where the Center in its discretion determines that, in view of all the circumstances of the case, a Tribunal composed of three members is appropriate.

Appointment Pursuant to Procedure Agreed Upon By the Parties

Article 15

A52–015 (a) If the parties have agreed on a procedure of appointing the arbitrator or arbitrators other than as envisaged in Articles 16 to 20, that procedure shall be followed.

(b) If the Tribunal has not been established pursuant to such procedure within the period of time agreed upon by the parties or, in the absence of such an agreed period of time, within 45 days after the commencement of the arbitration, the Tribunal shall be established or completed, as the case may be, in accordance with Article 19.

Appointment of a Sole Arbitrator

Article 16

A52–016 (a) Where a sole arbitrator is to be appointed and the parties have not agreed on a procedure of appointment, the sole arbitrator shall be appointed jointly by the parties.

(b) If the appointment of the sole arbitrator is not made within the period of time agreed upon by the parties or, in the absence of such an agreed period of time, within 30 days after the commencement of the arbitration, the sole arbitrator shall be appointed in accordance with Article 19.

Appointment of Three Arbitrators

Article 17

A52–017 (a) Where three arbitrators are to be appointed and the parties have not agreed upon a procedure of appointment, the arbitrators shall be appointed in accordance with this Article.

(b) The Claimant shall appoint an arbitrator in its Request for Arbitration. The Respondent shall appoint an arbitrator within 30 days from the date on which it receives the Request for Arbitration. The two arbitrators thus appointed shall, within 20 days after the appointment of the second arbitrator, appoint a third arbitrator, who shall be the presiding arbitrator.

(c) Notwithstanding paragraph (b), where three arbitrators are to be appointed as a result of the exercise of the discretion of the Center under Article 14(b), the Claimant shall, by notice to the Center and to the Respondent, appoint an arbitrator within 15 days after the receipt by it of notification by the Center that the Tribunal is to be composed of three arbitrators. The Respondent shall appoint an arbitrator within 30 days after the receipt by it of the said notification. The two arbitrators thus appointed shall, within 20 days after the appointment of the second arbitrator, appoint a third arbitrator, who shall be the presiding arbitrator.

(d) If the appointment of any arbitrator is not made within the applicable period of time referred to in the preceding paragraphs, that arbitrator shall be appointed in accordance with Article 19.

WIPO ARBITRATION RULES

Appointment of Three Arbitrators in Case of Multiple Claimants or Respondents

Article 18

(a) Where

(i) three arbitrators are to be appointed,
(ii) the parties have not agreed on procedure of appointment, and
(iii) the Request for Arbitration names more than one Claimant,

the Claimants shall make a joint appointment of an arbitrator in their Request for Arbitration. The appointment of the second arbitrator and the presiding arbitrator shall, subject to paragraph (b) of this Article, take place in accordance with Article 17(b), (c) or (d), as the case may be.

(b) Where

(i) three arbitrators are to be appointed,
(ii) the parties have not agreed on a procedure of appointment, and
(iii) the Request for Arbitration names more than one Respondent,

the Respondents shall jointly appoint an arbitrator. If, for whatever reason, the Respondents do not make a joint appointment of an arbitrator within 30 days after receiving the Request for Arbitration, any appointment of the arbitrator previously made by the Claimant or Claimants shall be considered void and two arbitrators shall be appointed by the Center. The two arbitrators thus appointed shall, within 30 days after the appointment of the second arbitrator, appoint a third arbitrator, who shall be the presiding arbitrator.

(c) Where

(i) three arbitrators are to be appointed,
(ii) the parties have agreed upon a procedure of appointment, and
(iii) the Request for Arbitration names more than one Claimant or more than one Respondent,

paragraphs (a) and (b) of this Article shall, notwithstanding Article 15(a), apply irrespective of any contractual provisions in the Arbitration Agreement with respect to the procedure of appointment, unless those provisions have expressly excluded the application of this Article.

Default Appointment

Article 19

(a) If a party has failed to appoint an arbitrator as required under Articles 15, 17 or 18, the Center shall, in lieu of that party, forthwith make the appointment.

(b) If the sole or presiding arbitrator has not been appointed as required under Articles 15, 16, 17 or 18, the appointment shall take place in accordance with the following procedure:

(i) The Center shall send to each party an identical list of candidates. The list shall comprise the names of at least three candidates in alphabetical order. The list shall include or be accompanied by a brief statement of each candidate's qualifications. If the parties have agreed on any particular qualifications, the list shall contain only the names of candidates [who] satisfy those qualifications.

(ii) Each party shall have the right to delete the name of any candidate or candidates to whose appointment it objects and shall number any remaining candidates in order of preference.

(iii) Each party shall return the marked list to the Center within 20 days after the date on which the list is received by it. Any party failing to return a marked list within that period of time shall be deemed to have assented to all candidates appearing on the list.

(iv) As soon as possible after receipt by it of the lists from the parties, or failing this, after the expiration of the period of time specified in the previous subparagraph, the Center shall, taking into account the preferences and objections expressed by the parties, invite a person from the list to be the sole or presiding arbitrator.

(v) If the lists which have been returned do not show a person who is acceptable as arbitrator to both parties, the Center shall be authorized to appoint the sole or presiding arbitrator. The Center shall similarly be authorized to do so if a person is not able or does not wish to accept the Center's invitation to be the sole or presiding arbitrator, or if there appear to be other reasons precluding that person from being the sole or presiding arbitrator, and there does not remain on the lists a person who is acceptable as arbitrator to both parties.

(c) Notwithstanding the provisions of paragraph (b), the Center shall be authorized to appoint the sole or presiding arbitrator if it determines in its discretion that the procedure described in that paragraph is not appropriate for the case.

Nationality of Arbitrators

Article 20

A52–020

(a) An agreement of the parties concerning the nationality of arbitrators shall be respected.

(b) If the parties have not agreed on the nationality of the sole or presiding arbitrator, such arbitrator shall, in the absence of special circumstances such as the need to appoint a person having particular qualifications, be a national of a country other than the countries of the parties.

Communication Between Parties and Candidates for Appointment as Arbitrator

Article 21

A52–021 No party or anyone acting on its behalf shall have any ex parte communication with any candidate for appointment as arbitrator except to discuss the candidate's qualifications, availability or independence in relation to the parties.

WIPO Arbitration Rules

Impartiality and Independence

Article 22

(a) Each arbitrator shall be impartial and independent.

(b) Each prospective arbitrator shall, before accepting appointment, disclose to the parties, the Center and any other arbitrator who has already been appointed any circumstances that might give rise to justifiable doubt as to the arbitrator's impartiality or independence, or confirm in writing that no such circumstances exist.

(c) If, at any stage during the arbitration, new circumstances arise that might give rise to justifiable doubt as to any arbitrator's impartiality or independence, the arbitrator shall promptly disclose such circumstances to the parties, the Center and the other arbitrators.

Availability, Acceptance and Notification

Article 23

(a) Each arbitrator shall, by accepting appointment, be deemed to have undertaken to make available sufficient time to enable the arbitration to be conducted and completed expeditiously.

(b) Each prospective arbitrator shall accept appointment in writing and shall communicate such acceptance to the Center.

(c) The Center shall notify the parties of the establishment of the Tribunal.

Challenge of Arbitrators

Article 24

(a) Any arbitrator may be challenged by a party if circumstances exist that give rise to justifiable doubt as to the arbitrator's impartiality or independence.

(b) A party may challenge an arbitrator whom it has appointed or in whose appointment it concurred only for reasons of which it becomes aware after the appointment has been made.

Article 25

A party challenging an arbitrator shall send notice to the Center, the Tribunal and the other party, stating the reasons for the challenge, within 15 days after being notified of that arbitrator's appointment or after becoming aware of the circumstances that it considers give rise to justifiable doubt as to that arbitrator's impartiality or independence.

Article 26

When an arbitrator has been challenged by a party, the other party shall have the right to respond to the challenge and shall, if it exercises this right, send, within 15 days after receipt of the notice referred to in Article 25, a copy of its response to the Center, the party making the challenge and the arbitrators.

Article 27

A52–027   The Tribunal may, in its discretion, suspend or continue the arbitral proceedings during the pendency of the challenge.

Article 28

A52–028   The other party may agree to the challenge or the arbitrator may voluntarily withdraw. In either case, the arbitrator shall be replaced without any implication that the grounds for the challenge are valid.

Article 29

A52–029   If the other party does not agree to the challenge and the challenged arbitrator does not withdraw, the decision on the challenge shall be made by the Center in accordance with its internal procedures. Such a decision is of an administrative nature and shall be final. The Center shall not be required to state reasons for its decision.

Release from Appointment

Article 30

A52–030   At the arbitrator's own request, an arbitrator may be released from appointment as arbitrator either with the consent of the parties or by the Center.

Article 31

A52–031   Irrespective of any request by the arbitrator, the parties may jointly release the arbitrator from appointment as arbitrator. The parties shall promptly notify the Center of such release.

Article 32

A52–032   At the request of a party or on its own motion, the Center may release an arbitrator from appointment as arbitrator if the arbitrator has become *de jure* or *de facto* unable to fulfill, or fails to fulfill, the duties of an arbitrator. In such a case, the parties shall be offered the opportunity to express their views thereon and the provisions of Articles 26 to 29 shall apply *mutatis mutandis*.

Replacement of an Arbitrator

Article 33

A52–033   (a) Whenever necessary, a substitute arbitrator shall be appointed pursuant to the procedure provided for in Articles 15 to 19 that was applicable to the appointment of the arbitrator being replaced.

(b) In the event that an arbitrator appointed by a party has either been successfully challenged on grounds which were known or should have been known to that party at the time of appointment, or has been released from appointment as arbitrator in accordance with Article 32, the Center shall have the discretion not to permit that party to make a new appointment. If it chooses to exercise this discretion, the Center shall make the substitute appointment.

(c) Pending the replacement, the arbitral proceedings shall be suspended, unless otherwise agreed by the parties.

Article 34

Whenever a substitute arbitrator is appointed, the Tribunal shall, having regard to any observations of the parties, determine in its sole discretion whether all or part of any prior hearings are to be repeated.

A52–034

Truncated Tribunal

Article 35

(a) If an arbitrator on a three-person Tribunal, though duly notified and without good cause, fails to participate in the work of the Tribunal, the two other arbitrators shall, unless a party has made an application under Article 32, have the power in their sole discretion to continue the arbitration and to make any award, order or other decision, notwithstanding the failure of the third arbitrator to participate. In determining whether to continue the arbitration or to render any award, order or other decision without the participation of an arbitrator, the two other arbitrators shall take into account the stage of the arbitration, the reason, if any, expressed by the third arbitrator for such non-participation, and such other matters as they consider appropriate in the circumstances of the case.

A52–035

(b) In the event that the two other arbitrators determine not to continue the arbitration without the participation of a third arbitrator, the Center shall, on proof satisfactory to it of the failure of the arbitrator to participate in the work of the Tribunal, declare the office vacant, and a substitute arbitrator shall be appointed by the Center in the exercise of the discretion defined in Article 33, unless the parties agree otherwise.

Pleas as to the Jurisdiction of the Tribunal

Article 36

(a) The Tribunal shall have the power to hear and determine objections to its own jurisdiction, including any objections with respect to form, existence, validity or scope of the Arbitration Agreement examined pursuant to Article 59(b).

A52–036

(b) The Tribunal shall have the power to determine the existence or validity of any contract of which the Arbitration Agreement forms part or to which it relates.

(c) A plea that the Tribunal does not have jurisdiction shall be raised not later than in the Statement of Defense or, with respect to a counterclaim or a setoff, the Statement of Defense thereto, failing which any such plea shall be barred in the subsequent arbitral proceedings or before any court. A plea that the Tribunal is exceeding the scope of its authority shall be raised as soon as the matter alleged to be beyond the scope of its authority is raised during the arbitral proceedings. The Tribunal may, in either case, admit a later plea if it considers the delay justified.

(d) The Tribunal may rule on a plea referred to in paragraph (c) as a preliminary question or, in its sole discretion, decide on such a plea in the final award.

(e) A plea that the Tribunal lacks jurisdiction shall not preclude the Center from administering the arbitration.

IV. Conduct of the Arbitration

Transmission of the File to the Tribunal

Article 37

A52–037 The Center shall transmit the file to each arbitrator as soon as the arbitrator is appointed.

General Powers of the Tribunal

Article 38

A52–038
(a) Subject to Article 3, the Tribunal may conduct the arbitration in such manner as it considers appropriate.

(b) In all cases, the Tribunal shall ensure that the parties are treated with equality and that each party is given a fair opportunity to present its case.

(c) The Tribunal shall ensure that the arbitral procedure takes place with due expedition. It may, at the request of a party or on its own motion, extend in exceptional cases a period of time fixed by these Rules, by itself or agreed to by the parties. In urgent cases, such an extension may be granted by the presiding arbitrator alone.

Place of Arbitration

Article 39

A52–039
(a) Unless otherwise agreed by the parties, the place of arbitration shall be decided by the Center, taking into consideration any observations of the parties and the circumstances of the arbitration.

(b) The Tribunal may, after consultation with the parties, conduct hearings at any place that it considers appropriate. It may deliberate wherever it deems appropriate.

(c) The award shall be deemed to have been made at the place of arbitration.

Language of Arbitration

Article 40

(a) Unless otherwise agreed by the parties, the language of the arbitration shall be the language of the Arbitration Agreement, subject to the power of the Tribunal to determine otherwise, having regard to any observations of the parties and the circumstances of the arbitration.

(b) The Tribunal may order that any documents submitted in languages other than the language of arbitration be accompanied by a translation in whole or in part into the language of arbitration.

Statement of Claim

Article 41

(a) Unless the Statement of Claim accompanied the Request for Arbitration, the Claimant shall, within 30 days after receipt of notification from the Center of the establishment of the Tribunal, communicate its Statement of Claim to the Respondent and to the Tribunal.

(b) The Statement of Claim shall contain a comprehensive statement of the facts and legal arguments supporting the claim, including a statement of the relief sought.

(c) The Statement of Claim shall, to as large an extent as possible, be accompanied by the documentary evidence upon which the Claimant relies, together with a schedule of such documents. Where the documentary evidence is especially voluminous, the Claimant may add a reference to further documents it is prepared to submit.

Statement of Defense

Article 42

(a) The Respondent shall, within 30 days after receipt of the Statement of Claim or within 30 days after receipt of notification from the Center of the establishment of the Tribunal, whichever occurs later, communicate its Statement of Defense to the Claimant and to the Tribunal.

(b) The Statement of Defense shall reply to the particulars of the Statement of Claim required pursuant to Article 41(b). The Statement of Defense shall be accompanied by the corresponding documentary evidence described in Article 41(c).

(c) Any counterclaim or setoff by the Respondent shall be made or asserted in the Statement of Defense or, in exceptional circumstances, at a later stage in the arbitral proceedings if so determined by the Tribunal. Any such counterclaim or setoff shall contain the same particulars as those specified in Article 41(b) and (c).

Further Written Statements

Article 43

A52–043 (a) In the event that a counter-claim or set-off has been made or asserted, the Claimant shall reply to the particulars thereof. Article 42(a) and (b) shall apply *mutatis mutandis* to such reply.

(b) The Tribunal may, in its discretion, allow or require further written statements.

Amendments to Claims or Defense

Article 44

A52–044 Subject to any contrary agreement by the parties, a party may amend or supplement its claim, counter-claim, defense or setoff during the course of the arbitral proceedings, unless the Tribunal considers it inappropriate to allow such amendment having regard to its nature or the delay in making it and to the provisions of Article 38(b) and (c).

Communication between Parties and Tribunal

Article 45

A52–045 Except as otherwise provided in these Rules or permitted by the Tribunal, no party or anyone acting on its behalf may have any *ex parte* communication with any arbitrator with respect to any matter of substance relating to the arbitration, it being understood that nothing in this paragraph shall prohibit *ex parte* communications which concern matters of a purely organizational nature, such as the physical facilities, place, date or time of the hearings.

Interim Measures of Protection; Security for Claims and Costs

Article 46

A52–046 (a) At the request of a party, the Tribunal may issue any provisional orders or take other interim measures it deems necessary, including injunctions and measures for the conservation of goods which form part of the subject matter in dispute, such as an order for their deposit with a third person or for the sale of perishable goods. The Tribunal may make the granting of such measures subject to appropriate security being furnished by the requesting party.

(b) At the request of a party, the Tribunal may, if it considers it to be required by exceptional circumstances, order the other party to provide security, in a form to be determined by the Tribunal, for the claim or counterclaim, as well as for costs referred to in Article 72.

(c) Measures and orders contemplated under this Article may take the form of an interim award.

(d) A request addressed by a party to a judicial authority for interim measures or for security for the claim or counterclaim, or for the implementation of any such measures or orders granted by the Tribunal, shall not be deemed incompatible with the Arbitration Agreement, or deemed to be a waiver of that Agreement.

Preparatory Conference

Article 47

The Tribunal may, in general following the submission of the Statement of Defense, conduct a preparatory conference with the parties for the purpose of organizing and scheduling the subsequent proceedings.

Evidence

Article 48

(a) The Tribunal shall determine the admissibility, relevance, materiality and weight of evidence.

(b) At any time during the arbitration, the Tribunal may, at the request of a party or on its own motion, order a party to produce such documents or other evidence as it considers necessary or appropriate and may order a party to make available to the Tribunal or to an expert appointed by it or to the other party any property in its possession or control for inspection or testing.

Experiments

Article 49

(a) A party may give notice to the Tribunal and to the other party at any reasonable time before a hearing that specified experiments have been conducted on which it intends to rely. The notice shall specify the purpose of the experiment, a summary of the experiment, the method employed, the results and the conclusion. The other party may by notice to the Tribunal request that any or all such experiments be repeated in its presence. If the Tribunal considers such request justified, it shall determine the timetable for the repetition of the experiments.

(b) For the purposes of this Article, "experiments" shall include tests or other processes of verification.

Site Visits

Article 50

The Tribunal may, at the request of a party or on its own motion, inspect or require the inspection of any site, property, machinery, facility, production line, model, film, material, product or process as it deems appropriate. A party may request such an inspection at any reasonable time prior to any hearing, and the Tribunal, if it grants such a request, shall determine the timing and arrangements for the inspection.

Agreed Primers and Models

Article 51

A52–051   The Tribunal may, where the parties so agree, determine that they shall jointly provide:

   (i) a technical primer setting out the background of the scientific, technical or other specialized information necessary to fully understand the matters in issue; and

   (ii) models, drawings or other materials that the Tribunal or the parties require for reference purposes at any hearing.

Disclosure of Trade Secrets and Other Confidential Information

Article 52

A52–052   (a) For the purposes of this Article, confidential information shall mean any information, regardless of the medium in which it is expressed, which is

   (i) in the possession of a party,
   (ii) not accessible to the public,
   (iii) of commercial, financial or industrial significance, and
   (iv) treated as confidential by the party possessing it.

(b) A party invoking the confidentiality of any information it wishes or is required to submit in the arbitration, including to an expert appointed by the Tribunal, shall make an application to have the information classified as confidential by notice to the Tribunal, with a copy to the other party. Without disclosing the substance of the information, the party shall give in the notice the reasons for which it considers the information confidential.

(c) The Tribunal shall determine whether the information is to be classified as confidential and of such a nature that the absence of special measures of protection in the proceedings would be likely to cause serious harm to the party invoking its confidentiality. If the Tribunal so determines, it shall decide under which conditions and to whom the confidential information may in part or in whole be disclosed and shall require any person to whom the confidential information is to be disclosed to sign an appropriate confidentiality undertaking.

(d) In exceptional circumstances, in lieu of itself determining whether the information is to be classified as confidential and of such nature that the absence of special measures of protection in the proceedings would be likely to cause serious harm to the party invoking its confidentiality, the Tribunal may, at the request of a party or on its own motion and after consultation with the parties, designate a confidentiality advisor who will determine whether the information is to be so classified, and, if so, decide under which conditions and to whom it may in part or in whole be disclosed. Any such confidentiality advisor shall be required to sign an appropriate confidentiality undertaking.

(e) The Tribunal may also, at the request of a party or on its own motion, appoint the confidentiality advisor as an expert in accordance with Article 55 in order to report to it, on the basis of the confidential information, on specific issues designated by the Tribunal without disclosing the confidential information either to the party from whom the confidential information does not originate or to the Tribunal.

Hearings

Article 53

(a) If either party so requests, the Tribunal shall hold a hearing for the presentation of evidence by witnesses, including expert witnesses, or for oral argument or for both. In the absence of a request, the Tribunal shall decide whether to hold such a hearing or hearings. If no hearings are held, the proceedings shall be conducted on the basis of documents and other materials alone.

(b) In the event of a hearing, the Tribunal shall give the parties adequate advance notice of the date, time and place thereof.

(c) Unless the parties agree otherwise, all hearings shall be in private.

(d) The Tribunal shall determine whether and, if so, in what form a record shall be made of any hearing.

A52–053

Witnesses

Article 54

(a) Before any hearing, the Tribunal may require either party to give notice of the identity of witnesses it wishes to call, as well as of the subject-matter of their testimony and its relevance to the issues.

(b) The Tribunal has discretion, on the grounds of redundance and irrelevance, to limit or refuse the appearance of any witness, whether witness of fact or expert witness.

(c) Any witness who gives oral evidence may be questioned, under the control of the Tribunal, by each of the parties. The Tribunal may put questions at any stage of the examination of the witnesses.

(d) The testimony of witnesses may, either at the choice of a party or as directed by the Tribunal, be submitted in written form, whether by way of signed statements, sworn affidavits or otherwise, in which case the Tribunal may make the admissibility of the testimony conditional upon the witnesses being made available for oral testimony.

(e) A party shall be responsible for the practical arrangements, cost and availability of any witness it calls.

(f) The Tribunal shall determine whether any witness shall retire during any part of the proceedings, particularly during the testimony of other witnesses.

A52–054

Experts Appointed by the Tribunal

Article 55

(a) The Tribunal may, after consultation with the parties, appoint one or more independent experts to report to it on specific issues designated by the Tribunal. A copy of the expert's terms of reference, established by the Tribunal, having regard to any observations of the parties, shall be communicated to the parties. Any such expert shall be required to sign an appropriate confidentiality undertaking.

A52–055

(b) Subject to Article 52, upon receipt of the expert's report, the Tribunal shall communicate a copy of the report to the parties, which shall be given the opportunity to express, in writing, their opinion on the report. A party may, subject to Article 52, examine any document on which the expert has relied in such a report.

(c) At the request of a party, the parties shall be given the opportunity to question the expert at a hearing. At this hearing, the parties may present expert witnesses to testify on the points at issue.

(d) The opinion of any expert on the issue or issues submitted to the expert shall be subject to the Tribunal's power of assessment of those issues in the context of all the circumstances of the case, unless the parties have agreed that the expert's determination shall be conclusive in respect of any specific issue.

Default

Article 56

A52–056 (a) If the Claimant, without showing good cause, fails to submit its Statement of Claim in accordance with Article 41, the Tribunal shall terminate the proceedings.

(b) If the Respondent, without showing good cause, fails to submit its Statement of Defense in accordance with Article 42, the Tribunal may nevertheless proceed with the arbitration and make the award.

(c) The Tribunal may also proceed with the arbitration and make the award if a party, without showing good cause, fails to avail itself of the opportunity to present its case within the period of time determined by the Tribunal.

(d) If a party, without showing good cause, fails to comply with any provision of, or requirement under, these Rules or any direction given by the Tribunal, the Tribunal may draw the inferences therefrom that it considers appropriate.

Closure of Proceedings

Article 57

A52–057 (a) The Tribunal shall declare the proceedings closed when it is satisfied that the parties have had adequate opportunity to present submissions and evidence.

(b) The Tribunal may, if it considers it necessary owing to exceptional circumstances, decide, on its own motion or upon application of a party, to reopen the proceedings it declared to be closed at any time before the award is made.

Waiver

Article 58

A52–058 A party which knows that any provision of, or requirement under, these Rules, or any direction given by the Tribunal, has not been complied with, and yet proceeds with the arbitration without promptly recording an objection to such non-compliance, shall be deemed to have waived its right to object.

V. Awards and Other Decisions

Laws Applicable to the Substance of the Dispute, the Arbitration and the Arbitration Agreement

Article 59

(a) The Tribunal shall decide the substance of the dispute in accordance with the law or rules of law chosen by the parties. Any designation of the law of a given State shall be construed, unless otherwise expressed, as directly referring to the substantive law of that State and not to its conflict of laws rules. Failing a choice by the parties, the Tribunal shall apply the law or rules of law that it determines to be appropriate. In all cases, the Tribunal shall decide having due regard to the terms of any relevant contract and taking into account applicable trade usages. The Tribunal may decide as *amiable compositeur* or *ex aequo et bono* only if the parties have expressly authorized it to do so.

(b) The law applicable to the arbitration shall be the arbitration law of the place of arbitration, unless the parties have expressly agreed on the application of another arbitration law and such agreement is permitted by the law of the place of arbitration.

(c) An Arbitration Agreement shall be regarded as effective if it conforms to the requirements concerning form, existence, validity and scope of either the law or rules of law applicable in accordance with paragraph (a), or the law applicable in accordance with paragraph (b).

Currency and Interest

Article 60

(a) Monetary amounts in the award may be expressed in any currency.

(b) The Tribunal may award simple or compound interest to be paid by a party on any sum awarded against that party. It shall be free to determine the interest at such rates as it considers to be appropriate, without being bound by legal rates of interest, and shall be free to determine the period for which the interest shall be paid.

Decision-making

Article 61

Unless the parties have agreed otherwise, where there is more than one arbitrator, any award, order or other decision of the Tribunal shall be made by a majority. In the absence of a majority, the presiding arbitrator shall make the award, order or other decision as if acting as sole arbitrator.

Form and Notification of Awards

Article 62

A52–062

(a) The Tribunal may make preliminary, interim, interlocutory, partial or final awards.

(b) The award shall be in writing and shall state the date on which it was made, as well as the place of arbitration in accordance with Article 39(a).

(c) The award shall state the reasons on which it is based, unless the parties have agreed that no reasons should be stated and the law applicable to the arbitration does not require the statement of such reasons.

(d) The award shall be signed by the arbitrator or arbitrators. The signature of the award by a majority of the arbitrators, or, in the case of Article 61, second sentence, by the presiding arbitrator, shall be sufficient. Where an arbitrator fails to sign, the award shall state the reason for the absence of the signature.

(e) The Tribunal may consult the Center with regard to matters of form, particularly to ensure the enforceability of the award.

(f) The award shall be communicated by the Tribunal to the Center in a number of originals sufficient to provide one for each party, the arbitrator or arbitrators and the Center. The Center shall formally communicate an original of the award to each party and the arbitrator or arbitrators.

(g) At the request of a party, the Center shall provide it, at cost, with a copy of the award certified by the Center. A copy so certified shall be deemed to comply with the requirements of Article IV(1)(a) of the Convention on the Recognition and Enforcement of Foreign Arbitral Awards, New York, June 10, 1958.

Time Period for Delivery of the Final Award

Article 63

A52–063

(a) The arbitration should, wherever reasonably possible, be heard and the proceedings declared closed within not more than nine months after either the delivery of the Statement of Defense or the establishment of the Tribunal, whichever event occurs later. The final award should, wherever reasonably possible, be made within three months thereafter.

(b) If the proceedings are not declared closed within the period of time specified in paragraph (a), the Tribunal shall send the Center a status report on the arbitration, with a copy to each party. It shall send a further status report to the Center, and a copy to each party, at the end of each ensuing period of three months during which the proceedings have not been declared closed.

(c) If the final award is not made within three months after the closure of the proceedings, the Tribunal shall send the Center a written explanation for the delay, with a copy to each party. It shall send a further explanation, and a copy to each party, at the end of each ensuing period of one month until the final award is made.

Effect of Award

Article 64

(a) By agreeing to arbitration under these Rules, the parties undertake to carry out the award without delay, and waive their right to any form of appeal or recourse to a court of law or other judicial authority, insofar as such waiver may validly be made under the applicable law.

(b) The award shall be effective and binding on the parties as from the date it is communicated by the Center pursuant to Article 62(f), second sentence.

Settlement or Other Grounds for Termination

Article 65

(a) The Tribunal may suggest that the parties explore settlement at such times as the Tribunal may deem appropriate.

(b) If, before the award is made, the parties agree on a settlement of the dispute, the Tribunal shall terminate the arbitration and, if requested jointly by the parties, record the settlement in the form of a consent award. The Tribunal shall not be obliged to give reasons for such an award.

(c) If, before the award is made, the continuation of the arbitration becomes unnecessary or impossible for any reason not mentioned in paragraph (b), the Tribunal shall inform the parties of its intention to terminate the arbitration. The Tribunal shall have the power to issue such an order terminating the arbitration, unless a party raises justifiable grounds for objection within a period of time to be determined by the Tribunal.

(d) The consent award or the order for termination of the arbitration shall be signed by the arbitrator or arbitrators in accordance with Article 62(d) and shall be communicated by the Tribunal to the Center in a number of originals sufficient to provide one for each party, the arbitrator or arbitrators and the Center. The Center shall formally communicate an original of the consent award or the order for termination to each party and the arbitrator or arbitrators.

Correction of the Award and Additional Award

Article 66

(a) Within 30 days after receipt of the award, a party may, by notice to the Tribunal, with a copy to the Center and the other party, request the Tribunal to correct in the award any clerical, typographical or computational errors. If the Tribunal considers the request to be justified, it shall make the correction within 30 days after receipt of the request. Any correction, which shall take the form of a separate memorandum, signed by the Tribunal in accordance with Article 62(d), shall become part of the award.

(b) The Tribunal may correct any error of the type referred to in paragraph (a) on its own initiative within 30 days after the date of the award.

(c) A party may, within 30 days after receipt of the award, by notice to the Tribunal, with a copy to the Center and the other party, request the Tribunal to make an additional award as to claims presented in the arbitral proceedings but not dealt with in the award. Before deciding on the request, the Tribunal shall give the parties an opportunity to be heard. If the Tribunal considers the request to be justified, it shall, wherever reasonably possible, make the additional award within 60 days of receipt of the request.

VI. Fees and Costs

Fees of the Center

Article 67

A52–067

(a) The Request for Arbitration shall be subject to the payment to the Center of a registration fee, which shall belong to the International Bureau of WIPO. The amount of the registration fee shall be fixed in the Schedule of Fees applicable on the date on which the Request for Arbitration is received by the Center.

(b) The registration fee shall not be refundable.

(c) No action shall be taken by the Center on a Request for Arbitration until the registration fee has been paid.

(d) If a Claimant fails, within 15 days after a second reminder in writing from the Center, to pay the registration fee, it shall be deemed to have withdrawn its Request for Arbitration.

Article 68

A52–068

(a) An administration fee, which shall belong to the International Bureau of WIPO, shall be payable by the Claimant to the Center within 30 days after the commencement of the arbitration. The Center shall notify the Claimant of the amount of the administration fee as soon as possible after receipt of the Request for Arbitration.

(b) In the case of a counterclaim, an administration fee shall also be payable by the Respondent to the Center within 30 days after the date on which the counterclaim referred to in Article 42(c) is made. The Center shall notify the Respondent of the amount of the administration fee as soon as possible after receipt of notification of the counterclaim.

(c) The amount of the administration fee shall be calculated in accordance with the Schedule of Fees applicable on the date of commencement of the arbitration.

(d) Where a claim or counterclaim is increased, the amount of the administration fee may be increased in accordance with the Schedule of Fees applicable under paragraph (c), and the increased amount shall be payable by the Claimant or the Respondent, as the case may be.

(e) If a party fails, within 15 days after a second reminder in writing from the Center, to pay any administration fee due, it shall be deemed to have withdrawn its claim or counterclaim, or its increase in claim or counterclaim, as the case may be.

(f) The Tribunal shall, in a timely manner, inform the Center of the amount of the claim and any counterclaim, as well as any increase thereof.

Fees of the Arbitrators

Article 69

(a) The amount and currency of the fees of the arbitrators and the modalities and timing of their payment shall be fixed, in accordance with the provisions of this Article, by the Center, after consultation with the arbitrators and the parties.

(b) The amount of the fees of the arbitrators shall, unless the parties and arbitrators agree otherwise, be determined within the range of minimum and maximum fees set out in the Schedule of Fees applicable on the date of the commencement of the arbitration, taking into account the estimated time needed by the arbitrators for conducting the arbitration, the amount in dispute, the complexity of the subject matter of the dispute, the urgency of the case and any other relevant circumstances of the case.

Deposits

Article 70

(a) Upon receipt of notification from the Center of the establishment of the Tribunal, the Claimant and the Respondent shall each deposit an equal amount as an advance for the costs of arbitration referred to in Article 71. The amount of the deposit shall be determined by the Center.

(b) In the course of the arbitration, the Center may require that the parties make supplementary deposits.

(c) If the required deposits are not paid in full within 30 days after receipt of the corresponding notification, the Center shall so inform the parties in order that one or other of them may make the required payment.

(d) Where the amount of the counterclaim greatly exceeds the amount of the claim or involves the examination of significantly different matters, or where it otherwise appears appropriate in the circumstances, the Center in its discretion may establish two separate deposits on account of claim and counterclaim. If separate deposits are established, the totality of the deposit on account of claim shall be paid by the Claimant and the totality of the deposit on account of counterclaim shall be paid by the Respondent.

(e) If a party fails, within 15 days after a second reminder in writing from the Center, to pay the required deposit, it shall be deemed to have withdrawn the relevant claim or counterclaim.

(f) After the award has been made, the Center shall, in accordance with the award, render an accounting to the parties of the deposits received and return any unexpended balance to the parties or require the payment of any amount owing from the parties.

Award of Costs of Arbitration

Article 71

A52–071 (a) In its award, the Tribunal shall fix the costs of arbitration, which shall consist of:

  (i) the arbitrators' fees,
  (ii) the properly incurred travel, communication and other expenses of the arbitrators,
  (iii) the costs of expert advice and such other assistance required by the Tribunal pursuant to these Rules, and
  (iv) such other expenses as are necessary for the conduct of the arbitration proceedings, such as the cost of meeting and hearing facilities.

(b) The aforementioned costs shall, as far as possible, be debited from the deposits required under Article 70.

(c) The Tribunal shall, subject to any agreement of the parties, apportion the costs of arbitration and the registration and administration fees of the Center between the parties in the light of all the circumstances and the outcome of the arbitration.

Award of Costs Incurred by a Party

Article 72

A52–072 In its award, the Tribunal may, subject to any contrary agreement by the parties and in the light of all the circumstances and the outcome of the arbitration, order a party to pay the whole or part of reasonable expenses incurred by the other party in presenting its case, including those incurred for legal representatives and witnesses.

VII. CONFIDENTIALITY

Confidentiality of the Existence of the Arbitration

Article 73

A52–073 (a) Except to the extent necessary in connection with a court challenge to the arbitration or an action for enforcement of an award, no information concerning the existence of an arbitration may be unilaterally disclosed by a party to any third party unless it is required to do so by law or by a competent regulatory body, and then only

  (i) by disclosing no more than what is legally required, and
  (ii) by furnishing to the Tribunal and to the other party, if the disclosure takes place during the arbitration, or to the other party alone, if the disclosure takes place after the termination of the arbitration, details of the disclosure and an explanation of the reason for it.

(b) Notwithstanding paragraph (a), a party may disclose to a third party the names of the parties to the arbitration and the relief requested for the purpose of satisfying any obligation of good faith or candor owed to that third party.

Confidentiality of Disclosures made during the Arbitration

Article 74

(a) In addition to any specific measures that may be available under Article 52, any documentary or other evidence given by a party or a witness in the arbitration shall be treated as confidential and, to the extent that such evidence describes information that is not in the public domain, shall not be used or disclosed to any third party by a party whose access to that information arises exclusively as a result of its participation in the arbitration for any purpose without the consent of the parties or order of a court having jurisdiction.

(b) For the purposes of this Article, a witness called by a party shall not be considered to be a third party. To the extent that a witness is given access to evidence or other information obtained in the arbitration in order to prepare the witness's testimony, the party calling such witness shall be responsible for the maintenance by the witness of the same degree of confidentiality as that required of the party.

Confidentiality of the Award

Article 75

The award shall be treated as confidential by the parties and may only be disclosed to a third party if and to the extent that

(i) the parties consent, or

(ii) it falls into the public domain as a result of an action before a national court or other competent authority, or

(iii) it must be disclosed in order to comply with a legal requirement imposed on a party or in order to establish or protect a party's legal rights against a third party.

Maintenance of Confidentiality by the Center and Arbitrator

Article 76

(a) Unless the parties agree otherwise, the Center and the arbitrator shall maintain the confidentiality of the arbitration, the award and, to the extent that they describe information that is not in the public domain, any documentary or other evidence

INSTITUTIONAL RULES

disclosed during the arbitration, except to the extent necessary in connection with a court action relating to the award, or as otherwise required by law.

(b) Notwithstanding paragraph (a), the Center may include information concerning the arbitration in any aggregate statistical data that it publishes concerning its activities, provided that such information does not enable the parties or the particular circumstances of the dispute to be identified.

VIII. MISCELLANEOUS

Exclusion of Liability

Article 77

A52–077   Except in respect of deliberate wrongdoing, the arbitrator or arbitrators, WIPO and the Center shall not be liable to a party for any act or omission in connection with the arbitration.

Waiver of Defamation

Article 78

A52–078   The parties and, by acceptance of appointment, the arbitrator agree that any statements or comments, whether written or oral, made or used by them or their representatives in preparation for or in the course of the arbitration shall not be relied upon to found or maintain any action for defamation, libel, slander or any related complaint, and this Article may be pleaded as a bar to any such action.

A52–079

SCHEDULE OF FEES
(All amounts are in United States dollars)

FEES OF THE CENTER

I. REGISTRATION FEE

(Article 67, WIPO Arbitration Rules)

Amount of Claim	*Registration Fee*
Up to $1,000,000	$1,000
$1,000,0001 to $10,000,000	$2,000
Over $10,000,000	$3,000

Notes

1. Where the amount of the claim is not specified at the time of submitting the Request for Arbitration, a registration fee of $1,000 shall be payable, subject to adjustment when the Statement of Claim is filed.

2. Where a claim is not for a monetary amount, a registration fee of $1,000 shall be

payable, subject to adjustment. The adjustment shall be made by reference to the registration fee that the Center, upon examination of the Request for Arbitration or the Statement of Claim, determines to be appropriate in the circumstances.

3. The amount of claims expressed in currencies other than United States dollars shall, for the purposes of calculating the registration fee, be converted to amounts expressed in United States dollars on the basis of the official United Nations exchange rate prevailing on the date of submission of the Request for Arbitration.

II. ADMINISTRATION FEE

(Article 68, WIPO Arbitration Rules)

A52–080

Amount of Claim or Counter-Claim	Administration Fee
Up to $100,000	$1,000
$100,001 to $1,000,000	$1,000 + 0.40% (of the amount above $100,000)
$1,000,001 to $5,000,000	$4,600 + 0.20% (of the amount above $1,000,000)
$5,000,001 to $20,000,000	$12,600 + 0.10% (of the amount above $5,000,000)
Over $20,000,000	$27,600 + 0.05% (of the amount above $20,000,000 up to a *maximum* administration fee of $35,000)

Notes

1. Where a claim or counterclaim is not for a monetary amount, the Center shall determine an appropriate administration fee.

2. For the purpose of calculating the administration fee, the percentage figures are applied to each successive part of the amount of claim or counterclaim. For example, if the amount of claim is $5,000,000, the administration fee would be calculated as follows:

$100,000		$1,000
$900,000 (difference between $100,000 and $1,000,000)	0.40%	$3,600
$4,000,000 (difference between $1,000,000 and $5,000,000)	0.20%	$8,000
$5,000,000		$12,600

3. The maximum administration fee payable is $35,000.

4. The amounts of claims or counterclaims expressed in currencies other than United States dollars shall, for the purposes of calculating the administration fee, be converted to amounts expressed in United States dollars on the basis of the official United Nations exchange rate prevailing on the date of submission of the claim or of the counterclaim, respectively.

ARBITRATORS' FEES

Arbitrators' Fees (Article 69, WIPO Arbitration Rules)

Amount of Claims	Fees			
	Minimum		Maximum	
	Sole Arbitrator	Three-person Tribunal	Sole Arbitrator	Three-person Tribunal
Up to $100,000	$2,000	$5,000	10.00%	25.00%
$100,001 to $500,000	$2,000 + 2.00% (of the amount above $100,000)	$5,000 + 5.00% (of the amount above $100,000)	$10,0000 + 4.00% (of the amount above $100,000)	$20,000 + 10.00% (of the amount above $100,000)
$500,001 to $1,000,000	$10,000 + 1.50% (of the amount above $500,000)	$25,000 + 3.75% (of the amount above $500,000)	$26,000 + 3.50% (of the amount above $500,000)	$65,000 + 8.75% (of the amount above $500,000)
$1,000,001 to $2,000,000	$17,500 + 1.00% (of the amount above $1,000,000)	$43,750 + 2.50% (of the amount above $1,000,000)	$43,500 + 2.00% (of the amount above $1,000,000)	$108,750 + 5.00% (of the amount above $1,000,000)
$2,000,001 to $5,000,000	$27,500 + 0.75% (of the amount above $2,000,000)	$68,750 + 1.90% (of the amount above $2,000,000)	$63,500 + 1.50% (of the amount above $2,000,000)	$158,750 + 3.75% (of the amount above $2,000,000)
$5,000,001 to $10,000,000	$50,000 + 0.50% (of the amount above $5,000,000)	$125,750 + 1.25% (of the amount above $5,000,000)	$108,500 + 1.00% (of the amount above $5,000,000)	$271,250 + 2.50% (of the amount above $5,000,000)
$10,000,001 to $25,000,000	$75,000 + 0.30% (of the amount above $10,000,000)	$188,250 + 0.75% (of the amount above $10,000,000)	$158,500 + 1.00% (of the amount above $10,000,000)	$396,250 + 2.50% (of the amount above $10,000,000)
Over $25,000,000	$120,000 + 0.25% (of the amount above $25,000,000)	$300,750 + 0.65% (of the amount above $25,000,000)	$308,500 + 1.00% (of the amount above $25,000,000)	$771,250 + 2.50% (of the amount above $25,000,000)

Notes

1. For the purpose of calculating the amount of claims, the value of any counterclaim is added to the amount of the claim.

2. For the purpose of calculating the minimum and maximum amounts of the arbitrators' fees, the percentage figures are applied to each successive part of the whole amount of claims. For example, if the amount of claim is $1,500,000, the minimum fees for a sole arbitrator would be calculated as follows:

$100,000		$2,000
$400,000 (difference between $100,000 and $500,000)	2.00%	$8,000
$500,000 (difference between $500,000 and $1,000,000)	1.50%	$7,500
$500,000 (difference between $1,000,000 and $1,500,000)	1.00%	$5,000
$1,500,000		$22,500

3. Where a claim or counterclaim is not for a monetary amount, the Center shall, in consultation with the arbitrators and the parties, determine an appropriate value for the claim or counterclaim for the purpose of determining the arbitrators' fees.

4. The amounts of claims or counter-claims expressed in currencies other than United States dollars shall, for the purpose of determining the arbitrators' fees, be converted to amounts expressed in United States dollars on the basis of the official United Nations exchange rate prevailing on the date of submission of the claim or of the counterclaim, respectively.

5. The amounts and percentage figures specified in the Table for a three-person Tribunal represent the total fees payable to such a Tribunal, and not the fees payable to each arbitrator. Such fees shall be distributed between the three persons in accordance with the unanimous decision of those three persons. In the absence of such a decision, the distribution shall be 40 per cent for the presiding arbitrator, and 30 per cent for each of the other two arbitrators.

6. Where, by the agreement of the parties, a number of arbitrators other than one or three is appointed to a Tribunal, the scale of minimum and maximum fees for the Tribunal in question shall be determined by the Center. That scale shall be so determined by multiplying the scale for a sole arbitrator by the number of arbitrators reduced by a factor that takes account of the sharing of work and responsibility among the arbitrators.

Annex 2 of the World Trade Organisation Agreement—Understanding on rules and procedures governing the settlement of disputes*

Members hereby *agree* as follows:

Article 1

Coverage and Application

A53–001   **1.** The rules and procedures of this Understanding shall apply to disputes brought pursuant to the consultation and dispute settlement provisions of the agreements listed in Appendix 1 to this Understanding (referred to in this Understanding as the "covered agreements"). The rules and procedures of this Understanding shall also apply to consultations and the settlement of disputes between Members concerning their rights and obligations under the provisions of the Agreement Establishing the World Trade Organization (referred to in this Understanding as the "WTO Agreement") and of this Understanding taken in isolation or in combination with any other covered agreement.

2. The rules and procedures of this Understanding shall apply subject to such special or additional rules and procedures on dispute settlement contained in the covered agreements as are identified in Appendix 2 to this Understanding. To the extent that there is a difference between the rules and procedures of this Understanding and the special or additional rules and procedures set forth in Appendix 2, the special or additional rules and procedures in Appendix 2 shall prevail. In disputes involving rules and procedures under more than one covered agreement, if there is a conflict between special or additional rules and procedures of such agreements under review, and where the parties to the dispute cannot agree on rules and procedures within 20 days of the establishment of the panel, the Chairman of the Dispute Settlement Body provided for in paragraph 1 of Article 2 (referred to in this Understanding as the "DSB"), in consultation with the parties to the dispute, shall determine the rules and procedures to be followed within 10 days after a request by either Member. The Chairman shall be guided by the principle that special or additional rules and procedures should be used where possible, and the rules and procedures set out in this Understanding should be used to the extent necessary to avoid conflict.

Article 2

Administration

A53–002   **1.** The Dispute Settlement Body is hereby established to administer these rules and procedures and, except as otherwise provided in a covered agreement, the consultation

---

* This document is reproduced with the kind permission of the World Trade Organisation.

and dispute settlement provisions of the covered agreements. Accordingly, the DSB shall have the authority to establish panels, adopt panel and Appellate Body reports, maintain surveillance of implementation of rulings and recommendations, and authorize suspension of concessions and other obligations under the covered agreements. With respect to disputes arising under a covered agreement which is a Plurilateral Trade Agreement, the term "Member" as used herein shall refer only to those Members that are parties to the relevant Plurilateral Trade Agreement. Where the DSB administers the dispute settlement provisions of a Plurilateral Trade Agreement, only those Members that are parties to that Agreement may participate in decisions or actions taken by the DSB with respect to that dispute.

2. The DSB shall inform the relevant WTO Councils and Committees of any developments in disputes related to provisions of the respective covered agreements.

3. The DSB shall meet as often as necessary to carry out its functions within the time-frames provided in this Understanding.

4. Where the rules and procedures of this Understanding provide for the DSB to take a decision, it shall do so by consensus.[1]

Article 3

General Provisions

1. Members affirm their adherence to the principles for the management of disputes heretofore applied under Articles XXII and XXIII of GATT 1947, and the rules and procedures as further elaborated and modified herein.

2. The dispute settlement system of the WTO is a central element in providing security and predictability to the multilateral trading system. The Members recognize that it serves to preserve the rights and obligations of Members under the covered agreements, and to clarify the existing provisions of those agreements in accordance with customary rules of interpretation of public international law. Recommendations and rulings of the DSB cannot add to or diminish the rights and obligations provided in the covered agreements.

3. The prompt settlement of situations in which a Member considers that any benefits accruing to it directly or indirectly under the covered agreements are being impaired by measures taken by another Member is essential to the effective functioning of the WTO and the maintenance of a proper balance between the rights and obligations of Members.

4. Recommendations or rulings made by the DSB shall be aimed at achieving a satisfactory settlement of the matter in accordance with the rights and obligations under this Understanding and under the covered agreements.

5. All solutions to matters formally raised under the consultation and dispute settlement provisions of the covered agreements, including arbitration awards, shall be consistent with those agreements and shall not nullify or impair benefits accruing to any Member under those agreements, nor impede the attainment of any objective of those agreements.

6. Mutually agreed solutions to matters formally raised under the consultation and

---

[1] The DSB shall be deemed to have decided by consensus on a matter submitted for its consideration, if no Member, present at the meeting of the DSB when the decision is taken, formally objects to the proposed decision.

dispute settlement provisions of the covered agreements shall be notified to the DSB and the relevant Councils and Committees, where any Member may raise any point relating thereto.

7. Before bringing a case, a Member shall exercise its judgement as to whether action under these procedures would be fruitful. The aim of the dispute settlement mechanism is to secure a positive solution to a dispute. A solution mutually acceptable to the parties to a dispute and consistent with the covered agreements is clearly to be preferred. In the absence of a mutually agreed solution, the first objective of the dispute settlement mechanism is usually to secure the withdrawal of the measures concerned if these are found to be inconsistent with the provisions of any of the covered agreements. The provision of compensation should be resorted to only if the immediate withdrawal of the measure is impracticable and as a temporary measure pending the withdrawal of the measure which is inconsistent with a covered agreement. The last resort which this Understanding provides to the Member invoking the dispute settlement procedures is the possibility of suspending the application of concessions or other obligations under the covered agreements on a discriminatory basis vis-à-vis the other Member, subject to authorization by the DSB of such measures.

8. In cases where there is an infringement of the obligations assumed under a covered agreement, the action is considered *prima facie* to constitute a case of nullification or impairment. This means that there is normally a presumption that a breach of the rules has an adverse impact on other Members parties to that covered agreement, and in such cases, it shall be up to the Member against whom the complaint has been brought to rebut the charge.

9. The provisions of this Understanding are without prejudice to the rights of Members to seek authoritative interpretation of provisions of a covered agreement through decision-making under the WTO Agreement or a covered agreement which is a Plurilateral Trade Agreement.

10. It is understood that requests for conciliation and the use of the dispute settlement procedures should not be intended or considered as contentious acts and that, if a dispute arises, all Members will engage in these procedures in good faith in an effort to resolve the dispute. It is also understood that complaints and counter-complaints in regard to distinct matters should not be linked.

11. This Understanding shall be applied only with respect to new requests for consultations under the consultation provisions of the covered agreements made on or after the date of entry into force of the WTO Agreement. With respect to disputes for which the request for consultations was made under GATT 1947 or under any other predecessor agreement to the covered agreements before the date of entry into force of the WTO Agreement, the relevant dispute settlement rules and procedures in effect immediately prior to the date of entry into force of the WTO Agreement shall continue to apply.[2]

12. Notwithstanding paragraph 11, if a complaint based on any of the covered agreements is brought by a developing country Member against a developed country Member, the complaining party shall have the right to invoke, as an alternative to the provisions contained in Articles 4, 5, 6 and 12 of this Understanding, the corresponding provisions of the Decision of 5 April 1966 (BISD 14S/18), except that where the Panel considers that the time-frame provided for in paragraph 7 of that Decision is insufficient to provide its report and with the agreement of the complaining party, that time-frame may be

---

[2] This paragraph shall also be applied to disputes on which panel reports have not been adopted or fully implemented.

extended. To the extent that there is a difference between the rules and procedures of Articles 4, 5, 6 and 12 and the corresponding rules and procedures of the Decision, the latter shall prevail.

Article 4

Consultations

1. Members affirm their resolve to strengthen and improve the effectiveness of the consultation procedures employed by Members.
2. Each Member undertakes to accord sympathetic consideration to and afford adequate opportunity for consultation regarding any representations made by another Member concerning measures affecting the operation of any covered agreement taken within the territory of the former.[3]
3. If a request for consultations is made pursuant to a covered agreement, the Member to which the request is made shall, unless otherwise mutually agreed, reply to the request within 10 days after the date of its receipt and shall enter into consultations in good faith within a period of no more than 30 days after the date of receipt of the request, with a view to reaching a mutually satisfactory solution. If the Member does not respond within 10 days after the date of receipt of the request, or does not enter into consultations within a period of no more than 30 days, or a period otherwise mutually agreed, after the date of receipt of the request, then the Member that requested the holding of consultations may proceed directly to request the establishment of a panel.
4. All such requests for consultations shall be notified to the DSB and the relevant Councils and Committees by the Member which requests consultations. Any request for consultations shall be submitted in writing and shall give the reasons for the request, including identification of the measures at issue and an indication of the legal basis for the complaint.
5. In the course of consultations in accordance with the provisions of a covered agreement, before resorting to further action under this Understanding, Members should attempt to obtain satisfactory adjustment of the matter.
6. Consultations shall be confidential, and without prejudice to the rights of any Member in any further proceedings.
7. If the consultations fail to settle a dispute within 60 days after the date of receipt of the request for consultations, the complaining party may request the establishment of a panel. The complaining party may request a panel during the 60-day period if the consulting parties jointly consider that consultations have failed to settle the dispute.
8. In cases of urgency, including those which concern perishable goods, Members shall enter into consultations within a period of no more than 10 days after the date of receipt of the request. If the consultations have failed to settle the dispute within a period of 20 days after the date of receipt of the request, the complaining party may request the establishment of a panel.

---

[3] Where the provisions of any other covered agreement concerning measures taken by regional or local governments or authorities within the territory of a Member contain provisions different from the provisions of this paragraph, the provisions of such other covered agreement shall prevail.

9. In cases of urgency, including those which concern perishable goods, the parties to the dispute, panels and the Appellate Body shall make every effort to accelerate the proceedings to the greatest extent possible.

10. During consultations Members should give special attention to the particular problems and interests of developing country Members.

11. Whenever a Member other than the consulting Members considers that it has a substantial trade interest in consultations being held pursuant to paragraph 1 of Article XXII of GATT 1994, paragraph 1 of Article XXII of GATS, or the corresponding provisions in other covered agreements,[4] such Member may notify the consulting Members and the DSB, within 10 days after the date of the circulation of the request for consultations under said Article, of its desire to be joined in the consultations. Such Member shall be joined in the consultations, provided that the Member to which the request for consultations was addressed agrees that the claim of substantial interest is well-founded. In that event they shall so inform the DSB. If the request to be joined in the consultations is not accepted, the applicant Member shall be free to request consultations under paragraph 1 of Article XXII or paragraph 1 of Article XXIII of GATT 1994, paragraph 1 of Article XXII or paragraph 1 of Article XXIII of GATS, or the corresponding provisions in other covered agreements.

Article 5

Good Offices, Conciliation and Mediation

1. Good offices, conciliation and mediation are procedures that are undertaken voluntarily if the parties to the dispute so agree.

2. Proceedings involving good offices, conciliation and mediation, and in particular positions taken by the parties to the dispute during these proceedings, shall be confidential, and without prejudice to the rights of either party in any further proceedings under these procedures.

3. Good offices, conciliation or mediation may be requested at any time by any party to a dispute. They may begin at any time and be terminated at any time. Once procedures for good offices, conciliation or mediation are terminated, a complaining party may then proceed with a request for the establishment of a panel.

4. When good offices, conciliation or mediation are entered into within 60 days after the date of receipt of a request for consultations, the complaining party must allow a period of 60 days after the date of receipt of the request for consultations before

---

[4] The corresponding consultation provisions in the covered agreements are listed hereunder: Agreement on Agriculture, Article 19; Agreement on the Application of Sanitary and Phytosanitary Measures, paragraph 1 of Article 11; Agreement on Textiles and Clothing, paragraph 4 of Article 8; Agreement on Technical Barriers to Trade, paragraph 1 of Article 14; Agreement on Trade-Related Investment Measures, Article 8; Agreement on Implementation of Article VI of GATT 1994, paragraph 2 of Article 17; Agreement on Implementation of Article VII of GATT 1994, paragraph 2 of Article 19; Agreement on Preshipment Inspection, Article 7; Agreement on Rules of Origin, Article 7; Agreement on Import Licensing Procedures, Article 6; Agreement on Subsidies and Countervailing Measures, Article 30; Agreement on Safeguards, Article 14; Agreement on Trade-Related Aspects of Intellectual Property Rights, Article 64.1; and any corresponding consultation provisions in Plurilateral Trade Agreements as determined by the competent bodies of each Agreement and as notified to the DSB.

requesting the establishment of a panel. The complaining party may request the establishment of a panel during the 60-day period if the parties to the dispute jointly consider that the good offices, conciliation or mediation process has failed to settle the dispute.

5. If the parties to a dispute agree, procedures for good offices, conciliation or mediation may continue while the panel process proceeds.

6. The Director-General may, acting in an *ex officio* capacity, offer good offices, conciliation or mediation with the view to assisting Members to settle a dispute.

Article 6

Establishment of Panels

1. If the complaining party so requests, a panel shall be established at the latest at the DSB meeting following that at which the request first appears as an item on the DSB's agenda, unless at that meeting the DSB decides by consensus not to establish a panel.[5]

2. The request for the establishment of a panel shall be made in writing. It shall indicate whether consultations were held, identify the specific measures at issue and provide a brief summary of the legal basis of the complaint sufficient to present the problem clearly. In case the applicant requests the establishment of a panel with other than standard terms of reference, the written request shall include the proposed text of special terms of reference.

Article 7

Terms of Reference of Panels

1. Panels shall have the following terms of reference unless the parties to the dispute agree otherwise within 20 days from the establishment of the panel:

> "To examine, in the light of the relevant provisions in (name of the covered agreement(s) cited by the parties to the dispute), the matter referred to the DSB by (name of party) in document ... and to make such findings as will assist the DSB in making the recommendations or in giving the rulings provided for in that/those agreement(s)."

2. Panels shall address the relevant provisions in any covered agreement or agreements cited by the parties to the dispute.

3. In establishing a panel, the DSB may authorize its Chairman to draw up the terms of reference of the panel in consultation with the parties to the dispute, subject to the

---

[5] If the complaining party so requests, a meeting of the DSB shall be convened for this purpose within 15 days of the request, provided that at least 10 days' advance notice of the meeting is given.

provisions of paragraph 1. The terms of reference thus drawn up shall be circulated to all Members. If other than standard terms of reference are agreed upon, any Member may raise any point relating thereto in the DSB.

Article 8

Composition of Panels

A53–008   **1.** Panels shall be composed of well-qualified governmental and/or non-governmental individuals, including persons who have served on or presented a case to a panel, served as a representative of a Member or of a contracting party to GATT 1947 or as a representative to the Council or Committee of any covered agreement or its predecessor agreement, or in the Secretariat, taught or published on international trade law or policy, or served as a senior trade policy official of a Member.

2. Panel members should be selected with a view to ensuring the independence of the members, a sufficiently diverse background and a wide spectrum of experience.

3. Citizens of Members whose governments[6] are parties to the dispute or third parties as defined in paragraph 2 of Article 10 shall not serve on a panel concerned with that dispute, unless the parties to the dispute agree otherwise.

4. To assist in the selection of panelists, the Secretariat shall maintain an indicative list of governmental and non-governmental individuals possessing the qualifications outlined in paragraph 1, from which panelists may be drawn as appropriate. That list shall include the roster of non-governmental panelists established on 30 November 1984 (BISD 31S/9), and other rosters and indicative lists established under any of the covered agreements, and shall retain the names of persons on those rosters and indicative lists at the time of entry into force of the WTO Agreement. Members may periodically suggest names of governmental and non-governmental individuals for inclusion on the indicative list, providing relevant information on their knowledge of international trade and of the sectors or subject matter of the covered agreements, and those names shall be added to the list upon approval by the DSB. For each of the individuals on the list, the list shall indicate specific areas of experience or expertise of the individuals in the sectors or subject matter of the covered agreements.

5. Panels shall be composed of three panelists unless the parties to the dispute agree, within 10 days from the establishment of the panel, to a panel composed of five panelists. Members shall be informed promptly of the composition of the panel.

6. The Secretariat shall propose nominations for the panel to the parties to the dispute. The parties to the dispute shall not oppose nominations except for compelling reasons.

7. If there is no agreement on the panelists within 20 days after the date of the establishment of a panel, at the request of either party, the Director-General, in consultation with the Chairman of the DSB and the Chairman of the relevant Council or Committee, shall determine the composition of the panel by appointing the panelists whom the Director-General considers most appropriate in accordance with any relevant special or additional rules or procedures of the covered agreement or covered agreements which are at issue in the dispute, after consulting with the parties to the dispute. The Chairman of the

---

[6] In the case where customs unions or common markets are parties to a dispute, this provision applies to citizens of all member countries of the customs unions or common markets.

DSB shall inform the Members of the composition of the panel thus formed no later than 10 days after the date the Chairman receives such a request.

8. Members shall undertake, as a general rule, to permit their officials to serve as panelists.

9. Panelists shall serve in their individual capacities and not as government representatives, nor as representatives of any organization. Members shall therefore not give them instructions nor seek to influence them as individuals with regard to matters before a panel.

10. When a dispute is between a developing country Member and a developed country Member the panel shall, if the developing country Member so requests, include at least one panelist from a developing country Member.

11. Panelists' expenses, including travel and subsistence allowance, shall be met from the WTO budget in accordance with criteria to be adopted by the General Council, based on recommendations of the Committee on Budget, Finance and Administration.

Article 9

Procedures for Multiple Complaints

1. Where more than one Member requests the establishment of a panel related to the same matter, a single panel may be established to examine these complaints taking into account the rights of all Members concerned. A single panel should be established to examine such complaints whenever feasible. **A53–009**

2. The single panel shall organize its examination and present its findings to the DSB in such a manner that the rights which the parties to the dispute would have enjoyed had separate panels examined the complaints are in no way impaired. If one of the parties to the dispute so requests, the panel shall submit separate reports on the dispute concerned. The written submissions by each of the complainants shall be made available to the other complainants, and each complainant shall have the right to be present when any one of the other complainants presents its views to the panel.

3. If more than one panel is established to examine the complaints related to the same matter, to the greatest extent possible the same persons shall serve as panelists on each of the separate panels and the timetable for the panel process in such disputes shall be harmonized.

Article 10

Third Parties

1. The interests of the parties to a dispute and those of other Members under a covered agreement at issue in the dispute shall be fully taken into account during the panel process. **A53–010**

2. Any Member having a substantial interest in a matter before a panel and having notified its interest to the DSB (referred to in this Understanding as a "third party") shall have an opportunity to be heard by the panel and to make written submissions to the panel. These submissions shall also be given to the parties to the dispute and shall be reflected in the panel report.

3. Third parties shall receive the submissions of the parties to the dispute to the first meeting of the panel.

4. If a third party considers that a measure already the subject of a panel proceeding nullifies or impairs benefits accruing to it under any covered agreement, that Member may have recourse to normal dispute settlement procedures under this Understanding. Such a dispute shall be referred to the original panel wherever possible.

Article 11

Function of Panels

A53–011 The function of panels is to assist the DSB in discharging its responsibilities under this Understanding and the covered agreements. Accordingly, a panel should make an objective assessment of the matter before it, including an objective assessment of the facts of the case and the applicability of and conformity with the relevant covered agreements, and make such other findings as will assist the DSB in making the recommendations or in giving the rulings provided for in the covered agreements. Panels should consult regularly with the parties to the dispute and give them adequate opportunity to develop a mutually satisfactory solution.

Article 12

Panel Procedures

A53–012 1. Panels shall follow the Working Procedures in Appendix 3 unless the panel decides otherwise after consulting the parties to the dispute.

2. Panel procedures should provide sufficient flexibility so as to ensure high-quality panel reports, while not unduly delaying the panel process.

3. After consulting the parties to the dispute, the panelists shall, as soon as practicable and whenever possible within one week after the composition and terms of reference of the panel have been agreed upon, fix the timetable for the panel process, taking into account the provisions of paragraph 9 of Article 4, if relevant.

4. In determining the timetable for the panel process, the panel shall provide sufficient time for the parties to the dispute to prepare their submissions.

5. Panels should set precise deadlines for written submissions by the parties and the parties should respect those deadlines.

6. Each party to the dispute shall deposit its written submissions with the Secretariat for immediate transmission to the panel and to the other party or parties to the dispute. The complaining party shall submit its first submission in advance of the responding party's first submission unless the panel decides, in fixing the timetable referred to in paragraph 3 and after consultations with the parties to the dispute, that the parties should submit their first submissions simultaneously. When there are sequential arrangements for the deposit of first submissions, the panel shall establish a firm time-period for receipt of the responding party's submission. Any subsequent written submissions shall be submitted simultaneously.

7. Where the parties to the dispute have failed to develop a mutually satisfactory solution, the panel shall submit its findings in the form of a written report to the DSB. In such cases, the report of a panel shall set out the findings of fact, the applicability of relevant provisions and the basic rationale behind any findings and recommendations that it makes. Where a settlement of the matter among the parties to the dispute has been found, the report of the panel shall be confined to a brief description of the case and to reporting that a solution has been reached.

8. In order to make the procedures more efficient, the period in which the panel shall conduct its examination, from the date that the composition and terms of reference of the panel have been agreed upon until the date the final report is issued to the parties to the dispute, shall, as a general rule, not exceed six months. In cases of urgency, including those relating to perishable goods, the panel shall aim to issue its report to the parties to the dispute within three months.

9. When the panel considers that it cannot issue its report within six months, or within three months in cases of urgency, it shall inform the DSB in writing of the reasons for the delay together with an estimate of the period within which it will issue its report. In no case should the period from the establishment of the panel to the circulation of the report to the Members exceed nine months.

10. In the context of consultations involving a measure taken by a developing country Member, the parties may agree to extend the periods established in paragraphs 7 and 8 of Article 4. If, after the relevant period has elapsed, the consulting parties cannot agree that the consultations have concluded, the Chairman of the DSB shall decide, after consultation with the parties, whether to extend the relevant period and, if so, for how long. In addition, in examining a complaint against a developing country Member, the panel shall accord sufficient time for the developing country Member to prepare and present its argumentation. The provisions of paragraph 1 of Article 20 and paragraph 4 of Article 21 are not affected by any action pursuant to this paragraph.

11. Where one or more of the parties is a developing country Member, the panel's report shall explicitly indicate the form in which account has been taken of relevant provisions on differential and more-favourable treatment for developing country Members that form part of the covered agreements which have been raised by the developing country Member in the course of the dispute settlement procedures.

12. The panel may suspend its work at any time at the request of the complaining party for a period not to exceed 12 months. In the event of such a suspension, the time-frames set out in paragraphs 8 and 9 of this Article, paragraph 1 of Article 20, and paragraph 4 of Article 21 shall be extended by the amount of time that the work was suspended. If the work of the panel has been suspended for more than 12 months, the authority for establishment of the panel shall lapse.

Article 13

Right to Seek Information

1. Each panel shall have the right to seek information and technical advice from any individual or body which it deems appropriate. However, before a panel seeks such information or advice from any individual or body within the jurisdiction of a Member it shall inform the authorities of that Member. A Member should respond promptly and fully to any request by a panel for such information as the panel considers necessary and appropriate. Confidential information which is provided shall not be revealed without formal authorization from the individual, body, or authorities of the Member providing the information.

2. Panels may seek information from any relevant source and may consult experts to obtain their opinion on certain aspects of the matter. With respect to a factual issue concerning a scientific or other technical matter raised by a party to a dispute, a panel may request an advisory report in writing from an expert review group. Rules for the establishment of such a group and its procedures are set forth in Appendix 4.

Article 14

Confidentiality

A53–014   **1.** Panel deliberations shall be confidential.
2. The reports of panels shall be drafted without the presence of the parties to the dispute in the light of the information provided and the statements made.
3. Opinions expressed in the panel report by individual panelists shall be anonymous.

Article 15

Interim Review Stage

A53–015   **1.** Following the consideration of rebuttal submissions and oral arguments, the panel shall issue the descriptive (factual and argument) sections of its draft report to the parties to the dispute. Within a period of time set by the panel, the parties shall submit their comments in writing.
2. Following the expiration of the set period of time for receipt of comments from the parties to the dispute, the panel shall issue an interim report to the parties, including both the descriptive sections and the panel's findings and conclusions. Within a period of time set by the panel, a party may submit a written request for the panel to review precise aspects of the interim report prior to circulation of the final report to the Members. At the request of a party, the panel shall hold a further meeting with the parties on the issues identified in the written comments. If no comments are received from any party within the comment period, the interim report shall be considered the final panel report and circulated promptly to the Members.
3. The findings of the final panel report shall include a discussion of the arguments made at the interim review stage. The interim review stage shall be conducted within the time-period set out in paragraph 8 of Article 12.

Article 16

Adoption of Panel Reports

1. In order to provide sufficient time for the Members to consider panel reports, the reports shall not be considered for adoption by the DSB until 20 days after the date they have been circulated to the Members.
2. Members having objections to a panel report shall give written reasons to explain their objections for circulation at least 10 days prior to the DSB meeting at which the panel report will be considered.
3. The parties to a dispute shall have the right to participate fully in the consideration of the panel report by the DSB, and their views shall be fully recorded.
4. Within 60 days after the date of circulation of a panel report to the Members, the report shall be adopted at a DSB meeting[7] unless a party to the dispute formally notifies the DSB of its decision to appeal or the DSB decides by consensus not to adopt the report. If a party has notified its decision to appeal, the report by the panel shall not be considered for adoption by the DSB until after completion of the appeal. This adoption procedure is without prejudice to the right of Members to express their views on a panel report.

Article 17

Appellate Review

Standing Appellate Body

1. A standing Appellate Body shall be established by the DSB. The Appellate Body shall hear appeals from panel cases. It shall be composed of seven persons, three of whom shall serve on any one case. Persons serving on the Appellate Body shall serve in rotation. Such rotation shall be determined in the working procedures of the Appellate Body.
2. The DSB shall appoint persons to serve on the Appellate Body for a four-year term, and each person may be reappointed once. However, the terms of three of the seven persons appointed immediately after the entry into force of the WTO Agreement shall expire at the end of two years, to be determined by lot. Vacancies shall be filled as they arise. A person appointed to replace a person whose term of office has not expired shall hold office for the remainder of the predecessor's term.
3. The Appellate Body shall comprise persons of recognized authority, with demonstrated expertise in law, international trade and the subject matter of the covered agreements generally. They shall be unaffiliated with any government. The Appellate Body membership shall be broadly representative of membership in the WTO. All persons serving on the Appellate Body shall be available at all times and on short notice, and shall stay abreast of dispute settlement activities and other relevant activities of the WTO.

---

[7] If a meeting of the DSB is not scheduled within this period at a time that enables the requirements of paragraphs 1 and 4 of Article 16 to be met, a meeting of the DSB shall be held for this purpose.

They shall not participate in the consideration of any disputes that would create a direct or indirect conflict of interest.

4. Only parties to the dispute, not third parties, may appeal a panel report. Third parties which have notified the DSB of a substantial interest in the matter pursuant to paragraph 2 of Article 10 may make written submissions to, and be given an opportunity to be heard by, the Appellate Body.

5. As a general rule, the proceedings shall not exceed 60 days from the date a party to the dispute formally notifies its decision to appeal to the date the Appellate Body circulates its report. In fixing its timetable the Appellate Body shall take into account the provisions of paragraph 9 of Article 4, if relevant. When the Appellate Body considers that it cannot provide its report within 60 days, it shall inform the DSB in writing of the reasons for the delay together with an estimate of the period within which it will submit its report. In no case shall the proceedings exceed 90 days.

6. An appeal shall be limited to issues of law covered in the panel report and legal interpretations developed by the panel.

7. The Appellate Body shall be provided with appropriate administrative and legal support as it requires.

8. The expenses of persons serving on the Appellate Body, including travel and subsistence allowance, shall be met from the WTO budget in accordance with criteria to be adopted by the General Council, based on recommendations of the Committee on Budget, Finance and Administration.

Procedures for Appellate Review

A53–018 9. Working procedures shall be drawn up by the Appellate Body in consultation with the Chairman of the DSB and the Director-General, and communicated to the Members for their information.

10. The proceedings of the Appellate Body shall be confidential. The reports of the Appellate Body shall be drafted without the presence of the parties to the dispute and in the light of the information provided and the statements made.

11. Opinions expressed in the Appellate Body report by individuals serving on the Appellate Body shall be anonymous.

12. The Appellate Body shall address each of the issues raised in accordance with paragraph 6 during the appellate proceeding.

13. The Appellate Body may uphold, modify or reverse the legal findings and conclusions of the panel.

Adoption of Appellate Body Reports

A53–019 14. An Appellate Body report shall be adopted by the DSB and unconditionally accepted by the parties to the dispute unless the DSB decides by consensus not to adopt the Appellate Body report within 30 days following its circulation to the Members.[8] This adoption procedure is without prejudice to the right of Members to express their views on an Appellate Body report.

---

[8] If a meeting of the DSB is not scheduled during this period, such a meeting of the DSB shall be held for this purpose.

Article 18

Communications with the Panel or Appellate Body

1. There shall be no *ex parte* communications with the panel or Appellate Body concerning matters under consideration by the panel or Appellate Body.   **A53–020**
2. Written submissions to the panel or the Appellate Body shall be treated as confidential, but shall be made available to the parties to the dispute. Nothing in this Understanding shall preclude a party to a dispute from disclosing statements of its own positions to the public. Members shall treat as confidential information submitted by another Member to the panel or the Appellate Body which that Member has designated as confidential. A party to a dispute shall also, upon request of a Member, provide a non-confidential summary of the information contained in its written submissions that could be disclosed to the public.

Article 19

Panel and Appellate Body Recommendations

1. Where a panel or the Appellate Body concludes that a measure is inconsistent with a covered agreement, it shall recommend that the Member concerned[9] bring the measure into conformity with that agreement.[10] In addition to its recommendations, the panel or Appellate Body may suggest ways in which the Member concerned could implement the recommendations.   **A53–021**
2. In accordance with paragraph 2 of Article 3, in their findings and recommendations, the panel and Appellate Body cannot add to or diminish the rights and obligations provided in the covered agreements.

Article 20

Time-frame for DSB Decisions

Unless otherwise agreed to by the parties to the dispute, the period from the date of establishment of the panel by the DSB until the date the DSB considers the panel or appellate report for adoption shall as a general rule not exceed nine months where the panel report is not appealed or 12 months where the report is appealed. Where either the   **A53–022**

---

[9] The "Member concerned" is the party to the dispute to which the panel or Appellate Body recommendations are directed.
[10] With respect to recommendations in cases not involving a violation of GATT 1994 or any other covered agreement, see Article 26.

panel or the Appellate Body has acted, pursuant to paragraph 9 of Article 12 or paragraph 5 of Article 17, to extend the time for providing its report, the additional time taken shall be added to the above periods.

Article 21

Surveillance of Implementation of Recommendations and Rulings

A53–023   1. Prompt compliance with recommendations or rulings of the DSB is essential in order to ensure effective resolution of disputes to the benefit of all Members.

2. Particular attention should be paid to matters affecting the interests of developing country Members with respect to measures which have been subject to dispute settlement.

3. At a DSB meeting held within 30 days[11] after the date of adoption of the panel or Appellate Body report, the Member concerned shall inform the DSB of its intentions in respect of implementation of the recommendations and rulings of the DSB. If it is impracticable to comply immediately with the recommendations and rulings, the Member concerned shall have a reasonable period of time in which to do so. The reasonable period of time shall be:

(a) the period of time proposed by the Member concerned, provided that such period is approved by the DSB; or, in the absence of such approval,

(b) a period of time mutually agreed by the parties to the dispute within 45 days after the date of adoption of the recommendations and rulings; or, in the absence of such agreement,

(c) a period of time determined through binding arbitration within 90 days after the date of adoption of the recommendations and rulings.[12] In such arbitration, a guideline for the arbitrator[13] should be that the reasonable period of time to implement panel or Appellate Body recommendations should not exceed 15 months from the date of adoption of a panel or Appellate Body report. However, that time may be shorter or longer, depending upon the particular circumstances.

4. Except where the panel or the Appellate Body has extended, pursuant to paragraph 9 of Article 12 or paragraph 5 of Article 17, the time of providing its report, the period from the date of establishment of the panel by the DSB until the date of determination of the reasonable period of time shall not exceed 15 months unless the parties to the dispute agree otherwise. Where either the panel or the Appellate Body has acted to extend the time of providing its report, the additional time taken shall be added to the 15-month period; provided that unless the parties to the dispute agree that there are exceptional circumstances, the total time shall not exceed 18 months.

5. Where there is disagreement as to the existence or consistency with a covered

---

[11] If a meeting of the DSB is not scheduled during this period, such a meeting of the DSB shall be held for this purpose.

[12] If the parties cannot agree on an arbitrator within ten days after referring the matter to arbitration, the arbitrator shall be appointed by the Director-General within ten days, after consulting the parties.

[13] The expression "arbitrator" shall be interpreted as referring either to an individual or a group.

agreement of measures taken to comply with the recommendations and rulings such dispute shall be decided through recourse to these dispute settlement procedures, including wherever possible resort to the original panel. The panel shall circulate its report within 90 days after the date of referral of the matter to it. When the panel considers that it cannot provide its report within this time frame, it shall inform the DSB in writing of the reasons for the delay together with an estimate of the period within which it will submit its report.

6. The DSB shall keep under surveillance the implementation of adopted recommendations or rulings. The issue of implementation of the recommendations or rulings may be raised at the DSB by any Member at any time following their adoption. Unless the DSB decides otherwise, the issue of implementation of the recommendations or rulings shall be placed on the agenda of the DSB meeting after six months following the date of establishment of the reasonable period of time pursuant to paragraph 3 and shall remain on the DSB's agenda until the issue is resolved. At least 10 days prior to each such DSB meeting, the Member concerned shall provide the DSB with a status report in writing of its progress in the implementation of the recommendations or rulings.

7. If the matter is one which has been raised by a developing country Member, the DSB shall consider what further action it might take which would be appropriate to the circumstances.

8. If the case is one brought by a developing country Member, in considering what appropriate action might be taken, the DSB shall take into account not only the trade coverage of measures complained of, but also their impact on the economy of developing country Members concerned.

Article 22

Compensation and the Suspension of Concessions

1. Compensation and the suspension of concessions or other obligations are temporary measures available in the event that the recommendations and rulings are not implemented within a reasonable period of time. However, neither compensation nor the suspension of concessions or other obligations is preferred to full implementation of a recommendation to bring a measure into conformity with the covered agreements. Compensation is voluntary and, if granted, shall be consistent with the covered agreements.

2. If the Member concerned fails to bring the measure found to be inconsistent with a covered agreement into compliance therewith or otherwise comply with the recommendations and rulings within the reasonable period of time determined pursuant to paragraph 3 of Article 21, such Member shall, if so requested, and no later than the expiry of the reasonable period of time, enter into negotiations with any party having invoked the dispute settlement procedures, with a view to developing mutually acceptable compensation. If no satisfactory compensation has been agreed within 20 days after the date of expiry of the reasonable period of time, any party having invoked the dispute settlement procedures may request authorization from the DSB to suspend the application to the Member concerned of concessions or other obligations under the covered agreements.

3. In considering what concessions or other obligations to suspend, the complaining party shall apply the following principles and procedures:

(a) the general principle is that the complaining party should first seek to suspend concessions or other obligations with respect to the same sector(s) as that in which the panel or Appellate Body has found a violation or other nullification or impairment;

(b) if that party considers that it is not practicable or effective to suspend concessions or other obligations with respect to the same sector(s), it may seek to suspend concessions or other obligations in other sectors under the same agreement;

(c) if that party considers that it is not practicable or effective to suspend concessions or other obligations with respect to other sectors under the same agreement, and that the circumstances are serious enough, it may seek to suspend concessions or other obligations under another covered agreement;

(d) in applying the above principles, that party shall take into account:

  (i) the trade in the sector or under the agreement under which the panel or Appellate Body has found a violation or other nullification or impairment, and the importance of such trade to that party;

  (ii) the broader economic elements related to the nullification or impairment and the broader economic consequences of the suspension of concessions or other obligations;

(e) if that party decides to request authorization to suspend concessions or other obligations pursuant to subparagraphs (b) or (c), it shall state the reasons therefor in its request. At the same time as the request is forwarded to the DSB, it also shall be forwarded to the relevant Councils and also, in the case of a request pursuant to subparagraph (b), the relevant sectoral bodies;

(f) for purposes of this paragraph, "sector" means:

  (i) with respect to goods, all goods;

  (ii) with respect to services, a principal sector as identified in the current "Services Sectoral Classification List" which identifies such sectors;[14]

  (iii) with respect to trade-related intellectual property rights, each of the categories of intellectual property rights covered in Section 1, or Section 2, or Section 3, or Section 4, or Section 5, or Section 6, or Section 7 of Part II, or the obligations under Part III, or Part IV of the Agreement on TRIPS;

(g) for purposes of this paragraph, "agreement" means:

  (i) with respect to goods, the agreements listed in Annex 1A of the WTO Agreement, taken as a whole as well as the Plurilateral Trade Agreements in so far as the relevant parties to the dispute are parties to these agreements;

  (ii) with respect to services, the GATS;

  (iii) with respect to intellectual property rights, the Agreement on TRIPS.

4. The level of the suspension of concessions or other obligations authorized by the DSB shall be equivalent to the level of the nullification or impairment.

---

[14] The list in document MTN.GNS/W/120 identifies eleven sectors.

5. The DSB shall not authorize suspension of concessions or other obligations if a covered agreement prohibits such suspension.

6. When the situation described in paragraph 2 occurs, the DSB, upon request, shall grant authorization to suspend concessions or other obligations within 30 days of the expiry of the reasonable period of time unless the DSB decides by consensus to reject the request. However, if the Member concerned objects to the level of suspension proposed, or claims that the principles and procedures set forth in paragraph 3 have not been followed where a complaining party has requested authorization to suspend concessions or other obligations pursuant to paragraph 3(b) or (c), the matter shall be referred to arbitration. Such arbitration shall be carried out by the original panel, if members are available, or by an arbitrator[15] appointed by the Director-General and shall be completed within 60 days after the date of expiry of the reasonable period of time. Concessions or other obligations shall not be suspended during the course of the arbitration.

7. The arbitrator[16] acting pursuant to paragraph 6 shall not examine the nature of the concessions or other obligations to be suspended but shall determine whether the level of such suspension is equivalent to the level of nullification or impairment. The arbitrator may also determine if the proposed suspension of concessions or other obligations is allowed under the covered agreement. However, if the matter referred to arbitration includes a claim that the principles and procedures set forth in paragraph 3 have not been followed, the arbitrator shall examine that claim. In the event the arbitrator determines that those principles and procedures have not been followed, the complaining party shall apply them consistent with paragraph 3. The parties shall accept the arbitrator's decision as final and the parties concerned shall not seek a second arbitration. The DSB shall be informed promptly of the decision of the arbitrator and shall upon request, grant authorization to suspend concessions or other obligations where the request is consistent with the decision of the arbitrator, unless the DSB decides by consensus to reject the request.

8. The suspension of concessions or other obligations shall be temporary and shall only be applied until such time as the measure found to be inconsistent with a covered agreement has been removed, or the Member that must implement recommendations or rulings provides a solution to the nullification or impairment of benefits, or a mutually satisfactory solution is reached. In accordance with paragraph 6 of Article 21, the DSB shall continue to keep under surveillance the implementation of adopted recommendations or rulings, including those cases where compensation has been provided or concessions or other obligations have been suspended but the recommendations to bring a measure into conformity with the covered agreements have not been implemented.

9. The dispute settlement provisions of the covered agreements may be invoked in respect of measures affecting their observance taken by regional or local governments or authorities within the territory of a Member. When the DSB has ruled that a provision of a covered agreement has not been observed, the responsible Member shall take such reasonable measures as may be available to it to ensure its observance. The provisions of the covered agreements and this Understanding relating to compensation and suspension of concessions or other obligations apply in cases where it has not been possible to secure such observance.[17]

---

[15] The expression "arbitrator" shall be interpreted as referring either to an individual or a group.
[16] The expression "arbitrator" shall be interpreted as referring either to an individual or a group or to the members of the original panel when serving in the capacity of arbitrator.
[17] Where the provisions of any covered agreement concerning measures taken by regional or local governments or authorities within the territory of a Member contain provisions different from the provisions of this paragraph, the provisions of such covered agreement shall prevail.

Article 23

Strengthening of the Multilateral System

A53–025 1. When Members seek the redress of a violation of obligations or other nullification or impairment of benefits under the covered agreements or an impediment to the attainment of any objective of the covered agreements, they shall have recourse to, and abide by, the rules and procedures of this Understanding.

2. In such cases, Members shall:

(a) not make a determination to the effect that a violation has occurred, that benefits have been nullified or impaired or that the attainment of any objective of the covered agreements has been impeded, except through recourse to dispute settlement in accordance with the rules and procedures of this Understanding, and shall make any such determination consistent with the findings contained in the panel or Appellate Body report adopted by the DSB or an arbitration award rendered under this Understanding;

(b) follow the procedures set forth in Article 21 to determine the reasonable period of time for the Member concerned to implement the recommendations and rulings; and

(c) follow the procedures set forth in Article 22 to determine the level of suspension of concessions or other obligations and obtain DSB authorization in accordance with those procedures before suspending concessions or other obligations under the covered agreements in response to the failure of the Member concerned to implement the recommendations and rulings within that reasonable period of time.

Article 24

Special Procedures Involving Least-Developed Country Members

A53–026 1. At all stages of the determination of the causes of a dispute and of dispute settlement procedures involving a least-developed country Member, particular consideration shall be given to the special situation of least-developed country Members. In this regard, Members shall exercise due restraint in raising matters under these procedures involving a least-developed country Member. If nullification or impairment is found to result from a measure taken by a least-developed country Member, complaining parties shall exercise due restraint in asking for compensation or seeking authorization to suspend the application of concessions or other obligations pursuant to these procedures.

2. In dispute settlement cases involving a least-developed country Member, where a satisfactory solution has not been found in the course of consultations the Director-General or the Chairman of the DSB shall, upon request by a least-developed country Member offer their good offices, conciliation and mediation with a view to assisting the

parties to settle the dispute, before a request for a panel is made. The Director-General or the Chairman of the DSB, in providing the above assistance, may consult any source which either deems appropriate.

Article 25

Arbitration

1. Expeditious arbitration within the WTO as an alternative means of dispute settlement can facilitate the solution of certain disputes that concern issues that are clearly defined by both parties.
2. Except as otherwise provided in this Understanding, resort to arbitration shall be subject to mutual agreement of the parties which shall agree on the procedures to be followed. Agreements to resort to arbitration shall be notified to all Members sufficiently in advance of the actual commencement of the arbitration process.
3. Other Members may become party to an arbitration proceeding only upon the agreement of the parties which have agreed to have recourse to arbitration. The parties to the proceeding shall agree to abide by the arbitration award. Arbitration awards shall be notified to the DSB and the Council or Committee of any relevant agreement where any Member may raise any point relating thereto.
4. Articles 21 and 22 of this Understanding shall apply *mutatis mutandis* to arbitration awards.

Article 26

Non-Violation Complaints of the Type Described in Paragraph 1(b) of Article XXIII of GATT 1994

1. Where the provisions of paragraph 1(b) of Article XXIII of GATT 1994 are applicable to a covered agreement, a panel or the Appellate Body may only make rulings and recommendations where a party to the dispute considers that any benefit accruing to it directly or indirectly under the relevant covered agreement is being nullified or impaired or the attainment of any objective of that Agreement is being impeded as a result of the application by a Member of any measure, whether or not it conflicts with the provisions of that Agreement. Where and to the extent that such party considers and a panel or the Appellate Body determines that a case concerns a measure that does not conflict with the provisions of a covered agreement to which the provisions of paragraph 1(b) of Article XXIII of GATT 1994 are applicable, the procedures in this Understanding shall apply, subject to the following:

   (a) the complaining party shall present a detailed justification in support of any complaint relating to a measure which does not conflict with the relevant covered agreement;

   (b) where a measure has been found to nullify or impair benefits under, or impede the attainment of objectives, of the relevant covered agreement without violation thereof, there is no obligation to withdraw the measure. However, in such cases, the panel or the Appellate Body shall recommend that the Member concerned make a mutually satisfactory adjustment;

(c) notwithstanding the provisions of Article 21, the arbitration provided for in paragraph 3 of Article 21, upon request of either party, may include a determination of the level of benefits which have been nullified or impaired, and may also suggest ways and means of reaching a mutually satisfactory adjustment; such suggestions shall not be binding upon the parties to the dispute;

(d) notwithstanding the provisions of paragraph 1 of Article 22, compensation may be part of a mutually satisfactory adjustment as final settlement of the dispute.

Complaints of the Type Described in Paragraph 1(c) of Article XXIII of GATT 1994

A53–029   2. Where the provisions of paragraph 1(c) of Article XXIII of GATT 1994 are applicable to a covered agreement, a panel may only make rulings and recommendations where a party considers that any benefit accruing to it directly or indirectly under the relevant covered agreement is being nullified or impaired or the attainment of any objective of that Agreement is being impeded as a result of the existence of any situation other than those to which the provisions of paragraphs 1(a) and 1(b) of Article XXIII of GATT 1994 are applicable. Where and to the extent that such party considers and a panel determines that the matter is covered by this paragraph, the procedures of this Understanding shall apply only up to and including the point in the proceedings where the panel report has been circulated to the Members. The dispute settlement rules and procedures contained in the Decision of 12 April 1989 (BISD 36S/61-67) shall apply to consideration for adoption, and surveillance and implementation of recommendations and rulings. The following shall also apply:

(a) the complaining party shall present a detailed justification in support of any argument made with respect to issues covered under this paragraph;

(b) in cases involving matters covered by this paragraph, if a panel finds that cases also involve dispute settlement matters other than those covered by this paragraph, the panel shall circulate a report to the DSB addressing any such matters and a separate report on matters falling under this paragraph.

Article 27

Responsibilities of the Secretariat

A53–030   1. The Secretariat shall have the responsibility of assisting panels, especially on the legal, historical and procedural aspects of the matters dealt with, and of providing secretarial and technical support.

2. While the Secretariat assists Members in respect of dispute settlement at their request, there may also be a need to provide additional legal advice and assistance in respect of dispute settlement to developing country Members. To this end, the Secretariat shall make available a qualified legal expert from the WTO technical cooperation services to any developing country Member which so requests. This expert shall assist the devel-

oping country Member in a manner ensuring the continued impartiality of the Secretariat.

3. The Secretariat shall conduct special training courses for interested Members concerning these dispute settlement procedures and practices so as to enable Members' experts to be better informed in this regard.

APPENDIX 1

AGREEMENTS COVERED BY THE UNDERSTANDING

(A) Agreement Establishing the World Trade Organization

(B) Multilateral Trade Agreements

    Annex 1A: Multilateral Agreements on Trade in Goods

    Annex 1B: General Agreement on Trade in Services

    Annex 1C: Agreement on Trade-Related Aspects of Intellectual Property Rights

    Annex 2: Understanding on Rules and Procedures Governing the Settlement of Disputes

(C) Plurilateral Trade Agreements

    Annex 4: Agreement on Trade in Civil Aircraft
           Agreement on Government Procurement
           International Dairy Agreement
           International Bovine Meat Agreement

The applicability of this Understanding to the Plurilateral Trade Agreements shall be subject to the adoption of a decision by the parties to each agreement setting out the terms for the application of the Understanding to the individual agreement, including any special or additional rules or procedures for inclusion in Appendix 2, as notified to the DSB.

APPENDIX 2

SPECIAL OR ADDITIONAL RULES AND PROCEDURES CONTAINED IN THE COVERED AGREEMENTS

Agreement	**Rules and Procedures**
Agreement on the Application of Sanitary and Phytosanitary Measures	11.2
Agreement on Textiles and Clothing	2.14, 2.21, 4.4, 5.2, 5.4, 5.6, 6.9, 6.10, 6.11, 8.1 through 8.12
Agreement on Technical Barriers to Trade	14.2 through 14.4, Annex 2
Agreement on Implementation of Article VI of GATT 1994	17.4 through 17.7
Agreement on Implementation of Article VII of GATT 1994	19.3 through 19.5, Annex II.2(f), 3, 9, 21
Agreement on Subsidies and Countervailing Measures	4.2 through 4.12, 6.6, 7.2 through 7.10, 8.5, footnote 35, 24.4, 27.7, Annex V

INSTITUTIONAL RULES

General Agreement on Trade in Services	XXII:3, XXIII:3
Annex on Financial Services	4
Annex on Air Transport Services	4
Decision on Certain Dispute Settlement Procedures for the GATS	1 through 5

The list of rules and procedures in this Appendix includes provisions where only a part of the provision may be relevant in this context.

Any special or additional rules or procedures in the Plurilateral Trade Agreements as determined by the competent bodies of each agreement and as notified to the DSB.

APPENDIX 3

WORKING PROCEDURES

1. In its proceedings the panel shall follow the relevant provisions of this Understanding. In addition, the following working procedures shall apply.

2. The panel shall meet in closed session. The parties to the dispute, and interested parties, shall be present at the meetings only when invited by the panel to appear before it.

3. The deliberations of the panel and the documents submitted to it shall be kept confidential. Nothing in this Understanding shall preclude a party to a dispute from disclosing statements of its own positions to the public. Members shall treat as confidential information submitted by another Member to the panel which that Member had designated as confidential. Where a party to a dispute submits a confidential version of its written submissions to the panel, it shall also, upon request of a Member, provide a non-confidential summary of the information contained in its submissions that could be disclosed to the public.

4. Before the first substantive meeting of the panel with the parties, the parties to the dispute shall transmit to the panel written submissions in which they present the facts of the case and their arguments.

5. At its first substantive meeting with the parties, the panel shall ask the party which has brought the complaint to present its case. Subsequently, and still at the same meeting, the party against which the complaint has been brought shall be asked to present its point of view.

6. All third parties which have notified their interest in the dispute to the DSB shall be invited in writing to present their views during a session of the first substantive meeting of the panel set aside for that purpose. All such third parties may be present during the entirety of this session.

7. Formal rebuttals shall be made at a second substantive meeting of the panel. The party complained against shall have the right to take the floor first to be followed by the complaining party. The parties shall submit, prior to that meeting, written rebuttals to the panel.

8. The panel may at any time put questions to the parties and ask them for explanations either in the course of a meeting with the parties or in writing.

9. The parties to the dispute and any third party invited to present its views in accordance with Article 10 shall make available to the panel a written version of their oral statements.

10. In the interest of full transparency, the presentations, rebuttals and statements referred to in paragraphs 5 to 9 shall be made in the presence of the parties. Moreover, each party's written submissions, including any comments on the descriptive part of the report and responses to questions put by the panel, shall be made available to the other party or parties.

11. Any additional procedures specific to the panel.

12. Proposed timetable for panel work:

(a) Receipt of first written submissions of the parties:
    (1) complaining Party: 3–6 weeks
    (2) Party complained against: 2–3 weeks
(b) Date, time and place of first substantive meeting with the parties; third party session: 1–2 weeks
(c) Receipt of written rebuttals of the parties: 2–3 weeks
(d) Date, time and place of second substantive meeting with the parties: 1–2 weeks
(e) Issuance of descriptive part of the report to the parties: 2–4 weeks
(f) Receipt of comments by the parties on the descriptive part of the report: 2 weeks
(g) Issuance of the interim report, including the findings and conclusions, to the parties: 2–4 weeks
(h) Deadline for party to request review of part(s) of report: 1 week
(i) Period of review by panel, including possible additional meeting with parties: 2 weeks
(j) Issuance of final report to parties to dispute: 2 weeks
(k) Circulation of the final report to the Members: 3 weeks

The above calendar may be changed in the light of unforeseen developments. Additional meetings with the parties shall be scheduled if required.

APPENDIX 4

Expert Review Groups

The following rules and procedures shall apply to expert review groups established in accordance with the provisions of paragraph 2 of Article 13.

1. Expert review groups are under the panel's authority. Their terms of reference and detailed working procedures shall be decided by the panel, and they shall report to the panel.

2. Participation in expert review groups shall be restricted to persons of professional standing and experience in the field in question.

3. Citizens of parties to the dispute shall not serve on an expert review group without the joint agreement of the parties to the dispute, except in exceptional circumstances when the panel considers that the need for specialized scientific expertise cannot be fulfilled otherwise. Government officials of parties to the dispute shall not serve on an expert review group. Members of expert review groups shall serve in their individual capacities and not as government representatives, nor as representatives of any organization. Governments or organizations shall therefore not give them instructions with regard to matters before an expert review group.

4. Expert review groups may consult and seek information and technical advice from any source they deem appropriate. Before an expert review group seeks such information or advice from a source within the jurisdiction of a Member, it shall inform the government of that Member. Any Member shall respond promptly and fully to any request by an expert review group for such information as the expert review group considers necessary and appropriate.

5. The parties to a dispute shall have access to all relevant information provided to an expert review group, unless it is of a confidential nature. Confidential information provided to the expert review group shall not be released without formal authorization from the government, organization or person providing the information. Where such information is requested from the expert review group but release of such information by the expert review group is not authorized, a non-confidential summary of the information will be provided by the government, organization or person supplying the information.

6. The expert review group shall submit a draft report to the parties to the dispute with a view to obtaining their comments, and taking them into account, as appropriate, in the final report, which shall also be issued to the parties to the dispute when it is submitted to the panel. The final report of the expert review group shall be advisory only.

APPENDIX 4

PRECEDENTS AND DRAFTING SUGGESTIONS

List of Precedents and Drafting Suggestions

Arbitration Agreements—Before a Dispute has arisen   **A54–001**

1   General arbitration clause—short form
2   Another longer form of general arbitration clause
3   Tailoring the powers of the tribunal to the wishes of the parties
4   Diminishing or enhancing the role of the court
5   *Scott v Avery* clause
6   Time limit
7   Place and law of the arbitration
8   Incorporating institutional rules
9   Chartered Institute of Arbitrators clause
10 London Court of International Arbitration clauses
11 BIMCO/London Maritime Arbitrators' Association clause
12 Clause referring disputes to arbitration by the Court of Arbitration of the International Chamber of Commerce
13 UNCITRAL Arbitration Rules—model clause
14 "Ad hoc" agreement
15 American Arbitration Association
16 Kuala Lumpur Regional Centre for Arbitration
17 Indian Council of Arbitration
18 Singapore International Arbitration Centre
19 Hong Kong International Arbitration Centre

Arbitration Agreements—After a Dispute has arisen

20 General form
21 To tailor an arbitration agreement to the wishes of the parties—see the suggestion at 9 above and the footnote to it
22 To diminish or enhance the role of the court in the contract for arbitration—see the suggestion at 10 above and the footnotes thereto
23 Agreement in advance (but post-dispute) for equal sharing of costs
24 Agreement varying the existing arbitration agreement

Appointments—Forms

25 Joint appointment of a sole arbitrator
26 Appointment of an arbitrator by a party

Precedents and Drafting Suggestions

27 Notice to concur in the appointment of a sole arbitrator
28 Notice requiring other party to appoint an arbitrator in the situation where the third arbitrator is an umpire
29 Appointment as sole arbitrator where other party fails to appoint to determine disputes currently existing
30 Appointment by two arbitrators of umpire or third arbitrator
31 Joint appointment of a substitute sole arbitrator
32 Appointment by an appointing body or person

Topics for Consideration

33 List of matters for possible consideration in organising arbitral proceedings

General—Initial Steps

34 Initial letter from sole arbitrator to the parties
35 Schedule of Fees
36 Letter appointing a preliminary meeting

Examples of initial Sets of Directions

37 Order for Directions No. 1
38 Another Order for Directions No. 1
39 Draft directions for consideration at preliminary meeting
40 Specimen letter following preliminary meeting sending [draft] directions
41 Notice to arbitrator of an application for leave to amend pleading or statement of case
42 Notice of intention to proceed *ex parte* after failure to comply with directions
43 Notice of intention to proceed *ex parte* after failure to attend hearing
44 Possible statement of case directions

Construction Cases

45 Clause for main or principal contract which also provides for determination of related sub-contract issues
46 Provision in sub-contract requiring concurrence with head arbitration if required
47 Construction directions
48 Another form of construction directions
49 Construction Scott Schedule Claim for extra work—stage one
50 Checklist for preliminary meeting
51 Construction Scott Schedule of defects—stage two
52 Claimant's Scott Schedule of defects

Arbitration Clauses relevant to Rent Review

53 Provision enabling rent review under underlease to be referred to same arbitrator as rent review under head lease
54 Provision in underlease of part enabling rent review to be referred to same arbitrator as rent review under head lease
55 Suggested draft directions for a rent review arbitration by written representation
56 Suggested draft directions for a rent review arbitration involving an oral hearing
57 Agreement to refer point of law for the decision of counsel

Precedents and Drafting Suggestions

Awards

- 58 Final award without reasons
- 59 Final award with reasons
- 60 Final award—reasons to be annexed—consumer dispute
- 61 Interim award
- 62 Interim awards reserving costs for later decision
- 63 Clause reserving costs and giving directions
- 64 Clause reserving costs but making an award "*nisi*" as to costs and giving directions
- 65 Final award incorporating alternative final award
- 66 Award by umpire
- 67 Clauses for awards—rent review—declaration that landlord has unreasonably withheld consent
- 68 Award for the delivery up of property, with alternative money award
- 69 Letter publishing award

Court Forms

Arbitration Award
- 70. N322A Application to enforce
- 71. PF 166 Certificate as to Finality

Arbitration Claims
- 72. N15 Acknowledgment of Service
- 73. N8 Claim Form
- 74. N8A Notes for the Claimant
- 75. N8B Notes for the Defendant

Arbitration Proceedings
- 76. No. 15A Acknowledgment of Service
- 77. No. 8A Claim Form
- 78. PF 167 Order to Stay Proceedings
- 79. Specimen letter—arbitrator's charges

Miscellaneous

- 80. ICC Arbitrator's Declaration of Acceptance and Statement of Independence
- 81. ICC Terms of Reference
- 82. Possible terms of engagement for a barrister/arbitrator
- 83. Dispute Board—Mediation—Arbitration clause
- 84. Communications Protocol

ADR Clauses

- 85. Suggested ICC ADR clauses
- 86. ADR clause combined with arbitration clause
- 87. Model Contract Clauses
- 88. Mediation UK Standards for Mediators (general mediation)

Precedents and Drafting Suggestions

INTRODUCTION

A health warning for your insurance policy

One of the areas where thought is most needed and least given is in the adaptation of precedents for the case in hand. Another is in the drafting of dispute resolution clauses. In the hope of encouraging adaptation rather than unthinking adoption, the title of this section of the Handbook has been changed to "Precedents and Drafting Suggestions". **A54–002**

Thought is particularly necessary in two situations. One is where the rules of an institution are being incorporated. These should not be incorporated blind; they should be read by the draughtsman; and can conveniently be annexed to the agreement. Even then, it is necessary to consider, which no drafting suggestion can, whether or not to provide for the automatic incorporation of changes in the rules made after the contract; or to incorporate only those rules as are extant at the date of the contract. In virtually no circumstances[1] should the draughtsman set out to redraft a set of rules. A situation that requires a redrafting requires a set of rules drafted from scratch.

The other is when dealing with the inclusion or exclusion of powers provided under the Act. The drafting suggestion herewith refers the draughtsman to Appendix 20. It would be a great waste of space, and also unnecessary (if the draughtsman is actually thinking as he should be) to set out individual drafting suggestions for as many times as there are powers to be included or excluded. And even that would not begin to address the vast range of combinations of powers that are available. Accordingly, here again, the draughtsman is well advised to set out in the clause, or even better in an annex to the clause, the express powers in full that are either incorporated or excluded. Where there are both inclusions and exclusions, he should then check specifically to make sure that one power or another has not got into both his inclusion and exclusion lists.

Another area which requires careful consideration is where the parties desire to have a form of dispute resolution prior to a formal arbitration. There are ADR drafting suggestions in the pages that follow; but linking them to formal arbitration clauses requires thought. It is recommended that any such procedure should be part of the arbitration clause procedure; and that there should be a limit on the time allowed to achieve an ADR solution, after which the time limits, if any, in the formal arbitration should kick in. This is to prevent a recalcitrant party from using the ADR procedure purely as a means of delay.

It should be borne in mind that even an unsuccessful ADR procedure may bring benefits, particularly in a complicated dispute. This can come about, for example, by way of clarification of the issues; identifying who are the parties more likely to carry responsibility; and who are the less potentially productive parties; which parties, if any have relevant finance and even, possibly, insurance; and so forth.

There are some footnotes to these drafting suggestions by way of comment. However, the principal texts of this book are where fuller discussions are to be found. The footnotes do not even begin to substitute them; and the absence of a footnote makes consulting the principal texts even more important.

---

[1] The authors cannot think of a situation which would justify this course, but we suppose that nothing is impossible.

Many, indeed most, of the suggestions that follow are grouped under headings relevant to an industry. It is of course permissible to use them, in whole or in part, for purposes other than those to which they have been allocated in these suggestions—but it needs thought, of course.

Drafting Suggestions

Arbitration Agreements—Before a Dispute has Arisen

1. General arbitration clause—short form

In the event of any dispute or difference arising between the parties to this agreement from or in connection with this agreement or its performance, construction or interpretation, such dispute shall be referred to arbitration by a single arbitrator in accordance with the provisions of the Arbitration Act 1996, or any amendments thereto, whose decision in relation to any such dispute or difference shall be final and binding on all the parties hereto.

A54–003

2. Another longer form of general arbitration clause

Any dispute or difference arising out of or in connection with this contract shall be determined by the arbitration of:

A single arbitrator who failing agreement shall be appointed by the President or a Vice-President for the time being[2] of the [Chartered Institute of Arbitrators].[3]

A54–004

OR

One arbitrator to be appointed by each party together (if they disagree) with an umpire who failing agreement between such arbitrators shall be appointed by the President or a Vice-President for the time being of the [Chartered Institute of Arbitrators][4] on the application of either party or either arbitrator.

OR

One arbitrator to be appointed by each party together with a third arbitrator (the chairman) who shall be appointed by such arbitrators or (if they cannot agree upon the appointment) by the President or a Vice-President for the time being of the [Chartered Institute of Arbitrators].[5] If on any matter in dispute the three arbitrators are not unanimous, the decision shall be given by the majority. If there is no majority the decision shall be given by the chairman.

Optional clauses that may be added to any of the clauses of 1 or 2 above are as follows—see 3 to 8, below:

3. Tailoring the powers of the tribunal to the wishes of the parties

In the conduct of any arbitration under this arbitration agreement, the arbitrator[6] [shall have][7] [shall not have] the following powers.[8]

A54–005

---

[2] It is wise to check that the chosen body does indeed have a President or Vice-President and that this relevant officer is prepared to appoint.

[3] Or other appointing institution as appropriate.

[4] See n.2, above.

[5] See n.2, above.

[6] Or "the Tribunal".

[7] If the parties intend simply to enlarge or reduce the powers of the tribunal, then the appropriate formulation should be used. If they desire to enlarge the powers in some respects and reduce them in others, separate clauses should be used—see the following footnotes for further comments.

[8] Under the 1996 Act, the arbitrator or tribunal will have all the powers listed in the text of Part 2. Accordingly, if the parties do not wish the arbitrator or tribunal to have any of these powers they will have to be expressly and specifically excluded. If the parties desire to give the arbitrator or tribunal further powers, the arbitration agreement will have to say so specifically. It is to be noted that the rules of most, but not all, arbitration institutions will address these matters. If, therefore, it is intended to incorporate such rules, they should be examined to see what powers they provide; and whether the "package" is what the parties desire. And see n.11 and The Role of Courts in Arbitration at para. A56–001, below.

4. Diminishing or enhancing the role of the court

A54–006 In respect of any arbitration arising under this agreement the role of the court[9] [shall not extend to the exercise of any of the following powers][10] [shall be enlarged as follows].[11]

5. *Scott v Avery* clause

A54–007 Where by this clause any dispute or difference is to be referred to arbitration the making of an award shall be a condition precedent to any right of action by either party against the other.

6. Time limit

A54–008 Any claim for damages for breach of this agreement shall be made in writing and shall be served upon the party whom the claim is made not more than X months from the date of the breach and in default any such claim shall be deemed to have been abandoned and shall be absolutely barred.

7. Place and law of the arbitration

A54–009 The arbitration shall be held in ... [12] and the dispute shall be decided in accordance with [English] law.

8. Incorporating institutional rules[13]

A54–010 The arbitration shall be conducted in accordance with the:

    (Rules of the Chartered Institute of Arbitrators)

    (Rules of the London Court of International Arbitration)

    (Rules of the London Maritime Arbitrators' Association)

    (London Bar Arbitration Scheme)

    (Rules of [Conciliation and][14] Arbitration of the International Chamber of Commerce)

    (Other scheme).[15]

---

[9] Or, where the context is international, "the High Court of England and Wales under the 1996 Arbitration Act".

[10] See n.7, above.

[11] The Role of Courts in Arbitration at para. A56-001 sets out in tabular form the role of the courts under the 1996 Act. The parties may wish to exclude some of these powers. The powers marked with an * may be excluded. If they are to be excluded, they should be specifically identified. *N.B.* Some of the powers of the courts are mandatory—those are the ones marked ●. There is no point in attempting to exclude them if English law is the procedural law of the arbitration. If it is wished to enhance the powers of the court, *e.g.* by an automatic right of appeal, not dependent on the leave of the court, again, this must be specifically set out.

[12] A venue needs to be filled in and it is sensible to opt for one where the local rules governing the conduct of arbitration are known by the draughtsman to be acceptable to the parties.

[13] See the third paragraph in the Introduction to this section. Parties are strongly advised against tinkering with an existing set of Rules.

[14] Delete if not required.

[15] The Institution and the correct name of the rules should be specified. Check that the Institution does in fact have a set of rules.

9. Chartered Institute of Arbitrators clause[16]

Any dispute or difference arising out of or in connection with this contract shall be determined by the appointment of a single arbitrator to be agreed between the parties, or failing agreement within fourteen days, after either party has given to the other a written request to concur in the appointment of an arbitrator, by an arbitrator to be appointed by the President or a Vice President of the Chartered Institute of Arbitrators.

A54–011

10. London Court of International Arbitration clauses[17]

Future disputes:

For contracting parties who wish to have future disputes referred to arbitration under the LCIA Rules, the following clause is recommended. Words/spaces in square brackets should be deleted/completed as appropriate.

A54–012

"Any dispute arising out of or in connection with this contract, including any question regarding its existence, validity or termination, shall be referred to and finally resolved by arbitration under the LCIA Rules, which Rules are deemed to be incorporated by reference into this clause.

The number of arbitrators shall be *[one/three]*.

The seat, or legal place, of arbitration shall be *[City and/or Country]*.

The language to be used in the arbitral proceedings shall be [   ].

The governing law of the contract shall be the substantive law of [   ]."

Existing disputes:

If a dispute has arisen, but there is no agreement between the parties to arbitrate, or if the parties wish to vary a dispute resolution clause to provide for LCIA arbitration, the following clause is recommended. Words/spaces in square brackets should be deleted/completed as appropriate.

"A dispute having arisen between the parties concerning [   ], the parties hereby agree that the dispute shall be referred to and finally resolved by arbitration under the LCIA Rules.

The number of arbitrators shall be *[one/three]*.

The seat, or legal place, of arbitration shall be *[City and/or Country]*.

The language to be used in the arbitral proceedings shall be [   ].

The governing law of the contract *[is/shall be]* the substantive law of [   ]."

---

[16] Reproduced with the kind permission of the copyright-holders, the Chartered Institute of Arbitrators.

[17] Reproduced with the kind permission of the London Court of International Arbitration.

11. BIMCO/LMAA Arbitration Clause[18]

A54–013 After consultation with the LMAA, BIMCO have adopted and are recommending the following amended arbitration clause, which the LMAA recommends for future use in place of the present LMAA Clause.

"(a) This Contract shall be governed by and construed in accordance with English law and any dispute arising out of or in connection with this Contract shall be referred to arbitration in London in accordance with the Arbitration Act 1996 or any statutory modification or re-enactment thereof save to the extent necessary to give effect to the provisions of this Clause.

The arbitration shall be conducted in accordance with the London Maritime Arbitrators Association (LMAA) Terms current at the time when the arbitration proceedings are commenced.

The reference shall be to three arbitrators. A party wishing to refer a dispute to arbitration shall appoint its arbitrator and send notice of such appointment in writing to the other party requiring the other party to appoint its own arbitrator within 14 calendar days of that notice and stating that it will appoint its arbitrator as sole arbitrator unless the other party appoints its own arbitrator and give notice that it has done so within the 14 days specified. If the other party does not appoint its own arbitrator and give notice that it has done so within the 14 days specified, the party referring a dispute to arbitration may, without the requirement of any further prior notice to the other party, appoint its arbitrator as sole arbitrator and shall advise the other party accordingly. The award of a sole arbitrator shall be binding on both parties as if he had been appointed by agreement.

Nothing herein shall prevent the parties agreeing in writing to vary these provisions to provide for the appointment of a sole arbitrator.

In cases where neither the claim nor any counterclaim exceeds the sum of US$50,000 (or such other sum as the parties may agree) the arbitration shall be conducted in accordance with the LMAA Small Claims Procedure current at the time when the arbitration proceedings are commenced.

(b) Notwithstanding (a) above, the parties may agree at any time to refer to mediation any difference and/or dispute arising out of or in connection with this Contract.

In the case of a dispute in respect of which arbitration has been commenced under (a), above, the following shall apply:—

(i) Either party may at any time and from time to time elect to refer the dispute or part of the dispute to mediation by service on the other party of a written notice (the "Mediation Notice") calling on the other party to agree to mediation.

(ii) The other party shall thereupon within 14 calendar days of receipt of the Mediation Notice confirm that they agree to mediation, in which case the parties shall thereafter agree a mediator within a further 14 calendar days, failing which on the application of either party a mediator will be appointed promptly by the Arbitration Tribunal ("the Tribunal") or such person as the Tribunal may designate for that purpose. The mediation shall be conducted in such place and in accordance with such procedure

---

[18] Reproduced with the kind permission of the London Maritime Arbitrators Association.

and on such terms as the parties may agree or, in the event of disagreement, as may be set by the mediator.
(iii) If the other party does not agree to mediate, that fact may be brought to the attention of the Tribunal and may be taken into account by the Tribunal when allocating the costs of the arbitration as between the parties.
(iv) The mediation shall not affect the right of either party to seek such relief or take such steps as it considers necessary to protect its interest.
(v) Either party may advise the Tribunal that they have agreed to mediation. The arbitration procedure shall continue during the conduct of the mediation but the Tribunal may take the mediation timetable into account when setting the timetable for steps in the arbitration.
(vi) Unless otherwise agreed or specified in the mediation terms, each party shall bear its own costs incurred in the mediation and the parties shall share equally the mediator's costs and expenses.
(vii) The mediation process shall be without prejudice and confidential and no information or documents disclosed during it shall be revealed to the Tribunal except to the extent that they are disclosable under the law and procedure governing the arbitration."[19]

12. Clause referring disputes to arbitration by the Court of Arbitration of the International Chamber of Commerce[20]

All disputes arising out of or in connection with the present contract shall be finally settled under the Rules of Arbitration of the International Chamber of Commerce by one or more arbitrators appointed in accordance with the said Rules[21]

A54–014

---

[19] Note: The parties should be aware that the mediation process may not necessarily interrupt time limits.
[20] Reproduced with the kind permission of the International Chamber of Commerce. Please also see the Rules of Arbitration of the International Chamber of Commerce at paras A39-001 to A39-054 of this Volume.
[21] The ICC comments:
"It may also be desirable for the parties to stipulate in the arbitration clause itself:
- the law governing the contract;
- the number of arbitrators;
- the place of arbitration; and
- the language of the arbitration.

Parties should also consider the possible need for special provisions in the event that arbitration is contemplated among more than two parties. In addition, the law in some countries may lay down certain requirements in respect of arbitration clauses. In principle, parties should also always ensure that the arbitration agreement is:
- *in writing*. The effectiveness of an arbitration clause first of all depends on proof of its existence. It should therefore generally be in writing. The 1958 New York Convention specifically states (Art. II) that Contracting States shall recognize arbitration agreements "in writing".
- *carefully drafted*. Time and again, the Court receives requests for arbitration based on ambiguous arbitration clauses. Badly worded clauses, at the very least, cause delay. At worst, they may impede the arbitration process."

13. UNCITRAL Arbitration Rules—model clause

A54–015 Any dispute, controversy or claim arising out of or relating to this contract, or the breach, termination, or invalidity thereof, shall be settled by arbitration in accordance with the UNCITRAL Arbitration Rules as at present in force.[22]

14. "Ad Hoc" Agreement

A54–016 By this agreement AB of   and XY of   hereby agree to refer [all disputes and differences between them[23]]
[all disputes and differences between them arising out of a contract dated *insert date*][24]
[the disputes and differences set out in the Schedule to this agreement][25] to arbitration by a single arbitrator [in *insert place in which arbitration to be conducted*] [under the Rules of   ].

15. American Arbitration Association[26]

A54–017 Either:

"Any controversy or claim arising out of or relating to this contract shall be determined by arbitration in accordance with the International Arbitration Rules of the International Centre for Dispute Resolution."

or

"Any controversy or claim arising out of or relating to this contract shall be determined by arbitration in accordance with the International Arbitration Rules of the American Arbitration Association."

---

[22] Reproduced with the kind permission of UNCITRAL. UNCITRAL also comments:
"The parties may wish to consider adding:
(a) the appointing authority shall be .... (name of institution or person);
(b) the number of arbitrators shall be .... (one or three);
(c) the place of arbitration shall be .... (town *and* country; if you simply put Paris, somebody with a desperate case or much in need of medical assistance will argue that you mean Paris, Texas!);
(d) the language(s) to be used in the arbitral proceedings shall be ....".

[23] Delete as appropriate.

[24] Delete as appropriate.

[25] Delete as appropriate.

[26] Copyright: the American Arbitration Association 2001. Reprinted with permission of the American Arbitration Association. As the International Centre for Dispute Resolution (ICDR) is a division of the American Arbitration Association (AAA), parties can arbitrate future disputes under these rules by inserting either of the clauses into their contracts. The parties may wish to consider adding:
(a) "The number of arbitrators shall be (one or three)";
(b) "The place of arbitration shall be (city and/or country)"; or
(c) "The language(s) of the arbitration shall be ....".

Precedents and Drafting Suggestions

16. Kuala Lumpur Regional Centre for Arbitration[27]

Any dispute, controversy or claim arising out of or relating to this contract, or the breach, termination or invalidity thereof, shall be decided by arbitration in accordance with the Rules for Arbitration of the Regional Centre for Arbitration Kuala Lumpur.[28]

A54–018

17. Indian Council of Arbitration[29]

Any dispute or difference whatsoever arising between the parties out of or relating to the construction, meaning, scope, operation or effect of this contract or the validity or the breach thereof shall be settled by arbitration in accordance with the Rules of Arbitration of the Indian Council of Arbitration and the award made in pursuance thereof shall be binding on the parties.

A54–019

18. Singapore International Arbitration Centre[30]

Any dispute arising out of or in connection with this contract, including any question regarding its existence, validity or termination, shall be referred to and finally resolved by arbitration in [Singapore] in accordance with the Arbitration Rules of Singapore International Arbitration Centre ("SIAC Rules") for the time being in force which rules are deemed to be incorporated by reference to this clause.[31]

A54–020

19. Hong Kong International Arbitration Centre[32]

Any dispute, controversy or claim arising out of or relating to this contract, or the breach termination or invalidity thereof, shall be settled by arbitration in accordance with the UNCITRAL Arbitration Rules as at present in force and as may be amended by the rest of this clause. The appointing authority shall be Hong Kong International Arbitration Centre. The place of arbitration shall be in Hong Kong at Hong Kong International Arbitration Centre (HKIAC). There shall be only one arbitrator.[33] Any such arbitration shall be administered by HKIAC in accordance with HKIAC Procedures for Arbitration in force at the date of this contract including such additions to the UNCITRAL Arbitration Rules as are therein contained.[34]

A54–021

---

[27] (First sentence) Reproduced with the kind permission of the Kuala Lumpur Regional Centre for Arbitration.

[28] K.L.R.C.A. comments: "NOTE: Parties may wish to consider adding: (a) The appointing authority shall be the Regional Centre for Arbitration Kuala Lumpur.
(b) The number of arbitrators shall be .... (one or three).
(c) The place of arbitration shall be ....(town or country).
(d) The language(s) to be used in the arbitration proceedings shall be ....
(e) The law applicable to this contract shall be that of ....".

[29] (First sentence) Reproduced with the kind permission of the Indian Council of Arbitration.

[30] (First sentence) Reproduced with the kind permission of the Singapore International Arbitration Centre.

[31] SIAC comments: "Parties may add: The Tribunal shall consist of .... arbitrator(s) to be appointed by the Chairman of SIAC.
The governing law of this contract shall be the substantive law of ....
The language of the arbitration shall be ...."

[32] (First sentence) Reproduced with the kind permission of the Hong Kong International Arbitration Centre.

[33] This sentence must be amended if a panel of three arbitrators is required.

[34] HKIAC notes that this sentence may be deleted if administration by HKIAC is not required. If it is retained the Centre will then act as a clearing house for communications between the parties and the arbitral tribunal and will liaise with the arbitral tribunal and the parties on timing of meetings, etc., will hold deposits from the parties and assist the tribunal with any other matters

Arbitration Agreements—After a Dispute has Arisen

20. General form[35]

A54–022 BY THIS AGREEMENT
A.B. of .... and
X.Y. of ....
HEREBY AGREE TO REFER
all disputes and differences whatsoever between them
        OR
all disputes and differences between them arising out of or in connection with a contract between them dated the ....
        OR
the disputes and differences set out in the Schedule to this Agreement
TO THE ARBITRATION OF
Mr John Smith
        OR
a single arbitrator who failing agreement shall be appointed by the President of the .... on the application of either party
        OR
Mr John Smith and Mr George Jones together, if they disagree, with an umpire to be appointed by them or, if they should disagree, by the President or a Vice-President for the time being of ....
        OR
Mr John Smith, Mr George Jones and Mr Robert Robinson
Dated this .... 20 ....
Signed on behalf of A.B   Signed on behalf of X.Y.

(By) .... (By) ....

(Name) .... (Name) ....

A54–023 21. **To tailor an arbitration agreement to the wishes of the parties—see the suggestion at 9 above and the footnotes to it**

A54–024 22. **To diminish or enhance the role of the court in the contract for arbitration—see the suggestion at 10 above and the footnotes thereto**

23. Agreement in advance (but post-dispute) for equal sharing of costs

A54–025 Each party shall bear its own costs of the arbitration and the costs of the arbitrator/arbitration tribunal shall be borne by the parties equally.

---

required. HKIAC also notes that if the language to be used in arbitration proceedings is likely to be in question, it may also be useful to include in contracts: "The language(s) to be used in the arbitral proceedings shall be ....".

[35] Please see the comments in the footnotes to the short-form clauses at 1 to 8 above.

Precedents and Drafting Suggestions

24. Agreement varying the existing arbitration agreement[36]

WHEREAS by clause XXX of a contract dated the .... and made between .... (hereinafter called the Vendor) and .... (Hereinafter called the Purchaser) certain differences or disputes therein mentioned were referred to arbitration.

AND WHEREAS certain disputes having arisen between the parties Mr A. N. OTHER has been appointed as arbitrator to determine them.

NOW THE PARTIES HEREBY AGREE to submit to the arbitration of the said arbitrator (in addition to the matters already referred to him) the following further matters, that is to say:

(example): Whether the said contract accurately sets out the terms agreed between the parties and intended to be contained in the said contract and if not whether and if so in what way the said contract should be rectified.

DATED THIS .... DAY OF ....

A54–026

Appointments—Forms

25. Joint appointment of a sole arbitrator

To A.B. of ....

A54–027

Disputes[37] have arisen between us arising out of or in connection with a contract between us dated the .... a copy of which is enclosed. We wish to have determined by arbitration by you all such disputes. We therefore nominate and appoint[38] you as sole arbitrator in respect of the said disputes.

Dated ....
(Signed) ....   (Signed) ....
(Name) ....   (Name) ....
for P.Q. plc of ....   for L.M. plc of ....

26. Appointment of an arbitrator by a party

To A.B. of ....

A54–028

By an agreement dated the .... and made between .... of the one part and .... of the other part it was agreed (*inter alia*) that any dispute or difference arising out of or in relation to the agreement should be referred to the arbitration of two arbitrators, one to be appointed by each party, together (if they disagree) with an umpire to be appointed by them. Disputes have arisen between the said parties. We, P.Q. plc hereby appoint[39] you as an arbitrator in accordance with the provisions of the said agreement.

Dated ....
(Signed) .... for P.Q. plc

---

[36] If the variation requires some adjustment (*e.g.* an enlargement of the Tribunal's powers) that needs to be put in here.

[37] These should be identified, *e.g.* by an annex, referred to in the clause thus: "Disputes as summarised on the attached annex".

[38] The appointee should insist on seeing the arbitration clause before accepting the appointment. Also if he accepts without agreeing fees, he may be unable to recover cancellation fees and the like as of right.

[39] See previous footnote.

27. Notice to concur in the appointment of a sole arbitrator

A54–029 To: A.B. plc of [etc.]

In pursuance of the provision for arbitration contained in clause .... of the agreement between us dated the .... we now require you to concur in the appointment of an arbitrator to resolve the disputes[40] that have arisen between us, namely .... Unless within [28][41] clear days after this notice is served upon you an arbitrator has been agreed between us we intend without further notice to apply to .... [42] for an appointment.

Dated ....

(Signed) ....

(Name) ....

For and on behalf of X.Y. plc

28. Notice requiring other party to appoint an arbitrator in the situation where the third arbitrator is an umpire

A54–030 To C.D. plc

The agreement between us dated the .... provides that any dispute or difference arising out of or in relation to the agreement shall be determined by two arbitrators, one to be appointed by each of us together (if they disagree) with an umpire to be appointed by them. We have today appointed Mr A.B. to act as arbitrator. We now require you, within [14][43] clear days after the service of this notice upon you, to appoint an arbitrator to determine the following dispute .... If you fail so to do we will appoint the said A.B. as sole arbitrator under the agreement.

Dated ....

(Signed) ....

(Name) ....

For and on behalf of E.F. plc

29. Appointment as sole arbitrator where other party fails to appoint to determine disputes currently existing

A54–031 To A.B.

We enclose a copy of a notice that was served on C.D. plc on .... day the .... They acknowledged receipt by a (letter) (telex) (telefax) dated the .... (OR They have not acknowledged receipt; a copy of our letter/telex is enclosed). They have not appointed an arbitrator. Pursuant to the power conferred upon us by section [ ] of the Arbitration Act 1996 we hereby appoint you as sole arbitrator.

Dated ....

(Signed) ....

(Name) ....

For and on behalf of E.F. plc

---

[40] Which should be specified in some manner. *e.g.* by an annex referred to in this notice.
[41] See s.16 of the Act.
[42] Insert name of appointer if one is specified in the arbitration agreement.
[43] See n.41, above.

30. Appointment by two arbitrators of umpire or third arbitrator[44]

To: L.M. Esq   A54–032

Under the provision for arbitration contained in the agreement made the .... between P.Q. plc of the one part and R.S. plc of the other party we the undersigned were appointed as arbitrators, with provision for [an umpire] OR [third arbitrator] to be appointed[45] by us. We hereby appoint you under the said provisions.

Dated ....
(Signed) ....
(Name) ....
(Signed) ....
(Name) ....

31. Joint appointment of a substitute sole arbitrator

By an appointment in writing dated the .... we the undersigned appointed A.B. to be the sole arbitrator to determine certain disputes under the agreement therein mentioned. A.B. has (died) (refused to act) (become incapable of acting). We hereby appoint C.D. to be the arbitrator in place of the said A.B.   A54–033

Dated ....
(Signed) ....   (Signed) ....
(Name) ....   (Name) ....
For and on behalf of L.M. plc   For and on behalf of P.Q. plc

32. Appointment by an appointing body or person

To C.D. plc of A54–034
and to E.F. plc of ....

By the arbitration clause contained in an agreement in writing dated the and made (between you) (between G.H. plc of the one part and the said E.F. plc .... of the other part) it was provided that any dispute arising out of or in relation to the agreement should be referred to the arbitration of a person who failing agreement should be appointed (by me) (by the President of the ....). By the letter dated the .... the said E.F. plc asserted that the disputes identified on the attached form had arisen between you and notified me that no person had been agreed between you and requested me to appoint an

---

[44] This precedent does not address the terms on which the umpire or third arbitrator is being appointed. Ideally, this will have been sorted out before this appointment is perfected. See n.46, below.
[45] See n.38, above.

arbitrator. Now I W.Y. (The person named as appointor as aforesaid) (being the President for the time being of the said ....) Do hereby appoint[46] A.B. of .... as arbitrator pursuant to the said agreement.

Dated ....

(Signed) ....

Topics for Consideration

33. List of matters for possible consideration in organising arbitral proceedings[47]

A54–035

1. Set of arbitration rules

    If the parties have not agreed on a set of arbitration rules, would they wish to do so.

2. Language of proceedings

    (a) Possible need for translation of documents, in full or in part.
    (b) Possible need for interpretation of oral presentations.
    (c) Cost of translation and interpretation.

3. Place of arbitration

    (a) Determination of the place of arbitration, if not already agreed upon by the parties.
    (b) Possibility of meetings outside the place of arbitration.

4. Administrative services that may be needed for the arbitral tribunal to carry out its functions

5. Deposits in respect of costs

    (a) Amount to be deposited.
    (b) Management of deposits.
    (c) Supplementary deposits.

6. Confidentiality of information relating to arbitration; possible agreement thereon

7. Routing of writing communications among the parties and the arbitrators

8. Telefax and other electronic means of sending documents

    (a) Telefax.
    (b) Other electronic means (*e.g.* electronic mail and magnetic or optical disk).

---

[46] See discussion in Pt 2 of Vol. 1 regarding the question of the terms the arbitrator is appointed under. The appointing institute must determine whether this is a complete and immediately effective appointment, a provisional appointment or a nomination. The appointee and the parties should also be clear about this.

[47] This list is part of the *UNCITRAL Notes on Organizing Arbitral Proceedings*, which the United Nations Commission on International Trade Law (UNCITRAL) adopted in 1996. The *Notes*, published as United Nations document V.96-84935, contain introductory explanations and annotations to the items that appear in this list (see paras A16-001 to A16-063, above).

9. Arrangements for the exchange of written submissions

    (a) Scheduling of written submissions.
    (b) Consecutive or simultaneous submissions.

10. Practical details concerning written submissions and evidence (*e.g.* method of submission, copies, numbering, references)

11. Defining points at issue; order of deciding issues; defining relief or remedy sought

    (a) Should a list of points at issue be prepared.
    (b) In which order should the points at issue be decided.
    (c) Is there a need to define more precisely the relief or remedy sought.

12. Possible settlement negotiations and their effect on scheduling procedures

13. Documentary evidence

    (a) Time-limits for submission of documentary evidence intended to be submitted by the parties; consequences of late submission.
    (b) Whether the arbitral tribunal intends to require a party to produce documentary evidence.
    (c) Should assertions about the origin and receipt of documents and about the correctness of photocopies be assumed as accurate.
    (d) Are the parties willing to submit jointly a single set of documentary evidence.
    (e) Should voluminous and complicated documentary evidence be presented through summaries, tabulations, charts, extracts or samples.

14. Physical evidence other than documents

    (a) What arrangements should be made if physical evidence will be submitted.
    (b) What arrangements should be made if an on-site inspection is necessary.

15. Witnesses

    (a) Advance notice about a witness whom a party intends to present; written witnesses' statements.
    (b) Manner or taking oral evidence of witnesses.
    (c) Order in which questions will be asked and the manner in which the hearing of witnesses will be conducted.
    (d) Whether oral testimony will be given under oath or affirmation and, if so, in what form an oath or affirmation should be made.
    (e) May witnesses be in the hearing room when they are not testifying.
    (f) The order in which the witnesses will be called.
    (g) Interviewing witnesses prior to their appearance at a hearing.
    (h) Hearing representatives of a party.

16. Experts and expert witnesses

    (a) Expert appointed by the arbitral tribunal.
    (b) The expert's terms of reference.

GENERAL—INITIAL STEPS

A54–036 **34. Initial letter from sole arbitrator to the parties**

Messrs
Name & address of party representative
[Means of communication][48]
Reference
For the attention of

Messrs
Name & address of party representative

Reference
For the attention of

....

Dear [   ][49]

My reference ....

Arbitration between AB plc and CD plc

I have been appointed[50] by (the President of the ....) to act in this arbitration. I have been sent the following documents:

....

....

Unless I am told in writing by both parties that they do not wish me to proceed for the time being, I propose convening a preliminary meeting at (this office). However, I am willing to arrange a telephone conference call if both parties think that we may thereby be able to dispense with a preliminary meeting. I would also be happy to deal with matters in writing provided that I am assured by both parties that this is very unlikely to lead to delay.

[If writing to principal]
If it is your intention to instruct representatives to act on your behalf, kindly ask them to get in touch with me.

OR

[If writing to solicitor or other agent]
Would you please confirm that you are authorised to deal with this arbitration on behalf of .... Please ensure that no document which is, or which refers to, a "without prejudice" matter is put before me, and that all communications to me are copied to the other party and marked accordingly. I enclose a Schedule setting out the fee basis[51] on which I propose to charge.

Yours faithfully,
Arbitrator

---

[48] The arbitrator should determine upon a specific method of communication (*e.g.* by fax, email and/or post) at an early stage, and stick to it, unless agreed otherwise with the parties.
[49] As appropriate.
[50] See n.38 above re agreeing fees.
[51] See n.38 above re agreeing fees.

35. Schedule of Fees

SCHEDULE OF FEES OF Mr (or Ms) ....

1.1 *Acceptance fee:*
(to include one preliminary meeting and up to five hours preliminary reading).

Payable:
On taking up the award, or three months after appointment, whichever is the earlier.

1.2 *Fees for hearing:*
£ .... per usual sitting day.
Part days charged at £ .... per hour with a minimum of £ ....
Payable:
On taking up the award, or 10 days after notification that the award is ready for collection, or 10 days after notice to the arbitrator that no award is required; whichever first occurs.

1.3 *Additional hours worked outside hearing;*
e.g. preliminary reading and interlocutory hearings not included in 1 above; views (if any): preparation of award: £ .... per hour.
Payable:
As in 2, or three months after the fee is earned (whichever is earlier).

1.4 *Cancellation fees:*
When a hearing date has been fixed I enter it into my diary, together with the appropriate number of additional days for the preparation of my award. If those dates are cancelled at less than .... months' notice, I reserve the right to charge a cancellation fee of the following proportions of the fees that would have been payable had it proceeded:
If cancelled at more than .... month's notice .... %
If cancelled at less than .... month's notice .... %
This fee will be payable 10 days after the first of the cancelled days.[52]

1.5 Travelling and hotel expenses, and all proper disbursements, will be charged at cost. [Air Travel will be .... class.]

1.6 VAT on the above as appropriate.

---

[52] Some arbitrators include the following clause: "In deciding whether to exercise this right I will have regard (*inter alia*) to whether I can fill the vacated days with remunerated work, and to whether the arbitration is abandoned or is to continue". However applying such a clause can be very difficult indeed. It is suggested that if an arbitrator is minded to waive these fees he do so on a voluntary ad hoc basis rather than make it a term in the agreement.

36. Letter appointing a preliminary meeting

A54–038 First Representative

....

....

.... *For the attention of*

and

Second Representative

....

....

.... *For the attention of*

Gentlemen,

Arbitration between .... and .... re ....

From the responses of both parties to my letter of .... it appears that they do not wish to have time for negotiations. I have not received from either party the confirmation requested in the second paragraph of my letter.[53] I propose to hold a preliminary meeting with the parties in the week commencing or .... in the week commencing .... If there are any dates or times during these weeks which would be inconvenient to you would you please let me know before .... At the preliminary meeting I would expect to ascertain the wishes of the parties so as to enable me to issue directions governing such matters as:

1.1 Whether the proceedings are to be by written representations only or whether there is to be an oral hearing.

1.2 The arrangements for either the submission of written representations or an oral hearing.

1.3 The nature of expert and any other evidence which the parties intend to submit or to call.

1.4 The preparation and the contents of a Statement of Agreed Facts relating to the issues in dispute or any of them.

1.5 Whether it may be desirable for a legal assessor to be appointed. If a party intends to be represented in the proceedings by solicitor or counsel it is highly desirable that the solicitor be present at the preliminary meeting.[54]

Please inform me and the other party of the names and status of those you will expect to attend the preliminary meeting; I should like to have this information by not later than ....

Yours truly,

---

[53] Confirmation that they do not wish the arbitrator to proceed—see suggestion No. 34, above.

[54] This clause is optional. Numerous firms of solicitors regard themselves as more than able to discuss preliminary directions without the help of counsel.

Precedents and Drafting Suggestions

Examples of Initial Sets of Directions

37. Order for Directions No. 1[55]

Upon hearing Counsel for both parties herein, I hereby direct as follows: **A54–039**

1.1 Claimant to prepare a bundle of principal documents and to include therein such documents as Respondent reasonably requests to be included.

1.2 Claimant to serve a comprehensive Statement of Case on liability. To the Case should be annexed a list of all documents relied upon by the Claimant. The Case is to be served by or before the [*date*]. The Case should finally identify who is or are said by the Claimant to be the Respondent/s. In so far as the Claimant does not accept that .... is the only proper Respondent, the Claimant should fully set out in the Case its submissions in support of its contentions.

1.3 Claimant may, if it so wishes, set out its case on Quantum in full.

1.4 Respondent to serve a comprehensive Statement of Defence (and of Counterclaim if so advised) by or before the expiry of six weeks from receipt of the Statement of Case. Respondent to annex to the Defence (and Counterclaim, if any) a list of the documents relied upon. The Statement of Defence (and Counterclaim, if any) shall include full submissions on the proper construction of any clause in the contract relied upon by the Respondent to defeat the claim. The Statement of Defence should also respond fully to any submissions to the effect that .... is not the proper Respondent or is not the only proper Respondent.

1.5 The Respondent may if it so wishes respond to the case on Quantum if such is put forward by the Claimant.

1.6 Claimant to serve a comprehensive Reply to the Defence (and a comprehensive Defence to the Counterclaim if a Counterclaim is served) by or before the expiry of six weeks from the date of receipt of the Defence (and Counterclaim). A list of any documents which are relied upon by the Claimant in connection with the Reply (and Defence to Counterclaim, if any) and which are not already listed shall be annexed.

1.7 At the same time as the Reply is served, the Claimant shall deliver to me, and to the Respondent if it so desires, a chronological bundle of the documents listed as relied upon by the parties. This bundle need not be finally paginated, since other documents may be added later.

1.8 Liberty to Restore.

1.9 Costs in the Reference.

---

[55] Both this precedent and the following one are taken from actual cases with specific issues. Accordingly neither will be wholly suitable for any other particular case—they are indications only.

38. Another Order for Directions No. 1[56]

A54–040 Having considered the correspondence and written and oral submissions in this matter the Tribunal hereby makes the following directions[57]:

BY CONSENT

TERMINOLOGY

A54–041 1.1 The .... Centre for Arbitration is hereinafter and in subsequent directions referred to as the "Centre".

1.2 The UNCITRAL Arbitration Rules, as amended for the use of the Centre are hereinafter and in subsequent directions referred to as the "Rules".

1.3 The amendments themselves are herein and hereafter referred to as the "Centre's Rules".[58]

TIME FOR ARBITRATION

A54–042 1.4 The parties agreed to the exercise by the Tribunal of the powers to extend for the completion of this arbitration by Rule 6 of the Centre's Rules. The Tribunal hereby extends the time for the completion of this arbitration under Rule 6 to [*date*].

PLEADINGS

A54–043 1.5 Each party is to file with the Tribunal and the other party a response to the claim of the other party by or before 18.00 hours on the [*date*].

EVIDENCE

A54–044 1.6 Each party is to file its evidence in chief, including witness statements containing the substance of the witness' evidence in chief and documentary evidence relied upon by or before 18.00 hours on the [*date*].

1.7 Along with its evidence in chief each party will file an initial *Dramatis Personae* identifying each individual and company referred to in its evidence in chief and the capacity and/or role of that individual or company. Likewise each party will file at the same time what it contends is a chronology of relevant events.

1.8 If either party is minded to file evidence in response, then the same is to be filed with the Tribunal and the other party by or before 18.00 hours on the [*date*].

---

[56] See previous footnote for a comment on the general (un)suitability of this precedent.
[57] Obviously this is just an exemplar of the kind of order for directions that might be generated. The matters which are consensual and the matters which are contested and require a decision will vary from arbitration to arbitration. Indeed they may all be contested or they may all be consensual.
[58] Some such distinction may be necessary where an institution has taken a standard set of rules and has added to them but has not adjusted the numbering.

1.9 If either party is minded to file evidence in reply, then the same is to be filed with the Tribunal and the other party by or before 18.00 hours on the [*date*]. Such evidence is to be limited to that necessary to deal with new matters contained in the evidence in response of the other party.[59]

1.10 Where a witness statement in the evidence in chief, in response or in reply refers to a document or documents, the place or places in the annexed or previously served files where the same can be found will also be indicated. If not previously served, the document will be served with the evidence referring to it, or an explanation given for non-service.

1.11 Once evidence, if any, in reply has been filed, the parties will seek to agree the *Dramatis Personae* and Chronology, taking into account any further matters arising from the evidence in response and in reply. The same will be served on the Tribunal on or before the [*date*], so far as agreed.

1.12 The evidence to be filed may include both factual and expert evidence.

DISCOVERY

1.13 Either party may seek discovery or class of documents at any time up to the [*date*]. Thereafter such an application may only be made by leave of the Tribunal.

1.14 Good cause for the discovery must be shown in all cases: and good cause for the lateness of the application must also be shown where the application is made after the [*date*].

HARD AND SOFT COPIES

1.15 As much as possible of the documentation supplied in accordance with the above orders should be supplied both in hard and soft form. The word-processing facilities of the Tribunal are as follows:

—Microsoft Word
—Word Perfect 6.1
—Word Perfect 7

LEGAL MATERIALS AND AUTHORITIES

1.16 Legal Materials and Authorities must be filed with the other party and the Tribunal by or before 18.00 hours on the [*date*].

DOSSIER

1.17 The documents filed in accordance with the above directions shall constitute the dossier for the principal hearings. Save for demonstrative exhibits, no new documents will be allowed to be introduced to the principal hearings save by leave of the Tribunal and for good cause.

---

[59] This is a third exchange of submission and goes further than is desirable—if possible the rounds should be kept to two.

PRECEDENTS AND DRAFTING SUGGESTIONS

INTERLOCUTORY APPLICATIONS

A54–049 1.18 Save for any matters which can conveniently be raised at the pre-hearing review—as to which, see below at 1.19(d)—and subject to the liberty to apply provided for below at 1.34, all interlocutory matters will be dealt with in writing. The parties should indicate whether they wish the decision on the application to be a decision of the whole Tribunal. In the absence of any such indication the matter will be dealt with by the chairman alone unless he sees fit to consult the co-arbitrators.

PRINCIPAL HEARINGS

A54–050 1.19 The principal hearings will be as follows:

(a) [*date*]–[*date*]—Evidence led by the Claimant and all relevant cross-examination and examination in reply.
(b) [*date*]–[*date*]—Evidence led by the Respondent and all relevant cross-examination and examination in reply.
(c) [*date*]–[*date*]—Closing oral submissions.
(d) Details of venue and organisation of the hearings will be determined in due course. However it should be noted that:

  (i) it is proposed to sit a five-day week, and a five-hour day;
  (ii) it is proposed to divide the available time between the parties;
  (iii) it is proposed to permit each party to make a short opening statement at the commencement of the first principal hearing;
  (iv) it is proposed to permit each party to lodge with the Tribunal a written opening, if it so desires;
  (v) examination in chief will be permitted but on a limited basis[60]
  (vi) it is proposed to direct the parties to identify the order in which witnesses will be called (without affecting the right to call them or not, as the party desires); and to seek a detailed schedule of how the hearing time will be expended;
  (vii) for the avoidance of doubt it is proposed to dispense with the common law rule that evidence not challenged is accepted; and to replace it by the principle that the weight to be given to any evidence of whatever nature is wholly a matter for the discretion of the Tribunal;
  (viii) there will be no extension of any of the hearing times save in very exceptional circumstances;
  (ix) it is to be hoped that a chronological bundle of the documentation to be used at the hearings will be put together; in the event that this is done, the references in witness statements to documents will have to have this chronological bundle reference added in due course;
  (x) it is to be hoped that a core bundle will be assembled.

(e) The parties are to consider the question of transcribing the proceedings at the principal hearings.

---

[60] This is more generous than many tribunals will be.

ADMINISTRATIVE

1.20 The parties have agreed to dispense with the requirement of Rule 5 of the **A54–051** Centre's Rules which provides for the Presiding Arbitrator to furnish records to the Director of the Centre.

1.21 All correspondence between the parties and the Tribunal shall be referenced and transmitted as follows:

    (a) The Tribunal's letters to the parties will have the reference 186. The letter commenting on these directions is 001. Each party will choose its own reference and then give each letter a consecutive number. Whether each party gives the letters to the Tribunal an independent sequence to that used for letters between the parties, or uses the same sequence for both series of letters is a matter for each party.[61]

    (b) Communications shall be effected by fax in the first place, and copied by air mail post. Important documents and ones where bulk militates against the use of the fax shall be transmitted by courier. Documents which are not in themselves letters shall have a covering letter.[62]

1.22 The proceedings and all documents shall be in the English language.

BY DECISION save where indicated by asterisk.

NUMBER OF ARBITRATIONS

1.23 There is to be a single arbitration.   **A54–052**

RELEVANT COMPANIES

1.24 The companies constituting the parties to the said arbitration will be specifically **A54–053** identified in the second Order for Directions to be issued in due course.

1.25 *The parties are to provide written submissions to the Tribunal and each other on the question of the identity of the parties to the arbitration as follows:

    (a) All initial submissions on or before 18.00 hours on the [*date*].
    (b) If so minded a submission in reply to the other party's initial submission on or before 18.00 hours on the [*date*].

CLAIMANT

1.26 In any event, ... will be Claimant.   **A54–054**

APPLICATIONS FOR PRELIMINARY ISSUES AND INTERIM RELIEF

1.27 The Tribunal does not accede to the applications for the hearing of preliminary **A54–055** issues, for the ordering of an audit or for the ordering of pre-hearing oral examinations of third-party witnesses.

---

[61] Whatever the choice, any without prejudice or similar letters should be treated separately—not included in the numbering system.
[62] And one can go into great detail—files to be two-hole ring binders, all stapling to be at top left and parallel to the long side of the page, and so on.

PRECEDENTS AND DRAFTING SUGGESTIONS

ANCILLARY

A54–056 1.28 For brevity and convenience, the Claimant may be referred to as .... and the Respondent as the ....

1.29 Where there is any reference to a time of day in these Directions, it is to be taken as the time of day in ....

1.30 Save where it is impracticable to do so, the parties should use two-ring lever arch files for filings with the Tribunal.

1.31 When serving its evidence in chief the Claimant will nominate its expert or, if there is more than one, then one of them, as its principal expert.

1.32 It will be the function of the principal expert to propose, once the evidence is complete, and seek to arrange, meetings between the various experts of like disciplines with a view to recording agreement where such agreement can be obtained; and isolating the principal issues of a technical nature. Such meetings will be without prejudice unless the parties agree otherwise. Once a statement, whether of agreement or principal issues or both, has been signed by the relevant experts for both parties, then the same is to be treated as an open document without the necessity for the agreement of the parties.

1.33 Unless the parties agree otherwise, discovery shall be effected by the transmission of copies by the discovering party to the inspecting party by whatever means chosen by and at the (reasonable according to the means chosen) cost of the inspecting party. At the instance and cost of the inspecting party, the copies can be notarised as true copies.

GENERAL

A54–057 1.34 Liberty to apply generally.

1.35 Costs in cause.

39. Draft directions for consideration at preliminary meeting

A54–058 1.1 .... plc shall be Claimant and .... plc shall be Respondent.

PLEADINGS

A54–059 1.2 Claimant to serve points of claim by the ....

(a) Respondent to serve point of defence within .... days after service of points of claim.
(b) Claimant to serve points of reply (if so desired) within .... days after service of points of defence.
(c) A copy of each pleading to be sent to the Arbitrator concurrently with service on the other party.

OR

STATEMENTS OF CASE

A54–060 1.3 Claimant to serve Statement of Case by the ....

Precedents and Drafting Suggestions

    (a) Respondent to serve Statement of Case within .... days after service of Claimant's Statement of Case.
    (b) Claimant to serve Reply (if so desired) within .... days after service of Respondent's Statement of Case.
    (c) Statements of Case shall [not exceed .... words],[63] and Statements in Reply shall [not exceed .... words].
    (d) Each Statement shall be accompanied by a copy of every document intended to be relied upon and not already delivered.

    [OR]
    (e) Claimant and Respondent each to serve on the other a Statement of Case, such Statements to be exchanged by the ....
    (f) Claimant and Respondent may each (if so desired) serve on the other a Statement in Reply, such Statements to be exchanged within .... days of exchange of Statements of Case.
    (g) Statements in Reply may contain evidence and submissions in rebuttal of material contained in the opposing party's Statements of Case, but may not otherwise introduce new material.
    (h) Each Statement is to be served in duplicate. The party receiving it shall within four working days either deliver to the Arbitrator one copy thereof or apply to the Arbitrator to strike out all or part of the same. Any such application shall state in broad terms the grounds of objection, e.g. that the same discloses without prejudice discussions.
    (i) Statements of Case shall not exceed .... words and Statements in Reply shall not exceed .... words.
    (j) as 1.3(d) above.

1.4 The parties agree that the arbitration shall proceed on documents only, with no oral evidence or oral submissions. But the Arbitrator reserves the right to convene a meeting and/or a hearing if the documents when lodged raise issues which in his opinion cannot be satisfactorily resolved on documents only.

    OR

1.5 A Statement of Agreed Facts shall be prepared by (Counsel) (Solicitors) (expert Witnesses) on each side, and a copy delivered to the Arbitrator by the ....

1.6 A copy of the written proof of any expert witness intended to be called shall be served on the other party by way of exchange by the ....

1.7 Where the proofs of experts conflict, a meeting shall be arranged between the experts concerned. It shall take place within .... days after exchange of proofs. It shall take place (with any legal adviser that a party wishes to be present) OR (without legal advisers). The discussions at such meeting shall be without prejudice. Before the end of such meeting the experts shall prepare, date and sign a note of the facts and opinions on which they are agreed and of the issues on which they cannot agree. This note will NOT be "without prejudice" and a copy of such note shall be delivered to the Arbitrator within .... days.

---

[63] A limitation is not essential, and should only be introduced when there is some justification for believing it to be necessary.

1.8 The provisional date for commencing the hearing is .... The parties shall on or before the .... 20 .... send to the Arbitrator an agreed estimate, or failing agreement each party's estimate, of the time required for the hearing and the numbers likely to attend the hearing.

1.9 The evidence will be given on oath or affirmation. If a party intends to call as a witness a person who wishes to take the oath otherwise than upon the Old or New Testaments, he shall make the appropriate arrangements to enable such witness to be sworn. If the party intends to call a witness to give evidence in a language other than English, he shall give notice to the Arbitrator so that the attendance of a suitable interpreter can be arranged.

1.10 A shorthand transcript of the hearing (will not be required) (will be required and will be arranged by the (claimant's) solicitors.) Unless the Arbitrator otherwise orders the expense thereof shall be borne equally by the parties.

1.11 (Discovery?)[64]

1.12 The arbitrator will make an interim award (dealing with the issue of liability only, and will thereafter arrange a further meeting to consider what further directions are needed).

OR

(dealing with all issues raised in the arbitration other than costs, and will thereafter take no action until one or both parties ask him to do so.)

1.13 Without prejudice discussions or correspondence are not to be disclosed to the Arbitrator in any form.

1.14 Communications to the arbitrator should where possible be made by telex/fax. In any event a copy of any communication to the Arbitrator should be sent to the other party/parties.

1.15 If any party wishes to ask for any other directions, he should give the maximum possible notice in writing to the other party/parties and to the Arbitrator. The costs of any adjournment necessitated by a party's avoidable failure to give reasonable notice are likely to be borne by that party.

40. Specimen letter following preliminary meeting sending [draft] directions[65]

A54–061 Gentlemen,

In the matter of an Arbitration
between ....

I have noted for the record the following matters discussed at the Preliminary Meeting held at .... on ....

1.1 The lessors of the premises are .... and they will be regarded as the Claimant in the proceedings.

1.2 The lessees of the premises are .... and they will be regarded as the Respondent in the proceedings.

---

[64] If there is to be an order for discovery, it should go here. The extent of the desired discovery should be considered—ranging from the old fashioned full common law style discovery (not desirable) to discovery limited to documents which can be specifically identified by the party seeking discovery and in respect of which that party can make out a strong case for the discovery.

[65] These are of course from a rent review arbitration.

1.3 The Claimant and the Respondent have retained Counsel.

1.4 Neither party has any point to raise on the rent review notice dated .... a copy of which was handed to me by the Respondent's solicitor.

1.5 Neither party has any point of law or matter of construction to be raised or which, at this stage, seems likely to arise and neither party thinks it necessary for a legal assessor to be appointed.

1.6 The parties agreed that pleadings are not necessary.

1.7 Both parties requested that there should be an oral Hearing and asked that the matter should not be dealt with by written representations.

1.8 At an oral Hearing each part would expect to call an expert valuation witness and, at this stage, neither part expects it to be necessary to call additional witnesses.

1.9 The Claimant thought that one day, possibly two days, would be sufficient for the Hearing. The Claimant's Counsel would be available on .... 20 .... for any two days. It was not known whether the Respondent's Counsel would be available. The parties' solicitors would liaise to reserve two consecutive days.

1.10 The Claimant's Solicitors would provide the Arbitrator with certified copies of the Underlease and any licences or other relevant documents, neither party thought it necessary for there to be an order for discovery.

1.11 The Respondent's view was that a transcript of the hearing was unnecessary. Counsel for the Claimant said that he would take instructions.

1.12 The Respondent requested that evidence should be taken on oath and the Claimant raised no objection.

1.13 Before the Preliminary Meeting the parties had discussed a timetable for the proceedings and, after further discussion the following timetable was agreed:

   (a) Statement of Agreed Facts relating to the subject premises. ....
   (b) Agreement of schedule of improvements and alterations and whether they should be disregarded or taken into account when determining the fair yearly rent. ....
   (c) Exchange of Schedule of comparable transactions ....
   (d) Exchange of Reports ....
   (e) Exchange of replies to Reports ....

1.14 It was agreed that the Claimant's expert witness should prepare a draft of the Statement of Agreed Facts and deliver it to the Respondent's expert witness within the two weeks following the date of the Preliminary Meeting and that the Statement should include the floor areas of the subject premises (and the method of measurement used to ascertain them) and such other matters as the respective expert witnesses considered to be relevant to the determination of the fair yearly rent and upon which they were able to agree, together with a set of agreed drawings of the subject premises.

1.15 It was agreed that the respective expert witnesses should each prepare a draft schedule of improvements and alterations and then endeavour to agree a Schedule.

Precedents and Drafting Suggestions

1.16 It was agreed that the respective expert witnesses should each prepare a draft schedule of comparable transactions included in the schedules. To the extent that relevant facts could not be agreed each party would be responsible for proving those facts at the Hearing. In respect of each transaction included in a Schedule there would be provided particulars of the premises; the lease covenants including term and rent payable; the floor areas (computed using the same method of measurement as used for the subject premises); a description of the premises; whether the rent thereof arose out of a market transaction or a rent review agreement or determination; and such other matters as were thought likely to affect the rental value of, or the rent payable for, the premises.

1.17 The parties agreed that they would like the Arbitrator to make a preliminary inspection which the Arbitrator would wish to make after the Hearing. The Arbitrator would wish to be accompanied by one representative of each party at both inspections.

1.18 It was not thought necessary for arrangements to be made for another Preliminary Meeting.

1.19 It was agreed that the Claimant's Solicitor would be responsible for making arrangements for the reservation of accommodation for the Hearing, in liaison with the Respondent's Solicitor, and would in due course inform the Arbitrator of the agreed arrangements for him to confirm.

1.20 Both parties requested that the Arbitrator should make a reasoned Award.

1.21 [It was agreed that the Arbitrator would send draft directions to the parties' Solicitors for comment.][66]

2.1 I enclose [a draft of] directions [which I propose to issue] to give effect to these arrangements. [Please let me know by not later than noon on .... whether you have any comments to make on the draft.]

2.2 It was indicated at the Preliminary Meeting that I would give consideration to the Arbitrator's costs of the Reference in the light of what transpired at that Meeting. I have now done so and propose to charge a basic fee of .... and, additionally, a time charge at a rate of .... per day and proportionately for part thereof. This would be exclusive of out-of-pocket expenses and disbursements and exclusive of VAT.[67]

2.3 Any costs incidental to the proceedings, *e.g.* hire of rooms; the taking of legal or other professional advice, etc., would be charged additionally as incurred.

2.4 In the event that the parties are themselves able to reach agreement at any stage before an Award is made my charges would be as follows:

---

[66] In complicated cases para. 21 of the letter would be included and directions in draft form issued.
[67] The part of the letter on fees could be varied to meet different circumstances. The amounts of the basic fee and the daily rate of charge are matters of judgment for the arbitrator having regard to all the facts.

(a)	Agreement reached at this stage with no further action required of the Arbitrator	£ .... Plus time charge
(b)	Agreement reached before exchange of Reports	One quarter of basic fee plus time charge
(c)	Agreement reached after exchange of Reports but before commencement of Hearing	One half of basic fee plus time charge
(d)	Agreement reached after completion of Hearing but before making my second inspection of the subject premises and any comparables	Three-quarters of basic fee plus time charge

Out-of-pocket expenses; costs incidental to the proceedings and VAT would be additional to the amounts mentioned in 2.4(a), 2.4(b), 2.4(c) and 2.4(d) above.
Would you please confirm that this basis is acceptable.
I enclose a copy of the Attendance List for the Preliminary Meeting.
Yours truly
Enclosure

[Draft] Directions
Gentlemen,

In the matter of an Arbitration
between ....

In accordance with the arrangements made at the Preliminary Meeting held on .... I **A54–062** now direct as follows:

3.1 That is these Arbitration proceedings the lessors, ..., shall be designated the Claimant and the lessees, ..., shall be designated the Respondent.

3.2 That there shall be an oral Hearing commencing on .... and continuing through to .... and if not then concluded to stand adjourned to such date as may then be agreed with the parties or determined by me and that the Claimant's Solicitors shall be responsible for liaison with the Respondent's Solicitor to agree and make provisional agreements for the venue for the Hearing.

3.3 That evidence given at the Hearing shall be given on oath.

3.4 That the parties shall each be permitted to call an expert valuation witness to give evidence at the Hearing.

3.5 That the Claimant's Solicitors shall provide me with certified copies of the Underlease and any licences or other documents relating to that Underlease.

3.6 That the parties expert witnesses shall each prepare a schedule describing the nature and extent of any improvements and of any alterations which have been carried out to the demised premises since the grant of the Underlease thereof indicating whether any such improvements or alterations have been carried out at the expense of the lessor or the lessee and whether they are to be disregarded or taken into account in assessing the fair yearly rent and indicating those items in respect of which the parties are in agreement such schedules to be settled by not later than noon on .... and copies thereof lodged with me by not later than one week thereafter.

3.7 That the Claimant's expert witness shall prepare the draft of a Statement of Agreed Facts relating to the demised premises and the parties' expert witnesses shall agree so much thereof as they are able by noon on .... and a copy of the Statement of Agreed Facts shall be signed by them on behalf of the parties and lodged with me by not later than one week thereafter.

3.8 That the Statement of Agreed Facts shall incorporate the floor areas of the subject premises and a statement of the method of measurement used to compute those areas and such other matters as the expert witnesses consider to be relevant to the determination of the fair yearly rent and that there shall be appended to that Statement a set of agreed plans of the subject premises.

3.9 That by not later than noon on .... the parties' expert witnesses shall exchange their Schedules of comparable transactions and shall thereafter, as soon as may be, endeavour to agree the facts contained in such Schedules so far as they are able.

3.10 That the schedules of comparable transactions shall, as far as is practicable, include particulars and a description of each property; the lease covenants including terms and rent payable and the floor areas thereof (computed using the same method of measurement as has been used for the subject premises) and whether the rent payable results from a market transaction or a rent review agreement or determination in such other matters as the expert witnesses consider likely to affect the rental value of, or the rent payable for, the premises listed in the schedules.

3.11 That the parties shall exchange copies of their expert witnesses' Reports by not later than noon on .... and that such reports shall contain copies of all valuations, plans, documents and correspondence upon which a party intends to rely at the hearing and each party shall lodge with me a copy of such Report not later than one week thereafter.

3.12 That the parties shall exchange their replies, if any, to such Reports by not later than noon on .... and each party shall lodge with me a copy of any such reply by not later than one week thereafter.

3.13 That each party shall be responsible for sending to the other party a copy of every letter, document, drawing or other material or communication sent by the party to me.
I reserve the right to issue further directions as may appear to me to necessary or desirable, with liberty to the parties to apply.

Yours truly,

41. Notice to arbitrator of an application for leave to amend pleading or statement of case

A.B.
Dear Sir,

.... plc v .... plc

A54–063 The Claimant desires to amend the Statement of Case dated the .... (by substituting for the words "By a contract in writing made on the 27th April 1981" the words "by a contract made partly in writing on the 27th April and partly in two telephone conversations between John Smith on behalf of the Claimant and Mark Brown on behalf of the Respondent on the 28th April 1981").

Precedents and Drafting Suggestions

OR

(as shown on the draft enclosed herewith.) The Respondent has declined to consent to this amendment. We therefore request an appointment for making the necessary application. Our client will be represented by ...., and he/she considers that .... (minutes) (hours) should be allowed.
Yours faithfully,
for the Claimant.

42. Notice of intention to proceed *ex parte* after failure to comply with directions

RECORDED DELIVERY OR BY MESSENGER[68]

To: L.M. plc   A54–064

In the matter of an arbitration between
.... plc and yourselves

I refer to my Directions herein dated the .... 20 .... and my letter to you dated the ....
You have failed to comply with the directions in that ....[69] and you have failed to give any effective answer to my letter dated [ ] which [ ].[70] The hearing is now fixed for the .... 19 .... in Room No .... at .... 10.00 hours.
If you fail to attend at the hearing it is my intention to proceed with the arbitration in your absence. In that event I will notify you when the award is ready for collection.[71]
Yours, etc.
Arbitrator

43. Notice of intention to proceed *ex parte* after failure to attend hearing

RECORDED DELIVERY OR BY MESSENGER

To: L.M. plc

In the matter of an arbitration between
J.K. plc and yourselves

I refer to my (letter) (Directions) dated the .... 20 .... in which I notified you that   A54–065
the hearing would take place at 10.00 hours at .... You failed to attend that hearing.
I accordingly adjourned it to the same place and time on .... day the .... 20 ....
If you do not attend the adjourned hearing it is my intention to proceed in your absence. In that event I will notify you when my award is ready for collection.
If you wish to attend an adjourned hearing but the date is inconvenient it is open to you to apply to me to change it. Any such application should be made promptly; notice of the application should be served upon me and upon J.K. plc; and you will be asked to explain why the date presently fixed is inconvenient. You should not assume in advance that any such application will be granted.
Yours, etc.
Arbitrator

---

[68] A receipt is essential.
[69] The direction and the failure must be spelt out.
[70] Purpose of letter.
[71] Of course the appropriate sanction for failure to comply with a direction may well not be for the arbitrator to proceed with a hearing—which may cause the defaulting party no inconvenience at all. Accordingly the text of the paragraph should relate sanction to disobedience— making the punishment fit the crime along the principle if not the particular style of the Mikado.

PRECEDENTS AND DRAFTING SUGGESTIONS

44. Possible statement of case directions

ORDER FOR DIRECTIONS

A54–066 Upon [hearing Counsel for both parties] [upon reading the written submissions] herein, I hereby direct as follows:

    1.1 Claimant to prepare a bundle of principal documents and to include therein such documents as Respondent requests to be included.

    1.2 Claimant to serve a comprehensive Statement of Case on liability. To the Case should be annexed a list of all documents relied upon by the Claimant. The Case is to be served by or before the [*date*]. The Case should finally identify who is or are said by the Claimant to be the Respondent/s. In so far as the Claimant does not accept that .... is the only proper Respondent, the Claimant should fully set out in the Case its submissions in support of its contentions.

    1.3 Claimant may, if it so wishes, set out its case on Quantum in full.

    1.4 Respondent to serve a comprehensive Statement of Defence (and of Counterclaim if so advised) by or before the expiry of six weeks from receipt of the Statement of Case. Respondent to annex to the Defence (and Counterclaim, if any) a list of the documents relied upon. The Statement of Defence (and Counterclaim, if any) shall include full submissions on the proper construction of any clause in the contract relied upon by the Respondent to defeat the claim. The Statement of Defence should also respond fully to any submissions to the effect that .... is not the proper Respondent or is not the only proper Respondent.

    1.5 The Respondent may if it so wishes respond to the case on Quantum if such is put forward by the Claimant.

    1.6 Claimant to serve a comprehensive Reply to the Defence (and a comprehensive Defence to the Counterclaim if a Counterclaim is served) by or before the expiry of six weeks from the date of receipt of the Defence (and Counterclaim). A list of any documents which are relied upon by the Claimant in connection with the Reply (and Defence to Counterclaim, if any) and which are not already listed shall be annexed.

    1.7 At the same time as the Reply is served, the Claimant shall deliver to me, and to the Respondent if it so desires, a chronological bundle of the documents listed as relied upon by the parties. This bundle need not be finally paginated, since other documents may be added later.

    1.8 Liberty to Restore.

    1.9 Costs in the Reference.

CONSTRUCTION CASES

45. Clause for main or principal contract which also provides for determination of related sub-contract issues[72]

A54–067   1.1 In the following provisions of this clause "Head Arbitration" means an arbitra-

---

[72] These provisions follow on a clause referring disputes to arbitration.

tion under this contract; "Related Arbitration" means an arbitration under any contract ("Related Contract") by one of the parties under this contract and a third party for the carrying out of, or services in connection with, any part of the works the subject of this contract; and "Head Arbitrator" means the arbitrator or the arbitration tribunal appointed in the Head Arbitration.

1.2 If within .... weeks prior to or after the commencement of a Head Arbitration, either party to a Related Contract commences a Related Arbitration in which the issues substantially overlap with issues raised or to be raised in the Head Arbitration the party to this contract who is also a party to the Related Contract may by notice in writing to the other party to this contract and to the party to the Related Arbitration require that the Related Arbitration be referred to the arbitration of the Head Arbitration and be consolidated with or heard together with the Head Arbitration. The other party to this contract shall consent to such a requirement.

1.3 Any dispute as to whether the Related Arbitration raises issues which substantially overlap issues raised in the Head Arbitration and any questions as to the order or manner in which the arbitrations or any issue in either of them are to be determined shall be decided by the Head Arbitrator.

46. Provision in sub-contract requiring concurrence with head arbitration if required

1.1 In the following provisions of this clause "Head Arbitration" means an arbitration under .... "Head Arbitrator" means the arbitration tribunal appointed in a "Head Arbitration"; and "Arbitration" means an arbitration under this contract.

1.2 Any arbitration under this contract shall be commenced by notice in writing to the other party.

1.3 If prior to or within .... weeks of the service of such notice a Head Arbitration is commenced in which the issues raised substantially overlap with the issues raised in the Arbitration the party to the Head Arbitration who is a party under this contract may by notice to the other party under this contract require that the Arbitration be referred to the determination of the Head Arbitrator and be consolidated with or heard together with the Head Arbitration and the other party shall consent to such a requirement.

1.4 Any dispute as to whether the issues respectively raised in the Arbitration and the Head Arbitration substantially overlap or as to whether the two arbitrations shall be heard or determined separately or together or as to the order or manner in which the two arbitrations or any issue in either of them shall be determined by the Head Arbitrator.

A54–068

47. Construction Directions

IN THE MATTER OF THE ARBITRATION ACT 1996 AND IN THE MATTER OF AN ARBITRATION BETWEEN:

Claimants

and

Respondents

A54–069 Upon hearing (Counsel) (the Solicitors) (on both sides) (and by consent) the following Directions are hereby given and it is Ordered that:

1.1 There be Pleadings in this Arbitration as follows:

(a) Points of Claim to be delivered to me and to the Respondent(s) Solicitor(s) within .... (days)/(weeks) from the date hereof;

(b) Points of Defence (and Counterclaim if any) to be delivered to me and to the Claimant(s) Solicitor(s) within .... (days)/(weeks) from the delivery of the Points of Claim; and

(c) Points of Reply (and Defence to Counterclaim) are to be delivered to me and to the Respondent(s) Solicitor(s) within .... (days)/(weeks) from delivery of the Points of Defence and Counterclaim; and

(d) Points of Reply of Defence to Counterclaim are to be delivered to me and to the Claimant(s) Solicitor(s) within .... (days)/(weeks) from the delivery of Points of Defence to Counterclaim; and

(e) Requests for Further information to be made within .... days from the receipt of any Pleading and to be answered within a further .... days; and

(f) Any such request for Further information will automatically extend the time for the delivery of the following Pleadings by a time equal to that which elapses between the request for such information and the answer thereto; and

1.2 After the close of the Pleadings the Claimants and the Respondents do respectively within .... (days)/(weeks) give standard disclosure of documents by delivery to the other of a List of Documents which sets out those documents required by CPR Part 31.6 (as if CPR Part 31 applies to the arbitration); and inspection be given within .... (days)/(weeks) thereafter; and

1.3 Correspondence, plans, photographs and figures be agreed as such as far as possible; and

1.4 Further Directions will be issued in due course controlling the preparation of "Agreed Bundles" but the Parties are advised now that such Agreed Bundles should consist solely of those documents which are relevant to the issues pleaded; and

1.5 The Parties are to consider the possibility of agreeing a limitation on the number of expert witnesses to be called and I am to be advised of the decision of the Parties on this point not later than .... (days) (weeks) after the close of Pleadings; and

1.6 The Parties do mutually disclose experts reports within .... (days) (weeks) (of the close of Pleadings) (prior to the start of the Hearing) and such reports be agreed if possible. Only such experts whose reports have been so disclosed may be called to give evidence at the Hearing; and

1.7 The Parties are to consider the possibility of agreeing to exchange proofs of evidence of witnesses of fact by some predetermined date prior to the Hearing and I am to be advised of the decision of the Parties on this possibility not later than 28 days after close of Pleadings; and

1.8 Not later than 28 days after the close of Pleadings the Claimants may serve on the Respondents a Notice to Admit Facts and the Respondents within a further 28 days are to reply to the Notice and if so advised, to serve their own Notice to Admit Facts such Notice to be replied to within 14 days; and

1.9 Not later than .... (weeks) after (close of Pleadings) (completion of discovery of documents) the Parties are to prepare and submit to me a statement setting forth in numbered paragraphs the various issues which I am called upon to decide such statement to be agreed if possible, failing which each Party to produce their own statement; and

1.10 (After the completion of the inspection of documents referred to in paragraph 2 above) (after the close of the Pleadings) the Parties are to consider and are to advise me as soon as possible thereafter of their best estimate of the duration of the Hearing and of dates when it is known that their witnesses etc. will not be available together with an expression of any preference a party may have regarding the venue for the Hearing; and

1.11 The Parties are to consider the necessity for a shorthand record of the Hearing being taken and of the extent and distribution of any transcript and I am to be advised of the decision of the Parties on this point not later than the close of the Pleadings (not less than .... (weeks) (months) before the start of the Hearing); and

1.12 If any communication is made to me by either Party a copy thereof is simultaneously to be sent to the other Party; and

1.13 Each Party is to advise the other Party if it is their intention to engage Counsel; and

1.14 The Parties are to consider the desirability of agreeing that Counsel's closing addresses be made in writing after the close of the Hearing, with a further Hearing after such written addresses have been received at which each party may make oral summaries not exceeding one half day in duration; and

1.15 The costs of this Order are costs in the arbitration, and

1.16 Liberty to either Party to apply.
Arbitrator.
Dated this .... day of .... 20 ....

48. Another form of construction directions

A54–070

ORDER FOR DIRECTIONS NO. 1

UPON CONSIDERING the matters raised at the initial interlocutory meeting in this matter and BY CONSENT, I direct as follows:

1.1 CIMA Rules are to apply to the conduct of this arbitration.

1.2 CIMA Rule 9 (Full Procedure) will be adopted, subject to the detailed directions given herein and in any subsequent order.

1.3 The Claimant shall serve, by or before the [date], a detailed Statement of Case.

1.4 The Respondents shall serve, by or before the [date], a detailed Statement of Defence, and any Statement of Counterclaim that they may be minded to make.

1.5 The Claimant shall be at liberty to serve a Statement of Reply to any duly served Statement of Defence, provided the same is served within 14 days of the service of the Statement of Defence.

1.6 If the Respondents duly serve a Statement of Counterclaim, the Claimant shall serve a Statement of Defence to Counterclaim within 28 days of service of the Statement of Counterclaim.

1.7 The Respondents shall be at liberty to serve a Statement of Reply to any Statement of Defence to Counterclaim that the Claimant may serve, provided the same is served within 14 days of the service of the Statement of Defence to Counterclaim.

1.8 With each of the above Statements, but principally with the Statements of Case, Defence and Counterclaim, the parties will include a list of any documents considered necessary by the serving party to support any part of the relevant Statement. In addition, each party shall serve of each of the principal documents upon which that party wishes to rely, save for any such document that has already been served by either party.

1.9 Each of the above statements should also comply with CIMA Rule 9.2.

1.10 Detailed directions for the conduct of the hearing are to be agreed by the parties by or before the [date]. Such directions must be constructed so as to ensure that the hearing finishes within the allotted time. If not agreed by the said date, specific directions on the matter will be issued.

1.11 Statements containing the evidence in chief of any witness whom it is proposed to call by either party shall be served by or before the [date]. These statements shall stand as evidence in chief. Oral evidence in chief from witnesses of fact will only be permitted on application, showing good cause. No statement so served shall be relied upon in the proceedings by either party until the witness is called and has formally proved the statement.

1.12 Liberty to the parties to adduce expert evidence. The identity of each expert whom a party proposes to call must be notified in writing to me and to the other party no later than the [date]. The notification must identify his or her discipline and enclose a copy of the relevant CV.

1.13 In respect of the following directions which deal with meetings and the like between the expert witnesses, the principal expert witness for the Claimant is to take on administrative responsibility for arranging or attempting to arrange the same; and is to chair any such meetings, and prepare the documents for circulation hereinafter referred to. The Claimant is to nominate his principal expert witness when identifying his experts.

1.14 The expert witnesses are to arrange at least one without-prejudice meeting before exchange of their reports and to be at liberty to arrange more than one. No reference to be made to the proceedings in such meetings, save by way of a written memorandum signed by each expert present, and containing such statements as all the signatories are content to have circulated.

1.15 Statements containing a full account of the relevant's expert's proposed evidence in chief are to be served by or before the [date].

1.16 After service of the said statements, the experts are to meet on a without-prejudice basis at least once before the [date] in an endeavour to reduce the issues and to clarify the contentious matters. The experts are to be at liberty to meet more than once. No reference to be made to the proceedings in such meetings, save by way of a written memorandum signed by each expert present, and containing such statements as all the signatories are content to have circulated. Any such memorandum to be produced by or before the [date].

1.17 A bundle to be agreed and served on or before the [date].

1.18 A written opening by the Claimant is to be served no later than [date].

1.19 A Site visit is to take place on the [date].

1.20 The Claimant is to organize the venue of the hearing. The Claimant may utilise its own offices for this purpose only if the Respondents agree.

1.21 There will be no transcript of the hearing.

1.22 Communications between the parties and myself will normally be by DX, but can be by fax in case of urgency.

1.23 Interlocutory applications will so far as possible be dealt with on paper and not by oral hearings.

1.24 Liberty to apply generally; and specifically by way of an application for specific disclosure.

1.25 Costs in the arbitration.

49. Construction Scott Schedule Claim for extra work—stage one

SCOTT SCHEDULE   A54–071

Served pursuant to Order of the Arbitrator

Dated the .... day of .... 20 ....

SCHEDULE

Part One

1. No. of Item	2. Full particulars of each item of extra work ordered by respondent and done by claimant	3. Date when order given and by whom on part of the respondent	4. Amount claimed by claimant	5. Amount, if any, admitted by respondent	6. Respondent's observations	7. For use of the arbitrator

50. Check list for preliminary meeting

A54–072

Item No.	Item	Notes
1.1	Confirm that arbitration is under the 1996 Act and not the 1950 Act.[73]	
1.2	Is there a binding arbitration agreement (see section 8 of the 1996 Act)? Obtain copies of all documents relied upon.	
1.3	Does the arbitration agreement contain any conditions precedent to an arbitration? (*e.g.* that work must be completed.) If so, have they been complied with?	
1.4	Have I seen a copy of the notice to concur or any other relevant document commencing the arbitration?	
1.5	Are there any grounds for disputing my jurisdiction? If so, how and when should I resolve them (section 30 of the 1996 Act)?[74]	
1.6	Are the terms of my appointment (including fees) agreed by the parties and have they signed my letter of appointment?	
1.7	What is this dispute about? 1. Who is the claimant? 2. Very brief review of nature of claim. 3. Very brief review of nature of likely defence if known to respondent. 4. Is there likely to be a counterclaim?	
1.8	General procedure for the arbitration 1. Does the arbitration agreement provide that the arbitration shall be in accordance with specified procedural rules (*e.g.* CIMA Rules)? 2. If there is choice of procedure, what sort of procedure do I think would be appropriate for this arbitration? 3. Do the parties have any view on overall procedure that I should take into account at this stage?	
1.9	My powers—what powers do the parties agree that I shall have and shall not have under the 1996 Act? What other powers do I have irrespective?	
1.10	Points of claim: what form should these take? When should they be served? Should the claimant attach any documents that they rely upon?[75]	

---

[73] It is unlikely that arbitrations with preliminary meetings being held now will be under the 1950 Act. Therefore references in this table are to the 1996 Act.

[74] The arbitrator may have to look at jurisdiction again later in the arbitration in relation to individual claims/counterclaims once they are known.

[75] The arbitrator may wish to raise this issue now but postpone discussing it until he deals with disclosure later on in the hearing.

Precedents and Drafting Suggestions

1.11	Points of defence/counterclaim.	
1.12	Reply to counterclaim.	
1.13	Is a Scott Schedule appropriate? If so, what should the headings be? Dates for completion.	
1.14	Disclosure: should there be full disclosure or not? Should disclosure be by lists or by simply attaching documents relied upon in the pleading? If there is not to be a full disclosure, what shall I shall say about applications for specific disclosure for particular documents?	
1.15	Date for exchange of list of documents/other mechanism for disclosure.	
1.16	Arrangements for inspection of documents.	
1.17	Expert witnesses—number and discipline, date for exchange of reports.	
1.18	Should I order without prejudice experts' meetings in order to try to limit issues for the hearing?	
1.19	Witness statements—anticipated number for each side, dates for exchange.	
1.20	Should I make an order for rebuttal statements now?	
1.21	Parties to try to agree plans and photographs.	
1.22	Parties to try to agree figures as figures.	
1.23	Anticipated length of hearing.	
1.24	Date of hearing.	
1.25	Venue of hearing—where and who to arrange.	
1.26	Will parties be represented at hearing? If so, by counsel or solicitor?	
1.27	Will any transcript be required?	
1.28	Will evidence be on oath?	
1.29	Claimants to prepare agreed bundle by given date.	
1.30	Should parties provide written opening statements in advance of hearing? If so, set dates.	
1.31	At the hearing, will evidence be on oath?	
1.32	Should parties provide written closing submissions?	
1.33	Contact between parties and arbitrator other than at hearings to be by fax or letter only, copy to be provided to the other side immediately and arbitrator's copy to be marked as having been so copied.	
1.34	Cost of the preliminary hearing to be costs in the arbitration.	

637

A54–073

51. Claimant's Scott Schedule of defects—Stage 1. Headings only

Scott Schedule item No.	Location of defect	Particulars of breach	Terms of contract/ specification breached	Remedial work required	Cost of remedial work required	Respondent's comments	Arbitrator's comments
1.							
2.							

1. This example Schedule adopts headings relevant to a defects claim in a construction case. The headings will not, however, be the same for every arbitration. Thought should always be given to what headings would be the most useful given the issues in dispute.
2. The Schedule should always be completed in stages. The headings should preferably be considered at the preliminary meeting and may be the subject of an Order. The Claimant should then complete his part of the Schedule. The Respondents should then fill in their comments. Finally, the Arbitrator can add his own comments.

52. Claimant's Scott Schedule of defects—Stage 2. Claimant's comments

	Location of defect		Particulars of breach	Terms of contract specification breached	Remedial work required	Cost of remedial work required	Respondent's comments	Arbitrator's comments
1.1	Room AB-2	V1214, jacket drain valve or V303	The jacket drain valve is difficult to access, which will cause operational problems.	Clause 3.2 of the General Conditions, requiring that the plant shall conform to good engineering service practice.	Extend and modifying piping.	£1,500		
2.1	Room AB-2	Line 3016	The line does not fall continuously to V1215 as required by the ELD. It will not be fully drainable and this will compromise cleaning and sterilization operations.	Clause 2 Section D of the Specification, requiring that the plant comply with European and American guidelines on GMP for Pharmaceuticals, which requires that system design facilitates cleaning and sterilization.	Modify piping/supports.	£3,000		

Arbitration Clauses Relevant to Rent Review

53. Provision enabling rent review under underlease to be referred to same arbitrator as rent review under head lease

A54–075

1.1 In the following provisions of this clause "Head Arbitration" means an arbitration under this lease; "Head Arbitrator" means the arbitrator or arbitration tribunal appointed in the Head Arbitration; and "Sub-arbitration" means an arbitration under any sub-lease created out of this lease.

1.2 Any Head Arbitration shall be commenced by written notice to the lessor or lessee requiring arbitration.

1.3 If whether before or after a Head Arbitration has commenced a Sub-arbitration is commenced in which the issues substantially overlap issues raised in the Head Arbitration or which in the opinion of the lessee are likely to be raised in a Head Arbitration the lessee may be notice in writing to the lessor and to the underlessee served within .... months of the written notice last mentioned required that the Sub-arbitration be referred to the arbitration of the Head Arbitrator.

1.4 Any dispute as to whether the Sub-arbitration raises issues which substantially overlap issues raised in the Head Arbitration or as to whether the two arbitrations shall be heard or determined separately or together or as to the order or manner in which the two arbitrations or any issue in either of them shall be determined by the Head Arbitrator.

1.5 Save for any dispute under 1.3 above, the Head Arbitrator shall be at liberty to treat the dispute or disputes under this lease and the dispute or disputes under the sub-lease as if they arose under this lease arbitration clause; to give directions accordingly; in particular, but without derogating from the generality of the foregoing, he shall be at liberty to hear all relevant parties at the same hearing, and to take into account any evidence led by any party so present when determining any of the said disputes.

54. Provision in underlease of part enabling rent review to be referred to same arbitrator as rent review under head lease

A54–076

1.1 In the following provisions of this clause "Head Arbitration" means an arbitration under the rent review provisions of the head lease out of which the estate hereby granted is created: "Head Arbitrator" means the arbitrator or arbitration tribunal appointed in the Head Arbitration; and "Sub-arbitration" means an arbitration under the rent review provision of this underlease.

1.2 Any Sub-arbitration shall be commenced by written notice requiring arbitration.

1.3 If whether before or after a Head Arbitration has commenced a Sub-arbitration is commenced under this sub-lease in which the issues substantially overlap issues raised in the Head Arbitration the under lessee may by notice in writing to the underlessee require that the Sub-arbitration be referred to the arbitration of the Head Arbitrator.

1.4 Any dispute as to whether the Sub-arbitration raises issues which substantially overlap issues in the Head Arbitration or as to whether the two arbitrations shall be heard together or separately or as to the order or manner in which the two arbitrations or any issue in either of them shall be determined by the Head Arbitrator.

55. Suggested draft directions for a rent review arbitration by written representations

DIRECTIONS NO: A54–077

In respect of

(ADDRESS)

IN THE MATTER OF
THE ARBITRATION ACT 1996
AND
IN THE MATTER OF AN ARBITRATION BETWEEN

Landlord/Tenant—Claimant

and

Landlord/Tenant—Respondent

FACTS:

By lease dated .... the above premises were demised by the .... to the ....
Under the terms of the lease, the rent fell to be reviewed on ....
The parties having failed to agree the revised rental value, I was by letter dated .... appointed by the President of the RICS to act as Arbitrator
A preliminary meeting was held at .... on .... as a result of which, by agreement, I now make the following directions:—

DIRECTIONS

1. The landlord is to be the Claimant/Respondent and the tenant is to be the Respondent/Claimant. The Claimant is to be represented by .... of .... The Respondent is to be represented by .... of ....

2. The parties have confirmed to me that there are no other matters dealing with procedure or evidence agreed between them which are not recorded in the arbitration agreement or in these directions.

3. I understand that no point of law affecting this rent review has been identified at this point. If subsequently the position changes in respect of a legal point or upon any other matter I will discuss with the parties the best procedure for settling the dispute.

4. The reference is to be by way of written representations from the respective surveyors. The procedure will comprise a statement of agreed facts including agreed comparable transactions, written representations and written replies.

5. The programme is to be as follows, adopting in each case the close of business at 17.00 on the appropriate date.

Action   Date

   (i) statement of agreed facts in relation to the subject premises
   (ii) schedule of agreed comparable transactions including agreed proformas
   (iii) initial representations
   (iv) replies

6. The Statement of Agreed Facts is to be a single document or bundle signed by both parties and is to include:—

   (a) An agreed copy of the lease and of the lease plan(s) coloured in accordance with the lease.
   (b) A schedule of tenant's improvements and alterations to the property and an indication whether any such improvements or alterations are to be taken into account or disregarded in assessing the open-market rental value.
   (c) Copy licences and other documents as appropriate.
   (d) A description of the demised premises.
   (e) An agreed statement of the hypothetical transaction.
   (f) The agreed floor areas (including agreed dimensions of a typical floor) measured in accordance with the RICS/ISVA Code of Measuring Practice and identifying any areas in respect of which there are differences of opinion.
   (g) Floor plans as available.
   (h) Rating assessment.
   (i) Service charge if any for the last three years.
   (j) VAT status of the building.
   (k) A note of any matters of fact upon which the parties are unable to agree and if possible the reasons for the disagreement.

7. Evidence supplied in respect of comparable transactions will include the following so far as is practical:—

   (a) Description of the property including floor areas (measured in accordance with the RICS/ISVA Code of Measuring Practice).
   (b) Type of transaction (for example open-market letting, rent review, third party determination, etc.).
   (c) The terms of the transaction including in the case of an open-market letting a note of the date when solicitors were instructed together with date of exchange of contracts and of possession and in the case of rent reviews or third-party determination, a copy of the rent review clause or if not possible a note of the main assumptions.
   (d) VAT status of the building.

(e) Any other matters which are considered likely to affect the open-market rental value or the rent payable for the property, including details of rent-free periods, capital payments etc.

8. As required under the RICS Practice Statement for surveyors acting as expert witnesses, the parties will make every effort to agree the facts of the comparable transactions and to produce as part of the statement of agreed facts agreed proformas in relation to each comparable transaction on which either party seeks to rely. If it is not possible to agree all the relevant facts relating to each comparable transaction, the parties should advise me as soon as possible whereupon I will consider what further action should be taken.

9. Arbitrator's awards and the determinations of independent experts shall be admissible as evidence in this arbitration but I will decide what weight to give them.

10. Unless otherwise agreed by the parties, privileged material will not be accepted, whether or not marked "without prejudice".

11. Replies are to be confined to matters of rebuttal only.

    If either party comes into possession of fresh evidence during the course of the reference application for leave to present that evidence may be made to me and I shall give such directions or make such orders as I think fit in all the circumstances.

12. Two copies of the representations and replies are to be exchanged privately between the parties on the dates set out above in paragraph 5 with each party forwarding the spare copy to me by close of business on the third working day thereafter. The interval is to allow any objections as to privileged or otherwise inadmissible material to be brought.

13. All paragraphs of the Statement of Agreed Facts, representations and replies shall be numbered. This requirement is required to assist both me and the parties in connection with the parties' counter-representations.

14. All proofs of evidence and replies are to comply with the RICS Practice Statement for surveyors acting as expert witnesses (second edition) and are to include a declaration in accordance with paragraphs 5.3 (e) & (f) of the Practice Statement. Each witness will also separately confirm that they comply with paragraph 3.1(a) of the Practice Statement.

15. I may direct questions to either or both parties on their representations or replies or on any other matter which I consider relevant. The other party will be informed of any such questions and the replies thereto.

16. I may wish to appoint experts or legal advisers or to take the advice of leading counsel and would give the parties notice accordingly. Any opinions, reports, or advice obtained will be made available to the parties and in that connection I shall give directions as to the time by which any representations or counter-representation shall be made. The costs involved in obtaining the opinions, reports, or advice shall form part of my costs and will be incorporated in my final award. Prior to taking any such advice, I will inform the parties of the identity of the advisers and of the estimated costs and will be willing to receive any representations.

17. The parties agree that I will be entitled to take the initiative in ascertaining the facts on a point. In doing so I will be acting as Arbitrator, not as an expert, and will inform the parties in advance of what I intend to do and give them the reasonable opportunity to make observations on my findings before making my award.

18. I shall reserve the right to call for a hearing if in my discretion the circumstances justify it or either party request it. All the costs incurred will form part of the cost of the award.

19. All correspondence with me is to be copied simultaneously to the other party by the same means and all letters are to be marked accordingly.

20. In due course I shall require the parties to make arrangements for me to inspect the subject premises and also the properties cited as comparables.

21. Following my consideration of the matter I shall notify the parties that my reasoned interim award is available and thereafter I shall give directions on submissions on costs.

22. My fees are to be agreed by way of separate correspondence. The award will be issued on receipt of my fees in full.

23. I reserve the right to issue further directions as may appear to me to be necessary and desirable with liberty to the parties to apply.

NAME AND SIGNATURE OF ARBITRATOR

DATE

56. Suggested draft directions for a rent review arbitration involving an oral hearing

A54–078

In respect of

DIRECTIONS NO:

(ADDRESS)

IN THE MATTER OF THE ARBITRATION ACT 1996
AND
IN THE MATTER OF AN ARBITRATION BETWEEN

Landlord/Tenant—Claimant

and

Landlord/Tenant—Respondent

FACTS:

By lease dated .... the above premises were demised by the .... to the .... Under the terms of the lease, the rent fell to be reviewed on ....

Precedents and Drafting Suggestions

The parties having failed to agree the revised rental value, I was by letter dated .... appointed by the President of the RICS to act as Arbitrator

A preliminary meeting was held at .... on .... as a result of which, by agreement, I now make the following directions.

DIRECTIONS

1. The landlord is to be the Claimant/Respondent and the tenant is to be the Respondent/Claimant. The Claimant is to be represented by .... of .... The Respondent is to be represented by .... of ....

2. The parties have confirmed to me that there are no other matters dealing with procedure or evidence agreed between them which are not recorded in the arbitration agreement or in these directions.

3. The reference is to be by way of statements of case, a statement of agreed facts including comparable evidence, written representations and replies and an oral hearing.

4. In respect of the statements of case, the Claimant shall serve points of claim on or before the date set out in the timetable attached to these directions and the Respondent shall serve points of defence in accordance with the timetable. The Claimant shall, if so required, serve points of reply in accordance with the timetable.

    The documents included in the statement of case shall as appropriate contain:—

    a) a summary of the terms of the hypothetical transaction as relied on by the party serving the same;
    b) a statement of any points in the hypothetical transaction specified by the other party which are disputed; and
    c) any point of principle or law which it could reasonably be anticipated should be brought to the attention of the other party.

    The documents need not contain any valuation.

5. By the first witness notification date set out in the timetable attached to these directions each of the parties shall serve on the other party and me notices specifying the names of each expert witness (or any other witness giving evidence of opinion) upon whom they intend to rely, and the areas of expertise in respect of which each such expert will give his evidence.

    By the second written notification date set out in the timetable attached to these directions each party may serve on the other party and me notices specifying the names of additional expert witnesses to be called in the same field as an expert witness notified by the other party as above to give evidence by way of rebuttal.

6. The Statement of Agreed Facts is to be a single document or bundle signed by both parties and is to include:—

    (a) An agreed copy of the lease and of the lease plan(s) coloured in accordance with the lease.

(b) A schedule of tenant's improvements and alterations to the property and an indication whether any such improvements or alterations are to be taken into account or disregarded in assessing the open-market rental value.
(c) Copy licences and other documents as appropriate.
(d) A description of the demised premises.
(e) The agreed floor areas (including agreed dimensions of a typical floor) measured in accordance with the RICS/ISVA Code of Measuring Practice and identifying any areas in respect of which there are differences of opinion.
(f) Floor plans as available.
(g) Rating assessment.
(h) Service charge if any for the last three years.
(i) VAT status of the building.
(j) A note of any matters of fact upon which the parties are unable to agree and if possible the reasons for the disagreement.

7. Evidence supplied in respect of comparable transactions will include the following so far as is practical:—

(a) Description of the property including floor areas (measured in accordance with the RICS/ISVA Code of Measuring Practice).
(b) Type of transaction (for example open-market letting, rent review, third-party determination, etc.).
(c) The terms of the transaction including in the case of an open-market letting a note of the date when solicitors were instructed together with date of exchange of contracts and of possession and in the case of rent reviews or third-party determination, a copy of the rent review clause or if not possible a note of the main assumptions.
(d) VAT status of the building.
(e) Any other matters which are considered likely to affect the open-market rental value or the rent payable for the property, including details of rent free periods, capital payments, etc.

8. As required under the RICS Practice Statement for surveyors acting as expert witnesses, the parties will make every effort to agree the facts of the comparable transactions and to produce as part of the statement of agreed facts agreed proformas in relation to each comparable transaction on which either party seeks to rely. If it is not possible to agree all the relevant facts relating to each comparable transaction, the parties should advise me as soon as possible whereupon I will consider what further action should be taken.

9. Arbitrator's awards and the determinations of independent experts shall be admissible as evidence in this arbitration but I will decide what weight to give them.

10. Unless otherwise agreed by the parties, privileged material will not be accepted, whether or not marked "without prejudice".

11. Replies are to be confined to matters of rebuttal only.

If either party comes into possession of fresh evidence during the course of the reference application for leave to present that evidence may be made to me and I shall give such directions or make such orders as I think fit in all the circumstances.

12. Copies of all specified documents are to be exchanged privately between the parties on the dates set out in the attached timetable with a copy being forwarded to me at the same time. I will not open my copy for three working days after receipt. The interval is to allow any objections as to privileged or otherwise inadmissible material to be brought.

13. All documents produced in this arbitration shall be in numbered paragraphs and all pages shall be numbered sequentially including the pages of appendices. All proofs and appendices shall contain a table of contents where it would be useful to do so.

14. All proofs of evidence and replies are to comply with the RICS Practice Statement for surveyors acting as expert witnesses (second edition) and are to include a declaration in accordance with paragraphs 5.3 (e) & (f) of the Practice Statement. Each witness will also confirm that they comply with paragraph 3.1 (a) of the Practice Statement.

15. I may wish to appoint experts or legal advisers or to take the advice of leading counsel and would give the parties notice accordingly. Any opinions, reports, or advice obtained will be made available to the parties and in that connection I shall give directions as to the time by which any representations or counter-representation shall be made. The costs involved in obtaining the opinions, reports, or advice shall form part of my costs and will be incorporated in my final award. Prior to taking any such advice, I will inform the parties of the identity of the advisers and of the estimated costs and will be willing to receive any representations.

16. The parties agree that I will be entitled to take the initiative in ascertaining the facts on a point. In doing so I will be acting as Arbitrator, not as an expert, and will inform the parties in advance of what I intend to do and give them the reasonable opportunity to make observations on my findings before making my award.

17. The proceedings will be conducted by way of an oral hearing commencing on the date set out in the timetable attached to these directions to be held at a venue to be arranged.
    Evidence at the proceedings will be taken on oath.
    A written transcript shall be prepared of each day's proceedings to be made available to each party and myself as soon as practical on that or the succeeding day.

18. All correspondence with me is to be copied simultaneously to the other party by the same means and all letters are to be marked accordingly.

19. In due course I shall require the parties to make arrangements for me to inspect the subject premises and also the properties cited as comparables.

20. Following my consideration of the matter I shall notify the parties that my reasoned interim award is available and thereafter I shall give directions on submissions on costs.

21. My fees are to be agreed by way of separate correspondence. The award will be issued on receipt of my fees in full.

22. I reserve the right to issue further directions as may appear to me to be necessary and desirable with liberty to the parties to apply.

TIMETABLE

The following should be served and delivered to me by 17.00 on the dates set out below:

Heading **Date**

1. Points of Claim

2. Points of Defence

3. Points of Reply (if any)

4. First Witness Notification

5. Agreed Statement of Facts

6. Second Witness Notification

7. Schedule of Agreed Evidence

8. Statement of Witnesses of Fact

9. Proofs of Evidence

10. Replies to Proofs

11. Oral Hearing

NAME AND SIGNATURE OF ARBITRATOR
DATE

57. Agreement to refer point of law for the decision of counsel

IN THE MATTER OF AN ARBITRATION
BETWEEN
L.M. plc   Claimants
and
P.Q. plc   Respondents

1.1 A contract between the above parties dated the .... 20 .... contained, in clause 6, provision for arbitration.

1.2 On the .... 20 .... Mr A.B. was appointed arbitrator (OR Mr A.B. and Mr C.D. have been appointed arbitrators by the claimants and the respondents respectively).

1.3 The matters in issue between the parties include the issue set out in the Schedule hereto.

1.4 The parties hereby agree:

(a) that the said issue shall be submitted, in the form of a Joint Case, for the Opinion of (Mr Y.Z. of Counsel)

OR

(b) (Counsel to be chosen by the Arbitrator(s) from a list of four names of which two shall be nominated by each party);

(c) that the Arbitrator(s) shall be bound to accept the Opinion of Counsel as correctly stating the law on the issue referred to him;
(d) (to be deleted if inapplicable) that any right of appeal under the Arbitration Act 1996 is hereby excluded in relation to the said issue;
(e) that the costs of obtaining the said opinion shall be in the discretion of the Arbitrator(s);

Dated ....

(Signed) .... (Signed) ....
(Name) .... (Name) ....
For L.M. plc   For P.Q. plc

58. Final award without reasons[76]

IN THE MATTER OF AN ARBITRATION A54–080
BETWEEN
P.Q. plc
Claimants
and
L.M. plc
Respondents

FINAL AWARD

1.1 I .... was appointed
(By letters respectively from the claimant dated the .... and from the respondent dated the .... 20 ....)

OR

(By letter from the President of the .... dated the .... 20 ....) to act as arbitrator under (an arbitration clause contained in a contract dated the .... 20 ....)

OR

(an arbitration agreement dated the .... 20 ....)

1.2 I have received and studied (a) the contract between the parties dated .... 19 .... and (b) the submissions of the parties hereto (made to me in written Statements of Case and Statements of Reply)

OR

(at a hearing on the .... and the .... 20 ....)

1.3 I have inspected ....

1.4 Neither party has asked for a reasoned award.

1.5 I DO HEREBY AWARD AND DETERMINE that the Respondent do pay to the claimant the sum of £ .... with interest thereon from the .... at the rate of .... per cent.

---

[76] An unmotivated award should be a very rare animal post the 1996 Act.

1.6 I further AWARD AND DIRECT
(that the .... do pay the .... my fees for this arbitration and award (which I hereby assess at £ ....) and the .... costs of the arbitration to be taxed (if not agreed))

OR

(that there be no order as to costs save that my fees for this arbitration and award shall be borne by the parties equally, and that if either party shall in the first instance pay more than one-half of my said fees the other party shall pay to him the amount of the excess).

1.7 I further award and direct that any taxation under the above provisions of my award shall be (by me)[77]

OR

(by the High Court) and shall be (on an indemnity basis)

OR

(on a party and party basis).

Dated ....
(Signed) ....
Arbitrator

59. Final award with reasons

A54–081

IN THE MATTER OF AN ARBITRATION
BETWEEN
P.Q. plc
Claimant
and
L.M. plc
Respondent
FINAL AWARD

1.1 I, A.B., was appointed by letters respectively from the claimant dated .... 20 .... and from the respondent dated the .... 20 ....

OR

by letter from the President of the .... dated the .... 20 .... to act as arbitrator under an arbitration clause contained in a contract dated .... 20 ....

OR

an arbitration agreement dated the .... 20 ....

1.2 The submissions of the parties hereto were made to me (in writing, by the claimant personally and by .... on behalf of the respondent)

OR

(at a hearing on the .... and the .... 20 .... at which the Claimant was represented by Miss X.Y. of Counsel and the Respondent by Mr W.R., a chartered quantity surveyor).

---

[77] To be preferred.

1.3 Three issues were put to me for determination. They were formulated (by Counsel) (by the advocates) (by the parties, with my assistance), as follows:
ISSUE 1: ....
ISSUE 2: ....
ISSUE 3: ....

1.4 (A Statement of Agreed Facts was put before me. It is annexed to and forms part of this Award.)
OR
(The following facts were not in dispute).

1.5 As to Issue 1: The case for the Claimant was ....
The case for the Respondent was ....
....
In my judgment .... therefore decide this issue in favour of the ....

1.6 As to Issue 2: [etc. as for Issue 1].

1.7 As to Issue 3: [etc. as for Issue 1].

1.8 The overall result of my determinations on these issues is ....

1.9 I therefore DO HEREBY AWARD AND DETERMINE that the Respondent pay to the claimant the sum of £ .... with interest thereon from the .... 20 .... at the rate of .... per cent.

1.10 I further AWARD AND DIRECT
(that the respondent do pay to the claimant my fees for this arbitration and award (which I hereby assess at £ ....) And the Claimant's costs of the arbitration to be taxed (if not agreed)
OR
(by me with the assistance if I think necessary of a Costs Assessor to be selected by me from the Costs Panel of the Chartered Institute of Arbitrators)
OR
(that there be no order as to costs save that my fees for this arbitration and award shall be borne by the parties equally, and that if either party shall in the first instance pay more than one-half of my said fees the other party shall pay to him the amount of the excess)
the taxation to be (on the standard basis)
OR
(on the indemnity basis).[78]

Dated ....

(Signed) ....
Arbitrator

---

[78] See Pt 2 of Vol. 1 re taxing costs, and who should do it.

60. Final award—reasons to be annexed—consumer dispute

A54–082 (Reference No.)

IN THE MATTER OF THE ARBITRATION ACT 1996
and
IN THE MATTER OF AN ARBITRATION UNDER THE
RULES OF THE .... SCHEME FOR THE .... INDUSTRY
(EDITION) BETWEEN:

(Name and address)

Claimant

and

(Name and address)

Respondent

ARBITRATOR'S AWARD

WHEREAS:

1.1 (On or about .... the Claimant entered into a contract with the Respondent whereby the Claimant would pay the total sum of £ and the Respondent would provide ....).

1.2 During the [*relevant circumstances and dates*] certain events occurred which resulted in a dispute arising between the parties.

1.3 Such dispute has not been amicably resolved and has been referred to arbitration in accordance with the Chartered Institute of Arbitrators' Arbitration Scheme for the .... Industry.

1.4 The parties to the arbitration have agreed to the Arbitrator deciding the case solely on documents which have been submitted by them.

1.5 On [*date of appointment*] the [*President or Vice President*] of the Chartered Institute of Arbitrators appoint me [*name, qualifications and reference to the particular panel of which arbitrator is a member*] to act as arbitrator in the Reference. This appointment I accepted on [*date*].

1.6 My reasons are set out in the annex to my Award, but they form part of my Award. Now I, the said (name), having carefully considered the submissions of the parties as set out in the documents provided to me, HEREBY AWARD AND DIRECT as follows:(Alternative forms of Award)

(A)

(a) The Claimant's claim succeeds.

(b) The Respondent shall pay to the Claimant in full and final settlement of his claim the sum of [£X] provided that if the Claimant has accepted all or any of the *ex gratia* payment offered by the Respondent the amount shall be reduced accordingly. For the avoidance of doubt, the sum of [£X] is to be paid net.

(c) The Respondent shall pay to the Claimant the sum of [£X] which sum represents the amount of the Claimant's Registration Fee payable under the Rules of the Scheme

(B)

(d) The Claimant's claim fails.

(e) The Claimant shall pay to the Respondent the sum of [£X] being the amount representing the Respondent's Registration Fee payable under the Rules of the Scheme.

Given under my hand this ( ) day of ( ) 20 ....
....
(Signature of arbitrator)
Witnessed by: ....

NOTES

1.7 It may not be necessary to specify the time within which payment is to be made since usually code arbitration Rules provide that payment is to be made within 21 days. The arbitrator should check the situation. The wording in parenthesis in note 1.6(b) will be appropriate in cases where the Respondent has already made an *ex gratia* payment.

1.8 In those exceptional cases where the arbitrator decides that a successful party should NOT recover his registration fee, the relevant paragraph would be omitted and the arbitrator would explain in his reasons why he has exercised his discretion in the way he has.

1.9 The annex referred to in paragraph 1.6 above would be headed "These reasons are given with and form part of my Award".

61. Interim award

[*Heading as in suggestion [60] but change "final award" to "interim award"*] A54–083
[*Paragraphs 1, 2, 3 and 4 as in suggestion [60], then continue:*]

1.1 (At the hearing) OR (By letters from the parties dated [*etc.*]) it was agreed between the parties that I should determine as a preliminary issue Issue 1, and publish an interim award upon it.

1.2 The Case for the Claimant on this issue was ....

1.3 The Case for the Respondent was ....

1.4 In my judgment ....

1.5 I therefore determine this preliminary issue in favour of the (Claimant) (Respondent) and I therefore DO AWARD AND DETERMINE that (*e.g.* the Respondent is liable to the Claimant for damages for the breach of contract alleged in paragraph .... of the Claimant's Statement of Case).

1.6 This award is made as my interim award. The question of the costs of this preliminary issue and of this interim award is reserved, as are all other issues in the arbitration.

Dated ....

(Signed) ....

62. Interim awards reserving costs for later decision

A54–084 Interim award, final as to all matters except costs
[*Heading as in suggestion [60], but change "final award" to "interim award"*]
[*Paragraphs 1 to 9 as in suggestion 60, then continue:*]

> 1.1 The parties have agreed that this award should be final as to all matters other than costs. I reserve my award as to the costs of the reference including liability for my fees as between the parties. In all other respects this award is my final award.
>
> Dated ....
> (Signed) ....
> Arbitrator

63. Clause reserving costs and giving directions

A54–085 [*Heading of award as in suggestion [60] but change "final award" to "interim award" (Final except as to costs)"*]
[*Paragraphs 1 to 9 as in suggestion [60], then continue:*]

> 1.1 This award is final as to all matters except costs.
>
> 1.2 I shall now proceed to make an award as to costs.

If either party wishes me to convene a hearing to receive submissions as to costs it should notify me, and the other party, in writing within [10] days of the date of this award. If neither party so notifies me, I will consider any written submissions as to costs (including information as to any *Calderbank* offer intender to be relied upon) received at the above address within a further 10 days.

64. Clause reserving costs but making an award "nisi" as to costs and giving directions

A54–086 [*Heading of award as in suggestion [60], but change "final award" to "interim award" (Final except as to costs)"*]
[*Paragraphs 1 to 9 as in Suggestion [60], then continue:*]

> 1.1 This award is final as to all matters except costs.
>
> 1.2 As to costs:
>
> 1.3 If neither party made any submissions to me as to costs I would determine and award that
> ....
> ....
>
> 1.4 If either party wishes to submit to me that I should make some order different from that indicated, or no order, it should notify me, and the other party, in writing within [10] days of the date of this award. Such notification should state what order it contends for, and
> *either* written submissions (including information as to any Calderbank offer

intended to be relied upon) showing why I should make the order asked for *or* notice requesting me to arrange an oral hearing on the question of costs. If upon the expiry of 10 days from the publication of this award I have not received such a notification, I will issue a final award in the terms set out in paragraph A above.

65. Final award incorporating alternative final award

[*Heading and paragraph 1 as suggestion [60], then continue:*]   A54–087

    1.1 I held a hearing on the .... 20 .... at which the Claimant were represented by Mr R.S. of Counsel and the respondents by Miss T.V. of Messrs. Smith and Jones, Solicitors. During the hearing a point of law was raised, which was formulated by agreement between the advocates as follows:
"Whether on a true construction of the contract dated the 27 June 1991 the obligation of the respondents was to deliver 220 tons not later than 1st November 1991 and the balance of 230 tons not later than 1st January 1992 (as the claimants contend) or whether the said obligation was to deliver 450 tons not later than 1st January 1992 (as the Respondent contends)."
The parties intimated that the unsuccessful party might wish to appeal against my decision on this issue, and they therefore requested me to make a final award but to include also an alternative final award to take effect if my decision upon the above issue were reversed by the Court.[79]

    1.2 The other issues put for my determination were agreed as follows:
Issue 2: ....
Issue 3: ....

    1.3 [*From here onwards as in paragraphs [   ] in suggestion [   ]*]

    1.4 If I had decided the first issue in favour of the .... I would have determined and awarded that .... and I would have award that the costs of this arbitration and award ....

Dated ....
(Signed) ....
Arbitrator

66. Award by umpire

IN THE MATTER OF AN ARBITRATION   A54–088
BETWEEN
L.M. plc
and
P.Q. plc
FINAL AWARD TO E.F. UMPIRE

---

[79] This format would be appropriate where there is a contract between the parties which permits appeals. Otherwise the arbitrator should invite submission as the appropriateness of this course, since it militates against finality.

1.1 By an arbitration clause in a contract made the .... 20 .... between the above named parties OR
(By an arbitration agreement made the .... 20 .... between the above named parties) it was provided that (copy from contract or agreement, *e.g.*: "Any dispute or difference should be referred to the arbitration of an arbitrator to be appointed by each party or if they disagreed by an umpire to be appointed by the arbitrators").

1.2 By letter dated the .... 20 .... L.M. plc appointed Mr A.B. as arbitrator and by letter dated the .... 20 .... P.Q. plc appointed Mr C.D. as arbitrator.

1.3 By a letter of appointment dated the .... 20 .... A.B. and C.D. having disagreed appointed me as Umpire pursuant to the said agreement.

[*Then continue as in award of single arbitrator, as appropriate.*]

67. Clauses for awards—rent review—declaration that landlord has unreasonably withheld consent

A54–089 I DO HEREBY AWARD AND DECLARE that the Respondent has unreasonably withheld its consent to the assignment to A.N. Other plc mentioned in paragraph X of the claimants Statement of Case.
AND I DO FURTHER AWARD AND DECLARE that the Claimant is now entitled to proceed with the assignment therein mentioned without the consent of the Respondent.

68. Award for the delivery up of property, with alternative money award

A54–090 I DO HEREBY AWARD AND DIRECT that the respondents do deliver up to the claimants not later than the .... 20 .... (or on such later date as the claimants may in their discretion allow) the property specified in paragraph X of the Statement of Claim, and that in default thereof the respondents do pay to the claimants the sum of £ ....

69. Letter publishing award

A54–091 Dear Sirs,
Arbitration between L.M. plc and P.Q. plc
I have now made my award in this arbitration. It may be taken up by either party at my office, on payment of my charges set out in the attached fee note. On the award being taken up by one party only, I will unless otherwise requested despatch a copy by first class post to the other party.
Yours faithfully,
Arbitrator

L.M. plc	P.Q. plc
Copy to: their (Solicitors)	Copy to: their (Solicitors)
(Other Representative)	(Other Representative)
Messrs	Messrs ....

Court Forms

Arbitration Award

70. Application to enforce an award A54–092

In the   Claim No.

County Court

                                                        Applicant

                                                        Respondent

The applicant applies to enforce, in this court, the award given on   20   by
the   under reference
and for an order that the respondent pay the costs of this application.
A copy of the award is attached.

1. Applicant   The **amount now owing** and the costs claimed are:
The Applicant is   The amount of the award   £
                                (including any costs)
whose address is
                                [Interest on £_____
                                from _____
            Postcode   to _____ 20 ___ at ____%]   £
Tel. No.   Ref.   **or**
                                [As shown in the attached   £_____
                                calculation]
Address for service (if different)
                                                sub-total £

            Postcode   Less amount paid   £_____

2. Respondent   Balance remaining unpaid   £
The Respondent is   Court fee   £
                                Solicitor's costs   £_____
whose address is   **Total**   £_____

            Postcode

Statement of Truth
*(I believe)(The applicant believes) that the facts stated in this application are true.
*I am duly authorised by the applicant to sign this statement.

signed _____ date _____
*(Applicant)(Litigation friend *(where applicant is a child or a patient)*)(Applicant's solicitor)
*delete as appropriate

Full name _____
Name of applicant's solicitor's firm _____
position or office held _____
            (if signing on behalf of firm or company)

N322A Application to enforce an award (March 2002)   Crown Copyright. Reproduced by Sweet & Maxwell Ltd

71. PF 166 Certificated as to finality, etc., of Arbitration Award for Enforcement Abroad (Arbitration Act 1996, s.58)

IN THE MATTER OF THE ARBITRATION ACT 1996
AND
IN THE MATTER OF AN ARBITRATION BETWEEN:

Claimant

Respondent

I, a Master of the Supreme Court [a District Judge of the High Court] of England and Wales, hereby certify:—

1. That the award made by *(name of arbitrator)* and published on *(date)* is not subject to any appeal or to any application to remit or set it aside and that the time for any such appeal or application has expired [*or* an appeal against the award was dismissed by the order of The Honourable Mr Justice *(name)* *(dated)*] (*or as may be*),

2. That the award is by virtue of the provisions of subsection (1) of section 58 of the Arbitration Act 1996 final and binding on the parties and any persons claiming through or under them.

Dated ....

(Signed) ....
a Master of the Supreme Court [a District Judge of the High Court] of England and Wales.

Arbitration Claims

72. Acknowledgment of Service (arbitration claim) A54–094

In the	
Claim No.	
Claimant (including ref)	
Defendant	

You should read the 'notes for defendant' attached to the claim form which will tell you how to complete this form, and when and where to sent it.

Tick and complete sections A–D as appropriate.
In all cases you must complete sections E and F

Section A

☐ I **do not** intend to contest this claim

Section B

☐ I intend to contest this claim
Give brief details of any different remedy you are seeking.

Section C

☐ I indent to dispute the court's jurisdiction
(Please note, any application must be filed within 14 days of the date on which you file this acknowledgment of service)

The court office at

When corresponding with the court, please address forms or letters to the Court Manager and quote the claim number.

N15 Acknowledgment of Service (arbitration) (March 2002)   Crown Copyright. Reproduced by Sweet & Maxwell Ltd

	Claim No.	

Section D

☐ I intend to rely on written evidence

My written evidence:
☐ is filed with this form
☐ will be filed and served within 21 days after the date by which I am required to file this acknowledgment of service.

Section E

Full name of defendant filing
this acknowledgment   _____

Section F

Signed (To be signed by you or by your solicitor)	*(I believe)(The defendant believes) that the facts stated in this form are true. *I am duly authorised by the defendant to sign this statement *delete as appropriate	**Position or office held** (if signing on behalf of firm or company)	

Date [   ]

Give an address in England or Wales to which notices about this case can be sent to you	 Postcode Tel. no.		if applicable
		Ref. no.	
		fax. no.	
		DX no.	
		e-mail	

73. Claim Form (arbitration)   A54–095

In the	
	for court use only
Claim No.	
Issue date	

In an arbitration claim between

Claimant

(SEAL)

Defendant(s)

In the matter of an [intended] arbitration between

Claimant

Respondent(s)   *Set out the names and addresses of persons to be served with the claim form stating their role in the arbitration and whether they are defendants.*

Defendant's name and address	☐ This claim will be heard on: at am/pm ☐ This claim is made without notice.

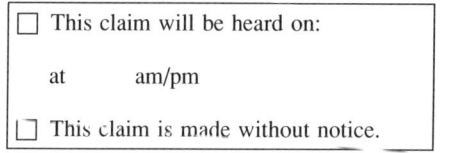

The court office at

When corresponding with the court, please address forms or letters to the Court Manager and quote the case number.

N8 Claim form (arbitration) (March 2002)   Crown Copyright. Reproduced by Sweet & Maxwell Ltd

| Claim No. | |

Remedy claimed and grounds on which claim is made

| Claim No. | |

The claimant seeks an order for costs against

Statement of Truth
*(I believe)(The claimant believes) that the facts stated these particulars of claim are true.
*I am duly authorised by the applicant to sign this statement.

Full name _____
Name of applicant's solicitor's firm _____

signed _____   position or office held _____
　　　　*(Claimant)(Claimant's solicitor)　　 (if signing on behalf of firm or company)

*delete as appropriate

Claimant's or claimant's solicitor's address to which documents should be sent if different from overleaf. If you are prepared to accept service by DX, fax or e-mail, please add details.

Precedents and Drafting Suggestions

74. Arbitration Claim—notes for the claimant

Please read these guidance notes before you begin completing the claim form

A54–096

The arbitration claim form may be used to start proceedings and make an application in existing proceedings, where an application is being made in existing proceedings, an acknowledgment of service form is not required and the references to an acknowledgment of service form in the Notes for the Defendant should be deleted.

With the exception of:
- applications under section 9 of the Arbitration Act 1996; and
- certain proceedings which may be started only in the High Court or only in a county court—see High Court and County Courts (Allocation of Arbitration Proceedings) Order 1996, arbitration proceedings may be started in the courts set out in the table opposite.

Court	List
Admiralty and Commercial Registry at the Royal Courts of Justice, London	Commercial
Technology and Construction Court Registry, St Dunstan's House, London	TCC
District Registry of the High Court *(where Mercantile court established)*	Mercantile
District Registry of the High Court *(where the Claim form marked 'Technology and Construction Court' in top right hand corner)*	TCC
Central London County Court	Mercantile

Heading

You must fill in the heading of the claim form with:
- the name of the court (High Court or county court); and
- if issued in a District Registry, the name of the District Registry

Claimant and defendant details

You must provide your full name and address and the full names and addresses of the defendants to be served. If a defendant is to be served outside England and Wales, the court's permission may need to be sought *(see Rule 62.5)*

Remedy claimed and grounds on which claim is made

You must:
- include a concise statement of
  — the remedy claimed; and
  — any questions on which you seek the decision of the court;
- give details of any arbitration award which you challenge, identifying which part or parts of the award are challenged and the grounds for the challenge;
- show that any statutory requirements have been met;

- specify under which section of the Act the claim is made;

Respondents

- if on notice, give the names and addresses of the persons on whom the arbitration claim form is to be served, stating their role in the arbitration and whether they are defendants; or
- state that the claim is made without notice under section 44(3) of the 1996 Act, and the grounds relied on.

Acknowledgment of service form

An acknowledgment of service form N15 must accompany the arbitration claim form. You should complete the heading on this form. Where the form is to be served out of the jurisdiction, you must amend the Notes for the Defendant to give the time within which the defendant must acknowledge service and file evidence. The claim form is valid for one month beginning with the date of its issue or, where required to be served out of the jurisdiction, for such period as the court may fix.

Address for documents

You must provide an address for service within England and Wales to which documents should be sent. That address must be either the business address of your solicitor, or your residential or business address.

Statement of Truth

The statement of truth must be signed by you or by your solicitor. Where the statement of truth is not signed by the solicitor and the claimant is a registed company or corporation, the statement of truth must be signed by either a director, the treasurer, secretary, chief executive, manager or other officer of the company and (in the case of a corporation) the mayor, chairman, president or town clerk.

You may rely on the matters set out in the claim form as evidence only if the claim form is verified by a statement of truth. You may also file an affidavit or witness statement in support of the arbitration claim, which must be served with the claim form.

N8A Arbitration claim – notes for claimant (March 2002)   Crown Copyright. Reproduced by Sweet & Maxwell Ltd

75. Arbitration Claim—notes for the defendant

A54–097 Please read these guidance notes before you respond to the arbitration claim form

Court staff can help you with proceedings but they cannot give legal advice. If you need legal advice, you should contact a solicitor or a Citizens Advice Bureau immediately.

Responding to the claim

If you are:
- named as a defendant in the claim form; and
- served with a copy of it,

you should respond by completing and returning to the court office the acknowledgment of service form which was enclosed with the claim form, within *(14 days) (   ) of the date it was served on you. At the same time you must serve a copy on the claimant and any other party shown on the claim form.

If the claim form was:
- sent by post, the *(14 days) (   ) starts 2 days from the date of the postmark on the envelope;
- delivered or left at your address, the *(14 days) (   ) starts on the day it was given to you;
- handed to you personally, the *(14 days) (   ) starts on the day it was given to you.

The acknowledgment of service

If you:
- fail to complete and file the acknowledgment of service within the time specified; or
- if you indicate that you do not intend to contest the claim.

If you later change your mind, you will not be entitled to contest the claim without the court's permission.

Evidence

If you wish to rely on evidence before the court, you must file and serve your written evidence within *(21 days) (   ) of the date the claim form was served on you.

Statement of truth

The acknowledgment of service myst be signed by you or by your solicitor. Where the acknowledgment of serice is not signed by your solicitor and you are a registered company or corporation, it must be signed by either a director, the treasurer, secretary, chief executive, manager or other officer of the company and (in the case of a corporation) the mayor, Chairman, president or town clerk.

Notes for arbitrators

If your are:
- an arbitrator; or
- ACAS (in a claim under the 1996 Act as applied with modification by the ACAS (England and Wales) Order 2001),

who has been named as a defendant in the claim form, the above notes apply to you as they do any other defendant.

If you were, or are:
- an arbitrator in the arbitration which led to this claim; and
- if you are not named as a defendant;

this claim form is sent to you for information

You may either;
- make a request (with notice only to the claimant) to be made a defendant
- may make representations to the court *(see paragraph 4.3 of practice direction to Part 62)*

N8B Arbitration claim – notes for defendant (March 2002)

Claimant should alter where appropriate if the claim form is to be served out of the jurisdiction (see CPR Part 6)

Crown Copyright. Reproduced by Sweet & Maxwell Ltd

PRECEDENTS AND DRAFTING SUGGESTIONS

ARBITRATION PROCEEDINGS

76. No. 15A (PT. 49G PD para. 11) Acknowledgement of service of arbitration claim form   A54–098

IN THE HIGH COURT OF JUSTICE
QUEEN'S BENCH DIVISION
COMMERCIAL COURT
[[   ]
            District Registry Mercantile List]
[In the Central London County Court
                              Business List]
                Claim No

In the matter of an [anticipated] Arbitration between:

Claimant

Respondent

Respondent/Arbitrator

If you wish to contest the claim you should complete section B.
If you wish to dispute the Court's jurisdiction you should complete section C.

Section A

Give your full name:

The court office is open between 10am and 4.30pm Monday to Friday. Please address all communications to the Court Manager quoting the claim number.

Section B
I intend to contest the arbitration claim.
I intend to contest the claim for costs.
I do not intend to contest either.

Section C
I intend to dispute the jurisdiction of the Court.

Signed _____   **position or office held** _____
*(Respondent)(Respondent's solicitor)   (if signing on behalf of firm or company)
*delete as approriate

Date _____

Give an address to which documents about this arbitration claim can be sent:

Ref: *DX:*
Tel: *Fax:*
Email:

A54–099 77. No. 8A (PT 49G PD para. 4) Claim Form (Arbitration application)

Royal Arms

IN THE HIGH COURT OF JUSTICE
QUEEN'S BENCH DIVISION
COMMERCIAL COURT
[[   ]
District Registry Mercantile List]
[In the Central London County Court
Business List]
Claim No

In an Arbitration application between:

Applicant

Respondent

Respondent

and

In the matter of an [anticipated] Arbitration between:

Claimant

Respondent

[*Give names and addresses of respondent(s) and any arbitrator(s) listed above as respondents or give full names and addresses or arbitrators not named above but to whom notice of this application is given.*]

To the Respondent(s):

Hearing

This arbitration application is made:

* without notice,   * on notice to the persons whose names are given above (*or set out names and addresses*).

* Tick as appropriate

This arbitration application will be heard by a Judge sitting in [public][private]*

* delete as appropriate

The hearing of this arbitration application will take place:

[in court/room no.   (*give address of court*) on (*date*) at (*time*).]

or

[on a date to be fixed.]

Grounds of application and details of what is being claimed:

The applicant seeks an order for costs against:

Set out the names of the person(s) against whom costs are sought:

Statement of Truth
*(I believe)(The Applicant/Claimant believes) that the facts stated in this arbitration application claim form are true.
*I am duly authorised by the Applicant/Claimant to sign this statement.

Full name _____

Name of Applicant/Claimant's solicitor's firm _____

signed _____ position or office held _____
*(Applicant/Claimant)(Applicant/Claimant's solicitor)   (if signing on behalf of firm or company)
*delete as approriate

This Claim Form was issued in the Commercial Registry, Room E 200 Royal Courts of Justice, Strand, London WC2A 2LL [DX 44450 STRAND]

or

in the [   ] District Registry of the High Court at (*give address*)

in the Central London County Court at (*give address*)

by the Applicant/Claimant whose address for service is (*give address*)

or

by (*Solicitor's name, address and reference***)**
Solicitor for the Applicant/Claimant whose address is (*give address*)

Guidance notes for the Applicant/Claimant

Please read these notes carefully before filling in the Arbitration Claim Form:—

A54–100   1. The Arbitration Claim Form may be used both to start proceedings and to make an application in existing proceedings. Applications which are not required by any provision of the Part 49G Practice Direction to be made by this form may be made in existing proceedings by application notice (N244 (or PF244 R.C.J. only)) or by a Part 8 Claim Form. Where an application is being made in existing proceedings, an acknowledgment of service form is not required and the references in the Guidance notes for the Respondent to an acknowledgement of service should be deleted.

2. Except for applications under section 9 of the Arbitration Act 1996, and in certain proceedings which may be started only in the High Court or only in a county court in accordance with the High Court and County Courts (Allocation of Arbitration Proceedings) Order 1996, arbitration proceedings may be started in;

(a) the Admiralty and Commercial Registry in the Royal Courts of Justice, to be entered in the Commercial list,

(b) in a district registry where a Mercantile Court has been established, to be entered in the Mercantile list, or

(c) in the Central London County Court, to be entered in the Business list.

If the application is not started in the Admiralty and Commercial Registry, the Judge in Charge of the List into which it is entered will consider whether the application should be transferred to the Commercial Court or any other list (see paragraph 5.4 of the Part 49G Practice Direction).

You must fill in the heading of the form with:

(a) the name of the Court (High Court or County Court)

(b) If issued in a District Registry, the name of the District Registry

(c) the full names of the parties.

3. The Claimant/Applicant must provide the full names and addresses of the respondent(s) to be served. If a respondent is to be served outside England and Wales, the court's permission may need to be sought. See paragraphs 7 and 8 of the Part 49G Practice Direction.

4. Grounds for application and details of the claim:
There must be included;

(a) a concise statement of

(i) the remedy claimed and
(ii) (where appropriate) the questions on which the Claimant/Applicant seeks the determination or direction of the Court,

(b) details of any arbitration award that is challenged by the Claimant/Applicant, showing the grounds for any such challenge,

(c) (where appropriate) the section of the Arbitration Act 1996 under which the claim/application is brought, and

Precedents and Drafting Suggestions

(d) an indication that any statutory requirements (incuding those set out in the Table at paragraph 4.2 of the Part 49G Practice Direction) have been satisfied.

5. The Claimant/ Applicant must provide an address for service within the jurisdiction. That address must be either the business address of his solicitor, or the residential or business address of the Claimant/Applicant.

6. An acknowledgment of service form in form No. 15A must accompany the Arbitration Claim Form. The Claimant/Applicant should complete the title on form No 15A. Where the Arbitration Claim Form is to be served out of the jurisdiction, the Claimant/Applicant must amend the Notes for the Respondent to give the time within which the Respondent must acknowledge service. The Arbitration Claim form is valid for one month beginning with the date of its issue or, where required to be served out of the jurisdiction, for such period as the Court may fix.

7. The statement of truth must be signed by the Claimant/Applicant or by his solicitor. Where the statement of truth is not signed by the solicitor and the Claimant/Applicant is a registered company or corporation, the statement of truth must be signed by either a director, the treasurer, secretary, chief executive, manager or other officer of the company and (in the case of a corporation) the mayor, chairman, president or town clerk.

8. A Claimant/Applicant may rely on the matters set out in the Arbitration Claim Form as evidence if the Arbitration Claim Form is verified by a statement of truth. A Claimant/Applicant may also file an affidavit or witness statement in support of the arbitration claim which must be served with the Arbitration Claim Form.

Notes for the Respondent

Please read these notes carefully before responding to the Arbitration Claim Form:—

1. If you are   **A54–101**

(a) named as a Respondent in the Arbitration Claim Form, and

(b) served with the Arbitration Claim Form,

you have 14 days from the date on which you were served with the Arbitration Claim Form in which to respond to the arbitration claim by completing and returning to the court office the acknowledgement of service form enclosed with the arbitration claim.

If the Arbitration Claim Form was

(a) sent by post, the 14 days begins 2 days from the date of the postmark on the envelope,

(b) delivered or left at your address, the 14 days begins the day after it was delivered, or

(c) handed to you personally, the 14 days begins on the day it was given to you.

Court staff can help you with procedures but they cannot give legal advice. If you need legal advice you should contact a solicitor or the Citizens Advice Bureau.

2. If you

(a) fail to complete the acknowledgement of service within the specified time, or

(b) if you indicate that you do not intend to contest the arbitration claim,

you will not be entitled to contest the arbitration claim without the permission of the Court, and, in respect of (a) above, you will not be given notice of the hearing of the arbitration claim.

3. To complete the acknowledgement of service form you should;

(a) set out your full name in section A,

(b) indicate in section B whether you intend to contest

   (i) the arbitration claim,
   (ii) (if applicable) the claim for costs, or
   (iii) neither, and

(c) indicate in section C whether you intend to dispute the jurisdiction of the Court.

4. The acknowledgement of service must be signed by you or your solicitor. Where the acknowledgement of service is not signed by the solicitor and the Respondent is a registered company or corporation, it must be signed by either a director, the treasurer, secretary, chief executive, manager or other officer of the company and (in the case of a corporation) the mayor, chairman, president or town clerk.

5. Notes for arbitrators:

If you are an arbitrator who has been named as a respondent in the Arbitration Claim Form, the above notes apply to you as they do to any other respondent.

If you were or are an arbitrator in the arbitration which gave rise to this arbitration claim and you are *not* named as a respondent, the Arbitration Claim Form has been sent to you for your information. You may either make a request (without notice to any party) to be made a respondent, or you may make representations to the court. See paragraph 12 of the Part 49G Practice Direction.

78. PF 167 Order to stay proceedings under Section 9 of the Arbitration Act 1996 (Part 49G PD para. 6)

A54–102

IN THE HIGH COURT OF JUSTICE
QUEEN'S BENCH DIVISION

Claim No.

Before (*Judge/Master/District Judge's name and title*) [sitting in Private]

Claimant

Defendant

An Application was made by [application notice/letter] dated *(date) or* by [Counsel][solicitor] for *(party)* and was attended by (   )

The [Judge][Master][District Judge] read the written evidence filed

IT IS ORDERED that:

1. all further proceedings in this claim be stayed under section 9 of the Arbitration Act 1996,
2. the costs of and caused by the claim [including the costs of this application] are [summarily assessed in the sum of £   ] [to be the subject of a detailed assessment] and to be paid by (party).

Dated ....

79. Specimen letter—arbitrator's charges

A54–103

Messrs   *For the attention of*
....
....
....
and
Messrs   *For the attention of*
....
....
....

Gentlemen,

In the matter of an Arbitration between
....
and
....
in respect of
....

It was indicated at the preliminary meeting which took place on .... that I would give consideration to the arbitrator's costs in the Reference in the light of what transpired at that meeting. I have now done so and propose to charge a fixed fee of .... % of the mean of the .... rental values contended for by the parties plus a time charge of £ .... per day, pro rata for part of a day, in excess of .... days, subject to a minimum fee of £ ....

In the event that the parties are themselves able to reach agreement at any stage before an award is made my charge would be as follows, depending on the period within which the parties reach an accord:—

Period 1	Up to and including the date of the Preliminary Meeting	£
Period 2	From the day after the end of Period 1 up to and including the date for exchanging statements of submissions	£
Period 3	From the day after the end of Period 2 up to and including the date of the preliminary inspection .... of the full fee subject to a minimum of	£
Period 4	From the day after the end of Period 3 up to and including the date of the full inspection .... of the full fee subject to a minimum of	£
Period 5	From the day after the end of Period 4 the full fee subject to a minimum of	£

Out-of-pocket expenses and disbursements; costs incidental to the proceedings, *e.g.* the hiring of rooms and the taking of legal and other professional advice and VAT will be charged additionally to the amounts mentioned above.

Yours truly,

Miscellaneous

80. ICC—Arbitrator's Declaration of Acceptance and Statement of Independence[79a]

A54–104 *(Please mark the relevant box or boxes)*

I, the undersigned,
Name .... First Name ....

Acceptance

☐ hereby declare that **I accept** to serve as arbitrator under the ICC Rules of Arbitration in the instant case. In so declaring, I confirm that I have familiarized myself with the requirements of the ICC Rules of Arbitration and am able and available to serve as an arbitrator in accordance with all of the requirements of those Rules and accept to be remunerated in accordance therewith.

Independence

*(**If you accept to serve as arbitrator**, please <u>also</u> check one of the two following boxes. The choice of which box to check will be determined after you have taken into account, <u>inter alia</u>, whether there exists any past or present relationship, direct or indirect, with any of the parties or their counsel, whether financial, professional or of another kind and whether the nature of any such relationship is such that disclosure is called for pursuant to the criteria set out below. <u>Any doubt should be resolved in favour of disclosure</u>.)*

☐ **I am independent** of each of the parties and intend to remain so; to the best of my knowledge, there are no facts or circumstances, past or present, that need be disclosed because they might be of such nature as to call into question my independence in the eyes of any of the parties.

OR

☐ **I am independent** of each of the parties and intend to remain so; **however**, in consideration of Article 7, paragraphs 2 & 3, of the ICC Rules of Arbitration,[80] I wish to call your attention to the following facts or circumstances which I hereafter disclose because they might be of such a nature as to call into question my independence in the eyes of any of the parties. (Use separate sheet if necessary.)

[79a] Reproduced with the kind permission of the copyright-holders, the International Chamber of Commerce.

[80] Article 7(2): "Before appointment or confirmation, a prospective arbitrator shall sign a statement of independence and disclose in writing to the Secretariat any facts or circumstances which might be of such a nature as to call into question the arbitrator's independence in the eyes of the parties. The Secretariat shall provide such information to the parties in writing and fix a time limit for any comments from them".

Article 7(3): "An arbitrator shall immediately disclose in writing to the Secretariat and to the parties any facts or circumstances of a similar nature which may arise during the arbitration".

Non-acceptance

☐ hereby declare that **I decline** to serve as arbitrator in the subject case. (If you wish to state the reasons for checking this box, please do so.)
Date: .... Signature: ....

81. ICC Terms of Reference

A54–105

⎡ International Court of Arbitration
⎢ of the International Chamber of Commerce
⎣ (ICC no.   ) ⎤⎦

ARBITRATION

BETWEEN

PARTY A,
Claimant,

AND

PARTY B,
Respondent.

TERMS OF REFERENCE

Arbitral Tribunal
X Q.C., arbitrator
Dr. Y, arbitrator
Mr. Z, chairman

[Date]

I. Names and Description of the Parties (Article 18.1(a) of the ICC Rules)

1. Claimant:

A54–106

PARTY A a company organized and existing under the laws of ...., with its principal office at ....,
hereinafter referred to as "Claimant" or "PARTY A", represented in this arbitration by their duly authorized attorneys, ...; Counsel: ...., with offices at ...., which offices have been chosen by Claimant as the venue for the service of process for the purpose of this arbitration.

2. Respondent:

PARTY B, a company organized and existing under the laws of ...., with its principal office at ....,
hereinafter referred to as "Respondent" or "PARTY B"
represented in this arbitration by its duly authorized attorneys, ...; Counsel: .... with offices at ...., which offices have been chosen by Respondent as the venue for the service of process for the purpose of this arbitration, and ...., with offices at ....;

3. Claimant and Respondent are herein referred to separately as a "Party" and collectively as the "Parties".

673

PRECEDENTS AND DRAFTING SUGGESTIONS

II. Notifications and Communications (Article 18.1(b) of the ICC Rules)

A54–107 4. All written notifications and communications arising in the course of this arbitration shall be deemed to have been validly made to each Party where they have been transmitted by (i) delivery against receipt, or (ii) courier service with notice of dispatch by facsimile, or (iii) facsimile transmission, if less than 30 pages, confirmed by ordinary mail or courier service or e-mail, or (iv) e-mail confirmed by ordinary mail, courier service or facsimile, to the arbitrators at the addresses indicated under section III para. 10 *infra* and to Counsel at the following addresses:

for Claimant, to:

[NAME]
[FIRM]
[ADDRESS]
Tel:
Fax:
e-mail:

for Respondent, to:

[NAME]
[FIRM]
[ADDRESS]
Tel:
Fax:
e-mail:

and to:

[NAME]
[FIRM]
[ADDRESS]
Tel:
Fax:
e-mail:

5. All written notifications and communications between the Parties or either of them and the arbitrators shall be made by one of the above-mentioned means to the respective addresses as set forth in this section and in section III.

6. A copy of any notification or communication by a Party to the arbitrators shall be simultaneously transmitted to the other Party and to the Secretariat of the International Court of Arbitration by same means (38, Cours Albert 1 er, 75008 Paris (France), phone: +33 1 49 53 28 13, fax: +33 1 49 53 29 33).

7. The provisions of article 3(3) and (4) of the ICC Rules (in force as of 1 January 1998) ("the ICC Rules" or the "Rules") shall apply to any notification or communication and period of time arising during the course of this arbitration, it being understood that the date of receipt by the Chairman shall be decisive in all respects.

8. Any change of name, description, address, telephone or fax number, or e-mail address, shall be immediately notified by the Party or the arbitrator concerned to all other addressees referred to in sections II and III. Failing such notification, notifications and communications sent in accordance with this section and section III shall be valid.

9. Detailed directions on the notifications and communications will be issued by the Arbitral Tribunal if and when the latter deems it appropriate.

III. Names and Addresses of the Arbitrators (Article 18.1(e) of the ICC Rules)

10. The Arbitral Tribunal is composed as follows: **A54–108**
X. Q.C.
at [ADDRESS]
Tel:
Fax:
e-mail:

proposed by Claimant

Dr Y
at [ADDRESS]
Tel:
Fax:
e-mail:

proposed by Respondent

Mr Z
at [ADDRESS]
Tel:
Fax:
e-mail:

jointly proposed as chairman by Mr X and Dr Y.

11. Pursuant to Article 9(2) of the ICC Rules, Mr X and Dr Y were confirmed as coarbitrators by the Secretary General of the International Court of Arbitration of the International Chamber of Commerce (the "Court") on .... and the chairman was confirmed by the Secretary General on ....

12. By the execution of these Terms of Reference, the arbitrators confirm the acceptance of their appointment.

13. By the execution of these Terms of Reference, the undersigning Parties confirm that, on the date hereof, they have no ground for objecting to the arbitrators.

IV. Background of the Dispute and Procedure to date

14. Under a contract entered into on .... ("Agreement for the construction of ....) **A54–109** between M.N. s.a. and O.P. s.a., Party B had agreed to design and construct ....

15. On ...., Party B entered into a contract no .... with Party A "for the delivery of .... "(the "the Party A Contract", the "Supply Contract" or the "Contract").

16. Under the Contract, Party A was to supply to Party B .... ("HK")

17. The .... in question were delivered by Party A at the beginning of .... and were installed at .... in late ....

18. After a few months, the .... installed at .... (as well as the .... installed at ...., under a contract between Party B and Q.R. "Contract no .... for the delivery of .... for .... "), started showing [defects]. In .... Party A undertook and completed wholesale replacement of all .... originally supplied.

19. A dispute arose between the Parties under the Party A Contract in respect of the financial consequences of the replacement of the defective valves.

20. Article 28 of the Party A Contract provides as follows:

675

"28. ARBITRATION

28.1 If at any time any question dispute or difference shall arise between the parties in connection with or arising out of this CONTRACT, which cannot be settled amicably, either party may give to the other one notice in writing of the existence of such questions dispute or difference specifying the nature and the point at issue, and the same shall be finally settled as an exclusive basis for resolution of disputes under the CONTRACT, by arbitration under and in accordance with the rules of Conciliation and Arbitration of the International Chamber of Commerce (ICC), which rules are deemed to be incorporated by reference into this Sub-article. The arbitration tribunal at the .... shall consist of three arbitrators, while each party shall appoint one arbitrator and the two in this manner appointed arbitrators shall appoint the leading arbitrator.

28.2 The arbitration proceedings to be conducted in the English language."

21. On .... , Party A filed a Request for Arbitration, which reached the Court on .... , together with exhibits .... to ....

22. Upon Respondent's application, the Secretariat of the Court fixed the date for the filing of the Answer to the Request for Arbitration at ....

23. Subject to its position as to the lack of jurisdiction of an ICC Arbitral Tribunal in this case, Party B agreed on a Tribunal of three arbitrators.

24. On .... , Party A appointed Mr .... , Q.C. as arbitrator.

25. On .... , Party B appointed Dr Y as arbitrator "[..........] if, notwithstanding Party B's objections, the ICC does proceed to set the arbitration motion [..........]".

26. On .... , Party B filed an Answer to the Request for Arbitration (the "Answer"), together with exhibits .... to .... with the Secretariat.

27. On .... , Party A filed an Amended Request for Arbitration with the Secretariat of the Court.

28. In subsequent correspondence exchanged with the Secretariat of the Court, the Parties argued, *inter alia*, on the jurisdiction issue and on the place of arbitration.

29. On .... , Counsel for Respondent filed Appendices .... to .... for insertion into exhibit ....

30. On .... , the Court fixed the place of arbitration at .... , pursuant to Article 14 of the ICC Rules.

31. On .... , the Court also decided that the matter shall proceed in accordance with Article 6(2) of the ICC Rules.

32. On .... , Party A filed a Submission on Jurisdiction with the Secretariat of the Court.

33. On .... , Party A filed exhibits .... to .... with the Secretariat of the Court.

34. Party B having taken the decision not to pay its share of the advance on costs requested by the Court, Party A informed the Secretariat of the Court, on 27 March 2002, of its decision to substitute Party B in this respect.

35. On .... , Claimant informed Respondent and the Secretariat of the Court of its intention to seek an interim award in respect of "Party A's financial covering of Party B's default".

36. At its session of .... , the Court decided not to reconsider its decision as to the place of arbitration.

37. On .... , Claimant filed a Reply and the attached documents.

38. On .... , at the request of the Tribunal, Claimant and Respondent filed a Summary Statement of Position and Relief Sought.

V. Summary of the Parties' Respective Positions and Claims/Defences and Reliefs sought (Article 18.1(c) of the ICC Rules)

39. The purpose of the following summaries, provided by the Parties, respectively, at the Tribunal's request, is to satisfy the requirements of Article 18.1(c) of the ICC Rules, without prejudice to any other or further allegations, arguments or contentions contained in the pleadings or submissions already filed, and in such submissions as will be made in the course of this arbitration. No statement or omission in the summary of either Party is to be interpreted as a waiver of any issue of fact or law. By signing the Terms of Reference, neither Party subscribes to or acquiesces in the summary of the other Parties set forth below. **A54–110**

V.A. *Summary of Claimant's position, claims and relief sought*

    (1) Claimant's position and claims ....

V.B. *Summary of Respondent's position, defences and relief sought*

    (1) Respondent's position and defences ....

VI. Amounts Claimed (Article 18.1 (c) of the ICC Rules)

45. The monetary amount of Claimant's claims can be estimated at € .... plus USD **A54–111**

VII. Issues to be Determined (Article 18.1 (d) of the ICC Rules)

46. Without prejudice to the provisions of article 19 of the ICC Rules, the Arbitral Tribunal shall decide upon all issues arising from the submissions, statements and pleadings of the Parties that are relevant to the adjudication of the Parties' respective claims and defences. **A54–112**

47. In a Preliminary Phase of the proceedings, the Arbitral Tribunal shall deal with Respondent's defence based on the alleged lack of jurisdiction of this Tribunal and, if it retains jurisdiction, with Claimant's request for provisional measures.

VIII. Applicable Substantive Law

48. Clause 25 of the Party A Contract provides that it shall be "governed by and interpreted pursuant to the .... law". **A54–113**

IX. Seat of the Arbitration (Articles 14 and 18.1(f) of the ICC Rules)

49. The seat of the arbitration is .... as decided by the Court at its session of **A54–114**

X. Applicable Procedural Rules and Miscellaneous Matters (Article 18.1(g) of the ICC Rules)

50. *Procedure* **A54–115**

    (i) The proceedings shall be governed by the ICC Rules and such other mandatory rules under the law of .... applicable to international arbitration taking place in .... , and, where these Rules are silent, by such other rules as may be agreed by the Parties or, failing the Parties' agreement, by the rules laid down by the Arbitral Tribunal.

(ii) The Arbitral Tribunal may, upon a motion made by one Party, instruct the Parties to file any documentary evidence which the Tribunal will deem relevant. The Tribunal shall draw inference as it shall deem appropriate, taking all prevailing circumstances into account, in case any Party fails to proceed with the filing as instructed.

(iii) If a documentary evidence which a Party is directed by the Arbitral Tribunal to file contains proprietary information or trade secrets, that Party shall so indicate to the Tribunal and to the other Parties. In that case, the Arbitral Tribunal shall determine, after consultation with the Parties, the appropriate measures to be implemented in order to respect the proprietary nature of the information while, to the extent possible, allowing the production of such evidence for the purpose of the arbitral proceedings.

51. *Language of the arbitration*

The language of the arbitration is English (Party A Contract, Article ....).

52. *Awards*

The Arbitral Tribunal shall have the authority to resolve the issues before it in partial or interim awards or to join them in a single award.

53. *Procedural measures by the Chairman*

Organizational measures shall be ordered by the Chairman on behalf of the Arbitral Tribunal after consultation with the co-arbitrators. Before making such decisions, the Arbitral Tribunal shall afford the Parties an adequate opportunity to make presentations in relation thereto, unless special circumstances render such presentations inappropriate. In case of urgency, the Chairman may order procedural measures alone. The Chairman shall have authority to sign procedural orders on behalf of the Arbitral Tribunal.

XI. Value Added Tax (VAT)

A54–116 54. The undersigning Parties agree that, if and to the extent that any of the arbitrators is required to collect VAT from one or both of the Parties, such Party or Parties, as determined by the Tribunal, shall pay the amount of such VAT to the arbitrator in addition to any fees also due to him.

SIGNED BY COUNSEL ON BEHALF OF THE PARTIES AND BY THE ARBITRATORS IN EIGHT ORIGINAL COPIES ON ....

On behalf of Respondent,   On behalf of Claimant,

....

THE ARBITRAL TRIBUNAL

....
Arbitrator   Arbitrator

....
Chairman

Attachments: —power of attorney given by Claimant to its Counsel
—power of attorney given by Respondent to its Counsel

82. Possible terms of engagement for a barrister/arbitrator

BASIS OF ENGAGEMENT A54–117

(January 1997 Edition)

To whom it may concern

1.1 *Fees and Disbursements*
I charge for my work by way of time charges. However, as will be seen from paragraph 3.1 below, I am happy to entertain different arrangements if preferred.

1.2 *The Hourly Rate*
Time expended on or in connection with this case is charged at the rate of £   per **A54–118**
hour. The phrase "in connection with" is intended to include both time expended in directly working upon a case as well as time otherwise expended—*e.g.* in travel connected with the case.

This can be an onerous obligation in some cases, and I am happy to consider or to make alternative proposals. In particular, if it is possible to relate more than one item of work to a particular journey, then, provided the arrangements are made prior to commencement of the travel, the travel time will be disposed between the items of work in what I consider to be a reasonable manner, or as agreed in advance of departure.

1.3 *Validity of Rate*
The rate quoted above is valid for time expended in 1997 I reserve the right to vary **A54–119**
the rate for time expended after [*date*]. This right may be exercised at any time, but if it is exercised after [*date*], then the varied rate will only apply to time expended after the date of variation. My right to charge the varied rate is not dependent upon prior notification to the client.

1.4 *Disbursements*
Disbursements are charged in addition. "Disbursements" includes such matters as **A54–120**
travel and accommodation charges, and fax, Lexis, courier and photocopying expenses.

2.1 *Advance Bookings*
I am happy to book time in my diary in advance. I am unwilling to follow the practice **A54–121**
of some clerks and double and treble book such time. Equally I am unhappy to have substantial amounts of time locked up which may never be used. Accordingly, booking charges will apply as follows:
   2.2 The first five consecutive calendar days of the first booking in a case do not attract a booking fee at all. For any other period there is a booking fee of £ ....
   per week, payable prior to the booking being entered into the diary.

PRECEDENTS AND DRAFTING SUGGESTIONS

2.3 This booking fee is only returnable if I am unable to hold the booking. (Bookings are accepted on the basis that I am not liable for any costs of whatsoever nature of or occasioned by my inability to keep the booking. "Inability" includes but is not limited to illness and overrun of other cases.) If the relevant week is actually utilized in whole or in part the booking fee for that week is treated as a credit on account of the fees for that week. This provision applies whatever the method of charging.

3.1 *Charging other than by hourly rates*

A54–122   If it is desired to have a more traditional arrangement with, for example, brief fees and refreshers rather than an hourly rate, please let me or my assistant know and we will be happy to give you a quotation. Please also let one of us know if a quotation in a different currency is required. Payment can be effected (perfectly legally so far as I am concerned!) to banks outside the UK if that too is desired.

4.1 *Arrangements through a Clerk*

A54–123   If it is preferred to deal through a clerk, please communicate with the clerk to my [   ] Chambers, as follows: ………. .

5.1 *Queries*

A54–124   I hope that the above is clear, but if it is not, please indicate the problem and I or my clerk (as appropriate) will endeavour to help.

6.1 *Value Added Tax*

A54–125   Where appropriate Value Added Tax is added to the above fees at the rate in force at the time the work is billed.

7.1 *Billing*

A54–126   7.2 Save as provided above and save as otherwise expressly agreed in writing, and whatever the method of charging, I reserve the right to bill fees and disbursements from time to time during the course of the case. Such billings will be in arrear, but will not be more frequently than monthly. Fees are payable within 28 days of billing and if not so paid give rise to a right on my part to cease further work on the case. This right is in addition to any other that I may have under these terms and/or the general law.
7.3 Interest will be charged on fees paid late at the rate of 10% per annum with quarterly rests.
7.4 When sitting as an arbitrator, each party is jointly and severally liable to me for all fees and disbursements and I shall be entitled to order, at any time, the provision of reasonable security.

A54–127 **8.1** *Signifying agreement*

A second copy of these terms is attached. While it is not necessary for each party to sign and return that copy to signify its agreement to them, it would make for good order if this were done by each party with a copy to the other side.

83. Dispute Board—Mediation—Arbitration clause

A54–128   If the Parties agree during the tender negotiations to rely on ADR (Alternative Dispute Resolution) techniques and especially to have a Dispute Board ("DB") procedure, it might be appropriate, for long-term projects, to integrate straight from the beginning a dispute resolution clause with two or even three stages, *i.e.* DB—arbitration or DB—mediation—arbitration.[81] The following clause could be suggested:

> "*In the event of a dispute arising between the Parties in connection with the contract or the execution of the works, the Parties agree, prior to any arbitration proceedings, to refer the case at first to a Dispute Board consisting of three experts. Such reference shall be made in accordance with the procedures set up in appendix XX. The written recommendation of the DB shall become final and binding upon both Parties, unless a notice of dissatisfaction has been given by either Party within 30 days after receiving such recommendation*".

In case the principle of a binding decision is selected, the last sentence of the previous paragraph would read:

> "*The written Decision has to be implemented without delay, regardless of any objection made by any Party. The decision will become final and binding unless a notice of dissatisfaction has been given by either Party within 30 days after receiving such decision. This decision may be then referred to arbitration.*
>
> *In the event of one Party disagreeing with the recommendation issued by the DB under the terms of the proceeding clause, such dissatisfied Party may decide, prior to any arbitration proceedings, to refer in a second stage the dispute to a mediation procedure. This mediation procedure will be conducted by two independent mediators. Such reference shall be made in accordance with the conditions set up in appendix YY. The written recommendation of the mediators shall become final and binding upon the Parties, unless a notice of dissatisfaction has been given by either Party within 30 days after receiving such recommendation.*
>
> *In the even that either the DRB procedure or both the DRB and the mediation procedure have failed and that the Parties have complied with the notification deadlines as set up in the previous two paragraphs, all disputes arising out of or in connection with the present contract shall be finally settled under the Rules of Arbitration of the International Chamber of Commerce by one or more arbitrators appointed in accordance with the said Rules*".

84. Communications Protocols

One way for the parties to deal with the legal uncertainties posed by electronic communications is to agree a communications protocol. This protocol should set out what methods of communication should be used in each stage of the procedure. In addition, it could state for each method of communication the standards and specifications to be observed. The protocol would enable the parties to agree the technology used to ensure compatibility, to decide on the level of security to be used and to deal with the issues of authentication and non-repudiation. This section provides a few examples and notes some considerations for the drafting of a Communications Protocol.[82]

A54–129

---

[81] Pierre M. Genton and François Vermeille, "Soft and Hard Arbitration" (1998): *International Business Law*.

[82] See also Richard Hill, "Changing Needs, Changing Rules: How the LCIA 1998 Rules meet Business Needs", in Andrew Berkeley and Jacqueline Mimms (eds), *International Commercial Arbitration: Practical Perspectives* (2001 Centre of Construction Law & Management, Kings College London) ISBN 1 902814-02-9, Annex; see also the Protocol of the Chartered Institute of Arbitrators: Christopher Dancaster, "A Protocol for the Use of Information Technology", 66 *Arbitration* 310-312 (November 2000).

The following procedural steps should be covered:

- Submissions and Supporting Documents
- Informal Communications (*e.g.* to arrange meetings)
- Hearing
- Deliberation between arbitrators (if applicable)
- Form of the award (U.K. law)
- Notification of award

The following methods of communication should be considered: fax, telephone, email, email with Word attachment, online filing, exchange of electronic documents on physical medium (CD-Rom), video or audio-conferencing.

Email (similar considerations may be used for online filing; some of the considerations are relevant for the exchange of documents on CD-Rom)

The parties may send all submissions by email to the other party at the address stated in the Request/Response. Documents sent by email should be attached as files not included within the body of the email. The submission should be attached in [*e.g.* Word for Windows 6.0] word-processing format. The parties agree to use the following software packages [email, spreadsheets, etc.] Email shall be deemed not to have been received until the putative recipient has acknowledged receipt of the email message and this acknowledgement has entered the mailbox of the original sender.[83] [The parties also agree to follow the sending of email by sending the email and any attachments in hard copy paper format by courier or registered mail or sending a CD-Rom or floppy containing the documents by courier or registered mail provided that it is ascertained that the recipient is able to read the file.][All diskettes, CD-Roms shall be clearly labelled with the name of the originator, the intended recipient, its contents, the format and if applicable the name and version of the compression software used.] [The parties agree to implement [BSI protocol BSI PD 0008:1999 and BSI PD 5000:1999] or other security protocols/recording procedures used]. [The parties shall maintain log files indicating the nature, time, length, content and name of the sender/recipient of all emails.][The parties shall identify themselves by using digital signatures [specify technology] [obligation to keep signature creation device or other means of authentication secure]]. [The parties agree to use the following encryption technology [specify]]. The parties shall be under an obligation to protect their computer bases against internal and external security attacks [specify technology]. The parties agree to inform each other without delay of any technical problems. The parties agree to use virus-checking software to check all electronic documents prior to their dispatch stating the anti-virus software and version used [specify]. If an electronic database contains privileged documents it shall be the duty of the recipient to treat them in the like manner as hard copy documents—they must be deleted as soon as it becomes clear that they are privileged documents. Revisions to documents shall be clearly marked as such and any conventions used for amendments should be observed.

Hearings

All documents related to the arbitration will be consolidated onto a single CD-Rom containing all software required to read, display and print the documents using a desktop

---

[83] See Article 14 (3) of the UNCITRAL Model Law on Electronic Commerce 1996.

using Windows 3.1 or later. The CD-Rom shall be sent by registered mail to the parties and the arbitrator [specify software and compression utility].

The parties will be notified of video-conferences and audio-conferences at least three weeks before they are scheduled [specify procedure & technology used: including the use of two cameras? Who will be present? Transcript? Which service provider? How to authenticate the identities of the speakers/witnesses?]. The parties agree to use [facility such as a law firm or arbitration centre]. Specify the technological requirements/compatibility.

ADR CLAUSES

85. Suggested ICC ADR clauses[84]

Optional ADR

"The parties may at any time, without prejudice to any other proceedings, seek to settle any dispute arising out of or in connection with the present contract in accordance with the ICC ADR Rules."

A54–130

Obligation to consider ADR

"In the event of any dispute arising out of or in connection with the present contract, the parties agree in the first instance to discuss and consider submitting the matter to settlement proceedings under the ICC ADR Rules."

Obligation to submit dispute to ADR with an automatic expiration mechanism

"In the event of any dispute arising out of or in connection with the present contract, the parties agree to submit the matter to settlement proceedings under the ICC ADR Rules. If the dispute has not been settled pursuant to the said Rules within 45 days following the filing of a Request for ADR or within such other period as the parties may agree in writing, the parties shall have no further obligations under this paragraph."

Obligation to submit dispute to ADR, followed by ICC arbitration[85] *as required*

"In the event of any dispute arising out of or in connection with the present contract, the parties agree to submit the matter to settlement proceedings under the ICC ADR Rules. If the dispute has not been settled pursuant to the said Rules within 45 days following the filing of a Request for ADR or within such other period as the parties may agree in writing, such dispute shall be finally settled under the Rules of Arbitra-

---

[84] Reproduced with the kind permission of the International Chamber of Commerce. Please also see the International Chamber of Commerce ADR Rules at paras A40-001 to A40-011 of this Volume. The ICC comments: "Four alternative ICC ADR clauses are suggested. They are not model clauses, but suggestions, which parties may adapt to their needs, if required. Their enforceability under the law applicable to the contract should be evaluated".

[85] Please also see the Rules of Arbitration of the International Chamber of Commerce at A39-001 to A39-054 of this Volume.

tion of the International Chamber of Commerce by one or more arbitrators appointed in accordance with the said Rules of Arbitration."

86. ADR clause combined with arbitration clause

A54–131   If any dispute or difference shall arise between the parties to this agreement from or in connection with this agreement or its performance, construction or interpretation, the parties shall endeavour to resolve it by agreement through negotiations [conducted in good faith].[86] If they are unable to agree, the issues shall in the first instance be dealt with by mediation with a mediator to be chosen jointly by them [or to be appointed by ………..]. Both parties reserve all their rights in the event that no agreed resolution shall be reached in the mediation [and neither party shall be deemed precluded from taking such interim formal steps as may be considered necessary to protect such party's position while the mediation or other procedure is pending]. If the dispute has not been resolved by mediation within [28] days of initiation thereof, or such extended period as the parties may agree, the dispute shall be referred to arbitration by a single arbitrator in accordance with the provisions of the Arbitration Act 1996, or any amendment thereto, whose decision in relation to any such dispute or difference shall be final and binding on the parties hereto.

87. Model Contract Clauses—Fast track drafting guide to key dispute resolution clauses[87]

How and why

A54–132   Including in a contract a clause which requires the parties to attempt to settle any dispute arising out of the contract by some form of ADR should increase the chances of settling any such dispute before, or notwithstanding that, the parties resort to court proceedings or arbitration.[88]

In the context of the 1999 Civil Procedure Rules, such a clause may give the parties the chance to pre-empt an order from the court requiring ADR and enable them to conduct any ADR on their own pre-agreed terms.

This document contains a "menu" of ADR contract clauses, with particular focus on mediation, which can be used individually or linked into "multi-step" dispute resolution provisions. The clauses are only model clauses and will need to be selected for, and adapted to, the circumstances and legal requirements of the particular contract.

---

[86] As to the effect of contracting to negotiate "in good faith", see Chap. 5 in Brown & Marriott's *ADR Principles & Practice* under the sub-heading "Good faith in negotiation", with particular reference to the House of Lords decision in *Walford v Miles* [1992] 2 W.L.R 174. However, the position remains to be resolved where the negotiation is expressed to take place within an ADR rather than traditional adversarial context. Arguably, in such event *Walford v Miles* will not be applicable because the parties have specifically agreed to work within a consensual process. There would also seem to be a distinction between conducting negotiations in good faith (importing certain principles of good faith into the substance of the negotiations) and attempting in good faith to arrive at a settlement agreement (which may require no more than a genuine good faith attempt to arrive at a settlement, even if the negotiations are conducted with individual self-interest).

[87] This document is reproduced with the kind permission of the copyright-holders, the Centre for Effective Dispute Resolution (CEDR). The CEDR Model Contract Clauses is one of the many model ADR documents from CEDR which can be found on their website at www.cedr.co.uk.

[88] The authors wish to acknowledge Mediation U.K. for permitting the reproduction of this Code.

Fast track drafting guide

A54–133

Type of clause required	Wording	Comment
Negotiation	See paragraph 1	Typical first stage of multi-step dispute resolution clause
Mediation—'boilerplate' / core wording	If any dispute arises out of this agreement the parties will attempt to settle it by mediation in accordance with the Centre for Effective Dispute Resolution (CEDR) Model Mediation Procedure	See paragraph 2. For optional additional wording see paragraphs 3–4. If part of multi-step dispute resolution clause see wording at end of paragraph 2
Mediation—dealing with disagreements on the mediation agreement	See paragraph 5	
Mediation—with the option of interim court remedies	See paragraph 7.4	For mediation in parallel with court proceedings / arbitration, see paragraphs 7.1 and 7.2
Mediation—obligatory; restriction on terminating the mediation	See paragraph 8	Overrides usual voluntary nature of mediation / paragraph 14 of Model Mediation Procedure
Arbitration—fallback	See paragraph 11	Typical stage of multi-step dispute resolution clause

Wording such as "the parties" and "this agreement" may need to be adapted to the definitions in the contract. Square brackets indicate wording on which a decision needs to be taken, *e.g.* as to how long a period should be specified, or as to whether to include the particular wording at all.

Negotiation

1 *If any dispute arises out of this agreement the parties will attempt to settle it by negotiation.* **A54–134**

[A party may not commence any ADR / court proceedings / an arbitration until [21] days after it has made a written offer to the other party(ies) to negotiate a settlement to the dispute.]

It is unlikely that this provision (even if it includes the second sentence) is legally enforceable (see comments in paragraph 2). It is also unlikely that it is effective in practice if one of the parties has no interest in settling the dispute. The argument for including it is that it provides a credible reason for one party approaching another in circumstances where otherwise that party might be concerned (rightly or wrongly) that such an approach would be interpreted as a sign of weakness.

The purpose of the wording in square brackets is to try and make negotiations obligatory in the sense that it operates as a temporary stay on ADR and court proceedings / arbitration.

A refinement on this is to specify who is to conduct the negotiations, the most usual requirements being that they:

- are of a certain seniority within the organisation; and
- have not previously been closely involved in the relevant matter/previous negotiations on the relevant dispute.

The rationale for these requirements is that those involved in the negotiations should have sufficient authority to settle and are able to be more objective and dispassionate than those who are close to the dispute. Wording along the following lines can be included:

Each of the parties is to be represented by a person who is a [director] or of equivalent executive authority with authority to settle the dispute and has had no direct day-to-day involvement in the relevant matter [and has not been directly involved in any previous negotiations in relation to the relevant dispute].

Mediation

'Boilerplate' / core wording

A54–135   2 *If any dispute arises out of this agreement, the parties will attempt to settle it by mediation in accordance with the Centre for Effective Dispute Resolution (CEDR) Model Mediation Procedure ("the Model Procedure").*

This clause by itself should be sufficient to give the parties the opportunity to attempt to settle any dispute by mediation/an executive tribunal (see paragraph 10). The Model Procedure provides clear guidelines on the conduct of the mediation and requires the parties to enter into an agreement based on the Model Mediation Agreement in relation to its conduct. This will deal with points such as the nature of the dispute, the identity of the mediator and where and when the mediation is to take place. There may however be advantages in including at least some of the optional/additional wording (particularly paragraph 3).

It may be argued that such a clause is an agreement to negotiate in good faith and lacks the necessary certainty to be enforceable. The counter-argument is that an ADR/ mediation clause, if it is sufficiently certain and clear as to the process to be used, is enforceable. The reference in the clause to a model procedure should give it that necessary certainty. Additional certainty would be given by the inclusion of the wording in paragraph 6 below.

This issue may be of little practical relevance. Most model ADR procedures/rules (see, *e.g.* CEDR Model Mediation Procedure paragraph 14) enable a party to terminate a mediation at any time. The concept of mediation being a consensual process can, however, be overridden, either by agreement (see paragraph 8 below) or by court order.

The reason for including an ADR clause is essentially the same for including a negotiation clause (see paragraph 1 above). The advantage, however, of an ADR clause is that:

Precedents and Drafting Suggestions

- it prompts the parties to consider a process which, unlike negotiation, would not necessarily occur to them;
- it introduces a specific process, which gives the parties a framework for exploring settlement; and
- ADR has other advantages over a typical negotiation (see guidance note to Model Procedure).

If paragraph 1 (negotiation) has been included, this wording needs to be revised so as to read:

If the parties are unable to settle any dispute by negotiation [within [21] days] the parties will ....

Optional / additional wording

Triggering / initiating the mediation

3 *To initiate a mediation, a party [by its Managing Director/ ....] must give notice in writing ("ADR notice") to the other party(ies) to the dispute [addressed to its/their respective Managing Director/ ....] requesting a mediation in accordance with clause 2. [A copy of the request should be sent to CEDR Solve.]* **A54–136**

This wording/clause is not essential but is recommended. It sets out what is to be done to initiate the mediation provided for in the core wording. As such, it should make it more straightforward for the parties to get the mediation off the ground. In some cases, that may mean the difference between a mediation and no mediation.

The main agreement may have a provision as to how notices are to be served. If not (or even possibly notwithstanding) there may be an advantage in the ADR notice coming from, and being addressed to, a relatively senior executive.

Copying the notice to CEDR Solve will enable CEDR Solve to start administering the process as quickly as possible, and to provide early advice to the parties where appropriate.

Amendments to Model Procedure

4 *The procedure in the Model Procedure will be amended to take account of:* **A54–137**

- *any relevant provisions in this agreement; or*
- *any other agreement which the parties may enter into in relation to the conduct of the mediation ("Mediation Agreement").*

This wording provides for the Model Procedure to be adapted to:

- any specific wording in the ADR contract clause(s) (see, *e.g.* paragraph 7.1); and
- whatever is agreed in the Mediation Agreement.

Apart from making the position clear, from a legal viewpoint this wording adds further certainty about the process (see commentary on paragraph 2).

Disagreement on Mediation Agreement

A54-138 **5** *If there is any point on the conduct of the mediation (including as to the nomination of the mediator) upon which the parties cannot agree within [14] days from the date of the [ADR notice], CEDR Solve will, at the request of any party, decide that point for the parties, having consulted with them.*

This wording almost mirrors paragraph 5 of the Model Procedure. It provides for a specific time from which CEDR Solve can take decisions and its inclusion in the contract may reinforce the point that mediation is not to be used as a delaying tactic. (The Model Procedure however does not stop a party commencing or continuing court proceedings/ an arbitration.)

This wording should help to speed up the commencement of the mediation by enabling an independent body (*e.g.* CEDR Solve) to decide points upon which the parties cannot agree. It may also, by providing a mechanism to reduce uncertainty as to the process, add weight to the argument that the ADR clause is enforceable (see commentary on paragraph 2).

Timing of mediation

A54-139 **6** *The mediation will start not later than [28] days after the date of the ADR notice.*

This wording is specifically addressed to the concern that any mediation should provide a quick solution. Without the wording in paragraph 5 above, it would in practice be difficult to enforce. The wording in paragraph 5 may, however, by itself be sufficient in that a party could refuse to agree to a late date for the mediation and CEDR Solve is unlikely to decide on a date which involves delay.

The best reason for including such wording may be simply that it evidences an intention that any mediation should happen quickly.

Juxtaposition with litigation / arbitration

Court proceedings in parallel

A54-140 **7.1** *The commencement of a mediation will not prevent the parties commencing or continuing court proceedings/an arbitration.*

Strictly this wording is not necessary as nothing in the mediation wording (paragraph 2) prevents court proceedings. Furthermore paragraph 15 of the Model Procedure states "Any litigation or arbitration .... may be commenced or continued .... unless the parties agree otherwise". The inclusion of this wording in the contract clause may however allay the concerns of a party who wishes to retain the ability to resort to court proceedings.

Mediation in parallel

A54-141 **7.2** *Any party which commences court proceedings/an arbitration must institute a mediation /serve an ADR notice on the other party(ies) to the court proceedings/arbitration within [21] days.*

This wording, which can be used with or without the wording in paragraph 7.1, is to provide for the situation where the parties wish to retain the ability to go to court but want to add force to the agreement to mediate by requiring the plaintiff party to take steps to institute the mediation within a specified time.

The defendant party can in any event initiate the mediation (*e.g.* by serving an ADR notice) at any time.

Unless wording along the lines of paragraph 7.3 (stay of litigation/arbitration) is included, the court proceedings can continue in parallel. If, however, a stay is provided for, then the plaintiff party will still have time to seek interim relief before serving the ADR notice.

Mediation before litigation

7.3 *No party may commence any court proceedings/arbitration in relation to any dispute arising out of this agreement until they have attempted to settle it by mediation and that mediation has terminated.*   **A54–142**

The rationale for this wording is that an ADR contract clause is intended to curtail court proceedings, etc., and that for them to be run in parallel is not conducive to an attempt to settle. The prospects of settlement may be higher before the lines of battle have been drawn by the hostile step of commencing court proceedings/arbitration.

This wording is the "agreement otherwise" in paragraph 15 of the Model Procedure (see commentary on a paragraph 7.1 above). If a party commences court proceedings/arbitration before attempting mediation it would be open to the other party(ies) to seek a stay pending the mediation.

If a party is concerned that the mediation is being used as a tactic to delay the commencement of court proceedings, it can (unless paragraph 8 wording has been included) withdraw from the mediation and thereby terminate it (see paragraph 14 of Model Procedure).

Stay of litigation after interim legal remedies

7.4 *Any party which commences court proceedings must institute a mediation/serve an ADR notice on the other party(ies) within [3] days or as soon as an order for interim relief has been made, whichever is later. The parties will take no further steps in the court proceedings until the mediation has terminated.*   **A54–143**

This clause provides for recourse to court proceedings only in so far as is necessary to obtain interim legal remedies, *e.g.* an interim injunction.

If this wording is not included in the contract clause, the parties can still agree to this course of action when a dispute is referred to mediation.

Specific terms may need to be included in this clause or at the time of the stay about the effect of such a stay on time limits in the litigation/arbitration.

Obligatory mediation—restriction on termination

8 *Neither party may terminate the mediation until each party has made its opening presentation and the mediator has met each party separately for at least [one hour]. Therefore paragraph 14 of the Model Procedure will apply.*   **A54–144**

Paragraph 14 of the Model Procedure states that "Any of the Parties may terminate the [ADR] at any time ....". It would therefore be open to a party to negative the intent of the core wording by withdrawing from the mediation as soon as it starts (see paragraph 2 above). Experience shows, however, that a skilful neutral/mediator may be able to increase the possibilities of a settlement if he/she is given the opportunity. The purpose of this wording is to give that opportunity, albeit to a limited extent, whilst not seriously undermining the intent of paragraph 14.

International contracts

A54–145   9 *The mediation will take place in [city/country of neither/none of the parties] and the language of the mediation will be .... [see Model Procedure guidance notes]. The Mediation Agreement referred to in the Model Procedure shall be governed by, and construed and take effect in accordance with [English] law. The courts of [England] shall have exclusive jurisdiction to settle any claim, dispute or matter of difference which may arise out of, or in connection with, the mediation.*

The model clauses above should be suitable for international contracts (*i.e.* contracts between parties in different jurisdictions) but consideration should be given to including provisions relating to the location and language of the mediation, as well as the governing law and jurisdiction applicable to the mediation agreement, along the lines of this paragraph.

Executive tribunal

A54–146   10 An Executive Tribunal (sometimes called a "mini trial") is essentially a mediation with a more structured opening presentation addressed to a panel comprising a senior executive from each party and a neutral. Appropriate contract clauses can easily be adapted from the wording for mediation clauses. In most cases this will simply involve substituting "executive tribunal" for "mediation".

There may also be consequential amendments to the cross-references to the paragraph numbers in the Model Executive Tribunal Procedure.

Arbitration

A54–147   11 *If the parties have not settled the dispute by the mediation within [42] days from when the mediation was instituted/ the date of the ADR notice, the dispute shall [be referred to, and finally resolved by, arbitration under the Rules of the London Court of International Arbitration/Chartered Institute of Arbitrators/ [relevant arbitral body] which Rules are deemed to be incorporated by reference to this clause.]*

If the parties to the agreement want the ultimate method of resolving a dispute to be arbitration rather than litigation/court proceedings, wording along these lines should be included. If no wording along the lines of paragraphs 7.1 or 7.3 has been included then strictly a straight arbitration clause, without the reference to mediation, would suffice.

The arbitration reference wording used should be the model/recommended wording of the arbitral body to which the reference is to be made (or whose rules are to be used).

If the "core" ADR/mediation clause does not include provision for service of an ADR notice (see paragraph 3 above), the wording should be amended to refer to the "initiation of the mediation" (although there is scope for dispute as to when initiation occurs, which is one reason why the wording in paragraph 3 is recommended).

Litigation

A54–148   12 If the parties to the agreement want the ultimate method of resolving any dispute to be court proceedings, rather than arbitration, there is no need for any additional wording to provide for this (although choice of law and jurisdiction clauses may need to be included).

88. Mediation U.K. Standards for Mediators (general mediation)

Standards for Mediators

Ethical Values:

A54–149
These values underpin all that mediators do when working with parties and in their relationships with other mediators, the mediation service, and other agencies. Reference is made to them in the National Vocational Qualification (NVQ) in Mediation (Community Mediation Evidence Route).

This ethical framework is based on ideals of: fairness, impartiality, justice, integrity, empowerment, trust, peace, excellence, growth and healing.

- People should always be treated with respect and without unfair discrimination.
- People should not be coerced into taking part or staying in the mediation process.
- The anonymity of all parties should be fully protected and confidentiality preserved within the service's published guidelines.
- Mediators should declare any conflict of interest which may put their neutrality into question.
- Mediators should maintain clear boundaries between mediation and other forms of intervention such as advice, counselling and advocacy.
- Mediators should seek to enhance the autonomy of parties and remain impartial regarding the objectives and outcomes of mediation.
- Mediators should treat each party fairly and endeavour to serve the best interests of all parties in conflict.
- Mediators should be aware of their own values and prejudices, and work to challenge discrimination in their own and others' behaviour.
- Mediators should recognise their own limitations regarding competence, values and experience and acknowledge that these could adversely affect their capacity to mediate in some circumstances.
- Mediators should evaluate their own practice regularly and be open to feedback from others.

Principles of Mediation

The Mediation Process: A54–150

- Encourages and maintains the voluntary participation of all parties.

- Encourages the participation and self-determination of all the parties involved so that they retain responsibility for both the content of the conflict and the outcome of the mediation.

- Encourages collaboration and working with people (rather than against them).

- Seeks creative and flexible approaches and solutions, within an ethnic framework.

- Encourages parties to recognise their abilities to work towards mutually acceptable and viable outcomes.

- Offer a structured and challenging approach to conflict resolution.

- Values the resources and skills of the participants and where possible uses and develops them.

- Creates the conditions for openness, participation, collaboration flexibility, tolerance, respect and non-violence.

- Acknowledges the value of "telling the story" (the past) first but encourages movement to focus on a positive outcome for the future.

- Seeks to help parties identify their own and others' feelings and interests, rather than defend positions.

Guidelines for putting Principles into practice
(These practice standards are reflected in the Mediation NVQ)

A54–151 All Mediators must:

- Know and understand the ethical values, principles and practice standards for mediation.

- Know and implement equal opportunity legislation and service policies and know how it relates to mediation.

- Possess the required skills and qualities and maintain them through regular mediation practice.

- Be committed to extending their knowledge of the community context within which they mediate.

- Be willing to take part in regular support and supervision sessions.

- Evaluate their own practice; seeking to up-date their knowledge and understanding; and be willing to develop their skills through further training.

A54–152 **WHEN PREPARING FOR A MEDIATION** mediators should:

- Check that all relevant and appropriate information relating to the proposed mediation has been received.

- Establish a working relationship with their co-mediator.

- Make all appropriate preparation and plans for their first contacts, taking account of access, equal opportunities and safety.

- Make contact with the party(ies) to establish communication, to create the right environment, ensure their understanding of the process and the potential of the mediation service.
- Listen actively and make an initial assessment of the appropriateness of mediation and other possible options for a way forward.
- Agree with parties the conditions and boundaries of mediation, including confidentiality and ways of working.
- Keep the co-ordinator/manager fully informed of progress (or lack of it).
- Plan each subsequent stage with minimum delay.

DURING THE MEDIATION mediators should: A54–153

- Develop interaction with the party(ies), encouraging voluntary participation in the process.
- Establish all the major issues with each party, promoting shared responsibility for the content of the mediation.
- Explore issues with each party, enabling them to express concerns and feelings.
- Facilitate exchanges between parties (face to face or indirectly)—fairly and without personal bias.
- Manage conflict and address power imbalances, recognising cultural differences which may influence the process.
- Help parties to clarify for themselves where their best interests lie.
- Help parties to identify and evaluate potential options for the future.
- Help parties move towards building and agreeing outcomes for themselves which are workable and can be reviewed as appropriate.
- Be confident to bring a session to a close if the above is not achieved.
- Aim to bring a session to a close to the satisfaction of all involved
- Aim for written agreements on outcomes, involving statements which incorporate some element of self-help and co-operation.
- Agree arrangements with parties for follow-up support to be offered by the mediation service.

AFTER THE MEDIATION mediators should: A54–154

- Complete all records to the standard required by the service.
- Review and evaluate the mediation independently, and then with the co-mediator and/or supervisor as appropriate.
- Seek to learn from each experience and plan to improve their practice.
- Maintain complete confidentiality regarding the parties involved in each mediation.

APPENDIX 5

MISCELLANEOUS

Chess Clock Arbitrations—Factors to consider when setting up and running time controls

CHESS CLOCK ARBITRATIONS

These are so called because each party is allocated a specific amount of time for its activities: and the time taken for any particular activity is deducted from the allocation. Theoretically a party can run out of time before its opponent and thus be left helpless to intervene while the opponent continues on. However, despite extensive experience of the procedure, neither of the authors has seen this happen, although it has come close. **A55–001**

The Tribunal must always retain the power to revise the timings, even after they have started to run. However, this is difficult to do without creating actual unfairness or at least an appearance of unfairness. Therefore revision should only be entertained for some very good reason, such as a quite unforeseeable turn of events in the hearing.

The form of the chess clock agreement can be as complicated or as simple as the parties wish. At one end is a simple agreement to split the hearing time equally between the parties. At the other is the complicated procedure set out below. In between there is an infinite number of possibilities.

This commentary will focus on the complicated procedure, since the discussion of these extensive provisions will throw up most of the points that are likely to occur in a less complicated arrangement.

The earlier the issues in the case can be identified and a draft bundle of working documents assembled, the better this type of arbitration works.

It is necessary to begin with some important points that apply to all forms of limited time arbitration and particularly hearings.

1. The primary benefits

1.1 It enables parties to estimate the extent and timing of their liability for costs with greater accuracy than is normally the case. **A55–002**

1.2 Likewise for the Tribunal who may be prepared to quote a lump sum payable in stages.

1.3 It avoids the (potentially very serious) diary problem, generated by overruns of hearings.

1.4 It provides a date at which an award can confidently be expected and permits a commercial organisation to plan its affairs appropriately.

2. Tribunal responsibilities

A55–003   It is essential that the Tribunal understands that a limited time hearing places very great strain on the advocates presenting the case. The Tribunal must conduct itself in such a way as to mitigate rather than aggravate that strain.

The Tribunal must be aware that even not very bright witnesses quickly realise that a long answer puts more pressure on the questioner than a short answer. Accordingly the Tribunal should make clear early on and repeat if necessary the warning that gratuitously long answers may damage credibility. The Tribunal must be prepared to intervene if even this does not work.

3. Recording the time

A55–004   In the case of a hearing that lasts longer than a day the time taken up during a day must be agreed at the end of the day and any dispute ruled on immediately. Each morning the parties should be told by the Tribunal the amount of time each one has left. To facilitate this exercise a particular individual on each side should be invested with the responsibility for noting the time taken and for agreeing it at the end of the day.

When there is to be a timed hearing the sitting hours and break timing must be spelt out and adhered to. Interlocutory disputes should be dealt with outside the appointed sitting hours.

A division of the time available to the parties, leaving them to decide how to use it is, perhaps, fairer than rather arbitrary decisions as to how long one can cross-examine for— *e.g.* the hour and a half for factual witnesses and the day for expert witnesses quoted elsewhere in the text.

4. The directions

A55–005   **4.1** These directions focus on a case with (by most standards) a very long hearing. However, in principle they work equally well for four days or 40: and indeed a very modified form would work for four hours.

They also start after the statement of case. Many such directions apply only to the hearing or hearings. On the other hand, a complete set of directions would include the statement of case and defence and would deal with other matters such as meetings of expert witnesses.

The original drafting work which led to these directions was done for a 90-day hearing in London in 1987. Those involved were Simon Tuckey Q.C.,[1] then instructed by Mr Park of Linklater & Paine; F. Bennett, Esq., and D. Kolkey, Esq.,[2] both of Gibson Dunn and Crutcher; and John Tackaberry. See also the paper given by Dr Robert Briner, "Experiences from the Iran-US Claims Tribunal" (London, 1994) which considers (among other matters) the question of timed hearings and how to operate them.

5. Draft order of directions

A55–006 *Recitals*
Whereas

---

[1] Now Lord Justice Tuckey, a member of the Court of Appeal in London.
[2] Now the Honorable Daniel M. Kolkey, an Associate Justice of the Court of Appeal in California.

5.1 40 working days commencing on [date] have been appointed for the hearing of this matter

40 days is a very long time for a chess clock hearing[3], and many jurisdictions would be horrified by the prospect of such a long hearing. However, as noted above, the directions work as well with a short hearing: and the longer the hearing the more important it is have the control given by this type of direction.

5.2 A period of 40 working days is a reasonable period to dispose of such elements of the claim as justify debate at a full oral hearing

This recital is useful if, in the relevant jurisdiction, there is any doubt about the power of the arbitrator to impose this kind of timescale. It is also useful to discourage later back sliding.

In a long hearing a key aim is to prevent the reinvention of the case of one side the other as matters continue. This can easily happen if one has a lot of good minds inadequately stretched by the proceedings. The reinvention leads to an application to amend. This is justified by the argument that it all sounds in costs and should therefore be allowed. The argument is flawed. It does not all sound in costs if the result is an award on a basis never floated before the hearing. Management time and resources for a company and the strain on an individual are not recoverable from a taxing master. Even more do costs fail to meet the situation if the result of the amendment/s is to force the parties into a further hearing. In a controlled time hearing there is little room for the traditional approach of Anglo-Saxon jurisdictions to amendment of cases.

5.3 In order that the hearing may be effective to dispose of all issues save those as to costs it is necessary to allocate the time available to the parties in a fair and equitable manner

5.4 It is also necessary to make ancillary arrangements to ensure that all matters in dispute can properly be dealt with

These two recitals state the obvious but there is no harm in that.

5.5 The following directions are made in order to achieve the above aims

> NOW I [JOHN ANTONY TACKABERRY] the duly appointed arbitrator in this matter, in the exercise of all relevant powers which I may have whether by operation of law or the agreement of the parties hereto, do DIRECT as follows:

Pre-hearing

5.6 Each party shall deliver to the other party and to each member of the Tribunal the written proof of any witness which it may wish to call

This direction deals with all witnesses—factual and expert.

Very often separate directions are used for the two different types of witness. In that event, the arbitrator should consider, by reference to the formulated cases, whether the expert or the factual evidence is likely to be the more important; and whether the expert evidence is likely to be affected by the factual evidence. If the expert evidence is both more important than and largely independent of the factual evidence, the exchange of that evidence should come first. If the expert evidence may be affected appreciably by the factual evidence, then the latter should come first and sufficiently in front of the expert evidence to afford the experts a good opportunity to consider it before finalizing their evidence. In many other cases the direction above does nicely. See below for experts' meetings.

---

[3] The Directions are in italics to distinguish these from the commentary.

5.7 *Such delivery shall be effected by or before 16.00 hours on [date]*

It is sensible to have a specific time. It is important to have a specific time if the parties are in different time zones. In that event the direction could add "local time at point of delivery" or "local time at seat of arbitration" or "local time at [Chairman]'s office at ....".

5.8 *Such proofs shall not exceed a total of [100,000] words in length*

There is no harm in restricting proofs to a set maximum. It is also worth asking for an index or other guide to long proofs.

The Tribunal should also consider whether documents may or must or must not be annexed to the proof. The suggested course is to get all documents relied upon into or referred to in the initial case formulation. This should reduce the number of new documents appearing at this stage. However more documents are likely to be identified as matters progress. Therefore give liberty to apply for the addition of the new ones.

As noted above, the formulation of a draft bundle a.s.a.p. is important for the smooth running of the arbitration.

5.9 *The delivery of a proof shall not oblige a party to call the witness who made it*

The direction is a straightforward one. What is more difficult to resolve, and has to be resolved straight away, is the status of the proofs prior to the calling of the witnesses. Court systems that call for delivery of proofs prior to calling the witnesses usually regard the proof as privileged until the witness is called. Thus the proof of a witness who is not called is always privileged whatever it says. This is therefore a respectable route that a Tribunal can take. However it can seem very artificial: and it is equally possible to say that the proof once served is to be treated as an open document, to which reference can be made by either party at any time.

It is suggested that this latter course is the more practical and down to earth which is what arbitration should be. It also forces parties to consider carefully what they put in their proofs. Also the less discovery the Tribunal orders, the more it ought to ensure that the parties are committed to their position in the documents that they do produce before the hearing.

A necessary concomitant of this approach is the outlawing of oral evidence in chief. If, on seeing the other side's evidence, or for some other good reason, a party decides it needs more evidence in chief, it should have to apply for leave to introduce it, in writing, at least a set time before the beginning of the hearing.

5.10 *If a party decides not to call as a witness any person whose proof has been delivered that party shall forthwith notify the other party of that decision*

Otherwise the opposing party, who may be relying on potential cross-examination of the particular witness, may be taken by surprise. However, the direction is difficult to police. How will you *know* that the notification is indeed at time of decision? In any case, a formal decision can be put off even though the likely course of conduct is well established. Of course a Tribunal can usually rely on the integrity of the advocates.

There may be an opportunity, depending on the jurisdiction, to invoke the assistance of a court—*e.g.* by *subpoena*—if the liberty given by the direction is used and a party is genuinely taken by surprise. Likewise there is the possibility of evidence on commission.

An alternative direction would be to direct that any witness whose statement is served shall be tendered for cross-examination, if not being otherwise formally called.

5.11 *Each party shall list the documents upon which it proposes to rely or to which it proposes to refer. A copy of such list shall be served upon the other party and upon me by or before 16.00 hours on the [date]*

These directions do not deal with the initial formulation of the case by either or both sides.

This direction does not involve discovery Anglo-Saxon style. The Tribunal must consider the question of documentation very carefully indeed if the case is paperheavy. This direction is the least burdensome variant that can properly be formulated. It probably does not go far enough: and it is suggested that the parties should be at liberty to call for specific documents for whose existence a reasonable case can be made out.

If such documents are called for and not produced, the Tribunal should consider carefully whether it goes down the "peremptory order" route. It may well be preferable simply to draw the most damaging inferences from the non production rather than have a head-on collision with a party about papers that may well be seen as very confidential—e.g. internal management records, profit details, techniques and methods of work or production, etc.

Once documents have been identified and produced, the sooner there is a draft bundle in existence the better. There should be an agreed bundle: and the parties must agree on the method by which it is to be presented to the Tribunal. The Tribunal should insist on this being addressed at an early stage, otherwise there is the small but real danger of each side constructing its bundle differently—e.g. one chronologically and one by topic. This makes the conduct of any hearing very tiresome.

5.12 *The hearing will commence upon [date] and shall continue for 40 working days thereafter. The sitting hours shall be 10.00 to 17.00 each day [with one hour for lunch and a morning and afternoon break of 15 minutes each]*

It is very important that the precise timing upon which the hearing has been planned **A55–010** is very clearly spelt out. Otherwise the parties will not be too clear as to what exactly is available to them. This is made worse if the Tribunal is relaxed about running into the lunch hour, or sitting late to finish a piece of evidence, or sitting early to accommodate someone's schedule. If the basic structure is uncertain such anomalies will provide a fruitful source of friction.

It is also important not to have too long a sitting day. Limited time hearings put a great strain on the presenting advocate: and he or she must have adequate time out of the hearing to rest, to prepare, to consult, to discuss. The continental habit of sitting hours such as 8 a.m. to 6 p.m. or even to 8 p.m. only works in the context of one or two day hearings.

5.13 *Time during the hearing shall be allotted as follows*

(a) *The Claimant shall have a total of 8 working days for its opening and closing speeches, to be allocated as the Claimant sees fit.*

(b) *The Respondent shall have a total of 6 days for any opening statement it may wish to make and for its closing speech.*

This was an old style hearing. Such "speeches" would now usually be in writing before/after the hearing as appropriate. The Tribunal should consider the order of delivery of such written openings and closings. Should they be consecutive or simultaneous? There is a good deal to be said for simultaneous: but if this route is adopted, each party should have a short opportunity for a brief written response to the other side's principal submission/s.

5.14 *The oral evidence time shall be divided into two equal halves—the first half for the presentation of the Claimant's evidence and the second half for the presentation of the Respondent's evidence*

5.15 *Within each such half, and subject to direction 16 below, each party shall have* **A55–011** *a maximum time of 13 days or [ ] working hours available for:*

699

(a) its evidence in chief and re-examination; and

(b) its cross-examination.

Again—an old style direction. Nowadays one would hope not to have any evidence in chief.

5.16 *Each party may deploy each said [ ] hours available to it as it sees fit*

This direction is the simplest one: and Directions 5.17 to 5.21 inclusive can be ignored if it is adopted. However, if the Tribunal or parties desire to have a tight control on all stages of the exercise the following directions can be considered.

5.17 *In the event that presentation of the Claimant's evidence takes less than half the witness time to complete, then the shortfall can be calculated*

5.18 *That shortfall shall be added to the time which would otherwise have been available to the Claimant during the presentation of the Respondent's evidence*

5.19 *In the event that during the presentation of the Respondent's evidence either party takes less than the total time which would in the event have been available to it (i.e. including any shortfall as provided for at Directions 5.17 and 5.18 above) then the saving by that party shall be added to the time available to that party for its closing speech*

5.20 *In the administration and calculation of the matters herein before provided for at Directions 5.16–5.18 inclusive, time reallocated from closing speeches (as hereinafter provided for) shall be wholly ignored*

5.21 *Either party may utilise the time hereinbefore provided for its speech or speeches to supplement the time otherwise available to it (pursuant to Directions 5.13 to 5.19 inclusive above) during the oral evidence stage. Such utilisation may be effected only after the time otherwise available to that party pursuant to the said Directions has been wholly used up*

See above, the comment in Direction 5.13.

Written submissions supplementing or in substitution for closing speeches

A55–012   **5.22** *Such written submissions may or shall be utilised (as the case may be) subject to the following Direction*

5.23 *Either party may deliver a submission in writing in substitution for or supplementing its closing speech. No such submission shall exceed 75,000 words in length. Such delivery shall be to me and to the other party and shall be by or before [16.45] hours on [date]*

No particular comment is necessary. Most such directions have no limit or length. Note the point above in the comment on Direction about simultaneous or consecutive addresses.

Matters ancilllary to the hearing

A55–013   **5.24** *Time taken during the working day, regarding procedural matters (which in any event are to be kept to a minimum and dealt with as far as possible outside the working day) and time taken in the questioning (if any) of witnesses by me at the end of the* *witnesses' testimony are to be allocated equally between the parties. Time taken in the questioning of witnesses by me during their testimony is to be treated as time taken by the party who was questioning the witness immediately prior to my question/s*

There are very few interlocutory matters indeed which HAVE to be dealt with the moment they arise. Nearly all of them can be adjourned until the normal working day hours have expired. What is more advocates should be strongly discouraged from interrupting each other more often than is absolutely essential. If admissibility of evidence is the problem, admit the material *de bene esse* and press on.

Another advantage of taking interlocutory disputes after the main work of the day is over is that, usually, few people will want to make a meal of the matter. Nonetheless it is wise to limit argument to an hour at maximum.

A rather different rule is necessary if the questioning is done by the Tribunal. In such a case it should allocate itself a specific time per witness or per side AND KEEP TO IT.

If the main questioning is done by the parties, the Tribunal should leave its questions right to the end of the re-examination, if there is such a stage; and should afford both sides the opportunity to follow up (but *only* to follow up) the Tribunal's question.

5.25 *A record of time taken by each party shall be kept and agreed at the end of each day. A note of such agreements is to be supplied to me from time to time*

Ensuring this is done each day is critical to the success of the exercise.

5.26 *Failure formally to challenge any evidence shall not be regarded as acceptance of that evidence*

If there is one direction that is essential to a chess-clock hearing it is this one. However it is only necessary at all where the procedural law treats as accepted any evidence that is not specifically challenged.

Such is the rule in England. In commercial matters, particularly paper-heavy matters, it is almost certainly otiose. It is quite out of place where time is limited and the aim is to get the parties to focus on the issues that actually matter.

The direction will also assist a party (and the Tribunal) faced with a situation where huge proofs of evidence are served, which deal at length with matters which appear peripheral to the issues.

Another version of this problem is the witness who is verbose beyond belief under cross-examination and admirably laconic when answering his own side.

A Tribunal should be astute to intervene if this is clearly happening—perhaps by way of polite hints that the time allocation may be challenged if it continues. Meanwhile the direction means that the questioner does not have to follow up the menagerie of hares, red herrings and wild geese started by the witness, or the other side's legal team.

The award

5.27 *My award dealing with all matters remaining in dispute in the reference (save as to any matter of costs) shall be published by or before the [date]*

This is a good discipline for the Tribunal and should be of assistance to the parties. Parties should insist upon it: and upon the Tribunal reserving time to achieve it. Of course such time, if reserved, may give rise to cancellation charges if the matter settles.

5.28 *The said award shall be a reasoned one*

This should be obligatory. It is now under English law, unless the parties agree otherwise. They should not so agree. A reasoned award is a good discipline for the Tribunal and enables the losing parties in particular to understand what happened.

Arbitrators should not be concerned about being appealed. Judges are appealed every day without the self-confidence of the judiciary being much affected—at least to judge by appearances.

5.29 *I may by notice in writing (such notice to be of not less than one calendar month) seek the assistance of the parties on any matter relevant to the said award at any time prior to the [date]*

5.30 *As and when all matters in dispute between the parties (save as to costs) have been finally determined (whether by settlement, award or court decision) either party may give written notice (such notice to be not less than one month) of its intention to seek directions as to the determination of all outstanding issues of costs*

5.31 *The costs of the hearing on [date] and of these Directions shall be costs in the cause. Lest it be relevant. the said hearing was fit for two counsel on each side*

5.32 *There shall be liberty to apply*

Save for direction 5.32 these directions do not need comment. Direction 5.32 does. It is very important to the Tribunal to retain, and to be seen to retain, control of the procedure, even to altering the time allocation half-way through, albeit only in very unusual circumstances.

General

6. Fairness

A55–015   In discussing directions, particularly where there are advocates from different countries and disciplines and even different cultures, the Tribunal should be astute to find a formula or procedure which all involved can see is reasonably fair. Any advocate who makes the leap (as some still do) from what he is used to what the best system is should be firmly reproved.

7. The equal split of hearing time

A55–016   The tendency is always to go for an equal split. This is both easy and looks equitable. However, the Tribunal should keep in mind the following points:

- If one side has to open a case orally, there will be an imbalance which may need correcting (*e.g.* a 3:2 or 7:6 split).
- In a case without an oral opening and without oral evidence in chief, the side that cross-examines first will have the harder task.
- By the time the other side of the case is cross-examining them the Parties and the Tribunal will (or should) be very much more familiar with the issue and the whole thing goes faster.
- A defendant may simply be concentrating on knocking down the claim without raising its own claim. This may be a shorter exercise than establishing the claim.
- It is sensible to keep a day in reserve, unallocated, for emergencies.

The Role of the Courts in Arbitrations

A56–001

Powers of the Court	UNCITRAL Model Law Article	New York Convention 1958	1950 Act, section	1975 Act, section	1979 Act, section	1996 Act section
Staying proceedings in court in order to give effect to an arbitration agreement	8		4(1) 5	1		9 ● 10 ● 11 ● 86 ●
Extension of time for commencement of arbitral proceedings			27			12 ● +
Power to modify limitation period						13●
Setting aside a "default" appointment of a sole arbitrator			7(b) 10(2b)			17 +
Power in support of the constitution of the arbitral tribunal including revocation of an appointment	11(4)		10(1), (2) and (3c) 25			18 +
Power to substitute an umpire for the original members of the tribunal			8(2), (3)			21 +
Power to remove an arbitrator	12–14		13(3) 23 24(1)			24 ● +
Powers consequential upon the resignation of an arbitrator	14					and (4) +
Powers to consider and adjust arbitration fees and expenses						28(2) to (4) ● +
Power to determine any questionas to the substantive jurisdiction of the tribunal		2				32 ● # (+)

Powers of the Court	UNCITRAL Model Law Article	New York Convention 1958	1950 Act, section	1975 Act, section	1979 Act, section	1996 Act section
Power to require a party to comply with a peremptory order made by the tribunal					5	42+ *
Power to secure the attendance of witnesses before the tribunal	27		12(4), (5)			43 ● +
General power in support of the arbitral proceedings	9 27	2	12(6)			44+ *
Power to determine a preliminary point of law					2	45* (+) #
Power to extend the time for the making of the award			13(2)			50+ *
Power to require delivery of a withheld award			19			56 ● +
Powers in connection with the determination of the amount of the recoverable costs of the arbitration and to disputes as to the recoverable costs part of fees and expenses of the tribunal			18(1), (2) 19			63 64*
Powers in connection with the enforcement of the award	35	3 5 6	26(1)			66 ●

704

Powers of the Court	UNCI-TRAL Model Law Article	New York Convention 1958	1950 Act, section	1975 Act, section	1979 Act, section	1996 Act section
Powers in connection with a challenge to an award on the basis of substantive jurisdiction or serious irregularity	16 34	5	22 23			67 + 68 ● +
Power to hear an appeal					1 3	69* (+) #
Powers to order a tribunal to state reasons for its award, to vary, remit or set aside awards or declaring them to be no effect			23(3) 22(2)		1(5), (6) 1(8)	70 # 71 ●
Power in respect of challenge by person taking no part in the arbitral proceedings						72 ●
Power to make orders securing the payment of solicitors' costs						
Powers in relation to service of documents						77+ *
Power to extend time limits within the arbitral proceedings						79* + 79(3) #
Stay of proceedings in the context of a domestic arbitration agreement			4(1)	1(1)		86
Enforcement of New York Convention awards		1		3		101

KEY: • Mandatory provisions under the 1996 Act.
  * Power of the court may be excluded by agreement of the parties.
  + Leave required to set to Court of First Instance.
  # Certificate required for leave to appeal to the Court of Appeal.
  ¡ There are other qualifications which the applicant must satisfy either to make the application or to obtain the order.
  ‡ The application to the court is subject to a threshold requirement of agreement from the other parties or leave to appeal from the court of first instance plus, in most cases, permission from the Tribunal.
  ■ Not in force.

Departmental Advisory Committee on Arbitration Law— Report on the Arbitration Bill

FEBRUARY 1996

MEMBERS OF THE COMMITTEE

The Rt Hon Lord Justice Saville (Chairman)

Professor J. M. Hunter (Deputy Chairman)

Miss C. R. Allen (Secretary)

Mr P. Bovey

Mr A. W. S. Bunch

Mr S. C. Boyd Q.C.

Dr K. G. Chrystie

Lord Dervaird

Mr J. B. Garrett

Professor R. M. Goode CBE, Q.C., FBA

Mr B. Harris

Mrs J. Howe

Mrs P. Kirby-Johnson

Mr R. A MacCrindle Q.C.

Mr A. L. Marriott

Mr K. S. Rokison Q.C.

Mr D. Sarre

Mr J. H. M. Sims

Professor D. R. Thomas

Professor J. Uff Q.C.

Mr V. V. Veeder Q.C.

The DAC has been greatly assisted by the invaluable work done by Mr T. T. Landau of counsel.

Chapter 1

Introduction

A57–002 1. In its Report of June 1989, the Departmental Advisory Committee on Arbitration Law (the DAC), under the chairmanship of Lord Justice Mustill (now Lord Mustill) recommended against England, Wales and Northern Ireland adopting the UNCITRAL Model Law on International Commercial Arbitration. Instead, the DAC recommended that there should be a new and improved Arbitration Act for England, Wales and Northern Ireland, with the following features (Paragraph 108):

> "*(1) It should comprise a statement in statutory form of the more important principles of the English law of arbitration, statutory and (to the extent practicable) common law.*
>
> *(2) It should be limited to those principles whose existence and effect are uncontroversial.*
>
> *(3) It should be set out in a logical order, and expressed in language which is sufficiently clear and free from technicalities to be readily comprehensible to the layman.*
>
> *(4) It should in general apply to domestic and international arbitrations alike, although there may have to be exceptions to take account of treaty obligations.*
>
> *(5) It should not be limited to the subject-matter of the Model Law.*
>
> *(6) It should embody such of our proposals for legislation as have by then been enacted: see paragraph 100 [of the 1989 Report].*
>
> *(7) Consideration should be given to ensuring that any such new statute should, so far as possible, have the same structure and language as the Model Law, so as to enhance its accessibility to those who are familiar with the Model Law.*"

2. In an Interim Report in April 1995, the DAC stated as follows:

> "*The original interpretation of [paragraph 108 of the 1989 Report] led to the draft Bill which was circulated in February 1994. Although undoubtedly a highly skilful piece of work, it now appears that this draft Bill did not carry into effect what most users in fact wanted. In the light of the responses, the view of the DAC is that a new Bill should still be grounded on the objectives set out in [paragraph 108 of the 1989 Report], but that, reinterpreted, what is called for is much more along the lines of a restatement of the law, in clear and 'user-friendly' language, following, as far as possible, the structure and spirit of the Model Law, rather than simply a classic exercise in consolidation.*"

3. The DAC's proposals in the Interim Report led to a new draft Bill which was circulated for public consultation in July 1995. This draft was very much the product of a fresh start. Indeed, it will be noted that whereas the February 1994 draft had the following long-title:

> "To consolidate, with amendments, the Arbitration Act 1950, the Arbitration Act 1975, the Arbitration Act 1979 and related enactments"

this was altered for the July 1995 draft, and now begins:

> "An Act to restate and improve the law relating to arbitration pursuant to an arbitration agreement ..."

4. The DAC remained of the view, for the reasons given in the Mustill Report, that the solution was not the wholesale adoption of the Model Law. However, at every stage in preparing a new draft Bill, very close regard was paid to the Model Law, and it will be seen that both the structure and the content of the July draft Bill, and the final draft, owe much to this model.

5. The task of the Committee has been made far easier by the extraordinary quantity and quality of responses we received both to the draft Bill published in February 1994 and to the draft Bill which was published in July 1995. A large number of people put substantial time and effort into responding to both drafts and putting forward suggestions, and we are very grateful to all of them. Indeed, both these consultation exercises have proved invaluable: the former showed that a new approach was required, while the latter showed that our April 1995 proposals seemed to be on the right track. Both sets of responses also contained carefully considered suggestions, many of which have been incorporated in the Bill. It should be emphasized that those suggestions which have not been adopted were only put on one side after lengthy consideration.

6. Among those who responded were a large number of institutions who offer arbitration services (such as the ICC) or who provide rules and administration for arbitrations concerning their members (such as the commodity associations). Both domestically and internationally institutions such as these play a very significant role in the field of arbitration. It seemed to us that the Bill should specifically recognize this, and that it should safeguard their spheres of operation. Consequently, there are many references to such institutions in the Bill, and, indeed, Clause 74 gives them what we believe to be a necessary degree of immunity from suit.

7. Given the extremely favourable response, the July 1995 draft was taken forward, with certain modifications, to form the basis of the final draft, which is explained in this Report.

8. As well as containing a guide to the provisions of the final draft, this Report also contains supplementary recommendations (in Chapter 6) on certain matters that have come to light since publication of the final draft, and since its second reading in the House of Lords.

Chapter 2

Part I of the Bill

9. The title to this Part is *Arbitration Pursuant to an Arbitration Agreement*. It is in A57–003 this Part that we have attempted to restate within a logical structure the basic principles of our law of arbitration, as it relates to arbitration under an agreement to adopt this form of dispute resolution. The Bill does not purport to provide an exhaustive code on the

subject of arbitration. It would simply not be practicable to attempt to codify the huge body of case law that has built up over the centuries, and there would be a risk of fossilizing the common law (which has the great advantage of being able to adapt to changing circumstances) had we attempted to do so. Rather, we have sought to include what we consider to be the more important common law principles, whilst preserving all others, in so far as they are consistent with the provisions of the Bill (see Clause 81).

10. A small number of key areas, however, have not been included, precisely because they are unsettled, and because they are better left to the common law to evolve. One such example concerns privacy and confidentiality in arbitrations, which deserves special mention here.

11. Privacy and confidentiality have long been assumed as general principles in English commercial arbitration, subject to important exceptions. It is only recently that the English courts have been required to examine both the legal basis for such principles and the breadth of certain of these exceptions, without seriously questioning the existence of the general principles themselves (see *e.g.* The Eastern Saga [1988] 2 Lloyd's Rep. 373, 379 (Leggatt L.J.); *Dolling-Baker v Merrett* [1990] 1 W.L.R. 1205, 1213 (Parker LJ); *Hassneh v Mew* [1993] 2 Lloyd's Rep. 243 (Colman J.); *Hyundai Engineering v Active* (unreported, 9 March 1994, Phillips J.); *Ins Company v Lloyd's Syndicate* [1995] 2 Lloyd's Rep. 272 (Colman J.); *London & Leeds Estates Limited v Parisbas Limited (No. 2)* (1995) E.G. 134 (Mance J.)).

12. In practice, there is also no doubt whatever that users of commercial arbitration in England place much importance on privacy and confidentiality as essential features of English arbitration (*e.g.* see survey of users amongst the "Fortune 500" US corporations conducted for the LCIA by the London Business School in 1992). Indeed, as Sir Patrick Neill Q.C. stated in his 1995 "Bernstein" Lecture, it would be difficult to conceive of any greater threat to the success of English arbitration than the removal of the general principles of confidentiality and privacy.

13. Last year's decision of the High Court of Australia in *Esso/BHP v Plowman* (see [1995] 11 *Arbitration International* 234) reinforced many people's interest in seeking to codify the relevant English legal principles in the draft Arbitration Bill. The implied term as the contractual basis for such principles was not in doubt under English law, and the English Courts were upholding these principles in strong and unequivocal terms. However, the Australian decision was to the effect that, as a matter of Australian law, this contractual approach was unsustainable as regards confidentiality. This has troubled users of commercial arbitration far outside Australia. The first response has been for arbitral institutions to amend their arbitration rules to provide expressly for confidentiality and privacy. The new WIPO Rules have sought to achieve this and we understand that both the ICC and the LCIA are currently amending their respective rules to similar effect.

14. In England, the second response was to consider placing these general principles on a firm statutory basis in the Arbitration Bill. This task was initially undertaken by the DAC mid-1995, and perhaps surprisingly, it soon proved controversial and difficult.

15. Whilst none could reasonably dispute the desirability of placing these general principles beyond all doubt on a firm statutory basis, applicable to all English arbitrations within the scope of the Bill (irrespective of the substantive law applicable to the arbitration agreement), grave difficulties arose over the myriad exceptions to these principles—which are necessarily required for such a statutory provision. There is of course no statutory guidance to confidentiality in the UNCITRAL Model Law whatever; and indeed, in a different context, Lord Mustill has recently warned against an attempt to give in the abstract an accurate exposition of confidentiality at large (see *Re D (Adoption Reports: Confidentiality)* [1995] 3 W.L.R. 483 at 496D: *"To give an accurate exposition* *of confidentiality at large would require a much more wide-ranging survey of the law and practice than has been necessary for a decision on the narrow issue raised by the appeal, and cannot in my opinion safely be attempted in the abstract"*).

16. For English arbitration, the exceptions to confidentiality are manifestly legion and unsettled in part; and equally, there are important exceptions to privacy (*e.g.* in *The Lena Goldfields Case* (1930), the arbitration tribunal in London opened the hearing to the press (but not the public) in order to defend the proceedings against malicious charges made by one of the parties, the USSR). As to the former, the award may become public in legal proceedings under the Arbitration Acts 1950–1979 or abroad under the 1958 New York Convention; the conduct of the arbitration may also become public if subjected to judicial scrutiny within or without England; and most importantly, several non-parties have legitimate interests in being informed as to the content of a pending arbitration, even short of an award: *e.g.* parent company, insurer, P+I Club, guarantor, partner, beneficiary, licensor and licensee, debenture-holder, creditors' committee etc., and of course even the arbitral institution itself (such as the ICC Court members approving the draft award). Whilst non-parties to the arbitration agreement and proceedings, none of these are officious strangers to the arbitration. Further, any provisions as to privacy and confidentiality would have to deal with the duty of a company to make disclosure of, *e.g.*, arbitration proceedings and actual or potential awards which have an effect on the company's financial position. The further Australian decision in *Commonwealth of Australia v Cockatoo Dockyard Pty Ltd* (1995) 36 NSWLR 662 suggests that the public interest may also demand transparency as an exception to confidentiality: "*Can it be seriously suggested that [the parties'] private agreement can, endorsed by a procedural direction of an arbitrator, exclude from the public domain matters of legitimate concern ...*" per Kirby J. This decision raises fresh complications, particularly for statutory corporations. We are of the view that it would be extremely harmful to English arbitration if any statutory statement of general principles in this area impeded the commercial good-sense of current practices in English arbitration.

17. Given these exceptions and qualifications, the formulation of any statutory principles would be likely to create new impediments to the practice of English arbitration and, in particular, to add to English litigation on the issue. Far from solving a difficulty, the DAC was firmly of the view that it would create new ones. Indeed, even if acceptable statutory guidelines could be formulated, there would remain the difficulty of fixing and enforcing sanctions for non-compliance. The position is not wholly satisfactory. However, none doubt at English law the existence of the general principles of confidentiality and privacy (though there is not unanimity as to their desirability). Where desirable, institutional rules can stipulate for these general principles, even where the arbitration agreement is not governed by English law. As to English law itself, whilst the breadth and existence of certain exceptions remains disputed, these can be resolved by the English courts on a pragmatic case-by-case basis. In due course, if the whole matter were ever to become judicially resolved, it would remain possible to add a statutory provision by way of amendment to the Bill. For these reasons, the DAC is of the view that no attempt should be made to codify English law on the privacy and confidentiality of English arbitration in the Bill. We would, however, draw attention to our supplementary recommendations on this topic in Chapter 6 below.

Clause 1. General Principles

18. The DAC was persuaded by the significant number of submissions which called for an introductory clause setting out basic principles. This Clause sets out three general

A57–004

principles. The first of these reflects what we believe to be the object of arbitration. We have not sought to define arbitration, since this poses difficulties that we discussed in our April 1995 Interim Report, and in the end we were not persuaded that an attempted definition would serve any useful purpose. We do, however, see value in setting out the object of arbitration. Fairness, impartiality and the avoidance of unnecessary delay or expense are all aspects of justice ie all requirements of a dispute resolution system based on obtaining a binding decision from a third party on the matters at issue. To our minds it is useful to stipulate that all the provisions of the Bill must be read with this object of arbitration in mind.

19. The second principle is that of party autonomy. This reflects the basis of the Model Law and indeed much of our own present law. An arbitration under an arbitration agreement is a consensual process. The parties have agreed to resolve their disputes by their own chosen means. Unless the public interest otherwise dictates, this has two main consequences. Firstly, the parties should be held to their agreement and secondly, it should in the first instance be for the parties to decide how their arbitration should be conducted. In some cases, of course, the public interest will make inroads on complete party autonomy, in much the same way as there are limitations on freedom of contract. Some matters are simply not susceptible of this form of dispute resolution (eg certain cases concerning status or many family matters) while other considerations (such as consumer protection) may require the imposition of different rights and obligations. Again, as appears from the mandatory provisions of the Bill, there are some rules that cannot be overridden by parties who have agreed to use arbitration. In general the mandatory provisions are there in order to support and assist the arbitral process and the stated object of arbitration.

20. So far as the third principle is concerned this reflects Article 5 of the Model Law. This Article provides as follows:—

"In matters governed by this Law, no court shall intervene except where so provided in this Law."

21. As was pointed out in the Mustill Report (pp. 50–52) there would be difficulties in importing this Article as it stands. However, there is no doubt that our law has been subject to international criticism that the Courts intervene more than they should in the arbitral process, thereby tending to frustrate the choice the parties have made to use arbitration rather than litigation as the means for resolving their disputes.

22. Nowadays the Courts are much less inclined to intervene in the arbitral process than used to be the case. The limitation on the right of appeal to the Courts from awards brought into effect by the Arbitration Act 1979, and changing attitudes generally, have meant that the Courts nowadays generally only intervene in order to support rather than displace the arbitral process. We are very much in favour of this modern approach and it seems to us that it should be enshrined as a principle in the Bill.

Clause 2. Scope of Application of Provisions

A57–005 **23.** International arbitrations can give rise to complex problems in the conflict of laws. A possible solution to some of these problems would have been to provide that all arbitrations conducted in England and Wales or in Northern Ireland should be subject to the provisions of the Bill, regardless of the parties' express or implied choice of some other system of law. We have not adopted this solution, which appears to us contrary to the basic principle that the parties should be free to agree how their disputes should be resolved. There appear to us to be no reasons of public policy to prevent the parties conducting an arbitration here under an agreement governed by foreign law or in accordance with a foreign procedural law. Clause 4(5) also follows the same basic principle. Of course, cases may well arise where considerations of our own concepts of public policy would lead to the refusal of the Court here to enforce an arbitration award. This, however, is covered by Clause 66(3).

24. The rules of the conflict of laws as they apply to arbitration are complex, and to some extent still in a state of development by the courts. It therefore seems to us inappropriate to attempt to codify the relevant principles, beyond the simple statements set out in clause 2(1). Thus, as clause 2(2) provides, matters referable to the arbitration agreement are governed by the law of England and Wales or of Northern Ireland, as the case may be, where that is the law applicable to the arbitration agreement, and matters of procedure are governed by that law where the seat of the arbitration is in England and Wales or in Northern Ireland: "seat" is defined in Clause 3. Beyond that we have not attempted to state the relevant rules of the conflict of laws, nor to embark on the issues of characterisation by which they are invoked.

25. Sub section (3) concerns the powers of the court to support the arbitration by staying proceedings brought in breach of an agreement to arbitrate, by compelling the attendance of witnesses, by granting those forms of interim relief which are set out in Clause 44, and by enforcing the award at common law by summary procedure. Such powers should obviously be available regardless of whether the seat of the arbitration is in England and Wales or in Northern Ireland, and regardless of what law is applicable to the arbitration agreement or the arbitral proceedings. Since we have used the expression "*whatever the law applicable . . . .*", it follows that Clause 2(3) is in no way restricted by Clause 2(1). It will be noted that in extending the power of the court to grant interim relief in support of arbitrations to arbitrations having a foreign seat we have given effect to our recommendation that section 25 of the Civil Jurisdiction and Judgments Act 1982 should be extended to arbitration proceedings. It should be appreciated that Rules of Court will have to be amended to give proper effect to the extension of the Court's jurisdiction in Clause 2(3) (*i.e.* so as to allow service out of the jurisdiction in cases where it is necessary). Sub-section (4) enables the court to refuse to exercise its power in such cases, where the fact that the arbitration has a foreign seat makes it inappropriate to exercise that power.

Clause 3. The seat of the arbitration

26. The definition of "*seat of the arbitration*" is required by Clause 2, and as part of the definition of "*domestic arbitration*" in Clause 85. The concept of the "seat" as the juridical seat of the arbitration is known to English law but may be unfamiliar to some users of arbitration. Usually it will be the place where the arbitration is actually conducted: but this is not necessarily so, particularly if different parts of the proceedings are held in different countries.

27. In accordance with the principle of party autonomy, Clause 3 provides that the seat may be designated by the parties themselves or in some other manner authorised by them. Failing that it must be determined objectively having regard to the parties' agreement and all other relevant circumstances. English law does not at present recognise the

concept of an arbitration which has no seat, and we do not recommend that it should do so. The powers of the court where the seat is in England and Wales or in Northern Ireland are limited to those necessary to carry into effect the principles enshrined in clause 1. Where the seat is elsewhere, the court's powers are further limited by Clause 2(4). The process of consultation identified no need for an arbitration which was "delocalised" to a greater extent than this.

Clause 4. Mandatory and Non-mandatory Provisions

A57–008   28. This provision is designed to make clear that the Bill has certain provisions that cannot be overridden by the parties; and for ease of reference these are listed in Schedule 1 to the Bill. The Clause also makes clear that the other provisions of this Part can be changed or substituted by the parties, and exist as "fall-back" rules that will apply if the parties do not make any such change or substitution, or do not provide for the particular matter in question. In this way, in the absence of any other contrary agreement, gaps in an arbitration agreement will be filled.

29. Sub-section (5). Although we believe that the choice of a foreign law would anyway have the effect set out in this provision, it seemed for the sake of clarity to be useful to state this expressly, so as to remind all concerned that a choice of a foreign law does amount to an agreement of the parties to which due regard should be paid.

30. It should be made clear that the phrase "*mandatory*" is not used in either of the two senses that it is used, for example, in Articles 3 and 7 of the Rome Convention (see Goode *Commercial Law*, 2nd Ed, at 1118): the mandatory provisions of Part 1 of the Bill are only mandatory in so far as the provisions of Part 1 apply (*i.e.* by virtue of Clause 2). The mandatory provisions would have no application if Part 1 does not apply.

Clause 5. Agreements to be in writing

(a) Arbitration Agreements

A57–009   31. Article 7 of the Model Law requires the arbitration agreement to be in writing. We have not followed the precise wording of this Article, for the reasons given in the Mustill Report (p. 52), though we have incorporated much of that Article in the Bill.

32. The requirement for the arbitration agreement to be in writing is the position at present under Section 32 of the Arbitration Act 1950 and Section 7 of the Arbitration Act 1975. If an arbitration agreement is not in writing then it is not completely ineffective, since the common law recognizes such agreements and is saved by Clause 81(2)(a).

33. We remain of the view expressed in the Consultative Paper issued with the draft Clauses published in July 1995, that there should be a requirement for writing. An arbitration agreement has the important effect of contracting out of the right to go to the court ie it deprives the parties of that basic right. To our minds an agreement of such importance should be in some written form. Furthermore the need for such form should help to reduce disputes as to whether or not an arbitration agreement was made and as to its terms.

34. We have, however, provided a very wide meaning to the words "*in writing*." Indeed this meaning is wider than that found in the Model Law, but in our view, is consonant with Article II.2 of the English text of the New York Convention. The non-

exhaustive definition in the English text ("*shall include*") may differ in this respect from the French and Spanish texts, but the English text is equally authentic under Article XVI of the New York Convention itself, and also accords with the Russian authentic text ("$$$"); see also the 1989 Report of the Swiss Institute of Comparative Law on Jurisdictional Problems in International Commercial Arbitration (by Adam Samuel), at pages 81 to 85. It seems to us that English Law as it stands more than justifies this wide meaning; see, for example, *Zambia Steel v James Clark* [1986] 2 Lloyd's Rep. 225. In view of rapidly evolving methods of recording we have made clear that "*writing*" includes recording by any means.

(b) Other agreements

35. These we have also made subject to a "writing" requirement. Had we not done so, we could envisage disputes over whether, for example, something the parties had agreed to during the conduct of the arbitration amounted to a variation of the arbitration agreement and required writing, or could be characterized as something else. By introducing some formality with respect to all agreements, the possibility of subsequent disputes (*e.g.* at the enforcement stage) is greatly diminished. Indeed it seemed to us that with the extremely broad definition we have given to writing, the advantages of requiring some record of what was agreed with regard to any aspect of an arbitration outweighed the disadvantages of requiring a specific form for an effective agreement.

A57–010

(c) Further points

36. Sub-section 5(3). This is designed to cover, amongst other things, extremely common situations such as salvage operations, where parties make an oral agreement which incorporates by reference the terms of a written form of agreement (*e.g.* Lloyd's Open Form), which contains an arbitration clause. Whilst greatly extending the definition of "writing", the DAC is of the view that given the frequency and importance of such activity, it was essential that it be provided for in the Bill. The reference could be to a written agreement containing an arbitration clause, or to a set of written arbitration rules, or to an individual written arbitration agreement. This provision would also cover agreement by conduct. For example, party A may agree to buy from party B a quantity of goods on certain terms and conditions (which include an arbitration clause) which are set out in writing and sent to party B, with a request that he sign and return the order form. If, which is by no means uncommon, party B fails to sign the order form, or send any document in response to the order, but manufactures and delivers the goods in accordance with the contract to party A, who pays for them in accordance with the contract, this could constitute an agreement "*otherwise than in writing by reference to terms which are in writing ...*", and could therefore include an effective arbitration agreement. The provision therefore seeks to meet the criticisms that have been made of Article 7(2) of the Model Law in this regard (see *e.g.* the Sixth Goff Lecture, delivered by Neil Kaplan QC in Hong Kong in November 1995, (1996) 12 *Arb. Int.* 35). A written agreement made by reference to separate written terms would, of course, be caught by Clause 5(2).

A57–011

37. Sub-section 5(4). There has been some concern that a writing requirement with respect to every agreement might unduly constrain the parties' freedom and flexibility with respect to, for example, minor matters of procedure during a hearing. This sub-section seeks to avoid this. An agreement will be evidenced in writing if recorded by, amongst others, a third party with the authority of the parties to the agreement. Given that this third party could of course be the tribunal, the parties are free during a hearing

to make whatever arrangements or changes to the agreed procedure they wish, as long as these are recorded by the tribunal. The DAC is of the view that this presents no serious hindrance to the parties' flexibility, and has the merit of reducing the risk of disputes later on as to what exactly was agreed. Clearly, this sub-section also has a wider effect, allowing for the recording of an oral agreement at stage.

38. Sub-section 5(5). This provision is based on Article 7(2) of the Model Law, but with certain important changes. The DAC has been careful to emphasize that for there to be an effective arbitration agreement for the purposes of this Part, it is not enough for one party to allege in a written submission that there is an arbitration agreement, in circumstances where the other party simply fails to respond at all. If this were enough, an unfair obligation would be placed on any party (including a stranger to the proceedings in question) to take the active step of serving a written submission in order to deny this allegation. Therefore, in order to satisfy this sub-section, there must be a failure to deny an allegation by a party who has submitted a response submission.

39. It has been suggested that the term *"written submissions"* is too narrow, and that this should be replaced by *"documents"*. The DAC does not agree with this, given that this would include the most informal of letters. It may well be unjust, for example, for one party to be able to point to one sentence in one letter in a long exchange with another party, in which there is an allegation that there exists an arbitration clause, and where this has not been denied.

40. Reference should also be made to sub-section 23(4). Whilst any agreement as to an arbitration must be in writing, the DAC is of the view that it is impracticable to impose a writing requirement on an agreement to terminate an arbitration. Parties may well simply walk away from proceedings, or allow the proceedings to lapse, and it could be extremely unfair if one party were allowed to rely upon an absence of writing at some future stage. Where a Claimant allows an arbitration to lapse, Clause 41(3) may be utilised.

The Arbitration Agreement

Clause 6. Definition of Arbitration Agreement

A57–012 **41.** The first sub-section reflects Article 7(1) of the Model Law and provides a more informative definition than that in Section 32 of the 1950 Act. We have used the word *"disputes"* but this is defined in Clause 82 as including *"differences"* since there is some authority for the proposition that the latter term is wider than the former; see *Sykes v Fine Fare Ltd* [1967] 1 Lloyd's Rep. 53.

42. The second sub-section reflects Article 7(2) of the Model Law. In English law there is at present some conflicting authority on the question as to what is required for the effective incorporation of an arbitration clause by reference. Some of those responding to the July 1995 draft Clauses made critical comments of the views of Sir John Megaw in *Aughton v M F Kent Services* [1991] 57 BLR 1 (a construction contract case) and suggested that we should take the opportunity of making clear that the law was as stated in the charter party cases and as summarized by Ralph Gibson LJ in *Aughton*. (Similar disquiet has been expressed about decisions following *Aughton*, such as *Ben Barrett v Henry Boot Management Ltd* [1995] Constr. Ind. Law Letter 1026). It seemed to us, however, that although we are of the view that the approach of Ralph Gibson LJ should prevail in all cases, this was really a matter for the Court to decide. The wording we have used certainly leaves room for the adoption of the charter party rules in all cases, since it refers to references to a document containing an arbitration clause as well as a reference to the arbitration clause itself. Thus the wording is not confined to cases where there is specific reference to the arbitration clause, which Sir John Megaw (but not Ralph Gibson LJ) considered was a requirement for effective incorporation by reference.

Clause 7. Separability of Arbitration Agreement

43. This Clause sets out the principle of separability which is already part of English law (see *Harbour Assurance v Kansa* [1993] QB 701), which is also to be found in Article 16(1) of the Model Law, and which is regarded internationally as highly desirable. However, it seems to us that the doctrine of separability is quite distinct from the question of the degree to which the tribunal is entitled to rule on its own jurisdiction, so that, unlike the Model Law, we have dealt with the latter elsewhere in the Bill (Clause 30).

44. In the draft Clauses published in July 1995 we inserted a provision to make clear that the doctrine of separability did not affect the question whether an assignment of rights under the substantive agreement carried with it the right or obligation to submit to arbitration in accordance with the arbitration agreement. This is now omitted as being unnecessary, since we have re-drafted sub-section (1) in order to follow the relevant part of Article 16 of the Model Law more closely, and to make clear that the doctrine of separability is confined to the effect of invalidity etc of the main contract on the arbitration agreement, rather than being, as it was in the July 1995 draft, a free-standing principle. Similarly, in being so restricted, this Clause is not intended to have any impact on the incorporation of an arbitration clause from one document or contract into another (which is addressed in Clause 6(2)).

45. A number of those responding to our drafts expressed the wish for the Bill to lay down rules relating to assignment, *e.g.* that the assignment of rights under the substantive agreement should be subject to any right or obligation to submit to arbitration in accordance with the arbitration agreement unless either of these agreements provided otherwise. Indeed we included such a provision in the illustrative draft published in April 1995. However, on further consideration, we concluded that it would not be appropriate to seek to lay down any such rules.

46. There were two principal reasons for reaching this view.

> i. In the first place, under English law the assignability of a contractual right is governed by the proper law of that right, while the effectiveness of the assignment is governed by the proper law of the assignment. However, where the law governing the substantive agreement (or the arbitration agreement) is not English law, different rules may well apply and there is an added problem in that those rules (under the foreign law in question) may be categorized as either substantive or procedural in nature. The Bill would therefore have to address such problems whilst simultaneously not interfering with substantive rights and obligations. We were not persuaded that it would be either practicable or of any real use to attempt to devise general rules which would deal satisfactorily with this matter.
>
> ii. In the second place, English law distinguishes between legal and equitable assignments, so that any rules we devised would have to take this into account.

A57–013

In our view, an attempt to devise rules relating to assignments where no foreign law elements are involved is more the subject of reform of the law of assignment generally than of a Bill relating exclusively to arbitration.

47. Finally, it should be noted that the substantive agreement of which the arbitration agreement forms part need not itself be in writing for the Bill to apply, provided of course that the arbitration agreement itself is in writing. This should be clarified as we suggest in our supplementary recommendations in Chapter 6 below.

Clause 8. Whether Agreement discharged by Death of a Party

A57–014   **48.** This Clause sets out the present statutory position. The common law was that an arbitration agreement was discharged by the death of a party. That rule was altered by the Arbitration Act 1934 as re-enacted by Section 2 of the Arbitration Act 1950. We have avoided using the technical expression "right of action" which is to be found in Section 2(3) of the 1950 Act and which could perhaps give rise to problems for the reasons given in the consultative paper published with the draft Clauses in July 1995. In line with party autonomy, we have provided that the parties can agree that death shall have the effect of discharging the arbitration agreement.

49. This Clause deals only with the arbitration agreement. The effect of the death of a party on the appointment of an arbitrator (also to be found in Section 2 of the 1950 Act) is now dealt with in that part of the Bill concerned with the arbitral tribunal (see Clause 26(2)).

STAY OF LEGAL PROCEEDINGS

Clause 9. Stay of Legal Proceedings

A57–015   **50.** We have proposed a number of changes to the present statutory position (section 4(1) of the 1950 Act and section 1 of the 1975 Act), having in mind Article 8 of the Model Law, our treaty obligations, and other considerations.

51. We have made it clear that a stay can be sought of a counterclaim as well as a claim. The existing legislation could be said not to cover counterclaims, since it required the party seeking a stay first to enter an "*appearance*", which a defendant to counterclaim could not do. Indeed, "*appearance*" is no longer the appropriate expression in the High Court in any event, and never was the appropriate expression in the county court. We have also made clear that an application can be made to stay part of legal proceedings, where other parts are not subject to an agreement to arbitrate.

52. Further, the Clause provides that an application is only to be made by a party against whom legal proceedings are brought (as opposed to any other party).

53. We have provided that an application may be made for a stay even where the matter cannot be referred to arbitration immediately, because the parties have agreed first to use other dispute resolution procedures. This reflects *dicta* of Lord Mustill *Channel Tunnel v Balfour Beatty* [1993] A.C. 334.

54. In this Clause we have made a stay mandatory unless the Court is satisfied that the arbitration agreement is null and void, inoperative, or incapable of being performed. This is the language of the Model Law and of course of the New York Convention on the Recognition and Enforcement of Foreign Arbitral Awards, presently to be found in the Arbitration Act 1975.

55. The Arbitration Act 1975 contained a further ground for refusing a stay, namely where the Court was satisfied that "*there was not in fact any dispute between the parties with regard to the matter agreed to be referred.*" These words do not appear in the New York Convention and in our view are confusing and unnecessary, for the reasons given in *Hayter v Nelson* [1990] 2 Lloyd's Rep. 265.

56. In Part II of the Bill these provisions are altered in cases of "*domestic arbitration agreements*" as there defined.

57. We have included a provision (sub-section (5)) that where the Court refuses to stay the legal proceedings, any term making an award a condition precedent to the bringing of legal proceedings (known as a *Scott v Avery* clause) will cease to have effect. This avoids a situation where the arbitration clause is unworkable, yet no legal proceedings can be successfully brought. Whilst one respondent suggested that this may go too far, it appears to be a matter of basic justice that a situation in which a party can neither arbitrate nor litigate must be avoided.

Clause 10. Reference of Interpleader Issue to Arbitration

58. This Clause is based on Section 5 of the 1950 Act. We have however taken the opportunity of making a stay mandatory so as to comply with the New York Convention, as well as trying to express the provision in simpler, clearer terms. The Clause is required because 'interpleader' arises where one party claiming no right himself in the subject matter, is facing conflicting claims from other parties and does not know to which of them he should account. English law allows such a party to bring those in contention before the Court which may order the latter to fight out the question between themselves. If they have agreed to arbitrate the matter then Clause 9 would not itself operate, since the party seeking interpleader relief would not be making a claim which he had agreed to arbitrate.

A57–016

59. We have not defined "*interpleader*", although some suggested that we should, given that this is a legal term of art, which goes far beyond arbitration contexts.

Clause 11. Retention of Security where Admiralty Proceedings stayed

60. This Clause is not intended to do more than re-enact the present statutory position as found in Section 26 of the Civil Jurisdiction and Judgments Act 1982.

A57–017

61. Clauses 9 to 11 are, of course, mandatory.

COMMENCEMENT OF ARBITRAL PROCEEDINGS

Clause 12. Power of Court to extend Time for beginning Arbitral Proceedings etc.

A57–018   62. We have proposed a number of changes to the existing law.

63. The major change concerns the test that the Court must apply before extending the time.

64. The power of the Court to extend a contractual time limit which would otherwise bar the claim first appeared in our law in Section 16(6) of the Arbitration Act 1934, which was re-enacted in Section 27 of the Arbitration Act 1950.

65. From paragraph 33 of the Report of the MacKinnon Committee presented to Parliament in March 1927 it can be seen that the reason for suggesting that the Court should have power to extend the time was that the vast majority of submissions to arbitration are contained in printed forms of contract, which cannot be carefully examined in the transaction of business and alteration of which it would be difficult for most people to secure. The Committee concluded that it might be sound policy to create a power to modify unconscionable provisions as regards common forms of submission in printed forms. It is also clear from Paragraph 34 of the Report that the Committee had in mind cases where the time limit was very short *i.e.* measured in days. The Committee suggested that the test should be whether the time limit created an "unreasonable hardship".

66. As can be seen from the Notes on Clauses to the 1934 Act, it was later felt that since the justification for giving the power was presumably either ignorance of the existence of the provision in the contract, or the acceptance of the provision through undue pressure by the other party, which could be the case whether or not the contract was in a common form, the power should not be limited to such forms.

67. Section 27 of the 1950 Act, with its test of undue hardship, seems to many to have been interpreted by the Courts in a way hardly envisaged by those who suggested the power in the first place. Indeed that interpretation seems to have changed over the years: see the discussion in Mustill and Boyd, *Commercial Arbitration*, 2nd Ed., pp. 201–215. Some responses indicated dissatisfaction with the way the Courts were using Clause 27 to interfere with the bargain that the parties had made. The present legal position would seem to owe much to a time, now some 20 years ago, when the Courts were flirting with the idea that they enjoyed some general power of supervisory jurisdiction over arbitrations.

68. The justification for time limits is that they enable commercial concerns (and indeed others) to draw a line beneath transactions at a much earlier stage than ordinary limitation provisions would allow. It should be mentioned, however, that other responses suggested that the position presently reached by the Courts should be maintained.

69. The present Committee re-examined Section 27 in the light of the underlying philosophy of the Bill, namely that of party autonomy. This underlying philosophy seems to have been generally welcomed in this country and abroad and of course it fits with the general international understanding of arbitration. Party autonomy means, among other things, that any power given to the Court to override the bargain that the parties have made must be fully justified. The idea that the Court has some general supervisory jurisdiction over arbitrations has been abandoned.

70. It seemed to us in today's climate that there were three cases where the power could be justified in the context of agreed time limits to bring a claim. These are, firstly,

where the circumstances are such as were outside the reasonable contemplation of the parties when they agreed the provision in question and that it would be fair to extend the time, secondly, where the conduct of one party made it unjust to hold the other to the time limit, and thirdly, where the respective bargaining position of the parties was such that it would again be unfair to hold one of them to the time limit.

71. The third of these cases seems to us to reflect the thinking of the MacKinnon Committee, while the other two have developed through the Courts' interpretation of Section 27. However this third category is really an aspect of what nowadays would be called "consumer protection". This part of the Bill is not concerned with consumer protection, for which provision is made elsewhere and in respect of which there is a growing body of European law.

72. In these circumstances it seemed to us to be appropriate to set out in this part of the Bill the first and second of the cases we have described. Apart from anything else, this will give the Courts the opportunity to reconsider how to proceed in the light of the philosophy underlying the Bill as a whole, namely that of party autonomy. As the Mac-Kinnon Committee itself intimated, great care must be taken before interfering with the bargain that the parties have made.

73. It was suggested to the DAC that the principal matter to be taken into account by the court should be the length of the contractual period in question. The DAC is of the view that this is only one of several relevant matters, another factor being, for example, the contemplation of the parties. For this reason, the DAC concluded that a simple test of *"substantial injustice"*, without more, would not suffice.

74. There are some other changes.

  i. Firstly, Clause 12(1)(b) contains a reference to other dispute resolution procedures. We understand that there is an increasing use of provisions which call for mediation and other alternative dispute resolution procedures to precede recourse to arbitration, so that we thought it proper to add this to the other step covered by the Clause, namely to begin arbitral proceedings. We do not intend to widen the scope of the Clause beyond this, so that unless the step in question is one of the two kinds described, the Clause will not operate. Thus this represents only a small but we think logical extension to the present law.

  ii. Secondly, it is made a pre-condition that the party concerned first exhausts any available arbitral process for obtaining an extension of time. In the view of the Committee it would be a rare case indeed where the Court extended the time in circumstances where there was such a process which had not resulted in an extension, for it would in the ordinary case be difficult if not impossible to persuade the Court that it would be just to extend the time or unjust not to do so, where by an arbitral process to which *ex hypothesi* the applying party had agreed, the opposite conclusion had been reached.

  iii. Thirdly, we have made any appeal from a decision of the Court under this Clause subject to the leave of that Court. It seems to us that there should be this limitation, and that in the absence of some important question of principle, leave should not generally be granted. We take the same view in respect of the other cases in the Bill where we propose that an appeal requires the leave of the Court.

iv. Fourthly, whereas the existing statutory provision refers to terms of an agreement that provide that claims shall be "*barred*", this has been extended to read "*barred, or the claimant's right extinguished*".

75. For obvious reasons, this Clause is mandatory.

Clauses 13 and 14. Application of Limitation Acts and Commencement of Arbitral Proceedings

A57–019   **76.** The first of these provisions is designed to restate the present law. The reference to the Foreign Limitation Periods Act 1984 avoids (subject to the provisions of that Act) the imposition of an English limitation period where an applicable foreign law imposes a different period. The second provision reflects to a degree Article 21 of the Model Law, but sets out the various cases, including one not presently covered by the law. It will be noted that we have used the word "*matter*" rather than the word "*disputes.*" This is to reflect the fact that a dispute is not the same as a claim; *c.f. Mustill and Boyd, op.cit.* at p. 29 and *Commission for the New Towns v Crudens* (1995) CILL 1035. The neutral word "*matter*" will cover both, so that an arbitration clause which refers to claims will be covered as well as one which refers to disputes.

77. Clause 13 is a mandatory provision.

THE ARBITRAL TRIBUNAL

Clause 15. The Arbitral Tribunal

A57–020   **78.** Article 10(1) of the Model Law provides that the parties are free to determine the number of arbitrators. We have included a like provision.

79. Article 10(2) of the Model Law stipulates that failing such determination, the number of arbitrators shall be three. This we have not adopted, preferring the existing English rule that in the absence of agreement the default number shall be one. The employment of three arbitrators is likely to be three times the cost of employing one, and it seems right that this extra burden should be available if the parties so choose, but not imposed on them. The provision for a sole arbitrator also accords both with common practice in this country, and the balance of responses the DAC received. The Model Law default does not, of course, cater for the situation where there are more than two parties to the arbitration.

Clause 16. Procedure for the Appointment of Arbitrators

A57–021   **80.** Again we have had the Model Law (Article 11) very much in mind in drafting these provisions, though we have attempted to cater for more cases and also for the fact that under our law, there can be either an umpire or a chairman. We should note that this has caused some confusion abroad, particularly in the United States, where what we would describe as a "chairman" is called an "umpire." In Clauses 20 and 21 we set out the differences between these two which (in the absence of agreement between the parties) is the present position under English law.

81. The time limits we have imposed for appointments we consider to be fair and reasonable. They can be extended by the Court under Clause 79, but the power of the Court in this regard is limited as set out in that Clause. In the ordinary case we would not expect the Court to allow a departure from the Clause 16 time limits.

82. It might be noted that periods of 28 days, rather than 30 days (as in the Model Law) have been used throughout the Bill, in order to reduce the likelihood of a deadline expiring on a weekend.

Clause 17. Power in case of default to appoint sole arbitrator

83. This Clause is intended to replace the present rules concerning the appointment of a sole arbitrator where the other party is in default (section 7(b) of the 1950 Act). It only applies to a two party case. We have stipulated that the party in default must not only appoint his arbitrator within the specified period but also inform the other party that he has done so. This in our view is a significant improvement on the present law, where the defaulting party was under no obligation to say that he had made an appointment. This was calculated to cause unnecessary delay, confusion and expense. **A57–022**

84. Some of those responding objected to this Clause. The DAC, however, remains of the view that this provision is an example of the Court supporting the arbitral process, and reducing the opportunities available for a recalcitrant party. The DAC is advised that section 7(b) of the 1950 Act is used a great deal, and that its very existence constitutes a deterrent to those contemplating dilatory tactics. The alternative would be to simply provide for recourse to Court. This would be overly burdensome in most cases, and is available, in any event, under the provisions of the Bill.

85. It has been suggested that the Bill should set out grounds upon which the Court should exercise its discretion in Clause 17(3). The DAC is of the view, however, that this is best left for the Courts to develop, given the specific circumstances of each case, and in the light of the overall philosophy of the Bill.

86. One respondent queried the use of the word *"refuses"* in Clause 17(1) The advantage of this is that if a party does actually refuse to appoint an arbitrator, rather than simply failing to do so, the non-defaulting party need not wait for the expiration of the relevant time period within which the defaulting party may make such an appointment, but could use the mechanism in Clause 17 straight away.

Clause 18. Failure of Appointment Procedure

87. Again we have had the Model Law in mind when drafting this provision, The starting point is any agreement the parties may have made to deal with a failure of the appointment procedure. In the absence of any such agreement, the Court is given the power to make appointments. This is a classic case of the Court supporting and helping to carry through the arbitration process. **A57–023**

88. It will be noted that we have given the Court power to revoke any appointments already made. This is to cover the case where unless the Court took this step it might be

suggested thereafter that the parties had not been fairly treated, since one had his own choice arbitrator while the other had an arbitrator imposed on him by the Court in circumstances that were no fault of his own. This situation in fact arose in France in the *Dutco* Case, where an award was invalidated for this reason.

89. The Model Law stipulates that there shall be no appeal from a decision of the Court. We have not gone as far as this, since there may well be questions of important general principle which would benefit from authoritative appellate guidance.

Clause 19. Court to have regard to Agreed Qualifications

A57–024   **90.** This comes from Article 11(5) of the Model Law, which itself seeks to preserve as much of the parties' agreement as possible.

Clauses 20 and 21. Chairman and Umpire

A57–025   **91.** The parties are, of course, free to make what arrangements they like about the functions and powers of Chairmen or Umpires. We have set out what we believe to be the position under English law in the absence of any such agreement. As we understand the current position, in the absence of an agreement between the parties, an umpire can neither take part nor attend an arbitration until the arbitrators have disagreed.

92. A cause of delay and expense often exists under our umpire system where the umpire does not attend the proceedings and it is only at an advanced stage (when the arbitrators disagree) that he takes over, for much that has gone on may have to be repeated before him. Equally, the time and expense of an umpire may be wasted if he attends but the arbitrators are able to agree on everything. We have decided that it would be preferable to stipulate that (in the absence of agreement between the parties) the umpire should attend the proceedings (as opposed to taking part in the proceedings) and be supplied with the same documents and materials as the other arbitrators. We hope, however, that common sense will prevail and that the parties will make specific agreement over this question, tailored to the circumstances of the particular case.

93. Sub-section 21(4) caused some concern amongst a few respondents, but this sub-section simply reflects what is understood to be the current position.

94. We should record that we considered whether the peculiarly English concept of an umpire should be swept away in favour of the more generally used chaired tribunal. As we have pointed out above, in the United States what we would describe as a chairman is called an umpire. In the end we decided not to recommend this, and to continue to provide default provisions for those who wanted to continue to use this form of arbitral tribunal.

Clause 22. Decision-making where no Chairman or Umpire

A57–026   **95.** We decided to include this situation for the sake of completeness, though the default provision can only work if there is unanimity or a majority. If there is neither, then it would appear that the arbitration agreement cannot operate, unless the parties can agree, or have agreed, what is to happen.

Clause 23. Revocation of arbitrator's authority

96. Statutory provisions making it impossible unilaterally to revoke the authority of an arbitrator have existed since 1833. The present Clause is designed to reflect the current position, save that we have imposed a writing requirement and thought it helpful to make express reference to arbitral institutions etc. These of course only have such powers as the parties have agreed they shall have, so that strictly this provision is not necessary, but we consider that an express reference makes for clarity.

97. Some of those responding suggested that the parties' right to agree to revoke an arbitral appointment should be limited (*e.g.* that Court approval should be required in every case). The DAC has not adopted these suggestions since any tribunal is properly regarded as the parties' tribunal and to do so would derogate from the principle of party autonomy.

98. It will be seen that various terms are used in the Bill with respect to the termination of an arbitral appointment, such as "*removal*" and "*revocation of authority*". Different terms have been adopted simply as a matter of correct English usage. The difference in terms is not intended to be of any legal significance.

99. Sub-section 23(4). Whilst any agreement as to an arbitration must be in writing, as defined earlier, the DAC is of the view that it is impracticable to impose a writing requirement on an agreement to terminate an arbitration. Parties may well simply walk away from proceedings, or allow the proceedings to lapse, and it could be extremely unfair if one party were allowed to rely upon an absence of writing at some future stage. Where a Claimant allows an arbitration to lapse, Clause 41(3) may be utilised.

Clause 24. Power of Court to Remove Arbitrator

100. We have set out the cases where the Court can remove an arbitrator.

101. The Model Law (Article 12) specifies justifiable doubts as to the independence (as well as impartiality) of an arbitrator as grounds for his removal. We have considered this carefully, but despite efforts to do so, no-one has persuaded us that, in consensual arbitrations, this is either required or desirable. It seems to us that lack of independence, unless it gives rise to justifiable doubts about the impartiality of the arbitrator, is of no significance. The latter is, of course, the first of our grounds for removal. If lack of independence were to be included, then this could only be justified if it covered cases where the lack of independence did **not** give rise to justifiable doubts about impartiality, for otherwise there would be no point including lack of independence as a separate ground.

102. We can see no good reason for including "non-partiality" lack of independence as a ground for removal and good reasons for not doing so. We do not follow what is meant to be covered by a lack of independence which does not lead to the appearance of partiality. Furthermore, the inclusion of independence would give rise to endless arguments, as it has, for example, in Sweden and the United States, where almost any connection (however remote) has been put forward to challenge the "independence" of an arbitrator. For example, it is often the case that one member of a barristers' Chambers appears as counsel before an arbitrator who comes from the same Chambers. Is that to be regarded, without more, as a lack of independence justifying the removal of the arbitrator? We are quite certain that this would not be the case in English law. Indeed the Chairman has so decided in a case in Chambers in the Commercial Court. We would also draw attention to the article *"Barristers' Independence and Disclosure"* by Kendall in (1992) 8 *Arb. Int.* 287. We would further note in passing that even the oath taken by those appointed to the International Court of Justice; and indeed to our own High Court, refers only to impartiality.

103. Further, there may well be situations in which parties desire their arbitrators to have familiarity with a specific field, rather than being entirely independent.

104. We should emphasize that we intend to lose nothing of significance by omitting reference to independence. Lack of this quality may well give rise to justifiable doubts about impartiality, which is covered, but if it does not, then we cannot at present see anything of significance that we have omitted by not using this term.

105. We have included, as grounds for removal, the refusal or failure of an arbitrator properly to conduct the proceedings, as well as failing to use all reasonable despatch in conducting the proceedings or making an award, where the result has caused or will cause substantial injustice to the applicant. We trust that the Courts will not allow the first of these matters to be abused by those intent on disrupting the arbitral process. To this end we have included a provision allowing the tribunal to continue while an application is made. There is also Clause 73 which effectively requires a party to "put up or shut up" if a challenge is to be made.

106. We have every confidence that the Courts will carry through the intent of this part of the Bill, which is that it should only be available where the conduct of the arbitrator is such as to go so beyond anything that could reasonably be defended that substantial injustice has resulted or will result. The provision is not intended to allow the Court to substitute its own view as to how the arbitral proceedings should be conducted. Thus the choice by an arbitrator of a particular procedure, unless it breaches the duty laid on arbitrators by Clause 33, should on no view justify the removal of an arbitrator, even if the Court would not itself have adopted that procedure. In short, this ground only exists to cover what we hope will be the very rare case where an arbitrator so conducts the proceedings that it can fairly be said that instead of carrying through the object of arbitration as stated in the Bill, he is in effect frustrating that object. Only if the Court confines itself in this way can this power of removal be justified as a measure supporting rather than subverting the arbitral process.

107. We have also made the exhaustion of any arbitral process for challenging an arbitrator a pre-condition to the right to apply to the Court. Again it will be a very rare case indeed where the Court will remove an arbitrator notwithstanding that that process has reached a different conclusion.

108. If an arbitrator is removed by the Court, we have given the Court power to make orders in respect of his remuneration. We would expect this power to be exercised where the behaviour of the arbitrator is inexcusable to the extent that this should be marked by depriving him of all or some of his fees and expenses. This sub-section is also the subject of a supplementary recommendation in Chapter 6 below.

109. As a matter of justice, we have stipulated that an arbitrator is entitled to be heard on any application for his removal.

110. This is a mandatory provision. It seems to us that an agreement to contract out of the cases we specify would really be tantamount to an agreement to a dispute resolution procedure that is contrary to the basic principles set out in Clause 1.

Departmental Advisory Committee on Arbitration Law

Clause 25. Resignation of Arbitrator

111. In theory it could be said that an arbitrator cannot unilaterally resign if this conflicts with the express or implied terms of his engagement. However, as a matter of practical politics an arbitrator who refuses to go on cannot be made to do so, though of course he may incur a liability for breach of his agreement to act. **A57–029**

112. In this Clause we have given an arbitrator who resigns the right to go to the Court to seek relief from any liability incurred through resigning and to make orders relating to his remuneration and expenses, unless the consequences of resignation have been agreed with the parties (*e.g.* by virtue of having adopted institutional rules).

113. We have chosen the words of sub-section (1) with care so that the agreement referred to is confined to an agreement as to the consequences of resignation. A simple agreement not to resign (or only to resign in certain circumstances) with no agreement as to what will happen if this promise is broken is not within the sub-section. This has to be so since otherwise (by virtue of sub-section (2)), sub-sections (3) and (4) would never or hardly ever operate, for the arbitrator will not be under any liability or at risk as to his fees or expenses unless he is in breach by resigning.

114. In the July draft we suggested a provision which would have entitled the Court to grant relief in all circumstances including those where the arbitrator had made an agreement as to the consequences of his resignation. However, as the result of a response that we received we have concluded that where the parties have agreed with an arbitrator on the consequences it would be wrong to give the Court a power to adjust the position.

115. The reason we propose this is that circumstances may well arise in which it would be just to grant such relief to a resigning arbitrator. For example, the arbitrator may (reasonably) not be prepared to adopt a procedure agreed by the parties (*i.e.* under Clause 34) during the course of an arbitration, taking the view that his duty under Clause 33 conflicts with their suggestions (the relationship between the duty of arbitrators in Clause 33 and the freedom of the parties in Clause 34, is discussed in more detail below). Again, an arbitration may drag on for far longer than could reasonably have been expected when the appointment was accepted, resulting in an unfair burden on the arbitrator. In circumstances where the Court was persuaded that it was reasonable for the arbitrator to resign, it seems only right that the Court should be able to grant appropriate relief.

Clause 26. Death of Arbitrator or Person appointing him

116. This Clause complements Clause 8 and is included for the same reason. Clause 26(1) is mandatory—it is difficult to see how parties could agree otherwise. **A57–030**

Clause 27. Filling of Vacancy etc.

117. This Clause reflects Article 15 of the Model Law, but also deals with certain other important ancillary matters. It should be noted that we do not propose to re-enact the power given to the Court under Section 25 of the Arbitration Act 1950 to fill a vacancy created by its removal of an arbitrator. It seems to us that (in the absence of agreement between the parties) it is preferable for the original appointment procedure to **A57–031**

be used, for otherwise (as in the *Dutco* case mentioned above) it might be argued that the parties were not being treated equally.

118. We have given the tribunal the right (when reconstituted) to determine to what extent the previous proceedings should stand, though we have also made clear that this does not affect any right a party may have to challenge what has happened.

119. Further, we have provided in Clause 27(5) that the fact of an arbitrator ceasing to hold office will not affect any appointment made by him (whether alone or jointly) of another arbitrator, unless the parties have otherwise agreed pursuant to Clause 27(1)(c).

Clause 28. Joint and Several Liability of Parties to Arbitrators for Fees and Expenses

120. Arbitration proceedings necessarily involve the incurring of expenditure. The arbitrators have to be paid, and the parties incur expense in presenting their cases to the tribunal. The issue of costs involves at least three quite discrete elements:

  i. As a matter of general contract law, arbitrators, experts, institutions and any other payees whatsoever are entitled to be paid what has been agreed with them by any of the parties. Therefore, for example, if a party appoints an arbitrator for an agreed fee, as a matter of general contract law (rather than anything in this Bill), that arbitrator is entitled to that fee.

  ii. It is generally accepted that all parties are jointly and severally liable for the fees of an arbitrator. This is an issue as to the entitlement of arbitrators, and as such is quite distinct from the third element.

  iii. As in court litigation, when one party is successful, that party should normally recover at least a proportion of his costs. This issue, being where the burden of costs should lie, is an issue as between the parties.

121. The Bill contains provisions as to costs and fees in two separate parts: the joint and several liability owed by the parties to the arbitrators (the second element) is addressed in this clause, whilst the third element (*i.e.* the responsibility for costs as between the parties) is addressed in Clauses 59–65. The first element, being a matter of general contract law, is not specifically addressed by either set of provisions, but is preserved in both. It is extremely important to distinguish between these provisions.

122. Clause 28 is concerned with the rights of the arbitrators in respect of fees and expenses. As sub-section (5) makes clear, and as explained above, this provision is not concerned with which of the parties should (as between themselves) bear these costs as the result of the arbitration, which is dealt with later in the Bill, nor with any contractual right an arbitrator may have in respect of fees and expenses.

123. As we understand the present law, the parties are jointly and severally liable to the arbitrator for his fees and expenses. The present position seems to be that if these are agreed by one party, the other party becomes liable, even if he played no part in making that agreement; and circumstances may arise in which that party is unable to obtain a reduction of the amount by taxation. It seems to us that whilst arbitrators should be protected by this joint and several liability of the parties, a potentially unfair result must be avoided: a party who never agreed to the appointment by another party of an exceptionally expensive arbitrator should not be held jointly and severally liable for that arbitrator's exceptional fees. To this end, we have stipulated, in Clause 28(1), that a party's joint and several liability to an arbitrator only extends to *"reasonable fees"*. Of course, if a party has agreed an exceptional fee with an arbitrator, that party may still be pursued by that arbitrator, under general contract law, which is preserved in Clause 28(5).

124. We have proposed a mechanism to allow a party to go to the Court if any question arises as to the reasonableness of the arbitrator's charges. The Court is empowered to adjust fees and expenses even after they have been paid, since circumstances may well arise in which a question about the level of fees and expenses only arises after payment has been made. For example, a large advance payment may be made at a time when it is considered that the arbitration will take a long time, but this does not turn out to be the case. However, the Court must be satisfied that it is reasonable in the circumstances to order repayment. Thus an applicant who delays in making an application is likely to receive short shrift from the Court, nor is the Court likely to order repayment where the arbitrator has in good faith acted in such a way that it would be unjust to order repayment. It seems to us that it is necessary to set out expressly in the Bill that the power of the Court extends to dealing with fees and expenses already paid, since otherwise there could be an argument that this power is confined to fees and expenses yet to be paid.

125. These provisions are extended by sub-section (6) to include an arbitrator who has ceased to act and an umpire who has not replaced the other arbitrators. An arbitrator may cease to act through the operation of Clauses 23 to 26, or if an umpire takes over following a disagreement.

126. The liability in Clause 28(1) is to *"the parties"*. It seems to us to follow that a person who has not participated at all, and in respect of whom it is determined that the arbitral tribunal has no jurisdiction, would not be a "party" for the purposes of this clause (*cf.* Clause 72). More difficult questions may well arise in respect of persons who have participated, for there the doctrine of *Kompetenz-Kompetenz* (Clauses 30 and 31) may have to be weighed against the proposition that a party can hardly be under any liability in respect of the fees and expenses of the tribunal which he has successfully established should not have been acting at all on the merits of the dispute.

127. It is to be noted that arbitrators' fees and expenses include, by virtue of Clause 37(2), the fees and expenses of tribunal appointed experts etc.

128. It seems that the present joint and several liability of the parties to an arbitrator for his fees may rest on some implied contract said to exist between them. Be this as it may, such an implied contract (in so far as it related to fees and expenses) would not survive by virtue of Clause 81 of this Bill, because this only saves rules of law which are consistent with Part I. Any implied contract imposing a liability for more than reasonable fees and expenses would clearly be inconsistent with Clause 28(1). Furthermore, since Clause 28(1) gives a statutory right there remains no good reason for any implied contractual right. As stated above, any specific contract would, however, of course be preserved by Clause 28(5).

129. Contrary to some suggestions made to us, it seems to us that rights of contribution between the parties in relation to their statutory liability under Clause 28(1) can best be left to the ordinary rules which relate to joint and several liability generally.

130. Clause 28 is made mandatory, since otherwise the parties could by agreement between themselves deprive the arbitrators of what seems to us to be a very necessary protection.

Clause 29. Immunity of Arbitrators

A57–033   131. Although the general view seems to be that arbitrators have some immunity under the present law, this is not entirely free from doubt. We were firmly of the view that arbitrators should have a degree of immunity, and most (though not all) the responses we received expressed the same view.

132. The reasons for providing immunity are the same as those that apply to Judges in our Courts. Arbitration and litigation share this in common, that both provide a means of dispute resolution which depends upon a binding decision by an impartial third party. It is generally considered that an immunity is necessary to enable that third party properly to perform an impartial decision making function. Furthermore, we feel strongly that unless a degree of immunity is afforded, the finality of the arbitral process could well be undermined. The prospect of a losing party attempting to re-arbitrate the issues on the basis that a competent arbitrator would have decided them in favour of that party is one that we would view with dismay. The Bill provides in our view adequate safeguards to deal with cases where the arbitral process has gone wrong.

133. This is a mandatory provision. Given the need and reason for immunity, it seems to us to follow that as a matter of public policy, this should be so.

134. The immunity does not, of course, extend to cases where it is shown that the arbitrator has acted in bad faith. Our law is well acquainted with this expression and although we considered other terms, we concluded that there were unlikely to be any difficulties in practice in using this test: see, for example, *Melton Medes Ltd v Securities and Investment Board* [1995] 3 All E.R.

135. Sub-section 29(3). There was a concern that if a provision such as this was not included, Clause 25, when read together with Clause 29, could be said to preclude a claim against an arbitrator for resigning in breach of contract and similarly a defence (based on resignation) to a claim by an arbitrator for his fees, unless "*bad faith*" is proved.

136. Since the publication of the final draft of the Bill, we have concluded that the Court should be given power to remove or modify the immunity as it sees fit when it removes an arbitrator. We consider this further in Chapter 6 below.

JURISDICTION OF THE ARBITRAL TRIBUNAL

Clause 30. Competence of tribunal to rule on its own Jurisdiction

A57–034   137. This Clause states what is called the doctrine of "*Kompetenz-Kompetenz*". This is an internationally recognized doctrine, which is also recognized by our own law (*e.g. Christopher Brown v Genossenschaft Osterreichlischer* [sic] *Waldbesitzer* [1954] 1 Q.B. 8), though this has not always been the case.

138. The great advantage of this doctrine is that it avoids delays and difficulties when a question is raised as to the jurisdiction of the tribunal. Clearly the tribunal cannot be the final arbiter of a question of jurisdiction, for this would provide a classic case of pulling oneself up by one's own bootstraps, but to deprive a tribunal of a power (subject to Court review) to rule on jurisdiction would mean that a recalcitrant party could delay

valid arbitration proceedings indefinitely by making spurious challenges to its jurisdiction.

139. The Clause and the following Clause are based on Article 16 of the Model Law, but unlike that model we have not made this provision mandatory so that the parties, if they wish, can agree that the tribunal shall not have this power. We have also spelt out what we mean by "substantive jurisdiction".

Clause 31. Objection to Substantive Jurisdiction of Tribunal

140. In this Clause we set out how a challenge to the jurisdiction can be made, and the circumstances in which it must be made (following Article 16 of the Model Law). This reflects much of the Model Law but we have, for example, refrained from using expressions like "submission of the statement of defence" since this might give the impression, which we are anxious to dispel, that every arbitration requires some formal pleading or the like.

A57–035

141. The Clause, in effect, sets out three ways in which the matter may proceed.

i. The first is that the tribunal may make an award on the question of jurisdiction. If it does so then that award may be challenged by a party under Clause 67.

ii. The second way is for the tribunal to deal with the question of jurisdiction in its award on the merits. Again on the jurisdiction aspect the award may be challenged under Clause 67.

We have provided these two methods because, depending on the circumstances, the one or the other may be the better course to take, bearing in mind the duty (in Clause 33) to adopt procedures suitable to the circumstances of the particular case, avoiding unnecessary delay or expense.

iii. The third way of proceeding is for an application to be made to the Court before any award (pursuant to Clause 32). Again this third course is designed to achieve the same objective (albeit in limited circumstances). For example, cases arise where a party starts an arbitration but the other party, without taking part, raises an objection to the jurisdiction of the tribunal. In such circumstances, it might very well be cheaper and quicker for the party wishing to arbitrate to go directly to the Court to seek a favourable ruling on jurisdiction rather than seeking an award from the tribunal. Such an approach would be very much the exception, and, to this end, Clause 32 is narrowly drawn. In this connection it must be remembered that a party who chooses not to take any part in an arbitration cannot in justice be required to take any positive steps to challenge the jurisdiction, for to do otherwise would be to assume against that party (before the point has been decided) that the tribunal has jurisdiction. We return to this topic when considering Clause 72.

142. Article 16(3) of the Model Law provides that the arbitral tribunal may rule on a plea as to jurisdiction either as a preliminary question or in an award on the merits. The DAC is of the view that it is unnecessary to introduce a new concept of a "preliminary ruling", which is somehow different from an award. Clause 31(4) therefore only refers to awards. This has the advantage that awards on jurisdiction will have the benefit of those provisions on awards generally (*e.g.* costs, lien, reasons, additional awards, etc), and, if appropriate, may be enforced in the same way as any other award.

143. A challenge to jurisdiction may well involve questions of fact as well as questions of law. Since the arbitral tribunal cannot rule finally on its own jurisdiction, it follows that both its findings of fact and its holdings of law may be challenged. The regime for challenging such awards is set out in Clause 67.

144. Clause 31(1) replaces the requirement set out in Article 16(2) of the Model Law (that a challenge to the overall jurisdiction of the tribunal must be raised no later than the submission of a statement of defence) with a requirement that such an objection be raised no later than the time a party takes the first step in the proceedings to contest the merits of any matter in relation to which he challenges the tribunal's jurisdiction. This allows for alternative procedures where there is no "statement of defence" as such.

145. Clause 31 is a mandatory provision. Under Clause 30, of course, the parties can agree that the tribunal shall not have power to rule on its own jurisdiction, but while this means (as sub-section (4) points out) that the tribunal cannot then make an award on jurisdiction, the compulsory nature of Clause 31 means that the objection must be raised as there stipulated. It seems to us that this is highly desirable by way of support for the object of arbitration as set out in Clause 1.

146. It has been suggested to the DAC that there should be a mechanism whereby an objecting party, or even a non-objecting party, could require the tribunal forthwith to make an award as to jurisdiction, rather than merely incorporating a ruling in an award on the merits. The DAC disagrees with this. Unless the parties agree otherwise, the choice as to which course to take will be left with the tribunal, who will decide what is to be done consistent with their duty under Clause 33 (see below). Indeed, in some cases it may be simply impracticable to rule on jurisdiction, before determining merits. If, however, the parties agree which course is to be taken, and if, of course, their agreement is effective (*i.e.* it does not require the tribunal to breach its mandatory duty under Clause 33) then the provision under discussion requires the tribunal to take the course chosen by the parties.

Clause 32. Determination of preliminary point of Jurisdiction

A57–036   **147.** In this Clause we have set out the procedure for the third of the possible ways of dealing with a challenge to the jurisdiction. As stated above, this Clause provides for exceptional cases only: it is not intended to detract from the basic rule as set out in Clause 30. Hence the restrictions in Clause 32(2), and the procedure in Clause 32(3). It will be noted that we have required either the agreement of the parties, or that the Court is satisfied that this is, in effect, the proper course to take. It is anticipated that the Courts will take care to prevent this exceptional provision from becoming the normal route for challenging jurisdiction. Since this Clause concerns a power exercisable by the Court in relation to the jurisdiction of the tribunal, it is in our view important enough to be made mandatory.

148. Under this Clause the tribunal may continue the arbitral proceedings and make an award whilst the application to the Court is pending. Thus a recalcitrant party will not be able to mount spurious challenges as a means of delaying the arbitral process. Under sub-section (5) of the preceding Clause the tribunal can, of course (and must if the parties agree) stay the arbitral proceedings whilst an application is made. Which course the tribunal takes (where it has power to choose) will of course depend once again on what it sees its Clause 33 duty to be.

149. The right of appeal from Court rulings is limited in the way set out in the Clause.

THE ARBITRAL PROCEEDINGS

Clause 33. General Duty of the Tribunal

150. This is one of the central proposals in our Bill (grounded on Article 18 of the Model Law). It is a mandatory provision, since, as is explained below, we fail to see how a proceeding which departed from the stipulated duties could properly be described as an arbitration. We endeavour to set out, in the simplest, clearest terms we have been able to devise, how the tribunal should approach and deal with its task, which is to do full justice to the parties. In the following Clauses we set out in detail the powers available to the tribunal for this purpose.

151. It has been suggested that the generality of Clause 33 may be problematic: that it may be an invitation to recalcitrant parties to launch challenges, or that vagueness will give rise to arguments. The advantage of arbitration is that it offers a dispute resolution system which can be tailored to the particular dispute to an extent which litigation finds it difficult to do. Thus depending on the nature of the dispute, there will be numerous ways in which the arbitration can be conducted. It is quite impossible to list all the possible variants and to set out what may or may not be done. Indeed any attempt to do so would defeat one of the main purposes of the Bill, which is to encourage arbitral tribunals not slavishly to follow court or other set procedures. It follows that the only limits can be those set out in the present clause. It is to be hoped that the Courts will take a dim view of those who try to attack awards because of suggested breaches of this clause which have no real substance. At the same time, it can hardly be suggested that awards should not be open to attack when the tribunal has not acted in accordance with the principles stated.

152. It has further been suggested that this part of the Bill will cause the demise of the amateur arbitrator. If by this is meant the demise of people who purport to act as arbitrators but who are either unable or unwilling (or both) to conduct the proceedings in accordance with what most would regard as self-evident rules of justice, then we indeed hope that this will be one of the results. But since these rules of justice are generally accepted in our democratic society, and are not merely theoretical considerations that concern lawyers alone, we can see no reason why the Bill should discourage anyone who is ready willing and able to apply them. Indeed we consider that the Bill will encourage and support all such people.

153. Sometimes the parties to an arbitration employ lawyers who seek, in effect, to bully a non-legal arbitrator into taking a course of action which is against his better instincts, by seeking to blind him with legal "science" to get their way. Again, in some circles it is thought that somehow the procedures in an arbitration should be modelled on Court procedures, and that to adopt other methods would be "misconduct" (an expression that the Bill does not use) on the part of the arbitrator. This part of the Bill is designed to prevent such bullying and to explode the theory that an arbitration has always to follow Court procedures. If an arbitrator is satisfied that the way he wants to proceed fulfils his duty under this Clause and that the powers he wants to exercise are available to him under the following Clauses, then he should have the courage of his own convictions and proceed accordingly, unless the parties are agreed that he should adopt some other course.

The relationship between Clauses 1(b), 33 and 34(1)

A57–038   154. It has been suggested to us there could be a conflict between:

i. the mandatory duty cast on arbitrators by Clause 33 and

ii the principle of party autonomy in Clause 1(b) and the proviso in Clause 34(1)).

As we explain below, the DAC does not consider that there is any inconsistency between these two principles.

155. Under the principle of party autonomy, the parties are free to agree upon anything to do with the arbitration, subject only to such safeguards as are necessary in the public interest (Clause 1(b)). The mandatory provisions set out those matters which have effect notwithstanding any agreement to the contrary: see Clause 4. It seems to us that the public interest dictates that Clause 33 must be mandatory *i.e.* that the parties cannot effectively agree to dispense with the duty laid on arbitrators under Clause 33. In other words, they cannot effectively agree that the arbitrators can act unfairly, or that the arbitrators can be partial, or that the arbitrators can decide that the parties (or one of them) should not have a reasonable opportunity of putting his case or answering that of his opponent, or indeed that the arbitrators can adopt procedures that are unsuitable for the particular circumstances of the case or are unnecessarily slow or expensive, so that the means for resolving the matters to be determined is unfair. It is, of course, extremely unlikely in the nature of things that the parties would wish deliberately to make such bizarre agreements, but were this to happen, then it seems to us that such agreements should be ineffective for the purposes of this Bill, *i.e.* not binding on the parties or the tribunal.

156. However, a situation could well arise in practice in cases where the parties are agreed on a method of proceeding which they consider complies with the first of the general principles set out in Clause 1 (and which therefore the tribunal could adopt consistently with its duty under Clause 33) but the tribunal takes a different view, or where they are agreed in their opposition to a method of proceeding which the tribunal considers should be adopted in order to perform its Clause 33 duty.

157. In our view it is neither desirable nor practicable to stipulate that the tribunal can override the agreement of the parties. It is not desirable, because the type of arbitration we are discussing is a consensual process which depends on the agreement of the parties who are surely entitled (if they can agree) to have the final say on how they wish their dispute to be resolved. It is not practicable, since there is no way in which the parties can be forced to adopt a method of proceeding if they are agreed that this is not the way they wish to proceed. The latter is the case even if it could be established that their agreement was ineffective since it undermined or prevented performance of the duty made mandatory by Clause 33.

158. A party would be unable to enforce an ineffective agreement against the other parties, nor would such an agreement bind the tribunal, but the problem under discussion only exists while the parties are *in fact* at one, whether or not their agreement is legally effective.

159. In circumstances such as these, the tribunal (assuming it has failed to persuade the parties to take a different course) has the choice of adopting the course preferred by

the parties or of resigning. Indeed, resignation would be the only course if the parties were in agreement in rejecting the method preferred by the tribunal, and no other way of proceeding was agreed by them or considered suitable by the tribunal.

160. We have stipulated elsewhere in the Bill that the immunity we propose for arbitrators does not extend to any liability they may be under for resigning (Clause 29) though under Clause 25 they may seek relief in respect of such liability from the Court. The reason for the limitation on immunity is that cases may arise where the resignation of the arbitrator is wholly indefensible and has caused great delay and loss. In our view Clause 25 would suffice to protect arbitrators who resigned because they reasonably believed that the agreement of the parties prevented them from properly performing their Clause 33 duty. Furthermore, arbitrators could always stipulate for a right to resign in such circumstances as a term of their appointment.

161. If, on the other hand, the tribunal adopted a method of proceeding agreed by the parties, it seems to us that none of the parties could afterwards validly complain that the tribunal had failed in its Clause 33 duty, since the tribunal would only have done what the parties had asked it to do. Again, the fact that as between the parties such an agreement may have been ineffective as undermining or preventing performance of the Clause 33 duties seems to us to be wholly irrelevant. It could of course be said that the tribunal had breached its Clause 33 duty, but this would have no practical consequences since the parties themselves would have brought about this state of affairs, and would therefore be unable to seek any relief in respect of it.

162. Some people have expressed concern that there is a danger that lawyers will agree between themselves a method of proceeding which the tribunal consider to be unnecessarily long or expensive. However, if a tribunal considered, for example, that lawyers were trying either deliberately to "churn" the case for their own private advantage or were simply but misguidedly seeking to adopt unnecessary procedures etc, the obvious solution would be to ask them to confirm that their respective clients had been made aware of the views of the tribunal but were nevertheless in agreement that the course proposed by their lawyers should be adopted. At the end of the day, however, the fact remains that the only sanction the arbitrators have is to resign.

163. In summary, therefore, we consider that the duty of the arbitrators under Clause 33 and the right of the parties to agree how the arbitration should be conducted do fit together. Under Clause 33 the tribunal have the specified duties. Under Clause 34 therefore, the tribunal must decide all procedural and evidential matters, subject to the right of the parties to agree any matter. If the parties reach an agreement on how to proceed which clashes with the duty of the tribunal or which the tribunal reasonably considers does so, then the arbitrators can either resign and have the protection of Clause 25, or can adopt what the parties want and will not afterwards be liable to the parties for doing so.

Further points

164. In this Clause we have provided that the tribunal shall give each party a "*reasonable opportunity*" of putting his case and dealing with that of his opponent. Article 18 of the Model Law uses the expression "*full opportunity*."

165. We prefer the word "*reasonable*" because it removes any suggestion that a party is entitled to take as long as he likes, however objectively unreasonable this may be. We are sure that this was not intended by those who framed the Model Law, for it would entail that a party is entitled to an unreasonable time, which justice can hardly require. Indeed the contrary is the case, for an unreasonable time would *ex hypothesi* mean unnecessary delay and expense, things which produce injustice and which accordingly would offend the first principle of Clause 1, as well as Clauses 33 and 40.

Clause 34. Procedural and evidential Matters

A57–040 166. We trust that the matters we have listed in this Clause (which are partly drawn from Articles 19, 20 22, 23 and 24 of the Model Law) are largely self-evident. We have produced a non-exhaustive check-list because we think it will be helpful both to arbitrating parties and to their arbitrators. We cannot emphasize too strongly that one of the strengths of the arbitral process is that it is able much more easily than any Court system to adapt its procedures to suit the particular case. Hence we have spelt this out as a duty under the preceding Clause. The list of powers helps the tribunal (and indeed the parties) to choose how best to proceed, untrammelled by technical or formalistic rules.

167. Some of those responding suggested that we should include a special code to deal with the arbitration of small claims. We have not adopted this suggestion for the very reason we have just stated. Any such code would have to have detailed rules, arbitrary monetary or other limits and other complicated provisions. In our view, proper adherence to the duties in Clause 33 will achieve the same result. A small claim will simply not need all the expensive procedural and other paraphernalia which might be required for the resolution of some huge and complicated international dispute.

168. Furthermore, we consider that associations and institutions concerned with specific areas of trade etc. can play a very significant part in formulating rules and procedures for arbitrating disputes concerning their members. Such bodies have the detailed knowledge and experience required to enable them properly to address this task, in relation both to small claims and otherwise. We feel strongly that it would be wrong for a Bill of the present kind to seek to lay down a rigid structure for any kind of case; and that different methods must be developed to suit different circumstances, by arbitral tribunals as well as those who have the necessary practical knowledge of those circumstances. Finally, of course, the Bill in no way impinges upon small claims procedures developed for use through the court system.

169. Sub-section (a). Whilst Article 20(1) of the Model law states that, in the absence of the agreement of the parties, "*the place of arbitration shall be determined by the arbitral tribunal **having regard to the circumstances of the case, including the convenience of the parties**"*, sub-section 34(2)(a) does not state that the tribunal should have the convenience of the parties in mind, given that this is a consideration that is really subsumed under the general duty of the Tribunal in Clause 33, and, further, because the DAC was of the view that like considerations apply to other parts of Clause 34, such as sub-section (b), even though the Model Law does not appear to reflect this. Unlike the Model Law, sub-section (a) also refers to "*when*", as well as "*where*".

170. Sub-section (f) makes it clear that arbitrators are not necessarily bound by the technical rules of evidence. In his 1993 Freshfields Lecture ((1994) 10 *Arbitration International* 1), Lord Steyn questioned why the technical rules of evidence should apply to arbitration, even if (as he doubted) there was authority for this. This provision clarifies the position. It is to be noted that Clause 34(2)(f) helps to put an end to any arguments that it is a question of law whether there is material to support a finding of fact.

171. Sub-section (g). Some anxiety was expressed at the power to act inquisitorially, to be found in sub-section (g), on grounds that arbitrators are unused to such powers and might, albeit in good faith, abuse them.

172. We do not share this view. Once again it seems to us that provided the tribunal in exercising its powers follows its simple duty as set out in Clause 33 (and sub-section (2) of this Clause tells the tribunal that this is what they must do) then in suitable cases an inquisitorial approach to all or some of the matters involved may well be the best way of proceeding. Clause 33, however, remains a control, such that, for example, if an arbitrator takes the initiative in procuring evidence, he must give all parties a reasonable opportunity of commenting on it.

173. A number of arbitrators who responded to our July 1995 draft suggested that the tribunal should be entitled to have the last word *i.e.* should be given the power to override the agreement of the parties to follow a different course. The interrelationship of the tribunal's duties and party autonomy has already been discussed above. As is clear from that discussion, we disagree with this view for the following reasons:

i. To give the tribunal such a power would be contrary to Article 19 of the Model Law. It would also be contrary to the present position under English law.

ii. To allow the tribunal to override the agreement of the parties would to our minds constitute an indefensible inroad into the principle of party autonomy, upon which the Bill is based.

iii. It is difficult to see how such a power could be backed by any effective sanction. If the parties agree not to adopt the course ordered by the tribunal, there is nothing the tribunal can do except resign.

iv. It seems to us that the problem is more apparent than real. In most cases the parties rely on the tribunal to decide how to conduct the case and do not sit down and agree between themselves how it is to be done. In order to reflect what actually happens in practice we have accordingly reversed the way many of the other Clauses begin and stated that it is for the tribunal to decide all procedural and evidential matters, subject to the right of the parties to agree any matter. In our view, however, since arbitration is the parties' own chosen method of dispute resolution, we cannot see why they should be deprived of the right to decide what form the arbitration should take.

174. As we have made clear above, it is of course open to those who frame rules for arbitration which the parties incorporate into their agreement, to stipulate that the tribunal is to have the last word, and likewise arbitrators can stipulate this as a term of their agreement to act, though once again there would be no means, apart from persuasion or the threat of resignation, of enforcing such a stipulation if the parties later jointly took a different view.

175. It has been suggested that there could be a conflict between the proviso in Clause 34(1) and Clause 40. This is said to arise, for example, where the parties have agreed a procedural or evidential matter which they are entitled to do under Clause 34(1), but the tribunal are intent on taking a different course. Does the parties' agreement override their duty under Clause 40?

The DAC considers that no such conflict exists:

i. The parties are free to agree on all procedural and evidential matters, pursuant to Clause 34(1).

ii. However, any such agreement will only be effective, if it is consistent with Clause 33, being a mandatory provision.

> iii. Any such agreement made pursuant to Clause 34(1), and consistent with Clause 33, will define the scope of Clause 40—*i.e.* the parties will have agreed on how the arbitration is to be conducted, or, in the words of Clause 40, what is to constitute the *"proper and expeditious conduct of the arbitral proceedings"*. The determinations of the tribunal should follow that agreement (which would not be the case if such an agreement was inconsistent with Clause 33) and *ex hypothesi* the parties should be obliged to comply.
>
> iv. If there are matters on which the parties have not agreed, then the tribunal will fill the gap under Clause 34(1) and Clause 40(1) will again operate without conflict.

176. It has also been suggested that the Bill should include a provision that the arbitrator should encourage the parties to use other forms of ADR when this was considered appropriate. This suggestion has not been adopted, since the Bill is concerned with arbitration where the parties have chosen this rather than any other form of dispute resolution.

Clause 35. Consolidation of Proceedings and Concurrent Hearings

177. This Clause makes clear that the parties may agree to consolidate their arbitration with other arbitral proceedings or to hold concurrent hearings.

178. During the consultation exercises, the DAC received submissions calling for a provision that would empower either a tribunal or the Court (or indeed both) to order consolidation or concurrent hearings. These were considered extremely carefully by the committee.

179. The problem arises in cases where a number of parties are involved. For example, in a construction project a main contractor may make a number of sub-contracts each of which contains an arbitration clause. A dispute arises in which a claim is made against one sub-contractor who seeks to blame another. In Court, of course, there is power to order consolidation or concurrent hearings, as well as procedures for allowing additional parties to be joined. In arbitrations, however, this power does not exist. The reason it does not exist is that this form of dispute resolution depends on the agreement of the contracting parties that their disputes will be arbitrated by a private tribunal, not litigated in the public courts. It follows that unless the parties otherwise agree, only their own disputes arising out of their own agreement can be referred to that agreed tribunal.

180. In our view it would amount to a negation of the principle of party autonomy to give the tribunal or the Court power to order consolidation or concurrent hearings. Indeed it would to our minds go far towards frustrating the agreement of the parties to have their own tribunal for their own disputes. Further difficulties could well arise, such as the disclosure of documents from one arbitration to another. Accordingly we would be opposed to giving the tribunal or the Court this power. However, if the parties agree to invest the tribunal with such a power, then we would have no objection.

181. Having said this, the DAC appreciates the common sense behind the suggestion. We are persuaded, however, that the problem is best solved by obtaining the agreement of the parties. Thus those who are in charge of drafting standard forms of contract, or who offer terms for arbitration services which the parties can incorporate into their agreements, (especially those institutions and associations which are concerned with situations in which there are likely to be numerous contracts and sub-contracts) could include suitable clauses permitting the tribunal to consolidate or order concurrent hearings in appropriate cases. For example, the London Maritime Arbitrators Association Rules have within them a provision along these lines. In order to encourage this, we have made clear in this Clause that with the agreement of the parties, there is nothing wrong with adopting such procedures.

182. It will be noted that whereas Clause 39 uses the expression "*[t]he parties are free to agree that the tribunal shall have power to order . . .* ", Clause 35 simpl[y] states that "*[t]he parties are free to agree . . .* ". This difference is easily explained. In both cases the parties are free to endow the tribunal with the power in question. This is implicit in Clause 35(1) by virtue of Clause 35(2). Under Clause 35(1), the parties may agree between themselves to consolidate two arbitrations, or to have concurrent hearings, before a tribunal has been appointed. This could, of course, have a bearing on how the tribunal is to be appointed in such a situation. Indeed the parties may agree on institutional rules that provide for this. However, an equivalent arrangement is difficult to imagine in the context of Clause 39. Overall, the difference in wording is not intended to impede the parties' freedom to agree what they like, when they like, in either case.

Clause 36. Legal or other Representation

183. It seems to us that this reflects a basic right, though of course the parties are free to dispense with it if they wish.

184. In the draft produced in July we used the phrase "*a lawyer or other person of his choice.*" We have changed this, because we felt that it might give the impression that a party could stubbornly insist on a particular lawyer or other person, in circumstances where that individual could not attend for a long time, thus giving a recalcitrant party a good means of delaying the arbitral process. This should not happen. "*A lawyer or other person chosen by him*" does not give this impression: if a party's first choice is not available, his second choice will still be "*a lawyer or other person chosen by him*". The right to be represented exists but must not be abused. Furthermore the right must be read with the first principle of Clause 1, as well as Clauses 33 and 40. If this is done then we trust that attempts to abuse the right will fail.

185. It has been suggested to the DAC that there should be some provision requiring a party to give advance notice to all other parties if he intends to be represented at a hearing. Whilst in some ways an attractive proposal, this would be difficult to stipulate as a statutory provision, given that it may be impossible in some circumstances, or simply unnecessary in others. Further, different sanctions may be appropriate depending on the particular case. It is clearly desirable that, as a general rule, such notice be given. If it is not, one sanction may be for the tribunal to adjourn a hearing at the defaulting party's cost. In the end, however, this must be a matter for the tribunal's discretion in each particular case.

186. It has been suggested that this Clause provides an opportunity of extending by statute the privilege enjoyed by legal advisers to non-legal advisers or representatives. We have not adopted this suggestion. It seems to us that it would be necessary to define with great precision which non-legal advisers or representatives are to be included (*e.g.* what relationship they must have to the arbitration and its conduct), and the precise classes of privilege which should be extended to them. Further, any such provision would necessarily have an impact on the position beyond arbitration. In short, it seems to us that this question cannot be confined to arbitrations and raises matters of general principle far beyond those of our remit.

MISCELLANEOUS

Clause 37. Power to appoint experts, legal advisers or assessors

A57–043 187. This to our minds would be a useful power in certain cases. We trust that the provisions we suggest are self-evident. Of course, the power can only be exercised if in the circumstances of the particular case its exercise falls within the scope of the duty of the tribunal set out in Clause 33.

188. Sub-section (2) is made mandatory, to avoid the risk of the parties agreeing otherwise and thus disabling the tribunal from recovering from the parties expenses properly incurred.

Clause 38. General Powers Exercisable by the Tribunal

A57–044 189. These provisions represent a significant re-drawing of the relationship between arbitration and the Court. Wherever a power could properly be exercised by a tribunal rather than the Court, provision has been made for this, thereby reducing the need to incur the expense and inconvenience of making applications to Court during arbitral proceedings.

190. The first of the powers in this Clause is one which enables the tribunal to order security for costs. The power presently given to the Court to order security for costs in arbitrations is removed in its entirety.

191. This is a major change from the present position where only the Court can order security for costs. The theory which lay behind the present law is that it is the duty of an arbitral tribunal to decide the substantive merits of the dispute referred to it and that it would not be performing this duty if it stayed or struck out the proceedings pending the provision of security: see for example, *Re Unione Stearinerie Lanza and Weiner* [1917] 2 K.B. 558.

192. We do not subscribe to this theory, which Parliament has already abandoned in the context of striking out a claim for want of prosecution. In our view, when the parties agree to arbitrate, they are agreeing that their dispute will be resolved by this means. To our minds (in the absence of express stipulations to the contrary) this does not mean that the dispute is necessarily to be decided on its substantive merits. It is in truth an agreement that it will be resolved by the application of the agreed arbitral process. If one party then fails to comply with that process, then it seems to us that it is entirely within what the parties have agreed that the tribunal can resolve the dispute on this ground.

193. Apart from this, the proposition that the Court should involve itself in such matters as deciding whether a claimant in an arbitration should provide security for costs has received universal condemnation in the context of international arbitrations. It is no exaggeration to say that the recent decision of the House of Lords in *S.A. Coppee Lavalin NV v Ken-Ren Chemicals and Fertilisers* [1994] 2 W.L.R. 631 was greeted with dismay by those in the international arbitration community who have at heart the desire to promote our country as a world centre for arbitration. We share those concerns.

194. It has been suggested to the DAC that the court should retain a power to order security for costs that may be incurred up to the appointment of the tribunal. We have not been persuaded, however, that this is really necessary.

195. It has been pointed out that in some cases an application for security before an arbitral tribunal might involve disclosing to that tribunal the fact that an offer of settle-

ment had been or was about to be made. Under the court system, such disclosure can be made to a court other than that which will try the merits of the case.

196. We are not disturbed by this. It seems to us that a tribunal, properly performing its duty under Clause 33, could and should not be influenced by such matters, if the case proceeds to a hearing on the merits, nor do we accept that the disclosure of such information could somehow disqualify the tribunal from acting.

197. Clause 38(3) has been the subject of significant criticism since the Bill was introduced. In the light of this, we have concluded that it must be redrawn. Chapter 6, to which reference should be made, contains a full discussion of the problems with this provision as currently drafted, and our recommendations for its amendment.

198. Whilst the sanction in court for a failure to provide security for costs is normally a stay of the action, this is inappropriate in arbitration: if an arbitrator stayed proceedings, the arbitration would come to a halt without there necessarily being an award which could be challenged (*e.g.* if a party seeks to continue the proceedings). We have therefore included a specific sanction with respect to a failure to provide security for costs, which is to be found in Clause 41(6). This provision also follows the practice of the English Commercial Court, which changed from the old practice of ordering a stay of proceedings if security was not provided. The disadvantage of the latter course was that it left the proceedings dormant but alive, so that years later they could be revived by the provision of security.

199. Clause 38 provides the tribunal with other powers in relation to the arbitration proceedings. We trust that these are self-explanatory.

Clause 39. Power to make Provisional Awards

200. In the July 1995 draft Clauses, this power did not require the agreement of the parties. As the result of responses, we have concluded on further consideration that this is necessary.

A57–045

201. In *The Kostas Melas* [1981] 1 Lloyd's Rep. 18 at 26, Goff J., as he then was, made clear that it was no part of an arbitrator's function to make temporary or provisional financial arrangements between the parties. Furthermore, as can be demonstrated by the abundance of court cases dealing with this subject (in the context of applications for summary judgment, interim payments, *Mareva* injunctions and the like) enormous care has to be taken to avoid turning what can be a useful judicial tool into an instrument of injustice. We should add that we received responses from a number of practising arbitrators to the effect that they would be unhappy with such powers, and saw no need for them. We should note in passing that the July 1995 draft would arguably (and inadvertently) have allowed arbitrators to order *ex parte Mareva* or even *Anton Piller* relief. These draconian powers are best left to be applied by the Courts, and the provisions of the Bill with respect to such powers have been adjusted accordingly.

202. There is a sharp distinction to be drawn between making provisional or temporary arrangements, which are subject to reversal when the underlying merits are finally decided by the tribunal; and dealing severally with different issues or questions at different times and in different awards, which we cover in Clause 47. It is for this reason that in this provision we draw attention to that Clause.

203. These considerations have led us firmly to conclude that it would only be desirable to give arbitral tribunals power to make such provisional orders where the parties have so agreed. Such agreements, of course, will have to be drafted with some care for the reasons we have stated. Subject to the safeguards of the parties' agreement and the arbitrators' duties (Clause 33), we envisage that this enlargement of the traditional jurisdiction of arbitrators could serve a very useful purpose, for example in trades and industries where cash flow is of particular importance.

Clause 40. General Duty of the Parties

A57–046   204. This is a mandatory provision, since it would seem that an ability to contract out of it would be a negation of the arbitral process.

205. We were asked what the sanction would be for non-compliance. The answer lies in other Clauses of the Bill. These not only give the tribunal powers in relation to recalcitrant parties (*e.g.* Clause 41), but stipulate time limits for taking certain steps (*e.g.* applications to the Court etc.) and (in Clause 73) making clear that undue delay will result in the loss of rights.

Clause 41. Powers of Tribunal in Case of Party's Default

A57–047   206. The first part of this Clause sets out the present law (section 13A of the 1950 Act, which was inserted by section 102 of the Courts and Legal Services Act 1990) giving the arbitral tribunal power to strike out for want of prosecution.

207. The second part makes clear that in the circumstances stipulated, a tribunal may proceed *ex parte*, though we have forborne from using this expression (or indeed any other legal Latin words or phrases) in the Bill. The Clause has its roots in Article 25 of the Model Law.

208. It is a basic rule of justice that a court or tribunal should give all parties an opportunity to put their case and answer that of their opponents. That is why this appears in Clause 33 of the Bill. Equally, however, and for reasons already mentioned, that opportunity should, again for reasons of justice, be limited to a reasonable one. If for no good reason such an opportunity is not taken by a party then to our minds it is only fair to the other party that the tribunal should be able to proceed as we have set out in this Clause.

209. The last part of this Clause sets out a system of peremptory orders. It will be noted that a peremptory order must be "*to the same effect*" as the preceding order which was disobeyed (sub-section (5)). It could be quite unfair for an arbitrator to be able to make any type of peremptory order, on any matter, regardless of its connection with the default in question.

210. For the reasons mentioned earlier, sub-section (6) provides that where a party fails to comply with a peremptory order to provide security for costs, the tribunal may make an award dismissing the claim, thereby following the practice of the English Commercial Court, and avoiding the danger that the proceedings are halted indefinitely, without there being anything to challenge before the Court.

211. So far as failure to comply with other peremptory orders is concerned, we have provided a range of remedies. They do not include a power simply to make an award against the defaulting party. The reason for this is that (unlike a failure to comply with a peremptory order to provide security) it seems to us that this is too draconian a remedy, and that the alternatives we have provided very much better fit the justice of the matter.

DEPARTMENTAL ADVISORY COMMITTEE ON ARBITRATION LAW

POWERS OF COURT IN RELATION TO ARBITRAL PROCEEDINGS

Clause 42. Enforcement of Peremptory Orders of Tribunal

212. Although in Clause 41 we have provided the tribunal with powers in relation to peremptory orders, it seemed to us that the Court should have power to order compliance with such orders, though (unless both parties have agreed) these can only be invoked with the permission of the tribunal. In our view there may well be circumstances where in the interests of justice, the fact that the Court has sanctions which in the nature of things cannot be given to arbitrators (*e.g.* committal to prison for contempt) will assist the proper functioning of the arbitral process. This Clause is a good example of the support the Court can give to that process. Sub-section (3) requires that any other available recourse within the arbitral process be first exhausted.   A57–048

Clause 43. Securing the Attendance of Witnesses

213. This Clause (which corresponds to Article 27 of the Model Law, and is derived from section 12(4) and (5) of the 1950 Act) is also designed to provide Court support for the arbitral process. It will be noted, in particular, that the agreement of the parties or the permission of the tribunal is required. The reason for this is to make sure that this procedure is not used to override any procedural method adopted by the tribunal, or agreed by the parties, for the arbitration. Thus, for example, if the tribunal has decided that there shall be no oral evidence, then (unless all parties agree otherwise) this procedure cannot be used to get round that decision.   A57–049

Clause 44. Court Powers Exercisable in Support of Arbitral Proceedings

214. This provision corresponds in part to Article 9 of the Model Law. As part of the redefinition of the relationship between arbitration and the Court, which was mentioned above, the powers we have given the Court are intended to be used when the tribunal cannot act or act effectively, as sub-section (5) makes clear. It is under this Clause that the Court has power to order *Mareva* or *Anton Piller* relief (*i.e.* urgent protective measures to preserve assets or evidence) so as to help the arbitral process to operate effectively. Equally, there may be instances where a party seeks an order that will have an effect on a third party, which only the Court could grant. For the same reason the Court is given the other powers listed.   A57–050

215. In order to prevent any suggestion that the Court might be used to interfere with or usurp the arbitral process, or indeed any attempt to do so, we have stipulated that except in cases of urgency with regard to the preservation of assets or evidence, the Court can only act with the agreement of the parties or the permission of the tribunal. We have excepted cases of urgency, since these often arise before the tribunal has been properly constituted or when in the nature of things it cannot act quickly or effectively enough.

216. Furthermore, under sub-section (6) the Court, after making an order, can in effect

hand over to the tribunal the task of deciding whether or not that order should cease to have effect. This is a novel provision, but follows from the philosophy behind these provisions: if a given power could possibly be exercised by a tribunal, then it should be, and parties should not be allowed to make unilateral applications to the Court. If, however, a given power could be exercised by the tribunal, but not as effectively, in circumstances where, for example, speed is necessary, then the Court should be able to step in.

Clause 45. Determination of Preliminary Point of Law

A57–051   217. This Clause preserves what used to be the old Consultative Case procedure, though its availability is limited as we have set out, in order not to interfere with the arbitral process. The Clause is based on section 2 of the 1979 Act, with certain important changes.

218. It seems to us that with the limitations we have provided, this procedure can have its uses. For example, an important point of law may arise which is of great general interest and potentially the subject of a large number of arbitrations. This not infrequently happens when some major event occurs, as, for example, the closure of the Suez Canal or the United States embargo on the export of soya beans. It may well be considered by those concerned that in such special circumstances it would be cheaper and better for all to obtain a definitive answer from the Court at an early stage.

219. However, under sub-section (1), unless the parties agree, the Court must now be satisfied that determination of the given question of law will substantially affect the rights of one or more of the parties. This last point is a departure from the 1979 Act, section 1 of which makes this precondition in relation to an appeal in respect of questions of law arising out of the award, but section 2 of which does not impose it in relation to the determination of a preliminary point of law.

220. Further, unless the parties agree, the Court will now have to be satisfied of the matters set out in sub-section (2) before considering an application, so that the procedure can only be used (even with the permission of the tribunal) in cases where its adoption will produce a substantial saving in costs to the parties or one of them. The condition in section 2(2) of the 1979 Act, which requires that the question of law be one in respect of which leave to appeal would be likely to be given under section 1(3)(b) of that Act, is not repeated.

221. It has been suggested to the DAC that the right to refer to the Court under this Clause be removed from all non-domestic arbitrations, unless the parties otherwise agree. For the reasons given above as to the value of this provision, and for the reasons given below with respect to preserving the right of appeal in Clause 69, we were not persuaded by this.

THE AWARD

Clause 46. Rules applicable to Substance of Dispute

A57–052   222. This Clause reflects much, though not all, of Article 28 of the Model Law. We have not, for example, directed the tribunal to "*take into account the usages of the trade applicable to the transaction.*" If the applicable law allows this to be done, then the provision is not necessary; while if it does not, then it could be said that such a direction overrides that law, which to our minds would be incorrect.

223. Sub-section (1)(b) recognizes that the parties may agree that their dispute is not to be decided in accordance with a recognized system of law but under what in this country are often called "equity clauses", or arbitration "*ex aequo et bono*", or "*amiable composition*" *i.e.* general considerations of justice and fairness etc. It will be noted that we have avoided using this description in the Bill, just as we have avoided using the Latin and French expressions found in the Model Law. There appears to be no good reason to prevent parties from agreeing to equity clauses. However, it is to be noted that in agreeing that a dispute shall be resolved in this way, the parties are in effect excluding any right to appeal to the Court (there being no "*question of law*" to appeal).

224. Sub-section (2) does, in effect, adopt the rule found in Article 28 of the Model Law, thereby avoiding the problems of *renvoi*.

225. Sub-section (3) caters for the situation where there is no choice or agreement. This again is the language of the Model Law. In such circumstances the tribunal must decide what conflicts of law rules are applicable, and use those rules in order to determine the applicable law. It cannot simply make up rules for this purpose. It has been suggested to the DAC that more guidance be given as to the choice of a proper law, but it appears to us that flexibility is desirable, that it is not our remit to lay down principles in this highly complex area, and that to do so would necessitate a departure from the Model Law wording.

Clause 47. Awards on Different Issues etc.

226. We regard this as a very important provision. Some disputes are very complex, **A57–053** raising a large number of complicated issues which, if they are all addressed and dealt with at one hearing, would necessarily take a very long time and be very expensive. Disputes concerning large scale construction contracts are a good example, though there are many other cases.

227. In recent years both the Commercial Court and the Official Referees Court in England (which deal with large cases) have adopted a different approach. The Judge plays much more of a managerial role, suggesting and indeed directing ways in which time and money can be saved. One of the ways is to select issues for early determination, not necessarily on the basis that they will be *legally* determinative of the entire litigation, but where they may well be *commercially* determinative, in the sense that a decision is likely to help the parties to resolve their other differences themselves without the need to spend time and money on using lawyers to fight them out. This has a further advantage. Cases fought to the bitter end often result in a permanent loss of goodwill between the warring factions, thus impeding or preventing future profitable relationships between them. The result is often in truth a loss to all the parties, whether or not they were the "winners" in the litigation.

228. In Court therefore, the old idea that a party is entitled to a full trial of everything at once has now largely disappeared; see, for example, the decision of the House of Lords in *Ashmore v Corporation of Lloyd's* [1992] 2 Lloyd's Rep. 1. Furthermore, this method of approach is reflected in the views expressed by Lord Woolf in his current consideration of how to improve our system of civil justice. The same reasoning, of course, applies to arbitrations.

229. As we have said earlier, arbitration enjoys an advantage over litigation, since the arbitral tribunal is appointed to deal with the particular dispute that has arisen, and is thus in a better position to tailor the procedure to suit the particular circumstances of that dispute. Furthermore, an arbitral tribunal is often able, for the same reason, to move much quicker than the Court.

230. For these reasons, we have tried to make clear in this Clause that the tribunal is empowered to proceed in this way. This is an aspect of the duty cast upon the tribunal to adopt procedures suitable to the circumstances of the particular case, which is set out in Clause 33(1)(a). We would encourage arbitrators to adopt this approach in any case where it appears that time and money will be saved by doing so, and where such an approach would not be at the expense of any of the other requirements of justice.

231. In this connection we would draw attention to the decision of Goff J. (now Lord Goff) in *The Kostas Melas, op. cit.* As we observed when considering Clause 39, the function of arbitrators is not to make temporary financial adjustments between the parties pending the resolution of the dispute, unless this is what they have agreed the arbitrators can do. As this case shows, there is a clear distinction between such arrangements and the right to make a permanent binding decision after considering the arguments, even though the later resolution of other issues (if this becomes necessary) may overall produce a different result.

232. We should emphasize that in this Clause we are not intending to give arbitral tribunals greater or different powers from those they presently have, but to emphasize how their powers should, in suitable cases, be exercised.

233. It might also be noted that we have been careful to avoid use of the term "*interim award*", which has become a confusing term, and in its most common use, arguably a misnomer.

Clause 48. Remedies

A57–054   234. We trust that the matters addressed in this Clause are self-evident. We have excluded specific performance of land contracts, so as not to change the law in this regard, but clarified the power of arbitrators to award injunctive relief. Given that the parties are free to agree on the remedies that a tribunal may order, there is nothing to restrict such remedies to those available at Court.

Clause 49. Interest

A57–055   235. The responses we received demonstrated to us that there was a general desire to give arbitral tribunals a general power to award compound interest.

236. There is no doubt that the absence of such a power adds to the delays (and thus the expense) of arbitrations and causes injustice, for it is often in a party's interest to delay the proceedings and the honouring of an award, since the interest eventually payable is less than can be made by holding on to funds which should be paid over to the other party, who of course is losing out by a like amount.

237. Some of those responding were fearful that arbitrators would abuse this power, and may, for example, award compound interest on a punitive rather than compensatory basis. We do not share those fears. To our minds any competent arbitrator seeking to

fulfil the duties laid on him by the Bill will have no more difficulty in making decisions about compound interest than he will in deciding in any other context what fairness and justice require. Anyone who has such difficulties demonstrates, in our view, that he is really not fit to act as an arbitrator. In such a case, the award and the arbitrator will be susceptible of challenge.

238. Clause 84 and 111 allow for transitional measures. In the context of this Clause, we understand that these may prove necessary in relation to the enforcement of awards through the county courts, who we are told are not presently equipped to calculate compound interest payable from the date of the award.

Clause 50. Extension of Time for making Award

239. This Clause re-enacts the existing law, though with two qualifications: **A57–056**

  i. arbitral procedures for obtaining an extension must be exhausted before recourse to the Court; and

  ii. the Court must be satisfied that substantial injustice would be done if the time were not extended.

It seems to us that these qualifications are needed so as to ensure that the Court's power is supportive rather than disruptive of the arbitral process. For the same reason, it seems to us that it would be a rare case indeed where the Court extended the time notwithstanding that this had not been done through an available arbitral process.

Clause 51. Settlement

240. This Clause reflects Article 30 of the Model Law. It enables an agreed settlement **A57–057** of the dispute to be given the status of an arbitral award, which could then be enforced as such.

241. Concern has been expressed that this provision (taken from Article 30 of the Model Law) might be used by the parties either to obtain an award in respect of matters which are simply not arbitrable (*e.g.* matters which under our law cannot be settled by agreement between the parties), or to mislead third parties (*e.g.* the tax authorities). It was suggested that any agreed award should have to state on its face that it is such.

242. Dealing first with deception, in our view there is no material difference between Clause 51 and our present law: *cf.* p.59 of the Mustill Report. As that Report observes, Article 30 and our present law recognize the right of the tribunal to refuse to make an award on agreed terms if it contains an objectionable feature, *e.g.* is structured to mislead third parties. Clause 51 preserves that right. Thus unless the tribunal is itself prepared to be a party to an attempted deception, we consider the risk that misleading awards will be made to be very small. If the tribunal is prepared to conspire with the parties, then nothing we could put in Clause 51 is likely to deter it. Furthermore, the whole of Clause 51 is based upon the assumption that there is a dispute between the parties which has been referred to arbitration and then settled. Nothing in the Clause would assist parties to mislead others where there was no genuine dispute or genuine reference or genuine settlement. The Clause would simply not apply to such a situation.

243. So far as arbitrability is concerned, this is a question that goes beyond agreed awards. We discuss this question when considering Clause 66 (see also the supplementary recommendations in Chapter 6 below).

244. We are not persuaded that we should require that any agreed award should state that it is such. Both under this Clause and Clause 52 the parties are free to agree on the form the award should take. In our view this is not only the position under the Model Law but also the position under our present law. A requirement that an agreed award should state that it is such would have to be made a mandatory provision to be effective. We are not aware of any problems arising under our present law and are reluctant to impose this formal requirement. Moreover, it would of course be open to the tribunal to record the agreement in the award if they thought it was appropriate to do so. However, at the enforcement stage we agree that the Court should be informed if the award is an agreed award, if this is not apparent from the award itself. We return to this point when considering Clause 66 below (see also Chapter 6).

Clause 52. Form of Award

A57–058 245. This Clause follows closely Article 31 of the Model Law. There are, however, two matters worthy of particular note.

246. In the first place, as in the Model Law, we have required the tribunal to give reasons, unless the award is an agreed award or the parties have agreed that reasons need not be given.

247. To our minds, it is a basic rule of justice that those charged with making a binding decision affecting the rights and obligations of others should (unless those others agree) explain the reasons for making that decision. This was also the view of the majority of those who commented on this.

248. It was suggested that having to give reasons would be likely to add to the cost of arbitrations and encourage applications for leave to appeal to the Court.

249. We do not agree. The need for reasons is that which we have explained above and has nothing to do with the question whether or not a Court should hear an appeal from an award. Further, we have introduced stricter conditions for the bringing of appeals in any event. As to cost, it is always open to the parties to agree to dispense with reasons if they wish to do so, though in the case of domestic arbitrations this can only be done after the dispute has arisen: see Clauses 69(1) and 87.

250. The second noteworthy point is that we have used the word "*seat*" instead of the Model Law phrase "*place of arbitration.*" We consider that the Model Law uses this phrase to mean the seat (there being no obvious legal reason to stipulate the geographical place where the award was made), and since we have used this word earlier in the Bill (see Clauses 2 and 3) it would in our view only cause confusion not to use it here. Of course the seat is only of importance in international arbitrations or where the question arises as to the enforcement of an award abroad. Therefore, in a purely domestic arbitration, if an arbitrator were to fail to state the "*seat*", or to state this incorrectly, it is extremely unlikely that the award could be challenged under Clause 68(2)(h), given that such a failure would be unlikely to result in "*substantial injustice*".

251. Sub-section (3) provides that the award shall be in writing and signed by all the arbitrators or, alternatively, by all those assenting to the award. An earlier draft of this sub-section had only stipulated that all arbitrators assenting to an award sign it. It was pointed out to the DAC, however, that (for whatever reason) some dissenting arbitrators

may not wish to be identified as such, and that the provision should therefore be amended to provide for this.

252. It has been suggested to the DAC that there should be a provision allowing for somebody to sign on behalf of an arbitrator. This could invoke complicated principles of agency, and, overall, is better left to be resolved in each particular case.

Clause 53. Place Where Award is Treated as Made

253. This Clause is designed to avoid disputes over where an award is made and (in cases where Part I of the Bill applies to the arbitration in question) it reverses the decision (although not the result) of the House of Lords in *Hiscox v Outhwaite* [1992] 1 A.C. 562.   A57–059

Clause 54. Date of Award

254. We trust this provision is self-explanatory.   A57–060

Clause 55. Notification of Award

255. This provision we also trust is self-explanatory. The obligation on the tribunal to notify the parties by service on them of copies of the award is important, given that certain time limits in the Bill for, *e.g.* challenging the award, run from the date of the award (which, under Clause 54, in the absence of any other agreement, is the date upon which it is signed). Time periods, of course, can be extended: see Clause 79. We have required the award to be notified to the "parties" so as to prevent one party from obtaining the award and sitting on it without informing the other party until the expiry of time limits for appeal etc, which we are aware has happened in practice.   A57–061

256. Clause 55(3) provides that nothing in this section affects the power to withhold an award in the case of non-payment. However, it should be noted that the duty to notify all parties would of course revive once the tribunal's "lien" has been satisfied.

Clause 56. Power to withhold Award in case of non-payment

257. These provisions enable a party to seek the assistance of the Court if he considers that the arbitrators are asking too much for the release of their award, though it is important to note from sub-section (4) that there is no recourse if there is already arbitral machinery for an appeal or review of the fees or expenses demanded.   A57–062

258. Sub-section (8) makes clear that this Clause does not affect the right to challenge fees and expenses under Clause 28 *i.e.* that paying them to get the award does not lose this right. The reason for this provision is that it may be important for a party to obtain the award quickly, rather than going to the Court for an order about fees and expenses before getting the award.

259. Unlike section 19 of the 1950 Act, this provision gives the Court a discretion to specify that a lesser amount than that claimed by the arbitrators be paid into Court, in order to have the award released. If this were not so, an arbitrator could demand an extortionate amount, in effect preventing a party from taking advantage of the mechanism provided for here.

260. For obvious reasons, this provision is mandatory.

Clause 57. Correction of Award or Additional Award

A57–063   261. This Clause reflects Article 33 of the Model Law. In our view this is a useful provision, since it enables the arbitral process to correct itself, rather than requiring applications to the Court. In order to avoid delay, we have stipulated time limits for seeking corrections etc.

Clause 58. Effect of Award

A57–064   262. This provision in effect simply restates the existing law.

263. It has been suggested that what is described as the other side of sub-section (1) should be spelt out in the Bill *i.e.* that whatever the parties may or may not agree, the award is of no substantive or evidential effect against any one who is neither a party nor claiming through or under a party.

264. Such a provision would, of course, have to be mandatory. It would have to confine itself to cases exclusively concerned with the laws of this country, for otherwise it could impinge on other applicable laws which have a different rule. Even where the situation was wholly domestic, it would also have to deal with all those cases (*e.g.* insurers) who are not parties to the arbitration but whose rights and obligations may well be affected by awards (agreed or otherwise) in one way or another. In our view it would be very difficult to construct an acceptable provision and we are not persuaded that it is needed.

COSTS OF THE ARBITRATION

A57–065

Clause 59. Costs of the Arbitration
Clause 60. Agreement to pay costs in any event
Clause 61. Award of Costs
Clause 62. Effect of Agreement or Award about costs
Clause 63. The recoverable costs of the arbitration
Clause 64. Recoverable fees and expenses of arbitrators
Clause 65. Power to limit recoverable costs

265. In these Clauses we have attempted to provide a code dealing with how the costs of an arbitration should be attributed between the parties. The question of the right of the arbitrators to fees and expenses is dealt with earlier in that part of the Bill concerned with the arbitral tribunal: see Clause 28.

266. Clause 59 defines costs.

267. Clause 60 is a mandatory provision preventing effective agreements to pay the whole or part of the costs in any event unless made after the dispute has arisen. The Clause is based on section 18(3) of the Arbitration Act 1950. The Committee are of the view that public policy continues to dictate that such a provision should remain.

268. Clause 62 empowers the arbitrators to make an award in relation to costs. Sub-section (2) sets out the general principle to be applied, which is the same principle that is applicable in Court.

269. It has been suggested that arbitral tribunals should not be fettered in this way, but to our minds it is helpful to state the principle, especially for those who may not be lawyers and who otherwise might not know how to proceed. Furthermore, it seems to us that there is no reason why the general principle should not apply to arbitrations: it certainly does under the present law. The parties are, of course, free to agree on other principles, subject to Clause 60.

270. Clauses 63 and 64 are we hope more or less self-explanatory. Clearly there has to be a special regime for the fees and expenses of the arbitrators, for otherwise they would be left with the power to decide for themselves whether or not they had overcharged!

271. Clause 64(4) preserves any contractual right an arbitrator may have to payment of his fees and expenses. If a party has agreed these, then it would in our view be wrong to allow the Court to adjust the amount *i.e.* to rewrite that agreement.

272. Clause 65 contains a new proposal. It gives the tribunal power to limit in advance the amount of recoverable costs. We consider that such a power, properly used, could prove to be extremely valuable as an aid to reducing unnecessary expenditure. It also represents a facet of the duty of the tribunal as set out in Clause 33. The Clause enables the tribunal to put a ceiling on the costs, so that while a party can continue to spend as much as it likes on an arbitration it will not be able to recover more than the ceiling limit from the other party. This will have the added virtue of discouraging those who wish to use their financial muscle to intimidate their opponents into giving up through fear that by going on they might be subject to a costs order which they could not sustain.

POWERS OF THE COURT IN RELATION TO AWARD

Clause 66. Enforcement of the Award

273. This reflects Article 35 of the Model Law. Enforcement through the Court provides the classic case of using the Court to support the arbitral process. Sub-section (3)(a) is intended to state the present law: see Mustill & Boyd, *Commercial Arbitration*, 2nd Ed., at p. 546. Sub-section (3)(b) is intended to cover cases where public policy would not recognize the validity of an award, for example awards purporting to decide matters which our law does not accept can be resolved by this means. For obvious reasons, this provision is mandatory.

274. Reference should be made to Chapter 6, where certain supplementary recommendations are made with respect to this Clause.

Clause 67. Challenging the Award: Substantive Jurisdiction

A57–067   **275.** Jurisdiction has already been considered in the context of that part of the Bill dealing with the jurisdiction of the arbitral tribunal: see Clauses 30 to 32.

276. Clause 31 allows the tribunal (where it has power to rule on its own jurisdiction) to make a "jurisdiction" award, either on its own, or as part of its award on the merits. Clause 67 provides the mechanism for challenging the jurisdiction rulings in such awards, and is a mandatory provision. It also provides a mechanism for challenges to the jurisdiction by someone who has taken no part in the arbitral proceedings. We deal with such persons below, when considering Clause 72.

277. To avoid the possibility of challenges to the jurisdiction causing unnecessary delay, the rights given by this Clause are subject to qualifications, which explains the reference in sub-section (1) to three other sections. In addition, sub-section (2) means that a challenge to jurisdiction does not stop the tribunal from proceeding with other aspects of the arbitration while the application is pending.

Clause 68. Challenging the Award: Serious Irregularity

A57–068   **278.** We have drawn a distinction in the Bill between challenges in respect of substantive jurisdiction (i.e. those matters listed in Clause 30) and challenges in respect of what we have called "*serious irregularity.*" We appreciate that cases may arise it which it might be difficult to decide into which category a particular set of circumstances should be placed, but since the time limits etc for both Clause 67 and Clause 68 are the same, this should cause no procedural difficulties. We are firmly of the view, however, that it is useful to have two categories.

279. The reason for this is that where jurisdiction is concerned, there can be no question of applying a test of "*substantial injustice*" or the like. An award of a tribunal purporting to decide the rights or obligations of a person who has not given that tribunal jurisdiction so to act simply cannot stand, though of course, if the party concerned has taken part in the arbitration, there is nothing wrong in requiring him to act without delay in challenging the award.

280. Irregularities stand on a different footing. Here we consider that it is appropriate, indeed essential, that these have to pass the test of causing "*substantial injustice*" before the Court can act. The Court does not have a general supervisory jurisdiction over arbitrations. We have listed the specific cases where a challenge can be made under this Clause. The test of "*substantial injustice*" is intended to be a applied by way of support for the arbitral process, not by way of interference with that process. Thus it is only in those cases where it can be said that what has happened is so far removed from what could reasonably be expected of the arbitral process that we would expect the Court to take action. The test is not what would have happened had the matter been litigated. To apply such a test would be to ignore the fact that the parties have agreed to arbitrate, not litigate. Having chosen arbitration, the parties cannot validly complain of substantial injustice unless what has happened simply cannot on any view be defended as an acceptable consequence of that choice. In short, Clause 68 is really designed as a long stop, only available in extreme cases where the tribunal has gone so wrong in its conduct of the arbitration that justice calls out for it to be corrected.

281. By way of example, there have been cases under our present law where the Court has remitted awards to an arbitral tribunal because the lawyers acting for one party failed (or decided not to) put a particular point to the tribunal: see, for example, *Indian Oil Corporation v Coastal (Bermuda) Ltd* [1990] 2 Lloyd's Rep. 407; *King v Thomas McKenna* [1991] 2 Q.B. 480; *Breakbulk Marine v Dateline*, 19 March 1992, unreported (jurisdiction recognised but not exercised).

282. The responses we received were critical of such decisions, on the grounds that they really did amount to an interference in the arbitral process agreed by the parties. We agree. The Clause we propose is designed not to permit such interference, by setting out a closed list of irregularities (which it will not be open to the Court to extend), and instead reflecting the internationally accepted view that the Court should be able to correct serious failure to comply with the "due process" of arbitral proceedings: *cf.* Article 34 of the Model Law.

283. This Clause is, of course, mandatory.

Clause 69. Appeal on Point of Law

284. We received a number of responses calling for the abolition of any right of appeal on the substantive issues in the arbitration. These were based on the proposition that by agreeing to arbitrate their dispute, the parties were agreeing to abide by the decision of their chosen tribunal, not by the decision of the Court, so that whether or not a Court would reach the same conclusion was simply irrelevant. To substitute the decision of the Court on the substantive issues would be wholly to subvert the agreement the parties had made.

285. This proposition is accepted in many countries. We have considered it carefully, but we are not persuaded that we should recommend that the right of appeal should be abolished. It seems to us, that with the safeguards we propose, a limited right of appeal is consistent with the fact that the parties have chosen to arbitrate rather than litigate. For example, many arbitration agreements contain an express choice of the law to govern the rights and obligations arising out of the bargain made subject to that agreement. It can be said with force that in such circumstances, the parties have agreed that that law will be properly applied by the arbitral tribunal, with the consequence that if the tribunal fail to do this, it is not reaching the result contemplated by the arbitration agreement.

286. In these circumstances what we propose is a right to apply to the Court to decide a point of law arising out of an award. This right is limited, however, in several ways.

  i. The point of law must substantially affect the rights of one or more of the parties. This limitation exists, of course, in our present law.

  ii. The point of law must be one that was raised before the tribunal. The responses showed that in some cases applications for leave to appeal have been made and granted on the basis that an examination of the reasons for the award shows an error on a point of law that was not raised or debated in the arbitration. This method of proceeding has echoes of the old and long discarded common law rules relating to error of law on the face of the award, and is in our view a retrograde step. In our view the right to appeal should be limited us we suggest.

iii. There have been attempts, both before and after the enactment of the Arbitration Act 1979, to dress up questions of fact as questions of law and by that means to seek an appeal on the tribunal's decision on the facts. Generally these attempts have been resisted by the Courts, but to make the position clear, we propose to state expressly that consideration by the Court of the suggested question of law is made on the basis of the findings of fact in the award.

iv. We have attempted to express in this Clause the limits put on the right to appeal by the House of Lords in *Pioneer Shipping Ltd v BTP Tioxide Ltd (The Nema)* [1982] A.C. 724.

287. With respect to the last point, we think it is very important to do this. Many of those abroad who do not have ready access to our case law were unaware that the Arbitration Act 1979 had been construed by the House of Lords in a way that very much limited the right of appeal, and which was not evident from the words of the Act themselves.

288. The test we propose is whether, in the ordinary case, the Court is satisfied that the decision of the tribunal is obviously wrong. The right of appeal is only available for such cases, for the reasons discussed above. Where the matter is one of general public importance, the test is less onerous, but the decision must still be open to serious doubt.

289. We propose a further test, namely whether, despite the agreement of the parties to resolve the matter by arbitration, it is just and proper in all the circumstances for the Court to determine the question.

290. We have been asked why we suggest this addition. The reason is that we think it desirable that this factor should be specifically addressed by the Court when it is considering an application. It seems to us to be the basis on which the House of Lords acted as it did in *The Nema, op. cit.* The Court should be satisfied that justice dictates that there should be an appeal; and in considering what justice requires, the fact that the parties have agreed to arbitrate rather than litigate is an important and powerful factor.

291. It will be noted that we have included a provision that the Court should determine an application without a hearing unless it appears to the Court that a hearing is required. This again reflects what was said in *The Nema, op. cit.* about the tendency for applications for leave being turned into long and expensive court hearings. In our view, the tests for leave (*i.e.* obviously wrong or open to serious doubt) are such that in most cases the Court will be able to decide whether to allow or reject the application on written material alone.

292. Finally, a question has been raised as to whether an agreement in advance of the proceedings (*i.e.* contained in an arbitration clause mor in the underlying contract) would satisfy Clause 69(2)(a). The Clause is intended to encompass such agreements, and in our view it plainly does so since the word agreement is not qualified. However, such an agreement will not automatically allow an appeal unless it complies with the other conditions set out in Clause 69 and 70.

Clause 70. Challenge or Appeal: supplementary Provisions

Clause 71. Challenge or Appeal: effect of Order of the Court

293. These provisions contain time-limits and other matters in relation to challenges to the award and applications and appeals. Some of these provisions are mandatory.

294. The time limit in Clause 70(3) runs from the date of the award, or, where applicable, the date when a party was notified of the result of any arbitral process of appeal or review. It has been suggested that difficulties might arise if an award is held back by the arbitrators, pending payment by the parties (*i.e.* under Clause 56). It is possible that the time limit in Clause 70(3) will have expired by the time an award is released. However, the DAC is of the view that the date of the award is the only incontrovertible date from which the time period should run. Any other starting point would result in great uncertainty (eg as to the exact point at which an award is "released" or "delivered"). Further, any difficulties arising from specific circumstances can be easily remedied by way of an extension of time under Clause 79.

MISCELLANEOUS

Clause 72. Saving for Rights of Person who takes no part in Proceedings

295. To our minds this is a vital provision. A person who disputes that an arbitral tribunal has jurisdiction cannot be required to take part in the arbitration proceedings or to take positive steps to defend his position, for any such requirement would beg the question whether or not his objection has any substance and thus be likely to lead to gross injustice. Such a person must be entitled, if he wishes, simply to ignore the arbitral process, though of course (if his objection is not well-founded) he runs the risk of an enforceable award being made against him. Those who do decide to take part in the arbitral proceedings in order to challenge the jurisdiction are, of course, in a different category, for then, having made that choice, such people can fairly and properly be required to abide by the time limits, etc that we have proposed.

296. This is a mandatory provision.

Clause 73. Loss of Right to Object

297. Recalcitrant parties or those who have had an award made against them often seek to delay proceedings or to avoid honouring the award by raising points on jurisdiction etc which they have been saving up for this purpose or which they could and should have discovered and raised at an earlier stage. Article 4 of the Model Law contains some provisions designed to combat this sort of behaviour (which does the efficiency of arbitration as a form of dispute resolution no good) and we have attempted to address the same point in this Clause. In particular, unlike the Model Law, we have required a party to arbitration proceedings who has taken part or continued to take part without raising the objection in due time, to show that at that stage he neither knew nor could with reason-

MISCELLANEOUS

able diligence have discovered the grounds for his objection (the latter being an important modification to the Model Law, without which one would have to demonstrate actual knowledge, which may be virtually impossible to do). It seems to us that this is preferable to requiring the innocent party to prove the opposite, which for obvious reasons it might be difficult or impossible to do.

298. For the reasons explained when considering Clause 72, the provision under discussion cannot, of course, be applied to a party who has chosen to play no part at all in the arbitral proceedings.

Clause 74. Immunity of arbitral Institutions etc.

A57–073   **299.** In this mandatory provision we have provided institutions and individuals who appoint arbitrators with a degree of immunity.

300. The reason for this proposal is that without such an immunity, there is in our view a real risk that attempts will be made to hold institutions or individuals responsible for the consequences of their exercise of the power they may be given to appoint or nominate arbitrators, or for what their appointed or nominate arbitrators then do or fail to do. This would provide a means of reopening matters that were referred to arbitration, something that might be encouraged if arbitrators were given immunity (as we have also proposed in Clause 29) but nothing was said about such institutions or individuals.

301. There is an additional point of great importance. Many organisations that provide arbitration services, including Trade Associations as well as bodies whose sole function it is to provide arbitration services, do not in the nature of things have deep pockets. Indeed much of the work is done by volunteers simply in order to promote and help this form of dispute resolution. Such organisations could find it difficult if not impossible to finance the cost of defending legal proceedings or even the cost of insurance against such cost. In our view the benefits which these organisations (and indeed individuals) have on arbitration generally fully justify giving them a measure of protection so that their good work can continue.

Clause 75. Charge to secure payment of Solicitors' costs

A57–074   **302.** This is a technical provision designed to maintain the present position.

SUPPLEMENTARY

Clause 76. Service of Notices etc.

A57–075   **303.** The subject matter of this Clause was touched on in the MacKinnon Report which led to the Arbitration Act 1934, but at that time no action was taken.

304. In this Clause we have attempted to do three things.

> i. We have stipulated that the parties can agree on how service of notices and other documents can be done.

ii. We have made clear that in the absence of agreement, service by *any* effective means will suffice.

iii. We have provided in sub-section (4) an option which can best be described as a "fail-safe" method, which a party may employ if he wishes, for example if he is not sure that other methods will be effective. We should emphasize that this fail-safe method is not a compulsory or preferred method for service, but merely a means which, if employed, will be treated as effective.

305. These provisions do not apply in respect of service in Court proceedings, for the obvious reason that such service must comply with the rules of the Court concerned.

Clause 77. Powers of Court in relation to service of documents

306. In this Clause we have given the Court powers to support the arbitral process so that it is not delayed or frustrated through difficulties over service. In the nature of human affairs, it is sadly the case that potential respondents to arbitration proceedings quite often go to considerable lengths to avoid service and thus to achieve this state of affairs, by making normal methods difficult or even impossible to use effectively. This Clause should, in appropriate cases, help to deal with such cases. **A57–076**

Clause 78. Reckoning Periods of Time

307. In our view it would be of great assistance to set out a code to deal with the reckoning of time, thus avoiding the need to refer to other sources. Hence this provision. **A57–077**

Clause 79. Power of Court to extend time limits relating to arbitral Proceedings

308. Here we propose that the Court should have a general right to extend time limits, except time limits for starting an arbitration, which is dealt with specifically in Clause 12. We propose that the wording of the Clause be clarified as set out in Chapter 6 below. **A57–078**

309. This power is limited in the ways set out in this Clause. In particular, no extension will be granted unless a substantial injustice would otherwise be done and any arbitral process for obtaining an extension must first be exhausted. As we have said in other contexts, it would be a rare case indeed where we would expect the Court to grant an extension where such has not been obtained through that process. With these limitations we take the view that this provision can properly be described as supporting the arbitral process.

MISCELLANEOUS

Clause 80. Notice and other Requirements in connection with legal Proceedings

A57–079   310. Legal proceedings must of course be subject to the rules of the Court concerned. We have made clear, therefore, that where the Bill provides for notice of legal proceedings to be given to others, this is a reference to such rules as the Court concerned may make; and is not a separate requirement over and above those rules.

Clause 81. Saving for certain Matters governed by Common Law

A57–080   311. As we have stated earlier, and as was stated in the Mustill Report, it would be neither practicable nor desirable to attempt to codify the whole of our arbitration law. Hence sub-sections (1) and (2) of this Clause.

312. It was suggested to us that a provision preserving the common law would enable arguments to be raised and accepted which were contrary to the spirit and intent of the Bill. We do not think that this will happen, in view of the opening words of the Clause and indeed the statements of principle in Clause 1. Equally, it seems to us to be necessary to make clear that the common law (so far as it is consistent with the Bill) will continue to make its great contribution to our arbitration law, a contribution that has done much to create and preserve the world wide popularity of arbitration in our country.

313. Sub-section (3) is technically necessary to make clear that the repeal of the existing statutes does not have the effect of reviving the common law rules relating to errors on the face of the award.

Clause 82. Minor Definitions

Clause 83. Index of defined Expressions: Part 1

A57–081   314. The first of these Clauses provides the definition of words and phrases which are often repeated in the body of the Bill, so that repetition of the meaning is avoided, as well as providing a ready means of discovering the meaning of certain important words and phrases. The second of these Clauses is also designed to help the reader by identifying the place where other important words and phrases are defined or explained.

Clause 84. Transitional Provisions

A57–082   315. This Clause sets out the general proposition, namely that the Bill will apply to arbitral proceedings commenced after the legislation comes into force, whenever the arbitration agreement is made. There are respectable precedents for this, since the Arbitration Acts 1889, and 1934 contained a like provision. The 1950 Act, of course, was not a precedent, since this was a consolidating measure. We consider this to be a useful provision, since some arbitration agreements have a very long life indeed (for example, rent review arbitration agreements under leases) and it would be most unsatisfactory if the existing law and the proposed legislation were to run in parallel (if that is the right expression) indefinitely into the future.

316. Reference should also be made to Clause 111.

Chapter 3

Part II of the Bill

OTHER PROVISIONS RELATING TO ARBITRATION

Domestic Arbitration Agreements

Clause 85. Modification of Part I in relation to Domestic Arbitration Agreements   A57–083

Clause 86. Staying of Legal Proceedings

Clause 87. Effectiveness of Agreement to exclude Court's Jurisdiction

Clause 88. Power to repeal or amend ss.85 to 87

317. Under our present law, a distinction is drawn between domestic and other arbitrations for two main purposes.

318. In the first place, the rules for obtaining a stay of legal proceedings differ. The reason for this is that under international Conventions, a stay in favour of an arbitration is mandatory except in certain specified circumstances. The current Convention is the New York Convention and the rules under that Convention we have now set out in Clause 9. With an exception that we have already discussed above, Clause 9 simply re-enacts the Arbitration Act 1975 so far as it concerns this matter.

319. Section 1 of the Arbitration Act 1975 does not apply to domestic arbitrations as there defined. These continue to be governed by Section 4(1) of the Arbitration Act 1950, which makes the grant of a stay discretionary.

320. It is our view that consideration should be given to abolishing this distinction and applying the New York Convention rules to all cases. It seems to us that these rules fit much more happily with the concept of party autonomy than our domestic rules, which were framed at a time when attitudes to arbitration were very different and the Courts were anxious to avoid what they described as usurpation of their process.

321. For example, there are cases justifying the refusal of a stay in cases where the Court considers that the party seeking to arbitrate has no defence to the claim and is merely seeking to delay the day of judgment. This has been explained on the basis that since there is no defence to the claim, there is no dispute that can be arbitrated. The difficulty with this argument is that it logically follows that only disputable matters can be arbitrated, or, in other words, that the arbitrators have no jurisdiction to deal with cases where there is no real defence. This in turn means that a claimant cannot refer a claim to arbitration where there is no real defence, since *ex hypothesi* the arbitrators would have no jurisdiction. In short, this argument leads to consequences that in our view have only to be stated to be rejected. As to delaying tactics, it has been our intention throughout the Bill to provide the means whereby an agreement to arbitrate can produce (in suitable cases) a very quick answer indeed. Indeed, if in truth there is no defence to a claim, then it should not take more than a very short time for an arbitral tribunal to deal with the matter and produce an award.

322. For these reasons, which are those discussed in *Nelson v Hayter* [1990] 2 Lloyd's Rep. 265, we consider that this ground for preserving the distinction between domestic and other arbitrations so far as stays are concerned is highly unconvincing.

323. The domestic rules have also been used to refuse stays where the disputes are likely to involve other parties, who could not be brought into the arbitration, since the agreement to arbitrate only binds those who were party to it. Here the justification for refusing to stay legal proceedings is that it would be much better for all the concerned parties to be brought into one proceeding, so that the whole matter can be sorted out between them all.

324. This reasoning of course is in one sense supported by common sense and justice, for in certain cases it would be better and fairer for all the disputes between all the parties involved to be dealt with by one tribunal, thereby avoiding delay and the possibility of inconsistent findings by different tribunals. However, as we observed in the context of considering whether there should be a power (without the agreement of the parties) to order consolidation or concurrent hearings in arbitrations (Clause 35), to refuse a stay because other parties are involved involves tearing up the arbitration agreement that the applicant for a stay has made. In other words, with the benefit of hindsight, the Court adjusts the rights and obligations of contracting parties.

325. We fully accept that for reasons of consumer protection, this on occasion can and should be done, but we are not persuaded that it should be a general rule in the context of stays of domestic arbitrations, for it sits uneasily with the principle of party autonomy and amounts to interference with rather than support for the arbitral process.

326. We should also note that the distinction drawn between domestic and other arbitrations produces odd results. An arbitration agreement between two English people is a domestic arbitration agreement, while an agreement between an English person and someone of a different nationality is not, even if that person has spent all his time in England. Furthermore, we are aware that it could be said that the distinction discriminates against European Community nationals who are not English, and is thus contrary to European law.

327. Notwithstanding the foregoing, we do not propose in this Bill to abolish the distinction. Some defend it and we have not had an opportunity to make all the soundings we would like on this subject. What we have done is to put the domestic arbitration rules in a separate part of the Bill, and provided in Clause 88 for a power of repeal through the mechanism of a positive joint resolution of each House of Parliament.

328. What we have felt able to do is to redraft the domestic rules on stays and to make two changes. Firstly we have removed the discretion and instead set out words which are wide enough to encompass the circumstances which the cases have developed as grounds for refusing a stay. Secondly and more importantly, we have reversed the existing burden of proof (and incidentally got rid of a double or perhaps treble negative in the previous legislation). It seemed to us that it was for the party seeking to litigate something which he had previously agreed to arbitrate to persuade the Court that he should be allowed to go back on his agreement.

329. The second purpose served by making a distinction between domestic and other arbitrations is to prevent the parties in a domestic case from effectively agreeing to exclude the jurisdiction of the Court to deal with preliminary points of law or with an appeal from an award on a point of law, until after the commencement of the arbitral

proceedings. This necessarily means that until the arbitration starts such parties cannot make an effective agreement to dispense with reasons, for that is treated as an agreement to exclude the jurisdiction of the Court—see, now, Clause 69(1).

330. Again we are not persuaded of the value or the validity of this, but we have preserved the existing law for the same reason as we have preserved the present position on stays. Our own view is that this distinction should disappear.

331. It should be noted that we have not preserved the "special categories" dealt with in Section 4 of the Arbitration Act 1979. These were intended as a temporary measure, and the weight of the responses received persuaded us that they should now go.

Consumer Arbitration Agreements

Clauses 89 to 93.

332. In these Clauses we have consolidated the provisions of the Consumer Arbitration Agreements Act 1988. We have suggested this in order to bring within the Bill all the current major enactments on arbitration, so as to provide as complete a code as possible.

333. We did not regard it as part of our remit to redraft this legislation, so we have not sought responses on it. However, we are aware that problems have arisen in construing this Act. For example, it has been suggested that what now appears as Clause 89 makes it far from clear whether a building contract made by a consumer falls outside the Act if the consumer has sought a number of quotes for the work.

334. We are also aware of a more fundamental problem. This country has recently implemented Council Directive 93/13 through the Unfair Terms in Consumer Contracts Regulations 1994 (SI 1994/3159). These Regulations came into force on 1st July 1995. Thus at the moment a situation exists where there are two parallel regimes for protecting consumer interests in the context of arbitration agreements.

335. To our minds this is an unsatisfactory state of affairs, likely to cause confusion and difficulties. Although we have not attempted to trespass into the field of consumer protection, it does seem to us that it would be unfortunate if the opportunity were not taken to clarify the position. On the face of it, the solution would seem to be to maintain the suggested repeal of the 1988 Act and to omit Clauses 89 to 92 of the Bill. If this were to be done, then we would welcome at least a cross-reference in the Bill to the Regulations, so that anyone reading the Bill will be made aware of them. As we understand it, the Regulations would not affect our international obligations regarding arbitrations (for example, the New York Convention) though doubtless those charged with the question of consumer protection will consider this aspect of the matter.

336. We would, however, emphasize that the arbitration community is extremely anxious that the Bill should not be delayed. The fact is that this country has been very slow to modernise its arbitration law and this has done us no good in our endeavour to retain our pre-eminence in the field of international arbitration, a service which brings this country very substantial amounts indeed by way of invisible earnings.

337. It is for these reasons that we have included in Clause 88 a power to amend or repeal Clauses 89 to 93. If the situation cannot be clarified or settled without delaying the progress of the Bill, then this mechanism could allow the Bill to go forward with the Consumer Arbitration Agreements Act in it, and the matter dealt with later.

MISCELLANEOUS

SMALL CLAIMS ARBITRATION IN THE COUNTY COURT

Clause 94. Exclusion of Part 1 in relation to small claims in the County Court

A57–085 338. There is an entirely separate regime for the arbitration of small claims in the County Court. The Bill is not intended to affect this.

339. As we observed earlier in the Report, we considered the suggestion that we should incorporate in the Bill another system for the arbitration of small claims, but for the reasons given, we have not adopted this suggestion and do not recommend it.

APPOINTMENT OF JUDGES AS ARBITRATORS

Clause 95. Appointment of Judges as Arbitrators

A57–086 340. In this Clause we have set out the existing provisions for the appointment of Commercial Judges and Official Referees as arbitrators.

341. We firmly of the view that provision should be made for any Judge to be appointed as an arbitrator, rather than limiting the power to the two kinds of Judge presently included. It was not, however, possible to obtain agreement to this proposal from the concerned departments in time to put it in the Bill.

342. We appreciate that in view of the court commitments of Judges generally, it is not possible to allow Judges to act as arbitrators whenever they are asked and are willing to do so. Hence the present requirement now set out in sub-sections (2) and (3). We would suggest that the same or a similar provision is used for all other Judges.

343. We are told that the problem is particularly acute in the field of patents and the like, where the parties are anxious to arbitrate but where the only acceptable arbitrators are Judges.

STATUTORY ARBITRATIONS

Clauses 96 to 101

A57–087 344. These provisions adapt Part 1 to statutory arbitrations. This exercise is not within our remit and we have played no part in it.

Chapter 4

Part III of the Bill

Clauses 102 to 107

345. The purpose of Part III is to re-enact the substance of the provisions relating to the recognition and enforcement of foreign arbitral awards contained in Part II of the Arbitration Act 1950 and the Arbitration Act 1975, which gave effect to the UK's treaty obligations under the Geneva and New York Conventions respectively.

346. The Geneva Convention only remains in force as between state parties to that Convention which have *not* subsequently become parties to the New York Convention. So far as the UK is concerned, it is believed that only a few states (*e.g.* Malta) remain in that category. Accordingly, in the interest of brevity, Clause 102 states simply that Part II of the Arbitration Act 1950 continues to apply to Geneva Convention awards which are not also New York Convention awards rather than restating or reframing the non-user friendly language of Part II of that Act.

347. The New York Convention on the Recognition and Enforcement of Foreign Arbitral Awards adopted by the UN Conference on International Arbitration on 10 June 1958 is not only the cornerstone of international dispute resolution; it is an essential ingredient more generally of world trade. If it did not exist, or even if it were not to have been widely adopted by the world's trading nations, contracting parties from different legal cultures might be reduced to resolving their disputes in the courts of a country which would be alien to either one or both of them (because of doubts as to the enforceability across national boundaries of arbitration awards made in a neutral country). Clauses 102 to 107 of the Bill restate the current implementing legislation (contained in the 1975 Act) in concise and simple language.

348. As we have indicated earlier in Chapter 2, we take the view that the definition of "*in writing*" is consonant with Article II.2 of the New York Convention. For clarity therefore, we consider that the Bill can be improved by including an express cross-reference to this definition in Clause 103(2). This would have the added advantage of ensuring that the enforcement of foreign awards under Clause 66 and enforcement under the New York Convention are in this respect in line with each other.

349. One intriguing question was highlighted by the decision of the House of Lords in *Hiscox v Outhwaite* [1992] 1 A.C. 562. This concerns the case of an arbitration with its "seat" in country A and an award that states expressly that it was "made" in country B. Country A might be a New York Convention country, and B not—or vice versa. (Article I.1 of the Convention provides that it shall apply to " . . . *awards made in the territory of a State other than the State in which recognition and enforcement of such awards are sought* . . . " (emphasis added)).

350. Distinguished authors (writing before the decision in *Hiscox*) are split on the question. Dr A.J. van den Berg in the first edition of his authoritative book on the Convention (at pp. 294/295) states: "*The award must be deemed to be made in the country which is indicated in the award as [the] place where the award was made.*" (emphasis added).

351. But the late Dr F.A. Mann Q.C. (in [1985] *Arb. Int.* 107/108) wrote, after recalling that little learning then existed on the question of where an award is made, "*It is submit-*

A57–088

ted that an award is 'made' at the place at which the arbitration is held, ie the arbitral seat .... admittedly the view suggested here attributes a somewhat strained meaning to the word 'made'. But for the reasons given the natural meaning of the word leads to such strange consequences that a less literal interpretation would seem to be justified".

352. In *Hiscox* the question arose as to whether, where the "*seat*" of the arbitration was in England and for all practical purposes it was a domestic "English" arbitration, the award became a "foreign" award for the purposes of the Convention merely because it stated expressly on its face that it was signed in Paris? According to the House of Lords, applying a literal interpretation of Article I.1 of the Convention, the answer was "Yes".

353. So far as arbitrations held in England, Wales or Northern Ireland are concerned, the "strange consequences" of this result have been removed by Clause 53 of the Bill (see above).

354. The DAC is of the view that this question should be resolved by incorporating into Part III of the proposed new legislation an equivalent provision to that contained in Clause 53—to the effect that an award shall be treated as made at the seat of the arbitration, regardless of where it was signed, despatched or delivered to any of the parties. It seems to us that this is consonant with the UK's treaty obligations under the New York Convention.

Chapter 5

Part IV of the Bill

A57–089   **355.** We have drawn attention to Clause 111 under Clause 84. The other Clauses in this Part we trust are self-evident, and were not within the remit of the DAC, although we do welcome the inclusion of Northern Ireland.

Chapter 6

Supplementary Recommendations

A57–090   **356.** The foregoing discussion is based on the text of the Bill as it was introduced in December 1995. Since that date we have had the advantage of considering the speeches made in the House of Lords on the Second Reading and some comments and suggestions from others, as well as looking once again at the text of the Bill in the course of preparing this Report. In consequence, we make the following recommendations.

Clause 2. Scope of Application

A57–091   **357.** A number of foreign readers have expressed the view that Clause 2(2)(a) does not sufficiently make clear that the applicable law referred to is the law applicable to the arbitration agreement, rather than the law applicable to the substantive agreement (which would have far reaching and wholly unintended consequences). For the sake of clarity, we would suggest an amendment along the following lines:

" ... where the applicable law **to that agreement is** the law of England and Wales or Northern Ireland; and ... "

Clause 7. Separability of Arbitration Agreement

358. In view of the definition of "agreement" in Clause 5, we suggest that the words *"(whether or not in writing)"* be inserted after the words *"another agreement"* in Clause 7, since otherwise it could be said that this Clause is only effective in relation to such other agreements as are in writing. This is not the intention. A57–092

Clause 14(5). Commencement of Arbitral Proceedings

359. It has been suggested that the words *"gives notice"* should be replaced by *"serves"*, in conformity with Clauses 14(3) and 14(4). This is a matter for Parliamentary Counsel to consider. A57–093

Clause 16(6)(b) and Clause 21(4)

360. The word *"any"* follows a negative and so could be read as meaning *"all."* This is not the intention. We therefore suggest that the words *"one or more matters"* follow the word *"any"* in these provisions. A57–094

Clause 24(4). Power of Court to Remove Arbitrator

361. We have explained in Chapter 1 above the reasoning behind Clause 29(3). Upon further reflection, it appears to us that Clause 24(4) needs to be altered for the same reason. As currently drafted, if an arbitrator resigns and is sued for his fees, he is not protected from such a breach of contract action by the immunity in Clause 29. Rather, he can apply to the Court for protection under Clause 25(3), and the Court may see fit to grant this, if appropriate. However, if an arbitrator does not resign, but is removed by the Court under Clause 24, it would appear that he will have the benefit of the immunity in Clause 29, come what may. In such circumstances, the parties could not sue him for breach of contract, unless they could demonstrate *"bad faith"*. This is anomalous. The DAC therefore recommends that Clause 24(4) be amended to provide that as well as making such order as it thinks fit with respect to an arbitrator's entitlement to fees, where the Court removes an arbitrator, it also be given a discretion to make such order as it thinks fit with respect to an arbitrator's immunity under Clause 29. Such wide words A57–095

would enable the Court, for example, to remove the immunity but impose a ceiling on the amount of any liability.

362. Arbitrators may also be removed by agreement of the parties. However, the DAC does not consider that a similar provision be made with respect to this, given that it would be contrary to the whole basis of Clause 29 for parties to be able to agree on the removal of an arbitrator's immunity.

Clause 25(2). Resignation of Arbitrator

A57–096   363. There is a rogue "*in writing*" in this sub-section, which should be deleted by virtue of Clause 5(1).

Clause 38(3). Security for Costs

A57–097   364. In the draft Clauses published in July 1995, the power to order security for costs was expressed in very general terms. This elicited a number of responses which expressed concern that there were no principles or guidelines for the exercise of this power. It is certainly the case that the power to order security for costs, unless exercised with great care, can all too easily work injustice rather than justice.

365. The rules and principles applied by the Courts with respect to security for costs have been carefully worked out over many years, and are contained in a large amount of case law that has developed alongside Order 23 of the Rules of the Supreme Court. Given the concerns referred to above, the DAC considered whether to set out these rules and principles in the Bill. In the end we decided that this would be simply impracticable: a codification of all the relevant case law would be extremely difficult, would result in very lengthy and complicated provisions, and may well have an unintended impact on how this area is approached by the Courts.

366. Clause 38(3) of the current draft of the Bill reflects what we initially concluded was the only solution to this difficulty: it provides that arbitrators are to have power to order a party to provide security for costs "*wherever the court would have power* . . . " and that this power is to be exercised: "*on the same principles as the court.*" In the light of many comments received since the Bill was introduced (including a significant number of criticisms of this sub-section from foreign arbitration specialists and institutions), we have had to reconsider this area, and, after much careful thought, we have concluded that Clause 38(3) requires amendment for the following reasons:

> i. As drafted, this sub-section is very far from being "user-friendly". Without referring to the Rules of the Supreme Court, and the case law referred to in the relevant part of the White Book, it would be impossible for any domestic or foreign user to determine what the nature and scope of the power conferred here is. Lay arbitrators may have difficulty locating or even, perhaps, understanding the relevant law (any error of law, of course, being a potential ground for appeal). In the case of a foreign arbitration that has its seat in this country for the sole reason that this is a neutral forum, it would be extremely undesirable for parties to have to instruct English lawyers in order to make sense of this provision. This alone could constitute a powerful disincentive to selecting this

country as an arbitral seat. Indeed, throughout the Bill, we have been very careful to avoid any such express cross-references to other legal sources.

ii. One of the grounds on which an order for security for costs may be made in Court is that the plaintiff is ordinarily resident out of the jurisdiction: see Order 23, Rule 1(1)(a) of the Rules of the Supreme Court. On further consideration of the matter, we have concluded that it would be very damaging to this country's position as the leading centre for international arbitrations to make this ground available to arbitral tribunals. It would reasonably appear to those abroad who are minded to arbitrate their claims here that foreigners were being singled out for special and undeserved treatment. (Of course if the parties agree to invest their tribunal with power to order security for costs on this ground, they are free to do so).

iii. On reflection, the concerns expressed above as to the potential scope of the power conferred by Clause 38(3) and the possibilities of injustice may be overstated. The other provisions of the Bill confer very far-reaching powers on arbitrators, and it has been made clear throughout that this is tempered, for example, by the mandatory duty in Clause 33. The same would be true of the power to order security for costs: in exercising the power, the tribunal would have to comply with Clause 33, and any serious irregularity could form the basis of a challenge. In agreeing to arbitration, parties in effect agree that their disputes could be decided differently from a Court, although in accordance with principles of justice. The fact that arbitrators may decide an issue as to security for costs differently from a judge appears to be no more than an aspect of this. It is true that if this power is improperly exercised, a claim could, for example, be stifled without justification. It is equally true, however, that the Bill contains mechanisms for parties to challenge any such injustice or improper conduct, and sufficient warnings to arbitrators as to their mandatory duties.

367. We remain of the view that the power to order security for costs is an important one, and should be given to arbitrators, and also that some basic restrictions should be set out in this Clause, in the light of the points made above. To this end, we recommend that Clause 38(3) be deleted, and replaced with a new provision along the following lines:

"*(3) The tribunal may order a claimant to provide security for the costs of the arbitration.*
Such power shall not be exercised on the grounds only that such party is—

(a) an individual ordinarily resident in a state other than the United Kingdom,
(b) a body corporate which was incorporated in or has its central management and control exercised in a state other than the United Kingdom."

368. Such a provision would allow arbitrators a flexibility in exercising this power, within the confines of their strict duty in Clause 33. The risk of an order on the sole ground that a party is from abroad, would be removed. Similarly, there would be no need for an arbitrator, whether domestic or foreign, to discern the English or Northern Irish law in this area, or, indeed, to instruct local lawyers in this respect. An arbitrator may well exercise this power differently from a Court (as with many other powers conferred by the Bill), but any misuse could be corrected under the other provisions of the Bill.

369. It is of course the case that orders for security are not to be made automatically, but only when the justice of the case so requires. We appreciate that cases are likely to arise when deciding what is just may be very difficult. For example, a claimant may contend that he might be prevented from continuing if he has to put up security, whilst at the same time a respondent is contending that unless security is provided, he is likely to be ruined. However, to our minds, this is merely an example of the balancing of factors in order to achieve the most just result possible which is part of the essential function of arbitrators.

370. The power to award security for costs under the proposed provision could be exercised against counter-claimants as well as claimants. This we have covered in the definition Clause (see Clause 82(1)).

Clause 66. Enforcement of Award

A57–098 **371.** In the present Bill, we have provided that leave by a Court to enforce an award may not be given if the award was so defective in form or substance that it is incapable of enforcement, if its enforcement would be contrary to public policy or if the tribunal lacked substantive jurisdiction.

372. These are what are described as "passive" defences to the enforcement of an award. The "positive" steps that may be taken are those we have set out in Clauses 67 to 69, together with the rights preserved in Clause 72 for someone who has taken no part in the arbitral proceedings.

373. In our view the way we have drafted Clause 66 sufficed to cover all the cases where enforcement should be refused. However, since the Bill was published it has been suggested to us that it would be advisable to spell out in more detail two particular cases, namely those where the arbitral tribunal has purported to decide matters which are simply not capable of resolution by arbitration, whatever the parties might have agreed (*e.g.* custody of a child) and those where the tribunal has made an award which (if enforced) would improperly affect the rights and obligations of those who were not parties to the arbitration agreement.

374. On the present wording, even if it could be said that either or both these cases fell outside the three categories where leave to enforce shall not be given, it does not follow that the Clause somehow sanctions enforcement in those cases. The reason for this is that the Clause does not require the Court to order enforcement, but only gives it a discretion to do so. That discretion is only fettered in a negative way *i.e.* by setting out certain cases where enforcement shall not be ordered. To our minds there is nothing to prevent a Court from refusing to enforce an award in other appropriate cases. Unlike, for example, Clause 68, there is no closed list of cases where leave to enforce an award may be refused. However, on reflection we consider that it would be preferable to set out the two cases as further instances where the discretion of the Court is negatively fettered, and we would suggest that a further category is added to sub-section (3) along the following lines:—

> "*it purports to decide matters which are not capable of resolution by arbitration or grants relief which (if enforced as a judgment or order of the court) would improperly affect the rights of persons other than the parties to the arbitration agreement.*"

375. Such a provision would best appear before the catch all case of public policy. It will be noted that this wording takes advantage of the definition of parties to an arbitration agreement to be found in Clause 82(2). Furthermore, to put the matter beyond any doubt, we would suggest that it is made clear that sub-section (3) is not a closed list, by inserting suitable words.

376. It is vital to include some such word as "*improperly*" since there is no doubt that there are many cases where third party rights and obligations are perfectly properly affected, such as guarantors or insurers who have agreed to pay the amount of an award to which they are not a party. Furthermore, it must always be borne in mind that the parties' rights and obligations may well be governed by a law other than our own, under which, for example, matters are arbitrable which would not be the case under our own law. In such cases it would not automatically follow that the Court would refuse to enforce the award, unless of course public policy dictated that course.

377. Apart from the enforcement procedure set out in this clause, under our law it is possible to bring an action on an award, in much the same way as an action is brought on an agreement. This method is expressly saved in Clause 81(2)(b). There is also an oblique reference to this in Clause 66(5) in the reference to "*rule of law*". On reflection, it seems to us that it would make for greater clarity to add the words "*or by an action on the award*" at the end of this sub-section.

378. There is one further point. It seems to us that there is much to be said for a suggestion that the Court must be informed on an application for enforcement if the award is an agreed award (see Clause 51) if this is not apparent from the award itself, and that any enforcement order or judgment of the Court should also state that it is made in respect of an agreed award, thus putting everyone concerned on notice of that fact and avoiding the risk that third parties might be misled into believing that the award was one made at arm's length. We suggest that these requirements be added to Clause 66.

Clause 69. Appeal on Point of Law

379. It has been pointed out that Clause 69(8) sets out the two pre-conditions to an **A57–099** appeal to the Court of Appeal as alternatives, whereas they should be cumulative (as with the similar pre-conditions in section 1(7) of the 1979 Act). We recommend that the Clause be amended accordingly.

Clause 70. Challenge or Appeal: supplementary provisions

380. We note that the power to order security or bring the money payable under the **A57–100** award into court only extends at present to applications under Clauses 67 or 68. This should be extended so that the Court can impose these requirements as a condition of granting leave to appeal under Clause 69. This is a tool of great value, since it helps to avoid the risk that while the appeal is pending, the ability of the losing party to honour the award may (by design or otherwise) be diminished.

Clause 74. Immunity of Arbitral Institutions etc.

A57–101 381. On reflection we consider that the wording of Clause 74(2) should be tightened so as to make clear that the institution or person concerned is not liable without more for anything done or omitted to be done by the arbitrator. Thus we suggest that the words *"by reason only of"* should be substituted for the word *"for"* in this sub-section.

Clause 79. Powers of Court to Extend Time Limits Relating to Arbitral Proceedings

A57–102 382. It has been pointed out to us that Clause 79(1) as presently drafted could be said to be inapplicable to, for example, Clause 70(3) where the time stipulated is not one having effect in default of agreement between the parties. We agree with this comment and suggest that Clause 79(1) be amended along the following lines:

> " ... the court may by order extend any time limit agreed by them in relation to any matter relating to the arbitral proceedings or **applicable by virtue of any provision of this Part**."

Clause 81. Saving for Certain Matters Governed by Common Law

A57–103 383. We suggest that two additions should be made to the specific cases mentioned in sub-section (2).

384. The first of these relates to confidentiality. For reasons we have explained, we have not included specific provisions dealing with this matter. However, it seems to us that it would be valuable to highlight the fact that our law does deal with it. Thus we suggest a further category which could perhaps be in the following words:—

> *"confidentiality and privacy in relation to arbitrations."*

385. The second addition we propose relates to arbitrability, which we have discussed in the context of Clause 66. Again there is a lot of important law on this topic. We suggest a further category which could perhaps be in the following words:—

> *"whether a matter is capable of resolution by arbitration."*

386. The title to this Clause is *"Saving for certain matters governed by common law."* We would prefer the expression *"other rules of law"* to the words *"common law"* as this would include legislation and be clearer to non-lawyers and those from abroad.

Clause 82. Minor Definitions

A57–104 387. The definition of *"question of law"* started life as part of the Clause dealing with appeals to the Court; now Clause 69. The objective was to make clear that there was no question of an appeal in respect of a matter of foreign law. Our law treats questions of foreign law as questions of fact. Furthermore, we can see no good reason for allowing an appeal on foreign law, since *ex hypothesi* the Court cannot give a definitive or authoritative ruling on such matters. The Courts have refused to grant leave to appeal on questions of foreign law, but attempts are still made and it would be desirable to put the matter beyond doubt.

388. The definition was moved to this Clause. It had, of course, to accommodate the fact that the Bill is expressed to apply to Northern Ireland as well as England and Wales. However the present definition, while it does this, also seems to indicate that where the seat of the arbitration is in neither of these places, the meaning of "question of law" is not confined to questions of (respectively) English law or the law of Northern Ireland. We would suggest that the definition be amended, so that "question of law" means a question of law of England and Wales where the application for leave to appeal is made to a Court in England and Wales, and a question of the law of Northern Ireland, where an application for leave to appeal is made to a Court in Northern Ireland.

Clause 85. Domestic Arbitration Agreements

389. It has been pointed out to us that the way "domestic arbitration agreements" is defined (which is taken from the existing legislation) means that agreements made by sovereign states which incorporate an arbitration clause fall into this category. We are sure that this was not the intention, so that if the distinction between domestic and non-domestic arbitrations is to remain, the opportunity should be taken to correct this anomaly. **A57–105**

Clause 95. Appointment of Judges as Arbitrators

390. For the reasons set out in our discussion of this Clause in Chapter 1, we recommend that this provision be extended to judges generally. **A57–106**

Clauses 96–100. Statutory Arbitrations

391. Although the application of Part 1 to statutory arbitrations is not part of our remit, we note that during the Second Reading Lord Lester suggested that it might be a requirement of European law in cases of compulsory arbitration that the arbitrators should be independent as well as impartial. We can offer no view on this point, but if it is felt appropriate to include any such requirement in the context of statutory arbitrations, great care should be taken to make clear that this requirement has no application to private or other consensual arbitrations, so as to avoid any risk of this concept being imported into other cases. This, for the reasons already given, would in our view be most damaging. We understand that Lord Lester shares our view that a requirement of independence for private or other consensual arbitrations is neither necessary nor desirable. **A57–107**

MISCELLANEOUS

Clause 103. New York Convention Awards

A57–108   392. For the reasons set out in our discussion in Chapter 3, this Clause should be amended so as to cross-refer to the definition of writing to be found in Part I of the Bill, and should also incorporate the recommendation that an award should be treated as made at the seat of the arbitration, regardless of where it was signed, despatched or delivered to any of the parties.

Clause 107. Saving for Other Bases of Recognition or Enforcement

A57–109   393. It has been pointed out that, as drafted, this Clause may not save enforcement under Part II of the 1950 Act. This is a matter for Parliamentary Counsel to consider.

CHAPTER 7

CONCLUSIONS

A57–110   394. The Arbitration Bill and this Report are the result of a long and wide-ranging process of consultation with interested parties, probably the most comprehensive for any Bill of this kind. Our recommendations are based on the many responses that we have received as well as our own researches and discussions. In a number of cases, of course, we have had to make decisions on matters where more than one point of view has been expressed. What we should emphasize, however, is that all were agreed that it is high time we had new legislation, to the extent that many people have stated to us that for this reason they were not disposed to delay progress by stubbornly insisting on their point of view on particular points; and have demonstrated that this is the case by being ready and willing to reach compromise solutions. We are convinced (as all are) that further delay will do grave and probably irretrievable damage to the cause of arbitration in this country, thus damaging our valuable international reputation as well as the promotion here of this form of dispute resolution.

395. We have attempted to produce a draft which can be read, understood and applied by everyone, not just lawyers learned in this branch of our law. Thus our aim has been to make the text "user-friendly" and the rules it contains clear and readily comprehensible, so that arbitration is available to all who wish to use it. This has not been an easy task, since in the nature of things this form of dispute resolution raises highly complex and sophisticated matters. We have attempted it, however, in the hope that our efforts will not only encourage and promote arbitration, but also help to achieve what we believe to be the true object of this form of dispute resolution, namely (in the words of Clause 1 of the Bill itself) to obtain the fair resolution of disputes by an impartial tribunal without unnecessary delay or expense.

Departmental Advisory Committee on Arbitration Law—Supplementary Report on the Arbitration Act 1996

January 1997

Chapter 1

Introduction

1. In our Report of February 1996 we discussed the provisions of the Arbitration Bill **A58–001** as introduced in the House of Lords in December 1995. In Chapter 6 of that Report we set out some recommendations for changes to some of the provisions of the Bill, having considered the speeches made in the House of Lords on the Second Reading and some comments and suggestions from others; and having also carried out our own re-examination of the Bill. This Report discusses the changes that were made to the Bill during its passage through Parliament and thus the differences between that Bill and the Arbitration Act 1996, which received the Royal Assent on 17 June 1996. All these changes were recommended by the Committee, though some differ from or are in addition to the suggestions originally made in Chapter 6. Not all the changes suggested in Chapter 6 were adopted, but again this met with the approval of the Committee, after yet further reflection and consideration of comments and suggestions made to us.

2. Certain decisions were also taken by the DAC after the Act received the Royal Assent, with respect to the commencement of its provisions. These are also discussed with respect to the particular sections affected, and in the context of the transitional provisions.

3. This Supplementary Report is to be read in conjunction with our Report of February 1996. The numbering of Sections corresponds to the Act in its final form. As several Sections were added to the Bill during its passage through Parliament, some of the references are slightly different from those in Chapter 6 of our February 1996 Report.

4. The new Order 73 of the Rules of the Supreme Court, together with the new Allocation Order (which stipulates the Courts to which arbitration applications may be made) have been included in Appendix A to this Report, together with a short commentary. The new Order 73 has been completely recast in order to reflect the changes brought about by the Act and to simplify the procedure for Court applications concerning arbitration. Although drafted in consultation with some members of the DAC, the new rules were not within the latter's remit, and are therefore included here simply for ease of reference.

5. By the Arbitration Act (Commencement No.1) Order 1996 (S.I. 1996 No. 3146), the Act (with the qualifications set out in that Order) comes into force on 31st January 1997. This Order also contains transitional provisions. The Order is reproduced in Appendix B, together with a short commentary.

Chapter 2

Part I of the Act

Section 2. Scope of Application

A58–002 6. Clause 2 of the Bill as introduced in the House of Lords in December 1995, read as follows:

> "2.—(1) The provisions of this Part apply where the law of England and Wales or Northern Ireland is applicable, or the powers of the court are exercisable, in accordance with the rules of the conflict of laws.
>
> (2) They apply, in particular—
>
> > (a) to matters relating to or governed by the arbitration agreement, where the applicable law is the law of England and Wales or Northern Ireland; and
> >
> > (b) to matters governed by the law applicable to the arbitral proceedings, where the seat of the arbitration is in England and Wales or Northern Ireland.
>
> (3) The following provisions apply whatever the law applicable to the arbitration agreement or the arbitral proceedings—
>
> > (a) sections 9 to 11 (stay of legal proceedings);
> >
> > (b) section 43 (securing the attendance of witnesses) and section 44 (court powers exercisable in support of arbitral proceedings); and
> >
> > (c) section 66 (enforcement of arbitral awards).
>
> (4) The court may refuse to exercise any power conferred by this Part if, in the opinion of the court, the fact that the seat of the arbitration is outside England and Wales or Northern Ireland, or that when designated or determined the seat is likely to be outside England and Wales or Northern Ireland, makes it inappropriate to exercise that power."

7. This provision was explained at paragraphs 23 to 25 of our Report of February 1996. The intention was to set out a clear statement identifying the scope of application of the Act, without attempting to codify any rules of the conflict of laws. The basic elements of this clause, as originally drafted, may be summarised as follows:

> i. Clause 2(1) simply provided that the Act applies wherever English law is found to be applicable to an arbitration, or where the powers of the English Court are exercisable in relation to an arbitration. Whether or not English law is applicable, and whether or not the powers of the English Court are exercisable, are both matters to be determined by reference to appropriate rules of the conflict of laws, which are to be found elsewhere.
>
> ii. Clause 2(2), as originally drafted, further refined this basic principle by recognising that different elements in an arbitration may well be governed by differ-

ent laws. The law governing the merits of the dispute (*e.g.* a choice of law clause in a contract) may not necessarily govern the arbitration clause itself, as the latter constitutes a separate agreement. Similarly, the law governing the procedure of the arbitration may well be a different law from that governing the merits of the dispute. Consequently, if the arbitration agreement was governed by English law, those provisions in the Act which concern arbitration agreements would apply (clause 2(2)(a)). Similarly, if the seat of the arbitration was in England and Wales or Northern Ireland, those parts of the Act which concern the arbitral procedure (as distinct from matters of substance) would apply (clause 2(2)(b)).

This further refinement was necessary in order to avoid the danger that all the provisions of Part I of the Act would be imported if English law is found to govern one particular aspect of an arbitration. For example, an arbitration may have a French seat, with French law governing the procedure, but English law governing the arbitration agreement. In such a situation, only those provisions of the Act which concern arbitration agreements should apply. It would be quite wrong to apply provisions of the Act which concern arbitral procedure, as this would be governed by French law. Indeed, if this were not the case, a choice of English law to govern an arbitration agreement would entitle a party to invoke the jurisdiction of the English Court wherever the seat of the arbitration might be, thereby endowing the English Court with an unacceptable extra-territorial jurisdiction.

iii. The remaining parts of the original Clause 2 made specific provision for the New York Convention (Clause 2(3)(a) and (b)—stays of legal proceedings and the enforcement of awards) and enacted Section 25 of the Civil Jurisdiction and Judgments Act 1982 (Clause 2(3)(b)—powers in support of foreign arbitrations).

8. In Chapter 6 of our February 1996 Report, at paragraph 357, we recommended that **A58–003** the original clause 2(2)(a) be slightly amended in order to make clear that the applicable law referred to there was the law applicable to the arbitration agreement, rather than the law applicable to the substantive agreement.

9. Following the introduction of the Bill into Parliament, we had the benefit of further detailed discussions with a number of leading arbitration experts from abroad, and took the opportunity of reconsidering this provision. It is fair to say that whilst there was unanimous support for the inclusion of such a provision identifying the scope of the Act, there was considerable disquiet as to the clause as drafted. It was felt that the provision was sound in principle, but unworkable in practice, for the following reasons:

i. The clause was complicated and extremely difficult to understand. To this end, it appeared to defeat its own object.

ii. In order to apply clause 2(2), it was necessary to be able to identify all those provisions of the Act which concerned the arbitration agreement, as distinct from all those that concerned the arbitral procedure. As explained above, if for example English law governed the arbitration agreement, but not the arbitral procedure, by virtue of clause 2(2) only those provisions in the Act which concerned the arbitration agreement (as opposed to the arbitral procedure) would apply. The provisions of the Act had therefore to be individually characterised and separated in this way.

However, the original clause made no attempt to characterise each provision of the Act, precisely because this had proved an extremely difficult and complex exercise. Many provisions concern both arbitration agreements and arbitral procedure, and there appeared to be a divergence of view with respect to many others.

> iii. There was a feeling amongst certain foreign experts that the original clause gave the wrong impression, in that it appeared to endow the English Court with inappropriate extra-territorial powers, when this was clearly not intended.

10. In the light of these difficulties, the DAC decided to recast the whole provision in a different form that would be far easier to understand and that would be entirely workable in practice. The policy behind the Section, however, was not materially altered. The final Section 2 provides a clear and simple scheme, which was welcomed by all those who had originally expressed concerns.

11. Section 2(1) states the basic rule: Part I of the Act applies to arbitrations which have their seat in England and Wales or Northern Ireland. The concept of a "seat" was referred to in our February 1996 Report, and is defined in Section 3 of the Act. The seat of an arbitration refers to its legal place, as opposed to its geographical location. It is, of course, perfectly possible to conduct an arbitration with an English seat at any convenient location, whether in England or abroad.

12. If the seat of an arbitration is in England and Wales or Northern Ireland, the arbitration will be governed by this Act. If, however, a foreign law has been chosen to govern any particular aspect of the arbitration, such as the arbitral procedure or the arbitration agreement, or is otherwise applicable to any such aspect, this is catered for by Section 4(5). Therefore, reference may be made to this Act in the first instance, and then back to another law with respect to a specific issue. Whilst a process of characterisation may still have to be done, the combination of Section 2 and Section 4(5) avoids the dangers that:

— a choice of English law with respect to one part of an arbitration will import other parts of the Act that concern other aspects of the arbitration;

— a choice of England as the seat of the arbitration will necessarily entail the imposition of every provision of the Act.

13. Sections 2(2) to (5) set out a series of deviations from the basic rule in Section 2(1).

14. Section 2(2) caters for the New York Convention. Under the terms of this Convention, the English Courts are obliged to recognise and enforce foreign arbitration agreements and foreign arbitral awards. Sections 9 to 11 (stays of legal proceedings etc) and Section 66 (enforcement) could not, therefore, be restricted to arbitrations with a seat in England and Wales or Northern Ireland. These particular Sections therefore apply even if the seat of an arbitration is abroad. Equally, these Sections will apply if no seat has been designated or determined.

15. Section 2(3) extends the power of the Court to grant interim relief in support of arbitrations with a foreign seat, thereby giving effect to Section 25 of the Civil Jurisdiction and Judgments Act 1982, as was intended by the original clause 2(3)(b). The power of the Court to exercise these powers is restricted in the last part of this Section to appropriate cases. There may well be situations in which it would be quite wrong for an English Court to make an interim order in support of a foreign arbitration, where this would result in a possible conflict with another jurisdiction.

16. Section 2(4) deals with those cases where a seat has still to be designated or determined, but where recourse to the Court is necessary in the meantime. For example, an arbitration agreement may provide that the tribunal, once constituted, will designate the seat of the arbitration. The agreement may also provide that any arbitration must be commenced within a specified time period. If that time period is exceeded, could a party make an application to the English Court pursuant to Section 12 of the Act for an Order extending time for the commencement of proceedings (eg in order that a seat may be designated)? See *e.g. International Tank & Pipe S.A.K. v Kuwait Aviation Fuelling Co. K.S.C.* [1975] Q.B. 224 (C.A.). Clearly this would not be possible under Section 2(1), as long as the arbitration was without an English or Northern Irish seat. It was our view, however, that the English Court should be able to exercise supportive powers if there is a sufficient connection with England and Wales or Northern Ireland such that this is appropriate (*i.e.* the requirement in Section 2(4)(b)), and if there will be no clash with a foreign jurisdiction. For example, there will be cases where it is extremely likely that once a seat is designated, that seat will be England and Wales or Northern Ireland.

17. Section 2(4) therefore gives the English Court powers where that Court is satisfied, as a matter of English law, that the arbitration in question does not have a seat elsewhere. As long as there is no seat elsewhere, there could be no possible conflict with any other jurisdiction.

18. Both Sections 2(3) and 2(4) are based on a very clear policy: the English Court should have effective powers to support an actual or anticipated arbitration that does not fall within Section 2(1). However, such powers should not be used where any other foreign Court is already, or is likely to be, seized of the matter, or where the exercise of such powers would produce a clash with any other more appropriate forum.

19. Section 2(5) provides that Section 7 (separability) and Section 8 (death of a party) apply whenever the law applicable to an arbitration agreement is English law, even if the seat of the arbitration is abroad. Without this provision, reference would have to be made to the old English common law with respect to separability and the effect of death in every arbitration where the arbitration agreement is governed by English law, but the seat is not in England and Wales or Northern Ireland, such as to be within Section 2(1). This would be an absurd result.

Section 7. Separability of Arbitration Agreement

20. As we said in Chapter 6, we suggested that the words "*(whether or not in writing)*" **A58–005** be inserted after the words "*another agreement*" in view of the definition of "agreement" in what is now Section 5, in order to preclude any argument that Section 7 only applies where the other agreement is in writing. This amendment was duly made.

Section 14(5). Commencement of Arbitral Proceedings

21. Parliamentary Counsel considered that it was not necessary to make the amendment **A58–006** suggested in Paragraph 359 of Chapter 6 and we accepted his advice.

Section 16(6)(b) and Section 21(4)

A58–007 22. The Bill used the word "*any*" after a negative which could thus be read as meaning "*all.*" This was not intended. We suggested a form of wording in Paragraph 360 of Chapter 6 but were persuaded that a neater solution was to replace "*any*" with "*a*", and this was done.

Section 24(4). Power of Court to Remove Arbitrator

A58–008 23. In Paragraph 361 of Chapter 6, we drew attention to the fact that the immunity of an arbitrator, under what is now Section 29, did not extend to protect an arbitrator from the consequences of resigning, though some protection is available under what is now Section 25(3). This we contrasted with what is now Section 24, since an arbitrator removed by the Court still enjoyed the Section 29 immunity. We thought that this was anomalous and that the Court should be given a discretionary power to make such order as it thought fit with regard to the immunity of an arbitrator it removed.

24. This suggestion was not adopted. After further consideration we concluded that the anomaly was more apparent than real and that the suggestion would undermine the reasons for providing arbitrators with the immunity expressed in Section 29. As will be seen from Paragraph 362 of Chapter 6, we were against adopting the same suggestion when the parties agreed to remove an arbitrator under what is now Section 23. What it seemed to us would be likely to happen if our original suggestion were adopted is that the parties, instead of privately agreeing to remove an arbitrator, would instead apply to the Court in the hope that the immunity would be wholly or partially removed. This seemed to us to be undesirable.

25. It should be remembered, of course, that while an arbitrator retains his immunity if removed by the Court, what is now Section 24(4) does give the Court the power to make orders about his fees and expenses, including those already paid.

Section 25(2). Resignation of Arbitrator

A58–009 26. At Paragraph 363 of Chapter 6 we noted that the words "*in writing*" appeared, though by virtue of Section 5(1) this was unnecessary. These words were duly removed by amendment.

Section 32, Section 45 and Section 69

A58–010 27. The Bill used the words "*unless the court certifies.*" These were changed by amendment to "*which shall not be given unless the court considers.*" This amendment was made to make clear that where an appeal is desired from a decision of the Court, leave must be obtained from that Court itself, and will always be required. Leave may not be obtained from the Court of Appeal. As originally drafted, the incorrect impression was given that leave of the Court may not be necessary where that Court certified the issue as being one of general importance or one which for some other special reason should be considered by the Court of Appeal.

Section 38(3). Security for Costs

28. The power for arbitrators to order security for costs was included in the Bill for the reasons set out at Paragraphs 189 to 199 of our February 1996 Report. In the Bill as introduced, we included a provision that the arbitral tribunal should apply the same principles as the Court in exercising this power. This was an attempt to meet the concerns of those who considered that since under the existing law arbitrators had no power to order security (unless the parties had expressly agreed to confer such a power), there was a need to set out some principles to guide arbitrators. However, as we explained at Paragraphs 364 to 370 of Chapter 6, we concluded in the end that this was not a good idea and that it would be better to amend this part of the Bill, by deleting the references to Court principles and by making clear that the fact that a claimant or counter-claimant came from abroad was not a ground for ordering security. Our suggestions were adopted. We proposed a specific amendment, but Parliamentary Counsel improved upon it, in particular by not using the word "*only*" since this might enable it to be argued that the fact that the claimant or counter-claimant came from abroad could be taken into account so long as there were other supporting factors as well. This, of course, was not our intention. **A58–011**

29. It should also be noted that the Bill as introduced used the word "*party*" in relation to orders for security for costs. This did not matter so long as there was a reference to Court principles, but once this was deleted, it was necessary to change this to "*claimant*", since it was not our intention to give arbitral tribunals the power to order respondents to provide security. Section 82 defines claimant as including counter-claimant.

Section 46(1)(b). "Equity Clauses"

30. Whilst the provisions of Part I of the Act apply to arbitrations commenced after the Act comes into force, regardless of when the arbitration agreement was made (by virtue of Section 84), strong representations were made to the DAC that Section 46(1)(b) should be commenced differently—in such a way as to preserve the existing law on the validity of "equity clauses" with respect to arbitration agreements that already exist and were made before the Act comes into force. Many existing contracts contain standard clauses which read as if they are "equity clauses", but which have been interpreted differently by the Courts. This is the case, for example, with so-called "honourable engagement" clauses in reinsurance treaties. It was thought that if Section 46(1)(b) were to apply to existing arbitration agreements, this would entail a retrospective substantive change in the meaning and effect of existing contracts, different from that which the contracting parties would have contemplated at the time of contracting. The DAC agreed with this view, and decided that Section 46(1)(b) should not apply to arbitration agreements that were made before the Act comes into force. Existing case law on the interpretation and effect of "equity clauses" will therefore continue to apply to such agreements. Transitional provisions have been put in place accordingly (see Appendix B). **A58–012**

Section 57. Correction of Award or Additional Award

A58–013   31. A minor drafting change was made to Section 57(3)(b).

Section 66. Enforcement of Award

A58–014   32. In Paragraphs 371 to 378 of Chapter 6 we made various suggestions for changes to the provision as it then appeared in the Bill. We were concerned that we had not covered enough of the cases where leave to enforce an award could be refused. We also suggested that it should be made clear that the list was not a closed list. However, on further reflection we concluded that it would be preferable, instead of having a list which would have to expressed as not closed, to have no list at all; instead relying on the fact (as noted at Paragraphs 373 and 374) that the opening words of the provision do not require the Court to order enforcement, but only give it a discretion to do so. Thus what was subsection (3) of the Bill was deleted by amendment. However, it will be noted that in what is now Section 81 it is made clear (by an amendment to the Bill as introduced) that any rule of law relating in particular to matters which are not capable of settlement by arbitration or to the refusal of recognition or enforcement of an arbitral award on the grounds of public policy continues to operate.

33. The suggestion that there should be an express reference to an action on the award was adopted and this reference is now to be found in Section 66(4) of the Act. This in turn meant that the reference to an action on an award in what is now Section 81 was unnecessary and this latter reference was accordingly removed by amendment.

34. In Paragraph 378 of Chapter 6 we suggested that where the application was to enforce an agreed award, the Court should be notified of that fact, which should also be recorded in any order for enforcement. Upon reflection, however, it seemed to us that such requirements would be better placed in the relevant Rules of Court, and this, we are informed, will be done.

Section 68. Challenging the Award: Serious Irregularity

A58–015   35. In the Bill, one of the grounds for challenging an award was expressed as "*uncertainty or ambiguity of the award.*" It was pointed out to us that this wording might encourage attempts to challenge an award under this provision on the grounds that the reasoning of the decision was uncertain or ambiguous. This was certainly not our intention. What we wanted to cover were cases where the result of the award was uncertain or ambiguous. Where the quality of the award was in question, there would only be recourse under the limited right to appeal under Section 69. To make matters clear, this part of the Section was amended and now reads "*uncertainty or ambiguity as to the effect of the award.*"

Section 70. Challenge or Appeal: Supplementary Provisions

36. In Paragraph 380 of Chapter 6 we suggested that the power to order security or that the amount of the award be brought into Court should be extended so as to apply to applications and appeals under what is now Section 69, as well as what are now Sections 67 and 68. This suggestion was adopted and the appropriate amendments made to Section 70. **A58–016**

37. Subsection 70(6) (security for costs) was further amended in order to bring this provision into line with the amended Section 38(3), which has been referred to above.

Section 74. Immunity of Arbitral Tribunals etc.

38. In Paragraph 381 of Chapter 6 we suggested tightening the wording of subsection 2. This suggestion was adopted by inserting into this subsection after the word "*liable*" the words "*by reason of having appointed or nominated him.*" Without this amendment it could have been suggested that an immunity existed even where, for example, an institution conspired with an arbitrator to act partially. **A58–017**

Section 76. Service of Notices etc.

39. Some minor textual amendments were made to the Bill as introduced, in order to tie this provision with others concerning the giving of notices. **A58–018**

Section 77. Powers of Court in Relation to Service of Documents

40. What was subsection (5) of Clause 77 in the Bill as introduced was deleted on amendment as being unnecessary. The point was already covered by Section 76(6). **A58–019**

Section 79. Power of Court to Extend Time Limits Relating to Arbitral Proceedings

41. In Paragraph 382 of Chapter 6 we noted that this provision did not cover cases where the time stipulated was not one having effect in default of agreement between the parties *e.g.* what is now Section 70(3). We suggested an amendment to what is now Section 79(1). This suggestion was not adopted, but the point was covered by adding the words "*the extending or abridging of periods*" to what is now Section 80(5). **A58–020**

Section 80.

42. The word "*appeal*" was added by amendment to this provision, so it would cover appeals as well as applications. **A58–021**

43. A minor change was also made to subsection (5) (insertion of the words "*the extending or abridging of periods*") in order to tie this provision in with relevant Rules of Court.

Section 81. Saving for Certain Matters Governed by Common Law

A58–022 44. In Paragraphs 383 to 386 of Chapter 6 we made a number of suggestions. First we suggested a reference to privacy and confidentiality. This suggestion was not adopted, since we finally concluded (especially as the law on this topic is in a stage of development) that it would be better to have no express reference at all, and to rely instead as necessary on the general opening words of this Section. The second suggestion (namely an express reference to whether a matter is capable of resolution by arbitration) was adopted and the words "*matters which are not capable of settlement by arbitration*" added by amendment. We also suggested changing the words "*common law*" in the title, but were persuaded that this was not really necessary.

Sections 82 to 83. Minor Definitions

A58–023 45. In Paragraphs 387 and 388 of Chapter 6 we raised a point of drafting on the definition of "*question of law.*" This was dealt with by deleting the words "*where the seat of the arbitration is*" and inserting in their place the words "*for a court.*"

46. Further minor amendments were made to Sections 82 and 83 in the light of the new Section 105 that was added (meaning of "court").

CHAPTER 3

PART II OF THE ACT

Sections 85–87. Domestic Arbitration Agreements

A58–024 47. In Paragraphs 317 to 331 of our February 1996 Report, we set out the reasons why the rules governing domestic arbitration agreements had been grouped together in Sections 85 to 87 of Part II of the Act, and our provisional view as to whether or not the distinction in English law between international and domestic arbitration should be maintained. In July 1996, the Department of Trade and Industry published a consultation document on the commencement of the Act in which, amongst other matters, views were sought on this issue. The majority of respondents were in favour of the abolition of this distinction, and the application of the international regime throughout (*i.e.* a mandatory stay of legal proceedings in all cases, and the ability to exclude the right to appeal on a point of law at any stage in all cases).

48. At about the same time as this consultation document was published, the Court of Appeal upheld the decision of Waller J. in *Philip Alexander Securities and Futures Lim-*

ited v Bamberger and others (unreported: 8 May 1996 [Commercial Court]; 12 July 1996 [Court of Appeal]), in which it was held (in the context of the Consumer Arbitration Agreements Act 1988) that the distinction between international and domestic arbitration is incompatible with European Community law because it amounts to a restriction on the freedom to provide services contrary to Article 59 of the Treaty of Rome and/or unlawful discrimination contrary to Article 6.

49. In the light of the responses to the consultation document, the decision of the Court of Appeal, and the factors we had originally set out in our February 1996 Report, the DAC has since decided that, as matters currently stand, there is no option but to abolish this distinction. Indeed, on one view, in the light of the *Philips Alexander* case, the distinction has already been removed from current English law. However, it is to be noted that (at the time of going to press) an application for leave to appeal the *Philips Alexander* is pending before the House of Lords, and there remains the possibility that the question will be referred to the European Court.

50. In these circumstances, Sections 85 to 87 have not been brought into force by the Commencement Order. The present intention is to repeal these Sections by an Order made pursuant to Section 88 of the Act, although this may now depend upon the outcome of the *Philips Alexander* case.

Section 85

51. In Paragraph 389 of Chapter 6 we noted an anomaly in the definition of "domestic **A58–025** arbitration agreement" and suggested that the opportunity should be taken to correct it. However, in view of the position with respect to the future of the distinction between domestic and non-domestic arbitration agreements, this suggestion was not adopted.

52. Various other minor textual amendments were also made to this Section, which now are of no consequence.

Section 88

53. A minor textual amendment was made to this Section, in order to reflect the **A58–026** amendments made to the consumer provisions of the Act (the new Sections 89 to 91).

Sections 89 to 91. Consumer Arbitration Agreements

54. Clauses 89 to 93 of the Bill as introduced into Parliament reproduced the Consumer **A58–027** Arbitration Agreements Act 1988. These provisions were removed by amendment, and replaced by what is now Sections 89 to 91, which refer to the Unfair Terms in Consumer Contracts Regulations 1994 (implementing EC Council Directive 93/13 EEC). The consumer provisions of the Act were beyond the remit of the DAC, and are therefore not commented upon here. For an explanation of these amendments, reference should be made to Hansard at HL Vol. 571 No. 72 Cols 152-5 (2 April 1996).

Section 93. Appointment of Judges as Arbitrators

A58–028　55. Our suggestion in Paragraph 390 of Chapter 6 was not adopted.

Sections 94–98. Statutory Arbitrations

A58–029　56. The issue that we noted at Paragraph 391 of Chapter 6 concerning the requirement of "independence" in statutory (compulsory) arbitration was debated in the House of Lords (see Hansard HL Vol. 569 No. 51 Col CWH 26-28 (28 February 1996)), but did not result in an amendment to the Bill.

57. The words "*or difference*" were inserted in Section 96(2) by way of tidying up.

CHAPTER 4

PART III OF THE ACT

Section 100(2). New York Convention Awards

A58–030　58. In Paragraph 392 of Chapter 6, we recommended that this provision be amended so as to cross-refer to the definition of writing to be found in Part I of the Act, and also to incorporate our recommendation that an award be treated as made at the seat of the arbitration, regardless of where it was signed, despatched or delivered to any of the parties. This recommendation was adopted.

Section 101

A58–031　59. A minor textual amendment was made to Section 101(2), in order to refer to the new Section 105, that was added.

Section 102. Evidence to be Produced

A58–032　60. The wording of this provision was amended in order to bring it back into line with the wording of the New York Convention itself.

Section 104. Saving for Other Bases of Recognition or Enforcement

A58–033　61. The concern recorded at Paragraph 393 of Chapter 6 did not lead to any amendment.

Chapter 5

Part IV of the Act

Section 105. Meaning of "the court": jurisdiction of High Court and county court

62. This is a new Section. It was added in order to confer order-making powers on the Lord Chancellor to allocate matters as between different Courts, thereby providing for more flexibility than was provided for by existing rules. Reference should be made to the Allocation Order set out at Appendix B.

Appendix A

The new RSC Order 73 & Allocation Order

Introduction by His Hon Judge Diamond QC

Scope of the Order

63. The Order had to govern not only applications to the Court under the Arbitration Act 1996, but also applications under the Arbitration Acts 1950 to 1979, which continue to apply to arbitrations commenced before 31st January 1997, the date when, by virtue of the Arbitration Act 1996 (Commencement No.1) Order 1996, the 1996 Act came into force. So as to cater for both classes of arbitration application, the new Order has been divided into three parts and a table has been inserted at the beginning of the Order to indicate to the user which part is appropriate, a matter which depends on the date when the relevant arbitration proceedings were commenced and the date of the application to the Court (see Chapter 7 of this Report). Part I is concerned with applications to the Court relating to arbitrations to which Part I of the 1996 Act applies. Part II of the Order preserves the procedure of the former Order 73 for arbitrations governed by the earlier statutes. Part III is concerned with all applications to enforce arbitration awards (save by action on the award), whether under the 1950, 1975 or 1996 Acts or under certain other enactments.

The General Scheme of Part I

64. Part I of the new Order completes and puts flesh on the general scheme set out in the 1996 Act governing applications to the Court. For example the Act provides that in some instances notice of an application is to be given "to the other parties" and in others "to the other parties and to the tribunal". The Order provides how that notice is to be given. In the case of parties (Rule 10(1)) this is to be done by making them respondents to the application and by effecting formal service of the proceedings upon them. In the case of arbitrators, notice of applications under Sections 24, 28 and 56 of the Act must be given in a similar manner (Rule 10(2)) but notice of all other applications to arbitrators

may be given by sending the papers to them at their last known address "for information" (Rule 10(3)). Similarly, the Order sets out the rights of parties and arbitrators who have been given notice of an application, to appear and be heard in the proceedings or, in the case of arbitrators who are given notice "for information", to make informal representations to the Court or to appear at their option.

Particular features of Part I

A58–037 65. While it was necessary for the Order to give some guidance as to whether arbitration applications should be heard in open Court or in Chambers, it was considered that this was a matter which depended essentially on the particular circumstances of each application. One consideration is the privacy of the arbitration process; another is whether the application raises points of principle which may be relevant in other cases. Rules 15(2) and 15(3) set out a *prima facie* presumption that all arbitration applications shall be heard in Chambers save for the determination of a preliminary point of law under Section 45 of the Act and an appeal on a question of law under Section 69 which should both be heard in open Court. The Court may however order that any arbitration application be heard in open Court or in Chambers depending on the particular circumstances.

66. Part I of the Order contains provisions designed to minimise the cost and delay involved in serving proceedings out of the jurisdiction. Where the respondent to the arbitration application is or was represented in the arbitration proceedings by a solicitor or other agent, the Court may give leave (on an *ex parte* application) for the proceedings to be served on that solicitor or agent (Rule 7(2)). While service out of the jurisdiction may still be necessary for the first application arising out of an arbitration or arbitration agreement, subsequent applications by either party can be served at the address for service within the jurisdiction given in the first application (Rule 7(4)).

67. When deciding in which Court to bring an arbitration application, the user needs to refer both to the High Court and County Courts (Allocation of Arbitration Proceedings) Order 1996 and also to Rule 5 of the new Order 73. Rule 5 also contains provisions designed to ensure that, wherever the application is issued, the Commercial Court is able to preserve some consistency of approach both to the application and to the interpretation of Order 73. All arbitration applications brought in the Royal Courts of Justice are, for this reason, to be issued out of the Admiralty and Commercial Registry (Rule 5(3)) so that the Commercial Court can act as a "filter" and the Judge in charge of the Commercial Court may transfer them elsewhere if he thinks fit (Rule 5(5)). In the case of applications brought in a Mercantile List or in the Central London County Court Business List, the control of the Commercial Court is preserved by provisions (Rules 5(5) and 5(6)) that the application will be reviewed by the Judge in charge of the list who, in consultation with the Judge in charge of the Commercial Court, may transfer the application to the Commercial Court or to another Court or List.

68. Rule 4(1) introduces a new form of originating process for applications governed by the 1996 Act, called simply an "arbitration application". This supersedes the two different forms of originating summons and the form of notice of motion used under the old procedure (which, however, is retained in Part II of the Order for applications governed by the old law).

General

A58–038 69. Though necessarily detailed, the new Order 73 is designed to be "user friendly". Users should be assisted by the table, to which reference has previously been made, indicating whether Part I or Part II of the Order is appropriate for a particular application. Similarly, rule 4 attempts to assist users by setting out in table form the most important statutory requirements that need to be satisfied and referred to in any arbitration application made under the 1996 Act.

The Rules of the Supreme Court (Amendment) 1996

(SI 1996/3219)

Made   *19th December 1996*
Laid before Parliament   *20th December 1996*
Coming into force   *31st January 1997*

We, the Supreme Court Rule Committee, having power under section 85 of the Supreme Court Act 1981 to make rules of court under section 60 of that Act and under section 84 of that Act for the purpose of regulating and prescribing the practice and procedure to be followed in the High Court and the civil division of the Court of Appeal, hereby exercise those powers as follows—   **A58–039**

Citation, commencement and interpretation

1.—(1) These Rules may be cited as the Rules of the Supreme Court (Amendment)   **A58–040**
1996 and shall come into force on 31st January 1997.

(2) In these Rules, an Order referred to by number means the Order so numbered in the Rules of the Supreme Court 1965 and a reference to Appendix A is a reference to Appendix A to those Rules.

Arbitration Act 1996

2. The Arrangement of Orders at the beginning of the Rules of the Supreme Court   **A58–041**
1965 shall be amended, by substituting for the title to Order 73, the following "Applications relating to Arbitration".

3. Order 11, rule 9(1) and (4) shall be amended by omitting the words "Subject to Order 73, rule 7,".

4. Order 59, rule 1A(7)(a) shall be amended by inserting, after "1979", the words "or under section 69(7) of the Arbitration Act 1996" and rule 1A(7)(b)(iii) shall be amended by inserting, after "section 1(2)", the words "or of section 69(7) of the said Act of 1996".

5. For Order 73 there shall be substituted the following—

THE RULES OF THE SUPREME COURT (AMENDMENT) 1996

"ORDER 73

APPLICATIONS RELATING TO ARBITRATION

Introduction

A58–042 This Order is divided into three Parts. Part I is concerned with applications to the Court relating to arbitration to which Part I of the Arbitration Act 1996 applies. Part II restates with some necessary adjustments provisions of the existing Order which are to be preserved. Part III is concerned with applications for enforcement under the earlier Arbitration Acts and under the 1996 Act.

The application of the Order to particular proceedings may be determined by reference to the following table. Column 1 shows the date on which arbitral proceedings (if any) were commenced. Column 2 shows the date of the application to the Court. Column 3 shows the appropriate Part of the Order for the application.

Column 1 *Date of arbitral proceedings*	*Column 2* *Date of application to the Court*	*Column 3* *Appropriate Part of Order 73*
not commenced	before 31st January 1997	Part II
before 31st January 1997	before 31st January 1997	Part II
not commenced	on or after 31st January 1997	Part I
before 31st January 1997	on or after 31st January 1997	Part II
on or after 31st January 1997	on or after 31st January 1997	Part I
on or after 31st January 1997	before 31st January 1997	Part II

The other provisions of these rules apply to applications relating to arbitration subject to the provisions of this Order and only to the extent that they do not conflict with it.

See, for example, the following provisions of these rules for the following matters—

    Order 10—service of originating process

    Order 12—acknowledgement of service

    Order 29—injunctions

    Order 32—proceedings in chambers

    Order 41—affidavits

    Order 65—service of documents.

DEPARTMENTAL ADVISORY COMMITTEE ON ARBITRATION LAW

Part I

The overriding objective

1. This Part of this Order is founded on the general principles in section 1 of the Arbitration Act and shall be construed accordingly. **A58–043**

Meaning of arbitration application

2.—(1) Subject to paragraph (2), "arbitration application" means the following— **A58–044**

   (a) an application to the Court under the Arbitration Act;

   (b) proceedings to determine—

   (i) whether there is a valid arbitration agreement;
   (ii) whether an arbitration tribunal is properly constituted;
   (iii) what matters have been submitted to arbitration in accordance with an arbitration agreement;

   (c) proceedings to declare that an award made by an arbitral tribunal is not binding on a party;

   (d) any other application affecting arbitration proceedings (whether instituted or anticipated) or to construe or affecting an arbitration agreement,

and includes the originating process by which an arbitration application is begun.

(2) In this Part of this Order, an arbitration application does not include proceedings to enforce an award—

   (a) to which Part III of this Order applies; or

   (b) by an action on the award.

Interpretation

3. In this Part— **A58–045**

   "applicant" means the party making an arbitration application and references to respondent shall be construed accordingly;
   "the Arbitration Act" means the Arbitration Act 1996 and any expressions used in this Order and in Part I of the Arbitration Act have the same meanings in this Order as they have in that Part of the Arbitration Act.

Form and content of arbitration application

4.—(1) An arbitration application must be in Form No. 8A in Appendix A. **A58–046**
(2) Every arbitration application must—

   (a) include a concise statement of

   (i) the remedy or relief claimed, and
   (ii) (where appropriate) the questions on which the applicant seeks the determination or direction of the Court;

(b) give details of any arbitration award that is challenged by the applicant, showing the grounds for any such challenge;

(c) where the applicant claims an order for costs, identify the respondent against whom the claim is made,

(d) (where appropriate) specify the section of the Arbitration Act under which the application is brought; and

(e) show that any statutory requirements have been satisfied including those set out, by way of example, in the Table Below.

Application made	Statutory requirements
section 9 (stay of legal proceedings)	see section 9(3)
section 12 (extensions of time for beginning arbitral proceedings)	see section 12(2)
section 18 (failure of appointment procedure)	see section 18(2)
section 21 (umpires)	see section 21(5)
section 24 (removal of arbitrators)	see section 24(2)
section 32 (preliminary point of jurisdiction)	see section 32(3)
section 42 (enforcement of peremptory orders)	see section 42(3)
section 44 (powers in support of arbitral proceedings)	see section 44(4), (5)
section 45 (preliminary point of law)	see section 45(3)
section 50 (extension of time for making award)	see section 50(2)
section 56 (power to withhold award)	see section 56(4)
sections 67, 68 (challenging the award)	see section 70(2), (3)
section 69 (appeal on point of law)	see section 69(2), (4), 70(2), (3)
section 77 (service of documents)	see section 77(3)

(3) The arbitration application must also state

(a) whether it is made *ex parte* or on notice and, if made on notice, must give the names and addresses of the persons to whom notice is to be given, stating their role in the arbitration and whether they are made respondents to the application;

(b) whether (having regard to rule 15) the application will be heard in open Court or in chambers; and

(c) the date and time when the application will be heard or that such date has not yet been fixed.

(4) Every arbitration application which is used as an originating process shall be indorsed with the applicant's address for service in accordance with Order 6, rule 5.

Issue of application

A58–047   5.—(1) This rule is to be read with the provisions of the High Court and County Courts (Allocation of Arbitration Proceedings) Order 1996 which allocates proceedings under the Arbitration Act to the High Court and the county courts and specifies proceedings which may be commenced or taken only in the High Court or in a county court.

(2) This rule does not apply to applications under section 9 of the Arbitration Act to stay legal proceedings.

(3) Any other arbitration application may be made—

 (a) in the Royal Courts of Justice, in which case it shall be issued out of the Admiralty and Commercial Registry;

 (b) in a district registry in which there is a mercantile list, in which case it shall be entered into that list.

(4) Except where an arbitration application is issued out of the Admiralty and Commercial Registry, the Judge in charge of the list shall

 (a) as soon as practicable after the issue of the application, and

 (b) in consultation with the Judge in charge of the commercial list,

consider whether the application should be transferred to the Commercial Court or to any another list.

(5) Where an arbitration application is issued out of the Admiralty and Commercial Registry, the Judge in charge of the commercial list may at any time after the issue of the application transfer the application to another list, court or Division of the High Court, to which he has power to transfer proceedings.

(6) In considering whether to transfer an application, the Judges referred to in paragraphs (4) and (5) shall have regard to the criteria specified in article 4(4) of the High Court and County Courts (Allocation of Arbitration Proceedings) Order 1996 and the application shall be transferred if those Judges so decide.

(7) In this rule "Judge in charge of the list" means—

 (a) a Commercial Judge, where the arbitration application is issued out of the Admiralty and Commercial Registry;

 (b) a Circuit mercantile Judge, where the arbitration application is entered in a mercantile list;

 (c) a Judge of the business list in the Central London County Court, where the arbitration application is commenced in the business list established at the Central London County Court by Order 48C of the County Court Rules 1981;

but nothing in this rule shall be construed as preventing the powers of a Commercial Judge from being exercised by any judge of the High Court.

Stay of legal proceedings

6.—(1) An application under section 9 of the Arbitration Act to stay legal proceedings shall be served—

 (a) in accordance with Order 65, rule 5, on the party bringing the relevant legal proceedings and on any other party to those proceedings who has given an address for service; and

 (b) on any party to those legal proceedings who has not given an address for service, by sending to him (whether or not he is within the jurisdiction) at his last known address or at a place where it is likely to come to his attention, a copy of the application for his information.

(2) Where a question arises as to whether an arbitration agreement has been concluded or as to whether the dispute which is the subject-matter of the proceedings falls within the terms of such an agreement, the Court may determine that question or give directions for its determination, in which case it may order the proceedings to be stayed pending the determination of that question.

Service of arbitration application

A58–049
7.—(1) Subject to paragraphs (2) and (4) below and to rules 6(1) and 8, an arbitration application shall be served in accordance with Order 10.

(2) Where the Court is satisfied on an *ex parte* application that

   (a) arbitral proceedings are taking place, or an arbitration award has been made, within the jurisdiction; and

   (b) an arbitration application is being made in connection with those arbitral proceedings or being brought to challenge the award or to appeal on a question of law arising out of the award; and

   (c) the respondent to the arbitration application (not being an individual residing or carrying on business within the jurisdiction or a body corporate having a registered office or a place of business within the jurisdiction)

      (i) is or was represented in the arbitral proceedings by a solicitor or other agent within the jurisdiction who was authorised to receive service of any notice or other document served for the purposes of those proceedings; and

      (ii) has not (at the time when the arbitration application is made) determined the authority of that solicitor or agent,

the Court may authorise service of the arbitration application to be effected on the solicitor or agent instead of the respondent.

(3) An order made under paragraph (2) must limit a time within which the respondent must acknowledge service and a copy of the order and of the arbitration application must be sent by post to the respondent at his address out of the jurisdiction.

(4) Where an arbitration application has been issued, any subsequent arbitration application made by the respondent and arising out of the same arbitration or arbitration agreement may be served on the applicant in accordance with Order 65, rule 5 (ordinary service: how effected) and similarly any subsequent arbitration application by any party may be served at the address for service given in the first arbitration application or in the acknowledgement of service.

(5) For the purposes of service, an arbitration application is valid in the first instance

   (a) where service is to be effected out of the jurisdiction, for such period as the Court may fix;

   (b) in any other case, for one month,

beginning with the date of its issue and Order 6, rule 8 shall apply with the substitution,

Departmental Advisory Committee on Arbitration Law

in paragraphs (2) and (2A), of "2 months" for "4 months" and "6 months" for "12 months".

Service out of the jurisdiction

8.—(1) Service out of the jurisdiction of an arbitration application is permissible with the leave of the Court if the arbitration application falls into one of the categories mentioned in the following table and satisfies the conditions specified. **A58–050**

Nature of application	*Conditions to be satisfied*
1. The applicant seeks to challenge, or to appeal to the Court on a question of law arising out of, an arbitration award.	Award must have been made in England and Wales. Section 53 of the Arbitration Act shall apply for determining the place where award is treated as made.
2. The application is for an order under section 44 of the Arbitration Act (Court powers exercisable in support of arbitral proceedings). Where the application is for interim relief in support of arbitral proceedings which are taking (or will take) place outside England and Wales, the Court may give leave for service out of the jurisdiction notwithstanding that no other relief is sought.	None.
3. The applicant seeks some other remedy or relief, or requires a question to be determined by the Court, affecting an arbitration (whether pending or anticipated), an arbitration agreement or an arbitration award.	The seat of the arbitration is or will be in England and Wales or the conditions in section 2(4) of the Arbitration Act are satisfied.

(2) An application for the grant of leave under this rule must be supported by an affidavit

(a) stating the grounds on which the application is made; and

(b) showing in what place or country the person to be served is, or probably may be found,

and no such leave shall be granted unless it shall be made sufficiently to appear to the Court that the case is a proper one for service out of the jurisdiction under this rule.

(3) Order 11, rules 5 to 8 shall apply to the service of an arbitration application under this rule as they apply to the service of a writ.

(4) Service out of the jurisdiction of any order made on an arbitration application is permissible with the leave of the Court.

Affidavit in support of arbitration application

A58–051   9.—(1) The applicant shall file an affidavit in support of the arbitration application which sets out the evidence on which he intends to rely and a copy of every affidavit so filed must be served with the arbitration application.

(2) Where an arbitration application is made with the written agreement of all the other parties to the arbitral proceedings or with the permission of the arbitral tribunal, the affidavit in support must

(a) give details of the agreement or, as the case may be, permission; and

(b) exhibit copies of any document which evidences that agreement or permission.

Requirements as to notice

A58–052   10.—(1) Where the Arbitration Act requires that an application to the Court is to be made upon notice to other parties notice shall be given by making those parties respondents to the application and serving on them the arbitration application and any affidavit in support.

(2) Where an arbitration application is made under section 24, 28 or 56 of the Arbitration Act, the arbitrators or, in the case of an application under section 24, the arbitrator concerned shall be made respondents to the application and notice shall be given by serving on them the arbitration application and any affidavit in support.

(3) In cases where paragraph (2) does not apply, an applicant shall be taken as having complied with any requirement to give notice to the arbitrator if he sends a copy of the arbitration application to the arbitrator for his information at his last known address with a copy of any affidavit in support.

(4) This rule does not apply to applications under section 9 of the Arbitration Act to stay legal proceedings.

Acknowledgement of service by respondent

A58–053   11.—(1) Service of an arbitration application may be acknowledged by completing an acknowledgement of service in Form No. 15A in Appendix A in accordance with Order 12 (as that Order applies by virtue of rule 9 of that Order).

(2) A respondent who

(a) fails to acknowledge service within the time limited for so doing; or

(b) having indicated on his acknowledgement of service that he does not intend to contest the arbitration application, then wishes to do so,

shall not be entitled to contest the application without the leave of the Court.

(3) The Court will not give notice of the date on which an arbitration application will be heard to a respondent who has failed to acknowledge service.

(4) The failure of a respondent to give notice of intention to contest the arbitration application or to acknowledge service shall not affect the applicant's duty to satisfy the Court that the order applied for should be made.

(5) This rule does not apply to—

(a) applications under section 9 of the Arbitration Act to stay legal proceedings; or

(b) subsequent arbitration applications.

Acknowledgement of service etc. by arbitrator

12.—(1) An arbitrator who is sent a copy of an arbitration application for his information may make

(a) a request *ex parte* in writing to be made a respondent; or

(b) representations to the Court under this rule,

and, where an arbitrator is ordered to be made a respondent, he shall acknowledge service within 14 days of the making of that order.

(2) An arbitrator who wishes to make representations to the Court under this rule may file an affidavit or make representations in writing to the Court.

(3) The arbitrator shall as soon as is practicable send a copy of any document filed or made under paragraph (2) to all the parties to the arbitration application.

(4) Nothing in this rule shall require the Court to admit a document filed or made under paragraph (2) and the weight to be given to any such document shall be a matter for the Court.

Automatic directions

13.—(1) Unless the Court otherwise directs, the following directions shall take effect automatically.

(2) A respondent who wishes to put evidence before the Court in response to any affidavit filed in support of an arbitration application shall serve his affidavit on the applicant before the expiration of 21 days after the time limited for acknowledging service or, in a case where a respondent is not required to file an acknowledgement of service, within 21 days after service of the arbitration application.

(3) An applicant who wishes to put evidence before the Court in response to an affidavit lodged under paragraph (2) shall serve his affidavit on the respondent within 7 days after service of the respondent's affidavit.

(4) Where a date has not been fixed for the hearing of the arbitration application, the applicant shall, and the respondent may, not later than 14 days after the expiration of the time limit specified in paragraph (2), apply to the Court for such a date to be fixed.

(5) Agreed indexed and paginated bundles of all the evidence and other documents to be used at the hearing shall be prepared by the applicant (with the co-operation of the respondent).

(6) Not later than 5 clear days before the hearing date estimates for the length of the hearing shall be lodged with the Court together with a complete set of the documents to be used.

(7) Not later than 2 days before the hearing date the applicant shall lodge with the Court—

(a) a chronology of the relevant events cross-referenced to the bundle of documents;

(b) (where necessary) a list of the persons involved;

(c) a skeleton argument which lists succinctly

(i) the issues which arise for decision,
(ii) the grounds of relief (or opposing relief) to be relied upon,

(iii) the submissions of fact to be made with the references to the evidence, and

(iv) the submissions of law with references to the relevant authorities,

and shall send a copy to the respondent.

(8) Not later than the day before the hearing date the respondent shall lodge with the Court a skeleton argument which lists succinctly

(a) the issues which arise for decision,

(b) the grounds of relief (or opposing relief) to be relied upon,

(c) the submissions of fact to be made with the references to the evidence, and

(d) the submissions of law with references to the relevant authorities,

and shall send a copy to the applicant.

Directions by the Court

A58–056   14.—(1) The Court may give such directions as to the conduct of the arbitration application as it thinks best adapted to secure the just, expeditious and economical disposal thereof.

(2) Where the Court considers that there is or may be a dispute as to fact and that the just, expeditious and economical disposal of the application can best be secured by hearing the application on oral evidence or mainly on oral evidence, it may, if it thinks fit, order that no further evidence shall be filed and that the application shall be heard on oral evidence or partly on oral evidence and partly on affidavit evidence, with or without cross-examination of any of the deponents, as it may direct.

(3) The Court may give directions as to the filing of evidence and as to the attendance of deponents for cross-examination and any directions which it could give in proceedings begun by writ.

(4) If the applicant makes default in complying with these rules or with any order or direction of the Court as to the conduct of the application, or if the Court is satisfied that the applicant is not prosecuting the application with due despatch, the Court may order the application to be dismissed or may make such other order as may be just.

(5) If the respondent fails to comply with these rules or with any order or direction given by the Court in relation to the evidence to be relied on, or the submissions to be made by that respondent, the Court may, if it thinks fit, hear and determine the application without having regard to that evidence or those submissions.

Hearing of applications: open Court or in chambers

A58–057   15.—(1) The Court may order that any arbitration application be heard either in open court or in chambers.

(2) Subject to any order made under paragraph (1) and to paragraph (3), all arbitration applications shall be heard in chambers.

(3) Subject to any order made under paragraph (1), the determination of a preliminary point of law under section 45 of the Arbitration Act or an appeal under section 69 on a question of law arising out of an award shall be heard in open court.

(4) Paragraph (3) shall not apply to

(a) the preliminary question whether the Court is satisfied of the matters set out in section 45(2)(b); or

(b) an application for leave to appeal under section 69(2)(b).

Securing the attendance of witnesses

16.—(1) A party to arbitral proceedings being conducted in England and Wales who wishes to rely on section 43 of the Arbitration Act to secure the attendance of a witness may apply for a writ of subpoena ad testificandum or of subpoena duces tecum to the Admiralty and Commercial Registry or, if the attendance of the witness is required within the district of a district registry, at that registry at the option of the party. A58–058

(2) A writ of subpoena shall not be issued until the applicant lodges an affidavit which shows that the application is made with the permission of the tribunal or the agreement of the other parties.

Security for costs

17. Subject to section 70(6) of the Arbitration Act, the Court may order any applicant (including an applicant who has been granted leave to appeal) to provide security for costs of any arbitration application. A58–059

Powers exercisable in support of arbitral proceedings

18.—(1) Where the case is one of urgency, an application for an order under section 44 of the Arbitration Act (Court powers exercisable in support of arbitral proceedings) may be made *ex parte* on affidavit (before the issue of an arbitration application) and the affidavit shall (in addition to dealing with the matters required to be dealt with by rule 9) state the reasons A58–060

(a) why the application is made *ex parte*; and

(b) (where the application is made without the permission of the arbitral tribunal or the agreement of the other parties to the arbitral proceedings) why it was not practicable to obtain the permission or agreement, and

(c) why the deponent believes that the condition in section 44(5) is satisfied.

(2) Where the case is not one of urgency, an application for an order under section 44 of the Arbitration Act shall be made on notice and the affidavit in support shall (in addition to dealing with the matters required to be dealt with by rule 9 and paragraph (1)(c) above) state that the application is made with the permission of the tribunal or the written agreement of the other parties to the arbitral proceedings.

(3) Where an application for an order under section 44 of the Arbitration Act is made before the issue of an arbitration application, any order made by the Court may be granted on terms providing for the issue of an application and such other terms, if any, as the Court thinks fit.

Applications under sections 32 and 45 of the Arbitration Act

19.—(1) This rule applies to the following arbitration applications:— A58–061

(a) applications for the determination of a question as to the substantive jurisdiction of the arbitral tribunal under section 32 of the Arbitration Act; and

(b) applications for the determination of a preliminary point of law under section 45 of the Arbitration Act.

(2) Where an application is made without the agreement in writing of all the other parties to the arbitral proceedings but with the permission of the arbitral tribunal, the affidavits filed by the parties shall set out any evidence relied on by the parties in support of their contention that the Court should, or should not, consider the application.

(3) As soon as practicable after the affidavits are lodged, the Court shall decide whether or not it should consider the application and, unless the Court otherwise directs, shall so decide without a hearing.

Applications for leave to appeal

A58–062 20.—(1) Where the applicant seeks leave to appeal to the Court on a question of law arising out of an arbitration award, the arbitration application shall identify the question of law and state the grounds on which the applicant alleges that leave should be granted.

(2) The affidavit in support of the application shall set out any evidence relied on by the applicant for the purpose of satisfying the Court of the matters mentioned in section 69(3) of the Arbitration Act and for satisfying the Court that leave should be granted.

(3) The affidavit lodged by the respondent to the application shall

(a) state the grounds on which the respondent opposes the grant of leave;

(b) set out any evidence relied on by him relating to the matters mentioned in section 69(3) of the Arbitration Act, and

(c) specify whether the respondent wishes to contend that the award should be upheld for reasons not expressed (or not fully expressed) in the award and, if so, state those reasons.

(4) As soon as practicable after the lodging of the affidavits, the Court shall determine the application for leave in accordance with section 69(5) of the Arbitration Act.

(5) Where leave is granted, a date shall be fixed for the hearing of the appeal.

Extension of time: applications under section 12

A58–063 21. An application for an order under section 12 of the Arbitration Act may include as an alternative an application for a declaration that such an order is not needed.

Time limit for challenges to or appeals from awards

A58–064 22.—(1) An applicant shall not be taken as having complied with the time limit of 28 days referred to in section 70(3) of the Arbitration Act unless the arbitration application has been issued, and all the affidavits in support have been sworn and filed, by the expiry of that time limit.

(2) An applicant who wishes

(a) to challenge an award under section 67 or 68 of the Arbitration Act; or

(b) to appeal under section 69 on a question of law arising out of an award,

may, where the time limit of 28 days has not yet expired, apply *ex parte* on affidavit for an order extending that time limit.

(3) In any case where an applicant seeks to challenge an award under section 67 or 68 of the Arbitration Act or to appeal under section 69 after the time limit of 28 days has already expired, the following provisions shall apply:
- (a) the applicant must state in his arbitration application the grounds why an order extending time should be made and his affidavit in support shall set out the evidence on which he relies;
- (b) a respondent who wishes to oppose the making of an order extending time shall file an affidavit within 7 days after service of the applicant's affidavit, and
- (c) the Court shall decide whether or not to extend time without a hearing unless it appears to the Court that a hearing is required,

and, where the Court makes an order extending the time limit, the respondent shall file his affidavit in response to the arbitration application 21 days after the making of the order.

Part II

Application of this Part

23.—(1) This Part of this Order applies to any application to the Court to which the old law applies and, in this rule, "the old law" means the enactments specified in section 107 of the Arbitration Act 1996 as they stood before their amendment or repeal by that Act.

(2) This Part of this Order does not apply to proceedings to enforce an award—

- (a) to which Part III of this Order applies; or
- (b) by an action on the award.

(3) Reference should be made to the other provisions of these rules (except Parts I and III of this Order) for the procedure for any application not expressly provided for in this Part.

Matters for a judge in court

24.—(1) Every application to the Court—

- (a) to remit an award under section 22 of the Arbitration Act 1950; or
- (b) to remove an arbitrator or umpire under section 23(1) of that Act; or
- (c) to set aside an award under section 23(2) of that Act; or
- (d) to determine, under section 2(1) of the Arbitration Act 1979, any question of law arising in the course of a reference,

must be made by originating motion to a single judge in court.

(2) Any appeal to the High Court under section 1(2) of the Arbitration Act 1979 shall be made by originating motion to a single judge in court.

(3) An application for a declaration that an award made by an arbitrator or umpire is not binding on a party to the award on the ground that it was made without jurisdiction

may be made by originating motion to a single judge in court, but the foregoing provision shall not be taken as affecting the judge's power to refuse to make such a declaration in proceedings begun by motion.

Matters for judge in chambers or master

A58–067   25.—(1) Subject to the foregoing provisions of this Order and the provisions of this rule, the jurisdiction of the High Court or a judge thereof under the Arbitration Act 1950 and the jurisdiction of the High Court under the Arbitration Act 1975 and the Arbitration Act 1979 may be exercised by a judge in chambers, a master or the Admiralty registrar.
(2) Any application

(a) for leave to appeal under section 1(2) of the Arbitration Act 1979, or

(b) under section 1(5) of that Act (including any application for leave), or

(c) under section 5 of that Act,

shall be made to a judge in chambers.
(3) Any application to which this rule applies shall, where an action is pending, be made by summons in the action, and in any other case by an originating summons which shall be in Form No. 10 in Appendix A.
(4) Where an application is made under section 1(5) of the Arbitration Act 1979 (including any application for leave) the summons must be served on the arbitrator or umpire and on any other party to the reference.

Applications in district registries

A58–068   26.—(1) An application under section 12(4) of the Arbitration Act 1950 for an order that a writ of subpoena ad testificandum or of subpoena duces tecum shall issue to compel the attendance before an arbitrator or umpire of a witness may, if the attendance of the witness is required within the district of a district registry, be made at that registry, instead of at the Admiralty and Commercial Registry, at the option of the applicant.

Time limits and other special provisions as to appeals and applications under the Arbitration Acts

A58–069   27.—(1) An application to the Court—

(a) to remit an award under section 22 of the Arbitration Act 1950; or

(b) to set aside an award under section 23(2) of that Act or otherwise, or

(c) to direct an arbitrator or umpire to state the reasons for an award under section 1(5) of the Arbitration Act 1979,

must be made, and the summons or notice must be served, within 21 days after the award has been made and published to the parties.
(2) In the case of an appeal to the Court under section 1(2) of the Arbitration Act 1979, the summons for leave to appeal, where leave is required, and the notice of originating motion must be served and the appeal entered, within 21 days after the award has been made and published to the parties.

Provided that, where reasons material to the appeal are given on a date subsequent to the publication of the award, the period of 21 days shall run from the date on which the reasons are given.

(3) An application, under section 2(1) of the Arbitration Act 1979, to determine any question of law arising in the course of a reference, must be made, and notice thereof served, within 14 days after the arbitrator or umpire has consented to the application being made, or the other parties have so consented.

(4) For the purpose of paragraph (3) the consent must be given in writing.

(5) In the case of every appeal or application to which this rule applies, the notice of originating motion, the originating summons or the summons, as the case may be, must state the grounds of the appeal or application and, where the appeal or application is founded on evidence by affidavit, or is made with the consent of the arbitrator or umpire or of the other parties, a copy of every affidavit intended to be used, or, as the case may be, of every consent given in writing, must be served with that notice.

(6) Without prejudice to paragraph (5), in an appeal under section 1(2) of the Arbitration Act 1979 the statement of the grounds of the appeal shall specify the relevant parts of the award and reasons, or the relevant parts thereof, shall be lodged with the court and served with the notice of originating motion.

(7) Without prejudice to paragraph (5), in an application for leave to appeal under section 1(2) of the Arbitration Act 1979, any affidavit verifying the facts in support of a contention that the question of law concerns a term of a contract or an event which is not a one-off term or event must be lodged with the court and served with the notice of originating motion.

(8) Any affidavit in reply to an affidavit under paragraph (7) shall be lodged with the court and served on the applicant not less than two clear days before the hearing of the application.

(9) A respondent to an application for leave to appeal under section 1(2) of the Arbitration Act 1979 who desires to contend that the award should be upheld on grounds not expressed or fully expressed in the award and reasons shall not less than two clear days before the hearing of the application lodge with the court and serve on the applicant a notice specifying the grounds of his contention.

Applications and appeals to be heard by Commercial Judges

28.—(1) Any matter which is required, by rule 24 or 25, to be heard by a judge, shall be heard by a Commercial Judge, unless any such judge otherwise directs. **A58–070**

(2) Nothing in the foregoing paragraph shall be construed as preventing the powers of a Commercial Judge from being exercised by any judge of the High Court.

Service out of the jurisdiction of summons, notice, etc.

29.—(1) Subject to paragraph (2), service out of the jurisdiction of— **A58–071**

(a) any originating summons or notice of originating motion under the Arbitration Act 1950 or the Arbitration Act 1979, or

(b) any order made on such a summons or motion,

is permissible with the leave of the Court provided that the arbitration to which the summons, motion or order relates is governed by English law or has been, is being or is to be held within the jurisdiction.

(2) Service out of the jurisdiction of an originating summons for leave to enforce an

award is permissible with the leave of the Court whether or not the arbitration is governed by English law.

(3) An application for the grant of leave under this rule must be supported by an affidavit stating the grounds on which the application is made and showing in what place or country the person to be served is, or probably may be found; and no such leave shall be granted unless it shall be made to appear to the Court that the case is a proper one for service out of the jurisdiction under this rule.

(4) Order 11, rules 5 to 8, shall apply in relation to any such summons, notice or order as is referred to in paragraph (1) as they apply in relation to a writ.

PART III

Application of this Part

A58–072   30. This Part of this Order applies to all enforcement proceedings (other than by an action on the award) regardless of when they are commenced and when the arbitral proceedings took place.

Enforcement of awards

A58–073   31.—(1) This rule applies to applications to enforce awards which are brought in the High Court and such an application may be made in the Royal Courts of Justice or in any district registry.

(2) An application for leave under—

(a) section 66 of the Arbitration Act 1996;

(b) section 101 of the Arbitration Act 1996;

(c) section 26 of the Arbitration Act 1950; or

(d) section 3(1)(a) of the Arbitration Act 1975;

to enforce an award in the same manner as a judgment or order may be made *ex parte* in Form No. 8A in Appendix A.

(3) The Court hearing an application under paragraph (2) may direct that the application is to be served on such parties to the arbitration as it may specify and service of the application out of the jurisdiction is permissible with the leave of the Court irrespective of where the award is, or is treated as, made.

(4) Where a direction is given under paragraph (3), rules 11 and 13 to 17 shall apply with the necessary modifications as they apply to applications under Part I of this Order.

(5) Where the applicant applies to enforce an agreed award within the meaning of section 51(2) of the Arbitration Act 1996, the application must state that the award is an agreed award and any order made by the Court shall also contain such a statement.

(6) An application for leave must be supported by affidavit—

(a) exhibiting

(i) where the application is made under section 66 of the Arbitration Act 1996 or under section 26 of the Arbitration Act 1950, the arbitration agreement and the original award or, in either case, a copy thereof;

(ii) where the application is under section 101 of the Arbitration Act 1996, the documents required to be produced by section 102 of that Act;

(iii) where the application is under section 3(1)(a) of the Arbitration Act 1975, the documents required to be produced by section 4 of that Act;

(b) stating the name and the usual or last known place of residence or business of the applicant and of the person against whom it is sought to enforce the award respectively,

(c) stating as the case may require, either that the award has not been complied with or the extent to which it has not been complied with at the date of the application.

(7) An order giving leave must be drawn up by or on behalf of the applicant and must be served on the respondent by delivering a copy to him personally or by sending a copy to him at his usual or last known place of residence or business or in such other manner as the Court may direct.

(8) Service of the order out of the jurisdiction is permissible without leave, and Order 11, rules 5 to 8, shall apply in relation to such an order as they apply in relation to a writ.

(9) Within 14 days after service of the order or, if the order is to be served out of the jurisdiction, within such other period as the Court may fix, the respondent may apply to set aside the order and the award shall not be enforced until after the expiration of that period or, if the respondent applies within that period to set aside the order, until after the application is finally disposed of.

(10) The copy of the order served on the respondent shall state the effect of paragraph (9).

(11) In relation to a body corporate this rule shall have effect as if for any reference to the place of residence or business of the applicant or the respondent there were substituted a reference to the registered or principal address of the body corporate.

Nothing in this rule shall affect any enactment which provides for the manner in which a document may be served on a body corporate.

Interest on awards

32.—(1) Where an applicant seeks to enforce an award of interest, the whole or any part of which relates to a period after the date of the award, he shall file a certificate giving the following particulars—

(a) whether simple or compound interest was awarded;

(b) the date from which interest was awarded;

(c) whether rests were provided for, specifying them;

(d) the rate of interest awarded, and

(e) a calculation showing the total amount claimed up to the date of the certificate and any sum which will become due thereafter on a *per diem* basis.

(2) The certificate under paragraph (1) must be filed whenever the amount of interest has to be quantified for the purpose of obtaining a judgment or order under section 66 of the Arbitration Act (enforcement of the award) or for the purpose of enforcing such a judgment or order by one of the means mentioned in Order 45, rule 1.

Registration in High Court of foreign awards

A58–075 33. Where an award is made in proceedings on an arbitration in any part of Her Majesty's dominions or other territory to which Part I of the Foreign Judgments (Reciprocal Enforcement) Act 1933 extends, being a part to which Part II of the Administration of Justice Act 1920 extended immediately before the said Part I was extended thereto, then, if the award has, in pursuance of the law in force in the place where it was made, become enforceable in the same manner as a judgment given by a court in that place, Order 71 shall apply in relation to the award as it applies in relation to a judgment given by that court, subject, however, to the following modifications—

(a) for references to the country of the original court there shall be substituted references to the place where the award was made; and

(b) the affidavit required by rule 3 of the said Order must state (in addition to the other matters required by that rule) that to the best of the information or belief of the deponent the award has, in pursuance of the law in force in the place where it was made, become enforceable in the same manner as a judgment given by a court in that place.

Registration of awards under the Arbitration (International Investment Disputes) Act 1966

A58–076 34.—(1) In this rule and in any provision of these rules as applied by this rule—"the Act of 1966" means the Arbitration (International Investment Disputes) Act 1966;

"award" means an award rendered pursuant to the Convention;
"the Convention" means the Convention referred to in section 1(1) of the Act of 1966;
"judgment creditor" and "judgment debtor" mean respectively the person seeking recognition or enforcement of an award and the other party to the award.

(2) Subject to the provisions of this rule, the following provisions of Order 71, namely, rules 1, 3(1) (except sub-paragraphs (c)(iv) and (d) thereof) 7 (except paragraph (3)(c) and (d) thereof), and 10(3) shall apply with the necessary modifications in relation to an award as they apply in relation to a judgment to which Part II of the Foreign Judgments (Reciprocal Enforcement) Act 1933 applies.

(3) An application to have an award registered in the High Court under section 1 of the Act of 1966 shall be made by originating summons which shall be in Form No. 10 in Appendix A.

(4) The affidavit required by Order 71, rule 3, in support of an application for registration shall—

(a) in lieu of exhibiting the judgment or a copy thereof, exhibit a copy of the award certified pursuant to the Convention; and

(b) in addition to stating the matters mentioned in paragraph 3(1)(c)(i) and (ii) of the said rule 3, state whether at the date of the application the enforcement of the award has been stayed (provisionally or otherwise) pursuant to the Convention and whether any, and if so what, application has been made pursuant to the Convention, which, if granted, might result in a stay of the enforcement of the award.

(5) There shall be kept in the Admiralty and Commercial Registry under the direction of the Senior Master a register of the awards ordered to be registered under the Act of 1966 and particulars shall be entered in the register of any execution issued on such an award.

(6) Where it appears to the Court on granting leave to register an award or an application made by the judgment debtor after an award has been registered—

(a) that the enforcement of the award has been stayed (whether provisionally or otherwise) pursuant to the Convention, or

(b) that an application has been made pursuant to the Convention, which, if granted, might result in a stay of the enforcement of the award,

the Court shall, or in the case referred to in sub-paragraph (b) may, stay execution of the award for such time as it considers appropriate in the circumstances.

(7) An application by the judgment debtor under paragraph (6) shall be made by summons and supported by affidavit.

Registration of awards under the Multilateral Investment Guarantee Agency Act 1988

35. Rule 34 shall apply, with the necessary modifications, in relation to an award rendered pursuant to the Convention referred to in section 1(1) of the Multilateral Investment Guarantee Agency Act 1988 as it applies in relation to an award rendered pursuant to the Convention referred to in section 1(1) of the Arbitration (International Investment Disputes) Act 1966.". **A58–077**

6. After Form No. 8 in Appendix A there shall be inserted the form in Schedule 1 to these Rules. **A58–078**

7. After Form No. 15 in Appendix A there shall be inserted the form in Schedule 2 to these Rules. **A58–079**

Hearsay evidence

8. For Order 38, rules 20 to 34, there shall be substituted the following— **A58–080**

"Application and interpretation

20.—(1) In this Part of this Order the '1995 Act' means the Civil Evidence Act 1995 and any expressions used in this Part of this Order and in the 1995 Act have the same meanings in this Part of this Order as they have in the Act. **A58–081**

(2) In this Part of this Order:

'hearsay evidence' means evidence consisting of hearsay within the meaning of section 1(2) of the 1995 Act;
'hearsay notice' means a notice under section 2 of the 1995 Act.

(3) This Part of this Order applies in relation to the trial or hearing of an issue or question arising in a cause or matter and to a reference, inquiry and assessment of damages, as it applies to the trial or hearing of a cause or matter.

Hearsay notices

A58–082   21.—(1) A hearsay notice must

(a) state that it is a hearsay notice;

(b) identify the hearsay evidence;

(c) identify the person who made the statement which is to be given in evidence;

(d) state why that person will (or may) not be called to give oral evidence; and

(e) if the hearsay evidence is contained in a witness statement, refer to the part of the witness statement where it is set out.

(2) A single hearsay notice may deal with the hearsay evidence of more than one witness.

(3) The requirement to give a hearsay notice does not apply to

(a) evidence which is authorised to be given by or in an affidavit; or

(b) a statement which a party to a probate action desires to give in evidence and which is alleged to have been made by the person whose estate is the subject of the action.

(4) Subject to paragraph (5), a party who desires to give in evidence at the trial or hearing of a cause or matter hearsay evidence shall

(a) in the case of a cause or matter which is required to be set down for trial or hearing or adjourned into Court, within 28 days after it is set down or so adjourned or within such other period as the Court may specify, and

(b) in any other case, within 28 days after the date on which an appointment for the first hearing of the cause or matter is obtained, or within such other period as the Court may specify,

serve a hearsay notice on every party to the cause or matter.

(5) Where witness statements are served under rule 2A of this Order, any hearsay notice served under this rule shall be served at the same time as the witness statements.

Power to call witness for cross-examination on hearsay evidence

A58–083   22.—(1) Where a party tenders as hearsay evidence a statement made by a person but does not propose to call the person who made the statement to give evidence, the court may, on application, allow another party to call and cross-examine the person who made the statement on its contents.

(2) An application under paragraph (1) shall be made on notice to all other parties not later than 28 days after service of the hearsay notice.

(3) Where the court allows another party to call and cross-examine the person who made the statement, it may give such directions as it thinks fit to secure the attendance of that person and as to the procedure to be followed.

Credibility

23.—(1) If   A58–084

(a) a party tenders as hearsay evidence a statement made by a person but does not call the person who made the statement to give oral evidence, and

(b) another party wishes to attack the credibility of the person who made the statement;

that other party shall notify the party tendering the hearsay evidence of his intention.

(2) A notice under paragraph (1) shall be given not later than 28 days after service of the hearsay notice.

Powers exercisable in chambers

24. The jurisdiction of the Court under rules 20 to 23 may be exercised in chambers.". A58–085

9. Nothing in rule 8 shall apply to proceedings   A58–086

(a) in which directions have been given, or orders have been made, as to the evidence to be given at the trial or hearing, or

(b) where the trial or hearing has begun

before 31st January 1997.

Miscellaneous amendments

10. Order 29, rule 11(2)(a) shall be amended by substituting for the words "as insurer" A58–087 the words "an insurer".

Mackay of Clashfern, C.,
Stephen Brown, P.,
Rattee, J.,
Colman, J.,
Bell, J.,
Jean Ritchie.

Dated 19th December 1996

THE RULES OF THE SUPREME COURT (AMENDMENT) 1996

SCHEDULE 1   Rule 6

Arbitration application

A58–088

No.8A
(O.73, r.4(1))
Guidance notes for Applicants

1. You should read the following notes carefully before completing the attached form. The form can be used to either:—
   (a) make an application in existing proceedings; or
   (b) begin proceedings (as an originating document).
   Notes 2 and 4 are relevant to an application as at 1(a); Notes 3 and 4 are relevant to an application as at 1(b).

2. **No** acknowledgement of service is required if the form is being used to make an application in existing proceedings. You should delete the notes relating to returning an acknowledgement of service. But you must still complete the address boxes at the end of the form as appropriate.

Service
3. (a) A completed acknowledgement of service must be served with the arbitration application. Notes for guidance attached to that form will tell you how to fill it in.
   (b) The application **may not** be served more than 1 month from the date of issue **unless**:—
       it is to be served on a party outside England and Wales, or
       the time for service has been extended by the Court.
   (c) You must write in the appropriate time limit for returning the acknowledgement of service. The relevant number of days should be given in the box below paragraph 6 of the notes about service.
   (d) If you are an applicant acting in person and you reside at an address which is not in England and Wales, you must give an address for service which is within the Court's jurisdiction.

4. Detach the guidance notes before this form is served.

DEPARTMENTAL ADVISORY COMMITTEE ON ARBITRATION LAW

Abitration application *Royal Arms* A58–089

In the High Court of Justice 19 NO
Queen's Bench Division
Commercial Court
       District Registry Mercantile List use black ink and capital letters

1. (i)   In an arbitration application between   **Applicant**

         and   **Respondent**

         of   **Respondent**

         of   **Respondent**

         of

(ii)   and in the matter of an (anticipated) arbitration between

    Claimant

    Respondent(s)

(iii)   The arbitrator(s) to whom notice of this application is given are:

give name of any arbitrator(s) listed above as respondents
or
give full names and addresses where not named as respondents

Hearing
(delete (i) or (ii) as applicable)

2.   [(i)]   This application is made on notice (ex parte).

     [(ii)]   The hearing of this application will take place in court (chambers)

on

at   o'clock,

(or on a date to be fixed)

at *(specify court)*

THE RULES OF THE SUPREME COURT (AMENDMENT) 1996

Grounds for application and details of what is being claimed
The grounds for making the application and details of what is being claimed should be set out either in the box below or on a separate sheet attached to this application. The details should include those required by Order 73.

(Set out below the grounds and details of your claim)

The applicant seeks an order for the costs of this application against:

(Set out below the name of the person(s) against whom costs are sought)

Dated ....

Returning the acknowledgement of service
(see also 'Notes for arbitrators,' at paragraph 5 below)

1. If you are (a) named as a respondent to this application, and
(b) served with a copy of this application

you should complete and return the accompanying acknowledgement of service to the court office which issued it. **You have only a limited time in which to do this.** Full details of the time allowed are set out in the notes for guidance to the form of acknowledgement. **Whether or not you complete the form, and how you complete it, if you decide to do so, will affect your right:**

- **to contest the application; and**
- **to be kept informed of any hearing or future hearings.**

DEPARTMENTAL ADVISORY COMMITTEE ON ARBITRATION LAW

2. If you **complete the form of acknowledgement** and **indicate that you intend to contest the application**, you will **be notified of all hearing dates** relating to this application and **will be entitled to put your case to the Court**. If you wish to put evidence before the Court in response to any affidavit filed by the applicant in support of the application, you must serve your affidavit on the applicant within 21 days after the time limited for acknowledging service (see time for acknowledging below).
3. If you **complete the form of acknowledgment** but **do not indicate that you intend to contest the application**, you will be notified of all hearing dates relating to the application but, unless the court gives permission, you **will not be allowed to put your case to the Court**. The Court will make whatever order it feels is just in the circumstances. If, after returning the acknowledgement, you decide you **do** wish to contest the application, you must **ask the Court's permission to do so**.
4. If you **do not return** the form of acknowledgement, you will **not be entitled to contest** the application, **or be notified of any hearing dates relating to it**. If you **fail to return** the form of acknowledgement within the time allowed for the purpose (see the notes for guidance on the form of acknowledgement) you must ask the Court's permission to return the form of acknowledgement after the proper time. Unless the Court gives permission, you will not be allowed to put your case to the Court. The Court will make whatever order it feels is just in the circumstances.

Notes for arbitrators

5. If you were or are an arbitrator in the arbitration which gave rise to this application and you are named as a respondent to the application, paragraphs 1 to 4 above apply to you as to any other respondent.
6. If you were or are an arbitrator in the arbitration which gave rise to this application and you are **not** named as a respondent, the application has been sent to you for your information. You need not complete or return the acknowledgement. You may, if you wish, file an affidavit or make representations in writing to the Court. If you wish to do this, you should do so as soon as practicable. You should send a copy of the document which you have sent to the Court to all parties to the arbitration application. Alternatively, you may apply to be made a respondent to the application. Any such application should be made to the Court in writing.

(write in 14 days, or where application is to be served out of the jurisdiction the time limit set by the Court)   The time limit for the respondents to acknowledge service is [ ] days

---

This summons was issued by

of

(Applicant) (Solicitor for the applicant)

(Complete only if you are an applicant acting in person and you reside at an address which is outside the Court's jurisdiction)
Applicant's address for service within the jurisdiction is

THE RULES OF THE SUPREME COURT (AMENDMENT) 1996

A58–090

SCHEDULE 2
No.15A
(O.73, r.11(1))

Rule 7

**Acknowledgment of Service of
Arbitration Application**

Guidance notes for the Applicant

Read these notes carefully
The notes explain what you have to do before this form is sent to ("served" on) the respondent

Form heading
You must fill in the heading of the form with:
- the number allocated to the application
- the name of the appropriate High Court Division, for example, Queen's Bench Division, (Commercial Court), or if the arbitration application was issued in a District Registry, the name of the District Registry, and
- the names of the parties (the "title") as they appear on the application.

Part 3 Please leave blank for respondent to complete

Part 4
Return address
Write in the full address of the District Registry or office in the Royal Courts of Justice to which the form should be returned.

On the reverse of acknowledgment form (Applicant's (Applicant's solicitor's) details.)
Fill in your name and the address to which papers about the case should be sent. Detach these guidance notes before the form is sent to the respondent.

DEPARTMENTAL ADVISORY COMMITTEE ON ARBITRATION LAW

Acknowledgement of Service of
Arbitration application
Guidance notes for the Respondent

Read these notes carefully.
They will help you to fill in the form attached and tell you what other steps you need to take.

Act quickly.
You have only a limited time to return the form.

Help and advice
You can get help and legal advice from:
- a solicitor, or
- a Citizens' Advice Bureau.

They will also tell you if you qualify for help with your legal costs ("legal aid"). Staff at any District Registry or office in the Royal Courts of Justice (Strand, London) will help you to fill in the form.

Time for returning the form
You have **14 days** from the day you receive the arbitration application to **return the completed form to the court**. The day on which the 14 day period begins depends on how you received the application (how it was "served" on you).
If the application was:
- handed to you personally, the 14 days begins on the day you were given the application;
- delivered by post, the 14 days begins 7 days from the date of the postmark;
- put through your letter box, the 14 days begins 7 days from the day this was done.

If you are a limited company and the application was delivered by post, the 14 days begins:
- on the second working day from the date of the postmark if first class post was used;
- on the fourth working day from the date of the postmark if the second class post was used.

Note: You may have less than 14 days to return the form in certain kinds of proceedings where an early hearing date has been fixed. If in doubt, seek advice.

If the arbitration application was served on you at an address outside England and Wales, the application will tell you how long you have to return the acknowledgement form.

The Rules of the Supreme Court (Amendment) 1996

Filling in the form

Read these notes carefully
They will help you to fill in the form opposite and tell you what other steps you need to take.

You can use the same form of acknowledgement for two (or more) respondents provided the form makes this clear and they all wish to reply in the same way.

If you are **under 18 or suffering certain mental disorders** ("under disability") you must ask another person to act for you. That person can be any friend or relative who is over 18 and not a co-defendant in the same claim. But they must act on your behalf with the help of a solicitor. **The solicitor must fill in the form of acknowledgement.**

Part 1 Write in your full name. If your name was incorrect on the summons, add the words "sued as" followed by the name stated on the application.

If you are: a person trading in a name other than your own, write in your name followed by the words "trading as" and the name under which you trade;

a partner in a firm, write in your name followed by the words "a partner in the firm of" and the name of the firm. **If you are sued as a partner but are not, say so.**

$\longrightarrow$

Part 2 Tick the appropriate box to show whether you intend to contest the application, the claim for costs, or neither. Read note 2 below.

$\longrightarrow$

Part 3 Unless your solicitor is filling in the form on your behalf, you must sign the form and give an address to which court documents should be sent, and any reference, telephone or fax numbers. If you are being sued as an individual (that is in your own name rather than of your firm or company) the address you give must be one in England and Wales. If you are a **limited company**, the form may be filled in by an **authorised officer** who must state his position in that company, or a solicitor. A solicitor may give his firm's address, an authorised officer must give the registered or principal office of the company.

$\longrightarrow$

Perforations

What to do when you have filled in the form.
1. Return the form
Detach these guidance notes and send or take the acknowledgement form to the office in the Royal Courts of Justice or the District Registry which issued the application.

2. Preparing your defence
If you are a respondent and wish to contest the application, you must set out your reasons in an affidavit (a sworn statement). You must send a copy of the affidavit to the applicant, the court and the other respondents. You must do this not more than 21 days after the last day for returning the acknowledgement of service, that is, 14 days after service.

If you are an arbitrator who is not named as a respondent, you may apply to be made a respondent or make representations to the court. If you wish to make representations, you may do so informally in writing or in an affidavit. You must send a copy to the court and all other parties as soon as practicable after you receive the application.

THE RULES OF THE SUPREME COURT (AMENDMENT) 1996

A58–091   Acknowledgement of servicing of originating summons
Arbitration application

In the High Court of Justice   19   NO

Queen's Bench Division

Commercial Court

Mercantile List   **District registry** Use black ink and capital letters

Respondent

Applicant

Part 1   (Your) (Respondent's) full name

Part 2   (Do you) (Does the respondent) intend to contest:

the application? ☐
the claim for costs (if applicable)? ☐
or neither? ☐

Part 3   I acknowledge that (I have) (the respondent has) been served with a copy of the arbitration application.

Signed _____ Date _____
Respondent (Solicitor for the respondent) (Authorised officer)

Address to which papers about this case should be sent.

Solicitor's ref.   Telephone no.   Fax no.

Part 4   When completed this form should be returned to:

DEPARTMENTAL ADVISORY COMMITTEE ON ARBITRATION LAW

Applicant's (Applicant's solicitor's) details)
Address to which papers about this case should be sent.

Solicitor's ref. ☐   Telephone no. ☐   Fax no. ☐

The High Court and County Courts (Allocation of Arbitration Proceedings) Order 1996

(SI 1996/3215)

Made	*19th December 1996*
Laid before Parliament	*20th December 1996*
Coming into force	*31st January 1997*

The Lord Chancellor, in exercise of the powers conferred on him by section 105 of the Arbitration Act 1996, hereby makes the following Order:

1.—(1) This Order may be cited as the High Court and County Courts (Allocation of Arbitration Proceedings) Order 1996 and shall come into force on 31st January 1997.

(2) In this Order, "the Act" means the Arbitration Act 1996.

2. Subject to articles 3 to 5, proceedings under the Act shall be commenced and taken in the High Court.

3. Proceedings under section 9 of the Act (stay of legal proceedings) shall be commenced in the court in which the legal proceedings are pending.

4. Proceedings under sections 66 and 101(2) (enforcement of awards) of the Act may be commenced in any county court.

5.—(1) Proceedings under the Act may be commenced and taken in the Central London County Court Business List.

(2) Where, in exercise of the powers conferred by sections 41 and 42 of the County Courts Act 1984 the High Court or the judge in charge of the Central London County Court Business List orders the transfer of proceedings under the Act which were commenced in the Central London County Court Business List to the High Court, those proceedings shall be taken in the High Court.

(3) Where, in exercise of its powers under section 40(2) of the County Courts Act 1984 the High Court orders the transfer of proceedings under the Act which were commenced in the High Court to the Central London County Court Business List, those proceedings shall be taken in the Central London County Court Business List.

(4) In exercising the powers referred to in paragraphs (2) and (3) regard shall be had to the following criteria—

(a) the financial substance of the dispute referred to arbitration, including the value of any claim or counterclaim;

(b) the nature of the dispute referred to arbitration (for example, whether it arises out of a commercial or business transaction or relates to engineering, building or other construction work);

(c) whether the proceedings are otherwise important and, in particular, whether they raise questions of importance to persons who are not parties, and

(d) the balance of convenience points to having the proceedings taken in the Central London County Court Business List,

and, where the financial substance of the dispute exceeds £200,000, the proceedings shall be taken in the High Court unless the proceedings do not raise questions of general importance to persons who are not parties.

(5) In this article—

"the Central London County Court Business List" means the business list established at the Central London County Court by Order 48C of the County Court Rules 1981;
"value" shall be construed in accordance with articles 9 and 10 of the High Court and County Courts Jurisdiction Order 1991.

6. Nothing in this Order shall prevent the judge in charge of the commercial list (within the meaning of section 62(3) of the Supreme Court Act 1981) from transferring proceedings under the Act to another list, court or Division of the High Court to which he has power to transfer proceedings and, where such an order is made, the proceedings may be taken in that list, court or Division as the case may be.

Mackay of Clashfern, C.

Dated 19th December 1996

Appendix B

Transitional Provisions

70. As we said in Paragraph 315 of our February 1996 Report, we decided to use the precedent of previous arbitration statutes so that the new Act applies to arbitrations commenced after it came into force, whenever the arbitration agreement was made. The transitional provisions reflect this, but of course also have to deal with arbitration agreements and arbitrations which are to remain governed by the pre-existing law.

71. Section 84(1) of the Act is a limiting provision, in that it stipulates that the Act does not apply to arbitrations commenced before the date on which Part I comes into force, and this is of course reflected in Paragraph 2(a) of Schedule 2 to the Commencement No.1 Order.

72. Section 84(2) is an enlarging provision, since it applies the Act to arbitrations commenced after Part I comes into force, even if the agreement is made at an earlier time.

73. The remaining transitional provisions in Paragraph 2 of Schedule 2 to the Commencement No.1 Order, deal with arbitration applications to the Court. Paragraph 2(b) is designed to ensure that the pre-existing law applies to all applications to Court made before Part I comes into force, and that this will remain the case even if an arbitration is commenced after Part I comes into force. Paragraph 2(c) is designed to ensure that applications relating to arbitral proceedings commenced before Part I comes into force are themselves governed by the pre-existing law so as to avoid one law applying to the arbitration proceedings and another to arbitration applications to the Court.

74. Paragraph 4 of Schedule 2 deals with the question of "Equity Clauses" in arbitration agreements, which we deal with in Paragraph 30 of this Report.

The Arbitration Act 1996 (Commencement No. 1) Order 1996

(SI 1996/3146)

Made   16th December 1996

A58–096   The Secretary of State, in exercise of the powers conferred on him by section 109 of the Arbitration Act 1996(a), hereby makes the following Order:

1. This Order may be cited as the Arbitration Act 1996 (Commencement No. 1) Order 1996.

2. The provisions of the Arbitration Act 1996 ("the Act") listed in Schedule 1 to this Order shall come into force on the day after this Order is made.

3. The rest of the Act, except sections 85 to 87, shall come into force on 31st January 1997.

4. The transitional provisions in Schedule 2 to this Order shall have effect.

John M. Taylor,
Parliamentary Under-Secretary of State
for Corporate and Consumer Affairs,
16th December 1996   Department of Trade and Industry

SCHEDULE 1   Article 2.

A58–097   Section 91 so far as it relates to the power to make orders under the section.
Section 105.
Section 107(1) and paragraph 36 of Schedule 3, so far as relating to the provision that may be made by county court rules.
Section 107(2) and the reference in Schedule 4 to the County Courts (Northern Ireland) Order 1980 so far as relating to the above matter.
Sections 108 to 110.

SCHEDULE 2   Article 4.

A58–098   **1.** In this Schedule:

(a) "the appointed day" means the date specified in Article 3 of this Order;

(b) "arbitration application" means any application relating to arbitration made by or in legal proceedings, whether or not arbitral proceedings have commenced;

(c) "the old law" means the enactments specified in section 107 as they stood before their amendment or repeal by the Act.

2. The old law shall continue to apply to:

(a) arbitral proceedings commenced before the appointed day;

(b) arbitration applications commenced or made before the appointed day;

(c) arbitration applications commenced or made on or after the appointed day relating to arbitral proceedings commenced before the appointed day

and the provisions of the Act which would otherwise be applicable shall not apply.

3. The provisions of this Act brought into force by this Order shall apply to any other arbitration application.

4. In the application of paragraph (b) of subsection (1) of section 46 (provision for dispute to be decided in accordance with provisions other than law) to an arbitration agreement made before the appointed day, the agreement shall have effect in accordance with the rules of law (including any conflict of laws rules) as they stood immediately before the appointed day.

United Nations Compensation Commission Governing Council—Report and Recommendations made by the Panel of Commissioners concerning the twenty-third instalment of "E3" claims; Annex: Summary of general propositions

Introduction

A59–001   1. In the Report and Recommendations Made by the Panel of Commissioners Concerning the Fourth Instalment of "E3" Claims (S/AC.26/1999/14) (the "Fourth Report"), this Panel set out some general propositions based on those claims which had come before it and the findings of other panels of Commissioners contained in their reports and recommendations. Those propositions, as well as some observations specific to the claims in the fourth instalment of "E3" claims, are to be found in the introduction to the Fourth Report (the "Preamble").

2. The Fourth Report was approved by the Governing Council in its decision 74 (S/AC.26/Dec.74 (1999)); and the claims that this Panel has subsequently encountered continue to manifest the same or similar issues. Accordingly, the Panel has revised the Preamble, so as to delete the specific comments, and thus present this Summary of General Propositions (the "Summary"). The Summary is intended to be annexed to, and to form part of, the reports and recommendations made by this Panel. The Summary should facilitate the drafting, and reduce the size, of this Panel's future reports, since it will not be necessary to set matters out *in extenso* in the body of each report.

3. As further issues are resolved, they may be added at the end of future editions of this Summary.

4. In this Summary, the Panel wishes to record:

(a) The procedure involved in evaluating the claims put before it and in formulating recommendations for the consideration of the Governing Council; and

(b) Its analyses of the recurrent substantive issues that arise in claims before the Commission relating to construction and engineering contracts.

5. In deciding to draft this Summary in a format which was separated out from the actual recommendations in the report itself, and in a way that was re-usable, the Panel was motivated by a number of matters. One was the desire to keep the substantive element of its reports to a manageable length. As the number of reports generated by the various panels increases, there seems to be a good deal to be said for what might be called economies of scale. Another matter was the awareness of the Panel of the high costs involved in translating official documents from their original language into each official language of the United Nations. The Panel is concerned to avoid the heavy costs of re-translation of recurrent texts, where the Panel is applying established principles to fresh claims. That re-translation would occur if the reasoning set out in this Summary had been incorporated into the principal text of each report at each relevant point. And, of course, that very repetition of principles seems unnecessary in itself, and this Summary avoids it. In sum, it is the intention of the Panel to shorten those reports and recommendations, wherever possible, and thereby to reduce the cost of translating them.

UNITED NATIONS COMPENSATION COMMISSION GOVERNING COUNCIL

I. THE PROCEDURE

A. *Summary of the process*

6. Each of the claimants whose claims are presented to this Panel is given the opportunity to provide the Panel with information and documentation concerning the claims. In its review of the claims, the Panel considers evidence from the claimants and the responses of Governments to the reports of the Executive Secretary issued pursuant to article 16 of the Provisional Rules for Claims Procedure (S/AC.26/1992/10) (the "Rules"). The Panel has retained consultants with expertise in valuation and in construction and engineering. The Panel has taken note of certain findings by other panels, approved by the Governing Council, regarding the interpretation of relevant Security Council resolutions and Governing Council decisions. The Panel is mindful of its function to provide an element of due process in the review of claims filed with the Commission. Finally, the Panel expounds in this Summary both procedural and substantive aspects of the process of formulating recommendations in its consideration of the individual claims. A59–002

B. *The nature and purpose of the proceedings*

7. The status and functions of the Commission are set forth in the report of the Secretary-General pursuant to paragraph 19 of Security Council resolution 687 (1991) dated 2 May 1991 (S/22559). A59–003

8. The Panel is entrusted with three tasks in its proceedings. First, the Panel is required to determine whether the various types of losses alleged by the claimants are within the jurisdiction of the Commission, *i.e.*, whether the losses were caused directly by Iraq's invasion and occupation of Kuwait. Second, the Panel has to verify whether the alleged losses that are in principle compensable have in fact been incurred by a given claimant. Third, the Panel is required to determine whether these compensable losses were incurred in the amounts claimed, and if not, the appropriate quantum for the loss based on the evidence before the Panel.

9. In fulfilling these tasks, the Panel considers that the vast number of claims before the Commission and the time limits in the Rules necessitate the use of an approach which is itself unique, but the principal characteristics of which are rooted in generally accepted procedures for claim determination, both domestic and international. It involves the employment of well established general legal standards of proof and valuation methods that have much experience behind them. The resultant process is essentially documentary rather than oral, and inquisitorial rather than adversarial. This method both realises and balances the twin objectives of speed and accuracy. It also permits the efficient resolution of the thousands of claims filed by corporations with the Commission.

C. *The procedural history of the "E3" Claims*

10. The claims submitted to the Panel are selected by the secretariat of the Commission from among the construction and engineering claims (the " 'E3' Claims") on the basis A59–004

823

of established criteria. These include the date of filing and compliance by claimants with the requirements established for claims submitted by corporations and other legal entities (the "category 'E' claims").

11. Prior to presenting each instalment of claims to the Panel, the secretariat performs a preliminary assessment of each claim included in a particular instalment in order to determine whether the claim meets the formal requirements established by the Governing Council in article 14 of the Rules.

12. Article 14 of the Rules sets forth the formal requirements for claims submitted by corporations and other legal entities. These claimants must submit:

(a) An "E" claim form with four copies in English or with an English translation;

(b) Evidence of the amount, type and causes of losses;

(c) An affirmation by the Government that, to the best of its knowledge, the claimant is incorporated in or organized under the law of the Government submitting the claim;

(d) Documents evidencing the name, address and place of incorporation or organization of the claimant;

(e) Evidence that the claimant was, on the date on which the claim arose, incorporated or organized under the law of the Government which has submitted the claim;

(f) A general description of the legal structure of the claimant; and

(g) An affirmation by the authorized official for the claimant that the information contained in the claim is correct.

13. Additionally, the "E" claim form requires that a claimant submit with its claim a separate statement in English explaining its claim ("Statement of Claim"), supported by documentary and other appropriate evidence sufficient to demonstrate the circumstances and the amount of the claimed losses. The following particulars are requested in the "INSTRUCTIONS FOR CLAIMANTS":

(a) The date, type and basis of the Commission's jurisdiction for each element of loss;

(b) The facts supporting the claim;

(c) The legal basis for each element of the claim; and

(d) The amount of compensation sought and an explanation of how the amount was calculated.

A59–005   **14.** If it is determined that a claim does not provide these particulars or does not include a Statement of Claim, the claimant is notified of the deficiencies and invited to provide the necessary information pursuant to article 15 of the Rules (the "article 15 notification"). If a claimant fails to respond to that notification, the claimant is sent a formal article 15 notification.

15. Further, a review of the legal and evidentiary basis of each claim identifies specific questions as to the evidentiary support for the alleged losses. It also highlights areas of the claim in which further information or documentation is required. Consequently, questions and requests for additional documentation are transmitted to the claimants pursuant to article 34 of the Rules (the "article 34 notification"). If a claimant fails to respond to the article 34 notification, a reminder notification is sent to the claimant. Upon receipt of the responses and additional documentation, a detailed factual and legal analysis of each claim is conducted. Communications with claimants are made through their respective governments.

16. It is the experience of the Panel in the claims reviewed by it to date that this analysis usually brings to light the fact that many claimants lodge little material of a genuinely probative nature when they initially file their claims. It also appears that many claimants do not retain clearly relevant documentation and are unable to provide it when asked for it. Indeed, some claimants destroy documents in the course of a normal administrative process without distinguishing between documents with no long term purpose and documents necessary to support the claims that they have put forward. Some claimants carry this to the extreme of having to ask the Commission, when responding to an article 15 or an article 34 notification, for a copy of their own claim. Finally, some claimants do not respond to requests for further information and evidence. The consequence is inevitably that for a large number of loss elements and a smaller number of claimants the Panel is unable to recommend any compensation.

17. The Panel performs a thorough and detailed factual and legal review of the claims. The Panel assumes an investigative role that goes beyond reliance merely on information and argument supplied with the claims as presented. After a review of the relevant information and documentation, the Panel makes initial determinations as to the compensability of the loss elements of each claim. Next, reports on each of the claims are prepared focusing on the appropriate valuation of each of the compensable losses, and on the question of whether the evidence produced by the claimant is sufficient in accordance with article 35(3) of the Rules.

18. The cumulative effect is one of the following recommendations: (a) compensation for the loss in the full amount claimed; (b) compensation for the loss in a lower amount than that claimed; or (c) no compensation.

II. Procedural Issues

A. Panel recommendations

19. Once a motivated recommendation of a panel is adopted by a decision of the **A59–006** Governing Council, it is something to which this Panel gives great weight.

20. All panel recommendations are supported by a full analysis. When a new claim is presented to this Panel it may happen that the new claim will manifest the same characteristics as the previous claim which has been presented to a prior panel. In that event, this Panel will follow the principle developed by the prior panel. Of course, there may still be differences inherent in the two claims at the level of proof of causation or quantum. Nonetheless the principle will be the same.

21. Alternatively, that second claim will manifest different characteristics to the first claim. In that event, those different characteristics may give rise to a different issue of principle and thus warrant a different conclusion by this Panel to that of the previous panel.

B. Evidence of loss

A59–007 22. Pursuant to article 35(3) of the Rules, corporate claims must be supported by documentary and other appropriate evidence sufficient to demonstrate the circumstances and amount of the claimed loss. The Governing Council has stated in paragraph 5 of decision 15 that, with respect to business losses, there "will be a need for detailed factual descriptions of the circumstances of the claimed loss, damage or injury" in order to justify a recommendation for compensation (S/AC.26/1992/15).

23. The Panel takes this opportunity to emphasise that what is required of a claimant by article 35(3) of the Rules is the presentation to the Commission of evidence that must go to both causation and quantum. The Panel's interpretation of what is appropriate and sufficient evidence will vary according to the nature of the claim. In implementing this approach, the Panel applies the relevant principles extracted from those within the corpus of principles referred to in article 31 of the Rules.

1. Sufficiency of evidence

A59–008 24. In the final outcome, claims that are not supported by sufficient and appropriate evidence fail. In the context of the construction and engineering claims that are before this Panel, the most important evidence is documentary. It is in this context that the Panel records a syndrome which it found striking when it addressed the first claims presented to it and which has continued to manifest itself in the claims subsequently encountered. This was the reluctance of claimants to make critical documentation available to the Panel.

25. Imperatively, the express wording of decision 46 of the Governing Council requires that " . . . claims received in categories 'D', 'E', and 'F' must be supported by documentary and other appropriate evidence sufficient to demonstrate the circumstances and amount of the claimed loss . . . " In this same decision, the Governing Council confirmed that " . . . no loss shall be compensated by the Commission solely on the basis of an explanatory statement provided by the claimant, . . . " (S/AC.26/Dec.46(1998)).

26. It is also the case that the Panel has power under the Rules to request additional information and, in unusually large or complex cases, further written submissions. Such requests usually take the form of procedural orders. Where such orders are issued, considerable emphasis is placed on this need for sufficient documentary and other appropriate evidence.

27. Thus there is an obligation to provide the relevant documentary evidence both on the first filing of a claim and on any subsequent steps.

28. What is more, the absence of *any* relevant contemporary record to support a particular claim means that the claimant is inviting the Panel to make an award, often of millions of dollars, on no foundation other than the assertion of the claimant. This would not satisfy the "sufficient evidence" rule in article 35(3) of the Rules and would go against the instruction of the Governing Council contained in decision 46. It is something that the Panel is unable to do.

2. Sufficiency under article 35(3): The obligation of disclosure

A59–009 29. Next in the context of documentary evidence, this Panel wishes to highlight an important aspect of the rule that claims must be supported by sufficient documentary and other appropriate evidence. This involves bringing to the attention of the Commission all material aspects of the claim, whether such aspects are seen by the claimant as beneficial to, or reductive of, its claims. The obligation is not dissimilar to good faith requirements under domestic jurisdictions.

3. Missing documents: The nature and adequacy of the paper trail

30. The Panel now turns to the question of what is required in order to establish an adequate paper trail.

31. Where documents cannot be supplied, their absence must be explained in a credible manner. The explanation must itself be supported by the appropriate evidence. Claimants may also supply substitute documentation for or information about the missing documents. Claimants must remember that the mere fact that they suffered a loss at the same time as the hostilities in the Persian Gulf were starting or were in process does not mean that the loss was directly caused by Iraq's invasion and occupation of Kuwait. A causative link must be established. It should also be borne in mind that it was not the intention of the Security Council in its resolutions to provide a "new for old" basis of reimbursement of the losses suffered in respect of tangible property. Capital goods depreciate. That depreciation must be taken into account and demonstrated in the evidence filed with the Commission. In sum, in order for evidence to be considered appropriate and sufficient to demonstrate a loss, the Panel expects claimants to present to the Commission a coherent, logical and sufficiently evidenced file leading to the financial claims that they are making.

32. Of course, the Panel recognises that in time of civil disturbances, the quality of proof may fall below that which would be submitted in a peace time situation. Persons who are fleeing for their lives do not stop to collect the audit records. Allowances have to be made for such vicissitudes.

33. Thus the Panel is not surprised that some of the claimants in the instalments presented to it to date seek to explain the lack of documentation by asserting that it is, or was, located in areas of civil disorder or has been lost or destroyed, or, at least, cannot be accessed. But the fact that offices on the ground in the region have been looted or destroyed would not explain why claimants have not produced any of the documentary records that would reasonably be expected to be found at claimants' head offices situated in other countries.

34. The Panel approaches the claims presented to it in the light of the general and specific requirements to produce documents noted above. Where there is a lack of documentation, combined with no or no adequate explanation for that lack, and an absence of alternative evidence to make good any part of that lack, the Panel has no opportunity or basis upon which to make a recommendation.

C. Amending claims after filing

35. In the course of processing the claims after they have been filed with the Commission, further information is sought from the claimants pursuant to the Rules. When the claimants respond they sometimes seek to use the opportunity to amend their claims. For example, they add new loss elements. They increase the amount originally sought in respect of a particular loss element. They transfer monies between or otherwise adjust the calculation of two or more loss elements. In some cases, they do all of these.

36. The Panel notes that the period for filing category "E" claims expired on 1 January 1996. The Governing Council approved a mechanism for these claimants to file unsolicited supplements until 11 May 1998. After that date a response to an inquiry for addi-

tional evidence is not an opportunity for a claimant to increase the quantum of a loss element or elements or to seek to recover in respect of new loss elements. In these circumstances, the Panel is unable to take into account such increases or such new loss elements when it is formulating its recommendations to the Governing Council. It does, however, take into account additional documentation where that is relevant to the original claim, either in principle or in detail. It also exercises its inherent powers to re-characterise a loss, which is properly submitted as to time, but is inappropriately allocated.

37. Some claimants also file unsolicited submissions. These too sometimes seek to increase the original claim in the ways indicated in the previous paragraph. Such submissions when received after 11 May 1998 are to be treated in the same way as amendments put forward in solicited supplements. Accordingly the Panel is unable to, and does not, take into account such amendments when it is formulating its recommendations to the Governing Council.

III. Substantive Issues

A. Applicable law

A59–012 38. As set forth in paragraphs 17 and 18 of the Fourth Report, paragraph 16 of Security Council resolution 687 (1991) reaffirmed the liability of Iraq and defined the jurisdiction of the Commission. Pursuant to article 31 of the Rules, the Panel applies Security Council resolution 687 (1991), other relevant Security Council resolutions, decisions of the Governing Council, and, where necessary, other relevant rules of international law.

B. Liability of Iraq

A59–013 39. When adopting resolution 687 (1991), the Security Council acted under chapter VII of the Charter of the United Nations which provides for maintenance or restoration of international peace and security. The Security Council also acted under chapter VII when adopting resolution 692 (1991), in which it decided to establish the Commission and the Compensation Fund referred to in paragraph 18 of resolution 687 (1991). Specifically, under resolution 687 (1991), the issue of Iraq's liability for losses falling within the Commission's jurisdiction is resolved and is not subject to review by the Panel.

40. In this context, it is necessary to address the meaning of the term "Iraq". In Governing Council decision 9 (S/AC.26/1992/9) and other Governing Council decisions, the word "Iraq" was used to mean the Government of Iraq, its political subdivisions, or any agency, ministry, instrumentality or entity (notably public sector enterprises) controlled by the Government of Iraq. In the Report and Recommendations Made by the Panel of Commissioners Concerning the Fifth Instalment of "E3" Claims (the "Fifth Report", S/AC.26/1999/2), this Panel adopted the presumption that for contracts performed in Iraq, the other contracting party was an Iraqi Government entity.

C. The "arising prior to" clause

41. The Panel recognises that it is difficult to establish a fixed date for the exclusion of its jurisdiction that does not contain an arbitrary element. With respect to the interpretation of the "arising prior to" clause in paragraph 16 of Security Council resolution 687 (1991), the Panel of Commissioners that reviewed the first instalment of "E2" claims concluded that the "arising prior to" clause was intended to exclude the foreign debt of Iraq which existed at the time of Iraq's invasion of Kuwait from the jurisdiction of the Commission. As a result, the "E2" Panel found that:

> "In the case of contracts with Iraq, where the performance giving rise to the original debt had been rendered by a claimant more than three months prior to 2 August 1990, that is, prior to 2 May 1990, claims based on payments owed, in kind or in cash, for such performance are outside of the jurisdiction of the Commission as claims for debts or obligations arising prior to 2 August 1990." (Report and Recommendations Made by the Panel of Commissioners Concerning the First Instalment of "E2" Claims, S/AC.26/1998/7, paragraph 90)).

42. That report was approved by the Governing Council. Accordingly, this Panel adopts the "E2" Panel's interpretation which is to the following effect:

(a) The phrase "without prejudice to the debts and obligations of Iraq arising prior to 2 August 1990, which will be addressed through normal mechanisms" was intended to have an exclusionary effect on the Commission's jurisdiction, i.e., such debts and obligations are not compensable by the Commission;

(b) The limitation contained in the clause "arising prior to 2 August 1990" was intended to leave unaffected the debts and obligations of Iraq which existed prior to Iraq's invasion and occupation of Kuwait; and

(c) The terms "debts" and "obligations" should be given the customary and usual meanings applied to them in ordinary discourse.

43. Thus, this Panel accepts that, in general, a claim relating to a "debt or obligation arising prior to 2 August 1990" means a debt or obligation that is based on work performed or services rendered prior to 2 May 1990.

D. Application of the "direct loss" requirement

44. Paragraph 21 of Governing Council decision 7 (S/AC.26/1991/7/Rev.1) is the seminal rule on "directness" for category "E" claims. It provides in relevant part that compensation is available for:

> "... any direct loss, damage, or injury to corporations and other entities as a result of Iraq's unlawful invasion and occupation of Kuwait. This will include any loss suffered as a result of:
>
> (a) Military operations or threat of military action by either side during the period 2 August 1990 to 2 March 1991;

(b) Departure of persons from or their inability to leave Iraq or Kuwait (or a decision not to return) during that period;

(c) Actions by officials, employees or agents of the Government of Iraq or its controlled entities during that period in connection with the invasion or occupation;

(d) The breakdown of civil order in Kuwait or Iraq during that period; or

(e) Hostage-taking or other illegal detention."

45. The text of paragraph 21 of decision 7 is not exhaustive and leaves open the possibility that there may be causes of "direct loss" other than those enumerated. Paragraph 6 of decision 15 of the Governing Council (S/AC.26/1992/15) confirms that there "will be other situations where evidence can be produced showing claims are for direct loss, damage or injury as a result of Iraq's unlawful invasion and occupation of Kuwait". Should that be the case, the claimants will have to prove specifically that a loss that was not suffered as a result of one of the five categories of events set out in paragraph 21 of decision 7 is nevertheless "direct". Paragraph 3 of decision 15 emphasises that for any alleged loss or damage to be compensable, the "causal link must be direct". (See also paragraph 9 of decision 9).

46. While the phrase "as a result of" contained in paragraph 21 of decision 7 is not further clarified, Governing Council decision 9 provides guidance as to what may be considered business "losses suffered as a result of" Iraq's invasion and occupation of Kuwait. It identifies the three main categories of loss types in the "E" claims: losses in connection with contracts, losses relating to tangible assets and losses relating to income-producing properties. Thus, decisions 7 and 9 provide specific guidance to the Panel as to how the "direct loss" requirement must be interpreted.

A59–016 **47.** In the light of the decisions of the Governing Council identified above, the Panel has reached certain conclusions as to the meaning of "direct loss". These conclusions are set out in the following paragraphs.

48. With respect to physical assets in Iraq or in Kuwait as at 2 August 1990, a claimant can prove a direct loss by demonstrating two matters. First, that the breakdown in civil order in these countries, which resulted from Iraq's invasion and occupation of Kuwait, caused the claimant to evacuate its employees. Second, as set forth in paragraph 13 of decision 9, that the claimant left physical assets in Iraq or in Kuwait.

49. With respect to losses relating to contracts to which Iraq was a party, *force majeure* or similar legal principles are not available as a defence to the obligations of Iraq.

50. With respect to losses relating to contracts to which Iraq was not a party, a claimant may prove a direct loss if it can establish that Iraq's invasion and occupation of Kuwait or the breakdown in civil order in Iraq or Kuwait following Iraq's invasion caused the claimant to evacuate the personnel needed to perform the contract.

51. In the context of the losses set out above, reasonable costs which have been incurred to mitigate those losses are direct losses. The Panel bears in mind that the claimant was under a duty to mitigate any losses that could have been reasonably avoided after the evacuation of its personnel from Iraq or Kuwait.

52. These findings regarding the meaning of "direct loss" are not intended to resolve every issue that may arise with respect to this Panel's interpretation of Governing Council decisions 7 and 9. Rather, these findings are intended as initial parameters for the review and evaluation of the claims.

53. Finally, there is the question of the geographical extent of the impact of events in Iraq and Kuwait outside these two countries. Following on the findings of the "E2" Panel in its first report, this Panel finds that damage or loss suffered as a result of (a) military operations in the region by either the Iraqi or the Allied Coalition Forces or (b) a credible and serious threat of military action that was connected to Iraq's invasion and occupation of Kuwait is compensable in principle. Of course, the further the project in question was from the area where military operations were taking place, the more the claimant may have to do to establish causality. On the other hand, the potential that an event such as the invasion and occupation of Kuwait has for causing an extensive ripple effect cannot be ignored. Each case must depend on its facts.

E. Date of loss

54. There is no general principle with respect to the date of loss. It needs to be addressed on an individual basis. In addition, the specific loss elements of each claim may give rise to different dates if analysed strictly. However, applying a different date to each loss element within a particular claim is impracticable as a matter of administration. Accordingly, the Panel has decided to determine a single date of loss for each claimant, which, in most cases, coincides with the date of the collapse of the project. A59–017

F. Currency exchange rate

55. While many of the costs incurred by the claimants were denominated in currencies other than United States dollars, the Commission issues its awards in that currency. Therefore the Panel is required to determine the appropriate rate of exchange to apply to losses expressed in other currencies. A59–018

56. The Panel finds that, as a general rule, where an exchange rate is set forth in the contract then that is the appropriate rate for losses under the relevant contracts because this was specifically agreed by the parties.

57. For losses that are not contract based, however, the contract rate is not usually an appropriate rate of exchange. For non-contractual losses, the Panel finds the appropriate exchange rate to be the prevailing commercial rate, as evidenced by the United Nations *Monthly Bulletin of Statistics*, at the date of loss.

G. Interest

58. On the issue of the appropriate interest rate to be applied, the relevant Governing Council decision is decision 16 (S/AC.26/1992/16). According to that decision, "[i]nterest will be awarded from the date the loss occurred until the date of payment, at a rate sufficient to compensate successful claimants for the loss of use of the principal amount of the award". In decision 16 the Governing Council further specified that "[i]nterest will be paid after the principal amount of awards", while postponing any decision on the methods of calculation and payment. A59–019

59. Accordingly, the Panel recommends that interest shall run from the date of loss.

H. Claim preparation costs

A59–020   60. Some claimants seek to recover compensation for the cost of preparing their claims. The compensability of claim preparation costs has not hitherto been ruled on and will be the subject, in due course, of a specific decision by the Governing Council. Therefore, this Panel has made and will make no recommendations with respect to claim preparation costs in any of the claims where they have been raised.

I. Contract losses

1. Claims for contract losses with non-Iraqi party

A59–021   61. Some of the claims relate to losses suffered as a result of non-payment by a non-Iraqi party. The fact of such a loss, *simpliciter*, does not establish it as a direct loss within the meaning of Security Council resolution 687 (1991). In order to obtain compensation, a claimant must lodge sufficient evidence that the entity with which it carried on business on 2 August 1990 was unable to make payment as a direct result of Iraq's invasion and occupation of Kuwait.

62. A good example of this would be that the party was insolvent and that the insolvency was a direct result of Iraq's invasion and occupation of Kuwait. At the very least a claimant should demonstrate that the other party had not renewed operations after the end of the occupation. In the event that there are multiple factors which have resulted in the failure to resume operations, apart from the proved insolvency of the other party, the Panel will have to be satisfied that the effective reason or *causa causans* was Iraq's invasion and occupation of Kuwait.

63. Any failure to pay because the other party was excused from performance by the operation of law which came into force after Iraq's invasion and occupation of Kuwait is in the opinion of this Panel the result of a *novus actus interveniens* and is not a direct loss arising out of Iraq's invasion and occupation of Kuwait.

2. Advance payments

A59–022   64. Many construction contracts provide for an advance payment to be made by the employer to the contractor. These advance payments are often calculated as a percentage of the initial price (initial, because many such contracts provide for automatic and other adjustments of the price during the execution of the works). The purpose of the advance payment is to facilitate certain activities which the contractor will need to carry out in the early stages.

65. Mobilisation is often one such activity. Plant and equipment may need to be purchased. A workforce will have to be assembled and transported to the work site, where facilities will be needed to accommodate it. Another such activity is the ordering of substantial or important materials which are in short supply and may, therefore, be available only at a premium or at a long lead time.

66. Advance payments are usually secured by a bond provided by the contractor, and are usually paid upon the provision of the bond. They are frequently repaid over a period of time by way of deduction by the employer from the sums which are payable at regular intervals (often monthly) to the contractor for work done. See, in the context of payments which are recovered over a period of time, the observations about amortisation at para-

graph 120, *infra*. Those observations apply *mutatis mutandis* to the repayment of advance payments.

67. The Panel notes that some claimants presenting claims have not clearly accounted for the amounts of money already paid to them by the employer. This Panel regularly sees evidence of advance payments amounting to tens of millions of United States dollars. Where advance payments have been part of the contractual arrangements between the claimant and the employer, the claimant must account for these payments in reduction of its claims, unless these payments can be shown to have been recouped in whole or in part by the employer. Where no explanation or proof of repayment is forthcoming, the Panel has no option but to conclude that these amounts paid in advance are due, on a final accounting, to the employer, and must be deducted from the claimant's claim.

3. Contractual arrangements to defer payments

(a) The analysis of "old debt"

68. Where payments are deferred under the contracts upon which the claims are based, **A59–023** an issue arises as to whether the claimed losses are "debts and obligations arising prior to 2 August 1990" and therefore outside the jurisdiction of the Commission.

69. In its first report, the "E2" Panel interpreted Security Council resolution 687 (1991) as intending to eliminate what may be conveniently called "old debt". In applying this interpretation to the claim before it the "E2" Panel identified, as "old debt", cases where the performance giving rise to the original debt had been rendered by a claimant more than three months prior to 2 August 1990, that is, prior to 2 May 1990. In those cases, claims based on payments owed, in kind or in cash, for such performance are outside the jurisdiction of the Commission as claims for debts or obligations arising prior to 2 August 1990. "Performance" as understood by the "E2" Panel for the purposes of this rule meant complete performance under a contract, or partial performance, so long as an amount was agreed to be paid for that portion of completed partial performance. In the claim the "E2" Panel was considering, the work under the contract was clearly performed prior to 2 May 1990. However, the debts were covered by a form of deferred payments agreement dated 29 July 1984. This agreement was concluded between the parties to the original contracts and postdated the latter.

70. In its analysis, the "E2" Panel found that deferred payments arrangements go to the very heart of what the Security Council described in paragraph 16 of resolution 687 as a debt of Iraq arising prior to 2 August 1990. It was this very kind of obligation which the Security Council had in mind when, in paragraph 17 of resolution 687 (1991), it directed Iraq to "adhere scrupulously" to satisfying "all of its obligations concerning servicing and repayment". Therefore, irrespective of whether such deferred payment arrangements may have created new obligations on the part of Iraq under a particular applicable municipal law, they did not do so for the purposes of resolution 687 (1991) and are therefore outside the jurisdiction of this Commission.

71. The arrangements that the "E2" Panel was considering were not arrangements that arose out of genuine arms' length commercial transactions, entered into by construction companies as part and parcel of their normal businesses. Instead the situation which the "E2" Panel was addressing was described as follows:

> "The negotiation of these deferred payment arrangements was typically conducted with Iraq not by the contractor or supplier itself, but rather by its Government. Typically, the Government negotiated on behalf of all of the contracting parties

833

from the country concerned who were in a similar situation. The deferred payment arrangements with Iraq were commonly entered into under a variety of forms, including complicated crude oil barter arrangements under which Iraq would deliver certain amounts of crude oil to a foreign State to satisfy consolidated debts; the foreign State then would sell the oil and, through its central bank, credit particular contractors' accounts." (S/AC.26/1998/7, paragraph 93).

"Iraq's debts were typically deferred by contractors who could not afford to 'cut their losses' and leave, and thus these contractors continued to work in the hope of eventual satisfaction and continued to amass large credits with Iraq. In addition, the payment terms were deferred for such long periods that the debt servicing costs alone had a significant impact on the continued growth of Iraq's foreign debt." (S/AC.26/1998/7, paragraph 94).

72. This Panel agrees.

(b) Application of the "old debt" analysis

A59–024 73. In the application of this analysis to claims other than those considered by the "E2" Panel, there are two aspects which are worth mentioning.

74. The first is that the problem does not arise where the actual work has been performed after 2 May 1990. The arrangement deferring payment is irrelevant to the issue. The issue typically resolves itself in these cases into one of proof of the execution of the work, the quantum, the non-payment and causation.

75. The second concerns the ambit of the above analysis. As noted above, the claims which led to the above analysis arose out of "non-commercial" arrangements. They were situations where the original terms of payment entered into between the parties had been renegotiated during the currency of the contract or the negotiations or renegotiations were driven by inter-governmental exchanges. Such arrangements were clearly the result of the impact of Iraq's increasing international debt.

76. Thus one can see underlying the "E2" Panel's analysis two important factors. The first was the subsequent renegotiation of the payment terms of an existing contract to the detriment of the claimant (contractor). The second was the influence on contracts of the transactions between the respective governments. In both cases, a key element underlying the arrangements must be the impact of Iraq's mountain of old debt.

77. In the view of this Panel, where either of these factors is wholly or partially the explanation of the "loss" suffered by the claimant, then that loss or the relevant part of it is outside the jurisdiction of the Commission and cannot form the basis of recommendation by a panel. It is not necessary that both factors be present. A contract that contained deferment provisions as originally executed would still be caught by the "arising prior to" rule if the contract was the result of an inter-governmental agreement driven by the exigencies of Iraq's financial problems. It would not be a commercial transaction so much as a political agreement, and the "loss" would not be a loss falling within the jurisdiction of the Commission.

4. Losses arising as a result of unpaid retention monies

A59–025 78. The claims before this Panel include requests for compensation for what could be described as another form of deferred payment, namely unpaid retention monies.

79. Under many if not most construction contracts, provision is made for the regular payment to the contractor of sums of money during the performance of the work under

the contract. The payments are often monthly, and often calculated by reference to the amount of work that the contractor has done since the last regular payment was calculated.

80. Where the payment is directly related to the work done, it is almost invariably the case that the amount of the actual (net) payment is less than the contractual value of the work done. This is because the employer retains in his own hands a percentage (usually 5 per cent or 10 per cent and with or without an upper limit) of that contractual value. (The same approach usually obtains as between the contractor and his subcontractors.) The retained amount is often called the "retention" or the "retention fund". It builds up over time. The less work the contractor carries out before the project comes to an early halt, the smaller the fund.

81. The retention is usually payable in two stages, one at the commencement of the maintenance period, as it is often called, and the other at the end. The maintenance period usually begins when the employer first takes over the project, and commences to operate or use it. Thus the work to which any particular sum which is part of the retention fund relates may have been executed a very long time before the retention fund is payable. It follows that a loss in respect of the retention fund cannot be evaluated by reference to the time when the work which gave rise to the retention fund was executed, as for instance is described at paragraph 74, *supra*. Entitlement to be paid the retention fund is dependent on the actual or anticipated overall position at the end of the project.

82. Retention fund provisions are very common in the construction world. The retention fund serves two roles. It is an encouragement to the contractor to remedy defects appearing before or during the maintenance period. It also provides a fund out of which the employer can reimburse itself for defects that appear before or during the maintenance period which the contractor has, for whatever reason, failed or refused to make good.

83. In the claims before this Panel, events – in the shape of Iraq's invasion and occupation of Kuwait – have intervened. The contract has effectively come to an end. There is no further scope for the operation of the retention provisions. It follows that the contractor, through the actions of Iraq, has been deprived of the opportunity to recover the money. In consequence the claims for retention fall within the jurisdiction of the Commission.

84. In the light of the above considerations it seems to this Panel that the situation in the case of claims for retention is as follows:

(a) The evidence before the Commission may show that the project was in such trouble that it would never have reached a satisfactory conclusion. In such circumstances, there can be no positive recommendation, principally because there is no direct causative link between the loss and the invasion and occupation of Kuwait.

(b) Equally the evidence may show that the project would have reached a conclusion, but that there would have been problems to resolve. Accordingly the contractor would have had to expend money resolving those problems. That potential cost would have to be deducted from the claim for retention; and accordingly the most convenient course would be to recommend an award to the contractor of a suitable percentage of the unpaid retention.

(c) Finally, on the evidence it may be the case that there is no reason to believe or conclude that the project would have gone other than satisfactorily. In those circumstances, it seems that the retention claim should succeed in full.

5. Guarantees, bonds, and like securities

A59–026   85. Financial recourse agreements are part and parcel of a major construction contract. Instances are (a) guarantees – for example given by parent companies or through banks; (b) what are called "on demand" or "first demand" bonds (hereinafter "on demand bonds") which support such matters as bidding and performance; and (c) guarantees to support advance payments. (Arrangements with government sponsored bodies that provide what might be called "fall-back" insurance are in a different category. As to these, see paragraphs 95 to 102, *infra*).

86. Financial recourse arrangements give rise to particular problems when it comes to determining the claims filed in the population of construction and engineering claims. A convenient and stark example is that of the on demand bond.

87. The purpose of an on demand bond is to permit the beneficiary to obtain monies under the bond without having to prove default on the part of the other party—namely, in the situations under discussion here, the contractor executing the work. Such a bond is often set up by way of a guarantee given by the contractor or its parent to its own bank in its home State. That bank gives an identical bond to a bank (the second bank) in the State of the employer under the construction contract. In its turn, the second bank gives an identical bond to the employer. This leaves the employer, at least theoretically, in the very strong position of being able, without having to prove any default on the part of the contractor, to call down a large sum of money which will be debited to the contractor.

88. Of course, the contractor's bank will have two arrangements in place. First, an arrangement whereby it is secured as to the principal sum, the subject of the bond, in case the bond is called. Second, it will have arranged to exact a service charge, typically raised quarterly, half-yearly or annually.

89. Many claimants have raised claims in respect of the service charges; and also in respect of the principal sums. The former are often raised in respect of periods of years measured from the date of Iraq's invasion and occupation of Kuwait. The latter have, hitherto at least, been cautionary claims, in case the bonds are called in the future.

90. This Panel approaches this issue by observing that the strength of the position given to the employer by the on demand bond is sometimes more apparent than real. This derives from the fact that the courts of some countries are reluctant to enforce payment of such bonds if they feel that there is serious abuse by the employer of its position. For example, where there is a persuasive allegation of fraud, some courts will be prepared to injunct the beneficiary from making a call on the bond, or one or other of the banks from meeting the demand. It is also the case that there may be remedies for the contractor in some jurisdictions when the bonds are called in circumstances that are clearly outside the original contemplation of the parties.

A59–027   91. The Panel notes that most if not all contracts for the execution of major construction works by a contractor from one country in the territory of another country will have clauses to deal with war, insurrection or civil disorder. Depending on the approach of the relevant governing law to such matters, these provisions, if triggered, may have a direct or indirect effect on the validity of the bond. Direct, if under the relevant legal regime, the effects of the clause in the construction contract apply also to the bond; indirect if the termination or modification of the underlying obligation (the construction contract) gives rise to the opportunity to seek a forum-driven modification or termination of the liabilities under the bond.

92. In addition, the simple passage of time is likely to give rise to the right to treat the bond obligation as expired or unenforceable, or to seek a forum-driven resolution to the same effect. In addition, it is necessary to bear in mind the existence of the trade

embargo and related measures.[1] The effect of the trade embargo and related measures was that an on demand bond in favour of an Iraqi party could not legally have been honoured after 6 August 1990. In those circumstances, it is difficult to see what benefit the issuing bank was providing in return for any service charges that it was paid once notice of the embargo had been widely disseminated. If the bank is providing no benefit, it is difficult to ascertain a juridical basis for any entitlement to receive the service charges.

93. In sum, and in the context of Iraq's invasion and occupation of Kuwait and the time which has passed since then, it seems to this Panel that it is highly unlikely that on demand bond obligations of the sort this Panel has seen in the instalments it has addressed are alive and effective.

94. If that analysis is correct, then it seems to this Panel that claims for service charges on these bonds will only be sustainable in very unusual circumstances. Equally, claims for the principal will only be sustainable where the principal has in fact been irrevocably paid out and where the beneficiary of the bond had no factual basis to make a call upon the bond.

6. Export credit guarantees

95. Arrangements with government sponsored bodies that provide what might be called "fall-back" insurance are in a different case to guarantees generally. These forms of financial recourse have names such as "credit risk guarantees". They are in effect a form of insurance, often underwritten by the government of the territory in which the contractor is based. They exist as part of the economic policy of the government in question, in order to encourage trade and commerce by its nationals abroad.

96. Such guarantees often have a requirement that the contractor must exhaust all local remedies before calling on the guarantee; or must exhaust all possible remedies before making a call.

97. Claims have been made by parties for:

(a) Reimbursement of the premia paid to obtain such guarantees; and also for

(b) Shortfalls between the amounts recovered under such guarantees and the losses said to have been incurred.

In the view of this Panel, one of these types of claim is misconceived; and the other is mis-characterised.

98. A claim for the premia is misconceived. A premium paid for any form of insurance is not recoverable unless the policy is avoided. Once the policy is in place, either the event that the policy is intended to embrace occurs, or it does not. If it does, then there is a claim under the policy. If it does not then there is no such claim. In neither case does it seem to the Panel that the arrangements—prudent and sensible as they are—give rise to a claim for compensation for the premia. There is no "loss" properly so called or any causative link with Iraq's invasion and occupation of Kuwait.

99. Further, where a contractor has in fact been indemnified in whole or in part by such a body in respect of losses incurred as a result of Iraq's invasion and occupation of

---

[1] The expression the "trade embargo and related measures" refers to the prohibitions in Security Council resolution 661 (1990) and relevant subsequent resolutions and the measures taken by the States pursuant thereto.

Kuwait, there is, to that extent, no longer any loss for which that contractor can claim to the Commission. Its loss has been made whole.

100. The second situation is that where a contractor claims for the balance between what are said to be losses incurred as a result of Iraq's invasion and occupation of Kuwait and what has been recovered from the guarantor.

101. Here the claim is mis-characterised. That balance may indeed be a claimable loss; but its claimability has nothing to do with the fact that the monies represent a shortfall between what has been recovered under the guarantee and what has been lost. Instead, the correct analysis should start from a review of the cause of the whole of the loss of which the balance is all that remains. The first step is to establish whether there is evidence to support that whole sum, that it is indeed a sum that the claimant has paid out or failed to recover; and that there is the necessary causation. To the extent that the sum is established, then to that extent the claim is *prima facie* compensable. However, so far as there has been reimbursement by the guarantor, the loss has been made good, and there is nothing left to claim for. It is only if there is still some qualifying loss, not made good, that there is room for a recommendation of this Panel.

102. Finally, there are the claims by the bodies granting the credit guarantees who have paid out sums of money. They entered into an insurance arrangement with the contractor. In consideration of that arrangement, they required the payment of premia. As before, either the event covered by the insurance occurred or it did not. In the former case, the Panel would have thought that the guarantor was contractually obliged to pay out; and in the latter case, not so. Whether any payments made in these circumstances give rise to a compensable claim is not a matter for this Panel. Such claims come within the population of claims allocated to the "E/F" Panel.

7. Frustration and force majeure clauses

A59–029   103. Construction contracts, both in common law and under the civil law, frequently contain provisions to deal with events that have wholly changed the nature of the venture. Particular events which are addressed by such clauses include war, civil strife and insurrection. Given the length of time that a major construction project takes to come to fruition and the sometimes volatile circumstances, both political and otherwise, in which such contracts are carried out, this is hardly surprising. Indeed, it makes good sense. The clauses make provision as to how the financial consequences of the event are to be borne; and what the result is to be so far as the physical project is concerned.

104. Such clauses give rise to two questions when it comes to the population of claims before this Panel. The first question is whether Iraq is entitled to invoke such clauses to reduce its liability. The second is whether claimants may utilise such clauses to support or enhance their recovery from the Commission.

105. As to the first question, the position seems to this Panel to be as follows. In the population of claims before the Commission, the frustrating or *force majeure* event will nearly always be the act or omission of Iraq itself. However, such a clause is designed to address events which, if they occurred at all, were anticipated to be wholly outside the control of both parties. It would be quite inappropriate for the causal wrongdoer to rely on such clause to reduce the consequences of its own wrongdoing.

106. But the second question then arises as to whether claimants can rely upon such clauses. An example of such reliance would be where the clause provides for the acceleration of payments which otherwise would not have fallen due. As to this question, one example of this sort of claim has been addressed and the answer categorically spelt out in the first report of the "E2" Panel as follows:

"Second, [the Claimants] direct the Commission's attention to the clauses relating to "frustration" in the respective underlying contracts. The Claimants assert that in the case of frustration of contract, these clauses accelerate the payments due under the contract, in effect giving rise to a new obligation on the part of Iraq to pay all the amounts due and owing under the contract regardless of when the underlying work was performed. The Panel has concluded that claimants may not invoke such contractual agreements or clauses before the Commission to avoid the 'arising prior to' exclusion established by the Security Council in resolution 687 (1991); consequently, this argument must fail." (S/AC.26/1998/7, paragraph 188).

107. The situation described above was one where the work that was the subject of the claim had been performed prior to Iraq's invasion and occupation of Kuwait, and, therefore, fell clearly foul of the "arising prior to" rule. However, the claimants, who had agreed on arrangements for delayed payment, sought to rely on the frustration clause to get over this problem. The argument was, as this Panel understands it, that the frustration clause was triggered by the events which had in fact occurred, namely Iraq's invasion and occupation of Kuwait. The frustration clause provided for the accelerated payment of sums due under the contract. Payment of the sums had originally been deferred to dates which were still in the future at the time of the invasion and occupation; but the frustrating event meant that they became due during the time of, or indeed at the beginning of, Iraq's invasion and occupation of Kuwait. Accordingly, the payments had, in the event, become due within the period covered by the jurisdiction established by Security Council resolution 687 (1991). Therefore, a claim for the reimbursement of these payments could be entertained by the "E2" Panel.

108. It was this claim that the "E2" Panel rejected. This Panel agrees.

109. There remains the situation where the frustration clause is being used by claimants to enhance a claim, other than by way of circumventing the "arising prior to" rule, for example, where the acceleration delivered by the frustration clause is put forward to seek to bring into the period within the jurisdiction of the Commission payments which would otherwise have been received, under the contract, well after the liberation of Kuwait, and therefore would not otherwise be compensable.

110. In the view of this Panel, such claims would similarly fail. In this case, as in the case addressed by the "E2" Panel, claimants are seeking to use the provisions of private contracts to enhance the jurisdiction granted by Security Council resolution 687 (1991) and defined by jurisprudence developed by the Commission. That is not an appropriate course. It is not open to individual entities by agreement or otherwise, to modify the jurisdiction of the Commission.

J. Claims for overhead and "lost profits"

1. General

111. Any construction project can be broken down into a number of components. All of these components contribute to the pricing of the works. In this Panel's view, it is helpful for the examination of these kinds of claims to begin by rehearsing in general terms the way in which many contractors in different parts of the world construct the prices that ultimately appear in the construction contracts they sign. Of course, there is no absolute rule as to this process. Indeed, it is unlikely that any two contractors will assemble their bids in exactly the same way. But the constraints of construction work and the realities of the financial world impose a general outline from which there will rarely be a substantial deviation.

112. Many of the construction contracts encountered in the claims submitted to this Panel contain a schedule of rates or a "bill of quantities". This document defines the amount to be paid to the contractor for the work performed. It is based on previously agreed rates or prices. The final contract price is the aggregate value of the work calculated at the quoted rates together with any variations and other contractual entitlements and deductions which increase or decrease the amount originally agreed.

113. Other contracts in the claims submitted to this Panel are lump sum contracts. Here the schedule of rates or bill of quantities has a narrower role. It is limited to such matters as the calculation of the sums to be paid in interim certificates and the valuation of variations.

114. In preparing the schedule of rates, the contractor will plan to recover all of the direct and indirect costs of the project. On top of this will be an allowance for the "risk margin". In so far as there is an allowance for profit it will be part of the "risk margin". However, whether or not a profit is made and, if made, in what amount, depends obviously on the incidence of risk actually incurred.

115. An examination of actual contracts combined with its own experience of these matters has provided this Panel with guidelines as to the typical breakdown of prices that may be anticipated on construction projects of the kind relevant to the claims submitted to this Panel.

A59–032

116. The key starting point is the base cost—the cost of labour, materials and plant—in French the "*prix secs*". In another phrase, this is the direct cost. The direct cost may vary, but usually represents 65 to 75 per cent of the total contract price.

117. To this is added the indirect cost—for example the supply of design services for such matters as working drawings and temporary works by the contractor's head office. Typically, this indirect cost represents about 25 to 30 per cent of the total contract price.

118. Finally, there is what is called the "risk margin"—the allowance for the unexpected. The risk margin is generally in the range of between barely above zero and five per cent of the total contract price. The more smoothly the project goes, the less the margin will have to be expended. The result will be enhanced profits, properly so called, recovered by the contractor at the end of the day. The more the unexpected happens and the more the risk margin has to be expended, the smaller the profit will ultimately be. Indeed, the cost of dealing with the unexpected or the unplanned may equal or exceed the risk margin, leading to a nil result or a loss.

119. In the view of the Panel, it is against this background that some of the claims for contract losses need to be seen.

2. Head office and branch office expenses

A59–033

120. These are generally regarded as part of the overhead. These costs can be dealt with in the price in a variety of ways. For example, they may be built into some or all of the prices against line items; they may be provided for in a lump sum; they may be dealt with in many other ways. One aspect, however, will be common to most, if not all, contracts. It will be the intention of the contractor to recover these costs through the price at some stage of the execution of the contract. Often the recovery has been spread through elements of the price, so as to result in repayment through a number of interim payments during the course of the contract. Where this has been done, it may be said that these costs have been amortised. This factor is relevant to the question of double-counting (see paragraph 123, *infra*).

121. If therefore any part of the price of the works has been paid, it is likely that some part of these expenses has been recovered. Indeed, if these costs have been built into items which are paid early, a substantial part or even all of these costs may have been recovered.

122. If these items were the subject of an advance payment, again they may have been recovered in their entirety at an early stage of the project. Here of course there is an additional complication, since the advance payments will be credited back to the employer—see paragraph 66, *supra*—during the course of the work. In this event, the Panel is thrown back onto the question of where in the contractor's prices payment for these items was intended to be.

123. In all of these situations, it is necessary to avoid double-counting. By this the Panel means the situation where the contractor is specifically claiming, as a separate item, elements of overhead which, in whole or in part, are already covered by the payments made or claims raised for work done.

124. The same applies where there are physical losses at a branch or indeed a site office or camp. These losses are properly characterised, and therefore claimable, if claimable at all, as losses of tangible assets.

3. Loss of profits on a particular project

125. Governing Council decision 9, paragraph 9, provides that where "continuation of the contract became impossible for the other party as a result of Iraq's invasion and occupation of Kuwait, Iraq is liable for any direct loss the other party suffered as a result, including lost profits".   **A59–034**

126. As will be seen from the observations at paragraphs 111 to 119, *supra*, the expression "lost profits" is an encapsulation of quite a complicated concept. In particular, it will be appreciated that achieving profits or suffering a loss is a function of the risk margin and the actual event.

127. The qualification of "margin" by "risk" is an important one in the context of construction contracts. These contracts run for a considerable period of time; they often take place in remote areas or in countries where the environment is hostile in one way or another; and of course they are subject to political problems in a variety of places—where the work is done, where materials, equipment or labour have to be procured, and along supply routes. The surrounding circumstances are thus very different and generally more risk prone than is the case in the context of, say, a contract for the sale of goods.

128. In the view of this Panel it is important to have these considerations in mind when reviewing a claim for lost profits on a major construction project. In effect one must review the particular project for what might be called its "loss possibility". The contractor will have assumed risks. He will have provided a margin to cover these risks. He will have to demonstrate a substantial likelihood that the risks would not occur or would be overcome within the risk element so as to leave a margin for actual profit.

129. This approach, in the view of this Panel, is inherent in the thinking behind paragraph 5 of Governing Council decision 15. This paragraph expressly states that a claimant seeking compensation for business losses such as loss of profits, must provide "detailed factual descriptions of the circumstances of the claimed loss, damage or injury" in order for compensation to be awarded.

130. In the light of the above analysis, and in conformity with the two Governing Council decisions cited above, this Panel requires the following from those construction and engineering claimants that seek to recover for lost profits. First, the phrase "continuation of the contract" imposes a requirement on the claimant to prove that it had an   **A59–035**

existing contractual relationship at the time of the invasion. Second, the provision requires the claimant to prove that the continuation of the relationship was rendered impossible by Iraq's invasion and occupation of Kuwait. This provision indicates a further requirement that profits should be measured over the life of the contract. It is not sufficient to prove that there would have been a "profit" at some stage before the completion of the project. Such a proof would only amount to a demonstration of a temporary credit balance. This can even be achieved in the early stages of a contract, for example where the pricing has been "front-loaded" for the express purpose of financing the project.

131. Instead, the claimant must lodge sufficient and appropriate evidence to show that the contract would have been profitable as a whole. Such evidence would include projected and actual financial information relating to the relevant project, such as audited financial statements, budgets, management accounts, turnover, original bids and tender sum analyses, time schedules drawn up at the commencement of the works, profit/loss statements, finance costs and head office costs prepared by or on behalf of the claimant for each accounting period from the first year of the relevant project to March 1993. The claimant should also provide: original calculations of profit relating to the project and all revisions to these calculations made during the course of the project; management reports on actual financial performance as compared to budgets that were prepared during the course of the project; evidence demonstrating that the project proceeded as planned, such as monthly/periodic reports, planned/actual time schedules, interim certificates or account invoices, details of work that was completed but not invoiced by the claimant, details of payments made by the employer and evidence of retention amounts that were recovered by the claimant. In addition, the claimant should provide evidence of the percentage of the works completed at the time work on the project ceased.

4. Loss of profits for future projects

A59–036   132. Some claimants say they would have earned profits on future projects, not let at the time of Iraq's invasion and occupation of Kuwait. Such claims are of course subject to the sorts of considerations set out by this Panel in its review of claims for lost profits on individual projects. In addition, it is necessary for such a claimant to overcome the problem of remoteness. How can a claimant be certain that it would have won the opportunity to carry out the projects in question? If there was to be competitive tendering, the problem is all the harder. If there was not to be competitive tendering, what is the basis of the assertion that the contract would have come to the claimant?

133. Accordingly, in the view of this Panel, for such a claim to warrant a recommendation, it is necessary to demonstrate by sufficient documentary and other appropriate evidence a history of successful (*i.e.*, profitable) operation, and a state of affairs which warrants the conclusion that the hypothesis that there would have been future profitable contracts is well founded. Among other matters, it will be necessary to establish a picture of the assets that were being employed so that the extent to which those assets would continue to be productive in the future can be determined. Balance sheets for previous years will have to be produced, along with relevant strategy statements or like documents which were in fact utilised in the past. The current strategy statement will also have to be provided. In all cases, this Panel will be looking for contemporaneous documents rather than ones that have been formulated for the purpose of the claim; although the latter may have a useful explanatory or demonstrational role.

134. Such evidence is often difficult to obtain; and accordingly in construction cases such claims will only rarely be successful. And even where there is such evidence, the

K. Loss of monies left in Iraq

1. Funds in bank accounts in Iraq

135. Numerous claimants seek to recover compensation for funds on deposit in Iraqi banks. Such funds were of course in Iraqi dinars and were subject to exchange controls.

136. The first problem with these claims is that it is often not clear that there will be no opportunity in the future for the claimant to have access to and to use such funds. Indeed, many claimants, in their responses to interrogatories or otherwise have modified their original claims to remove such elements, as a result of obtaining access to such funds after the initial filing of their claim with the Commission.

137. Second, for such a claim to succeed it would be necessary to establish that in the particular case, Iraq would have permitted the exchange of such funds into hard currency for the purposes of export. For this, appropriate evidence of an obligation to this effect on the part of Iraq is required. Furthermore, this Panel notes that the decision to deposit funds in banks located in particular countries is a commercial decision, which a corporation engaged in international operations is required to make. In making this decision, a corporation would normally take into account the relevant country or regional risks involved.

138. This Panel, in analysing the claims presented to it to date concludes that, in most cases, it will be necessary for a claimant to demonstrate (in addition to such matters as loss and quantum) that:

(a) The relevant Iraqi entity was under a contractual or other specific duty to exchange those funds for convertible currencies;

(b) Iraq would have permitted the transfer of the converted funds out of Iraq; and

(c) This exchange and transfer was prevented by Iraq's invasion and occupation of Kuwait.

139. Absent proof of these aspects of the matter, it is difficult to see how the claimant can be said to have suffered any "loss". If there is no loss, this Panel is unable to recommend compensation.

2. Petty cash

140. Exactly the same considerations apply to claims for petty cash left in Iraq in Iraqi dinars. These monies were left in the offices of claimants when they departed from Iraq. The circumstances in which the money was left behind vary somewhat; and the situation which thereafter obtained also varies—some claimants contending that they returned to Iraq but the monies were gone; and others being unable to return to Iraq and establish the position. In these different cases, the principle seems to this Panel to be the same. Claimants in Iraq needed to have available sums (which could be substantial) to meet liabilities which had to be discharged in cash. These sums necessarily consisted of Iraqi dinars. Accordingly, absent evidence of the same matters as are set out in paragraph 138,

supra, it will be difficult to establish a "loss", and in those circumstances, this Panel is unable to recommend compensation.

3. Customs deposits

A59–039   141. In this Panel's understanding, these sums are paid, nominally at least, as a fee for permission to effect a temporary importation of plant, vehicles or equipment. The recovery of these deposits is dependent on obtaining permission to export the relevant plant, vehicles and equipment.

142. The Panel further understands that such permission was hard to obtain in Iraq prior to Iraq's invasion and occupation of Kuwait. Accordingly, although defined as a temporary exaction, it was often permanent in fact, and no doubt contractors experienced in the subtleties of working in Iraq made suitable allowances. And no doubt they were able to, or expected to, recover these exactions through payment for work done. Once the invasion and occupation of Kuwait had occurred, obtaining such permission to export became appreciably harder. Indeed, given the trade embargo, a necessary element would have been the specific approval of the Security Council.

143. In the light of the foregoing, it seems to the Panel that claims to recover these duties need to be supported by sufficient evidentiary material, going to the issue of whether, but for Iraq's invasion and occupation of Kuwait, such permission would, in fact or on a balance of probabilities, have been forthcoming.

144. Absent such evidence and leaving aside any question of double-counting (see paragraph 123, *supra*), the Panel is unlikely to be able to make any positive recommendations for compensating unrecovered customs deposits made for plant, vehicles and equipment used at construction projects in Iraq.

L. Tangible property

A59–040   145. With reference to losses of tangible property located in Iraq, decision 9 provides that where direct losses were suffered as a result of Iraq's invasion and occupation of Kuwait with respect to tangible assets, Iraq is liable for compensation (decision 9, paragraph 12). Typical actions of this kind would have been the expropriation, removal, theft or destruction of particular items of property by Iraqi authorities. Whether the taking of property was lawful or not is not relevant for Iraq's liability if it did not provide for compensation. Decision 9 furthermore provides that in a case where business property had been lost because it had been left unguarded by company personnel departing due to the situation in Iraq and Kuwait, such loss may be considered as resulting directly from Iraq's invasion and occupation (decision 9, paragraph 13).

146. Many of the construction and engineering claims that come before this Panel are for assets that were confiscated by the Iraqi authorities in 1992 or 1993. Here the problem is one of causation. By the time of the event, Iraq's invasion and occupation of Kuwait was over. Liberation was a year or more earlier. Numerous claimants had managed to obtain access to their sites to establish the position that obtained at that stage. In the cases the subject of this paragraph, the assets still existed. However, that initially satisfactory position was then overtaken by a general confiscation of assets by Iraqi authorities. While it sometimes seems to have been the case that this confiscation was triggered by an event which could be directly related to Iraq's invasion and occupation of Kuwait, in the vast majority of the claims that this Panel has seen, this was not the case. It was simply the result of a decision on the part of the authorities to take over these assets.

This Panel has difficulty in seeing how these losses were caused by Iraq's invasion and occupation of Kuwait. On the contrary, it appears that they stem from an wholly independent event and accordingly are outside the jurisdiction of the Commission.

M. Payment or relief to others

147. Paragraph 21(b) of decision 7 specifically provides that losses suffered as a result of "the departure of persons from or their inability to leave Iraq or Kuwait" are to be considered the direct result of Iraq's invasion and occupation of Kuwait. Consistent with decision 7, therefore, the Panel finds that evacuation and relief costs incurred in assisting employees in departing from Iraq are compensable to the extent proven.

148. Paragraph 22 of Governing Council decision 7 provides that "payments are available to reimburse payments made or relief provided by corporations or other entities to others—for example, to employees, or to others pursuant to contractual obligations—for losses covered by any of the criteria adopted by the Council".

149. In the Fourth Report, this Panel found that the costs associated with evacuating and repatriating employees between 2 August 1990 and 2 March 1991 are compensable to the extent that such costs are proven by the claimant and are reasonable in the circumstances. Urgent temporary liabilities and extraordinary expenses relating to evacuation and repatriation, including transportation, food and accommodation, are in principle, compensable.

150. Many claimants do not provide a documentary trail detailing to perfection the expenses incurred in caring for their personnel and transporting them (and, in some instances, the employees of other companies who were stranded) out of a theatre of hostilities.

151. In these cases this Panel considers it appropriate to accept a level of documentation consistent with the practical realities of a difficult, uncertain and often hurried situation, taking into account the concerns necessarily involved. The loss sustained by claimants in these situations is the very essence of the direct loss suffered which is stipulated by Security Council resolution 687 (1991). Accordingly, the Panel uses its best judgement, after considering all relevant reports and the material at its disposal, to arrive at an appropriate recommendation for compensation.

N. Final awards, judgments and settlements

152. In the case of some of the projects in which claimants are seeking compensation from the Commission, there have been proceedings between the parties to the project contract leading to an award or a judgment; or there has been a settlement between the claimant and another party to the relevant contract. In all such cases, one is concerned with finality. The award, judgment or settlement must be final—not subject to appeal or revision.

153. The claim that is then raised with the Commission is either for sums said not to have been included in the award or judgment or for sums said not to have been included in the settlement.

154. It follows that it will be a prerequisite to establish that that is in fact the case, namely that, for some reason, the claim resulting in the award, judgment or settlement did not raise or resolve the subject matter of the claim being put before the Commission. Sufficient evidence of this will be needed. The absence of an identifiable element in the award, judgment or settlement relating to the claim before the Commission does not necessarily mean that that it has not been addressed. The Tribunal that issued the award or judgment or the parties that concluded the settlement may have reached a single sum to cover a number of claims, including the claim in question; or the Tribunal may have considered that the claim was not maintainable. Equally, the claim may have been abandoned in, and as part of, the settlement. In such an event it would appear that the claim has been resolved and there is no loss left to be compensated. At that stage, it will be necessary to review the file to see if there is any special circumstance or material that would displace this initial conclusion. Absent such circumstance or material, no loss has been established. Sufficient evidence of an existing loss is essential if this Panel is to recommend compensation.

155. If, on the other hand, it is clear that the particular claim has not been adjudicated or settled, then it may be entertained by the Commission.

Convention on the settlement of investment disputes between States and Nationals of other States

Preamble

The Contracting States

Considering the need for international cooperation for economic development, and the role of private international investment therein;

A60–001

Bearing in mind the possibility that from time to time disputes may arise in connection with such investment between Contracting States and nationals of other Contracting States;

Recognizing that while such disputes would usually be subject to national legal processes, international methods of settlement may be appropriate in certain cases;

Attaching particular importance to the availability of facilities for international conciliation or arbitration to which Contracting States and nationals of other Contracting States may submit such disputes if they so desire;

Desiring to establish such facilities under the auspices of the International Bank for Reconstruction and Development;

Recognizing that mutual consent by the parties to submit such disputes to conciliation or to arbitration through such facilities constitutes a binding agreement which requires in particular that due consideration be given to any recommendation of conciliators, and that any arbitral award be complied with; and

Declaring that no Contracting State shall by the mere fact of its ratification, acceptance or approval of this Convention and without its consent be deemed to be under any obligation to submit any particular dispute to conciliation or arbitration,

Have agreed as follows:

Chapter I

International Centre for Settlement of Investment Disputes

Section 1

Establishment and Organization

Article 1

(1) There is hereby established the International Centre for Settlement of Investment Disputes (hereinafter called the Centre).

A60–002

(2) The purpose of the Centre shall be to provide facilities for conciliation and arbitration of investment disputes between Contracting States and nationals of other Contracting States in accordance with the provisions of this Convention.

Article 2

A60–003   The seat of the Centre shall be at the principal office of the International Bank for Reconstruction and Development (hereinafter called the Bank). The seat may be moved to another place by decision of the Administrative Council adopted by a majority of two-thirds of its members.

Article 3

A60–004   The Centre shall have an Administrative Council and a Secretariat and shall maintain a Panel of Conciliators and a Panel of Arbitrators.

Section 2

The Administrative Council

Article 4

A60–005   (1) The Administrative Council shall be composed of one representative of each Contracting State. An alternate may act as representative in case of his principal's absence from a meeting or inability to act.

(2) In the absence of a contrary designation, each governor and alternate governor of the Bank appointed by a Contracting State shall be *ex officio* its representative and its alternate respectively.

Article 5

A60–006   The President of the Bank shall be *ex officio* Chairman of the Administrative Council (hereinafter called the Chairman) but shall have no vote. During his absence or inability to act and during any vacancy in the office of President of the Bank, the person for the time being acting as President shall act as Chairman of the Administrative Council.

Article 6

A60–007   (1) Without prejudice to the powers and functions vested in it by other provisions of this Convention, the Administrative Council shall:

   (a) adopt the administrative and financial regulations of the Centre;

   (b) adopt the rules of procedure for the institution of conciliation and arbitration proceedings;

   (c) adopt the rules of procedure for conciliation and arbitration proceedings (hereinafter called the Conciliation Rules and the Arbitration Rules);

   (d) approve arrangements with the Bank for the use of the Bank's administrative facilities and services;

   (e) determine the conditions of service of the Secretary-General and of any Deputy Secretary-General;

(f) adopt the annual budget of revenues and expenditures of the Centre;

(g) approve the annual report on the operation of the Centre.

The decisions referred to in sub-paragraphs (a), (b), (c) and (f) above shall be adopted by a majority of two-thirds of the members of the Administrative Council.

(2) The Administrative Council may appoint such committees as it considers necessary.

(3) The Administrative Council shall also exercise such other powers and perform such other functions as it shall determine to be necessary for the implementation of the provisions of this Convention.

Article 7

(1) The Administrative Council shall hold an annual meeting and such other meetings as may be determined by the Council, or convened by the Chairman, or convened by the Secretary-General at the request of not less than five members of the Council. **A60–008**

(2) Each member of the Administrative Council shall have one vote and, except as otherwise herein provided, all matters before the Council shall be decided by a majority of the votes cast.

(3) A quorum for any meeting of the Administrative Council shall be a majority of its members.

(4) The Administrative Council may establish, by a majority of two-thirds of its members, a procedure whereby the Chairman may seek a vote of the Council without convening a meeting of the Council. The vote shall be considered valid only if the majority of the members of the Council cast their votes within the time limit fixed by the said procedure.

Article 8

Members of the Administrative Council and the Chairman shall serve without remuneration from the Centre. **A60–009**

Section 3

The Secretariat

Article 9

The Secretariat shall consist of a Secretary-General, one or more Deputy Secretaries-General and staff. **A60–010**

Article 10

(1) The Secretary-General and any Deputy Secretary-General shall be elected by the Administrative Council by a majority of two-thirds of its members upon the nomination of the Chairman for a term of service not exceeding six years and shall be eligible for re-election. After consulting the members of the Administrative Council, the Chairman shall propose one or more candidates for each such office. **A60–011**

(2) The offices of Secretary-General and Deputy Secretary-General shall be incom-

patible with the exercise of any political function. Neither the Secretary-General nor any Deputy Secretary-General may hold any other employment or engage in any other occupation except with the approval of the Administrative Council.

(3) During the Secretary-General's absence or inability to act, and during any vacancy of the office of Secretary-General, the Deputy Secretary-General shall act as Secretary-General. If there shall be more than one Deputy Secretary-General, the Administrative Council shall determine in advance the order in which they shall act as Secretary-General.

Article 11

A60–012   The Secretary-General shall be the legal representative and the principal officer of the Centre and shall be responsible for its administration, including the appointment of staff, in accordance with the provisions of this Convention and the rules adopted by the Administrative Council. He shall perform the function of registrar and shall have the power to authenticate arbitral awards rendered pursuant to this Convention, and to certify copies thereof.

Section 4

The Panels

Article 12

A60–013   The Panel of Conciliators and the Panel of Arbitrators shall each consist of qualified persons, designated as hereinafter provided, who are willing to serve thereon.

Article 13

A60–014   (1) Each Contracting State may designate to each Panel four persons who may but need not be its nationals.

(2) The Chairman may designate ten persons to each Panel. The persons so designated to a Panel shall each have a different nationality.

Article 14

A60–015   (1) Persons designated to serve on the Panels shall be persons of high moral character and recognized competence in the fields of law, commerce, industry or finance, who may be relied upon to exercise independent judgment. Competence in the field of law shall be of particular importance in the case of persons on the Panel of Arbitrators.

(2) The Chairman, in designating persons to serve on the Panels, shall in addition pay due regard to the importance of assuring representation on the Panels of the principal legal systems of the world and of the main forms of economic activity.

Article 15

A60–016   (1) Panel members shall serve for renewable periods of six years.

(2) In case of death or resignation of a member of a Panel, the authority which designated the member shall have the right to designate another person to serve for the remainder of that member's term.

(3) Panel members shall continue in office until their successors have been designated.

Article 16

(1) A person may serve on both Panels. A60–017

(2) If a person shall have been designated to serve on the same Panel by more than one Contracting State, or by one or more Contracting States and the Chairman, he shall be deemed to have been designated by the authority which first designated him or, if one such authority is the State of which he is a national, by that State.

(3) All designations shall be notified to the Secretary-General and shall take effect from the date on which the notification is received.

Section 5

Financing the Centre

Article 17

If the expenditure of the Centre cannot be met out of charges for the use of its facilities, A60–018 or out of other receipts, the excess shall be borne by Contracting States which are members of the Bank in proportion to their respective subscriptions to the capital stock of the Bank, and by Contracting States which are not members of the Bank in accordance with rules adopted by the Administrative Council.

Section 6

Status, Immunities and Privileges

Article 18

The Centre shall have full international legal personality. The legal capacity of the A60–019 Centre shall include the capacity:

(a) to contract;

(b) to acquire and dispose of movable and immovable property;

(c) to institute legal proceedings.

Article 19

To enable the Centre to fulfil its functions, it shall enjoy in the territories of each A60–020 Contracting State the immunities and privileges set forth in this Section.

Article 20

The Centre, its property and assets shall enjoy immunity from all legal process, except A60–021 when the Centre waives this immunity.

Article 21

A60–022   The Chairman, the members of the Administrative Council, persons acting as conciliators or arbitrators or members of a Committee appointed pursuant to paragraph (3) of Article 52, and the officers and employees of the Secretariat:

> (a) shall enjoy immunity from legal process with respect to acts performed by them in the exercise of their functions, except when the Centre waives this immunity;
>
> (b) not being local nationals, shall enjoy the same immunities from immigration restrictions, alien registration requirements and national service obligations, the same facilities as regards exchange restrictions and the same treatment in respect of travelling facilities as are accorded by Contracting States to the representatives, officials and employees of comparable rank of other Contracting States.

Article 22

A60–023   The provisions of Article 21 shall apply to persons appearing in proceedings under this Convention as parties, agents, counsel, advocates, witnesses or experts; provided, however, that sub-paragraph (b) thereof shall apply only in connection with their travel to and from, and their stay at, the place where the proceedings are held.

Article 23

A60–024   (1) The archives of the Centre shall be inviolable, wherever they may be.

(2) With regard to its official communications, the Centre shall be accorded by each Contracting State treatment not less favourable than that accorded to other international organizations.

Article 24

A60–025   (1) The Centre, its assets, property and income, and its operations and transactions authorized by this Convention shall be exempt from all taxation and customs duties. The Centre shall also be exempt from liability for the collection or payment of any taxes or customs duties.

(2) Except in the case of local nationals, no tax shall be levied on or in respect of expense allowances paid by the Centre to the Chairman or members of the Administrative Council, or on or in respect of salaries, expense allowances or other emoluments paid by the Centre to officials or employees of the Secretariat.

(3) No tax shall be levied on or in respect of fees or expense allowances received by persons acting as conciliators, or arbitrators, or members of a Committee appointed pursuant to paragraph (3) of Article 52, in proceedings under this Convention, if the sole jurisdictional basis for such tax is the location of the Centre or the place where such proceedings are conducted or the place where such fees or allowances are paid.

CHAPTER II

JURISDICTION OF THE CENTRE

Article 25

A60–026   (1) The jurisdiction of the Centre shall extend to any legal dispute arising directly out of an investment, between a Contracting State (or any constituent subdivision or agency of a Contracting State designated to the Centre by that State) and a national of another Contracting State, which the parties to the dispute consent in writing to submit to the Centre. When the parties have given their consent, no party may withdraw its consent unilaterally.

(2) "National of another Contracting State" means:

(a) any natural person who had the nationality of a Contracting State other than the State party to the dispute on the date on which the parties consented to submit such dispute to conciliation or arbitration as well as on the date on which the request was registered pursuant to paragraph (3) of Article 28 or paragraph (3) of Article 36, but does not include any person who on either date also had the nationality of the Contracting State party to the dispute; and

(b) any juridical person which had the nationality of a Contracting State other than the State party to the dispute on the date on which the parties consented to submit such dispute to conciliation or arbitration and any juridical person which had the nationality of the Contracting State party to the dispute on that date and which, because of foreign control, the parties have agreed should be treated as a national of another Contracting State for the purposes of this Convention.

(3) Consent by a constituent subdivision or agency of a Contracting State shall require the approval of that State unless that State notifies the Centre that no such approval is required.

(4) Any Contracting State may, at the time of ratification, acceptance or approval of this Convention or at any time thereafter, notify the Centre of the class or classes of disputes which it would or would not consider submitting to the jurisdiction of the Centre. The Secretary-General shall forthwith transmit such notification to all Contracting States. Such notification shall not constitute the consent required by paragraph (1).

Article 26

Consent of the parties to arbitration under this Convention shall, unless otherwise stated, be deemed consent to such arbitration to the exclusion of any other remedy. A Contracting State may require the exhaustion of local administrative or judicial remedies as a condition of its consent to arbitration under this Convention.

Article 27

(1) No Contracting State shall give diplomatic protection, or bring an international claim, in respect of a dispute which one of its nationals and another Contracting State shall have consented to submit or shall have submitted to arbitration under this Convention, unless such other Contracting State shall have failed to abide by and comply with the award rendered in such dispute.

(2) Diplomatic protection, for the purposes of paragraph (1), shall not include informal diplomatic exchanges for the sole purpose of facilitating a settlement of the dispute.

Chapter III

Conciliation

Section 1

Request for Conciliation

Article 28

A60–029 (1) Any Contracting State or any national of a Contracting State wishing to institute conciliation proceedings shall address a request to that effect in writing to the Secretary-General who shall send a copy of the request to the other party.

(2) The request shall contain information concerning the issues in dispute, the identity of the parties and their consent to conciliation in accordance with the rules of procedure for the institution of conciliation and arbitration proceedings.

(3) The Secretary-General shall register the request unless he finds, on the basis of the information contained in the request, that the dispute is manifestly outside the jurisdiction of the Centre. He shall forthwith notify the parties of registration or refusal to register.

Section 2

Constitution of the Conciliation Commission

Article 29

A60–030 (1) The Conciliation Commission (hereinafter called the Commission) shall be constituted as soon as possible after registration of a request pursuant to Article 28.

(2) (a) The Commission shall consist of a sole conciliator or any uneven number of conciliators appointed as the parties shall agree.

(b) Where the parties do not agree upon the number of conciliators and the method of their appointment, the Commission shall consist of three conciliators, one conciliator appointed by each party and the third, who shall be the president of the Commission, appointed by agreement of the parties.

Article 30

A60–031 If the Commission shall not have been constituted within 90 days after notice of registration of the request has been dispatched by the Secretary-General in accordance with paragraph (3) of Article 28, or such other period as the parties may agree, the Chairman shall, at the request of either party and after consulting both parties as far as possible, appoint the conciliator or conciliators not yet appointed.

Article 31

A60–032 (1) Conciliators may be appointed from outside the Panel of Conciliators, except in the case of appointments by the Chairman pursuant to Article 30.

(2) Conciliators appointed from outside the Panel of Conciliators shall possess the qualities stated in paragraph (1) of Article 14.

Section 3

Conciliation Proceedings

Article 32

(1) The Commission shall be the judge of its own competence. A60–033
(2) Any objection by a party to the dispute that that dispute is not within the jurisdiction of the Centre, or for other reasons is not within the competence of the Commission, shall be considered by the Commission which shall determine whether to deal with it as a preliminary question or to join it to the merits of the dispute.

Article 33

Any conciliation proceeding shall be conducted in accordance with the provisions of this Section and, except as the parties otherwise agree, in accordance with the Conciliation Rules in effect on the date on which the parties consented to conciliation. If any question of procedure arises which is not covered by this Section or the Conciliation Rules or any rules agreed by the parties, the Commission shall decide the question. A60–034

Article 34

(1) It shall be the duty of the Commission to clarify the issues in dispute between the parties and to endeavour to bring about agreement between them upon mutually acceptable terms. To that end, the Commission may at any stage of the proceedings and from time to time recommend terms of settlement to the parties. The parties shall cooperate in good faith with the Commission in order to enable the Commission to carry out its functions, and shall give their most serious consideration to its recommendations. A60–035
(2) If the parties reach agreement, the Commission shall draw up a report noting the issues in dispute and recording that the parties have reached agreement. If, at any stage of the proceedings, it appears to the Commission that there is no likelihood of agreement between the parties, it shall close the proceedings and shall draw up a report noting the submission of the dispute and recording the failure of the parties to reach agreement. If one party fails to appear or participate in the proceedings, the Commission shall close the proceedings and shall draw up a report noting that party's failure to appear or participate.

Article 35

Except as the parties to the dispute shall otherwise agree, neither party to a conciliation proceeding shall be entitled in any other proceeding, whether before arbitrators or in a court of law or otherwise, to invoke or rely on any views expressed or statements or admissions or offers of settlement made by the other party in the conciliation proceedings, or the report or any recommendations made by the Commission. A60–036

Chapter IV

Arbitration

Section 1

Request for Arbitration

Article 36

A60–037 (1) Any Contracting State or any national of a Contracting State wishing to institute arbitration proceedings shall address a request to that effect in writing to the Secretary-General who shall send a copy of the request to the other party.

(2) The request shall contain information concerning the issues in dispute, the identity of the parties and their consent to arbitration in accordance with the rules of procedure for the institution of conciliation and arbitration proceedings.

(3) The Secretary-General shall register the request unless he finds, on the basis of the information contained in the request, that the dispute is manifestly outside the jurisdiction of the Centre. He shall forthwith notify the parties of registration or refusal to register.

Section 2

Constitution of the Tribunal

Article 37

A60–038 (1) The Arbitral Tribunal (hereinafter called the Tribunal) shall be constituted as soon as possible after registration of a request pursuant to Article 36.

(2) (a) The Tribunal shall consist of a sole arbitrator or any uneven number of arbitrators appointed as the parties shall agree.

(b) Where the parties do not agree upon the number of arbitrators and the method of their appointment, the Tribunal shall consist of three arbitrators, one arbitrator appointed by each party and the third, who shall be the president of the Tribunal, appointed by agreement of the parties.

Article 38

A60–039 If the Tribunal shall not have been constituted within 90 days after notice of registration of the request has been dispatched by the Secretary-General in accordance with paragraph (3) of Article 36, or such other period as the parties may agree, the Chairman shall, at the request of either party and after consulting both parties as far as possible, appoint the arbitrator or arbitrators not yet appointed. Arbitrators appointed by the Chairman pursuant to this Article shall not be nationals of the Contracting State party to the dispute or of the Contracting State whose national is a party to the dispute.

Article 39

The majority of the arbitrators shall be nationals of States other than the Contracting State party to the dispute and the Contracting State whose national is a party to the dispute; provided, however, that the foregoing provisions of this Article shall not apply if the sole arbitrator or each individual member of the Tribunal has been appointed by agreement of the parties.

A60–040

Article 40

(1) Arbitrators may be appointed from outside the Panel of Arbitrators, except in the case of appointments by the Chairman pursuant to Article 38.
(2) Arbitrators appointed from outside the Panel of Arbitrators shall possess the qualities stated in paragraph (1) of Article 14.

A60–041

Section 3

Powers and Functions of the Tribunal

Article 41

(1) The Tribunal shall be the judge of its own competence.
(2) Any objection by a party to the dispute that that dispute is not within the jurisdiction of the Centre, or for other reasons is not within the competence of the Tribunal, shall be considered by the Tribunal which shall determine whether to deal with it as a preliminary question or to join it to the merits of the dispute.

A60–042

Article 42

(1) The Tribunal shall decide a dispute in accordance with such rules of law as may be agreed by the parties. In the absence of such agreement, the Tribunal shall apply the law of the Contracting State party to the dispute (including its rules on the conflict of laws) and such rules of international law as may be applicable.
(2) The Tribunal may not bring in a finding of *non liquet* on the ground of silence or obscurity of the law.
(3) The provisions of paragraphs (1) and (2) shall not prejudice the power of the Tribunal to decide a dispute *ex aequo et bono* if the parties so agree.

A60–043

Article 43

Except as the parties otherwise agree, the Tribunal may, if it deems it necessary at any stage of the proceedings,

A60–044

(a) call upon the parties to produce documents or other evidence, and
(b) visit the scene connected with the dispute, and conduct such inquiries there as it may deem appropriate.

Article 44

Any arbitration proceeding shall be conducted in accordance with the provisions of this Section and, except as the parties otherwise agree, in accordance with the Arbitration

A60–045

Rules in effect on the date on which the parties consented to arbitration. If any question of procedure arises which is not covered by this Section or the Arbitration Rules or any rules agreed by the parties, the Tribunal shall decide the question.

Article 45

A60–046 (1) Failure of a party to appear or to present his case shall not be deemed an admission of the other party's assertions.

(2) If a party fails to appear or to present his case at any stage of the proceedings the other party may request the Tribunal to deal with the questions submitted to it and to render an award. Before rendering an award, the Tribunal shall notify, and grant a period of grace to, the party failing to appear or to present its case, unless it is satisfied that that party does not intend to do so.

Article 46

A60–047 Except as the parties otherwise agree, the Tribunal shall, if requested by a party, determine any incidental or additional claims or counterclaims arising directly out of the subject-matter of the dispute provided that they are within the scope of the consent of the parties and are otherwise within the jurisdiction of the Centre.

Article 47

A60–048 Except as the parties otherwise agree, the Tribunal may, if it considers that the circumstances so require, recommend any provisional measures which should be taken to preserve the respective rights of either party.

Section 4

The Award

Article 48

A60–049 (1) The Tribunal shall decide questions by a majority of the votes of all its members.

(2) The award of the Tribunal shall be in writing and shall be signed by the members of the Tribunal who voted for it.

(3) The award shall deal with every question submitted to the Tribunal, and shall state the reasons upon which it is based.

(4) Any member of the Tribunal may attach his individual opinion to the award, whether he dissents from the majority or not, or a statement of his dissent.

(5) The Centre shall not publish the award without the consent of the parties.

Article 49

A60–050 (1) The Secretary-General shall promptly dispatch certified copies of the award to the parties. The award shall be deemed to have been rendered on the date on which the certified copies were dispatched.

(2) The Tribunal upon the request of a party made within 45 days after the date on which the award was rendered may after notice to the other party decide any question which it had omitted to decide in the award, and shall rectify any clerical, arithmetical

or similar error in the award. Its decision shall become part of the award and shall be notified to the parties in the same manner as the award. The periods of time provided for under paragraph (2) of Article 51 and paragraph (2) of Article 52 shall run from the date on which the decision was rendered.

Section 5

Interpretation, Revision and Annulment of the Award

Article 50

(1) If any dispute shall arise between the parties as to the meaning or scope of an award, either party may request interpretation of the award by an application in writing addressed to the Secretary-General.

(2) The request shall, if possible, be submitted to the Tribunal which rendered the award. If this shall not be possible, a new Tribunal shall be constituted in accordance with Section 2 of this Chapter. The Tribunal may, if it considers that the circumstances so require, stay enforcement of the award pending its decision.

Article 51

(1) Either party may request revision of the award by an application in writing addressed to the Secretary-General on the ground of discovery of some fact of such a nature as decisively to affect the award, provided that when the award was rendered that fact was unknown to the Tribunal and to the applicant and that the applicant's ignorance of that fact was not due to negligence.

(2) The application shall be made within 90 days after the discovery of such fact and in any event within three years after the date on which the award was rendered.

(3) The request shall, if possible, be submitted to the Tribunal which rendered the award. If this shall not be possible, a new Tribunal shall be constituted in accordance with Section 2 of this Chapter.

(4) The Tribunal may, if it considers that the circumstances so require, stay enforcement of the award pending its decision. If the applicant requests a stay of enforcement of the award in his application, enforcement shall be stayed provisionally until the Tribunal rules on such request.

Article 52

(1) Either party may request annulment of the award by an application in writing addressed to the Secretary-General on one or more of the following grounds:

(a) that the Tribunal was not properly constituted;

(b) that the Tribunal has manifestly exceeded its powers;

(c) that there was corruption on the part of a member of the Tribunal;

(d) that there has been a serious departure from a fundamental rule of procedure; or

(e) that the award has failed to state the reasons on which it is based.

(2) The application shall be made within 120 days after the date on which the award

was rendered except that when annulment is requested on the ground of corruption such application shall be made within 120 days after discovery of the corruption and in any event within three years after the date on which the award was rendered.

(3) On receipt of the request the Chairman shall forthwith appoint from the Panel of Arbitrators an *ad hoc* Committee of three persons. None of the members of the Committee shall have been a member of the Tribunal which rendered the award, shall be of the same nationality as any such member, shall be a national of the State party to the dispute or of the State whose national is a party to the dispute, shall have been designated to the Panel of Arbitrators by either of those States, or shall have acted as a conciliator in the same dispute. The Committee shall have the authority to annul the award or any part thereof on any of the grounds set forth in paragraph (1).

(4) The provisions of Articles 41–45, 48, 49, 53 and 54, and of Chapters VI and VII shall apply *mutatis mutandis* to proceedings before the Committee.

(5) The Committee may, if it considers that the circumstances so require, stay enforcement of the award pending its decision. If the applicant requests a stay of enforcement of the award in his application, enforcement shall be stayed provisionally until the Committee rules on such request.

(6) If the award is annulled the dispute shall, at the request of either party, be submitted to a new Tribunal constituted in accordance with Section 2 of this Chapter.

Section 6

Recognition and Enforcement of the Award

Article 53

A60–054 (1) The award shall be binding on the parties and shall not be subject to any appeal or to any other remedy except those provided for in this Convention. Each party shall abide by and comply with the terms of the award except to the extent that enforcement shall have been stayed pursuant to the relevant provisions of this Convention.

(2) For the purposes of this Section, "award" shall include any decision interpreting, revising or annulling such award pursuant to Articles 50, 51 or 52.

Article 54

A60–055 (1) Each Contracting State shall recognize an award rendered pursuant to this Convention as binding and enforce the pecuniary obligations imposed by that award within its territories as if it were a final judgment of a court in that State. A Contracting State with a federal constitution may enforce such an award in or through its federal courts and may provide that such courts shall treat the award as if it were a final judgment of the courts of a constituent state.

(2) A party seeking recognition or enforcement in the territories of a Contracting State shall furnish to a competent court or other authority which such State shall have designated for this purpose a copy of the award certified by the Secretary-General. Each Contracting State shall notify the Secretary-General of the designation of the competent court or other authority for this purpose and of any subsequent change in such designation.

(3) Execution of the award shall be governed by the laws concerning the execution of judgments in force in the State in whose territories such execution is sought.

Article 55

Nothing in Article 54 shall be construed as derogating from the law in force in any Contracting State relating to immunity of that State or of any foreign State from execution.

Chapter V

Replacement and Disqualification of Conciliators and Arbitrators

Article 56

(1) After a Commission or a Tribunal has been constituted and proceedings have begun, its composition shall remain unchanged; provided, however, that if a conciliator or an arbitrator should die, become incapacitated, or resign, the resulting vacancy shall be filled in accordance with the provisions of Section 2 of Chapter III or Section 2 of Chapter IV.

(2) A member of a Commission or Tribunal shall continue to serve in that capacity notwithstanding that he shall have ceased to be a member of the Panel.

(3) If a conciliator or arbitrator appointed by a party shall have resigned without the consent of the Commission or Tribunal of which he was a member, the Chairman shall appoint a person from the appropriate Panel to fill the resulting vacancy.

Article 57

A party may propose to a Commission or Tribunal the disqualification of any of its members on account of any fact indicating a manifest lack of the qualities required by paragraph (1) of Article 14. A party to arbitration proceedings may, in addition, propose the disqualification of an arbitrator on the ground that he was ineligible for appointment to the Tribunal under Section 2 of Chapter IV.

Article 58

The decision on any proposal to disqualify a conciliator or arbitrator shall be taken by the other members of the Commission or Tribunal as the case may be, provided that where those members are equally divided, or in the case of a proposal to disqualify a sole conciliator or arbitrator, or a majority of the conciliators or arbitrators, the Chairman shall take that decision. If it is decided that the proposal is well-founded the conciliator or arbitrator to whom the decision relates shall be replaced in accordance with the provisions of Section 2 of Chapter III or Section 2 of Chapter IV.

Chapter VI

Cost of Proceedings

Article 59

The charges payable by the parties for the use of the facilities of the Centre shall be determined by the Secretary-General in accordance with the regulations adopted by the Administrative Council.

Article 60

A60–061   (1) Each Commission and each Tribunal shall determine the fees and expenses of its members within limits established from time to time by the Administrative Council and after consultation with the Secretary-General.

(2) Nothing in paragraph (1) of this Article shall preclude the parties from agreeing in advance with the Commission or Tribunal concerned upon the fees and expenses of its members.

Article 61

A60–062   (1) In the case of conciliation proceedings the fees and expenses of members of the Commission as well as the charges for the use of the facilities of the Centre, shall be borne equally by the parties. Each party shall bear any other expenses it incurs in connection with the proceedings.

(2) In the case of arbitration proceedings the Tribunal shall, except as the parties otherwise agree, assess the expenses incurred by the parties in connection with the proceedings, and shall decide how and by whom those expenses, the fees and expenses of the members of the Tribunal and the charges for the use of the facilities of the Centre shall be paid. Such decision shall form part of the award.

Chapter VII

Place of Proceedings

Article 62

A60–063   Conciliation and arbitration proceedings shall be held at the seat of the Centre except as hereinafter provided.

Article 63

A60–064   Conciliation and arbitration proceedings may be held, if the parties so agree,

> (a) at the seat of the Permanent Court of Arbitration or of any other appropriate institution, whether private or public, with which the Centre may make arrangements for that purpose; or
>
> (b) at any other place approved by the Commission or Tribunal after consultation with the Secretary-General.

Chapter VIII

Disputes between Contracting States

Article 64

A60–065   Any dispute arising between Contracting States concerning the interpretation or application of this Convention which is not settled by negotiation shall be referred to the

International Court of Justice by the application of any party to such dispute, unless the States concerned agree to another method of settlement.

Chapter IX

Amendment

Article 65

Any Contracting State may propose amendment of this Convention. The text of a proposed amendment shall be communicated to the Secretary-General not less than 90 days prior to the meeting of the Administrative Council at which such amendment is to be considered and shall forthwith be transmitted by him to all the members of the Administrative Council.

Article 66

(1) If the Administrative Council shall so decide by a majority of two-thirds of its members, the proposed amendment shall be circulated to all Contracting States for ratification, acceptance or approval. Each amendment shall enter into force 30 days after dispatch by the depositary of this Convention of a notification to Contracting States that all Contracting States have ratified, accepted or approved the amendment.

(2) No amendment shall affect the rights and obligations under this Convention of any Contracting State or of any of its constituent subdivisions or agencies, or of any national of such State arising out of consent to the jurisdiction of the Centre given before the date of entry into force of the amendment.

Chapter X

Final Provisions

Article 67

This Convention shall be open for signature on behalf of States members of the Bank. It shall also be open for signature on behalf of any other State which is a party to the Statute of the International Court of Justice and which the Administrative Council, by a vote of two thirds of its members, shall have invited to sign the Convention.

Article 68

(1) This Convention shall be subject to ratification, acceptance or approval by the signatory States in accordance with their respective constitutional procedures.

(2) This Convention shall enter into force 30 days after the date of deposit of the twentieth instrument of ratification, acceptance or approval. It shall enter into force for each State which subsequently deposits its instrument of ratification, acceptance or approval 30 days after the date of such deposit.

Article 69

A60–070   Each Contracting State shall take such legislative or other measures as may be necessary for making the provisions of this Convention effective in its territories.

Article 70

A60–071   This Convention shall apply to all territories for whose international relations a Contracting State is responsible, except those which are excluded by such State by written notice to the depositary of this Convention either at the time of ratification, acceptance or approval or subsequently.

Article 71

A60–072   Any Contracting State may denounce this Convention by written notice to the depositary of this Convention. The denunciation shall take effect six months after receipt of such notice.

Article 72

A60–073   Notice by a Contracting State pursuant to Articles 70 or 71 shall not affect the rights or obligations under this Convention of that State or of any of its constituent subdivisions or agencies or of any national of that State arising out of consent to the jurisdiction of the Centre given by one of them before such notice was received by the depositary.

Article 73

A60–074   Instruments of ratification, acceptance or approval of this Convention and of amendments thereto shall be deposited with the Bank which shall act as the depositary of this Convention. The depositary shall transmit certified copies of this Convention to States members of the Bank and to any other State invited to sign the Convention.

Article 74

A60–075   The depositary shall register this Convention with the Secretariat of the United Nations in accordance with Article 102 of the Charter of the United Nations and the Regulations thereunder adopted by the General Assembly.

Article 75

A60–076   The depositary shall notify all signatory States of the following:

   (a) signatures in accordance with Article 67;

   (b) deposits of instruments of ratification, acceptance and approval in accordance with Article 73;

   (c) the date on which this Convention enters into force in accordance with Article 68;

   (d) exclusions from territorial application pursuant to Article 70;

   (e) the date on which any amendment of this Convention enters into force in accordance with Article 66; and

   (f) denunciations in accordance with Article 71.

DONE at Washington, in the English, French and Spanish languages, all three texts being equally authentic, in a single copy which shall remain deposited in the archives of the International Bank for Reconstruction and Development, which has indicated by its signature below its agreement to fulfil the functions with which it is charged under this Convention.

Arbitration Act 1950

(14 Geo. 6 c.27)

An Act to consolidate the Arbitration Acts 1889 to 1934

[28th July 1950]

Part I

General Provisions as to Arbitration

Effect of Arbitration Agreements, etc.

Authority of arbitrators and umpires to be irrevocable

A61–001   1. The authority of an arbitrator or umpire appointed by or by virtue of an arbitration agreement shall, unless a contrary intention is expressed in the agreement, be irrevocable except by leave of the High Court or a judge thereof.

Death of party

A61–002   2.—(1) An arbitration agreement shall not be discharged by the death of any party thereto, either as respects the deceased or any other party, but shall in such an event be enforceable by or against the personal representative of the deceased.

(2) The authority of an arbitrator shall not be revoked by the death of any party by whom he was appointed.

(3) Nothing in this section shall be taken to affect the operation of any enactment or rule of law by virtue of which any right of action is extinguished by the death of a person.

Bankruptcy

A61–003   3.—(1) Where it is provided by a term in a contract to which a bankrupt is a party that any differences arising thereout or in connection therewith shall be referred to arbitration, the said term shall, if the trustee in bankruptcy adopts the contract, be enforceable by or against him so far as relates to any such differences.

(2) Where a person who has been adjudged bankrupt had, before the commencement of the bankruptcy, become a party to an arbitration agreement, and any matter to which the agreement applies requires to be determined in connection with or for the purposes of the bankruptcy proceedings, then, if the case is one to which subsection (1) of this section does not apply, any other party to the agreement or, with the consent of the [creditors' committee established under section 301 of the Insolvency Act 1986], the trustee in bankruptcy, may apply to the court having jurisdiction in the bankruptcy proceedings for an order directing that the matter in question shall be referred to arbitration in accordance with the agreement, and that court may, if it is of opinion that, having regard to all the circumstances of the case, the matter ought to be determined by arbitration, make an order accordingly.

Staying court proceedings where there is submission to arbitration

4.—(1) If any party to an arbitration agreement, or any person claiming through or under him, commences any legal proceedings in any court against any other party to the agreement, or any person claiming through or under him, in respect of any matter agreed to be referred, any party to those legal proceedings may at any time after appearance, and before delivering any pleadings or taking any other steps in the proceedings, apply to that court to stay the proceedings, and that court or a judge thereof, if satisfied that there is no sufficient reason why the matter should not be referred in accordance with the agreement, and that the applicant was, at the time when the proceedings were commenced, and still remains, ready and willing to do all things necessary to the proper conduct of the arbitration, may make an order staying the proceedings.

(2) [. . .]

A61–004

Reference of interpleader issues to arbitration

5. Where relief by way of interpleader is granted and it appears to the High Court that the claims in question are matters to which an arbitration agreement, to which the claimants are parties, applies, the High Court may direct the issue between the claimants to be determined in accordance with the agreement.

A61–005

Arbitrators and Umpires

When reference is to a single arbitrator

6. Unless a contrary intention is expressed therein, every arbitration agreement shall, if no other mode of reference is provided, be deemed to include a provision that the reference shall be to a single arbitrator.

A61–006

Power of parties in certain cases to supply vacancy

7. Where an arbitration agreement provides that the reference shall be to two arbitrators, one to be appointed by each party, then, unless a contrary intention is expressed therein:

A61–007

(a) if either of the appointed arbitrators refuses to act, or is incapable of acting, or dies, the party who appointed him may appoint a new arbitrator in his place;

(b) if, on such a reference, one party fails to appoint an arbitrator, either originally, or by way of substitution as aforesaid, for seven clear days after the other party, having appointed his arbitrator, has served the party making default with notice to make the appointment, the party who has appointed an arbitrator may appoint that arbitrator to act as sole arbitrator in the reference and his award shall be binding on both parties as if he had been appointed by consent:

Provided that the High Court or a judge thereof may set aside any appointment made in pursuance of this section.

Umpires

8.—Unless a contrary intention is expressed therein, every arbitration agreement shall, where the reference is to two arbitrators, be deemed to include a provision that the two

A61–008

arbitrators [may appoint an umpire at any time] after they are themselves appointed [and shall do so forthwith if they cannot agree].

(2) Unless a contrary intention is expressed therein, every arbitration agreement shall, where such a provision is applicable to the reference, be deemed to include a provision that if the arbitrators have delivered to any party to the arbitration agreement, or to the umpire, a notice in writing stating that they cannot agree, the umpire may forthwith enter on the reference in lieu of the arbitrators.

(3) At any time after the appointment of an umpire, however appointed, the High Court may, on the application of any party to the reference and notwithstanding anything to the contrary in the arbitration agreement, order that the umpire shall enter upon the reference in lieu of the arbitrators and as if he were a sole arbitrator.

Majority award of three arbitrators

A61–009   9. Unless the contrary intention is expressed in the arbitration agreement, in any case where there is a reference to three arbitrators, the award of any two of the arbitrators shall be binding.

Power of court in certain cases to appoint an arbitrator or umpire

A61–010   10.—(1) In any of the following cases:

  (a) where an arbitration agreement provides that the reference shall be to a single arbitrator, and all the parties do not, after differences have arisen, concur in the appointment of an arbitrator;

  (b) if an appointed arbitrator refuses to act, or is incapable of acting, or dies, and the arbitration agreement does not show that it was intended that the vacancy should not be supplied and the parties do not supply the vacancy;

  (c) where the parties or two arbitrators are [required or are] at liberty to appoint an umpire or third arbitrator and do not appoint him . . . ;

  (d) where an appointed umpire or third arbitrator refuses to act, or is incapable of acting, or dies, and the arbitration agreement does not show that it was intended that the vacancy should not be supplied, and the parties or arbitrators do not supply the vacancy;

any party may serve the other parties or the arbitrators, as the case may be, with a written notice to appoint or, as the case may be, concur in appointing, an arbitrator, umpire or third arbitrator, and if the appointment is not made within seven clear days after the service of the notice, the High Court or a judge thereof may, on application by the party who gave the notice, appoint an arbitrator, umpire or third arbitrator who shall have the like powers to act in the reference and make an award as if he had been appointed by consent of all parties.

(2) In any case where:

  (a) an arbitration agreement provides for the appointment of an arbitrator or umpire by a person who is neither one of the parties nor an existing arbitrator (whether the provision applies directly or in default of agreement by the parties or otherwise); and

(b) that person refuses to make the appointment or does not make it within the time specified in the agreement or, if no time is so specified, within a reasonable time,

any party to the agreement may serve the person in question with a written notice to appoint an arbitrator or umpire and, if the appointment is not made within seven clear days after the service of the notice, the High Court or a judge thereof may, on the application of the party who gave the notice, appoint an arbitrator or umpire who shall have the like powers to act in the reference and make an award as if he had been appointed in accordance with the terms of the agreement.

[(3) In any case where:

(a) an arbitration agreement provides that the reference shall be to three arbitrators, one to be appointed by each party and the third to be appointed by the two appointed by the parties or in some other manner specified in the agreement; and

(b) one of the parties ("the party in default") refuses to appoint an arbitrator or does not do so within the time specified in the agreement or, if no time is specified, within a reasonable time,

the other party to the agreement, having appointed his arbitrator, may serve the party in default with a written notice to appoint an arbitrator.

(3A) A notice under subsection (3) must indicate whether it is served for the purposes of subsection (3B) or for the purposes of subsection (3C).

(3B) Where a notice is served for the purposes of this subsection, then unless a contrary intention is expressed in the agreement, if the required appointment is not made within seven clear days after the service of the notice:

(a) the party who gave the notice may appoint his arbitrator to act as sole arbitrator in the reference; and

(b) his award shall be binding on both parties as if he had been appointed by consent.

(3C) Where a notice is served for the purposes of this subsection, then, if the required appointment is not made within seven clear days after the service of the notice, the High Court or a judge thereof may, on the application of the party who gave the notice, appoint an arbitrator on behalf of the party in default who shall have the like powers to act in the reference and make an award (and, if the case so requires, the like duty in relation to the appointment of a third arbitrator) as if he had been appointed in accordance with the terms of the agreement.

(3D) The High Court or a judge thereof may set aside any appointment made by virtue of subsection (3B).]

[(4) Except in a case where the arbitration agreement shows that it was intended that the vacancy should not be supplied, paragraph (b) of each of subsection (2) and (3) shall be construed as extending to any such refusal or failure by a person as is there mentioned arising in connection with the replacement of an arbitrator who was appointed by that person (or, in default of being so appointed, was appointed under that subsection) but who refuses to act, or is incapable of acting or has died.]

Power of official referee to take arbitrations

A61–011 **11.** (1) An official referee may, if in all the circumstances he thinks fit, accept an appointment as sole arbitrator, or as umpire, by or by virtue of an arbitration agreement.

(2) An official referee shall not accept appointment as arbitrator or umpire unless the Lord Chief Justice has informed him that, having regard to the state of official referees' business, he can be made available to do so.

(3) The fees payable for the services of an official referee as arbitrator or umpire shall be taken in the High Court.

(4) Schedule 3 to the Administration of Justice Act 1970 (which modifies this Act in relation to arbitration by judges, in particular by substituting the Court of Appeal for the High Court in provisions whereby arbitrators and umpires, their proceedings and awards are subject to control and review by the court) shall have effect in relation to official referees appointed as arbitrators or umpires as it has effect in relation to judge-arbitrators and judge-umpires (within the meaning of that Schedule).

(5) Any jurisdiction which is exercisable by the High Court in relation to arbitrators and umpires otherwise than under this Act shall, in relation to an official referee appointed as arbitrator or umpire, be exercisable instead by the Court of Appeal.

(6) In this section "official referee" means any person nominated under section 68(1)(a) of the Supreme Court Act 1981 to deal with official referees' business.

(7) Rules of the Supreme Court may make provision for:

(a) cases in which it is necessary to allocate references made under or by virtue of arbitration agreements to official referees; and

(b) the transfer of references from one official referee to another.

Conduct of Proceedings, Witnesses, etc.

Conduct of proceedings, witnesses, etc.

A61–012 **12.**—(1) Unless a contrary intention is expressed therein, every arbitration agreement shall, where such a provision is applicable to the reference, be deemed to contain a provision that the parties to the reference, and all persons claiming through them respectively, shall, subject to any legal objection, submit to be examined by the arbitrator or umpire, on oath or affirmation, in relation to the matters in dispute, and shall, subject as aforesaid, produce before the arbitrator or umpire all documents within their possession or power respectively which may be required or called for, and do all other things which during the proceedings on the reference the arbitrator or umpire may require.

(2) Unless a contrary intention is expressed therein, every arbitration agreement shall, where such a provision is applicable to the reference, be deemed to contain a provision that the witnesses on the reference shall, if the arbitrator or umpire thinks fit, be examined on oath or affirmation.

(3) An arbitrator or umpire shall, unless a contrary intention is expressed in the arbitration agreement, have power to administer oaths to, or take the affirmations of, the parties to and witnesses on a reference under the agreement.

(4) Any party to a reference under an arbitration agreement may sue out a writ of *subpoena ad testificandum* or a writ of *subpoena duces tecum*, but no person shall be compelled under any such writ to produce any document which he could not be compelled to produce on the trial of an action, and the High Court or a judge thereof may order that a writ of *subpoena ad testificandum* or of *subpoena duces tecum* shall issue to

compel the attendance before an arbitrator or umpire of a witness wherever he may be within the United Kingdom.

(5) The High Court or a judge thereof may also order that a writ of *habeas corpus ad testificandum* shall issue to bring up a prisoner for examination before an arbitrator or umpire.

(6) The High Court shall have, for the purpose of and in relation to a reference, the same power of making orders in respect of:

    (a) security for costs;

    (b) [. . .]

    (c) the giving of evidence by affidavit;

    (d) examination on oath of any witness before an officer of the High Court or any other person, and the issue of a commission or request for the examination of a witness out of the jurisdiction;

    (e) the preservation, interim custody or sale of any goods which are the subject matter of the reference;

    (f) securing the amount in dispute in the reference;

    (g) the detention, preservation or inspection of any property or thing which is the subject of the reference or as to which any question may arise therein, and authorising for any of the purposes aforesaid any persons to enter upon or into any land or building in the possession of any party to the reference, or authorising any samples to be taken or any observation to be made or experiment to be tried which may be necessary or expedient for the purpose of obtaining full information or evidence; and

    (h) interim injunctions or the appointment of a receiver;

as it has for the purpose of and in relation to an action or matter in the High Court;

Provided that nothing in this subsection shall be taken to prejudice any power which may be vested in an arbitrator or umpire of making orders with respect to any of the matters aforesaid.

Provisions as to Awards

Time for making award

13.—(1) Subject to the provisions of subsection (2) of section twenty-two of this Act, and anything to the contrary in the arbitration agreement, an arbitrator or umpire shall have power to make an award at any time.

(2) The time, if any, limited for making an award, whether under this Act or otherwise, may from time to time be enlarged by order of the High Court or a judge thereof, whether that time has expired or not.

(3) The High Court may, on the application of any party to a reference, remove an arbitrator or umpire who fails to use all reasonable despatch in entering on and proceeding with the reference and making an award, and an arbitrator or umpire who is removed by the High Court under this subsection shall not be entitled to receive any remuneration in respect of his services.

For the purposes of this subsection, the expression "proceeding with a reference" includes, in a case where two arbitrators are unable to agree, giving notice of that fact to the parties and to the umpire.

Want of prosecution

A61–014 13A.—(1) Unless a contrary intention is expressed in the arbitration agreement, the arbitrator or umpire shall have power to make an award dismissing any claim in a dispute referred to him if it appears to him that the conditions mentioned in subsection (2) are satisfied.

(2) The conditions are:

   (a) that there has been inordinate and inexcusable delay on the part of the claimant in pursuing the claim; and
   (b) that the delay:
      (i) will give rise to a substantial risk that it is not possible to have a fair resolution of the issues in that claim; or
      (ii) has caused, or is likely to cause or to have caused, serious prejudice to the respondent.

(3) For the purpose of keeping the provision made by this section and the corresponding provision which applies in relation to proceedings in the High Court in step, the Secretary of State may by order made by statutory instrument amend subsection (2) above.

(4) Before making any such order the Secretary of State shall consult the Lord Chancellor and such other persons as he considers appropriate.

(5) No such order shall be made unless a draft of the order has been laid before, and approved by resolution of, each House of Parliament.

Interim awards

A61–015 14. Unless a contrary intention is expressed therein, every arbitration agreement shall, where such a provision is applicable to the reference, be deemed to contain a provision that the arbitrator or umpire may, if he thinks fit, make an interim award, and any reference in this Part of this Act to an award includes a reference to an interim award.

Specific performance

A61–016 15. Unless a contrary intention is expressed therein, every arbitration agreement shall, where such a provision is applicable to the reference, be deemed to contain a provision that the arbitrator or umpire shall have the same power as the High Court to order specific performance of any contract other than a contract relating to land to land or any interest in land.

Awards to be final

A61–017 16. Unless a contrary intention is expressed therein, every arbitration agreement shall, where such a provision is applicable to the reference, be deemed to contain a provision that the award to be made by the arbitrator or umpire shall be final and binding on the parties and the persons claiming under them respectively.

Arbitration Act 1950

Power to correct slips

17. Unless a contrary intention is expressed in the arbitration agreement, the arbitrator or umpire shall have power to correct in any award any clerical mistake or error arising from any accidental slip or omission.

A61–018

Costs, Fees and Interest

Costs

18.(1) Unless a contrary intention is expressed therein, every arbitration agreement shall be deemed to include a provision that the costs of the reference and award shall be in the discretion of the arbitrator or umpire, who may direct to and by whom and in what manner those costs or any part thereof shall be paid, and may tax or settle the amount of costs to be so paid or any part thereof, and may award costs to be paid as between solicitor and client.

A61–019

(2) Any costs directed by an award to be paid shall, unless the award otherwise directs, be taxable in the High Court.

(3) Any provision in an arbitration agreement to the effect that the parties or any party thereto shall in any event pay their or his own costs of the reference or award or any part thereof shall be void, and this Part of this Act shall, in the case of an arbitration agreement containing any such provision, have effect as if that provision were not contained therein;

Provided that nothing in this subsection shall invalidate such a provision when it is part of an agreement to submit to arbitration a dispute which has arisen before the making of that agreement.

(4) If no provision is made by an award with respect to the costs of the reference, any party to the reference may, within fourteen days of the publication of the award or such further time as the High Court or a judge thereof may direct, apply to the arbitrator for an order directing by and to whom those costs shall be paid, and thereupon the arbitrator shall, after hearing any party who may desire to be heard, amend his award by adding thereto such directions as he may think proper with respect to the payment of the costs of the reference.

(5) Section sixty-nine of the Solicitors Act 1932 (which empowers a court before which any proceeding is being heard or is pending to charge property recovered or preserved in the proceeding with the payment of solicitors' costs) shall apply as if an arbitration were a proceeding in the High Court, and the High Court may make declarations and orders accordingly.

Taxation of arbitrator's or umpire's fees

19.—(1) If in any case an arbitrator or umpire refuses to deliver his award except on payment of the fees demanded by him, the High Court may, on an application for the purpose, order that the arbitrator or umpire shall deliver the award to the applicant on payment into court by the applicant of the fees demanded, and further that the fees demanded shall be taxed by the taxing officer and that out of the money paid into court there shall be paid out to the arbitrator or umpire by way of fees such sum as may be found reasonable on taxation and that the balance of the money, if any, shall be paid out to the applicant.

A61–020

(2) An application for the purposes of this section may be made by any party to the

reference unless the fees demanded have been fixed by a written agreement between him and the arbitrator or umpire.

(3) A taxation of fees under this section may be reviewed in the same manner as a taxation of costs.

(4) The arbitrator or umpire shall be entitled to appear and be heard on any taxation or review of taxation under this section.

Power of arbitrator to award interest

A61–021   19A.—(1) Unless a contrary intention is expressed therein, every arbitration agreement shall, where such a provision is applicable to the reference, be deemed to contain a provision that the arbitrator or umpire may, if he thinks fit, award simple interest at such rate as he thinks fit:

> (a) on any sum which is the subject of the reference but which is paid before the award, for such period ending not later than the date of the payment as he thinks fit; and
>
> (b) on any sum which he awards, for such period ending not later than the date of the award as he thinks fit.

(2) The power to award interest conferred on an arbitrator or umpire by subsection (1) above is without prejudice to any other power of an arbitrator or umpire to award interest.

Interest on awards

A61–022   20. A sum directed to be paid by an award shall, unless the award otherwise directs, carry interest as from the date of the award and at the same rate as a judgment debt.

Special cases, Remission and Setting aside of Awards, etc.

A61–023   21. [. . .]

Power to remit award

A61–024   22.—(1) In all cases of reference to arbitration the High Court or a judge thereof may from time to time remit the matters referred, or any of them, to the reconsideration of the arbitrator or umpire.

(2) Where an award is remitted, the arbitrator or umpire shall, unless the order otherwise directs, make his award within three months after the date of the order.

Removal of arbitrator and setting aside of award

A61–025   23.—(1) Where an arbitrator or umpire has misconducted himself or the proceedings, the High Court may remove him.

(2) Where an arbitrator or umpire has misconducted himself or the proceedings, or an arbitration or award has been improperly procured, the High Court may set the award aside.

(3) Where an application is made to set aside an award, the High Court may order that any money made payable by the award shall be brought into court or otherwise secured pending the determination of the application.

Power of court to give relief where arbitrator is not impartial or the dispute involves question of fraud

24.—(1) Where an agreement between any parties provides that disputes which may arise in the future between them shall be referred to an arbitrator named or designated in the agreement, and after a dispute has arisen any party applies, on the ground that the arbitrator so named or designated is not or may not be impartial, for leave to revoke the authority of the arbitrator or for an injunction to restrain any other party or the arbitrator from proceeding with the arbitration, it shall not be a ground for refusing the application that the said party at the time when he made the agreement knew, or ought to have known, that the arbitrator, by reason of his relation towards any other party to the agreement or of his connection with the subject referred, might not be capable of impartiality.

(2) Where an agreement between any parties provides that disputes which may arise in the future between them shall be referred to arbitration, and a dispute which so arises involves the question whether any such party has been guilty of fraud, the High Court shall, so far as may be necessary to enable that question to be determined by the High Court, have power to order that the agreement shall cease to have effect and power to give leave to revoke the authority of any arbitrator or umpire appointed by or by virtue of the agreement.

(3) In any case where by virtue of this section the High Court has power to order that an arbitration agreement shall cease to have effect or to give leave to revoke the authority of an arbitrator or umpire, the High Court may refuse to stay any action brought in breach of the agreement.

A61–026

Power of court where arbitrator is removed or authority of arbitrator is revoked

25.—(1) Where an arbitrator (not being a sole arbitrator), or two or more arbitrators (not being all the arbitrators), or an umpire who has not entered on the reference is or are removed by the High Court [or the Court of Appeal], the High Court [or the Court of Appeal, as the case may be] may, on the application of any party to the arbitration agreement, appoint a person or persons to act as arbitrator or arbitrators or umpire in place of the person or persons so removed.

(2) Where the authority of an arbitrator or arbitrators or umpire is revoked by leave of the High Court [or the Court of Appeal], or a sole arbitrator or all the arbitrators or an umpire who has entered on the reference is or are removed by the High Court [or the Court of Appeal], the High Court [or the Court of Appeal, as the case may be] may, on the application of any party to the arbitration agreement, either:

(a) appoint a person to act as sole arbitrator in place of the person or persons removed; or

(b) order that the arbitration agreement shall cease to have effect with respect to the dispute referred.

(3) A person appointed under this section by the High Court [or the Court of Appeal] as an arbitrator or umpire shall have the like power to act in the reference and to make an award as if he had been appointed in accordance with the terms of the arbitration agreement.

(4) Where it is provided (whether by means of a provision in the arbitration agreement or otherwise) that an award under an arbitration agreement shall be a condition precedent to the bringing of an action with respect to any matter to which the agreement applies, the High Court [or the Court of Appeal], if it orders (whether under this section or under

A61–027

Enforcement of Award

Enforcement of award

A61–028   26.—(1) An award on an arbitration agreement may, by leave of the High Court or a judge thereof, be enforced in the same manner as a judgment or order to the same effect, and where leave is so given, judgment may be entered in terms of the award.

(2) If a county court so orders, the amount sought to be recovered shall be recoverable (by execution issued from the county court or otherwise) as if payable under an order of that court and shall not be enforceable under subsection (1) above.

(3) An application to the High Court under this section shall preclude an application to a county court and an application to a county court under this section shall preclude an application to the High Court.

(4) [. . .]

Miscellaneous

Power of court to extend time for commencing arbitration proceedings

A61–029   27. Where the terms of an agreement to refer future disputes to arbitration provide that any claims to which the agreement applies shall be barred unless notice to appoint an arbitrator is given or an arbitrator is appointed or some other step to commence arbitration proceedings is taken within a time fixed by the agreement, and a dispute arises to which the agreement applies, the High Court, if it is of opinion that in the circumstances of the case undue hardship would otherwise be caused, and notwithstanding that the time so fixed has expired, may, on such terms, if any, as the justice of the case may require, but without prejudice to the provisions of any enactment limiting the time for the commencement of arbitration proceedings, extend the time for such period as it thinks proper.

Terms as to costs, etc.

A61–030   28. Any order made under this Part of this Act may be made on such terms as to costs or otherwise as the authority making the order thinks just.

Extension of section 496 of the Merchant Shipping Act 1894

A61–031   29.—(1) In subsection (3) of section 496 of the Merchant Shipping Act 1894 (which requires a sum deposited with a wharfinger by an owner of goods to be repaid unless legal proceedings are instituted by the shipowner), the expression "legal proceedings" shall be deemed to include arbitration.

(2) For the purposes of the said section 496, as amended by this section, an arbitration shall be deemed to be commenced when one party to the arbitration agreement serves on the other party or parties a notice requiring him or them to appoint or concur in appointing an arbitrator, or, where the arbitration agreement provides that the reference shall be to a person named or designated in the agreement, requiring him or them to submit the dispute to the person so named or designated.

(3) Any such notice as is mentioned in subsection (2) of this section may be served either:

   (a) by delivering it to the person on whom it is to be served; or

   (b) by leaving it at the usual or last known place of abode in England of that person; or

   (c) by sending it by post in a registered letter addressed to that person at his usual or last known place of abode in England;

as well as in any other manner provided in the arbitration agreement; and where a notice is sent by post in manner prescribed by paragraph (c) of this subsection, service thereof shall, unless the contrary is proved, be deemed to have been effected at the time at which the letter would have been delivered in the ordinary course of post.

Crown to be bound

30. This Part of this Act [. . .] shall apply to any arbitration to which His Majesty, either in right of the Crown or of the Duchy of Lancaster or otherwise, or the Duke of Cornwall, is a party. **A61–032**

Application of Part I to statutory arbitrations

31.—(1) Subject to the provisions of section thirty-three of this Act, this Part of this Act, except the provisions thereof specified in subsection (2) of this section, shall apply to every arbitration under any other Act (whether passed before or after the commencement of this Act) as if the arbitration were pursuant to an arbitration agreement and as if that other Act were an arbitration agreement, except in so far as this Act is inconsistent with that other Act or with any rules or procedure authorised or recognised thereby. **A61–033**

(2) The provisions referred to in subsection (1) of this section are subsection (1) of section two, section three, [. . .] section five, subsection (3) of section eighteen and sections twenty-four, twenty-five, twenty-seven and twenty-nine.

Meaning of "arbitration agreement"

32. In this Part of this Act, unless the context otherwise requires, the expression "arbitration agreement" means a written agreement to submit present or future differences to arbitration, whether an arbitrator is named therein or not. **A61–034**

Operation of Part I

33. This Part of this Act shall not affect any arbitration commenced (within the meaning of subsection (2) of section twenty-nine of this Act) before the commencement of this Act, but shall apply to an arbitration so commenced after the commencement of this Act under an agreement made before the commencement of this Act. **A61–035**

Extent of Part I

34. [. . .] none of the provisions of this Part of this Act shall extend to Scotland or Northern Ireland. **A61–036**

Miscellaneous

Part II

Enforcement of Certain Foreign Awards

Awards to which Part II applies

A61–037 35.—(1) This Part of this Act applies to any award made after the twenty-eighth day of July, nineteen hundred and twenty-four:—

    (a) in pursuance of an agreement for arbitration to which the protocol set out in the First Schedule to this Act applies; and

    (b) between persons of whom one is subject to the jurisdiction of some one of such Powers as His Majesty, being satisfied that reciprocal provisions have been made, may by Order in Council declare to be parties to the convention set out in the Second Schedule to this Act, and of whom the other is subject to the jurisdiction of some other of the Powers aforesaid; and

    (c) in one of such territories as His Majesty, being satisfied that reciprocal provisions have been made, may by Order in Council declare to be territories to which the said convention applies;

and an award to which this Part of this Act applies is in this Part of this Act referred to as "a foreign award".

(2) His Majesty may by a subsequent Order in Council vary or revoke any Order previously made under this section.

(3) Any Order in Council under section one of the Arbitration (Foreign Awards) Act 1930 which is in force at the commencement of this Act shall have effect as if it had been made under this section.

Effect of foreign awards

A61–038 36.—(1) A foreign award shall, subject to the provisions of this Part of this Act, be enforceable in England either by action or in the same manner as the award of an arbitrator is enforceable by virtue of [section twenty-six of this Act].

(2) Any foreign award which would be enforceable under this Part of this Act shall be treated as binding for all purposes on the persons as between whom it was made, and may accordingly be relied on by any of those persons by way of defence, set off or otherwise in any legal proceedings in England, and any references in this Part of this Act to enforcing a foreign award shall be construed as including references to relying on an award.

Conditions for enforcement of foreign awards

A61–039 37.—(1) In order that a foreign award may be enforceable under this Part of this Act it must have:—

    (a) been made in pursuance of an agreement for arbitration which was valid under the law by which it is governed;

    (b) been made by the tribunal provided for in the agreement or constituted in manner agreed upon by the parties;

(c) been made in conformity with the law governing the arbitration procedure;

(d) become final in the country in which it was made;

(e) been in respect of a matter which may lawfully be referred to arbitration under the law of England;

and the enforcement thereof must not be contrary to the public policy or the law of England.

(2) Subject to the provisions of this subsection, a foreign award shall not be enforceable under this Part of this Act if the court dealing with the case is satisfied that:—

(a) the award has been annulled in the country in which it was made; or

(b) the party against whom it is sought to enforce the award was not given notice of the arbitration proceedings in sufficient time to enable him to present his case, or was under some legal incapacity and was not properly represented; or

(c) the award does not deal with all the questions referred or contains decisions on matters beyond the scope of the agreement for arbitration:

Provided that, if the award does not deal with all the questions referred, the court may, if it thinks fit, either postpone the enforcement of the award or order its enforcement subject to the giving of such security by the person seeking to enforce it as the court may think fit.

(3) If a party seeking to resist the enforcement of a foreign award proves that there is any ground other than the non-existence of the conditions specified in paragraphs (a), (b) and (c) of subsection (1) of this section, or the existence of the conditions specified in paragraphs (b) and (c) of subsection (2) of this section, entitling him to contest the validity of the award, the court may, if it thinks fit, either refuse to enforce the award or adjourn the hearing until after the expiration of such period as appears to the court to be reasonably sufficient to enable that party to take the necessary steps to have the award annulled by the competent tribunal.

Evidence

38.—(1) The party seeking to enforce a foreign award must produce:— **A61–040**

(a) the original award or a copy thereof duly authenticated in manner required by the law of the country in which it was made; and

(b) evidence proving that the award has become final; and

(c) such evidence as may be necessary to prove that the award is a foreign award and that the conditions mentioned in paragraphs (a), (b) and (c) of subsection (1) of the last foregoing section are satisfied.

(2) In any case where any document required to be produced under subsection (1) of this section is in a foreign language, it shall be the duty of the party seeking to enforce the award to produce a translation certified as correct by a diplomatic or consular agent of the country to which that party belongs, or certified as correct in such other manner as may be sufficient according to the law of England.

(3) Subject to the provisions of this section, rules of court may be made under section

[84 of the Supreme Court Act 1981] with respect to the evidence which must be furnished by a party seeking to enforce an award under this Part of this Act.

Meaning of "final award"

A61–041 39. For the purposes of this Part of this Act, an award shall not be deemed final if any proceedings for the purpose of contesting the validity of the award are pending in the country in which it was made.

Saving for other rights, etc.

A61–042 40. Nothing in this Part of this Act shall:—

(a) prejudice any rights which any person would have had of enforcing in England any award or of availing himself in England of any award if neither this Part of this Act nor Part I of the Arbitration (Foreign Awards) Act 1930 had been enacted; or

(b) apply to any award made on an arbitration agreement governed by the law of England.

41. [. . .]

Application of Part II to Northern Ireland

A61–043 42.—(1) The following provisions of this section shall have effect for the purpose of the application of this Part of this Act to Northern Ireland.

(2) For the references to England there shall be substituted references to Northern Ireland.

(3) For subsection (1) of section thirty-six there shall be substituted the following subsection:

"(1) A foreign award shall, subject to the provisions of this Part of this Act, be enforceable either by action or in the same manner as the award of an arbitrator under the provisions of the Common Law Procedure Amendment Act (Ireland) 1856 was enforceable at the date of the passing of the Arbitration (Foreign Awards) Act 1930".

(4) [. . .]

A61–044 43. [. . .]

Part III

General

Short title, commencement and repeal

A61–045 44.—(1) This Act may be cited as the Arbitration Act 1950.

(2) This Act shall come into operation on the first day of September, nineteen hundred and fifty.

(3) The Arbitration Act 1889, the Arbitration Clauses (Protocol) Act 1924 and the Arbitration Act 1934 are hereby repealed except in relation to arbitrations commenced (within the meaning of subsection (2) of section twenty-nine of this Act) before the commencement of this Act, and the Arbitration (Foreign Awards) Act 1930 is hereby repealed; and any reference in any Act or other document to any enactment hereby repealed shall be construed as including a reference to the corresponding provision of this Act.

SCHEDULES

Section 35   FIRST SCHEDULE

Protocol on Arbitration Clauses Signed on Behalf of His Majesty at a Meeting of the Assembly of the League of Nations held on the Twenty-Fourth Day of September, Nineteen-Hundred and Twenty-Three

The undersigned, being duly authorised, declare that they accept, on behalf of the countries which they represent, the following provisions:—

1. Each of the Contracting States recognises the validity of an agreement whether relating to existing or future differences between parties, subject respectively to the jurisdiction of different Contracting States by which the parties to a contract agree to submit to arbitration all or any differences that may arise in connection with such contract relating to commercial matters or to any other matter capable of settlement by arbitration, whether or not the arbitration is to take place in a country to whose jurisdiction none of the parties is subject. Each Contracting State reserves the right to limit the obligation mentioned above to contracts which are considered as commercial under its national law. Any Contracting State which avails itself of this right will notify the Secretary-General of the League of Nations, in order that the other Contracting States may be so informed.

2. The arbitral procedure, including the constitution of the arbitral tribunal, shall be governed by the will of the parties and by the law of the country in whose territory the arbitration takes place.

The Contracting States agree to facilitate all steps in the procedure which require to be taken in their own territories, in accordance with the provisions of their law governing arbitral procedure applicable to existing differences.

3. Each Contracting State undertakes to ensure the execution by its authorities and in accordance with the provisions of its national laws of arbitral awards made in its own territory under the preceding articles.

4. The tribunals of the Contracting Parties, on being seized of a dispute regarding a contract made between persons to whom Article 1 applies and including an arbitration agreement whether referring to present or future differences which is valid in virtue of the said article and capable of being carried into effect, shall refer the parties on the application of either of them to the decision of the arbitrators.

Such reference shall not prejudice the competence of the judicial tribunals in case the agreement or the arbitration cannot proceed or become inoperative.

5 The present Protocol, which shall remain open for signature by all States, shall be ratified. The ratifications shall be deposited as soon as possible with the Secretary-General of the League of Nations, who shall notify such deposit to all the signatory States.

A61–046

6. The present Protocol shall come into force as soon as two ratifications have been deposited. Thereafter it will take effect, in the case of each Contracting State, one month after the notification by the Secretary-General of the deposit of its ratification.

7. The present Protocol may be denounced by any Contracting State on giving one year's notice. Denunciation shall be effected by a notification addressed to the Secretary-General of the League, who will immediately transmit copies of such notification to all the other signatory States and inform them of the date of which it was received. The denunciation shall take effect one year after the date on which it was notified to the Secretary-General, and shall operate only in respect of the notifying State.

8. The Contracting States may declare that their acceptance of the present Protocol does not include any or all of the under-mentioned territories: that is to say, their colonies, overseas possessions or territories, protectorates or the territories over which they exercise a mandate.

The said States may subsequently adhere separately on behalf of any territory thus excluded. The Secretary-General of the League of Nations shall be informed as soon as possible of such adhesions. He shall notify such adhesions to all signatory States. They will take effect one month after the notification by the Secretary-General to all signatory States.

The Contracting States may also denounce the Protocol separately on behalf of any of the territories referred to above. Article 7 applies to such denunciation.

Section 35   SECOND SCHEDULE

CONVENTION ON THE EXECUTION OF FOREIGN ARBITRAL AWARDS SIGNED AT GENEVA ON BEHALF OF HIS MAJESTY ON THE TWENTY-SIXTH DAY OF SEPTEMBER, NINETEEN-HUNDRED AND TWENTY-SEVEN

Article 1

A61–047   In the territories of any High Contracting Party to which the present Convention applies, an arbitral award made in pursuance of an agreement, whether relating to existing or future differences (hereinafter called "a submission to arbitration") covered by the Protocol on Arbitration Clauses, opened at Geneva on September 24, 1923 shall be recognised as binding and shall be enforced in accordance with the rules of the procedure of the territory where the award is relied upon, provided that the said award has been made in a territory of one of the High Contracting Parties to which the present Convention applies and between persons who are subject to the jurisdiction of one of the High Contracting Parties.

To obtain such recognition or enforcement, it shall, further, be necessary:—

(a) That the award has been made in pursuance of a submission to arbitration which is valid under the law applicable thereto;

(b) That the subject-matter of the award is capable of settlement by arbitration under the law of the country in which the award is sought to be relied upon;

(c) That the award has been made by the Arbitral Tribunal provided for in the submission to arbitration or constituted in the manner agreed upon by the parties and in conformity with the law governing the arbitration procedure;

(d) That the award has become final in the country in which it has been made, in the sense that it will not be considered as such if it is open to *opposition, appel* or *pourvoi en cassation* (in the countries where such forms of procedure exist) or if it is proved that any proceedings for the purpose of contesting the validity of the award are pending;

(e) That the recognition or enforcement of the award is not contrary to the public policy or to the principles of the law of the country in which it is sought to be relied upon.

Article 2

Even if the conditions laid down in Article 1 hereof are fulfilled, recognition and enforcement of the award shall be refused if the Court is satisfied: **A61–048**

(a) That the award has been annulled in the country in which it was made;

(b) That the party against whom it is sought to use the award was not given notice of the arbitration proceedings in sufficient time to enable him to present his case; or that, being under a legal incapacity, he was not properly represented;

(c) That the award does not deal with the differences contemplated by or falling within the terms of the submission to arbitration or that it contains decisions on matters beyond the scope of the submission to arbitration.

If the award has not covered all the questions submitted to the arbitral tribunal, the competent authority of the country where recognition or enforcement of the award is sought can, if it think fit, postpone such recognition or enforcement or grant it subject to such guarantee as that authority may decide.

Article 3

If the party against whom the award has been made proves that, under the law governing the arbitration procedure, there is a ground other than the grounds referred to in Article 1(a) and (c), and Article 2(b) and (c), entitling him to contest the validity of the award in a Court of Law, the Court may, if it thinks fit, either refuse recognition or enforcement of the award or adjourn the consideration thereof, giving such party a reasonable time within which to have the award annulled by the competent tribunal. **A61–049**

Article 4

The party relying upon an award or claiming its enforcement must supply, in particular: **A61–050**

(1) The original award or a copy thereof duly authenticated, according to the requirements of the law of the country in which it was made;

(2) Documentary or other evidence to prove that the award has become final, in the sense defined in Article 1(d), in the country in which it was made;

(3) When necessary, documentary or other evidence to prove that the conditions laid down in Article 1, paragraph 1 and paragraph 2(a) and (c) have been fulfilled.

A translation of the award and of the other documents mentioned in this Article into the official language of the country where the award is sought to be relied upon may be demanded. Such translation must be certified correct by a diplomatic or consular agent of the country to which the party who seeks to rely upon the award belongs or by a sworn translator of the country where the award is sought to be relied upon.

Article 5

A61–051 The provisions of the above Articles shall not deprive any interested party of the right of availing himself of an arbitral award in the manner and to the extent allowed by the law or the treaties of the country where such award is sought to be relied upon.

Article 6

A61–052 The present Convention applies only to arbitral awards made after the coming into force of the Protocol on Arbitration Clauses, opened at Geneva on September 24, 1923.

Article 7

A61–053 The present Convention, which will remain open to the signature of all the signatories of the Protocol of 1923 on Arbitration Clauses, shall be ratified.

It may be ratified only on behalf of those Members of the League of Nations and non-Member States on whose behalf the Protocol of 1923 shall have been ratified. Ratifications shall be deposited as soon as possible with the Secretary-General of the League of Nations, who will notify such deposit to all the signatories.

Article 8

A61–054 The present Convention shall come into force three months after it shall have been ratified on behalf of two High Contracting Parties. Thereafter, it shall take effect, in the case of each High Contracting Party, three months after the deposit of the ratification on its behalf with the Secretary-General of the League of Nations.

Article 9

A61–055 The present Convention may be denounced on behalf of any Member of the League or non-Member State. Denunciation shall be notified in writing to the Secretary-General of the League of Nations, who will immediately send a copy thereof, certified to be in conformity with the notification, to all the other Contracting Parties, at the same time informing them of the date on which he received it.

The denunciation shall come into force only in respect of the High Contracting Party which shall have notified it and one year after such notification shall have reached the Secretary-General of the League of Nations.

The denunciation of the Protocol on Arbitration Clauses shall entail *ipso facto*, the denunciation of the present Convention.

Article 10

A61–056 The present Convention does not apply to the Colonies, Protectorates or territories under suzerainty or mandate of any High Contracting Party unless they are specially mentioned.

The application of this Convention to one or more of such Colonies, Protectorates or territories to which the Protocol on Arbitration Clauses, opened at Geneva on September

24, 1923, applies, can be effected at any time by means of a declaration addressed to the Secretary-General of the League of Nations by one of the High Contracting Parties.

Such declaration shall take effect three months after the deposit thereof.

The High Contracting Parties can at any time denounce the Convention for all or any of the Colonies, Protectorates or territories referred to above. Article 9 hereof applies to such denunciation.

Article 11

A certified copy of the present Convention shall be transmitted by the Secretary-General of the League of Nations to every Member of the League of Nations and to every non-Member State which signs the same.

Arbitration Act 1975

(1975 c.3)

An Act to give effect to the New York Convention on the Recognition and Enforcement of Foreign Arbitral Awards.

[25TH FEBRUARY, 1975]

Effect of arbitration agreement on court proceedings

Staying court proceedings where party proves arbitration agreement

A62–001 1.—(1) If any party to an arbitration agreement to which this section applies, or any person claiming through or under him, commences any legal proceedings in any court against any other party to the agreement, or any person claiming through or under him, in respect of any matter agreed to be referred, any party to the proceedings may at any time after appearance, and before delivering any pleadings or taking any other steps in the proceedings, apply to the court to stay the proceedings; and the court, unless satisfied that the arbitration agreement is null and void, inoperative or incapable of being performed or that there is not in fact any dispute between the parties with regard to the matter agreed to be referred, shall make an order staying the proceedings.

(2) This section applies to any arbitration agreement which is not a domestic arbitration agreement; and neither section 4(1) of the Arbitration Act 1950 nor section 4 of the Arbitration Act (Northern Ireland) 1937 shall apply to an arbitration agreement to which this section applies.

(3) [. . .]

(4) In this section "domestic arbitration agreement" means an arbitration agreement which does not provide, expressly or by implication, for arbitration in a State other than the United Kingdom and to which neither:

(a) an individual who is a national of, or habitually resident in, any State other than the United Kingdom; nor

(b) a body corporate which is incorporated in, or whose central management and control is exercised in, any State other than the United Kingdom,

is a party at the time the proceedings are commenced.

Enforcement of Convention awards

Replacement of former provisions

A62–002 2. Sections 3 to 6 of this Act shall have effect with respect to the enforcement of Convention awards; and where a Convention award would, but for this section, be also a foreign award within the meaning of Part II of the Arbitration Act 1950, that Part shall not apply to it.

ARBITRATION ACT 1975

Effect of Convention awards

3.—(1) A Convention award shall, subject to the following provisions of this Act, be enforceable: **A62–003**

(a) in England and Wales, either by action or in the same manner as the award of an arbitrator is enforceable by virtue of section 26 of the Arbitration Act 1950;

(b) [. . .];

(c) in Northern Ireland, either by action or in the same manner as the award of an arbitrator is enforceable by virtue of section 16 of the Arbitration Act (Northern Ireland) 1937.

(2) Any Convention award which would be enforceable under this Act shall be treated as binding for all purposes on the persons as between whom it was made, and may accordingly be relied on by any of those persons by way of defence, set off or otherwise in any legal proceedings in the United Kingdom; and any reference in this Act to enforcing a Convention award shall be construed as including reference to relying on such an award.

Evidence

4. The party seeking to enforce a Convention award must produce: **A62–004**

(a) the duly authenticated original award or a duly certified copy of it; and

(b) the original arbitration agreement or a duly certified copy of it; and

(c) where the award or agreement is in a foreign language, a translation of it certified by an official or sworn translator or by a diplomatic or consular agent.

Refusal of enforcement

5.—(1) Enforcement of a Convention award shall not be refused except in the cases mentioned in this section. **A62–005**

(2) Enforcement of a Convention award may be refused if the person against whom it is invoked proves:

(a) that a party to the arbitration agreement was (under the law applicable to him) under some incapacity; or

(b) that the arbitration agreement was not valid under the law to which the parties subjected it or, failing any indication thereon, under the law of the country where the award was made; or

(c) that he was not given proper notice of the appointment of the arbitrator or of the arbitration proceedings or was otherwise unable to present his case; or

(d) (subject to subsection (4) of this section) that the award deals with a difference not contemplated by or not falling within the terms of the submission to arbitration or contains decisions on matters beyond the scope of the submission to arbitration; or

(e) that the composition of the arbitral authority or the arbitral procedure was not in accordance with the agreement of the parties or, failing such agreement, with the law of the country where the arbitration took place; or

(f) that the award has not yet become binding on the parties, or has been set aside or suspended by a competent authority of the country in which, or under the law of which, it was made.

(3) Enforcement of a Convention award may also be refused if the award is in respect of a matter which is not capable of settlement by arbitration, or if it would be contrary to public policy to enforce the award.

(4) A Convention award which contains decisions on matters not submitted to arbitration may be enforced to the extent that it contains decisions on matters submitted to arbitration which can be separated from those on matters not so submitted.

(5) Where an application for the setting aside or suspension of a Convention award has been made to such competent authority as is mentioned in subsection (2)(f) of this section, the court before which enforcement of the award is sought may, if it thinks fit, adjourn the proceedings and may, on the application of the party seeking to enforce the award, order the other party to give security.

Saving

A62–006 6. Nothing in this Act shall prejudice any right to enforce or rely on an award otherwise than under this Act or Part II of the Arbitration Act 1950.

General

Interpretation

A62–007 7.—(1) In this Act:

> "arbitration agreement" means an agreement in writing (including an agreement contained in an exchange of letter or telegrams) to submit to arbitration present or future differences capable of settlement by arbitration;
> "Convention award" means an award made in pursuance of an arbitration agreement in the territory of a State, other than the United Kingdom, which is a party to the New York Convention; and
> "the New York Convention" means the Convention on the Recognition and Enforcement of Foreign Arbitral Awards adopted by the United Nations Conference on International Commercial Arbitration on 10th June 1958.

(2) If Her Majesty by Order in Council declares that any State specified in the Order is a party to the New York Convention the Order shall, while in force, be conclusive evidence that that State is a party to that Convention.

(3) An Order in Council under this section may be varied or revoked by a subsequent Order in Council.

Short title, repeals, commencement and extent

A62–008 8.—(1) This Act may be cited as the Arbitration Act 1975.

(2) The following provisions of the Arbitration Act 1950 are hereby repealed, that is to say:

(a) section 4(2);

(b) in section 28 the proviso;

(c) in section 30 the words "(except the provisions of subsection (2) of section 4 thereof)";

(d) in section 31(2) the words "subsection (2) of section 4"; and

(e) in section 34 the words from the beginning to "save as aforesaid".

(3) This Act shall come into operation on such date as the Secretary of State may by order made by statutory instrument appoint.

(4) This Act extends to Northern Ireland.

Arbitration Act 1979

(1979 c.42)

An Act to amend the law relating to arbitrations and for purposes connected therewith

[4TH APRIL, 1979]

Judicial review of arbitration awards

A63–001   **1.**—(1) In the Arbitration Act 1950 (in this Act referred to as "the principal Act") section 21 (statement of case for a decision of the High Court) shall cease to have effect and, without prejudice to the right of appeal conferred by subsection (2) below, the High Court shall not have jurisdiction to set aside or remit an award on an arbitration agreement on the ground of errors of fact or law on the fact of the award.

(2) Subject to subsection (3) below, an appeal shall lie to the High Court on any question of law arising out of an award made on an arbitration agreement; and on the determination of such an appeal the High Court may by order:

(a) confirm, vary or set aside the award; or

(b) remit the award to the reconsideration of the arbitrator or umpire together with the court's opinion on the question of law which was the subject of the appeal,

and where the award is remitted under paragraph (b) above the arbitrator or umpire shall, unless the order otherwise directs, make his award within three months after the date of the order.

(3) An appeal under this section may be brought by any of the parties to the reference:

(a) with the consent of all the other parties to the reference; or

(b) subject to section 3 below, with the leave of the court.

(4) The High Court shall not grant leave under subsection (3)(b) above unless it considers that, having regard to all the circumstances, the determination of the question of law concerned could substantially affect the rights of one or more of the parties to the arbitration agreement; and the court may make any leave which it gives conditional upon the applicant complying with such conditions as it considers appropriate.

(5) Subject to subsection (6) below, if an award is made and, on an application made by any of the parties to the reference:

(a) with the consent of all the other parties to the reference; or

(b) subject to section 3 below, with the leave of the court,

it appears to the High Court that the award does not or does not sufficiently set out the reasons for the award, the court may order the arbitrator or umpire concerned to state the reasons for his award in sufficient detail to enable the court, should an appeal be brought under this section, to consider any question of law arising out of the award.

(6) In any case where an award is made without any reason being given, the High Court shall not make an order under subsection (5) above unless it is satisfied:

(a) that before the award was made one of the parties to the reference gave notice to the arbitrator or umpire concerned that a reasoned award would be required; or

(b) that there is some special reason why such a notice was not given.

[(6A) Unless the High Court gives leave, no appeal shall lie to the Court of Appeal from a decision of the High Court:

(a) to grant or refuse leave under subsection (3) (b) or (5) (b) above; or

(b) to make or not to make an order under subsection (5) above.]

(7) No appeal shall lie to the Court of Appeal from a decision of the High Court on an appeal under this section unless:

(a) the High Court or the Court of Appeal gives leave; and

(b) it is certified by the High Court that the question of law to which its decision relates either is one of general public importance or is one which for some other special reason should be considered by the Court of Appeal.

(8) Where the award of an arbitrator or umpire is varied on appeal, the award as varied shall have effect (except for the purposes of this section) as if it were the award of the arbitrator or umpire.

Determination of preliminary point of law by court

2.—(1) Subject to subsection (2) and section 3 below, on an application to the High Court made by any of the parties to a reference:

(a) with the consent of an arbitrator who has entered on the reference or, if an umpire has entered on the reference, with his consent; or

(b) with the consent of all the other parties,

the High Court shall have jurisdiction to determine any question of law arising in the course of the reference.

(2) The High Court shall not entertain an application under subsection (1) (a) above with respect to any question of law unless it is satisfied that:

(a) the determination of the application might produce substantial savings in costs to the parties; and

(b) the question of law is one in respect of which leave to appeal would be likely to be given under section 1(3)(b) above.

(2A) Unless the High Court gives leave, no appeal shall lie to the Court of Appeal from a decision of the High Court to entertain or not to entertain an application under subsection (1) (a) above.

(3) A decision of the High Court under [subsection (1) above] shall be deemed to be a judgment of the court within the meaning of section [16 of the Supreme Court Act 1981] (appeals to the Court of Appeal), but no appeal shall lie from such a decision unless:

(a) the High Court or the Court of Appeal gives leave; and

(b) it is certified by the High Court that the question of law to which its decision relates either is one of general importance or is one which for some other special reason should be considered by the Court of Appeal.

Exclusion agreements affecting rights under sections 1 and 2

A63–003 3.—(1) Subject to the following provision of this section and section 4 below:

(a) the High Court shall not, under section 1 (3) (b) above, grant leave to appeal with respect to a question of law arising out of an award, and

(b) the High Court shall not, under section 1 (5) (b) above, grant leave to make an application with respect to an award, and

(c) no application may be made under section 2 (1) (a) above with respect to a question of law,

if the parties to the reference in question have entered into an agreement in writing (in this section referred to as an "exclusion agreement") which excludes the right of appeal under section 1 above in relation to that award or, in a case falling within paragraph (c) above, in relation to an award to which the determination of the question of law is material.

(2) An exclusion agreement may be expressed so as to relate to a particular award, to awards under a particular reference or to any other description of awards, whether arising out of the same reference or not; and an agreement may be an exclusion agreement for the purposes of this section whether it is entered into before or after the passing of this Act and whether or not it forms part of an arbitration agreement.

(3) In any case where:

(a) an arbitration agreement, other than a domestic arbitration agreement, provides for disputes between the parties to be referred to arbitration, and

(b) a dispute to which the agreement relates involves the question whether a party has been guilty of fraud, and

(c) the parties have entered into an exclusion agreement which is applicable to any award made on the reference of that dispute,

then, except in so far as the exclusion agreement otherwise provides, the High Court shall not exercise its powers under section 24 (2) of the principal Act (to take steps necessary to enable the question to be determined by the High Court) in relation to that dispute.

(4) Except as provided by subsection (1) above, sections 1 and 2 above shall have effect notwithstanding anything in any agreement purporting:

(a) to prohibit or restrict access to the High Court; or

(b) to restrict the jurisdiction of that court; or

(c) to prohibit or restrict the making of a reasoned award.

(5) An exclusion agreement shall be of no effect in relation to an award made on, or

Arbitration Act 1979

a question of law arising in the course of a reference under, a statutory arbitration, that is to say, such an arbitration as is referred to in subsection (1) of section 31 of the principal Act.

(6) An exclusion agreement shall be of no effect in relation to an award made on, or a question of law arising in the course of a reference under, an arbitration agreement which is a domestic arbitration agreement unless the exclusion agreement is entered into after the commencement of the arbitration in which the award is made or, as the case may be, in which the question of law arises.

(7) In this section "domestic arbitration agreement" means an arbitration agreement which does not provide, expressly or by implication, for arbitration in a State other than the United Kingdom and to which neither:

- (a) an individual who is a national of, or habitually resident in, any State other than the United Kingdom; nor
- (b) a body corporate which is incorporated in, or whose central management and control is exercised in, any State other than the United Kingdom,

is a party at the time the arbitration agreement is entered into.

Exclusion agreements not to apply in certain cases

4.—(1) Subject to subsection (3) below, if an arbitration award or a question of law **A63–004** arising in the course of a reference relates, in whole or in part, to:

- (a) a question or claim falling within the Admiralty jurisdiction of the High Court, or
- (b) a dispute arising out of a contract of insurance, or
- (c) a dispute arising out of a commodity contract,

an exclusion agreement shall have no effect in relation to the award or question unless either:

- (i) the exclusion agreement is entered into after the commencement of the arbitration in which the award is made or, as the case may be, in which the question of law arises, or
- (ii) the award or question relates to a contract which is expressed to be governed by a law other than the law of England and Wales.

(2) In subsection (1)(c) above "commodity contract" means a contract:

- (a) for the sale of goods regularly dealt with on a commodity market or exchange in England or Wales which is specified for the purposes of this section by an order made by the Secretary of State; and
- (b) of a description so specified.

(3) The Secretary of State may by order provide that subsection (1) above:

- (a) shall cease to have effect; or

(b) subject to such conditions as may be specified in the order, shall not apply to any exclusion agreement made in relation to an arbitration award of a description so specified;

and an order under this subsection may contain such supplementary, incidental and transitional provisions as appear to the Secretary of State to be necessary or expedient.

(4) The power to make an order under subsection (2) or subsection (3) above shall be exercisable by statutory instrument which shall be subject to annulment in pursuance of a resolution of either House of Parliament.

(5) In this section "exclusion agreement" has the same meaning as in section 3 above.

Interlocutory orders

A63–005   5.—(1) If any party to a reference under an arbitration agreement fails within the time specified in the order or, if no time is so specified, within a reasonable time to comply with an order made by the arbitrator or umpire in the course of the reference, then, on the application of the arbitrator or umpire or of any party to the reference, the High Court may make an order extending the powers of the arbitrator or umpire as mentioned in subsection (2) below.

(2) If an order is made by the High Court under this section, the arbitrator or umpire shall have power, to the extent and subject to any conditions specified in that order, to continue with the reference in default of appearance or of any other act by one of the parties in like manner as a judge of the High Court might continue with proceedings in that court where a party fails to comply with an order of that court or a requirement of rules of court.

(3) Section 4(5) of the Administration of Justice Act 1970 (jurisdiction of the High Court to be exercisable by the Court of Appeal in relation to judge-arbitrators and judge-umpires) shall not apply in relation to the power of the High Court to make an order under this section, but in the case of a reference to a judge-arbitrator or judge-umpire that power shall be exercisable as in the case of any other reference to arbitration and also by the judge-arbitrator or judge-umpire himself.

(4) Anything done by a judge-arbitrator or judge-umpire in the exercise of the power conferred by subsection (3) above shall be done by him in his capacity as judge of the High Court and have effect as if done by that court.

(5) The preceding provisions of this section have effect notwithstanding anything in any agreement but do not derogate from any powers conferred on an arbitrator or umpire, whether by an arbitration agreement or otherwise.

(6) In this section "judge-arbitrator" and "judge-umpire" have the same meaning as in Schedule 3 to the Administration of Justice Act 1970.

A63–006   6. [...]

Application and interpretation of certain provisions of Part I of principal Act

A63–007   7.—(1) References in the following provisions of Part I of the principal Act to that Part of that Act shall have effect as if the preceding provisions of this Act were included in that Part, namely:

(a) section 14 (interim awards);

(b) section 28 (terms as to costs of orders);

(c) section 30 (Crown to be bound);

(d) section 31 (application to statutory arbitrations); and

(e) section 32 (meaning of "arbitration agreement").

(2) Subsections (2) and (3) of section 29 of the principal Act shall apply to determine when an arbitration is deemed to be commenced for the purposes of this Act.

(3) For the avoidance of doubt, it is hereby declared that the reference in subsection (1) of section 31 of the principal Act (statutory arbitrations) to arbitration under any other Act does not extend to arbitration under [section 64 of the County Courts Act 1984] (cases in which proceedings are to be or may be referred to arbitration) and accordingly nothing in this Act or in Part 1 of the principal Act applies to arbitration under the said [section 64].

Short title, commencement, repeals and extent

8.—(1) This Act may be cited as the Arbitration Act 1979.

(2) This Act shall come into operation on such day as the Secretary of State may appoint by order made by statutory instrument; and such an order:

(a) may appoint different days for different provisions of this Act and for the purposes of the operation of the same provision in relation to different descriptions of arbitration agreement; and

(b) may contain such supplementary, incidental and transitional provisions as appear to the Secretary of State to be necessary or expedient.

(3) In consequence of the preceding provisions of this Act, the following provisions are hereby repealed, namely:

(a) in paragraph (c) of section 10 of the principal Act the words from "or where" to the end of the paragraph;

(b) section 21 of the principal Act;

(c) in paragraph 9 of Schedule 3 to the Administration of Justice Act 1970, in sub-paragraph (1) the words "21(1) and (2)" and sub-paragraph (2).

(4) This Act forms part of the law of England and Wales only.

Late Payment of Commercial Debts (Interest) Act 1998

(1998 c.20)

A64–001 An Act to make provision with respect to interest on the late payment of certain debts arising under commercial contracts for the supply of goods or services; and for connected purposes

[11TH JUNE, 1998]

PART I

STATUTORY INTEREST ON QUALIFYING DEBTS

Statutory interest

1.—(1) It is an implied term in a contract to which this Act applies that any qualifying debt created by the contract carries simple interest subject to and in accordance with this Part.

(2) Interest carried under that implied term (in this Act referred to as "statutory interest") shall be treated, for the purposes of any rule of law or enactment (other than this Act) relating to interest on debts, in the same way as interest carried under an express contract term.

(3) This Part has effect subject to Part II (which in certain circumstances permits contract terms to oust or vary the right to statutory interest that would otherwise be conferred by virtue of the term implied by subsection (1)).

Contracts to which Act applies

A64–002 **2.**—(1) [. . .] This Act applies to a contract for the supply of goods or services where the purchaser and the supplier are each acting in the course of a business, other than an excepted contract.

(2) In this Act "contract for the supply of goods or services" means—

   (a) a contract of sale of goods; or

   (b) a contract (other than a contract of sale of goods) by which a person does any, or any combination, of the things mentioned in subsection (3) for a consideration that is (or includes) a money consideration.

(3) Those things are—

   (a) transferring or agreeing to transfer to another the property in goods;

   (b) bailing or agreeing to bail goods to another by way of hire or, in Scotland, hiring or agreeing to hire goods to another; and

   (c) agreeing to carry out a service.

(4) For the avoidance of doubt a contract of service or apprenticeship is not a contract for the supply of goods or services.

(5) The following are excepted contracts—

(a) a consumer credit agreement;

(b) a contract intended to operate by way of mortgage, pledge, charge or other security [.]

[...]

(7) In this section—

"business" includes a profession and the activities of any government department or local or public authority; "consumer credit agreement" has the same meaning as in the Consumer Credit Act 1974; "contract of sale of goods" and "goods" have the same meaning as in the Sale of Goods Act 1979; "government department" includes any part of the Scottish Administration; "property in goods" means the general property in them and not merely a special property.

Application of the Act to Advocates

2A. [The provisions of this Act apply to a transaction in respect of which fees are paid for professional services to a member of the Faculty of Advocates as they apply to a contract for the supply of services for the purpose of this Act.]   **A64–003**

Qualifying debts

3.—(1) A debt created by virtue of an obligation under a contract to which this Act applies to pay the whole or any part of the contract price is a "qualifying debt" for the purposes of this Act, unless (when created) the whole of the debt is prevented from carrying statutory interest by this section.   **A64–004**

(2) A debt does not carry statutory interest if or to the extent that it consists of a sum to which a right to interest or to charge interest applies by virtue of any enactment (other than section 1 of this Act).

This subsection does not prevent a sum from carrying statutory interest by reason of the fact that a court, arbitrator or arbiter would, apart from this Act, have power to award interest on it.

(3) A debt does not carry (and shall be treated as never having carried) statutory interest if or to the extent that a right to demand interest on it, which exists by virtue of any rule of law, is exercised.

[...]

Period for which statutory interest runs

4.—(1) Statutory interest runs in relation to a qualifying debt in accordance with this section (unless section 5 applies).   **A64–005**

(2) Statutory interest starts to run on the day after the relevant day for the debt, at the rate prevailing under section 6 at the end of the relevant day.

(3) Where the supplier and the purchaser agree a date for payment of the debt (that is, the day on which the debt is to be created by the contract), that is the relevant day unless the debt relates to an obligation to make an advance payment.

A date so agreed may be fixed one or may depend on the happening of an event or the failure of an event to happen.

(4) Where the debt relates to an obligation to make an advance payment, the relevant day is the day on which the debt is treated by section 11 as having been created.

(5) In any other case, the relevant day is the last day of the period of 30 days beginning with—

    (a) the day on which the obligation of the supplier to which the debt relates is performed; or

    (b) the day on which the purchaser has notice of the amount of the debt or (where that amount is unascertained) the sum which the supplier claims is the amount of the debt,

whichever is the later.

(6) Where the debt is created by virtue of an obligation to pay a sum due in respect of a period of hire of goods, subsection (5)(a) has effect as if it referred to the last day of that period.

(7) Statutory interest ceases to run when the interest would cease to run if it were carried under an express contract term.

(8) In this section "advance payment" has the same meaning as in section 11.

Remission of statutory interest

A64–006   5.—(1) This section applies where, by reason of any conduct of the supplier, the interests of justice require that statutory interest should be remitted in whole or part in respect of a period for which it would otherwise run in relation to a qualifying debt.

(2) If the interests of justice require that the supplier should receive no statutory interest for a period, statutory interest shall not run for that period.

(3) If the interests of justice require that the supplier should receive statutory interest at a reduced rate for a period, statutory interest shall run at such rate as meets the justice of the case for that period.

(4) Remission of statutory interest under this section may be required—

    (a) by reason of conduct at any time (whether before or after the time at which the debt is created); and

    (b) for the whole period for which statutory interest would otherwise run or for one or more parts of that period.

(5) In this section "conduct" includes any act or omission.

Compensation arising out of late payment

A64–007   5A.—(1) Once statutory interest begins to run in relation to a qualifying debt, the supplier shall be entitled to a fixed sum (in addition to the statutory interest on the debt).

(2) That sum shall be—

    (a) for a debt less than £1,000, the sum of £40;

    (b) for a debt of £1,000 or more, but less than £10,000, the sum of £70;

    (c) for a debt of £10,000 or more, the sum of £100.

(3) The obligation to pay an additional fixed sum under this section in respect of a qualifying debt shall be treated as part of the term implied by section 1(1) in the contract creating the debt. [. . .]

Rate of statutory interest

6.—(1) The Secretary of State shall by order made with the consent of the Treasury set the rate of statutory interest by prescribing—

(a) a formula for calculating the rate of statutory interest; or

(b) the rate of statutory interest.

(2) Before making such an order the Secretary of State shall, among other things, consider the extent to which it may be desirable to set the rate so as to—

(a) protect suppliers whose financial position makes them particularly vulnerable if their qualifying debts are paid late; and

(b) deter generally the late payment of qualifying debts.

PART II

CONTRACT TERMS RELATING TO LATE PAYMENT OF QUALIFYING DEBTS

Purpose of Part II

7.—(1) This Part deals with the extent to which the parties to a contract to which this Act applies may by reference to contract terms oust or vary the right to statutory interest that would otherwise apply when a qualifying debt created by the contract (in this Part referred to as "the debt") is not paid.

(2) This Part applies to contract terms agreed before the debt is created; after that time the parties are free to agree terms dealing with the debt.

(3) This Part has effect without prejudice to any other ground which may affect the validity of a contract term.

Circumstances where statutory interest may be ousted or varied

8.—(1) Any contract terms are void to the extent that they purport to exclude the right to statutory interest in relation to the debt, unless there is a substantial contractual remedy for late payment of the debt.

(2) Where the parties agree a contractual remedy for late payment of the debt that is a substantial remedy, statutory interest is not carried by the debt (unless they agree otherwise).

(3) The parties may not agree to vary the right to statutory interest in relation to the debt unless either the right to statutory interest as varied or the overall remedy for late payment of the debt is a substantial remedy.

(4) Any contract terms are void to the extent that they purport to—

(a) confer a contractual right to interest that is not a substantial remedy for late payment of the debt, or

(b) vary the right to statutory interest so as to provide for a right to statutory interest that is not a substantial remedy for late payment of the debt,

unless the overall remedy for late payment of the debt is a substantial remedy.

(5) Subject to this section, the parties are free to agree contract terms which deal with the consequences of late payment of the debt.

Meaning of "substantial remedy"

A64–011   9.—(1) A remedy for the late payment of the debt shall be regarded as a substantial remedy unless—

(a) the remedy is insufficient either for the purpose of compensating the supplier for late payment or for deterring late payment; and

(b) it would not be fair or reasonable to allow the remedy to be relied on to oust or (as the case may be) to vary the right to statutory interest that would otherwise apply in relation to the debt.

(2) In determining whether a remedy is not a substantial remedy, regard shall be had to all the relevant circumstances at the time the terms in question are agreed.

(3) In determining whether subsection (1)(b) applies, regard shall be had (without prejudice to the generality of subsection (2)) to the following matters—

(a) the benefits of commercial certainty;

(b) the strength of the bargaining positions of the parties relative to each other;

(c) whether the term was imposed by one party to the detriment of the other (whether by the use of standard terms or otherwise); and

(d) whether the supplier received an inducement to agree to the term.

Interpretation of Part II

A64–012   10—(1) In this Part—

"contract term" means a term of the contract creating the debt or any other contract term binding the parties (or either of them); "contractual remedy" means a contractual right to interest or any contractual remedy other than interest; "contractual right to interest" includes a reference to a contractual right to charge interest; "overall remedy", in relation to the late payment of the debt, means any combination of a contractual right to interest, a varied right to statutory interest or a contractual remedy other than interest; "substantial remedy" shall be construed in accordance with section 9.

(2) In this Part a reference (however worded) to contract terms which vary the right to statutory interest is a reference to terms altering in any way the effect of Part I in relation to the debt (for example by postponing the time at which interest starts to run or by imposing conditions on the right to interest).

(3) In this Part a reference to late payment of the debt is a reference to late payment of the sum due when the debt is created (excluding any part of that sum which is prevented from carrying statutory interest by section 3).

Part III

General and Supplementary

Treatment of advance payments of the contract price

11.—(1) A qualifying debt created by virtue of an obligation to make an advance payment shall be treated for the purposes of this Act as if it was created on the day mentioned in subsection (3), (4) or (5) (as the case may be).

(2) In this section "advance payment" means a payment falling due before the obligation of the supplier to which the whole contract price relates ("the supplier's obligation") is performed, other than a payment of a part of the contract price that is due in respect of any part performance of that obligation and payable on or after the day on which that part performance is completed.

(3) Where the advance payment is the whole contract price, the debt shall be treated as created on the day on which the supplier's obligation is performed.

(4) Where the advance payment is a part of the contract price, but the sum is not due in respect of any part performance of the supplier's obligation, the debt shall be treated as created on the day on which the supplier's obligation is performed.

(5) Where the advance payment is a part of the contract price due in respect of any part performance of the supplier's obligation, but is payable before that part performance is completed, the debt shall be treated as created on the day on which the relevant part performance is completed.

(6) Where the debt is created by virtue of an obligation to pay a sum due in respect of a period of hire of goods, this section has effect as if—

(a) references to the day on which the supplier's obligation is performed were references to the last day of that period; and

(b) references to part performance of that obligation were references to part of that period.

(7) For the purposes of this section an obligation to pay the whole outstanding balance of the contract price shall be regarded as an obligation to pay the whole contract price and not as an obligation to pay a part of the contract price.

Conflict of laws

12.—(1) This Act does not have effect in relation to a contract governed by the law of a part of the United Kingdom by choice of the parties if—

(a) there is no significant connection between the contract and that part of the United Kingdom; and

(b) but for that choice, the applicable law would be a foreign law.

(2) This Act has effect in relation to a contract governed by a foreign law by choice of the parties if—

(a) but for that choice, the applicable law would be the law of a part of the United Kingdom; and

(b) there is no significant connection between the contract and any country other than that part of the United Kingdom.

(3) In this section—

"contract" means a contract falling within section 2(1); and "foreign law" means the law of a country outside the United Kingdom.

Assignments, etc.

A64–015   13.—(1) The operation of this Act in relation to a qualifying debt is not affected by—

(a) any change in the identity of the parties to the contract creating the debt; or

(b) the passing of the right to be paid the debt, or the duty to pay it (in whole or in part) to a person other than the person who is the original creditor or the original debtor when the debt is created.

(2) Any reference in this Act to the supplier or the purchaser is a reference to the person who is for the time being the supplier or the purchaser or, in relation to a time after the debt in question has been created, the person who is for the time being the creditor or the debtor, as the case may be.

(3) Where the right to be paid part of a debt passes to a person other than the person who is the original creditor when the debt is created, any reference in this Act to a debt shall be construed as (or, if the context so requires, as including) a reference to part of a debt.

(4) A reference in this section to the identity of the parties to a contract changing, or to a right or duty passing, is a reference to it changing or passing by assignment or assignation, by operation of law or otherwise.

Contract terms relating to the date for payment of the contract price

A64–016   14.—(1) This section applies to any contract term which purports to have the effect of postponing the time at which a qualifying debt would otherwise be created by a contract to which this Act applies.

(2) Sections 3(2)(b) and 17(1)(b) of the Unfair Contract Terms Act 1977 (no reliance to be placed on certain contract terms) shall apply in cases where such a contract term is not contained in written standard terms of the purchaser as well as in cases where the term is contained in such standard terms.

(3) In this section "contract term" has the same meaning as in section 10(1).

Orders and regulations

A64–017   15.—(1) Any power to make an order or regulations under this Act is exercisable by statutory instrument.

(2) Any statutory instrument containing an order or regulations under this Act, other than an order under section 17(2), shall be subject to annulment in pursuance of a resolution of either House of Parliament.

Late Payment of Commercial Debts (Interest) Act 1998

Interpretation

16.—(1) In this Act—

"contract for the supply of goods or services" has the meaning given in section 2 (2); "contract price" means the price in a contract of sale of goods or the money consideration referred to in section 2(2)(b) in any other contract for the supply of goods or services; "purchaser" means (subject to section 13(2)) the buyer in a contract of sale or the person who contracts with the supplier in any other contract for the supply of goods or services; "qualifying debt" means a debt falling within section 3(1); "statutory interest" means interest carried by virtue of the term implied by section 1(1); and "supplier" means (subject to section 13(2)) the seller in a contract of sale of goods or the person who does one or more of the things mentioned in section 2(3) in any other contract for the supply of goods or services.

(2) In this Act any reference (however worded) to an agreement or to contract terms includes a reference to both express and implied terms (including terms established by a course of dealing or by such usage as binds the parties).

Short title, commencement and extent

17.—(1) This Act may be cited as the Late Payment of Commercial Debts (Interest) Act 1998.

(2) This Act (apart from this section) shall come into force on such day as the Secretary of State may by order appoint; and different days may be appointed for different descriptions of contract or for other different purposes.

An order under this subsection may specify a description of contract by reference to any feature of the contract (including the parties).

(3) The Secretary of State may by regulations make such transitional, supplemental or incidental provision (including provision modifying any provision of this Act) as the Secretary of State may consider necessary or expedient in connection with the operation of this Act while it is not fully in force.

(4) This Act does not affect contracts of any description made before this Act comes into force for contracts of that description.

(5) This Act extends to Northern Ireland.

Contracts (Rights of Third Parties) Act 1999

(1999 c.31)

A65–001 An Act to make provision for the enforcement of contractual terms by third parties.
[11TH NOVEMBER 1999]

Right of third party to enforce contractual term

1.—(1) Subject to the provisions of this Act, a person who is not a party to a contract (a "third party") may in his own right enforce a term of the contract if—

(a) the contract expressly provides that he may, or

(b) subject to subsection (2), the term purports to confer a benefit on him.

(2) Subsection (1)(b) does not apply if on a proper construction of the contract it appears that the parties did not intend the term to be enforceable by the third party.

(3) The third party must be expressly identified in the contract by name, as a member of a class or as answering a particular description but need not be in existence when the contract is entered into.

(4) This section does not confer a right on a third party to enforce a term of a contract otherwise than subject to and in accordance with any other relevant terms of the contract.

(5) For the purpose of exercising his right to enforce a term of the contract, there shall be available to the third party any remedy that would have been available to him in an action for breach of contract if he had been a party to the contract (and the rules relating to damages, injunctions, specific performance and other relief shall apply accordingly).

(6) Where a term of a contract excludes or limits liability in relation to any matter references in this Act to the third party enforcing the term shall be construed as references to his availing himself of the exclusion or limitation.

(7) In this Act, in relation to a term of a contract which is enforceable by a third party—

"the promisor" means the party to the contract against whom the term is enforceable by the third party, and "the promisee" means the party to the contract by whom the term is enforceable against the promisor.

Variation and rescission of contract

A65–002 **2.**—(1) Subject to the provisions of this section, where a third party has a right under section 1 to enforce a term of the contract, the parties to the contract may not, by agreement, rescind the contract, or vary it in such a way as to extinguish or alter his entitlement under that right, without his consent if—

(a) the third party has communicated his assent to the term to the promisor,

(b) the promisor is aware that the third party has relied on the term, or

(c) the promisor can reasonably be expected to have foreseen that the third party would rely on the term and the third party has in fact relied on it.

(2) The assent referred to in subsection (1)(a)—

(a) may be by words or conduct, and

(b) if sent to the promisor by post or other means, shall not be regarded as communicated to the promisor until received by him.

(3) Subsection (1) is subject to any express term of the contract under which—

(a) the parties to the contract may by agreement rescind or vary the contract without the consent of the third party, or

(b) the consent of the third party is required in circumstances specified in the contract instead of those set out in subsection (1)(a) to (c).

(4) Where the consent of a third party is required under subsection (1) or (3), the court or arbitral tribunal may, on the application of the parties to the contract, dispense with his consent if satisfied—

(a) that his consent cannot be obtained because his whereabouts cannot reasonably be ascertained, or

(b) that he is mentally incapable of giving his consent.

(5) The court or arbitral tribunal may, on the application of the parties to a contract, dispense with any consent that may be required under subsection (1)(c) if satisfied that it cannot reasonably be ascertained whether or not the third party has in fact relied on the term.

(6) If the court or arbitral tribunal dispenses with a third party's consent, it may impose such conditions as it thinks fit, including a condition requiring the payment of compensation to the third party.

(7) The jurisdiction conferred on the court by subsections (4) to (6) is exercisable by both the High Court and a county court.

Defences, etc, available to promisor

3.—(1) Subsections (2) to (5) apply where, in reliance on section 1, proceedings for **A65–003** the enforcement of a term of a contract are brought by a third party.

(2) The promisor shall have available to him by way of defence or set-off any matter that—

(a) arises from or in connection with the contract and is relevant to the term, and

(b) would have been available to him by way of defence or set-off if the proceedings had been brought by the promisee.

(3) The promisor shall also have available to him by way of defence or set-off any matter if—

(a) an express term of the contract provides for it to be available to him in proceedings brought by the third party, and

(b) it would have been available to him by way of defence or set-off if the proceedings had been brought by the promisee.

(4) The promisor shall also have available to him—

(a) by way of defence or set-off any matter, and

(b) by way of counterclaim any matter not arising from the contract,

that would have been available to him by way of defence or set-off or, as the case may be, by way of counterclaim against the third party if the third party had been a party to the contract.

(5) Subsections (2) and (4) are subject to any express term of the contract as to the matters that are not to be available to the promisor by way of defence, set-off or counterclaim.

(6) Where in any proceedings brought against him a third party seeks in reliance on section 1 to enforce a term of a contract (including, in particular, a term purporting to exclude or limit liability), he may not do so if he could not have done so (whether by reason of any particular circumstances relating to him or otherwise) had he been a party to the contract.

Enforcement of contract by promisee

A65–004 4. Section 1 does not affect any right of the promisee to enforce any term of the contract.

Protection of promisor from double liability

A65–005 5. Where under section 1 a term of a contract is enforceable by a third party, and the promisee has recovered from the promisor a sum in respect of—

(a) the third party's loss in respect of the term, or

(b) the expense to the promisee of making good to the third party the default of the promisor,

then, in any proceedings brought in reliance on that section by the third party, the court or arbitral tribunal shall reduce any award to the third party to such extent as it things appropriate to take account of the sum recovered by the promisee.

Exceptions

A65–006 6.—(1) Section 1 confers no rights on a third party in the case of a contract on a bill of exchange, promissory note or other negotiable instrument.

(2) Section 1 confers no rights on a third party in the case of any contract binding on a company and its members under section 14 of the Companies Act 1985.

(2A) Section 1 confers no rights on a third party in the case of any incorporation document of a limited liability partnership or any limited liability partnership agreement as defined in the Limited Liability Partnerships Regulations 2001 (S.I. No. 2001/).

(3) Section 1 confers no right on a third party to enforce—

(a) any term of a contract of employment against an employee,

(b) any term of a worker's contract against a worker (including a home worker), or

(c) any term of a relevant contract against an agency worker.

(4) In subsection (3)—

(a) "contract of employment", "employee", "worker's contract", and "worker" have the meaning given by section 54 of the National Minimum Wage Act 1998,

(b) "home worker" has the meaning given by section 35(2) of that Act,

(c) "agency worker" has the same meaning as in section 34(1) of that Act, and

(d) "relevant contract" means a contract entered into, in a case where section 34 of that Act applies, by the agency worker as respects work falling within subsection (1)(a) of that section.

(5) Section 1 confers no rights on a third party in the case of—

(a) a contract for the carriage of goods by sea, or

(b) a contract for the carriage of goods by rail or road, or for the carriage of cargo by air, which is subject to the rules of the appropriate international transport convention,

except that a third party may in reliance on that section avail himself of an exclusion or limitation of liability in such a contract.

(6) In subsection (5) "contract for the carriage of goods by sea" means a contract of carriage—

(a) contained in or evidenced by a bill of lading, sea waybill or a corresponding electronic transaction, or

(b) under or for the purposes of which there is given an undertaking which is contained in a ship's delivery order or a corresponding electronic transaction.

(7) For the purposes of subsection (6)—

(a) "bill of lading", "sea waybill" and "ship's delivery order" have the same meaning as in the Carriage of Goods by Sea Act 1992, and

(b) a corresponding electronic transaction is a transaction within section 1(5) of that Act which corresponds to the issue, indorsement, delivery or transfer of a bill of lading, sea waybill or ship's delivery order.

(8) In subsection (5) "the appropriate international transport convention" means—

(a) in relation to a contract for the carriage of goods by rail, the Convention which has the force of law in the United Kingdom under section 1 of the International Transport Conventions Act 1983,

(b) in relation to a contract for the carriage of goods by road, the Convention which has the force of law in the United Kingdom under section 1 of the Carriage of Goods by Road Act 1965, and

(c) in relation to a contract for the carriage of cargo by air—

(i) the Convention which has the force of law in the United Kingdom under section 1 of the Carriage by Air Act 1961, or

(ii) the Convention which has the force of law under section 1 of the Carriage by Air (Supplementary Provisions) Act 1962, or

(iii) either of the amended Conventions set out in Part B of Schedule 2 or 3 to the Carriage by Air Acts (Application of Provisions) Order 1967.

Supplementary provisions relating to third party

A65–007   7.—(1) Section 1 does not affect any right or remedy of a third party that exists or is available apart from this Act.

(2) Section 2(2) of the Unfair Contract Terms Act 1977 (restriction on exclusion, etc. of liability for negligence) shall not apply where the negligence consists of the breach of an obligation arising from a term of a contract and the person seeking to enforce it is a third party acting in reliance on section 1.

(3) In sections 5 and 8 of the Limitation Act 1980 the references to an action founded on a simple contract and an action upon a specialty shall respectively include references to an action brought in reliance on section 1 relating to a simple contract and an action brought in reliance on that section relating to a specialty.

(4) a third party shall not, by virtue of section 1(5) or 3(4) or (6), be treated as a party to the contract for the purposes of any other Act (or any instrument made under any other Act).

Arbitration provisions

A65–008   8.—(1) Where—

(a) a right under section 1 to enforce a term ("the substantive term") is subject to a term providing for the submission of disputes to arbitration ("the arbitration agreement"), and

(b) the arbitration agreement is an agreement in writing for the purposes of Part I of the Arbitration Act 1996,

the third party shall be treated for the purposes of that Act as a party to the arbitration agreement as regards disputes between himself and the promisor relating to the enforcement of the substantive term by the third party.

(2) Where—

(a) a third party has a right under section 1 to enforce a term providing for one or more descriptions of dispute between the third party and the promisor to be submitted to arbitration ("the arbitration agreement"),

(b) the arbitration agreement is an agreement in writing for the purposes of Part I of the Arbitration Act 1996, and

(c) the third party does not fall to be treated under subsection (1) as a party to the arbitration agreement,

the third party shall, if he exercises the right, be treated for the purposes of that Act as a party to the arbitration agreement in relation to the matter with respect to which the right is exercised, and be treated as having been so immediately before the exercise of the right.

CONTRACTS (RIGHTS OF THIRD PARTIES) ACT 1999

Northern Ireland

9.—(1) In its application to Northern Ireland, this Act has effect with the modifications **A65–009** specified in subsections (2) and (3).

(2) In section 6(2), for "section 14 of the Companies Act 1985" there is substituted "Article 25 of the Companies (Northern Ireland) Order 1986".

(3) In section 7, for subsection (3) there is substituted—

"(3) In Articles 4(a) and 15 of the Limitation (Northern Ireland) Order 1989, the references to an action founded on a simple contract and an action upon an instrument under seal shall respectively include references to an action brought in reliance on section 1 relating to a simple contract and an action brought in reliance on that section relating to a contract under seal.".

(4) In the Law Reform (Husband and Wife) (Northern Ireland) Act 1964, the following provisions are hereby repealed—

(a) section 5, and

(b) in section 6, in subsection (1)(a), the words "in the case of section 4" and "and in the case of section 5 the contracting party" and in subsection (3), the words "or section 5".

Short title, commencement and extent

10.—(1) This Act may be cited as the Contracts (Rights of Third Parties) Act 1999. **A65–010**

(2) This Act comes into force on the day on which it is passed but, subject to subsection (3), does not apply in relation to a contract entered into before the end of the period of six months beginning with that day.

(3) The restriction in subsection (2) does not apply in relation to a contract which—

(a) is entered into on or after the day on which this Act is passed, and

(b) expressly provides for the application of this Act.

(4) This Act extends as follows—

(a) section 9 extends to Northern Ireland only;

(b) the remaining provisions extend to England and Wales and Northern Ireland only.

Federation of Oils, Seeds and Fats Associations Ltd (FOSFA International) Rules of Arbitration and Appeal[1]

REVISED AND EFFECTIVE FROM 1 JANUARY 2001

A66–001 Any dispute arising out of a contract or contracts subject to these Rules, including any questions of law arising in connection therewith, shall be referred to arbitration in London (or without prejudice to the juridical seat elsewhere if so agreed) in accordance with the Arbitration Act 1996 and any statutory modification or re-enactment thereof for the time being in force.

The juridical seat of the arbitration shall be, and is hereby designated pursuant to Section 3 of the Arbitration Act 1996 as, England.

Each party engaging in an arbitration or an appeal pursuant to these Rules, whether or not a Member of the Federation, is deemed therefore to abide by these Rules and to agree with the Federation to be liable to the Federation (jointly and severally with the other parties to the arbitration or appeal) for all fees and expenses incurred in connection with the arbitration or appeal, which said fees and expenses shall, upon notification by the Federation under the provisions of Rules 1(*b*), 1(*f*), 6(*b*) and 9, be and become a debt due to the Federation.

1. Appointment of Arbitrators/Umpire

A66–002
(*a*) Each party shall appoint an arbitrator who shall have accepted the appointment. However the two parties may by agreement appoint a sole arbitrator who shall have accepted the appointment. Any reference to arbitrators in these Rules shall also be taken to refer to a sole arbitrator. Each party shall advise the Federation promptly of the name of any arbitrator which that party has appointed.

(*b*) If two arbitrators have been appointed they shall, if and when they disagree, appoint an umpire. If the arbitrators fail to agree on the appointment of an umpire, they shall notify the Federation which shall appoint an umpire. The Federation shall charge a fee, to be fixed by the Council from time to time, on such appointment.

(*c*) Only Trading, Full Broker and Full Non-Trading Members or their nominated representative/s to the Federation shall have the right to act as arbitrators or umpires subject to retirement at age 75, if still active in the trade, or two years after retirement, whichever comes first. No person shall be eligible to act who, or whose company or firm has any direct or indirect interest in the transaction in the dispute. No person shall be eligible to proceed as an arbitrator or umpire who is already proceeding as an arbitrator or umpire in 10 disputes, excluding arbitrations on quality and/or condition and any arbitration stayed by Order of the Court. Any arbitration other than on quality and/or condition that is being held as between the first Seller and the last Buyer in a string shall be counted as single dispute.

(*d*) If the party claiming arbitration has notified the other party and the Federation

---

[1] This document is reproduced with the kind permission of the Federation of Oil, Seeds and Fats Associations Ltd.

in accordance with Rule 2(a) or 2(b) and that party fails to appoint an arbitrator within the time specified, or in the event that an arbitrator refuses to act, becomes incapable of acting or ineligible to act, or delays unduly, and the party who made the appointment omits to appoint a substitute, then the other party may apply to the Federation in accordance with Rule 1(f) for the appointment of an arbitrator to act on behalf of the party who failed to appoint an arbitrator or substitute as the case may be.

(e) Any application to the Federation as mentioned under Rule 1(b) and 1(d) shall be accompanied by a copy of the notice of claim for arbitration together with a copy of the contract.

(f) The Federation on receiving an application to appoint under Rule 1(d) shall charge the appropriate fee fixed by the Council from time to time. The Federation will notify the party who has failed to make an appointment or a substitution of its arbitrator, as the case may be, that the Federation intends to make such an appointment unless that party makes its own appointment within 14 consecutive days of notice being dispatched to it by the Federation. In the absence of an appointment being notified to the Federation within the stipulated period the Federation shall make such an appointment.

2. Procedure for claiming arbitration and time limits

(a) Claims on quality and/or condition:

(i) If the claim is not to be supported by certificate/s of contractual analysis/ses, the party claiming arbitration shall despatch the notice of claim with the name of his appointed arbitrator to the other party within 21 consecutive days from the date of completion of discharge of the goods and shall at the same time notify the Federation and despatch sealed sample/s to the office of the Federation, where such sample/s shall be held at the disposal of the arbitrators and/or umpire. The other party shall nominate an arbitrator and notify his name to the Federation within 7 consecutive days from receipt of such notice. Notwithstanding the above, if the claimant requires a supporting analysis then a further sample shall have been dispatched to the analyst within 21 consecutive days from the date of completion of discharge of the goods.

For FOB, ex tank, ex mill and ex store contracts under 2(a) the word 'delivery' shall be read in place of 'discharge'.

(ii) If the claim is to be supported by certificate/s of contractual analysis/ses, the notice under 2(a)(i) shall be dispatched and the Federation notified within 14 consecutive days from the date of the final analysis certificate. The other party shall nominate an arbitrator and notify his name to the Federation within 7 consecutive days from the receipt of such notice.

(iii) If the claim relates to goods sold as fair average quality and the contract provides for a standard average for the month of shipment being made, the notice shall be dispatched and the Federation notified within 14 consecutive days of the publication in the trade lists that the standard has been or will not be made. The other party shall nominate an arbitrator and notify his name to the Federation within 7 consecutive days from the receipt of such notice.

A66–003

If the arbitration is not proceeded with within 14 consecutive days of the appointment of the arbitrator acting for the respondent, then either party may apply to the Federation in accordance with Rule 1(*d*) for the appointment of a substitute.

(*b*) Claims other than on quality and/or condition shall be notified by the claimant with the name of an arbitrator to the other party and to the Federation within the time limits stipulated in this Rule:

  (i) For goods sold

    (1) On CIF, CIFFO, C&F and similar contract terms: not later than 120 consecutive days after the expiry of the contract period of shipment or of the date of completion of final discharge of the goods whichever period shall last expire. The other party shall nominate an arbitrator and notify his name to the Federation within 30 consecutive days from receipt of such notice.

    (2) On FOB terms: not later than 120 consecutive days after the expiry of the contract period of shipment. The other party shall nominate an arbitrator and notify his name to the Federation within 30 consecutive days from receipt of such notice.

    (3) On any other terms: not later than 120 consecutive days after the last day of the contractual delivery period. The other party shall nominate an arbitrator and notify his name to the Federation within 30 consecutive days from receipt of such notice.

  (ii) In respect of any monies due by one party to the other, not later than 60 consecutive days after the dispute has arisen. The other party shall nominate an arbitrator and notify his name to the Federation within 30 consecutive days from receipt of such notice.

(*c*) Claims for arbitration shall be made by any means of rapid written communication (facsimile machines excluded unless acknowledgement is received). All notices shall be under reserve for errors in transmission. Notices shall be passed on with due despatch by intermediate Buyers and Sellers. Any notice received after 16.00 hours on a business day shall be deemed to have been received on the following business day. Notice from a broker shall be a valid notice under these Rules.

Should the time limit for doing any act or giving any notice expire on a Saturday, Sunday or any public holiday in the country where the party required to do the act or give the notice resides or carries on business or in the country where the act has to be done or the notice has to be received or on any day which the Federation shall declare to be a non-business day the time so limited shall be extended until the first business day thereafter. All business days shall be deemed to end at 16.00 hours Mondays to Fridays inclusive.

(*d*) In the event of non-compliance with any of the preceding provisions of this Rule, and of such non-compliance being raised by the respondents as a defence, claims shall be deemed to be waived and absolutely barred unless the arbitrators, umpire or Board of Appeal referred to in these Rules, shall, in their absolute discretion, otherwise determine. Either party has a right of appeal against the arbitrators'/umpire's decision, in which case the Board of Appeal have the same rights as the arbitrators under this clause.

(e) Failure to notify the Federation as required by Rule 1(a) 2(a) or 2(b) shall not in itself debar a claim for arbitration nor prevent an arbitration proceeding but shall be taken into account by arbitrators, umpire or Board of Appeal in exercising their discretion under Rule 2(d).

3. Lapse of claim

If neither the claimant nor the respondent submits any documentary evidence or submissions to the arbitrator appointed by or for him with the copy to the other party within the period of one year from the date of appointment of the first named arbitrator, then the claim to arbitration shall be deemed to have lapsed on expiry of the said period of one year unless before that date the claim is renewed by a further claim for arbitration to be made by either party notifying the other before the expiry date. Any such renewal shall be for a period of one year from the date of the giving of notice of renewal when it shall lapse again unless renewed in the like manner as the first renewal or unless by then documentary evidence or submissions have been submitted by either the claimant or the respondent. In the event of failure to renew a claim as provided in this Rule such claim shall be deemed to have been withdrawn and abandoned unless the arbitrator/s shall in his/their absolute discretion otherwise determine upon such terms as he/they may think fit.

4. Procedure for arbitrations

All submissions, interlocutory applications and related correspondence referred to under this Rule shall be dispatched within any of the specified time limits to:

one copy to each of the appointed arbitrators;
one copy to the Federation;
one copy to the other party.

(a) Claims under Rule 2(a) (quality and/or condition):

- (i) The party claiming arbitration shall despatch in writing his submission together with supporting documents within 10 consecutive days of the claim for arbitration.
- (ii) If the party against whom a claim is made wishes to reply to the claimants submission, such reply together with supporting documents shall be dispatched in writing within 14 consecutive days of the receipt thereof. Failing receipt of such reply, the arbitrators shall proceed with the arbitration without delay.
- (iii) In arbitration under Rule 2(a)(i) and 2(a)(iii), the Award of the arbitrator/s or umpire shall be dispatched to FOSFA International for typing within 28 consecutive days from the date of the claim or the date of the publication of the standard.

(b) Claims under 2(b) (other than on quality and/or condition):

- (i) The party claiming arbitration shall despatch in writing his submission together with supporting documents without delay.
- (ii) If the party against whom a claim is made wishes to reply, such reply together with supporting documents shall be dispatched in writing without delay. Failing receipt of such reply, the arbitrators shall proceed with the arbitration without delay.

(c) When arbitrators appoint an umpire they shall also notify the Federation.

(d) A sole arbitrator or the arbitrators, by mutual agreement, or the umpire, or the Board of Appeal, as the case may be, shall have discretion to extend the time limits under Rule 4(a).

(e) If one party has submitted any document to the arbitrator/s which has not been submitted to the other party, then a copy thereof shall be supplied to that party by the arbitrator/s prior to the hearing.

(f) The arbitrator/s or the umpire, as the case may be, shall have the power to request further information or documents from either of the parties, to hear oral submissions or evidence if they or he so desire and to make such directions relating to the conduct of the arbitration as they or he think fit. The parties shall be entitled to a reasonable period within which to comply with any such request but the arbitrators or the umpire, as the case may be, having given reasonable notice, may make an Award if such requests have not been complied with.

(g) If either party has expressed a wish to be present, the arbitrators or the umpire shall give reasonable notice to the parties of the date, time and place when any oral evidence or additional submissions may be heard and both parties to the arbitration or their authorised representatives may attend any such hearing but may not have present or be represented by counsel, solicitor or any member of the legal profession wholly or principally engaged in legal practice.

(h) The arbitrator/s or the umpire at their absolute discretion may require the claimant to lodge a deposit with the Federation on account of the fees, costs and expenses of the arbitration before proceeding. If after the expiration of 14 consecutive days after the notification to the claimant of the deposit required the claimant not having paid such deposit, the arbitration shall be stayed until such time as the deposit is paid. In the event that the deposit is not paid within 28 consecutive days the arbitration shall be deemed to be permanently stayed unless the arbitrator/s or umpire in the exercise of their absolute discretion decide to continue the arbitration.

(i) If any party to an arbitration considers that either arbitrator or the umpire is failing to exercise all reasonable despatch in entering on or proceeding with the arbitration then that party may notify the Federation accordingly in writing with full details. Upon receipt of such notice the Federation shall call upon the arbitrator or umpire to explain the reasons for the delay. The arbitrator or umpire must furnish the Federation with such an explanation within 7 days of the Federation's request for such an explanation. If the Federation is not satisfied with the arbitrators' or umpire's explanation the Federation shall fix a 7 day period in which the arbitrator or umpire is to take the next step required to be done in proceeding with the arbitration. Should the arbitrator or umpire fail to respond to the Federation's request for an explanation or fail to take the next step required to be done in proceeding with the arbitration, within the 7 day period then the Federation shall have the right to require the arbitrator or umpire to resign his position as arbitrator or umpire in that particular arbitration. The arbitrator or umpire shall be deemed to have resigned his position 14 consecutive days after despatch to him of the Federation's written requirement that he resigns his appointment unless otherwise decided by the Federation.

An arbitrator or umpire who is called upon to resign his position as arbitrator or umpire under this provision shall not be entitled to receive any remuneration in respect of his services provided in the particular arbitration in question unless otherwise decided by the Federation. Where an arbitrator resigns his position under this provision then the party who appointed the arbitrator shall appoint another duly qualified arbitrator in his place within 14 days of the notice being dispatched in accordance with the provisions of Rule 1. If that party does not so appoint then the Federation shall make such an appointment and shall charge the defaulting party the appropriate fee fixed by the Council from time to time being in force.

Where an umpire resigns his position under this provision then the two arbitrators who have appointed him shall appoint another umpire in his place, within 7 days of being notified of the resignation of the umpire. If the arbitrators do not so appoint then the Federation shall make such an appointment in accordance with its powers under Rule 1(b).

In circumstances where an arbitrator or umpire is removed from an arbitration by the Federation as provided for above, the Federation may, by a decision of the Council, also suspend or remove that person's right to act as an arbitrator or umpire and to serve on the Appeal Panel.

5. Jurisdiction

(a) The arbitrators may rule on their own jurisdiction as to whether there is a valid arbitration agreement. If arbitrators agree that they have no jurisdiction they shall jointly advise the parties in writing.

(b) If the arbitrators cannot agree that they have jurisdiction they shall appoint an umpire under Rule 1(b) who shall first determine the question of jurisdiction.

(c) If the umpire decides that he has no jurisdiction then he shall advise the arbitrators in writing who shall advise the parties in writing.

(d) If the umpire decides that he does have jurisdiction, he shall proceed with the arbitration without delay.

(e) A right of appeal to the Appeal Panel of the Federation shall apply to Rules 5(a) and 5(c).

6. Procedure for arbitration awards

(a) Awards, which shall incorporate the reasons therefore, shall be in writing on the official form of the Federation and the arbitrators or the umpire shall have the power to assess and award their fees and award by whom these and other fees and expenses of the arbitration shall be paid. The Federation's fees shall be those in force as prescribed by the Council of the Federation.

(b) When an Award has been signed it shall be the duty of the arbitrators or the umpire to lodge the original and one copy with the Federation who shall date them and give notice to the parties named in the award that the award is at their disposal upon payment of the fees and expenses of the arbitration. Such payment must be received by the Federation within 42 days of the date of the award or the parties shall forfeit their right to appeal against the award under Rule 7. On receipt of payment, the Federation shall immediately send the original award to the party who has paid and send a copy to the other party. Until payment has been made, the contents of the award shall under no circumstances be divulged.

(c) Should the contract form part of a string of contracts which are in all material points identical in terms, except as to the date and price, then:

(i) In any arbitration for quality and/or condition, as mentioned in Rule 2(a), the arbitration shall be held as between the first Seller and the last Buyer in the string as though they were contracting parties.

Any Award so made (in these Rules called the String Award) shall, subject to the right of appeal as provided in these Rules, be binding on all the intermediate parties in the string, and may be enforced by any intermediate party against his immediate contracting party as though a separate award has been made under each contract.

(ii) In other cases arbitration shall only be held as between the first Seller and the last Buyer in a string as though they were contracting parties if all parties in the string agree in writing and provided each intermediate party shall have submitted his contract and all relevant information to the arbitrators. A separate Award shall be made in respect of each contract.

7. Procedure for claiming appeal and time limits

(a) Any party to an award of arbitration shall have the right to appeal to the Appeal Panel of the Federation provided that payment of the fees and expenses of the arbitration was made to the Federation within 42 days of the date of the award as per Rule 6(b) and that notice of appeal is received by the Federation not later than 12.00 hours on the 28th consecutive day after the date on which the award is sent to the parties, in accordance with Rule 6(b).

(b) The appellant when giving notice of appeal to the Federation shall at the same time send a copy to the other principal to the contract and arrange to pay to the Federation a deposit as prescribed by the Council of the Federation on account of fees, costs and expenses of the appeal, which is to be received by the Federation not later than 7 consecutive days after receipt of the notice of appeal. If due to currency regulations payment of the deposit is not possible within the 7 day time limit an extension of 14 consecutive days shall be granted for the payment of the deposit provided that the appellant has produced satisfactory evidence from a bank that the application for the transfer of the deposit has been made.

(c) Every notice given to a party to any string Award shall be passed on with due despatch by that party and such passing on, provided it is done with due despatch shall be deemed to be in compliance with the procedure for claiming appeal.

(d) Should it not be possible to perform any of the foregoing acts within the time limits stipulated, application may be made to the Federation for an extension of the time limit, which extension may be granted at the absolute discretion of the Federation.

(e) The appellant shall within 21 days of lodging the appeal, provide the Federation and the other party with an outline of the reasons for appeal.

FOSFA International Rules of Arbitration and Appeal

8. Procedure for appointment of Boards of Appeal

(*a*) The appeal shall be determined by a Board of Appeal consisting of five members appropriately appointed by the Federation from the Appeal Panel. No member of the Panel who, or whose company or firm, has any direct or indirect interest in the transaction in dispute or who has acted as arbitrator or umpire in the case, nor any member of the same company or firm to which either of the arbitrators or the umpire belong, shall be entitled to be appointed a member of the Board of Appeal. **A66–009**

(*b*) In the case of illness or death, or refusal, or incapacity, or inability to act, of any member appointed to serve on a Board of Appeal, the Federation shall appoint a substitute from the Appeal Panel in his place. Nevertheless if only four members of the Board are able to serve on the day of the substantive hearing, they may, subject to the agreement of the parties or of their duly authorised representatives, exercise all the powers of the Board of Appeal.

(*c*) In the event of appeals lodged by more than one party in relation to the same Award, the Federation shall consolidate such appeals for hearing by the same Board of Appeal.

9. Procedure at appeals

(*a*) Each party may state their case orally and/or in writing and may appear either personally or be represented by a listed representative in the appropriate section of a Trading, Full Broker or Full Non-Trading member of the Federation and duly appointed in writing, but shall not be represented by or have present at the hearing of such appeal, Counsel or Solicitor, or any member of the legal profession wholly or principally engaged in legal practice, unless, at the sole discretion of the Board of Appeal, the case is of special importance, and in such cases the other party shall have the same rights. **A66–010**

(*b*) The Board of Appeal shall issue a reasoned Award signed by the Chairman on behalf of the Board and counter-signed by the Secretary to the Board of Appeal after confirmation that the majority agree the Award, and when so signed shall be the Award of the Board of Appeal which shall be final and binding.

(*c*) In respect of any String Award made by a Board of Appeal such String Award shall be binding on the first Sellers, the last Buyers, and all the intermediate parties in the string and may be enforced by any intermediate party against his immediate contracting party as though a separate award had been made under each contract.

(*d*) The Board of Appeal shall have the power to require from time to time a further deposit/s to be made by either party and shall award the payment of appeal fees, costs and expenses of, and incidental to, the appeal. If an Award is remitted to a Board of Appeal by Order of the Court the Board shall have the power to require a deposit to be made by the party/ies that made application to the Court on account of the fees, costs and expenses of any hearing by the Board of submissions by the parties or of any meeting of the Board occasioned by such remission. No interest shall be payable on any deposit or further deposit made by any party to an appeal under the provisions either of this Rule or Rule 7.

(*e*) If the appellant, on receiving from the Board of Appeal notice of the date fixed for the hearing of the appeal, requests a postponement of more than 14 days or at the first or any subsequent hearing of the appeal requests an adjournment, then in such events the Board of Appeal may at their absolute discretion direct that as a condition of granting a postponement or an adjournment all or any part of the money required by the terms of the award of arbitration to be paid by either party to the other shall be deposited in a bank (either in England or abroad) as the Board of Appeal may direct. Such money shall be held by such bank in an account in the name of the Federation and otherwise in such terms as the Board of Appeal directs.

The Board of Appeal shall, where such money has been deposited, in their Award direct how and to which of the parties the amount so held shall be paid out. Provided that, if in the opinion of the Board of Appeal after hearing the parties, the appellant shall have delayed unduly the proceedings of his appeal, he shall after due warning and if the Board of Appeal so decides, be deemed to have withdrawn his appeal in which case the money on deposit (with interest, if any, less tax) shall immediately become due and payable to the party or parties entitled thereto under the terms of the Award of Arbitration.

10. Withdrawal of appeals

A66–011   (*a*) An appellant shall have the right at any time before the hearing of the appeal to withdraw his appeal subject to payment of such costs, if any, as the Federation or the Board of Appeal may determine:

    (i) On notice being received from the appellant at least 24 hours before the appointment of the Board of Appeal half of the deposit shall be returned.
    (ii) On notice being received at least 72 hours before the time fixed for the hearing by the Board of Appeal one quarter shall be returned.
    (iii) If such notice of withdrawal is received after that time no part of the deposit shall be returned.
    (iv) When an appeal is withdrawn before any action has been taken by the Federation the deposit shall be refunded.

(*b*) In the event of such withdrawal as aforesaid any other party to an Award of Arbitration shall have a right of appeal against that award to the Appeal Panel of the Federation in accordance with the provisions of Rule 6 save that the time limit for giving notice of appeal laid down in Rule 7(*a*) shall be 12.00 hours on the 21st consecutive day after the date of the Federation's notice to that party of the aforesaid withdrawal.

11. General

A66–012   (*a*) (i) Any objection to the membership of a Board of Appeal on the ground that a member of the Board of Appeal was not eligible to serve must be made in writing and established to the satisfaction of the Council of the Federation before the hearing of the substantive case has commenced.
    (ii) If such objection is made the Federation in its absolute discretion shall have the power to appoint a substitute member or members of a Board of Appeal from the Appeal Panel up to the beginning of the hearing of the substantive case.
    (iii) No Award of a Board of Appeal shall be questioned or invalidated on the ground of any irregularity in the appointment of the Board of Appeal or

any of its members or on the ground that any member of the Board of Appeal was not eligible to serve.

(*b*) Any notice may be delivered personally or left at the place where the party to whom it is to be delivered is carrying on business or (by reason of the provisions of the contract) is to be considered to be carrying on business. A copy shall be delivered to the Federation.

(*c*) If an Arbitration or an Appeal Award is not taken up by any of the parties to the dispute within 28 consecutive days after the date of the Award, the Federation shall call upon the claimant or the appellant, as the case may be, to take up the Award. If the claimant or the appellant fail to take up the Award, the Council of the Federation may post on the Federation's notice board and/or circularise to members in any way thought fit a notification to that effect. The parties to any such arbitration or appeal held under these Rules shall be deemed to have consented to the Council taking such action.

(*d*) In the event of any party to an arbitration or appeal held under these Rules neglecting or refusing to carry out or abide by an Award of arbitrators or umpire or Board of Appeal made under these Rules, the Council of the Federation may post on the Federation's Notice Board and/or circularise to members in any way thought fit a notification to that effect. The parties to any such arbitration or appeal shall be deemed to have consented to the Council taking such action.

Sports Dispute Resolution Panel ("SDRP") Arbitration Rules[1]

1. Introduction

A67–001 1.1 The following Rules (as amended by the SDRP from time to time) ("the Rules") shall apply where any agreement, submission or reference provides in writing for arbitration, hearing or resolution under the Rules of the SDRP or by the SDRP. In such event the parties shall be taken to have agreed that the arbitration shall be conducted in accordance with these Rules.

1.2 In relation to arbitrations under these Rules, the role of the SDRP is:

(a) to establish or assist in establishing tribunals with power to resolve sports disputes in accordance with these Rules; and

(b) to assist in the smooth running of the associated proceedings.

1.3 The responsibility of such tribunals is (amongst other things) to resolve:

(a) the disputes referred to them under the Appeal Arbitration Procedure; or

(b) the disputes referred to them under the Full Arbitration Procedure.

1.4 The Director of the SDRP shall decide in case of doubt which of the two procedures is to be followed. Such decision may not be challenged or raised as a cause of irregularity.

2. Appeal Arbitration Procedure

A67–002 2.1 A party (the "Appellant") may appeal from a disciplinary, doping, selection or other decision of a sports federation, governing body, club, association or other body in so far as the regulations of the relevant body or a specific arbitration agreement provide for the appeal to be heard under the Rules of the SDRP or by the SDRP and, unless the parties otherwise agree, insofar as the Appellant has exhausted all other procedures available under any applicable regulations.

Notice of Appeal

A67–003 2.2 The Appellant shall submit to the SDRP and serve on the Respondent a notice of appeal containing or accompanied by (collectively referred to as the "Notice of Appeal"):

(a) the names and addresses and the relevant contact details of all the parties and notification if any are under the age of eighteen (with their date of birth (if known));

(b) details, and where available a copy, of the decision appealed from;

(c) the Appellant's request for relief or remedy;

(d) if applicable an application to stay the execution of the decision appealed from together with the reasons;

---

[1] This document is reproduced with the kind permission of the Sports Dispute Resolution Panel. The new Rules were adopted on October 16, 2002.

Sports Dispute Resolution Panel ("SDRP") Arbitration Rules

(e) a copy of the regulations or the specific written agreement of both parties providing for appeal arbitration under the Rules of the SDRP or by the SDRP; and

(f) any non-refundable deposit as set by the SDRP from time to time.

Time-limit

2.3 In the absence of a time-limit set in the regulations of the sports body concerned or of a previous subsisting agreement, the time-limit for the receipt by the SDRP and for the service by the Appellant on the Respondent of the Notice of Appeal shall be twenty-one (21) days from the date of the decision from which the appeal is made or to be made. **A67–004**

Statement of Appeal

2.4 Within ten (10) days of the expiry of the time-limit as set out in 2.3 above, the Appellant shall submit to the SDRP and serve on the Respondent a Statement of Appeal (failing which the appeal shall be deemed to be withdrawn) containing or accompanied by (collectively referred to as the "Statement of Appeal"): **A67–005**

(a) a statement of the facts and any law giving rise to the appeal and upon which the Appellant is relying;

(b) copies of all documents upon which the Appellant is relying;

(c) a statement of any procedural matters upon which the parties have already agreed or proposals in relation to such procedure, including but not limited to apportioning costs, the location of the arbitration, any variations from the existing Rules relating to any timetable, decision-making powers, confidentiality, the number and qualification of the arbitrator(s) or any other matters.

Reply

2.5 Within fourteen (14) days of receipt by the Respondent of the Statement of Appeal, the Respondent shall submit to the SDRP and serve on the Appellant a reply containing or accompanied by (collectively referred to as the "Reply"): **A67–006**

(a) confirmation or denial of all or part of the Appellant's Statement of Appeal, setting out as fully as possible the facts and any law in the claim which the Respondent admits or denies, on what grounds and any other facts and law upon which the Respondent relies;

(b) copies of all documents on which the Respondent is relying unless the document has been previously submitted by the Appellant;

(c) any proposals in relation to the appeal procedure.

Further written submissions

2.6 Unless the Tribunal permits or directs otherwise, the parties shall not submit further written argument(s) after the time limited for the submission of the Statement of Appeal or the Reply as the case may be. **A67–007**

2.7 If the Respondent fails to submit its Reply within the time-limit set, the Tribunal may nevertheless proceed with the arbitration and deliver its award.

Communication of the decision

A67–008 2.8 The written decision and its reasons shall be communicated by the Tribunal to the parties and a copy sent to the SDRP as soon as possible and ordinarily within two (2) months after the receipt by the SDRP of the Notice of Appeal, unless the parties otherwise agree.

3. Full Arbitration Procedure

A67–009 3.1 If any party wishes to bring a matter to arbitration under this Full Arbitration Procedure that party or parties ("the Applicant") shall submit to the SDRP and serve on the Respondent a written notice to arbitrate under this Full Arbitration Procedure containing or accompanied by (collectively referred to as the "Notice"):

>   (a) the names and addresses and the relevant contact details of all the parties to the arbitration and notification if any are under the age of eighteen (with their date of birth (if known));
>
>   (b) a copy of the contractual documents in which the arbitration clause is contained or the specific written agreement of the parties providing for arbitration under the Rules of the SDRP or by the SDRP;
>
>   (c) a statement describing the nature and circumstances of the dispute, and specifying the Applicant's claim(s) against the other party/parties to the arbitration (the "Respondent") and the relief claimed or the remedy sought;
>
>   (d) any non-refundable deposit as set by the SDRP from time to time.

3.2 The date of receipt by the SDRP of the Notice shall be the date the arbitration commenced ("the Commencement Date").

Statement of Claim

A67–010 3.3 Within twenty-one (21) days of the Commencement Date the Applicant shall submit to the SDRP and serve on the Respondent a Statement of Claim (failing which the arbitration shall be deemed to be withdrawn) containing or accompanied by (collectively referred to as the "Statement of Claim"):

>   (a) a statement of the facts and any law giving rise to the arbitration and upon which the Applicant is relying;
>
>   (b) copies of all documents upon which the Applicant is relying;
>
>   (c) a statement of any procedural matters upon which the parties have already agreed or proposals in relation to such procedure, including but not limited to apportioning costs, the location of the arbitration, any variations from the existing Rules relating to any timetable, decision-making powers, confidentiality, the number and qualification of the arbitrator(s) or any other matters.

Sports Dispute Resolution Panel ("SDRP") Arbitration Rules

Reply of the Respondent

3.4 Within twenty-one (21) days of the receipt by the Respondent of the Statement of Claim the Respondent shall send to the SDRP a reply containing or accompanied by (collectively referred to as the "Reply"):

(a) confirmation or denial of all or part of the Applicant's Statement of Claim, setting out as fully as possible the facts and any law in the claim which the Respondent admits or denies, on what grounds and any other facts and law upon which the Respondent relies;

(b) a statement of the nature and circumstances of any counterclaims specifying the Respondent's counterclaim(s) against the Applicant, the relief claimed or the remedy sought and the facts and law upon which the Respondent is relying ("the Counterclaim");

(c) copies of all documents on which the Respondent is relying unless the document has been previously submitted by the Applicant;

(d) any proposals in relation to the arbitration procedure.

Further written submissions

3.5 The Applicant may within twenty-one (21) days of the receipt by it of any Counterclaim, submit to the SDRP and serve on the Respondent a defence to such Counterclaim (the "Defence to Counterclaim"). Unless the Tribunal permits or directs otherwise, the parties shall not submit further written argument(s) after the submission of the Statement of Appeal, the Reply, the Counterclaim or the Defence to Counterclaim as the case may be.

3.6 If the Respondent fails to submit or serve its Reply or any Counterclaim or the Applicant any Defence to Counterclaim within the time-limit set, the Tribunal may nevertheless proceed with the arbitration and deliver its award.

Communication of the decision

3.7 The written decision and its reasons shall be communicated by the Tribunal to the parties and a copy sent to the SDRP as soon as possible and ordinarily within four (4) months after the receipt by the SDRP of the Notice unless the parties otherwise agree.

4. Communications

4.1 The parties and the Tribunal shall communicate through the SDRP on procedural matters (save for documents required under these Rules to be served on another party). The Director of the SDRP may direct that communication shall take place directly between the Tribunal and the parties with copies of all correspondence and documents to be sent at the same time to the SDRP.

4.2 Any communication from one party to the SDRP or to the Tribunal, must be accompanied by a copy for the Tribunal or the SDRP (as the case may be), and a copy sent to the other party.

4.3 All communications shall be delivered or sent by first class post, fax or email to the parties at the addresses set out for each in the Notice of Appeal or Notice, or at such address as any party may have previously notified the SDRP, the Tribunal and the other parties.

5. Conciliation

A67–015 5.1 The Director of the SDRP before the formation of the Tribunal, and thereafter the Tribunal, may encourage the parties to seek to resolve the dispute by conciliation.

6. Formation of the Tribunal

A67–016 6.1 Any dispute submitted to the SDRP shall be decided by a one or three member tribunal ("the Tribunal") appointed by the Director of the SDRP unless the parties have otherwise agreed in writing (within any timescale notified by the Director of the SDRP) that they wish to make their respective nomination(s) in accordance with Rule 6.2 or 6.3. The Director of SDRP shall decide whether to appoint a one or three member tribunal as he considers appropriate in all the circumstances and in discussion with the parties unless the parties have agreed in writing whether the Tribunal should consist of one or three members.

6.2 Where the parties have agreed that the Tribunal is to consist of one arbitrator and that the parties wish to agree a nomination, the Director of the SDRP shall propose to the parties the name(s) of potential arbitrators. The parties shall seek to agree on one, whom they shall nominate to be appointed by the Director of the SDRP. That one Arbitrator shall constitute a valid Tribunal. If the parties fail to agree, the Director of the SDRP shall appoint the Arbitrator.

6.3 Where the parties agree that the Tribunal shall consist of three arbitrators and that the parties wish to nominate an arbitrator each they shall notify the Director of the SDRP accordingly. Each party shall be permitted to nominate one arbitrator. The Director of the SDRP shall propose to the parties the names of potential arbitrators from whom the parties shall seek to make their respective nominations to the Director of the SDRP for him to appoint.

6.4 If either party fails to nominate an arbitrator in accordance with these Rules, the arbitrator for that party shall be chosen by the Director of the SDRP. If the parties nominate the same individual, that nomination shall remain and the Director of the SDRP shall choose the second arbitrator. The Arbitrators selected by (or on behalf of) the parties shall seek to choose the third Arbitrator from the list of potential Chairperson arbitrators as proposed by the Director of the SDRP (which arbitrator will act as Chairperson of the Tribunal). In the absence of agreement or if the parties so request the third Arbitrator shall be chosen by the Director of the SDRP from the SDRP's list of Chairperson arbitrators.

6.5 The SDRP shall notify the parties of the name(s) of the Arbitrator(s) who are to constitute the Tribunal and in the case of a three member Tribunal, which Arbitrator has been appointed Chairperson.

6.6 A party may challenge the appointment of an Arbitrator where there are justifiable doubts as to the Arbitrator's impartiality or independence or where the party raises any material objection(s). If a party intends to challenge any appointment that party shall, within seven days of notification by the Director of the SDRP of the appointment, submit in writing to the Chairman of the SDRP Panel Appointments Board (the "PAB") (with a copy to the Tribunal and the SDRP) the reasons why that party is challenging the Arbitrator. Unless the challenged Arbitrator withdraws or the other party agrees to the challenge, the Chairman of the PAB shall decide on the challenge in accordance with the SDRP's procedures for the appointment and removal of Arbitrators and that decision shall be final.

6.7 If any Arbitrator, after appointment to a Tribunal dies, gives written notice of the desire to resign, is removed, refuses to act, or in the opinion of the Chairman of the PAB becomes unable or unfit to act, the Director of the SDRP shall, in accordance with the SDRP's procedures for the appointment and removal of Arbitrators appoint another Arbitrator to the Tribunal in his/her place (to act as Chairperson if the circumstances require) and shall so inform the parties and any remaining members of the Tribunal. Alternatively, if the parties so agree, the remaining members of any three member Tribunal may proceed in the Arbitrator's absence.

6.8 If in the opinion of the majority of the Tribunal, any Arbitrator has refused or failed to comply with the Rules or any applicable law relating to the making of the decision and/or award, having been given a reasonable opportunity to do so, the other Arbitrator(s) (if any) may remove him and the remaining Arbitrator(s) shall proceed in his absence.

6.9 Any appointment or removal required to be made by the Director of the SDRP or the Chairman of the PAB under these Rules shall be made in accordance with the SDRP's procedures for the appointment and removal of Arbitrators and after giving full consideration to the nature and circumstances of the matter, the location of the parties and any other relevant factor(s). Every Arbitrator conducting an arbitration under these Rules shall be independent, impartial, suitably qualified and capable and shall not act as advocate for any party.

6.10 In the case of any former member of the Tribunal, the Chairman of the PAB shall decide on the amount of the former Arbitrator's fees and expenses (if any). The remaining member(s) and any replacement member(s) of the Tribunal (or if the Tribunal is unable to decide the Chairman of the PAB in accordance with the SDRP's procedures for the appointment and removal of Arbitrators), shall decide upon the status of any prior decisions or existing proceedings of the Tribunal.

7. Jurisdiction of the Tribunal

7.1 The Tribunal may decide on its own jurisdiction, including whether the Tribunal **A67–017** is properly constituted, what matters have been submitted and any objections with respect to the existence or validity of an arbitration agreement. For that purpose, an arbitration clause which forms part of a contract or part of the rules and/or procedures of a sports body in the United Kingdom shall be treated as an agreement independent of the other terms of the contract or rules and/or procedures. If the Tribunal decides that the contract is void or the rules and/or procedures invalid or otherwise unenforceable this shall not prejudice the validity of the arbitration clause.

8. Conduct of the Proceedings

8.1 The Tribunal shall conduct the proceedings of the arbitration in such manner as it **A67–018** considers fit and may follow any arbitral procedure agreed by the parties if it is in the Tribunal's opinion reasonably practicable so to do. The Tribunal shall act in accordance with these Rules and any other applicable regulations. With the consent of the parties, the Tribunal may proceed in an expedited manner for which it shall issue appropriate directions. Any decision of the Tribunal in relation to the conduct of the proceedings shall be consistent with its duties at all times to act fairly and impartially, to allow the parties reasonable opportunity to put their respective cases and to deal with that of their opponent and to avoid unnecessary delay or expense, so as to provide a fair and efficient means for resolving the dispute.

9. Hearings

A67–019 9.1 The Tribunal shall subject to any agreement of the parties fix the date, time and place of any hearings in the arbitration and shall give the parties as much notice as practicable either directly or via the SDRP of the date, time and place of any hearing.

9.2 Any party requesting an oral hearing has the right to be heard in front of the Tribunal. In the absence of any such request, the Tribunal shall endeavour to reach a decision without a hearing on the basis of the written evidence.

9.3 Any such hearings shall be in private unless the parties agree otherwise or unless the Tribunal directs.

10. Witnesses

A67–020 10.1 The parties must notify the Tribunal and other parties as soon as practicable and within any time limits set by the Tribunal of the identity of any witnesses they wish to call and, if the Tribunal requires it, each party shall disclose the subject matter and content of the evidence on which each such witness will be relying and how that evidence relates to the points at issue and the Tribunal shall have power to decide whether such witness shall be required to attend or be called to give evidence at any hearing.

10.2 The Tribunal may question a witness at any stage and shall control the questioning of a witness by the other parties.

11. Experts

A67–021 11.1 The Tribunal may, provided it shall have notified the parties, appoint one or more experts acting independently and impartially of the parties to report to the Tribunal on specific issues and may require a party to give such an expert any relevant information or to produce, or to provide access to, any relevant documents, goods or property for inspection by the expert.

11.2 The Tribunal may (unless the parties shall otherwise agree) direct an expert witness to give evidence either before a hearing in the form of a written report and/or at the hearing in the form of an oral report, and may also require an expert witness to attend a hearing so that the Tribunal or the parties may question him or her.

11.3 The fees and expenses of any expert appointed by the Tribunal shall form part of the costs of the arbitration.

11.4 The parties must notify the Tribunal and other parties as soon as practicable and within any time limits set by the Tribunal of the identity of any expert they wish to call and, if the Tribunal requires it, each party shall disclose the subject matter and content of the evidence on which each such expert will be relying and how that evidence relates to the points at issue and the Tribunal shall have power to decide whether such expert shall be required to attend or be called to give evidence at any hearing.

11.5 The Tribunal may question any expert at any stage and shall control the questioning of any expert by the other parties.

12. Decisions and Powers of the Tribunal

A67–022 12.1 The decision and/or award of the Tribunal shall be in writing and shall be dated and signed by the Arbitrator(s), and shall state the reasons on which it is based.

12.2 Where there are three arbitrators, the Tribunal shall decide on any issue by a majority and if the Tribunal fails to reach a majority decision on any issue, the decision of the Chairperson of the Tribunal shall be final.

12.3 The sole arbitrator or Chairperson of the Tribunal shall arrange for the decision and/or award to be delivered to the SDRP and the SDRP shall transmit certified copies to the parties.

12.4 All decisions and/or awards of the Tribunal shall be final and binding on the parties and on any party claiming through or under them and the parties agree, by submitting to arbitration under these Rules, to waive irrevocably their right to any form of appeal, review or recourse to any state court or other judicial authority, subject to any applicable statutory or other rights.

12.5 The Tribunal shall have the powers as set out in the Act, including the powers to make a declaration on any matter to be determined in the proceedings, to order the payment of a sum of money by way of damages or otherwise including the award of simple or compound interest on the whole or part of any amount, to order a party to do or refrain from doing anything, to order specific performance of a contract (except one relating to land), and to order the rectification, setting aside or cancellation of a deed.

12.6 In addition, the Tribunal shall have the power:

(a) to allow any party to amend its written case and/or to submit further evidence;

(b) to extend or abbreviate any time-limit provided by these Rules or any arbitration agreement;

(c) to conduct enquiries;

(d) to order any party to make any property under its control available for inspection by the Tribunal;

(e) to order the production to the Tribunal and the other party/parties for inspection, copies of any documents in a party's control which the Tribunal considers relevant;

(f) to decide which rules of evidence on admissibility, relevance and/or weight shall apply;

(g) to dismiss a claim or to proceed in the absence of one or more of the parties, in the event of a failure to comply with any directions of the Tribunal;

(h) to consolidate proceedings subject to the consent in writing of all the parties concerned;

(i) to join any other party to the proceedings on the application of a party, subject to the consent in writing of such third party; and

(j) to order on an interim basis, subject to final determination in a decision and/or award, any relief or remedy which the Tribunal would have the power to grant in a final decision and/or award including a provisional order for security for costs, any deposit, the payment of any other money, to order a party to do or refrain from doing anything, and/or in any appeal, staying execution of the decision below. The Tribunal may not make any interim order or grant any provisional award unless and until the Notice of Appeal or the Notice as the case may be have been properly submitted and served.

13. Costs

13.1 The amount of the costs of the arbitration (i.e. the costs of the SDRP, the Tribunal and any experts appointed by the Tribunal) shall be determined by the Director of the SDRP in accordance with the SDRP's procedures in force at the time. Unless the parties otherwise agree or unless the Tribunal otherwise directs or unless any applicable regulations otherwise provide each party shall be liable to the SDRP for an equal share of the costs of the arbitration.

13.2 The parties shall be responsible for their own legal and other costs unless the parties otherwise agree or unless the Tribunal otherwise directs or unless any applicable regulations otherwise provide. The Tribunal shall also have the power unless the parties otherwise agree or any applicable regulations otherwise provide to order that all or part of the legal costs and any other costs incurred by a party be paid by another party.

14. Confidentiality

A67–024 14.1 Subject to Rule 9.3 above, the proceedings shall be confidential. The parties, the SDRP and the Tribunal undertake to keep confidential all documents and any other materials produced for the purpose of the arbitration by any party and/or participant in the arbitration—except to the extent that disclosure may be required by a legal duty, to pursue or protect a legal right, to enforce or challenge an award in bona fide legal proceedings or that such documents may already be in the public domain (otherwise than in breach of this undertaking).

14.2 Notwithstanding Rule 14.1 the SDRP may publish the Tribunal's award or decision and its reasons in any appeal arbitration conducted under these Rules unless the parties expressly agree prior to the Tribunal making its award or decision that they should remain confidential. In the case of any arbitration conducted under these Rules the SDRP may publish generic, non-identifying information relating to that arbitration.

15. Applicable Law

A67–025 15.1 The seat of the arbitration shall be London, unless otherwise determined by the Tribunal. However, the Tribunal may at its discretion hold a hearing in another place.

15.2 Procedurally, arbitrations under these Rules shall be governed by the Arbitration Act 1996 ("the Act") unless otherwise determined by the Tribunal, and shall incorporate all the provisions of the Act (save for non-mandatory provisions expressly excluded or modified by these Rules or by the agreement of the parties).

15.3 Substantively, arbitrations under these Rules shall be decided in accordance with the law of England and Wales unless otherwise agreed in writing by the parties or unless otherwise directed by the Tribunal.

16. General Rules

A67–026 16.1 If a party proceeds with an arbitration notwithstanding the fact that a provision of, or requirement under these Rules has not been complied with without promptly stating its objection that party shall have waived its right to object.

As amended 16 October 2002.

Consumer ODR Schemes

Arbitration

The following ODR providers offer arbitration for consumers: **A68–001**

    Chartered Institute of Arbitrators (www.arbitrators.org/WebTrader/index.htm)
    The Internet Ombudsman (www.ombudsman.at)
    MARS (www.resolvemydispute.com)
    NovaForum (www.novaforum.com)
    WebAssured (www.webassured.com)
    IntelliCOURT (http://www.intellicourt.com/how_it_works.html)

Evaluation

The following providers offer online evaluation for consumers: **A68–002**

    ECODIR (www.ecodir.org)
    The Virtual Magistrate (www.vmag.org)

Mock Trial

iCourthouse offers mock trials (www.i-courthouse.com) **A68–003**

Mediation

The following ODR providers offer online mediation for consumers: **A68–004**

    Squaretrade (http://www.squaretrade.com/cnt/jsp/index.jsp)
    E-Mediator (http://www.consensus.uk.com/e-mediator.html)
    Internet Neutral (http://www.internetneutral.com/)
    The Internet Ombudsmann (http://www.ombudsman.at)
    MARS Fair & Square Program (www.resolvemydispute.com)
    NovaForum (www.novaforum.com)
    ECODIR (www.ecodir.org)
    Online Resolution (http://www.onlineresolution.com/index-om.cfm)
    Resolution Forum Inc (http://www.resolutionforum.org/services.html)
    WebAssured (www.webassured.com)

Automated Settlement Assistance

The following ODR providers offer Automated Settlement Systems: **A68–005**

    ClickNSettle (http://www.clicknsettle.com)
    Cybersettle (http://www.cybersettle.com)
    MARS (www.resolvemydispute.com)
    SettleOnline (www.settleonline.com)
    SettleSmart (http://www.settlesmart.com)

Complaints Assistance

The following ODR providers offer complaints assistance: **A68–006**

    UK Citizens Advice Bureaux, Online Advice & Advice per email

(http://www.nacab.org.uk/dir_emws.ihtml)
(http://www.adviceguide.org.uk/nacab/plsql/nacab.homepage)
US Better Business Bureaus (http://www.bbbonline.org)
Austria: The Internet Ombudsman (http://www.ombudsman.at)
NovaForum (www.novaforum.com)
Squaretrade (http://www.squaretrade.com/cnt/jsp/index.jsp)
WebAssured (www.webassured.com)
Which? Webtrader (http://whichwebtrader.which.net/webtrader/index.html)
Trusted Shops (http://www.trustedshops.de/en/home/index.html)
TrustUK (http://www.trustuk.org.uk)
Econsumer scheme (http://www.econsumer.gov)
Howtocomplain.com (http://www.howtocomplain.com)

Online Dispute Resolution Providers

A69–001

Name and web-page and country	Types of disputes	ADR techniques offered	Communication or online technology	Security provisions or technology	Short description	Procedure or filing	Cost or funding
Allsette (US) www.allsettle.com	Insurance claims.	Blind bidding.	Completely online, no initial contact with third party.	Password protected secure web page.	Median amount if offer and demand are within one third of each other.	Parties make confidential offers considering highest demand and bottom line.	US $200 only in case of successful settlement.
Chartered Institute of Arbitrators (UK) www.arbitrators.org	B2C—online— scheme only for: (Ford—car selling) (ABTA—travel) (Webtrader— e-commerce). Also B2B.	Arbitration.	Completely online or mix between postal and email communication.	Encrypted communication. Secure web pages.	Established non-profit organisation offering arbitration for all types of B2B and B2C disputes.	Online application, allows electronic evidence as well as original documents.	Min. £100 registration fee. Arbitrators fee paid by company.
Claimresolver (US) www.claimresolver.com	All disputes involving US $.	Blinding bidding and supporting interactive negotiation/ mediation option.	Generates personal web page to control the process, teleconference.	Encrypted communication. Secured data storage.	Supported by Ernst & Young LLC Dynamic offer and demand management system. Median amount if 90% matching.	Filing and management via personal homepage.	US $35 registration fee + success fee of $250 < $10,000 $350 > $10,000
e-mediator (UK) www.consensus.uk.com	All disputes.	Mediation.	Mainly email exchange but every other form of communication if suitable and technology provided by parties.	Encrypted communication.	Private company offering online service as well as face-to-face mediation.	Online filing. Mainly email exchange.	£75 for each party.

A69–002

Name and web-page and country	Types of disputes	ADR techniques offered	Communication or online technology	Security provisions or technology	Short description	Procedure or filing	Cost or funding
eNeutral (US) www.eneutral.com	B2B disputes.	Mediation, arbitration, evaluation.	Video-conference. Electronic document transfer.	TRUSTe seal about privacy and confidentiality.	Private company offering mainly video-conferencing supported services.	Online filing form, scheduled video-conference.	US $250 first two hours, then US $200.
Mediation America (US) www.mediationamerica.com	All kinds of B2B and B2C disputes.	Mediation.	Video-conference, interactive multiparty negotiations with neutral third party, document exchange, simultaneously view option.	Encrypted communication.	Totally online based mediation service which offers advanced technology and specialised neutrals.	Online filing form.	Unclear.
Mediation Arbitration Resolution Service (MARS) (US) www.resolvemydispute.com	All types of disputes but just one pure online scheme for (Fair & Square for e-commerce)	Blind bidding, mediation, arbitration.	Email, tele- and video-conferencing, public chat rooms, message boards and news groups.	No mentioned security measures.	Offers several schemes combining different on- and offline communication forms. Offers trustseal program.	Complete online scheme. Online supported schemes using internet for assistance.	US $25 advance filing fee + US $50–650 depends on selected service.
Nova Forom (Can) www.novaforum.com	Commercial disputes.	Mediation, arbitration, early neutral evaluation.	Voice- and video-conference, conference rooms, chat, message board.	Encrypted communication.	Commercial ODR-provider with advanced technology and several strategic alliances, e.g. IBM.	"8-Step Methodology" mediation before arbitration, translation service.	US $2,500 each party, additional costs for special services, e.g. translation.

Online Dispute Resolution Providers

Name and web-page and country	Types of disputes	ADR techniques offered	Communication or online technology	Security provisions or technology	Short description	Procedure or filing	Cost or funding
Online Resolution (US) www.onlineresolution.com	All types of disputes.	Negotiation, mediation, arbitration, expert evaluation.	ERoom technology, online presentation of evidence as text, image, audio or video files.	Secure web technology. Firewall, system monitored by staff.	Offers nearly all forms of ADR at a very high standard.	Online filing form.	Each party for disputes <$10,000–$50/h <$50,000–$75/h <$50,000–$100/h min. 2 hours
Resolution Forum (US) www.resolut.onforum.org	All forms of B2C and B2B disputes.	Mediation, arbitration.	CAN-WIN conference system (text based only, implementation of video conferencing is in progress).	Password protected access. Other aspects unclear.	Non-profit educational organisation with the aim to make ODR widely accessible.	Online filing, use of CAN-WIN system for communication.	Unclear.
Square Trade (US) www.squaretrade.com	E-commerce disputes between buyers and sellers (consumer orientated).	Negotiation tool, mediation, limited arbitration services.	Negotiation tool, case page.	Encrypted communication.	Widely-used consumer orientated dispute resolution scheme related to online-market platforms.	Online filing form. First free use of negotiation tool but optional involvement of mediator (arbitrator).	Negotiation tool is free. Mediation cost depends on used marketplace and value of dispute. US $15–2500.
The Claimroom—TCR (UK) www.theclaimroom.com	B2C as well as B2B disputes. Mainly financial disputes.	Blind bidding, mediation.	Could be incorporated in existing web services.		Online scheme alongside or supporting of traditional negotiation. Strategic alliance with UK ADR-Group.		Blind betting fee when settlement achieved <£2,000–£100 <£5,000–£200 <£10,000–£300 <£10,000–£400 fees for mediation.

A69–004

Name and web-page and country	Types of disputes	ADR techniques offered	Communication or online technology	Security provisions or technology	Short description	Procedure or filing	Cost or funding
The Virtual Magistrate (US) www.vmag.org	Scheme for online-related B2C and B2B disputes.	Arbitration.	Listserver/ newsgroup for every case. Email communication.	Confidentiality rulings.	Scheme for online related disputes supported by NCAIR, American Arbitrators Association (AAA) and the Cyberspace Law Institute (CLI).	Online filing form. Vmag contact other party and assigns arbitrator. Decisions published on the web.	No cost for participants. Arbitrators get US $250/dispute. External funding by different sources including NCAIR.
WebMediate (US) www.webmediate.com	Insurance, B2B-disputes.	Blind bidding, mediation, arbitration.	Completely web-based communication. Virtual common and private conference rooms.	Encrypted communication.	Independent ODR-provider offering web-based service without public disclosure. They can arrange face-to-face mediation and arbitration as well.	Online filing. Controlling of all possible schemes through a so-called "My Matters page".	US $30 registration fee. Payment by successful settlement divided by both parties. 5% < US $5,000 2% > US $5,000, US $250/h for mediator/arbitrator.
WeCanSettle (UK) www.wecansettle.com	Disputes involving payment of money.	Blind bidding.	Negotiation tool.	Encrypted communication. Verification by digital certificates.	Confidential offers, settlement at median with selected default percentage of 10%, 20% or 30%.	Login to control web page. Online filing and bidding.	Payment only by successful settlement but by each party <£1,000–£25 <£3,000–£50 <£10,000–£100 <£10,000–£150
Word&Bond www.wordandbond.com	Dispute resolution for buyers and sellers on online marketplaces.	Arbitration.	Interactive Arbitration System.		Documents-only procedure.	Fast procedure.	£40–£150

The World Bank, Washington, D.C. Standard Bidding Documents, Procurement of Works[1]

MAY 2000

REVISED MARCH 2002

SECTION XIII. DISPUTES SETTLEMENT PROCEDURE[2]

(Version 1)

Disputes Review Board's Rules and Procedures

(see Clause 67 of the Conditions of Particular Application) A70–001

1. Except for providing the services required hereunder, the Board Members shall not give any advice to either party or to the Engineer concerning conduct of the Works. The Board Members:

   (a) shall have no financial interest in any party to the Contract, or the Engineer, or a financial interest in the Contract, except for payment for services on the Board;

   (b) shall have had no previous employment by, or financial ties to, any party to the Contract, or the Engineer, except for fee-based consulting services on other projects, all of which must be disclosed in writing to both parties prior to appointment to the Board;

   (c) shall have disclosed in writing to both parties prior to appointment to the Board any and all recent or close professional or personal relationships with any director, officer, or employee of any party to the Contract, or the Engineer, and any and all prior involvement in the project to which the Contract relates;

   (d) shall not, while a Board Member, be employed whether as a consultant or otherwise by either party to the Contract, or the Engineer, except as a Board Member, without the prior consent of the parties and the other Board Members;

   (e) shall not, while a Board Member, engage in discussion or make any agreement with any party to the Contract, or with the Engineer, regarding employment whether as a consultant or otherwise either after the Contract is completed or after service as a Board Member is completed;

   (f) shall be and remain impartial and independent of the parties and shall disclose

---

[1] This document is reproduced with the kind permission of the copyright-holders, the International Bank for Reconstruction and Development/The World Bank.
[2] This Section XIII contains alternative Rules and Procedures and Declaration of Acceptance for the Disputes Review Board and Disputes Review Expert, respectively. The Employer shall select the version of the Rules and Procedures corresponding to the version of Sub-Clause 67.1 that was selected in the Conditions of Particular Application (and delete the other version from the final bidding documents).

in writing to the Employer, the Contractor, the Engineer, and one another any fact or circumstance that might be such as to cause either the Employer or the Contractor to question the continued existence of the impartiality and independence required of Board Members; and

(g) shall be fluent in the language of the Contract.

A70–002 2. Except for its participation in the Board's activities as provided in the Contract and in this Agreement none of the Employer, the Contractor, or the Engineer shall solicit advice or consultation from the Board or the Board Members on matters dealing with the conduct of the Works.

A70–003 3. The Contractor shall:

(a) Furnish to each Board Member one copy of all documents that the Board may request including Contract documents, progress reports, variation orders, and other documents pertinent to the performance of the Contract.

(b) In cooperation with the Employer, coordinate the Site visits of the Board, including conference facilities, and secretarial and copying services.

A70–004 4. The Board shall begin its activities following the signing of a Board Member's Declaration of Acceptance by all three Board Members, and it shall terminate these activities as set forth below:

(a) The Board shall terminate its regular activities when either (i) the Defects Liability Period referred to in Sub-Clause 49.1 (or, if there are more than one, the Defects Liability Period expiring last) has expired, or (ii) the Employer has expelled the Contractor from the Site pursuant to Sub-Clause 63.1, and when, in either case, the Board has communicated to the parties and the Engineer its Recommendations on all disputes previously referred to it.

(b) Once the Board has terminated its regular activities as provided by the previous paragraph, the Board shall remain available to process any dispute referred to it by either party. In case of such a referral, Board Members shall receive payments as provided in paragraphs 7 (a) (ii), (iii), and (iv).

A70–005 5. Board Members shall not assign or subcontract any of their work under these Rules and Procedures. However, the Board may in its discretion decide to seek independent expert advice on a particular specialized issue to assist in reaching a Recommendation, and the cost of obtaining any such expert opinion(s) shall be shared equally by the Employer and the Contractor in accordance with the procedure specified in paragraph 7 (d) below.

A70–006 6. The Board Members are independent contractors and not employees or agents of either the Employer or the Contractor.

A70–007 7. Payments to the Board Members for their services shall be governed by the following provisions:

(a) Each Board Member will receive payments as follows:

(i) A retainer fee per calendar month equivalent to three times the daily fee established from time to time for arbitrators under the Administrative and Financial Regulations of the International Centre for Settlement of

Investment Disputes (the ICSID Arbitrator's Daily Fee), or such other retainer as the Employer and Contractor may agree in writing. This retainer shall be considered as payment in full for:

    (A) Being available, on seven days' notice, for all hearings, Site visits, and other meetings of the Board.
    (B) Being conversant with all project developments and maintaining relevant files.
    (C) All office and overhead expenses such as secretarial services, photocopying, and office supplies (but not including telephone calls, faxes, and telexes) incurred in connection with the duties as a Board Member.
    (D) All services performed hereunder except those performed during the days referred to in paragraph (ii) below.

(ii) A daily fee equivalent to the ICSID Arbitrator's Daily Fee, or such other daily fee as the Employer and Contractor may agree in writing. This daily fee shall only be payable in respect of the following days and shall be considered as payment in full for:

    (A) Each day up to a maximum of two days of travel time in each direction for the journey between the Board Member's home and the Site or other location of a Board meeting.
    (B) Each day on Site or other locations of a Board meeting.

(iii) Expenses. In addition to the above, all reasonable and necessary travel expenses (including less than first-class air fare, subsistence, and other direct travel expenses) as well as the cost of telephone calls, faxes, and telexes incurred in connection with the duties as Board Member shall be reimbursed against invoices. Receipts for all expenses in excess of US$25.00 (U.S. Dollars Twenty Five) shall be provided.

(iv) Reimbursement of any taxes that may be levied in the country of the Site on payments made to the Board Member (other than a national or permanent resident of the country of the Site) pursuant to this paragraph 8.

(b) Escalation. The retainer and fees shall remain fixed for the period of each Board Member's term.

(c) Phasing out of monthly retainer fee. Beginning with the next month after the Taking-Over Certificate referred to in Clause 48 (or, if there are more than one, the one issued last) has been issued, the Board Members shall receive only one-third of the monthly retainer fee. Beginning with the next month after the Board has terminated its regular activities pursuant to paragraph 4 (a) above, the Board members shall no longer receive any monthly retainer fee.

(d) Payments to the Board Members shall be shared equally by the Employer and the Contractor. The Contractor shall pay Members' invoices within 30 calendar days after receipt of such invoices and shall invoice the Employer (through the monthly statements to be submitted in accordance with Sub-Clause 60.1 of the General Conditions) for one-half of the amounts of such invoices. The Employer shall pay such Contractor's invoices within the time period specified in the Construction Contract for other payments to the Contractor by the Employer.

(e) Failure of either the Employer or the Contractor to make payment in accordance with this Agreement shall constitute an event of default under the Contract, entitling the nondefaulting party to take the measures set forth, respectively, in Clause 63 or Clause 69.

(f) Notwithstanding such event of default, and without waiver of rights therefrom, in the event that either the Employer or the Contractor fails to make payment in accordance with these Rules and Procedures, the other party may pay whatever amount may be required to finance the operation of the Board. The party making such payments, in addition to all other rights arising from such default, shall be entitled to reimbursement of all sums paid in excess of one-half of the amount required to maintain operation of the Board, plus all costs of obtaining such sums.

A70–008 8. Board Site Visits:

(a) The Board shall visit the Site and meet with representatives of the Employer and the Contractor and the Engineer at regular intervals, at times of critical construction events, at the written request of either party, and in any case not less than three times in any period of 12 months. The timing of Site visits shall be as agreed among the Employer, the Contractor, and the Board, but failing agreement shall be fixed by the Board.

(b) Site visits shall include an informal discussion of the status of the construction of the Works, an inspection of the Works, and the review of any Requests for Recommendation made in accordance with paragraph 10 below. Site visits shall be attended by personnel from the Employer, the Contractor, and the Engineer.

(c) At the conclusion of each Site visit, the Board shall prepare a report covering its activities during the visit and shall send copies to the parties and to the Engineer.

A70–009 9. Procedure for Dispute Referral to the Board:

(a) If either party objects to any action or inaction of the other party or the Engineer, the objecting party may file a written Notice of Dispute to the other party with a copy to the Engineer stating that it is given pursuant to Clause 67 and stating clearly and in detail the basis of the dispute.

(b) The party receiving the Notice of Dispute will consider it and respond in writing within 14 days after receipt.

(c) This response shall be final and conclusive on the subject, unless a written appeal to the response is filed with the responding party within 7 days after receiving the response. Both parties are encouraged to pursue the matter further to attempt to amicably settle the dispute.

(d) When it appears that the dispute cannot be resolved without the assistance of Board, or if the party receiving the Notice of Dispute fails to provide a written response within 14 days after receipt of such Notice, either party may refer the dispute to the Board by written Request for Recommendation to the Board. The Request shall be addressed to the Chairman of the Board, with copies to the other Board Members, the other party, and the Engineer, and it shall state that it is made pursuant to Clause 67.

(e) The Request for Recommendation shall state clearly and in full detail the specific issues of the dispute to be considered by the Board.

(f) When a dispute is referred to the Board, and the Board is satisfied that the dispute requires the Board's assistance, the Board shall decide when to conduct a hearing on the dispute. The Board may request that written documentation and arguments from both parties be submitted to each Board Member before the hearing begins. The parties shall submit insofar as possible agreed statements of the relevant facts.

(g) During the hearing, the Contractor, the Employer, and the Engineer shall each have ample opportunity to be heard and to offer evidence. The Board's Recommendations for resolution of the dispute will be given in writing to the Employer, the Contractor, and the Engineer as soon as possible, and in any event not less than 56 days after receipt by the Chairman of the Board of the written Request for Recommendation.

10. Conduct of Hearings:

(a) Normally hearings will be conducted at the Site, but any location that would be more convenient and still provide all required facilities and access to necessary documentation may be utilized by the Board. Private sessions of the Board may be held at any cost-effective location convenient to the Board.

(b) The Employer, the Engineer, and the Contractor shall be given the opportunity to have representatives at all hearings.

(c) During the hearings, no Board Member shall express any opinion concerning the merit of the respective arguments of the parties.

(d) After the hearings are concluded, the Board shall meet privately to formulate its Recommendations. All Board deliberation shall be conducted in private, with all Members' individual views kept strictly confidential. The Board's Recommendations, together with an explanation of its reasoning, shall be submitted in writing to both parties and to the Engineer. The Recommendations shall be based on the pertinent Contract provisions, applicable laws and regulations, and the facts and circumstances involved in the dispute.

(e) The Board shall make every effort to reach a unanimous Recommendation. If this proves impossible, the majority shall decide, and the dissenting Member may prepare a written minority report for submission to both parties and to the Engineer.

11. In all procedural matters, including the furnishing of written documents and arguments relating to disputes, Site visits, and conduct of hearings, the Board shall have full and final authority. If a unanimous decision on any such matter proves impossible, the majority shall decide.

12. After having been selected and, where necessary, approved, each Board Member shall sign two copies of the following declaration and make one copy available each to the Employer and to the Contractor:

[BOARD MEMBER'S DECLARATION OF ACCEPTANCE]

A70–013 WHEREAS

(a) a Construction Contract (the Contract) for the *[name of project]* project has been signed on *[fill in date]* between *[name of Employer]* (the Employer) and *[name of Contractor]* (the Contractor);

(b) Clause 67 of the Conditions of Particular Application of the Construction Contract provides for the establishment and operation of a Disputes Review Board (the Board);

(c) the undersigned has been selected (and where required, approved) to serve as a Board Member on said Board;

NOW THEREFORE, the undersigned Board Member hereby declares as follows:

1. I accept the selection as a Board Member and agree to serve on the Board and to be bound by the provisions of Clause 67 of the Conditions of Particular Application of the Contract and the Disputes Review Board's Rules and Procedures attached to the Conditions of Particular Application.
2. With respect to paragraph 1 of said Disputes Review Board's Rules and Procedures, I declare

   (a) that I have no financial interest of the kind referred to in subparagraph (a);
   (b) that I have had no previous employment nor financial ties of the kind referred to in subparagraph (b); and
   (c) that I have made to both parties any disclosures that may be required by subparagraphs (b) and (c).

BOARD MEMBER

_____

_____ *[print name of Board Member]*

Date: _____

The Refined Sugar Association Rules Relating to Arbitration[1]

Recommended Arbitration Clause

Parties to a White Sugar Contract who wish to have any disputes referred to arbitration under the following Rules are recommended to insert in the Contract an arbitration clause in the following form: **A71–001**

> "Any disputes arising out of or in connection with this Contract shall be referred to arbitration before The Refined Sugar Association for settlement in accordance with the Rules Relating to Arbitration. Such arbitration shall be conducted in accordance with English Law. This contract shall be governed by and construed in accordance with English Law".

Rules

1. Any dispute arising out of or in connection with a Contract which the Parties have agreed (either in the Contract or otherwise) to refer to arbitration by The Refined Sugar Association shall be determined in accordance with the following Rules.   **A71–002**

2. Any party wishing to commence an arbitration concerning a dispute falling within Rule 1 shall give to the other party seven clear days notice of his intention to claim arbitration.   **A71–003**

After the expiry of the seven clear days notice period a written request for arbitration shall be sent to the Secretary. The Arbitration Rules of the Association in force at the time such request is received and any subsequent amendments to them will apply to the reference.

The Claimant shall, together with the request for arbitration or within 30 days thereafter or such extended time as the Council or Secretary shall in its or his absolute discretion allow, forward to the Secretary the following:—

(a) a clear and concise statement of his case, in duplicate;

(b) copies of the contractual documents, in duplicate, in which the arbitration clause is contained or under which the arbitration arises;

(c) any supporting documentary evidence, in duplicate, he thinks proper;

(d) the names, addresses, telexes and facsimile numbers (if appropriate) of the parties to the arbitration;

(e) a non-returnable registration fee (see Rule 3);

(f) if required (and without prejudice to the provisions of the Arbitration Act 1996, relating to security for costs) an advance payment on account of the Association's fees, costs and expenses (see Rule 3).

---

[1] This document is reproduced with the kind permission of the Refined Sugar Association. Please note that the Arbitration Rules of the Sugar Association of London are identical to these Rules.

The Council shall thereupon have power to determine, as hereinafter provided, any such matter in dispute. The Secretary shall have power to make decisions on behalf of the Council on procedural and administrative matters which may arise in the course of a reference, in accordance with the provisions of these Rules. Without prejudice to the provisions of the Arbitration Act 1996 relating to jurisdiction, where both parties to a dispute are members, the Council shall have the jurisdiction to determine whether a contract has been made, whether there is a valid arbitration agreement and what matters have been submitted to arbitration in accordance with such agreement.

The Respondent shall, not later than thirty days after dispatch to his last known address by the Secretary of a copy of the Claimant's statement of case and supporting documents, or such extended time as the Council or Secretary shall in its or his absolute discretion allow, submit in duplicate to the Secretary a clear and concise statement of his defence together with a copy of such other documentary evidence in duplicate as he thinks proper. A copy of this statement of defence and supporting documents shall be forwarded by the Secretary to the Claimant.

The Claimant and the Respondent will in turn be permitted a period of twenty-one days, or such extended time as the Council or Secretary shall in its or his absolute discretion allow, within which to submit further written comments and/or documents in reply to the other party's last submission, until the Council or Secretary shall in its or his absolute discretion decide that the Council should proceed to make its award.

All statements, contracts and documentary evidence must be submitted in the English language. Whenever documentary evidence is submitted in a foreign language this must be accompanied by an officially certified English translation.

A71–004 3. A non-returnable registration fee of such amount as shall be decided by the Council from time to time shall be paid to the Secretary upon any reference to arbitration. The Council or Secretary may if it or he thinks fit at any time order either party to the arbitration to make one or more advance payments on account of the Association's fees, costs and expenses in connection with or arising out of the arbitration. Such power shall be without prejudice to the power of the Council to order security for costs in accordance with the Arbitration Act 1996.

A71–005 4. Any notice, document or other correspondence to be served on any party in connection with an arbitration under these Rules may be effected either by (a) courier, (b) first class post, (c) post in a registered letter, (d) telex, (e) cable or (f) facsimile in each case to the usual or last known address or place of business of any party. In the case of a facsimile such notice, document or correspondence shall also be served in accordance with one of the provisions under (a) to (e) above.

A71–006 5. Should a party in dispute with another party refuse to concur in the reference to arbitration as herein provided, the party referring the matter to arbitration may forthwith obtain an award of the Council on the question in dispute. The Council may at its discretion refuse to arbitrate on any reference made by a Member who has been suspended from the Association or whose Membership has been revoked.

A71–007 6. Unless the Council shall as hereinbefore provided have refused to arbitrate, neither the Buyer, Seller, Trustee in Bankruptcy, liquidator nor any other person claiming under any of them, shall bring any action against any party to the contract in respect of any dispute arising out of such contract, until such dispute shall have been adjudicated upon in arbitration under these Rules; and the obtaining of an award under these Rules shall be a condition precedent to the right of either contracting party to sue the other in respect of any claim arising out of the contract.

A71–008 7. When the subject matter and terms of contract are identical, except as to date and price, arbitration may in the Council's absolute discretion and subject to the written agreement of all parties be held as between first Seller and last Buyer as though they were contracting parties and the award made in pursuance thereof shall be binding on all intermediate parties, provided that this Rule shall not apply where a question or dispute shall arise between intermediate parties, not affecting both first Seller and last Buyer, and in such case the arbitration may be held as between the two parties affected by the dispute or, subject as aforesaid in the event of there being more than two such parties, as between the first and last of such parties as though they were contracting parties, and the award made in pursuance thereof shall be binding on all parties affected by the dispute.

8. For the purpose of all proceedings in arbitration, the contract shall be deemed to **A71–009** have been made in England, any correspondence in reference to the offer, the acceptance, the place of payment or otherwise, notwithstanding, and England shall be regarded as the place of performance. Disputes shall be settled according to the law of England wherever the domicile, residence or place of business of the parties to the contract may be or become. The seat of the Arbitration shall be England and all proceedings shall take place in England. It shall not be necessary for the award to state expressly the seat of the arbitration. Unless the contract contains any statement expressly to the contrary, the provisions of neither the Convention relating to a Uniform Law on the International Sale of Goods, of 1964, nor the United Nations Convention on Contracts for the International Sale of Goods, of 1980, shall apply thereto. Unless the Contract contains any statement expressly to the contrary, a person who is not a party to the Contract has no right under the Contract (Rights of Third Parties) Act 1999 to enforce any term of it.

9. For determination of a dispute the Council or Secretary shall appoint not less than **A71–010** three and no more than five persons from the Panel of Arbitrators to act on behalf of the Council. The number of persons appointed to determine a dispute shall be in the absolute discretion of the Council or Secretary. No such person shall act in an arbitration where he is, or becomes, directly or indirectly interested in the subject matter in dispute. In the event of a person becoming so interested, dying or becoming in any other way in the view of the Council or Secretary incapacitated from acting prior to the first meeting, the Council or Secretary may appoint another person from the Panel of Arbitrators to take his place, and the arbitration shall thereupon proceed as if that other person had been originally appointed in lieu of the first person. If subsequently an Arbitrator discovers that he is directly involved in the subject matter in dispute, dies or becomes in any other way in the view of the Council or Secretary incapacitated from acting, then the hearing shall, unless the Council or Secretary in its or his absolute discretion decides otherwise, proceed without the necessity of appointing another person from the Panel of Arbitrators. The decision of the persons so appointed to act on behalf of the Council shall be by a majority and, in the event of an equality of votes, the Chairman, who shall have been previously elected by such persons, shall have a second or casting vote. The award of such persons shall be signed by the said Chairman (and it shall not be necessary for any of the other persons appointed from the Panel of Arbitrators to sign it) and when so signed shall be deemed to be the award of the Council and shall be final and binding in all cases.

10. The Council may in its discretion decide the case on the written statements and **A71–011** documents submitted to it without an oral hearing (without the attendance of the parties or their representatives and witnesses). The Council may however, call the parties before it, and request the attendance of witnesses, or the provision of further documents, or information in written form.

Should either or both parties require an oral hearing they shall make their request, in writing, to the Secretary. The Council may grant or refuse such request in its absolute discretion and without assigning any reason.

Without prejudice to the provisions of the Arbitration Act 1996 relating to legal representation, in the event of an oral hearing, with or without witnesses, each party shall appear either personally or by any agent duly appointed in writing and may be represented at the oral hearing by counsel or solicitor. One party shall not, however, make an oral statement in the absence of the other, excepting in the case of his opponent failing to appear after notice has been given to him by the Secretary.

The Council or Secretary may also, on its or his own behalf, whether in relation to a case decided on documents or an oral hearing, consult the legal advisers of the Association and unless otherwise agreed by the Council any information, opinion or advice offered by such person/s whether or not in writing shall be for the sole use of the Council and shall not be made available to the parties.

Without prejudice to the provisions of section 34 of the Arbitration Act 1996, the Council shall not be bound by the strict rules of evidence and shall be at liberty to admit and consider any material whatsoever notwithstanding that it may not be admissible under the law of evidence.

Unless both parties notify the Secretary in writing, to the contrary, the Council shall issue a Reasoned Award.

The Council shall have the power to make more than one award at different times on different issues in accordance with section 47 of the Arbitration Act 1996, but shall not have the power to make provisional awards pursuant to section 39 of the Arbitration Act 1996.

A71–012 11. If a party wishes to withdraw a claim or counterclaim, he shall give notice to that effect to the Secretary. On receipt of such a notice, the Secretary shall inform the other party and shall cancel any arrangements for the hearing of that claim or counterclaim (unless any other claim or counterclaim remains to be dealt with at the same hearing). The other party shall be entitled to an award dismissing the withdrawn claim or counterclaim with costs, provided that a written request for such an award is received by the Secretary within 28 days after such other party has been informed by the Secretary of the withdrawal. If no such request is received by the Secretary within the said period of 28 days the arbitration shall be deemed to have been terminated by consent so far as it relates to such claim or counterclaim. Such award or termination shall not affect any other claim or counterclaim which is the subject of the same arbitration proceedings, or the Council's or Secretary's right to recover the Council's and the Association's fees, costs and expenses.

A71–013 12. Subject to any agreement to the contrary, the Council shall, in addition to the powers under section 49 of the Arbitration Act 1996, have the power if it thinks fit:

> (a) to award interest on any sum which becomes due in respect of a contract whether by way of debt or damages and which is paid before the commencement of arbitration proceedings at such rate as it thinks fit and for such period as it thinks fit ending not later than the date of payment;
>
> (b) where a sum is due in respect of a contract whether by way of debt or damages, to award general damages in respect of the late payment of such sum.

A71–014 13. The Arbitration fees shall be in the discretion of the Council or Secretary in every case, and shall be paid by whom the Council or Secretary shall determine.

Any expenses incurred by the Association or by the Council, including the expenses incurred in obtaining legal assistance, copies of documents or evidence, shorthand notes, etc., may be added to such fees.

The Council may also make an award or order as to payment of the costs of the parties to the arbitration. In accordance with section 63 of the Arbitration Act 1996, the Council may also determine by award the recoverable costs of the parties on such basis as it thinks fit.

14. A book shall be kept in which all cases shall be noted, together with the award **A71–015** and fees and expenses charged. The Secretary shall notify the parties as soon as the award is signed and it shall be held by the Secretary at the disposal of either party against payment of the fees, costs and expenses incurred by the Association or by the Council. A copy of the Award shall be given to the party who does not take up the original. If the award is not taken up within ten days, the Council or Secretary may order either of the parties to take up the award, and in such case the party so ordered shall take up the award and pay the fees, costs and expenses as directed. The Secretary, on behalf of the Council, shall have the right to invoke arbitration Rule 16, if any party neglects or refuses to abide by any such order.

15. The Award must be honoured within twenty-eight days from the date on which it **A71–016** is taken up.

16. In the event of a party to an arbitration neglecting or refusing to carry out or abide **A71–017** by any award or order made under Arbitration Rule 14, the Secretary on behalf of the Council may circularise to Members of the Association in any way thought fit a notification to that effect. The parties to any such arbitration shall be deemed to have consented to the Council taking such action as aforesaid. The information contained in any such notice shall be issued to a member only on the understanding that neither the member nor any of its employees or any authorised representative of it shall use such information for anything other than the members own commercial knowledge and purposes and that it shall remain privy to that member, its employees or any authorised representative of it at all times. Any member failing to adhere to this Rule shall immediately cease to receive the aforesaid notice and Constitution Rules 7 and 8 may be invoked by the Council.

17. In the event of both parties consenting in writing to the publication to Members **A71–018** of the Association of an Award or any part thereof or summary of its contents, the Council or Secretary may make available the same to Members of the Association in a form approved by the parties. The Council or Secretary shall be entitled to charge a fee to Members for the provision of such information.

AAA Supplementary Procedures for Online Arbitration of July 1, 2001[1]

Introduction

A72–001   The purpose of the Supplementary Procedures for Online Arbitration is to permit, where the parties have agreed to arbitration under these Supplementary Procedures, arbitral proceedings to be conducted and resolved exclusively via the Internet. The Supplementary Procedures provide for all party submissions to be made online, and for the arbitrator, upon review of such submissions, to render an award and to communicate it to the parties via the Internet. These Supplementary Procedures further authorize the parties and the arbitrator in certain circumstances to use methods of communication other than the Internet.

Definitions

A72–002   (a) **Administrative Site** refers to the internet site www.adr.org. At the Administrative Site, parties may initiate arbitration under the Supplementary Procedures and pay filing fees and other administrative costs. The Administrative Site also provides schedules of applicable fees and costs, technical guidelines regarding the format of submissions, as well as other important information and resources.

(b) **Arbitrator** refers to a sole arbitrator or a three person panel appointed according to the Supplementary Procedures.

(c) **Case Site** refers to the Internet site established to maintain the case files and submissions. All of the parties' written submissions shall be posted on the Case Site, and no one other than the AAA, the parties, and the Arbitrator shall have access to the Case Site.

(d) **Hearing**, whether used in the singular or plural, refers to any meeting or meetings of the parties before the Arbitrator, whether conducted in-person or by telephone, video-conference, or other means.

(e) **Internet** and **online** are used interchangeably to refer to the world-wide electronic online medium.

(f) **Portal Terms** shall refer to the terms and conditions of use of the Case Site and Administrative Site, as may be amended from time to time by the AAA.

(g) **Submit** refers to (i) the electronic transmittal of pleadings, exhibits, communications, or other documents to the Case Site, or (ii) such other method of transmitting pleadings, exhibits, communications, or other documents as may be authorized by the Arbitrator under Section 12(a). **Submissions** refers to all such pleadings, exhibits, communications, or other documents, however transmitted.

---

[1] Copyright: the American Arbitration Association 2001. Reprinted with the kind permission of the American Arbitration Association.

(h) **Writing** refers not only to the customary definition of "writing" but also to an "electronic record" as the term is defined the Uniform Electronic Transactions Act (U.L.A.), § 2.

Procedures

1. Agreement to Arbitrate under these Supplementary Procedures

(a) The parties shall be deemed to have made these Supplementary Procedures a part of their arbitration agreement whenever they have provided for arbitration by the American Arbitration Association (the "AAA") under its Supplementary Procedures for online Arbitration. These Supplementary Procedures may also be used, by agreement of the parties and Arbitrator, in arbitrations initiated under other sets of rules. The Supplementary Procedures and any amendment to them shall apply in the form in effect at the time of commencement of the arbitration. The parties, by agreement in writing, may vary the procedures set forth in these Supplementary Procedures.

(b) The Supplementary Procedures are supplemental to the AAA's Commercial Dispute Resolution Procedures, or any other set of applicable AAA rules, which shall remain applicable except where modified by the Supplementary Procedures.

(c) The AAA may decide that an arbitration shall not be conducted under the Supplementary Procedures where a party lacks the capacity to participate in the arbitration in accordance with these Procedures, or where the AAA otherwise finds, in its discretion, that an arbitration should not be conducted under these Procedures. In the event that the AAA makes such a determination, the arbitration shall be conducted in accordance with the Commercial Dispute Resolution Procedures or other applicable AAA rules.

(d) By agreeing to the Supplementary Procedures, the parties also agree to the Portal Terms in effect at the time of commencement of the arbitration.

(e) When the parties agree to arbitrate under the Supplementary Procedures, they thereby authorize the AAA to administer the arbitration.

2. Serving of Notices and Calculation of Time Periods

(a) Except as otherwise agreed by the parties and approved by the Arbitrator, all submissions provided for under the Supplementary Procedures shall be deemed to have been made when received at the Case Site. The date and time of receipt shall be that stated in the confirmatory e-mail sent from the Case Site to the party making the submission.

(b) For the purposes of calculating a period of time under the Supplementary Procedures, such period shall begin to run from the date of receipt at the Case Cite.

3. The Claim in Arbitration

(a) The Claimant shall initiate the arbitration by submitting to the Administrative Site a claim in arbitration (the "Claim"), which shall include: the parties' arbitration agreement; any agreement between the parties regarding the number, identity, qualifications, and/or the manner of selection of the Arbitrator; basic documents insofar as reasonably susceptible to electronic transmittal; and a statement of the nature of the dispute, the legal arguments which support the Claim, the amount involved, if any, and the remedy sought.

(b) In addition to the foregoing, the Claim shall provide the following information:

(1) the e-mail address at which the Claimant will receive e-mail communications from the Case Site;

(2) the last known valid e-mail address of the Respondent; and

(3) the names, postal addresses, and telephone and facsimile numbers of the parties.

(c) The Claimant shall pay the appropriate filling fee within five days of submitting the Claim to the Administrative Site. Such fee may be paid electronically or by any other method prescribed by the AAA.

4. Notification of Complaint

A72–006 (a) Upon receipt of the appropriate filing fee from the Claimant, the AAA shall review the Claim to ascertain whether it complies with Section 3. Once the AAA has satisfied itself of the foregoing, the AAA shall, within five business days, establish a Case Site upon which the Claim shall immediately be made available. The AAA shall notify the parties by e-mail of the Internet address for the Case Site. The arbitration shall be deemed commenced on the date upon which the Case Site was established, as reflected in the confirmatory e-mails sent by the AAA to the parties.

(b) If the AAA finds that notification to the Respondent via e-mail is not possible, the AAA may decide that the Supplementary Procedures should not apply.

(c) If the AAA determines that the Claim is administratively deficient, the AAA shall not create a Case Site and shall promptly notify the Claimant of the deficiencies identified.

5. Response to Claim

A72–007 Within thirty calendar days following the establishment of the Case Site, the Respondent shall submit to the Case Site a response, which shall include:

(1) the response to the Claim, together with the facts, documents, and legal arguments supporting such response;

(2) any objection to the jurisdiction of the Arbitrator, to the number, identity, qualifications, and/or manner of selection of the Arbitrator, or to the applicability of the Supplementary Procedures;

(3) the e-mail address at which the Respondent will receive e-mail communications from the Case Site; and

(4) if the Respondent has a counterclaim, a submission satisfying the requirements for a Claim set out in Section 3.

AAA SUPPLEMENTARY PROCEDURES FOR ONLINE ARBITRATION

6. Response to Counterclaim

Where the Respondent has submitted a counterclaim, the Claimant shall submit to the Case Site a response within thirty calendar days from the date upon which the Respondent's counterclaim was submitted to the Case Site. The response shall include the information sufficient to meet the requirements of a response to a Claim set out in Section 5.

7. Extensions of Time

The AAA or the Arbitrator may, for good cause shown, extend the period of time for the Respondent to submit its response to the Claim or for the Claimant to submit its response to any counterclaim. Any such request made to the Arbitrator shall be submitted to the Case Site. Any such request made to the AAA shall be both submitted to the Case Site and sent by e-mail to the AAA as provided in Section 12(b).

8. Language of the Arbitration

Unless otherwise agreed by the parties, the language of the arbitration shall be that of the document(s) containing the arbitration agreement, subject to the power of the Arbitrator to determine otherwise.

9. Hearings

(a) Unless either party requests and the Arbitrator agrees to a Hearing, the Arbitrator will make the award based on the submissions. In the absence of a request for a Hearing, the Arbitrator will render the award within thirty days of the closing of the proceeding.

(b) At a Hearing, witness testimony may be received, cross-examination of witnesses may be conducted, and additional documentary evidence may be received as approved by the Arbitrator.

10. Place of Award

The parties may agree in writing upon the place of the award, and the Arbitrator shall designate this as the place of the award in the award. In the absence of such an agreement between the parties, the Arbitrator shall decide and shall designate the place of the award in the award.

11. Communication of the Award to the Parties

The Arbitrator shall submit the award to the Case Site. The award shall be deemed to have been made when submitted, which date shall be stated in the confirmatory e-mail sent from the Case Site to the parties notifying them that the award has been submitted. The Case Site shall remain available to the parties for thirty days from the date upon which the award was submitted.

12. Additional Methods of Communication

(a) The Arbitrator may authorize a method of communicating with the Arbitrator other than the above-described use of the Case Site.

(b) The AAA shall provide to the parties and to the Arbitrator an e-mail address for those communications between the parties and the AAA or between the Arbitrator and the AAA which are not to be made available to all parties and the Arbitrator through submission to the Case Site (e.g., administrative queries).

Hong Kong International Arbitration Centre Electronic Transaction Arbitration Rules[1]

(ADOPTED TO TAKE EFFECT FROM 1 JANUARY 2002)

Preamble

Where any agreement, submission or reference provides for arbitration under the Electronic Transaction Arbitration Rules of the Hong Kong International Arbitration Centre (the Rules), the parties shall be taken to have agreed that the arbitration shall be conducted in accordance with the following Rules, or such amended Rules as Hong Kong International Arbitration Centre (HKIAC) may have adopted to take effect before the commencement of the arbitration. The Rules are subject to such modifications as the parties may agree in writing at any time.

Article 1

Commencement of Arbitration

1.1 Any party wishing to commence an arbitration under these Rules (the Claimant) shall send to the other party (the Respondent) a written Notice of Arbitration as per Form N requiring the Respondent to appoint or concur in appointing the Arbitrator.

1.2 A copy of the Notice of Arbitration and verification of service to the Respondent at the Respondent's last known address shall be sent to the Secretary General of the HKIAC (the Secretary General) together with a filing fee as detailed in Appendix A ("Arbitration Costs and Administrative Fees Schedule"). For the purposes of this subrule, registered post shall constitute good service.

1.3 The date on which the Notice of Arbitration and verification of service to the Respondent is received by the HKIAC shall, for all purposes, be deemed to be the date of the commencement of the arbitral proceedings.

1.4 For the purpose of facilitating the choice of the Arbitrator, within 14 days of receipt of the Notice of Arbitration, the Respondent shall send to the Claimant a Response (Response to the Notice of Arbitration) as per Form R.

1.5 A copy of the Response and verification of service to the Claimant at the latter's last known address shall be sent to the Secretary General or his designate. For the purposes of this subrule, registered post shall constitute good service.

1.6 The Secretary General or his designate may grant the Respondent an extension of time of not more than 7 days for filing the Response, if the HKIAC deems it to be necessary upon the request of the Respondent.

1.7 Failure to send a Response within the required timeframe shall neither preclude the Respondent from denying the claim nor from setting out a counterclaim in its Statement of Defence.

1.8 For the avoidance of doubt, where these Rules require any notice, pleading, submission or any other communication to be in writing, then, unless the parties agree or the Arbitrator orders otherwise, a communication delivered by facsimiles, telex, email, electronic or computer transmission shall satisfy that requirement together with a record of the sending thereof.

---

[1] Reproduced with the kind permission of the Hong Kong International Arbitration Centre.

Article 2

Appointing Authority

A73–003   **2.1** The HKIAC shall be the Appointing Authority*.

2.2 Any application to the Appointing Authority to act in accordance with these Rules shall be accompanied by:

(a) a duly completed Appointment Submission Form (Form A);

(b) copies of the Notice of Arbitration (Form N) and Response to the Notice of Arbitration (Form R) and any other related correspondence, in particular, the arbitration agreement;

(c) confirmation in writing that a copy of the application has been sent to or received by the other party; and

(d) payment of the necessary appointment fees as detailed in Appendix A ("Arbitration Costs and Administrative Fees Schedule").

Article 3

Appointment of Arbitrator

A73–004   **3.1** The Arbitrator may be appointed by agreement of the parties. Failing such agreement within 28 days of the commencement of the arbitration in accordance with Article 1, the Arbitrator shall, upon the application of either party in accordance with Article 2.2, be appointed by the HKIAC.

3.2 The application to the HKIAC to appoint an Arbitrator pursuant to Article 3.1 shall be made within 42 days of the commencement of the Arbitration, failing which the case in question shall be closed without prejudice to the right of the Claimant to submit another Notice of Arbitration in respect of the same case.

3.3 For an arbitration under these Rules, there shall be a sole Arbitrator.

3.4 The Arbitrator shall ensure that each party has a reasonable opportunity to present its case. In doing so, the Arbitrator shall act fairly and shall remain at all times wholly independent and impartial, and shall not act as advocate for any party.

3.5 Prior to appointment of a proposed Arbitrator as well as after appointment, the Arbitrator shall disclose to the parties any circumstance likely to create an impression of bias or prevent a prompt resolution of the dispute between the parties. Except by consent of the parties, no person shall serve as Arbitrator in any dispute in which that person has any interest which, if a party knew of it, might lead such party to think that the Arbitrator might be biased.

3.6 In connection with Article 3.5, prior to appointment a prospective Arbitrator shall confirm in writing to the HKIAC any facts or circumstances which might be of such a nature as to call into question the Arbitrator's independence in the eyes of the parties. The HKIAC shall provide such information to the parties in writing and the parties shall have 7 days to provide comments upon the prospective Arbitrator proposed.

3.7 The decisions of the HKIAC as to the appointment, challenge or replacement of

---

* The HKIAC will require payment of an appointment fee for the use of its services as Appointing Authority as set out in the Arbitration Costs and Administrative Fees Schedule.

an Arbitrator shall be final and the reasons for such decisions shall not be communicated.

3.8 If the Arbitrator dies, is unable to act, or refuses to act, the HKIAC will, upon request by either party, appoint another Arbitrator.

Article 4

Communication between Parties, the Arbitrator and the HKIAC

4.1 The Secretary General of the HKIAC (the Secretary General) or his designate will act as the administrator of the arbitration. All communications and notices between a party and the Arbitrator in the course of the arbitration (except at meetings and hearings) will be addressed through the Secretary General or his designate.

4.2 Where the Secretary General or his designate sends any communication to one party, he shall send a copy to the other party at the same time.

4.3 Where a party sends any communication (including statements and documents under Article 6) to the Secretary General, it shall be copied to the other party and verification of service thereof should be forwarded to the Secretary General.

4.4 The addresses of the parties for the purpose of all communications arising under the Rules shall be those set out in the Notice of Arbitration, or as either party may at any time notify the Secretary General and the other party.

4.5 Unless the contrary is proved, any communication by post shall be deemed to be received in the ordinary course of mail. Any instantaneous means of communication (e.g. fax, telex or email) shall be deemed to be received on the same day as transmitted.

4.6 The HKIAC will charge an Administrative fee in accordance with the "Arbitration Costs and Administrative Fees Schedule" as detailed in Appendix A for the services of the Secretary General or his designate acting as arbitration administrator.

Article 5

Conduct of the Proceedings

5.1 The Arbitrator shall have the power to adopt wherever possible a simplified or expedited procedure and in any case shall have the widest discretion allowed by law to conduct the proceeding so as to ensure the just, expeditious, economical, and final determination of the dispute.

5.2 Unless the Arbitrator is of the opinion that a preliminary meeting is necessary, all procedural matters in the arbitration shall, failing agreement between the parties, be settled by directions of the Arbitrator set out in written communications.

Article 6

Submission of Written Statements and Documents

6.1 Subject to any procedural rules agreed by the parties or determined by or requested from the Arbitrator under Article 5, written statements and supporting documents shall be exchanged as set out in this Article (and in accordance with Article 4).

6.2 Within 14 days of receipt by the Claimant of notification of the Arbitrator's acceptance of the appointment, the Claimant shall send to the Secretary General or his designate a Statement of Claim setting out a full description in narrative form of the nature and circumstances of the dispute specifying all factual matters and, if necessary for the proper understanding of the claim, a summary of any contentions of law relied upon and the relief claimed.

6.3 As soon as practicable after the Secretary General or his designate receives a Statement of Claim, he shall transmit the Statement of Claim to the Respondent and a copy thereof to the Arbitrator.

6.4 Within 14 days of receipt of the Statement of Claim, the Respondent shall send to the Secretary General or his designate a Statement of Defence setting out a full description in narrative form the factual matters and contentions of law in the Statement of Claim which he admits or denies, on what grounds, and specifying any other factual matters and, if necessary for the proper understanding of the defence, a summary of any contentions of law relied upon. Counterclaims, if any, shall be submitted with the Statement of Defence in the same manner as claims set out in the Statement of Claim.

6.5 As soon as practicable after the Secretary General or his designate receives a Statement of Defence, he shall transmit the Statement of Defence to the Claimant and a copy thereof to the Arbitrator.

6.6 Within 14 days of receipt of the Statement of Defence, the Claimant may send to the Secretary General or his designate a Statement of Reply which, where there are Counterclaims, shall include a Defence to Counterclaims.

6.7 As soon as practicable after the Secretary General or his designate receives a Statement of Reply, he shall transmit the Statement of Reply to the Respondent and a copy thereof to the Arbitrator.

6.8 If the Statement of Reply contains a Defence to Counterclaims, the Respondent may within a further 14 days send to the Secretary General or his designate a Statement of Reply regarding Counterclaims.

6.9 As soon as practicable after the Secretary General or his designate receives a Statement of Reply regarding Counterclaims, he shall transmit the Statement of Reply regarding Counterclaims to the Claimant and a copy thereof to the Arbitrator.

6.10 All Statements referred to in this Article shall be accompanied by copies (or, if they are especially voluminous and by leave of the Arbitrator, lists) of all essential documents on which the party concerned relies and which have not previously been submitted by any party, and (where appropriate) by any relevant samples.

6.11 The Arbitrator may order the parties to produce any additional documents he may specify.

6.12 As soon as practicable following completion of the submission of the Statements specified in this Article, the Secretary General or his designate shall forward the supporting information to the Arbitrator in order for him to proceed pursuant to his authority under the Rules unless otherwise agreed by the parties.

Article 7

Documents-Only Arbitration

7.1 Unless the Arbitrator is of the opinion that a hearing is necessary or the parties otherwise agree, the arbitration shall be conducted on a documents-only basis in accordance with this Article.

7.2 Where a documents-only arbitration procedure has been adopted, the parties shall not be entitled to a hearing and the testimony of any witness shall be presented in written form and shall be submitted in accordance with Article 6. If the Arbitrator feels unable to make an award on the basis of the documents submitted, he shall be entitled to require further evidence or submissions whether oral or in writing.

7.3 If a party fails to submit any statement in accordance with Article 6, the Arbitrator may make an award on the substantive issues and an award as to costs without a hearing.

Article 8

Representation

A party may conduct his case in person or be represented throughout or in part by lawyers or other advisers or representatives of his choice (Representative). A party shall notify the Secretary General and the other parties of any change of Representative and his address (and telephone, telex, fax numbers and email addresses) as soon as practicable after any such change.

Article 9

Hearings

9.1 Hearings may, without limitation, be conducted in person, by videolink, by telephone or on-line (by email or by other electronic or computer communication).

9.2 The Arbitrator shall fix the date, time, place (if applicable) and manner of meetings and hearings in the arbitration, and shall give the parties reasonable notice thereof.

9.3 The Arbitrator may in advance of hearings provide the parties with a list of matters or questions to which he wishes them to give special consideration.

9.4 The Arbitrator may also order opening and closing statements to be in writing and shall fix the periods of time for communicating such statements and the replies that may be necessary.

9.5 The Arbitrator may also order a transcript of any hearing or part of any hearing.

9.6 All meetings and hearings shall be in private unless the parties agree otherwise.

9.7 HKIAC shall make all reasonable endeavours to provide security for the transmission of data on-line between the parties, the Arbitrator, Secretary General or his designate and the HKIAC shall use its best endeavour to see to it that the date is inaccessible or accessible only in an encrypted form to other persons.

9.8 Notwithstanding Article 9.7, HKIAC accept no liability whatsoever for breach of contract, tort, negligence or otherwise for any damage arising as a result of any data transmitted on-line in the course of an Arbitration be disclosed to persons other than the intended recipient(s).

Article 10

Witnesses

10.1 Subject to Article 5, the calling of witnesses and the giving of evidence by witnesses at any hearing shall be governed by this Article.

10.2 The Arbitrator may at any time require any party to give notice of the identity of witnesses he intends to call and a short summary of the subject matter of their testimony and its relevance to the issues. The Arbitrator may also require the exchange of witnesses' statements and of expert reports.

10.3 The Arbitrator has discretion to allow, limit, or refuse to allow the appearance of witnesses, whether witnesses of fact or expert witnesses.

10.4 Any witness who gives oral evidence may be questioned by each party or its Representative, under the control of the Arbitrator, and may be required by the Arbitrator to testify under oath or affirmation in accordance with the Arbitration Ordinance. The Arbitrator may put questions to the witnesses at any stage of the examination.

10.5 The Arbitrator may, if he consider is necessary or expedient for the just disposal of the Arbitration or for the saving of costs or otherwise, order that a witness may give oral evidence by videolink or by telephone or may give written evidence on-line and be cross-examined thereon.

10.6 The testimony of witnesses may be presented in written form, either as signed statements or by duly sworn affidavits, and the Arbitrator may order that such statements or affidavits shall stand as evidence-in-chief. Subject to Article 10.3 any party may request that such a witness should attend for oral examination at a hearing. If the witness fails to attend, the Arbitrator may place such weight on the written testimony as he thinks fit, or may exclude it altogether.

Article 11

Assessor* Appointed by the Arbitrator

A73–012   Unless otherwise agreed by the parties, the Arbitrator may:

(a) appoint an Assessor to assist him;

(b) require a party to give any Assessor any relevant information or to produce, or to provide access to any relevant documents, goods or property for inspection by the Assessor.

Article 12

Powers and Jurisdiction of the Arbitrator

A73–013   **12.1** Without prejudice to the generality of Article 5.1 and unless the parties at any time agree otherwise, the Arbitrator shall have the power and/or jurisdiction to:

(a) allow any party, upon such terms (as to costs and otherwise) as the Arbitrator shall determine, to amend any document submitted under Article 6;

(b) extend or abbreviate any time limits provided by the Rules or by his directions;

(c) conduct such enquiries as may appear to the Arbitrator to be necessary or expedient;

---

* As defined under "The New Shorter Oxford English Dictionary, Edition 1993" as (1) A person who sits as assistant or adviser to a judge or magistrate on technical points. (2) A person who sits beside another; a person who shares another's position.

HKIAC ELECTRONIC TRANSACTION ARBITRATION RULES

(d) order the parties to make any property or thing available for inspection, in their presence, by the Arbitrator or any Assessor;

(e) order any party to produce to the Arbitrator, and to the other parties for inspection, and to supply copies of any documents or classes of documents in their possession, custody or power which the Arbitrator determines to be relevant;

(f) order the rectification in any contract or arbitration agreement of any mistake which he determines to be common to the parties;

(g) rule on the existence, validity or termination of the contract;

(h) rule on his own jurisdiction, including any objections with respect to the existence or validity of the arbitration agreement to the validity of his appointment or to his terms of reference;

(i) determine any question of law arising in the arbitration;

(j) determine any question of good faith, dishonesty or fraud arising in the dispute, if specifically asserted by a party in one of their Statements;

(k) receive and take into account such written or oral evidence as he shall determine to be relevant and shall not be bound by the rules of evidence;

(l) proceed in the arbitration and make an award notwithstanding the failure or refusal of any party to comply with these Rules or with the Arbitrator's written orders or written directions, or to exercise its right to present its case, but only after giving that party written notice that he intends to do so;

(m) order the making by one party to another of an interim payment of monies alleged to be due where, in the opinion of the Arbitrator, payment is undoubtedly due;

(n) order any party to provide security for the legal or other costs of any other party including without limitation the fees of the Arbitrator by way of deposit or bank guarantee or in any other manner the Arbitrator thinks fit; and

(o) order any party to provide security for all or part of any amount in dispute in the arbitration.

12.2 By agreeing to arbitration under the Rules, the parties hereby agree to apply to the Arbitrator, and not to any court of law or other judicial authority, for any order which, but for the Rules, would normally be made by a court of law or other judicial authority.

12.3 For the purpose of Article 12.1(h) above, an arbitration clause which forms part of a contract shall be treated as an agreement independent of the other terms of the contract. A decision by the Arbitrator that the contract is null and void shall not entail the invalidity of the arbitration clause.

12.4 A plea that the Arbitrator does not have jurisdiction shall be raised not later than the time for service of the Statement of Defence. A plea that the Arbitrator is exceeding the scope of his authority shall be raised promptly after the Arbitrator has indicated his intention to decide on the matter alleged to be beyond the scope of his authority. In either case the Arbitrator may nevertheless admit a late plea under this paragraph if the Arbitrator considers the delay justified.

Article 13

Default of Appearance by a Party

A73–014   If the Claimant fails to attend any hearing of which due notice has been given, the Arbitrator may make an award on the substantive issues and an award as to costs, with or without a hearing. If the Respondent fails to submit a Statement of Defence or to attend any hearing after due notice has been given, the Arbitrator may conduct the hearing in the absence of the Respondent and make an Award on the evidence.

Article 14

Seat of Arbitration

A73–015   The seat of the arbitration will be Hong Kong SAR but the Arbitrator may decide for the purpose of expediting any hearing or saving costs to hear witnesses or oral argument or consult with an Assessor (if appointed) at any place the Arbitrator deems appropriate having regard to the circumstances of the arbitration.

Article 15

Language

A73–016   **15.1** The language of the arbitration shall be English and all written communications and statements, and all hearings shall be conducted in the English language unless the parties and the Arbitrator otherwise agree.

15.2 The Arbitrator may order that any documents other than written statements which are produced in the course of the arbitration in their original language shall be accompanied by a translation into the language of the arbitration, such translation to be certified if not agreed.

15.3 Unless the Arbitrator otherwise orders, witnesses shall be entitled to give their evidence in the language of their choice and the Arbitrator may order the translation of that evidence into the language of the arbitration by a suitably qualified person.

15.4 The cost of translating documents pursuant to Article 15.2 and oral testimony pursuant to Article 15.3 shall, in the first instance, unless the Arbitrator orders otherwise, be borne by the party seeking to rely upon the relevant document or testimony. Nothing in this Article shall derogate from the powers of the Arbitrator pursuant to Article 20.

Article 16

Deposits and Security

A73–017   **16.1** The Secretary General or his designate may direct the parties, in such proportions as he deems just, to make one or more deposits to secure the Arbitrator's fees and expenses and those of the HKIAC. Such deposits shall be made to and held by the HKIAC and may be drawn from as required by the Arbitrator and the HKIAC. Interest on sums deposited, if any, shall be accumulated to the deposits.

16.2 In the event that a party fails to make a deposit directed by the Secretary General or his designate in accordance with Article 16.1, it shall be open to any other party to make that deposit.

16.3 When a direction to make a deposit has not been complied with, and after consultation with the Arbitrator, the Secretary General or his designate may direct the Arbitrator to suspend its work and set a time limit, which must be not less than 14 days, on the expiry of which the relevant claims, or counterclaims, shall be deemed to be withdrawn. Should any party wish to object to this measure it must make a request within the aforementioned period for the matter to be decided by the Secretary General or his designate. A party shall not be prevented on the ground of such deemed withdrawal from relying upon the same claims or counterclaims in other proceedings or from issuing a new Notice of Arbitration in respect of the same claims or counterclaims.

Article 17

The Award

17.1 The Arbitrator shall make his award in writing and, unless all the parties agree otherwise, shall state the reasons upon which the award is based. The award shall be dated and signed by the Arbitrator. The award shall be deemed to be made in Hong Kong SAR.

17.2 The Arbitrator shall notify the Secretary General or his designate who shall notify the parties as soon as the award is ready for collection but shall not be obliged to deliver the award unless appropriate fees and expenses have been paid by the parties or by one of them.

17.3 The Arbitrator may make interim awards including separate awards on different issues at different times.

17.4 If, before an award/ interim award is made, the parties agree on a settlement of the dispute, the Arbitrator shall either issue an order for termination of the arbitration or, if requested by both parties and accepted by the Arbitrator, record the settlement in the form of a consent award. The Arbitrator shall then be discharged and the reference to arbitration concluded, subject to payment by the parties of all outstanding fees and expenses of the Arbitrator and the HKIAC.

17.5 The time limit within which the Arbitrator must render a final Award under these Rules is six months from the date the Arbitrator is appointed. The Secretary General or his designate may extend this time limit pursuant to a reasoned request from the Arbitrator or on its own initiative if he decides it is necessary to do so.

17.6 An original of each Award made in accordance within these Rules shall be deposited with the HKIAC.

17.7 Every Award shall be binding on the parties. By submitting the dispute to arbitration under the Rules, the parties undertake to carry out any Award without delay and shall be deemed to have waived their right to any form of recourse in so far as such waiver can validly be made.

Article 18

Interpretation of Awards, Correction of Awards and Additional Awards

18.1 Within 14 days of receiving an award, unless another period of time has been agreed upon by the parties, a party may by written notice to the Secretary General or his designate and the other party request the Arbitrator to give an interpretation of the award. Such party may also request the Arbitrator to correct in the award any errors in computation, any clerical or typographical errors or any errors of a similar nature. If the Arbitrator considers the request to be justified, he shall provide an interpretation or correction within 14 days of receiving the request. Any interpretation or correction shall be given in writing and shall be notified in writing to the Secretary General or his designate who shall transmit the same to the parties. Any interpretation or correction shall take the form of an addendum and shall become part of the award.

18.2 The Arbitrator may correct any error of the type referred to in Article 17.1 on his own initiative within 14 days of the date of the award.

18.3 Unless otherwise agreed by the parties, a party may by notice to the Secretary General or his designate, request the Arbitrator, within 14 days of the date of the award, and with written notice to the other party, to make an additional award as to claims presented in the reference to arbitration but not dealt with in the award. If the Arbitrator considers the request to be justified, he shall notify the Secretary General or his designate within 7 days who shall transmit such notification to the parties. The Arbitrator shall make the additional award within 28 days.

18.4 The provisions of Article 17 shall apply to any interpretation or correction of the award and to any additional award.

Article 19

Payment into Court

A73–020 Any party may at any time avail himself of the procedure for payment into court pursuant to the provisions of Order 73 of the Rules of the High Court of Hong Kong, although the Arbitrator may take account of any written offer of settlement where a payment into court could have been made.

Article 20

Costs

A73–021 **20.1** The costs of arbitration shall include the fees and expenses of the Arbitrator and the Secretary General or his designate administrative expenses fixed by the HKIAC which shall be determined having regard to the Fee Schedule as shown in Appendix A ("Arbitration Costs and Administrative Fees Schedule") together with the costs of any Assessor, transcriber or translator, save that the HKIAC may, having regard to the complexity and circumstances of the case, fix the fees of the Arbitrator at a sum higher or lower than that indicated by the Fee Schedule.

20.2 The Arbitrator shall specify in the award the total amount of the costs of the Arbitration. Unless the parties shall agree otherwise after the dispute has arisen, the Arbitrator shall determine the proportions in which the parties shall pay such costs, provided that the parties will be jointly and severally liable to the HKIAC for payment of all such costs until they have been paid in full. If the Arbitrator has determined that all or any of such costs be paid by any party other than a party which has already paid them to the Arbitrator or the HKIAC, the latter party shall have the right to recover the appropriate amount from the former.

20.3 Unless the parties shall agree otherwise after the dispute has arisen, the Arbitrator may order in the award that all or a part of the legal or other costs of one party reasonable in amount and reasonably incurred shall be paid by the other party. The Arbitrator also has power to tax these costs and shall do so if requested by the parties.

20.4 If an arbitration is abandoned, suspended or concluded, by agreement or otherwise, before the final award is made, the parties shall be jointly and severally liable to pay to the HKIAC the costs of the Arbitration as determined by the Arbitrator.

Article 21

Interest

Unless otherwise agreed by the parties, the Arbitrator may order that compound interest be paid.

A73–022

Article 22

Exclusion of Liability

22.1 Without prejudice to any existing rule of law, the Arbitrator shall not be liable to any party for any act or omission in connection with any arbitration conducted under the Rules, save for the consequences of fraud or dishonesty.

A73–023

22.2 The HKIAC and its Secretary General shall not be liable to any party for any act or omission in connection with any arbitration conducted under the Rules, save for the consequences of fraud or dishonesty.

22.3 After an award has been made and the possibilities of interpretation, correction and additional awards referred to in Article 17 have lapsed or been exhausted, the Arbitrator, the HKIAC and its Secretary General shall not be under any obligation to make any statement to any person about any matter concerning the arbitration, and no party shall seek to make the Arbitrator, the HKIAC or its Secretary General or his designate a witness in any legal proceedings arising out of the arbitration.

Article 23

Waiver

A party which knew or ought to have known of non-compliance with the Rules and yet proceeds with the arbitration without promptly stating its objection to such non-compliance, shall be deemed to have waived its right to object. The Arbitrator shall determine any issue which may arise as to whether a party has waived its right to object to the non-compliance by any other party.

A73–024

Article 24

Destruction of Documents

The HKIAC may destroy all documents served on it pursuant to the Rules after the expiry of a period of one year after the date of the last correspondence received by the HKIAC relating to the arbitration.

A73 025

Article 25

Interpretation and General Clauses Ordinance

A73–026   The Interpretation and General Clauses Ordinance (or any statutory modification or re-enactment thereof for the time being in force) shall apply to these Rules.

Article 26

Confidentiality

A73–027   No information relating to the arbitration shall be disclosed by any person without the written consent of each and every party to the arbitration.

Article 27

Amendments

A73–028   The HKIAC may amend the Rules from time to time at its sole discretion.

China International Economic and Trade Arbitration Commission Arbitration Rules[1]

(REVISED AND ADOPTED BY CHINA COUNCIL FOR THE PROMOTION OF INTERNATIONAL TRADE/CHINA CHAMBER OF INTERNATIONAL COMMERCE ON SEPTEMBER 5, 2000. EFFECTIVE AS FROM OCTOBER 1, 2000.)

CHAPTER I

GENERAL PROVISIONS

Section 1. Jurisdiction

Article 1

These Rules are formulated in accordance with the Arbitration Law of the People's Republic of China and the provisions of other relevant laws, as well as the "Decision" of the former Administration Council of the Central People's Government and the "Notice" and the "Official Reply" of the State Council.

A74–001

Article 2

China International Economic and Trade Arbitration Commission (originally named the Foreign Trade Arbitration Commission of the China Council for the Promotion of International Trade, later renamed the Foreign Economic and Trade Arbitration Commission of the China Council for the Promotion of International Trade, and currently called the China International Economic and Trade Arbitration Commission, hereinafter referred to as the "Arbitration Commission") independently and impartially resolves, by means of arbitration, disputes arising from economic and trade transactions of a contractual or non-contractual nature.

A74–002

The disputes stated in the preceding paragraph include:

(1) international or foreign-related disputes;

(2) disputes related to the Hong Kong SAR or the Macao SAR or the Taiwan region;

(3) disputes between foreign investment enterprises or between a foreign investment enterprise and a Chinese legal person, physical person and/or economic organization;

(4) disputes arising from project financing, invitations to tender and bidding submissions, project construction or other activities conducted by a Chinese legal person, physical person and/or other economic organization which utilize

---

[1] This document is reproduced with the kind permission of the China International Economic and Trade Arbitration Commission.

capital, technology or services from foreign countries, international organizations or from the Hong Kong SAR, the Macao SAR and the Taiwan region;

(5) disputes that may be taken cognizance of by the Arbitration Commission in accordance with special provisions of, or upon special authorization from, the laws or administrative regulations of the People's Republic of China; and

(6) any other domestic disputes that the parties have agreed to arbitrate by the Arbitration Commission.

The Arbitration Commission does not accept the cases over the following disputes:

(1) marital, adoption, guardianship, support and succession disputes;

(2) administrative disputes that laws require to be handled by administrative authorities;

(3) labor disputes and disputes within the agricultural collective economic organizations over contracted management in agriculture.

Article 3

A74–003   The Arbitration Commission will, upon the written application by one of the parties, accept a case in accordance with the arbitration agreement concluded between the parties, either before or after the occurrence of the dispute, in which it is provided that disputes are to be submitted to the Arbitration Commission for arbitration.

An arbitration agreement means an arbitration clause in a contract concluded between the parties or any other form of written agreement providing for settlement of dispute by arbitration.

Article 4

A74–004   The Arbitration Commission has the power to decide on the existence and validity of an arbitration agreement and on jurisdiction over an arbitration case. If the parties concerned dispute the validity of an arbitration agreement, with one party requesting the Arbitration Commission to make a decision and the other party requesting the people's court to make a ruling, the people's court will make such a ruling.

Article 5

A74–005   An arbitration clause contained in a contract shall be regarded as existing independently and separately from the other clauses of the contract, and an arbitration agreement attached to a contract shall be treated as a part of the contract existing independently and separately from the other parts of the contract. The validity of an arbitration clause or an arbitration agreement shall not be affected by any modification, rescission, termination, expiry, invalidity, or non-existence of the contract.

Article 6

A74–006   Any objection to an arbitration agreement and/or the jurisdiction over an arbitration case shall be raised before the first hearing conducted by the arbitration tribunal. Where a case is examined on the basis of documents only, an objection to jurisdiction should be raised before submission of the first substantive defense.

Any objection to an arbitration agreement and/or the jurisdiction over an arbitration case shall not affect the hearing of the case according to the arbitration procedures.

Article 7

If the parties agree to submit their dispute to the Arbitration Commission for arbitration, it will be taken that they have agreed to the case being arbitrated under these Rules. However, if the parties have agreed otherwise, and subject to consent by the Arbitration Commission, the parties' agreement will prevail. **A74–007**

Section 2. Organization

Article 8

The Arbitration Commission has one honorary Chairman and several advisers. **A74–008**

Article 9

The Arbitration Commission consists of one Chairman, several Vice-Chairmen and a number of Commission members. The Chairman performs the functions and duties vested in him by these Rules and the Vice-Chairmen may also perform the Chairman's functions and duties with the Chairman's authorization. **A74–009**

The Arbitration Commission has a secretariat to handle its day-to-day work under the leadership of the Secretary-General of the Arbitration Commission.

Article 10

The Arbitration Commission establishes a Panel of Arbitrators. The arbitrators are selected and appointed by the Arbitration Commission from among Chinese and foreign persons with professional knowledge and practical experience in the fields of law, economics and trade, science and technology, etc. **A74–010**

Article 11

The Arbitration Commission is based in Beijing. The Arbitration Commission has a Shenzhen Sub-Commission in Shenzhen Special Economic Zone and a Shanghai Sub-Commission in Shanghai. These Sub-Commissions are an integral part of the Arbitration Commission. **A74–011**

The Sub-Commissions have their respective secretariats to handle their day-to-day work under the leadership of the Secretaries-General of the respective Sub-Commissions.

These Rules uniformly apply to the Arbitration Commission and its Sub-Commissions. When arbitration proceedings are conducted in the Sub-Commissions, the functions and duties under these Rules to be carried out by the Chairman, the secretariat and the Secretary-General of the Arbitration Commission shall be performed by the Vice-Chairmen as authorized by the Chairman, the secretariats and the Secretaries-General of the Sub-Commissions respectively, except for the circumstances provided for in Article 30 of these Rules.

Article 12

The parties may agree to have their dispute arbitrated by the Arbitration Commission in Beijing or by the Shenzhen Sub-Commission in Shenzhen or by the Shanghai Sub-Commission in Shanghai. **A74–012**

In the absence of such an agreement, the Claimant will have option to submit the case to be arbitrated by the Arbitration Commission in Beijing or by the Shenzhen Sub-commission in Shenzhen or by the Shanghai Sub-Commission in Shanghai.

When deciding on where the case should be arbitrated, the first choice should be final. In case of any dispute, the Arbitration Commission will make a decision accordingly.

Chapter II

Arbitration Proceedings

Section 1. Application for Arbitration, Defense and Counter-claim

Article 13

A74–013   The arbitration proceedings will commence from the date on which the Notice of Arbitration is issued by the Arbitration Commission or its Sub-Commissions.

Article 14

A74–014   A Claimant submitting an Application for Arbitration must:

(1) Submit an Application for Arbitration in writing, which shall, inter alia, contain:

(a) the names and addresses of the Claimant and the Respondent, including the zip code, telephone, telex, fax, and cable numbers or any other means of electronic telecommunications, if any;
(b) the arbitration agreement relied upon by the Claimant;
(c) the facts of the case and the main points of dispute; and
(d) the Claimant's claim and the facts and reasons on which his claim is based.

The Application for Arbitration shall be signed by, and/or affixed with the seal of, the Claimant and/or the authorized agent of the Claimant.

(2) Attach to the Application for Arbitration the relevant documentary evidence which supports the facts on which the Claimant's claim is based.

(3) Pay an arbitration fee in advance to the Arbitration Commission according to the Arbitration Fee Schedule of the Arbitration Commission.

Article 15

A74–015   Upon receipt of the Application for Arbitration and its attachments, if the secretariat of the Arbitration Commission, after examination, finds that the Claimant has not yet completed the formalities required for arbitration, it will request the Claimant to complete them. If it finds that the Claimant has completed such formalities, the secretariat should promptly send to the Respondent a Notice of Arbitration, together with one copy each of the Claimant's Application for Arbitration and its attachments as well as the Arbitration Rules, the Panel of Arbitrators and the Arbitration Fee Schedule of the Arbitration Commission. At the same time, the Notice of Arbitration, the Arbitration Rules, the Panel of Arbitrators and Arbitration Fee Schedule should be sent to the Claimant as well.

The secretariat of the Arbitration Commission, after sending the Notice of Arbitration to the Claimant and Respondent, shall appoint one of its staff-members to take charge of procedural administration of the case.

Article 16

The Claimant and the Respondent shall, within 20 days as from the date of receipt of the Notice of Arbitration, each appoint an arbitrator from among the Panel of Arbitrators of the Arbitration Commission or authorize the Chairman of the Arbitration Commission to make such appointment. A74–016

Article 17

The Respondent shall, within 45 days from the date of receipt of the Notice of Arbitration, submit his written defense and relevant documentary evidence to the secretariat of the Arbitration Commission. A74–017

Article 18

The Respondent shall, at the latest within 60 days from the date of receipt of the Notice of Arbitration, file with the secretariat of the Arbitration Commission his counterclaim in writing, if any. The arbitration tribunal may extend that time limit if it deems that there are justified reasons. A74–018

When filing a counterclaim, the Respondent must state in his written statement of counterclaim his specific claim and facts and reasons upon which his claim is based, and attach to his written statement of counterclaim any relevant documentary evidence.

When filing a counterclaim, the Respondent must pay an arbitration fee in advance according to the Arbitration Fee Schedule of the Arbitration Commission.

Article 19

The Claimant may request to amend his claim and the Respondent may request to amend his counterclaim. However, the arbitration tribunal may refuse such an amendment if it considers that the request has been raised too late and may affect the progress of the arbitration proceedings. A74–019

Article 20

When submitting application for arbitration, written defense, statement of counterclaim, documentary evidence and other documents, the parties shall submit them in quintuplicate. If the number of the parties is more than two, additional copies shall be provided accordingly. If the arbitration tribunal is composed of only one arbitrator, the number of copies submitted may be reduced by two. A74–020

Article 21

The progress of arbitration proceedings shall not be affected notwithstanding the failure of the Respondent to file his defense in writing or the failure of the Claimant to submit his written defense against the Respondent's counterclaim. A74–021

Article 22

A74–022 The parties may authorize arbitration agents to deal with the matters relating to arbitration; the authorized arbitration agent must produce a Power of Attorney to the Arbitration Commission.

Both Chinese and foreign citizens can be authorized to act as arbitration agents.

Article 23

A74–023 When a party applies for property preservative measures, the Arbitration Commission shall submit the party's application to the people's court for a ruling in the place where the domicile of the party against whom the property preservative measures are sought is located or in the place where the property of the said party is located.

When a party applies for taking interim measures of protection of evidence, the Arbitration Commission shall submit the party's application to the people's court in the place where the evidence is located for a ruling.

Section 2. Formation of Arbitration Tribunal

Article 24

A74–024 Each of the parties shall appoint one arbitrator from among the Panel of Arbitrators of the Arbitration Commission or entrust the Chairman of the Arbitration Commission to make such appointment. A third arbitrator shall be jointly appointed by the parties or appointed by the Chairman of the Arbitration Commission upon the parties' joint authorization.

In case the two parties fail to jointly appoint a third arbitrator or fail to jointly entrust the Chairman of the Arbitration Commission to appoint a third arbitrator within 20 days from the date on which the Respondent receives the Notice of Arbitration, the third arbitrator will be appointed by the Chairman of the Arbitration Commission. The third arbitrator will act as the presiding arbitrator.

The presiding arbitrator and the two appointed arbitrators will jointly form an arbitration tribunal to jointly hear the case.

Article 25

A74–025 The Claimant and the Respondent may jointly appoint or jointly authorize the Chairman of the Arbitration Commission to appoint a sole arbitrator to form an arbitration tribunal to hear the case alone.

If both parties agree to having a sole arbitrator to hear their case but are unable to agree on the choice of such a sole arbitrator within 20 days from the date on which the Respondent receives the Notice of Arbitration, the Chairman of the Arbitration Commission will make the appointment.

Article 26

A74–026 If the Claimant or the Respondent fails to appoint or authorize the Chairman of the Arbitration Commission to appoint an arbitrator according to Article 16 of these Rules, the Chairman of the Arbitration Commission will appoint an arbitrator for the Claimant or the Respondent.

Article 27

Where there are two or more Claimants and/or Respondents involved in an arbitration case, the Claimants' side and/or the Respondents' side each shall, through consultation, appoint or entrust the Chairman of the Arbitration Commission to appoint one arbitrator from among the Panel of Arbitrators of the Arbitration Commission.

If the Claimants' side or the Respondents' side fails to make such appointment or entrustment within 20 days as from the date on which the Respondents' side receives the Notice of Arbitration, the appointment will be made by the Chairman of the Arbitration Commission.

Article 28

Any appointed arbitrator having a personal interest in the case shall himself disclose such circumstance to the Arbitration Commission and request a withdrawal from his office.

Article 29

Any party who has justified reasons to suspect the impartiality and independence of an appointed arbitrator may make a request in writing to the Arbitration Commission for that arbitrator's withdrawal. In the request, the facts and reasons on which the request is based shall be stated with the supporting evidence provided.

A challenge against an arbitrator must be put forward in writing no later than the first oral hearing. If the grounds for the challenge come out or are made known after the first oral hearing, the challenge may nevertheless be raised before the conclusion of the last hearing.

Article 30

The Chairman of the Arbitration Commission shall decide whether an arbitrator should be withdrawn.

Before any decision is made by the Chairman of the Arbitration Commission, the challenged arbitrator shall continue to perform the duties of an arbitrator.

Article 31

If an arbitrator is unable to perform the duties owing to his/her withdrawal, demise, removal from the Panel of Arbitrators or any other reasons, a substitute arbitrator shall be appointed in accordance with the procedure pursuant to which the original arbitrator was appointed.

After the appointment of the substitute arbitrator, the arbitration tribunal has discretion to decide whether to repeat the whole or a part of the previous procedures.

Section 3. Hearing

Article 32

The arbitration tribunal will hold oral hearings. At the request of the parties or with their consent, the arbitration tribunal may, if it also considers oral hearings unnecessary, hear and decide a case on the basis of documents only.

Article 33

A74–033   The date of the first oral hearing shall be decided by the arbitration tribunal in consultation with the secretariat of the Arbitration Commission. The secretariat shall notify the two parties of the decision 30 days before the date of the hearing. Any party having justified reasons may request a postponement of the hearing, but a written request must be submitted to the secretariat of the Arbitration Commission 12 days before the date of the hearing. The arbitration tribunal will then decide whether to postpone the hearing or not.

Article 34

A74–034   The notice of the date of hearing subsequent to the first hearing is not subject to the 30-day time limit.

Article 35

A74–035   Where the parties have agreed on the place of arbitration, the case shall be arbitrated in that place. Unless the parties agree otherwise, the cases accepted by the Arbitration Commission shall be heard in Beijing, or in other places with the approval of the Secretary-General of the Arbitration Commission. The cases accepted by a Sub-Commission of the Arbitration Commission shall be heard in the place where the Sub-Commission is located, or in other places with the approval of the Secretary-General of that Sub-Commission.

Article 36

A74–036   The arbitration tribunal shall not hear cases in open session. However, if both parties request that an open session hearing be held, the arbitration tribunal shall decide whether to do so or not.

Article 37

A74–037   For cases heard in closed session, the parties, their arbitration agents, witnesses, arbitrators, experts consulted by the arbitration tribunal and appraisers appointed by the arbitration tribunal and the relevant staff-members of the secretariat of the Arbitration Commission shall not disclose to outsiders the substantive or procedural matters of the case.

Article 38

A74–038   The parties shall produce evidence in support of the facts on which their claim, defense or counterclaim is based. The arbitration tribunal may, on its own initiative, undertake investigations and collect evidence as it considers necessary.

When investigating and collecting evidence by itself, the arbitration tribunal shall promptly inform the parties to be present if it considers necessary. Should one party or both parties fail to appear, the investigation and collection of evidence shall not be affected.

Article 39

A74–039   The arbitration tribunal may consult an expert or appoint an appraiser for clarification of the specific issues relating to a case. Such an expert or appraiser may be either a Chinese or foreign organization or citizen.

The arbitration tribunal has the power to order the parties to submit or produce to the expert or appraiser any relevant materials, documents, or properties and goods for check-up, inspection and/or appraisal, and the parties are so obliged as well.

Article 40

The expert's report and the appraiser's report shall be copied to the parties so that the parties may have the opportunity to give their opinions thereon. At the request of any party to the case and with the approval of the arbitration tribunal, the expert and appraiser may be present at the hearing, and, if considered necessary and appropriate by the arbitration tribunal, be required to give explanations of their reports.

Article 41

The evidence submitted by the parties will be examined and evaluated by the arbitration tribunal. The arbitration tribunal shall decide whether to adopt the expert's report and the appraiser's report.

Article 42

Should one of the parties fail to appear at the hearing, the arbitration tribunal may proceed with the hearing and make an award by default.

Article 43

During the hearing, the arbitration tribunal may make a record in writing and/or by tape-recording. The arbitration tribunal may, when it considers necessary, make a minute stating the main points of the hearing and ask the parties and/or their arbitration agents, witnesses and/or other persons involved to sign and/or affix their seal to it.

The record in writing or by tape-recording is only available for use and reference by the arbitration tribunal.

Article 44

If the parties reach an amicable settlement agreement by themselves, they may either request the arbitration tribunal to conclude the case by making an award in accordance with the contents of their amicable settlement agreement, or request a dismissal of the case.

The Secretary-General of the Arbitration Commission shall decide on the dismissal of an arbitration case if the decision on dismissal is made before the formation of the arbitration tribunal, and the arbitration tribunal shall decide thereon if the decision on dismissal is made after the formation of the arbitration tribunal.

If the party or the parties refer the dismissed case again to the Arbitration Commission for arbitration, the Chairman of the Arbitration Commission shall decide whether to accept the reference or not.

If the parties reach a settlement agreement by themselves through conciliation without involvement of the Arbitration Commission, any of them may, based on an arbitration agreement concluded between them providing for arbitration by the Arbitration Commission and their settlement agreement, request the Arbitration Commission to appoint a sole arbitrator to render an arbitration award in accordance with the contents of the settlement agreement.

Article 45

A74–045 If both parties have a desire for conciliation or one party so desires and the other party agrees to it when consulted by the arbitration tribunal, the arbitration tribunal may conciliate the case under its cognizance in the process of arbitration.

Article 46

A74–046 The arbitration tribunal may conciliate cases in the manner it considers appropriate.

Article 47

A74–047 The arbitration tribunal shall terminate conciliation and continue the arbitration proceedings when one of the parties requests a termination of conciliation or when the arbitration tribunal believes that further efforts to conciliate will be futile.

Article 48

A74–048 If the parties have reached an amicable settlement outside the arbitration tribunal in the course of conciliation conducted by the arbitration tribunal, such settlement shall be taken as one which has been reached through the arbitration tribunal's conciliation.

Article 49

A74–049 The parties shall sign a settlement agreement in writing when an amicable settlement is reached through conciliation conducted by the arbitration tribunal, and the arbitration tribunal will close the case by making an arbitration award in accordance with the contents of the settlement agreement unless otherwise agreed by the parties.

Article 50

A74–050 Should conciliation fail, any statement, opinion, view or proposal which has been made, raised, put forward, acknowledged, accepted or rejected by either party or by the arbitration tribunal in the process of conciliation shall not be invoked as grounds for any claim, defense and/or counterclaim in the subsequent arbitration proceedings, judicial proceedings or any other proceedings.

Article 51

A74–051 The party who knows or should have known that any provision or requirement of these Rules has not been complied with and yet proceeds with the arbitration proceedings without explicitly raising in writing his objection to non-compliance in a timely manner shall be taken to have waived his right to object.

Section 4. Award

Article 52

A74–052 The arbitration tribunal shall render an arbitral award within 9 months as from the date on which the arbitration tribunal is formed. The Secretary-General of the Arbitration Commission may extend this time limit at the request of the arbitration tribunal if the Secretary-General of the Arbitration Commission considers that it is really necessary and the reasons for extension are truly justified.

Article 53

The arbitration tribunal shall independently and impartially make its arbitral award on the basis of the facts, in accordance with the law and the terms of the contracts, with reference to international practices and in compliance with the principle of fairness and reasonableness.

A74–053

Article 54

Where a case is heard by an arbitration tribunal composed of three arbitrators, the arbitral award shall be decided by the majority of the arbitrators and the minority opinion may be recorded and placed on file.

When the arbitration tribunal cannot attain a majority opinion, the arbitral award shall be decided in accordance with the presiding arbitrator's opinion.

A74–054

Article 55

The arbitration tribunal shall state in the arbitral award the claims, the facts of the dispute, the reasons on which the arbitral award is based, the result of the arbitral award, the allocation of the arbitration costs, the date on which and the place at which the arbitral award is made. The facts of the dispute and the reasons on which the arbitral award is based may not be stated in the arbitral award if the parties have agreed not to state them in the arbitral award, or the arbitral award is made in accordance with the contents of the settlement agreement reached between the parties.

A74–055

Article 56

Unless the arbitral award is made in accordance with the opinion of the presiding arbitrator or the sole arbitrator, the arbitral award shall be signed by a majority of arbitrators. An arbitrator who has a dissenting opinion may sign or not sign his name on the arbitral award.

The arbitrators shall submit the draft arbitral award to the Arbitration Commission before signing the award. The Arbitration Commission may remind the arbitrator of any issue related to the form of the arbitral award on condition that the arbitrator's independence of decision is not affected

The Arbitration Commission's stamp shall be affixed to the arbitral award.

The date on which the arbitral award is made is the date on which the arbitral award comes into legal effect.

A74–056

Article 57

An interlocutory award or partial award may be made on any issue of the case at any time in the course of arbitration before the final award is made if considered necessary by the arbitration tribunal, or if the parties make such a proposal and it is agreed to by the arbitration tribunal. Either party's failure to perform the interlocutory award will not affect the continuation of the arbitration proceedings, nor will it prevent the arbitration tribunal from making a final award.

A74–057

Article 58

The arbitration tribunal has the power to determine in the arbitral award the arbitration fee and other expenses to be paid by the parties to the Arbitration Commission.

A74–058

Article 59

A74–059 The arbitration tribunal has the power to decide in the arbitral award that the losing party shall pay the winning party as compensation a proportion of the expenses reasonably incurred by the winning party in dealing with the case. The amount of such compensation shall not in any case exceed 10% of the total amount awarded to the winning party.

Article 60

A74–060 The arbitral award is final and binding upon both disputing parties. Neither party may bring a suit before a law court or make a request to any other organization for revising the arbitral award.

Article 61

A74–061 Either party may request in writing that a correction be made to any writing, typing, calculating errors or any errors of a similar nature contained in the arbitral award within 30 days from the date of receipt of the arbitral award; if there is really an error in the arbitral award, the arbitration tribunal shall make a correction in writing within 30 days form the date of receipt of the written request for correction. The arbitration tribunal may likewise correct any errors in writing on its own initiative within 30 days from the date on which the arbitral award is issued. The correction in writing forms a part of the arbitral award.

Article 62

A74–062 If anything claimed or counterclaimed is found to have been omitted in the arbitral award, either of the parties may make a request in writing to the arbitration tribunal for an additional award within 30 days from the date on which the arbitral award is received. If there is really something omitted, the arbitration tribunal shall make an additional award within 30 days from the date of receipt of the written request. The arbitration tribunal may likewise make an additional award on its own initiative within 30 days from the date on which the arbitral award is issued. The additional award forms a part of the arbitral award previously issued.

Article 63

A74–063 The parties must automatically execute the arbitral award within the time limit specified in the arbitral award. If no time limit is specified in the arbitral award, the parties shall carry out the arbitral award immediately.

In case one party fails to execute the arbitral award, the other party may apply to the Chinese court for enforcement of the arbitral award pursuant to Chinese law or apply to the competent foreign court for enforcement of the arbitral award according to the 1958 Convention on Recognition and Enforcement of Foreign Arbitral Awards or other international treaties that China has concluded or acceded to.

Chapter III. Summary Procedure

Article 64

Unless otherwise agreed by the parties, this Summary Procedure shall apply to any case in dispute where the amount of the claim totals not more than RMB 500,000 yuan, and to any case in dispute where the amount of the claim totals more than RMB 500,000 yuan provided that one party applies for arbitration under this Summary Procedure and the other party agrees in writing.

Article 65

When an application for arbitration is submitted to the Arbitration Commission, the secretariat of the Arbitration Commission shall, if such application is examined and found to be acceptable and qualified for application of the Summary Procedure, send a Notice of Arbitration immediately to the parties.

Unless both parties have jointly appointed one sole arbitrator from among the Panel of Arbitrators of the Arbitration Commission, they shall jointly appoint or jointly entrust the Chairman of the Arbitration Commission to appoint one sole arbitrator within 15 days from the date on which the Notice of Arbitration is received by the Respondent. Should the parties fail to make such appointment or entrustment, the Chairman of the Arbitration Commission shall immediately appoint one sole arbitrator to form an arbitration tribunal to hear the case.

Article 66

The Respondent shall, within 30 days from the date of receipt of the Notice of Arbitration, submit his defense and relevant documentary evidence to the secretariat of the Arbitration Commission; a counterclaim, if any, shall be filed with documentary evidence within the said time limit.

Article 67

The arbitration tribunal may hear the case in the way it considers appropriate. The arbitration tribunal may in its full discretion decide to hear the case only on the basis of the written materials and evidence submitted by the parties or to hold an oral hearing as well.

Article 68

The parties must hand in written materials and evidence required for arbitration in compliance with the requirements of the arbitration tribunal within the time limit given by the arbitration tribunal.

Article 69

For a case which needs an oral hearing, the secretariat of the Arbitration Commission shall, after the arbitration tribunal has fixed a date for hearing, inform the parties of the date of the hearing 15 days before the date of the hearing.

Article 70

If the arbitration tribunal decides to hear the case orally, only one oral hearing shall be held. However, the arbitration tribunal may hold two oral hearings if really necessary.

Article 71

A74–071 Should one of the parties fail to act in compliance with this Summary Procedure during summary proceedings, such failure shall not affect the arbitration tribunal's conduct of the proceedings and the arbitration tribunal's power to render an arbitral award.

Article 72

A74–072 The conduct of the summary proceedings shall not be affected by any amendment of the claim or by the filing of a counterclaim, except that the disputed amount of the revised arbitration claim or counterclaim is in conflict with the provision of Article 64.

Article 73

A74–073 Where a case is heard orally, the arbitration tribunal shall make an arbitral award within 30 days from the date of the oral hearing if one hearing is to be held, or from the date of the second oral hearing if two oral hearings are to be held. Where a case is examined on the basis of documents only, the arbitration tribunal shall render an arbitral award within 90 days from the date on which the arbitration tribunal is formed. The Secretary-General of the Arbitration Commission may extend the said time limit if such extension is necessary and justified.

Article 74

A74–074 For matters not covered in this Chapter, the relevant provisions in the other Chapters of these Rules shall apply.

Chapter IV. Special Provisions for Domestic Arbitration

Article 75

A74–075 The provisions of this Chapter apply to the domestic arbitration cases accepted by the Arbitration Commission in respect of the disputes listed in Item (3), (4), (5) and (6) of paragraph 2, Article 2 of these Rules.

The provisions of Summary Procedure of Chapter III shall apply if the domestic arbitration cases fall within the scope of Article 64 of these Rules.

Article 76

A74–076 After receipt of the Application for Arbitration, the Arbitration Commission, if considered that the application formalities stated in Article 14 of these Rules have been complied with, shall initiate the arbitration proceedings within 5 days and give notification to the parties. Or alternatively, the Arbitration Commission will initiate the arbitration proceedings immediately and notify the parties accordingly. If the Arbitration Commission considers that the application formalities have not been completed, it shall notify the applicant party in writing of its refusal and explain the reasons thereof.

Article 77

A74–077 Upon receipt of the Application for Arbitration, if the Arbitration Commission considers that the Application does not fulfill the requirements set out in Article 14, it may ask the party to rectify it within a specified time limit. If no required rectification is made within that time limit, such Application for Arbitration will be rejected.

Article 78

When the Claimant or the Respondent is required to appoint or authorize the Chairman of the Arbitration Commission to appoint arbitrator(s) according to Article 16, 24, 25 and 27, the time limits provided for by each of the above-mentioned articles shall be 15 days.

Article 79

The Respondent shall, within 30 days from the date of receipt of the Notice of Arbitration, submit his written defense and relevant documentary evidence to the secretariat of the Arbitration Commission.

The Respondent shall, at the latest within 45 days from the date of receipt of the Notice of Arbitration, file with the Arbitration Commission his counterclaim in writing, if any. The arbitration tribunal may extend this time limit if it considers that there are justified reasons.

Article 80

For cases requiring oral hearing(s), the secretariat of the Arbitration Commission shall notify the parties involved of the hearing date at least 15 days in advance. The arbitration tribunal may, with consent from both parties, hold the hearing ahead of schedule. Any party may request a postponement of the hearing if it has justified reasons, but a written request must be submitted to the arbitration tribunal at least 7 days before the date of the hearing. The tribunal will then decide whether to postpone the hearing or not.

The notice of the date of hearing subsequent to the first hearing is not subject to the 15-day time limit stipulated by the preceding paragraph.

Article 81

If a case is heard orally, evidences shall be presented during the hearing(s) and be submitted within the time limit set by the arbitration tribunal.

Article 82

The arbitration tribunal shall make a record of the hearing(s) in writing. Any party or participant in the arbitration may apply for correction if any omission or mistake is found in the record of his own statement. If the arbitration tribunal refuses to correct, such an application shall nevertheless be recorded.

The written record shall be signed or sealed by the arbitrator(s), the person who takes the notes, the parties, and other participants to the arbitration, if any.

Article 83

The arbitration tribunal shall render an arbitral award within 6 months as from the date on which the arbitration tribunal is formed. At the request of the arbitration tribunal, the Secretary-General of the Arbitration Commission may extend this time limit as he considers necessary and justifiable.

Article 84

For matters not covered in this Chapter, the relevant provisions in the other Chapters of these Rules shall apply.

Chapter V. Supplementary Provisions

Article 85

A74–085   The Chinese language is the official language of the Arbitration Commission. If the parties have agreed otherwise, their agreement shall prevail.

At the hearing, if the parties or their arbitration agents or witnesses require language interpretation, the secretariat of the Arbitration Commission may provide an interpreter for them. Or the parties may bring with them their own interpreter.

The arbitration tribunal and/or the secretariat of the Arbitration Commission may, as it considers necessary, request the parties to hand in the corresponding translation copies in Chinese language or other languages of the documents and evidential materials submitted by the parties.

Article 86

A74–086   All the arbitration documents, notices and materials may be sent to the parties and/or their arbitration agents in person, or by registered letter or express airmail, telefax, telex, cable or by any other means considered proper by the secretariat of the Arbitration Commission.

Article 87

A74–087   Any written correspondence to the parties and/or their arbitration agents shall be taken to have been properly served if it is delivered to the addressee or delivered at his place of business, habitual residence or mailing address, or if, after reasonable inquiries, none of the aforesaid addresses can be found, the written correspondence is sent to the addressee's last known place of business, habitual residence or mailing address by registered letter or by any other means which provides a record of the attempt to deliver it.

Article 88

A74–088   Apart from charging arbitration fees from the parties according to the arbitration Fee Schedule of the Arbitration Commission, the Arbitration Commission may collect from the parties other extra, reasonable and actual expenses including arbitrators' special remuneration and their travel and boarding expenses for dealing with the case, as well as the fees and expenses for experts, appraisers and interpreters appointed by the arbitration tribunal, etc.

If a case is withdrawn after the parties have reached between themselves an amicable settlement or is concluded with an arbitral award made according to paragraph 4 of Article 44, the Arbitration Commission may charge a certain amount of fees from the parties in consideration of the quantity of work and the amount of the actual expenses incurred by the Arbitration Commission.

Article 89

A74–089   Where an arbitration agreement or an arbitration clause contained in the contract provides for arbitration to be conducted by China International Economic and Trade Arbitration Commission or its Sub-Commissions or by the formerly named Foreign Trade Arbitration Commission or Foreign Economic and Trade Arbitration Commission of the China Council for the Promotion of International Trade, it shall be taken that the parties have unanimously agreed that the arbitration shall be conducted by China International Economic and Trade Arbitration Commission or by its Sub-Commissions.

Where an arbitration agreement or an arbitration clause contained in the contract provides for arbitration by China Council for the Promotion of International Trade/China Chamber of International Commerce or by the arbitration commission or court of arbitration of China Council for the Promotion of International Trade/China Chamber of International Commerce, it shall be taken that the parties have unanimously agreed that the arbitration shall be conducted by China International Economic and Trade Arbitration Commission.

Article 90

These Rules shall come into force as from October 1st, 2000. For cases accepted by the Arbitration Commission or by its Sub-Commissions before the date on which these Rules become effective, the Rules of Arbitration effective at the time of acceptance shall apply. However, these Rules will be applied if the parties so agree.

Article 91

The power to interpret these Rules is vested in the Arbitration Commission.

B v Dentists Disciplinary Tribunal[1]

HIGH COURT AUCKLAND 26, 27 MAY 1993 WILLIAMS J

A75–001 *Practice and procedure—Jurisdiction—Challenge to procedural orders made by Dentists Disciplinary Tribunal—Whether procedural orders appealable as of right—Whether jurisdiction to appeal only in relation to final orders—Whether application for judicial review appropriate procedure—Dental Act 1988, ss 39, 55 and 64.*

Practice and procedure—Jurisdiction—Jurisdiction of Dentists Disciplinary Tribunal to hear complaints—Source of tribunal's jurisdiction—Whether inherent jurisdiction to adopt own procedure—Dental Act 1988, ss 39, 55 and 64—Commissions of Inquiry Act 1908, ss 4, 48—District Courts Rules 1992, rr 4, 9, 434, 495 and 506.

Administrative law—Tribunals and boards—Judicial review of procedural decision of Dentists Disciplinary Tribunal—Whether tribunal permitted to receive evidence by means of video conference—Whether evidence given by video conference complied with rules of natural justice—Judicature Amendment Act 1972, s 4—Dental Act 1988, ss 61, 63.

Evidence—Admissibility—Witness overseas—Whether grounds existed for witness not attending hearing in person—Whether evidence by video conference appropriate—Whether possibility of prejudice by using video conference—Whether credibility of witness able to be assessed—Guidelines to safeguard principles of natural justice—Commissions of Inquiry Act 1908, s 4B—District Courts Rules 1992, r 434(4)(i).

A75–002   **Editorial note:** The learned Judge points out that r 495 of the District Courts Rules 1992 was "derived" from R 496 of the High Court Rules, and that r 434(4)(i) "appears to have been derived" from R 438(4)(i) of the High Court Rules. In so far as Williams J has construed those District Courts Rules, his findings may also be relevant to the comparable High Court Rules.

This proceeding related to an appeal by a dental surgeon or, alternatively, an application for judicial review, challenging the jurisdiction of the Dentists Disciplinary Tribunal to make interlocutory orders that evidence be received by way of a satellite video link-up, whether such orders were appropriate and complied with the rules of natural justice, and as to timetable orders. The application for such orders had been made by the complainant because her principal medical witness was an overseas expert who was unable to attend the hearing in person, but could give viva voce evidence and be cross-examined by means of a satellite video conference. There was also a preliminary issue as to whether the challenge was properly by way of appeal or must be made by judicial review of the tribunal's decision.

A75–003 **Held:** 1 There was no jurisdiction to bring an appeal on procedural matters. The scheme of the Dental Act 1988 and the powers of the Dentists Disciplinary Tribunal under that Act and under the Commissions of Inquiry Act 1908 indicated that the tribunal had the jurisdiction to control its own procedures, subject only to the requirement to observe the rules of natural justice. The better interpretation of the appeal provision of the Dental Act was that it only applied to final orders or decisions of the tribunal. Such an approach

---

[1] Reproduced with the kind permission of LexisNexis Butterworths.

was similar to that which applied to other disciplinary bodies which were subject only to judicial review proceedings on procedural matters, including jurisdictional matters which arose before a final determination could be made (see p 100 line 5, p 100 line 22).
Duncan v Medical Practitioners Disciplinary Committee [1986] 1 NZLR 513 (CA) applied.

2 The Dentists Disciplinary Tribunal had the jurisdiction to make an order permitting evidence to be given by video link. The ambit of the tribunal's jurisdiction had formerly been circumscribed by the incorporation of the District Court's powers in the exercise of its civil jurisdiction, but that had been terminated by the Commissions of Inquiry Amendment Act 1980. The tribunal's powers to summon witnesses, administer oaths and hear evidence were therefore wholly derived from the Dental Act 1988 and the Commissions of Inquiry Act 1908, together with the inherent powers which the common law associated by inference with Commissions of Inquiry (see p 100 line 50, p 102 line 15). A75–004
Browne v Minister of Immigration [1990] NZAR 67 referred to.

3 In the circumstances of this case, there were no factors sufficient to outweigh the desirability, in fairness to the complainant, of receiving viva voce evidence from the primary expert witness by means of a video conference, provided guidelines were followed to ensure compliance with the rules of natural justice. The interests of both parties had to be balanced, and it was therefore preferable to have the ability to cross-examine, rather than to have to rely on affidavit evidence. Further, there were public interest factors involved in ensuring that complaints were fully and properly considered, and that the credibility of the disciplinary procedures was not put in question by excluding direct expert evidence (see p 109 line 3, p 109 line 26, p 109 line 37). A75–005
R v Board of Visitors of Hull Prison, ex parte St Germain (No 2) [1979] 1 WLR 1401; [1979] 3 All ER 545 referred to.
Appeal dismissed; application for judicial review declined; declarations accordingly.

Observations: (i) Even if the District Courts Rules were relevant to the jurisdiction of the Dentists Disciplinary Tribunal, the provisions of r 434(4)(i) allow for a combination of modes of testifying, provided there is opportunity for cross-examination. Since video conferencing can be brought within the ambit of viva voce evidence, it is very much the same thing as hearing evidence in Court, and in any case the Courts are able to adopt innovative new procedures that will improve the efficiency of the Court (see p 102 line 47, p 103 line 53, p 104 line 37). A75–006
Myers v Director of Public Prosecutions [1965] AC 1001; [1964] 2 All ER 881 referred to.

(ii) As to whether it was appropriate to permit the reception of evidence by means of a video conference, overseas this technique has gained wide acceptance in the context of viva voce evidence, and positive statements have been made by the New Zealand Courts as to its usefulness. There is no reason not to embrace the new technology, provided it is used to serve the interests of justice and fairness (see p 105 line 15, p 107 line 9).
Pacific Fundraising Ltd v Universal Australia Pty Ltd (1990) 3 PRNZ 372, *Bayer AG v Blewett (Minister for Health of the Commonwealth)* (1988) 96 FLR 50; 13 IPR 225 (NSW:SC), *Garcin v Amerindo Investment Advisers Ltd* [1991] 1 WLR 1140; [1991] 4 All ER 655 and *Re San Juan Dupont Plaza Hotel Fire Litigation* 129 FRD 424 (D Puerto Rico 1989) referred to.

Other cases mentioned in judgment *B v B* (High Court, Auckland, HC 4/92, 6 April 1993, Blanchard J). A75–007

Henderson v SBS Realisations Ltd (Court of Appeal, England, 13 April 1992) noted at (1992) 108 LQR 561.
Keith v Television New Zealand Ltd (High Court, Auckland, CP 780/91, 30 October 1992, Robertson J).
R v Accused (CA 32/91) [1992] 1 NZLR 257 (CA).
Scott v Scott [1913] AC 417.
Washington Public Power Supply System Securities Litigation, Re (9 August 1988, Browning CJ, United States District Court for the District of Arizona).

A75–008 **Application** These proceedings were an appeal against interlocutory orders of a tribunal or alternatively an application for judicial review.

A H Waalkens for the appellant/plaintiff.
R E Harrison for the first respondent/first defendant.
M McLelland and *Susan Bridger* for the second respondent/second defendant.

Cur adv vult

A75–009 **WILLIAMS J.** There are presently two proceedings before this Court. The first is an appeal, which purports to be brought pursuant to s 64 of the Dental Act 1988. The second is an application for judicial review. As a preliminary matter, this Court makes an order that the identity of the parties not be revealed until further order of the Court, the reason being that the Dentists Disciplinary Tribunal has found it appropriate to make such orders and this Court has no wish to undermine that ruling in any way.

In the appeal the first respondent was initially named as the Dental Council of New Zealand. Mr Harrison, who appeared for the tribunal, suggested, that in the appeal the proper party should have been the Dentists Disciplinary Tribunal. All other parties agreed. I record that I made an order substituting that tribunal for the council as first defendant/respondent. I should record that no party had any objection to counsel for the tribunal making submissions in this case. Since the matters in issue go to the tribunal's jurisdiction and to procedural matters, there is, in my view, nothing inappropriate in submissions being made by the tribunal itself.

In both proceedings the appellant/applicant (the surgeon) seeks to challenge various procedural orders made by the Dentists Disciplinary Tribunal (the tribunal) in relation to the forthcoming hearing of allegations made against him. The second defendant/respondent (the complainant) has lodged a complaint in accordance with the provisions of the Dental Act 1988, alleging professional misconduct, and acts or omissions on the part of the surgeon during the course of dental treatment and surgery in late 1988. The surgeon denies each of the allegations made against him. The complaints are scheduled to be heard by the Dentists Disciplinary Tribunal at Auckland in the two weeks commencing Monday 31 May 1993. That hearing date was notified to the parties last February. The original timetable was subsequently amended by order of the tribunal dated 11 May which provided that the surgeon's affidavits be filed and served on 17 May.

A75–010 The evidence filed and served on behalf of the complainant comprises affidavits from herself and five witnesses. Much of the evidence relates to medical and dental expert evidence. One of the expert witnesses for the complainant is Dr Ian Munro of Dallas, Texas, United States of America. I am told that he is the principal expert medical witness on behalf of the complainant, his evidence being critical to the conduct of her case. A draft of Dr Munro's 21-page affidavit was received by the surgeon on 8 April 1993. The surgeon's evidence at this stage consists of seven affidavits.

On 19 May the complainant sought various orders from the tribunal including an adjournment of the hearing or in the alternative, an order that Dr Munro's evidence be received by means of a satellite video link. Video conferencing is now able to be achieved in this country and the position would be that Dr Munro would be present in a telecommunication studio in Dallas, Texas, while the tribunal and the parties and counsel would be in a similar studio in Auckland. By means of a satellite video link, the parties in both centres could not only communicate instantaneously but Dr Munro would be visible during both examination-in-chief and cross-examination. The complainant requested that that video link take place on Tuesday 8 June at 10 am which, bearing in mind Queen's Birthday weekend, would mean that it would be on the first hearing day of the second week of the hearing.

The surgeon opposed both the adjournment and the video link applications. The tribunal was convened to consider both applications on Friday 21 May and heard submissions from the parties on that day by way of a telephone conference. It also had assistance from its own legal advisor, Dr Harrison. Later that afternoon the tribunal gave notice to the parties that video link evidence would be permitted for Dr Munro's evidence and that the adjournment application had been declined. Although there was some suggestion that the tribunal had firmly fixed the time for the taking of that evidence as being 8 June, that does not appear to have been the case. Indeed on that subject the written reasons of the tribunal which were supplied later confirmed that there is to be a meeting on 28 May at 10 am, to discuss timetabling and other procedural matters. I should say, however, that counsel for the surgeon raised various matters concerning the time at which the video link is to take place if that order is upheld by the Court, and there is no opposition from the other parties to this matter of timing being considered by this Court at least in a preliminary way. This seemed sensible in order to try to avoid a situation where, with the hearing commencing next Monday, the surgeon, if dissatisfied with the timetable, might be compelled to come back to the Court again. However, as I shall say later, the limited remarks I propose to make on the timetabling matter must be regarded as provided simply for the broad guidance of the tribunal. Even if I was minded to do so I could hardly issue directions when the tribunal itself has not first had the chance to deliberate further on the matter.

Returning to the narrative, the reasons for the orders or directions of the tribunal include the following:

> "Adjournment:
> The complainant seeks adjournment of the hearing on the ground that the complainant will otherwise 'suffer serious and insurmountable prejudice in the prosecution of her case and this will seriously impinge on the Tribunal's ability to conduct a fair and balanced inquiry'.
>
> The applicant alleges that affidavits filed by Dr B raise new matters she had not anticipated, and there will be insufficient time to call or brief further witnesses to respond to those matters.
>
> The Tribunal has heard detailed argument from both counsel, particularly on the question of which of them is more at fault for delays in complying with earlier directions to file affidavits.
> . . .
> Video Link-up:
> The applicant's case is that Dr Ian Munro is unable to attend the hearing in person, but is prepared to give evidence and be cross-examined by way of video conference.
>
> The respondent opposes, saying first, that the Tribunal has no jurisdiction to hear

evidence in this manner and secondly, that it seriously prejudices the conduct of his cross-examination.

The Tribunal's Legal Assessor advises that there is jurisdiction for a video link-up, relying [inter alia] on section 4B(1) of the Commissions of Inquiry Act 1908 (although respondent's counsel disputes his interpretation of these provisions). The Legal Assessor notes, quite properly, that the proposed method of receiving evidence may well bear on the weight of that evidence, and that the benefit of any reduction in its weight must go to the respondent.

The Tribunal is not entirely satisfied with the adequacy of Dr Munro's reasons for declining to attend in person. Further, the Tribunal has sympathy for respondent's submissions that cross-examination by video disadvantages the respondent in his conduct of the case.

In the circumstances, however, the Tribunal reluctantly takes the view that evidence and cross-examination by video are preferable to no cross-examination at all. The Tribunal considers it does have jurisdiction to hear evidence in this manner, but it has no jurisdiction to subpoena an overseas witness.

Accordingly, the Tribunal rules that Dr Munro may give evidence and be cross-examined by way of video link-up between Auckland and Dallas, Texas. The complainant must bear any risk attaching to the weight or credibility of Dr Munro's evidence arising from his non-appearance in person.

There is some suggestion that timetabling difficulties may arise in respect of the expert witnesses. The Tribunal therefore proposes that counsel meet with the Chairperson and the Legal Assessor on Friday 28 May at 10 am in the Dental Association's rooms in Auckland to schedule witnesses and to settle timetable and any outstanding procedural matters. It will be acceptable, and probably appropriate, for Kensington Swan to instruct a solicitor from its Auckland office to attend this meeting."

Appeal from an order of the tribunal

A75–013 The first matter which needs to be considered is jurisdiction in respect of the appeal. The surgeon relies upon s 64 of the Dental Act 1988 which is concerned with appeals from decisions of the Dental Council, the Dental Technicians Board and Dentists Disciplinary Tribunals and lists a number of situations in which an appeal is available. The particular subsection relied upon is s 64(1)(d) which states that:

> **64. Appeals from decisions of Council, Board, and Tribunals**—(1) Every person who is dissatisfied with the whole or any part of—
>
> . . .
>
> (d) Any order of the Tribunal made under this Act relating to that person; or
>
> . . .
>
> may, within 28 days after the notice of the decision, direction, or order has been served on him or her or by the Secretary or within such further time as the High Court may allow on application made before or after the expiration of that period, appeal to the High Court against the decision, direction, or order, as the case may be.

Counsel for the surgeon contends that the order allowing evidence by way of video conference is an "order of the Tribunal". The written reasons are headed "Orders of the

Tribunal". He submits that it is also an order "relating to that person" who is appealing, namely the surgeon. That is certainly true in a general sense, because the whole of the proceedings relate to the surgeon who is the respondent to the complaint.

However, I raised with counsel for the surgeon the question as to whether it was intended that procedure rulings of this tribunal should be appealable as of right. The scheme of the Act suggests that the tribunal is intended to be in total control, the master of its own procedure, particularly in view of the inquisitorial powers given to it by cross-referencing to the Commissions of Inquiry Act 1908. These extensive powers are subject only to certain specific provisions within the Dental Act 1988 itself, such as the requirement in s 61(5) that the council and tribunal are to observe the rules of natural justice.

It is one construction of s 64(1)(d) that the "orders" referred to therein are only intended to encompass final orders, such as the range of orders that can be made under s 55, (penalties which may be imposed on a practitioner who has been found guilty of misconduct) and orders as to costs and expenses pursuant to s 56. Final orders obviously justify an appeal because they concern matters of such consequence as the removal of a practitioner's name from the register. Section 39(10) of the Dental Act 1963 certainly seems to have restricted the right to appeal to final orders, referring as it does to an "order of suspension or censure or the imposition of a penalty or of a liability to pay costs and expenses".

Bearing in mind the remaining subsections in s 64, I have serious doubts as to whether it was intended by the general language of s 64(1)(d) to enable parties involved in dental disciplinary proceedings to be able to come to this Court on each occasion when a procedural order or direction is made which affects them in an indirect sense. In my view, the much more likely interpretation is that the orders referred to are those with the serious consequences described in s 55. If my view is correct, the position would be similar to that of other such disciplinary bodies, where the parties are confined by statute to appeal against final orders or decisions of such tribunals, and are left to take judicial review proceedings in cases where major procedural issues, including matters of jurisdiction, arise before a final determination: see *Duncan v Medical Practitioners Disciplinary Committee* [1986] 1 NZLR 513, at p 539.

Because of my concerns I gave counsel for the surgeon an opportunity to lodge judicial review proceedings which mirrored the appeal. This was done without opposition from the other parties, who sensibly took the view that the guidance of the Court was important and the matter should not be dismissed at the threshold. I therefore propose to proceed to consider the matter on the basis of the judicial review proceedings.

Judicial review: challenges to the order of the tribunal

The challenge to the order of the tribunal permitting the video conferencing is based **A75–014** on three grounds. First, that there is no jurisdiction to make such an order. Secondly, that the presentation of evidence by video link would be inappropriate or unduly prejudicial to the surgeon and thirdly that the tentative timing for the link-up is unsuitable and unreasonable. It is said that in these three ways the tribunal both erred in law and breached the rules of natural justice.

Jurisdiction

I deal first with the issue of jurisdiction. As a preliminary to that it is necessary to **A75–015** consider the scheme of Part III of the Dental Act. The recent judgment of Blanchard J in *B v B* (High Court, Auckland, HC 4/92, 6 April 1993) at pp 4–6 provides a helpful outline:

> "*Scheme of Part III of Dental Act*
> Section 52 of the Dental Act 1988 requires that a person seeking to complain about the conduct of a dentist must make the complaint in writing to the secretary of the Dental Council of New Zealand as constituted by s 69 of the Act. Where the secretary of the council receives the complaint it is referred to the chairperson of the council 'who shall appoint a Complaints Assessment Committee in accordance with s 45 of this Act and refer the complaint to that Committee'.
>
> A Complaints Assessment Committee for cases involving a dentist consists of two dentists and one person who is not a dentist: s 45. Such a committee is a body established in relation to a specific complaint rather than a standing body. In contrast, the Dental Disciplinary Tribunal is established under s 46 as a standing body. It consists of three dentists appointed by the council and two persons who are not dentists. The members of the tribunal are appointed for a term of three years: s 49. So it is a permanent body to deal with all matters referred to it. The quorum of the tribunal is three members: s 51.
>
> The tribunal is empowered to appoint a legal assessor, who may be present at any proceedings of the tribunal and may then, or at any time previously or subsequently, advise the tribunal on matters of law, procedure and evidence relating thereto. However, no legal assessor is entitled to be present during the deliberations of the tribunal: s 68.
>
> Under s 53 a Complaints Assessment Committee must determine whether or not in its opinion the complaint which has been referred to it should be considered by the tribunal and must report its finding to the chairperson of the tribunal. Where the committee has reported that in its opinion the matter should be considered by the tribunal, the chairperson of the tribunal must forthwith cause a notice to be served on the dentist in accordance with s 61(1) of the Act. So the function of the committee is limited to reporting on whether or not it thinks that the tribunal should consider a complaint. The responsibility for framing a notice under s 61 is given by statute to the chairperson of the very body which will conduct the hearing and determine the guilt or innocence of the dentist and impose, or decide not to impose, penalties. The statute thus intermingles some prosecutorial functions with the judicial functions but, at the same time, it does not actually provide for a prosecutor. Obviously, therefore, administrative law questions relating to the activities of the tribunal must be considered in light of this statutory conflation of roles.
>
> Section 61(1) specifies that the tribunal must not exercise its disciplinary powers before its chairperson causes to be served on the dentist a notice:
>
> - stating that the committee has reason to believe that a ground exists entitling the tribunal to exercise its disciplinary powers and
> - containing such particulars as will inform the dentist of the substance of the grounds believed to exist and
> - specifying a date, being not less than 28 days after the date of service of the notice, on which the tribunal intends to hear the matter.
>
> In the same section there is also a direction that the tribunal must observe the rules of natural justice: subs (5). That must be read in the context to which I have just referred.
>
> The disciplinary powers of the tribunal are exercisable only after it has conducted

a hearing. If it is satisfied that the dentist has been guilty of any act or omission in the course of or associated with the practice of dentistry that was or could have been detrimental to the welfare of any patient or other person, or if it is satisfied that the dentist has been guilty of professional misconduct (including, without limiting the generality of the foregoing, professional negligence), the tribunal may exercise certain disciplinary powers: s 54. It may:

- order that the name of the dentist be removed from the register
- order that the registration of the dentist be suspended for a period not exceeding 12 months
- order that the dentist may, for a period not exceeding three years, practice only subject to such conditions as to employment, supervision or otherwise as the tribunal may specify in the order
- order the dentist to pay a fine not exceeding $5000
- order that the dentist be censured: s 55(1).

The power to impose a fine is cumulative upon the power to make an order for removal, suspension or practising subject to conditions. Under s 56 the tribunal may also order the dentist to pay any costs and expenses of and incidental to the hearing by the tribunal and any Inquiry made by the committee."

The argument against jurisdiction was that pursuant to s 63 of the Dental Act 1988 **A75–017** the tribunal has, for the purposes of its hearing, the powers of a commission of inquiry and ss 4 to 9 of the Commissions of Inquiry Act 1908 apply. In relation to the conduct of the hearing, s 4 of the latter Act provides that for the purposes of an inquiry the commission has "the powers of a District Court in the exercise of its civil jurisdiction, in respect of citing parties ... and conducting and maintaining order at the inquiry". Thus the starting point of counsel for the surgeon was the contention that the only powers which this tribunal possessed are those which are available to District Courts. This interpretation was challenged by counsel for the complainant, and indeed by counsel for the tribunal. The opposing argument was that the 1980 amendments to the Commissions of Inquiry Act, which eliminated the words "summoning witnesses, administering oaths, hearing evidence", had terminated the incorporation of the District Court's powers with respect to these matters, with the result that the tribunal's powers to summon witnesses, administer oaths and hear evidence, were now wholly derived from the Dental Act 1988 and in the Commissions of Inquiry Act 1908. These powers are coupled with the inherent powers which the common law has held to be associated inferentially with Commissions of Inquiry. In my view, this latter argument is correct and I note that Eichelbaum CJ in *Browne v Minister of Immigration* [1990] NZAR 67 was of the same view, although he did not finally decide the point.

However, out of an abundance of caution, I propose to consider the question of jurisdiction both under the Commissions of Inquiry Act 1908 and under the District Courts Act 1947. In my view, for the reasons I will give shortly, the result is the same in each case.

The Commissions of Inquiry Act, gives the tribunal control of its own procedure. Section 4(b)(i) of the Commissions of Inquiry Act 1908 states "that the Commission may receive as evidence any statement, document, information or matter that in its opinion may assist it to deal effectively with the subject matter of the inquiry". This evidence may be received "whether or not it would be admissible in a Court of law". It seems to me that the language of this section is broad enough to encompass the jurisdiction to receive oral evidence by means of a video link.

A75–018 But even if the District Courts Act is still pertinent, it is my view that the answer would be no different. The relevant provisions in this case are the District Courts Rules 1992. These rules came into force on 1 January 1992, and were introduced as part of measures to bring that Court more in line with the procedures of the High Court following the increase in its civil jurisdiction. I mention this because the rules at issue in the present case have their origins in the High Court Rules. Any relevant case law involving the latter may be of assistance.

The argument against jurisdiction was based primarily on r 495 of the District Courts Rules 1992, which is derived from R 496 of the High Court Rules. It was argued that the District Courts Rules clearly contemplate the physical presence of a witness in Court for the purpose of giving evidence both in-chief and by cross-examination. Rule 495 provides:

> **R 495. Evidence to be given orally**—Except where otherwise directed by the Court or required or authorised by these rules or any Act, disputed questions of fact arising at the hearing of any proceeding shall be determined on evidence given by means of witnesses examined orally in open Court.

It was submitted by counsel for the surgeon that the few exceptions to this long-established practice of compelling a witness to be physically present in Court to give evidence have been specifically provided for either in the rules themselves or by statute or regulation. As to the rules, reference was made to r 506, which rule contemplates that where affidavit evidence is challenged the deponent must be physically present in Court for cross-examination, and to r 434(4)(i), which empowers a Judge at any prehearing conference to direct that evidence be given in any one of a number of ways. It was submitted that in each of these cases the rule specifically requires that any party shall have the opportunity of cross-examining any witness. As to statutes or regulations, there was reference to the way in which parliament has enacted specific regulations dealing with the evidence of child complainants in sexual abuse cases, namely in the Evidence (Videotaping of Child Complainants) Regulations 1990 (SR 1990/164). That was said to demonstrate that Parliament has had to deal with such special cases by legislating to authorise videotaping of certain evidence. Against this background it was argued that the absence of statutory provisions for video link evidence was of significance.

Against this background it was submitted that, under the District Courts Rules, the only relevant provision was r 434(4)(n) which entrusted the Court with a general discretion to order that evidence be given in any manner *provided the parties agreed*. In the absence of agreement, as in the present case, it was submitted that there was no such jurisdiction.

A75–019 I do not read the rules in that way. First, even if r 495 is to be considered, it provides in the introductory words that it applies "[e]xcept where otherwise directed by the Court or required or authorised by these rules or by any Act". As *McGechan on Procedure* states at p 3–600, the general rule requiring oral evidence in open Court is subject to three exceptions, where (a) the Court otherwise directs; (b) the rules or any Act otherwise requires; or (c) the rules or any Act otherwise authorises. Counsel for the complainant submitted that other Acts are of relevance here, namely the Dental Act 1988 and the Commissions of Inquiry Act 1908. The latter specifically authorises the admission of a variety of forms of evidence, and permits both written and oral evidence.

In any case, to the extent that r 434(4)(n) is said to be the only rule that is relevant, it is to be noted that r 434(3) states in relation to directions affecting the hearing, that "the Court may make such orders and give such directions (whether sought by the party applying or not) as appear best adapted to secure the just, expeditious, and economical disposal of the proceeding". The opening language of sub r 4 provides that "[i]n particular, but without limiting the generality of the foregoing provision, the Court may by its order ... " make various directions or orders. Thus the provisions of r 434(4)(n) are not to cut down the broad ability of the Court to give the order that is best suited to secure the just, expeditious and economical disposal of the proceedings. As *McGechan* has noted at p 3–483, the power in the rule is general, although particular powers are listed. A Court still has room to move within the general power but outside of the specific instances delineated by the rule.

In any event, in view of the procedure that is proposed here, it seems to me that r 434(4)(i), rather than r 434(4)(n), would cover the position:

R 434. Directions affecting the hearing—

...

(4) In particular, but without limiting the generality of the foregoing provision, the Court may by its order—

...

(i) Direct that the evidence, or the evidence of any particular witness or witnesses shall be given by examination viva voce in open Court, or by affidavit, or by pre-recorded statement or report duly sworn by the witness before or at the hearing, or partly by one and partly by another or others of such modes of testifying:

"Provided that in every case any opposite party shall (if that party so requires) have the opportunity of cross-examining any witness:.

This rule, which appears to have been derived from R 438(4)(i) of the High Court Rules, allows for a combination of modes of testifying, with the proviso that the opposite party shall have the opportunity of cross-examining any witness in any case. Clearly video link evidence is not an affidavit nor is it a "pre-recorded statement or report" for the purposes of this rule, because of its contemporaneity. However, in my opinion, the evidence available through video link is effectively viva voce evidence. I note that Lord Donaldson MR seems to have reached a similar conclusion in *Henderson v SBS Realisations Ltd* (Court of Appeal, England, 13 April 1992) noted at (1992) 108 LQR 561 a decision to which I shall return shortly. It is sufficient for present purposes to note that the Master of the Rolls considered that "[a] video link is, for all practical purposes, very much the same as hearing evidence in court". That the rule refers to examination "viva voce *in open Court*", is only to reiterate the usual preference for open Court, rather than in camera hearings. This certainly seems to be the stance taken in *McGechan on Procedure*, at p 3–600(a) in relation to the "open Court" requirement in R 496 of the High Court Rules.

Even if that construction was thought inadequate there are other relevant provisions in the District Courts Rules. Rule 4 is a general injunction to construe the rules to secure the "just, speedy and inexpensive determination of any proceeding ... ". Rule 9 provides that in cases not explicitly provided for, the Court is to follow "as nearly as may be practicable ... the High Court Rules". If there are no such provisions, the Court is to act "in such manner as the Court thinks best calculated to promote the ends of justice".

So in my view the challenge to jurisdiction based on the suggested absence of empowering provisions in the District Courts Rules must fail no matter which route is taken especially since, in matters of procedure as opposed to matter of substantive law, the Courts have always felt able to adopt innovative new procedures that will improve the efficiency of the Court. Even if the rules could not be construed so as to create the necessary jurisdiction, this Court would not be left impotent to act without legislative intervention. I am reminded of the words of Lord Donovan in *Myers v Director of Public Prosecutions* [1965] AC 1001, at p 1047:

> "The common law is moulded by the judges and it is still their province to adapt it from time to time so as to make it serve the interests of those it binds. Particularly is this so in the field of procedural law."

A75–021 Cooke P, in *R v Accused (CA 32/91)* [1992] 1 NZLR 257 at p 262 a decision concerning the videotaping of children's evidence considered that the inherent jurisdiction of the Court could be invoked to authorise closed circuit evidence and probably to videotape evidence also. Citing Viscount Haldane's judgment in *Scott v Scott* [1913] AC 417, 437–438, Cooke P referred to the need to:

> " ... keep in the forefront Viscount Haldane LC's emphasis ... on the paramount duty of the Court to adapt its procedure to ensure that justice is done. This adaptability should enable the adjustment of Court procedure to take advantage of technological advances."

There is every reason for that approach to be taken not only in relation to the District Court and the High Court, but also in relation to a specialist tribunal such as the Dentists Disciplinary Tribunal. I do not doubt that occasions will arise from time to time where there will be overseas experts involved in disciplinary hearings. Subject to appropriate safeguards, I believe that it would be beneficial to allow such tribunals to be informed and assisted by overseas experts in the field without the need for the cost and expense of bringing expert witnesses to New Zealand. Indeed such bodies have the potential to be at the forefront of the introduction of video link technology into this country.

Video link evidence overseas

A75–022 Accepting that the tribunal possessed jurisdiction to allow evidence by way of video link the next question is whether it was appropriate to make the orders it did. The first question is whether there is a sufficiently good "track record" with this form of evidence to make its use appropriate. Here an analysis of overseas practice is instructive. Counsel referred me to decisions on this topic in this and other jurisdictions namely *Pacific Fundraising Ltd v Universal Australia Pty Ltd* (1990) 3 PRNZ 372; *Bayer AG v Blewett (Minister for Health of the Commonwealth)* (1988) 96 FLR 50, at p 116 and *Garcin v Amerindo Investment Advisers Ltd* [1991] 4 All ER 655. In addition, through my own inquiries, I have been able to locate some others.

In this country, Tompkins J in *Pacific Fundraising Ltd v Universal Australia Pty Ltd* made positive statements about video link evidence in the context of taking evidence abroad. The parties were encouraged to consider video link as an option. Tompkins J referred to the decision of the Supreme Court of New South Wales in *Bayer AG v Blewett (Minister for Health of the Commonwealth)*. In that case Young J noted that evidence had been successfully received by video link. Young J highlighted possible difficulties concerning the administration of the oath abroad and the question of whether there could be a prosecution for perjury in Australia where the evidence was received but considered that overall the exercise had been a success, given that the demeanour of witnesses could be easily assessed.

In Australia, and in Victoria in particular, a progressive stance has been taken on video links. The High Court of Australia has given a practice direction enabling appellants seeking special leave to appeal in civil matters to appear by way of "video tele-hearing". Teleconferencing has been permitted both in Court, and within tribunals; see [1991] Law Institute Journal September, pp 862–863. For example, in 1991, the Melbourne Accident Compensation Tribunal had its first interstate teleconferencing hearing, and four doctors gave evidence by this means.

In Canada, video-conferencing has been encouraged by the Supreme Court of Canada since 1983; see *Goldstein on Video-tape and Photographic Evidence Case Law & Reference Manual* (1986) at p 16.

The position in the United States varies between individual states. Hertzberg, *"Clever Tool or Dirty Pool?: WPPSS, Closed Circuit Testimony and the Rule 45(e) Subpoena Power"* (1989) 21 Arizona State LJ 275, provides a helpful discussion of the treatment of this topic by the American Courts. The author explains that there is no specific rule within the US Federal Rules of Civil Procedure which authorises such evidence. Rule 30(b)(4) permits video depositions, but these are a pre-recorded, rather than a live means of giving evidence. Resort has been had to R 45(e), which limits the Court's power to subpoena witnesses to those within a one hundred mile radius, and to the guiding principle of the Federal Rules—that "they shall be construed to secure the just, speedy and inexpensive determination of every action". Where a witness is outside of this 100 mile range, the Courts have held that video link evidence is permissible. *Re Washington Public Power Supply System Securities Litigation*, unreported (9 August 1988, Browning CJ, United States District Court for the District of Arizona), and *Re San Juan Dupont Plaza Hotel Fire Litigation* 129 FRD 424 (D Puerto Rico 1989) are both examples of cases where video link evidence has been permitted at trial, pursuant to the subpoena power of a foreign District Court. The comments of Acosta J of the US District Court, District of Puerto Rico in the latter case are pertinent. In response to a submission by the defendants who opposed the video link evidence on the basis that such a technique was "untried, unauthorised, and unworkable", he said at pp 425–426:

" ... the futuristic aspects of the PSC proposal need not be perceived as a threat. It is a well-known aphorism that 'professions are the enemy of change'. Yet no profession can remain indefinitely sheltered from the maelstrom of modernism that in recent years has completely changed the communications landscape. One need only consider that computers were once thought to be strictly secretarial tools, yet now many lawyers carry their stylish lap-top computers in addition to their briefcases. With this increased acceptance and personalised use of sophisticated technology has come the belated realisation that just because some mechanism or process is 'untried' does not mean that it should be disregarded; rather, it should be used if it contains at least a well-founded promise of some important benefit and causes little or no prejudice. In short, the use of this type of technology in the courtroom, as with other types already in use, will not create a sort of 'brave new world' as feared by defendants. The Court has little doubt that the presentation of live testimony by satellite is a viable, and even refreshing, alternative to the deadening recitation of numerous depositions. It would also be most helpful to the jury in the fulfilment of their sworn duties. After all, the purpose of a trial is precisely to ensure the truth-seeking process which, to a great extent, is based on the demeanour of witnesses. In addition, the use of satellite transmitted testimony avoids the burdens and problems inherent in the arranging of travel schedules, conflicting obligations, and extended stays in the transferee district because of the uncertainties of trial schedules."

A75–024 In England, legislation has been specifically enacted to permit video link evidence in certain types of criminal cases namely those involving murder, manslaughter or complex fraud: s 32 of the Criminal Justice Act 1988. Similar enabling legislation was not considered to be necessary in civil matters, where the English equivalent of the High Court Rules was seen as sufficiently broad as to permit video link evidence. Thus in *Garcin v Amerindo Investment* Morritt J considered that the English Courts had the necessary jurisdiction to receive such evidence pursuant to RSC Order 38, r 3 which provides the Court with the power to determine how evidence is to be given at the trial of any action.

A recent decision of the English Court of Appeal in *Henderson v SBS Realisations Ltd* pp 561–565, considers the availability of video link testimony within the County Court setting. Both Lord Donaldson MR and Balcombe LJ made general statements in favour of the admission of this form of evidence. Lord Justice Balcombe stated that:

" . . . this Court should be very loath to construe the statutory provisions relating to jurisdiction or so to exercise its powers under the rules as to preclude the use of technological improvements which the law ought to be minded to accept wherever possible."

The Master of the Rolls, when confronted with a precedent relating to the admissibility of documentary evidence, sought to distinguish evidence given by video link at p 564:

"' . . . If you have a critical matter to be proved, it is most unsatisfactory that it should be done by documents. A video link is quite different. A video link is, for all practical purposes, very much the same as hearing evidence in court. I agree that there are technical problems about it and it may be that it is marginallly preferable that the evidence should be heard in court. But it is in no way comparable with seeking to prove matters by the production of documents.' "

A75–025 To conclude, it appears that video linking, or teleconferencing, is gaining acceptance as a means of presenting legal argument and the evidence of witnesses in Canada, (the Supreme Court), Australia (the High Court), England (the Court of Appeal) and the United States. In view of this considerable body of opinion and experience there is no reason not to embrace this new technology. However, that the Court or tribunal has the jurisdiction to employ this technology does not eliminate the need to ensure that it is used fairly. The words of Justice Estey, in the foreword to *Goldstein* at p viii, should be heeded:

"The ends of justice may well be served by material developments which enable the assembly and analysis of evidence in a timely and economic manner so as to reveal with accuracy the truth of the relationship between the parties. *The countervailing need, of course, is to ensure that the whole of this process is carried out in a way that will as well serve the interests of justice and fairness.*" (Emphasis added.)

Is video link evidence appropriate in this case?

A75–026 Bearing this caution in mind, I turn now to the question as to whether it was appropriate for the tribunal to make the video link order. The first matter that was raised by the surgeon was that the reasons advanced as to why the doctor could not give evidence in person were inadequate.

The tribunal was supplied with information from the complainant to the effect that Dr Munro, who is an eminent medical specialist, was simply unable to leave his practice for a week and that the expense that would be involved in his spending a week in New Zealand was not something which the complainant could reasonably be expected to meet. While I would have preferred to see direct evidence on these issues, I do not consider that it was at all unreasonable for the tribunal to draw the inference that it was impracticable to secure the personal attendance of the doctor. I note in that respect that the tribunal said it was not entirely satisfied with the adequacy of Dr Munro's reasons for his unavailability but sensibly it took the view that evidence-in-chief and cross-examination by video link were preferable to no cross-examination at all. It seems to me that if the doctor was unable to attend it would have been permissible for his affidavit to be received although the tribunal would then have had the further difficulty of deciding what weight, if any, should be given to the untested opinions of an expert. In my view, the reasoning of the tribunal on the appropriateness of the video link in the present case was sound.

However, the matter of prejudice to the surgeon needs consideration. If the submissions on this point are cumulatively sufficient to show that the end result would be unfair or prejudicial, then the decision to allow video link evidence would have to be revisited. This is a most important matter for the surgeon whose reputation and livelihood is at risk. In considering these matters that factor always must be borne in mind.

The submissions advanced by counsel for the surgeon focused upon the potential for prejudice in the conduct of cross-examination. First, the witness was likely to gain some comfort "behind" the television screen rather than being before the tribunal. The point is directed at supposed benefits to the witness in that he or she will not be subjected to the same pressures as he would if appearing in person. I doubt whether the "video witness" would be more composed than the live witness, but even if it might be so in some cases, it could not, in a case before a specialist tribunal, make such a dramatic difference as to warrant excluding the technique altogether.

The second contention was that the spontaneity of cross-examination would be prejudiced. Once again, I cannot see that this is a sufficiently serious disqualifying factor. It may be true that the video link requires a short gap between the announcement of the question and its reception, but it is virtually simultaneous. Indeed, it may be that there will be greater spontaneity because of the fact that the cross-examiner will not have to keep pace with stenographers or typists since the whole examination will be recorded.

Thirdly, it was claimed that the ability of counsel for the surgeon to put exhibits, three-dimensional models, superimposed slides, photographs and video evidence before the witness would be hampered. I believe that this objection can be met largely by appropriate organisation on the part of counsel. First, there is to be an "agreed bundle" of exhibits (comprising x-rays, photographs and hospital records) which is to be made available to Dr Munro prior to the commencement of the proceedings. In addition each party will have possession of the video taken while the complainant was in hospital in New Zealand. Secondly, if the need arises to put to Dr Munro additional documents not in the agreed bundle, then as counsel for the complainant has indicated, such documents can be transmitted instantaneously by facsimile machines which will be ready in each studio. Thirdly, to the extent that anatomical models are required, standard medical models of the head and skull would doubtless be available to both parties at either end of the link. Once again I do not see that any serious difficulty is likely to be encountered provided that counsel undertake sufficient advance preparation.

The final contention was that as credibility will be an issue in this case there would be a real potential for difficulty in assessment of the demeanour of the witness. I am not persuaded by this argument. First, this is not a case involving a simple conflict of credibility on primary facts. It is the standard situation where there are differing opinions expressed by expert witnesses, including Dr Munro. Secondly, even if credibility was in issue, I fail to see how the system that is to be employed would prevent the assessment of the demeanour of the witness because as already noted, the witness will be seen giving his evidence to the same extent, or to no significantly lesser extent, than if present in a Court or in a hearing room. Some overseas articles suggest that the video link technique may enhance credibility—the so called "TV effect". This was a concern expressed by Robertson J in *Keith v Television New Zealand Ltd* (High Court. Auckland, CP 780/91, 30 October 1992). There an application was made in a defamation case to be tried before a jury for consent to video the evidence of an overseas witness and play the resulting videotape to the jury. The alternative was to require the witness to return from overseas to give viva voce evidence. Robertson J said at pp 6–7:

> "I am of the view that there is little or no accurate knowledge of or experience in the effect on a jury of material introduced by video. I am conscious of the power of the silver screen within the homes of this country. I suspect that there is a degree of authority attaching to evidence when it is seen not in the flesh, but on a receiver. Mr Waalken's submission was that the jury would be in no different position if they saw a video recording of the entire examination and cross-examination than if Dr Volkerling was present in the Court. I am not persuaded that such is a valid submission. I rather suspect that the evidence has the potential to make a greater impact if transmitted by video than would otherwise be the case."

A75–028 I do not consider that the same concern arises with a "live" performance especially before a specialist tribunal as opposed to a jury. It is unlikely that tribunal members will be unduly swayed by a live video presentation of evidence especially on complex matters of medical opinion.

In my view, none of the reasons advanced amount to prejudice, let alone to the type of prejudice that would be sufficient to outweigh the desirability, in fairness to the complainant, of allowing her primary medical expert witness to "appear" before the tribunal on the video link. One has to remember that a balancing exercise is required here. There are not just the interests of the surgeon at stake. The complainant's interests are entitled to proper weight. There are public interest factors in ensuring that complaints are properly and fully considered. The credibility of the disciplinary procedures under the Dental Act 1988 might come into question if the tribunal or this Court was to rule that this kind of evidence could not be presented. So I find no substance in the argument that there would be prejudice, less still prejudice sufficient to outweigh all other considerations and lead to this evidence being excluded.

I should record that the case of the *R v Board of Visitors of Hull Prison, ex parte St Germain (No 2)* [1979] 1 WLR 1401, 1409 was relied upon by counsel for the surgeon for the proposition that where a tribunal has power to receive hearsay evidence which would otherwise not be admissible, and the evidence is crucial, there is still an overriding obligation to provide the accused with a fair hearing and therefore direct evidence should be insisted upon. In my view the case is distinguishable because, as was submitted by counsel for the tribunal, the present case is not dealing with hearsay evidence. The proposed evidence will be direct evidence.

Safeguards where evidence is received by video link

However, having reached that conclusion I do want to say that it is entirely appropriate where video link techniques are to be used that there be appropriate safeguards to ensure that the process is conducted fairly and aligned as closely as possible to the situation which applies where a witness is present in Court for cross-examination. In this respect, counsel for the tribunal indicated that any guidance given by this Court would be welcome. Therefore I propose to provide some guidelines, acknowledging, however, that ultimately it is for the tribunal to establish an appropriate procedure. For example, if it was thought that the quality of the picture from the video link was inadequate, then nothing that I have said in this decision is to be construed as obliging the tribunal to continue. In the end, the tribunal will have to make such decisions when the video link occurs.

I indicated in the course of argument that if I upheld the tribunal's order, certain conditions or guidelines should be imposed and I outlined some of them. In the *San Juan* case the Court appended a protocol to its judgment containing comprehensive details as to the precise manner in which the video link evidence was to be taken before the jury. In the present case, involving an expert tribunal, I do not consider that such exhaustive detail is necessary. The seven conditions which follow seem to me to provide adequate safeguards, although they are not to be seen as exclusive, If as the matter develops, the tribunal considers that there are further procedures that would be beneficial, it should consider itself free to add them. These seven procedures are:

1. The video conference system in Dallas must be such as to allow a reasonable part of the interior of the room in which Dr Munro is situated to be shown on screen, yet retaining sufficient proximity to depict Dr Munro himself.

2. Dr Munro is to give his evidence either sitting at a plain desk or standing at a lectern.

3. All written materials or exhibits already discovered between the parties that Dr Munro is to be referred to in the course of his evidence must be clearly identified: a paginated agreed bundle of documents is to be made available and the exhibits are to be numbered for identification purposes.

4. Unless agreed otherwise, normal Court sitting times should be observed in the course of Dr Munro's evidence, with adjournments of 15 min in the morning and afternoon sessions, and 1 hr 15 min for lunch, together with such other adjournments as are acceptable to the tribunal and the parties.

5. A facsimile machine is to be located in both the Dallas and Auckland venues for the video conference.

6. At all times during the course of the video conference the tribunal may terminate the video conference if it is so unsatisfactory that it is unfair to either party to continue.

7. The only persons present in the Dallas facility (other than Dr Munro) are to be those operating the video and facsimile facilities. Any other person present at the video conference in Dallas is to be identified upon entry into the video room facility.

These procedures are self-explanatory, except perhaps for the fourth requirement. It is designed solely to ensure that cross-examining counsel is not obliged to conduct a non-stop cross-examination until the matter is concluded. He or she should retain the advantage of having the usual intervals that the tribunal provides.

The only other matter not dealt with in the preceding list is the question of the administration of the oath. I note that in *Bayer,* the oath administered was the oath of the country where the witness was present. That probably is in line with what happens when evidence is taken on commission. Here, since the tribunal has the power to administer an oath it would be my suggestion that the tribunal administer the oath to indicate the formality of the occasion even though any sanctions, if there were ever any problems of perjury, would probably be impossible of achievement.

Timing of the video link

A75–030 Finally there is the matter of the timing of the evidence. Counsel for the surgeon makes the very valid point that he does not want to be put in a position where he is obliged to open his case before the complainant's case is concluded, and then have Dr Munro's evidence after his opening. He requires the completion of the case for the plaintiff before he commences on behalf of the surgeon. His concerns have arisen in part because of the fact that the tribunal had indicated previously that it only had two weeks available for this case to be heard. However, counsel assisting the tribunal indicated that the matter could go into a third week, should this be necessary. An additional concern was the question as to how the surgeon's overseas witness could be coordinated with Dr Munro's evidence, and there were other timing matters raised by the parties.

For the reasons given earlier I cannot and should not rule on this matter. All I will say, for the guidance of the tribunal, is that as far as reasonably possible the standard procedures should be followed so that the surgeon's counsel is not asked to begin his case and then revert to cross-examining Dr Munro. I am sure that in the conference tomorrow matters can be arranged satisfactorily. In saying this I am not meaning to suggest that the surgeon's requirements should necessarily be satisfied in every possible respect. As is usual in these cases, the tribunal will strive to achieve the fairest and most practicable outcome, but in the end it will be driven by the need to ensure that there is no further adjournment of this case.

In case any difficulties arise in relation to the video link or its timing, I reserve leave to the parties to apply further. In doing that I stress that I am not wanting to offer the services of this Court as a way of challenging every "mechanical" order made by the tribunal. Rather, leave is reserved lest some major issue arises which all parties, including the tribunal, consider is appropriate to have returned to this Court.

Conclusion and final orders

A75–031 I dismiss the appeal for want of jurisdiction. As to the formal orders of the Court in the judicial review matter, I declare (I) that the tribunal had jurisdiction to make the order for Dr Munro's evidence to be given by video link and (2) that provided that the seven listed conditions are adhered to, there would be no breach of natural justice. Out of an abundance of caution I should say that in making that second declaration I do not mean to convey the impression that additions to the list given, or modifications of it in part, would create such a breach. So long as the spirit of these procedural guidelines is adopted, natural justice will be accorded to the surgeon.

As to costs, even if there had been an application for costs against the surgeon I would not have granted it. This was a novel issue and there were proper grounds for bringing the matter before this Court for clarification. Therefore I make no costs order.

Appeal dismissed; application for judicial review declined; declarations accordingly.

Solicitors for the appellant/plaintiff: *Bell Gully Buddle Weir* (Auckland). Solicitors for the first respondent/first defendant: *Kensington Swan* (Auckland).

Reported by: Briar Gordon, *Barrister*

ICSID Rules of Procedure for the Institution of Conciliation and Arbitration Proceedings (Institution Rules)

A76–001 *The Rules of Procedure for the Institution of Conciliation and Arbitration Proceedings (the Institution Rules) of ICSID were adopted by the Administrative Council of the Centre pursuant to Article 6(1)(b) of the ICSID Convention.*

The Institution Rules are supplemented by the Administrative and Financial Regulations of the Centre, in particular by Regulations 16, 22(1), 23, 24, 30 and 34(1).

The Institution Rules are restricted in scope to the period of time from the filing of a request to the dispatch of the notice of registration. All transactions subsequent to that time are to be regulated in accordance with the Conciliation and the Arbitration Rules.

Rule 1

The Request

A76–002 (1) Any Contracting State or any national of a Contracting State wishing to institute conciliation or arbitration proceedings under the Convention shall address a request to that effect in writing to the Secretary-General at the seat of the Centre. The request shall indicate whether it relates to a conciliation or an arbitration proceeding. It shall be drawn up in an official language of the Centre, shall be dated, and shall be signed by the requesting party or its duly authorized representative.

(2) The request may be made jointly by the parties to the dispute.

Rule 2

Contents of the Request

A76–003 (1) The request shall:

(a) designate precisely each party to the dispute and state the address of each;

(b) state, if one of the parties is a constituent subdivision or agency of a Contracting State, that it has been designated to the Centre by that State pursuant to Article 25(1) of the Convention;

(c) indicate the date of consent and the instruments in which it is recorded, including, if one party is a constituent subdivision or agency of a Contracting State, similar data on the approval of such consent by that State unless it had notified the Centre that no such approval is required;

(d) indicate with respect to the party that is a national of a Contracting State:

   (i) its nationality on the date of consent; and
   (ii) if the party is a natural person:

   (A) his nationality on the date of the request; and
   (B) that he did not have the nationality of the Contracting State party to the dispute either on the date of consent or on the date of the request; or

(iii) if the party is a juridical person which on the date of consent had the nationality of the Contracting State party to the dispute, the agreement of the parties that it should be treated as a national of another Contracting State for the purposes of the Convention;

(e) contain information concerning the issues in dispute indicating that there is, between the parties, a legal dispute arising directly out of an investment; and

(f) state, if the requesting party is a juridical person, that it has taken all necessary internal actions to authorize the request.

(2) The information required by subparagraphs (1)(c), (1)(d)(iii) and (1)(f) shall be supported by documentation.

(3) "Date of consent" means the date on which the parties to the dispute consented in writing to submit it to the Centre; if both parties did not act on the same day, it means the date on which the second party acted.

Rule 3

Optional Information in the Request

The request may in addition set forth any provisions agreed by the parties regarding the number of conciliators or arbitrators and the method of their appointment, as well as any other provisions agreed concerning the settlement of the dispute.   **A76–004**

Rule 4

Copies of the Request

(1) The request shall be accompanied by five additional signed copies. The Secretary-General may require such further copies as he may deem necessary.   **A76–005**

(2) Any documentation submitted with the request shall conform to the requirements of Administrative and Financial Regulation 30.

Rule 5

Acknowledgement of the Request

(1) On receiving a request the Secretary-General shall: **A76–006**

(a) send an acknowledgement to the requesting party;

(b) take no other action with respect to the request until he has received payment of the prescribed fee.

(2) As soon as he has received the fee for lodging the request, the Secretary-General shall transmit a copy of the request and of the accompanying documentation to the other party.

Rule 6

Registration of the Request

A76–007 (1) The Secretary-General shall, subject to Rule 5(1)(b), as soon as possible, either:

(a) register the request in the Conciliation or the Arbitration Register and on the same day notify the parties of the registration; or

(b) if he finds, on the basis of the information contained in the request, that the dispute is manifestly outside the jurisdiction of the Centre, notify the parties of his refusal to register the request and of the reasons therefor.

(2) A proceeding under the Convention shall be deemed to have been instituted on the date of the registration of the request.

Rule 7

Notice of Registration

A76–008 The notice of registration of a request shall:

(a) record that the request is registered and indicate the date of the registration and of the dispatch of that notice;

(b) notify each party that all communications and notices in connection with the proceeding will be sent to the address stated in the request, unless another address is indicated to the Centre;

(c) unless such information has already been provided, invite the parties to communicate to the Secretary-General any provisions agreed by them regarding the number and the method of appointment of the conciliators or arbitrators;

(d) invite the parties to proceed, as soon as possible, to constitute a Conciliation Commission in accordance with Articles 29 to 31 of the Convention, or an Arbitral Tribunal in accordance with Articles 37 to 40;

(e) remind the parties that the registration of the request is without prejudice to the powers and functions of the Conciliation Commission or Arbitral Tribunal in regard to jurisdiction, competence and the merits; and

(f) be accompanied by a list of the members of the Panel of Conciliators or of Arbitrators of the Centre.

Rule 8

Withdrawal of the Request

A76–009 The requesting party may, by written notice to the Secretary-General, withdraw the request before it has been registered. The Secretary-General shall promptly notify the other party, unless, pursuant to Rule 5(1)(b), the request had not been transmitted to it.

Rule 9

Final Provisions

(1) The texts of these Rules in each official language of the Centre shall be equally authentic.

(2) These Rules may be cited as the "Institution Rules" of the Centre.

ICSID Rules of Procedure for Arbitration Proceedings (Arbitration Rules)

A77–001   The Rules of Procedure for Arbitration Proceedings (the Arbitration Rules) of ICSID were adopted by the Administrative Council of the Centre pursuant to Article 6(1)(c) of the ICSID Convention.

The Arbitration Rules are supplemented by the Administrative and Financial Regulations of the Centre, in particular by Regulations 14–16, 22–31 and 34(1).

The Arbitration Rules cover the period of time from the dispatch of the notice of registration of a request for arbitration until an award is rendered and all challenges possible to it under the Convention have been exhausted. The transactions previous to that time are to be regulated in accordance with the Institution Rules.

Chapter I

Establishment of the Tribunal

Rule 1

General Obligations

A77–002   (1) Upon notification of the registration of the request for arbitration, the parties shall, with all possible dispatch, proceed to constitute a Tribunal, with due regard to Section 2 of Chapter IV of the Convention.

(2) Unless such information is provided in the request, the parties shall communicate to the Secretary-General as soon as possible any provisions agreed by them regarding the number of arbitrators and the method of their appointment.

(3) The majority of the arbitrators shall be nationals of States other than the State party to the dispute and of the State whose national is a party to the dispute, unless the sole arbitrator or each individual member of the Tribunal is appointed by agreement of the parties. Where the Tribunal is to consist of three members, a national of either of these States may not be appointed as an arbitrator by a party without the agreement of the other party to the dispute. Where the Tribunal is to consist of five or more members, nationals of either or these States may not be appointed as arbitrators by a party if appointment by the other party of the same number of arbitrators of either of these nationalities would result in a majority of arbitrators of these nationalities.

(4) No person who had previously acted as a conciliator or arbitrator in any proceeding for the settlement of the dispute may be appointed as a member of the Tribunal.

Rule 2

Method of Constituting the Tribunal in the Absence of Previous Agreement

A77–003   (1) If the parties, at the time of the registration of the request for arbitration, have not agreed upon the number of arbitrators and the method of their appointment, they shall, unless they agree otherwise, follow the following procedure:

(a) the requesting party shall, within 10 days after the registration of the request, propose to the other party the appointment of a sole arbitrator or of a specified uneven number of arbitrators and specify the method proposed for their appointment;

(b) within 20 days after receipt of the proposals made by the requesting party, the other party shall:

   (i) accept such proposals; or
   (ii) make other proposals regarding the number of arbitrators and the method of their appointment;

(c) within 20 days after receipt of the reply containing any such other proposals, the requesting party shall notify the other party whether it accepts or rejects such proposals.

(2) The communications provided for in paragraph (1) shall be made or promptly confirmed in writing and shall either be transmitted through the Secretary-General or directly between the parties with a copy to the Secretary-General. The parties shall promptly notify the Secretary-General of the contents of any agreement reached.

(3) At any time 60 days after the registration of the request, if no agreement on another procedure is reached, either party may inform the Secretary-General that it chooses the formula provided for in Article 37(2)(b) of the Convention. The Secretary-General shall thereupon promptly inform the other party that the Tribunal is to be constituted in accordance with that Article.

Rule 3

Appointment of Arbitrators to a Tribunal Constituted in Accordance with Convention Article 37(2)(b)

(1) If the Tribunal is to be constituted in accordance with Article 37(2)(b) of the Convention:

(a) either party shall in a communication to the other party:

   (i) name two persons, identifying one of them, who shall not have the same nationality as nor be a national of either party, as the arbitrator appointed by it, and the other as the arbitrator proposed to be the President of the Tribunal; and
   (ii) invite the other party to concur in the appointment of the arbitrator proposed to be the President of the Tribunal and to appoint another arbitrator;

(b) promptly upon receipt of this communication the other party shall, in its reply:

   (i) name a person as the arbitrator appointed by it, who shall not have the same nationality as nor be a national of either party; and
   (ii) concur in the appointment of the arbitrator proposed to be the President of the Tribunal or name another person as the arbitrator proposed to be President;

(c) promptly upon receipt of the reply containing such a proposal, the initiating party shall notify the other party whether it concurs in the appointment of the arbitrator proposed by that party to be the President of the Tribunal.

(2) The communications provided for in this Rule shall be made or promptly confirmed in writing and shall either be transmitted through the Secretary-General or directly between the parties with a copy to the Secretary-General.

Rule 4

Appointment of Arbitrators by the Chairman of the Administrative Council

A77–005 (1) If the Tribunal is not constituted within 90 days after the dispatch by the Secretary-General of the notice of registration, or such other period as the parties may agree, either party may, through the Secretary-General, address to the Chairman of the Administrative Council a request in writing to appoint the arbitrator or arbitrators not yet appointed and to designate an arbitrator to be the President of the Tribunal.

(2) The provision of paragraph (1) shall apply *mutatis mutandis* in the event that the parties have agreed that the arbitrators shall elect the President of the Tribunal and they fail to do so.

(3) The Secretary-General shall forthwith send a copy of the request to the other party.

(4) The Chairman shall use his best efforts to comply with that request within 30 days after its receipt. Before he proceeds to make an appointment or designation, with due regard to Articles 38 and 40(1) of the Convention, he shall consult both parties as far as possible.

(5) The Secretary-General shall promptly notify the parties of any appointment or designation made by the Chairman.

Rule 5

Acceptance of Appointments

A77–006 (1) The party or parties concerned shall notify the Secretary-General of the appointment of each arbitrator and indicate the method of his appointment.

(2) As soon as the Secretary-General has been informed by a party or the Chairman of the Administrative Council of the appointment of an arbitrator, he shall seek an acceptance from the appointee.

(3) If an arbitrator fails to accept his appointment within 15 days, the Secretary-General shall promptly notify the parties, and if appropriate the Chairman, and invite them to proceed to the appointment of another arbitrator in accordance with the method followed for the previous appointment.

Rule 6

Constitution of the Tribunal

A77–007 (1) The Tribunal shall be deemed to be constituted and the proceeding to have begun on the date the Secretary-General notifies the parties that all the arbitrators have accepted their appointment.

(2) Before or at the first session of the Tribunal, each arbitrator shall sign a declaration in the following form:

"To the best of my knowledge there is no reason why I should not serve on the Arbitral Tribunal constituted by the International Centre for Settlement of Investment Disputes with respect to a dispute between _____ and _____.

"I shall keep confidential all information coming to my knowledge as a result of my participation in this proceeding, as well as the contents of any award made by the Tribunal.

"I shall judge fairly as between the parties, according to the applicable law, and shall not accept any instruction or compensation with regard to the proceeding from any source except as provided in the Convention on the Settlement of Investment Disputes between States and Nationals of Other States and in the Regulations and Rules made pursuant thereto.

"A statement of my past and present professional, business and other relationships (if any) with the parties is attached hereto."

Any arbitrator failing to sign a declaration by the end of the first session of the Tribunal shall be deemed to have resigned.

Rule 7

Replacement of Arbitrators

At any time before the Tribunal is constituted, each party may replace any arbitrator appointed by it and the parties may by common consent agree to replace any arbitrator. The procedure of such replacement shall be in accordance with Rules 1, 5 and 6.

A77–008

Rule 8

Incapacity or Resignation of Arbitrators

(1) If an arbitrator becomes incapacitated or unable to perform the duties of his office, the procedure in respect of the disqualification of arbitrators set forth in Rule 9 shall apply.

A77–009

(2) An arbitrator may resign by submitting his resignation to the other members of the Tribunal and the Secretary-General. If the arbitrator was appointed by one of the parties, the Tribunal shall promptly consider the reasons for his resignation and decide whether it consents thereto. The Tribunal shall promptly notify the Secretary-General of its decision.

Rule 9

Disqualification of Arbitrators

(1) A party proposing the disqualification of an arbitrator pursuant to Article 57 of the Convention shall promptly, and in any event before the proceeding is declared closed, file its proposal with the Secretary-General, stating its reasons therefor.

A77–010

(2) The Secretary-General shall forthwith:

(a) transmit the proposal to the members of the Tribunal and, if it relates to a sole arbitrator or to a majority of the members of the Tribunal, to the Chairman of the Administrative Council; and

(b) notify the other party of the proposal.

(3) The arbitrator to whom the proposal relates may, without delay, furnish explanations to the Tribunal or the Chairman, as the case may be.

(4) Unless the proposal relates to a majority of the members of the Tribunal, the other members shall promptly consider and vote on the proposal in the absence of the arbitrator concerned. If those members are equally divided, they shall, through the Secretary-General, promptly notify the Chairman of the proposal, of any explanation furnished by the arbitrator concerned and of their failure to reach a decision.

(5) Whenever the Chairman has to decide on a proposal to disqualify an arbitrator, he shall use his best efforts to take that decision within 30 days after he has received the proposal.

(6) The proceeding shall be suspended until a decision has been taken on the proposal.

Rule 10

Procedure during a Vacancy on the Tribunal

A77–011 (1) The Secretary-General shall forthwith notify the parties and, if necessary, the Chairman of the Administrative Council of the disqualification, death, incapacity or resignation of an arbitrator and of the consent, if any, of the Tribunal to a resignation.

(2) Upon the notification by the Secretary-General of a vacancy on the Tribunal, the proceeding shall be or remain suspended until the vacancy has been filled.

Rule 11

Filling Vacancies on the Tribunal

A77–012 (1) Except as provided in paragraph (2), a vacancy resulting from the disqualification, death, incapacity or resignation of an arbitrator shall be promptly filled by the same method by which his appointment had been made.

(2) In addition to filling vacancies relating to arbitrators appointed by him, the Chairman of the Administrative Council shall appoint a person from the Panel of Arbitrators:

(a) to fill a vacancy caused by the resignation, without the consent of the Tribunal, of an arbitrator appointed by a party; or

(b) at the request of either party, to fill any other vacancy, if no new appointment is made and accepted within 45 days of the notification of the vacancy by the Secretary-General.

(3) The procedure for filling a vacancy shall be in accordance with Rules 1, 4(4), 4(5), 5 and, *mutatis mutandis*, 6(2).

Rule 12

Resumption of Proceeding after Filling a Vacancy

As soon as a vacancy on the Tribunal has been filled, the proceeding shall continue from the point it had reached at the time the vacancy occurred. The newly appointed arbitrator may, however, require that the oral procedure be recommenced, if this had already been started.   A77–013

CHAPTER II

WORKING OF THE TRIBUNAL

Rule 13

Sessions of the Tribunal

(1) The Tribunal shall hold its first session within 60 days after its constitution or such other period as the parties may agree. The dates of that session shall be fixed by the President of the Tribunal after consultation with its members and the Secretary-General. If upon its constitution the Tribunal has no President because the parties have agreed that the President shall be elected by its members, the Secretary-General shall fix the dates of that session. In both cases, the parties shall be consulted as far as possible.   A77–014

(2) The dates of subsequent sessions shall be determined by the Tribunal, after consultation with the Secretary-General and with the parties as far as possible.

(3) The Tribunal shall meet at the seat of the Centre or at such other place as may have been agreed by the parties in accordance with Article 63 of the Convention. If the parties agree that the proceeding shall be held at a place other than the Centre or an institution with which the Centre has made the necessary arrangements, they shall consult with the Secretary-General and request the approval of the Tribunal. Failing such approval, the Tribunal shall meet at the seat of the Centre.

(4) The Secretary-General shall notify the members of the Tribunal and the parties of the dates and place of the sessions of the Tribunal in good time.

Rule 14

Sittings of the Tribunal

(1) The President of the Tribunal shall conduct its hearings and preside at its deliberations.   A77–015

(2) Except as the parties otherwise agree, the presence of a majority of the members of the Tribunal shall be required at its sittings.

(3) The President of the Tribunal shall fix the date and hour of its sittings.

Rule 15

Deliberations of the Tribunal

A77–016 (1) The deliberations of the Tribunal shall take place in private and remain secret.
(2) Only members of the Tribunal shall take part in its deliberations. No other person shall be admitted unless the Tribunal decides otherwise.

Rule 16

Decisions of the Tribunal

A77–017 (1) Decisions of the Tribunal shall be taken by a majority of the votes of all its members. Abstention shall count as a negative vote.
(2) Except as otherwise provided by these Rules or decided by the Tribunal, it may take any decision by correspondence among its members, provided that all of them are consulted. Decisions so taken shall be certified by the President of the Tribunal.

Rule 17

Incapacity of the President

A77–018 If at any time the President of the Tribunal should be unable to act, his functions shall be performed by one of the other members of the Tribunal, acting in the order in which the Secretary-General had received the notice of their acceptance of their appointment to the Tribunal.

Rule 18

Representation of the Parties

A77–019 (1) Each party may be represented or assisted by agents, counsel or advocates whose names and authority shall be notified by that party to the Secretary-General, who shall promptly inform the Tribunal and the other party.
(2) For the purposes of these Rules, the expression "party" includes, where the context so admits, an agent, counsel or advocate authorized to represent that party.

CHAPTER III

GENERAL PROCEDURAL PROVISIONS

Rule 19

Procedural Orders

A77–020 The Tribunal shall make the orders required for the conduct of the proceeding.

ICSID Arbitration Rules

Rule 20

Preliminary Procedural Consultation

(1) As early as possible after the constitution of a Tribunal, its President shall endeavor to ascertain the views of the parties regarding questions of procedure. For this purpose he may request the parties to meet him. He shall, in particular, seek their views on the following matters:

    (a) the number of members of the Tribunal required to constitute a quorum at its sittings;

    (b) the language or languages to be used in the proceeding;

    (c) the number and sequence of the pleadings and the time limits within which they are to be filed;

    (d) the number of copies desired by each party of instruments filed by the other;

    (e) dispensing with the written or the oral procedure;

    (f) the manner in which the cost of the proceeding is to be apportioned; and

    (g) the manner in which the record of the hearings shall be kept.

(2) In the conduct of the proceeding the Tribunal shall apply any agreement between the parties on procedural matters, except as otherwise provided in the Convention or the Administrative and Financial Regulations.

Rule 21

Pre-Hearing Conference

(1) At the request of the Secretary-General or at the discretion of the President of the Tribunal, a pre-hearing conference between the Tribunal and the parties may be held to arrange for an exchange of information and the stipulation of uncontested facts in order to expedite the proceeding.

(2) At the request of the parties, a pre-hearing conference between the Tribunal and the parties, duly represented by their authorized representatives, may be held to consider the issues in dispute with a view to reaching an amicable settlement.

Rule 22

Procedural Languages

(1) The parties may agree on the use of one or two languages to be used in the proceeding, provided, that, if they agree on any language that is not an official language of the Centre, the Tribunal, after consultation with the Secretary-General, gives its approval. If the parties do not agree on any such procedural language, each of them may select one of the official languages (i.e., English, French and Spanish) for this purpose.

(2) If two procedural languages are selected by the parties, any instrument may be filed in either language. Either language may be used at the hearings, subject, if the

Tribunal so requires, to translation and interpretation. The orders and the award of the Tribunal shall be rendered and the record kept in both procedural languages, both versions being equally authentic.

Rule 23

Copies of Instruments

A77–024   Except as otherwise provided by the Tribunal after consultation with the parties and the Secretary-General, every request, pleading, application, written observation, supporting documentation, if any, or other instrument shall be filed in the form of a signed original accompanied by the following number of additional copies:

(a) before the number of members of the Tribunal has been determined: five;

(b) after the number of members of the Tribunal has been determined: two more than the number of its members.

Rule 24

Supporting Documentation

A77–025   Supporting documentation shall ordinarily be filed together with the instrument to which it relates, and in any case within the time limit fixed for the filing of such instrument.

Rule 25

Correction of Errors

A77–026   An accidental error in any instrument or supporting document may, with the consent of the other party or by leave of the Tribunal, be corrected at any time before the award is rendered.

Rule 26

Time Limits

A77–027   (1) Where required, time limits shall be fixed by the Tribunal by assigning dates for the completion of the various steps in the proceeding. The Tribunal may delegate this power to its President.

(2) The Tribunal may extend any time limit that it has fixed. If the Tribunal is not in session, this power shall be exercised by its President.

(3) Any step taken after expiration of the applicable time limit shall be disregarded unless the Tribunal, in special circumstances and after giving the other party an opportunity of stating its views, decides otherwise.

Rule 27

Waiver

A party which knows or should have known that a provision of the Administrative and Financial Regulations, of these Rules, of any other rules or agreement applicable to the proceeding, or of an order of the Tribunal has not been complied with and which fails to state promptly its objections thereto, shall be deemed—subject to Article 45 of the Convention—to have waived its right to object.

Rule 28

Cost of Proceeding

(1) Without prejudice to the final decision on the payment of the cost of the proceeding, the Tribunal may, unless otherwise agreed by the parties, decide:

(a) at any stage of the proceeding, the portion which each party shall pay, pursuant to Administrative and Financial Regulation 14, of the fees and expenses of the Tribunal and the charges for the use of the facilities of the Centre;

(b) with respect to any part of the proceeding, that the related costs (as determined by the Secretary-General) shall be borne entirely or in a particular share by one of the parties.

(2) Promptly after the closure of the proceeding, each party shall submit to the Tribunal a statement of costs reasonably incurred or borne by it in the proceeding and the Secretary-General shall submit to the Tribunal an account of all amounts paid by each party to the Centre and of all costs incurred by the Centre for the proceeding. The Tribunal may, before the award has been rendered, request the parties and the Secretary-General to provide additional information concerning the cost of the proceeding.

CHAPTER IV

WRITTEN AND ORAL PROCEDURES

Rule 29

Normal Procedures

Except if the parties otherwise agree, the proceeding shall comprise two distinct phases: a written procedure followed by an oral one.

Rule 30

Transmission of the Request

As soon as the Tribunal is constituted, the Secretary-General shall transmit to each member a copy of the request by which the proceeding was initiated, of the supporting documentation, of the notice of registration and of any communication received from either party in response thereto.

Rule 31

The Written Procedure

A77–032 (1) In addition to the request for arbitration, the written procedure shall consist of the following pleadings, filed within time limits set by the Tribunal:

(a) a memorial by the requesting party;

(b) a counter-memorial by the other party;

and, if the parties so agree or the Tribunal deems it necessary:

(c) a reply by the requesting party; and

(d) a rejoinder by the other party.

(2) If the request was made jointly, each party shall, within the same time limit determined by the Tribunal, file its memorial and, if the parties so agree or the Tribunal deems it necessary, its reply; however, the parties may instead agree that one of them shall, for the purposes of paragraph (1), be considered as the requesting party.

(3) A memorial shall contain: a statement of the relevant facts; a statement of law; and the submissions. A counter-memorial, reply or rejoinder shall contain an admission or denial of the facts stated in the last previous pleading; any additional facts, if necessary; observations concerning the statement of law in the last previous pleading; a statement of law in answer thereto; and the submissions.

Rule 32

The Oral Procedure

A77–033 (1) The oral procedure shall consist of the hearing by the Tribunal of the parties, their agents, counsel and advocates, and of witnesses and experts.

(2) The Tribunal shall decide, with the consent of the parties, which other persons besides the parties, their agents, counsel and advocates, witnesses and experts during their testimony, and officers of the Tribunal may attend the hearings.

(3) The members of the Tribunal may, during the hearings, put questions to the parties, their agents, counsel and advocates, and ask them for explanations.

Rule 33

Marshalling of Evidence

A77–034 Without prejudice to the rules concerning the production of documents, each party shall, within time limits fixed by the Tribunal, communicate to the Secretary-General, for transmission to the Tribunal and the other party, precise information regarding the

Rule 34

Evidence: General Principles

(1) The Tribunal shall be the judge of the admissibility of any evidence adduced and of its probative value.

(2) The Tribunal may, if it deems it necessary at any stage of the proceeding:

   (a) call upon the parties to produce documents, witnesses and experts; and

   (b) visit any place connected with the dispute or conduct inquiries there.

(3) The parties shall cooperate with the Tribunal in the production of the evidence and in the other measures provided for in paragraph (2). The Tribunal shall take formal note of the failure of a party to comply with its obligations under this paragraph and of any reasons given for such failure.

(4) Expenses incurred in producing evidence and in taking other measures in accordance with paragraph (2) shall be deemed to constitute part of the expenses incurred by the parties within the meaning of Article 61(2) of the Convention.

Rule 35

Examination of Witnesses and Experts

(1) Witnesses and experts shall be examined before the Tribunal by the parties under the control of its President. Questions may also be put to them by any member of the Tribunal.

(2) Each witness shall make the following declaration before giving his evidence:

> "I solemnly declare upon my honour and conscience that I shall speak the truth, the whole truth and nothing but the truth."

(3) Each expert shall make the following declaration before making his statement:

> "I solemnly declare upon my honour and conscience that my statement will be in accordance with my sincere belief."

Rule 36

Witnesses and Experts: Special Rules

Notwithstanding Rule 35 the Tribunal may:

   (a) admit evidence given by a witness or expert in a written deposition; and

(b) with the consent of both parties, arrange for the examination of a witness or expert otherwise than before the Tribunal itself. The Tribunal shall define the subject of the examination, the time limit, the procedure to be followed and other particulars. The parties may participate in the examination.

Rule 37

Visits and Inquiries

A77–038 If the Tribunal considers it necessary to visit any place connected with the dispute or to conduct an inquiry there, it shall make an order to this effect. The order shall define the scope of the visit or the subject of the inquiry, the time limit, the procedure to be followed and other particulars. The parties may participate in any visit or inquiry.

Rule 38

Closure of the Proceeding

A77–039 (1) When the presentation of the case by the parties is completed, the proceeding shall be declared closed.

(2) Exceptionally, the Tribunal may, before the award has been rendered, reopen the proceeding on the ground that new evidence is forthcoming of such a nature as to constitute a decisive factor, or that there is a vital need for clarification on certain specific points.

CHAPTER V

PARTICULAR PROCEDURES

Rule 39

Provisional Measures

A77–040 (1) At any time during the proceeding a party may request that provisional measures for the preservation of its rights be recommended by the Tribunal. The request shall specify the rights to be preserved, the measures the recommendation of which is requested, and the circumstances that require such measures.

(2) The Tribunal shall give priority to the consideration of a request made pursuant to paragraph (1).

(3) The Tribunal may also recommend provisional measures on its own initiative or recommend measures other than those specified in a request. It may at any time modify or revoke its recommendations.

(4) The Tribunal shall only recommend provisional measures, or modify or revoke its recommendations, after giving each party an opportunity of presenting its observations.

(5) Nothing in this Rule shall prevent the parties, provided that they have so stipulated in the agreement recording their consent, from requesting any judicial or other authority

to order provisional measures, prior to the institution of the proceeding, or during the proceeding, for the preservation of their respective rights and interests.

Rule 40

Ancillary Claims

(1) Except as the parties otherwise agree, a party may present an incidental or additional claim or counter-claim arising directly out of the subject-matter of the dispute, provided that such ancillary claim is within the scope of the consent of the parties and is otherwise within the jurisdiction of the Centre.

(2) An incidental or additional claim shall be presented not later than in the reply and a counter-claim no later than in the counter-memorial, unless the Tribunal, upon justification by the party presenting the ancillary claim and upon considering any objection of the other party, authorizes the presentation of the claim at a later stage in the proceeding.

(3) The Tribunal shall fix a time limit within which the party against which an ancillary claim is presented may file its observations thereon.

Rule 41

Objections to Jurisdiction

(1) Any objection that the dispute or any ancillary claim is not within the jurisdiction of the Centre or, for other reasons, is not within the competence of the Tribunal shall be made as early as possible. A party shall file the objection with the Secretary-General no later than the expiration of the time limit fixed for the filing of the counter-memorial, or, if the objection relates to an ancillary claim, for the filing of the rejoinder—unless the facts on which the objection is based are unknown to the party at that time.

(2) The Tribunal may on its own initiative consider, at any stage of the proceeding, whether the dispute or any ancillary claim before it is within the jurisdiction of the Centre and within its own competence.

(3) Upon the formal raising of an objection relating to the dispute, the proceeding on the merits shall be suspended. The President of the Tribunal, after consultation with its other members, shall fix a time limit within which the parties may file observations on the objection.

(4) The Tribunal shall decide whether or not the further procedures relating to the objection shall be oral. It may deal with the objection as a preliminary question or join it to the merits of the dispute. If the Tribunal overrules the objection or joins it to the merits, it shall once more fix time limits for the further procedures.

(5) If the Tribunal decides that the dispute is not within the jurisdiction of the Centre or not within its own competence, it shall render an award to that effect.

Rule 42

Default

(1) If a party (in this Rule called the "defaulting party") fails to appear or to present its case at any stage of the proceeding, the other party may, at any time prior to the

discontinuance of the proceeding, request the Tribunal to deal with the questions submitted to it and to render an award.

(2) The Tribunal shall promptly notify the defaulting party of such a request. Unless it is satisfied that that party does not intend to appear or to present its case in the proceeding, it shall, at the same time, grant a period of grace and to this end:

(a) if that party had failed to file a pleading or any other instrument within the time limit fixed therefor, fix a new time limit for its filing; or

(b) if that party had failed to appear or present its case at a hearing, fix a new date for the hearing.

The period of grace shall not, without the consent of the other party, exceed 60 days.

(3) After the expiration of the period of grace or when, in accordance with paragraph (2), no such period is granted, the Tribunal shall resume the consideration of the dispute. Failure of the defaulting party to appear or to present its case shall not be deemed an admission of the assertions made by the other party.

(4) The Tribunal shall examine the jurisdiction of the Centre and its own competence in the dispute and, if it is satisfied, decide whether the submissions made are well-founded in fact and in law. To this end, it may, at any stage of the proceeding, call on the party appearing to file observations, produce evidence or submit oral explanations.

Rule 43

Settlement and Discontinuance

A77–044 (1) If, before the award is rendered, the parties agree on a settlement of the dispute or otherwise to discontinue the proceeding, the Tribunal, or the Secretary-General if the Tribunal has not yet been constituted, shall, at their written request, in an order take note of the discontinuance of the proceeding.

(2) If the parties file with the Secretary-General the full and signed text of their settlement and in writing request the Tribunal to embody such settlement in an award, the Tribunal may record the settlement in the form of its award.

Rule 44

Discontinuance at Request of a Party

A77–045 If a party requests the discontinuance of the proceeding, the Tribunal, or the Secretary-General if the Tribunal has not yet been constituted, shall in an order fix a time limit within which the other party may state whether it opposes the discontinuance. If no objection is made in writing within the time limit, the other party shall be deemed to have acquiesced in the discontinuance and the Tribunal, or if appropriate the Secretary-General, shall in an order take note of the discontinuance of the proceeding. If objection is made, the proceeding shall continue.

Rule 45

Discontinuance for Failure of Parties to Act

If the parties fail to take any steps in the proceeding during six consecutive months or such period as they may agree with the approval of the Tribunal, or of the Secretary-General if the Tribunal has not yet been constituted, they shall be deemed to have discontinued the proceeding and the Tribunal, or if appropriate the Secretary-General, shall, after notice to the parties, in an order take note of the discontinuance.

CHAPTER VI

THE AWARD

Rule 46

Preparation of the Award

The award (including any individual or dissenting opinion) shall be drawn up and signed within 120 days after closure of the proceeding. The Tribunal may, however, extend this period by a further 60 days if it would otherwise be unable to draw up the award.

Rule 47

The Award

(1) The award shall be in writing and shall contain:

    (a) a precise designation of each party;

    (b) a statement that the Tribunal was established under the Convention, and a description of the method of its constitution;

    (c) the name of each member of the Tribunal, and an identification of the appointing authority of each;

    (d) the names of the agents, counsel and advocates of the parties;

    (e) the dates and place of the sittings of the Tribunal;

    (f) a summary of the proceeding;

    (g) a statement of the facts as found by the Tribunal;

    (h) the submissions of the parties;

    (i) the decision of the Tribunal on every question submitted to it, together with the reasons upon which the decision is based; and

    (j) any decision of the Tribunal regarding the cost of the proceeding.

(2) The award shall be signed by the members of the Tribunal who voted for it; the date of each signature shall be indicated.

(3) Any member of the Tribunal may attach his individual opinion to the award, whether he dissents from the majority or not, or a statement of his dissent.

Rule 48

Rendering of the Award

A77–049   (1) Upon signature by the last arbitrator to sign, the Secretary-General shall promptly:

    (a) authenticate the original text of the award and deposit it in the archives of the Centre, together with any individual opinions and statements of dissent; and

    (b) dispatch a certified copy of the award (including individual opinions and statements of dissent) to each party, indicating the date of dispatch on the original text and on all copies.

(2) The award shall be deemed to have been rendered on the date on which the certified copies were dispatched.

(3) The Secretary-General shall, upon request, make available to a party additional certified copies of the award.

(4) The Centre shall not publish the award without the consent of the parties. The Centre may, however, include in its publications excerpts of the legal rules applied by the Tribunal.

Rule 49

Supplementary Decisions and Rectification

A77–050   (1) Within 45 days after the date on which the award was rendered, either party may request, pursuant to Article 49(2) of the Convention, a supplementary decision on, or the rectification of, the award. Such a request shall be addressed in writing to the Secretary-General. The request shall:

    (a) identify the award to which it relates;

    (b) indicate the date of the request;

    (c) state in detail:

        (i) any question which, in the opinion of the requesting party, the Tribunal omitted to decide in the award; and

        (ii) any error in the award which the requesting party seeks to have rectified; and

    (d) be accompanied by a fee for lodging the request.

(2) Upon receipt of the request and of the lodging fee, the Secretary-General shall forthwith:

(a) register the request;

(b) notify the parties of the registration;

(c) transmit to the other party a copy of the request and of any accompanying documentation; and

(d) transmit to each member of the Tribunal a copy of the notice of registration, together with a copy of the request and of any accompanying documentation.

(3) The President of the Tribunal shall consult the members on whether it is necessary for the Tribunal to meet in order to consider the request. The Tribunal shall fix a time limit for the parties to file their observations on the request and shall determine the procedure for its consideration.

(4) Rules 46–48 shall apply, *mutatis mutandis*, to any decision of the Tribunal pursuant to this Rule.

(5) If a request is received by the Secretary-General more than 45 days after the award was rendered, he shall refuse to register the request and so inform forthwith the requesting party.

CHAPTER VII

INTERPRETATION, REVISION AND ANNULMENT OF THE AWARD

Rule 50

The Application

(1) An application for the interpretation, revision or annulment of an award shall be addressed in writing to the Secretary-General and shall:

(a) identify the award to which it relates;

(b) indicate the date of the application;

(c) state in detail;

    (i) in an application for interpretation, the precise points in dispute;

    (ii) in an application for revision, pursuant to Article 51(1) of the Convention, the change sought in the award, the discovery of some fact of such a nature as decisively to affect the award, and evidence that when the award was rendered that fact was unknown to the Tribunal and to the applicant, and that the applicant's ignorance of that fact was not due to negligence;

    (iii) in an application for annulment, pursuant to Article 52(1) of the Convention, the grounds on which it is based. These grounds are limited to the following:

        — that the Tribunal was not properly constituted;

        — that the Tribunal has manifestly exceeded its powers;

        — that there was corruption on the part of a member of the Tribunal;

- that there has been a serious departure from a fundamental rule of procedure;
- that the award has failed to state the reasons on which it is based;

(d) be accompanied by the payment of a fee for lodging the application.

(2) Without prejudice to the provisions of paragraph (3), upon receiving an application and the lodging fee, the Secretary-General shall forthwith:

(a) register the application;

(b) notify the parties of the registration; and

(c) transmit to the other party a copy of the application and of any accompanying documentation.

(3) The Secretary-General shall refuse to register an application for:

(a) revision, if, in accordance with Article 51(2) of the Convention, it is not made within 90 days after the discovery of the new fact and in any event within three years after the date on which the award was rendered (or any subsequent decision or correction);

(b) annulment, if, in accordance with Article 52(2) of the Convention, it is not made:

(i) within 120 days after the date on which the award was rendered (or any subsequent decision or correction) if the application is based on any of the following grounds:

- the Tribunal was not properly constituted;
- the Tribunal has manifestly exceeded its powers;
- there has been a serious departure from a fundamental rule of procedure;
- the award has failed to state the reasons on which it is based;

(ii) in the case of corruption on the part of a member of the Tribunal, within 120 days after discovery thereof, and in any event within three years after the date on which the award was rendered (or any subsequent decision or correction).

(4) If the Secretary-General refuses to register an application for revision, or annulment, he shall forthwith notify the requesting party of his refusal.

Rule 51

Interpretation or Revision: Further Procedures

A77–052 (1) Upon registration of an application for the interpretation or revision of an award, the Secretary-General shall forthwith:

(a) transmit to each member of the original Tribunal a copy of the notice of registration, together with a copy of the application and of any accompanying documentation; and

(b) request each member of the Tribunal to inform him within a specified time limit whether that member is willing to take part in the consideration of the application.

(2) If all members of the Tribunal express their willingness to take part in the consideration of the application, the Secretary-General shall so notify the members of the Tribunal and the parties. Upon dispatch of these notices the Tribunal shall be deemed to be reconstituted.

(3) If the Tribunal cannot be reconstituted in accordance with paragraph (2), the Secretary-General shall so notify the parties and invite them to proceed, as soon as possible, to constitute a new Tribunal, including the same number of arbitrators, and appointed by the same method, as the original one.

Rule 52

Annulment: Further Procedures

(1) Upon registration of an application for the annulment of an award, the Secretary-General shall forthwith request the Chairman of the Administrative Council to appoint an *ad hoc* Committee in accordance with Article 52(3) of the Convention.

(2) The Committee shall be deemed to be constituted on the date the Secretary-General notifies the parties that all members have accepted their appointment. Before or at the first session of the Committee, each member shall sign a declaration conforming to that set forth in Rule 6(2).

Rule 53

Rules of Procedure

The provisions of these Rules shall apply *mutatis mutandis* to any procedure relating to the interpretation, revision or annulment of an award and to the decision of the Tribunal or Committee.

Rule 54

Stay of Enforcement of the Award

(1) The party applying for the interpretation, revision or annulment of an award may in its application, and either party may at any time before the final disposition of the application, request a stay in the enforcement of part or all of the award to which the application relates. The Tribunal or Committee shall give priority to the consideration of such a request.

(2) If an application for the revision or annulment of an award contains a request for a stay of its enforcement, the Secretary-General shall, together with the notice of registration, inform both parties of the provisional stay of the award. As soon as the Tribunal or Committee is constituted it shall, if either party requests, rule within 30 days on whether such stay should be continued; unless it decides to continue the stay, it shall automatically be terminated.

(3) If a stay of enforcement has been granted pursuant to paragraph (1) or continued pursuant to paragraph (2), the Tribunal or Committee may at any time modify or terminate the stay at the request of either party. All stays shall automatically terminate on the date on which a final decision is rendered on the application, except that a Committee granting the partial annulment of an award may order the temporary stay of enforcement of the unannulled portion in order to give either party an opportunity to request any new Tribunal constituted pursuant to Article 52(6) of the Convention to grant a stay pursuant to Rule 55(3).

(4) A request pursuant to paragraph (1), (2) (second sentence) or (3) shall specify the circumstances that require the stay or its modification or termination. A request shall only be granted after the Tribunal or Committee has given each party an opportunity of presenting its observations.

(5) The Secretary-General shall promptly notify both parties of the stay of enforcement of any award and of the modification or termination of such a stay, which shall become effective on the date on which he dispatches such notification.

Rule 55

Resubmission of Dispute after an Annulment

A77–056   (1) If a Committee annuls part or all of an award, either party may request the resubmission of the dispute to a new Tribunal. Such a request shall be addressed in writing to the Secretary-General and shall:

    (a) identify the award to which it relates;

    (b) indicate the date of the request;

    (c) explain in detail what aspect of the dispute is to be submitted to the Tribunal; and

    (d) be accompanied by a fee for lodging the request.

(2) Upon receipt of the request and of the lodging fee, the Secretary-General shall forthwith:

    (a) register it in the Arbitration Register;

    (b) notify both parties of the registration;

    (c) transmit to the other party a copy of the request and of any accompanying documentation; and

    (d) invite the parties to proceed, as soon as possible, to constitute a new Tribunal, including the same number of arbitrators, and appointed by the same method, as the original one.

(3) If the original award had only been annulled in part, the new Tribunal shall not reconsider any portion of the award not so annulled. It may, however, in accordance with the procedures set forth in Rule 54, stay or continue to stay the enforcement of the unannulled portion of the award until the date its own award is rendered.

(4) Except as otherwise provided in paragraphs (1)–(3), these Rules shall apply to a proceeding on a resubmitted dispute in the same manner as if such dispute had been submitted pursuant to the Institution Rules.

Chapter VIII

General Provisions

Rule 56

Final Provisions

(1) The texts of these Rules in each official language of the Centre shall be equally authentic.

(2) These Rules may be cited as the "Arbitration Rules" of the Centre.

ICSID Rules of Procedure for Conciliation Proceedings (Conciliation Rules)

A78–001   *The Rules of Procedure for Conciliation Proceedings (the Conciliation Rules) of ICSID were adopted by the Administrative Council of the Centre pursuant to Article 6(1)(c) of the ICSID Convention.*

The Conciliation Rules are supplemented by the Administrative and Financial Regulations of the Centre, in particular by Regulations 14–16, 22–31 and 34(1).

The Conciliation Rules cover the period of time from the dispatch of the notice of registration of a request for conciliation until a report is drawn up. The transactions previous to that time are to be regulated in accordance with the Institution Rules.

Chapter I

Establishment of the Commission

Rule 1

General Obligations

A78–002   (1) Upon notification of the registration of the request for conciliation, the parties shall, with all possible dispatch, proceed to constitute a Commission, with due regard to Section 2 of Chapter III of the Convention.

(2) Unless such information is provided in the request, the parties shall communicate to the Secretary-General as soon as possible any provisions agreed by them regarding the number of conciliators and the method of their appointment.

Rule 2

Method of Constituting the Commission in the Absence of Previous Agreement

A78–003   (1) If the parties, at the time of the registration of the request for conciliation, have not agreed upon the number of conciliators and the method of their appointment, they shall, unless they agree otherwise, follow the following procedure:

(a) the requesting party shall, within 10 days after the registration of the request, propose to the other party the appointment of a sole conciliator or of a specified uneven number of conciliators and specify the method proposed for their appointment;

(b) within 20 days after receipt of the proposals made by the requesting party, the other party shall:

   (i) accept such proposals; or
   (ii) make other proposals regarding the number of conciliators and the method of their appointment;

(c) within 20 days after receipt of the reply containing any such other proposals, the requesting party shall notify the other party whether it accepts or rejects such proposals.

(2) The communications provided for in paragraph (1) shall be made or promptly confirmed in writing and shall either be transmitted through the Secretary-General or directly between the parties with a copy to the Secretary-General. The parties shall promptly notify the Secretary-General of the contents of any agreement reached.

(3) At any time 60 days after the registration of the request, if no agreement on another procedure is reached, either party may inform the Secretary-General that it chooses the formula provided for in Article 29(2)(b) of the Convention. The Secretary-General shall thereupon promptly inform the other party that the Commission is to be constituted in accordance with that Article.

Rule 3

Appointment of Conciliators to a Commission Constituted in Accordance with Convention Article 29(2)(b)

(1) If the Commission is to be constituted in accordance with Article 29(2)(b) of the Convention:

    (a) either party shall, in a communication to the other party:

        (i) name two persons, identifying one of them as the conciliator appointed by it and the other as the conciliator proposed to be the President of the Commission; and

        (ii) invite the other party to concur in the appointment of the conciliator proposed to be the President of the Commission and to appoint another conciliator;

    (b) promptly upon receipt of this communication the other party shall, in its reply:

        (i) name a person as the conciliator appointed by it; and

        (ii) concur in the appointment of the conciliator proposed to be the President of the Commission or name another person as the conciliator proposed to be President;

    (c) promptly upon receipt of the reply containing such a proposal, the initiating party shall notify the other party whether it concurs in the appointment of the conciliator proposed by that party to be the President of the Commission.

(2) The communications provided for in this Rule shall be made or promptly confirmed in writing and shall either be transmitted through the Secretary-General or directly between the parties with a copy to the Secretary-General.

Rule 4

Appointment of Conciliators by the Chairman of the Administrative Council

(1) If the Commission is not constituted within 90 days after the dispatch by the Secretary-General of the notice of registration, or such other period as the parties may

agree, either party may, through the Secretary-General, address to the Chairman of the Administrative Council a request in writing to appoint the conciliator or conciliators not yet appointed and to designate a conciliator to be the President of the Commission.

(2) The provision of paragraph (1) shall apply *mutatis mutandis* in the event that the parties have agreed that the conciliators shall elect the President of the Commission and they fail to do so.

(3) The Secretary-General shall forthwith send a copy of the request to the other party.

(4) The Chairman shall use his best efforts to comply with that request within 30 days after its receipt. Before he proceeds to make an appointment or designation, with due regard to Article 31(1) of the Convention, he shall consult both parties as far as possible.

(5) The Secretary-General shall promptly notify the parties of any appointment or designation made by the Chairman.

Rule 5

Acceptance of Appointments

A78–006 (1) The party or parties concerned shall notify the Secretary-General of the appointment of each conciliator and indicate the method of his appointment.

(2) As soon as the Secretary-General has been informed by a party or the Chairman of the Administrative Council of the appointment of a conciliator, he shall seek an acceptance from the appointee.

(3) If a conciliator fails to accept his appointment within 15 days, the Secretary-General shall promptly notify the parties, and if appropriate the Chairman, and invite them to proceed to the appointment of another conciliator in accordance with the method followed for the previous appointment.

Rule 6

Constitution of the Commission

A78–007 (1) The Commission shall be deemed to be constituted and the proceeding to have begun on the date the Secretary-General notifies the parties that all the conciliators have accepted their appointment.

(2) Before or at the first session of the Commission, each conciliator shall sign a declaration in the following form:

> "To the best of my knowledge there is no reason why I should not serve on the Conciliation Commission constituted by the International Centre for Settlement of Investment Disputes with respect to a dispute between _____ and _____ .
>
> "I shall keep confidential all information coming to my knowledge as a result of my participation in this proceeding, as well as the contents of any report drawn up by the Commission.
>
> "I shall not accept any instruction or compensation with regard to the proceeding from any source except as provided in the Convention on the Settlement of Investment Disputes between States and Nationals of Other States and in the Regulations and Rules made pursuant thereto.

"A statement of my past and present professional, business and other relationships (if any) with the parties is attached hereto."

Any conciliator failing to sign such a declaration by the end of the first session of the Commission shall be deemed to have resigned.

Rule 7

Replacement of Conciliators

At any time before the Commission is constituted, each party may replace any conciliator appointed by it and the parties may by common consent agree to replace any conciliator. The procedure of such replacement shall be in accordance with Rules 1, 5 and 6.

Rule 8

Incapacity or Resignation of Conciliators

(1) If a conciliator becomes incapacitated or unable to perform the duties of his office, the procedure in respect of the disqualification of conciliators set forth in Rule 9 shall apply.

(2) A conciliator may resign by submitting his resignation to the other members of the Commission and the Secretary-General. If the conciliator was appointed by one of the parties, the Commission shall promptly consider the reasons for his resignation and decide whether it consents thereto. The Commission shall promptly notify the Secretary-General of its decision.

Rule 9

Disqualification of Conciliators

(1) A party proposing the disqualification of a conciliator pursuant to Article 57 of the Convention shall promptly, and in any event before the Commission first recommends terms of settlement of the dispute to the parties or when the proceeding is closed (whichever occurs earlier), file its proposal with the Secretary-General, stating its reasons therefor.

(2) The Secretary-General shall forthwith:

(a) transmit the proposal to the members of the Commission and, if it relates to a sole conciliator or to a majority of the members of the Commission, to the Chairman of the Administrative Council; and

(b) notify the other party of the proposal.

(3) The conciliator to whom the proposal relates may, without delay, furnish explanations to the Commission or the Chairman, as the case may be.

(4) Unless the proposal relates to a majority of the members of the Commission, the other members shall promptly consider and vote on the proposal in the absence of the conciliator concerned. If those members are equally divided, they shall, through the Sec-

retary-General, promptly notify the Chairman of the proposal, of any explanation furnished by the conciliator concerned and of their failure to reach a decision.

(5) Whenever the Chairman has to decide on a proposal to disqualify a conciliator, he shall use his best efforts to take that decision within 30 days after he has received the proposal.

(6) The proceeding shall be suspended until a decision has been taken on the proposal.

Rule 10

Procedure during a Vacancy on the Commission

A78–011 (1) The Secretary-General shall forthwith notify the parties and, if necessary, the Chairman of the Administrative Council of the disqualification, death, incapacity or resignation of a conciliator and of the consent, if any, of the Commission to a resignation.

(2) Upon the notification by the Secretary-General of a vacancy on the Commission, the proceeding shall be or remain suspended until the vacancy has been filled.

Rule 11

Filling Vacancies on the Commission

A78–012 (1) Except as provided in paragraph (2), a vacancy resulting from the disqualification, death, incapacity or resignation of a conciliator shall be promptly filled by the same method by which his appointment had been made.

(2) In addition to filling vacancies relating to conciliators appointed by him, the Chairman of the Administrative Council shall appoint a person from the Panel of Conciliators:

(a) to fill a vacancy caused by the resignation, without the consent of the Commission, of a conciliator appointed by a party; or

(b) at the request of either party, to fill any other vacancy, if no new appointment is made and accepted within 45 days of the notification of the vacancy by the Secretary-General.

(3) The procedure for filling a vacancy shall be in accordance with Rules 1, 4(4), 4(5), 5 and, *mutatis mutandis*, 6(2).

Rule 12

Resumption of Proceeding after Filling a Vacancy

A78–013 As soon as a vacancy on the Commission has been filled, the proceeding shall continue from the point it had reached at the time the vacancy occurred. The newly appointed conciliator may, however, require that any hearings be repeated in whole or in part.

CHAPTER II

WORKING OF THE COMMISSION

Rule 13

Sessions of the Commission

(1) The Commission shall hold its first session within 60 days after its constitution or such other period as the parties may agree. The dates of that session shall be fixed by the President of the Commission after consultation with its members and the Secretary-General. If upon its constitution the Commission has no President because the parties have agreed that the President shall be elected by its members, the Secretary-General shall fix the dates of that session. In both cases, the parties shall be consulted as far as possible.

(2) The dates of subsequent sessions shall be determined by the Commission, after consultation with the Secretary-General and with the parties as far as possible.

(3) The Commission shall meet at the seat of the Centre or at such other place as may have been agreed by the parties in accordance with Article 63 of the Convention. If the parties agree that the proceeding shall be held at a place other than the Centre or an institution with which the Centre has made the necessary arrangements, they shall consult with the Secretary-General and request the approval of the Commission. Failing such approval, the Commission shall meet at the seat of the Centre.

(4) The Secretary-General shall notify the members of the Commission and the parties of the dates and place of the sessions of the Commission in good time.

Rule 14

Sittings of the Commission

(1) The President of the Commission shall conduct its hearings and preside at its deliberations.

(2) Except as the parties otherwise agree, the presence of a majority of the members of the Commission shall be required at its sittings.

(3) The President of the Commission shall fix the date and hour of its sittings.

Rule 15

Deliberations of the Commission

(1) The deliberations of the Commission shall take place in private and remain secret.

(2) Only members of the Commission shall take part in its deliberations. No other person shall be admitted unless the Commission decides otherwise.

Rule 16

Decisions of the Commission

A78–017 (1) Decisions of the Commission shall be taken by a majority of the votes of all its members. Abstention shall count as a negative vote.

(2) Except as otherwise provided by these Rules or decided by the Commission, it may take any decision by correspondence among its members, provided that all of them are consulted. Decisions so taken shall be certified by the President of the Commission.

Rule 17

Incapacity of the President

A78–018 If at any time the President of the Commission should be unable to act, his functions shall be performed by one of the other members of the Commission, acting in the order in which the Secretary-General had received the notice of their acceptance of their appointment to the Commission.

Rule 18

Representation of the Parties

A78–019 (1) Each party may be represented or assisted by agents, counsel or advocates whose names and authority shall be notified by that party to the Secretary-General, who shall promptly inform the Commission and the other party.

(2) For the purposes of these Rules, the expression "party" includes, where the context so admits, an agent, counsel or advocate authorized to represent that party.

Chapter III

General Procedural Provisions

Rule 19

Procedural Orders

A78–020 The Commission shall make the orders required for the conduct of the proceeding.

Rule 20

Preliminary Procedural Consultation

A78–021 (1) As early as possible after the constitution of a Commission, its President shall endeavor to ascertain the views of the parties regarding questions of procedure. For this purpose he may request the parties to meet him. He shall, in particular, seek their views on the following matters:

(a) the number of members of the Commission required to constitute a quorum at its sittings;

(b) the language or languages to be used in the proceeding;

(c) the evidence, oral or written, which each party intends to produce or to request the Commission to call for, and the written statements which each party intends to file, as well as the time limits within which such evidence should be produced and such statements filed;

(d) the number of copies desired by each party of instruments filed by the other; and

(e) the manner in which the record of the hearings shall be kept.

(2) In the conduct of the proceeding the Commission shall apply any agreement between the parties on procedural matters, except as otherwise provided in the Convention or the Administrative and Financial Regulations.

Rule 21

Procedural Languages

(1) The parties may agree on the use of one or two languages to be used in the proceeding, provided that, if they agree on any language that is not an official language of the Centre, the Commission, after consultation with the Secretary-General, gives its approval. If the parties do not agree on any such procedural language, each of them may select one of the official languages (i.e., English, French and Spanish) for this purpose. A78–022

(2) If two procedural languages are selected by the parties, any instrument may be filed in either language. Either language may be used at the hearings, subject, if the Commission so requires, to translation and interpretation. The recommendations and the report of the Commission shall be rendered and the record kept in both procedural languages, both versions being equally authentic.

CHAPTER IV

CONCILIATION PROCEDURES

Rule 22

Functions of the Commission

(1) In order to clarify the issues in dispute between the parties, the Commission shall hear the parties and shall endeavor to obtain any information that might serve this end. The parties shall be associated with its work as closely as possible. A78–023

(2) In order to bring about agreement between the parties, the Commission may, from

time to time at any stage of the proceeding, make—orally or in writing—recommendations to the parties. It may recommend that the parties accept specific terms of settlement or that they refrain, while it seeks to bring about agreement between them, from specific acts that might aggravate the dispute; it shall point out to the parties the arguments in favor of its recommendations. It may fix time limits within which each party shall inform the Commission of its decision concerning the recommendations made.

(3) The Commission, in order to obtain information that might enable it to discharge its functions, may at any stage of the proceeding:

   (a) request from either party oral explanations, documents and other information;

   (b) request evidence from other persons; and

   (c) with the consent of the party concerned, visit any place connected with the dispute or conduct inquiries there, provided that the parties may participate in any such visits and inquiries.

Rule 23

Cooperation of the Parties

A78–024   (1) The parties shall cooperate in good faith with the Commission and, in particular, at its request furnish all relevant documents, information and explanations as well as use the means at their disposal to enable the Commission to hear witnesses and experts whom it desires to call. The parties shall also facilitate visits to and inquiries at any place connected with the dispute that the Commission desires to undertake.

(2) The parties shall comply with any time limits agreed with or fixed by the Commission.

Rule 24

Transmission of the Request

A78–025   As soon as the Commission is constituted, the Secretary-General shall transmit to each member a copy of the request by which the proceeding was initiated, of the supporting documentation, of the notice of registration and of any communication received from either party in response thereto.

Rule 25

Written Statements

A78–026   (1) Upon the constitution of the Commission, its President shall invite each party to file, within 30 days or such longer time limit as he may fix, a written statement of its position. If, upon its constitution, the Commission has no President, such invitation shall be issued and any such longer time limit shall be fixed by the Secretary-General. At any stage of the proceeding, within such time limits as the Commission shall fix, either party may file such other written statements as it deems useful and relevant.

(2) Except as otherwise provided by the Commission after consultation with the parties

and the Secretary-General, every written statement or other instrument shall be filed in the form of a signed original accompanied by additional copies whose number shall be two more than the number of members of the Commission.

Rule 26

Supporting Documentation

(1) Every written statement or other instrument filed by a party may be accompanied by supporting documentation, in such form and number of copies as required by Administrative and Financial Regulation 30.

(2) Supporting documentation shall ordinarily be filed together with the instrument to which it relates, and in any case within the time limit fixed for the filing of such instrument.

Rule 27

Hearings

(1) The hearings of the Commission shall take place in private and, except as the parties otherwise agree, shall remain secret.

(2) The Commission shall decide, with the consent of the parties, which other persons besides the parties, their agents, counsel and advocates, witnesses and experts during their testimony, and officers of the Commission may attend the hearings.

Rule 28

Witnesses and Experts

(1) Each party may, at any stage of the proceeding, request that the Commission hear the witnesses and experts whose evidence the party considers relevant. The Commission shall fix a time limit within which such hearing shall take place.

(2) Witnesses and experts shall, as a rule, be examined before the Commission by the parties under the control of its President. Questions may also be put to them by any member of the Commission.

(3) If a witness or expert is unable to appear before it, the Commission, in agreement with the parties, may make appropriate arrangements for the evidence to be given in a written deposition or to be taken by examination elsewhere. The parties may participate in any such examination.

Chapter V

Termination of the Proceeding

Rule 29

Objections to Jurisdiction

A78–030 (1) Any objection that the dispute is not within the jurisdiction of the Centre or, for other reasons, is not within the competence of the Commission shall be made as early as possible. A party shall file the objection with the Secretary-General no later than in its first written statement or at the first hearing if that occurs earlier, unless the facts on which the objection is based are unknown to the party at that time.

(2) The Commission may on its own initiative consider, at any stage of the proceeding, whether the dispute before it is within the jurisdiction of the Centre and within its own competence.

(3) Upon the formal raising of an objection, the proceeding on the merits shall be suspended. The Commission shall obtain the views of the parties on the objection.

(4) The Commission may deal with the objection as a preliminary question or join it to the merits of the dispute. If the Commission overrules the objection or joins it to the merits, it shall resume consideration of the latter without delay.

(5) If the Commission decides that the dispute is not within the jurisdiction of the Centre or not within its own competence, it shall close the proceeding and draw up a report to that effect, in which it shall state its reasons.

Rule 30

Closure of the Proceeding

A78–031 (1) If the parties reach agreement on the issues in dispute, the Commission shall close the proceeding and draw up its report noting the issues in dispute and recording that the parties have reached agreement. At the request of the parties, the report shall record the detailed terms and conditions of their agreement.

(2) If at any stage of the proceeding it appears to the Commission that there is no likelihood of agreement between the parties, the Commission shall, after notice to the parties, close the proceeding and draw up its report noting the submission of the dispute to conciliation and recording the failure of the parties to reach agreement.

(3) If one party fails to appear or participate in the proceeding, the Commission shall, after notice to the parties, close the proceeding and draw up its report noting the submission of the dispute to conciliation and recording the failure of that party to appear or participate.

Rule 31

Preparation of the Report

A78–032 The report of the Commission shall be drawn up and signed within 60 days after the closure of the proceeding.

ICSID Conciliation Rules

Rule 32

The Report

(1) The report shall be in writing and shall contain, in addition to the material specified in paragraph (2) and in Rule 30:

    (a) a precise designation of each party;

    (b) a statement that the Commission was established under the Convention, and a description of the method of its constitution;

    (c) the names of the members of the Commission, and an identification of the appointing authority of each;

    (d) the names of the agents, counsel and advocates of the parties;

    (e) the dates and place of the sittings of the Commission; and

    (f) a summary of the proceeding.

(2) The report shall also record any agreement of the parties, pursuant to Article 35 of the Convention, concerning the use in other proceedings of the views expressed or statements or admissions or offers of settlement made in the proceeding before the Commission or of the report or any recommendation made by the Commission.

(3) The report shall be signed by the members of the Commission; the date of each signature shall be indicated. The fact that a member refuses to sign the report shall be recorded therein.

Rule 33

Communication of the Report

(1) Upon signature by the last conciliator to sign, the Secretary-General shall promptly:

    (a) authenticate the original text of the report and deposit it in the archives of the Centre; and

    (b) dispatch a certified copy to each party, indicating the date of dispatch on the original text and on all copies.

(2) The Secretary-General shall, upon request, make available to a party additional certified copies of the report.

(3) The Centre shall not publish the report without the consent of the parties.

Chapter VI

General Provisions

Rule 34

Final Provisions

A78–035 (1) The texts of these Rules in each official language of the Centre shall be equally authentic.

(2) These Rules may be cited as the "Conciliation Rules" of the Centre.

INDEX

AAA. *See* AMERICAN ARBITRATION ASSOCIATION INTERNATIONAL ARBITRATION RULES
ABANDONMENT OF ARBITRATION,
  remuneration of arbitrator, 2–348
ABROAD, WITNESSES. *See* WITNESSES
ABTA, 8–011, 8–012
  evidence, 8–036
  internal appeal procedures, 8–052
ACCEPTANCE OF SETTLEMENT OFFER. *See* SETTLEMENT
ACCIDENTAL SLIP,
  agricultural property arbitration, 3–082
ACCOMPANIED INSPECTIONS, 13–052
ACKNOWLEDGMENT OF SERVICE, A54–094
AD HOC ARBITRATION,
  arbitration clause, A54–016
  fees, 9–049—9–051
  international arbitration. *See* International arbitration
  maritime arbitration, 11–007
  remuneration of arbitrator,
    express contract, 2–349
    quantum, 2–389
ADDITIONAL AWARD,
  Arbitration Act 1996, A6–058
  construction industry arbitration, 6–104
  LCIA arbitration, 9–029, A44–028
  Model Law, A14–033
  representations, 2–512
  time limits, 2–512
  UNCITRAL Arbitration Rules, A15–038
  WIPO arbitration, A52–066
ADJOURNMENTS, 2–686—2–688
  agricultural property arbitration, 3–058
  application, 2–686
  new law, 2–687
  old law, 2–687
  short hearings, 2–688
ADJUDICATION, 5–001—5–113
  CEDR Rules for Adjudication. *See* CEDR Rules for Adjudication
  construction industry disputes, 2–003, 6–027
  Government Contract GC/Works/1, 6–050, 6–062
  Housing Grants, Construction and Regeneration Act 1996. *See* Housing Grants, Construction and Regeneration Act 1996
  meaning, 4–048
  NEC forms, 6–059

ADMINISTERED SCHEMES. *See* CODE OF PRACTICE ARBITRATIONS
ADMINISTRATIVE FEES,
  American Arbitration Association International Arbitration Rules, A18–038—A18–041
ADMIRALTY COURT, 11–002
ADMIRALTY PROCEEDINGS,
  retention of security, 2–176
  security, retention of, 2–176
  stay of legal proceedings, 2–173, A6–012
ADMISSIBLE EVIDENCE. *See* EVIDENCE
ADMISSION OF FACTS OR DOCUMENTS, 2–771
ADR, 4–001—4–058
  See also Mediation
  adjudicatory processes distinguished, 4–001
  advantages, 4–004, 4–016
  alternative, meaning of, 4–001
  arbitration,
    Arbitration Act 1996, 4–024, 4–028
    differences between ADR and, 4–029—4–034
  arbitrator, participation of, 4–049—4–051
  attitude, 4–017
    mediator, 4–005—4–009
  Australia, 4–003, 4–056
  basis of decisions, 4–032
  case management, 4–046—4–052
  categorisation, 4–001
  Civil Procedure rules, 4–018—4–020
  clauses,
    combined with arbitration clause, A54–131
  conceptual questions, 4–058
  costs, 4–016
  court-attached schemes, 4–035—4–037
  definition, 4–001
  European Commission Green Paper, 4–014, 4–015
  European Union, access in, 4–014, 4–015
  forms, 4–004
  Government, approach of, 4–057
  ICC clauses, A54–1430
  ICC rules. *See* ICC ADR rules
  independence, 4–002
  Leggatt Report, 4–054, 4–055
  mandatory references, 4–043—4–045
  Med-Arb. *See* Med-Arb
  mediation. *See* Mediation
  negotiation within structured context, 4–001
  objective, 4–016
  online dispute resolution, 12–004

1037

ADR—cont.
  practice, in, 4–004
  private sector, 4–038
  recent court decisions, 4–040—4–042
  root of, 4–001
  settlement, promotion of, 4–016—4–034
  suitable uses, 4–003
  techniques, 4–001, 4–004
  USA, 4–003, 4–046, 4–056
  use in UK, 4–002
  Woolf Report, 4–016, 4–046
ADVICE,
  See also under Powers of arbitrator
  agricultural property arbitration, 3–041, 3–052
  confidentiality, 2–347
  dispute boards, 7–034
  farm business tenancy arbitration, 3–108
  ICE arbitration, A43–015
  natural justice, 2–347
  property valuation arbitration, 13–023
  rent review arbitration, 13–022
  resignation of arbitrator, 2–297
  RSA, 16–057
  selection of evidence for hearing, 2–720
  technical, 8–039
ADVOCATE, 2–820—2–844
  See also Barristers
  adversarial system, role in, 2–820
  agricultural property arbitration, 3–066
  arbitration, 2–820
  arbitrator, duty to, 2–821, 2–844
  choosing, 2–830—2–835
    available choices, 2–830
    combined witness/advocate, 2–832
    directors, 2–831
    employee, 2–831
    generally, 2–830
    lawyer, 2–835
    lay advocate, 2–834
    person, party in, 2–832
    restrictions, 2–830
  correctness of contentions, 2–821
  deceiving court, 2–821
  direct access, 2–822
  directors, 2–831
  duty to arbitrator, 2–821
  employee, 2–831
  expert witness,
    distinguished, 2–846
  facts, getting right, 2–829
  function, 2–823
  identification of issues, 2–825
  investigation, 2–824
  lawyer, 2–835
  lay, 2–834
  litigation, 2–821
  meaning, 2–823
  misleading court, 2–821
  person, party in, 2–832

ADVOCATE—cont.
  pleadings, 2–826
  preparation for hearing, 2–790
  presentation of case, 2–827, 2–828
  reliance on statements made by, 2–821
  role of, 2–820, 2–823—2–292
  simplicity aimed for, 2–827
  summary of position, 2–836
  task of, 2–823—2–829
  technology, use of, 2–843
  tenable argument, 2–828
  weeding out "bad points", 2–828
  written representations, 2–837—2–844
    addressing argument, 2–839
    appendices, 2–841
    arbitrator's duty to, 2–844
    beginning, 2–838
    "blue pencil", 2–841
    brevity, 2–840
    clarity, 2–840
    compelling nature, 2–842
    concise, 2841, 2–841
    cross-headings, 2–840
    heading of arguments, 2–840
    logic, 2–837
    preparation, 2–844
    principles, 2–837
    Table of Contents, 2–840
    technology, use of, 2–843
    understanding case, 2–837
AFTER THE EVENT INSURANCE, 4–023
AGREEMENT. See ARBITRATION AGREEMENT
AGRICULTURAL HOLDINGS,
  Act of 1986,
    appointment of arbitrator, A2–001
    arbitrations, A2–001
    award, A2–003
    conduct of proceedings, A2–002
    costs, A2–006
    interest on awards, A2–005
    miscellaneous matters, A2–008
    reasons for award, A2–004
    remission, A2–007
    remuneration of arbitrator, A2–001
    setting aside, A2–007
    special case, A2–007
    witnesses, A2–002
  award,
    form of award, A3–001—A3–006
    interest, A2–005
    reasons, A2–004, A3–007
AGRICULTURAL PROPERTY ARBITRATION, 3–001—3–109
  1986 Act arbitrations,
    agreement to resolve disputes under, 3–015, 3–016
    appointment of arbitrators, 3–018—3–023
      agreement, by, 3–018
      date of appointment, 3–027

1038

INDEX

AGRICULTURAL PROPERTY ARBITRATION—*cont.*
1986 Act arbitrations—*cont.*
  appointment of arbitrators—*cont.*
    President, by, 3–019—3–021
    revocation of appointment, 3–023
  dispute resolved under, 3–013
  jurisdiction, 3–013—3–017
  method of reference, 3–014
  revocation of appointment, 3–023
  Statement of case. *See* Statement of case *below*
1995 Act. *See* Farm business tenancy arbitration
accidental slip, 3–082
action on appointment, 3–027—3–029
adjournments, 3–058
advocates, 3–066
amendment of case, 3–036—3–039
appointment of arbitrators,
  action on, 3–027—3–028
  agreement, 3–018
  date of, 3–022
  notice of appointment, 3–027
  President, by, 3–019—3–021
  revocation, 3–023
arbitrator,
  action on appointment, 3–027—3–029
  appointment. *See* appointment of arbitrator *above*
  challenges to jurisdiction, 3–030—3–032
  enforcement of order, 3–049, 3–050
  jurisdiction, 3–028, 3–029
  legal advice, taking, 3–052
  notice of appointment, 3–027
  powers, 3–033
  removal, 3–023
  revocation of appointment, 3–023
award, 3–068—3–089
  accidental slip, 3–082
  Calderbank offer, 3–072
  challenging. *See* Challenging award *below*
  clerical mistakes, 3–082
  correction, 3 082
  costs, 3–076—3–078
  date of, 3–079
  delivery of award, 3–079
  departing from parties' cases, 3–068
  error on the face of, 3–087, 3–088
  extension of time to make up, 3–069, 3–070
  final and binding, 3–082
  form of, 3 074
  interest, 3–075
  interim, 3–075
  lien on, 3–080
  making up, 3–069
  reasons for, 3–081
  running out of time for delivery, 3–069
  sealed offer, 3–072
  setting aside, 3–088
  time for, 3–035, 3–069, 3–070

AGRICULTURAL PROPERTY ARBITRATION—*cont.*
background, 3–001—3–003
bundles, 3–044
Calderbank offer, 3–072
challenges to jurisdiction, 3–030—3–032
challenging award, 3–082—3–089
  accidental slips, 3–082
  basic rule, 3–082
  case stated procedure, 3–087, 3–088
  clerical mistakes, 3–082
  correction of award, 3–082
  error on the face, 3–087—3–088
  misconduct, 3–083—3–086
  omissions, 3–082
  procedure, 3–088, 3–089
  setting aside award, 3–088
  slip rule, 3–082
clerical errors, 3–082
correction of award, 3–082
costs, 3–076—3–078
date of award, 3–079
date of hearing, 3–057
delivery of award, 3–079
discovery, 3–042, 3–043
disputes, 3–010—3–012
disqualification of arbitrator, 3–030
documents only arbitration, 3–040
documents used at hearing, 3–045
enforcement of order, 3–049—3–050
error on face of award, 3–087, 3–088
errors, 3–082
examination of witnesses, 3–064
expert evidence, 3–046
farm business tenancies. *See* Farm business tenancies
farm inspection. *See* Farm inspection
final and binding award, 3–082
form of award, 3–074
forms of letting land, 3–001
hearing,
  advocates, 3–066
  date of, 3–057
  evidence, 3–065
  experts as advocates, 3–066
  generally, 3–040
  oath, evidence on, 3–064
  order of events, 3–063
  place of, 3–057
  post-hearing events, 3–067
  requirement, 3–040
  rules of evidence, 3–065
historical background, 3–001
inspection. *See* Farm inspection
interest, 3–075
interim awards, 3–071—3–073
invalidity of appointment, 3–030
jurisdiction, 3–028, 3–029
legal advice, taking, 3–052
milk quotas. *See* Milk quota arbitrations
misconduct, 3–083—3–086
notice of appointment, 3–027

AGRICULTURAL PROPERTY ARBITRATION—cont.
  notice to quit, 3–001
  oath, evidence on, 3–064
  oral hearing, 3–040
  partnerships, 3–010
  place of hearing, 3–057
  points of law, 3–051, 3–052, 3–053
  powers of arbitrator, 3–033
  procedure,
    adjournments, 3–058
    bundles, 3–045
    date of hearing, 3–057
    discovery, 3–042, 3–043, 3–044
    document used at hearing, 3–045
    enforcement order, 3–049, 3–050
    expert evidence, 3–045, 3–046
    general advice, 3–041
    legal advice, taking, 3–052
    milk quota arbitration, 3–099
    place of hearing, 3–057
    records, 3–044
    stating a case, 3–053—3–055
    witnesses, 3–047, 3–048
  reasonable disbursements, 3–024
    debt, as, 3–026
    President, appointment by, 3–025
  reasons for award, 3–081
  remuneration of arbitrator, 3–024—3–026
    agreement, appointment by, 3–024
    default of agreement, 3–024
    fair rate, 3–024
    milk quota arbitration, 3–099
  rent review, 3–003
  revocation of appointment, 3–023
  rules of evidence, 3–065
  sealed offer, 3–072
  setting aside award, 3–088
  share-farming, 3–010
  slip rule, 3–082
  special case, 3–053—3–056
  statement of claim, 3–027, 3–034—3–039
    additions to, 3–036—3–039
    "all necessary particulars", 3–034, 3–039
    amendments, 3–036—3–039
    criticism of 1986 Act, 3–034
    making award after, 3–035
    onus of proof, 3–038
    parallel preparation, 3–035
    procedure for delivery, 3–034
    sketchy, 3–039
    time of delivery, 3–034
    uninformative, 3–039
  stating case, 3–053—3–056
  statutory arbitrations, 3–003
  summonses, witness, 3–047—3–048
  termination of tenancies, 3–002
  time for award, 3–069, 3–070
  time limits, 3–035
  wills, 3–010
  witness summonses, 3–047, 3–048
  witnesses, 3–047, 3–048

ALTERNATIVE DISPUTE RESOLUTION. *See* ADR; MEDIATION
AMALGAMATION OF ADJUDICATIONS, 2–630—2–633
AMENDMENT OF CLAIM OR DEFENCE,
  agricultural property arbitration, 3–036—3–039
  American Arbitration Association International Arbitration Rules, A18–005
  causing substantial delay, 2–682
  claimant seeking, 2–684
  consideration of applications for leave, 2–679
  negligence claims, adding, 2–680
  new issues of fact, not introducing, 2–685
  not causing substantial delay, 2–681
  notice to arbitrator of application, A54–063
  pleadings, 2–679
  presumption, 2–683
  UNCITRAL Arbitration Rules, A15–021
  WIPO arbitration, A52–044
AMERICAN ARBITRATION ASSOCIATION INTERNATIONAL ARBITRATION RULES, A18–001—A18–041
  administrative fees, A18–038—A18–041
  amendment of claim or defence, A18–005
  applicable laws, A18–029
  appointment of arbitrator, 9–102, A18–007
  arbitration clause, A54–017
  arbitrators,
    appointment, 9–102, A18–007
    compensation, A18–033
    impartiality, A18–008
    independence, A18–008
  award, A18–027—A18–032
    correction of award, A18–031
    effect, A18–028
    form, A18–028
    interpretation, A18–031
  challenging arbitrators, A18–009
  conduct of arbitration, A18–017
  confidentiality, A18–035
  correction of award, A18–031
  costs, A18–032
  counterclaim, A18–004
  decisions, A18–027
  defence, A18–004
  deposit of costs, A18–034
  evidence, A18–020
  exclusion of liability, A18–036
  experts, A18–023
  general conditions, A18–013—A18–037
  hearings, A18–021
  ICD Arbitration, A18–002—A18–037
  impartiality of arbitrators, A18–008
  independence of arbitrators, A18–008
  interim measures, A18–022
  interpretation, A18–031
  introduction, A18–001
  jurisdiction, A18–016

INDEX

AMERICAN ARBITRATION ASSOCIATION
INTERNATIONAL ARBITRATION
RULES—*cont.*
language of proceedings, A18–015
notice of arbitration, A18–003
notices, A18–019
number of arbitrators, A18–006
online dispute resolution, 12–090—12–093, A72–001—A72–014
place of arbitration, A18–014
representation, A18–013
settlement, A18–030
statement of claim, A18–003
waiver of rules, A18–026
written statements, A18–018
AMERICAN CYANAMID DECISION, 4–021, 4–022
AMIABLE COMPOSITEUR, 9–089—9–092
arbitrator acting, 2–727
UNCITRAL Arbitration Rules, A15–034
ANNULMENT OF AWARD,
ICSID arbitration, A60–053
resubmission of dispute after annulment, A77–055
APPEALS,
Arbitration Act 1996, A6–070, A6–071, A6–072
action by arbitrator, 2–936
control of awards, 2–930, 2–931
DAC Report, 2–928
exclusion agreements, 2–925
fact, questions of, 2–927
jurisdictional challenges, 2–932—2–934
leave, appeal, 2–926
losing right, 2–930
obviously wrong, decision, 2–928
options available to court, 2–926
permission to appeal, 2–926
point of law, on, 2–925
reasons for award, 2–929
remedying irregularity, 2–930
restrictions, 2–926, 2–927
results of remission and setting aside, 2–935—2–937
serious irregularity, 2–927, 2–928
substantial injustice, 2–928
time limits, 2–927
Chartered Institute of Arbitrators Commercial Arbitration Scheme, A23–012, A23–013
costs, A23–013
Chartered Institute of Arbitrators "Surveyors Arbitration" Scheme Rules,
Appeal Tribunal, A25–009
costs, A25–010
court, A25–011
Civil Procedure Rules, A5–012
costs, 2–922, 2–923
Court of Arbitration for Sport (CAS), A29–038—A29–050
expert determination, 2–056

APPEALS—*cont.*
GAFTA, A34–018
appeal awards, A34–023
boards of appeal, A34–019
composition of Board of Appeal, 16–104
deadline for lodging, 16–103
delays by appellant, 16–108
objections to qualification of board, 16–109
powers of Board, 16–107
procedure, A34–020
representation, 16–106
string contracts, A34–022
timetable, 16–105
withdrawal, A34–021
withdrawal of appeal, 16–110
High Court, to, 2–949
ICE arbitration, A43–031
leave, 1–005, 2–926, 2–943, 2–949
LMAA small claims procedure, 11–102, A47–004
point of law, on,
generally, 2–099
small claims in county court, 14–094—14–101
costs, 14–101
further appeal, 14–100
two jurisdictions, 2–924
APPLICABLE LAW,
American Arbitration Association International Arbitration Rules, A18–029
arbitration agreement, A54–009
Chartered Institute of Arbitrators Arbitration Scheme for the Travel Industry, A21–012
Chartered Institute of Arbitrators Rules of the Mortgage Code Arbitration, A24–006
Chartered Institute of Arbitrators "Surveyors Arbitration" Scheme Rules, A25–012
ICC arbitration, A39–019
ICSID arbitration, 10–023—10–025
investment treaty arbitration, 10–022—10–025
host state law, 10–023—10–025
ICSID arbitration, 10–023—10–025
international law, 10–021
LMAA terms, 11–076
maritime arbitration, 11–076
precedent, A54–009
Sport Dispute Resolution Panel, 15–034, A67–025
UNCITRAL Arbitration Rules, A15–034
APPLICATIONS TO COURT, 2–938—2–941
balance of convenience, 2–938
Central London County Court, 2–940
Civil Procedure Rules, 2–939
consent of parties, 2–510
County Court, 2–938
evidence secured through application to, 2–507

1041

INDEX

APPLICATIONS TO COURT—*cont.*
financial level of dispute, 2–938
High Court, 2–938
jurisdiction, 2–938
nature of dispute, 2–938
Practice Direction, 2–939—2–941
peremptory orders, 2–938
preservation of evidence, 2–508
procedural timetable, 2–941
procedure for arbitration applications, 2–939—2–941
supervisory powers, 2–938
supportive powers, 2–938
threshold issue, 2–938
transfer of proceedings, 2–938
APPOINTMENT OF ADJUDICATOR,
Housing Grants, Construction and Regeneration Act 1996, 5–036—5–040
appointee, 5–042, 5–043
nominating bodies, 5–041
APPOINTMENT OF ARBITRATOR,
AAA arbitration, 9–102
See also Challenging appointment; Disqualification of arbitrator; Revocation of appointment; Three person tribunal; Two arbitrators and an umpire; Two arbitrators and a chairman
action by arbitrator on, 2–314—2–318
conditions of appointment, 2–317
copy of agreement, 2–314
fees, 2–317
first meeting, terms at, 2–318
imposition of terms, 2–317
jurisdiction, 2–316
terms of appointment, 2–315
widening of powers, 2–315
adjudication, 2–227
Agricultural Holdings Act 1986, under, A2–001
agricultural property arbitration,
action on, 3–027—3–028
agreement, 3–018
date of, 3–022
notice of appointment, 3–027
President, by, 3–019—3–021
American Arbitration Association International Arbitration Rules, A18–007
ancillary matters, 2–266
Arbitration Act 1996, A6–017
failure of appointment procedure, A6–019
procedure, A6–017
qualifications, A6–020
sole arbitrator, A6–018
arbitration agreement, 2–125—2–141
"beauty parade", 2–246
characteristics required, 2–228
Chartered Institute of Arbitrators Arbitration Rules, A20–005
Chartered Institute of Arbitrators Commercial Arbitration Scheme, A23–004

APPOINTMENT OF ARBITRATOR—*cont.*
CIMAR, 6–037, A28–002
contract, 2–306
Court of Arbitration for Sport (CAS), A29–023
date of,
agricultural property arbitration, 3–022
default, 2–268
Dispute Board, 2–226
farm business tenancy arbitration, 3–104, 3–106
FOSFA, 16–020, A66–002
GAFTA, 16–089—16–091, A35–003
ICC arbitration, 9–102
ICE Conditions of Contract, 6–075, 6–087
institutional appointment, 2–126
international arbitration, 9–101—9–119
ad hoc arbitration, 9–103
appointment of arbitrator,
bias, appearance of, 9–111—9–114
disqualifying factors, 9–118
factors affecting, 9–106
grey area, 9–120, 9–121
ICC arbitration, 9–102
independence, 9–107—9–116
non-disqualifying factors, 9–119
number of arbitrators, 9–101
party-appointed arbitrators, 9–115, 9–116
sole arbitrator, 9–102, 9–103
three-member tribunal, 9–103
JCT Standard Form Contract, 6–065
LCIA arbitration, 9–105
LMAA small claims procedure, 11–102, A47–002
LME, 16–019, 16–020
method, 2–125—2–141
misleading appointment, 2–310
Model Law, A14–011
notice of appointment,
agricultural property arbitration, 3–027
precedents,
appointing body or person, appointment by, A54–034
joint appointment as sole arbitrator, A54–027
notice to concur in appointment, A54–029
party, appointment of arbitrator by, A54–028
sole arbitrator, A54–031
substitute sole arbitrator, joint appointment of, A54–033
third party as umpire, notice requiring appointment where, A54–030
two arbitrators appointing umpire or third arbitrator, A54–032
preliminary dialogue, 2–657
procedural rules, 2–127

1042

APPOINTMENT OF ARBITRATOR—cont.
  property valuation arbitration, 13–008—
      13–013
    arbitration agreement, 13–008
    RICS appointments, 13–009
  qualifications, agreement on, 2–228
  quality of arbitrators,
    institutions maintaining, 2–319
    transparency, 2–320
  rent review arbitration, 13–008—13–013
    arbitration agreement, 13–008
    RICS appointments, 13–009
  Royal Institute of British Architects, by,
      6–086
  RSA, 16–041—16–045, 16–056
  substantive contract, nomination in, 2–225—
      2–228
  terms of appointment, 2–246, 2–315
  time limits,
    contractual, 2–270
    statutory, 2–269
    stop running, time, 2–271, 2–272
    third party commencing appointment,
        2–272
  UNCITRAL Arbitration Rules, A15–007—
      A15–009
  widening of powers on, 2–315
  WIPO arbitration, A52–015—A52–019
    default appointment, A52–019
    multiple claimants or respondents, where,
        A52–018
    procedure, A52–015
    sole arbitrator, A52–016
    three arbitrators, A52–017
APPOINTMENT OF MEDIATOR,
  City Disputes Panel Mediation Rules, A27–
      002
  Court of Arbitration for Sport (CAS)
      mediation, A31–006, A31–007
  GAFTA mediation, A37–003
ARBITRAL PROCEEDINGS,
  acknowledgment of service, A54–094, A54–
      098
  amendment of claim or defence,
    UNCITRAL Arbitration Rules, A15–021
  commencement. See Commencement of
      arbitration
  court assistance in taking evidence,
    Model Law, A14–027
  default of party,
    Model Law, A14–025, A14–053
  defence. See Defence
  equal treatment of parties,
    Model Law, A14–018
  hearings,
    See also Hearings
    ICC arbitration, A39–023
    Model Law, A14–024
    UNCITRAL Arbitration Rules, A15–025,
        A15–026

ARBITRAL PROCEEDINGS—cont.
  ICC arbitration,
    applicable law, A39–019
    closing proceedings, A39–024
    conservatory measures, A39–025
    establishing facts of case, A39–022
    hearings, A39–023
    interim measures, A39–025
    language of proceedings, A39–18
    new claims, A39–021
    place of arbitration, A39–016
    rules governing proceedings, A39–017
    terms of reference, A39–020
    timetable, A39–020
    transmission of file to arbitral tribunal,
        A39–015
  language,
    Model Law, A14–022
  Model Law,
    commencement, A14–021
    conduct, A14–050—A14–053
    court assistance in taking evidence, A14–
        027
    default of party, A14–14.025, A14–053
    defence, A14–023
    determination of rules of procedure, A14–
        019, A14–052
    equal treatment of parties, A14–018
    expert appointed by arbitral tribunal,
        A14–026
    hearings, A14–024
    language, A14–022
    place of arbitration, A14–020
    procedural rights of party, A14–051
    statement of claim, A14–023
    written proceedings, A14–024
  place of arbitration,
    Model Law, A14–020
    UNCITRAL Arbitration Rules, A15–017
  precedents,
    issues to consider, A54–035
  statement of claim,
    Model Law, A14–023
    UNCITRAL Arbitration Rules, A15–019
  stay of proceedings,
    precedent order, A54–102
  UNCITRAL Arbitration Rules,
    amendment of claim or defence, A15–021
    defence, A15–020
    evidence, A15–025
    further written statements, A15–023
    general provisions, A15–016
    hearings, A15–025, A15–026
    language, A15–018
    periods of time, A15–024
    place of arbitration, A15–017
    statement of claim, A15–019
    waiver of rules, A15–031
  written proceedings,
    Model Law, A14–024

1043

INDEX

ARBITRAL TRIBUNAL,
  Arbitration Act 1996, A6–016—A6–030
    appointment of arbitrators, A6–017—A6–019
    chairman, A6–021
    competence to rule on own jurisdiction, A6–031
    death of arbitrator or person appointing, A6–027
    decision-making where no chairman or umpire, A6–023
    failure of appointment procedure, A6–019
    general duty, A6–034
    immunity of arbitrator, A6–030
    joint and several liability of parties, A6–029
    jurisdiction, A6–031—A6–033
    objections to substantive jurisdiction, A6–032
    powers, A6–039
    principles of arbitration, application of, 2–068
    qualifications, A6–020
    removal of arbitrator, A6–025
    resignation of arbitrator, A6–026
    revocation of authority, A6–024
    sole arbitrator, appointment of, A6–018
    umpire, A6–022
    vacancies, A6–028
  chairman,
    Arbitration Act 1996, A6–021
  choice of, 2–016
  City Disputes Panel Arbitration Rules, A26–004
    additional powers, A26–010
    duty, A26–011
    jurisdiction, A26–009
    procedural freedom, A26–012
  composition,
    Model Law, A14–010—A14–015
    UNCITRAL Arbitration Rules, A15–006—A15–015
  general duty,
    Arbitration Act 1996, A6–034
  ICC arbitration,
    general provisions, A39–009
    number of arbitrators, A39–010
  immunity of arbitrator,
    Arbitration Act 1996, A6–030
  interim measures,
    Model Law, A14–017, A14–049
    UNCITRAL Arbitration Rules, A15–027
  international arbitration,
    preliminary applications, 9–122—9–150
  joint and several liability of parties,
    Arbitration Act 1996, A6–029
  jurisdiction,
    Arbitration Act 1996, A6–031—A6–033
    LCIA arbitration, A44–024
    LMAA terms, A46–004

ARBITRAL TRIBUNAL—cont.
  jurisdiction—cont.
    Model Law, A14–016, A14–017, A14–048
    UNCITRAL Arbitration Rules, A15–022
  LCIA arbitration,
    additional powers, A44–023
    communications, A44–014
    deposits, A44–025
    expedited formation, A44–010
    formation, A44–006
    jurisdiction, A44–024
  LMAA terms, A46–003
    jurisdiction, A46–004
    reconstitution, A46–027
  mixed disciplines, 2–018
  Model Law,
    appointment of arbitrators, A14–011
    challenge, A14–012, A14–013
    composition, A14–010—A14–015
    failure or impossibility to act, A14–014
    interim measures, A14–017, A14–049
    jurisdiction, A14–016, A14–017, A14–048
    number of arbitrators, A14–010
    substitute arbitrator, A14–015
  number of arbitrators,
    Arbitration Act 1996, A6–016
    ICC arbitration, A39–010
    Model Law, A14–010
    UNCITRAL Arbitration Rules, A15–006
  own evidence of, 13–031—13–033
  powers under Arbitration Act 1996, A6–039
  seat of arbitration determined by, 2–072
  umpire,
    Arbitration Act 1996, A6–022
  UNCITRAL Arbitration Rules,
    composition, A15–006—A15–015
    interim measures, A15–027
    jurisdiction, A15–022
    number of arbitrators, A15–006
ARBITRATION,
  ad hoc. See Ad hoc arbitration
  agreement. See Arbitration agreement
  arbitrability, 2–004
  civil disputes, resolution of, 2–009
  concurrent. See Concurrent arbitration
  consolidated. See Consolidated arbitration
  definition, 2–010
  function, 2–009, 2–010
  Government Contract GC/Works/1, 6–051
  international. See International arbitration
  legal definition, 2–010
  ligitation,
    compared, 2–011—2–015
    differences between, 2–016—2–022
  motivation where parties cannot agree on tribunal, 2–019
  parallel claims. See Parallel arbitration
  pressure from the courts, 2–002
  public service, as, 2–012
  role, 2–012

1044

INDEX

ARBITRATION—cont.
  statutory. *See* Statutory arbitration
  technical evidence, 2–022
  wide range of choice, 2–001
ARBITRATION ACT 1950, A61–001—A61–057
  arbitration agreements, A61–001—A61–005
  arbitrator, A61–006—A61–011
  awards, A61–013—A61–018
  bias of arbitrator, A61–026
  conduct of proceedings, A61–012
  costs, A61–019, A61–030
  enforcement of award, A61–028
  extension of time-limits, A61–029
  fees, A61–020
  foreign awards, enforcement of, A61–037—A61–044
  interest, A61–021, A61–022
  miscellaneous provisions, A61–029—A61–036
  remission of award, A61–024
  removal of arbitrator, A61–025, A61–027
  revocation of authority of arbitrator, A61–027
  setting aside award, A61–025
  umpires, A61–006—A61–011
  witnesses, A61–012
ARBITRATION ACT 1975, A62–001—A62–008
  Convention awards, effect of, A62–003
  evidence, A62–004
  interpretation, A62–007
  refusal of enforcement, A62–005
  replacement of former provisions, A62–002
  staying court proceedings, A62–001
ARBITRATION ACT 1979, A63–001—A63–008
  exclusion agreements, A63–003, A63–004
  interlocutory orders, A63–005
  judicial review of arbitration awards, A63–001
  preliminary point of law, determination by court of, A63–002
ARBITRATION ACT 1996,
  additional award, A6–058
  appeals, A6–070, A6–071, A6–072
    action by arbitrator, 2–936
    control of awards, 2–930, 2–931
    DAC Report, 2–928
    exclusion agreements, 2–925
    fact, questions of, 2–927
    jurisdictional challenges, 2–932—2–934
    leave, appeal, 2–926
    losing right, 2–930
    obviously wrong, decision, 2–928
    options available to court, 2–926
    permission to appeal, 2–926
    point of law, on, 2–925
    reasons for award, 2–929
    remedying irregularity, 2–930
    restrictions, 2–926, 2–927
    results of remission and setting aside, 2–935—2–937
    serious irregularity, 2–927, 2–928

ARBITRATION ACT—cont.
  appeals—cont.
    serving summons on arbitrator, 2–937
    substantial injustice, 2–928
    time limits, 2–927
  application of, 2–058
  appointment of arbitrator,
    failure of appointment procedure, A6–019
    procedure, A6–017
    qualifications, A6–020
    sole arbitrator, A6–018
  arbitral proceedings,
    assessors, appointment of, A6–038
    concurrent hearings, A6–036
    consolidation of proceedings, A6–036
    default of parties, A6–042
    experts, appointment of, A6–038
    extension of time by court, A6–080
    general duty of tribunal, A6–034
    legal advisers, appointment of, A6–038
    legal representation, A6–037
    parties, duty of, A6–041
    peremptory orders of tribunal, enforcement of, A6–043
    powers of tribunal, A6–039
    procedural and evidential matters, A6–035
    provisional awards, A6–040
  arbitral tribunal, A6–016—A6–030
    appointment of arbitrators, A6–017—A6–019
    chairman, A6–021
    competence to rule on own jurisdiction, A6–031
    death of arbitrator or person appointing, A6–027
    decision-making where no chairman or umpire, A6–023
    failure of appointment procedure, A6–019
    general duty, 4–026, 4–027, A6–034
    immunity of arbitrator, A6–030
    joint and several liability of parties, A6–029
    jurisdiction, A6–031—A6 033
    number of arbitrators, A6–016
    objections to substantive jurisdiction, A6–032
    powers, A6–039
    preliminary point of jurisdiction, determination of, A6–033
    qualifications, A6–020
    removal of arbitrator, A6–025
    resignation of arbitrator, A6–026
    revocation of authority, A6–024
    sole arbitrator, appointment of, A6–018
    umpire, A6–022
    vacancies, A6–028
  arbitration agreement,
    death of party, A6–009
    definition, A6–007
    separability, A6–008
  assessment of effect, 1–004

ARBITRATION ACT—cont.
   attendance of witnesses, securing, A6–044
   award, A6–047—A6–059
      additional award, A6–058
      appeal on point of law, A6–070, A6–071, A6–072
      challenging, A6–068, A6–069, A6–071, A6–072
      correction of award, A6–058
      court's powers, A6–067—A6–072
      date of award, A6–055
      different issues, awards on, A6–048
      effect of award, A6–059
      enforcement by court, A6–067
      extension of time for making, A6–051
      form, A6–053
      interest, A6–050
      notification of award, A6–056
      place of award, A6–054
      remedies, A6–049
      rules applicable to substance of dispute, A6–047
      serious irregularity, A6–069
      settlement, A6–052
      substantive jurisdiction, challenging, A6–068
      withholding award for non-payment, A6–057
   challenging award, A6–068, A6–069
   charge to secure payment of solicitor's costs, A6–076
   codification of law through, 2–059
   commencement, 1–004, 2–058
   commencement of arbitral proceedings, A6–013—A6–015
      commencement, A6–015
      extension of time, A6–013
      Limitation Acts, application of, A6–014
   commencement orders, A7–001—A7–003
   common law, matters governed by, A6–082
   concurrent hearings, A6–036
   consequential amendments, A6–125—A6–186
   consolidation of law through, 2–059
   consolidation of proceedings, A6–036
   consumer arbitration agreements,
      legal person, consumer as, A6–091
      modest amount sought, A6–092
      unfair contract terms, A6–090
   correction of award, A6–058
   costs of arbitration, 1–012, 4–024, A6–060—A6–066
      agreement to pay costs in any event, A6–061
      award, A6–062
      effect of agreement or award, A6–063
      fees and expenses of arbitrator, A6–065
      limiting recoverable costs, A6–066
      recoverable costs, A6–064
   DAC, 2–060
   date of award, A6–055

ARBITRATION ACT—cont.
   death of arbitrator or person appointing, A6–027
   definitions, A6–083
   domestic arbitration agreements,
      excluding court's jurisdiction,
         effectiveness of agreement to, A6–088
      international arbitration distinguished, 2–071
      meaning, 2–071
      modifications, A6–086
      staying of legal proceedings, A6–087
   drafting of, 2–059
   extension of time relating to arbitral proceedings, A6–080
   foreign awards,
      evidence, A6–103
      Geneva Convention awards, A6–100
      New York Convention awards, A6–101
      recognition and enforcement, A6–102
      refusal of recognition or enforcement, A6–104
   general principles, A6–002
   general provisions, A6–106—A6–111
   Geneva Convention awards, A6–100
   immunity of arbitral institutions, A6–075
   immunity of arbitrator, A6–030
   index of defined expressions, A6–084
   interest on awards, A6–050
   judges appointed as arbitrators, A6–113—A6–124
   law, issues of, 2–727
   legal proceedings, A6–081
   legal representation, A6–037
   mandatory provisions, A6–005, A6–112
   New York Convention awards, A6–101
   non-mandatory provisions, A6–005
   notices, service of, A6–077
   notification of award, A6–056
   object, loss of right to, A6–074
   objective, 4–025
   origins, 2–060
   overview, 1–003, 2–104
   parties, duty of, A6–041
   party autonomy, 4–025
   peremptory orders of tribunal, enforcement of, A6–043
   persons taking no part in proceedings, A6–073
   place of award, A6–054
   powers of court,
      attendance of witnesses, securing, A6–044
      peremptory orders of tribunal, enforcement of, A6–043
      preliminary point of law, determination of, A6–046
      supporting arbitral proceedings, A6–045
   pre-commencement arbitrations, 2–058
   precedent, use of, 2–104
   principle based system, 2–066

Index

ARBITRATION ACT—*cont.*
  principles of arbitration, 1–003
    applicability of, 2–068
    foundation of statute, 2–068
    generally, 2–067
    meaning, 2–067
    nature of, 2–069
    parties, application to, 2–070
    purpose of, 2–068
    tribunal, application to, 2–069
  procedure,
    assessment of, 2–077
    freedom to choose, 2–077, 2–078
    innovation in, 2–078
    suitability, 2–077
  provisional awards, A6–040
  reckoning periods of time, A6–079
  refusal of recognition, A14–036
  removal of arbitrator, A6–025
  repeals, A6–187
  resignation of arbitrator, A6–026
  scope, 2–058
  scope of application of provisions, A6–003, A6–004
  seat of arbitration, A6–004
  service,
    documents, A6–078
    notices, A6–077
  small claims arbitration in county court, A6–093
  statutory arbitration, A6–095—A6–099
  stay of legal proceedings, A6–010
    Admiralty proceedings, A6–012
    reference of interpleader issue to arbitration, A6–011
  structure, 2–065—2–070
  transitional provisions, A6–085
  vacancies, A6–028
  withholding award for non-payment, A6–057
  writing, agreements to be in, A6–006
ARBITRATION AGREEMENT,
  aim, 2–110
  applicable law, A54–009
  Arbitration Act 1996,
    death of party, A6–009
    definition, A6–007
    separability, A6–008
    stay of legal proceedings, A6–010—A6–012
  "arbitrator not to be bound by the law" clauses, 2–134
  basic clause, 2–116
  choice of law, 9–067
  clauses, 2–108
  commodity trade arbitrations. *See* Commodity trade arbitration
  confidentiality, 2–803
  constituents, 2–116—2–124
    "arbitrator not to be bound by the law" clauses, 2–134
    award condition precedent to litigation, 2–128

ARBITRATION AGREEMENT—*cont.*
  constituents—*cont.*
    basic clause, 2–116
    extreme levels of complication, 2–132
    foreign law, contract governed by, 2–117
    institutional bodies' rules, 2–120
    method of appointment, 2–125—2–141
    national law to be applied, 2–129
    number of arbitrators, 2–121—2–124
    procedural disputes, 2–133
    qualifications of arbitrators, 2–136
    seat of arbitration, 2–135
    substantive law of arbitration agreement, 2–130
    time limits, 2–137—2–141
    trade rules incorporated, 2–119
    venue, 2–135
  construction industry arbitration, 6–081
  consumer disputes, 2–115
  contract terms including arbitration clauses, incorporation of, 2–119
  costs, 2–106
  death of party, A6–009
  definition, 2–111—2–115
    Model Law, A14–007, A14–045
  "disputes to be settled by arbitration", 2–116
  drafting, 2–110, 2–118, 2–142
  evidence, 2–762
  existing disputes, 2–105
  extending jurisdiction in on-going arbitrations, 2–114
  foreign law, contract governed by, 2–117
  form,
    Model Law, A14–007, A14–045
  form of, 2–112
  future disputes, 2–105, 2–106
  host agreement and, 2–108
  institutional bodies' rules, 2–120
  invalid clauses, 2–118
  JCT Standard Form Contract, 6–046
  meaning, 2–108, 2–111
  method of appointment, 2–125—2–141
  mistakes, 2–142
  Model Law, A14–007—A14–009
    courts, A14–046
    definition, A14–007, A14–045
    form, A14–007, A14–045
    interim measures by court, A14–009
    substantive claim before court, A14–008
  national law to be applied, 2–129
  number of arbitrators, 2–121—2–124
  online dispute resolution, 12–027—12–041
    enforcement of awards, 12–039—12–041
    evidence, 12–031—12–038
    nature of electronic communications, 12–029, 12–030
    validity, 12–027, 12–028
  oral arbitration agreement, 2–113
  pathological clauses, 2–118
  place of arbitration, A54–009

ARBITRATION AGREEMENT—*cont.*
  precedents,
    advance agreement for sharing of costs, A54–023
    applicable law, A54–007
    arbitration clause, A54–001—A54–026
    CIA clause, A54–009
    court's role, A54–006, A54–022
    general form, A54–020
    institutional rules, incorporating, A54–010
    place of arbitration, A54–009
    pre-dispute, A54–003—A54–021
    Scott v. Avery clause, A54–007
    tailoring powers of arbitrator to wishes of parties, A54–005, A54–021
    time limit, A54–008
    variation of existing arbitration agreement, A54–024
  problematic drafting, 2–118
  qualifications of arbitrator, 2–136
  recording, 2–112
  reference in an arbitration agreement, 2–112
  rules of procedure, 2–762
  seat of arbitration, 2–135
  sharing costs, 2–106
  signatures, 2–112
  small claims arbitration in county court where, 14–009
  statutory definition, 2–111—2–115
  substantive law of arbitration agreement, 2–130
  tape recordings, 2–112
  termination of primary arbitration agreement, 2–108
  time limits, 2–137—2–141
  trade rules incorporated, 2–120
  venue, 2–135
  writing requirement, 2–112
ARBITRATION CLAUSE,
  "ad hoc" agreement, A54–016
  American Arbitration Association International Arbitration Rules, A54–017
  Asbatankvoy Clause, 11–024
  Baltime Clause, 11–020
  Centrocon Clause, 11–021
  CIA clause, A54–09
  CIETAC, 16–062
  court proceedings overriding, 2–641
  GAFTA, 16–085
  Hong Kong International Arbitration Centre, A54–021
  ICC arbitration, A54–014
  Indian Council of Arbitration, A54–019
  Kuala Lumpur Regional Centre for Arbitration, A54–018
  LCIA arbitration, A54–012
  LMAA terms, 11–028, A54–013
  long form, A54–004
  New York Produce Exchange Form Clause, 11–022, 11–023

ARBITRATION CLAUSE—*cont.*
  Norwegian Saleform Clause, 11–026, 11–027
  RSA, 16–039
  settlements term, 2–754
  short form, A54–003
  Singapore International Arbitration Centre, A54–020
  UNCITRAL Arbitration Rules, A54–015
ARBITRATOR,
  adjournment by, 2–311
  advice sought by. *See* Advice
  advocate's duty to, 2–821
  agricultural property arbitration,
    action on appointment, 3–027—3–029
    challenges to jurisdiction, 3–030—3–032
    enforcement of order, 3–049, 3–050
    jurisdiction, 3–028, 3–029
    legal advice, taking, 3–052
    notice of appointment, 3–027
    powers, 3–033
    removal, 3–023
    revocation of appointment, 3–023
  amiable composituer, acting as, 2–134
  appointment. *See* Appointment of arbitrator
  "arbitrator not to be bound by the law" clauses, 2–103, 2–134
  autonomy, 2–465
  busy, 2–312
  cancellation charges, 2–313
  challenging appointment. *See* Challenging arbitrator
  competence to rule on own jurisdiction. *See* Competence to rule on own jurisdiction
  conforming to own directions, 2–516
  construction industry arbitration. *See* Construction industry arbitration
  contract out powers, 2–475, 2–476
  correction of award, 2–485
  court applications, sanctioning, 2–506—2–511
  death, 2–307
  discovery, 2–469
  disqualification. *See* Disqualification of arbitrator; Removal of arbitrator
  duties. *See* Duties of arbitrator
  even number, 2–122, 2–218
  evidence, responsibilities relating to, 2–714
  ex aequo et bono, acting, 2–727
  exceeding powers, 2–514
  expenses. *See* Expenses
  farm business tenancy arbitration,
    experience, 3–100
    remuneration, 3–107
  fees. *See* Fees
  fraudulent awards, 2–513
  health, 2–307
  immunity, 2–074
  insurance against failure of duties, 2–308
  JCT Standard Form Contract, jurisdiction, 6–065

INDEX

ARBITRATOR—*cont.*
  judging techniques. *See* Judging techniques
  look-sniff arbitration, 2–044
  master of own procedure, 2–470—2–472
  material used, 2–042
  medical records, access to, 2–308
  notes, 2–816
  notice of appointment,
    agricultural property arbitration, 3–027
  number of,
    agreement, 2–121—2–124
    even, 2–122, 2–218
    freedom to choose, 2–121
    ICC arbitration, 9–014
    maximum, 2–217
    no agreement on, 2–123
  obligations of, 2–512
  obligations to complete, 2–307
  own evidence of, 13–031—13–033
  partnership, in, 2–814
  possession of file, 2–814
  powers. *See* Powers of arbitrator
  publication of file, 2–815
  removal. *See* Removal of arbitrator
  remuneration. *See* Remuneration of arbitrator
  representative, obligation to hear, 2–512
  resignation. *See* Resignation of arbitrator
  revocation of appointment,
    agricultural property arbitration, 3–023
  sole. *See* Sole arbitrator
  statutory immunity, 2–074, 2–075
  taking charge of proceedings. *See* Powers of arbitrator
  terms of engagement,
    precedent, A54–117—A54–127
  voluntary withdrawal, 2–291
"ARBITRATOR NOT TO BE BOUND BY THE LAW" CLAUSES, 2–134
ARBITRATORS,
  American Arbitration Association International Arbitration Rules,
    challenge, A18–009
    compensation, A18–033
    impartiality, A18–008
    independence, A18–008
    replacement, A18–011, A18–012
  appointment. *See* Appointment of arbitrators
  arbitrators,
    revocation of authority, A26–008
  bias, appearance of,
    international arbitration, 9–111—9–114
  challenging,
    City Disputes Panel Arbitration Rules, A26–008
    Court of Arbitration for Sport (CAS), A29–016
    ICC arbitration, A39–013
    UNCITRAL Arbitration Rules, A15–010—A15–013
    WIPO arbitration, A52–024—A52–029

ARBITRATORS—*cont.*
  Chartered Institute of Arbitrators Arbitration Rules,
    appointment, A20–005
    communications, A20–006
    powers, A20–008
  Chartered Institute of Arbitrators Commercial Arbitration Scheme,
    appointment, A23–004
    communications, A23–005
  CIMAR,
    appointment, A28–002
  City Disputes Panel Arbitration Rules,
    challenging, A26–008
    impartiality, A26–005
    revocation of authority, A26–008
  compensation,
    American Arbitration Association International Arbitration Rules, A18–033
  Court of Arbitration for Sport (CAS), A29–006
    appointment, A29–023
    challenging, A29–016
    confirmation, A29–024
    independence, A29–015
    qualifications, A29–015
    removal, A29–017
    replacement, A29–018
  declaration of acceptance, A54–104
  disqualification,
    ICSID arbitration, A60–058, A60–059
  ICC arbitration,
    appointment, A39–011
    challenge, A39–013
    confirmation, A39–011
    replacement, A39–014
  ICSID arbitration,
    disqualification, A60–058, A60–059
    replacement, A60–057
  impartiality,
    American Arbitration Association International Arbitration Rules, A18–008
    international arbitration, 9–107—9–116
    WIPO arbitration, A52–022
  independence,
    American Arbitration Association International Arbitration Rules, A18–008
    Court of Arbitration for Sport (CAS), A29–015
    international arbitration, 9–107—9–116
    WIPO arbitration, A52–022
  international arbitration,
    approach, 9–095
    bias, appearance of, 9–111—9–114
    discretion, 9–093
    impartiality, 9–107—9–116
    independence, 9–107—9–116
    party-appointed, 9–115, 9–116

ARBITRATORS—*cont.*
LCIA arbitration,
communications, A44–014
nationality, A44–007
nomination, A44–008, A44–009, A44–012
party nomination, A44–008
replacement, A44–012
revocation of appointment, A44–011
three or more parties, nomination by, A44–009
nationality,
LCIA arbitration, A44–007
WIPO arbitration, A52–020
number,
international arbitration, 9–101
number of arbitrators,
American Arbitration Association International Arbitration Rules, A18–006
Arbitration Act 1996, A6–016
ICC arbitration, A39–010
Model Law, A14–010
UNCITRAL Arbitration Rules, A15–006
WIPO arbitration, A52–014
powers. *See* Powers of arbitrators
removal,
American Arbitration Association International Arbitration Rules, A18–011, A18–012
Arbitration Act 1996, A6–025
Court of Arbitration for Sport (CAS), A29–017
remuneration. *See* Remuneration of arbitrators
replacement,
Court of Arbitration for Sport (CAS), A29–018
ICC arbitration, A39–014
ICSID arbitration, A60–057
LCIA arbitration, A44–012
UNCITRAL Arbitration Rules, A15–014, A15–015
resignation,
Arbitration Act 1996, A6–026
revocation of appointment,
Arbitration Act 1996, A6–024
LCIA arbitration, A44–011
sole. *See* Sole arbitrator
UNCITRAL Arbitration Rules,
challenging, A15–010—A15–013
number of arbitrators, A15–006
repetition of hearings when arbitrator replaced, A15–015
replacement, A15–014, A15–015
WIPO arbitration,
acceptance, A52–023
availability, A52–023
challenging, A52–024—A52–029
impartiality, A52–022
independence, A52–022
nationality, A52–020

ARBITRATORS—*cont.*
WIPO arbitration—*cont.*
notification, A52–023
number, A52–014
release from appointment, A52–030—A52–032
replacement, A52–033, A52–034
ARCHITECTS,
construction industry arbitration, 6–027
ASBATANKVOY CLAUSE, 11–024
ASEAN AGREEMENT FOR THE PROMOTION AND PROTECTION OF INVESTMENTS, 10–010
ASIAN DOMAIN NAME DISPUTE RESOLUTION CENTRE (ADNDRC), 12–111
ASSESSORS,
ICE arbitration, A43–015
property valuation arbitration, 13–023
rent review arbitration, 13–023
ASSISTANCE,
UNCITRAL Arbitration Rules, A15–005
ASSOCIATION OF BRITISH TRAVEL AGENTS. *See* ABTA
ASSOCIATIONS. *See* Commodity trade associations
AUSTRALIA,
ADR, 4–003, 4–056
AUTHORITY. *See* REVOCATION OF ARBITRATION POWERS
AUTOMATED BLIND-BIDDING, 12–013
AUTOMATED SETTLEMENT SYSTEMS, 12–137
AUTONOMY,
arbitrator, 2–465
party, 2–067
AWARD, 2–873—2–890
accidental slips, 2–885, 2–886
additional. *See* Additional award
agreement on form, 2–873
agricultural holdings,
interest, A2–005
reasons, A2–004
agricultural property arbitration, 3–068—3–089
accidental slip, 3–082
Calderbank offer, 3–072
clerical mistakes, 3–082
correction, 3–082
costs, 3–076—3–078
date of, 3–079
delivery of award, 3–079
departing from parties' cases, 3–068
error on the face of, 3–087, 3–088
extension of time to make up, 3–069, 3–070
final and binding, 3–082
form of, 3–074
interest, 3–075
interim, 3–075
lien on, 3–080
making up, 3–069
reasons for, 3–081

1050

AWARD—*cont.*
   agricultural property arbitration—*cont.*
      running out of time for delivery, 3–069
      sealed offer, 3–072
      setting aside, 3–088
      time for, 3–069, 3–070
   ambiguous, 2–513
   American Arbitration Association
      International Arbitration Rules, A18–027—A18–032
      correction of award, A18–031
      effect, A18–028
      form, A18–028
      interpretation, A18–031
   annulment,
      ICSID arbitration, A60–053
   Arbitration Act 1950, A61–013—A61–018
   Arbitration Act 1996, A6–047—A6–059
      additional award, A6–058
      appeal on point of law, A6–070, A6–071, A6–072
      challenging, A6–068, A6–069, A6–071, A6–072
      correction of award, A6–058
      date of award, A6–055
      different issues, awards on, A6–048
      effect of award, A6–059
      enforcement by court, A6–067
      extension of time for making, A6–051
      form, A6–053
      interest, A6–050
      notification of award, A6–056
      place of award, A6–054
      remedies, A6–049
      rules applicable to substance of dispute, A6–047
      serious irregularity, A6–069
      settlement, A6–052
      substantive jurisdiction, challenging, A6–068
      withholding award for non-payment, A6–057
   arbitrator's power,
      correction of award, 2–485
      date of award, 2–484
      form of award, 2–512
      partial awards, 2–512
      reason for award, 2–512
      refusal to deliver award, 2–484
   certainty, 2–877
   challenging. *See* Challenging award; Serious irregularity
   charter party arbitration, A36–013
   Chartered Institute of Arbitrators Arbitration Rules, A20–010
   Chartered Institute of Arbitrators Arbitration Scheme for the Travel Industry,
      finality, A21–007
      review, A21–010
   Chartered Institute of Arbitrators Commercial Arbitration Scheme, A23–009

AWARD—*cont.*
   Chartered Institute of Arbitrators "Surveyors Arbitration" Scheme Rules,
      appeal to Appeal Tribunal, A25–009
      costs, A25–009
      review, A25–008
   CIETAC, 16–069, A74–052—A74–063
   CIMAR, 6–042, A28–012
   City Disputes Panel Arbitration Rules, A26–022
   clerical mistakes, 2–485, 2–876
   commodity trade arbitration,
      CIETAC, 16–069
      LME, 16–032—16–034
      RSA, 16–052
   condition precedent to litigation, 2–128
   confidentiality, 2–804, 2–818, 2–819
   correction of award,
      agricultural property arbitration, 3–082
      American Arbitration Association
         International Arbitration Rules, A18–031
      Arbitration Act 1996, A6–058
      ICE arbitration, A43–030
      LCIA arbitration, A44–028
      Model Law, A14–033
      WIPO arbitration, A52–066
   costs, A15–039—A15–041
   Court of Arbitration for Sport (CAS), 15–079, 15–089, A29–037
   DAC Report, 2–873
   date,
      agricultural property arbitration, 3–079
      Arbitration Act 1996, A6–055
   date of award,
      form of award, 2–875, 2–876
      interest, 2–898
      power of arbitrator, 2–484
   decisions,
      Model Law, A14–029
      UNCITRAL Arbitration Rules, A15–032
   delivery,
      agricultural property arbitration, 3–079
      construction industry arbitration, 6–103
      farm business tenancy arbitration, 3–108
   different issues, awards on,
      Arbitration Act 1996, 2–874, A6–048
   disclosure, 2–804
   draft, 13–053—13–061
      circulating, 2–443—2–445
      natural justice, 2–443—2–445
      reasons, 2–883—2–886
   effect of award,
      American Arbitration Association
         International Arbitration Rules, A18–028
      Arbitration Act 1996, A6–059
   enforcement. *See* Enforcement of awards; New York Convention
   error on the face of,
      agricultural property arbitration, 3–087, 3–088

1051

AWARD—cont.
  errors in, 2–885, 2–886
  estoppel arising out of, 2–887
    cause of action, 2–290, 2–888, 2–889
    issue, 2–888, 2–889, 2–890
    judgement, estoppel by, 2–887
    new point, raising, 2–890
  expedition, 2–554
    programming writing, 2–555
  extension of time for making,
    Arbitration Act 1996, A6–051
  farm business tenancy arbitration, 3–108
    delivery, 3–108
  finality,
    agricultural property arbitration, 3–082
    certificate as to, A54–093
  foreign. *See* Foreign awards
  form,
    agricultural property arbitration, 3–074
    American Arbitration Association
      International Arbitration Rules, A18–028
    Arbitration Act 1996, A6–053
    Model Law, A14–031
    UNCITRAL Arbitration Rules, A15–033
  form of, 2–875
    absence of agreement, 2–875
    agreement on, 2–512, 2–873
    arbitrator's power, 2–512
    construction industry arbitration, 6–102
    correction, 2–876
    date of award, 2–875, 2–876
    institutional rules, 2–875
    Model Law, 2–875
    notification of award, 2–876
    omissions, 2–876
    place of award, 2–875
    requirements as to, 2–875
    seat of arbitration, 2–875
    signatures, 2–875
    slip rule, 2–876
  FOSFA, A66–007
  fraud, obtained by, 2–515
  fraudulent, 2–515
  GAFTA, A34–017
    different aspects, on, A34–016
  ICC arbitration,
    consent, award by, A39–0283
    correction of award, A39–031
    deposit of costs, A39–030
    enforceability, A39–030
    interpretation of award, A39–031
    making award, A39–027
    notification, A39–030
    scrutiny of award by court, A39–029
    time limit, A39–026
  ICE arbitration, A43–024—A43–031
    appeals, A43–031
    correction of award, A43–030
    costs, A43–027
    interest, A43–026

AWARD—cont.
  ICE arbitration—cont.
    making award, A43–029
    provisional relief, A43–025
    reasons, A43–028
  ICSID arbitration, 10–056, A60–049, A60–050
    annulment, A60–053
    enforcement of award, 10–058, A60–054—A60–056
    interpretation, A60–051
    recognition of award, A60–054—A60–056
    revision, A60–052
  implementation 2–942. *See also* Enforcement of award
  interest. *See* Interest
  interim. *See* Interim award
  interpretation,
    American Arbitration Association
      International Arbitration Rules, A18–031
    ICSID arbitration, A60–051
    Model Law, A14–033
    UNCITRAL Arbitration Rules, A15–036
  judicial review, A63–001
  LCIA arbitration, A44–027
    correction, A44–028
  legal effect, 2–942
  lien on,
    agricultural property arbitration, 3–080
  LMAA small claims procedure, 11–102, A47–007
  LMAA terms, A46–012
  LME, 16–032—16–034
  making up,
    agricultural property arbitration, 3–069
  Model Law, 2–875
    additional award, A14–033
    content, A14–031
    correction, A14–033
    decision by panel of arbitrators, A14–029
    form, A14–031
    interpretation, A14–033
    making of award, A14–055
    recognition of award, A14–059—A14–062
    recourse against award, A14–034, A14–056
    setting aside, A14–034, A14–057, A14–058
    settlement, A14–030
    substance of dispute, A14–028, A14–054
    termination of proceedings, A14–032
  New York Convention. *See* New York Convention
  notification, 2–512, 2–876
  notification of award,
    Arbitration Act 1996, A6–056
  online dispute resolution, 12–062—12–072
    delivery, 12–073
    electronic signatures, 12–062—12–072
    enforcement, 12–074

INDEX

AWARD—cont.
  online dispute resolution—cont.
    notification, 12–073
    signature of award, 12–062—12–072
  partial, 2–512, 2–874
  place of award, 2–875
    Arbitration Act 1996, A6–054
  precedents,
    alternative final award, A54–087
    certificate as to finality, A54–093
    consumer disputes, A54–082
    delivery up, A54–090
    enforce, application to, A54–092
    final award with reasons, A54–081
    final award without reasons, A54–080
    interim award, A54–083
    publication of award, A54–091
    rent review, A54–089
    reservation of costs, A54–085, A54–086
    umpire, award by, A54–088
  provisional. See Provisional awards
  publication. See Publication of award
  reasons for award,
    accidental slip, 2–885, 2–886
    arbitrator's power, 2–512
    consumer disputes, 8–050, 8–051
    discipline of, 2–882
    dispensing with requirement, 2–512
    documents only arbitration in consumer
      disputes, 8–049—8–052
    drafting, 2–883—2–886
    generally, 2–875
    maritime arbitration, 11–088—11–091
    misconduct, 2–880
    part of award, 2–881
    public interest, 2–880
    rent review arbitration, 13–056—13–057
    short structure, 2–884
    sketching out unpublished, 2–882
    statement for reasons, 2–880
    structure, 2–884
  reasons for,
    agricultural property arbitration, 3–081
    recitals, 2–879
  recognition,
    ICSID arbitration, A60–054—A60–056
    Model Law, A14–059—A14–062
    New York Convention. See New York
      Convention
  recourse against award,
    Model Law, A14–034, A14–056
  revision,
    ICSID arbitration, A60–052
  RSA, 16–052
  running out of time for delivery,
    agricultural property arbitration, 3–069
  seat of arbitration, 2–512, 2–875
  serious irregularity,
    Arbitration Act 1996, A6–069

AWARD—cont.
  setting aside,
    agricultural property arbitration, 3–088
    Model Law, A14–034, A14–058, A14–057
    New York Convention, A17–006
  signatures, 2–875
  slip rule, 2–876
  statement for reasons, 2–880
  substantive requirements, 2–877—2–882
    certainty, 2–877
    final award, 2–878
    interim award, 2–878
    partial awards, 2–878
    recitals, 2–879
  suspension,
    New York Convention, A17–006
  time for,
    agricultural property arbitration, 3–069, 3–070
  types, 2–873
  umpire,
    precedent, A54–088
  uncertain, 2–098
  UNCITRAL Arbitration Rules,
    additional award, A15–038
    amiable compositeur, A15–034
    applicable law, A15–034
    correction of award, A15–037
    costs, A15–039—A15–041
    decisions, A15–032
    effect, A15–033
    form, A15–033
    interpretation, A15–036
    settlement, A15–035
    termination, A15–035
  WIPO arbitration, A52–059—A52–066
    additional award, A52–066
    correction, A52–066
    currency, A52–060
    decision-making, A52–061
    final award, A52–063
    form, A52–062
    interest, A52–060
    notification, A52–062
    time period for delivery, A52–063
  withholding award for non-payment,
    Arbitration Act 1996, A6–057

B V DENTISTS DISCIPLINARY TRIBUNAL, A75–001—A75–031
BALTIC EXCHANGE, 11–004, 11–005
BARRISTERS,
  See also Legal Services Ombudsman;
    Professional conduct of barristers and
    solicitors
  access, 2–027
  Adjudication Panel,
    decisions, 18–030, 18–031
    investigations, 18–028, 18–029

1053

BARRISTERS—*cont.*
  Adjudication Panel—*cont.*
    procedure, 18–028, 18–029
    referral to, 18–027
  Code of Conduct for the Bar of England and Wales, 18–016—18–079
    principal obligations, 18–07
  Complaints Commissioner, 18–019
    Annual Report 2001, 18–025
  dealing with complains, 18–018
  Direct Access Rules, 2–027, 18–004
  Disciplinary Tribunal proceedings,
    adjournments, 18–062
    amendments, 18–062
    convening orders, 18–060
    directions, 18–057, 18–059
    documents, 18–056, 18–069
    evidence, 18–069
    finality, 18–072
    findings, 18–063
    formulation of sentences and reports, 18–065
    guilty pleas, 18–058
    hearing, 18–061
    hearing before the Visitors, 18–070, 18–071
    Interim Suspension Rules, 18–073—18–076
    IPS, appeal against finding of, 18–067
    penalties, 18–064
    petition, 18–069
    preliminary hearings, 18–057
    preliminary steps, 18–052, 18–053
    recording of sentences, 18–065
    requests to admit facts, 18–058
    sanctions, 18–064
    sentencing, 18–063
    service of documents, 18–060
    suspension pending appeal, 18–066
    witness statements, 18–056
  Disciplinary Tribunal proceedings,
    membership, 18–054, 18–055
    proceedings, 18–051
    results, 18–026
  evaluation of disciplinary regime, 18–078
  future of disciplinary procedures, 18–079
  Inadequate Professional Service (IPS),
    Adjudication Panel. *See* Adjudication Panel *above*
    appeals against finding of, 18–032—18–034, 18–067
    definition, 18–023
    meaning, 18–018
  Informal Hearing Panel, 18–035—18–039
    investigations, 18–037
    sanctions, 18–038, 18–039
  Legal Services Ombudsman, review of complaints handling by, 18–077
  overlaps with work of solicitors, 18–033

BARRISTERS—*cont.*
  Professional Conduct and Complaints Committee (PCC),
    function, 18–020
    membership, 18–020, 18–054, 18–055
    powers, 18–021, 18–022
  professional misconduct, 18–018
    appeals against findings of, 18–068
    definition, 18–024
  Summary Hearing Panel, 18–040
    ancillary powers, 18–046
    appeals, 18–048, 18–049
    attendance of defendant, 18–044
    costs, 18–047
    findings, 18–045
    procedure, 18–043
    publication of findings, 18–050
    reporting of findings, 18–050
    sanctions, 18–045
  Summary Procedure Rules, 18–040
    determination of complaints, 18–041, 18–042
  suspension panels, 18–073—18–076
    appeals, 18–076
    expedited hearing, 18–076
    powers, 18–075
    review of suspension, 18–076
  terms of engagement,
    precedent, A54–117—A54–127
BEAUTY PARADE, 2–246
BEETROOT SUGAR ASSOCIATION OF LONDON. *See* SUGAR ASSOCIATION
BELGIUM,
  international arbitration, 9–064
BERMUDA,
  Med-Arb, 4–029
BIAS OF ARBITRATOR,
  natural justice, 2–414
  property valuation arbitration, 13–013
  rent review arbitration, 13–013
BOOKING FEES, 2–384
  maritime arbitration, 11–096
BREACH OF CONTRACT,
  interest, 2–893
BREACH OF DUTY,
  expert evidence, 2–849—2–853
BRUSSELS CONVENTION, 9–074
BUILD-OPERATE-TRANSFER CONTRACTS,
  dispute boards, 7–007
BUNDLES,
  agricultural property arbitration, 3–044
BURDEN OF PROOF,
  documents only arbitration in consumer disputes, 8–041
  judging techniques, 2–869
  WTO dispute settlement, 17–030

CALCULATION ERRORS,
  judging techniques, 2–870
CALDERBANK OFFER,
  agricultural property arbitration, 3–072

INDEX

CALDERBANK OFFER—cont.
  costs, 2–906, 2–907
  effect, 2–741
  expansion, 2–906
  meaning, 2–741, 2–906
  method, 2–758
  property valuation arbitration, 13–064, 13–065
  purpose, 2–741, 2–758
  security for costs, as, 2–492
CANCELLATION CHARGES, 2–313
  remuneration of arbitrator, 2–348, 2–384
CAPPING COSTS, 2–909—2–912
  timing, 2–913
CAS. See COURT OF ARBITRATION FOR SPORT (CAS)
CASE DIRECTIONS,
  possible statement of, A54–066
CASE MANAGEMENT,
  ADR, 4–046—4–052
  Civil Procedure Rules, 2–566, 4–019, 4–021, 4–022
CASE STATED PROCEDURE,
  abuse, 1–002
  agricultural property arbitration, 3–087, 3–088
CATTLE FOOD TRADE ASSOCIATION, 16–084
CAUSE OF ACTION ESTOPPEL, 2–290, 2–888, 2–889
CCPIT, 16–061
CEDR RULES FOR ADJUDICATION, A19–001—A19–010
  commencement of adjudication, A19–001
  conduct of adjudication, A19–002
  costs, A19–005
  decision of adjudicator, A19–003
  enforcement, A19–004
  fees, A19–006
  law, A19–010
  mediation, 4–009, A19–008
  model contract clauses, A54–132—A54–148
  nomination of adjudicator, A19–001
  other provisions, A19–009
  resignation of adjudicator, A19–007
CENTRE FOR EFFECTIVE DISPUTE RESOLUTION. See CEDR RULES FOR ADJUDICATION
CENTROCON CLAUSE, 11–021
CERTIFICATES,
  look-sniff arbitration, 16–005
CHAIRMAN,
  Arbitration Act 1996, A6–021
  ICC arbitration, 2–241
  legally qualified, 2–730
  remuneration of, 2–390, 2–391
  role, 2–241
  statutory role, 2–241
CHALLENGING ARBITRATOR,
  appointing party's response to, 2–287
  CIETAC, 16–065
  Court of Arbitration for Sport (CAS), 15–051, 15–052, A29–017

CHALLENGING ARBITRATOR—cont.
  LME, 16–023
  removal,
    See also Removal of arbitrator
    appointing party, 2–287
    appointment in place, 2–287
    prospective arbitrator, by, 2–287, 2–288
    time limit, 2–285
    waiver of time limit, 2–285
CHALLENGING AWARD,
  agricultural property arbitration, 3–082—3–089
  accidental slips, 3–082
  basic rule, 3–082
  case stated procedure, 3–087, 3–088
  clerical mistakes, 3–082
  correction of award, 3–082
  error on the face, 3–087—3–088
  misconduct, 3–083—3–086
  omissions, 3–082
  procedure, 3–088, 3–089
  setting aside award, 3–088
  slip rule, 3–082
  American Arbitration Association International Arbitration Rules, A18–009
  Arbitration Act 1996, A6–068, A6–069, A6–071, A6–072
  case stated procedure,
    agricultural property arbitration, 3–087, 3–088
  clerical mistakes,
    agricultural property arbitration, 3–082
  correction of award. See Correction of award
  farm business tenancy arbitration, 3–108
  ICSID arbitration, 9–034
  misconduct, 2–098
    agricultural property arbitration, 3–083—3–086
  serious irregularity. See Serious irregularity
  setting aside. See Setting aside award
  slip rule. See Slip rule
  stay of enforcement pending, 2–948—2–950
CHARTER PARTY ARBITRATION,
  award, A36–013
  concurrent hearings, A36–009
  consolidated arbitrations, A36–009
  costs, A36–014
  GAFTA,
    appointment of tribunal, A36–003—A36–007
    award, A36–013
    awards on different aspects, A36–012
    concurrent hearings, A36–009
    consolidated arbitration, A36–009
    costs, A36–014
    default of party, A36–021
    evidence, A36–015
    fees, A36–016
    non-compliance with time limits and rules, A36–020

1055

CHARTER PARTY ARBITRATION—cont.
  GAFTA—cont.
    notices, A36–017—A36–019
    preliminary issues, A36–001
    procedure, A36–002, A36–008
    provisional orders, A36–011
    representation, A36–014
    substantive jurisdiction, issues of, A36–010
    time limits, A36–002
  representation, A36–014
CHARTERED INSTITUTE OF ARBITRATORS,
  administration of Code of Practice arbitrations, 8–022, 8–023, 8–028
  arbitration clause, A54–011
  Arbitration Rules. *See* Chartered Institute of Arbitrators Arbitration Rules
  Code of Practice arbitrations, 8–021, 8–023, 8–028
  Commercial Arbitration Scheme. *See* Chartered Institute of Arbitrators
  COMMERCIAL ARBITRATION SCHEME
    dispute resolution services, A22–001—A22–006
  remuneration of arbitrator, 2–393
  Rules of the Mortgage Code Arbitration. *See* Chartered Institute of Arbitrators Rules of the Mortgage Code Arbitration
  surveyors arbitration scheme rules. *See* Chartered Institute of Arbitrators "Surveyors Arbitration" Scheme Rules
  training by, 11–033
  travel industry. *See* Chartered Institute of Arbitrators Arbitration Scheme for the Travel Industry
CHARTERED INSTITUTE OF ARBITRATORS ARBITRATION RULES, A20–001—A20–016
  appointing authority, A20–004
  appointment of arbitrators, A20–005
  arbitrators,
    appointment, A20–005
    communications, A20–006
    powers, A20–008
  award, A20–010
  commencement of arbitration, A20–003
  communications between parties and arbitrator, A20–006
  costs, A20–011
  definitions, A20–013
  form of procedure, A20–009
  general provisions, A20–012
  powers of arbitrators, A20–008
  procedure for arbitration, A20–007
  purpose, A20–002
  Short Form Procedure, A20–014—A20–016
CHARTERED INSTITUTE OF ARBITRATORS ARBITRATION SCHEME FOR THE TRAVEL INDUSTRY,
  applicable law, A21–012

CHARTERED INSTITUTE OF ARBITRATORS ARBITRATION SCHEME FOR THE TRAVEL INDUSTRY—cont.
  award,
    finality, A21–007
    review, A21–010
  commencement of arbitration, A21–003
  confidentiality, A21–011
  costs, A21–006
  finality of award, A21–007
  powers of arbitrator, A21–005
  procedure for arbitration, A21–003
  review procedures, A21–008
    conditions, A21–010
    costs, A21–009
  scope of scheme, A21–002
  statement of claim, A21–004
  submissions for arbitration, A21–004
  substituting arbitrator, A21–012
CHARTERED INSTITUTE OF ARBITRATORS COMMERCIAL ARBITRATION SCHEME,
  appeal, A23–012, A23–013
  appeals against award, A23–012, A23–013
  costs, A23–013
  appointment of arbitrators, A23–004
  arbitrators,
    appointment, A23–004
    communications, A23–005
  award, A23–009
    appeal to Appeal Tribunal, A23–012, A23–013
    review, A23–011
  commencement of arbitration, A23–003
  communications between parties and arbitrator, A23–005
  costs, A23–010
  definitions, A23–015
  form of procedure, A23–008
  generally, A23–002
  powers of arbitrator, A23–007
  procedures, A23–006
  representation, A23–014
  review of award, A23–011
  Short Form Procedure, A23–016—A23–018
CHARTERED INSTITUTE OF ARBITRATORS RULES OF THE MORTGAGE CODE ARBITRATION,
  applicable law, A24–006
  commencement of arbitration, A24–002
  costs, A24–005
  defence, A24–004
  generally, A24–001
  miscellaneous issues, A24–006
  procedure, A24–003
  scope, A24–001
  statement of claim, A24–004
  submissions for arbitration, A24–004

Index

Chartered Institute of Arbitrators "Surveyors Arbitration" Scheme Rules,
appeal,
  Appeal Tribunal, A25–009
  costs, A25–010
  court, A25–011
applicable law, A25–012
award,
  appeal to Appeal Tribunal, A25–009
  costs, A25–009
  review, A25–008
commencement of arbitration, A25–003
costs, A25–007
  appeal, A25–010
counterclaim, A25–006
defence, A25–006
generally, A25–002
powers of arbitrator, A25–005
procedure, A25–004
review of award, A25–008
scope, A25–002
statement of claim, A25–006
submissions for arbitration, A25–006
Charterparty, 11–001, 11–004
maritime arbitration,
  Baltic Exchange, 11–004
Chat, online, 12–010, 12–019, 12–082
Chess clock arbitrations,
expedition, 2–544—2–547
factors to consider, 2–545, A55–001—A55–016
meaning, 2–544
monopoly of questioning by tribunal, 2–547
potential misunderstandings by tribunals, 2–546
variety of schemes, 2–545
Children,
small claims in county court, 14–051
China,
China Council for the Promotion of International Trade (CCPIT), 16–061
China International Economic and Trade Arbitration Commission. *See* CIETAC
Med-Arb, 4–034
Choice of law,
Court of Arbitration for Sport (CAS), 15–076—15–078
sports arbitration, 15–008
unfair contract terms, A1–028
CIETAC, 16–015, 16–061—16–083
advantages, 16–082
application for arbitration, A74–013—A74–023
arbitration clause, 16–062
arbitrators, 16–063, 16–064
  challenging, 16–065
assessment of system, 16–082
availability of the award, 16–079
award, 16–069, A74–052—A74–063
challenging arbitrators, 16–065

CIETAC—*cont.*
commencement of arbitration, 16–066, 16–067
conciliation, 16–073, 16–074
confidentiality, 16–081
domestic arbitration, A74–075—A74–084
establishment, 16–061
execution of award, 16–071
expenses, 16–077
final and binding award, 16–069
formation of tribunal, A74–024—A74–031
hearing, A74–032—A74–051
importance of rules, 16–085
initiative of the Tribunal, 16–075
jurisdiction, A74–001—A74–007
language, 16–076
lawyers, role of, 16–068
non-Chinese nationals, role of, 16–078
organisation, A74–008—A74–013
property preservation, 16–071
summary procedure, A74–064—A74–073
unless otherwise agreed, 16–072
validity of arbitration agreement, 16–070
WTO and, 16–083
CIMAR, 6–036—6–044
adoption, A29–003
amendment of rules, 6–037
application, A28–001
appointment of arbitrators, 6–037, A28–002
arbitrators,
  appointment, A28–002
  assessment, 6–044
award, 6–042, A28–012
commencement of arbitration, A28–002
common purpose in, 6–037
conflicting procedures, 6–037
consolidation of proceedings, 2–652, 6–038, A28–003
costs, 6–043, A29–019—A29–021
  allocation, 6–043, A29–023, A29–024
  counterclaims, 6–043
  non-monetary claims, 6–043, A29–025
  recoverable, 6–043, 6–044, A29–025
default of party, 6–041, A28–011
definition of terms, A28–015
directions, 6–039, A28–006
documents only arbitration, 6–040, A28–008
evidence, 6–039, A28–005
full procedure, A28–009
hearing,
  documents only arbitration, 6–040, A28–008
  full procedure, 6–040, A28–009
  short, 6–040, A28–007
JCT Standard Form Contract, incorporation into, 6–065
joinder of disputes, 6–038, A28–003
Notes, A29–001—A29–025
  adoption of CIMAR, A29–003
  background, A29–001
  drafting, A29–002

CIMAR—*cont.*
  Notes—*cont.*
    Rules, on, A29–004—A29–018
    security for costs, A29–019—A29–021
  objective, A28–001
  powers of arbitrator, A28–004
  procedure, A28–005
    directions, 6–039, A28–006
    form, 6–039, 6–040, A28–006
  provisional relief, 6–041, A28–010
  publication, 6–037
  reasons for decision, 6–039
  remedies, 6–042, A28–012
  representation, A28–014
  sanctions, A28–011
  security for costs, 2–502, 6–039, A29–019—A29–021
  short hearing, A28–007
  Society of Construction Arbitrators Notes, A29–001—A29–025
  specific performance, 6–042, A29–022
  standard decisions under, whether, 6–036
  Supplementary and Advisory Procedures, 6–065
  use, 6–037
CITY DISPUTES PANEL,
  Arbitration Rules. *See* City Disputes Panel Arbitration Rules
  Mediation Rules. *See* City Disputes Panel Mediation Rules
CITY DISPUTES PANEL ARBITRATION RULES,
  aim, A26–001
  alternative dispute resolution procedures, A26–011
  arbitral tribunal, A26–004
    additional powers, A26–010
    duty, A26–011
    jurisdiction, A26–009
    procedural freedom, A26–012
  arbitrators,
    challenging, A26–008
    impartiality, A26–005
  award, A26–022
  cessation of arbitrator's authority, A26–008
  challenging arbitrator, A26–008
  commencement of arbitration, A26–003
  communications, A26–007
  completion of appointment, A26–006
  costs, A26–025
  decision without hearing, A26–029
  defining issues, A26–017
  exclusion of liability, A26–026
  experts, A26–020
  first management meeting, A26–014
    rapid decision, A26–015
  further management meetings, A26–018
  hearings, A26–021
  impartiality of arbitrators, A26–005
  interest, A26–024

CITY DISPUTES PANEL ARBITRATION RULES—*cont.*
  management meetings,
    first, A26–014, A26–016
    further, A26–018
  parties, duty of, A26–013
  remedies, A26–023
  request for arbitration, A26–002
  Scotland, A26–027
  simplified hearing procedure, A26–028
  witnesses, A26–019
CITY DISPUTES PANEL MEDIATION RULES,
  appointment of mediator, A27–002
  approach, A27–001
  confidentiality, A27–005
  legal advisers, A27–004
  privilege, A27–005
  procedure, A27–003
CIVIL PROCEDURE RULES, 1–001
  active case management, 2–566, 4–019
  ADR, 4–018—4–020
  aims, 2–565
  applications to court, 2–939
  arbitration claims (Part 62), A4–001—A4–021
    applications to judge, A4–012
    case management, A4–007
    claim form, A4–004
    District Registries, claims in, A4–014
    hearings, A4–010
    interest on award, A4–019
    interpretation, A4–002
    notice, A4–006
    old law, application of, A4–011—A4–016
    registration,
      Arbitration (International Investment Disputes) Act 1966, A4–021
      High Court of foreign awards, A4–020
    service out of jurisdiction, A4–005, A4–016
    starting the claim, A4–003, A4–013
    stay of legal proceedings, A4–008
    time limits, A4–015
    variation of time, A4–009
  case management, 2–566, 4–019, 4–021, 4–022
  commencement, 2–565
  construction industry arbitration, 6–034, 6–035
  costs, 2–901
  enforcement of award, 2–943
  influence, 4–024
  overriding objective, 2–565, 2–566, 4–018, 14–022
  Part 20 claims, 2–630—2–633
  Practice Direction on arbitration, A5–001—A5–018
    acknowledgment of service, A5–004, A5–018
    applications under ss 32 and 45 of 1996 Act, A5–009

INDEX

CIVIL PROCEDURE RULES—*cont.*
  Practice Direction on arbitration—*cont.*
    Arbitration (International Investment Disputes) Act 1966, A5–016
    attendance of witnesses, securing, A5–007
    case management, A5–006
    claim form, A5–003, A5–017
    decision without hearing, A5–010
    interim remedies, A5–008
    permission to appeal, applications for, A5–012
    starting the claim, A5–002, A5–014
    supply of documents, A5–005
    variation of time, A5–011
  practitioners following procedures of, 1–011
  pre-action protocols, 2–567
  proactive role of courts, 2–565
  settlement, promotion of, 4–020
  small claims arbitration in county court, 14–005, 14–006
  small claims in county court,
    addition of parties, 14–049
    amendments, 14–048
    applications, 14–053
    children, 14–051
    counterclaims, 14–050
    injunctions, 14–056—14–058
    overriding objective, 14–022
    patients, 14–051
    statements of truth, 14–052
    summary judgment, 14–054, 14–055
    third party claims, 14–050
    witnesses, 14–059
  stages of litigation, 2–568
  summary judgment, 14–054, 14–055
CLAIM FORM,
  notes for claimant, A54–096
  notes for defendant, A54–097
  precedent, A54–095, A54–099
CLASS ACTIONS, LITIGATION, 2–038
CLERICAL ERRORS,
  agricultural property arbitration, 3–082
CLERICAL MISTAKES,
  award, 2–485, 2–876
  LCIA arbitration, 9–029
CLOSURE OF HEARING,
  experts, A18–025
CODE ARBITRATION. *See* CODE OF PRACTICE ARBITRATIONS
CODE OF PRACTICE ARBITRATIONS,
  See also Consumer disputes; Documents only arbitrations in consumer disputes
  ABTA, 8–011, 8–012
  additional evidence, 8–026, 8–027
  administration of schemes, 8–022, 8–023, 8–028
  Chartered Institute of Arbitrators, 8–022, 8–023
  consumer choice, 8–020
  costs, 8–060—8–063
  development, 8–011

CODE OF PRACTICE ARBITRATIONS—*cont.*
  difficult questions of law, 8–032
  disregarding law, no power to, 8–029—8–032
  duties of arbitrator, 8–026—8–035
    disregarding law, no power to, 8–029—8–032
    mandatory duty, 8–030
    point of law, 8–033—8–035
    travel claims, 8–030
  election to enter arbitration agreement, 8–021
  examples, 8–012
  existing schemes, 8–012
  features of, 8–010
  formal arbitration and, 8–020
  further evidence, 8–026, 8–027
  generally, 8–010
  Glass and Glazing Federation, 8–011
  liberty to litigate, 8–018
  National Association of Retail Furnishers, 8–011
  National House Building Council, 8–011
  NHBC, 8–011
  obligation to arbitrate, 8–018
  oral hearing, 8–020
  pleadings, 8–025
  point of law, 8–033
  procedure, 8–023—8–028
  seeking further evidence, 8–026, 8–027
  setting down machinery to resolve consumer disputes, 8–010
  setting up scheme, 8–012
  simple procedure suing documents only, 8–011
  structure of schemes, 8–018—8–020
  Surveyors & Valuers Arbitration Scheme, 8–011
  tourism, 8–013
  Waltham Forest Leaseholders Arbitration Scheme, 8–010
COLLISIONS BETWEEN SHIPS, 11–002
COLONIAL AND BUENOS AIRES INVESTMENT PROTOCOLS OF MERCOSUR, 10–010
COMBINED WITNESS/ADVOCATE, 2–832
COMMENCEMENT OF ADJUDICATION,
  CEDR Rules for Adjudication, A19–001
COMMENCEMENT OF ARBITRATION, 2–196
  Agios Lazaros, 2–200—2–202
  Arbitration Act 1996, A6–013—A6–015
  commencement, A6–015
  extension of time, A6–013
  Limitation Acts, application of, A6–014
  Chartered Institute of Arbitrators Arbitration Rules, A20–003
  Chartered Institute of Arbitrators Arbitration Scheme for the Travel Industry, A21–003
  Chartered Institute of Arbitrators Commercial Arbitration Scheme, A23–003

1059

COMMENCEMENT OF ARBITRATION—*cont.*
Chartered Institute of Arbitrators Rules of the Mortgage Code Arbitration, A24–002
Chartered Institute of Arbitrators "Surveyors Arbitration" Scheme Rules, A25–003
CIETAC, 16–066, 16–067
CIMAR, A28–002
City Disputes Panel Arbitration Rules, A26–003
extension of time limits, 2–205—2–213
  conflicting documents, 2–210
  effect, 2–205
  lack of access to documentation, 2–208
  length of extension, 2–212
  protective extensions, 2–211
  relevant circumstances, 2–207
  retrospective extensions, 2–213
  silence not unjust, 2–209
  terms upon which granted, 2–212
  threshold criteria, 2–206
GAFTA, 16–092
ICC arbitration, A39–006—A39–008
ICE arbitration, A43–002
LME, 16–021, 16–022
Model Law, A14–021
party autonomy, 2–196
power, 2–205—2–213
RSA, 16–046, 16–047
simple arbitration clause, 2–198
subject matter of reference, identifying, 2–199
substantive effect of time limits, 2–214, 2–215
WIPO arbitration, A52–006—A52–013
  answer to request, A52–011, A52–012
  representation, A52–013
  request for arbitration, A52–006—A52–010

COMMERCIAL ARBITRATION,
Chartered Institute of Arbitrators Scheme. *See* Chartered Institute of Arbitrators Commercial Arbitration Scheme

COMMERCIAL COURT, 2–013

COMMERCIAL JUDGE,
sole arbitrator, as, 2–230

COMMODITY TRADE ARBITRATION, 16–001—16–111
See also Commodity trade associations
appeals,
  GAFTA, 16–103—16–111
appointment of arbitrators,
  FOSFA, 16–020
  GAFTA, 16–089—16–091
  LME, 16–019, 16–020
  RSA, 16–041—16–045, 16–056
arbitration clause,
  CIETAC, 16–062
  GAFTA, 16–085

COMMODITY TRADE ARBITRATION—*cont.*
arbitrators,
  CIETAC, 16–063, 16–064
  GAFTA, 16–087, 16–088
  LME, 16–017—16–018
  RSA, 16–040
award,
  CIETAC, 16–069
  LME, 16–032—16–034
  RSA, 16–052
Beetroot Sugar Association of London. *See* Sugar Association
challenging arbitrator,
  CIETAC, 16–065
  LME, 16–023
China International Economic and Trade Arbitration Commission. *See* CIETAC
commencement of arbitration,
  CIETAC, 16–066, 16–067
  GAFTA, 16–092
  LME, 16–021, 16–022
  RSA, 16–046, 16–047
communications,
  LME, 16–037
costs,
  RSA, 16–058
courts, role of,
  CIETAC, 16–070, 16–071
directions,
  LME, 16–026
discretion,
  GAFTA, 16–095
  LME, 16–036
documents,
  LME, 16–024—16–026
  RSA, 16–060
Federation of Oils, Seeds and Fats Association (FOSFA). *See* FOSFA
final and binding award, 16–069
FOSFA Rules. *See* FOSFA
Grain and Feed Trade Association (GAFTA). *See* GAFTA
hearing,
  LME, 16–026
lawyers, role of, 16–011, 16–012
  CIETAC, 16–068
  GAFTA, 16–096, 16–097
  LME, 16–027—16–029
  RSA, 16–048—16–051
LME. *See* LME
London Metal Exchange (LME). *See* LME
London Rice Brokers' Association (LRBA), 16–002
look-sniff arbitration. *See* Look-sniff arbitration
LRBA, 16–002
mediation, 16–013, 16–014
powers of tribunal,
  LME, 16–030, 16–031
Refined Sugar Association. *See* RSA
RSA Rules. *See* RSA

INDEX

COMMODITY TRADE ARBITRATION—*cont.*
Scott-Avery clause,
  GAFTA, 16–085, 16–086
seat of arbitration,
  GAFTA, 16–086
Secretariat,
  GAFTA, 16–098, 16–099
settlement,
  LME, 16–026
single-tier arbitration,
  RSA, 16–059
  use, 16–007
submissions,
  LME, 16–024—16–026
technical arbitrations, 16–006
time limits,
  GAFTA, 16–092, 16–094
  LME, 16–035
two-tier arbitration,
  costs, 16–009
  experience of arbitrators on appeal, 16–008
  FOSFA, 16–008
  GAFTA, 16–008
  lawyer participation, 16–010
  practice, 16–007
  tactics, 16–007
  theory, 16–007
  use, 16–007
COMMODITY TRADE ASSOCIATIONS,
  See also Commodity trade arbitration
  Beetroot Sugar Association of London. *See* Sugar Association
  composition, 16–003
  English character, 16–004
  Federation of Oils, Seeds and Fats Association (FOSFA). *See* FOSFA
  FOSFA. *See* FOSFA
  function, 16–003, 16–004
  Grain and Feed Trade Association (GAFTA). *See* GAFTA
  LME, 16–001
  LME. *See* LME
  London Metal Exchange (LME). *See* LME
  London, role of, 16–003, 16–004
  LRBA, 16–002
  promotion, 16–03
  role, 16–003, 16–004
  world trade bodies and, 16–004
  WTO, promotion at, 16–003
COMMUNICATIONS,
  protocols, A54–129
COMPENSATION,
  arbitrators,
    American Arbitration Association
      International Arbitration Rules, A18–033
    investment treaty arbitration, 10–061—10–063

COMPETENCE TO RULE ON OWN JURISDICTION,
  Arbitration Act 1996, A6–031
  construction industry arbitration, 6–089
  WIPO arbitration, 9–040
CONCILIATION,
  CIETAC, 16–073, 16–074
  construction industry, 6–030
  Court of Arbitration for Sport (CAS), A29–029
  ICSID, A60–029—A60–036
  Sport Dispute Resolution Panel, 15–023, A67–015
  WTO dispute settlement, A53–005
CONCURRENT HEARINGS, 2–637
  Arbitration Act 1996, A6–036
  charter party arbitration, A36–009
  claimant's rights, 2–646
  GAFTA, A34–013
  ICE arbitration, A43–013
  no general power to order, 2–644—2–651
  same person appointed for all claims, whether, 2–645
CONDITIONAL FEES,
  costs, 2–913
CONDUCT OF HEARING, 1–015, 2–792—2–802
  closing submissions, 2–801
  cross-examination, 2–795
    interventions by the arbitrator, 2–798, 2–799
  evidence in chief, 2–794
    interventions by the arbitrator, 2–797
  final submissions, 2–801
    interventions by the arbitrator, 2–802
  interventions by the arbitrator, 2–797—2–802
    cross-examination, 2–798, 2–799
    evidence in chief, 2–797
    final submissions, 2–802
    re-examination, 2–800
  list of issues, 2–793
  opening for the claimant, 2–792
  opening statement for the respondent, 2–793
  re-examination, 2–796
    interventions by the arbitrator, 2–800
CONFIDENTIALITY,
  See also Privacy; Privilege
  advice sought by arbitrator, 2–347
  American Arbitration Association
    International Arbitration Rules, A18–035
  application to use confidential documents, 2–723
  arbitration agreement, 2–803
  assumption in arbitration, 2–803
  award, 2–804, 2–818, 2–819
  Chartered Institute of Arbitrators Arbitration Scheme for the Travel Industry, A21–011
  CIETAC, 16–081
  City Disputes Panel Mediation Rules, A27–005

1061

CONFIDENTIALITY—cont.
compulsorily produced documents, 2–803
Court of Arbitration for Sport (CAS), 15–057, A29–030
court proceedings, documents produced in, 2–804
DAC Report, 1–010, 2–103, 2–819
documents produced in arbitration, 2–808
exceptions, 2–806
express agreement, 2–803, 2–806
implied term, 2–803—2–805
injunctions to restrain publication, 2–808
interests of justice requiring disclosure, 2–806
LCIA arbitration, A44–031
LCIA mediation, A45–011
limits of, 2–103
LMAA mediation terms, A48–010
notes of arbitrator, 2–816
online dispute resolution, 12–046—12–050
others, disclosure to, 2–813
partner, arbitrator as, 2–814
persons bound by duty, 2–817
possession of file by arbitrator, 2–814
principles, 2–103
proofs of evidence, 2–770
property in arbitrator's notes, 2–816
public interest, 2–805, 2–818, 2–819
publication of award, 2–815
reasonable necessity, 2–805
Scheme for Construction Contracts, 5–095
Sport Dispute Resolution Panel, A67–024
sports arbitration, 15–007
supervisory jurisdiction of court, invoking, 2–804, 2–818
terms imposed on order for disclosure, 2–810
use of documents produced in arbitration outside proceedings, 2–804, 2–805
uses, 2–770
WIPO arbitration, 9–041, A52–073—A52–076
witness asked to disclose confidential information, 2–811, 2–812
WTO dispute settlement, A53–014
CONFLICTS OF INTEREST,
disqualification of arbitrator, 2–274
property valuation arbitration, 13–013
rent review arbitration, 13–013
CONSENT AWARD,
settlements incorporated into, 2–752
CONSERVATORY MEASURES,
Court of Arbitration for Sport (CAS), 15–053—15–056
courts, 2–553
ICC arbitration, A39–025
international arbitration, 9–125—9–128
LCIA arbitration, 9–027, A44–026

CONSOLIDATED ARBITRATION,
See also Multi-party arbitration
agreement of parties, 2–631—2–633
alternatives, 2–634
Arbitration Act 1996, A6–036
assignment of rights, 2–652
charter party arbitration, A36–009
CIMAR, 2–652, 6–038, A28–003
claimant's rights, 2–646
construction industry arbitration, 6–095, 6–096
costs, 2–639
countries allowing, 2–035
DAC Report, 2–101
English law, 2–035
freedom of parties, 2–101
future amendment of law, 2–102
GAFTA, A34–013, A36–009
generally, 2–101
Hong Kong, 2–102, 2–652
institutional provision, 2–652
LME, 16–034
meaning, 2–635
no general power to order, 2–644—2–651
same person appointed for all claims, whether, 2–645
statement of principle, 2–101
statutory provision, 2–652
CONSTRUCTION CONTRACTS,
CIMAR. See CIMAR
dispute boards. See Dispute boards
Housing Grants, Construction and Regeneration Act 1996. See Housing Grants, Construction and Regeneration Act 1996
Scheme for Construction Contracts (England and Wales) Regulations. See Scheme for Construction Contracts (England and Wales) Regulations
CONSTRUCTION INDUSTRY ARBITRATION,
accountability of public sector settlements, 6–026
additional award, 6–104
adjudication, 6–003
first-tier method, as, 6–029
appointment of arbitrator, 6–075
choice of method, 6–085
ICE appointments, 6–087
method, 6–085
publication of potential arbitrators, 6–086
RIBA, 6–086
RICS appointments, 6–088
appropriate procedures, 6–080
arbitration agreement, 6–081
arbitration clauses, 6–004
JCT Standard Form Contract, 6–005
published forms of contract, 6–008
arbitrator,
choosing tribunal, 6–084
generally, 6–082, 6–083

INDEX

CONSTRUCTION INDUSTRY ARBITRATION—*cont.*
arbitrator—*cont.*
   identity, 6–083
   number, 6–083, 6–084
architect's power, 6–027
arguments for, 6–033
award,
   additional award, 6–104
   correction of award, 6–104
   delivery of award, 6–104
   drafting, 6–102
   form of, 6–102
   notification of award, 6–103
   publication of award, 6–103
case management, 4–048
cash-flow, 6–025
characteristics, 6–016
CIMAR 6–036—6–044. *See also* CIMAR
Civil Procedure Rules, 6–034, 6–035
clause for main or principle contract, A54–067
commercial supplies distinguished, 6–015
competence to rule on own jurisdiction, 6–089
conclusiveness preventing disputes, 6–027
concurrence with head contract, subcontract provision requiring, A54–068
concurrent hearings, 6–078
consolidation of proceedings, 6–095, 6–096
construction industry model arbitration rules 6–036—6–044. *See also* CIMAR
contract administrator's opinion, 6–011
correction of award, 6–104
DAC Reports, 6–095
de facto use of, 6–009
decline of, 6–001
delivery of award, 6–103
directions, A54–069, A54–070
dispute resolution procedures,
   adjudication, 6–027
   architect's power, 6–027
   conciliation, 6–030
   conclusiveness, 6–027
   dispute review boards, 6–032
   engineer's power, 6–028, 6–031
   expert determination, 6–031
   mediation, 6–030
   multi-stage procedure, 6–030, 6–032
dispute review boards, 6–032
distinctive feature of construction contracts, 6–014—6–023
diversity of evidence, 6–018
domestic stay, 6–091
engineer,
   first-tier dispute resolver, as, 6–028
   power, 6–027
evidence, 6–018, 6–078
expert determination, 6–031
FIDC forms, 6–052—6–056
Government Contract GC/Works/1. *See* Government Contract GC/Works/1

CONSTRUCTION INDUSTRY ARBITRATION—*cont.*
hearing,
   alternative types, 6–099
   choice of procedure, 6–099
   flexibility, 6–099
   generally, 6–098
   questions from tribunal, 6–100
   time limits, 6–101
interactivity in, 6–017
interim measurement, 6–021
International Federation of Consulting Engineers. *See* FIDIC Conditions
mediation, 6–030
multi-party arbitration, 6–024, 6–093, 6–096
multi-stage procedures, 6–030, 6–032
NEC forms, 6–007, 6–057—6–060
notification of award, 6–103
payment arrangements, 6–019
payment regimes under HGCRA 1996, 6–022, 6–023
post-1996 challenges, 6–013, 6–080
procurement of construction, 6–015
provisional awards, 6–097
public sector settlements, 6–030
publication of award, 6–103
reform, 6–080
remeasurement system, 6–019, 6–020
RIBA appointment of arbitrator, 6–086
Scott schedule,
   precedents, A54–071—A54–074
secondary market for technical specialists, 6–012
servicing, 6–040
Society of Construction Arbitrators, 6–036
Society of Construction Law, 6–036
   Delay and Disruption Protocol, 6–036, 6–105—6–109
standard form contracts, 6–004—6–008, 6–036
stay of proceedings, 6–090
support for pre-arbitral methods, 6–092
technical disputes, requirements, 6–010—6–013
Technology and Construction Court (TCC), 6–002, 6–035
time limits, 6–101
turnkey projects, 6–017
unusual characteristics, 6–016
Woolf reforms, 6–034, 6–080
CONSTRUCTION INDUSTRY DISPUTES,
adjudication, 2–003, 6–027
arbitration. *See* Construction industry arbitration
CONSTRUCTION INDUSTRY MODEL ARBITRATION RULES. *See* CIMAR
CONSUMER ARBITRATION AGREEMENTS,
Arbitration Act 1996,
   unfair contract terms, A6–090
   legal person, consumer as, A6–091
   modest amount sought, A6–092
   unfair contract terms, A6–090

1063

INDEX

CONSUMER DISPUTES,
  arbitration agreement, 2–115
  European law, 8–006, 8–007
  package holiday directive, 8–013
  protection for consumer,
    England, in, 8–007, 8–008
    outside England, 8–009
  reasoned awards, 8–050, 8–051
CONTINGENT FEES,
  costs, 2–913
CONTRACT,
  appointment of arbitrator, 2–306
  arbitrator and appointing party, between, 2–304
  investment treaty arbitration and, 10–046, 10–047
  negligence claim added, 2–680
CONTRACTS (RIGHTS OF THIRD PARTIES) ACT 1999, A65–001—A65–010
  arbitration provisions, A65–008
  defences, A65–003
  double liability, protection of promisor from, A65–005
  exceptions, A65–006
  Northern Ireland, A65–009
  promisee, enforcement of contract by, A65–004
  rescission of contract, A65–002
  right of third party to enforce contractual term, A65–002
  supplementary provisions, A65–007
  variation of contract, A65–002
CONVENTION FOR THE PROTECTION OF HUMAN RIGHTS AND FUNDAMENTAL FREEDOMS,
  fair trial, right to, A13–001
CONVENTIONS,
  Brussels, 9–074
  Geneva, 9–070—9–073
  Rome, 9–069—9–071
  Washington, 9–070
CORRECTION OF AWARD,
  agricultural property arbitration, 3–082
  American Arbitration Association International Arbitration Rules, A18–031
  Arbitration Act 1996, A6–058
  ICC arbitration, A39–031
  LCIA arbitration, 9–029, A44–028
  power, 2–485, 2–876
  representations on, 2–512
  time limits, 2–512
  UNCITRAL Arbitration Rules, A15–037
  WIPO arbitration, A52–066
COSTS, 2–901—2–923
  ADR, 4–016
  advance agreement for sharing, A54–023
  advantage of arbitration, 2–030—2–034
  agreement, 2–903
    pay costs in any event, A6–061
  agricultural property arbitration, 3–076—3–078

COSTS—*cont.*
  American Arbitration Association International Arbitration Rules, A18–032
  appeals, 2–922, 2–923
  apportionment, 2–905
  Arbitration Act 1950, A61–019, A61–030
  Arbitration Act 1996, 1–012, 2–903, A6–060—A6–066
    agreement to pay costs in any event, A6–061
    award, A6–062
    effect of agreement or award, A6–063
    fees and expenses of arbitrator, A6–065
    limiting recoverable costs, A6–066
    recoverable costs, A6–064
  arbitrator's powers, 2–504
  assessment by arbitrator, 2–915—2–921
    advantages, 2–920
    Costs Assessor, 2–921
    CPR, 2–917
    detailed assessment, 2–917, 2–918
    fixed sum without detail, 2–919
  award, A6–062
  Calderbank offer, 2–906, 2–907
  capping, 2–909—2–912
    timing, 2–913
  CEDR Rules for Adjudication, A19–005
  charter party arbitration, A36–014
  Chartered Institute of Arbitrators Arbitration Rules, A20–011
  Chartered Institute of Arbitrators Arbitration Scheme for the Travel Industry, A21–006
  Chartered Institute of Arbitrators Commercial Arbitration Scheme, A23–010
  Chartered Institute of Arbitrators Rules of the Mortgage Code Arbitration, A24–005
  Chartered Institute of Arbitrators "Surveyors Arbitration" Scheme Rules, A25–007
  CIMAR, 6–043, A29–019—A29–021
    allocation, 6–043, A29–023, A29–024
    counterclaims, 6–043
    non-monetary claims, 6–043, A29–025
    recoverable, 6–043, 6–044, A29–025
  City Disputes Panel Arbitration Rules, A26–025
  Civil Procedure Rules, 2–901
  Code of Practice arbitrations, 8–060—8–063
  conditional fees, 2–913
  consolidated arbitration, 2–639
  contingent fees, 2–913
  Court of Arbitration for Sport (CAS), A29–055—A29–057
    Appeals Arbitration Division, 15–092
  DAC report, 2–903
  deposit,
    UNCITRAL Arbitration Rules, A15–042
  discretion exercised by arbitrators, 2–907

COSTS—*cont.*
  documents only arbitration in consumer disputes, 8–060—8–063
  effect of agreement or award, A6–063
  exclusion of liability, A26–026
  expert determination, 2–052
  fees and expenses of arbitrator, A6–065
  following the event, 2–902, 2–903
  GAFTA, A35–006
  GAFTA mediation, A37–005
  ICC ADR rules, A40–007
  ICC arbitration, 9–020, 9–021
    advance to cover, A39–032, A39–051
    decision as to costs, A39–033
    fees, A39–052
  ICC DOCDEX Rules, A40–010
  ICE arbitration, A43–027
  ICSID arbitration, A60–060—A60–062
  increasing, 2–901
  indemnity basis, 2–914
  LCIA arbitration, A44–029
  LCIA mediation, A45–009
  litigants in person, 14–091
  LMAA mediation terms,
    mediator's, A48–013
    parties', A48–014
  LMAA small claims procedure, 11–102, A47–008
  look-sniff arbitration, 2–052
  lump sum fee agreed, 2–031
  mediation, 4–052
  multi-party arbitration, 2–639
  open offer, in, 2–747, 2–748
  Part 36 offer, 2–906, 2–907
  partial success in claim, 2–904, 2–905
  peremptory orders, 2–478, 2–600
  pre-1996 position, 2–902
  reasonable, 2–30
  recoverable, 2–908, A6–064
  reducing, 2–785
  rent review arbitration, 13–019
  RSA, 16–058
  sanctions, 2–585, 2–588
  Scheme for Construction Contracts, 5–081, 5–087, 5–088
  sealed offers, 2–906, 2–907
  set-off, 2–904
  settlement, 2–906
  small claims in county court, 14–083—14–093
    appeals, 14–101
    consent, cases allocated by, 14–090
    general rule, 14–083
    litigants in person, 14–091
    no costs rule, 14–088, 14–089
    principles, 14–084—14–087
  Solicitor's Disciplinary Tribunal, 18–138
  Sport Dispute Resolution Panel, 15–033, A67–023
  standard basis, 2–914
  Summary Hearing Panel, 18–047

COSTS—*cont.*
  taxation, 13–070
  three person tribunal, 2–238
  umpire's powers, 2–505
  UNCITRAL Arbitration Rules, A15–039—A15–041
    deposit of costs, A15–042
    winning or losing case, 2–904
  WIPO arbitration, A52–067—A52–069
  Woolf reforms, 2–901
COUNTERCLAIM,
  American Arbitration Association International Arbitration Rules, A18–004
  Chartered Institute of Arbitrators "Surveyors Arbitration" Scheme Rules, A25–006
  proofs of evidence, 2–768
COUNTY COURT,
  allocation of arbitration proceedings, A8–001, 8–002
  applications to court, 2–938
  role, 14–001
  small claims. *See* Small claims in the county court
COURT OF ARBITRATION FOR SPORT (CAS), 15–039—15–096
  See also Sports arbitration
  answer, A29–021
  appeal, 15–094, A29–038—A29–050
  Appeals Arbitration Division, 15–044, 15–045, 15–080—15–089
    award, 15–089
    costs, 15–092
    exhaustion of remedies, 15–080
    hearing, 15–088
    limits on new legal arguments/evidence, 15–085
    number of arbitrator, 15–086
    provision for appeal, 15–080
    respondent's obligations, 15–084
    scope of review, 15–087
    selection of arbitrator, 15–086
    statement of appeal, 15–081
    time-limits, 15–082, 15–083
  appointment of arbitrators, A29–023
  arbitrator, A29–006
    appointment, A29–023
    challenging, 15–051, 15–052, A29–016, A29–017
    confirmation, A29–024
    independence, A29–015
    number, 15–060—15–063, 15–086
    qualifications, 15–044, A29–015
    removal, 15–051, 15–052, A29–017
    replacement, A29–018
    selection, 15–060—15–063, 15–086
  assignment of proceedings, 15–045
  Atlanta Olympic games, 15–040
  award, 15–079, 15–089, A29–037
  challenging arbitrator, 15–051, 15–052, A29–017

INDEX

COURT OF ARBITRATION FOR SPORT
(CAS)—*cont.*
choice of law, 15–076—15–078
code, 15–041
conciliation, A29–029
confidentiality, 15–057, A29–030
confirmation of arbitrators, A29–024
connection with sport, 15–048, 15–049
conservatory measures, 15–053—15–056
consultation, 15–090, A29–051—A29–053
costs, A29–055—A29–057
   Appeals Arbitration Division, 15–092
   Ordinary Arbitration Division, 15–091
creation, A30–001
enforcement of decision, 15–096
establishment, 15–039
expedited procedure, 15–075
hearing disputes, 15–046—15–049, 15–074
history, 15–039—15–041
initiation of arbitration by CAS, A29–021
interim remedies, 15–053—15–056
International Council of Arbitration for Sport,
   membership, 15–043
   role, 15–042
International Court of Arbitration for Sport. *See* International Court of Arbitration for Sport
interpretation, A29–054
IOC, links with, 15–039
   funding, 15–039
jurisdiction, 15–046—15–049
language of proceedings, A29–011
length of arbitration, 15–093
mediation, A31–001—A31–015
   appointment of mediator, A31–006, A31–007
   commencement of mediation, A31–005
   conduct of mediation, A31–009
   confidentiality, A31–011
   costs, A31–015
   definitions, A31–002, A31–003
   failure to settle, A29–014
   representation, A31–008
   role of mediator, A31–010
   scope of application of rules, A31–004
   settlement, A31–013
   termination, A31–012
merits, law applicable to the, A29–036
miscellaneous provisions, A29–008, A29–058
mission, A29–005
multi-party arbitration, 15–064—15–068, A29–025—A29–028
national courts, relationship with, 15–095
notifications, A29–013
Ordinary Arbitration Division, 15–044, 15–045, 15–058—15–079
   award, 15–079
   choice of law, 15–076—15–078
   costs, 15–091

COURT OF ARBITRATION FOR SPORT
(CAS)—*cont.*
Ordinary Arbitration Division—*cont.*
   expedited procedure, 15–075
   hearing, 15–074
   multi-party arbitrations, 15–064—15–068
   number of arbitrator, 15–060—15–063
   request, 15–058
   respondent's obligations, 15–059
   selection of arbitrator, 15–060—15–063
organisation, A29–007
panel, A29–022
procedure before, 15–070—15–073, A29–031—A29–035
President, 15–044
procedural rules,
   application of rules, A29–009
   independence of arbitrators, A29–015
   language of proceedings, A29–011
   challenging arbitrators, A29–016
   notifications, A29–013
   provisional measures, A29–019
   qualifications of arbitrators, A29–015
   removal of arbitrator, 15–051, 15–052, A29–017
   replacement of arbitrators, A29–018
   representation, A29–012
   seat of arbitration, A29–010
   time-limit, 15–050, A29–014
provisional measures, 15–053—15–056
refusal to hear dispute, 15–048
removal of arbitrator, 15–051, 15–052, A29–017
representation, A29–012
request for arbitration, A29–020
seat of arbitration, A29–010
sports-related disputes, 15–047
Statutes of the Bodies Working for the Settlement of Sports-related Disputes, International Council for Arbitration for Sport. *See* International Council of Arbitration for Sport (ICAS)
joint dispositions, A29–001
structure, 15–044, 15–045
time-limit, A29–014
transfer of file, A29–024
urgent cases, 15–093
COURTS,
appeal on point of law, 2–099
applications to. *See* Applications to court
consent of parties to application, 2–510
conservatory orders, 2–553
continuation of arbitration whilst court proceedings are in train, 2–092
evidence secured through application to, 2–508
expedition, 2–092
improving management, 2–529
injunctions, 2–553
interim questions of law, 2–091
jury trial, influence of, 2–526—2–529

COURTS—*cont.*
  pending applications, 2–092
  preservation of evidence, 2–508
  role in arbitration, A56–001
  role of, 2–089, 2–090
  securing attendance through, 2–507
  speedy, where, 2–553
  supervision,
    farm business tenancy arbitration, 3–108
  supervisory role, 2–089, 2–095—2–100
    definition, 2–844
    enforcement of award, 2–095
    serious irregularity, 2–096, 2–097
    supportive role, 2–089, 2–090
CPR INSTITUTE FOR DISPUTE RESOLUTION, 12–111
CREDIT CARD CHARGE BACK, 12–139
CROSS-EXAMINATION, 2–795
  expert evidence, 2–852
  interventions by the arbitrator, 2–798, 2–799
  proofs of evidence, 2–769
CYBERSQUATTING, 12–115

DAC REPORT, 1–010
  confidentiality, 1–010, 2–103, 2–819
  consolidated arbitration, 2–101, 6–095
  construction industry arbitration, 6–095
  costs, 2–903
  immunity, 2–076
  influences, 2–062
  intermediate solution proposed by, 2–062, 2–064
  Model law and, 2–059—2–064
  multi-party arbitration, 2–627
  privacy, 2–103
  recommendations, 2–062
  rejection of Model Law, 2–062
  statutory reform recommended, 2–062
DATABASES,
  online dispute resolution, 12–008
DATE OF AWARD,
  agricultural property arbitration, 3–079
  Arbitration Act 1996, A6–055
DATE OF HEARING,
  fixing, 2–425, 11–073
  maritime arbitration, 11–073
  natural justice, 2–425
DEATH,
  arbitrator, 2–307
    Arbitration Act 1996, A6–027
    person appointing arbitrator, A6–027
  witness, 2–769
DEATH OF PARTY,
  arbitration agreement, A6–009
DECISION-MAKING,
  arbitration, 2–023
  diary, 2–023
  interlocutory decisions, 2–024
  litigation, 2–023

DECISIONS,
  American Arbitration Association International Arbitration Rules, A18–027
DECLARATION,
  arbitrator, made by, 2–481
  enforcement of award, 2–945
DEFAULT JUDGMENTS,
  small claims arbitration in county court, 14–017
DEFAULT OF PARTY,
  CIMAR, 6–041, A28–011
  experts, A18–024
  GAFTA, A34–032
  LMAA terms, 11–081
  maritime arbitration, 11–081
  Model Law, A14–025
  WIPO arbitration, A52–056
DEFENCE,
  American Arbitration Association International Arbitration Rules, A18–004
  Chartered Institute of Arbitrators Rules of the Mortgage Code Arbitration, A24–004
  Chartered Institute of Arbitrators "Surveyors Arbitration" Scheme Rules, A25–006
  clubs, 11–015, 11–016, 11–0135
  documents only arbitration in consumer disputes, 8–042, 8–043
  enforcement of award, 2–946, 2–947
    election, 2–947
    estoppel, 2–947
    no jurisdiction to make award, 2–946
    waiver, 2–947
  maritime arbitration, 11–064
  Model Law, A14–023
  UNCITRAL Arbitration Rules, A15–020
  WIPO arbitration, A52–042
DEFENCE CLUBS,
  maritime arbitration, 11–012
DELAY,
  See also Expedition; Target programming
  inordinate and inexcusable, striking out, 2–088
  procedure controlled by arbitrator, 2–464
  sanctions against,
    costs, 2–588
    displeasure of arbitrator, 2–587
    interest, 2–588
    proceeding to a hearing, 2–589
  striking out for, 2–088
DELIVERY OF AWARD,
  agricultural property arbitration, 3–079
  construction industry arbitration, 6–103
  online dispute resolution, 12–073
DEPARTMENTAL ADVISORY COMMITTEE ON ARBITRATION LAW, A58–004—A58–091

DEPOSIT OF COSTS,
American Arbitration Association International Arbitration Rules, A18–034
LCIA arbitration, A44–025
UNCITRAL Arbitration Rules, A15–042
UNCITRAL Notes on Organizing Arbitral Proceedings, A15–017—A15–019
WIPO arbitration, A52–070
DIRECT ACCESS RULES, 2–027, 2–822, 18–004
DIRECTIONS,
CIMAR, 6–039, A28–006
construction arbitration, 6–039, A54–069, A54–070
documents only arbitration, 8–035—8–036
expert evidence, 2–777
identification of issues, 2–787, 2–788
LME, 16–026
non-compliance with,
striking out for want of prosecution, 2–088
order for,
precedent, A54–040—A54–062
preliminary dialogue, 2–658
proofs of evidence, 2–768, 2–771
property valuation arbitration, 13–019
rent review arbitration, 13–019, A54–077, A54–078
selection of evidence for hearing, 2–789
small claims in county court, 14–033, 14–035, 14–036
striking out for want of prosecution, 2–088
DIRECTORS,
advocate, 2–831
DISCLOSURE, 2–695—2–712
See also Confidentiality; Privacy
arbitrator,
discretion, 2–696
power, 2–695
categorisation of documents, 2–704
discretion of arbitrator, 2–696
ICE arbitration, A43–012
internal documents, 2–705
legal professional privilege, 2–700, 2–701
LMAA small claims procedure, A47–006
natural justice, 2–286
others, to, 2–813
powers of arbitrator, 2–695, 2–810
privilege, 2–697
communications with other persons, 2–706
inadvertent disclosure, 2–703
legal professional privilege, 2–700, 2–701
self-incrimination, privilege against, 2–699
public policy, 2–697
public policy immunity, 2–698
related person, documents in possession of, 2–707
rent review arbitration, 13–036—13–038
self-incrimination, privilege against, 2–699

DISCLOSURE—cont.
small claims in county court, 14–038
statutory power, 2–695
terms imposed on order for, 2–810
DISCOVERY,
agricultural property arbitration, 3–042, 3–043
availability, 2–469
denying requests, 2–469
full, 2–469
international arbitration, 9–129—9–134
powers of arbitrators, 2–469
DISPUTE ADJUDICATION BOARD, 7–010
FIDIC Conditions, 6–054
DISPUTE BOARDS, 7–001—7–085
adjusted dispute contract clause, 7–043, 7–044, 7–045
ADR procedures distinguished, 7–081
advantages, 7–084
advice, 7–034
agreements considered, 7–043—7–046
alternative forms, 7–025—7–027
alternative to litigation, 7–004
appointment of panel, 7–048, 7–049
approach, 7–009—7–015
arbitration and, 7–080
assignment, 7–051
assistance from, 7–081
background, 7–001—7–008
build-operate-transfer contracts, 7–007
cases in which approach adopted, 7–020
Combined Dispute Board, 7–034
comparison of approaches, 7–028—7–031
complimentary nature, 7–015
compulsory use, 7–012
conciliating legitimate interests of buyer and seller, 7–003
confidentiality of report, 7–068, 7–069
construction industry arbitration, 6–032
consultation of DB outside DB procedure, 7–058
context of application, 7–009—7–015
contracts using, 7–007
criteria for designation of DB, 7–052—7–054
DAB approach, 7–019
daily fee, 7–050
deadline for recommendation/decision, 7–060, 7–061
decisions, 7–034, 7–035, 7–036
binding, 7–062
objections, 7–079
semi-binding, 7–062
decisive approach, 7–019
development, 7–016—7–024
disadvantages, 7–084
domestic markets, 7–007
early stage, selection at an, 7–033
effectiveness, 7–081
Europe, use in, 7–021, 7–022
evaluation, 7–083, 7–084

INDEX

DISPUTE BOARDS—cont.
  expectations of business community, 7–001—7–008
  fees, 7–050
  FIDIC, 7–006, 7–014, 7–017
  flexibility, 7–084
  flexible and formal advisory panel, 7–027
  formal advisory panel, 7–025
  formal referral of disputes, 7–073—7–078
    deliberation, 7–077
    hearing, 7–076
    notice requesting recommendation/decision, 7–074
    position paper, 7–075
    reporting, 7–078
  forms, 7–025
  future of, 7–006
  ICC, 7–006
  joint venture contracts, 7–007
  litigation and, 7–080
  members prevented from acting in legal proceedings, 7–070
  methods of setting up, 7–047
  milestones in development, 7–018
  monthly retainer fee, 7–050
  NEC forms, 7–017
  non-compliance by party, 7–064
  number of members, 7–047
  objections, 7–079
  objectives, 7–012
  obstruction by party, 7–066
  origins, 7–017
  potential disputes, 7–071, 7–072
  pre-arbitration and deciding panel, 7–026
  pre-arbitration step, 7–015
  prevention of litigation, 7–005
  procedural rules, 7–043
  procedure, 7–052—7–070
    automatic start of legal proceedings, 7–067
    binding decision or non-binding recommendation, 7–062, 7–063
    consultation of DB outside DB procedure, 7–058
    criteria for designation of DB, 7–052—7–054
    deadline for recommendation/decision, 7–060, 7–061
    defining procedure, 7–059
    formulation of request for recommendation or decision, 7–057
    non-compliance by party, 7–064
    obstruction by party, 7–066
    renewal of mandate, 7–066
    subdivisions, 7–059
    truncation, 7–065
    when should referral be made, 7–055, 7–056
  recommendations, 7–034, 7–035, 7–036, 7–062
    binding, when, 7–079

DISPUTE BOARDS—cont.
  remuneration, 7–050
  rigidity, avoiding, 7–084
  role, 7–012
  selection of approach, 7–023—7–036
  semi-binding decision, 7–062
  setting up mechanism, 7–037—7–051
  site visits, 7–051
  standard construction contracts, 7–006
  statistical data, 7–020
  success, factors affecting, 7–023, 7–032
  terminology, 7–013
  Three Party Agreement, 7–043
  training, 7–084
  truncated, 7–065
    renewal of mandate, 7–066
  type of system selected, 7–041, 7–042
  when should procedure be used, 7–037—7–040
DISPUTE RESOLUTION,
  arbitrability, 2–004
  binding and non-binding decisions, 2–005
  choice, 2–001
  courts, pressure from the, 2–002
  methods, 2–001
  variety, 2–002
DISPUTE REVIEW BOARD, 7–010, 7–013
DISQUALIFICATION OF ARBITRATOR,
  ability to do job, 2–273
  agricultural property arbitration, 3–030
  basic test, 2–279
  conflict of interest, 2–274
  degree of conflict, 2–274
  Human Rights Act 1998, 2–275
  ICSID arbitration, A60–058, A60–059
  prior adoption of a point of view, 2–278
  prior connection with a similar dispute, 2–277
  prior decision on same issue, 2–276
  reasons for, 2–273
  test, 2–279
  undertakings, 2–206
DOCUMENTS,
  See also Disclosure; Discovery; Documents only arbitration; Selection of evidence for hearing
  farm business tenancy arbitration, 3–108
DOCUMENTS ONLY ARBITRATION,
  advantages, 8–016
  CIMAR, 6–040, A28–008
  consumer disputes See Documents only arbitration in consumer disputes
  directions, 8–035—8–036
  ICE arbitration, A43–020
  inappropriate uses, 8–017
  JCT Standard Form Contract, 6–067
  powers of arbitrators, 2–466
  preliminary dialogue, 2–656, 2–657
  procedure,
    available choices, 2–466
    property valuation arbitration, 13–021

1069

DOCUMENTS ONLY ARBITRATION—*cont.*
rent review arbitration, 13–021
RSA, 16–060
DOCUMENTS ONLY ARBITRATION IN CONSUMER DISPUTES, 8–014—8–063
1988 Act, 8–002, 8–003
additional evidence, 8–026, 8–027
administered arbitrations, 8–014
administered schemes, 8–014
advantages, 8–016
award, 8–048—8–052
  general principles, 8–048
  reasons, 8–049—8–051
awareness of rights, consumer, 8–038
background, 8–001
burden of proof, 8–041
claimant, 8–037
clarification of issues, 8–040
compensation,
  assessment, 8–053
  damages,
    factors affecting, 8–056
    general damages, 8–056
    holiday cases, 8–057
    limits on, 8–053
    loss of enjoyment and disappointment in holiday cases, 8–057
    quantum, 8–055
    special, 8–056
  foreseeability, 8–043
  interest, 8–058—8–059
  limits, 8–053
  quantum of damages, 8–055
"consumer", 8–004, 8–005
"consumer disputes", 8–006
costs, 8–060—8–063
county court, 8–014
defence, failure to submit, 8–042, 8–043
definition of consumer, 8–004, 8–005
directions, 8–035—8–036
disregard law, no power to, 8–029
duties of arbitrator,
  disregarding law, no power to, 8–029—8–032
  point of law, 8–033
  travel claims, 8–030
evidence, 8–036
ex gratia payments, 8–045
exaggerated claims, 8–051
excluded claims, 8–017
failure to claim, 8–051
form of award, 8–049
frivolous claims, 8–051
further evidence, 8–026, 8–027
generally, 8–001
inappropriate uses, 8–017
inarticulate claimant, 8–037
independent technical advice, 8–039
inexperienced claimant, 8–037
interest, 8–057, 8–059
internal appeal procedures, 8–052

DOCUMENTS ONLY ARBITRATION IN CONSUMER DISPUTES—*cont.*
lawyers' intervention, 8–046
lump sums including interest, 8–059
outside administered or code schemes, 8–015
physical injury, 8–017
pleadings, 8–025
point of law, 8–033
privilege, 8–044
procedure, 8–023—8–028
protection, consumer, 8–007—8–009
reasons for award, 8–049—8–051
representation, 8–046, 8–047
technical advice, independent, 8–039
unnecessary delay or expense, 8–038
unsupported allegations, 8–041
"without prejudice" correspondence, 8–044
DOMESTIC ARBITRATION,
international arbitration distinguished, 2–071
meaning, 2–071
DRAFT AWARD,
calculations in, 2–443
circulating, 2–294
maritime arbitration, 11–087
natural justice, 2–294
DUTIES OF ARBITRATOR,
advocate, to, 2–821, 2–844
Code of Practice arbitration. *See* Code of Practice arbitrations
conduct of arbitration, 2–206
confidentiality. *See* Confidentiality
deciding dispute according to chosen law, 2–512
economic and expeditious means of dispute resolution, 2–759, 2–760
expert evidence, 2–512
form of award, 2–512
non-compliance, 2–513
notification of award, 2–512
obligation to complete, 2–307
partial awards, 2–512
property valuation arbitration, 13–012
reasons for award, 2–512
rent review arbitration, 13–012
representative, hearing chosen, 2–512
seat of arbitration stated in award, 2–512
settlements, 2–512, 2–735

E-COMMERCE DISPUTES, 12–125, 12–126
  confidence in e-commerce, 12–140—12–146
  online dispute resolution, 12–005
E-RESOLUTION, 12–111
ELECTRONIC FILE MANAGEMENT, 12–015, 12–016
ELECTRONIC SIGNATURES, 12–062—12–072
EMPLOYEES,
  advocate, 2–831
ENERGY CHARTER TREATY 1994, 9–075, 10–01

INDEX

ENFORCEMENT,
  award. *See* Enforcement of award; New York Convention
  settlements, 2–753
ENFORCEMENT OF AWARD, 2–942—2–950
  agreement between parties, award as, 2–943
  Arbitration Act 1996, A6–067
    election, 2–947
    estoppel, 2–947
    waiver, 2–947
  calculations necessary, where, 2–945
  CCR, 2–943
  Civil Procedure Rules, 2–94, 2–944
  conditions imposed on leave to appeal to High Court, 2–949
  consequences of award, 2–943
  court, by, A6–067
    meaning of courts, 2–943
  cross-application for leave to enforce, 2–950
  declaratory awards, 2–945
  defences, 2–946, 2–947
    election, 2–947
    estoppel, 2–947
    no jurisdiction to make award, 2–946
    waiver, 2–947
  ease of, 2–034
  estoppel, 2–947
  Human Rights Act 1998, 2–595
  ICSID arbitration, A60–054—A60–056
  lack of jurisdiction to make award, 2–943, 2–946
  leave of court, 2–943
  legal effect of award, 2–942
  Model Law, A14–035, A14–036
  New York Convention. *See* New York Convention
  online dispute resolution, 12–039—12–041, 12–074
  reforms, 2–943
  RSC, 2–943
  rules governing, 2–943
  stay of enforcement pending challenge, 2–948—2–950
  summary enforcement, 2–943—2–945
    calculations necessary, where, 2–945
    declaratory awards, 2–945
    leave of court, 2–943
    methods, 2–944
    nature of award, 2–942
    where not available, 2–945
  transition, process in, 2–943
  waiver, 2–947
ENGINEER,
  See also NEC forms
  construction industry arbitration, 6–027, 6–053
  FIDIC Conditions, 6–052
  first-tier dispute resolver, 6–028
  ICE Conditions of Contract, reference under, 6–048
EQUITY CLAUSES, 9–089—9–092

ERROR ON FACE OF AWARD,
  agricultural property arbitration, 3–087, 3–088
ERRORS,
  accidental slips in award, 2–885, 2–886
  award, correcting, 2–885, 2–886
ESTOPPEL,
  award, arising out of, 2–887—2–890, 2–947
  cause of action, 2–290, 2–888, 2–889
  enforcement of award, 2–947
  issue, 2–888, 2–889, 2–890
  judgment, by, 2–887
  law, issues of, 2–732
EUROPEAN LAW,
  consumer protection, 8–006, 8–007
  Market Access Strategy, 17–072, 17–073
  Trade Barriers Regulation. *See* Trade Barriers Regulation
EUROPEAN UNION,
  ADR, access to, 4–014, 4–015
EVEN NUMBER OF ARBITRATORS, 2–122, 2–218
EVIDENCE,
  See also Conduct of hearing; Expert evidence; Hearing; Proofs of evidence; Witnesses
  ABTA scheme, 8–036
  admissibility,
    Arbitration Act 1996, 2–716
    general rule, 2–716
    IBA Rules, A38–017
    privilege. *See* Privilege
    relevance, 2–717
  admission of facts or documents, 2–771
  American Arbitration Association International Arbitration Rules, A18–020
  arbitration agreement, relevance of, 2–762
  arbitrator, of, 13–031—13–033
  assessment,
    IBA Rules, A38–017
  CIMAR, 6–039, A28–005
  comparables, 13–039
  confidentiality, 13–045—13–047
  construction industry arbitration, 6–018, 6–078
  copying, unnecessary, 2–715
  costs of objecting to, 2–719
  cross-examination, 2–792
  de bene esse, to be given, 2–718
  documents only arbitration in consumer disputes, 8–036
  electronic signatures, 12–068—12–072
  examination in chief, 2–794
  farm business tenancy arbitration, 3–108
  GAFTA, A34–025
  hearsay, 13–027
  IBA Rules. *See* IBA Rules
  ICE arbitration, A43–018
    hearing, 6–077, A43–018
  ICE Conditions of contract, 6–078
  inadmissible. *See* Privilege

1071

Index

EVIDENCE—cont.
international arbitration, 9–150
irrelevant, 2–717
late evidence, 13–028
LCIA arbitration, 9–028
notice to admit facts or documents, 2–771
online dispute resolution, 12–031—12–038
physical property identification, 13–035, 13–036
privilege 2–717. *See also* Privilege
property valuation arbitration, 13–026—13–049
   application of rules, 13–026—13–030
   art of valuation, 13–041
   assumptions, 13–040
   comparables, 13–039, 13–041
   confidentiality, 13–045—13–047
   consistency of evidence, 13–048, 13–049
   disclosure, 13–036—13–038
   expert evidence, 13–048, 13–049
   hearsay, 13–027
   irrelevant, 13–044
   late evidence, 13–028
   other awards, 13–043
   own evidence, arbitrator's, 13–031—13–033
   physical property identification, 13–034, 13–035
   principles, statutory, 13–025
   reported cases, 13–042
   serious irregularities, 13–030
re-examination, 2–796
reception of, 2–762
relevance, 2–717
resignation of arbitrator after disclosure of "without prejudice" negotiations, 2–724, 2–725
selection for hearing 2–713—2–725. *See also* Selection of evidence for hearing
UNCITRAL Arbitration Rules, A15–025
WIPO arbitration, A52–048
EVIDENCE IN CHIEF, 2–794
interventions by the arbitrator, 2–797
EX AEQUO ET BONO, ARBITRATOR ACTING, 2–727
EX GRATIA PAYMENTS DOCUMENTS ONLY ARBITRATION IN CONSUMER DISPUTES, 8–045
EX PARTE PROCEEDINGS,
natural justice, 2–439
notice, A54–064, A54–065
EXCLUSION OF LIABILITY,
American Arbitration Association International Arbitration Rules, A18–036
City Disputes Panel Arbitration Rules, A26–026
costs, A26–026
ICC arbitration, A39–036
ICE arbitration, A43–034
LCIA arbitration, A44–032

EXCLUSION OF LIABILITY—cont.
privilege, A27–007
WIPO arbitration, A52–077
EXECUTION OF AWARD,
CIETAC, 16–071
EXPEDITION,
See also Oral hearing ; Target programming
arbitration practice compared to court practice, 2–530—2–533
both parties wanting delay, 2–578
both parties wanting speed, 2–576
chess clock arbitrations, 2–544—2–547
Civil Procedure Rules. *See* Civil Procedure Rules
claimant wanting delay and respondent wanting speed, 2–579
claimant wants speed and respondent wants delay, 2–582
discrete issues, finding, 2–571
early request for issues, 2–573
fair hearing, 2–548—2–551
   discretion, 2–548
   minimum requirements, 2–549
   present position, 2–550
fast track procedures, 2–607—2–616
   absence of agreement by parties, 2–609
   consent, summary procedure by, 2–607
   dangers, 2–612
   enforcement of fast track award, 2–614
   interim awards, 2–615
   liability, 2–616
   matters to consider, 2–610
   methods of agreement, 2–608
   possible approach, 2–613
   provisional awards, 2–611
   quantum, 2–616
Human Rights Act 1998, 2–617—2–625
   Article 6, 2–624
   impact, 2–617
   Mousaka, 2–620, 2–621
   North Range, 2–619
   permissible method of dispute resolution, arbitration as, 2–623
   purposive construction of statutes, 2–622
   Re Swaptronics, 2–618
   waiver of right to challenge arbitrator, 2–625
interim awards, 2–615
issue of award, 2–554
long advance dates, 2–574
objective of arbitrator, 2–570
oral hearing. *See* Oral hearing
peremptory orders. *See* Peremptory orders
programming the award writing, 2–555
progress of arbitration, 2–556—2–560
   appointing bodies, role of, 2–559
   delay, 2–556
   diaries, 2–558, 2–559
   diary, arbitrator's, 2–558
   removal of arbitrator, 2–560

EXPEDITION—*cont.*
  progress of arbitration—*cont.*
    responsibility, 2–556
    statutory duties, 2–557
    provisional awards, 2–611
    recalcitrant party, dealing with, 2–590—
      2–595
      common law, 2–590
      courts and, 2–594
      default powers in arbitration, 2–591
      due process, 2–595
      Human Rights Act 1998, 2–595
      late case, excluding, 2–593
      short notice hearing, 2–592
    sanctions,
      costs, 2–585, 2–588
      delay, 2–587—2–589
      displeasure of arbitrator, 2–587
      interest, 2–588, 32–586
      proceeding to a hearing, 2–588
      reluctant debtor, 2–584—2–586
    settlement, 2–533
    speed, importance of, 2–552—2–555
    target dates, 2–572
    trial by jury, influence of, 2–526—2–529
    unavoidable delay, 2–581
    want of prosecution. *See* Want of
      prosecution
  WIPO arbitration, 9–042
  Woolf reforms, 2–529
EXPENSES,
  arbitrator's, 2–384, 2–387
  payment, 2–387
  resignation of arbitrator, 2–298
  Scheme for Construction Contracts, 5–081
EXPERIMENTS,
  WIPO arbitration, A52–049
EXPERT DETERMINATION, 2–041—2–057
  advantages, 2–041—2–057
  appeals, 2–056
  arbitration distinguished, 2–041—2–057
  arbitration statutes not applying, 2–042
  auxiliary powers of court, 2–055
  clear rules of procedure, 2–054
  construction industry disputes, 6–031
  costs, 2–052
  decision-making process, 2–047
  determination of own jurisdiction by
    arbitrator, 2–049, 2–050
  dispute resolution clause, 2–048
  enforcement, 2–046
  examples of use, 2–041
  investigations, 2–043
  jurisdiction, 2–051
  material on which decision made, 2–043
  nature of determination, 2–045
  negligence, 2–057
  New York Convention, 2–045
  point of law, decision on, 2–056
  procedure, 2–047, 2–054
  provision for, 2–041

EXPERT DETERMINATION—*cont.*
  speed, 2–044
  thoroughness, 2–053
  uses, 2–041
EXPERT EVIDENCE, 2–772—2–779
  advocate distinguished, 2–846
  American Arbitration Association
    International Arbitration Rules, A18–
      023
  appointment, 2–772
    arbitrator's participation in choosing,
      2–859
    costs, 2–859
    guidelines, 2–858
    institutional, 2–858
    tribunal, by, 2–858
  assumptions upon which based, 2–852
  both parties instructing, 2–776
  breach of duty, 2–849—2–853
  calling, 2–779
  change of roles, 2–848
  changing mind, expert, 2–852
  City Disputes Panel Arbitration Rules, A26–
    020
  closure of hearing, A18–025
  commenting on, 2–512
  conferencing, 2–542
  conflicting, 2–871
  conflicts, resolution of, 2–852—2–857
    different conclusions deriving from
      different facts, 2–855
    exaggerations, 2–856
    general conflicts of opinion, 2–857
    types of conflict, 2–854
  costs, 2–559
  cross-examination, 2–852
  declaration, 13–048, 13–049
  default of party, A18–024
  directions, 2–777
  disadvantage to client, 2–850
  discussion with client about opinions, 2–851
  duties to arbitrator, 2–512
  duty of expert to tribunal, 2–849
  entitlement to call, 2–772
  exaggerations, 2–856
  exchanging proofs, 2–773
  expertise of expert, 2–772
  faulty assumptions, 2–852
  IBA Rules, A38–013
    party-appointed experts, A38–013
    report, 9–146, 9–148
    tribunal-appointed experts, 9–148, A38–
      014
  ICC arbitration, 9–144
  ICC DOCDEX Rules, A40–006
    procedure, A40–007
  ICC Rules for Expertise, A42–001—A42–
    026
    administration of expertise proceedings,
      A42–010—A42–016
    appointment of experts, A42–006—A42–
      009

EXPERT EVIDENCE—cont.
ICC Rules for Expertise—cont.
exclusion of liability, A42–018
general rule, A42–019
proposal of experts, A42–003—A42–005
Statutes of the Standing Committee of the International Centre for Expertise, A42–020—A42–023
waiver, A42–017
ICE arbitration, A43–022, A43–023
international arbitration, 9–143—9–149
approaches, 9–143, 9–144
battle of expert evidence, 9–143
IBA Rules of Evidence, 9–146, 9–148
ICC arbitration, 9–144
LCIA arbitration, 9–144
report, 9–146
technical issues, 9–145
tribunal-appointed, 9–147, 9–148
UNCITRAL Model Law, 9–149
LCIA arbitration, 9–144, A44–022
limiting, 2–772
meetings,
arranging, 2–775
basis of, 2–775
binding agreements reached, 2–775
directions, 2–777
lawyers attendance at, 2–775
marking statements, 2–777
open, 2–775
productive, making, 2–777, 2–778
purpose, 2–775
recording, 2–775
refusal to co-operate, 2–777
repetitive evidence, 2–779
statement of agreed facts, 2–778
summary of, 2–777
usefulness, 2–777
without prejudice, 2–775
Model Law, A14–026
nature of expert's role, 2–772
need for, 2–772
negotiator distinguished, 2–846
opinion evidence, 2–845
preliminary dialogue, 2–772
proofs of evidence, 2–774
property valuation arbitration, 13–048, 13–049
reasonable opportunity to comment on, 2–512
rent review arbitration, 13–048, 13–049
repetitive, 2–779
role of witness, 2–845—2–859
Royal Institute of Chartered Surveyors, 2–845
simultaneous instructions, 2–776
small claims in county court, 14–041, 14–042
Sport Dispute Resolution Panel, 15–030, A67–021
statement of agreed facts, 2–778

EXPERT EVIDENCE—cont.
testing validity, 2–852
truthfulness of evidence, 2–416, 2–417
UNCITRAL Model Law, 9–149
WIPO arbitration, A52–055
Woolf Report, 2–845

FARM BUSINESS TENANCY ARBITRATION, 3–008—3–009, 3–100—3–109
1996 Act excluded, 3–100
action on appointment, 3–104, 3–105
appointment of arbitrator, 3–104, 3–106
arbitrator,
experience, 3–100
new arbitrator appointed, 3–106
remuneration, 3–107
revocation of appointment, 3–106
award, 3–108
delivery, 3–108
challenging award, 3–108
commencing, 3–104
conduct of proceedings, 3–108
disputes, 3–102
documents, 3–108
enforcement of orders, 3–108
evidence, 3–108
excluded disputes, 3–103
experience of arbitrator, 3–100
form of award, 3–108
framework of legislation, 3–102, 3–103
hearing, 3–108
initiating, 3–104
interest, 3–108
interim awards, 3–108
jurisdiction, 3–108
legal advice, 3–108
line on award, 3–108
meaning, 3–008
new arbitrator appointed, 3–106
oral hearing, 3–108
powers of arbitrator, 3–108
purpose, 3–008
reform of legislation, 3–008
remuneration, 3–107
revocation of arbitration powers, 3–106
statement of claim, 3–108
statutory arbitrations, 3–009, 3–011
statutory regulation, 3–008
supervision by court, 3–108
FARM INSPECTION, 3–060—3–062
assistance in, 3–060
date of, 3–059
disclosure observations, 3–062
early, 3–059
experience of arbitrator, 3–061
importance, 3–059
impressions obtained on, 3–061, 3–062
lobbying in advance, 3–060
matters taken into account, 3–062
objectives, 3–059

FARM INSPECTION—*cont.*
  relevant matters, 3–062
  timing, 3–059
  unaccompanied, 3–060
FEDERATION OF OILS, SEEDS AND FATS ASSOCIATION (FOSFA). *See* FOSFA
FEES,
  See also Remuneration of arbitrator; VAT
  ad hoc arbitration, 9–049—9–051
  Arbitration Act 1950, A61–020
  booking, 2–384, 11–096, 11–097
  CEDR Rules for Adjudication, A19–006
  dispute boards, 7–050
  GAFTA, A34–026, A35–006
  GAFTA mediation, A37–005
  ICC ADR rules, A40–007
  institutional, 2–487
  interim, 2–359, 2–360
  LMAA small claims procedure, 11–102, A47–003
  LMAA terms, A46–005
  property valuation arbitration, 13–010
  raising issue, 2–317
  rent review arbitration, 13–010
  resignation of arbitrator, 2–298, 2–304
  RSA, 16–052
  schedule, A54–037
  Scheme for Construction Contracts, 5–081, 5–089—5–091
  security for, 2–413
  WIPO arbitration, A52–067—A52–069
FIDIC CONDITIONS, 6–052—6–056
  amicable settlement, 6–055
  arbitration, 6–056
  Dispute Adjudication Board, 6–054, 7–006, 7–014, 7–017
  engineer, reference to, 6–053
  settlement, 6–055
  types of dispute, 6–056
FINAL SUBMISSIONS,
  conduct of hearing, 2–801
FINALITY OF AWARD,
  agricultural property arbitration, 3–082
FINALITY OF PROCEEDINGS,
  acceptance of decision, 2–032
  advantages of arbitration, 2–032, 2–033
FIXING DATES,
  natural justice, 2–426
FOREIGN AWARDS,
  Arbitration Act 1996,
    evidence, A6–103
    Geneva Convention awards, A6–100
    New York Convention awards, A6–101
    recognition and enforcement, A6–102
    refusal of recognition or enforcement, A6–104
  evidence,
    Arbitration Act 1996, A6–103
  Geneva Convention awards,
    Arbitration Act 1996, A6–100

FOREIGN AWARDS—*cont.*
  New York Convention awards,
    Arbitration Act 1996, A6–101
  recognition and enforcement,
    Arbitration Act 1996, A6–102
  refusal of recognition or enforcement,
    Arbitration Act 1996, A6–104
FOREIGN LAW, CONTRACT GOVERNED BY,
  agreement, 2–117
FORM OF AWARD. *See* Award
FOSFA, A66–001—A66.012
  appeals, A66–008—A66–011
  appointment of arbitrator, 16–020, A66–002
  awards, A66–007
  establishment, 16–001
  jurisdiction, A66–006
  lapse of claim, A66–004
  procedure, A66–003, A66–005
  time-limits, A66–003
  two-tier arbitration, 16–008
  umpire, appointment of, 16–020, A66–002
FRAUDULENT AWARDS, 2–515
FREEDOM OF EXPRESSION,
  Human Rights Act 1998, A11–013
FREEDOM OF THOUGHT, CONSCIENCE AND RELIGION,
  Human Rights Act 1998, A11–014
FURTHER AND BETTER PARTICULARS, 2–674—2–677
  disadvantages, 2–676
  presentation, 2–677
  reasons for requesting, 2–674
  test for, 2–677
  when to direct, 2–675

GAFTA, 16–015, 16–084—16–111
  appeals against award, 16–103—16–111, A34–018
    appeal awards, A34–023
    boards of appeal, A34–019
    composition of Board of Appeal, 16–104
    deadline for lodging, 16–103
    delays by appellant, 16–108
    objections to qualification of board, 16–109
    powers of Board, 16–107
    procedure, A34–020
    representation, 16–106
    signing appeal award, 16–111
    string contracts, A34–022
    timetable, 16–105
    withdrawal, A34–021
    withdrawal of appeal, 16–110
  appointment of arbitrator, 16–089—16–091, A35–003
  appointment of tribunal, A34–005—A34–008
  arbitration agreement, A35–011
  arbitration clause, 16–085

1075

GAFTA—cont.
  awards, A34–017
    different aspects, on, A34–016
    simple dispute rules, A35–007
  charter party arbitration,
    appointment of tribunal, A36–003—A36–007
    awards, A36–013
    awards on different aspects, A36–012
    concurrent hearings, A36–009
    consolidated arbitration, A36–009
    costs, A36–014
    default of party, A36–021
    evidence, A36–015
    fees, A36–016
    non-compliance with time limits and rules, A36–020
    notices, A36–017—A36–019
    preliminary issues, A36–001
    procedure, A36–002, A36–008
    provisional orders, A36–011
    representation, A36–014
    substantive jurisdiction, issues of, A36–010
    time limits, A36–002
  China Committee, 16–004
  CIF terms, 16–094
  commencement of arbitration, 16–092
  concurrent hearings, A34–013
  condition, disputes as to, 16–093
  consolidated arbitrations, A34–013, A36–009
  contracts issued by, 16–084
  costs, A35–006
  currency regulations, A34–027
  default of party, A34–032
  discretion, 16–095
  establishment, 16–002
  evidence, A34–025
  fees, A34–026, A35–006
  FOB terms, 16–094
  hearing, A35–004
  lapse of claim, 16–102
  mediation, 16–013
  non-compliance with time-limits and rules, A34–031
  notices, A34–028—A34–030
  place of arbitration, 16–086, A35–001
  preliminary issues, A34–001
  principal activities, 16–084
  procedure, 16–100, 16–101, A34–002—A34–004
  provisional orders, A34–015
  purpose of organisation, 16–084
  quality, disputes as to, 16–093
  representation, 16–096, 16–097, A34–024, A35–005
  "Rye Terms" clause, 16–093, A34–012
  samples, A34–011
  Scott-Avery clause, 16–085, 16–086
  seat of arbitration, 16–086

GAFTA—cont.
  Secretariat, 16–098, 16–099
  simple dispute rules,
    appointment of arbitrator, A35–003
    award, A35–007
    claim, A35–002
    costs, A35–006
    definition, A35–009
    fees, A35–006
    general provisions, A35–008
    hearing, A35–004
    notices, A35–010
    place of arbitration, A35–001
    representation, A35–005
  string arbitrations, A34–013, A34–022
  substantive jurisdiction, A34–014
  time-limits, 16–092, 19–094
  tribunal, appointment of, 9–070—9–073
  two-tier arbitration, 16–008
GAFTA MEDIATION,
  agreement, A37–007
  agreement resulting from, A37–006
  appointment of mediator, A37–003
  costs, A37–005
  fees, A37–005
  general, A37–001
  place of mediation, A37–002
  procedure, A37–004
GC/WORKS CONTRACT,
  natural justice, 2–447, 2–448
GENEVA CONVENTION, 9–006, 9–007, 9–070—9–073
  Arbitration Act 1996, A6–100
GGF, 8–011
GLASS AND GLAZING FEDERATION, 8–011
GOVERNMENT CONTRACT GC/WORKS/1,
  adjudication, 6–050, 6–062
  arbitration, 6–051, 6–063
  forms of dispute resolution, 6–061—6–063
GRAIN AND FEED TRADE ASSOCIATION. *See* GAFTA; GAFTA Mediation

HAGUE CONVENTION, 2–781
HEALTH OF ARBITRATOR, 2–307, 2–308
HEARING,
  See also Adjournments; Consolidated arbitration; Evidence; Expedition; Oral hearing; Natural justice; Pre-hearing review; Representation; Selection of evidence for hearing
  advocates,
    See also Barristers; Representation
    agricultural property arbitration, 3–066
  agricultural property arbitration,
    advocates, 3–066
    date of, 3–057
    evidence, 3–065
    experts as advocates, 3–066
    generally, 3–040
    oath, evidence on, 3–064

INDEX

HEARING—*cont.*
  agricultural property arbitration—*cont.*
    order of events, 3–063
    place of, 3–057
    post-hearing events, 3–067
    requirement, 3–040
    rules of evidence, 3–065
  American Arbitration Association International Arbitration Rules, A18–021
  chess clock arbitrations, 2–544—2–547
  CIETAC, A74–032—A74–051
  CIMAR,
    documents only arbitration, 6–040, A28–008
    full procedure, 6–040, A28–009
    short, 6–040, A28–007
  City Disputes Panel Arbitration Rules, A26–021
  date of,
    agricultural property arbitration, 3–057
  effective conduct of, 2–784
  evidence, selection of 2–713—2–725. *See also* Evidence; Selection of evidence for hearing
  farm business tenancy arbitration, 3–108
  fixed period allocated to, 2–784
  fixing, 2–425, 2–426
  GAFTA, A35–004
  ICE arbitration, 6–078
    evidence, A43–018
    powers at hearing, 6–078, A43–017
    procedure, 6–078, A43–017, A43–018
  LCIA arbitration, A44–020
  long, disadvantages of, 2–783, 2–784
  Model Law, A14–024
  natural justice, 2–425, 2–426
  oath, evidence on,
    agricultural property arbitration, 3–064
  online dispute resolution, 12–054—12–056
  place of,
    choice of arbitrator, 2–466
    powers of arbitrator, 2–466
  preparation for. *See* Preparation for hearing
  series of, 2–782—2–788
  single, 2–782—2–788
  Sport Dispute Resolution Panel, 15–028, A67–019
  time limits, 2–784
  WIPO arbitration, A52–053
  written statements of case, 6–040, A28–009
HEARSAY EVIDENCE, 13–027
HIGH COURT,
  allocation of arbitration proceedings, A8–001, 8–002
  applications to court, 2–938
  conditions imposed on leave to appeal to, 2–949
  Rules of Court, 2–460

HONG KONG,
  consolidated arbitration, 2–102, 2–652
  Med-Arb, 4–029
HONG KONG INTERNATIONAL ARBITRATION CENTRE, 12–094—12–097, A73–001—A73–028
HOUSING GRANTS, CONSTRUCTION AND REGENERATION ACT 1996,
  adjudication, A9–005
  amounts involved in adjudication, 5–020
  appointment of adjudicator, 5–036—5–040
    appointee, 5–042, 5–043
    nominating bodies, 5–041
  assistance to parties, 5–021
  bars to adjudication, 5–020
  binding decisions, 5–001
  case law, 5–005
  changes effected by, 5–002
  commencement, 5–001
  compliant contracts, 5–001, 5–005, 5–006, 5–007, 5–009—5–020
  conditional payment provisions, A9–010
  construction contract, 5–015, 5–016
  construction operations, 5–017—5–020
    exclusions, 5–018, 5–019, 5–020
  Crown application, A9–014
  dates for payment, A9–007
  decision of arbitrator, 5–002
  default by parties, 5–056
  determination of underlying contract, 5–020
  express requirement for adjudication, 5–002
  foreign law, 5–009
  general duties of adjudicator, 5–046—5–048
  Human Rights Act 1998, 5–061
  jurisdiction, 5–062—5–070
  meaning, A9–001, A9–002
  mediator, assuming role of, 5–055
  notice of intention to seek adjudication, 5–022
    formal requirements, 5–034, 5–035
  notice of intention to withhold payment, 5–003, A9–008
    "at any time", 5–023, 5–024
    existence of a dispute, 5–025—5–029
    scope of dispute, 5–030—5–033
  oral agreements, 5–012, 5–013
  pay-when-paid clauses, 5–003
  payment provisions, 5–003
  place of construction operations, 5–009
  post-May 1st 1998 contracts, 5–002
  procedure after referral, 5–049—5–054
  process of adjudication, 5–006, 5–007
  purpose of regime, 5–004
  reckoning periods of time, A9–013
  referral notice, 5–044, 5–045
  regime, 5–002
  representation, 5–021
  residential occupier, contract with, A9–003
  right to refer dispute for adjudication, 5–001, 5–017
  s 110 notice, 5–003

1077

INDEX

HOUSING GRANTS, CONSTRUCTION AND
REGENERATION ACT—*cont*.
s.111 notice, 5–003, A9–008
Scheme for Construction Contracts. *See*
Scheme for Construction Contracts
scope of claims, 5–017
scope of dispute, 5–030—5–033
service of notices, A9–012
stage payments, A9–006
survivorship of underlying contract, 5–020
suspension of performance for non-payment,
A9–009
timetable, 5–071—5–073
not achieved, 5–074
variation of contract, 5–010
writing, provisions applicable to agreements
in, 5–011—5–014, A9–004
HUMAN RIGHTS ACT 1998, 1–007—1–009,
A11–001—A11–056
Convention rights, A11–024—A11–043
interpretation, A11–003
derogations, A11–015, A11–017, A11–050
disqualification of arbitrator, 2–275
enforcement of award, 2–595
European Court of Human Rights,
appointment to, A11–019
expedition, 2–617—2–625
impact, 2–617
Mousaka, 2–620, 2–621
North Range, 2–619
permissible method of dispute resolution,
arbitration as, 2–623
purposive construction of statutes, 2–622
Re Swaptronics, 2–618
freedom of expression, A11–013
freedom of thought, conscience and religion,
A11–014
Housing Grants, Construction and
Regeneration Act 1996, 5–061
interpretation, A11–022
legislation,
Crown intervention, A11–006
declaration of incompatibility, A11–005
interpretation, A11–004
orders under, A11–021
Parliamentary procedure, A11–020
professional conduct of barristers and
solicitors, 18–005—18–012
fair and public hearing, right to, 18–007
independence, 18–011
investigation of complaints, 18–009
property, protection of, 18–008
self-incrimination, 18–010
sufficiency of appeal, 18–012
public authorities,
acts of, A11–007
judicial acts, A11–010
judicial remedies, A11–009
proceedings, A11–008
remedial action, power to take, A11–011
remedial orders, A11–044—A11–049

HUMAN RIGHTS ACT—*cont*.
reservations, A11–016, A11–018, A11–052
safeguard for existing human rights, A11–012
statements of compatibility, A11–020

IBA RULES,
See also International arbitration
admissibility of evidence, A38–017
adoption, 9–099
Arbitration and ADR Committee, A38–002—A38–006
assessment of evidence, A38–017
definitions, A38–009
documents, A38–011
evidentiary hearing, A38–016
experts,
party-appointed experts, A38–013
report, 9–146, 9–148
tribunal-appointed experts, 9–148, A38–014
party-appointed experts, A38–013
preamble, A38–008
purpose, 9–099
scope, A38–010
on site inspection, A38–015
tribunal-appointed experts, A38–014
witnesses, A38–012
ICANN, 12–104—12–124
management of domain names, 12–105
registration of domain names, 12–105, 12–106
responsibility, 12–106
Uniform Domain Name Dispute Resolution
Procedure. *See* UDRP
ICAS. *See* INTERNATIONAL COURT OF
ARBITRATION FOR SPORT (ICAS)
ICC ADR RULES,
automatic expiration mechanism, A40–002
commencement of proceedings, A40–005
conduct of procedure, A40–008
costs, A40–007
fees, A40–007
general provisions, A40–010
obligation to consider ADR, A40–002
optional ADR, A40–002
preamble, A40–003
precedent clauses, A54–130
schedule of costs, A40–011
scope, A40–004
selection of the neutral, A40–006
suggested clauses, A40–002, A54–130
termination of ADR proceedings, A40–009
ICC ARBITRATION, 9–013—9–031
applicable law, A39–019
appointment of arbitrators, 9–102, A39–011
approval of award, 9–018

INDEX

ICC ARBITRATION—cont.
  arbitral proceedings,
    applicable law, A39–019
    closing proceedings, A39–024
    conservatory measures, A39–025
    establishing facts of case, A39–022
    hearing, A39–023
    interim measures, A39–025
    language of proceedings, A39–018
    new claims, A39–021
    place of arbitration, A39–016
    rules governing proceedings, A39–017
    terms of reference, A39–020
    timetable, A39–020
    transmission of file to arbitral tribunal, A39–015
  arbitral tribunal,
    general provisions, A39–009
    number of arbitrators, A39–010
  arbitration clause, A54–014
  arbitrators,
    appointment, A39–011
    challenge, A39–013
    confirmation, A39–011
    replacement, A39–014
  award,
    approval, 9–018
    clarification, 9–018
    consent, award by, A39–028
    correction of award, A39–031
    deposit of costs, A39–030
    enforceability, A39–030
    interpretation of award, A39–031
    making award, A39–027
    notification, A39–030
    redrafting, 9–019
    scrutiny, 9–018, 9–019, A39–029
    time limit, A39–026
  background, 9–013—9–014
  case load, 9–013
  chairman, 2–241
  challenging arbitrators, A39–013
  clarification of award, 9–018
  closing proceedings, A39–024
  commencement of arbitration, A39–006—A39–008
  communication of award, 9–018
  communications, A39–005
  confirmation of arbitrators, A39–011
  conservatory measures, A39–025
  correction of award, A39–031
  costs, 9–020, 9–021
    advance to cover, A39–032, A39–051
    decision as to costs, A39–033
    fees, A39–052
  creation of ICC, 9–013
  definitions, A39–004
  exclusion of liability, A39–036
  experts, 9–144
  general rule, A39–037

ICC ARBITRATION—cont.
  International Court of Arbitration, A39–003
    internal rules, A39–045—A39–050
    Statutes, A39–038—A39–044
  interpretation of award, A39–031
  jurisdiction, 2–325
  language of proceedings, A39–018
  modified time limits, A39–034
  multiple parties, A39–012
  national committee, 9–014
  nationality of parties, 9–013
  new claims, A39–021
  number of arbitrators, 9–014, A39–010
  online arbitration, 12–083—12–086
  oral hearing, 9–153
  place of arbitration, 9–014, A39–016
  pre-arbitral reference procedure, 9–022
  procedural rules, 9–015, 9–017
  redrafting award, 9–019
  remuneration of arbitrator, 2–395
  replacement of arbitrators, A39–014
  rules governing proceedings, A39–017
  scrutiny of award, 9–018, 9–019
  seat of court, 9–013
  sole arbitrator, 9–014
  standard clause, A39–002
  statistics, 9–013, 9–021
  terms of reference, 9–015—9–017, A39–020
    criticism, 9–016
    procedural rules, 9–015, 9–017
  three person tribunal, 9–014
  time limits, A39–005
  timetable, A39–020
  venue, 9–014
  waiver of rules, A39–035
  written notifications, A39–005
  written statements, 9–137
ICC DOCDEX RULES,
  acknowledgements, A40–005
  answer, A40–003
  costs, A40–010
  decision, A40–008
  deposit of decision, A40–009
  dispute resolution service, A41–001
  experts, A40–006
    procedure, A40–007
  fees, A40–102, A40–103
  general, A40–011
  payment, A40–014
  publication of decision, A40–009
  rejections, A40–005
  request, A40–002
  supplements, A40–004
  transmission, A40–015
ICE ARBITRATION,
  aims, A43–001
  appeals, A43–031
  application of procedure, A43–033

ICE ARBITRATION—*cont.*
appointment of sole arbitrator,
agreement, by, A43–003
agent, by, A43–003
President, by, A43–004
arrangements for the arbitration, A43–006
assessors, A43–015
award, A43–024—A43–031
appeals, A43–031
correction of award, A43–030
costs, A43–027
interest, A43–026
making award, A43–029
provisional relief, A43–025
reasons, A43–028
commencement of arbitration, A43–002
concurrent hearings, A43–013
costs, A43–027
definitions, A43–032
disclosure of documents, A43–012
documents only arbitration, A43–020
evidence, A43–018
hearing, 6–077, A43–018
exclusion of liability, A43–034
experts, A43–022, A43–023
hearing, 6–078
powers at hearing, 6–078, A43–017
procedure, 6–078, A43–017, A43–018
interest, A43–026
notice of further disputes or differences, A43–005
objectives, A43–001
outside advice, seeking, A43–015
powers of arbitrator, 6–077, A43–007—A43–011
evidence, 6–077
limiting recoverable costs, A43–009
procedure, 6–077, A43–008
protective measures, A43–011
ruling on own jurisdiction, 6–077, A43–007
security, ordering, A43–010
pre-hearing procedures, A43–012—A43–016
preliminary meeting, A43–006
preparation for hearing, A43–016
procedural meetings, A43–014
protective measures, A43–011
provisional awards, A43–025
short procedure, A43–019—A43–021
special procedure for experts, A43–022, A43–023
statement of case, A43–012
ICE CONDITIONS OF CONTRACT, 6–047—6–051
appointment of arbitrator, 6–075, 6–087
commencement of arbitration, 6–077
conciliation, 6–044
concurrent hearings, 6–078
construction industry arbitration, 6–006
contractor's claims, A32–001

ICE CONDITIONS OF CONTRACT—*cont.*
Dispute Adjudication Agreement,
default of member, A33–008
definitions, A33–001
disputes, A33–009
general provisions, A33–002
obligations of employer and contractor, A33–005
obligations of member, A33–005
payment, A33–006
termination, A33–007
warranties, A33–003
Dispute Adjudication Board,
amicable settlement, A32–005
appointment, A32–002
arbitration, A32–006
expiry of appointment, A32–008
failure to agree, A32–003
failure to comply with decision, A32–007
obtaining decision, A32–004
engineer, reference to, 6–048
evidence, 6–078
first stage, 6–044
hearing procedure, 6–048
influences on, 6–012
Notice of Dispute, 6–048
optional conciliation, 6–049
powers of arbitrator, 6–077, 6–078
pre-arbitral stages, 6–048
procedural rules, A33–010
procedure for arbitration,
appointment of arbitrator, 6–077
arrangements for arbitration, 6–077
commencement of arbitration, 6–067
objectives, 6–076
powers of arbitrator, 6–077, 6–078
preparation, 6–076
rules, arbitration, 6–047—6–051
warranties, A33–003
ICSID,
Administrative Council, A60–005—A60–009
arbitration. *See* ICSID arbitration
conciliation, A60–029—A60–036
Rules, A78–001—A78–035
conciliation procedures, A78–023—A78–029
establishment of the Commission, A78–002—A78–013
final provisions, A78–035
procedural provisions, A78–020—A78–022
termination of the proceeding, A78–030—A78–034
working of the Commission, A78–014—A78–020
Convention, A60–002—A60–076
establishment, A60–002—A60–004
financing centre, A60–018
immunities, A60–019—A60–025

ICSID—cont.
  Institution Rules, A76–001—A76–010
    acknowledgement of the request, A76–006
    contents of request, A76–003
    copies of the request, A76–005
    final provisions, A76–010
    notice of registration, A76–008
    optional information in the request, A76–004
    registration of request, A76–007
    request, A76–002
    withdrawal of request, A76–009
  jurisdiction of centre, A60–026—A60–028
  panels, A60–013—A60–017
  privileges, A60–019—A60–025
  Secretariat, A60–010—A60–012
  status, A60–019—A60–025
ICSID ARBITRATION, 9–032—9–038
  See also ICSID; Investment treaty arbitration
  acceptance of convention, 9–033
  advantages, 9–037
  amendment of Convention, A60–066, A60–067
  annulment of award, A60–053
  applicable law, 10–023, 10–024
  arbitrators,
    disqualification, A60–058, A60–059
    replacement, A60–057
  availability, 10–055
  award, 10–056, A60–049, A60–050
    annulment, A60–053
    enforcement of award, 10–058, A60–054—A60–056
    interpretation, A60–051
    recognition of award, A60–054—A60–056
    revision, A60–052
  caseload, 10–64
  chairman, review by, 9–038
  challenging award, 9–034
  choosing, 10–058, 10–059
  constitution of tribunal, 10–056, A60–038—A60–041
  Convention, 9–032, A60–002—A60–076
  costs, A60–060—A60–062
  creation, 9–032
  disputes between contracting states, A60–065
  disqualification of arbitrators, A60–058, A60–059
  enforcement of award, 10–058, A60–054—A60–056
  exclusion of challenge, 9–034
  first session of tribunal, 10–056
  functions, A60–042—A60–048
  further proceedings, 10–056
  importance of, 9–035—9–037
  jurisdiction, objections to, 10–056
  numbers of arbitrations, 9–035
  objections to jurisdiction, 10–056
  operation, 9–033
  oral hearing, 10–056

ICSID ARBITRATION—cont.
  place of arbitration, A60–063, A60–064
  powers of tribunal, A60–042—A60–048
  pre-hearing conference, 10–056
  preliminary procedural consultation, 10–056
  procedure, 10–056
  public knowledge of existence of arbitration, 10–059
  recognition of award, A60–054
  registration, 10–056, A60–037
  request, 10–056, A60–037
  review by chairman, 9–038
  revision of award, A60–052
  Rules of Procedure, A77–001—A77–056
    ancillary claims, A77–041
    annulment of award, A77–053
    award, A77–047—A77–050
    default, A77–043
    discontinuance, A77–044—A77–046
    establishment of the Tribunal, A77–002—A77–013
    final provisions, A77–056
    general provisions, A77–020—A77–029
    interpretation or revision of award, A77–051, A77–052
    objections to jurisdiction, A77–042
    provisional measures, A77–040
    resubmission of dispute after annulment, A77–055
    settlement, A77–044
    stay of enforcement of award, A77–054
    workings of the Tribunal, A77–014—A77–019
    written and oral procedures, A77–030—A77–039
  unavailable, 10–059
  World Bank, 9–033
  written statements, 9–140, 10–056
IDENTIFICATION OF ISSUES, 2–665—2–694
  adjournment of hearing, 2–686—2–688
  advocate, 2–825
  amendment,
    aim, 2–683
    causing substantial delay, 2–682
    claimant seeking, 2–684
    consideration of application, 2–679
    negligence claim added to contract claim, 2–680
    new issues of fact, not introducing, 2–685
    not causing substantial delay, 2–681
    pleadings, 2–678
    presumption, 2–683
    statements of case, 2–678
  directions, 2–787, 2–788
  early identification, importance of, 2–665, 2–666
  further and better particulars, 2–674—2–677
    disadvantages, 2–676
    presentation, 2–677
    reasons for requesting, 2–674

1081

IDENTIFICATION OF ISSUES—*cont.*
further and better particulars—*cont.*
test for, 2–677
when to direct, 2–675
list of issues. *See* List of issues
lodging of claim and defence, 2–666
methods, 2–667—2–673
pleadings, 2–667, 2–668
amendment, 2–678
reasons for, 2–665
schedules, 2–672, A4–222
Statements of Case, 2–670, 2–671
amendment, 2–678
correspondence as, 2–673
technical issues, 2–665
IMMUNITY,
arbitrator, 2–074, 2–075
Arbitration Act 1996, A6–030
DAC Report, 2–076
institutions, 2–074, 2–075
IMPARTIALITY OF ARBITRATOR,
See also Maritime arbitration; Natural justice
American Arbitration Association International Arbitration Rules, A18–008
international arbitration, 9–107—9–116
online dispute resolution, 12–150
WIPO arbitration, A52–022
INDEPENDENCE OF ARBITRATOR,
American Arbitration Association International Arbitration Rules, A18–008
international arbitration, 9–107—9–116
WIPO arbitration, A52–022
INDIA,
Med-Arb, 4–029
INDIAN COUNCIL OF ARBITRATION,
arbitration clause, A54–019
INJUNCTIONS,
courts, 2–553
publication of documents produced in arbitration restrained by, 2–808
small claims in county court, 14–056—14–058
INSPECTION, 13–050—13–052
accompanied inspections, 13–052
information obtained on, 2–432
natural justice, 2–432
new evidence obtained from, 13–051
object of, 13–050
own evidence of arbitrator, 13–050
property valuation arbitration, 13–050—13–052
purpose, 13–050
rent review arbitration, 13–050—13–052
uses, 13–050
INSTALMENT PAYMENTS,
remuneration of arbitrator, 2–358
small claims in county court, 14–082

INSTITUTIONS,
agreement, incorporated into arbitration, 2–120
immunity, 2–074—2–075
importance, 2–073
power, 2–073
role, 2–073—2–076
statutory immunity, 2–074, 2–075, 2–076
timetables set by, 2–426
INSURANCE,
arbitrator failing in duties, 2–308
INTEREST, 2–891—2–900
agreement of parties, 2–892
agricultural property arbitration, 3–075
Arbitration Act 1950, A61–021, A61–022
Arbitration Act 1996, A6–050
arbitrator's power to award, 2–483, 2–892
borrowing money to pay, 2–900
breach of contract, 2–894
City Disputes Panel Arbitration Rules, A26–024
Civil Procedure Rules, A4–019
claims for, 2–891
compound, 2–892, 2–900
date of award, 2–898
debt,
paid, 2–893, 2–894
unpaid, 2–895—2–897
documents only arbitration in consumer disputes, 8–058, 8–059
exercise of discretion to award, 2–897
farm business tenancy arbitration, 3–108
ICE arbitration, A43–026
payment of debt,
before arbitration commenced, 2–893
unpaid at commencement of arbitration, 2–895—2–897
power to award, 2–483, 2–892
property valuation arbitration, 13–071
rate of, 2–899
sanctions, 2–586, 2–588
simple, 2–892, 2–900
small claims in county court, 14–082
sum awarded, on, 2–896
INTERIM AWARD,
agricultural property arbitration, 3–071—3–073, 3–075
expedition, 2–615
farm business tenancy arbitration, 3–108
judging techniques, 2–870
maritime arbitration, 11–084—11–086
precedent, A54–083, A54–084
precedents, A54–083, A54–084
property valuation arbitration, 13–053
rent review arbitration, 13–053
stating that, 2–878
substantive requirements, 2–878

INDEX

INTERIM MEASURES,
  American Arbitration Association
    International Arbitration Rules, A18–022
  arbitral tribunal,
    Model Law, A14–017, A14–049
    UNCITRAL Arbitration Rules, A15–027
  ICC arbitration, A39–025
  international arbitration, 9–125—9–128
  LCIA arbitration, 9–027, A44–026
  Model Law, A15–017, A15–019
  UNCITRAL Arbitration Rules, A15–027
  WIPO arbitration, A52–046
INTERIM REVIEW,
  WTO dispute settlement, A53–015
INTERLOCUTORY STAGES,
  courts, in, 2–021
  involvement of arbitrator in, 2–020
INTERNATIONAL ARBITRATION, 9–001—9–171
  ad hoc arbitration, 9–044—9–051
    appointment arrangements, 9–048
    difficulties, 9–045, 9–046
    fees, 9–049—9–051
    gaps in agreement, 9–046
    generally, 9–044
    meaning, 9–044
    UNCITRAL rules, 9–046, 9–048, 9–049
  amiable composition, 9–089—9–092
  applicable law. *See* choice of law *below*
  appointment of arbitrators, 9–101—9–119
    AAA arbitration, 9–102
    bias, appearance of, 9–111—9–114
    disqualifying factors, 9–118
    factors affecting, 9–106
    grey area, 9–120, 9–121
    impartiality, 9–107—9–116
    independence, 9–107—9–116
    LCIA arbitration, 9–102, 9–105
    non-disqualifying factors, 9–117, 9–118
    number of arbitrators, 9–101
    party-appointed arbitrators, 9–115, 9–116
    sole arbitrator, 9–102, 9–103
    three-member tribunal, 9–103
  arbitral tribunal,
    appointment, 9–101—9–119
    preliminary applications, 9–122—9–150
  arbitration agreement,
    ad hoc arbitration, 9–046
    arbitral institution, 9–056
    avoided, provisions to be, 9–056
    drafting, 9–052—9–056
    equivocation, 9–056
    indispensable elements, 9–053
    model clauses, changing, 9–056
    occasionally useful elements, 9–055
    procedural laws, 9–056
    recommended contents, 9–054
  arbitrators,
    appointment, 9–101—9–119
    approach, 9–095
    bias, appearance of, 9–111—9–114

INTERNATIONAL ARBITRATION—*cont.*
  arbitrators—*cont.*
    discretion, 9–093
    impartiality, 9–107—9–116
    independence, 9–107—9–116
    party-appointed, 9–115, 9–116
  Belgium, 9–064
  benefits, 9–002
  challenges to jurisdiction, 9–123, 9–124
  choice of law, 9–065—9–092
    amiable composition, 9–089—9–092
    arbitration agreement, 9–067
    capacity, 9–066
    concurrent laws, 9–078, 9–079
    equity clauses, 9–089—9–092
    freezing law, clauses, 9–080—9–082
    general principles of law, 9–076, 9–077
    lex mercatoria, 9–083—9–085
    national law, 9–072—9–075
    no choice of law in contract, 10–107—10–110
    private contracts, 9–082
    procedure, 9–066
    relevant systems, 9–065
    Rome Convention, 9–069—9–071
    rules of law, implied, 9–075
    stabilisation clause, 9–081
    state contracts, 9–080
    substance of dispute, law governing, 9–068—9–071
    systems, relevant, 9–086—9–088
    trade usage, 9–086—9–088
    Washington Convention, 9–079
  conclusions, 9–167—9–171
  concurrent laws, 9–078, 9–079
  conduct of hearing, 2–784
  consent, 9–093
  consequences of involvement in, 9–001—9–004
  conservatory measures, 9–125—9–128
  de-localised arbitration, 9–059
  disadvantages, 9–002
  discovery, 9–129—9–134
  discretion of arbitrators, 9–093
  equity clauses, 9–089—9–092
  evidence, 9–150
  experts, 9–143—9–149
    approaches, 9–143, 9–144
    battle of experts, 9–143
    IBA Rules of Evidence, 9–146, 9–148
    ICC arbitration, 9–144
    LCIA arbitration, 9–144
    report, 9–146
    technical issues, 9–145
    tribunal-appointed, 9–147, 9–148
    UNCITRAL Model Law, 9–149
  factual witnesses, 9–141, 9–142
  fees, *ad hoc* arbitration, 9–049—9–051
  FIDIC. *See* FIDIC Conditions
  flexibility, need for, 9–094, 9–095
  freezing law, clauses, 9–080—9–082

1083

INTERNATIONAL ARBITRATION—cont.
   Geneva Convention, 9–006, 9–007
   Hague Conference on Private International Law, 9–004
   IBA Rules of Evidence, 9–099
   ICC arbitration. See ICC arbitration
   ICC. See ICC arbitration
   ICSID. See ICSID arbitration
   institutional arbitration, 9–012
   interim measures, 9–125—9–128
   International Centre for the Settlement of Investment Disputes. See ICSID
   International Chamber of Commerce. See ICC arbitration
   International Federation of Consulting Engineers. See FIDIC Conditions
   Kompetenz-Kompetenz, 9–123
   law governing procedure of arbitration, 9–058
   LCIA. See LCIA arbitration
   lex mercatoria, 9–083—9–085
   London Court of International Arbitration. See LCIA
   maritime arbitration. See Maritime arbitration
   meaning, 2–071
   multi-party arbitrations, 9–164—9–166
      challenges, 9–166
      horizontal, 9–165
      ICC Report on, 9–165
      precautions, 9–165
      procedural difficulties, 9–164
      reasons for, 9–164
      UNCITRAL Notes, 9–166
      vertical, 9–165
   nationality of parties, 9–095
   New York Convention, 9–005
   norms, international, 9–096, 9–097
   number of arbitrators, 9–101
   oral hearing,
      decision-making, 9–152
      examination of witnesses, 9–160
      IBA Rules, 9–162
      ICC arbitration, 9–153
      limited submissions, 9–158
      order of witnesses, 9–159
      presence of witnesses when not testifying, 9–161, 9–162
      purpose, 9–151—9–154
      timescale, 9–155—9–157
      UNCITRAL Notes, 9–155, 9–161
   order of proceedings, 9–156—9–163
      generally, 9–156, 9–157
   place of arbitration, 9–057
      Belgium, 9–064
      choosing, 9–060—9–062
      leading venues, 9–064
      traditional situs, advantages of, 9–063
   practice, in, 9–093—9–171

INTERNATIONAL ARBITRATION—cont.
   preliminary applications, 9–122—9–136
      challenges to jurisdiction, 9–123, 9–124
      conservatory measures, 9–125—9–128
      generally, 9–122
      interim measures, 9–125—9–128
      reasons for the production of documents, 9–129—9–134
      scope, 9–122
      substantive issues, 9–135, 9–136
   procedural norms, 9–100—9–171
   reasons for agreeing to, 9–002, 9–005
   role of, 9–001—9–008
   Rome Convention, 9–069—9–071
   success of, 9–003
   Treaties. See Treaties
   types, 9–009—9–011
   VAT, 2–397
   Washington Convention on the Settlement of Investment Disputes, 9–006, 9–079
   WIPO arbitration. See WIPO arbitration
   witnesses, 9–141, 9–142
   World Intellectual Property Organisation. See WIPO arbitration
   written statements, 9–137—9–140
      factual witnesses, 9–141, 9–142
   written submissions, 9–138—9–140
INTERNATIONAL BAR ASSOCIATION RULES. See IBA Rules
INTERNATIONAL CENTRE FOR EXPERTISE, A42–002
INTERNATIONAL CHAMBER OF COMMERCE,
   ADR. See ICC ADR Rules
   arbitration. See ICC Arbitration
   International Centre for Expertise, A42–002
   mediation. See ICC mediation
   Rules for Expertise, A42–001—A42–026
      administration, A42–010—A42–016
      appointment of experts, A42–006—A42–009
      costs, A42–024—A42–026
      exclusion of liability, A42–018
      proposal of experts, A42–003—A42–005
      spirit of rules, acting in, A42–019
      Statutes of the Standing Committee of the International Centre for Expertise, A42–020—A42–023
      waiver, A42–017
INTERNATIONAL COURT OF ARBITRATION, A39–003
   See also ICC arbitration
   internal rules, A39–045—A39–050
   removal of arbitrator, 15–052
   Statutes, A39–038—A39–044
INTERNATIONAL COURT OF ARBITRATION FOR SPORT (ICAS), 15–039
   attributions, A29–003
   composition, 15–043, A29–002
   functions, 15–042, 15–043, A29–003

INDEX

INTERNATIONAL COURT OF ARBITRATION FOR
  SPORT (ICAS)—cont.
  membership, 15–043, A29–002
  operation, A29–004
  role, 15–042
INTERNATIONAL FEDERATION OF CONSULTING
    ENGINEERS. See FIDIC Conditions
INTERNATIONAL SUPPLY CONTRACTS,
  unfair contract terms, A1–027
INTERPLEADER PROCEEDINGS,
  meaning, 2–173
  staying court proceedings, 2–173—2–175
INTERPRETATION OF AWARD,
  American Arbitration Association
      International Arbitration Rules, A18–031
  UNCITRAL Arbitration Rules, A15–036
INTERROGATORIES, 2–712
INVESTMENT TREATY ARBITRATION,
  applicable law, 10–022—10–025
    host state law, 10–023—10–025
    ICSID arbitration, 10–023—10–025
    international law, 10–021
  arbitrary or discriminatory measures
      impairing investment, no, 10–032, 10–033
  ASEAN Agreement for the Promotion and
      Protection of Investments, 10–010
  availability, 10–001
  bilateral investment treaties (BITs), 10–002
    appeal, 10–007—10–009
    awards, 10–006
    cases, 10–006
    innovation, 10–009
    rise on, 10–006
  breach of obligations by host state, 10–021—10–042
    applicable law, 10–022—10–025
    arbitrary or discriminatory measures
        impairing investment, no, 10–032, 10–033
    fair and equitable treatment, 10–027—10–029
    free transfer of funds related to
        investments, 10–042
    full protection and security, 10–030, 10–031
    generally, 10–021
    most favoured nation treatment, 10–035—10–037
    national treatment, 10–035—10–037
    prompt, adequate and effective
        compensation, no expropriation
        without, 10–038—10–041
    protection, overview of, 10–026—10–047
  Chorzów Factory rule, 10–060
  Colonia and Buenos Aires Investment
      Protocols of Mercosur, 10–010
  compensation, 10–061—10–063
  conclusions on, 10–064, 10–065

INVESTMENT TREATY ARBITRATION—cont.
  conditions for exercise of rights, 10–048—10–052
    bypassing procedural requirements on
        basis of MFN clause, 10–052
    consultation period, 10–048—10–052
    negotiation period, 10–048—10–050
    prior recourse to host state courts, 10–051
    consultation period, 10–048—10–050
    contract remedies and, 10–046, 10–047
    covered investor, whether investment
        belongs to, 10–019, 10–020
    customary international law, 10–008
    direct access, 10–043—10–047
      contract remedies and, 10–046, 10–047
      "fork in the road" provision, 10–044, 10–045
      option under treaty, arbitration as, 10–043
    direct control of investing company, 10–013—10–015
    Energy Charter Treaty 1994, 10–01
    fair and equitable treatment, 10–027—10–029
      general notion, 10–027
      international case law, 10–028
      international minimum standard, 10–029
      NAFTA arbitration, 10–028, 10–029
    first case, 10–004, 10–005
    free transfer of funds related to investments,
        10–042
    full protection and security,
      due diligence, 10–030
      meaning, 10–030
      physical and legal protection of
          investments, 10–031
      strict liability standard, 10–030
    Group of Three Agreement 1990, chapter 17
        of, 10–010
    growth in, 10–064
    ICSID. See ICSID arbitration
    identification of potentially applicable treaty,
        10–011
    indirect control of investing company, 10–013—10–015
    investment, 10–016, 10–017, 10–018
    investors entitled to rely on, 10–012
    monetary compensation, 10–061—10–063
    most favoured nation treatment, 10–035—10–037, 10–052
    multilateral investment treaties (MITs), 10–002
      advent, 10–010
      ASEAN Agreement for the Promotion and
          Protection of Investments, 10–010
      Colonia and Buenos Aires Investment
          Protocols of Mercosur, 10–010
      Energy Charter Treaty 1994, 10–010
      Group of Three Agreement 1990, chapter
          17 of, 10–010
      NAFTA arbitration 10–002. See also
          NAFTA arbitration

1085

INDEX

INVESTMENT TREATY ARBITRATION—cont.
  national treatment, 10–035—10–037
  negotiation period, 10–048—10–050
  new territory of, 10–001—10–003
  overview, 10–004—10–010
  prior recourse to host state courts, 10–051
  proliferation, 10–064
  prompt, adequate and effective
      compensation, no expropriation without,
      10–038—10–041
    direct and indirect takings, 10–039—
      10–041
  protected investment,
    definition, 10–016
    meaning, 10–016
  reparation, 10–060—10–063
    Chorzów Factory rule, 10–060
    monetary compensation, 10–061—10–063
    restitution, 10–062
  restitution, 10–062
  selecting arbitration option,
    factors affecting choice, 10–058—10–059
    institutional options, 10–054—10–056
    non-institutional options, 10–057
    treaty provisions, 10–053
  significance, 9–008
  specific investment undertakings, observance
    of, 10–034
  without privity, 10–001, 10–002
ISSUES,
  defining, 2–788
ISSUES OF LAW. *See* Law, issues of

JCT MANAGEMENT CONTRACT, 6–072
JCT STANDARD FORM CONTRACT, 6–005,
  6–046, 6–065—6–078
  Appendix, 6–046, 6–065
  appointment of arbitrator, 6–065
  arbitration agreement, 6–046
  arbitrator,
    jurisdiction, 6–065
  articles of agreement, 6–046
  CIMAR, incorporation of, 6–065
    mandatory procedures, 6–066
    optional procedures, 6–067, 6–068
  conditions, 6–035
  documents only arbitration, 6–067
  elements of arbitration agreement, 6–046
  Final Certificate, 6–071
  full procedure, 6–067
  influences on, 6–012
  jurisdiction, 6–065
  powers of arbitrator, 6–068
  procedures, 6–065—6–070
  rules, arbitration,
    incorporation, 6–046
  short hearing, 6–067
JCT WORKS CONTRACT, 6–072
JOINDER OF DISPUTES,
  CIMAR, 6–038, A28–003

JOINDER OF PARTIES,
  LCIA arbitration, 9–028
JOINT AND SEVERAL LIABILITY,
  Arbitration Act 1996, A6–029
  remuneration of arbitrator, 2–345
JUDGEMENT, ESTOPPEL BY, 2–887
JUDGES,
  arbitrators, appointed as, A6–113—A6–124
JUDGING TECHNIQUES, 2–860—2–872
  admissibility of evidence, 2–872
  burden of proof, 2–869
  calculation errors, 2–870
  conflicts of fact, 2–865, 2–866
  demeanour, judgments based on, 2–866
  errors, calculation, 2–870
  experience of judging, 2–860—2–872
  fact, deciding issues of, 2–865, 2–866
  interim awards, 2–870
  interventions, 2–864
  intra-cranial jury room, 2–868
  knowledge and experience of arbitration,
    2–863
  law, deciding issues of, 2–871
  obvious version of events, 2–865
  "team spirit", 2–867
  understanding judicial process, 2–861
  unequal representation, 2–864
  using advocates, 2–862
  written evidence, 2–865
JUDICIAL REVIEW,
  award, A63–001
JURISDICTION,
  agricultural property arbitration, 3–028,
    3–029
  American Arbitration Association
    International Arbitration Rules, A18–
    016
  Arbitration Act 1996, A6–031—A6–033
    competence to rule on own jurisdiction,
      A6–031
    objections to substantive jurisdiction, A6–
      032
    preliminary points, determination of, A6–
      033
  challenging, 2–079, 2–084—2–086
    absence of agreement by the parties, 2–
      329
    addressing the issue, 2–331
    aim of 1996 Act, 2–324
    arbitral tribunal, 2–328
    consequences, 2–327
    cost savings argument, 2–327
    ex parte proceedings, 2–334
    Harbour Assurance v Kansa, moving on
      from, 2–323, 2–338
    ICC arbitration, 2–325
    Kompetenz Kompetenz, 2–329
    LCA Rules, 2–325
    Model Law, 2–325
    options available to tribunal, 2–331
    party autonomy, 2–332

INDEX

JURISDICTION—cont.
  challenging—cont.
    procedure, 2–322—2–334
    timing, 2–330, 2–333
  claim or procedure outside agreement, 2–335
  Court of Arbitration for Sport (CAS), 15–046—15–049
  deciding on own,
    establishment of principle, 2–083
    power to the arbitrators, 2–087
  default provisions, 2–088
  defence where lacking, 2–946
  farm business tenancy arbitration, 3–108
  ICC arbitration, 2–325
  ICSID arbitration,
    objections, 10–056
  JCT Standard Form Contract, 6–065
  Kompetenz Kompetenz, 2–083, 2–326, 2–329
  LCIA arbitration, 2–325, A44–024
  LMAA arbitration, A46–004
  Sport Dispute Resolution Panel, 15–024
  sports arbitration, 15–008
  staying court proceedings, 2–144
  widening ambit of arbitrator's jurisdiction, 2–334—2–336
  WIPO arbitration, A52–036
  writing, outcome of issues recorded in, 2–336
  WTO dispute settlement, 17–005
JURY TRIAL,
  influence, 2–526—2–529
JUSTICE,
  private, 2–014
  public, 2–014

KOMPETENZ KOMPETENZ, 9–123
  establishment of principle, 2–083
  meaning, 2–329
  Sport Dispute Resolution Panel, 15–026
  staying court proceedings, 2–180—2–186
KUALA LUMPUR REGIONAL CENTRE FOR ARBITRATION,
  arbitration clause, A54–018

LAND,
  specific performance of contracts relating to, no, 2–337
LANGUAGE OF PROCEEDINGS,
  American Arbitration Association International Arbitration Rules, A18–015
  Court of Arbitration for Sport (CAS), A29–011
  ICC arbitration, A39–18
  LCIA arbitration, A44–018
  Model Law, A14–022
  UNCITRAL Arbitration Rules, A15–018
  WIPO arbitration, A52–040

LAPSE OF CLAIM,
  GAFTA, 16–102
LATE PAYMENT OF COMMERCIAL DEBTS (INTEREST) ACT 1998, A64–001—A64–019
  advance payments of the contract price, A64–013
  advocates, application of Act to, A64–003
  assignments, A64–015
  compensation arising out of late payment, A64–007
  conflict of laws, A64–014
  contracts to which Act applies, A64–003
  date of payment of the contract price, A64–011
  interpretation, A64–012, A64–018
  orders and regulations, A64–017
  qualifying debts, A64–004
  statutory interest, A64–001
    ouster, A64–010
    period for which runs, A64–005
    rate, A64–008
    remission, A64–006
    variation, A64–010
  substantial remedy, A64–011
LAW, ISSUES OF, 2–726—2–732
  amiable compositeur, arbitrator acting, 2–727
  Arbitration Act 1996, s.46, 2–727
  contract, meaning of, 2–871
  deciding, 2–871
  estoppel, 2–732
  ex aequo et bono, arbitrator acting, 2–727
  formulating the issue, 2–728
  judging techniques, 2–871
  legal advice, taking, 2–731
  legally qualified chairman or umpire, 2–730
  meaning, 2–726
  resolution of issue, 2–729
  substantive law, 2–726
  voie directe, 2–727
LCIA ARBITRATION, 9–023—9–031
  additional award, 9–029, A44–028
  additional powers of arbitral tribunal, A44–023
  appointment of arbitrators, 9–102, 9–105
  approval of award, 9–029
  arbitral tribunal,
    additional powers, A44–023
    communications, A44–014
    expedited formation, A44–010
    formation, A44–006
    jurisdiction, A44–024
  arbitration clause, A54–012
  arbitrators,
    communications, A44–014
    nationality, A44–007
    nomination, A44–008, A44–009, A44–012
    party nomination, A44–008
    revocation of appointment, A44–011
    three or more parties, nomination by, A44–009

1087

LCIA ARBITRATION—*cont.*
award, A44–027
additional, A44–028
correction, A44–028
background, 9–023
case load, 9–023
challenging arbitrators, 9–029
clerical mistakes, 9–029
communications between parties and arbitral tribunal, A44–014
conduct of proceedings, A44–015
confidentiality, A44–031
conservatory measures, 9–027, A44–026
correcting mistakes, 9–029
correction of award, 9–028, A44–028
costs, A44–029
deposits, A44–025
evidence, 9–028
exclusion of liability, A44–032
expedited formation, 9–027
experts, 9–144, A44–022
general rules, A44–033
governing law, 9–024
hearing, A44–020
interim measures, 9–027, A44–026
joinder of parties, 9–028
jurisdiction, 2–325, A44–024
language, 9–023
language of arbitration, A44–018
LCIA Court, A44–004
decisions, A44–030
majority power to continue proceedings, A44–013
membership, 9–024
multi-party disputes, 6–096
nationality of arbitrators, 9–024, 9–025, A44–007
nomination of arbitrators, A44–012
notice of arbitration, A44–005
online dispute resolution, 12–087—12–089
party-nomination process, 9–026
periods of time, A44–005
place of arbitration, A44–017
presumption of sole arbitrator, 9–026
proceedings, 9–028
purpose, 9–023
Registrar, A44–004
remuneration of arbitrator, 2–394, 9–030
replacement of arbitrators, A44–012
representation, A44–019
request for arbitration, A44–002
response to request, A44–003
revocation of appointment, A44–011
seat of arbitration, A44–017
sole arbitrator, 9–026
submission of written statements and documents, A44–016
terms of reference, 9–029
witnesses, A44–021
written statements, 9–137, A44–016

LCIA MEDIATION,
appointment of mediator, A45–004
commencement of mediation,
no prior agreement, A45–003
prior existing agreements to mediate, A45–002
conclusion of mediation, A45–007
conduct of mediation, A45–006
confidentiality, A45–011
costs, A45–009
exclusion of liability, A45–012
generally, A45–001
judicial or arbitral proceedings, A45–010
prior existing agreements to mediate, A45–002
privacy, A45–011
settlement agreement, A45–008
statements by the parties, A45–005
LEGAL ADVICE,
property valuation arbitration, 13–023
rent review arbitration, 13–023
LEGAL PROFESSIONAL PRIVILEGE,
litigation/arbitration is contemplated or pending, 2–701
whether or not litigation/arbitration contemplated or pending, 2–700
LEGAL REPRESENTATION,
See also Representation
Arbitration Act 1996, A6–037
LEGAL SERVICES OMBUDSMAN, 18–013—18–015
exclusions from remit, 18–117
function, 18–116
generally, 18–013
investigatory powers, 18–014
Office for the Supervision of Solicitors, 18–116—18–118
recommendations, 18–015, 18–118
LEGGATT REPORT, 4–054, 4–055
LENGTH OF ARBITRATION,
adjournment, 2–312
cancellation charges, 2–313
overrunning, 2–312
preparation time, 2–313
LEX MERCATORIA, 9–083—9–085
LIEN,
remuneration of arbitrator, 2–344
LINER SHIPPING, 11–008
LIST OF ISSUES, 2–689—2–694
alteration, 2–691
benefits, 2–691
enlargement, 2–691
index, as, 2–694
modification, 2–691
note management, 2–694
pre-hearing review, 2–693
preparation, 2–689
tribunal approach, 2–690
LITIGANTS IN PERSON,
costs, 14–091
small claims in county court, 14–091

INDEX

LITIGATION,
  advantages, 2–035—2–040
  advocate, 2–822
  alternative to arbitration, 2–009
  arbitration,
    compared, 2–011—2–015
    differences between, 2–016—2–022
  authoritive decision required, 2–039
  award condition precedent to, 2–128
  Civil Procedure Rules. *See* Civil Procedure Rules
  class actions, 2–038
  commercial litigation, problems of, 2–017
  construction industry and, 2–037
  costs, 2–030
  decision-making, 2–023
  enforcement, 2–034
  fast track procedures, 2–607
  function, 2–009
  interlocutory stages, 2–020
  meaning, 2–011
  multi-party disputes, 2–035, 2–036
  pleadings, 2–668
  pre-action protocols, 2–567
  preferable, when, 2–035—2–040
  preparations for hearing, 2–020
  publicity, 2–014
  representation, 2–025
  role of court, 2–569
  settlement, as incentive to, 2–734
  states, 2–568
  summary judgment, 2–607
  technical evidence, 2–022
LMAA,
  applicable law, 11–076
  appointment fees, 11–095
  arbitration clause, 11–028
  availability of arbitrator, 11–054
  booking fees, 11–096, 11–097
  chain arbitration, 11–078—11–080
  Clause, 11–028
  confidential reasons, 11–089, 11–090
  establishment, 11–032
  functions, 11–033, 11–034
  meaning, 11–032
  mediation. *See* LMAA mediation terms
  membership, 11–034
  powers of arbitrators, 11–077
  purpose, 11–032
  qualifications of arbitrators, 11–034
  seat of arbitration, 11–076
  small claims procedure. *See* LMAA small claims procedure
  supporting membership, 11–034
  terms. *See* LMAA terms
LMAA MEDIATION TERMS,
  admissibility of evidence in other proceedings, A48–016
  application, A48–002
  appointment of mediator, A48–005
  co-operation of pars, A48–008

LMAA MEDIATION TERMS—*cont.*
  commencement of mediation, A48–004
  confidentiality, A48–010
  costs,
    mediator's, A48–013
    parties', A48–014
  duties of mediator, A48–007
  exchange of information, A48–006
  number of mediators, A48–003
  other proceedings, role of mediator in, A48–015
  powers of mediator, A48–007
  purpose, A48–002
  resort of arbitration or judicial proceedings, A48–012
  settlement agreement, A48–009
  termination of mediation procedure, A48–011
LMAA SMALL CLAIMS PROCEDURE,
  appeals, 11–102, A47–004
  appointment of arbitrator, 11–102, A47–002
  award, 11–102, A47–007
  commentary, A47–010—A47–018
  costs, 11–102, A47–008
  disclosure of documents, A47–006
  features, 11–102
  fees, 11–102, A47–003
  generally, A47–009
  oral hearing, 11–102
  procedure, A47–005
  recommended use, 11–101
  suitability, 11–101
  timetable, 11–102
  use, 11–101
LMAA TERMS, 11–035, 11–036, 11–057
  See also Maritime arbitration
  accommodation, A46–021
  adjournment, A46–010
  applicable law, 11–076
  application, A46–002
  application of, 11–075
  appointment fees, 11–095
  arbitral tribunal, A46–003
    jurisdiction, A46–004
    powers of tribunal, A46–008
    reconstitution, A46–027
  arbitration clause, A54–013
  availability of arbitrators, A46–011
  award, A46–012
  booking fees, 11–096, 11–097
  busy arbitrator, 11–061, 11–062
  chain arbitration, 11–078—11–080
  commentary, A46–028
  dispensing with reasons, 11–090
  fees, A46–015—A46–020
  generally, A46–014
  hearing date, 11–073
  interlocutory proceedings, A46–007
  jurisdiction, A46–004
  powers of arbitrators, 11–077
  powers of tribunal, A46–008

1089

LMAA TERMS—*cont.*
  preliminary matters, A46–001
  preliminary meetings, A46–024—A46–026
  procedure, A46–006, A46–022
  questionnaire, A46–023
  seat of arbitration, 11–076
  service of documents, A46–013
  settlement, A46–010
  string arbitration, 11–078—11–080
LME, 16–001, 16–015, 16–016—16–037
  administrative simplicity, 16–034
  appointment of arbitrators, 16–019, 16–020
  arbitrators,
    application to be, 16–017
    background, 16–017
    nomination, 16–017
    prerequisites, 16–018
    qualifications, 16–017, 16–018
  award, 16–032—16–034
  base metals traded on, 16–016
  challenging arbitrator, 16–023
  commencement of arbitration, 16–021, 16–022
  communications, 16–037
  consolidation, 16–034
  directions, 16–026
  discretion, 16–036
  disputes, 16–016
  documents, 16–024—16–026
  hearing, 16–026
  lawyers, role of, 16–027—16–029
  notice to arbitrate, 16–021, 16–022
  points of claim, 16–024, 16–025
  powers of tribunal, 16–030, 16–031
  role, 16–016
  settlement, 16–026
  submissions, 16–024—16–026
  time limits, 16–035
LONDON,
  influence of, 2–062
  maritime arbitration, 11–006
LONDON CORN TRADE ASSOCIATION, 16–084
LONDON COURT OF INTERNATIONAL ARBITRATION,
  arbitration rules. *See* LCIA arbitration
  mediation. *See* LCIA mediation
LONDON MARITIME ARBITRATORS ASSOCIATION,
  mediation. *See* LMAA mediation terms
  small claims. *See* LMAA small claims procedure
  terms. *See* LMAA terms
LONDON METAL EXCHANGE (LME). *See* LME
LONDON RICE BROKERS' ASSOCIATION (LRBA), 16–002
LOOK-SNIFF ARBITRATION,
  arbitrator, 2–044
  certificates, 16–005
  costs, 2–052
  disputes, 16–005
  free average quality, 16–005

LOOK-SNIFF ARBITRATION—*cont.*
  meaning, 16–005
  powers of arbitrators, 2–466
  procedure, available, 2–466
  technical disputes, 16–005
LRBA, 16–002

MARITIME ARBITRATION,
  ad hoc arbitration, 11–007
  administered arbitration, 11–007
  Admiralty Court, 11–002
  applicable law, 11–076
  appointment of arbitrator,
    "all disputes arising", 11–037
    arbitration clause, 11–037
    commercial men, requirement that, 11–045
    default in appointment, 11–041
    identity, 11–044, 11–045
    notice of appointment, 11–040
    sole arbitrator, 11–038
    third arbitrator, 11–042, 11–043
    umpire, 11–043
  arbitration clauses, 11–019—11–031
    appointment of arbitrator, 11–037
    Asbatankvoy Clause, 11–025
    Baltime Clause, 11–020
    Centrocon Clause, 11–021
    choosing between clauses, 11–029—11–031
    LMAA Clause, 11–028
    New York Produce Exchange form Clause, 11–022, 11–023
    Norwegian Saleform Clause, 11–026, 11–027
    standard form contracts, 11–019
  Asbatankvoy Clause, 11–025
  awards, 11–084—11–092
    confidential reasons, 11–089, 11–090
    dispensing with reasons, 11–090
    draft, 11–087
    interim, 11–084—11–086
    open reasons, 11–091
    publication of award, 11–092
    reasons, 11–088—11–091
    writing, 11–087
  Baltic Exchange, 11–005
  Baltime Clause, 11–020
  booking fees, 11–096, 11–097
  busy arbitrator, 11–061, 11–062
  Centrocon Clause, 11–021
  chain arbitration, 11–078—11–080
  charterparty, 11–004
  club managers, 11–017, 11–018
  collisions between ships, 11–002
  common, why arbitration is, 11–008—11–011
  communication, mode of, 11–074
  confidential reasons, 11–089, 11–090
  contracts, arising under, 11–001

INDEX

MARITIME ARBITRATION—cont.
  date of hearing, 11–073
  default in appointment, 11–041
  default cases, 11–081
  defence, 11–064
  defence clubs, 11–012
  disclosure of documents, 11–068
  dispensing with reasons, 11–090
  disponent owner, meaning, 11–011
  draft award, 11–087
  extension of time for starting, 11–039
  fees of arbitrator,
    appointment fees, 11–095
    basis, 11–093, 11–094
    booking fees, 11–096, 11–097
    scales, 11–094
  fixing hearing dates, 11–073
  hearing date, 11–073
  impartiality, 11–046—11–054
    availability of arbitrator, 11–054
    formalities, 11–047
    "my arbitrator", 11–048, 11–049
    problem of, 11–046
    three-member tribunals, 11–050—11–053
  institutions involved in, 11–007
  interim awards, 11–084—11–086
  interlocutory applications, 11–069
    unnecessary costs, 11–070
  international, 11–005
  lawyers, representation by, 11–017, 11–018
  lay claim handlers, 11–018
  liner shipping, 11–008
  LMAA. See LMAA terms
  London, 11–006
  London Maritime Arbitrators Association.
    See LMAA terms
  meaning, 11–001, 11–002
  New York, 11–104—11–106
  New York Produce Exchange form Clause, 11–022, 11–023
  Norwegian Saleform Clause, 11–026, 11–027
  notice of appointment, 11–040, 11–042
  number, 11–010
  open reasons, 11–091
  outside U.K, 11–103—11–113
    generally, 11–103
    New York, 11–104—11–106
  P&I Associations, 11–012, 11–014
  Paris, 11–107—11–110
  parties, 11–011
  payments on account, 11–098
  place of, 11–005—11–007
  popularity, 11–008—11–011
  powers of arbitrators, 11–077
  preliminary meetings, 11–065
  proceedings with, 11–055—11–074
    busy arbitrator, 11–061, 11–062
    freedom to choose procedure, 11–056
    procedure, 11–055
  publication of award, 11–092

MARITIME ARBITRATION—cont.
  purpose, 11–003, 11–004
  questionnaire, 11–065, 11–067
  reasons for award, 11–088—11–091
  representation,
    club managers, 11–017
    defence clubs, 11–012, 11–015, 11–016
    lawyers, by, 11–017, 11–018
    P&I Associations, 11–013, 11–014
  resignation of arbitrator, 11–099
  salvage arbitrations, 11–002
  scope of text, 11–002
  seat of arbitration, 11–005, 11–076
  security for costs, 11–072, 11–074, 11–100
  Small Claims Procedure, 11–036
  sole arbitrator, 11–038
  standard form contracts, 11–0219
  starting, 11–037—11–045
    appointment of arbitrator, 11–037
    default in appointment, 11–041
    extension of time for, 11–039
    notice of appointment, 11–040
    sole arbitrator, 11–038
    third arbitrator, appointment, 11–042, 11–043
    umpire, appointment of, 11–043
  third arbitrator, appointment of, 11–042, 11–043
  three-member tribunals, impartiality, 11–050—11–053
  Tokyo, 11–111—11–113
  tramp shipping, 11–008, 11–009
  umpire, appointment of, 11–043
  uses, 11–003, 11–004
  writing award, 4–978, 11–087
  written submissions, 11–063, 11–064
    procedure following, 11–065
MED-ARB,
  Bermuda, 4–029
  China, 4–034
  forms, 4–033
  Hong Kong, 4–029
  India, 4–029
  meaning, 4–033
  practical use, 2–738, 2–739
  settlements, 2–738, 2–739
  Singapore, 4–029
  use, 4–029
MEDIATION,
  See also ADR
  agreement to mediate, 4–008
  alternative to arbitration, 2–009
  arbitration clause, A54–128
  arbitration distinguished, 4–030
  attitude of mediator, 4–005—4–009
  balance of power, 4–012
  basis of decisions, 4–032
  categories of dispute expected to go to, 2–002
  CEDR Rules for Adjudication, 4–009, A19–008

MEDIATION—cont.
City Disputes Panel. *See* City Disputes Panel Mediation Rules
commodity trade arbitration, 16–013, 16–014
conduct, 4–010—4–013
construction industry, 6–030
costs, 4–052
Court of Arbitration for Sport (CAS), A31–001—A31–015
  appointment of mediator, A31–006, A31–007
  commencement of mediation, A31–005
  conduct of mediation, A31–009
  confidentiality, A31–011
  costs, A31–015
  definitions, A31–002, A31–003
  failure to settle, A31–014
  representation, A31–008
  role of mediator, A31–010
  scope of application of rules, A31–004
  settlement, A31–013
  termination, A31–012
duty of mediator, 4–031
evaluative, 4–011
facilitative, 4–011
GAFTA. *See* GAFTA mediation
good faith, 4–031
impartiality of mediator, 4–010
increasing use, 1–013
London Court of International Arbitration. *See* LCIA mediation
meaning, 2–009
medical records, access to, arbitrator, of, 2–308
natural justice, 4–031
objective, 4–031
online dispute resolution, 12–009—12–013, 12–136
role of mediator, 4–005
settlement, 4–013
shadow of the law, in, 4–002
stages, 4–007
USA, 4–006, 4–015
Walford v Miles, 4–053
WTO dispute settlement, 17–014, A53–005
MILK QUOTA ARBITRATIONS, 3–004—3–007, 3–090—3–099
action on appointment, 3–097, 3–098
appointment of arbitrator, 3–004, 3–092, 3–094, 3–095
apportionment of, 3–005, 3–011
asset, as, 3–004
changes in occupation, 3–004
circumstances of claim, 3–006
Common Agricultural Policy, 3–004
compensation claims, 3–007
conduct, 3–090
creation, 3–004
death of arbitrator, 3–096
formalities, 3–096

MILK QUOTA ARBITRATIONS—cont.
holding, 3–006, 3–007
joinder of parties, 3–097, 3–098
legal status, 3–004
multi-party proceedings, 3–093
parts of holding, changes in occupation of, 3–004
procedure, 3–099
quitting part of land whilst retaining other part, 3–007
reference quantity, 3–004
registration, 3–004
regulations, 3–090
remuneration of arbitrator, 3–099
revocation of appointment, 3–096
statutory arbitrations, 3–005
summary of provisions on, 3–004
supervision of court, 3–099
technical disputes, 3–091
types of dispute, 3–091
writing requirements, 3–096
MISCONDUCT,
agricultural property arbitration, 3–083—3–086
public interest, disclosed in, 2–880
MISREPRESENTATION,
unfair contract terms, A1–009
MISTAKES IN AWARD,
correcting, 2–885, 2–886
MOCK TRIALS, 12–135
MODEL LAW, A14–001—A14–062
additional award, A14–033
adoption, 2–015
appointment of arbitrators, A14–011
arbitral proceedings,
  commencement, A14–021
  conduct, A14–050—A14–053
  court assistance in taking evidence, A14–027
  default of party, A14–14.025, A14–053
  defence, A14–023
  determination of rules of procedure, A14–019, A14–052
  equal treatment of parties, A14–018
  expert appointed by arbitral tribunal, A14–026
  hearings, A14–024
  language, A14–022
  place of arbitration, A14–020
  procedural rights of party, A14–051
  statements of claim, A14–023
  written proceedings, A14–024
arbitral tribunal,
  appointment of arbitrators, A14–011
  challenge, A14–012, A14–013
  composition, A14–010—A14–015
  interim measures, A14–017, A14–049
  jurisdiction, A14–016, A14–017, A14–048
  number of arbitrators, A14–010
  substitute arbitrator, A14–015

MODEL LAW—*cont.*
  arbitration agreement, A14–007—A14–009
    courts, A14–046
    definition, A14–007, A14–045, A14–0451
    form, A14–007, A14–045, A14–0451
    interim measures by court, A14–009
    substantive claim before court, A14–008
  award, 2–875
    additional award, A14–033
    content, A14–031
    correction, A14–033
    decision by panel of arbitrators, A14–029
    enforcement, A14–035, A14–036
    form, A14–031
    interpretation, A14–033
    making of award, A14–055
    recognition of award, A14–059—A14–062
    recourse against award, A14–034, A14–056
    refusal of recognition, A14–036
    setting aside, A14–034, A14–057, A14–058
    settlement, A14–030
    substance of dispute, A14–028, A14–054
    termination of proceedings, A14–032
  background, A14–038—A14–040
  correction of award, A14–033
  court intervention, extent of, A14–005, A14–043
  criticisms of, 2–062, 2–063
  DAC Report and, 2–059—2–064
  default of party, A14–14.025
  defence, A14–023
  definitions, A14–002
  enforcement of award, A14–035, A14–036
  expert appointed by arbitral tribunal, 9–149, A14–026
  explanatory note, A14–037
  functions of arbitration assistance and supervision, court for, A14–006
  hearings, A14–024
  impact, 2–015, 2–061
  importance, 9–076
  interim measures, A15–017, A15–019
  interpretation, A14–002
    award, A14–033
  jurisdiction, 2–325, A14–042, A14–048
  language, A14–022
  place of arbitration, A14–020
  purpose, 2–061, 9–076
  receipt of written communications, A14–003
  recognition of award, A14–059—A14–062
  recourse against award, A14–034
  refusal of recognition of award, A14–036
  regime established by, 2–061
  salient features, A14–041—A14–062
  scope of application, A14–001
  setting aside award, A14–034, A14–057, A14–058
  settlement, A14–030
  special procedural regime, A14–041

MODEL LAW—*cont.*
  statements of claim, A14–023
  termination of proceedings, A14–032
  territorial scope, A14–042
  three person tribunal, 2–238
  waiver of right to object, A14–004
MORTGAGES,
  Chartered Institute of Arbitrators Rules of the Mortgage Code Arbitration. *See* Chartered Institute of Arbitrators Rules of the Mortgage Code Arbitration
MOST FAVOURED NATION TREATMENT,
  investment treaty arbitration, 10–035—10–037, 10–052
MULTI-PARTY ARBITRATION, 2–626—2–652
  alternatives, 2–634
  concerns, 2–626
  concurrent arbitrations, 2–637
  consecutive arbitrations before same arbitrator, 2–640
  consolidated arbitration. *See* Consolidated arbitration
  construction industry arbitration, 6–024, 6–093, 6–096
  contract and sub-contract, 2–629
  costs, 2–639
  Court of Arbitration for Sport (CAS), 15–064—15–068, A29–025—A29–028
  court proceedings overriding arbitration clause, 2–641
  DAC, 2–627
  development of approaches, 2–627
  independent arbitrations before separate arbitrator, 2–634, 2–638
  LCIA Rules, 6–096
  networks of contracts, 2–628
  New York Convention, 2–626
  parallel claims against same respondent, 2–642, 2–643
    appointment of common arbitrator, 2–648
    contractual provision for third party situations, 2–649
    courts, attitude of, 2–643
    interlocking arbitration clauses, 2–650
    respondent's rights, 2–647
    string contracts, 2–651
  party autonomy, 2–627
  solutions, possible, 2–628
  UNCITRAL Notes on Organizing Arbitral Proceedings, 9–166, A15–005
MULTI-PARTY LITIGATION, 2–035, 2–036, 2–636
MULTILATERAL TREATIES, 9–068, 9–069
MUSTILL REPORT,
  See also DAC Report
  objectives, 1–001

NATIONAL ARBITRATION FORUM, 12–111
NATIONAL ASSOCIATION OF RETAIL FURNISHERS, 8–011

INDEX

NATIONAL HOUSE BUILDING COUNCIL, 8–011, 8–014
NATIONAL TREATMENT,
  investment treaty arbitration, 10–035—10–037
NATIONALITY,
  international arbitration, 9–095
  LCIA arbitration, A44–007
  WIPO arbitration, A52–021
NATURAL JUSTICE, 2–414—2–455
  advice, arbitrator seeking, 2–347
  ambushes, 2–427
  beliefs, conflicting, 2–431
  bias of arbitrator, 2–414
  Calderbank offer, 2–445
  circulating draft award, 2–443
  communications to arbitrator, 2–417
  conflicting beliefs, 2–431
  date of hearing, 2–425
  disclosure, 2–430
  disinterested and unbiased arbitrator,
    generally, 2–414
    reasonable man test, 2–416
    statutory provisions, 2–415
    test for, 2–275
  Doherty, 2–454
  draft award, 2–443—2–445
    Calderbank offer, 2–445
  Egmatra case, 2–451
  evidence properly before the tribunal, 2–436
  ex parte hearing, 2–439
  fair opportunity to present case, 2–421—2–422
  fixing dates, 2–425
  Fletamentos case, 2–453
  fundamental requirements, 2–414—2–420
  Gbangbola case, 2–450
  GC/Works contract, 2–447, 2–448
  "helpful" contributions from the tribunal, 2–440
  impartially, duty to act, 2–416
  inappropriate behaviour, 2–417
  independence, 2–419
  information obtained on inspection, 2–432
  inspection, 2–432
    institutional timetables, 2–426
  knowledge of case, 2–422, 2–423
  knowledge and experience of arbitrator, 2–428—2–442
    beliefs, conflicting, 2–431
    chosen for, arbitrator, 2–429
    conflicting beliefs, 2–287
    disclosure, 2–430
    duty to notify of concerns, 2–433
    ex parte hearing, 2–439
    information obtained on inspection, 2–433
    inspection, 2–433
    opportunity to answer opposing case, 2–428
    own view, failure to disclose, 2–437—2–438

NATURAL JUSTICE—*cont.*
  knowledge and experience of arbitrator—*cont.*
    self, giving evidence to, 2–435—2–442
    unchallenged evidence, 2–434, 2–435—2–442
  legitimate expectation, 2–446
  leisurely claimant, 2–427
  mediation, 4–031
  opportunity to answer opposing case, 2–284
  oral hearing, 2–423, 2–424
  outstanding issues at end of hearing, 2–441
  Pacol case, 2–452, 2–453
  requirements, 2–414—2–420
  Scheme for Construction Contracts, 5–057—5–060
  seen to act impartially, duty to be, 2–417
  statutory provisions, 2–415
  summary of law, 2–455
  The Smaro, 2–453
  timetables set by institutions, 2–426
  transparency, 2–420
  unchallenged evidence, accepting, 22–435—22–442
NEC FORMS,
  adjudication, 6–059
  avoidance of disputes, 6–058
  construction industry arbitration, 6–007, 6–057—6–060
  dispute boards, 7–017
  forms of dispute resolution, 6–058—6–060
  review by a tribunal, 6–060
  settlement of disputes, 6–058
NEGLIGENCE,
  expert determination, 2–057
  removal of arbitrator, 2–411
NEGOTIATOR,
  expert witness distinguished, 2–846
NEW YORK,
  Convention. *See* New York Convention
  maritime arbitration, 11–104—11–106
NEW YORK CONVENTION, 9–005
  accession, A17–009
  agreement in writing, A17–002
  application, A17–004, A17–014
  arbitral awards, A17–001
  Arbitration Act 1996, A6–101
  authentic texts, A17–016
  commencement, A17–012
  denunciation, A17–013
  disadvantages of, 9–069
  effects, 9–068
  federal States, A17–011
  general rule, A17–002, A17–003
  impact, 2–016
  importance, 9–069
  multilateral or bilateral agreements, A17–007
  non-unitary States, A17–011
  notifications, A17–015
  online dispute resolution, 12–022

1094

INDEX

NEW YORK CONVENTION—cont.
  purpose, 9–069
  ratification, 9–069, A17–008
  refusal of recognition and enforcement, A17–005
    setting aside award, A17–006
  scope, 2–034, A17–001
  success of, 9–069
  territorial scope, A17–010
NEW YORK PRODUCE EXCHANGE FORM CLAUSE, 11–022, 11–023
NEW ZEALAND,
  staying court proceedings, 1–006
NHBC, 8–011, 8–015
NORTH AMERICAN FREE TRADE AGREEMENT, 9–075
NORWEGIAN SALEFORM CLAUSE, 11–026, 11–027
NOTES OF ARBITRATOR,
  confidentiality, 2–816
  property in, 2–816
NOTICE OF APPOINTMENT,
  agricultural property arbitration, 3–027
NOTICE OF ARBITRATION,
  American Arbitration Association International Arbitration Rules, A18–003
  LCIA arbitration, A44–005
NOTICE TO QUIT,
  agricultural property arbitration, 3–001
NOTICES,
  admit facts or documents, 2–771
  American Arbitration Association International Arbitration Rules, A18–019
  GAFTA, A34–028—A34–030
  UNCITRAL Arbitration Rules, A15–004
NOTIFICATION OF AWARD, 2–512
  Arbitration Act 1996, A6–056
  construction industry arbitration, 6–103
  online dispute resolution, 12–073

ODR. See ONLINE DISPUTE RESOLUTION
OFFICE FOR THE SUPERVISION OF SOLICITORS,
  correspondence from, 18–098
  establishment, 18–095
  grants from Solicitor's Compensation Fund, applications for, 18–111—18–113
    maintenance of fund, 18–111
    grants, 18–113
    purpose of fund, 18–112
  investigation of complaints, complainants, 18–102
    handling of complaints, complaints about, 18–107
  IPS, complaints of, 18–103—18–107
    procedure, 18–103—18–107
    professional misconduct, 18–108—18–110
  IPS, complaints of,
    decision, 18–105

OFFICE FOR THE SUPERVISION OF SOLICITORS—cont.
  IPS, complaints of—cont.
    investigation, 18–105
    preliminary requirements, 18–103
    pursuing claim, 18–104
    review of decision, 18–106
    sanctions, 18–110
  jurisdiction, 18–098—18–101
  lay members, 18–095
  Legal Services Ombudsman, 18–116—18–118
  monitoring, 18–095
  objectives, 18–097
  ordering production of a file, 18–099
  powers, 18–098—18–101
  professional misconduct, 18–108—18–110
    criteria used to progress complaints, 18–109
    sanctions, 18–110
  remit for handling complaints, 18–096
  remuneration certificate procedure, 18–114
    determination, 18–115
  sanction for non-compliance with decision, 18–100, 18–110
  Solicitor's Compensation Fund, 18–111—18–113
  Solicitor's Disciplinary Tribunal and, 18–101
OMISSIONS IN AWARD, 2–876
ONLINE DISPUTE RESOLUTION, 12–001—12–159
  ADR, 12–004
  advantages, 12–004, 12–005
  American Arbitration Association International Arbitration Rules, 12–090—12–093, A72–001—A72–014
  arbitration agreement, 12–027—12–041
    enforcement of awards, 12–039—12–041
    evidence, 12–031—12–038
    nature of electronic communications, 12–029, 12–030
    validity, 12–027, 12–028
  arbitration, online, 12–022—12–074
    conduct of proceedings, 12–023—12–026
    confidentiality, 12–046—12–050
    deliberations between arbitrator, 12–057—12–061
    foreign awards, 12–043
    formal requirements for award, 12–062—12–072
    hearings, 12–054—12–056
    international arbitration, 12–022
    legal issues, 12–022
    New York Convention, 12–022
    non-repudiation, 12–051—12–053
    privacy, 12–046—12–050
    seat of arbitration, 12–044, 12–045
    service of documents, 12–051—12–053
    unequal access to technology, 12–042, 12–043

1095

ONLINE DISPUTE RESOLUTION—*cont.*
  arbitration, online—*cont.*
    writing for purposes of arbitration
      agreement, 12–027—12–041
  arbitration, supporting, 12–014—12–019
  automated blind-bidding, 12–013
  automated settlement systems, 12–137
  award, 12–062—12–072
    delivery, 12–073
    electronic signatures, 12–062—12–072
    enforcement, 12–074
    notification, 12–073
    signature of award, 12–062—12–072
  business to consumer transactions, 12–125—12–139
    arbitration, 12–129—12–133
    automated settlement systems, 12–137
    complaints assistance, 12–138
    consumer disputes, 12–129—12–133
    credit card charge back, 12–139
    evaluation, 12–134
    mediation, 12–136
    mock trials, 12–135
    nature of consumer disputes, 12–126, 12–127
    types of mechanism offered, 12–128—12–139
  chat, online, 12–010, 12–019, 12–082
  commercial disputes, 12–006, 12–020—12–074
    confidentiality, 12–046—12–050
    electronic signatures, 12–062—12–072
    generally, 12–020
    institutional. *See* institutional arbitration providers *below*
    interests of parties, 12–020
    online arbitration. *See* arbitration, online *above*
    seat of arbitration, 12–044, 12–045
    trust, 12–101, 12–102
    unequal access to technology, 12–042, 12–043
  communication tools, 12–004
  complaints assistance, 12–138
  confidence in consumer e-commerce, 12–140—12–146
  confidentiality, 12–046—12–050
  consumer, 12–006, A68–001—A68–006
    See also business to consumer transactions *above*
    confidence, 12–140—12–146
    due process considerations, 12–147—12–149
    emergence of standards, 12–153—12–155
    impartiality, 12–150
    independence, 12–150
    market place provision of dispute resolution service, 12–145, 12–146
    money back guarantees, 12–144—12–146
    publicity, 12–151, 12–152

ONLINE DISPUTE RESOLUTION—*cont.*
  consumer—*cont.*
    transparency, 12–151, 12–152
    trustmark schemes, 12–141—12–144
  convenience, 12–005
  credit card charge back, 12–139
  databases, 12–008
  deliberations between arbitrator, 12–057—12–061
  delivery of award, 12–073
  document management, 12–008
  domain names,
    ICANN. *See* ICANN
    meaning, 12–105
    trade marks and, 12–107, 12–108
    Uniform Domain Name Dispute Resolution Procedure. *See* UDRP
  drafting documents, 12–008
  e-commerce, 12–005, 12–125, 12–126
  efficiency, 12–005
  electronic file management, 12–015, 12–016
  electronic signatures, 12–062—12–072
    biometric signatures, 12–066
    evidence, 12–068—12–072
    methods of signing electronically, 12–065, 12–066
    Public Key Infrastructure, 12–066
    validity, 12–067
  enforcement of award, 12–039—12–041, 12–074
  evaluation, 12–134
  evidence, 12–031—12–038
    electronic signatures, 12–068—12–072
  exclusively conducted online, proceedings, 12–006
  filing documentation, 12–017, 12–080
  hearings, 12–054—12–056
  Hong Kong International Arbitration Centre, 12–094—12–097, A73–001—A73–028
  ICANN. *See* ICANN
  ICC arbitration, 2–083—2–086
  information management, 12–004
  institutional arbitration providers, 12–075—12–102
    American Arbitration Association, 12–090—12–093, A72–001—A72–014
    approach of institutions, 12–075
    CD-Rom, use of, 12–076
    email, 12–077—12–079
    filing, online, 12–080
    Hong Kong International Arbitration Centre, 12–094—12–097, A73–001—A73–028
    ICC International Court of Arbitration, 12–083—12–086
    LCIA arbitration, 12–087—12–089
    WIPO Arbitration and Mediation Center, 12–098—12–100
  LCIA arbitration, 12–087—12–089
  legal information websites, 12–008
  meaning, 12–004—12–007

1096

ONLINE DISPUTE RESOLUTION—cont.
mediation, 12–009—12–013, 12–136
mock trials, 12–135
negotiation software, 12–013
New York Convention, 12–022
notification of award, 12–073
online technology, 12–004
platform, online, 12–009, 12–010, 12–080, 12–081
precedents, use of, 12–008
privacy, 12–046—12–050
purpose, 12–001
scanning, 12–016
schemes, 12–003, A68–001, A69–001
seat of arbitration, 12–044, 12–045
service of documents, 12–051—12–053
settlement, 12–013
spectrum of, 12–006
supporting proceedings, 12–006
techniques, 12–006, 12–007
   general, 12–008
   mediation, 12–009—12–013
   supporting mediation, 12–009—12–013
translation software, 12–008
travelling drafts, 12–008
trust, creation of, 12–101, 12–102
trustmark schemes, 12–141—12–144
unequal access to technology, 12–042, 12–043
Uniform Domain Name Dispute Resolution Procedure. *See* UDRP
uptake of, 12–157—12–159
usefulness, 12–1556
video-conferencing, 12–018, 12–082
virtual meetings, 12–011
visual expression, forms of, 12–012
WIPO Arbitration and Mediation Center, 12–098—12–100
ORAL AGREEMENT TO ARBITRATE, 2–113
ORAL HEARING,
accuracy of evidence, 2–538
advantages, 2–537—2–544
agricultural property arbitration, 3–040
Code of Practice arbitrations, 8–020
diaries, 2–536
disadvantages, 2–535
evidence, 2–539
examination of witnesses,
   international arbitration, 9–160
fair hearing, 2–548—2–551
   discretion, 2–548
   minimum requirements, 2–549
   practical approach, 2–551
   present position, 2–550
farm business tenancy arbitration, 3–108
generally, 2–534
ICC arbitration, 9–153
ICSID arbitration, 10–056
interchange between tribunal and party, effective, 2–540

ORAL HEARING—cont.
international arbitration, 9–151—9–154
   examination of witnesses, 9–160
   IBA Rules, 9–162
   ICC arbitration, 9–153
   limited submissions, 9–158
   order of witnesses, 9–159
   presence of witnesses when not testifying, 9–161, 9–162
   purpose, 9–151—9–154
   timescale, 9–155—9–157
   UNCITRAL Notes, 9–155, 9–161
LMAA small claims procedure, 11–102
natural justice, 2–423, 2–424
no right to, 2–423, 2–424
order of witnesses,
   international arbitration, 9–159
peace of mind for loser, 2–543
perceived difficulties, pointing out, 2–541
presence of witnesses when not testifying,
   international arbitration, 9–161, 9–162
presentation of cases, 2–540
reconciliation of diaries, 2–536
witness conferencing, 2–542
OVERRIDING OBJECTIVE,
Civil Procedure Rules, 2–565, 2–566, 4–018, 14–022

P&I ASSOCIATIONS, 11–013, 11–014
PACKAGE HOLIDAY DIRECTIVE, 8–013
PARIS,
maritime arbitration, 11–107—11–110
PART 36 OFFER,
costs, 2–906, 2–907
PARTIAL AWARDS, 2–874
PARTIES,
Arbitration Act 1996,
   principles of arbitration, application of, 2–070
autonomy. *See* Party autonomy Arbitration Act 1996
maritime arbitration, 11–011
PARTNERSHIPS,
agricultural property arbitration, 3–010
arbitrator in, 2–814
PARTY AUTONOMY, 1–002
Arbitration Act 1996, 4–025
challenging jurisdiction, 2–332
commencement of proceedings, 2–196
meaning, 2–067
multi-party arbitration, 2–627
principle of, 2–067
PATIENTS,
small claims in county court, 14–051
PAYMENT INTO COURT,
remuneration of arbitrator, 2–399, 2–400
statutory provisions for, 2–399, 2–400
PEREMPTORY ORDERS,
adverse inferences, 2–599
applications to court, 2–601, 2–938

PEREMPTORY ORDERS—*cont.*
  available orders, 2–478
  costs, 2–478, 2–600
  court enforcement, 2–091
  debarring reliance, 2–598
  ignoring, 2–088
  meaning, 2–596
  non-compliance, 2–088, 2–596, 2–597
  own initiative, arbitrator acting on, 2–603
  parties, application by, 2–602
  powers of arbitrators, 2–088
  reinforcing order, as, 2–596
  Scheme for Construction Contracts, 5–080
  security for costs, 2–478, 2–596
PERMANENT COURT OF ARBITRATION,
  appointing authority, intervention by, A51–001—A51–003
  basic documents, A49–001—A49–005
    conventions, A49–001
    model clauses, A49–003
    rules of procedure, A49–002
    UNCITRAL rules and procedures, A49–004
  UNCITRAL rules and procedures, A50–001—A50–009
PLACE OF ARBITRATION,
  American Arbitration Association International Arbitration Rules, A18–014
  arbitration agreement, A54–009
  GAFTA, 16–086, A35–001
  ICC arbitration, 9–014, A39–016
  ICSID arbitration, A60–063, A60–064
  international arbitration, 9–057
    choosing, 9–060—9–062
    leading venues, 9–064
    traditional situs, advantages of, 9–063
  LCIA arbitration, A44–017
  Model Law, A14–020
  precedent, A54–009
  UNCITRAL Arbitration Rules, A15–017
  WIPO arbitration, A52–039
PLACE OF AWARD,
  Arbitration Act 1996, A6–054
PLATFORM, ONLINE, 12–009, 12–010, 12–080
PLEADINGS,
  See also Statement of case
  advocate preparing, 2–826
  amendment, 2–679
  Code of Practice arbitrations, 8–025
  documents only arbitration, consumer disputes, 8–025
  function, 2–826
  identification of issues, 2–667, 2–668
  litigation, 2–668
POWERS OF ARBITRATOR, 2–456—2–525
  advice, seeking, 2–518—2–525
    advance approval of parties, 2–522
    colleagues, 2–525
    confidentiality, 2–519
    difficulties with, 2–519

POWERS OF ARBITRATOR—*cont.*
  advice, seeking—*cont.*
    disclosure to parties, 2–519
    express statutory power, 2–520
    institutional rules, 2–524
    natural justice, 2–519
    payment for, 2–518
    procedural points, 2–524
    safeguards, 2–522—2–524
    sources, 2–518
    taking advice before appointment, 2–523
  agricultural property arbitration, 3–033
  autonomy of arbitrator, 2–465
  award,
    additional, 2–485
    ambiguities, 2–485
    clerical mistakes, 2–485
    correction, 2–485
    date of, 2–484
    form of, 2–512
    partial, 2–512
    reasons for, 2–512
    refusal to deliver, 2–484
  categories, 2–475
  Chartered Institute of Arbitrators Arbitration Rules, A20–008
  Chartered Institute of Arbitrators Arbitration Scheme for the Travel Industry, A21–005
  Chartered Institute of Arbitrators Commercial Arbitration Scheme, A23–007
  Chartered Institute of Arbitrators "Surveyors Arbitration" Scheme Rules, A25–005
  CIMAR, A28–004
  conforming to own directions, 2–516
  construction industry arbitration, 6–077, 6–078
  contract out powers, 2–475, 2–476
  contract in powers, 2–475
  correction of award, 2–485
  costs, 2–504
  court applications, sanctioning, 2–506—2–511
  court powers, corresponding to, 2–482
  declaration, power to make, 2–481
  default, acting in, 2–088
  documents only arbitration, 2–466
  domestic and international practice, interaction of, 2–456
  evidence,
    ICE arbitration, A43–008
  exceeding, 2–514
  exercise, 2–532, 2–533
  express terms, 2–457—2–449
  farm business tenancy arbitration, 3–108, 13–012
  follow through, failure to, 2–517
  form of award, 2–512
  fraudulent awards, 2–515

POWERS OF ARBITRATOR—*cont.*
ICE arbitration, 6–077, A43–007—A43–011
  evidence, 6–077, A43–008
  limiting recoverable costs, A43–009
  procedure, 6–077, A43–008
  protective measures, A43–011
  ruling on own jurisdiction, 6–077, A43–007
  security, ordering, A43–010
ICE Conditions of Contract, 6–077, 6–078
implied terms, 2–457—2–459
innovative exercise, 2–532
interest, 2–483
JCT Standard Form Contract, 6–068—6–070
jurisdiction, deciding, 2–083, 2–087
limiting recoverable costs,
  ICE arbitration, A43–009
LMAA, 11–077
LME, 16–030, 16–031
maritime arbitration, 11–077
master of own procedure, 2–470—2–472
multiple awards, 2–480
place of hearing, 2–466
procedures,
  See also Expedition
  adoption by arbitrator, 2–463
  adoption of rules by parties, 2–461
  autonomy of arbitrator, 2–465
  available choices, 2–466
  choice available to arbitrator, 2–466—2–469
  conforming to own procedure, 2–516
  delay and, 2–464
  discovery, 2–469
  documents only arbitration, 2–466
  exercising powers, 2–532, 2–533
  freedom, 2–462
  informality, 2–463
  innovative, 2–533
  look-sniff arbitration, 2–466
  master of procedure, arbitrator, 2–462—2–463
  newly available, 2–468
  place of hearing, 2–466
  range available, 2–460—2–464
protective measures,
  ICE arbitration, A43–011
public policy, 2–515
quality of decision making, 2–473
rent review arbitration, 13–012
ruling on own jurisdiction,
  ICE arbitration, A43–007
sanctioning applications to court, 2–506—2–511
security, ordering,
  ICE arbitration, A43–010
sources,
  arbitration agreement, 2–457—2–459
  contracting out of statutory provisions, 2–457—2–459
  express agreement, 2–458

POWERS OF ARBITRATOR—*cont.*
sources—*cont.*
  implied terms, 2–458
  institutional terms, 2–458
  statutory, 2–457—2–459
specific, 2–477
striking out, 2–088
taking charge of proceedings, 2–470—2–476
  agreement of parties to procedure, 2–471
  decisions, role to take, 2–471
  firmness required, 2–472
  first meeting, 2–474
  master of own procedure, 2–470—2–472
  preliminary discussions, 2–473
  quality of decision making, 2–473
POWERS OF ARBITRATORS,
interest, 2–892
PRE-ACTION PROTOCOLS,
Civil Procedure Rules, 2–567
evaluation, 4–023
PRE-HEARING CONFERENCE,
ICSID arbitration, 10–056
PRE-HEARING REVIEW,
list of issues, 2–693
PRELIMINARY DIALOGUE, 2–653—2–664
appointment of arbitrator, 2–657
directions, 2–658
documents only arbitration, 2–656, 2–657
expert evidence, 2–772
informal exchanges, 2–663
matters to be considered, 2–604
need for, 2–656, 2–657
preliminary meeting, 2–662
taking charge of proceedings, 2–659, 2–660
  draft directions, 2–661—2–663
  draft issues in advance, 2–660
  old approach, 2–659
telecommunications, 2–656
transformation of procedure, 2–653—2–655
PRELIMINARY MEETING,
considering whether to hold, 2–655
draft directions for consideration at, A54–039
letter appointing, A54–038
preliminary dialogue, 2–662
property valuation arbitration, 13–017
rent review arbitration, 13–017
PREPARATION FOR HEARING, 2–759—2–791
admission of facts or documents, 2–771
arbitration agreement, relevance of, 2–762
control, 2–020
costs, reducing, 2–785
duties of arbitrator, economic and expeditious means of dispute resolution, 2–759, 2–760
economic and expeditious means of dispute resolution, 2–759, 2–760
evidence,
  admission of facts or documents, 2–771
  arbitration agreement, 2–762

1099

PREPARATION FOR HEARING—*cont.*
  evidence—*cont.*
    notice to admit facts or documents, 2–771
    reception of, 2–762
  notice to admit facts or documents, 2–771
  number of hearings, 2–782—2–788
    effective conduct, 2–784
    key options, 2–782
    long hearings, 2–783, 2–784
    series of hearings, 2–782
    time limits, 2–784
    traditional hearing, 2–782
  oral evidence,
    economic and expeditious presentation, 2–763
    methods of reducing, 2–763—2–767
    notice to admit facts or documents, 2–771
    reducing volume of, 2–763—2–767
    written and oral, balance between, 2–763
  reducing costs, 2–785
PREPARATORY CONFERENCE,
  WIPO arbitration, A52–047
PRESENTATION OF CASE,
  advocate, 2–827, 2–828
PRESERVATION OF EVIDENCE,
  court application for, 2–508
PRIVACY,
  See also Confidentiality
  assumption in arbitration, 2–803
  DAC Report, 2–103
  infringing, 2–014
  limits of, 2–103
  online dispute resolution, 12–046—12–050
  principles, 2–103
  proceedings, 2–807
PRIVILEGE,
  categorisation of documents, 2–704
  City Disputes Panel Mediation Rules, A27–005
  communications with other persons, 2–706
  disclosure, 2–697
  documents only arbitration in consumer disputes, 8–044
  exclusion of evidence, 2–717
  exclusion of liability, A27–007
  inadmissible evidence, 2–721—2–725
    contested application to use confidential documents, 2–713
    general rule, 2–721
    waiver of protection, 2–722
  inadvertent disclosure, 2–703
  internal documents, 2–705
  legal professional privilege, 2–700, 2–701
  post-mediation functions, A27–009
  public policy, 2–697
  recording agreements, A27–006
  related person, documents in possession of, 2–707
  resignation of arbitrator after disclosure of without prejudice offer, 2–724

PRIVILEGE—*cont.*
  self-incrimination, against, 2–699
  termination of mediation, A27–008
PROCEDURE,
  arbitration agreement, in, 2–762
  delay, on, 2–464
  expert determination, 2–047, 2–054
  resignation of arbitrator, 2–297
  settlements, 2–735
PROFESSIONAL CONDUCT OF BARRISTERS AND SOLICITORS,
  See also Barristers; Legal Services Ombudsman; Solicitors
  Human Rights Act 1998, 18–005—18–012
    fair and public hearing, right to, 18–007
    independence, 18–011
    investigation of complaints, 18–009
    property, protection of, 18–008
    self-incrimination, 18–010
    sufficiency of appeal, 18–012
  maintenance of two distinct bodies, 18–002
PROOFS OF EVIDENCE,
  advance exchange, 2–790
  arbitrator, delay before delivery to, 2–767
  confidentiality, 2–770
  consecutive delivery, 2–766
  counterclaims, 2–768
  cross examination, 2–769
  death of witness after, 2–769
  degree of details required, 2–768
  delay before delivery to arbitrator, 2–767
  directions, 2–768, 2–771
  exchange,
    advance, 2–790
    arbitrator, to, 2–790
    counterclaims, 2–770
    degree of details required, 2–768
    directions, 2–768, 2–771
    effect of, 2–790
    expert evidence, 2–772
    methods, 2–763—2–767
    novel methods, 2–766, 2–776
    order, 2–765—2–766
    provision for, 2–764
    rebuttal evidence, 2–766
    simultaneous exchange, 2–765
    timing, 2–765
  expert evidence, 2–772, 2–774
  late presentation, 2–768
  not calling witness, 2–770
  not limited to, parties, 2–768—2–770
  order of exchange, 2–765, 2–766
  rebuttal evidence, 2–766
  simultaneous exchange, 2–776
  skeleton, 2–776
  status, 2–769
  weight attached to, 2–769
  witness not called, 2–770
PROPERTY PRESERVATION,
  CIETAC, 16–071

INDEX

PROPERTY VALUATION ARBITRATION,
  accompanied inspections, 13–052
  advice on procedure, 13–022
  agreeing directions, 13–019
  alternative tribunals, 13–003
  appointment of arbitrator, 13–008—13–013
    RICS appointments, 13–009
  arbitrator,
    appointment, 13–008—13–013
    arbitration agreement, 13–008
    bias, 13–013
    conflicts of interest, 13–013
    duties, 13–012
    fees, 13–010
    independent expert distinguished, 13–004
    powers, 13–012
    removal, 13–014
    serious irregularity, 13–015
    style, 13–011
  art of valuation, 13–041
  assessors, 13–023
  award,
    clarification of issues, 13–054
    drafting, 13–053—13–061
    final award, 13–053
    interim award, 13–053
    own knowledge of arbitrator, 13–055
    publication, 13–060
    reasons, 13–056—13–057
    without reasons, 13–061
  background, 13–001—13–002
  bias of arbitrator, 13–013
  Calderbank offers, 13–064, 13–065
  clarification of issues, 13–054
  comparables, 13–039, 13–041
  conduct of reference, 13–018
  confidentiality, 13–045—13–047
  conflicts of interest, 13–013
  costs, 13–020, 13–061—13–071
    allocation, 13–062
    amount, 13–069
    Calderbank offers, 13–064, 13–065
    "event", 13–063
    fractional awards, 13–066, 13–068
    generally, 13–062
    interest, 13–071
    not following event, 13–068
    taxation, 13–070
  directions, 13–019
  disclosure, 13–036—13–038
  documents only arbitration, 13–021
  duties of arbitrator, 13–012
  expert evidence, 13–048, 13–049
  fees, 13–010
  fractional award, 13–066, 13–067
  guidelines on procedure, 13–016
  hearsay evidence, 13–027
  independent expert and, 13–004
  interest, 13–071
  interim award, 13–053
  irrelevant evidence, 13–044

PROPERTY VALUATION ARBITRATION—cont.
  late evidence, 13–028
  legal advisers, 13–023
  other awards, 13–043
  own knowledge of arbitrator, 13–055
  physical property identification, 13–035
  powers of arbitrator, 13–012
  preliminary meeting, 13–017
  preliminary point of law, 13–024
  procedure,
    advice on, 13–022
    agreeing directions, 13–019
    agreeing on, 13–022
    assessors, 13–023
    conduct of reference, 13–018
    costs, 13–020
    directions, 13–019
    documents only arbitration, 13–021
    guidelines, 13–016
    legal advisors, 13–023
    preliminary meeting, 13–017
    preliminary point of law, 13–024
  publication of award, 13–060
  purpose, 13–002
  reasons for award, 13–056—13–057
  removal of arbitrator, 13–014
  reported cases, 13–042
  representation, 13–023
  serious irregularity, 13–015
  style of arbitrator, 13–011
  taxation of costs, 13–070
  uses, 13–001
  without reasons, award, 13–061
  witness summons, 13–045—13–049
PROTECTIVE MEASURES,
  ICE arbitration, A43–011
PROVISIONAL AWARDS,
  Arbitration Act 1996, A6–040
  construction industry arbitration, 6–097
  expedition, 2–611
  ICE arbitration, A43–025
PROVISIONAL MEASURES,
  Court of Arbitration for Sport (CAS), 15–053—15–056
PROVISIONAL ORDER,
  security for costs, 2–503
PROVISIONAL RELIEF,
  CIMAR, 6–041, A28–010
PUBLIC INTEREST,
  confidentiality, 2–805, 2–818, 2–819
PUBLIC POLICY,
  settlements, 2–735
PUBLIC SERVICE,
  arbitration as, 2–012
PUBLICATION OF AWARD, A54–091
  confidentiality, 2–815
  construction industry arbitration, 6–103
  maritime arbitration, 11–092
  method, 2–398
  property valuation arbitration, 13–060
  remuneration of arbitrator, 2–395

1101

INDEX

PUBLICATION OF AWARD—*cont.*
  rent review arbitration, 13–060
  RSA, 16–052

QUALIFICATION OF ARBITRATOR,
  agreement, 2–136, 2–222

RE-EXAMINATION, 2–796
  interventions by the arbitrator, 2–800
RECITALS,
  award, 2–879
  contents, 2–879
  importance, 2–879
  length, 2–879
  scope, 2–879
RECOGNITION OF AWARD,
  ICSID arbitration, A60–054
  Model Law, A14–059—A14–062
  New York Convention. *See* New York Convention
REFINED SUGAR ASSOCIATION. *See* RSA
RELATED CONTRACTS. *See* Concurrent arbitration; Consolidated arbitration
REMEASUREMENT SYSTEM,
  construction industry arbitration, 6–019, 6–020
REMEDIES,
  CIMAR, 6–042, A28–012
REMOVAL OF ARBITRATOR,
  adoption of point of view, 2–278
  Arbitration Act 1950, A61–025
  Arbitration Act 1996, 2–560, A6–025
  breach of obligations, 2–409
  business connection with party, 2–283
  change in nature of arbitration, 2–309, 2–310
  Court of Arbitration for Sport (CAS), 15–051, 15–052, A29–017
  court, by,
    adoption of point of view, 2–278
    business connection with party, 2–283
    grounds, 2–280, 2–560
    institutional remedy exhausted, 2–281
    prior connection with similar dispute, 2–277
    refusal by institution to exercise power, 2–282
    subject-matter of arbitration, connection with, 2–284
  grounds, 2–280, 2–560
  incapacity, 2–408
  institutional remedy exhausted, 2–281
  irregularity in proceedings, 2–285
  nature of arbitration changed, 2–310
  negligence, 2–411
  partially qualified arbitrator, 2–410
  parties in the picture, keeping, 2–412
  physical or mental incapacity, 2–408
  point of view adopted by arbitrator, 2–278

REMOVAL OF ARBITRATOR—*cont.*
  prior connection with similar dispute, 2–277
  property valuation arbitration, 13–014
  remuneration of arbitrator, 2–407—2–412
  rent review arbitration, 13–014
  response to challenge,
    appointing party, of, 2–287
    appointment already in place, 2–290
    prospective arbitrator, 2–288
    resignation, 2–291
    written particulars of challenge, 2–289
  similar dispute, prior connection with, 2–277
  subject-matter of arbitration, connection with, 2–284
  taking part without objection or reservation, 2–286
  time for challenge, 2–285, 2–286
  unqualified arbitrator, 2–040
  waiver of time limit, 2–286
  "without prejudice" objection, 2–303
REMUNERATION OF ARBITRATOR, 2–339—2–413
  abandonment of arbitration, 2–348
  absence of agreement, 2–345, 2–378
  ad hoc arbitration,
    express contract, 2–349
    quantum, 2–389
  agreement, 2–342
  Agricultural Holdings Act 1986, under, A2–001
  agricultural property arbitration, 3–024—3–026
    agreement, appointment by, 3–024
    default of agreement, 3–024
    fair rate, 3–024
    milk quota arbitration, 3–099
  alternative methods, 2–382
  approach, 2–339
  bases, possible, 2–382
  bias, 2–360
  booking fees, 2–384
  cancellation charges, 2–384
  cases,
    old legislation, 2–358—2–363
  chairman, 2–390
  Chartered Institute of Arbitrators, 2–393
  churning, 2–383
  compromise, 2–348
  contractual position, 2–345
  court determination, statutory provisions, 2–239
  court proceedings and arbitration, 2–373
  DAC, 2–355
  delivery, payment on, 2–398
  difference between recoverable fees, 2–232
  dilatory tribunal, 2–379
  dilemma facing arbitrators, 2–377
  drafting suggestion, 2–353
  enforcing right, 2–398—2–403
    delivery, payment on, 2–398
    disadvantages of disputes, 2–402

1102

REMUNERATION OF ARBITRATOR—*cont.*
  enforcing right—*cont.*
    disputes, disadvantages of, 2–402
    exhaustion of remedies, 2–401
    payment into court, 2–399, 2–400
    publication of award, 2–398
  exhaustion of remedies, 2–401
  expenses, 2–387
  express contract, 2–342, 2–349—2–357
    ad hoc arbitration, 2–349
    alteration after, 2–358
    alternative methods, 2–382
    bases, 2–382
    cancellation fees, 2–384
    commitment fees, 2–358
    construction, 2–361
    contents, 2–381—2–387
    expenses, 2–387
    factors affecting method, 2–382
    implied terms, 2–360, 2–361—362, 2–361—2–380
    instalment payments, 2–359
    institutional appointment, 2–350
    lump sum, 2–381
    party appointed arbitrator, 2–350
    percentage of amount in issue, 2–383
    preliminary dialogue, 2–350
    prescribed, 2–351
    rates of remuneration, 2–352
    rent review, 2–383
    status of arbitrator, 2–358
    time for payment, 2–387
    timing of agreement, 2–350
    trilateral agreement, 2–358
  extravagant charges, 2–239, 2–348
  factors affecting method, 2–382
  fair rate,
    agricultural property arbitration, 3–024
  farm business tenancy arbitration, 3–107
  free, acting for, 2–341
  guidance, 2–394
  ICC Arbitrations, 2–395
  instalment payments, 2–359
  institutional appointment, 2–376, 2–393
  institutional payment, 2–343
  interim payment, 2–360
  interim fees, 2–368
    work to date, for, 2–380
  interim payment, 2–342
  joint and several liability, 2–345
  jurisdiction, fees without, 2–355—2–357
  lack of case law, 2–340
  LCIA, 2–394
  LCIA arbitration, 9–030
  lien, 2–344
  limitations on implied right, 2–347
  lump sum, 2–381
  methods, possible, 2–382
  milk quota arbitration, 3–099
  misconduct, 2–360
  parties, disputes between, 2–403

REMUNERATION OF ARBITRATOR—*cont.*
  payment,
    before award, 2–340
    into court, 2–399, 2–400
    time for, 2–387
  percentage of amount in issue, 2–383
  physical or mental incapacity, 2–408
  prolonged arbitration, 2–361
  publication of award, 2–392
  quantum, 2–388—2–392
    ad hoc arbitration, 2–389
    administered arbitration, 2–393—2–395
    administration, 2–388
    chairman, 2–390, 2–392
    Chartered Institute of Arbitrators, 2–393
    different rates, 2–391
    factors affecting, 2–388
    guidance, 2–388
    ICC Arbitrations, 2–395
    institutional appointments, 2–393
    LCIA, 2–395
    three person tribunal, 2–389
    two or more arbitrators, where, 2–389
    umpire, 2–392
  rates of remuneration, express contract, 2–352
  recovery from parties, 2–346
  removal of arbitrator, 2–407—2–412
  resignation of arbitrator, 2–406
  review for removal, 2–375
  right, 2–340—2–348
  security for fees, 2–374, 2–413
  settlements, 2–753
  statutory provisions, 2–345
  "such reasonable fee as is appropriate . . . ", 2–345
  third arbitrator appointed by two-party appointed arbitrators, 2–354
  three person tribunal, 2–389
  time for payment, 2–387
  umpire, 2–354, 2–392
  VAT, 2–396—2–397
RENT REVIEW,
  agricultural property arbitration, 3–003
  arbitration. *See* Rent review arbitration
RENT REVIEW ARBITRATION,
  accompanied inspections, 13–052
  advice on procedure, 13–022
  agreeing directions, 13–019
  appointment of arbitrator, 13–008—13–013
    arbitration agreement, 13–008
    RICS appointments, 13–009
  arbitrator,
    appointment, 13–008—13–013
    bias, 13–013
    conflicts of interest, 13–013
    duties of arbitrator, 13–012
    fees, 13–010
    independent expert distinguished, 13–004
    powers, 13–012
    removal, 13–014

Rent review arbitration—*cont.*
  arbitrator—*cont.*
    serious irregularity, 13–015
    style, 13–011
  art of valuation, 13–041
  assessors, 13–023
  award,
    clarification of issues, 13–054
    content, 13–058
    drafting, 13–053—13–061
    final award, 13–053
    interim, 13–053
    own knowledge of arbitrator, 13–055
    publication of award, 13–060
    reasons for, 13–056—13–057
    style of, 13–059
    without reasons, 13–061
  bias of arbitrator, 13–013
  clarification of issues, 13–054
  comparables, 13–039, 13–041
  conduct of reference, 13–018
  confidentiality, 13–045—13–049
  conflicts of interest, 13–013
  content of award, 13–058, 13–059
  costs, 13–020
  directions, 13–019, A54–077, A54–078
  disclosure, 13–036—13–038
  documents only arbitration, 13–021
  duties of arbitrator, 13–012
  expert evidence, 13–049
  fees, 13–010
  growth in, 13–005
  guidelines on procedure, 13–016
  hearsay evidence, 13–027
  hypothetical characteristics, 13–007
  independent expert and, 13–004
  interim awards, 13–053
  irrelevant evidence, 13–044
  late evidence, 13–028
  legal advisers, 13–023
  other awards, 13–043
  own knowledge of arbitrator, 13–055
  physical property identification, 13–035
  powers of arbitrator, 13–012
  precedents,
    agreement to refer point of law for the decision of counsel, A54–079
    directions, A54–077, A54–078
    underlease of part referred to head lease arbitrator, A54–076
    underlease provisions to be referred to same arbitrator, A54–075
  preliminary meeting, 13–017
  preliminary point of law, 13–024
  procedure, 13–016—13–024
    advice on, 13–022
    agreeing directions, 13–019
    assessors, 13–023
    conduct of reference, 13–018
    costs, 13–020
    directions, 13–019

Rent review arbitration—*cont.*
  procedure—*cont.*
    documents only arbitration, 13–021
    guidelines, 13–016
    legal advisers, 13–023
    preliminary meeting, 13–017
    preliminary point of law, 13–024
    saving time, 13–020
  publication of award, 13–060
  reasons for award, 13–056—13–057
  removal of arbitrator, 13–014
  reported cases, 13–042
  representation, 13–023
  saving time, 13–020
  scope of text, 13–006
  serious irregularity, 13–015
  style of arbitrator, 13–011
  without reasons, award, 13–061
  witness summons, 13–045—13–049
Replacement of arbitrator,
  UNCITRAL Arbitration Rules, A15–014, A15–015
  WIPO arbitration, A52–033, A52–034
Representation,
  advantage of arbitration, 2–025, 2–026
  American Arbitration Association International Arbitration Rules, A18–013
  charter party arbitration, A36–014
  Chartered Institute of Arbitrators Commercial Arbitration Scheme, A23–014
  choice of, 2–025, 2–026
  CIETAC, 16–068
  CIMAR, A28–014
  continuity, 2–029
  Court of Arbitration for Sport (CAS), A29–012
  documents only arbitration in consumer disputes, 8–046, 8–047
  GAFTA, 16–096, 16–097, A34–024, A35–005
  Housing Grants, Construction and Regeneration Act 1996, 5–021
  LCIA arbitration, A44–019
  LME, 16–027—16–029
  obligation of arbitrator to hear, 2–512
  property valuation arbitration, 13–023
  rent review arbitration, 13–023
  RSA, 16–048—16–051
  Scheme for Construction Contracts, 5–021
  solicitors, advocacy by, 2–028
  UNCITRAL Arbitration Rules, A15–005
  unequal, 2–864
  WIPO arbitration, A52–013
Resignation,
  adjudicator,
    CEDR Rules for Adjudication, A19–007
  arbitrator. *See* Resignation of arbitrator

INDEX

RESIGNATION OF ARBITRATOR,
  advice on, 2–297
  alternative appointments, 2–299
  Arbitration Act 1996, 2–557, A6–026
  availability, 2–291
  busy arbitrator, 2–311
  change in nature of arbitration, 2–309, 2–310
  consultation on, 2–297
  court's powers on, 2–293—2–296
  delays, 2–293
  difficulties caused by, 2–294
  disclosure of without prejudice offer, after, 2–724
  exercise of rights, 2–198
  expenses, 2–298
  fees, 2–298, 2–304
  limited immunity, 2–295
  maritime arbitration, 11–099
  misleading appointment, 2–310
  mutual request, 2–304
  nature of arbitration changed, 2–309, 2–310
  new appointment challenged, 2–300
  objectionable behaviour, 2–295
  post-appointment factors, 2–299
  powers of court on, 2–293—2–296
  procedure for, 2–296
  relief from liability, 2–295
  remuneration of arbitrator, 2–406
  replacement, 2–300
  requesting, 2–301
  terms of engagement of arbitrator, 2–292
  waiver, 2–303
  withdrawing challenge, 2–299
  without challenge, 2–302
  "without prejudice" objection, 2–303
RESTITUTION,
  investment treaty arbitration, 10–062
RETIREMENT OF ARBITRATOR,
  change in nature of arbitration, 2–309, 2–310
  constraints on right, 2–305
  contract of appointment, 2–305
  duties of arbitrator, 2–305
  implied power, 2–306
  misleading appointment, 2–310
  nature of arbitration changed, 2–309, 2–310
  power, 2–306
  term against, 2–306
REVISION OF AWARD,
  ICSID arbitration, A60–052
REVOCATION OF APPOINTMENT,
  agricultural property arbitration, 3–023
  farm business tenancy arbitration, 3–106
REVOCATION OF AUTHORITY,
  Arbitration Act 1950, A61–027
  Arbitration Act 1996, A6–024
  arbitrator, A26–008
  City Disputes Panel Arbitration Rules, A26–008
RIBA, 6–086

RICS, 6–088
ROME CONVENTION, 9–069—9–071
ROYAL INSTITUTION OF BRITISH ARCHITECTS,
  appointment of arbitrator, 6–086
ROYAL INSTITUTION OF CHARTERED SURVEYORS,
  appointment of arbitrator, 6–088
  expert evidence, 2–845
RSA, 16–001, 16–015, 16–038—16–060
  advice, availability of, 16–057
  appointment of arbitrators, 16–041—16–045, 16–056
  arbitration clause, 16–039, A71–001
  arbitrators, 16–040
  assessment of system, 16–054
  award, 16–052
  commencement of arbitration, 16–046, 16–047
  communications, 16–055
  costs, 16–058
  day-to-day management, 16–039
  documents only arbitration, 16–060
  establishment of RSA, 16–038
  fees, 16–052
  lawyers, role of, 16–048—16–051
  legal assessor, 16–050
  number of arbitrators, 16–052
  publication of award, 16–052
  role, 16–038
  rules, A71–003—A71–018
  Secretariat, 16–052—16–054
  single-tier arbitration, 16–059
  substitute arbitrator, 16–052
  time limits, 16–035
  withdrawal of claim, 16–052
"RYE TERMS" CLAUSE,
  GAFTA, 16–093, A34–012

SAL, 16–038
SALVAGE ARBITRATIONS, 11–002
SAMPLES,
  GAFTA, A34–011
SANCTIONS,
  CIMAR, A28–011
SCANNING,
  online dispute resolution, 12–016
SCHEME FOR CONSTRUCTION CONTRACTS, 5–002, A10–001—A10–013
  appointment of adjudicator, 5–036—5–040
  appointee, 5–042, 5–043
  nominating bodies, 5–041
  case law, 5–005
  ceasing to be adjudicator, 5–093
  confidentiality, 5–095
  costs, 5–081, 5–087, 5–088
  decision of adjudicator, 5–076—5–081, A10–006
  costs, 5–081
  declaratory, 5–078
  duty of adjudicator, 5–076

1105

INDEX

SCHEME FOR CONSTRUCTION
  CONTRACTS—*cont.*
  decision of adjudicator—*cont.*
    parties, 5–084—5–086
    powers of adjudicator, 55–077
    reasons, 5–082
    rectification of contract, 5–079
    slips, 5–083
  default by parties, 5–055—5–056
  discharge of duties of adjudicator, 5–111
  effects of decision, A10–007
  enforcement of payment, 5–096—5–103
    adjudicator and, 5–109, 5–110
  eventual litigation/arbitration, 5–112
  existence of a dispute, 5–032
  expenses, 5–081
  fees, 5–081, 5–089—5–091
  fresh adjudication, 5–075
  functus officio, 5–111
  future of, 5–113
  human rights, 5–061
  liability of adjudicator, 5–092
  natural justice, 5–057—5–060
  non-compliant contracts, 5–008
  non-compulsory areas, 5–005
  notice of adjudication, 5–008
  party to the contract, 5–008
  party to the dispute, 5–008
  payment, 5–003, A10–008—A10–013
  peremptory orders, 5–080
  powers of adjudicator, A10–005
  procedure after referral, 5–049—5–054
  reasons for decision, 5–082
  rectification of contract, 5–079
  referral notice, 5–044, 5–045
  representation, 5–021
  resignation of adjudicator, 5–094
  slip rule, 5–083
  statutory demand, 5–108
  stay of execution, 5–104—5–107
  summary judgment, 5–096—5–103
  timetable, 8–071—8–073
    not achieved, 5–074
SCOTLAND,
  City Disputes Panel Arbitration Rules, A26–027
SCOTT V. AVERY CLAUSE, 2–128
  GAFTA, 16–085, 16–086
  precedent, A54–007
SDRP. *See* SPORT DISPUTE RESOLUTION
  PANEL
SEA CARRIAGE OF PASSENGERS,
  unfair contract terms, A1–029
SEALED OFFER,
  agricultural property arbitration, 3–072
  costs, 2–906, 2–907
SEAT OF ARBITRATION,
  abroad, witnesses, 2–780
  agreement, 2–135
  Arbitration Act 1996, A6–004
  award, 2–512, 2–875

SEAT OF ARBITRATION—*cont.*
  determination,
    express, 2–072
    tribunal, 2–072
  GAFTA, 16–086
  importance, 2–072
  LMAA, 11–076
  maritime arbitration, 11–005, 11–076
  meaning, 2–072
  Sport Dispute Resolution Panel, 15–034
  statutory provision, 2–072
  witnesses abroad, 2–570
SECRETARIAT,
  GAFTA, 16–098, 16–099
  ICSID, A60–010—A60–012
  RSA, 16–052—16–054
  WTO dispute settlement, A53–030
    RSA, 16–052—16–054
SECURITY,
  costs, for. *See* Security for costs
  fees, for, 2–487
SECURITY FOR COSTS, 2–486—2–503
  agreement on, 2–487
  Arbitration Act 1996, 2–094
  arbitrator's powers, 2–486—2–503
    acting of his own motion, 2–490
    CIMAR, 2–502
    court position and, 2–488
    fees, 2–487
    institutional fees, 2–487
    institutional rules, 2–502
    international arbitration, 2–489
    ordering, 2–486—2–503
    provisional order, 2–503
    quantum, 2–499—2–503
    restrictions on power, 2–487
    scope of power, 2–487
    stages, ordering by, 2–500
    weaknesses in system, 2–491
  Calderbank offers, 2–492, 2–493, 2–496, 2–497
    respondent's who want security, 2–495
  CIMAR, 2–502, 6–039, A29–019—A29–021
  court power, 2–486, 2–488
  determining quantum, 2–499—2–503
  generally, 2–093
  international arbitration, 2–489
  Ken-Ren, 2–093
  manner of providing, 2–501
  maritime arbitration, 11–072, 11–074, 11–100
  penniless claimants, 2–498
  peremptory orders, 2–478, 2–596
  provisional order, 2–503
  quantum, 2–499—2–503
SELECTION OF EVIDENCE FOR HEARING,
  2–713—2–725
  See also Evidence
  arbitrator, by, 2–714
  copying, controlling the cost of, 2–715
  costs, 2–719

1106

SELECTION OF EVIDENCE FOR HEARING—*cont.*
  de bene esse, evidence to be given, 2–718
  documents, 2–788
  legal advice, 2–720
  parties, by, 2–713
SELF-INCRIMINATION, PRIVILEGE AGAINST, 2–699
SEPARABILITY,
  difficulty of English courts with, 2–326
  establishment of principle, 2–080
  invalidity or defect in host contract, 2–081
  staying court proceedings, 2–177—2–179
SERIOUS IRREGULARITY,
  ambiguous award, 2–096
  award,
    Arbitration Act 1996, A6–069
  court supervision, 2–093
  declaration that award ineffective, 2–096
  definition, 2–096
  discretion of court, 2–096
  effect of, 2–096
  exercise of powers, 2–097
  ineffective award, 2–097
  meaning, 2–096
  opportunity to answer case, 13–023
  own evidence of arbitrator, 13–032
  property valuation arbitration, 13–015
  remission of award, 2–097, 2–098
  rent review arbitration, 13–015, 13–017
  scope, 2–096
  setting aside award, 2–097, 2–098
  supervision by court, 2–097
  technical misconduct, 2–098
  uncertain award, 2–097
SERVICE,
  Arbitration Act 1996,
    documents, A6–078
    notices, A6–077
SETTING ASIDE AWARD,
  agricultural property arbitration, 3–088
  Arbitration Act 1950, A61–025
  Model Law, A14–034, A14–057, A14–058
  New York Convention, A17–006
  serious irregularity, 2–097
SETTLEMENTS, 2–733—2–758
  acceptance, 2–750—2–754
    arbitration clause, 2–754
    binding contract, 2–750
    confidentiality requirement, 2–753
    consent award, 2–752
    dispute as to, 2–750
    "subject to contract", 2–751
    Tomlin order, 2–753
    undisclosed terms, 2–753
  adoption of procedures for, 2–735
  advantages, 2–734
  American Arbitration Association
    International Arbitration Rules, A18–030
  arbitration clause, 2–754
  arbitration as incentive to, 2–734

SETTLEMENTS—*cont.*
  Calderbank offer, 2–741, 2–758
  confidentiality requirement, 2–753
  consent award, 2–752
  construction industry disputes, 6–026
  costs, 2–906
  desirability of, 2–733
  duties of arbitrator, 2–512, 2–735
  enforcement, 2–753
  expressing view on case, arbitrator, 2–739
  FIDIC Conditions, 6–055
  help from arbitrator, 2–738
  incentive to, 2–734
  incorporation into consent award, 2–752
  jurisdiction as incentive to, 2–734
  LMAA terms, A46–010
  LME, 16–026
  Med-Arb, 2–738, 2–739
  mediation, 4–013
  Model Law, A14–030
  online dispute resolution, 12–013
  open offers, 2–743—2–749
    arbitrator role, 2–745, 2–746
    consideration, 2–749
    costs dealt with, 2–747, 2–748
    effect of, 2–745, 2–746
    entitlement to make, 2–744
    keeping offer open, 2–749
    length kept open in, 2–749
    making, 2–744
    meaning, 2–743
    purpose, 2–743
    reasonable time to consider, 2–749
    tactics, 2–743
    terms of, 2–743
    time to consider, 2–749
    weight attached to, 2–749
    writing, 2–744
  part dispute, 2–755, 2–756
  public policy, 2–735
  public sector, 6–026
  questions raised by, 2–739
  rejection of offer, 2–757
  remuneration of arbitrator, 2–753
  role of arbitrator, 2–745, 2–746
  "subject to contract", acceptance, 2–751
  termination of proceedings, 2–512
  Tomlin order, 2–753
  UNCITRAL Arbitration Rules, A15–035
  undisclosed terms on, 2–753
  without prejudice offers, 2–740
  Woolf report, 2–733
SHARE-FARMING, 3–010
SHORT FORM PROCEDURE,
  Chartered Institute of Arbitrators Arbitration Rules, A20–014—A20–016
SINGAPORE,
  Med-Arb, 4–029
SINGAPORE INTERNATIONAL ARBITRATION CENTRE,
  arbitration clause, A54–020

1107

SITE INSPECTION,
  on IBA Rules, A38–015
SITE VISITS,
  dispute boards, 7–051
  WIPO arbitration, A52–050
SKELETON PROOFS,
  advantage, 2–776
  exchange, 2–776
SLIP RULE,
  agricultural property arbitration, 3–082
  award, 2–876
  power to correct, 2–885, 2–886
  Scheme for Construction Contracts, 5–083
SMALL CLAIMS IN COUNTY COURT, 11–036, 14–001—14–103
  acknowledgment of service, 14–013
  addition of parties, 14–049
  admissions, 14–014
  advantages, 2–040
  allocation,
    counterclaims, 14–027
    exercise of discretion, 14–022
    financial value, 14–021, 14–023—14–025
    jurisdiction of Small Claims Track, 14–020
    notice of, 14–031, 14–032
    overriding objective, 14–022
    procedure, 14–019
    re-allocation, 14–032
    test cases, 14–028
    transfer, 14–0198
    wishes of parties, 14–029
  amendments, 14–048
  appeals, 14–094—14–101
    costs, 14–101
    further appeal, 14–100
  Arbitration Act 1996, A6–093
  arbitration agreement, where, 14–009
  attendance at the hearing, 14–063—14–066
    disposal without a hearing, 14–064
    non-attendance by one or both parties, 14–065, 14–066
    paper adjudication, 14–063
  children, 14–051
  Civil Procedure Rules, 14–005, 14–006
    addition of parties, 14–049
    amendments, 14–048
    application of provisions, 14–046—14–059
    applications, 14–053
    children, 14–051
    counterclaims, 14–050
    disapplication, 14–037—14–045
    injunctions, 14–056—14–058
    overriding objective, 14–022
    patients, 14–051
    statements of truth, 14–052
    summary judgment, 14–054, 14–055
    third party claims, 14–050
    witnesses, 14–059
  claim, 14–011

SMALL CLAIMS IN COUNTY COURT—*cont.*
  claim form, 14–011
  commencing proceedings, 14–010, 14–011
  conduct of hearing, 14–060—14–082
    adducing the evidence, 14–075, 14–076
    attendance at the hearing, 14–063—14–066
    expert evidence, 14–077, 14–078
    judge, 14–061
    lay representatives, 14–062
    order of evidence, 14–074
    practice, 14–071—14–082
    Practice Direction, 14–068—14–070
    representation, 14–062
    rules, 14–067
    submissions, 14–079
  costs, 14–083—14–093
    appeals, 14–101
    consent, cases allocated by, 14–090
    general rule, 14–083
    litigants in person, 14–091
    no costs rule, 14–088, 14–089
    principles, 14–084—14–087
  counterclaims, 14–050
  decision, 14–080—14–082
  default judgments, 14–017
  defence,
    contents, 14–016
    time for, 14–015
  directions, 14–033, 14–035, 14–036
  disapplication of CPR, 14–037
  disclosure, 14–038
  enforcement of judgment, 14–102
  evidence, 14–039, 14–040
  expert evidence, 14–041, 14–042
  financial value, 14–021, 14–023—14–025
    cases exceeding £500, 14–030, 14–036
    claims with no, 14–026
  further information, 14–043
  historical background, 14–001, 14–002
  injunctions, 14–056—14–058
  instalment orders, 14–082
  interest, 14–082
  judge, 14–061
  lay representatives, 14–062
  litigants in person, 14–091
  mainstream arbitration, relationship with, 14–008
  nature of hearings, 14–007
  notes for guidance, 14–103
  notice of allocation, 14–031
  offers to settle, 14–044
  patients, 14–051
  Practice Direction, 14–068—14–070
  pre-hearing procedure, 14–033—14–036
    claims exceeding £500, 14–036
    directions, 14–033, 14–035, 14–036
    preliminary hearing, 14–034
  preliminary hearing, 14–034

INDEX

SMALL CLAIMS IN COUNTY COURT—*cont.*
  present regime, 14–003—14–006
    Civil Procedure Rules, 14–005, 14–006
    County Court Act 1984, 14–003
    County Court Rules, 14–004
  public hearings, 14–045
  re-allocation, 14–03
  representatives, 14–062
  responding to claim, 14–013
  service of claim, 14–012
  setting aside judgment, 14–093
  Small Claims Track, 14–005, 14–006
    exercise of discretion, 14–022
    financial value, 14–021, 14–23–14–25
    jurisdiction, 14–020
  statements of truth, 14–052
  stay of court proceedings, 14–009
  test cases, 14–028
  third party claims, 14–050
  witnesses, 14–059
SOCIETY OF CONSTRUCTION ARBITRATORS, 6–036
  Notes on CIMAR, A29–001—A29–025
SOCIETY OF CONSTRUCTION LAW, 6–036
  Delay and Disruption Protocol, 6–036, 6–105—6–109
    aims, 6–109
    compensation, 6–108
    core principles, 6–107, 6–108
    drafting, 6–106
    incorporation, 6–105
    publication, 6–105
    record-keeping, 6–106
    use, 6–105
    variations, 6–108
SOLE ARBITRATOR,
  agreement, 2–124
  appointing body, 2–221
  appointment, 2–217
    agreed method, 2–248, 2–253
    appeals, 2–251
    application to court, 2–249
    appointed arbitrator transformed into sole arbitrator, 2–260—2–264
    candidates, 2–221
    commercial judge, 2–230
    completion of appointment, 2–256
    confirmation of sole arbitrator, 2–259
    contrary intention, 2–219
    court's powers, 2–249, 2–252
    date of agreement, 2–253
    deemed agreement, 2–250
    default notice, 2–257, 2–258
    default procedure, 2–221
    delay in court application, 2–252
    formal procedure, 2–229—2–233
    help from the institutions, 2–224
    inaction by the respondent, 2–256
    institutional, 2–221
    interpretation of agreement, 2–219
    parties' agreement on, 2–220

SOLE ARBITRATOR—*cont.*
  appointment—*cont.*
    parties, by, 2–248
    procedure, 2–229—2–233
    professional bodies, responsibility of, 2–223
    rejection, 2–221
    requesting party not seeking sole arbitrator's appointment, 2–264
    seeking sole arbitrator's appointment, 2–260—2–264
    Technology and Construction Court judge, 2–232, 2–233
    third person by, 2–221
    time allowed for, 2–249
    transformation of appointed arbitrator into sole arbitrator, 2–160—2–164
    use of knowledge of institutions, 2–222
  candidates, 2–221
  commercial judge as, 2–230
  contrary intention, 2–219
  deciding on, 2–124
  default procedure, 2–221
  express provision, 2–220
  formal procedure for appointment, 2–229—2–233
  ICC arbitration, 9–014
  institutional appointment, 2–221
  interpretation of agreement, 2–219
  LCIA arbitration, 9–026
  letter to parties, A54–036
  maritime arbitration, 11–038
  parties' agreement on, 2–220, 2–221
  presumption that intended, 2–219—2–224
  procedure for choosing, 2–228—2–233
  rejection of appointment, 2–221
  Technology and Construction Court judge as, 2–232, 2–233
  terms of reference,
    preparation, 9–029
  third person, appointment by, 2–221
  usual procedure, 2–233
SOLICITORS,
  See also Legal Services Ombudsman; Professional conduct of barristers and solicitors
  barristers distinguished, 18–002
  Compliance Board, 18–091, 18–092—18–094
  Consumer Redress Scheme, 18–085
  Customer Assistance Unit, 18–087, 18–088
  essential features, 18–087
  court, disciplinary powers of, 18–145
  evaluation of disciplinary processes, 18–146
  Law Society, 18–083, 18–084
    Compliance Board, 18–091, 18–092—18–094
    investigation of complaints, 18–089
  Office for the Supervision of Solicitors. *See* Office for the Supervision of Solicitors (OSS)

1109

SOLICITORS—*cont.*
  Law Society—*cont.*
    Practice Standards Unit, 18–086
    Regulations Directorate, 18–086
    remuneration certificate applications, 18–090
    structure of professional conduct system, 18–091
  Legal Services Complaints Commissioner, 18–084
  Office for the Supervision of Solicitors. *See* Office for the Supervision of Solicitors (OSS)
  overlap with work of barristers, 18–003
  principal professional obligations, 18–080
  Solicitor's Compensation Fund, 18–111—18–113
  Solicitor's Disciplinary Tribunal,
    affidavit evidence, 18–130
    amendments to applications, 18–132
    appeals, 18–142—18–144
    applications, 18–123
    costs, 18–138
    decisions, 18–137
    disciplinary findings, 18–129
    documents, 18–127
    failure of party to attend hearing, 18–134
    filing of findings and orders, 18–140
    formal requirements, 18–143
    further evidence, 18–128
    hearings, 18–133
    independence, 18–119
    interlocutory steps, 18–125
    judgments, 18–129
    jurisdiction, 18–120
    late evidence, 18–131
    membership, 18–121
    notice to admit facts, 18–128
    outcomes, 18–141
    penalties, 18–139
    practice, 18–122
    preparatory steps, 18–125
    previous convictions, 18–129
    primary evaluation, 18–124
    procedure, 18–122
    references to the Law Society or the OSS, 18–135
    sanctions, 18–139
    timetabling, 18–126
    withdrawal of application, 18–136
  Solicitors Practice Rules, 18–080—18–082
SPECIFIC PERFORMANCE,
  CIMAR, 6–042, A29–022
  land, contracts relating to, 2–337
SPORT DISPUTE RESOLUTION PANEL, A67–001—A67–026
  See also Sports arbitration
  appeal arbitration procedure, 15–017, 15–018, A67–002—A67–008
  applicable law, 15–034, A67–025
  arbitration procedures, 15–015, A67–001—A67–026

SPORT DISPUTE RESOLUTION PANEL—*cont.*
  communications, A67–014
  conciliation, 15–023, A67–015
  conduct of proceedings, 15–027, A67–018
  confidentiality, A67–024
  costs, 15–033, A67–023
  current rules, 15–013
  death of arbitrator, 15–026
  decisions, 15–031, A67–022
  development of practice, 15–038
  experts, 15–030, A67–021
  formulation of the Tribunal, A67–016
  full arbitration procedure, 15–019—15–022, A67–009—A67–013
  hearing, 15–028, A67–019
  history, 15–012
  Human Rights Act 1998, 15–037
  jurisdiction, 15–024, A67–017
  Kompetenz Kompetenz, 15–026
  new rules, 15–013, 15–035
  nomination of arbitrator, 15–024, 15–025
  powers of tribunal, 15–031, 15–032
  purpose of rules, 15–035
    growth of "challenge" culture, 15–037
  referral of disputes to, 15–016
  resignation of arbitrator, 15–026
  role, 15–014
  seat of arbitration, 15–034
  witnesses, 15–029, A67–020
SPORTS ARBITRATION, 15–001—15–114
  advantages, 15–004—15–011
  choice of law, 15–008
  confidentiality, 15–007
  Court of Arbitration for Sport (CAS). *See* Court of Arbitration for Sport (CAS)
  expense, 15–005
  expertise, 15–004
  finality, 15–111—15–114
  generally, 15–001—15–011
  harmonisation, lack of, 15–097—15–099
  human rights, 15–107—15–110
  International Court of Arbitration for Sport (ICAS). *See* International Court of Arbitration for Sport (ICAS)
  international nature, 15–009
  jurisdiction, 15–008
  on-field controversies, 15–103—15–106
  post-competition publicity, 15–102
  preservation of relationships, 15–006
  publicity, 15–102
  specific schemes, 15–011
  speed, 15–005
    pre-competition cases, 15–100, 15–101
  Sports Dispute Resolution Panel (SDRP). *See* Sports Dispute Resolution Panel (SDRP)
  time, 15–005
SPORTS DISPUTE RESOLUTION PANEL (SDRP), 15–010
STANDARD FORM CONTRACTS,
  maritime arbitration, 11–019

INDEX

STATEMENT OF CASE. *See* Statement of claim
STATEMENT OF CLAIM,
  additions to,
    agricultural property arbitration, 3–036—3–039
  agricultural property arbitration, 3–027, 3–034—3–039
    additions to, 3–036—3–039
    "all necessary particulars", 3–034, 3–039
    amendments, 3–036—3–039
    criticism of 1986 Act, 3–034
    making award after, 3–035
    onus of proof, 3–038
    parallel preparation, 3–035
    procedure for delivery, 3–034
    sketchy, 3–039
    time of delivery, 3–034
    uninformative, 3–039
  amendment, 2–678
  American Arbitration Association International Arbitration Rules, A18–003
  Chartered Institute of Arbitrators Arbitration Scheme for the Travel Industry, A21–004
  Chartered Institute of Arbitrators Rules of the Mortgage Code Arbitration, A24–004
  Chartered Institute of Arbitrators "Surveyors Arbitration" Scheme Rules, A25–006
  correspondence as, 2–673
  farm business tenancy arbitration, 3–108
  ICE arbitration, A43–012
  identification of issues, 2–670, 2–671
    correspondence as, 2–673
  Model Law, A14–023
  precedent, A54–095, A54–099
  sketchy,
    agricultural property arbitration, 3–039
  time of delivery,
    agricultural property arbitration, 3–034
  UNCITRAL Arbitration Rules, A15–019
  uninformative,
    agricultural property arbitration, 3–039
  WIPO arbitration, A52–041
STATUTORY ARBITRATION,
  agricultural property arbitration, 3–003
  Arbitration Act 1996, A6–095—A6–099
  farm business tenancy arbitration, 3–009, 3–011
STATUTORY ARBITRATIONS,
  meaning, 2–010
STATUTORY IMMUNITY,
  arbitrator, 2–074, 2–075, 2–076
  DAC Report, 2–076
  institutions, 2–074, 2–075, 2–076
STAY OF PROCEEDINGS,
  adjudication, 2–162
  construction industry arbitration, 6–090

STAYING COURT PROCEEDINGS, 2–143—2–194
  actively seeking stay, 2–147
  admiralty proceedings, 2–176, A6–012
  anti-suit injunction, stay by, 2–149
  appeals, 2–172
  Arbitration Act 1975, A62–001
  Arbitration Act 1996, A6–010
    Admiralty proceedings, A6–012
    reference of interpleader issue to arbitration, A6–011
    spirit of the Act, 2–156
  arbitration clause, validity of, 2–144
  award as condition precedent, 2–170, 2–175
  challenging jurisdiction, 2–187—2–194
    considerations, 2–192
    no straitjacket for courts, 2–193
    parties' understanding at time of agreement to arbitrate, 2–191
    preferred approach, 2–189
    unenforceable host agreement, 2–188
  completion of works, 2–169
  conditional relief, party seeking, 2–157
  consecutive dispute resolution procedures, 2–167
  construction agreements, 2–169—2–171
    award as condition precedent, 2–170
    condition precedent, 2–170, 2–171
    late application, 2–116
    no application to stay, 2–171
    provision for stay in, 2–168
    waiver of condition precedent, 2–171
  consumer disputes, 2–166
  definition of a dispute, 2–164
  disputes, 2–160
  Halki Shipping v Sopex, 2–161
  inherent jurisdiction, 2–148—2–150
    1996 Act, under, 2–151, 2–152
    basic rule, 2–152
    power, 2–148
    reasons for, 2–148
    timing of application, 2–153
  initiating the stay investigation, 2–174
  interpleader proceedings, 2–173—2–175
  issues arising out of application, 2–144
  jurisdiction, 2–143, 2–144
  kinds of jurisdiction, 2–143, 2–144
  Kompetenz Kompetenz, 2–180—2–186
  mandatory, 2–143, 2–159
  multiple proceedings in court, existence of, 2–163
  neither side calling for arbitration, 2–145
  New Zealand, 1–006
  order for, 2–144
  Patel' case, 2–154—2–157
  policy, 2–143
  precedent order, A54–102
  recording an argument to rescind in writing, 2–146
  seeking, 2–147
  separability, 2–177—2–179
  small claims in county court, 14–009

1111

STAYING COURT PROCEEDINGS—cont.
　stand-alone ADR clauses, 2–168
　step in the action, 2–153—2–158
　time bars, impact of, 2–165
　trends, 1–006
　unqualified defence, 2–158
STRIKING OUT,
　want of prosecution. See Want of
　　prosecution
STRING ARBITRATIONS,
　GAFTA, A34–013, A34–022
　LMAA terms, 11–078—11–080
　maritime arbitration, 11–078—11–080
STRING CONTRACTS, 2–651
SUBMISSION AGREEMENT,
　meaning, 2–109
SUBSTANTIVE LAW,
　agreement, of, 2–130
SUGAR ASSOCIATION,
　establishment, 16–002
SUGAR ASSOCIATION OF LONDON (SAL),
　16–038
SUMMARY JUDGMENT, 2–607
　Civil Procedure Rules, 14–054, 14–055
SUMMARY PROCEDURE,
　CIETAC, A74–064—A74–073
　fast track procedures, 2–607
SURVEYORS,
　Chartered Institute of Arbitrators Scheme
　　Rules. See Chartered Institute of
　　Arbitrators "Surveyors Arbitration"
　　Scheme Rules
SURVEYORS & VALUERS ARBITRATION
　SCHEME, 8–011
SUSPENSION OF AWARD,
　New York Convention, A17–006

TAPE RECORDINGS,
　agreement, 2–112
TARGET PROGRAMMING,
　arbitration,
　　both parties wanting delay, 2–578
　　both parties wanting speed, 2–576
　　claimant wanting delay and respondent
　　　wanting speed, 2–579
　　claimant wants speed and respondent
　　　wants delay, 2–582
　　dates, target, 2–572
　　diary, arbitrator's, 2–577
　　discrete issues, finding, 2–571
　　early request for issues, 2–573
　　long advance dates, 2–574
　　objective, 2–570
　　possibilities, 2–575
　　speed of resolution as measure of system,
　　　2–583
　　unavoidable delay, 2–581
　Civil Procedure Rules. See Civil Procedure
　　Rules

TARGET PROGRAMMING—cont.
　old practice, 2–561
　　choice of advocate, 2–564
　　consequences of, 2–562
　　hearing cut off, no, 2–563
　　speed of resolution, 2–564
　present position, 2–565—2–595
TAXATION OF COSTS,
　property valuation arbitration, 13–070
TECHNICAL EVIDENCE,
　form of, 2–022
TECHNOLOGY AND CONSTRUCTION COURT,
　2–013, 6–002, 6–035
　judges,
　　courts, 2–232
　　sole arbitrator, as, 2–232
　　umpire, as, 2–232
TERMINATION OF PROCEEDINGS,
　Model Law, A14–032
　settlements, 2–512
TEST CASES,
　small claims in county court, 14–028
THIRD PARTIES,
　expert determination. See Expert
　　determination
　WTO dispute settlement, 17–028, 17–029,
　　A53–010
THREE PERSON TRIBUNAL,
　advantages, 2–235—2–238
　agreement, 2–124
　appointment, 2–235
　　absence of agreed procedure, 2–255—
　　　2–257
　　"beauty parade", 2–246
　　contractual, 2–270
　　court's role, 2–266
　　default, 2–268
　　difficulties, 2–247
　　stop running time, 2–271, 2–272
　　terms of appointment, 2–246
　　third party commencing appointment, 2–
　　　272
　　time limits, 2–269
　　umpire or third party, 2–265
　costs, 2–238
　cultural objections, 2–238
　drawbacks, 2–237
　ICC arbitration, 9–014
　maritime arbitration, 11–050—11–053
　Model Law, 2–238
　remuneration of arbitrator, 2–389
　selection difficulties, 2–236
　technical qualifications, 2–235
　two arbitrator and an umpire. See Two
　　arbitrator and an umpire
　two arbitrator and a chairman. See Two
　　arbitrator and a chairman
TIME,
　See also Time limits
　agricultural property arbitration, 3–069,
　　3–070

INDEX

TIME—*cont.*
reckoning periods of,
  Arbitration Act 1996, A6–079
  Housing Grants, Construction and Regeneration Act 1996, A9–013
TIME LIMITS, 2–195—2–215
  agreement, 2–137—2–141
  commencement of proceedings, 2–196, 2–197
  construction industry arbitration, 6–101
  correction of award, 2–512
  drafting, 2–204
  GAFTA, 16–092, 19–094
  hearing, uses, 2–787
  LME, 16–035
  non-compliance, 2–203
  RSA, 16–035
  substantive effects, 2–214, 2–215
  use of, 2–787
TOKYO,
  maritime arbitration, 11–111—11–113
TOMLIN ORDER, 2–753
TRADE BARRIERS REGULATION, 17–074—17–091
  Community interest test, 17–088—17–091
  governmental measures, 17–075
  individual community enterprises, 17–081, 17–082
  initiation of WTO proceedings, 17–087
  locus standi, 17–077
  market definition for complaints, 17–076
  Member State complaints, 17–078—17–080
  outcome, 17–086
  permitted subject-matter, 17–075—17–077
  post complaints procedure, 17–084, 17–085
  threatened injury, 17–083
TRADE RULES,
  agreement, incorporated into arbitration, 2–120
TRADE SECRETS,
  WIPO arbitration, A52–052
TRAINING,
  Chartered Institute of Arbitrators, 11–033
TRAMP SHIPPING, 11–008, 11–009
TRANSCRIPT,
  abroad, witnesses, 2–782
TRANSLATION SOFTWARE, 12–008
TRAVEL INDUSTRY. *See* ABTA SCHEMES; DOCUMENTS ONLY ARBITRATION IN CONSUMER DISPUTES; CHARTERED INSTITUTE OF ARBITRATORS ARBITRATION SCHEME FOR THE TRAVEL INDUSTRY
TRAVELLING DRAFTS, 12–008
TREATIES,
  bilateral, 9–077—9–079
  bilateral investment treaties, 9–079
  Brussels Convention, 9–074
  Energy Charter Treaty, 9–075
  generally, 9–064—9–067
  Geneva Convention, 9–070—9–073
  importance of, 9–064—9–079

TREATIES—*cont.*
  multilateral, 9–068, 9–069
  North American Free Trade Agreement, 9–075
  signatory states, action against, 9–075
  UNCITRAL, 9–076
  Washington convention, 9–070
TRIBUNAL. *See* ARBITRAL TRIBUNAL
TRUSTMARK SCHEMES, 12–141—12–144
TURNKEY PROJECTS,
  construction industry arbitration, 6–017
TWO ARBITRATORS AND AN UMPIRE,
  appointment,
    arbitrators, 2–244
    "beauty parade", 2–246
    contractual, 2–270
    court's role, 2–266
    difficulties, 2–247
    stop running, time, 2–271, 2–272
    terms of appointment, 2–247
    third party commencing appointment, 2–272
    third party, umpire or, 2–265
    time limits, statutory, 2–269
    umpire, 2–243
  appointment of umpire, 2–243
  delayed appointment of umpire, 2–243
  party appointed arbitrators', role of, 2–244
  role of umpire, 2–242
  three arbitrator tribunal compared, 2–242
TWO ARBITRATORS AND A CHAIRMAN,
  appointment,
    absence of agreed procedures, 2–255—2–257
    agreement on, 2–254
    "beauty parade", 2–247
    contractual, 2–270
    court's role, 2–266
    difficulties, 2–247
    failure to appoint, 2–254
    independence of each party, 2–240
    methods, 2–239
    stopping time running, 2–271, 2–272
    terms of, 2–247
    third party, commencement of appointment by, 2–272
    time limits, 2–174
  chairman's role, 2–241
  independence of each party, 2–240
  use, 2–239
TWO OR MORE PERSONS, TRIBUNAL OF,
  appointment,
    absence of agreed procedures, 2–255—2–257
    "beauty parade", 2–247
    difficulties, 2–247
    terms of, 2–247
    three arbitrator. *See* Three person tribunal
  appointment of arbitrator, 2–234
  three arbitrator. *See* Three person tribunal

1113

TWO OR MORE PERSONS, TRIBUNAL OF—*cont.*
two arbitrator and an umpire. *See* Two arbitrator and an umpire
two arbitrator and a chairman. *See* Two arbitrator and a chairman

UDRP,
approved service providers, 12–111
Asian Domain Name Dispute Resolution Centre (ADNDRC), 12–111
binding, 12–106
CPR Institute for Dispute Resolution, 12–111
cybersquatting, 12–115
defences, 12–115, 12–116
E-Resolution, 12–111
evaluation of scheme, 12–118—12–123
extensive interpretation, 12–117
implementation, 12–124
incorporation, 12–106
meaning, 12–1105
National Arbitration Forum, 12–111
rationale, 12–106
registration of domain names, 12–106
remedies, 12–112—12–114
start of proceedings, 12–109, 12–110
WIPO, 12–111
UMPIRE,
See also Two arbitrator and an umpire
appointment, 2–243
Arbitration Act 1950, A61–006—A61–011
Arbitration Act 1996, A6–022
award, A54–088
definition, 2–243
FOSFA, 16–020
legally qualified, 2–730
remuneration of, 2–392
role, 2–243
Technology and Construction Court judge as, 2–232
UNCERTAIN AWARD, 2–097
notes on organising arbitral proceedings treaties, 9–076
UNCITRAL,
Arbitration Rules. *See* UNCITRAL Arbitration Rules
Model Law. *See* Model Law
Notes on Organizing Arbitral Proceedings, 9–098, A16–001—A16–063
administrative services, A15–016
confidentiality, A15–020
decision-making process, A15–006
defining points at issue, A15–028—A15–030
delivering award, A15–062, A15–063
deposits in respect of costs, A15–017—A15–019
discretion in conduct of proceedings, A15–004

UNCITRAL—*cont.*
Notes on Organizing Arbitral Proceedings—*cont.*
documentary evidence, A15–032—A15–036
electronic means of communication, A15–023
exchange of written submissions, A15–024—A15–026
experts, A15–048—A15–052
filing award, A15–062, A15–063
hearings, A15–053—A15–060
interpretation of oral presentation, A15–012, A15–013
language of proceedings, A15–010
matters for possible consideration, A15–007, A15–008
multi-party arbitration, 9–166, A15–005, A15–061
non-binding character, A15–003
physical evidence, A15–037—A15–039
place of arbitration, A15–014, A15–015
practical details, A15–027
preface, A15–001
procedure, 9–098
purpose, 9–098, A15–002
routing of written communications, A15–021
set of arbitration rules, A15–009
settlement negotiations, A15–031
telefax, A15–022
timely decisions, usefulness of, A15–004
translations, A15–011,, A15–013
witnesses, A15–040—A15–047
UNCITRAL ARBITRATION RULES, A15–001—A15–042
additional award, A15–038
amendment of claim or defence, A15–021
amiable compositeur, A15–034
applicable law, A15–034
appointment of arbitrators, A15–007—A15–009
arbitral proceedings,
amendment of claim or defence, A15–021
defence, A15–020
evidence, A15–025
further written statements, A15–023
general provisions, A15–016
hearings, A15–025, A15–026
interim measures, A15–027
language, A15–018
periods of time, A15–024
place of arbitration, A15–017
statement of claim, A15–019
waiver of rules, A15–031
arbitral tribunal,
appointment of arbitrators, A15–007
challenging arbitrators, A15–010—A15–013
composition, A15–006—A15–015
jurisdiction, A15–022

INDEX

UNCITRAL ARBITRATION RULES—*cont.*
  arbitral tribunal—*cont.*
    number of arbitrators, A15–006
    replacement of arbitrator, A15–014, A15–015
  arbitration clause, A54–015
  assistance, A15–005
  award,
    additional award, A15–038
    amiable compositeur, A15–034
    applicable law, A15–034
    correction of award, A15–037
    costs, A15–039—A15–041
    decisions, A15–032
    effect, A15–033
    form, A15–033
    interpretation, A15–036
    settlement, A15–035
    termination, A15–035
  calculation of periods of time, A15–003
  challenging arbitrators, A15–010—A15–013
  correction of award, A15–037
  costs, A15–039—A15–041
  costs of arbitration,
    deposit of costs, A15–042
  defence, A15–020
  deposit of costs, A15–042
  evidence, A15–025
  General Assembly, A15–001
  interim measures, A15–027
  interpretation of award, A15–036
  language of proceedings, A15–018
  Notes on Organizing Arbitral Proceedings, 9–098, 9–166, A15–005
  notice, A15–003
  notice of arbitration, A15–004
  place of arbitration, A15–017
  replacement of arbitrator, A15–014, A15–015
  representation, A15–005
  scope of application, A15–002
  settlement, A15–035
  statement of claim, A15–019
UNDERTAKINGS,
  disqualification from completing arbitration, 2–306
UNFAIR CONTRACT TERMS,
  Act of 1977,
    breach, effect of, A1–010
    choice of law clauses, A1–028
    Consumer Protection Acts, obligations under, A1–031
    contracts under which goods pass, A1–008
    contractual liability, A1–004
    dealing as consumer, A1–013
    evasion by means of secondary contract, A1–011
    guarantee of consumer goods, A1–006
    international supply contracts, A1–027
    interpretation, A1–015

UNFAIR CONTRACT TERMS—*cont.*
  Act of 1977—*cont.*
    misrepresentation, A1–009
    negligence liability, A1–003
    reasonableness test, A1–012, A1–035
    sale and hire-purchase, A1–007
    savings, A1–030
    scope, A1–002
    Scotland, A1–016—A1–026
    sea carriage of passengers, A1–029
    unreasonable indemnity clause, A1–005
    varieties of exemption clause, A1–014
  Arbitration Act 1996, A6–090
  choice of law clauses, A1–028
  international supply contracts, A1–027
  misrepresentation, A1–009
  reasonableness test, A1–012, A1–035
  Regulations 1999, A12–001—A12–021
    advice, A12–016
    assessment of unfair terms, A12–007
    choice of law clauses, A12–010
    complaints, A12–011, A12–012
    documents and information, power to obtain, A12–014
    effect of unfair term, A12–009
    FSA, functions of, A12–017
    information, A12–016
    injunction to prevent continued use, A12–013
    interpretation, A12–004
    list of terms, A12–020
    notification of undertakings and orders to Director, A12–015
    publication, A12–16
    qualifying bodies, A12–018
    terms to which regulations apply, A12–005
    unfair terms, A12–006
    written contracts, A12–008
  sea carriage of passengers, A1–029
UNIFORM DOMAIN NAME DISPUTE RESOLUTION PROCEDURE. *See* UDRP
UNITED NATIONS COMPENSATION COMMISSION GOVERNING COUNCIL,
  "E3" claims, A59–001——A59–048
USA,
  ADR, 4–003, 4–046, 4–056
  Dispute Review Board, 7–010
  mediation, 4–006, 4–015

VACANCIES,
  Arbitration Act 1996, A6–028
VALUATION ARBITRATION. *See* Property valuation arbitration
VAT,
  approval of arrangement reached, 2–397
  domestic arbitration, 2–396
  international arbitration, 2–397
  remuneration of arbitrator, 2–396—2–397

Index

VIDEO TAPE,
  abroad, witnesses, 2–782
VIDEO-CONFERENCING, 12–018, 12–082
VIRTUAL MEETINGS, 12–011
VOIE DIRECTE, 2–727

WAIVER,
  American Arbitration Association International Arbitration Rules, A18–026
  enforcement of award, 2–947
  ICC arbitration, A39–035
  UNCITRAL Arbitration Rules, A15–031
  WIPO arbitration, A52–058, A52–078
WALFORD V MILES, 4–053
WANT OF PROSECUTION, 2–604—2–606
  applications for extension of time, 2–606
  grounds for striking out, 2–605
  power to strike out for, 2–604
WARRANTIES,
  ICE Conditions of Contract, A33–003
WASHINGTON CONVENTION, 9–006, 9–079
WILLS,
  agricultural property arbitration, 3–010
WIPO ARBITRATION, 9–039—9–044
  additional award, A52–066
  agreed primers and models, A52–051
  amendment of claim or defence, A52–044
  anti-cybersquatting policy, 9–043
  appointment of arbitrators, A52–015—A52–019
    default appointment, A52–019
    multiple claimants or respondents, where, A52–018
    procedure, A52–015
    sole arbitrator, A52–016
    three arbitrators, A52–017
  Arbitration center, 9–040
  arbitrators,
    acceptance, A52–023
    availability, A52–023
    challenging, A52–024—A52–029
    communications, A52–021
    impartiality, A52–022
    independence, A52–022
    nationality, A52–020
    notification, A52–023
    number, A52–014
    release from appointment, A52–030—A52–032
    replacement, A52–033, A52–034
  award, A52–059—A52–066
    additional award, A52–066
    correction, A52–066
    currency, A52–060
    decision-making, A52–061
    effect of award, A52–064
    final award, A52–063
    form, A52–062
    interest, A52–060

WIPO ARBITRATION—*cont.*
  award—*cont.*
    notification, A52–062
    settlement, A52–065
    time period for delivery, A52–063
  closure of proceedings, A52–057
  commencement of arbitration, A52–006—A52–013
    answer to request, A52–011, A52–012
    representation, A52–013
    request for arbitration, A52–006—A52–010
  communications, A52–021, A52–045
  competence, 9–040
  conduct of arbitration, A52–037—A52–058
  confidentiality, 9–041, A52–073—A52–076
  correction of award, A52–066
  costs, A52–067—A52–069
  default of party, A52–056
  defence, A52–042
  deposit of costs, A52–070
  documents, A52–005
  domain name disputes, 9–043
  evidence, A52–048
  exclusion of liability, A52–077
  expedition, 9–042
  experiments, A52–049
  experts, A52–055
  fees, A52–079—A52–081
  further written statements, A52–043
  general powers of tribunal, A52–038
  general provisions, A52–001
  hearing, A52–053
  impartiality of arbitrators, A52–022
  inauguration, 9–039
  independence of arbitrators, A52–022
  interim measures, A52–046
  jurisdiction, A52–036
  language of arbitration, A52–040
  notices, A52–004
  online dispute resolution, 12–098—12–100
  periods of time, A52–004
  place of arbitration, A52–039
  preparatory conference, A52–047
  purpose, 9–039
  replacement of arbitrator, A52–033, A52–034
  representation, A52–013
  request for arbitration, A52–006—A52–010
  scope of rules, A52–002
  security for claims, A52–046
  settlement, A52–065
  site visits, A52–050
  staff, 9–043
  statement of claim, A52–041
  termination of arbitration, A52–065
  trade secrets, A52–052
  transmission of file to tribunal, A52–037
  truncated Tribunal, A52–035
  waiver of rules, A52–058, A52–078
  witnesses, A52–054

INDEX

WITHDRAWAL OF CLAIM,
  RSA, 16–052
WITHHOLDING AWARD FOR NON-PAYMENT,
  Arbitration Act 1996, A6–057
"WITHOUT PREJUDICE" NEGOTIATIONS,
  Calderbank offer, 2–741
  meaning, 2–740, 2–741
  rejection of offer to settle, 2–757
  settlements, 2–740
"WITHOUT PREJUDICE" NEGOTIATIONS,
  documents only arbitration in consumer
    disputes, 8–044
  resignation of arbitrator after disclosure of,
    2–724, 2–725
WITNESS SUMMONS,
  agricultural property arbitration, 3–047,
    3–048
  production of documents required by,
    2–709—2–711
    arbitrator having no power to apply for
      summons, 2–709
    focused disclosure, 2–711
    return date, 2–710
  rent review arbitration, 13–045—13–049
WITNESSES, 15–029
  abroad, 2–780—2–781
    agreement of parties, 2–782
    court ordering examination, 2–781
    essential witnesses, 2–780
    examination, 2–780—2–781
    Hague Convention, 2–781
    seat of arbitration, 2–780
    taking evidence, 2–780
    transcripts, 2–780
    video, 2–780
  advocacy combined with, 2–832
  agricultural property arbitration, 3–047,
    3–048
  Arbitration Act 1950, A61–012
  Arbitration Act 1996, A6–044
  City Disputes Panel Arbitration Rules, A26–019
  combined witness/ advocate, 2–832
  compelling to answer, 2–812
  compelling witness to answer, 2–812
  conferencing, 2–542
  confidential information, 2–811, 2–812
  death, 2–769
  disclosing confidential information, 2–811—2–813
  examination,
    See also Conduct of hearing
    international arbitration, 9–160
  Hague Convention, 2–781
  IBA Rules, A38–012
  LCIA arbitration, A44–021
  misconduct, 2–184
  production of documents, 2–811
  small claims in county court, 14–059
  Sport Dispute Resolution Panel, 15–029,
    A67–020

WITNESSES—*cont.*
  videotaping, 2–780
  WIPO arbitration, A52–054
WOOLF REPORT, 1–001, 2–529
  ADR, 4–016, 4–046
  assessment, 4–023
  case management, 4–021, 4–022
  costs, 2–901
  expert evidence, 2–845
  objectives, 1–002
  realisation of reforms, 4–023
  settlements, 2–733
WORLD BANK, 9–033, 9–037
  disputes settlement procedure, A70—001—A70–013
WORLD INTELLECTUAL PROPERTY
  ORGANIZATION. *See* WIPO arbitration
WRITTEN STATEMENTS,
  American Arbitration Association
    International Arbitration Rules, A18–018
  factual witnesses, 9–141, 9–142
  ICC arbitration, 9–137
  ICSID arbitration, 9–140, 10–056
  international arbitration, 9–137—9–140
  LCIA arbitration, 9–137, A44–016
WTO DISPUTE SETTLEMENT,
  administration, A53–002
  adoption of panel reports, 17–046—17–048,
    A53–016
  agreement rules and procedures, A53–032
  agreements covered by understanding, A53–031
  amicus briefs, 17–025—17–027
  appellate body, 17–038—17–045, A53–017
    adoption of reports, A53–019
    membership, 17–038
    procedures, 17–040, A53–018
    process, 17–041—17–044
    recommendations, A53–021
    right of appeal, 17–039
    ruling, 17–045
  arbitration, 17–012, 17–013, A53–027
  burden of proof, 17–030
  bypassing system, 17–012—17–014
  commencement of operations, 17–001
  compensation, A53–024
  complaints under EC law, 17–072—17–092
    Article 133 Committee, 17–092
    Market Access Strategy, 17–072, 17–073
    Trade Barriers Regulation. *See* Trade
      Barriers Regulation
  compliance review panel, 17–056, 17–057
  composition of panels, A53–008
  conciliation, A53–005
  confidentiality, A53–014
  consultations, 17–016, 17–017, A53–004
  good offices, A53–005

WTO DISPUTE SETTLEMENT—cont.
European legal order, status within, 17–003, 17–068—17–092
complaints mechanism 17–072—17–092. See also complaints under EC law below
compliance review by Community courts, 17–069—17–071
private enforcement, 17–068
expert review groups, A53–034
function of panels, A53–011
fundamental features, 17–009
GATT,
non-violation complaints, A53–028
general provisions, A53–003
implementation of reports, 17–049—17–052
monitoring of compliance, 17–052
notification of intentions, 17–049
reasonable period of time, 17–050, 17–051
review, 17–055
information,
right to seek, A53–013
sources, 17–010
institutions, 17–006—17–008
interim review, A53–015
jurisdiction, 17–005
least-developed country members, special procedures involving, A53–026
legally binding results, 17–009
litigation report, 17–010
mediation, 17–014, A53–005
membership of WTO, 17–009
multilateral system, suspension of, A53–025
multiple complainants, A53–009
non-compliance, 17–058—17–062
novel features, 17–009
overview, 17–015
panels,
adoption of panel reports, 17–046—17–048, A53–016
amicus briefs, 17–025—17–027
composition, A53–008

WTO DISPUTE SETTLEMENT—cont.
panels—cont.
establishment, 17–020, A53–006
evidence, 17–024
final panel report, 17–037
first interim panel report, 17–034
first written submissions, 17–031, 17–032
full interim panel report, 17–036
function, 17–023, A53–011
information, right to seek, A53–013
procedures, 17–031—17–037, A53–012
recommendations, A53–021
request, 17–018, 17–019
second meeting of the panel, 17–035
second written submissions, 17–033
selection of panel, 17–021
terms of reference, 17–022, A53–007
time-frame for DSB decisions, A53–022
practical results of proceedings, 17–011
recommendations as to manner of compliance, 17–054
remedies, 17–053
retaliation, 17–063—17–067
scope, A53–001
Secretariat, responsibilities of, A53–030
sources of information, 17–010
surveillance of implementation of recommendations and rulings, A53–023
suspension of concessions, 17–063—17–067, A53–024
arbitration to determine, 17–067
cross-retaliation, 17–065
determination of level, 17–066
request for authorisation, 17–064
same sector, 17–065
terms of reference of panels, A53–007
third parties, 17–028, 17–029, A53–010
Trade Barriers Regulation. *See* Trade Barriers Regulation
unitary system, 17–009
use, 17–001
working procedures, A53–033